THE POETIC WORKS OF
HELIUS EOBANUS HESSUS

VOLUME 2

RENAISSANCE TEXT SERIES

VOLUME 20

THE RENAISSANCE SOCIETY OF AMERICA

MEDIEVAL AND RENAISSANCE TEXTS AND STUDIES

VOLUME 333

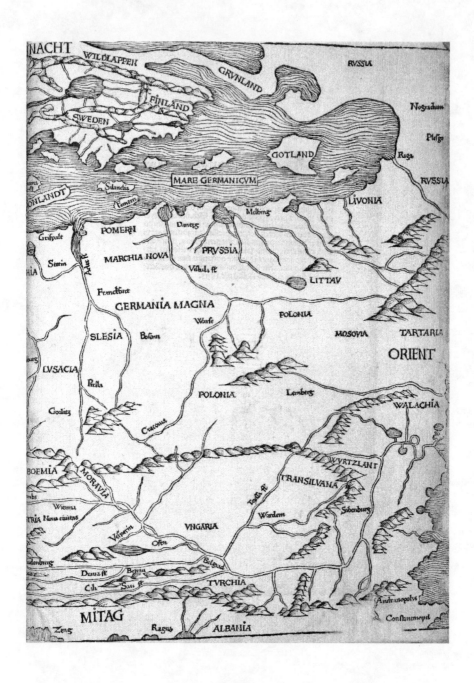

Northeastern Europe. Detail from Hieronymus Münzer's
map at the end of Hartmann Schedel's *Liber chronicarum* (Nuremberg, 1493)
Rare Books and Manuscripts Library of The Ohio State University Libraries

THE POETIC WORKS OF
HELIUS EOBANUS HESSUS

Edited, translated, and annotated by

Harry Vredeveld

Volume 2
JOURNEYMAN YEARS, 1509–1514

Published by: Arizona Center for Medieval and Renaissance Studies. PO Box 874402, Tempe, AZ 85287-4402.

MRTS Volume 333
Renaissance Text Series Volume 20

ISBN: 978-0-86698-381-5

Hessus, Helius Eobanus, 1488–1540
   [Poems. English & Latin]
   The Poetic Works of Helius Eobanus Hessus / edited, translated, and annotated by Harry Vredeveld.
      v. cm. — (Medieval and Renaissance Texts and Studies ; 333)
   Contents: v. 2. Journeyman Years, 1509–1514
   ISBN: 978-0-86698-381-5 (alk. paper)
   1. Hessus, Helius Eobanus, 1488–1540 — Translations into English. 2. Latin poetry, Medieval and modern — Germany — Prussia — Epithalamia — Christian saints — women saints — Translations into English. 3. Vredeveld, Harry. II. Title. III. Medieval & Renaissance Texts & Studies (Series); v. 333.

PA8527.H4A28 2004
971'.04—dc22

2003070860

Digitally printed on acid-free paper by Yurchak Printing, Inc. of Lancaster, PA.

For Vera Mae

Es enim tu, dulcissima coniunx,

tam nomine quam rerum pondere

Vera mea.

TABLE OF CONTENTS

ACKNOWLEDGMENTS

It is a pleasure to open this volume with a heartfelt thanks to the many colleagues, friends, and organizations that helped bring it into the world. A research fellowship from The National Endowment for the Humanities — generously matched by the College of Humanities at The Ohio State University — allowed me to complete a first draft of the book in 1999–2000. I am also indebted to The Renaissance Society of America and the Arizona Center for Medieval and Renaissance Studies for jointly shouldering the burden of publication. A special thank-you is due to the libraries here and in Europe that have so graciously provided the foundation on which this edition stands. Let me conclude by paying a warm tribute to Timothy Krause, who cheerfully brought all his editorial prowess to bear on my manuscript and with admirable patience insisted on bringing it up to the style standards of *Renaissance Quarterly*. Bravo, Tim!

CORRIGENDA AND ADDENDA TO VOLUME 1

In volume 1 of this edition I unquestioningly accepted Carl Krause's argument that the anonymously published satire *De generibus ebriosorum et ebrietate vitanda* (Erfurt, 1515) may be attributed to Eobanus' close friend Petrejus Eberbach. See Krause, *HEH*, 1:202–18; cf. Martin von Hase, *Bibliographie der Erfurter Drucke von 1501–1550* (Nieuwkoop, 1968³), no. 357; Kleineidam, 2:205. After studying the work more closely, I now recognize that Petrejus could have had nothing to do with it. The true author is none other than Eobanus himself. An edition of the mock speech is planned for volume 3.

Reprinted by Migne in *PL* 19, cols. 385–88, as an appendix to Juvencus' biblical epic, the anonymous poem *Triumphus Christi heroicus* has been variously assigned to Juvencus himself or to some patristic, medieval, or humanistic author. The poem is in fact the work of the Lutheran preacher Johann Spangenberg (1484–1550), as I have just now discovered. I shall have more to say about Spangenberg's poem in volume 3, introduction to *Victoria Christi ab inferis* (1517). For now it will suffice to say that it is Spangenberg who plunders Eobanus' epyllion, and not the other way around, as I had feared.

To the copies of the *Bucolicon* mentioned on p. 269 add the copy in Munich, Bayerische SB (P. o. lat. 1686 g). This text can be viewed online at the library's website.

In the notes to *Buc.* 3.26 and 8.121 correct "Gianfrancesco Pico" to "Giovanni Pico."

The headnote to *Buc.* B 5 (Supplementary Notes, p. 543) ascribes the epigram "Πρόγνωσις in Venetos anni noni supra sesquimillesimum" to Eobanus Hessus. I did not notice that Karl Gillert had earlier attributed the same verses (here taken from *Epp.* 4, sig. H3ʳ) to Konrad Mutianus Rufus and edited them as *Ep.* 159. The distichs, however, are neither by Mutianus nor by Eobanus. They are extracted from Zaccaria Ferreri's *Ad Venetos . . . elegia* (1508), printed at Erfurt by Johann Knappe the Elder in 1509. I owe this correction to Gisela Möncke, "Zwei Erfurter Drucke mit unbekannten Gedichten von Eobanus Hessus," *Gutenberg-Jahrbuch* 79 (2004), 150.

Let me take this opportunity to add a few commentary notes.

The phrase "Permessidos undas" at *Laud.* 249 does indeed go back to a variant reading of Mart. 1.76.11, where some mss. and early eds. read either "Permessidos unda" or "Permessidis unda."

While writing *De amantium infoelicitate*, Eobanus must have been reading Antonio Urceo, *In hoc Codri volumine haec continentur: Orationes seu sermones ut ipse appellabat, epistolae, silvae, satyrae, eglogae, epigrammata* (Bologna, 1502). For at *Ama.* 22.1–23.1 he closely follows two passages in Urceo's "Sermo quartus, utrum ducenda sit uxor." At sig. H1ᵛ Urceo writes: "Sane viros castos, virgines qui nunquam Venereis rebus operam dederunt, videmus esse formosos, virides, odorem quendam suavem, qualis in pueris esse solet antequam sint hirquitalli, spirantes, contra viros libidinosos deformes cito fieri et senes et odore hircino, qualem quondam Lemnii viri dicuntur habuisse fetentes. Quare recte illa de innocentibus pueris cantata sunt: 'Hi sunt qui cum mulieribus non sunt coinquinati, virgines enim sunt,' et quae sequuntur. Quare allegorizantes merito Chimaeram finxerunt, quoniam libidinosus iuvenis tanquam leo furens non parcit matri, non parcit sororibus et tanquam capra humorem quendam fetidum sudat, et post factam a conscientia sceleris tanquam a draconis cauda verberatur." And at sig. H6ᵛ Urceo adds: "Germani, ut Caesar in Commentariis memoriae mandavit, intra annum vigesimum feminae noticiam habuisse in turpissimis habebant rebus. Nostri pueri non dico intra vigesimum annum sed intra decimum sciunt turpia, dicunt turpia, faciunt turpia."

The pungent phrase "venenosus Amor" at *Ama.* 36.4 derives from Mant. *c. Am.*, fol. 177ʳ: "Longa venenosus tempora vivit amor."

At *Buc.* 2.36–40 Eobanus appears to have remembered "Sermo primus" in the above-mentioned work by Antonio Urceo, sig. A5ᵛ–A6ʳ. There Urceo describes the expensive tastes of fashionable women: "haec segmentis, illa corallis . . . onerata conspicabilis est. . . . Emantur smaragdi, . . . iaspides, . . . dactylothecae."

ENCOMIUM NUPTIALE

DIVO SIGISMUNDO,

REGI POLONIAE

A NUPTIAL ENCOMIUM

FOR THE GODLIKE SIGISMUND,

KING OF POLAND

Encomiū Nuptiale

diuo Sigismūdo Regi Po
loniae Scriptū. Anno
Christiani calculi
M.D.XII.
Magistri Eobani Vessi
diligentia.

Ad Librum.

Scripte liber gelida:gelida placiture sub arcto
Non poteras titulo candidiore legi
Si tamen z celebri de miserit Istula Rheno
Ista:sed ex nostro pectore verba refer
Parte mei:nulla gp par sum fratribus:haec est
Causa:fere nullo tempore scriptus eram.

3

Title page of *Encomium nuptiale*
Cracow: Johann Haller, 1512
Ratsschulbibliothek, Zwickau

ENCOMIUM NUPTIALE

Introduction

In October of 1509 the now twenty-one-year-old Eobanus Hessus saw himself forced to break the pledge required of all newly-minted MAs at Erfurt to continue teaching at the university for two years after graduation. Cutting short his *biennium* after just half a year, he turned his back on Erfurt and made his way to Leipzig. Many years later he explained to Joachim Camerarius that he had acted "not so much . . . upon careful reflection as upon impulse."[1]

Certainly he left in a great hurry, without saying good-bye to his old friend and mentor Ludwig Christiani. A month or two later, however, he made amends in a rueful verse letter, eventually published as *Sylv.* 3.4. Departing with a few comrades on a cold, blustery day, he recalls, he had looked back at the town through a mist of tears, just as Ovid had done when forced to leave Rome for exile in Tomis. For even though Erfurt had proved a kind mother to him during his student years, that ungrateful city, he laments, failed in the end to provide for her adopted son. On the fourth morning after setting out he had finally arrived in the Mark of Meissen. Now it is late autumn. Soon he will be leaving again, though he cannot yet tell exactly when. He has accepted a position at court. Dressed in the courtier's scarlet cloak, he has learned to speak in polished phrases and to bend the knee. Still, he concludes, here at least the Muses are loved and revered.

From this poetic account we gather that our humanist had become so disheartened by the conditions at Erfurt that he felt morally justified in breaking his commitment to teach for the required *biennium*. The town was indeed in dire straits. In May 1509 the city council had finally admitted that Erfurt was hopelessly mired in debt.[2] Blaming the disaster on the plutocrats who dominated the government, the citizens revolted and took control. Riots and unrest continued to flare up throughout the summer. At the university, morale plummeted. Eobanus himself had already vented his frustration in the fourth eclogue of his *Bucolicon* (1509). By the early autumn, as magisters and students were increasingly defecting to more hospitable climes, he could see no point to staying any longer. Learning that several friends of his were setting out for Leipzig, he decided on the spur of the

---

[1]Camerarius, *Nar.* 7.4. Cf. Eob. *Sylv. duae* 1.188, referring to his spur-of-the-moment decision to leave Erfurt: "Alas, how impetuously did my vessel set sail!"

[2]On the so-called "Mad Year" in Erfurt's history see Theodor Neubauer, *Das tolle Jahr von Erfurt*, ed. Martin Waehler (Weimar, 1948); R. W. Scribner, "Civic Unity and the Reformation in Erfurt," *Past and Present* 66 (1975), 30–38.

moment to join them. And why not? Even if Ulrich von Hutten was no longer at Leipzig, he would still be able to meet such humanists as Johannes Rhagius Aesticampianus and Veit Werler and to put out feelers for a lectureship at the university. But when no position materialized there, Eobanus signed on as chief secretary to Job von Dobeneck, Bishop of Pomesania, who was then attending the Grand Master of the Teutonic Order, Frederick of Saxony, at the latter's residence in nearby Rochlitz.[3] The man who introduced Eobanus to the bishop may well have been Sebastian Myricius of Königsberg, who had close contacts with the Order.[4]

Before the year was out Eobanus made his way north to the episcopal residence at Riesenburg in Prussia (now Prabuty, Poland), possibly together with Myricius. The bishop himself had to stay in Saxony for another year. Eobanus would continue to serve him as chancellor and private secretary until April 1513, constantly traveling on diplomatic missions in Prussia, Livonia, Poland, and Germany. It is not known if he was present at the Congress of Posen in July 1510, though he does allude to preparations for it in a letter to Ludwig Platz of February 18. He certainly attended the Congress of Thorn in December 1511. By early January of 1512 he must have been in Kulmbach, where the bishop reported on that congress to Grand Master Albert. He spent February in Cracow. The next month he was in Leipzig, and by Easter he was back in Riesenburg. He was expecting to return to Cracow in June, for (as he confided to his friend Georg Spalatin) he had a role to play at the upcoming diet there (Mutian. *Ep.*, 2:368). However, this diet had to be postponed until November and was then held in Piotrków. There Eobanus addressed King Sigismund of Poland in a long elegy defending the rights of the Teutonic Order (*Sylv.* 1.1). It was not the first time he had addressed himself to the king. At Sigismund's wedding in early February that same year Eobanus had personally presented him with a *Nuptial Encomium*. He told the king that he had composed the epithalamium, not "in the heat of the moment" as Statius had done for Stella and Violentilla, but rather at the command of his lord, Bishop Job von Dobeneck.

The Wedding

Sigismund I (1467–1548) was the youngest son of Casimir IV and Elizabeth of Habsburg. After the death of his brother King Alexander on 19 August 1506 Sigismund was acclaimed Grand Duke of Lithuania in October and crowned king in January 1507. The early years of his reign were troubled by constant frontier wars with Muscovy, a war with Moldavia in 1509, and Turkish invasions in 1510 and 1512. At the demand of the Polish Diet, Sigismund had agreed in 1509 to take a wife, but then put off the matter until a time of peace. In March 1511 negotiations began for the hand of Barbara Zápolyai of Hungary (1495–1515),

---

[3] For Job von Dobeneck see 1:25, n. 22.
[4] For Myricius see p. 71 below (n. 1 at *Sylv. duae*, liminary poem).

the daughter of Prince Stephen Zápolyai (d. 1499). The marriage contract was signed on December 2.

Accompanied by her mother Hedwig of Teschen, her brother John (the future King of Hungary), her great-uncle Duke Casimir of Teschen, and a retinue of 800 horsemen, the bride-to-be arrived at an estate two miles outside of Cracow on Thursday, February 5. The next morning Sigismund, escorted by his invited guests, orators, legates, and his sister Elizabeth, among others, went out in a long cavalcade to meet her. Because of the intense cold and deep snow, the king himself rode in the royal coach and then awaited his bride in a great tent. Some time later Barbara stepped out of the coach that had been given to her by King Vladislav II of Hungary and walked on the red carpet into the tent. After the Archbishop of Gnesen, Jan Łaski, had greeted her in Polish and the papal legate Giovanni Stafileo had spoken in Latin to wish her a happy married life, the king invited the future queen into his carriage, and the whole party returned to Cracow. Here the university faculty, the city council, and the people all cheered her arrival. As daylight waned, Barbara came to Wawel Cathedral. In a solemn ceremony she was welcomed by the Bishop of Przemyśl, Matthias Drzewicki. The wedding and coronation took place in the cathedral church on the following Sunday, February 8. Jan Łaski officiated; Giovanni Stafileo delivered the sermon. The ceremonies were followed by receptions, dances, tournaments, and all manner of popular amusements.[5]

The Encomium nuptiale *and its Aftermath*

No grand wedding in the Renaissance could be complete without poems written especially for the occasion.[6] King Sigismund's, indeed, was graced with no fewer than five epithalamia that were personally offered to the king at a formal ceremony, no doubt in deluxe presentation manuscripts.[7] Besides Eobanus' own contribution, which was printed at Cracow on February 29, we can mention:

> 1. Johannes Dantiscus (Jan Dantyszek), *Epithalamium in nuptiis inclyti Sigismundi regis Poloniae invictissimi ac illustrissimae principis Barbarae filiae praeclari quondam Stephani comitis perpetui Czepusiensis et regni Ungariae Palatini* (Cracow: Johann Haller,

---

[5]See Jodocus Ludovicus Decius, *De Sigismundi regis temporibus liber 1521*, ed. Wiktor Czermak (Cracow, 1901), 50–59; and *Acta Tomiciana*, vol. 2, ed. W. Ketrzynski (Poznań, 1852), 1–40.

[6]On the genre see: Virginia Tufte, *The Poetry of Marriage: The Epithalamium in Europe and its Development in England* (Los Angeles, 1970); Jozef IJsewijn and Dirk Sacré, *Companion to Neo-Latin Studies*, vol. 2 (Louvain, 1998), 100–02; Sabine Horstmann, *Das Epithalamium in der lateinischen Literatur der Spätantike*, Beiträge zur Altertumskunde 197 (Munich, 2004). Eobanus himself was to write two more epithalamia later in his career: *Venus triumphans, ad Ioachimum Cam. Qu. . . . In nuptiis Ioachimi Cam. epithalamion seu ludus Musarum* (Nuremberg, 1527) and *Epithalamion seu ludus gratulatorius in nuptiis et receptione insigniorum Doctoratus Iurium humanissimi et eruditissimi viri, D. Iusti Studaei* (Frankfurt am Main, 1539).

[7]Cf. *Sylv.* 1.1.21–34.

12 February 1512), ed. W. Ketrzynski in *Acta Tomiciana*, vol. 2
(Poznań, 1852), 30–38, and Stanisław Skimina in *Ioannis Dantisci
poetae laureati carmina* (Cracow, 1950), 41–58

2. Andreas Cricius (Andrzej Krzycki), *In augustissimum
Sigismundi regis Poloniae et reginae Barbarae connubium . . . carmen*
(Cracow: Johann Haller, 18 February 1512), ed. W. Ketrzynski in
Acta Tomiciana, vol. 2 (Poznań, 1852), 21–27, and by Kazimierz
Morawski in *Andreae Cricii carmina* (Cracow, 1888), 20–28

3. Paulus Crosnensis (Paweł z Krosna), *Epithalamion, hoc est
carmen connubiale in nuptias illustrissimi ac invictissimi principis et
domini, domini Sigismundi regis Poloniae, nobilissimaeque ac
pudicissimae Barbarae filiae inclyti et magnifici domini Stephani
Palatini Pannoniae Cepusiique comitis perpetui* (Cracow: Florian
Ungler, 1 March 1512), ed. Maria Cytowska in *Pauli Crosnensis
Rutheni carmina* (Warsaw, 1962), 151–67

4. Johann Lohmüller of Danzig, *Epithalamion . . . in nuptias
Divi Sigismundi . . . Poloniae regis necnon . . . reginae Barbarae.*
Paper ms., sixteenth century, 96 leaves, 4°. See August Bertling,
Katalog der Danziger Stadtbibliothek, vol. 1 (Danzig, 1892), 312–13,
no. 530. Though personally prepared for publication, with a limi-
nary epigram by Johannes Dantiscus to the reader and an autograph
letter by Lohmüller to his patron, the Danzig councilman Matz
Lange, this poem never appeared in print.[8]

Unlike his Polish counterparts, who had evidently come to the wedding with
their epithalamia in hand and (with the exception of the MA candidate
Lohmüller) had arranged to have them printed shortly afterwards, Eobanus did
not start writing his nuptial encomium until after the ceremony. As he told the
king in the dedicatory letter, dated February 17, the composition had taken him
all of four days.

Even before the work was completed, its introductory lines stirred up controversy. For at the start of the poem Eobanus proclaims that he, as a Christian poet
writing for a Christian king, rejects the inspiration of Phoebus and the Muses and
invokes Christ instead. The reaction to this invocation was swift and vehement.
Almost immediately an unnamed poet at Cracow got wind of the opening verses
and ridiculed them in an epigram that called on Apollo to flay this "second

---

[8]Johann Lohmüller (Lomolner, Lomoller) was born at Danzig around 1490. Very little is known
about his early life. After studying in Cracow, he became chancellor of the Bishop of Ösel in 1515. In
1517 he entered the service of the Archbishop of Riga, Jasper Linde. Appointed municipal scribe of
Riga in 1520, he was named syndic in 1532. He died sometime before 1560. See Hans Quednau,
"Johannes Lohmüller, Stadtsyndikus von Riga, ein Träger deutscher Reformation in Nordosteuropa,"
Archiv für Reformationsgeschichte 36 (1939), 51–67, 253–69. See also the introduction to *Sylvae duae*,
n. 8, p. 47 below. I am grateful to Georg N. Knauer for introducing me to Lohmüller. According to a
private communication from Tomasz Ososinski, the Danzig ms. containing Lohmüller's *Epithalamion*
was lost during World War II.

Marsyas." Eobanus defended himself in a mocking elegy of his own, preserved in the *Sylvarum libri* of 1535/39 as *Sylv.* 1.10. Hotly challenging his anonymous rival to a poetic competition, he told him "*You* will carry Apollo's tripods, *I* the cross of Christ." So incensed was Eobanus, in fact, that he alludes to the disparagement several times in the *Encomium nuptiale* itself — not only in the dedicatory letter, but also at the end of the poem (ll. 358–65) and in a postscript.

The attack rankled in his mind for many years to come. He brings it up in the dedicatory letter to the *Heroidum Christianarum epistolae* (ded. 10.1–5), addressed to Bishop Job von Dobeneck. And in his *In poetam Sarmatam* — an invective against an anonymous Polish poet who had taunted the Germans for retreating from Danzig in November 1520 — he again recalls the incident. Identifying this unnamed poet with his old Cracow antagonist, Eobanus addresses him as follows in 1523:

> As much as you might have wanted to, you weren't able to hide from me: I've known your atrociously bad muse for a long time already. You sense that yourself, I'm sure! You conceded defeat once before, when you were struck by these thunderbolts of mine.
>
> If only you weren't so stubborn in refusing to try to please those who ought to have been spared this abomination! Then I'd have less to complain about you, and your loyal friendship to me might still exist as it once did. Scoundrel! Born of German parents, you now presume to set the Poles above your own people in war. If you had left it at that, however, I could have forgiven you. As it is, your impudent muse spouts nothing but taunts.[9]

What are we to make of that tempest-in-a-teacup that took place at Cracow in mid-February 1512? And who was the anonymous rival who, in Eobanus' telling, first stirred it up?

Although he consistently portrayed himself as the victim of a scurrilous attack, Eobanus can hardly have been as innocent as he made himself out to be. In truth, he doth protest too much. The poem's opening verses seem just a little too sanctimonious for an epithalamium, just a little too ostentatiously pious for a poet who, good Christian though he was, could scarcely write a verse without some allusion to the myths of antiquity.[10] And indeed, no sooner has he rejected

---

[9]*Sarmat.* 15–26. Eobanus last alludes to the controversy in *Calum.* 9–10, published in 1538 and again in 1539: "Pinximus hanc [*sc.* Calumniam] olim dum nos populosa teneret / Subdita Sarmaticis Prussia sideribus."

[10]In *Laud.* 13–14 and *Buc.* 11.14–22, Eobanus also calls on Christ and the heavenly Muses, but only via their mythical counterparts Phoebus and the Pierides. In *De laudibus* the allusion to Christ is so discreet that one has to read the passage twice to catch the meaning: "Phoebus, you who hold sway over the heights of heaven." In the *Bucolicon* passage the Christian invocation appropriately introduces a rustic paean to the Virgin Mary: "Put on a last show, Pierian Maidens — not those heathen deities who are supposed to have defeated nine magpies in a singing match, but you, celestial souls, who breathe divine inspiration on us from on high, you Muses of the holy bards" (*Buc.* 11.16–19). It is worth noting that Eobanus' later epithalamia (1527, 1538) introduce not only Apollo and the Muses, but also a whole panoply of pagan gods and goddesses, including Venus, Hymen, and Cupid.

Phoebus and the Muses in favor of Christ than he once more speaks of the "Latin Muses" and "Helicon's fountains" that helped him cool the ardor brought on by "Cupid's arrow." Towards the end of the poem (ll. 360–61) he even declares that it was Phoebus who inspired him to counterattack the Polish rival in elegiac rather than heroic verse: "Phoebus did not move me then to write in an exalted strain." Why then did Eobanus flaunt his Christianity at the very start of his nuptial encomium?

To answer this question we must look at the poems written by Eobanus' Polish colleagues — in particular the priest Andreas Cricius (1482–1537), chancellor of the cathedral chapter of Posen and soon-to-be chancellor to the new queen. Cricius opens his epithalamium by calling on Phoebus to inspire the poet, bring the Muses to him, and wash his breast with Helicon's water:

> Phoebe decus vatum, pulcherrime Phoebe deorum,
> Conspiciende coma plectroque insignis et arcu,
> Huc ades et numeros tecum turbamque novenam
> Affer et Aoniis mea pectora prolue lymphis. . . .

> Phoebus, glory of poets, Phoebus, most beautiful of the gods, conspicuous by your locks and recognizable by your plectrum and bow, come hither and bring with you the ninefold choir and drench my breast with Aonian water. . . .

These motifs, of course, are precisely the ones that Eobanus rejects at the start of his own epithalamium. The parallel can hardly be accidental. Eobanus must have known Cricius' wedding poem well before he started writing his own. Most probably he heard it recited at one of the gala events that accompanied the royal nuptials.[11] So even as his rival's contribution was being printed (it was published on February 18) Eobanus decided on a different, more Christian tack to set himself off from the Polish cleric.

If this analysis is correct, Eobanus' opening lines were motivated less by religious fervor, as he would later claim, than by the spirit of rivalry. As it happened, however, the holier-than-thou invocation also struck a blow at the other two Poles. The epithalamium by Paulus Crosnensis opens with a long parade of ancient deities, led by Apollo and the Muses, all of whom have assembled for the royal

---

[11]Cricius, who was a member of the Polish delegation that brought Barbara to Poland, had written the epithalamium (161 hexameters) in advance of the wedding. After a lengthy invocation, followed by a second invocation to the Muse Calliope, Cricius lauds Bishop Jan Lubrański and the other two Polish representatives who voyaged to Hungary in January 1512 to conduct the bride to Cracow. At this point the poet feels sufficiently inspired by the Muse to praise the bride and to declare her fortunate to have obtained so great a husband. The second half of the poem offers Barbara a foretaste of the glories of Cracow and Poland and, indeed, of the king himself. The poem ends with an epilogue calling on the king to embrace his bride and beget a young Sigismund who will take after his father in looks and character and eventually succeed him to the throne. The nuptial refrain "O felix virgo tantum sortita maritum" ("O happy virgin to have obtained so marvelous a husband") reappears in the oration that Giovanni Stafileo delivered on the wedding day. See *Acta Tomiciana*, vol. 2., ed. W. Ketrzynski (Poznań, 1852), 21.

wedding. Like Statius in *Silv.* 1.2.47–49, the poet then invokes the Muse Erato to inspire him with a worthy song. Crosnensis' student, the royal secretary and notary Johannes Dantiscus, also calls on Erato. The Muse obliges him by recounting how Juno and Venus have agreed to lay aside their ancient enmity in order to unite the noblest of kings with the fairest of virgins. And so, as Amor pierces Sigismund's heart with a gold-tipped arrow, Venus sets Barbara's marrow on fire.

Thus, with his invocation to Christ and his showy rejection of Phoebus and the Muses, Eobanus had affronted the three most prominent humanists then at Cracow. As soon as the verses became known — our hard-drinking poet may well have bragged about them in his cups — one of the Poles circulated an epigram ridiculing the German's pretensions. Eobanus, as we have seen, replied at once in elegiac verses and challenged his anonymous opponent to a poetic duel, to be fought out before the scholars of Cracow.

But who was this unnamed rival?

That Eobanus complains about his antagonist and asserts his own innocence in both the dedicatory letter to King Sigismund as well as at the end of the epithalamium is an unmistakable indication that he knew the Pole to be a royal favorite who was sure to bring the matter up before the king. Furthermore, from Eobanus' *In poetam Sarmatam invectiva* of 1523 we learn that the two rivals had long since buried the hatchet and become the best of friends. When we remember finally that the "Sarmatian" poet was actually a German by birth — in fact, a native of Danzig[12] — the mystery is solved. Eobanus' antagonist in 1512 and again in 1523 was none other than Johannes Dantiscus (1485–1548), who would go on to become not only a celebrated humanist in his own right but also the Bishop of Chełmno (Kulm) and Warmia (Ermland). As Joachim Camerarius remarks in his biography of Eobanus Hessus:

> There was a certain companion of his, a native of Danzig, who was about the same age as Eobanus, in physical appearance not far infe-rior to him, but inferior nonetheless, and likewise his inferior in mental endowment, who called himself Dantiscanus after his home town. Between these men there arose a noble rivalry in talent and erudition, as each challenged the other to poetic works, initially at least, as I have heard, in a rather too hotheaded manner. But being a sensible man, Dantiscanus quickly realized how far Eobanus out-stripped him in this arena and frankly conceded Eobanus' superior-ity and entered upon another path to renown and preeminence.[13]

---

[12]See *Sarmat.* 55–56: "Hic, ubi castra locant Dantisci ad moenia clari / Et patriam cingunt obse-dione tuam." Forstreuter, 58–59, 135, argues that the anonymous rival was Andreas Cricius. But Cricius was a native of Silesia, not of Danzig, and never became friends with Eobanus.

[13]Camerarius, *Nar.* 10.1–3, where see n. 29 (1:30–33). The poem that Eobanus wrote in compe-tition with Johannes Dantiscus can be identified as *Victoria Christi ab inferis*, first published at Erfurt in 1517. See my article, "Eobanus Hessus in Krakau," in *Humanismus in Erfurt*, Akademie gemein-nütziger Wissenschaften zu Erfurt. Acta Academiae Scientiarum 7, Humanismusstudien 1, ed. Gerlinde Huber-Rebenich and Walther Ludwig (Rudolstadt and Jena, 2002), 161–76.

Printing History

Eobanus' epithalamium for King Sigismund was published in Cracow by Johann Haller on 29 February 1512:

A

[*Fraktur:*] Encomiũ Nuptiale | diuo Sigifmũdo Regi Po | loniae Scriptũ. Anno | Chriftiani calculi | M.D.XII. | Magiftri Eobani Heffi | diligentia. | Ad Librum. | [*3 distichs*]

Colophon:	Cracouiae Jmprimebat Johan	nes Haller Regnāte inclyto Si-	gifmũdo Rege Poloniae. P. P.	Pridie Kalēdas Martias Anni	M.D.XII.	[*printer's device*]
Collation:	4°: 6 unsigned leaves
Contents:	*1ʳ* title page; *1ᵛ* dedicatory letter; *2ʳ–6ʳ* epithalamium; *6ʳ* colophon; *6ᵛ* blank
Copytext:	Zwickau, Ratsschulbibliothek Call number: 24.7.24/3

The entire book is set in Fraktur. I have also consulted the copy in Cracow, Biblioteka Czartoryskich (call number: Cim. 170/II), and in Wrocław, Ossolineum Library (call number: XVI. Qu. 3712).[14] In the latter copy, folios 3 and 4 are bound in reverse order. Carl Krause knew the work by title only (*HEH*, 1:101, n. 1). It was first rediscovered in Zwickau by Otto Clemen. See his "Bibliographisches zu Helius Eobanus Hessus und Biblio-Biographisches zum Verfasser der 'Katzipori,'" *Archiv für Schreib- und Buchwesen* 3 (1929–30), 7.

---

[14]According to Karol J. T. Estreicher, *Bibliografia Polska*, section 3, vol. 5 (Cracow, 1898), 64, there was a further copy in the Krasinski Estate Library. Much of this collection was destroyed or removed to Germany in World War II; the rest was incorporated into the Polish National Library. Another copy, according to Estreicher, was located in the St. Petersburg Public Library.

ENCOMIUM NUPTIALE
DIVO SIGISMUNDO,
REGI POLONIAE,
scriptum anno Christiani calculi M.D.XII
Magistri Eobani Hessi
diligentia

AD LIBRUM

Scripte, liber, gelida, gelida placiture sub Arcto,
  Non poteras titulo candidiore legi.
Si tamen et celebri te miserit Istula Rheno,
  Ista, sed ex nostro pectore, verba refer:
5 "Parte meis nulla quod par sum fratribus, haec est
  Causa: fere nullo tempore scriptus eram."

A NUPTIAL ENCOMIUM
FOR THE GODLIKE SIGISMUND,
KING OF POLAND,
written in the year 1512 of the Christian era
through the attentiveness of
Magister Eobanus Hessus

TO THE BOOK

Written in the dead of winter, my book, you're bound to be a hit up here in the frozen North. Certainly you couldn't ask for a catchier title! Should the Vistula, however, send you also to the celebrated Rhine,[1] speak the following words for me, but straight from the heart: "If I'm in no way up to my brothers' standard,[2] it's because I was written in practically no time at all."

---

[1] If the printer at Cracow should send copies of the book to Germany.
[2] That is, up to the standard of Eobanus' earlier publications.

[13]

SERENISSIMO POTENTISSIMOQUE PRINCIPI SIGIS-MUNDO, REGI POLONIAE, MAGNO DUCI LITHU-ANIAE, RUSSIAE PRUSSIAEQUE DOMINO ET HE-REDI, DOMINO SUO CLEMENTISSIMO, EOBANUS HESSUS S. D.

Papinium Statium imitatus, Serenissime Rex Sigismunde, scripsi
encomium potius quam epithalamium nuptiarum tuarum. **2** Sed
bone Deus, quam precipitanter absolutum! **3** Quod non tam
"subito" mihi (ut ait ille) "calore" effluxerat quam mandato et
authoritate principis mei Iobi, Pomesaniensis presulis, viri profecto Tuae Celsitudinis et Gloriae studiosissimi amantissimique,
quasi invita (ut aiunt) Minerva deductum. **4** Qui etiamnum cum
tantam tamque pene incredibilem Tuae Maiestatis in peragendis
istis nuptiarum tuarum cerimoniis magnificentiam liberali-
tatemque animadvertisset, dignam putavit quae et litteratioribus
litteris commendaretur et poaetico stilo futurae posteritati transmissa aeternitati consecraretur. **5** Quod ubi per me fieri posse
confideret, hanc Serenitatis Tuae nuptiarum scribendarum provinciam ingeniolo meo ad id negocii iamdudum impense aspiranti
demandavit, quo et Tuae gloriosae Celsitudini de tam splendido
apparatu princeps ille gratificaretur aliisque quibusdam de sua
quantulacunque liberalitate supra modum gloriosis nauseam
iniiceret, ut indulgentissimae tuae magnificentiae testimonium
velut exemplar quoddam intuentes suae eos angustiae cum tua
amplitudine collatae poeniteat. **6** Et profecto quis te principum
magnificentior? Quis opibus splendidior? Quis cultu lautior? Quis
regno latior? Quis armis potentior? **7** Certe nemo, nisi ad uni-
versitatem quandam et collegium Christianae communitatis
respicias. **8** Qui vero in tuenda orthodoxae fidei religione te uno
sit occupatior exercitatiorque, quocunque respexeris, offendes
neminem. **9** Quid enim ensis ille tuus continua infidelium caede
rubens nisi pro pietate Christiana, nisi pro Catholica societate
tam servanda quam partim occupata redimenda invictum sese
flagrantemque et semper expeditum ostendit? **10** Testes sunt
(etsi nollent) toties fusi Tartari, toties strati totque gravissimis per
te antecessoresque tuos cladibus affecti Valachi, toties fugati
Moschi, toties profligata Turcarum perfidia.

11 Sed quae istuc Pallas in mentem misit tuarum virtutum
excellentiam vel titulotenus attingere? **12** Quibus pleniter exe-
quendis non hoc quod in me est ingenii (quod sentio quam sit

---

[1]Like his Renaissance contemporaries, Eobanus regarded Statius' "Epithalamium in Honor of
Stella and Violentilla" (*Silv.* 1.2) as the very model of a wedding poem.

TO HIS MOST SERENE AND PUISSANT HIGHNESS PRINCE SIGISMUND, KING OF POLAND, GRAND DUKE OF LITHUANIA, HEREDITARY LORD OF RUSSIA AND PRUSSIA, HIS MOST GRACIOUS LORD, EOBANUS HESSUS SENDS GREETINGS.

Following the lead of Papinius Statius,[1] Your Most Serene Highness King Sigismund, I have written more an encomium of your nuptials than an epithalamium. But good heavens, how hurriedly was it brought to completion! The poem did not (as that same author put it[2]) spring forth "in the heat of the moment" but rather at the behest and command of my lord Job, the Bishop of Pomesania, a man assuredly most devoted and attached to Your Glorious Highness.[3] As a matter of fact, it was composed (as they say) practically against the grain. For when my lord once again had occasion to observe the enormous and indeed almost unbelievable sumptuousness and munificence with which Your Majesty celebrated those wedding ceremonies of yours, he deemed them worthy of being committed to writing in an elegant work, handed down to future generations in a poetic style, and consecrated to eternity. Having assured himself that this was something I could carry out for him, he entrusted the task of describing Your Serenity's nuptials to my feeble talent. It was, in truth, a commission to which I had been eagerly aspiring for some time already, and with good reason: It would give my lord an opportunity to demonstrate his gratitude to Your Glorious Highness for such splendid pomp. To be sure, some other princes who unduly vaunt their paltry liberality are liable to get sick to their stomachs when they read the account of your most gracious munificence. Still, if they look at your comportment as a kind of exemplar, they may see fit to compare their tightfistedness with your own openhandedness and change their ways accordingly. For truly, who among the sovereigns is more magnificent than you? Who more dazzling in riches? Who more resplendent in adornments? Who more far-reaching in power? Who mightier in battle? Certainly no one, unless you look at Christian society, so to speak, in its totality and aggregate. Look all around you, indeed, and you will not find anyone more engaged and better versed in defending the religion of the orthodox faith than you. For why is that sword of yours constantly red with the blood of the infidels? Why does it show itself invincible and blazing and always at the ready, if not for the sake of Christian piety and the Catholic community, as much to save our religion from danger as to reconquer the territories we have lost? Witnesses, whether they like it or not, are the Tartars, whom you have routed so often, the Walachians, upon whom you and your predecessors have so often visited death and destruction, the Muscovites, whom you have so often put to flight, the Turks, whose perfidy you have so often overwhelmed.

But what Pallas put it into my head to touch on the excellence of your virtues, if only summarily? To rehearse them in detail, this talent that is within me (and I am only too keenly aware how puny it is) would be wholly inadequate.

---

[2]In the preface to bk. 1 of Statius' *Silvae*.
[3]On Bishop Job von Dobeneck see Camerarius, *Nar.* 7.5, with n. 22 (1:25).

exiguum), sed ne illustre quidem aliquod satis sufficere quis non videat? **13** Habes tamen, inclyte rex, et meae fidelitatis et principis mei in te pietatis et observantiae exemplum in encomio, in mediis nuptiarum tuarum celebritatibus a nobis non tam laboriose quam tumultuanter effuso magis quam excogitato. **14** Toto enim quadriduo libellum hunc, quasi foetum immaturum, excussimus. **15** Quem et Tuae Maiestati nuncupatum dedicatumque emittere totque Aristarchis non secus ac cupaedias quasdam exoticas obiicere decrevimus nihiloque sumus veriti, sperantes et libellum ipsum sub tui praeclarissimi nominis tutela a circumforaneis quibusdam criticis tutum fore nosque tuo patrocinio magis posse innocentiam nostram tueri. **16** Quem si placuisse Tuae Celsitudini cognovero, nec operae me nec impensae poenitebit. Vale.

17 Cracoviae, decimotertio Kalendas Martias, anno Christianorum M.D.XII.

But then, who does not see that even a man of genius could not do justice to them? Nevertheless, illustrious king, you possess in this encomium a concrete example both of my own faithfulness to you and of my prince's respect and deferential regard for you, even though the work admittedly came into being amid the celebrations occasioned by your nuptials and was hence not so much laboriously thought out by me as hastily thrown together. In fact, it took me all of four days to shake this little book down, like an unripe fruit. All the same, I have decided not only to publish it inscribed with your name and dedicated to Your Majesty, but also to throw it like some exotic tidbits before the many aristarchs of this world. Far from being afraid of them, I am confident that under the aegis of your most lustrous name the booklet will be safe from certain blustering critics[4] and that your patronage will let me defend my innocence even more effectively. Once I learn that the work has found favor with Your Highness, I shall regret neither my labor nor my expense. Farewell.

Cracow, February 17 in the year 1512 of the Christian era.

[4]Alluding to Johannes Dantiscus and his friends. The king's secretary had mocked Eobanus for starting his epithalamium by rejecting the inspiration of Apollo and the Muses and invoking Christ instead. See the introduction, pp. 6–9 above.

2^r

Regalis thalami pompam taedasque iugales
Coniugiique datam pro conditione coronam
Canturo non, Phoebe, veni, sed, numina forsan
Si licet in parvis rebus tua, Christe, vocare.

5   Et te iamdudum per mille poemata falsis
Praetulimus divis veterumque insignia, Musas,
Sprevimus et Clariis nunquam innatavimus undis.
Sed neque nunc Latias refero per pascua Musas
Ut quondam baculo pastor contentus agresti,

10   Pectora nec Paphia percussus arundine nitor
Concoeptum Aoniis extinguere fontibus ignem.
Nulla iterum hic molli canitur mihi Flavia versu.
Denique non scriptis diversa epigrammata sylvis
Qualia florenti tot milia lusimus aevo.

15   Quicquid id est quod prima aetas iuveniliter ausa est
Et quod adhuc teneris nondum desuescimus annis,
Interea paulatim abeat. Requiescite, nuper
Sudantes elegi, dum grandia plectra moventur,
Sed paucis heroa modis referentia magnum.

20   Terra Lycaoniam late protensa sub Arcton
Sarmaticae princeps operosa Polonia gentis
Immensum complexa iacet. Quam plurima circum
Bella sonant infesta cruci Christumque perosi
Christicolis populi insultant. Quos Tartarus inter

25   Epoto satiatus equo celeresque Valachi
Fortibus arma movent diverso Marte Polonis,
Qui toties victi nondum cognoscere pacem
Aut nolunt aut non possunt — tam barbara gens est.
Hinc Russi vicina tenent, hinc Teutona pubes.

30   Martia terra viris, Cerealibus inclyta pratis,
Dives inexhausti pecoris, generosa metallis,
Christiferae tutela crucis, quam sepe ruentem
Restituit stravitque armis victricibus hostem.

Hanc igitur Scythico praelatam viribus orbi,

35   Tempore iam Caesar quo Maximus Aemilianus
Fulminat in Venetos contra socia arma moventes

---

[5]Claros, a small coastal town in Ionia, was sacred to Apollo.

[6]These lines serve not only to establish Eobanus' credentials with his Polish audience but are also intended to build up to the poem's main theme. Cf. the proem to Vergil's *Aeneid* (*A.* 1.1a–1e). The works to which Eobanus refers are his *Bucolicon* (in ll. 8–9), *De amantium infoelicitate* (in ll. 10–11), his love poetry to "Flavia" (in l. 12), and his as yet unpublished *Sylvae* (in ll. 13–14). For Flavia, see *Ama.* B 2, with n. 43 (1:253). For the *Sylvae*, see the introduction to *Sylvae duae*, p. 55 below.

Inspire me as I sing the solemn procession of the royal wedding
and the nuptial torches and the crowning of the bride in
fulfillment of the marriage compact. Come hither — no, not you,
Phoebus, but you, Christ, if perhaps I may be allowed to invoke
your divine power in matters of small moment. For a long time
now and in countless poems I have exalted you above the false gods.
I have spurned those emblems of antiquity, the Muses, and have
never swum the waters of Claros.[5] Now, however, I am not leading
the Latin Muses back to the meadows, as I did some time ago when
I was a shepherd content with my rustic crook. [10] Nor, my breast
pierced with Cupid's arrow, do I struggle here to douse the fire of
passion in Helicon's fountains. Here I am not about to sing of
Flavia again in amatory verse. Finally, I am not writing a forest of
diverse epigrams like the ones I have been inditing by the
thousands, while still in the flower of life.[6] Whatever it is that my
adolescence in its youthful exuberance has ventured to produce and
that I, still in tender years, have not yet laid aside, let it take a bow
for the nonce and gradually leave center stage. Take a breather, you
elegiacs that were sweating so hard just now,[7] while I take up an
epic theme and, if only in a few measures, tell of a mighty hero.

[20] In the far North, beneath the Lycaonian Bear,[8] lies the
industrious and immense country of Poland, the chief home of the
Sarmatian people. Her borders resound with the tumult of many
wars, because nations hostile to the cross and with a deep hatred for
Christ never cease harassing her Christian population. Among
those who war against the valiant Poles in far-flung battles are the
Tartars, who gorge themselves on draughts of horses' blood, as well
as the fleet Walachians, who, defeated time after time, have thus
far shown themselves either unwilling or unable to understand
peace — so barbarous a people are they. On the one flank are the
Russians, on the other the Germans. [30] The country is renowned
for her warriors, celebrated for her grainfields, inexhaustibly rich in
livestock, abounding in metals. Protectress of the Christ-bearing
cross, she has repeatedly saved it from toppling as she overwhelmed the enemy with her conquering arms.

This kingdom, then, is now the strongest power in the
Scythian East. And even as Emperor Maximus Aemilian[9] hurls his
thunderbolts at the Venetians, who with their allies are attacking

---

[7]Eobanus alludes to his *Heroidum Christianarum epistolae*, begun at Riesenburg in 1510 and
published at Leipzig in 1514.

[8]The constellation Great Bear is called "Lycaonian" because of its supposed connection to
Callisto, a daughter of the Arcadian king Lycaon. After Callisto became the mother of Arcas by Jupiter,
the jealous Juno changed her into a she-bear. Jupiter then placed her among the stars as Ursa Major.

[9]The humanists liked to call Emperor Maximilian by this flattering name in order to associate
him with two of Rome's greatest generals: Q. Fabius Maximus Cunctator, who outlasted Hannibal in
the Second Punic War, and P. Cornelius Scipio Africanus Aemilianus, the hero of the Third Punic War.

Rhomanas aquilas et fortis lilia Galli,
Sceptriger Augusta princeps in pace regebat:
Flore Sigismundus iuvenili in regna vocatus,
40   Maximus ingenio iuvenis, fortissimus armis,
Militiae nulli veterum virtute secundus,
Hannibal ingenio vincendi, Caesar in armis,
Ad facta expedienda celer Pompeius alter,
Consilio Fabius, frangendos Scipio in hostes,
45   Denique Alexander bellis utcunque regendis.
2ᵛ   Hiis aliae accedunt virtutes agmine facto
Continuo magnum stipantes ordine regem
Inque sacro admissae tandem omnes corde residunt.
Sicut apum redolenti errans examen in Hybla
50   Nunc hos, nunc illos florum scrutatur odores,
Pallentes violas et purpureos hyacinthos,
Atque ubi praeteriit fruticum tot milia, tandem
Invento stridens apiastri in flore resedit:
Non secus in tanti concordat pectore regis
55   Virtutum chorus heroidum. Sed cuncta molestum est
Colligere in numeros, quando gravitate Catonem,
Relligione Numam, generoso pectore Achillem,
Quando omnes veteres virtutibus omnibus aequat,
Quando omnes omni superat virtute coevos,
60   Naturae meritis plus quam regalibus auctus,
Formosus simul et sapiens. In principe rarum
Sit licet hoc, tamen hoc rarum se gaudet adeptum,
Nobilis ex atavis, de stirpe propaginis ortus
Caesareae, factis titulisque insignis avorum,
65   Quos memor ad superas evexit gloria sedes.
     Talis hic et tantus, cui nec desideret addi
Gratia quicquam hominis sibi convenientis ad unguem,
Talis hic et tantus, magnorum gloria regum,
Heres imperii defuncto fratre relictus,
70   In regnum (ut memini) iuvenili in flore vocatus,
Iam vir inaudaces aliquatenus exuit annos,
Regia iam celebs sine coniuge sceptra gerebat,
Maturusque aevo taedasque subire iugales
Dignior et regni laturam insignia prolem
75   Sufficere intereaque aliquos promittere reges.

75 promittere *scripsi*: praemittere **A**.

the Roman eagles and the fleurs-de-lis of the valiant French,[10] Poland enjoys Augustan peace under the rule of her sceptered prince Sigismund.[11] Called to the kingship while still in the flower of his youth, [40] he is a young man of brilliant intellect, a doughty hero in battle. Indeed, in military prowess he is second to none of the ancients, a Hannibal in his genius for conquest, a Caesar in tactics, another Pompey in the swift attainment of his objectives, a Fabius in counsel, a Scipio in crushing his enemies, and, to sum up, by all means an Alexander in the conduct of his campaigns. To these qualities he joins a multitude of other virtues. They throng around the great king in unbroken ranks, gain admission into his sacred heart, and at length take up residence there one and all. As a swarm of bees roams the redolent slopes of Hybla, [50] exploring now these, now those fragrant flowers, the pale violets and purple hyacinths, and passes over so many thousands of shrubs until it finally alights with whirring wings on the flowering balm it has found: just so the choir of heroic virtues congregates harmoniously within the breast of that eminent king. But to put everything into verse would be tiresome, inasmuch as he is a Cato in moral rectitude, a Numa in religious devotion, an Achilles in nobility of soul. Talent for talent he is a match for each and every one of the ancients. As for his contemporaries, he surpasses them all in every conceivable virtue. [60] Blessed by nature with more than kingly merits, he is at once handsome and wise. Though such perfection may be rare in a prince, he nevertheless rejoices that he has attained this rare perfection. He is, after all, noble by ancestry, descended from a family of imperial stock, and distinguished through the exploits and achievements of his forefathers, whom all-remembering glory has exalted to the skies.

This paragon, to whom Grace has granted such consummate charm that he leaves nothing to be desired, this paragon, this ornament of great kings, was left heir to the throne at his brother's death.[12] [70] He was called to the kingship, as I mentioned, while still in the flower of youth. Though already a man who, to some extent, had put his diffident years behind him, he remained a bachelor, holding the royal scepter without a spouse. Still, he was mature in years and truly deserved to be married, to beget offspring who would bear the insignia of the realm and, in the meantime, to hold

---

[10]In October 1511 Pope Julius II, Spain, Switzerland, and Venice formed the Holy League to drive the French out of Italy. The attacks on the French began the following January and lasted until June 1512. Maximilian was allied with King Louis XII of France, but signed an armistice with Venice on April 1.

[11]The peace that currently prevails under King Sigismund recalls the Pax Romana under Caesar Augustus.

[12]Alexander I (1461–1506), the third son of King Casimir IV, became Grand Duke of Lithuania in 1492 and King of Poland in 1501. He died on 19 August 1506.

Ergo ubi consilio procerum sententia stabat
Quaerere consortem thalami sociamque coronae
Dignam cui tanto liceat convivere regi,
Legitimo esse parem genialis foedere lecti,
80   Tantaque non rudibus circumdare colla lacertis
Quae reges, quae regna timent, quae Tartarus audax
Expertus metuit tot cladibus, altaque gentes
Ad Thanaim quaecunque colunt deserta nivalem.
    Illis digna tamen tandem est inventa per omnes
85   Saemideum quaesita nurus, dignissima certe
Regales ire in thalamos, regalibus uti
Deliciis, quam blanda Venus, quam Gratia ridens,
Quam facilis rectum Natura polivit ad unguem,
Quam Phrygia si forte Paris vidisset in Ida
90   Aurea non Veneri stupefactus poma dedisset,
Quam sibi nec Iuno nec Pallas glauca doleret
Praelatam — tantum formosior omnibus illa est,
Barbara, Pannonicis de regibus aedita, quamvis
Paulatim titulos abolevit longa vetustas,
95   Ut solet in reges etiam exercere superbum
Imperium omnigenum rerum mutabilis ordo.
Sola tamen titulos virtus et clara meretur
Nomina; de sola potior virtute paratur
Nobilitas quam nulla potest abolere vetustas.
100 Sic te, digna deas heroidas inter haberi,
Nobilis ex atavis regi transmisit habendam,
Nobilior virtute, parens, quem gloria coelo
Bellica sublimem tollit tituloque coronat
Egregio Stephanum, quo nomine dicta corona est.
105   Ergo ubi iam promissa dies foelicibus astris
Advenit qua nupta erat excipienda marito
Speratosque diu primum tactura lacertos,
Hic procerum collecta cohors, quae nuper ab omni
Confluxit parte insignem visura triumphum,
110 Conveniunt nuptamque parant deducere in urbem,
Regibus ut mos est. Ludum subeuntibus istum
Protinus exultant animis ingentibus, omnes
Clamantes Hymenaea. Sonant Hymenaea per urbem.
Fervet Hymen. Hymenaea sonant, Hymenaea frequentant,

3^r

98 potior *scripsi*: patior *A*.   **106** qua *scripsi*: quo *A*.

out the promise of a line of kings. Upon the advice of the diet,
therefore, it was decided to search for a consort to share the king's
bed and crown, a spouse who would be worthy of living with so
great a king, of being his equal by the legitimate bonds of matrimony, [80] and of flinging her graceful arms around the mighty
neck that kings, that kingdoms fear, that the audacious Tartars have
learned to dread from bitter experience in so many defeats — and
not just they, but everyone of the peoples that dwell in the high
steppes along the snowy Don.

After a search among all the daughters of the demigods,
however, she was discovered at last: a maiden worthy of him, certainly most worthy of entering the royal bedroom and enjoying
the delights of kingly love, a maiden whom charming Venus,
smiling Grace, and kindly Nature have polished to absolute perfection. Had Paris chanced to see her on Phrygian Ida, [90] he
would have been too awestruck to award the golden apple to
Venus.[13] Neither Juno nor brighteyed Pallas would have felt
pained to see her preferred to themselves — so much more beautiful is she than all others, Barbara, descended from Hungarian
kings, albeit the passing ages have gradually erased those titles, as
if to demonstrate that omnipresent Changeability is accustomed
to wield her proud power also over kings. But only virtue
deserves titles and lustrous fame; only virtue can bestow that
higher nobility that no length of time can efface. [100] And so it
was that you, worthy of being reckoned among the goddess-
heroines, were given in marriage to the king by your father,
himself noble by his ancient lineage, more noble by his virtue,
a man whom martial glory exalts to the stars and crowns with a
splendid title and whose very name *Stephen* means "crown."[14]

Accordingly, when the promised day has arrived under propitious stars, the day when the bride is to be welcomed by her
husband and she will first touch the arms that she has looked forward to so long, a great host of nobles gathers here. Having recently
flocked together from all sides to witness the magnificent procession, [110] they assemble and prepare to conduct the bride into the
city, as is the custom with kings. Now that this spectacle is fast
approaching, their heroic hearts leap for joy. They all burst out in
wedding songs. Wedding songs resound throughout the city.
Nuptial hymns fill the air. They sing marriage songs; they chant

[13]Paris of Troy awarded a golden apple to Venus in a beauty contest with Juno and Pallas on
Mount Ida. The story is told, for example, in Ov. *Ep.* 16. Eobanus offers the same compliment to
another lady in *Buc.* B 2.40–42.

[14]The name *Stephen* comes from the Greek word for "crown." Stephen Zápolyai, elected Palatine
of Hungary in 1490, died in 1499. Eobanus thus errs in stating that it was Stephen who gave Barbara
in marriage to the king.

115 Qualiter umbrosis Phrygiae sub vallibus Idae
Intonuit celebratus Hymen Simoentis ad undam,
Cum senior magnum Protheus praedixit Achillem
Formosae Thetidi ruiturum maenia Troiae.
    Fit clamor pulsatque leves tuba ductilis auras,
120 Tergora tensa crepant. Concurritur undique ad arcem
Regalem. Lectas populo impediente cohortes,
Certatur quis nobilibus praestantior armis
Exeat et reliquis preciosius induat aurum.
Sicut ubi radiis nubes discussit et imbrem
125 Sol pater; agminibus fervent per compita densis
Formicae parvisque trahunt ingentia rostris
Grana, nec assiduo caedunt utcunque labori:
Sarmatica haud aliter consurgit in arma iuventus,
Gaudia, non luctum facientia. Qualibus aiunt
130 Troades abductam quondam excoepisse Lacaenam,
Cum fureret Phrygios fax incensura penates.
Iamque novis properata cohors fulgebat in armis,
Non qualem Rhomanus eques sub signa coegit,
Sed qualem claudant vix milia multa cohortem.
135 Qualis Dardanios exercitus ibat in hostes,
Magnanimum quoties Hector metuisset Achillem.
    Ergo eques insignes auro phaleratus habenas
Egreditur tecto et paulatim deserit arcem,
Non solus patrio spectandus honore Polonus,
140 Sed qui diverso nuper confluxit ab orbe
Regales spectator opes visurus, ut olim
Ludicra cum populo mollis spectacula Caesar
Aederet et strata miles gestiret harena.
Belliger ante alios, duro ferus ense, Polonus
145 Agmine progreditur longo, sublimis et auro,
Gemmifero sublimis equo, sublimis et ostro,
Qualis non Tyrias miretur purpura conchas,
Cui ruber antiquum murex concedat honorem.
Talis apud nullas est magnificentia gentes
150 Promptior in gemmis nusquam nec largior usus,
Gemmiferas quamvis Indus despumet harenas
Et vagus undanti Pactolus fluctuet auro.

3ᵛ (left margin, at line 135)

---

115 Idae *scripsi*: Ideae **A**.

marriage songs without end. Just so the nuptial hymns kept on resounding in the shady vales of Phrygian Ida, on the banks of the Simois River, after aged Proteus had prophesied to the lovely Thetis that mighty Achilles would overthrow the walls of Troy.[15]

Shouts are raised; the coiling trumpet assails the light breezes; [120] the stretched cowhides boom. From every quarter people rush to the royal castle. And as the crowd jostles the elite cohorts, the competition is on to see who rides forth in grander armor and who has donned more expensive gold than the others. As when Father Sun with his beams of light has scattered the clouds and the rain; at the crossroads the ants busily march in dense columns and drag huge grains with their tiny mandibles and, as best they can, keep at their assiduous work: just so the Polish youths rise up in arms — to bring joy, however, not grief. It was with arms like these, they say, [130] that the Trojans of old greeted the abducted woman of Sparta,[16] while the flame that would set their Phrygian homes ablaze was burning madly. And now the cohort is massing swiftly, aglint in brand-new armor, not the kind of cohort that the Roman cavalry used to collect under its standards,[17] but one so expanded as to comprise many thousands of horsemen. They resembled the army that did battle against the Trojan enemy, as often as Hector dreaded the greathearted Achilles.

These horsemen, then, richly caparisoned, their reins all studded with gold, exit the courtyard and gradually leave the castle behind — not just the Poles, impressive in their native finery, [140] but also the guests who only recently flocked here from all over the world to see the king's opulence for themselves, just as in bygone times when effeminate emperors put on entertainments for the people and gladiators fought in the arena. The warlike Poles, ferocious-looking with their cruel swords, ride at the head in a long procession. They look imposing in their gold, imposing on their bejeweled steeds, imposing also in their purple, a purple that does not marvel at the mollusks of Tyre, a purple to which the scarlet murex would concede her antique honor. Among no other people on earth will you find sumptuousness on such a large scale; [150] nowhere else will you see jewels put more readily or more lavishly to use, no matter how many gem-bearing sands the Indus may skim, no matter how much gold the winding Pactolus may carry

[15]The sea god Proteus prophesied to Thetis, chief of the Nereids, that she would someday bear a son who would surpass his father in heroism. After Peleus had gained her as his bride, she gave birth to Achilles. See Ov. *Met.* 11.221–23. Eobanus misremembers the locale of the wedding. Peleus and Thetis were married in Thessaly, not Troy.

[16]King Menelaus' wife Helen, who was carried off to Troy by Paris.

[17]The Roman *cohors* was one of the ten infantry units in a legion, each with between four hundred and six hundred men.

Venerat et gravibus cataphrattus Teuton in armis,
Precipue armipotens quos misit Slesia tellus,
155 Slesia, confini nimium vicina Polono,
Et quos laudato generosa Moravia Baccho.
Magnanimi venere duces non unus et alter,
Sed plures. Numerare piget nec forte necesse est.
Pannonico pugnax venit gravis Ungarus auro,
160 Regalem patriis nuptam comitatus ab oris.
Venit et Herciniae quondam bonus incola sylvae,
Teutonico doctus ritu pugnare Bohemus.
Oraque frigoribus rigidi squalentia Russi,
Sarmaticoque ruens pannosus ab aequore Livo
165 Venerat et Scythica canus nive. Venit et alti
Accola Bosphoreos, et qui vada frigida potat
Undosi Tanais, iuxta Maeotin et Hebrum,
Et quot preterea populos numerare molestum est.
      Et iam tempus erat, vernum nix alta decorem
170 Abstulit et Mariae celebrabant Februa mystae.
Iamque omnis portis exercitus ibat apertis,
Ordine quo ductor turmas eduxit Achivum
Aut aliquis magnae ruiturus moenia Troiae,
Cum subito ecce aderat tantum decus illud, amore
175 Digna tuo coniunx, te digna futura marito
Pulchra prole parens, quamvis tu dignior illa,
O et Sarmatici moderator maxime sceptri,
Rex, et Christicolae fidei sanctissime tutor.
Illa aderat nuribus merito praelata Polonis,
180 Barbara non vultu, sed nomine Barbara tantum,
Nobilium quam lecta manus stipantia circum
Agmina densabat longisque effulsit in armis,
Non secus ac nymphae quondam sub gurgite vasto
Nudam Cyrenem vel glaucam Cymodocaeam
185 Immenso circum famulantes agmine stipant,
Milia sive equitum formosa Semiramis inter
Oppressam impexo capiat Babilona capillo.
Quid memorem effusos in tot dispendia sumptus?
Quid gemmas, quid tot preciosa monilia dicam?
190 Quid loquar in multo radiantes pectore bullas?
Quos labor est numerare idem et contendere frustra,
Quid memorem auratos, memoranda insignia, currus?

4ʳ

---

[18]That is, men from the Khanate of Crimea. The Strait of Kerch (Cimmerian Bosphorus) connects the Black Sea and the Sea of Azov.

in its waves. The Germans had come too, clad in mail and heavy armor, particularly the ones sent by Silesia, mighty in war — Silesia, that shares a border with Poland — but also those sent by Moravia, teeming with excellent wines. Not a few noble-spirited dukes came, so many in fact that it would be irksome and probably unnecessary to enumerate them all. The combative Hungarians, laden with Pannonian gold, came [160] to accompany the royal bride from her native land. The inhabitants of the Hercynian Forest, the formerly loyal Bohemians who are expert at fighting in the German style, came there too. So did the hard-bitten Russians, their faces raw from the cold climate back home, as well as the tattered Livonians, hoary with Scythian snow, who had hurried here from the Baltic Sea. There also came men who live along the deep Strait of Kerch,[18] men who drink the frigid waters of the billowy Don, men who dwell by the Sea of Azov and the Hebrus River, and so many others besides that it would be tedious to list them.

It was now that time of year when deep snow has robbed the land of its vernal beauty [170] and the priests have celebrated the Purification of Mary.[19] Drawn up in formation, as if one or another Greek commander were leading his squadrons into the field to overthrow the walls of mighty Troy, the whole army was already passing through the wide-open gates, when suddenly, lo, there she was, that dazzling beauty, the bride worthy of your love, worthy of marrying you and becoming the mother of beautiful children — though you, O king, mightiest ruler of the Sarmatian realm and holiest protector of the Christian faith, are even worthier of her. There she was, the one you rightly preferred to all the young women of Poland, [180] a Barbara only in name, not in her features. Around her the chosen band of nobles crowded in serried ranks, resplendent in their long armor, just as in days of old the attendant nymphs beneath the boundless sea would cluster in a huge throng around the naked Cyrene or the bluegreen Cymodoce, or as thousands of horsemen massed round the beautiful Semiramis, her hair unkempt, as she was taking Babylon by storm.[20] Need I say how much money was poured into this occasion? Need I mention how many jewels, how many costly chains were to be seen? [190] Need I speak of the lockets that flashed on many a chest? Need I talk of the gilded carriages, emblazoned with memorable coats of arms? Any

---

[19]The wedding invitations specifically mention that the guests were to arrive in Cracow "for the feast of the Purification of the Blessed Virgin Mary" (February 2). See *Acta Tomiciana*, vol. 2, ed. W. Ketrzynski (Poznań, 1852), 5.

[20]Cyrene, mother of the mythical hero Aristaeus, was a Thessalian nymph. Cymodoce was one of the daughters of the sea god Nereus. Semiramis, the legendary queen of Babylon, was having her hair done when she heard that the city had revolted. Leaving half of her hair loose, she ran off to storm the city. It was not until the city was recaptured that she consented to finish her coiffure. See V. Max. 9.3, ext. 4.

Qualibus Andromache vecta est et adultera coniunx,
Connubium ut patriae Paris exitiale coegit.
195   Iam prope constiterant, curru cum regia virgo
Exit inaurato regem amplexura maritum,
Virgineas ornata comas, ornata lacertos.
Dii superi, quales vultus! Quam candida colla!
Qualis in ore rubor! Quae fax in lumine utroque?
200   Certe ea quae tanti possit succendere regis
Pectora et ardentes iaculare in viscera flammas.
Quam tener exiguo pulvis spirabat in ore!
O etiam quaerenda Iovi constanter olori
Oscula, vel si quis superum descendit in auro!
205   Denique talis erat, talem se laeta ferebat,
Qualis Athlantiaco Pallantias exit ab astro
Cum redit et rebus reddit lux alma colorem.
Nec minus innata rex maiestate verendus
Contra progreditur, molli quem lubrica lapsu
210   Esseda portabat plenoque advexit in auro.
Hic vero, postquam est congressum parte ab utraque,
Quam sit regali, quam pleno excoepta favore
Dicere non patitur presens angustia, nanque
Haec res est alicui graviter dicenda Maroni.
215   Nos humiles puerique sumus sine numine vates.
Ne tamen incoepto, properata Thalia, labori
Parce. Refer parvis ingentia facta Camaenis.
       Affuit ante omnes lingua facundus Ulysses
Quem sacra nuper presul Rhomanus ab urbe
220   Miserat. Illustrem venientem in regna puellam
Excipere et longam pro se mandare salutem
Ianitor aethereae iussit, pater optimus, aulae.
Post quem Pannonio presul de rege legatus
Cui celebris clarum dat Vratislavia nomen,
225   Commissam patriis nuptam comitatus ab oris.
4ᵛ   Tertius et merito sequeris, pater optime, nigra

---

²¹Andromache was the wife of the Trojan hero Hector. The "adulterous wife," of course, is Helen of Troy.

²²Jupiter visited Leda in the form of a swan: cf. *Her. Chr.* 1.150. The princess Danaë was locked away in a bronze tower, but the father of gods and men fell on her in a shower of gold: cf. Ov. *Met.* 4.611; Eob. *Her. Chr.* 1.149, 10.121–22. Eobanus' model in the present passage is Stat. *Silv.* 1.2.135–36.

attempt to enumerate them would be labor lost. It was in a carriage like these that Andromache once rode, as did that adulterous wife when Paris entered upon the marriage that would prove disastrous for his native city.[21]

When they had drawn close together and were standing still, the royal maiden stepped out of her gilded coach to embrace her bridegroom the king. Richly adorned were her virginal locks, richly adorned her arms. Gods above, what a beauteous face! What a marvelously white neck! What a blush on her cheeks! What is that spark in both her eyes? [200] Surely the spark that could set the breast of so mighty a king on fire and throw the ardent flames into his heart of hearts. What tender strife breathes on her tiny mouth! Ah, those kisses, which even Jupiter would steadfastly pursue as a swan or (if any of the gods ever did descend that way) in a shower of gold![22] In short, she looked as radiant and carried herself as joyfully as Aurora rising from the starry daughters of Atlas,[23] when quickening daylight returns and brings color back to the world. The king, inspiring no less awe with his inborn majesty, advanced from the opposite side. He had ridden in a carriage that glided on smooth-rolling wheels [210] and conveyed him in a profusion of gold. To describe here, however, with what truly regal and warmhearted favor he welcomed his bride after they had come together from each side, this the brevity of the present poem does not permit. Indeed, that is a theme worthy of some Vergil singing in lofty strains. I am only a youth, a humble poet, not divinely inspired. But that does not mean you may now hurry along, Thalia, and desist from the work you began. In a few verses recount the momentous events.

At the head of the whole company was the silvertongued Ulysses whom the Bishop of Rome had lately sent from the Holy City.[24] [220] The gatekeeper of the heavenly court, the best of fathers, had bidden him welcome the illustrious maiden at her arrival in the kingdom and wish her a long and happy life for him. Behind him came the prelate whom the King of Hungary had sent as his envoy and to whom the famed city of Breslau lends her glorious name.[25] The bride having been entrusted to his care, he had accompanied her from her native land. You, eminent father, followed in third place — and rightly so! — your white mantle

[24]The papal nuncio who greeted the bride and preached an elegant sermon at the wedding was Giovanni Stafileo (1472–1528), elected Bishop of Sebenico in 1512. Eobanus calls him a "silvertongued Ulysses" because that far-wandering hero was famed for his eloquence.

[25]Peter Beriszlo (Berislavus), Bishop of Veszprim in Hungary from 1513 to 1520. He came as the emissary of Vladislav II (ca. 1456–1516), King of Bohemia since 1471 and King of Hungary since 1490.

Pallia signatus cruce candida, Presul Iobe,
Inclyta cui celebres titulos Pomesania foecit,
Teutonicae ductor fortissime militiai.
230 Stipabat sponsum, venerabilis infula, regem
Pontificum chorus, ante alios qui primus habetur
Per regnum, vir consilio maturus et annis,
Presul Iohannes, quo principe Gnisna superba est,
Aurea cui puppis signum est. Quem nulla laborum
235 Curarumve unquam moles ita fregit ut esset
Tardus ad utilibus firmanda negocia rebus
Publica, precipue si quid pro nomine Christi
Servando fuit audendum. Se prebet in omnes
Invictum casus. Qualem Thoronia nuper
240 Christicola vidit pro relligione molestum.
     Qui simul accepta dictaque salute vicissim
Sic fatur vultusque in se convertit et ora
Plaudentis populi et verbis Hymenaea vocantis:
     "Barbara, virginei flos inviolate pudoris,
245 Pannonicas formosa nurus interque Polonas,
Magnanimo regi quae nubere digna reperta es,
Nobilis ingentem regni latura coronam,
Te sibi promissam comitem sociamque futuram
Excipit et gaudet venisse faventibus astris
250 Rex, populis pietate pater, qui te sibi solam
Delegit, cui sola places, cui sola futura es.
Ingredere et fausto pede rura Polonica tange.
Ingredere adventuque tuo data sceptra secunda.
Ingredere et magno foelix coniungere regi.
255 Iam tibi foelicem spondet Venus aurea cursum.
Fervet Hymen. Hymenaea sonant, Hymenaea frequentant
Sexus uterque tibi et vulgi promiscuus ordo.
Missa bono auspicio gelidam, regina, sub Arcton,
Et nos et tua regna adeas pede dextra secundo."
260   Sic breviter fatus tacuit. Cui regia virgo,
Quantum virgineus potuit pudor, annuit ultro.
     Te quoque regali Ruthena Leopolis urbi

---

[26]The white mantle and black cross of the Teutonic Order.
[27]Jan Łaski (1455/56–1531) served as royal grand chancellor of Poland from 1503 to 1510.
Thereafter he was Archbishop of Gnesen and primate of the Polish Church. In December 1511 he

blazoned with the black cross,[26] O Bishop Job, to whom renowned Pomesania has granted your distinguished title, powerful Commander of the Teutonic Order. [230] Round about the royal bridegroom thronged a venerable band of mitered bishops. They were led by their primate Jan, a man mature in judgment and years, the archbishop of whom Gnesen is proud.[27] His device is a golden ship. The burden of work and cares never wearies him to the extent that he is slow to promote the affairs of state with purposeful action, particularly if something has to be ventured to preserve the name of Christ from danger. He always rises to the occasion. Just recently the city of Thorn [240] saw for herself how formidable he can be when he defends the Christian religion.

After they had exchanged greetings, he drew the faces and eyes of the applauding, cheering people toward himself and spoke as follows:

"Barbara, inviolate flower of maidenly honor, beauteous among the young women of Hungary and Poland, you who have been found worthy of marrying the greathearted king and are about to wear the lofty crown of his celebrated realm: the king greets you as his betrothed companion and future consort. He rejoices that you have arrived safely under favoring stars. [250] A devoted father to his people, he has chosen you alone to be his bride. You are the only one he loves; you will always be the only one in his heart. We bid you welcome and offer you our best wishes as you step on Polish soil. We bid you welcome and hope that your coming will be a blessing to the kingdom that is being given to you. We bid you welcome and pray that your marriage to the mighty king will be a happy one indeed. Golden Venus is already vouchsafing you Godspeed. Everyone is bursting out in wedding songs. Wedding songs resound everywhere. Nuptial hymns fill the air, as people of both sexes and all ranks rejoice with you. Sent under happy auspices to us here in the icy North, O queen, look on us with favor and enter upon your realms with propitious step!"

[260] After this brief speech he fell silent. The princess, as far as maidenly modesty allowed, graciously nodded her assent to him.

Among the mitered heads in attendance was also the archbishop whom Lemberg in Ruthenia had sent to the royal city.[28] The

---

headed the Polish delegation at the Congress of Thorn (see ll. 239–40 below); Bishop Job von Dobeneck represented the Teutonic Order. As the bishop's secretary, Eobanus was present at those meetings. Laski's device was a golden ship, adorned at the prow and stern with a lion's head and bearing a tower instead of a mast and sail: cf. Cricius, *Carm.* 4.59.1–2, 4.60.1–2.

[28]Bernard Wilczek, Archbishop of Lemberg from 1505 to 1540.

Metrarcha misit caput insignite tiara.
Sed neque Sarmaticae mihi cancellarius aulae
265 Praetereundus erat, magna sed voce Mathias
Cantandus, qui nunc Premislia templa gubernat,
Quemque patrem tonsae Cracovia docta coronae
Praetulit et sacris rarum decus addidit aris,
Preterea Erasmus Plocensis episcopus, omni
270 Laude vir insignis, quantum se Stoica vulgo
Laudari virtus patitur, tuque optime doctos
Pontifices inter Ludbranti gloria, quem nunc
Dives honorata Posnania sede tuetur,
Et cui clara subest Prutheno Varmia Lucae.
275   Musa, etiam meritos presenti defer honores
Et qui preterea plures insigne ferebant
Pontificale viri. Quos et numerare volebam,
Ni se contemni Brevitas causata fuisset
Temporaque in longum non sufficientia carmen
280 Claudere in occiduas properaret lucifer undas.
Ergo ubi dicta salus utrimque et reddita, iamque
Duxit anhelantes prono temone iugales
Vesper in Oceanum coelumque nigrescere coepit,
Audisses sonitu terreri summa tubarum
285 Sydera percussamque melos resonare sub auram.
Fit reditus stratoque iterum procaeditur ostro
Et patulas iterum longo subit ordine portas
Iam duplicata acies. Ibi primum Hymenaeus ad arcem
Regalem sonat exultans. Tum regia luxu
290 Magnifico domus instruitur pictisque recumbunt
Nobilium pars multa thoris. Pars ordine mensas
Instruit apponuntque epulas atque ordine longo
Plena coronato libant carchesia Baccho.
Illic multifori non unus arundine Triton,
295 Non unus Misenus erat, sufflare monaulon
Doctus et argutam pleno ore lacessere buxum.
Non etiam unus erat cythara spectandus Iopas,
Non unus faciles chordas tangebat Arion.
Multus ibi aequabat multos Amphionas Orpheus.
300 Denique Syrenum non vox erat una, sed omnes.
Auditis quibus ipse ratem reflectat Ulysses.

chancellor of the Polish court, Matthias, who now directs the cathedral of Przemyśl, ought not to be passed over either in my poem.[29]
Indeed, he deserves to be extolled in a loud voice, as does the father
whom scholarly Cracow has elevated to her bishopric and who lends
rare distinction to her sacred altars.[30] I should also mention Erazm,
the Bishop of Plock,[31] [270] a man who is praiseworthy in every
virtue (to the extent that Stoic virtue allows itself to be praised by the
masses), you too, excellent Lubrański, an ornament among learned
bishops, whom wealthy Posen now maintains on her seat of honor,[32]
and you, Lukas of Prussia, to whom illustrious Warmia is subject.[33]

Muse, do spare us the other worthies, the many other men
who wear the bishop's miter. I would have enumerated them
too, had not Brevity objected to being snubbed and had not
the sun, cutting off the time for a lengthy poem, [280] been
hastening toward the western waves.

Well then, after they had exchanged greetings and the evening
star was already leading the sun's panting team headlong into the
ocean and the sky was beginning to blacken, you could hear trumpet blasts alarm the highest stars and the bugle calls resound in the
echoing air. The paraders turn back, once again riding over carpets
of purple, and once more pass through the wide-open gates in a
long procession, a host twice its former size. As soon as they assemble in front of the king's castle, they burst out in an exultant wedding hymn. And now the royal [290] palace is being prepared with
magnificent sumptuousness. A good many of the nobles lean back
on the embroidered couches. Others set the banquet tables in order.
They serve up course after course and fill goblet after goblet with
the wines of garlanded Bacchus.[34] In that hall more than one Triton
played the perforated flute, more than one Misenus too, skilled in
blowing the recorder and challenging the tuneful boxwood with
bulging cheeks. There was also more than one Iopas, virtuoso on
the cittern. More than one Arion plucked the melodious strings.
Many an Orpheus there could match many an Amphion.[35] [300]
Finally, there was not just one Siren singing there, but all of them.
If he could have heard them, Ulysses himself would have turned his

[29]Matthias Drzewicki (1467–1535), Bishop of Przemyśl from 1504 to 1513.

[30]Jan Konarski (1447–1525), Bishop of Cracow from 1503 to 1523.

[31]Erazm Ciołek (ca. 1474–1522), Bishop of Płock from 1503 to 1522.

[32]Jan Lubrański (1456–1520), Bishop of Posen since 1498. It was he whom the king sent in
January to conduct his bride to Poland.

[33]Lukas Watzelrode of Thorn, Bishop of Warmia (Ermland) from 1489 to 1512, and the maternal uncle of Nicolaus Copernicus.

[34]Bacchus traditionally wore a crown of vineleaves or a garland made of clusters of ivy-berries.

[35]Each of these names represents a type of the virtuoso musician. The sea god Triton and Aeneas'
trumpeter Misenus played wind instruments (cf. *Pug.* 13–14, with n. 3), while Iopas (the lyrist at
Queen Dido's court), Arion, Amphion, and Orpheus all played stringed instruments.

Atque ut plura brevi complectar: ibi omnibus omnis
Gratia Laeticiis commixta sororibus ibat.
Et tamen haec veris quasi progymnasmata ludis
305   Maiorem pompam maioraque festa manebant.
          Iamque polo humentes lux postera dispulit umbras.
Ad sacra conveniunt rex et regina, iugalem
Iam primum in copulam coituri. Hic flamen utrunque
Corripiens utraque manu sic maximus infit:
310   "Quod faustum foelixque et vobis caedat et orbi
Quem regitis frigente sub axe Lycaonis Ursae,
Vos ego coniungo Christo sponsore iugatos
Foedere legitimo, mentem duo pectora in unam.
Ite pares igitur, nec brachia vestra sequaci
315   Concaedant hederae, Paphiis non ora columbis,
Foecundique genus numerosa extendite prole
Et date semideos spaciosa in regna nepotes
Prolificoque thoro generosas vincite vires.
Sic facilis castae faveat Lucina puellae
320   Nullaque sit rigido cutis exponenda Luperco.
Omnes sic vobis currant foeliciter anni
Nullaque sit vestro labes obnoxia regno."
          Finierat presul. Facile in suffragia vulgus
Acclamat gratum sonitu testante favorem:
325   "Dii faciles coeptis faveant nuptaeque viroque!
Rex bone, vive diu! Longum vive, optima coniunx!"
Tum strepitus clamorque virum clangorque tubarum
Exoritur. Rursusque instant nova gaudia, rursus
Aurea regales velant aulaea diaetas
330   Discumbuntque altis, procerum stipante corona,
Nuptaque virque thoris. Sed iam post rite peractam
Coniugiique datam pro conditione coronam,
Tempus erat quo rex placido frueretur amatae
Virginis amplexu. In primo iam frigida cursu

5ᵛ

---

318 vires *scripsi*: vites **A**.

ship back.[36] And to sum it all up in a few words: there each of the Graces walked arm-in-arm with every one of their sisters, the Delights. And yet these celebrations were, so to speak, only a warm-up to the real entertainments, a promise of even greater pomp and even greater festivities to come.

And now the following day was dispersing the dank shades of night from the sky. The king and queen arrived for the ceremony in which they were to be joined for the first time in holy matrimony. Thereupon the archbishop,[37] taking each of them by the hand, began to speak as follows:

[310] "In the hope that all may turn out propitiously and happily, both for you and for the land you rule in the frigid North beneath the Lycaonian Bear, I now unite you, under the sponsorship of Christ, as man and wife yoked in lawful wedlock, two hearts, one single soul. Go as partners, therefore. Let not your arms yield to the trailing ivy or your lips to Venus' doves. Be fruitful and prolong your stock with many children. Provide your spacious realms with demigod descendants and surpass your own noble powers in prolific union. May gracious Lucina smile upon the chaste maiden. [320] May her skin never need to be exposed to the stern Luperci.[38] May all the years of your life pass in good fortune and your rule be free from disaster."

When the archbishop had finished speaking, the crowd expressed its enthusiastic approval in shouts of gratitude and goodwill: "May God bless this marriage and smile on the bride and groom! Long live our good king! Long live his most excellent consort!" Then a great clamor arose, as men cheered and trumpets blared. And once again new joys await; once again golden tapestries deck the royal halls [330] and the bride and groom recline on the high couches, with a great crowd of nobles around them. But now, after the bride has been crowned with all due ceremony in accordance with the marriage compact, the time has come for the king to enjoy the gentle embrace of the beloved virgin. Cold night had

---

[36]According to a medieval and Renaissance commonplace, wise Ulysses stopped his own ears to avoid hearing the Sirens' song. See n. 20 at *Ama.* 27.2 (1:234–35).

[37]Jan Łaski. See n. 27 above (pp. 30–31).

[38]Eobanus follows Ov. *Fast.* 2.425–52: may you conceive a child easily, without the dubious aid of the pagan Luperci; and may you have an easy delivery with the help of Lucina, the goddess of childbirth. At the fertility festival known as the Lupercalia, Roman women who wanted to become pregnant held out their palms to be struck by priests (Luperci) wielding thongs of goatskin. See, for example, Juv. 2.142.

335   Nox erat ut primum ad dominum deducta puella est
        Regalem in thalamum castoque oblata cubili.
        Regia tum incensis lucebant atria taedis.
        Omnia laeticiis, celebri plena omnia luxu
        Nox ea reddiderat, qua nec formosior esset
340   Ulla dies, licet aestivum sol colligat ignem.
        Postquam est ingressum in thalamos clausaeque negabant
        Ire fores quenquam ulterius, ibi Musa pudicos
        Demisit vultus retroque ignava recessit.
          Caetera, quae longo dici vix carmine possent,
345   Non uno, verum multis celebrata diebus
        Gaudia, Caesareo non inferiora triumpho.
        Ut sit robustis concursum protinus hastis,
        Ut cursu certatum in equis, dicenda poaetis
        Quos habet insignes Cracovia docta relinquo.
350   Rem mihi summatim satis est tetigisse, nec omnem
        Hystoriam tantae scripsisse ab origine pompae.
        Vos, quibus est tranquilla quies maiorque facultas
        Divitis ingenii meliorque aspirat Apollo,
        Dicite quae superant nobis intacta, poaetae,
355   Certatimque alacres regem celebrate potentem
        Et nobis, si quid versu peccamus inepto,
        In veniam faciles ignoscite. Non ego vobis
        Ista (deos testor) scripsi contrarius. At me
        Hic non defuerat qui cogeret esse poetam
360   Qualemcunque tamen, nec enim mihi grandia Phoebus
        Plectra movet, nec me gravitas heroica coelo
        Sublimem rapit attollens. Sed parvula forsan
        Connectentem elegos commendat gratia molles.
        Et mihi fama etiam scriptis est parta libellis,
365   Nostra nec exiguum Germania respuit Hessum.
          Iam satis est. Hymenaee, fave nuptaeque viroque
        Quos breviter cecini subitis utcunque Camaenis.

        Nunc age, qui nuper mihi Zoilus esse solebas,
          Insani! Nos te novimus esse nihil.

        Conscientia mille testes

6^r

---

366 nuptaeque *scripsi*: nuptae **A**.

already begun its course, when the maiden was first escorted to her lord in the royal apartment and brought before his chaste bed. Then the king's palace gleamed with the light of kindled torches. That night too was packed with all manner of delights, all manner of sumptuous celebrations. No day could be more beautiful than that night, [340] even if the sun were gathering the heat of summer. But since the couple has now entered the bridal chamber and the closed doors forbid us to go any further, my Muse here modestly lowers her eyes and bashfully draws back.

The remaining festivities, to which even a long epic could hardly do justice, were not celebrated in one single day, but rather over many days — festivities that were in no wise inferior to an imperial triumph. How the knights galloped at each other with stout lances, how they ran races on horseback, that I leave for the outstanding poets of scholarly Cracow to describe. [350] It is enough for me to touch on the matter summarily instead of writing the whole story of these magnificent games from beginning to end. You poets who enjoy tranquil leisure and can boast a richer talent, you whom Apollo inspires with finer verse: sing of those things that I have left untouched and eagerly compete with one another in extolling the mighty king. Kindly forgive me if I make a blunder in some ill-shaped verse. As God is my witness, I did not compose these verses to spite you. All the same, there was someone here who provoked me to be a poet, [360] though not much of one, to be sure. Phoebus did not move me then to write in an exalted strain, nor did the majesty of epic verse lift me up to the sky.[39] Still, the small charm that those tender elegiacs exhibit may perhaps suffice to commend him who wove them. I too have gained fame in the writing of books, and our Germany does not spurn anything offered by the "smallminded" Hessus.

But this will do. Hymen, smile on the bride and groom whom I have celebrated briefly, as best I could, in extemporaneous verses.

You who made it a habit of late to pick me to pieces,
    just go berserk! I know you for the nil that you are.[40]

A clear conscience is worth a thousand witnesses.

---

[39]For the allusions to Eobanus' hot-headed rivalry with Johannes Dantiscus see the introduction, pp. 6–9.

[40]Here too Eobanus alludes to his rival Johannes Dantiscus. See the introduction, pp. 6–9.

SYLVAE DUAE NUPER AEDITAE:
"PRUSSIA" ET "AMOR"

TWO IMPROMPTUS OF RECENT VINTAGE:
"PRUSSIA" AND "LOVE"

Helii. Eobani.

Hessi. Sylvae duae nug
arbitar Prussia et
Amor.

Sebastiani Myricii Regiomontani ad
Patriam Prussiam Ο,δαρρ/γκοι.

Quamuis multiplici naturę dotę beata
Non cedas vlli patrię chara loco
Hoc tamen his solum qui te videre patebat
Vix alijs ipso nomine nota prius
Reddidit illustrem cunctis nunc Helius oris
Carminibus Vates te celebrando suis
Nunc igitur foelix mea dulcis Prussia gaude
Quod te tam celebri contigit ore cani,

Title page of *Sylvae duae nuper aeditae*
[Leipzig: Melchior Lotter, 1514]
Ratsschulbibliothek, Zwickau

HELII EOBA

NI HESSI SYLVARVM LIBRI VI.

Nuper primum æditi Anno
M. D. XXXIII.

LECTORI

Alcinoi legimus, miramur Adonidis hortos
Inuenit Hesperidum succina sylua fidem
Quæ tandem inuidia est, non his permittere syluis
Ficticij saltem nominis esse decus?
Fallor, an hûc aliquis tamen ingredietur amicus
Quem noua querceti diuitis umbra iuuet?

Ιωαχείμου τῷ Καμεραρίου.

ὕλω τινδ' ἐλθὼν εἰς ἄξυλον ἔργ᾽ ὐ ἀθρήσις
οὐχ ὅτε τῆσ᾽ ἄρξων ἀλλ᾽ ὅτι λήξόμμῳ.
ᾗ ↑ τ᾽εἰ πᾶσα μυρι᾽ἔασι κάλ᾽ ἀλλά τε τέρψιν
ἔξι ὁμῶσ᾽ πρότερον πᾶν πελεκι ασάμῳμον.
μᾶλλ᾽ δ᾽ οὔ ᾽πόνυ κόρος οὔ᾽ ὅτι ἔασε τ᾽ ἔρεωὲ
πρὶν Ίαλ᾽ ἀ̓αναγνώσι δινδρεὰ πάνζα πίση

HELII EOBA

NI HESSI SYLVARVM LIBRI VI,
Nuper primum ædiri Anno
M. D. XXXV.

LECTORI

Alcinoi legimus, miramur Adonidis hortos
Inuenit Hesperidum succina sylua fidem
Quæ tandem inuidia est, non his permittere syluis
Ficticij saltem nominis esse decus?
Fallor, an huc aliquis tamen ingredietur amicus
Quem noua querceti diuitis umbra iuuet?

Ἰωαχείμου τοῦ Καμεραρίου.

Ὤλω Τινδ᾽ ἐλθὼν εἰς ἄξυλον ἔργα ἀθρήσαις
οὐχ ὅτι βῆσ᾽ ἄρξων ἀλλ᾽ ὅτι ληξόμενΘ.
ἢ Τ᾽ εἰ πάσα μυρί᾽ ἔασι κάλ᾽ ἀλλά πε τέρτιψ
ἔξι ὁμῶσ πρότερον πᾶν πελεκι σα μύνορ.
μᾶλλ᾽ δ᾽ οὐ πόνṷ κόρος οὐ σοι ἔασε τ᾽ ἐρωὴ
πρὶν Τάδ᾽ ἀνανύσαι δενδρεὰ πάντα πέση

Title page of *Sylvarum libri VI* (second state)
Haguenau: Peter Braubach, 1535
Washington University Libraries, Department of Special Collections, St. Louis

OPERVM

HELII EOBA

NI HESSI FARRAGINES DVAE, NV
per ab eodem qua fieri potuit diligentia contractæ, et
in hanc, quam uides formam coactæ, quibus
etiam non parum multa acceßerunt
nunc primum et nata &
edita.

Catalogum operum ipforum uerfa pa=
gella oftendet.

Acceßit unicuiqʒ farragini fuus etiam index, explicãs
quid in fingulis libris contineatur, & ad
quos potißimum autor fcribat.

HALAE SVEVORVM
ANNO XXXIX.

Title page of *Operum farragines duae*
Schwäbisch Hall, 1539
Herzog August Bibliothek, Wolfenbüttel

SYLVAE DUAE

Introduction

At the behest of Bishop Job von Dobeneck, Eobanus left Riesenburg in April 1513 to study law at Frankfurt an der Oder. Joachim Camerarius explains the move: "It was the bishop's plan to put Eobanus in charge of his correspondence and of those affairs that require statesmanship and to have him conduct embassies whenever someone had to be sent to the neighboring princes. He therefore arranged to purchase a set of lawbooks for him . . . , first the ones encompassing imperial law, then those containing the imitation made by the Roman popes, which on that account came to be termed civil and pontifical law. In addition, he provided Eobanus with plenty of money and sent him . . . to study these subjects."[1]

To Eobanus the bishop's proposal must have seemed a godsend. Already in 1510–11 he was lamenting to his friend and fellow poet Temonius that court life has all but sapped their creative energies. Only when drunk can they still dream of their old life of scholarship and of escaping to some Italian university like Bologna (*Sylv.* 4.5). Conducting the episcopal correspondence was a tedious and burdensome business. The frequent embassies, the extravagant banquets and drinking bouts, were beginning to take their toll. By the spring of 1512 Eobanus' weariness had turned into loathing. He can no longer endure living among the "barbarians" in Prussia, he tells Georg Spalatin, who by now was working at the Saxon court in Wittenberg. To avoid wasting his youth in utter misery, he must return as soon as possible to the scholarly environment of a university. Almost desperately, therefore, he appeals to his influential friend to help him obtain a lectureship at Wittenberg.[2]

Riesenburg was assuredly not the idyllic sanctuary of the Muses that later writers have made it out to be. Job von Dobeneck was stingy in his support of the arts and failed to reward Eobanus with adequate raises. The episcopal library was

---

[1] *Nar.* 7.10–12.
[2] See Mutian. *Ep.*, 2:367–69 (letter of 12 April 1512).

too meager for serious work.[3] Worse, the number of humanistically-minded peers at Riesenburg remained distressingly small. Indeed, the extant correspondence reveals just three good friends during the entire Riesenburg period, all of them Erfurt alumni. Besides the already-mentioned Temonius, we know only of Georg Bonemilch of Laasphe and Bartholomew Götz of Treisa in Hesse.[4]

Eobanus, of course, jumped at the bishop's offer. Here was his chance to withdraw from the court for a few years, to live the life of a student again, to finish his *Heroides* and have them published in some university town![5] On May 2, shortly after his arrival in Frankfurt an der Oder, he wrote Georg Spalatin in Wittenberg to tell him about the move. He is planning to study law here for the next two years, he says, and then return to Prussia with a degree in hand. In truth, he allows, had his friend not discouraged him, he would much rather have gone to Wittenberg. Still, he is doing extremely well ("perbelle") here.[6]

[3]In *Her. Chr.*, ded. 8.2, Eobanus insinuates that Riesenburg lacks an adequate "supply of the very best books, especially on Church History." In the same letter he hints that Bishop Dobeneck has not been the most generous of patrons (ded. 4.1–5) and that his only real contribution to learning has been the founding of a grammar school at Riesenburg (ded. 17.3). Eobanus is far more blunt about the bishop's stinginess in a private letter to Georg Spalatin of 12 April 1512. After complaining about having to live among the "barbarians" at Riesenburg, he writes: "The bishop is . . . good to me, by God, but not generous enough. For example, after nearly three years with him I still don't earn more than thirty gold florins per year" ("Princeps mihi est . . . bonus, per Deum, sed non satis liberalis, puta apud quem nunc pene triennium non amplius triginta nummum auri signati stipendio annuatim mereo"). See Mutian. *Ep.*, 2:367. From other sources we know that Bishop Dobeneck diverted a large endowment for the support of Prussian students at Leipzig to his own personal use: see Forstreuter, 55. Nevertheless, the hoary myth that the bishop fostered a humanistic idyll, a *sodalitas* of poets, at Riesenburg continues to flourish unabated. See, for example, Hermann Freytag, "Der preussische Humanismus bis 1550," *Zeitschrift des Westpreußischen Geschichtsvereins* 47 (1907), 51–52; Wilhelm Meyer, "Bartholomäus Götz," *Altpreußische Forschungen* 4 (1927), 119; Schoenborn, 15–16; Heinz Otto Burger, *Renaissance, Humanismus, Reformation: Deutsche Literatur im europäischen Kontext* (Bad Homburg v. d. H., 1969), 403. Though more skeptical, Forstreuter, 53–59, still speaks of "the Riesenburg circle" and "that idyllic court of the Muses in Riesenburg." Arnold, 104, also refers to Eobanus' "humanist circle."
[4]For Temonius, see pp. 58–59 below.
Georg Bonemilch (presumably a relative of Eobanus' former patron, Bishop Johann Bonemilch) matriculated at Erfurt in 1501, earning the BA in the autumn of 1507. Probably in 1510 Eobanus addressed a poem to him (*Sylv.* 1.6), in which he avers that he is still deeply in love with Flavia and not at all serious about his new girlfriend. After his stay in Prussia, Bonemilch taught in Fulda. In 1523 he returned to Erfurt. Eobanus addressed a letter to him on 1 April 1524, inviting him over for lunch. By 1526 Bonemilch was in Königsberg.
Bartholomew Götz, who matriculated at Erfurt in the winter semester of 1504–05, became BA in 1507 and MA in 1512. Not long afterwards he moved to Riesenburg, where he eventually succeeded Eobanus as chancellor to Bishop Dobeneck. Eobanus wrote him a verse letter from Leipzig, probably in the early spring of 1514 (*Sylv.* 2.7). When the bishop died on 25 May 1521, Götz moved to Königsberg and served as legal counsel to Grand Master Albert. In November 1523 he visited Eobanus in Erfurt and prevailed on him to write a poem in defense of the Teutonic Order, *In poetam Sarmatam invectiva*. From 1524 until his death in 1531 he occupied various government posts in Königsberg. See Wilhelm Meyer, "Bartholomäus Götz," *Altpreußische Forschungen* 4 (1927), 117–27.
[5]See *Sylv. duae*, ded. 2–3; *Her. Chr.*, ded. 2.1.
[6]See Mutian. *Ep.*, 2:369. No doubt Eobanus chose Wittenberg first for the same reason that he later moved to Leipzig: to publish his *Heroides* and then lobby for a lectureship. Besides, at Wittenberg he would enjoy the company of several old friends: Justus Jonas (now studying law), Johann Lang, Georg Spalatin, and Balthasar Phachus (Fabricius) of Vacha in Hesse. Eobanus greets the latter two as

It is easy to see why Eobanus settled on Frankfurt an der Oder as his second choice. Obviously, it was close to Prussia. More importantly, like Wittenberg, the University of Frankfurt was a recent foundation and enjoyed a reputation for openness to humanistic learning. As it happened, three highly respected teachers of the humanities at Frankfurt were also students of law when Eobanus arrived. They were Fabian Funck of Haynau (Silesia), who was elected dean of liberal arts that same semester;[7] Achatius Freund of Elbing, who had just completed a term as the university's rector and quickly welcomed our poet in a verse letter, despite the bad fortune which he himself was then suffering;[8] and Eobanus' old friend Hermann Trebelius, the poet laureate who had been teaching the humanities and studying law at Frankfurt since the autumn of 1508.[9] Another old acquaintance, who became professor of poetry at Frankfurt that very semester, was the Dalmatian Riccardo Sbruglio — the same man whom Eobanus had excoriated for his arrogance in the tenth eclogue of the *Bucolicon*.

Though our poet, as can be imagined, would have nothing to do with Sbruglio, he joyously renewed his friendship with Hermann Trebelius. In a springtime elegy (*Sylv.* 1.9) we see him inviting himself over for lunch at the latter's house and looking forward to the simple fare and delightful conversation. He also enjoyed the company of two of Trebelius' students, the Pomeranian noblemen Johann and Alexander von der Osten,[10] for whom Ulrich von Hutten had earlier

---

"amicos summos" in his letter to Lang of 4 July 1513. Phachus was also good friends with Ulrich von Hutten: see Hutten, *Opera*, 1:26–27 (letter 11).

[7]Fabian Funck matriculated at Cracow in the winter semester of 1499–1500 (BA 1502). Together with his younger brother Mathias he moved to Frankfurt an der Oder in 1506. There he received his MA in December 1507. Before long he was professor of liberal arts, and from 1508 to 1511 also secretary of the university. At the same time time he studied law. In 1508 he became bachelor of civil and canon law, in 1514 licentiate. After leaving the university in 1514 he was at the court of the electoral prince in Berlin. By 1520 he was a priest. He retired to Wrocław in 1551 and died the following year. See further Höhle, 83–85.

[8]Achatius Freund (Frunt, Frundt, Philostorgus) of Elbing matriculated at Leipzig in 1501, earning the BA in 1502 and the MA in early 1505. That same winter he matriculated at Cracow. In the summer semester of 1511 he became professor of the humanities at Frankfurt an der Oder. At the same time he studied law. In the winter semester of 1512–13 he served as rector of the university. Achatius introduced himself to Eobanus in a short verse letter, in which he says that is now starting his third decade of life, but has just suffered a severe reversal of fortune. Eobanus responds at length in *Sylv.* 1.4. Not long after venting his distress to Eobanus, Achatius left Frankfurt and became a canon in Frauenburg. Johann Lohmüller of Danzig mentions him in a dedicatory letter of 13 April 1514, addressed to Bishop Fabian of Ermland and preserved in Biblioteka Kórnicka Polskiej Akademii Nauk, Kórnik, syn. 632, cart., s. XVI (1511). At the end of this letter (fol. 6ʳ) Lohmüller appeals to the bishop to have the erudite Achatius publish the copy of an anonymous translation of Homer's *Odyssey* that he, Lohmüller, had discovered in a royal library (in Cracow): "hilariter suscipe, deinde tui nominis studiosissimo Acatio, viro multis litteris erudito, ut impressoriae officinae tradatur, commenda, qui illud pro sua in te observantia, et ut tuo titulo, quam felicissime et emendatissime exeat, procurabit diligenter." Lohmüller's ms., however, was never published. (For Lohmüller see the introd. to *Encomium nuptiale*, n. 8, p. 6 above. I am grateful to Georg N. Knauer for sharing this information with me from his forthcoming survey of Latin Homer-translations, s.v. "Leontius Pilatus.") In 1525–26 Achatius represented the bishop in negotiations with Duke Albert. He died in 1533. See further Höhle, 88–89.

[9]For his life see 1:308–09, n. 40 (*Buc.* 4).

[10]The brothers had matriculated at Frankfurt in the winter semester of 1507–08. The elder brother Johann died at Wittenberg in January 1519.

written his *Art of Versification* (1511). Three contemporary poems to Johann have come down to us as *Sylv.* 1.12, 4.17, and 4.19.[11] Eobanus may also have befriended Mathias Funck, Fabian's younger brother.[12] In the early spring of 1513 Mathias had published a short epic on the birth of the Virgin Mary, *Primitie carminum in genethlium salutifere virginis Marie* (Frankfurt an der Oder, 1513), to which Trebelius contributed two laudatory epigrams. The following year he would come out with an epyllion on Christ's descent into hell, entitled *Triumphus Christianus*. Since Eobanus had himself written a little epic on the theme in 1512 (published as *Victoria Christi ab inferis* in 1517), it is conceivable that it was he who first prompted Mathias to write his own narrative poem.

In this congenial atmosphere Eobanus felt inspired not only to throw himself into his studies,[13] but also to finish the *Heroides*, on which he had been working fitfully for so long already. To the fifteen letters he had brought with him from Riesenburg he added nine new ones over the summer — as well as the dedicatory letter to Job von Dobeneck — and then lightly revised the entire work for publication. But at this juncture Eobanus suffered a misfortune, the details of which are not revealed in the extant correspondence. Mutianus, however, alludes to it in a letter to Urbanus, dated 12 September 1513: "Your most recent letter about the ill fortune that befell Eobanus . . . dismayed and perturbed me deeply."[14] The letters that Eobanus himself wrote about the calamity are no longer extant. All we have from him is what he tells Sebastian Myricius in the dedicatory letter to the *Sylvae duae*, dated 1 January 1514. His sudden departure from Frankfurt, he says, was due to his overwhelming "disgust at some of the people there."

What could have occasioned this "disgust"? As we have seen, Eobanus had been happy and productive at the university. A letter to Johann Lang of 4 July 1513 still shows him to be his old carefree self. It is not until the late summer that the tone suddenly changes to one of severe distress. Fortunately, as Gustav Bauch has pointed out, the university's *Liber conclusorum* for 11 December 1513 appears to shed light on this

---

[11]*Sylv.* 1.12 was first published at the end of *De vera nobilitate* (Erfurt, 1515), under the title "Ad Ioannem Osthenium Equitem cur vocetur Helius."

[12]On Mathias Funck, see Höhle, 86–88, and my article in *VLDH*, 1:844–48.

[13]While at Frankfurt and Leipzig, Eobanus seems to have taken the opportunity to take courses not only in law but also in medicine. We can glean that bit of information from a verse letter he sent to Bartholomew Götz in the early spring of 1514. There our poet, now living in Leipzig, declares that he has abandoned his studies of law and medicine and is working full time on the *Heroides*. See *Sylv.* 2.7.45–48: "Hic ego nec bifidi perplexa aenigmata Iuris / Nec sequor ambages, magne Galene, tuas, / Sed sacra Musarum Phoebique aeterna professus / Numina, sed quorum nomina Christus amet."

[14]*Ep.* 316: "Confudit me ac magnopere perturbavit epistola tua nuperrima de malo fato Eobani." Cf. *Ep.* 311, an undated letter (1513) that alludes to some rumors reported three months earlier by Johann Lang in Wittenberg, to the effect that Eobanus was in trouble because of some scandalous love affair. The letter cannot date from August, as Gillert has it, because Mutianus alludes to the judgment of the Erfurt theological faculty on Reuchlin that was issued on September 3. However, he has only heard about it, not yet seen the actual report. He would not actually read it until early October (*Ep.* 320). Hence *Ep.* 311 must have been written sometime in September, probably a week or two after *Ep.* 316. Mutianus, however, dismisses Lang's report "de fututione culpabili" as rubbish, because Eobanus, who wrote him two weeks earlier, never did mention that trouble ("infortunium").

mystery.[15] For there we learn that Eobanus Hessus, Alexander von der Osten, and the otherwise unidentified Andreas had been so cruelly abused by a local citizen that they were contemplating revenge. Having been advised to address themselves to the rector and not to take matters into their own hands, they had refused the university's mediation. Hereupon they had been summoned to the Franciscan cloister, where, in the presence of the rector, the university council, and the municipal councillors, they were formally enjoined to take their case to the rector, the bishop, or the Electoral Prince. Since Alexander had threatened not to leave the matter unavenged, he was forbidden to leave the city until the case was settled.

Feeling powerless and enraged, Eobanus took his leave on the spot. Traveling by way of Wittenberg, where he called on Georg Spalatin,[16] he continued on to Leipzig. As if to demonstrate that he was still serious about his diplomatic career, he quickly enrolled at the university.[17] At the same time he wasted no time contacting old friends.[18] Now, however, his overriding goal was to have the *Heroides* published as soon as possible, and in the meantime to start lobbying discreetly for an academic position. But here a new disappointment awaited him. Almost immediately he was warned that publishing such an impressive poem would send the wrong signal to the anti-humanist faction at the university and undermine whatever prospects he had of landing a lectureship here. Faced with this unexpected obstacle, he decided to ingratiate himself first with a more modest publication. To this end he retrieved two shorter poems from his papers, revised them in a hurry, and brought them out in January 1514 as *Helii Eobani Hessi Sylvae duae*. It was the first time that he used the name *Helius* in print.[19]

Printing History

The *Sylvae duae* was published by Melchior Lotter at Leipzig in January 1514, but without indication of place, printer, or date:

A (1514)

[*Fraktur:*] Helij. Eobani. | Heſſi. Syluae duae nuᴘ | aeditae Pruſſia et | Amor. | [*roman:*] Sebaſtiani Myricij Regiomontani ad | Patriam Pruſſiam Ογδοαστιχον. | [*4 distichs*]

---

[15]See *Liber conclusorum*, Brandenburgisches Landeshauptarchiv, Potsdam, Rep. 86, no. 10, fol. 12ʳ (formerly fol. 14); Gustav Bauch, *Die Anfänge der Universität Frankfurt a. O. und die Entwicklung des wissenschaftlichen Lebens an der Hochschule (1506–1540)*, Texte und Forschungen 3 (Berlin, 1900), 119–20; Höhle, 115.

[16]See *Sylv.* 2.25.

[17]The university register records his name as "Dominus Eobanus de Franckenberck magister Erfordensis."

[18]Though few, his friends at Leipzig were of the best, as Eobanus tells Mutianus Rufus on 4 August 1514 (Mutian. *Ep.* 408): "amicos, quibus quam paucis, sed optimis certe Lypsi usus sum." Some of them were old friends like Sebastian Myricius, Veit Werler, and Georg Helt. Among the new friends he could count Johannes Sturnus as well as Karl Schenk von Limpurg, Paul von Schwarzenberg, and Gregor Aubanus.

[19]Eobanus explains the full appellation in *Nob.* B 1, an elegy addressed to Johann von der Osten. The poem reappears in revised form as *Sylv.* 1.12.

Collation: 4°: A–B⁶, [$3 signed], 12 leaves
Contents: A1ʳ title page; A1ᵛ dedicatory letter; A2ʳ–A6ᵛ *Generalis Prussiae*
                        descriptio; A6ᵛ–B6ʳ *Illiciti amoris antidotarium*; B6ᵛ blank
Copytext: Zwickau, Ratsschulbibliothek
                        Call number: 24.7.24/2

The Zwickau copy (*A¹*) contains a great mass of interlinear and marginal notes, evidently written down during Eobanus' lectures on the book in Leipzig. Carl Krause owned a copy similarly filled with student's notes: see *HEH*, 1:121; "Beiträge," 37–40 (with critical apparatus). I have checked the copytext against the copies in Frankfurt am Main, Stadt- und UB (Bibliothek Gustav Freytag, XIX, 65; catalogue no. 4127), indicated in the apparatus criticus as *A²*; Giessen/Lahn, UB (Ink E 10760/3); Jena, UB (4 Phil. X 14/4); and London, BL (11408. f. 22). The London copy is indicated in the apparatus criticus as *A³*. Like the Zwickau copy, it contains copious manuscript notes taken during Eobanus' lectures on the book. There are further copies in Dresden, Sächsische Landesbibliothek; Thorn, University Library; Wittenberg, Lutherhalle; and Wrocław, Biblioteka Ossolineum.

The poems "Prussia" and "Amor" have also come down to us as *Sylv.* 1.2 and 1.3 in *Sylvarum libri VI* (Haguenau, 1535), sigs. AA8ʳ–BB6ᵛ, reprinted in *Sylvarum libri IX*, as part of the *Operum farragines duae* (Schwäbisch Hall, 1539), sigs. ²A1ᵛ–A8ʳ.

Eobanus seems to have completed the manuscript for *Sylvarum libri VI* at Nuremberg in the summer of 1532. He tells Johannes Dantiscus in the dedicatory letter to book 1 that assembling all these poems proved difficult, partly because they were scattered about in his files, on little sheets of paper or scraps of parchment, and partly because the originals were often so "mutilated and acephalous" that he had to reconstitute them laboriously. Of the juvenilia, he adds, nothing remains. After spending a couple of days rereading the manuscript in the late summer, he was ready to have it published. Since he had known as early as 10 March 1532 (*Epp. fam.*, 47) that Johann Setzer, his Haguenau printer, had died earlier that year, he sent the book instead to Setzer's associate Peter Braubach, then visiting Frankfurt am Main for the autumn book fair. Toward the end of September, however, Eobanus wrote an urgent letter to Jakob Micyllus at Frankfurt about the manuscript. Micyllus was to retrieve it from Braubach and check it over for any words or phrases that Eobanus — who really had been in too much of a hurry when rechecking it himself — might have omitted in copying out the originals.[20] Braubach apparently began the printing in the spring of 1533. At any rate, all five of Eobanus' dedicatory letters bear the date March 1533, even though they must have been part of the manuscript delivered in the previous summer. The book's title page, as first printed, also bore the expected publication date "1533." However, in other copies this title page is replaced with one showing the actual year of publication, 1535.

---

[20]*Epp. fam.*, 50–51, written at Nuremberg. The date "14 August 1533" printed at the end of this letter is erroneous. In the same letter Eobanus informs Micyllus that he has decided to leave Nuremberg and return to Erfurt on 1 May 1533. A letter of 3 October 1532, also to Micyllus, has very similar wording and refers back to this letter as written "superioribus diebus." See *Epp. fam.*, 50.

The *Sylvarum libri VI*, then, was brought out by Peter Braubach at Haguenau in two states, the title pages of which differ in the publication date ("XXXIII" / "XXXV") and in line 5 of Eobanus' liminary epigram ("hūc" / "huc"). Two further differences appear on later pages: a catchword printed on sig. AA4ᵛ in *S¹* is lacking in *S²*; and the form "curis" on sig. BB4ᵛ in *S¹* is truncated to "cur" in *S²* (see the variant reading at *Sylv. duae* 2.91–96).

S¹ (1535)

HELII EOBA | NI HESSI SYLVARVM LIBRI VI. | Nuper primum æditi Anno | M. D. XXXIII. | [*vine leaf*] | LECTORI | *Alcinoi legimus, miramur Adonidis hortos* | *Inuenit Hefperidum fuccina fylua fidem* | *Quæ tandem inuidia est, non his permittere* | *fylvis* | *Ficticii faltem nominis effe decus?* | *Fallor, an hūc aliquis tamen ingredietur* | *amicus* | *Quem noua querceti diuitis umbra iuuet?* | [*cloverleaf*] | Ιωαχείμου τοῦ Καμεραρίου. | [*three Greek distichs*]

Colophon:	HAGANOAE EX OFFICI	NA PETRI BRV	BACCHII	Anno Domini Millefimo	Quingentefimo trice	fimo quinto,	Menfe	Iulio.	
Collation:	8°: AA–PP⁸, [$5 signed], 120 leaves
Contents:	AA1ʳ title page; AA1ᵛ blank; AA2ʳ–AA4ʳ dedicatory letter to book 1; AA4ᵛ–CC7ᵛ book 1; CC8ʳ–DD1ʳ dedicatory letter to book 2; DD1ʳ–FF2ʳ book 2; FF2ᵛ–FF3ʳ dedicatory letter to book 3; FF3ᵛ–HH4ʳ book 3; HH4ᵛ–HH5ᵛ dedicatory letter to book 4; HH6ʳ–LL4ʳ book 4; LL4ʳ–LL4ᵛ dedicatory letter to book 5; LL5ʳ–NN6ᵛ book 5; NN7ʳ–PP6ʳ book 6; PP6ᵛ blank; PP7ʳ colophon; PP7ᵛ printer's device; PP8 blank
Catchwords:	Used on versos only; lacking on sigs. AA6ᵛ, HH5ᵛ, HH6ᵛ, HH7ᵛ, KK1ᵛ, LL3ᵛ, LL4ᵛ, and NN5ᵛ; miscatching "Tu quoque" as "Mors" on BB4ᵛ
Running titles:	The dedicatory letters have the running title "EPISTOLA". For the books of poetry the running title is "SYLVARUM LIBER I [II, III, IIII, V, VI]." Sig. LL2ʳ prints "LIBER V" instead of "LIBER IIII".
Location:	Munich, Bayerische Staatsbibliothek Call number: P.o. lat. 1661/g

S² (1535)

HELII EOBA | NI HESSI SYLVARVM LIBRI VI. | Nuper primum æditi Anno | M. D. XXXV. | [*vine leaf*] | LECTORI | *Alcinoi legimus, miramur Adonidis hortos* | *Inuenit Hefperidum fuccina fylua fidem* | *Quæ tandem inuidia est, non his permittere* | *fylvis* | *Ficticii faltem nominis effe decus?* | *Fallor, an huc aliquis tamen ingredietur* | *amicus* | *Quem noua querceti diuitis umbra iuuet?* | [*cloverleaf*] | Ιωαχείμου τοῦ Καμεραρίου. | [*three Greek distichs*]

Location:	Munich, Universitätsbibliothek Call number: 8° P. lat. rec. 910

There are further copies of S^1 in Milan, Biblioteca Nazionale Braidense; Stuttgart, Württembergische Landesbibliothek; Trier, StadtB; Vienna, ÖNB; Zwickau, Ratsschulbibliothek. Of S^2 there are further copies in Basel, UB; Dresden, Sächsische Landesbibliothek; Haguenau, Bibliothèque municipale; Halle, UB; Jena, UB; Paris, Sorbonne; Soest, StadtB; St. Louis, Washington University; Strasbourg, BNU; Vatican City, Vatican Library; and Vienna, ÖNB.

Augmented with three more books, the *Sylvarum libri VI* was reprinted at Schwäbisch Hall in 1539, in part 1 of *Operum Helii Eobani Hessi farragines duae* (*Two Medleys of Helius Eobanus Hessus' Works*). The title *farragines* places the work in a tradition that includes Erasmus' *Farrago nova epistolarum* (Basel, 1519), Martin Luther's *Epistolarum farrago* (Haguenau, 1525), and Philip Melanchthon's *Farrago aliquot epigrammatum* (Haguenau, 1528).

O (1539)

OPERVM | HELII EOBA | NI HESSI FARRAGINES DVAE, NV | *per ab eodem qua fieri potuit diligentia contractæ, et | in hanc, quam uides formam coactæ, quibus | etiam non parum multa acceßerunt | nunc primum et nata & | ædita.* | *Catalogum operum ipsorum uersa pa =* | *gella ostendet.* | *Acceßit unicuiq; farragini suus etiam index, explicãs | quid in singulis libris contineatur, & ad | quos potißimum autor scribat.* | HALAE SVEVORVM | ANNO XXXIX. | [*without indication of printer (Peter Braubach)*]

Colophon:	Lacking
Collation:	8°: A⁸, a–z⁸, ²A–V⁸, ³A–Q⁸, [\$5 signed (–A2, a1, ²K5, ³C3, C4, O5; z3 missigned z5; ²N3 missigned M3; ²O3 missigned O5)], 480 leaves, (part 1) fols. [*1–8*], 1–192, 195–340 (misprinting 35 as "27," 54 as "45," 149 as "148," 222 as "122," 236 as "239," 254–58 as "256–60," and 329 as "326"); (part 2) [*1–6*], 1–128 (misprinting 51 as "52")
Contents:	A1ʳ title page; A1ᵛ table of contents for the entire work; A2ʳ–A8ʳ detailed table of contents for the *Heroides, Epicedia*, and *Sylvarum libri IX*; A8ᵛ blank; a1ʳ title page for the first farrago; a1ᵛ general table of contents for the first farrago; a2ʳ–g7ʳ *Bucolicorum idyllia XVII*; g7ᵛ title page for *Heroidum libri tres*; g8ʳ blank; g8ᵛ–t1ʳ *Heroidum libri tres*; t1ᵛ–z2ʳ *Epicedia XII*; z2ᵛ blank; z3ʳ–²V2ʳ *Sylvarum libri IX*; V2ᵛ general table of contents for the second farrago; V3ʳ–V4ᵛ detailed table of contents for the second farrago; V5ʳ–³D5ʳ *Urbs Noriberga*; D5ᵛ blank; D6ʳ title page for *De victoria Wirtembergensi*; D6ᵛ blank; D7ʳ–F2ʳ *De victoria Wirtembergensi*; F2ᵛ–G7ʳ *Coluthi de raptu Helenes*; G7ᵛ–K5ʳ *Homericae aliquot icones insigniores*; K5ᵛ blank; K6ʳ title page for *Bonae valetudinis conservandae rationes aliquot*; K6ᵛ blank; K7ʳ–M7ʳ *Bonae valetudinis conservandae rationes aliquot*; M7ᵛ–N7ᵛ *Medicinae laus*; N8ʳ–O3ᵛ *Chorus illustrium medicorum*; O4ʳ–O4ᵛ *Chorus Musarum*; O5ʳ–P4ʳ *Elegiae tres*; P4ᵛ–Q8ᵛ *Elegiae quaedam pro assertione Lutherani dogmatis*

Catchwords: Used on versos only; lacking on a1ᵛ, b7ᵛ, c8ᵛ, e1ᵛ, e6ᵛ, f1ᵛ, h3ᵛ, h6ᵛ, k1ᵛ, o2ᵛ, u3ᵛ, z5ᵛ, ²B6ᵛ, B7ᵛ, C5ᵛ, D7ᵛ, G5ᵛ, I1ᵛ, K5ᵛ, M8ᵛ, P4ᵛ, P7ᵛ, Q1ᵛ, V2ᵛ, V4ᵛ, ³D7ᵛ, F2ᵛ, G7ᵛ, O3ᵛ, O4ᵛ, Q2ᵛ; miscatching "Iamque" as "Qua" on l7ᵛ; "Hic tu" as "Hic tu," on o8ᵛ; "Nulli" as "Nulla" on t5ᵛ; "Nam duo" as "Num duo" on ²A1ᵛ; "Iam ver" as "Iam pu" on H2ᵛ; "Insunt" as "Insunt," on K3ᵛ; "Et, nisi" as "Et nisi" on P5ᵛ

Running titles: Each work contained in the book has its own running title, misprinting "IDYLLION XI" as "IDYLLION IX" on d8ʳ; "IDYLLION XI" as "IDYLLION V" on e1ʳ; "IDYLLION XIIII" as "IDYLLION XIII" on f3ʳ; "IDYLLION XV" as "IDYLION XV" on f5ʳ; "IDYLLION XVII" as "IDYLLION XVI" on g5ʳ; "HEROIDVM EPIST." as "HEROIDVM APIST." on i7ᵛ; "LIBER III" as "LIER III" on o5ʳ and q5ʳ; "LIBER III" as "LIBER II" on q3ʳ; "ILLVSTRI. VIROR." as "ILLVSTRI. VITOR." on x8ᵛ; "LIBER III" as "LIBER II" on E6ʳ and F4ʳ; "LIBER IIII" as "LIBER III" on H1ʳ; "LIBER IIII." as "LIBER III.I" on H2ʳ; "LIBER IIII" as "LIBER III" on I1ʳ and I4ʳ; "LIBER V" as "LIBER IIII" on M5ʳ; "LIBER VII" as "LIBER VI" on Q3ʳ; "LIBER VIII" as "LIBER VII" on Q8ʳ; "ILLVSTRATA" as "ILLVSSTRATA" on A7ʳ; "NORIBERGA" as "NORIAERGA" on B6ᵛ and C5ᵛ; "DE VICTOR. VVIRTEM." as "DE VICTOR. VVIRTEN." on D7ᵛ and D8ᵛ and as "DE VICTO. VVITTEM." on E8ᵛ; "DE RAP. HELE." as "ARGVMENTVM" on G7ʳ; and "MEDICI-NAE LAVS" as "MEDICINE LAVS" on N6ᵛ

Location: Wolfenbüttel, Herzog August Bibliothek
Call number: 143 Poetica

I have also consulted the copy in Mannheim, UB (Sch 073/049; Notation: L 334 D 092), as well as the one in the National Library of Medicine, Washington (WZ 240.H587 1539; title page lacking). In the Mannheim and Washington copies, some textual loss in the marginalia has occurred because of cropping. In the same two copies the title page for *Heroidum libri tres* is printed correctly on sig. g8ʳ while sig. g7ᵛ is left blank; the folio number on sig. t5ʳ is correctly printed as "149". In the Washington copy, the signature "K3" (third series) is inverted. The folio numbering in the Mannheim copy at sig. I4ʳ–I8ʳ is: 254, 257, 256, 259, 258.

The three copies also differ occasionally from one another in their readings. At *Idyl.* 5.92, for example, the Wolfenbüttel copy prints "menses" for "messes"; at *Idyl.* 6.71, it has "Extinctas" instead of "Extinctus"; and at *Idyl.* 7.160 it reads "Exempla . . . amore", rather than "Exemplo . . . amare". In each case the other two copies offer the correct readings. At *Nor.* 430 and 561 the Mannheim copy erroneously prints "Atlantico" and "fluxu" respectively; the Washington and Wolfenbüttel copies have the correct forms "Atlantiaco" and "flexu".

There are further copies of *O* in Augsburg, SB (three copies); Austin, University of Texas; Bamberg, SB; Bretten, Bibliothek des Melanchthonhauses; Cambridge

University; Cambridge, MA, Harvard University Medical School; Chicago, Newberry Library; Copenhagen, Kongelige Bibliotek; Cracow, Biblioteka Czartoryskich; Dresden, Sächsiche Landesbibliothek; Eßlingen, Evangelische Kirchenbibliothek; Göttingen, UB; 's-Gravenhage, Koninklijke Bibliotheek; Halle/Saale, UB; Heidelberg, UB; Innsbruck, UB; Jena, UB; Lausanne, Bibliothèque cantonale et universitaire (incomplete); Leipzig, UB; London, BL; Lund, University Library; Munich, SB; Munich, UB (two copies); Münster in Westfalen, UB; Nashville, Vanderbilt University; New Haven, Yale University; Nuremberg, Germanisches Museum; Nuremberg, StadtB (two copies); Paris, BN (two incomplete copies); Philadelphia, University of Pennsylvania; Princeton, Princeton University; Providence, Brown University; San Francisco, California State Library; Strasbourg, BNU; Stuttgart, Württembergische Landesbibliothek; Tübingen, UB (two copies, one of them incomplete); Ulm, StadtB; Urbana-Champaign, University of Illinois; Vienna, ÖNB; Warsaw, Biblioteka Narodowa; Wiesbaden, LB; Wittenberg, Lutherhalle (two copies); Wolfenbüttel, Herzog August Bibliothek (another copy); Wrocław, University Library (two copies); Würzburg, UB; Zürich, Zentralbibliothek.

The *Operum farragines duae* was reprinted by Peter Braubach at Frankfurt am Main in 1549 and 1564.

Of the two "Impromptus," the "Description of Prussia" was reprinted several more times, in each case according to the text of *Sylv.* 1.2:

1. Johannes Andreas Pomeranus, *Historia de solenni convivio quod in arce Regiomontana Senatui et civibus Cneiphovianis quot annis in Die Ascensionis Domini exhibetur, bucolico carmine descripta a Iohanne Andrea Pomerano. Addita est Elegia Eobani Hessi continens descriptionem Prussiae* (Königsberg, 1552)

2. [Michael Lilienthal], *Erleutertes Preußen, Oder Auserlesene Anmerckungen, Ueber verschiedene Zur Preußischen Kirchen-, Civil- und Gelehrten-Historie gehörige besondere Dinge . . .* , vol. 5 (Königsberg, 1742), 638–42

3. Hermann Cramer, "Geschichte des vormaligen Bisthums Pomesanien," *Zeitschrift des historischen Vereins für den Regierungs–Bezirk Marienwerder* 13 (1884), 289–93

4. Karl Gillert, among the correspondence of Mutianus Rufus as *Ep.* 343 (1 January 1514)

5. Wilhelm Kühlmann and Werner Straube, "Zur Historie und Pragmatik humanistischer Lyrik im alten Preußen: Von Konrad Celtis über Eobanus Hessus zu Georg Sabinus," in *Kulturgeschichte Ostpreußens in der Frühen Neuzeit*, Frühe Neuzeit 56, ed. Klaus Garber, Manfred Komorowski, and Axel E. Walter (Tübingen, 2001), 657–736 (with an introduction, text, translation, and commentary on 677–82, 702–11). The article also offers a close reading and annotated edition-translation of *Sylv.* 1.1 (Eobanus' appeal to King Sigismund at the Diet of Piotrków in November 1512): see 669–77, 693–702.

Origins and Transformations

On 1 October 1506 Mutianus Rufus urged Eobanus to select some of the more finished occasional poems from his files and publish them in one volume (*Ep.* 45; cf. *Ep.* 46). Eobanus took the advice to heart. Already in *De laudibus* (1507) he tells his readers that he will soon bring out a collection of extemporaneous poems entitled *Sylvae* ("rough-hewn pieces," or, in an alternative translation, "forests").[21] By 1508 the manuscript had grown to several books: "The books of *Sylvae* that I have written here in Erfurt (and have promised you so often) should be leaving my literary workshop and reaching you any day now," he says at the end of *De amantium infoelicitate* (B 1.2). Indeed, he had already decided that he would dedicate the large volume ("grande volumen") to his patron Bishop Johann Bonemilch (*Epp. fam.*, 11). In *Encomium nuptiale* 13–14 he again alludes to a "*sylva* of diverse epigrams like the ones I've been inditing by the thousands." And the letter to Posterity that concludes his *Heroidum Christianarum epistolae* (24.115–18) reports: "A good many unpublished pieces still need more polishing; in fact, quite a *sylva* of them is tucked away in my drawer."

It was to these bulging files that Eobanus turned when he realized in late December 1513 that he would have to propitiate the Leipzig professors with "some minuscule first fruits" before coming out with the *Heroides*. He explains his decision in the dedicatory letter to *Sylvae duae*: "Because I was advised not to rush headlong into publication — and sound advice it was too — it occurred to me that I ought to assay the taste of the scholarly public by offering up, as it were, some minuscule first fruits beforehand. For if I went ahead and brought out the magnum opus regardless, I might have to pay the price for my temerity and find disgrace instead of favor. From the multitude of my verse, therefore, I have selected two poems, though not necessarily the best ones."

The two *Sylvae* published at Leipzig in January 1514 — "A Description of Prussia in General" and "An Antidotary for Illicit Love" — are both written in the manner of a verse letter, the first one being addressed to Mutianus Rufus, the second to the priest Theodore Collucius. Curiously, the same elegies reappear two decades later in Eobanus' *Sylvarum libri VI* (1535; reprinted, with three new books, in the *Farragines* of 1539). Here, however, the topographical poem (*Sylv.* 1.2) is sixty lines shorter than the 1514 version and is entitled "A Letter to Mutianus Rufus Containing a Description of Prussia." The poem against illicit love (*Sylv.* 1.3), some fifty-six lines shorter than the 1514 version, is now entitled, "To the Love-struck Temonius, Concerning Love."

Relying on this publication history, Carl Krause and others have taken it for granted that the 1514 edition (*A*) represents the original version of the poems and that the elegies printed in the *Sylvarum libri* of 1535/39 (*S O*) are a later,

---

[21]See *Laud.* 5–8, 280. First used by Statius, the title *Sylvae* was later adopted by Angelo Polizziano, Baptista Mantuanus, and others.

much-abbreviated redaction.[22] Closer examination, however, shows that the critics have it backwards. Though published first, **A** is in fact an expanded revision of the original poems. The texts eventually published in **S** and **O**, by contrast, either represent the archetype or, at the least, more closely approximate the original manuscripts that Eobanus found among his papers in the early 1530s.

(1) *Generalis Prussiae descriptio.* Let us begin by examining the "Description of Prussia in General." In the 1514 redaction the title signals that the poem is primarily topographical in intent and theme. The elegy will introduce readers to a part of the world quite foreign, even exotic to them. Sebastian Myricius' liminary epigram reinforces that message: "Even though you, dear homeland, are blessed with such manifold gifts of nature that no country on earth can rival you, this fact is nonetheless known only to those who have seen you. Until today, the others barely knew you, even by name. But the bard Helius has now made you illustrious all over the world by celebrating you in his verse." Eobanus too presents the poem that way in his dedicatory letter to Myricius, namely as "a topographical description of your homeland." He takes the same tack in his public lecture on the *Sylvae duae*, delivered in late January 1514: "I took my theme from the geography, customs, culture, and history of the lands that I had entered: I described Prussia, not, as other topographers do, with precise facts and figures, but rather in my own, that is to say, poetic manner, by way of a description in the form of a letter."[23] That he wrote his topography in the form of a letter to Mutianus Rufus seems in the 1514 redaction little more than a literary device, the purpose of which is to pay homage to a great friend and to the circle of humanists that our poet has left behind at Erfurt.[24]

In the 1535/39 version, on the other hand, the emphasis is quite different. Here the poem is presented, not as a topography per se, but as "A Letter to Mutianus Rufus Containing a Description of Prussia." In other words, it is a personal communication to a friend, the purpose of which is to let him know where the writer is now staying and how he is doing — a verse letter of the kind that Eobanus dashed off to his friends on all occasions, in great numbers, throughout his life. Some of them, like this one, were later gathered up in his *Sylvarum libri*, others were collected by his friends and published posthumously, but many more were lost without a trace.[25]

Unlike the Leipzig redaction, the 1535/39 version starts off as a true letter: "It is Hessus, until recently a regular fixture in your circle of friends, who is sending you this greeting from the seacoast. Here where Prussia, half-seared by hyperborean frost,

[22]See Krause, *HEH*, 1:99–100, 104–05. See also Krause's edition *Der Briefwechsel des Mutianus Rufus*, Zeitschrift des Vereins für hessische Geschichte und Landeskunde, NF, IX. Supplement (Kassel, 1885), no. 604, pp. 637–38, where he dates the elegy "early 1514," and his "Beiträge," 37–40; Kühlmann and Straube, 677, n. 47. Gillert was unable to locate the 1514 redaction; see Mutian. *Ep.* 343, 2:1, n. 1. Reprinting the 1535 version (*Sylv.* 1.2), he dates the poem 1 January 1514. However, its opening lines lead him to believe that the letter was "begun" in Prussia, that is, before the spring of 1513. Krause, "Beiträge," 37–40, supplies the readings of **A** lacking in Gillert's text.
[23]See pp. 64, 66 below.
[24]See Kühlmann and Straube, 678–80. Krause, *HEH*, 1:99, also does not see the elegy as a true letter to Mutianus, and will say of it only: "dem Gothaer Freunde Mutian gewidmet."
[25]See the dedicatory letter to the *Sylvarum libri* of 1535/39.

sees the arctic sky from close up, here where a flank of the sea that even today bears its name from the Germans washes the Sarmatian lands, here is where that Hessus of yours is now living — the very one you often used to praise as he sang melodious words to the golden lyre."[26] Despite the vast distance between them, he continues, he still feels close to his friend and thinks of him often. But there is no going back any more. If only Mutianus lived here, this barbarous land would be paradise!

The 1535/39 version, in brief, has the look and feel of a letter that was actually sent to Mutianus in Gotha in midwinter of 1510, perhaps only a month or two after Eobanus arrived in Prussia.[27] Here we need point only to the adverb "recently" ("modo"), and to the emphasis on "hyperborean frost," both of which are lacking in *A*. At the end of the letter, after describing the distant country to which he has moved, Eobanus again addresses Mutianus directly. Alluding to his *Bucolicon* of late September 1509, he wants Mutianus to tell him how his "flock" has been getting along without its shepherd. How has the book's dedicatee (Johann Englender) reacted? And what about the Erfurt friends Crotus Rubianus, Georg Spalatin, and Petrejus Eberbach? Is "Phileremus" (Herbord von der Marthen) still residing in his "holy dale" (the monastery of Georgenthal)? These, of course, are precisely the kind of questions that one expects at the end of a true letter. In this case, they confirm not just the epistolary genre but also the poem's composition date (early in 1510). Crotus, after all, did not move to Fulda until the late autumn of 1510, while Herbord was to remain at Georgenthal until the end of 1511. But we are not confined to inference alone. In his inaugural lecture on the *Sylvae duae* Eobanus himself avers that he wrote the poem almost immediately ("primo statim") after arriving in Prussia.[28]

If the 1535/39 version represents (or at least approximates) the original letter sent to Mutianus in early 1510, then all the passages occurring in *A* but not in *S O* must be Eobanus' revisions as he prepared the poem for publication in December 1513. As it turns out, several inserted passages are virtually identical to lines first found in the elegy (*Sylv.* 1.1) that Eobanus addressed to Sigismund I at the Diet of Piotrków in November 1512, in particular ll. 49–58, 63–64, and 161–78. Other revisions embroider on the original verse letter to Mutianus (ll. 19–26, 31–32, 89–92, 115–18, and 121–22) or provide details about life in Prussia that Eobanus could not yet have known in the early winter of 1510 (ll. 79–80 and 99–108). The interjected verses 131–34 show Eobanus in his more recently assumed role as propagandist for the Teutonic Order. In ll. 155–58 he introduces a praise of the little town of Riesenburg, now being enhanced by the bishop, and of its superbly fortified castle. This praise must have been added at Leipzig, for when Eobanus wrote Mutianus in early 1510 the bishop was still in Saxony and would not return to his residence until December. It is no coincidence that the bishop's defensive works and building projects at Riesenburg are also lauded in the dedication to Eobanus' *Heroidum Christianarum epistolae* (ded. 18.6–9), a letter dating from the late summer of 1513.

[26]Cf. *Sylv. duae* 1.19–26.

[27]Cf. *Sylv.* 3.4.55–56, where Eobanus, in a verse letter of ca. November 1509, promises to send Ludwig Christiani a poem to tell him where he is now living, what he is doing, and what friends he has made: "Verum ubi sit, quid agat, quibus et cum vivat amicis, / Si vivet, Musa liberiore leges."

[28]See pp. 64, 66 below.

(2) *Illiciti amoris antidotarium.* Like the "Description of Prussia," the "Antidotary for Illicit Love" began its career as a verse letter (preserved for us in *Sylv.* 1.3). Eobanus wrote it for a friend at Riesenburg, probably already in 1510, and then revised it for publication at Leipzig in 1514. The latter version differs from the former not only in its greater length but also in the poem's title and in the name and profession of the addressee. In the Leipzig redaction the title is "To the Priest Theodore Collucius: An Antidotary for Illicit Love." In the *Sylvae* of 1535/39 the heading reads simply "To the Love-struck Temonius, Concerning Love."

Puzzled by the change in the addressee's names, Carl Krause could explain them only as humanistic pseudonyms for one and the same person (*HEH*, 1:105). But though we never again hear of Theodore Collucius, the name *Temonius* reappears in the contemporary poems *Sylv.* 1.5 and *Sylv.* 4.5, both composed during Eobanus' first year at Riesenburg. More significantly, as Krause points out, the name *Temonius* occurs also in Ulrich von Hutten's *Querelae* 2.10.87–88, in an elegy written and published in 1510. Hutten, in fact, gives the young man's full name as "Ioannes Temonius" and ranks him among the best poets of Erfurt. Temonius, then, was a humanist who, while now totally forgotten, was still relatively well known in 1514. Accordingly we might theorize that Eobanus changed his friend's name to "Collucius" just to spare him the embarrassment of seeing his name publicly associated with passionate love. But why should Temonius feel discomfited at being caught in the toils of love when Eobanus himself shows no embarrassment at admitting his own love for Flavia in ll. 31–37? There must have been another reason for the switch in names. This reason becomes apparent when we compare the two versions of the poem. In the 1535/39 version there is no hint whatsoever that Temonius has taken holy orders. In the 1514 redaction, by contrast, the addressee is now a priest, who is upbraided for engaging in "illicit" love. Had Temonius perhaps entered the priesthood in the meantime? If so, Eobanus would have had no choice but to use a pseudonym to hide his friend's identity in the Leipzig revision. Of course, having obliterated all tell-tale clues to Temonius, Eobanus was free to seize on the man's priesthood to "update" his poem and lend it satiric spice by reproaching a celibate for what was now obviously an "illicit" passion.

The little that is presently known about Temonius derives from the three poems that Eobanus wrote for him at Riesenburg and from the brief hints in Hutten's *Querelae.* He was a native of Thuringia (*Sylv.* 1.3.85, 1.5.7–8; *Sylv. duae* 2.1). Since Hutten seems to have known him personally, Temonius probably studied with him at Erfurt (from ca. 1503 to 1505). Later he studied with Eobanus (*Sylv.* 1.3.1–2). Eobanus agrees with Hutten that their mutual friend was a gifted poet (*Sylv.* 1.3.169–72; *Sylv. duae* 2.171–76, 223). Sometime after completing his studies at Erfurt, Temonius entered the service of Bishop Job von Dobeneck at Riesenburg. This must have occurred well before Eobanus' arrival, for in early 1510, when Eobanus was still becoming acclimatized to Prussia, Temonius was already being sent to the Vatican, perhaps as an emissary for the Teutonic Order. At Temonius' departure, Eobanus presented him with a poem (*Sylv.* 1.5) in which he reviews the famed cities that his friend would be passing through along the way. He warns Temonius, however, not to stay long in Padua, still reeling from

Maximilian's siege that lasted from August to early October 1509. During his journey Temonius may have spent some time in Bologna, for in later conversations with Eobanus he praised its university to the skies (*Sylv.* 4.5.29–32). After returning to Riesenburg, Temonius fell so deeply in love that our poet felt moved to cure him of his passion in the same way he had cured Fronto Fundinus (and himself) in *De amantium infoelicitate*: with the Muses' help. Sometime between 1510 and 1514 he appears to have taken holy orders.

To these sparse indications, gleaned from Hutten's and Eobanus' writings, we can now add some new information. The "Register of Bachelors and Masters in the Faculty of Arts at the University of Erfurt" lists sixteen students who received their MA in February of 1516. Among them were not only Eobanus' friend and compatriot Euricius Cordus but also "Frater Johannes theomonius salczensis."[29] Now the name *Theomonius* is so similar to the equally unusual name *Temonius* that one cannot help but associate the two, all the more so, as this Theomonius also has the first name *Johannes*. Even more remarkably, Theomonius is said to be a "friar" who hails from the Thuringian town of Salza (Langensalza), not far from Erfurt. Since Salza was a small town that never sent many students to Erfurt, let alone two named Johannes who happened to be at Erfurt within a span of twelve years, the historians Rainer C. Schwinges and Klaus Wriedt tentatively identify Frater Johannes Theomonius Salczensis with the Johannes Gesselman de Salcza (Gysselman Saltzensis) who matriculated at Erfurt in the summer semester of 1503 (perhaps together with Hutten?) and earned his BA as "Joannes Gyselman Salsensis" in the early autumn of 1506, together with Eobanus.[30] This tentative identification becomes a near certainty when we realize that in Thuringian dialect the name *Gesselman* or *Gyselman* means "Geissel-mann" ("whip-man," hence "wagoner"). It thus has precisely the same meaning as *Temonius* (formed from *temo*, "yoke-beam of a wagon," hence, by synecdoche, "wagon"). As for the form *Theomonius* found in the Erfurt register for 1516, it can be explained either as a variant spelling or as the name Temonius adopted after he became a friar (*Theos*, "God" + *monius*, by analogy to Middle Latin *sanctimonia, sanctimonium*).

Sources and Models

(1) *Generalis Prussiae descriptio.* As we have seen, Eobanus composed his letter to Mutianus Rufus within a month or two after arriving at Riesenburg. With a newcomer's eye he observes how the locals use silver everywhere, even in everyday utensils and clothing; and as a seasoned bibbler, he takes special note of the country's beers and imported wines (ll. 113–24): "Nowhere else do they use silver more liberally or lavishly than here; back home, our country barely has that much lead. . . . Plump Ceres laces Achelous' draughts with barley; there is no country on earth where they love their beer more. . . . Merchants also import [wines] from overseas — new wines from Crete along with casks from Rhodes." Of the Prussian towns, he had

---

[29]Kleineidam, 2:371.
[30]*Das Bakkalarenregister der Artistenfakultät der Universität Erfurt 1392–1521* (Jena, 1995), 285.

already visited some five or six. He must have stopped at Thorn on his way north; and once at Riesenburg, he no doubt made trips on chancellery business to Danzig, Königsberg, and Elbing, perhaps also to Marienburg. At any rate, these are the cities that he briefly describes in ll. 127–54. He alludes to them also in a letter of 18 February 1510 to Ludwig Platz in Erfurt: "It is amazing how many magnificent cities [there are] in this region . . . , [cities] that a long time ago could not abide the over-bearing arrogance and insolence of their Teutonic overlords and hence defected to the king [of Poland]."[31] The phrase "magnificent cities" ("praeclarae urbes") used in this letter reappears in the same context in Eobanus' verse letter to Mutianus (l. 127).

The passages just discussed (ll. 113–54) form the second half of the description of Prussia in the original letter to Mutianus. Their selection and detail betray firsthand observation. The first half of the letter, by contrast, brings together information on Prussia that our poet could not possibly have gained through personal exploration during that first winter: knowledge about the region's neighbors, its rich harvests, its amber, fish, and honey, its wild game and cattle, its history. Here, of course, he would have had to rely on his authorities.

Which authorities? Students' notes, written during Eobanus' lectures at Leipzig in 1514, give us the answer: "Eneas Sylvius in Europa et Raphael Volaterranus in Commentariis urbanis geographii liber 7."[32] Completed in 1458, Enea Silvio's De Europa had been printed repeatedly, for example, at Venice in 1477, at Memmingen in 1490, and at Paris in 1509. By the winter of 1509–10 it had long since become the standard chorography of Europe. Its chapters on Livonia and Prussia (nos. 28 and 29) were the foundation of all humanistic descriptions of the German northeast. There can be no doubt that Eobanus had those sections in front of him when he wrote his description of Prussia. In this he follows the example of Raphael Volaterranus (Raffaele Maffei), to whose Commentariorum urbanorum octo et triginta libri (Rome, 1506) Eobanus alludes at the start of his course in Leipzig. In fact, it is fair to say that Volaterranus' treatment of Prussia in book 7 (fol. 97ʳ) is little more than a synopsis of the corresponding section in Enea Silvio's De Europa.[33]

Another humanist who closely studied De Europa for his own topography of Prussia was Erasmus Stella (Stüler) of Leipzig. After matriculating at Leipzig in 1470 (BA 1480, MA 1483) Stella taught at the university until at least 1488 and then traveled to Bologna to pursue his medical studies. Thereafter he became a physician in Zwickau. From 1501 to 1507 he was in Prussia as personal physician

---

[31]Epp. fam., 11: "Mirum quam praeclarae in hac regione urbes [sunt] . . . , quae olim, cum nimiam superbiam et insolentiam Teutonicorum dominorum ferre non possent, ad regem defecerunt."

[32]See sig. A1ᵛ of the London copy. The Zwickau copy has virtually the same note, also on sig. A1ᵛ. The students' notes go on to quote a passage from Volaterranus, book 7 (fol. 97ʳ). Despite the explicit reference in his lecture, Eobanus did not in fact use Volaterranus as a source for his description of Prussia.

[33]Like Eobanus, Johannes Cochlaeus mentions both Enea Silvio and Volaterranus as topographical authorities in his Brevis Germanie descriptio (Nuremberg, 1512). See Johannes Cochlaeus, Brevis Germanie descriptio (1512), ed. Karl Langosch (Darmstadt, 1976). Assuming that Cochlaeus' fourfold reference to "Volaterranus" points to Jacopo da Volterra, Langosch (p. 21) was unable to identify the true source.

For a general introduction to the history and practice of German topography in the Renaissance (though without mention of Prussia) see Gerald Strauss, Sixteenth-Century Germany: Its Topography and Topographers (Madison, 1959); for Enea Silvio's influence, see 12–17.

to Grand Master Frederick of Saxony. While in Prussia he maintained close contacts with the humanists in Königsberg and with the Bishop of Pomesania, Job von Dobeneck. When Frederick left Prussia in the late spring of 1507, Stella returned with him to Saxony. By the autumn he was back in Zwickau. Here he was to serve as physician, later also as mayor until his death in 1521.

In 1518 Stella published a topographical and historical account of Prussia that he entitled *De Borussiae antiquitatibus libri duo* (Basel: Joh. Froben).[34] Since it is dedicated to Frederick, who died on 14 December 1510, the manuscript must have been composed well before that date. Stella himself explains in the dedicatory letter that he began the book at the urging of Job von Dobeneck (bishop from 1501 to 1521). Elsewhere he adds that he wrote it at Frederick's court in Prussia, that is to say, sometime before May 1507.[35] From the additional circumstance that he asked Sebastian Myricius and Hieronymus Emser to contribute commendatory epigrams we may deduce that Stella intended to publish *De Borussiae antiquitatibus* shortly after his return to Saxony in 1507. Certainly both of those men were still active at Leipzig during this time. Myricius, who received his MA at Leipzig in early 1505, taught at the university until the late summer of 1509. After a stay in Prussia he was back at Leipzig from 1511 to 1514. Thereafter he lived in Prussia. Emser taught humanistic courses at Leipzig off and on from 1504 to 1510, even after becoming private secretary to Duke George of Saxony at Dresden, and until 1514 he often contributed epigrams to works by Leipzig humanists and theologians. For example, he wrote three epigrams for Johannes Rhagius Aesticampianus' *Septem divi Hieronymi epistole* (Leipzig, 1508). Other scholars who contributed epigrams for this book include Ulrich von Hutten, Veit Werler, and Sebastian Myricius.[36] Emser and Myricius

---

[34]For the text, see *Scriptores rerum Prussicarum: Die Geschichtsquellen der Preußischen Vorzeit bis zum Untergange der Ordensherrschaft*, ed. Theodor Hirsch, Max Töppen, and Ernst Strehlke, vol. 4 (Leipzig, 1870; repr. Frankfurt am Main, 1965), 282–98, with an introduction by Hirsch on 275–82. On Stella and his book see also Schoenborn, especially 29–30, 58–77; Arnold, 93–106; Mentzel-Reuters, 600–09.

[35]See Stella's letter to Andreas Althamer, dated 15 December 1519 ("XVIII. Kal. Januar. 1520"), in Stella, *Boruss.*, 281, n. 3 (rather carelessly reprinted in Mentzel-Reuters, 603–04): "Cum superioribus annis in comitatu illustris Principis, ducis Friderici, qui in ea provincia principatum gessit, agerem. . . ." The letter goes on to say that the work published at Basel in 1518 was to have formed the introduction to a history of the Teutonic Order in ten books, all of them written in Prussia. Stella had hoped to publish the remaining eight books with Froben also, but the distressing number of printing errors in the first two books as well as the critics' hostility had deterred him: "ab eorum [librorum] tamen editione hactenus abstinui, vel quod primi illi commentarioli a typographis haut curiose fuerant excusi, vel quod morsibus quoque colubrinis [haud] omnino caruerunt." There is no evidence, incidentally, to suggest that the original manuscript of *De Borussiae antiquitatibus* was in any way different from the version actually published in 1518, as Mentzel-Reuters, 603–04, suggests. The above-quoted phrase "haut curiose fuerant excusi" hardly suggests that the printers altered, abbreviated, or edited the text. Rather, it berates them for their carelessness in setting the book in type — that is, for the many typographical errors they introduced. The critical apparatus to Hirsch's edition of the text shows that Stella's complaint was only too well-founded.

[36]See Gustav Kawerau, *Hieronymus Emser: Ein Lebensbild aus der Reformationsgeschichte*, Schriften des Vereins für Reformationsgeschichte 15 (Halle, 1898), 24, 118; Gustav Bauch, *Geschichte des Leipziger Frühhumanismus, mit besonderer Rücksicht auf die Streitigkeiten zwischen Konrad Wimpina und Martin Mellerstadt* (Leipzig, 1899), 173.

later joined forces with Eobanus and others in writing commendatory epigrams for Hieronymus Dungersheim's *Confutatio apologetici cuiusdam sacre scripture falso inscripti* (Leipzig, 1514).

Given his closeness to both Sebastian Myricius and Job von Dobeneck, we can easily surmise that Eobanus too had an opportunity to peruse Stella's manuscript, either in the autumn of 1509 at Leipzig or in the following winter at Riesenburg.[37] And indeed, when we compare the two descriptions of Prussia, we quickly find parallels to the dedicatory letter and first book of *De Borussiae antiquitatibus*. Prussia's abundance of crops, cattle, game, and fish, summarily mentioned by Enea Silvio, is amplified by Stella and then — unmistakably via Stella — by Eobanus in ll. 77–108 of his poem. It is only in Stella that he could have found Prussia specifically associated with each of the following in turn: amber (ll. 73–76); wild honey (81–92); deer, wild boar, bison, elk, and aurochs (99–104). Eobanus himself, of course, could not have had any firsthand knowledge of these natural bounties in the winter of 1509–10. Just as tellingly, the unusual phrase "hanc scribendi provinciam," which Stella uses at the end of his dedicatory letter to Duke Frederick,[38] returns in the dedicatory letter of Eobanus' *Encomium nuptiale* as "nuptiarum scribendarum provinciam" (ded. 5) and as "scribendarum heroidum provintiam" in the dedication of *Heroidum Christianarum epistolae* (ded. 8.1).

Though it sometimes said that Eobanus' poem served as the inspiration for Georg Joachim Rheticus' prose "Encomium Prussiae,"[39] I see no evidence whatsoever to back this claim. The parallels between the two works — and there are indeed some — all derive from a common source: the first book of Erasmus Stella's *De Borussiae antiquitatibus*. Rheticus' encomium, written in 1539, was first published as an addendum to *De libris revolutionum . . . Nicolai Copernici . . . narratio prima* (Gdańsk, 1540), sig. H3r–I3r. It was reprinted at Basel in 1541 under the title "Encomium Borussiae." For an annotated edition, with translation into French, see *Georgii Joachimi Rhetici Narratio prima*, Studia Copernicana 20, ed. and trans. Henri Hugonnard-Roche and Jean-Pierre Verdet (Wrocław, 1982), 82–87, 140–45.

(2) *Illiciti amoris antidotarium*. We can be much briefer in detailing the models for Eobanus' "Antidotary for Illicit Love." As in *De amantium infoelicitate* (to which he alludes in *Sylv. duae* 2.31–38) our humanist places himself squarely in the tradition of cures for unbridled passion. This tradition, which starts with Ovid's *Remedia amoris* (*Cures for Love*), continues, for example, with Enea Silvio's oft-printed "Amoris illiciti medela" ("A Remedy for Illicit Love") — a letter to an older man who has desperately fallen in love with a prostitute.[40] The central premise of the tradition is

[37]This possibility is left open by Arnold, 104. *Pace* Arnold, however, Schoenberg does not discuss the question on pp. 15–16 of his dissertation. He only denies that Eobanus and Stella could have met at Riesenburg.

[38]Stella, *Boruss.*, 285: "Ego autem hanc scribendi provinciam non tam mea sponte quam iussu venerandi antistitis Iobi Pomesaniensis a nullo antea tentatam accepi." This sentence seems to have impressed Eobanus, for he also imitates it in *Nup.*, ded. 3: "Quod non tam 'subito' mihi (ut ait ille) 'calore' effluxerat quam mandato et authoritate principis mei Iobi, Pomesaniensis presulis, . . . deductum."

[39]See Leopold Prowe, *Nicolaus Coppernicus* (1883–84; repr. Osnabrück, 1967), 1.2:446; Karl Heinz Burmeister, *Georg Joachim Rhetikus, 1514–1574: Eine Bio-Bibliographie*, vol. 1 (Wiesbaden, 1967), 45–46; Arnold, 104.

that passionate love is a disease or poison that can be successfully treated only if the patient first recognizes it as such. The poet or narrator plays the role of physician who prescribes medicines for the disease or antidotes for the poison. A recent German example that Eobanus may well have known is Wolfgang Cyclopius' elegiac poem *Antidotarius contra furiosam Veneris frenesim . . . de vulgari in Latinum translatus* (*An Antidotary against the Frenzied Madness of Venus, Translated from the Vernacular into Latin*). First published at Erfurt in 1511, the elegy was reprinted at Wittenberg in 1512 and at Heidelberg in ca. 1515.[41] For several other late medieval and Renaissance examples see *Poetic Works*, 1:435. See further Mary Frances Wack, *Lovesickness in the Middle Ages: The* Viaticum *and Its Commentaries* (Philadelphia, 1990) and *A Treatise on Lovesickness: Jacques Ferrand*, ed. and trans. Donald A. Beecher and Massimo Ciavolella (Syracuse, 1990).

Eobanus' Inaugural Lecture on Sylvae duae

As soon as his *Sylvae duae* was published in mid-January, Eobanus applied to the philosophical faculty at Leipzig for permission to teach a course on the work. On January 23 the professors gave their qualified assent. He would be permitted to teach the course "until he reached the end of that poem." If he observed the university and college rules thereafter, he could continue with another course, but only at scheduled times.[42] Having promised to abide by these conditions, Eobanus posted a notice of the upcoming course and delivered a short lecture to introduce it to the students. Though Eobanus never published the speech himself, he kept a copy of it among his papers. Johann Drach found it there after his friend's death and edited it in *Helii Eobani Hessi, poetae excellentiss., et amicorum ipsius epistolarum familiarium libri XII* (Marburg, 1543), 246–48. Because it throws interesting light not only on the two poems but also on Eobanus' aspirations during this period, I append the lecture here, with translation:

HELII EOBANI HESSI ORATIO IN PRAELECTIONE SYLVA-RUM, OLIM LYPSIAE HABITA

Nihil minus hoc tempore sperabam, optimi auditores, quam in hoc celebratis-simo pulcherrimoque Lypsensi Gymnasio, ubi tot artes bonae, tot disciplinae honestae, tot rectissima studia, tot denique praestantissima ingenia velut

[40]Reprinted as letter 106 in his *Opera quae extant omnia* (Basel, 1571), 607–10. Enea wrote it long before he became Pope Pius II.

[41]See *VLDH*, 1:540–41. The elegy, ninety-eight distichs long, was originally written in German verse by Johann Heß of Nuremberg. I have consulted both the Erfurt and the Wittenberg prints. The latter includes, among other things, an elegy on drunkenness by Eobanus' friend Georg Spalatin and an elegy by Cyclopius in praise of poets. Eobanus is hailed as the pride of Hesse, along with Hermann Trebelius and Mutianus Rufus.

[42]See *Die Matrikel der Universität Leipzig*, ed. Georg Erler, vol. 2 (1897; repr. Nendeln, 1976), 492: "secunda feria post Agnetis concluserunt domini seniores, ut mgr. Eobanus, qui voluit legere pu-blice, admitteretur, donec istud carmen in finem deduceret. Si autem postea se conformaret statutis nostre universitatis et magistrorum de concilio facultatis respondendo, postea iterum legere posset horis tamen admissis. Quod idem dns. Eobanus promisit se facturum."

publico merent stipendio, quicquam me professurum, imo nec suggestum hoc unquam ad dicendum conscensurum, qui hoc exercitationis genus iam annos aliquot ex aulica desuetudine intermiseram, multoque magis ad theoricen quam practicam me philosophiam (quis enim et haec studia philosophiam non appellaverit?) converteram. **2** Postquam enim ex Erfurdensi Gymnasio, acceptis probatae eruditionis insigniis, in Prussiam ad liberalissimum et humanissimum pontificem meum Pomesaniensem venissem, statui omnem ingenii vim et potentiam, omnem (si qua esset) eruditionis[43] diu multumque laboratae virtutem, omne denique ocium, quantum videlicet per occupationes publicas quibus apud eum principem praefectus eram liceret, scribendis operibus impendere. **3** Itaque primo statim velut ingenii periculum facturus quid sub frigido isto et duriore coelo possem, qui antea quoque bucolica, quod ante me fere nullus in Germania, aliaque multa aediddissem, coepi ex ipso terrarum, quas ingressus eram, situ, moribus, cultu, et antiquitatibus argumentum, descripsi Prussiam, non ut reliqui solent topographi absoluta definitione, sed meo, hoc est, poetico more in epistolam coacta descriptione. **4** Cum vero dico poetico more, optimi auditores, nolim intelligat ex vobis quisquam mendacia me conscripsisse.[44] **5** Nostis enim modum hunc, quemadmodum res ipsa ad historicae[45] filum contexta, adiectis quibusdam velut parergis veterum nugamentorum amoenitatibus, exprimi soleat. **6** Quod qui non faciunt, extra poeticae venerationis album sine contentione relinquuntur. **7** Exemplo nobis ex multis unus est Lucanus, qui ob idipsum a multis tanquam poeticae appellationis indignus inter historicos cathalogo refertur.[46]

8 Sed ne extra praefinitas limites digrediar, optimi viri,[47] adnexum est huic topographo Prussiensi carmen contra Venerei amoris impotentiam dehortativum, ex eadem chorda lyratum et plane (ut dici solet) eiusdem farinae,[48] sed argumento longe diversissimo, quod amico quondam eo malo laboranti velut antidotum quoddam salutare ex plenissimo Musarum myropolio sanus ipse aegroto composui, mixtum [*p. 247*] diversis pulveribus, innumeris speciebus aromaticis. **9** Ex quo, si qui sunt ex vobis ad istas communis iuventutis illecebras paulo procliviores, remedium salutare licet consequi. **10** Eatenus tamen (ut sciatis) hoc officium agimus, quatenus amorem, istum blandissimum operosissimumque humanae naturae affectum, non destruere, non detestari, non prohibere, sed admissum lenire et mitigare velle videamur. **11** Haec intentio, hoc propositum, "hoc opus, hic labor est."[49] **12** Quis enim, Deus bone, tam alienatus ab humanis affectibus, tam durus, tamque audax, ut bonum hoc malum (sic enim dicere libet)

[43]For the modesty topos cf. *Nup.*, ded. 12, n.

[44]Cf. Erasmus, *Adag.* 2.2.98; Otto 1444; Eob. *Gen. ebrios.* 24.8: "Dicerent enim statim, poetam me esse . . . atque ideo mentiri, quoniam persuasum habent, ad mendacia dumtaxat natos poetas."

[45]For this form (instead of "historiae"), cf. *Eleg.* 1.115, referring to the study of history at Nuremberg: "Quaeris an historicae sit et hic locus, est quoque, siqua / Nomina res Macedum regis habere putas."

[46]Cf. *Her. Chr.*, ded. 14.3, n.

[47]Drach's text prints "optimi N." instead of "optimi V."

[48]Cf. Erasmus, *Adag.* 3.5.44.

[49]Verg. *A.* 6.129.

prorsus damnet, insectetur, excutiat, quandoquidem nemo unquam has Syrtes, has Charybdes, hos scopulos, hunc Sphynga, hunc denique inextricabilem Labyrinthum[50] effugerit? **13** Teneriori aetati ludus iste ab summis viris impune admittitur, ut videlicet in Amoris officina rudis adhuc aetas et inculta velut artificio quodam expoliatur et non secus ac informe aliquod corpus adiectis quibusdam liniamentis perficiatur. **14** Artifex enim Amor est (duriores amusoteri[51] "carnificem" vocant). **15** Artifex, inquam, est; artificium pulcherrimum exercet. **16** Quod vero illud, rogaverit quispiam? **17** Dicam, sed apud vos, hoc est candidissimi et non perturbati iudicii homines, auditores iucundissimi. **18** Mores docet, formam componit, gestus indicat, humanitatem ostendit, frontem variat, animum levat, denique ex stultis sapientes reddit. **19** Quorum omnium exemplum in uno Cymone Boccatii videre licet.[52]

20 Quod si qui critici verba haec mea in peiorem partem interpretaturi contra sentient, dicam sanctissimi cuiusdam hominis verba, qui sic in hymno quodam, "Amorem sive divinum sive angelicum sive spiritualem sive animalem sive naturalem dixerimus, unitivam quandam et commiscentem intelligimus virtutem," et quae sequuntur. **21** Virtutem (ut videtis) appellat vir ille amorem, nec immerito. **22** Virtus enim est, quamdiu nos in vitium non convertimus. **23** Fit enim plaerunque, dum effusis continentiae habenis[53] virtutem hanc amplectimur, ut in vitium decidamus. **24** Quicquid enim nimium est, ut dici solet, fertur in vitium.[54] **25** Unde enim tot mortes, tot fata infoelicia, tot miserandi amantium exitus? **26** Unde, nisi ex insani amoris nimia indulgentia? **27** Qui profecto, si temperantiam tenere potuissent, nunquam in vitium tam praeclaram virtutem convertissent, non tot tragoediis, tot epigrammatis, tot denique poematibus de se conscriptis materiam praebuissent. **28** Quod malum ut sapienter evitare possitis, eruditi iuvenes, capessite, haurite, imbibite quae in proposito vobis carmine a me dicentur. **29** Puto nec vos impensarum nec me operae poeni- [*p. 248*] tebit, tametsi nulla, vel certe quam exigua erit haec opera, quam nullius spe lucri, nullius cupiditate gloriae, nullius invidiae (quae in magno animo locum non habet) stimulo excitatus aggredior, sed ut his minutulis ad maiora viam aperiam. **30** Constitueram namque, ut ex eulogio nostro foribus affixo intelligere potuistis, Heroidas meas Christianas, quatuor annorum lucubrationem, multis vigiliis,

---

[50]Cf. *Ama.* 12.11, n.

[51]For "amusoteri" Drach's text has "amusatri." Cf. Filippo Beroaldo, "Oratio proverbialis," in *Varia Philippi Beroaldi opuscula* (Basel, 1513), fol. 47ʳ: "omnes tam amusoteri quam litterati." For the thought, cf. Pl., *Cist.* 203: "Credo ego Amorem primum apud homines carnificinam commentum."

[52]In his praise of love, Filippo Beroaldo expresses the same thoughts, though without mentioning the example of Boccaccio's Cimon. See "Oratio habita in principio enarrationis Propertii continens laudes amoris," in *Varia Philippi Beroaldi opuscula* (Basel, 1513), fol. 4ᵛ. Cf. further Eob. *Ama.* B 2.17–18; *Gen. ebrios.* 20.21–23: "amor enim . . . instruit, informat, mores docet. Componit sese ad benevolentiam qui amat, ut fiat amabilis. Videte Cimonem Boccaccii, qui ex fatuo sapiens, ex rudi doctus, ex rustico urbanus, ex agresti civilis solo amoris beneficio factus est."

[53]*Ama.* 12.8, n. The phrase occurs also in *Gen. ebrios.* 12.1.

[54]For the proverb see Walther 7687 and 19859: "Omne quod est nimium, vertitur in vitium"; 19837: "omne nimium vertitur in vitium." In his praise of love (fol. 4ᵛ) Beroaldo likewise counsels against immoderate love.

magno labore, summo vero studio congestum opus, cum primum hoc Lycaeum attigissem, publicis characteribus transformatum dimittere et evulgari. **31** Mutavi tamen propositum, ratus convenire et esse non undequaque male consultum si prius, velut praenuntium aliquod, duo haec quae nunc in manibus sunt carmina praemitterem, ne post absolutum et expressum opus quoquo modo periclitarer et tum demum post facta consilium capesserem.[55] **32** Nec me fefellit opinio, quotus enim quisque vestrum est qui nesciat ab hoc quoque meo pio et bono proposito me esse deterritum. **33** Spero tamen innocentiam meam olim vel apud hos homines gratiam inventuram, qui non mercedem posco, non decipulas tendo, non vane glorior, non intumesco, non extollor, sed (quae mea semper fuit hodieque est mediocritas) ut huic Gymnasio florentissimo, his hominibus doctissimis, vobis quoque commilitonibus meis eatenus gratificari possim, ut fidelium laborum meorum mercedem mediocrem, duntaxat famam apud vos inveniam.

Dixi.

A LECTURE BY HELIUS EOBANUS HESSUS, WHICH HE HELD A LONG TIME AGO IN LEIPZIG TO INTRODUCE A COURSE ON HIS *SYLVAE*

The last thing I expected at this time, distinguished members of the audience, was to give a lecture at this world-renowned and first-rate university of Leipzig, where so many liberal arts, so many honorable disciplines, so many superb courses, and, lastly, so many brilliant minds are, as it were, earning their keep at public expense. In fact, I never expected even to mount this podium to say a few words. During the past several years, after all, I had stopped doing this kind of exercise, owing to a lack of opportunity at court, and had applied myself far more to theory than to practical philosophy (for who would not extend the term philosophy to these pursuits too?). Indeed, after graduating from the University of Erfurt with the distinctions granted to proven erudition and arriving in Prussia to serve my most magnanimous and gracious lord the Bishop of Pomesania, I resolved to devote all the vigor and power of my mind, all the merit (if any there be) of my hard-won erudition, and, finally, all my leisure time — that is to say, as much as was allowed me by the public affairs of which I was in charge at the court of that prince — to the writing of literary works. Accordingly, wishing right from the start to put my mind, so to speak, to the test, in order to see what I could accomplish under that frigid and rather harsh sky, as one who had even published bucolics (which virtually nobody in Germany had done until then) and many other things besides, I took my theme from the geography, customs, culture, and history of the lands that I had entered: I described Prussia, not, as other topographers do, with precise facts and figures, but rather in my own, that is to say, poetic manner, by way of a description in the form of a letter. Now when I say "poetic manner," distinguished members of the audience, I do not want any of you to think that I composed a pack of lies. For you are well acquainted with

---

[55]Cf. *Sylv. duae*, ded. 1–4.

this style, in which the topic itself, though woven together with the thread of history, tends to be expressed by adding some charming antique touches, by way of embroidery, so to speak. Anyone who fails to do this is unceremoniously dropped from the honor roll of poets. From the many we may take as our example Lucan, who for this very reason is widely deemed unworthy of the title *poet* and is hence classified among the historians instead.

[8] But lest I digress from the topic I have set myself, distinguished gentlemen: adjoined to this topographical description of Prussia is a poem dissuading the reader from the unbridled force of passionate love. It is harped on the same string and obviously (as they say) baked from the same flour,[56] but deals with a completely different theme. Having been cured of the disease myself,[57] I wrote the poem for an ailing friend who quite some time ago was suffering from that very malady, as a sort of therapeutic antidote taken from the well-stocked pharmacy of the Muses and made up of diverse powders and innumerable aromatic drugs. From it, if any of you happen to be a bit too prone to those allurements that entice young people of both sexes, you can obtain an efficacious remedy. However (just so you know) I perform that benefit only to the extent that I don't come across as wishing to eradicate, denounce, or proscribe love, that most charming and troublesome emotion of the human heart, but to accept, allay, and mitigate it. This is my intention, this my purpose, "this the task, this the labor." For who, good Lord, is so estranged from human emotions, so hard-hearted, and so presumptuous as to utterly condemn, censure, and banish this beneficent evil (for that is what I like to call it), considering that nobody has ever escaped these shoals, these whirlpools, these reefs, this Sphinx, in fine, this inextricable Labyrinth? To teenagers that sport has always been permitted with impunity by the foremost authorities, who realize that this as yet rude and unsophisticated season of life is, by some ingenious process, polished in the workshop of Love and, like some shapeless mass, perfected by the addition of certain lineaments. For Love is a craftsman (surly philistines call him a "hangman"). He is a craftsman, I say; he practices the most beautiful craftsmanship. Is there someone who asks what that might be? I'll say it, but just among you, that is, among the most upright of men, untroubled in judgment, a most delightful audience. He teaches manners, creates good looks, instills poise, demonstrates culture, varies the brow, elevates the mind, and, finally, turns fools into wise men. If you want an example for all these benefits, you need look only at Boccaccio's Cimon.[58]

[20] Now if there are critics out there who, taking these words of mine in ill part, are of the opposite opinion, I'll quote the words of a certain most holy man,

---

[56]That is, it is written in the same meter (elegiac distich).

[57]See *Ama.* B 2; *Nup.* 10–11.

[58]See Giovanni Boccaccio, *The Decameron*, fifth day, first story (opening pages). After falling in love with the beautiful Iphigenia, the highborn but uncouth Cimon is transformed into a polished, gallant gentleman. The story was translated into Latin prose by Filippo Beroaldo and thence into elegiac distichs by Heinrich Bebel. For the former see "Mythica historia in Latinum e vernaculo sermone conversa" in *Varia Philippi Beroaldi opuscula* (Basel, 1513), fol. 33ʳ–36ᵛ; for the latter see *In hoc libro continentur haec Bebeliana opuscula nova et adolescentiae labores* (Strasbourg, 1508), sig. P6ʳ–Q7ʳ.

who in one hymn or other wrote, "Whether we speak of love as something divine
or angelic or intellectual or psychic or natural, we understand it as a kind of unify-
ing and binding virtue," and so forth.[59] As you can see, that man calls love a
virtue, and justly so. It is indeed a virtue — as long as we ourselves do not turn it
into a vice. For it often happens, when we slacken the reins of self-control in
embracing this virtue, that we fall into vice. Indeed, every excess, as they say,
becomes a vice. For what else has brought about so many deaths, so many
unhappy fates, so many lovers' catastrophes? What else but the excessive indulging
in frenzied love? Without question, if they could have exercised restraint, they
would never have turned so brilliant a virtue into a vice or furnished the theme for
so many tragedies, so many epigrams — in short, so many poems written about
them. So you can wisely keep clear of this evil, young scholars, I recommend that
you grab, get your fill of, imbibe what I have to say in the poem that I am laying
before you. You, I think, will not regret the expense nor I the work involved, even
though the work involved will be nothing, or certainly as good as nothing, seeing
that I am not undertaking it spurred by the hope of any wealth, the desire for any
glory, the goad of any malice (which has no place in a generous soul), but rather
by means of these minuscule works to open the way to greater ones. For as you
can tell from the commendation that I posted on the door, I had decided that my
Christian Heroides — four years' worth of lucubrations, a book put together by
dint of many vigils, much labor, and in truth the utmost enthusiasm — should be
set in type and published here the moment I reached this university. However, I
changed this plan, thinking it appropriate and by no means ill-advised if I should
first, as a kind of harbinger, so to speak, send out the two poems that are now in
your hands, for fear that after completing and printing the big book I might run
some kind of risk and not take counsel until it was too late. Nor was I mistaken in
this opinion; for most of you are aware that I have been strongly discouraged also
from this honorable and good intention of mine. I hope, however, that my innocence will find favor someday even among those men, seeing that I am not asking
for pay, not setting any snares, not ostentatiously pluming myself, not swelling
with pride, not putting myself on a pedestal. Rather, it has always been and still is
my humble aim to be able to oblige this most flourishing university, these most
learned scholars, and you too, my fellow students, to such a degree that in modest
payment for my faithful labors I shall find fame among you.

I am done.

---

[59]The "most holy man" is Hierotheus — most probably a literary fiction. See Ps.-Dionysius, *De
divinis nominibus* 4.15, translated into Latin by Marsilio Ficino and quoted as follows by Konrad
Celtis in *Quatuor libri amorum* (Nuremberg, 1502), sig. m2ʳ: "Verba Ierothei sanctissimi ex eius hym-
nis amatoriis: 'Amorem sive divinum sive angelicum sive spiritualem sive animalem sive naturalem
dixerimus: unitivam quandam et commiscentem intelligimus virtutem.'" For the translation I have
adapted John D. Jones' phrasing in his *Pseudo-Dionysius Areopagite: The Divine Names and Mystical
Theology* (Milwaukee, 1980), 147. In Hierotheus' definition, love is a "power," not a "virtue," as
Eobanus interprets it.

Helii Eobani Hessi
SYLVAE DUAE NUPER AEDITAE:
"PRUSSIA" ET "AMOR"

SEBASTIANI MYRICII REGIOMONTANI
AD PATRIAM PRUSSIAM ΟΓΔΟΑΣΤΙΧΟΝ

Quamvis multiplici naturae dote beata
   Non caedas ulli, patria chara, loco,
Hoc tamen his solum qui te videre patebat,
   Vix aliis ipso nomine nota prius.
5 Reddidit illustrem cunctis nunc Helius oris
   Carminibus vates te celebrando suis.
Nunc igitur foelix, mea dulcis Prussia, gaude,
   Quod te tam celebri contigit ore cani.

Tit. et epigramma Myricii. *Add. A.*

Helius Eobanus Hessus
TWO IMPROMPTUS OF RECENT VINTAGE: "PRUSSIA" AND "LOVE"

AN EIGHT-LINE EPIGRAM TO HIS NATIVE PRUSSIA BY SEBASTIAN MYRICIUS OF KÖNIGSBERG[1]

Even though you, dear homeland, are blessed with such manifold gifts of nature that no country on earth can rival you, this fact is nonetheless known only to those who have seen you. Until today, the others barely knew you, even by name. But the bard Helius has now made you illustrious all over the world by celebrating you in his verse.[2] Now then, be glad, my sweet Prussia! Rejoice that you have the good fortune to be sung by so distinguished a voice.

---

[1]Sebastian Myricius (von der Heide), a native of Königsberg, matriculated at Leipzig in 1499 (BA 1502, MA 1505). Later he taught at the university, serving as promoter during the summer semesters of 1508 and 1509. In 1508 he was among those who vigorously supported the humanist Johannes Rhagius Aesticampianus. Eobanus appears to have met Myricius in Leipzig in the autumn of 1509. In view of his close contacts with the Teutonic Order, it may well have been he who introduced Eobanus to Bishop Job von Dobeneck, then attending the Grand Master in nearby Rochlitz. Myricius went back to Prussia in late 1509, probably with Eobanus in tow. Having received a benefice in Cremitten, near Königsberg, Myricius returned to Leipzig in 1511 to continue his law studies. Eobanus refers to him as a mutual friend ("Miritium nostrum") in a letter to Georg Spalatin of 12 April 1512 (Mutian. *Ep.*, 2:369). During the winter semester of 1512–13 Myricius served as rector of the university, earning a bachelor's degree in canon and civil law around the same time. He returned to Prussia in the spring of 1514 to serve the Teutonic Order (Mutian. *Ep.*, 2:371, a letter from Eobanus to Georg Spalatin of 22 June 1514). In 1515 he carried out an embassy to Reval on behalf of the order. Thereafter he was pastor at Pobethen, later at Cremitten. After the Reformation he is said to have become an evangelic preacher in Löbenicht. He died in 1531.

During his stays at Leipzig, Myricius often wrote complimentary epigrams for his colleagues' books, including two for Erasmus Stella's *De Borussiae antiquitatibus libri duo* (printed at Basel in 1518, but written well over a decade earlier) and another one for Hieronymus Dungersheim's *Confutatio apologetici cuiusdam sacre scripture falso inscripti* (Leipzig, 1514), to which Eobanus also contributed.

[2]Myricius puns on Eobanus' newly-assumed name *Helius* (*helios*, "sun"): the sun-poet Helius has shed light on hitherto obscure Prussia and made it "illustrious" throughout the world. In an earlier epigram he had paid the same compliment to Erasmus Stella (*stella*, "star").

**HELIUS EOBANUS HESSUS SEBASTIANO MYRICIO
REGIOMONTANO SUO FOELICITATEM.**

Quartus iam annus agitur, mi Sebastiane, postquam Heroidas
Christianas (opus ut inventione novum, ita argumentis varium et
multiplex) scribere sum aggressus. **2** Quas cum in Prussia, quae
tibi patria est, superiori anno absolvissem, statui ex aula ad gymnasium aliquod ubi publico charactere transcriberentur secedere.
3 Itaque ad ripam Oderae aliquandiu remoratus, taedio quorundam hominum Lypsim tandem — hic, ubi optimarum literarum
optimum diversorium — concessi, eo animo ut quamprimum
Heroidas meas e sinu meo in vulgus dimitterem, facturus periculum possent ne gratiam sibi et immortalitatem polliceri. **4** Quod
ubi non statim et omnino bene consultum visum est, venit in
mentem minutulo aliquo prius velut praemetio multitudinis eru-
ditae iudicium experiri, ne opus alioqui magnum inconsulto
aedens temeritatis poenam ignominiam fortasse pro gratia
invenirem.

5 Ex multis itaque duo tametsi non optima selegi carmina
quae velut praeexercitamenta quaedam praemitterem, gladiatores
palestritas imitatus, qui in arenam descendentes levibus quibusdam et ludicris velitationibus praeludunt spectatorumque in se et
animos et oculos rapiunt. **6** Ita et mihi his duobus carminibus
faciundum putavi, quorum unum patriae tuae topographum,
alterum vero illiciti amoris est velut antidotarium. **7** Utrunque
vero tibi nuncupare statui, cum eam ob rem ut Prussiae descriptionem non nisi eius nationis homini et ei quidem doctissimo
dedicarem, tum etiam ut multis tuis in me beneficiis iamdudum
ut nunc quoque collocatis ex aliqua saltem, licet exigua parte
responderem. **8** Es enim tu (quod verum est) ut eruditus et eruditis omnibus vel naturae tuae beneficio singulari quadam pietate
affectus, ita et hoc munere et bonorum omnium favore, gratia, et
observantia dignus. **9** Bene vale.

10 Lypsi, Kalendis Ianuariis, M.D.XIIII.

Ded. *Add. A.*

HELIUS EOBANUS HESSUS TO HIS DEAR FRIEND SEBASTIAN MYRICIUS OF KÖNIGSBERG, BEST WISHES.

This is already the fourth year, my dear Sebastian, since I began writing the *Christian Heroides*, a work as original in invention as it is varied and ever-changing in theme. After finishing those letters last year in your native Prussia, I decided to take my leave from court and go to some university town where they could be printed. To this end I stayed for a while on the banks of the Oder. But overcome with disgust at some of the people there,[3] I ended up moving here to Leipzig — the best of lodgings for the best of books — with an eye to unveiling my *Heroides*, bringing them before the public as soon as possible, and determining if they could indeed win favor and immortality for themselves. Because I was advised not to rush headlong into publication — and sound advice it was too — it occurred to me that I ought to assay the taste of the scholarly public by offering up, as it were, some minuscule first fruits beforehand. For if I went ahead and brought out the magnum opus regardless, I might have to pay the price for my temerity and find disgrace instead of favor.

From the multitude of my verse, therefore, I have selected two poems, though not necessarily the best ones, which I am sending out ahead of the main action, so to speak, in imitation of the master gladiators, who, as they went down into the arena, used to warm up with some light and amusing displays of swordsmanship and so drew the hearts and eyes of the spectators onto themselves. To my mind, that is exactly what these two poems are intended to do. The first is a topographical description of your homeland; the other, figuratively speaking, is an antidotary for illicit love. If I have resolved to offer both of them to you, it is partly because I wanted to dedicate the description of Prussia to none but a native of that country, and a most learned one too; and more importantly, because I wanted to repay you, in some small way at least, for the many kindnesses you have shown me for such a long time already and are still showing me today. For you (and this is the truth) are a scholar who, through a remarkable endowment of your nature, are possessed of a special respect for all other scholars. It is these qualities that make you worthy, not only of this tribute of mine, but also of the favor, gratitude, and respect of all men of good will. Farewell.

Leipzig, 1 January 1514.

---

[3] See the introduction, pp. 48–49 above.

1 **HELII EOBANI HESSI AD DOCTISSIMUM VIRUM MUTIANUM RUFUM GENERALIS PRUSSIAE DESCRIPTIO**

Quam legis, hanc Hessus mittit tibi, Rufe, salutem
  Hinc ubi in aequoreas Vistula fertur aquas.
Qui licet et tantis et tot regionibus absit,
  Est tamen et praesens contiguusque tibi.
5 Nam duo quae ratio distantia corpora fecit,
  Haec animos vinclo proximiore ligat.
Et loca si nullum simul in diversa feratur
  Corpus, ad hoc animum vincula nulla ligant.
Liber ut est, partes ita derivatur in omnes,
10 Mobiliusque nihil maximus orbis habet.
Non mare, non terrae, non astra, nec igneus aether
  Clauditur huic. Penetrat corpora, numen habet.
Numen habet — si se partem de semine caeli
  Inclusam lutea sentiat esse domo.
15 Sentit et ex istis ad te spatiatur arenis,
  Pars eadem nostri maxima, quando libet.
Ergo et adhuc animo non deficiente valemus.
  Fortunae dominae caetera credidimus.
Ut tamen accipias, nobis charissime Rufe,
20 Res nostrae quo sint ordine quove loco,
Scito Lycaoniam nos processisse sub Arcton —
  Maior in has etiam despicit Ursa plagas.
Hic, ubi Prussiacum latus aequoris occupat orbem,
  Quod de Germanis nunc quoque nomen habet,
25 Hic tuus ille Hessus vivit quem saepe probabas
  Ludere ad auratam verba canora chelim.
Vivimus hic certe non retroeuntibus astris.
  Uno te nobis posse carere grave est.
Omnia praestiterit si te fortuna, mihique
30 Barbara quae visa est terra Latina foret.
Barbara sit licet, haec terrarum uberrima vincit
  Et Rhodon et Cretam, Lydia regna, Paphum.

Sylv. duae **1**. *Cf. Sylv. 1.2 in* **SO**.   *Tit.* Helii — descriptio *A*: Ad Mutianum Rufum epistola Prussiae descriptionem continens **SO**.   **1–2** Quam — aquas *A*: Mittit ab aequoreo tibi littore, Rufe, salutem / Hessus, amicitiae pars modo iusta tuae, / Hinc [Hic **SO**], ubi Parrhasium vicinior aspicit axem / Prussia, Hyperboreo semiperusta gelu, / Hinc, ubi Sarmaticum latus aequoris alluit orbem, / Quod de Germanis nunc quoque nomen habet. / Hic tuus ille Hessus vivit quem saepe probabas / Ludere ad auratam verba canora chelim **SO** [*cf. vv. 21–26*].   **4** Est — tibi *A*: Nunquam non praesens est tamen ille tibi **SO**.   **9** derivatur *A*: se dimittit **SO**.   **10** Mobiliusque nihil *A*: Quo nil mobilius **SO**.   **19–26** Ut tamen — chelim. *add. A*.   **27** certe *A*: igitur **SO**.   **30** terra Latina *A*: patria terra **SO**.   **31–32** Barbara — Paphum. *add. A*.   **31** sit licet *A*: scilicet *Krause*.

1 A DESCRIPTION OF PRUSSIA IN GENERAL, ADDRESSED BY HELIUS EOBANUS HESSUS TO THAT MOST LEARNED OF SCHOLARS MUTIANUS RUFUS[1]

The greetings that you're reading, Hessus sends them to you, Rufus, from here where the Vistula empties into the sea. Though he is separated from you by such vast spaces and so many regions, he is nevertheless present with you and nearby. After all, the same circumstance that sunders two bodies also ties souls together with a closer bond. For while the body can never be in several places at once, the mind is not tied down like that. Unfettered as it is, it can fly off in all directions. [10] Indeed, in the whole wide world there is nothing quite so nimble. Neither sea nor land, neither the stars nor the fiery ether are off-limits to the mind. It can pass through bodies; it has divine power. It has divine power — so long as it recognizes that it is part of the seed of heaven, imprisoned in a house of clay. This it recognizes; and so, as the greatest part of my being, it leaves these sandy coasts behind and ambles off to you, whenever it feels the urge.

As you can see, I'm in good spirits and sound health. The rest I've entrusted to Lady Luck. However, so that you, my dearest Rufus, [20] can learn how I'm getting along and where I'm staying at present, know that I have traveled north to the lands beneath the Lycaonian Bear.[2] Yes, Ursa Major looks down on these regions too! Here where Prussia lies by that sea that even today takes its name from the Germans,[3] here is where that Hessus of yours is now living, the one you often used to praise as he sang melodious words to the golden lyre. This is where I intend to stay. There is no turning back now, that's for sure. My only regret is having to do without you. Fortune would fulfill my every wish if she could contrive to bring you here! Then [30] this country, which just now seemed so barbarous, would be a second Italy to me.

Barbarous though it may be, this country is exceedingly fertile, more so even than Rhodes, Crete, Lydia, and Cyprus. Except for

---

[1] For Mutianus Rufus' life, see Camerarius, *Nar.* 12–13, with n. 36 (1:37–39).

[2] See n. 8 at *Nup.* 20.

[3] In Eobanus' day the Baltic was known as the Mare Germanicum (German Sea), as one can learn not only from Hieronymus Münzer's map printed at the end of Hartmann Schedel's *Liber Chronicarum* (Nuremberg, 1493) and Celtis, *Germania* 132–33, but also from a manuscript gloss in the Zwickau and London copies. Raphael Volaterranus, *Commentariorum urbanorum octo et triginta libri* (Rome, 1506), bk. 7, fol. 98ʳ, likewise refers to the Baltic Sea as "mari Germanico." Cf. Plin. *Nat.* 4.103 (often interpreted to mean the Baltic): "Germanicum mare." In Eob. *Gen. ebrios.* 16.6, the Baltic is called "Oceanus Germanicus."

Haec est Christiferae regio crucis ultima cultrix,
    Preter quam merito, Livo comose, tenes.
35   Regna dein servant pharetrati proxima Rhussi,
    Gens fera, sed nigrae saepe subacta cruci.
Prussia et insignis magno Livonia Christo,
    Sunt duo Teutonicae subdita regna cruci.
Parte orientalem qua Prussia vergit in Eurum,
40   Livonum gentes et Lythuana iacent.

A3ʳ

Proxima nymbosis quae flatibus irrigat Auster
    Mazovita et durus rura Polonus arat.
Occiduum Saxones habent. Latus unde remugit
    Hirsutus Boreas Balthica stagna tenent.
45   Tam late, tam vasta patet Pruthenica tellus,
    Inclyta, plena, potens, cultibus, aere, manu.
Hanc cruce signatus nigra pallaque nivali
    Teutonicus partam sanguine miles habet.
Caesarea sedit Fridericus in arce Secundus,
50   Prussia adhuc Stygia nocte sepulta fuit.
Cum Mahometigenae capta Ptholomaide Turcae
    Teutonicam Syria destituere crucem,
Tum quod erat propior, quod adhuc idola colebat,
    Hec a Teutonicis terra petita fuit.
55   Annuit et summo summus cum rege sacerdos
    Et titulum optati iussit habere soli.
Quaesitam obtinuit cruce munitissimus ordo;
    Teutonicum subiit gens superata iugum.
Scit vagus et magno fluvio par Vistula Rheno,
60   Sanguine quem totum subrubuisse ferunt.
(Vistula Pannoniis oriens e montibus, omnem,
    Quam longa est, terram hanc perluit amne vago.)

A3ᵛ

Hinc urbes positaeque altae victoribus arces
    Firmaque ductilibus oppida cincta vadis.
65   Hic etiam (ut noris quo nunc sim fine quietus)
    Omnibus ad victum rebus habundat ager.
Dum sinit et melior cum sole revertitur annus,
    Has Cererem terras incoluisse putes.
Atque adeo plenis hos messibus aggravat agros,
70   Ut queat hoc credi Copia nata loco.

---

42 durus *A*: fortis *SO*.   45 Tam — tellus *A*: Prussia tam latas terrarum possidet oras *SO*.
49–58 Caesarea — iugum. *add. A*.   53 Tum *A*: Iam *Krause*.   55 summo *A*: summos *Krause*.
61–62 omnem . . . terram hanc *A*: omnem hanc . . . terram *SO*.   62 amne *AO*: omne *S*.
63–64 Hinc — vadis *A*: Inde vago lapsu magnum se condit in aequor, / Quod variis totam flexibus
ambit humum *SO*.   65 (ut noris — quietus) *A*: vario naturae munere laetus *SO*.   66 habundat
A: abundet *SO*.   69 Atque *A*: Usque *SO*.

the area rightfully held by the long-haired Livonians,[4] this is the easternmost territory that reveres the cross of Christ. The neighboring realms belong to the quiver-bearing Russians, a fierce people, but often subdued by the black cross.[5] Both Prussia and Livonia — herself noted for her trust in Christ's power — are countries subject to the Teutonic cross. On the flank where Prussia faces the East wind [40] dwell the peoples of Livonia and Lithuania. The nearby fields that the South wind drenches with its rainstorms are farmed by the Mazovites and the hardy Poles. To the west live the Saxons. The shore whence the bristling North wind bellows is lapped by the Baltic Sea. That is the immense length and breadth of Prussia's domain, famed for its agriculture, rich in ores, mighty in battle.

It was the Teutonic Knights, marked with the black cross and snow-white cloak, who shed their blood to carve out this country of theirs. When Frederick the Second occupied the imperial throne, [50] Prussia was still buried in Stygian darkness. But then the Mohammedan Turks captured Acre, and Syria turned its back on the Teutonic cross. Accordingly, because it was closer by, because it still worshiped idols, the Teutonic Knights aimed to conquer this region instead. Together with the emperor, the supreme pontiff gave his blessing to their enterprise and gave them title to the lands they coveted. Thoroughly safeguarded by the cross, the order seized the territory it wanted; the vanquished population submitted to the Teutonic yoke.[6] The winding Vistula knows all about that. Though it is as large a river as the Rhine, [60] it is said to have run completely red with blood. (Rising in the mountains of Hungary, the Vistula in its wandering course washes the entire length of this country.) Their mission accomplished, the victors founded cities and towering castles and fortified towns, ringed with moats.

This country (just so you'll know where I have settled down now) is also rich in all kinds of foodstuffs. As long as the growing season permits and the sun is warm enough again, you would think that Ceres herself dwells in this countryside. In fact, she burdens these fields with such abundant harvests [70] that one might well

---

[4]Livonia, a territory now in Latvia and Estonia, was Christianized in the thirteenth century by Bishop Albert of Livonia and the order of Brothers of the Sword that he founded (absorbed by the Teutonic Order in 1237).

[5]That is, by the Teutonic Order, whose symbol was a black cross on a white background.

[6]This brief, if somewhat unchronological history of Prussia, was first added in 1514. Originally founded by merchants of Lübeck and Bremen in 1190–91 to take care of the sick, the Teutonic Order became an order of German knights during the Third Crusade in 1198. The Grand Master had his seat in Acre, Palestine, while the German Master (*Deutschmeister*) led the order in Germany. In 1226 Emperor Frederick II granted the order permission to claim any territories it could wrest from the pagan Prussi. The conquest of Prussia began in 1229 and was complete in 1283. Pope Gregory IX gave his blessing to the operations in 1234, provided that the order agree to receive the conquered lands from him as a fief. After the fall of Acre in 1291, the Grand Master moved his seat to Venice and in 1308 to Marienburg.

Horrea saepe suo non sunt satis ampla colono,
　　Lataque vix messis frugibus arva patent.
Est mare nobilibus plenum atque insigne lapillis;
　　Electrum primae nomina laudis habet.
75　Saepius hoc puerique legunt timidaeque puellae,
　　Nec stupet a prima pes madefactus aqua.
Est mare, sunt fluvii, sunt stagna immensa lacusque.
　　Non magis est vario pisce superba Pharos.
Salmo, lupus, sturio, murenae, rhombus, et esox
80　Vix uno, quamvis sit gravis, asse venit.
Sunt et apum pulchris tenerarum examina sylvis,
　　Qualia non unquam Sicelis Hybla tulit.
Non illis (res mira) loci satis esse probatum est,
　　Quo dulces possint accumulare favos.
A4r　85　Saepe sub arboribus mollique in graminis herba
　　Flava laborifero poplite mella locant.
Conferat huic Rhodopen Panchaeaque rura Lyaeus,
　　Nesciet inventos se docuisse favos.
Huc mihi si veniat pando Silenus asello,
90　Crabronum calva milia fronte feret.
Spicula sed nec apum calcemve timebit aselli,
　　Quin avido gratum devoret ore cibum.
Sunt nemora et saltus, est multae gloria sylvae
　　Idaliis lucis Thessalicisque prior:
95　Pinguibus alta feris stabula et venatio dives.
　　Maenalon oderit hic ipsa Diana suum.
Hic poteras spreta, iuvenis Thesaee, noverca,
　　Innocuos alio claudere fine dies.
Hic damae capreaeque leves cervique fugaces,
100　Hic cadit adversa cuspide fossus aper.
Hic sua dant canibus villosi terga bisontes,
　　Hic plenum est vastis alcibus omne nemus.
Sunt etiam immanes horrendis cornibus uri —
　　Regna quoque Hercinium contigit ista nemus.
105　Non plura Hyrcani novere cubilia saltus,
　　Non Pyrenaeus, non leporosus Athos,
A4v　Non Garamas, non fuscus Arabs, non decolor Indus,
　　Non Geta, non crudo Sarmata pastus equo.

73–74 nobilibus — habet A: laudatae lucrosum munere gemmae; / Germanus glessum, succina Roma vocat SO.　75 hoc A: hanc SO.　76 madefactus A: tamen udus SO.　79–80 Salmo — venit. add. A.　82 non A: vix SO.　83 Non . . . probatum est A: Saepe . . . negatur SO.　87 huic A: huc SO.　89–92 Huc — cibum. add. A.　93–94 est multae — prior A: sunt non deformia Tempe, / Thessala cum fluvio dixeris esse suo SO.　99–108 Hic damae — equo. add. A.

imagine that the goddess of Plenty was born in this place. The granaries are often not big enough for the farmer who owns them, and the broad fields are scarcely visible beneath the shocks of grain. The sea is remarkable for being full of precious stones; indeed, its amber is reputed to be first-class. Quite often boys and timid girls go out to gather this treasure. Soaking wet, their feet don't stop at the water's edge. There is the sea, there are rivers, there are immense pools and lakes. Egypt herself cannot glory in a greater variety of fish. Salmon, bass, sturgeon, eel, turbot, and pike, [80] no matter how heavy, are on sale here for just a penny apiece. In the lovely forests, moreover, there are swarms of tender bees, the likes of which Mount Hybla in Sicily never brought forth. And what is truly amazing, it is a proven fact that there isn't room enough for them to pile up all those sweet honeycombs of theirs. And so, their legs toiling away, they often store the golden honey under trees or in the soft greensward. Were Bacchus to compare Rhodope and the fields of Pangaea with this country, he wouldn't know that he had taught the art of keeping bees. If Silenus came to me here on his swaybacked ass, [90] he'd have to endure thousands of hornets on his bald pate.[7] But neither bee stings nor the hoof of his ass would deter him from gorging himself on the delectable food. There are copses and woodlands, there are vast forests more beautiful than the groves of Idalium and Thessaly: deep lairs of sleek beasts and rich hunting grounds. Here Diana herself would have become disenchanted with her haunts on Mount Maenalus. Here Theseus' son could have spurned his stepmother and ended his days blameless and unharmed.[8] Here swift-footed deer and roes and flighty stags, [100] here wild boars fall pierced by the hunter's spear. Here the shaggy bison turn tail and run from the hounds; here the whole forest is full of huge elk. There are even enormous aurochs with dreadful horns — the Hercynian Forest stretches into these realms too. The woods of Hyrcania or the Pyrenees have never known as many dens as these, not Mount Athos either, despite its countless hares, not the Africans, not the swarthy Arabs, not the dark-skinned Indians, not the Thracians, not the Sarmatians, fed on draughts of horses' blood.[9] What should I say about the

[7]Accompanied by the satyrs, Bacchus accidentally discovered honey in the mountains of western Thrace (Rhodope) and Macedonia (Pangaea). Once they had tasted it, the satyrs and their baldpated companion Silenus started looking for it everywhere, despite the inevitable bee stings. See Ov. *Fast.* 3.735–56.

[8]When Phaedra discovered that her stepson Hippolytus would rather hunt than make love to her, she falsely accused him of attempted rape. Cursed by his father Theseus, he was torn to pieces by his own horses.

[9]The Sarmatians of antiquity reportedly sustained themselves by drinking their horses' blood.

Quid loquar ingentem pecorum vim? Qualia nunquam
110   Armenta Arcadico germine pasta liquet,
Qualia non unquam colles videre Lycaei,
    Non, quamvis dives, Delphice pastor, eras.
Maior in argento nusquam nec largior usus;
    Vix tantum plumbi patria nostra tenet.
115 Argentum phialae, lances, cochlearia, disci:
    Qui fecit, credo non didicisse modum.
Vestibus argentum teritur vulgaribus; exit
    Nulla nisi argento foemina plena foras.
Pocula crassa Ceres Acheloia miscet aristis;
120   Hic bibitur nullo gratior orbe liquor.
Vina Teraphnaeis non inferiora racemis
    Hic aeris minimo pondere constat emi.
Advehit huc etiam peregrinis vector ab oris
    Per mare cum Rhodiis Cretica musta cadis.
125 Denique ad humanos quicquid convertitur usus,
    Hic velut ex cornu liberiore fluit.
Sunt etiam preclarae urbes opibusque superbae.
    Vix habet his (mirum) Teutonis ora pares.
In mare qua tacito demergitur Istula flexu,
130   Nobile Dantiscum littora prima tenet.
Urbs dominis ingrata suis nisi forte fuisset,
    Fortunis certe visa beata suis.
Quae postquam sacro defecit ab ordine, summa
    Excisa nigram propulit arce crucem.
135 Classibus haec portus et mercibus inclyta magnis,
    Et minor est Venetis Noriciisque prior.
Altera divitiis Monsregius, hanc opulentam
    Velifera ditat Bregela vastus aqua.
Quam nunc militiae sedem tenet Archimagister
140   (Hoc in eo princeps ordine nomen habet).
Structuris domuum reliquas Thuronia vincit,
    Pulchra quidem, sed non dives ut ante fuit.
Illa quoque excisae vestigia continet arcis,
    Quam vagus undanti Vistula lambit aqua.
145 Praeterea Albingum reliquas imitata ruinas,
    Eximium captae diruit arcis opus.

A5ʳ

115–18 Argentum — foras. *add. A.*   **121–22** Vina — emi. *add. A.*   **124** musta *A*: mista *SO*.
127 opibusque *SO*: opibus *A*, *sed corr. manus vetus in A¹, A²*, et *A³*.   **129** flexu *A*: lapsu *SO*.
131–34 Urbs — crucem. *add. A.*   **135–36** et mercibus — prior *A*: domus inclyta mercibus,
haec est / Urbs maris imperii parte beata sui *SO*.   **137–39** opulentam — Archimagister *A*: quoque
ditat / In mare velifera Bregela versus aqua. / Haec modo militiae sedes est alta Magistri *SO*.
143 Illa quoque *A*: Haec vetera *SO*.

prodigious number of cattle? [110] The slopes of Mount Lycaeus, certainly, never saw herds fatted on Arcadian pastures quite as good-looking as these — I don't care how rich you may have been, Delphian shepherd![10]

Nowhere else do they use silver more liberally or lavishly than here; back home, our country barely has that much lead.[11] Silver saucers, plates, spoons, dishes: whoever made them all presumably never heard of restraint. Silver is worn on everyday clothes. No woman goes out of doors unless she is decked out with silver. Plump Ceres laces Achelous' draughts with barley;[12] [120] there is no country on earth where they love their beer more. Wines that are in no way inferior to those of Corsican vintage can be bought here for a song. Merchants also import them from overseas — new wines from Crete along with casks from Rhodes. In short, whatever can be made to serve human needs flows bounteously here, as if from the horn of Plenty.

There are magnificent cities too, glorying in their wealth. Germany herself, believe it or not, has scarcely any to match these. Where the Vistula in noiseless loops spills into the sea, [130] celebrated Danzig occupies the shorefront. If that city hadn't been ungrateful to her rulers, she could certainly be considered blessed with good fortune. After breaking with the holy order, she demolished the towering castle and expelled the black cross.[13] The city is renowned as a bustling port and a great center of trade, ranking behind Venice but ahead of Nuremberg. Second in terms of wealth is Königsberg, an opulent city that the desolate Pregel enriches with sail-bearing stream. It is now the seat of the Grand Master of the Teutonic Knights [140] (that is what they call the head of this order).[14] In the magnificence of its houses Thorn outstrips the others. Still beautiful, she is no longer as wealthy as in days past. This city too contains the remnants of a demolished castle, which the roaming Vistula laps with billowing stream.[15] Like the other towns, Elbing has her share of ruins, for she captured the citadel and razed its splendid fortifications.

[10]Apollo. As punishment for killing the Cyclopes, Zeus ordered him to pasture the cattle of Admetus, the King of Pherae in Thessaly.

[11]A gloss in the Zwickau and London copies indicates that Eobanus hyperbolically refers to Hesse, well known for its lead-mines. (Both Mutianus and Eobanus were natives of Hesse.)

[12]Ceres is the goddess of cereal crops; the Achelous River stands for water. So (to put it prosaically) the Prussians use barley and water to brew beer.

[13]Danzig broke with the Teutonic Order in 1454 and became a "free city" under Polish sovereignty in 1466. Thereafter it enjoyed great prosperity as the main port of Poland.

[14]After losing Marienburg Castle to Poland in 1457, the Teutonic Order relocated its headquarters to Königsberg in East Prussia.

[15]Like Danzig, Thorn revolted against the Teutonic Order in 1454.

Hinc Marieburgum, quondam domus inclyta Magnis
　　　Principibus, nullo crimine facta nocens.
Sed tamen infoelix regi data serva Polono,
150　　Cum reliquis misere, sed sine labe iacet.

Ubere laeta solo, Noganum sita propter amaenum,
　　　Extructa in terris non habet arce parem.
Non procul inde meis Riseburgum nobile Musis
　　　Pinguia foecundi possidet arva soli.
155　Moenia parva quidem, sed quae nunc Presul Iobus
　　　Auget et aeternum nomen habere facit.
Hic quoque praeclaram merito laudaveris arcem,
　　　Aggeribus cinctam, turribus, atque lacu.
Hactenus, unde legas properatam, Rufe, salutem,
160　　Carminibus facta est Prussia nota meis.
Prussia, Teutonicae merces data militiei,
　　　Prussia, Christiferae Virginis hospitium,
Floruit et plures late dominata per annos
　　　Deliciis tandem languit ipsa suis.
165　Atque ut cunctarum rerum est mutabilis ordo,
　　　Fortunae instabilem sensit et illa rotam.
Sic illa, emerito cum iam polleret honore
　　　Deflueretque opibus molliter ipsa suis,
Magnarum veteres rerum est imitata ruinas,
170　　Visa nec exemplo est interiisse novo.
Martia sic rerum cum Rhoma potita vigeret
　　　Lapsa est. Caecropiae sic cecidistis opes,

Sic Thebae, sic Troia potens, sic alta Corinthus,
　　　Punica sic Tyria moenia structa manu.
175　Sic patrium amisit Iudaea potentia sceptrum,
　　　Non semel excisam sic Babilona ferunt.
Sic urbes, sic regna cadunt, sic omnia mutat
　　　Haec dea quae certum nescit habere locum.
Omnia quis referat? Sed et haec, quae pauca videtis,
180　　Vix quoque sunt minima parte relata mihi.
Vivit in his igitur baculo qui primus agresti
　　　Teutona Rhomanum duxit in arva gregem.

---

154 Pinguia — soli *A*: Arx vetus in parvo condita colle iacet *SO*.　　**155–78** Moenia — locum.
add. A.　　**155** Iobus *manus vetus in A¹, A², et A³*: Iob *A*.　　**179** videtis *A*: canebam *SO*.
180 quoque *A*: ea *SO*.

Next is Marienburg, which was once famed as the residence of the Grand Masters, but has since incurred guilt through no fault of her own. Given in bondage to the King of Poland nevertheless, [150] the ill-fated city now lies prostrate with her fellows, miserable but not disgraced.[16] Delighting in her fertile soil, founded along the charming Nogat, she boasts a castle without equal on earth. Not far from there lies Riesenburg. Known for my Muses, the town possesses fields rich with fertile soil. It is a small place, to be sure; but Bishop Job[17] is now enhancing it and causing it to have a name for all time. Here too you may justly praise the superb castle, girdled with ramparts, towers, and a moat.

This is all I can tell you, Rufus, [160] in my poem about Prussia, from where I sent the hurried greetings you're reading. Prussia, granted as a reward to the Teutonic Knights, hospice for the Christ-bearing Virgin,[18] Prussia flourished for many years; but after exercising her dominion far and wide, she at last grew soft in her luxury. And as all things are liable to change, she too experienced the turning of Fortune's wheel. So, just when she was basking in her well-earned glory and comfortably sinking back in her riches, she followed the great empires of old in their decline and fall; [170] for her collapse is by no means unparalleled in history. That is how Mars' Rome fell into ruin, at the very moment she was thriving as mistress of the world. That is how your power crumbled, Athens. The same fate befell Thebes and mighty Troy and lofty Corinth and that Phoenician colony, founded by a Tyrian hand.[19] That is how powerful Judea lost her ancestral sovereignty. Babylon too, they say, was destroyed like this, and not just once either. That is how cities and kingdoms fall; that is how that fickle-minded goddess[20] transforms all things.

Who could describe everything? Indeed, with the few things I've mentioned to you [180] I have just barely scratched the surface. This, then, is where that herdsman lives who with his shepherd's crook first led a Roman flock to German pastures.[21] But you, my

[16]Though Marienburg withstood a Polish siege in 1454, the order was finally forced to pawn the magnificent castle to its unpaid mercenaries. The latter then handed it over to Poland in 1457. The city itself remained loyal to the order and defended itself until 1460. Like the other West Prussian cities, Marienburg was ceded to Poland in the Peace of Thorn of 1466.

[17]For Eobanus' patron, Bishop Job von Dobeneck, see Camerarius, *Nar.* 7.5, with n. 22 (1:25).

[18]The Teutonic Order, originally a north German order of hospitalers, was soon attached to the German Church of St. Mary the Virgin at Jerusalem. Hence its members were also known as the Teutonic Knights of St. Mary's Hospital at Jerusalem.

[19]Carthage, founded by Queen Dido of Tyre (Phoenicia), was destroyed by Rome in the Punic Wars.

[20]The goddess Fortune.

[21]Eobanus alludes to his *Bucolicon*, published in late September 1509. In that pastoral work he celebrates his circle of friends, including Mutianus Rufus.

At tu, noster amor, consors patriaeque lyraeque,
Rufe, Latinorum docte sonare tubam,
185 Quid facit amisso grex errabunda magistro?
Quam timeo saevos, monstra cruenta, lupos!
Quid facit is, merito cui pagina nostra dicata est?
Hei mihi, quam praeceps nostra carina fuit!
Quid mihi mentito Phileremus nomine dictus?
190 Cessit? An in sacra valle moratur adhuc?
Vivite, deliciae nostrae, dum vester amicus
Longius a vobis quam decuisset abest.
Is tamen ut vultis vivitque valetque, videtque
Quam non vobiscum vivere triste nihil.
A6ᵛ 195 Quem precor ut solita semper virtute colatis.
Ipse sub hoc etiam sydere vester erit.

183–84 noster amor — tubam *A*: Rufe, meae formator prime iuventae, / Per te vocalis debita fama lyrae *SO*.   *Post* **190** *in SO*: Quid Crotus ingenio plus quam florente beatus? / Haerens principibus quid Spalatinus agit? / Nobilis hunc animum Petrei cura relinquet, / Cum flammae glaciem, cum dabit unda faces.   **193** Is *A*: Qui *SO*.

bosom friend, my compatriot and fellow poet, Rufus, virtuoso on the Latin trump: What is my roving herd doing, now that it has lost its shepherd? How I fear the savage wolves, those bloodthirsty monsters![22] And what is he doing, the man to whom I deservedly dedicated my book?[23] Alas, how impetuously did my vessel set sail![24] What about the one to whom I gave the fictitious name Phileremus? [190] Has he left? Or is he still living in that holy dale?[25]

Farewell, my favorites, while that friend of yours lives farther away from you than he should. Still, he is alive and well, just as you wanted; and besides missing you he has no regrets at all. Please keep him in your hearts, as always. He himself will remain yours truly, even up here in the North.

[22]The critics who will carp at his pastorals. Cf. *Buc.* B 11.11.
[23]Johann Englender, the dedicatee of Eobanus' *Bucolicon.*
[24]That is: How impetuously I left Erfurt (in the autumn of 1509)!
[25]Phileremus, whom Eobanus introduces in *Buc.* 4, is his good friend Herbord von der Marthen. He taught at the monastery of Georgenthal ("Saint George's dale") from 1508 to late 1511.

2 EIUSDEM AD THEODORUM COLLUCIUM SACERDOTEM ILLICITI AMORIS ANTIDOTARIUM

Quae tibi, dum patria tecum frueretur eadem,
  Incelebri lusit carmina multa cheli,
Quae tibi clavigeri visuro numen Iuli,
  "Sic redeas," ausa est dicere, "sicut abis,"
5 Haec eadem optata te conditione potitum
  Musa fere criticis audet adire modis.
Quid velit, unde ferat properatam inopina salutem,
  Protinus ex ipsa fronte videre licet.
Et si fronte minus patefacta aut crine soluto,
10 Esse tibi ex ipso nota colore potest.
Excipe consueta residem pietate Thaliam,
  Colluci, et vacua quid ferat aure nota.
Vestibus ingreditur Tyrium referentibus ostrum,
  Qualis et in veste est, talis in ore color.
15 Nulla, vides, niveo rutilant gestamina collo,
  Nulla sub arctato pectore bulla tumet.
Plus formosa quidem poterit quam pulchra videri,
  Et mihi neglecta simplicitate placet.
Sic mea iampridem devicit pectora, quamvis
20 Claudicet ex uno semirecincta pede.
Cur tamen in dextra laurum quam fronte solebat?
  Cur gerit effusis myrtea serta comis?
Ad te qur aliquo comitata Cupidine venit?
  Veste Venus posita sic tibi visa foret.
25 Quid sit amor charum venit instructura sodalem,
  Qui sedet et nullum sentit in igne malum.
"Quid tibi cum Paphio, castissima Pieris, aestu?
  Turpe est virginibus dicere quid sit amor."

B1ʳ

Sylv. duae 2. *Cf. Sylv. 1.3 in SO.*   **Tit.** Eiusdem — antidotarium *A*: Ad Temonium amantem. De amore *SO*.   **1** tibi *A*: ubi *SO*; patria . . . eadem *A*: studiis . . . eisdem *SO*.   **2** Incelebri . . . cheli *A*: Ad patriam . . . chelim *SO*.   **3** numen *A*: limen *SO*.   **Post 6** *in SO*: Excipe consueta residem pietate Thaliam, / Temoni, et vacua quid ferat aure nota. [*cf. vv. 11–12*]   **9** Et *A*: Quod *SO*; soluto *A*: soluta *SO*.   **11–12** Excipe — nota. *add. A.*   **16** arctato *A*: angusto *SO*. **17–20** Plus — pede. *add. A.*   **17** videri *manus vetus in A¹ et A³*: vidire *A*.   **24** tibi *A*: ubi *SO*.

---

[1]The Latin term *antidotarium* (handbook of antidotes) recurs in the late Middle Ages and Renaissance as a title for pharmacological compendia. Theodore Collucius is a pseudonym for Johannes Temonius (Gesselman, Gyselman) of Salza (Thuringia). After studying at Erfurt with Eobanus, he entered the service of Bishop Job von Dobeneck in Riesenburg, Prussia. See the introduction (pp. 58–59). The first name *Theodore* is perhaps a nod to *Theomonius*, the name Temonius seems to have adopted after taking holy orders. The surname Collucius associates him with the famed humanist and papal secretary Coluccio Salutati, who lived from 1331 to 1406.

2   BY THE SAME POET TO THE PRIEST THEODORE
COLLUCIUS: AN ANTIDOTARY FOR ILLICIT LOVE[1]

The Muse who enjoyed living with you in your homeland, she who sang many a song for you to the accompaniment of her undistinguished lyre, she who ventured to tell you, as you were about to set out for the godlike majesty of the key-bearer Julius,[2] "May you come back the same way you left," this very same Muse presumes to address you on a rather critical note, now that you've indeed come back safe and sound. What she has in mind, for what reason she offers you this hurried greeting out of the blue, that ought to be obvious, for it's written all over her face. And even if her face weren't such an open book, even if her hair didn't hang loose, [10] you'd still recognize her by her very complexion.

Do welcome my idle Thalia with your usual kindness, Collucius, and when you have a free moment, listen carefully to what she has to say. She approaches you in a gown reminiscent of Tyrian purple; and the same color you see in her gown also stains her cheeks. Look, no ornaments glitter upon her snowy neck; no locket swells beneath her straitlaced chest. True, the lovely lady could look more glamorous; but I rather prefer her like this, in her unstudied simplicity. This is how she has long since won my heart, even if, [20] half ungirt, she limps in one foot.[3] Still, why is the laurel that normally graces her brow now in her hand? Why does she wear a myrtle garland in her flowing locks?[4] Why does she come to you accompanied by some Cupid? Were she unrobed, you'd have sworn she was Venus.

She has come to teach you what love means — you, her dear comrade, who is sitting in a fire, yet feels no pain.

"What business have you to talk about the flames of passion, most chaste Muse? It is disgraceful for virgins to explain what love means."

---

[2]Pope Julius II (1503–13) is the "key-bearer," because as Bishop of Rome he is the successor of Peter, to whom Christ gave the keys of the kingdom (Matthew 16.19). Temonius seems to have been on a diplomatic mission to the Vatican, on behalf of the bishop or the Teutonic Order. As he was setting out for Rome in early 1510, Eobanus addressed a farewell poem to him (*Sylv.* 1.5).

[3]Eobanus' Muse "limps in one foot" because she writes elegiac couplets, in which a hexameter is followed by the shorter-footed pentameter.

[4]She has replaced her laurel wreath, sacred to Apollo, with a garland of myrtle leaves, sacred to Venus. And her hair, which is normally kept chastely bound, now is allowed to flow free.

Non ita, Colluci! Quid enim de virgine Musa
30   Quod de Vestali turpe referre putes?
Illa, Cytheriacos cum torqueremur ad aestus,
    Ignibus in mediis mite levamen erat.
Hessiaco legitur notissima Flavia versu,
    Cum dolet et vatem Musa dolere vetat.
35   Arsimus et tacitum — dii, quam grave! — sensimus ignem.
    Per mala tot victor te duce, Musa, fui.
Illa meas flammas et vidit et ipsa sequta est.
    Quid dubitas castam turpia posse loqui?

B1ᵛ

Quis pudor est igitur? Quid lumina contegis? Aut quid
40   Virgine te tacito conveniente rubes?
Illa tibi insanum non exprobrat ante tribunal,
    Per fora nec stricto publica fune trahit.
Oportuna diu quaesivit tempora. Postquam
    Sunt data quae voluit, vult sine teste loqui.
45   Aeger es, heu, medicas vix iam sanande per artes.
    Dii faciant nequeas esse, fuisse queas.
Aeger es, an papulis? an febribus? anne podagra?
    Quis dolor est? Palles. Hoc erat illud, amas!
Morbus is est, novi, quia te pallere videbam.
50   Quid, precor, est quare palleat omnis amans?
Hac ego iamdudum laesum te peste notabam.
    Talia qui sensit vulnera nosse potest!
Sanus adhuc nullis constrictus legibus ibas.
    Effreni licuit quolibet ire tibi.
55   Convenisse tuos poteras si quando sodales,
    Laeticia nemo te potiore fuit.
Arguit invictam facies tam florida mentem.
    Heu, quantum compos desinis esse tui!
Vincula captivus coniectus in impia langues,
60   Victima placandos ut solet ante deos.

B2ʳ

Pectore mens abiit, color est mutatus in ore,
    Vix tenuis restat spiritus ipse tibi.
Non tamen hic in te, speculo sed vivit in illo
    In quo te vitam posse videre putas.
65   Victus es et durae subiisti pondera legis;
    Non licet, ut quondam, quolibet ire tibi.
Convenisse potes charos si quando sodales,
    Tristitia nemo te potiore manet.
Lumina demittis, suspiria longa frequentas;
70   Multa sub obscura nubila fronte sedent.

---

29 Colluci *A*: Temoni *SO*.   **38** castam *A*: castum *SO*.   **66** quondam *A*: nuper *SO*.

Not so fast, Collucius! For how could you impute to the virgin Muse [30] what would be shameful to say about a Vestal? When I myself was tormented with fiery passion, she was a gentle solace in the midst of my flames.[5] Everybody has read about Flavia, celebrated in Hessus' verse when he was pining for her and the Muse told the poet to stop aching. Gods, how I burned, how I felt the hidden fire! Under the Muse's guidance I emerged victorious from all those troubles. Yes, she saw my flames; but then she did something about them. How can you imagine that the chaste Maid could say anything disgraceful?

Well? What is making you so bashful? Why are you covering your eyes? Or why [40] are you blushing in silence as this virgin draws near? She won't haul you before a tribunal and rail at you like mad; she won't drag you by a rope through the public squares. For quite some time she has looked for a suitable opportunity. Now that she has found what she wanted, she just wants a quiet talk with you.

You're sick. Alas, you can scarcely be cured by the medical arts anymore. May the gods grant you a cure, so you can put this disease behind you. You're sick. Is it with the pox? With fevers? With podagra? What's bothering you? You're awfully pale. That's it! You're in love! That's your ailment. I know, because I saw you looking wan. [50] What is it, I wonder, that makes every lover turn pale? I've observed you afflicted with this plague for a long time already. A man who has himself felt such wounds can be counted on to recognize the symptoms! When you were still in sound health, you were not tied down in any way. You could come and go as you pleased. Whenever you had the chance to get together with friends, you were always the life of the party. Your ruddy face beamed with confidence. Alas, how much self-control have you lost! Cruelly enchained, you languish in prison, [60] just as a victim in the olden days awaited sacrifice to the gods. You've taken leave of your senses. You've lost the glow in your cheeks. You're just a shadow of your former self. Yet your mind doesn't live in you, but rather in that mirror in which you fancy you can see life itself. Vanquished, you've submitted to a harsh, oppressive law. You can't move about freely, the way you used to. Now, whenever you have the chance to get together with dear friends, you're just a wet blanket. You stare at the ground; you keep letting out long sighs, [70] while a big cloud knits your gloomy brow.

---

[5]Eobanus alludes to *Ama*. B 2, where the Muse Calliope cures him of his passionate love. For his girlfriend Flavia ("Blonde") see n. 43 at *Ama*. B 2.1 (1:253).

Fallor? An expertum necquicquam intelligo amorem?
　　Non ita. Signa sui talia prebet amor.
Miles in hac multos annos iam versor arena.
　　Quam teris, ah, nimium nota palestra mihi est.
75　Et licet hunc totis attraxeris ossibus ignem
　　Altaque iam prima vulnera tabe fluant,
Ne tamen in saniem possint consurgere, perfer
　　Auxiliatrices applicuisse manus.
Sed prius ex alto morbi natura videnda est;
80　　Saepe minus iuste pharmaca sumpta nocent.
Flamma latens amor est sapidumque per ossa venenum
　　Tormentumque iuvans exitiumque placens.
B2ᵛ　Qui simul icta levi penetrarit corda sagitta,
　　Quem tetigit memorem non sinit esse sui.
85　Hinc oblitus amans proprii per crimen honoris
　　Dedecus omne sibi posse licere putat.
Dumque exempla nequit votis per honesta potiri,
　　Fraude intentatum nil sinit esse sua.
Gargaricae potius messis numerabis aristas,
90　　Quam quot possideat crimina turpis amor —
Cura, labor, gemitus, lachrymae, suspiria, febres,
　　Sollicitae noctes sollicitaeque dies,
Iusticiae fuga, paupertas, dispendia rerum,
　　Stulticia in prima sede pudenda sedet,
95　Multaque quae miseras turbant insomnia noctes
　　Pluraque tam brevibus non referenda modis.
Tot mala cum videas et tanta in amore, quid audes
　　In tam sollicita longius ire via?
Est puer, at puerum quisquis devicit Amorem,
100　　Hic decus ex meritis Hercule maius habet.
Nam quid Naemaeum clava stravisse leonem,
　　Quid fuit Aetolum devoluisse suem,
Infernum traxisse canem, vicisse draconem
　　Quasque tulit volucres Stymphalis unda feras,
B3ʳ　105　Omnia quid vastae superasse pericula terrae?
　　Quem puer infami vulnere vicit Amor.

---

73 Miles . . . multos annos *A*: Pugil . . . annos aliquot *SO*.　　78 applicuisse *A*: apposuisse *SO*.
85 per crimen *A*: vesanus *SO*.　　86 Dedecus — licere *A*: Esse sibi licitum dedecus omne *SO*.
89 Gargaricae *A*: Thuringae *SO*.　　91–96 Cura — modis *A*: Ut taceam gemitus, lachrymas, suspiria, curis [cur *S² O*] / Sollicitas noctes sollicitosque dies, / Num rationis agit puer hic oblivia et altos /
A seipsis animos degenerare docet? / Consilia evertit, iustum aversatur et odit, / Exiguo magnas tempore perdit opes. / Sunt comites huic paupertas, infamia, morbi. / Stulticia in prima sede pudenda
sedet, / Mors quoque nonnunquam. Quis enim tot nescit amantum / Saxa, ignes, laqueos, flumina,
tela, cruces? [*cf. vv. 221–22*] *SO*.　　97 Tot mala . . . et tanta *A*: Quae tu . . . et plura *SO*.
101 Naemaeum — stravisse *A*: erat vastum Nemeae sub rupe *SO*.　　102 Aetolum [Aetolam *A*] —
suem *A*, aeripedi praevaluisse ferae *SO*.　　104 Quasque — feras *A*: Nubigenas clava perdomuisse
viros *SO*.　　105 Omnia quid vastae *A*: Cuncta quid ambitae *SO*.

Well, am I wrong? As one who's been in love himself, did I misdiagnose your condition? Of course not. Those are the classic symptoms of love. I've fought this battle for many years myself. The struggle you're engaged in, alas, is all too familiar to me. And though you're inflamed to the very marrow with love and your gaping wounds are already starting to ooze with pus, don't let them get infected. Have a physician apply a helping hand. First of all, however, you must get a bird's-eye view of this disease; [80] for medicines taken the wrong way often do more harm than good.

Love is a hidden flame, a savory poison coursing through the bones, a delightful torment, an agreeable death. As soon as it pierces the stricken heart with its fleet arrow, the person it touches stops being mindful of himself. That is why a lover in the throes of passion forgets about his own honor and thinks he can get away with all kinds of disgraceful behavior. And when he cannot make his wishes come true by honorable means, he stops at nothing in his delusion. Sooner will you count the ears of grain in Gargara's harvest[6] [90] than the taints of degrading love — worry, distress, groans, tears, sighs, fevers, anxious nights and anxious days, injustice, poverty, the dissipation of wealth, shameful folly lording it over the lot, swarms of bad dreams that disturb the cheerless nights, and far more things than I can recount in this brief poem. Since you see all the great evils that love brings in its train, how dare you continue on a path as thorny as this?

Amor is just a boy. But anyone who vanquishes this boy [100] is entitled to greater glory than Hercules. For what good did it do *him* to club the Nemean lion to death or bring down the Aetolian boar, drag the dog out of the underworld, conquer the serpent and the savage birds of Lake Stymphalus, and overcome all sorts of dangers throughout the whole wide world? The boy Amor conquered him with a shameful wound.[7] The same goes

[6]The slopes of Gargara, not far from Troy, were famed for their grain crops. Cf. Verg. *G.* 1.103; Ov. *Ars* 1.57. In the original version of this line, however (*Sylv.* 1.3.85), Eobanus refers instead to the harvests in Temonius' native Thuringia — another indication that the 1514 text was revised to obliterate all hints concerning the addressee's identity.

[7]Like his model, Ov. *Her.* 9.1–26, Eobanus first alludes to the twelve labors of Hercules and then to Hercules' love affair with Iole of Oechalia, the daughter of King Eurytus. For the labors of Hercules, see, for example, Ov. *Met.* 9.182–99.

Tu quoque, cum superes reliquae ludibria sortis,
    Turpiter imbelli victus Amore iaces.
Sentis? An ignoras quam sis delapsus ab alto,
110   Quam vel ab excelso trusus ad ima loco?
Respicis? An simulas summo loca proxima caelo?
    Hinc es ad infernae lapsus opaca domus!
Qualiter incautus dubia sub nocte viator
    Antra die claro non adeunda subit,
115   Sic te per Paphiae discrimina noctis euntem
    Materna arcitenens duxit in antra puer.
Praetulit exterius claram Venus aurea lucem;
    Limine nox horrens interiore sedet.
At tibi luce solet nox clarior illa videri,
120   Et magis hoc optas posse dolere malo.
Iste dolor tibi non dolor est, sed blanda voluptas,
    Vulneraque, ut doleas, te iuvat ista pati.
Qualis cum miseris dementia mentibus adsit,
    Dum calet, hoc omneis igne perire iuvat.
125   "Omnes," dicebam, "quot sunt in amore pusilli,
    Ludus enim fortes non capit iste viros."

Fortis enim tenues stipulas ut flamma perurit,
    Nec facili durus flectitur igne chalybs,
Sic amor est timido muliebria pectora morsu,
130   Fortia non aliquo rodere dente potest.
Quoque magis credas, pauca est narrare voluptas.
    Est vetus, at multa fabula plena fide.
Liquerat Idalium volucri comitata puello
    Sacraque Pieridum venit in arva Venus.
135   Constitit aereo Parnassi vertice montis;
    Musarum in viridi valle chorea fuit.
Movit atrox pharetram prompturus taela Cupido.
    Quem peteret mater dum rogat, ille refert:
"Vicimus his iaculis totumque subegimus orbem;
140   Haec taela in superos ius habuere deos.
Movimus his manes dominumque coegimus Orci
    Curribus insolitis ad nova furta vehi.
Sensit in aequoreo qui servat regna profundo,
    Aequoreaeque nurus aereumque genus.
145   Sola meas nondum sensit percussa sagittas,
    Quam turbam in viridi ludere valle vides.

---

108 imbelli . . . Amore *A*: imberbi . . . ab hoste *SO*.   **109** ignoras *A*: dubitas *SO*.   **118** Limine —
sedet *A*: Nox intus nigro te tulit atra sinu *SO*.   **120** magis — malo *A*: cuperes nullum rursus adire
diem *SO*.   **121** Iste — non dolor *A*: Sed furor hic tibi non furor *SO*.   **123** cum *O*: em̄ *A*, enim *S*.
130 rodere *A*: laedere *SO*.   **135** vertice *A*: in vertice *SO*.   **140** Haec — ius *A*: In superos vires haec
SO.   **146** Quam — vides *A*: Turba sub hoc ducens culmine laeta choros *SO*.

for you. After surmounting the mockeries of fortune everywhere else, you have been shamefully brought low by unwarlike Love.

Don't you feel this? Don't you know how you've gone downhill [110] or how low you've fallen? Do you ever look back? Or do you still pretend you're in seventh heaven? You've sunk all the way down to the blackness of hell! As an unwary traveler at dusk enters a cave he would never go near in broad daylight, so you stroll through the dangers of Paphian night while that bowboy leads you into his mother's grotto. On the outside, golden Venus radiates brightness; horrid night broods within. But to you this night appears to be more radiant than daylight, [120] and all you want is to suffer this disease some more. That pain isn't a pain to you at all, but a sweet pleasure; and though you feel the hurt, you enjoy suffering those wounds. When such madness afflicts wretched minds, while this fire burns hot, they are all eager to perish in its blaze. "Everyone who's in love," I used to say, "is a milksop; for that silly game doesn't enthrall real men." Indeed, just as a lusty flame consumes slender straw, while hard steel can't be bent in casual heat, so love timidly gnaws at the effeminate, [130] but doesn't have the pluck to snap at manly hearts.

To clinch my case, I'd like to tell you a little story. It's an old tale, but utterly trustworthy.

After leaving Idalium in the company of her winged son, Venus arrived in the holy fields of the Pierian Sisters. There she stood, on the soaring peak of Mount Parnassus, while the Muses danced together in the green valley below. Cupid shook his quiver fiercely and started to take out the arrows. When his mother asked him at whom he was aiming, he replied: "With these darts I've conquered and subdued the whole world. [140] These arrows have power over the gods on high. With them I've moved the spirits of the dead; I've forced the lord of Orcus to make an exception and ride his chariot into the upper world to kidnap a bride.[8] The god who keeps to the ocean depths has felt them; so have the nymphs of the sea and the airy tribe. The only ones that haven't yet felt the sting of my arrows is the group you see dancing in the green valley below. In fact, the

---

[8]Pluto, the god of the underworld, was moved by love to abduct Proserpina. The story is told at length in Claudian's *De raptu Proserpinae*.

Nostra quidem steriles contemnunt spicula Musae.
Heu, quid in his nostrum languit imperium?"

B4^r
Tum Venus ex alto suspiria pectore ducens,
150   "Tam quoque constantes aggrediamur," ait.
Et simul aereo de culmine lapsa resedit,
Virginibus Musis taliter orsa loqui:
"Quid iuvat usque adeo sterilem deducere vitam,
Contemptrix nati turba novena mei?
155 Marcet inutiliter sine me consumpta iuventus;
Crescit muneribus largiter aucta meis.
Ocia quid miserae numeratis inania vitae,
O bona Castalio turba liquore potens?
Aut igitur mea sacra piae celebrate sorores,
160   Aut meus haec vobis inferet arma puer."
Contra quam breviter fata est cui nomen Amantis
(Sic iussit sacri regia virgo chori):
"Marti taela, Venus, Marti, Venus, arma minare!
Quem regis inter nos non volat iste puer.
165 Pierides castae, castorum numina vatum,
Turbaque bellipotens in tua regna sumus."
Palluit ut sperni vidit sua regna Cupido,
Quem Venus ad patriam sustulit alma Paphum.
Nunc iacet et castis moeret superata puellis,
170   Vincere quam superi non potuere dei.

B4^v
Tu vir es et tales vidisti sepe puellas,
Nec solum culta est Pieris una tibi.
Ardua Phocaicae tetigisti culmina Cyrrhae,
Musicus Aonio pulvere factus eques.
175 Ecquid adhuc igitur, tantis exercite sacris,
Ludicra non cessas ista prophana sequi?
Nec, quamvis poteras, audes vitare quod urget
Passaque degeneri damna timore iuvas,
Ceu puer ostensi pavidus terrore flagelli
180   Concidit et certam iurat adesse necem?
Quo ruis, ah, duris operate laboribus olim?
Tene levis mulier fortior una fuit?

---

149 alto *A*: imo *SO*.   153 deducere *A*: producere *SO*.   156 Crescit — meis *A*: Me duce quo melior germine fiat habet *SO*.   157–58 Ocia — potens? *add A*.   164 Quem regis *A*: Torpet et *SO*. 167 regna *A*: tela *SO*.   168 ad *A*: in *SO*; alma *A*: alta *SO*.   169–70 iacet — superi *A*: quoque se castis victum dolet esse puellis / Vincere quem fortes *SO*.   172 solum *A*: tantum *SO*. 173–74 Ardua — eques. *add. A*.   180 certam — necem *A*: certum credit adesse mori *SO*.

barren Muses hold my darts in contempt. Alas, why does my mastery wilt when I deal with them?"

Hereupon Venus, heaving a sigh from the depth of her breast, [150] said, "Steadfast though they are, let's have at them too." At once she glided down from the airy summit, sat down, and began to address the virgin Muses as follows: "What is the point of leading so barren a life, you ninefold choir who despise my son? Spent without me, youth wilts to no purpose; but it thrives when blessed with my gifts. Why do you insist on living in wretched boredom, O excellent nymphs of the Castalian spring? Therefore, either celebrate my rites, gentle sisters, [160] or my son will shoot his arrows at you."

The Muse who bears the name *Ladylove* answered her briefly (for this is what the maidenly queen of that sacred band bade her say):[9] "Oh, come on, Venus, go brandish those darts at Mars! Threaten Mars with those weapons, Venus! We won't have that boy of yours flying in our midst. We are the Pierian Maidens, the goddesses of chaste bards, a throng mighty in war against your realms."

When he saw his dominion spurned like that, Cupid grew pale. Bountiful Venus had to take him back to her homeland of Paphos. Even now she lies prostrate, grieved at the thought that she, [170] whom the gods above have never been able to defeat, was herself defeated by chaste maidens.

You're a man who has often seen such maidens; indeed, you've devoted yourself to more than one Muse.[10] You've climbed the arduous peaks of Parnassus in Phocis and as a knight of the Muses won your spurs on the Helicon. Why on earth, then, does a poet like you, versed in such sacred mysteries, not stop chasing after those unholy amusements? And why (though you're perfectly capable of it) can't you bring yourself to keep clear of love's urgings? Why go on wallowing in the losses incurred by your unmanly fear? You remind me of a boy who, threatened with a whipping, [180] falls to his knees in terror and swears it will surely be the death of him. Ah, to what lows can you sink — you, a man who used to keep his nose to the grindstone! Was then one fickle woman stronger than you?

[9]"Ladylove" is the Muse Erato. The "queen" of the Muses is Calliope; see *Laud.* 246, n.
[10]Temonius has written poetry in more than one genre and meter.

Paucane te infami clauserunt verba catasta,
 Verba dari ficta qualia voce solent?
185 Hauserunt animam tibi suavia pauca sequacem;
 Suxerunt animum dulcia labra tuum.
Ah, pudet et turpe est scelus enarrare nefandum:
 Sydera nequitia polluis alta tua.
Heu, sacra contrectas quo pollice turpia tangis.
190 Oscula quo sumis, sumis et ore Deum.
Improbe, pro sacris iam non stature sacerdos,
 Vade, piae nomen relligionis habe!

B5^r Atria tu dominaeque fores et limina serva;
 Maneque compositum vespere profer "Ave."
195 Pura Deum casti sumant libamina mystae;
 Sancta prophanatas non amat ara manus.
An tibi, cum niveo steteris vestitus amictu,
 Foemina praesentem non subit ante Deum?
Ebrius epoto consumpti sanguine Christi,
200 Sub memori dominae pectore nomen habes.
Scilicet huic tacita misereri mente precaris,
 Quem tu Christophago colligis ore Deum!
Parce, locus precibus non convenit iste nefandis,
 Quas sine polluta fundere mente nequis.
205 His tua nequitiis absolvi debuit aetas
 Vitaque quam sacram tonsa corona facit.
Consulat erranti populo de lege sacerdos;
 Non ita cum pueris insipienter amet.
Sordida cum Veneris nusquam sit honesta libido,
210 Plus tamen in sacro pectore sordis habet.
Et neque delictum punit Deus acrius ullum
 Quam grave pollutae relligionis opus.
Multa exempla tibi praebet Iudaea vetustas,
 Sed nequeunt elegi multa referre breves.

B5^v 215 Doctus ut es studiis, potes haec cognoscere, in illis
 Se ignorans quicquam si modo scire potest.
Aspice praeterea veterum sacra carmina vatum
 (Non est propositi cuncta referre mei).
Aspice quoscunque et veteres ubicunque libellos,
220 Prebeat et faustum si quid amare vide.
Obruor exemplis. Quis enim tot nescit amantum
 Saxa, ignes, laqueos, flumina, taela, cruces?

183–224 Paucane — fores? *add. A.*

Did a few words doom you to ignominious slavery, the sort of words that are apt to be uttered in a put-on voice? A few sweet nothings have swallowed your docile soul; honeyed lips have sucked up your mind.

Ah, it's shameful and disgusting to explain every detail of an abominable sin: with your wantonness you defile the stars on high. Alas, with the same thumb with which you handle the sacraments you also engage in filthy behavior. [190] With the same mouth with which you receive kisses you also receive God. Impious priest who no longer lives up to the priesthood, go now and make yourself a reputation for pious devotion! Haunt the home and door and threshold of your mistress; then, at matins and vespers, blandly offer your Ave Maria. Priests should be chaste when they partake of the pure wine, the blood of God. The sacred altar does not care for polluted hands. Come on now, when you stand there robed in your snow-white vestment, in the presence of God, doesn't that woman steal into your mind? Exhilarated by taking and drinking the blood of Christ, [200] you think of nothing but your mistress' name. It is really to her, then, that you silently pray to take pity on you! She is the God you receive with Christ-eating mouth!

Enough! That is not the place for impious prayers — the kind that can only pour out of a filthy mind. You are at an age where you ought to be forswearing these depravities; you ought to be leading the life of holiness that your tonsure suggests. A consecrated priest should take thought for his errant flock, not be foolishly in love like some teenager. Though sordid lust is despicable wherever it is found, [210] it is even more sordid when it crops up in a hallowed heart. Indeed, God punishes no transgression quite so severely as the grave sin of desecrating religion. Jewish antiquity provides you with numerous examples, but brief elegiacs cannot recount that many. Since you're a well-read scholar, you can look them up your-self — if indeed someone who fails to understand himself can also take them to heart. While you are at it, also take a look at the sacred songs of the ancient bards (I really don't intend to bring them all up myself). Also glance at as many of the old books as you can lay your hands on [220] and see if love has ever brought anyone good luck. I'm overwhelmed with examples. For who hasn't heard of all those lovers' cliffs, flames, nooses, floods, swords, torments?[11]

---

[11]Glosses in the Zwickau and London copies show that Eobanus had very specific examples in mind. All of them are the subject of poems in Ovid's *Heroides*. In the order in which Eobanus lists them, they are: Sappho (who threw herself over a cliff); Hercules (who died on a pyre) and Jason (who had to kill a fire-breathing dragon); Phyllis (who hanged herself); Byblis (who was turned into a spring), Sappho (who leaped into the sea), and Hero (who threw herself into the Hellespont after Leander drowned); and Dido (who fell on the sword given to her by Aeneas).

Ad propiora vocor. Quis te, charissime Musis,
　　Ereptum Paphias alligat ante fores?
225　Frange truces laqueos, retinacem frange cathenam!
　　Vincitum est fortem dedecus esse virum.
Quid retineris adhuc? Quid adhuc non pessima frangis
　　Vincula? Fac fortes experiare manus.
Surge luto, suibus commixte. Quid inter olentes
230　Esuriens hyrcos aesopa spurca voras?
Quid facies? Quod amas, alio cras forsan abibit.
　　Num velles aliquo posse dolore mori?
Absentem, heu, quoties tu suspirabis amicam!
　　Heu, quam (si pateris dicere) stultus eris!
235　Tormentum quod te cruciet tibi flebis ademptum.
　　O mentem Stygia pigricitate gravem!
B6ʳ　Frena tibi imponi. Non amplius ista dolebis
　　Teque voles semper posse manere suem.
Exue, si quid habes quod non decet; indue quod te
240　Esse hominem faciat, non sinat esse feram.
Cum brutis tibi communis fuit illa voluptas.
　　Quae, precor, ut noceat esse, fuisse iuvet.
Carmina sic olim tibi nostra fidelius ibunt,
　　Si modo (quod debes) carmina nostra probas.
245　Iam tibi, quod longo voluisti tempore carmen,
　　Antidotum morbo fecimus ecce tuo.
Quod si prisca manet sub pectore flamma calenti,
　　Iam virtus, Musae, vestra iacebit iners.
Vincere sed castae Venerem potuere sorores,
250　Cum quateret castis taela minatus Amor.
Et modo si solitae superant in carmine vires,
　　Fertis ab immiti rapta trophea deo.
Ite, triumphali rediturae fronde Camenae,
　　Ite. Fugam timidus iam meditatur Amor.
255　At tu, qui nimio doluisti perditus aestu,
　　Iam nunquid quod ames displicet omne tibi?
Vive, decus vatisque tui fratrumque tuorum,
　　Atque gravi — o utinam! — salvus amore, vale.

Finis

229–38 Surge — suem. *add. A.*　　**241** illa *A*: ista *SO*.　　**246** fecimus *A*: misimus *SO*.
258 gravi . . . salvus amore *A*: hoc . . . liber ab igne *SO*.　　**Subscriptio** Finis *add. A*.

But let's get back to you. Darling of the Muses, who was it that swept you off your feet and left you tied hand and foot in front of Love's door? Break the cruel snares, smash the chain that holds you fast! It's a disgrace for a brave man to remain in bondage. What is still keeping you back? Why haven't you broken those detestable shackles yet? Show them what strong hands can do. Get up out of the muck, for you've been mingling with swine. Why [230] do you ravenously devour nauseating grease amid the stinking goats? What are you going to do? The one you love will perhaps leave you tomorrow for another man. You wouldn't want to die of a broken heart, would you? How often, alas, will you sigh for your truant sweetheart! Alas (if you'll forgive me for saying it), what a fool you will be! You'll weep that you've been robbed of the torment that racks you. Oh, the mind burdened with Stygian sloth!

Put the bridle on yourself. Stop grieving for those things and wishing you could remain a swine for the rest of your life. Get rid of anything about you that isn't right; get used to whatever lets you [240] be a man, not a beast. The lust in your heart is something you have in common with the brutes. Since it is harming you, please put this infatuation behind you. If you do that, I promise to be more reliable sending you songs of mine — assuming, of course, that you still appreciate my poems. (You owe me that much at least!) For now, here's the poem you've been looking forward to so long. Look, it's an antidote I've prepared specifically for your malady. But if the old flame keeps on blazing in your heart, then the Muses are really at their wits' end. However the chaste Sisters did succeed in conquering Venus [250] when Amor threatened the Maidens and brandished his arrows at them. And if they've retained their customary powers in verse, you will snatch a trophy from that merciless god.

Go, Muses. You'll soon be back, wreathed in triumphal laurel! Go. Amor is already nervously contemplating retreat. You, on the other hand, who've been forlornly suffering the pangs of unrestrained passion, don't you hate everything you were in love with just now?

Good luck, pride and joy of your bard and your brethren. And now that you're cured of your frenzied love (oh, how I wish!), farewell!

The End

HEROIDUM CHRISTIANARUM EPISTOLAE

LETTERS OF CHRISTIAN HEROINES

Helij Eobani Hes
si Heroidũ Christianarum Epistolae. opus Nouitium nuper aeditum. Anno M.D.xiiij.

HESSI DE SE EVLOGIVM,

Sunt quibus omne iocis teritur iuuenilibus aeuũ,
  Musaq́ſeruandos perdit inepta dies
At mea, cui debet, Christo deuota Iuuenta est
  Huic ero deuotus, ſi volet ipſe, ſenex
Cedite gentiles meritis, non arte, Poetę
  Materia Vates nos meliore ſumus

Title page of *Heroidum Christianarum epistolae*
Leipzig: Melchior Lotter, 1514
Universitätsbibliothek, Munich

HEROIDUM CHRISTIANARUM EPISTOLAE

Introduction

After settling into his duties as chancellor at Riesenburg in early 1510, Eobanus cast about for a project whereby he could win not only immortal fame for himself but also — and no less importantly — advancement at the episcopal court. His first thought was a poetic treatment of the liturgical calendar, a Christian answer to Ovid's *Fasti*.[1] It soon dawned on him, however, that such an undertaking, which would demand a huge amount of religious, historical, and astronomical research, would take far too long to complete and moreover require a far better library than the meager one available to him in Riesenburg. Upon further reflection, therefore, he hit upon an idea that, while still ambitious and agreeably novel, could be completed in his leisure hours, yet would be no less suitable for presentation to Bishop Job von Dobeneck: a book of Christian heroic epistles, in emulation of Ovid's *Heroides*. Like Ovid's, Eobanus' heroines would write letters to beloved men. But unlike Ovid's mythical-pagan women, Eobanus' writers would be Christian heroines: wives and mothers, virgins and sisters in Christ. Their elegies would recall Ovid's in form, but surpass them in spirit.[2]

Court life, with its tedious labors and splendid diversions, gave him little time for serious poetry. Nevertheless, Eobanus worked at his book whenever he could. As he would tell Camerarius later, "he composed the bulk of it in his head and finished it on horseback, while he was accompanying the bishop perhaps or riding out to hunt or traveling on diplomatic missions."[3] It is no wonder, then, that it took him three years to finish the first fifteen letters. Once set free at Frankfurt an der Oder, he managed to write nine more in just a single semester, lightly revise the earlier ones, and add a long dedicatory letter to Job von Dobeneck.[4]

---

[1]See *Her. Chr.*, ded. 8.1–2. The first to complete this ambitious project was Baptista Mantuanus. His *De sacris diebus* (Lyons, 1516) was reprinted at Strasbourg in 1518 as *Fastorum libri duodecim*. Eobanus began a version of his own in 1540: see Camerarius, *Nar.* 26.4, with n. 127 (1:77). Even then he needed a strong push from his friend Philip Melanchthon. See his letter to Melanchthon of 2 July 1539 (*Epp. fam.*, 204). After Eobanus' death Melanchthon asked Johann Stigel to take on the project together with him. Despite encouragement and offers of help from Melanchthon and occasional bursts of writing, the project proved too difficult for Stigel. See Walther Ludwig, "Musenkult und Gottesdienst — Evangelischer Humanismus der Reformationszeit," *Die Musen im Reformationszeitalter*, ed. W. Ludwig (Leipzig, 2001), 45–46, n. 133.

[2]*Her. Chr.*, ded. 7.1–9.3
[3]Camerarius, *Nar.* 7.9.
[4]See *Her. Chr.*, ded. 8.3–5.

Though the book was sure to promote his career at Riesenburg, Eobanus was astute enough to realize that it could open doors for him elsewhere too, should he ever grow tired of life in that cultural backwater. And grow tired he did. Indeed, in a letter of 12 April 1512, a few weeks after returning from Cracow, Eobanus is so desperate to escape from the "barbarism" of Prussia that he appeals to his friend Georg Spalatin, now mentoring two nephews of Duke Frederick, to do everything in his power to help him obtain a lectorship at the University of Wittenberg. If Spalatin could use his influence at the Saxon court, Eobanus would present him not only with the newly-published *Encomium nuptiale*, but also with many other works — in particular the *Christian Heroides*, on which he has been working for over two years already. In any case, Eobanus concludes, he is not likely to hold out much longer in Prussia. He will leave no stone unturned to obtain his leave from the bishop.[5]

In the early spring of the German Renaissance, however, with conservative hostility to the humanists coming to a boil everywhere, it was difficult for a poet, even for a rising star like Eobanus, to establish himself at a university. Accordingly, when no position materialized at Wittenberg, Eobanus jumped at the bishop's request in the early spring of 1513 that he study law at some German university. Without having to give up his current post, he would now be able to leave Riesenburg, finish his *Heroides*, and at the same time lobby discretely for the teaching position that he was hankering for. But which university should he choose?

His first choice naturally fell on Wittenberg. But when Spalatin strongly counseled against this plan, Eobanus settled on Frankfurt an der Oder.[6] There, with plenty of free time left over from his studies, he made rapid progress on the *Heroides*. By the early autumn of 1513 the book was ready for the printer. But then, as we have seen, disaster struck.[7] Eobanus and two of his friends were so cruelly maltreated by a local citizen that they contemplated revenge and refused the legal remedies open to them. When the university finally enjoined them on December 11 to forswear taking the matter into their own hands and instead appeal their case to the highest authorities, Eobanus stormed out in high dudgeon and headed first to Wittenberg, where he consulted with Spalatin, and thence to Leipzig. Here he matriculated almost at once as "Dominus Eobanus de Franckenberck, magister Erfordensis." His immediate goal was to publish the *Heroides* and make himself visible at the university. Wisely, however, he continued to wear the courtier's scarlet cloak. This, indeed, is how Joachim Camerarius first saw him at Georg Helt's house later that December.[8]

But Eobanus' hopes were quickly dashed. Almost at once he learned that the anti-humanist faction at Leipzig was too powerful to be overcome with a headlong charge. In fact, he was warned outright against publishing the *Heroides Christianae*

---

[5]Mutian. *Ep.*, 2:367–69.
[6]See pp. 46–47 above.
[7]See pp. 48–49 above.
[8]Camerarius, *Nar.* 7.13–14.

here, at least for the time being. From the available evidence it appears that the conservatives, who in 1511 had succeeded in relegating Johannes Rhagius Aesticampianus from Leipzig, were deathly afraid that the humanist upstarts would draw off too many students from the traditional curriculum. On 5 January 1514 the philosophical faculty passed a resolution that expressly prohibited Johannes Sturnus and the other magisters from teaching classes in private homes throughout the city, lest these courses undermine the university "in a novel and sinister way."[9] Faced with these realities, Eobanus postponed publication of the *Heroides* and sought to smooth his way instead with the much more modest *Sylvae duae*, printed in early January 1514. This is how he explained his decision in the work's dedicatory letter, dated January 1: "Because I was advised not to rush headlong into publication — and sound advice it was too — it occurred to me that I ought to assay the taste of the scholarly public by offering up, as it were, some minuscule first fruits beforehand. For if I went ahead and brought out the magnum opus regardless, I might have to pay the price for my temerity and find disgrace instead of favor."

Eobanus' conciliatory gesture did not go unrewarded. On January 23 the faculty approved his request to teach a course on the *Sylvae duae*, provided that he obey the university rules and not continue teaching on his own after he had finished with the poem. In his inaugural lecture to the course he gingerly hints at all the backstage maneuvering:[10]

You, I think, will not regret the expense nor I the work involved, even though the work involved will be nothing, or certainly as good as nothing, seeing that I am not undertaking it spurred by the hope of any wealth, the desire for any glory, the goad of any malice (which has no place in a generous soul), but rather by means of these minuscule works to open the way to greater ones. For as you can tell from the commendation that I posted on the door, I had decided that my *Christian Heroides* — four years' worth of lucubrations, a book put together by dint of many vigils, much labor, and in truth the utmost enthusiasm — should be set in type and published here the moment I reached this university. However I changed this plan, thinking it appropriate and by no means ill-advised if I should first, as a kind of harbinger, so to speak, send out the two poems that are now in your hands, for fear that after completing and printing the big book I might run some kind of risk and not take counsel until it was too late. Nor was I mistaken in this opinion; for most of you are aware

[9] *Die Matrikel der Universität Leipzig*, ed. Georg Erler, vol. 2 (1897; repr. Nendeln, 1976), 492: "In eadem convocatione concluserunt omnes magistri, ut dns. Stornus ceterique magistri in domibus civium legentes prohiberentur, ne aliquid in preiudicium collegiorum, magistrorum, lectorum ordinarie legencium, complencium et tocius facultatis nova et sinistra quadam via attemptaretur." Johannes Sturnus (Staar) of Schmalkalden matriculated at Leipzig in the winter semester of 1510–11 as "Dominus Iohannes Stornus de Schmalkaldia, poeta laureatus." When Eobanus arrived in Leipzig, Sturnus welcomed him with a verse letter. Eobanus replied in the poem later printed as *Sylv.* 1.11.

[10] See pp. 63–68 above.

that I have been strongly discouraged also from this honorable and good intention of mine. I hope, however, that my innocence will find favor someday even among those men, seeing that I am not asking for pay, not setting any snares, not ostentatiously pluming myself, not swelling with pride, not putting myself on a pedestal.

All these gambits notwithstanding, it gradually became obvious that Eobanus had no chance of landing a lectureship at Leipzig. At the same time, his renewed immersion in academic life made it unthinkable for him to return to his law books and an eventual career as a diplomat in "barbarous" Prussia. Therefore, upon the advice of Mutianus Rufus he addressed himself to prominent scholars in Germany and Austria to enlist their help in obtaining a post at their universities. In one of these letters, dated 20 March 1514, Eobanus introduces himself to the humanist Joachim Vadian (1484–1551) at Vienna. All the works he has written thus far, he tells Vadian, will bear witness that he is a Christian poet to the core, but none more so than his *Christian Heroides* — "a work that I trust will prove not only pleasing but also sufficiently great, a book I have been gestating for four years already and am now eager to send out into the world." As a sample of his verse he is also sending Vadian a copy of the *Sylvae duae* and longs to hear his colleague's judgment. He concludes by imploring Vadian to see if there is any chance of obtaining a teaching position for him at Vienna.[11]

As Eobanus had foreseen, there could be no career advancement without the *Heroides*. By the spring, with neither a lectureship nor an impressive book to show for his efforts, he had nothing to gain from waiting any longer. He set aside the elegy "On True Nobility" that he had been composing at Spalatin's request and now spent all his waking moments on readying the magnum opus for publication. By June 13 it was ready for the printer. A week later, on June 22, Eobanus was able to tell Spalatin that the work was now in press and would come out in two or three weeks.[12] By July 21, his book in hand, he was back in Erfurt, where so much had changed since the "Mad Year" of 1509–10. Yet even there, despite the efforts of Mutianus Rufus and other friends, despite his hard-won reputation as the most distinguished poet in Germany, Eobanus was not to obtain a faculty position at the university until the summer of 1518.

Reception

Even though the *Heroides Christianae* did not have the immediate effect of launching Eobanus' academic career, the work did bring him the fame he thirsted for. Congratulations arrived from admirers all over Germany. Mutianus Rufus, to whom he sent a copy on August 4, lauds the book in letter after letter (*Epp.* 409,

---

[11]See *Die Vadianische Briefsammlung der Stadtbibliothek St. Gallen*, ed. Emil Arbenz, vol. 1 (St. Gallen, 1890), no. 31. To all appearances Vadian did not reply to this appeal.

[12]The book's dedicatory letter is dated June 13. For the letter to Spalatin see Mutian. *Ep.*, 2:370–71.

410, 412–14, 416, 436, 446, and 460). Already on August 8 he marvels at his friend's "almost Homeric grandiloquence" and praises the poem's incredible clarity, fluidity, and charm, its beautiful marriage of classical form with Christian content, such that it will surely find favor with scholastics and humanists alike (*Ep.* 410). He exults in another letter that Eobanus' "queens" — his heroines — "plainly show him to be the greatest poet of our time and, so to speak, divine" (*Ep.* 409). On August 13 he tells Eobanus that the work has not only made made him immortal, it has also propelled him into the ranks of the most eloquent poets, right between Ovid and Baptista Mantuanus (*Ep.* 412). He repeats the compliment in a letter of September 26 (*Ep.* 436), declaring that Eobanus is nothing less than a cross between Ovid and Mantuanus, "but so close to the former that one cannot tell whether he is walking in his own shoes or Ovid's." And to Duke Frederick the Wise of Saxony, to whom he presented a copy, Mutianus praises the work on August 13 as a "very lovely and beautiful book" that will surely give the duke much pleasure (*Ep.* 413). Ten days later he is happy to report that the duke's librarian Georg Spalatin now speaks of Eobanus in all earnest as "the Vergil of Germany" (*Ep.* 421). Other friends and colleagues — among them Crotus Rubianus, Ulrich von Hutten, Petrejus Eberbach, and Michael Hummelberg — were equally generous.[13] The celebrated trilinguist Johann Reuchlin extols Eobanus in a letter of 26 October 1514 as "the prince of literature — the noblest of them all, lacking any rival," and crowns him "king," because "among the Christian poets of your generation you yourself are the king."[14] Reuchlin later presented his own copy to the young humanist Johannes Alexander Brassicanus (1500–39), who in 1526 wrote Eobanus from Vienna to tell him how much he still loved the poet of the *Christian Heroides* (*Epp. fam.*, 31–32). Beatus Rhenanus too, in a letter of 26 March 1522, recalls that at his first reading of the *Heroides* he thought to himself: "Germany ought to hold this man in the highest esteem."[15] No less stinting in his praise was Beatus' friend Erasmus of Rotterdam. After Eobanus had come to visit him at Louvain in October 1518, the great Dutch humanist wrote: "I thought I knew my Germany well and had sought out all its distinguished minds. I was devoted to the abilities of Beatus Rhenanus, found Philippus Melanchthon's character delightful, admired Reuchlin's dignity, and was much taken with Hutten's charming conversation. And here is Hessus all of a sudden, uniting in himself all I had previously loved or admired in others separately. What does one think of in your *Heroides* but a Christian Ovid? Who is so happy

---

[13]Cf. pp. 120–21 below. For Crotus' praise, see also his letter to Johann Reuchlin, 25 January 1515, in Hutten, *Opera*, 1:29. For Hutten, Eberbach, and Hummelberg, see Adalbert Horawitz, "Zur Biographie und Correspondenz Johannes Reuchlin's," *Sitzungsberichte der kaiserlichen Akademie der Wissenschaften, Philosophisch-Historische Classe* 85 (1877), 142–43, 145.

[14]See William Hamilton, *Discussions on Philosophy and Literature, Education and University Reform* (1853), repr. in *Works of William Hamilton*, ed. Savina Tropea (Bristol, 2001), 1:237–38, from the autograph; Johann Reuchlin, *Briefwechsel*, vol. 3, ed. Matthias Dall'Asta and Gerald Dörner (Stuttgart, 2007), 120–21, no. 252, unfortunately from an inaccurate, incomplete apograph.

[15]"Nam primum Heroidas tuas vidi, quod accidit annos ab hinc aliquot, statim dixi: 'hic dignus est, quem Germania plurimi faciat.'" See *Epp. fam.*, 289; *Briefwechsel des Beatus Rhenanus*, ed. Adalbert Horawitz and Karl Hartfelder (1886; repr. Hildesheim, 1966), no. 219.

in plain prose as you are in verse of every kind? Your learning balances your gifts of expression, and your Christian piety enhances both. In prose you are already so successful that one would think you had no poetry in you. Yours is a truly golden vein of talent."[16]

Innovation and Models

When he lauded Eobanus as "Christian Ovid" in the autumn of 1518, Erasmus could hardly have failed to recall how, two decades before, he had assigned the similar title "Christian Vergil" to the famed Italian poet Baptista Mantuanus (1447–1516).[17] If so, he was by no means alone in creating this nexus of associations. Mutianus Rufus and Georg Spalatin, after all, had made the very same connection as early as 1514, and rightly so. For just as Mantuanus' *Parthenicae* and other hagiographic epics imitate Vergil's *Aeneid* to recount the lives of such saints as the Virgin Mary (1481), Catherine (1489), and George (1507), so Eobanus' *Heroides Christianae* follows Ovid's *Heroides* in form, but replaces his mythical, pagan women with Christian heroines, beginning with Mary, Mary Magdalene, and Catherine of Alexandria.[18] In Eobanus' work, Paris' wooing letter and Helen's reluctant assent are supplanted by Emmanuel's wooing letter to the Blessed Virgin and her humble, but joyous, acceptance. Laodamia's letter to her doomed husband Protesilaus is superseded with Elizabeth's anxious letter to her husband Ludwig, whom she would never see alive again. The faithful Penelope is outdone by the Christian wife Sabina, who — after a full twenty years have passed — now pleads with Alexius to return home at last. Eobanus' Martha goes so far as to reject the Ovidian heroines outright and associates herself instead with the Mother of God: "This is the way weeping eyes are apt to write — not the eyes, to be sure, with which Briseis wept for the enraged Achilles or Laodamia for her absent husband, but the eyes with which she who became pregnant with superhuman seed wept at the cruel death of her Son" (*Her. Chr.* 22.14–18). And St. Ursula, writing to her fiancé Ethereus, first contrasts her pure love with the sordid passions of Ovidian "heroines like Phyllis, Hermione, Briseis, and Hypsipyle" (*Her. Chr.* 17.41–44) and then admonishes her beloved (ll. 129–45):

> If you have a hankering for love poetry, pick out what is useful,
> throw out what is noxious. As you skim through the disgraceful lies
> of the old poets, keep telling yourself while you read that they con-
> tain potent venom. Don't let some Thisbe of Babylon move you to

---

[16]Erasmus, *Ep.* 874, letter of 19 October 1518. The translation is by R. A. B. Mynors and D. F. S. Thomson, *Collected Works of Erasmus*, vol. 6 (Toronto, 1982), 142.

[17]Erasmus, *Ep.* 49 (ed. Allen, 1:163).

[18]For an admirable history and analysis of the heroic epistle, see Heinrich Dörrie, *Der heroische Brief: Bestandsaufnahme, Geschichte, Kritik einer humanistisch-barocken Literaturgattung* (Berlin, 1968). Dörrie discusses Baptista Mantuanus and Eobanus Hessus on 363–74.

tears here, no poetess [*Sappho*] dying at the behest of some god. Don't be grieved at the death of some abandoned Phyllis or at a girl left stranded in barbarous Naxos [*Ariadne*]. Don't sympathize with anyone who burns with forbidden love for her brother [*Canace*] or plunges the cruel sword into her side [*Dido*]. Don't picture Paris or Achilles to yourself, nor the one who was poisoned with Nessus' blood [*Hercules*]. Don't let some Acontius incline your ears. Whoever he is, let Protesilaus love without you. Also don't marvel at Leander swimming in the swollen waves or at the girl from Sestos as she drifts in the strait near her home. Rather, keep your eyes on us, stormtossed as we are on all the seas. . . .

Ursula's catalogues expand on the one in Mantuanus' second *Parthenice*, where Catherine lists ten ancient heroines whose amours plunged them into grief and death. Of Mantuanus' exempla, six come from Ovid's *Heroides*.[19]

Eobanus, of course, had no trouble acknowledging his debt to Ovid and Mantuanus. Already in the private letter to Spalatin of 12 April 1512 he self-deprecatingly calls himself "Ovid's monkey" as he toiled at his *Heroides*.[20] Adopting a more dignified tone in the book's dedicatory letter he tells Job von Dobeneck: "In writing them I did not so much imitate Ovidius Naso as admire him. The former, certainly, is something I could do with some success; the latter is something I could never do enough of" (ded. 7.1–2). And at the end of the work he confesses with engaging modesty: "In writing these letters, my Muse presumed more to admire the genius of the Pelignian poet than to smack of it" (24.133–34). He is equally forthright in pointing to Mantuanus as his model (ded. 15.5–7): "In our own time the consummately learned poet Baptista Mantuanus has portrayed saintly heroines in a series of *Parthenicae*, as he himself called them, albeit in a different genre from mine. . . . The same poet composed an epic about Saint George, cast in the heroic mold, to be sure, and yet far removed from the way he is traditionally presented. It is after Mantuan's image of him that I too, in a manner of speaking, have modeled my own likeness of the saint. From him I also borrowed the name of my heroine 'Alcyone.'"

As he had done earlier with *De amantium infoelicitate* (1508) and *Bucolicon* (1509), Eobanus insinuates on the title page of his *Heroides Christianae* that the book represents a new kind of work ("opus novitium") — a fresh genre in German literature that neatly blends Ovid with Mantuanus. Eobanus' claim to innovation is certainly justified, but with the same qualification that we made earlier about his claims regarding the prosimetric satire and the pastoral cycle.[21] He was indeed the first German to write sacred heroides and the very first poet anywhere to write

---

[19]They are Briseis, Dido, Phyllis, Oenone, Helen, and Medea. See A. P. Orbán, ed., *Vitae Sanctae Katharinae: Pars secunda*, CCCM 119 A (Turnhout, 1992), 399, ll. 451–56. The parallels to Ursula's letter were first noted and interpreted by Dörrie, 368–69.

[20]See Mutian. *Ep.*, 2:368: "simiam Ovidii."

[21]See *Ama.*, ded., n. 3 (1:202–03), and *Buc.*, lim. 5, n. (1:453).

an entire set of them. The genre's originator, however, was not Eobanus, but the Dutch humanist Jakob of Gouda, called Magdalius.[22]

Jakob, who took the name Magdalius after he became a Dominican, was born at Gouda around 1470. After matriculating at Cologne in 1489, he earned his BA in the winter semester of 1490–91, his MA in 1495. By 1497 he had entered a Dominican monastery at Cologne and was studying theology. He continued to teach courses in poetics at the university, however. In 1501 and 1503 he published two textbooks on the art of poetry and versification that proved successful enough to merit reprinting: *Erarium aureum poetarum, omnibus Latinae linguae . . . professoribus accommodum* (Cologne, 1501; repr. 1502, 1503, 1506, and 1515) and *Stichologia Gaudensis. Enchiridion poetarum. Homeomata eorundem. Naumachia ecclesiastica* (Cologne, 1503; repr. 1506 and 1508). To each of these handbooks Magdalius appended a small collection of his own verse. Ulrich von Hutten, who may have studied with him at Cologne in 1505–06, could therefore rightly laud Magdalius in 1510 as a scholar who combined instruction in versification with poetry of his own — indeed, as the premier poet of Cologne: "The first place of honor [at Cologne] belongs to Jakob of Gouda, who unites the sacred rites of the Muses with his own sacred songs. Few are more expert in these arts of ours or write elegies in a purer vein."[23]

Only a few years after Hutten wrote these lines, humanist admiration turned to scorn. Yielding to heavy pressure from his prior, inquisitor Jakob of Hoogstraten, Magdalius published an epigram in 1513 railing at Johann Reuchlin in his fight against Johann Pfefferkorn. Though Magdalius soon signaled his regret, Reuchlin

---

[22]The first to draw attention to Magdalius as the genre's originator was Jozef IJsewijn. See his review of Dörrie in *Leuvense Bijdragen* 59 (1970), 67 (no. 5). IJsewijn points to Magdalius also in later publications: see "Humanism and Humanist Literature in the Low Countries before 1500," in *Classical Influences on European Culture A.D. 500–1500*, ed. R. R. Bolgar (Cambridge, 1971), 117–18; "The Coming of Humanism to the Low Countries," in *Itinerarium Italicum: The Profile of the Italian Renaissance in the Mirror of its European Transformations* (Leiden, 1975), 280; and *Companion to Neo-Latin Studies*, part 2, Supplementa Humanistica Lovaniensia 14 (Leuven, 1998), 77.

The best presentation of Magdalius' life and works is Gabriel M. Löhr, "Der Kölner Dominikanerhumanist Jacobus Magdalius Gaudanus und seine Naumachia ecclesiastica," *Archivum Fratrum Praedicatorum* 18 (1948), 281–302, with an edition of the poems in *Naumachia*. Heinrich Grimm's article in *Neue Deutsche Biographie* (Berlin, 1953–), 10:317–18, unfortunately draws on outdated scholarship.

For a detailed history of the genre, in particular the *Heroides sacrae*, see Dörrie. For the veneration of saints in humanist literature before the Reformation, see Angelika Dörfler-Dierken, *Die Verehrung der heiligen Anna in Spätmittelalter und früher Neuzeit* (Göttingen, 1992); Roland Stieglecker, *Die Renaissance eines Heiligen: Sebastian Brant und Onuphrius eremita* (Wiesbaden, 2001), 17–122. See also Andrzej Budzisz, "Helius Eobanus Hessus' *Heroides* as an Example of Renaissance Religious Elegy," in *Ad Litteras: Latin Studies in Honour of J. H. Brouwer*, ed. A. P. Orbán and M. G. M. van der Poel (Nijmegen, 2001), 273–81.

[23]Hutten, *Querel.* 2.10.181–84 (a poem written and published in 1510): "Prima est ante alios Iacobo gloria Gaudae, / Qui miscet sacris Musica sacra suis. / Vix alius nostras callet studiosior artes, / Vix elegos vena candidiore facit." Ever since Ludwig Geiger, *Johann Reuchlin: Sein Leben und seine Werke* (Leipzig, 1871), 359–60, the phrase "miscet sacris Musica sacra suis" has been misunderstood to indicate that Magdalius also taught music at Cologne. For the phrase "Musica sacra" in the sense translated here, see Eob. *Laud.* 330, n.

never forgave him.[24] In the *Letters of Obscure Men* (1.11) Magdalius is grouped with other Dominican obscurantists and ironically dismissed as "a most subtle poet" ("poeta subtilissimus"). His reputation in tatters, his poetic and scholarly work forgotten, Magdalius died not long after 1518.

As I have mentioned, Magdalius appended a small collection of verse to each of his textbooks on the art of poetry. The poem of interest to us occurs in the oft-reprinted *Erarium aureum poetarum* (sig. H2^r–H3^r). Entitled "Letter from Saint Mary Magdalene to Christ, concerning the Illness of her Brother Lazarus," the elegy is based on the familiar biblical story of Mary and Martha's brother Lazarus (John 11.1–44). As Lazarus lay dying, his sisters sent the news to Christ. However, Christ tarried and did not come to Bethany until Lazarus had been in the tomb for four days already. Moved by Mary's tears, he went to the tomb and brought her brother back to life.

In Magdalius' fiction, Mary writes her letter to Christ several days after the master has first been told of Lazarus' illness. She has been waiting for him with ever-growing fears. Each time the dog barks, she runs to the door, only to be disappointed. She keeps climbing up to the roof to see if Christ is coming yet. Unable to stand the strain any longer, she now shares her grief with him and describes how Lazarus is dying before her eyes. Bone-weary from the waking and writing, she concludes her letter in the same way she began: by asking Christ to grant Lazarus the health and welfare that she herself cannot send in salutation or farewell.

But here is the poem itself, as it appears in the editio princeps (1501):

H2^r **EPISTOLA DIVE MARIE MAGDALENE AD**
           CHRISTUM IN INFIRMITATE LAZARI FRATRIS

>   Quam, mea vita, legis, infauste nuncia sortis,
>   Est raptim tremula charta notata manu.[25]
>   Querere forte velis, fixis paulisper ocellis,
>   Quur habeat truncum littera missa caput.
>   5   Accipe plura brevi, nec te stupor occupet ullus,
>   Mentio si capiti nulla salutis inest:
>   Quod mihi non licuit, dare te decuisse putavi,
>   Sole sub est rapido quo sine nulla salus,
>   Me rata scribentem, si mens tam ceca fuisset,
>   10   Omnia callenti prodere velle, levem.
>   Nam tua lachrymulis vestigia sepe rigantem
>   Non arbitrabar posse latere manum.[26]

---

[24]See Ludwig Geiger, *Johann Reuchlin: Sein Leben und seine Werke* (1871; repr. Nieuwkoop, 1964), 293, 359–60. For an account of Reuchlin's dispute with Pfefferkorn and the Cologne Dominicans, see Erika Rummel, *The Case against Johann Reuchlin: Religious and Social Controversy in Sixteenth-Century Germany* (Toronto, 2002).

[25]Cf. Ov. *Ep.* 3.1–2. Magdalius continues the imitation at ll. 29–34 below.

[26]For the motif cf. Ov. *Ep.* 15.1–4.

Quid mihi nunc animi,[27] quid fratri quidve sorori,
    Signa docent spacio non bene tracta suo,
15 Nam dolor immodicus memori sub mente repostus[28]
    Flexit ab intento tramite sepe stilum.
Tantus, crede mihi, teneros dolor occupat artus,
    Sepius a digitis repserit ille meis.
Flamine qui quondam calamus tremefactus aquoso
20   Ex omni didicit parte movere caput,
Quo non debuerat (longo fortassis ab usu)
    Iam licet evulso cespite carpsit iter.
Summisere comam suspiria anhela tenellam
    Ambigue parti pectore tracta cavo.
25 Forte videbatur fluidis madefactus ocellis
    Amne paludoso rursus habere pedem.
Consona si fidei videar minus esse locuta,
    Testis adest lachrymis littera feda meis.
Ecce notis pigeat si non conferre lituras,
30   Vix in eis numerus qui superabit erit.
Nocte dieque vigil gemitu quo verser anhelo,
    Signa satis possent ore tacente loqui.
Nil opus est igitur digitos lassare reduncos,
    Pondera quum vocis queque litura ferat.[29]
35 Levia diffusis circum precordia flammis
    Ne tamen obductus seviat ignis edax
Solaque ne patiar, tecum communico penam,
    Utque fiet levius divido tristis onus.
Perdit enim magnas divisa potentia vires;
40   Fervida quum fuerit sparsa tepescit aqua.
Me Fortuna videt vultu malefida sinistro
H2ᵛ   Et retrahit placidam quam dedit ante manum.
Sidera quaeque vigent tristes spondentia morbos,
    Inque meum vulnus stelliger axis agit.
45 Bellicus horrisonis Mavors crudescit in armis,
    Et furit in tardo falcifer orbe senex.
Ecce mihi quondam Lachesis quos texuit annos,
    Nititur adversans rumpere Parca soror.
Lethifera exiguo pecori quid spicula tendis?
50   Fac tua Thespiadum tela cruore micent!
Quid iuvat insidias viridi posuisse iuvente
    Duraque prevalida saxa rotasse manu?

[27]Cf. Ov. *Ep.* 11.87.
[28]Verg. *A.* 1.26.
[29]Cf. Ov. *Ep.* 3.3–4.

Candida parce quibus serpit lanugo per ora,
    Et cadat annoso cum seniore nurus.
55 Unguibus obstrinos[30] laceret Pallantias artus
    Et cubet in gelido sola relicta toro.
Grandia turrite regat alter menia Troie;
    Cysseis Priamum defleat orba suum.
Intempestivi secedat staminis hora,
60   Et fugiat nostros Mors procul acta lares.
Tela retardetur paulisper, rosida noxque
    Furetur nitido fila retorta die.
Sollicitasse Iovem mage quum decuisset, in ore
    Volvere quid Parcas, docta Thalia, studes?
65 Ne pigeat revocare gradum, precor, unde parumper
    Calle pererrato flectere visa pedem es.
Ecce tibi lachrymis Dominoque Deoque profusis
    Quamlibet indignas offero, Christe, preces.
Ad tua fraternos miserans vestigia morbos
70   Pectoris internas mesta recludo fores.
Nulla Cytheinis fratri quum spes sit in herbis,
    Quod spectat, superest, preter obire, nihil.
Gramina sufficiunt nihil Anticyrea salutis
    Nilque Machaonia potio mixta manu.
75 Pectora nam Cereri stomacho suadente repugnant,
    Ossaque vix tenui pelle sepulta iacent.
Lingua, corymbiferi multum calefacta Lyei,
    Flagitat invitis pocula sepe labris.
Ebria pluma mero quamquam relevare calorem
80   Nititur, aligeri corpore vulsa gregis,
Rauca tamen (dictu si fas) precordia Iacchum
    Et prius infusas eiaculantur aquas.
Ad caput ipsa locor flavis discincta capillis.[31]
    Martha fere gelidos sistitur ante pedes.
H3^r 85 Utraque disiecti speculantes lumina vultus
    Miramur tacitas mortis in ora notas.
Oscula purpureo quondam suffusa colore
    Sunt velut educto pallida cera favo.
Sepius attonitos tenuit que lingua disertos
90   Barbaricos bleso cudit in ore sonos.
Frigore crura rigent; nares tenuantur aquose;
    Orbe restringuntur lumina mesta suo.
Ah, quotiens dixi Marthe, "Dilecta," sorori,
    "Que, cedo, iam Christi causa moratur iter?"

[30]A variant spelling of *ostrinos*.
[31]Cf. Ov. *Ep.* 6.89.

95   Quo trahis usque moram? Lachrymis inflectere nostris
           Daque salutiferam (nam potes) ultro manum.
        Te soror et frater, te fletibus ipsa profusis,
           Te domus omnis avens nocte dieque manet.
        Te puto presentem quotiens canis ostia servans
100   Aurea terrificos fundit ad astra sonos.
        Me licet expassis tenuis sopor occupet alis,
           Pervigil emoto vecte recludo fores.
        Undique coniectis ubi non spectaris ocellis,
           Pulsantur pugnis pectora nuda meis.
105   Et quum membra toro rursus iam lassa reclino,
           Mesta novaturus lumina somnus abest.
        Me miseram, quotiens positis sine lege lacertis
           Parte caput recubat qua iacuere pedes!
        Memnonis alma parens[32] ubi summa cacumina lustrans
110   Lucem puniceis provocat acta rotis,
        Protinus ethereas iterum levo corpus ad auras,
           Certior ut fiam quid velit eger opis.
        Fumida saepe domus laquearia scando, ut ab omni
           Parte mihi pateat qua veniatur iter.
115   Triste fenestellis caput effero saepe solutis,
           Destituunt oculos sed iuga celsa meos.
        Inde torum repetens ubi summa pericula specto,
           Ante pedem lecti labor utroque genu.
        Lumina sicco manu gelido suffusa liquore,
120   Compingens tacitis tristia verba meis.
        Plura canenda forent, sed lassat epistola corpus,[33]
           Parca satis spatii vixque papyrus habet.
        Littera principio qua missa salute carebat,
           Iam ratione pari finis inesse nequit.
125   Tu largire velim quod abest cum fine titellum,[34]
           Te siquidem solum finis et alpha decent.

LETTER FROM SAINT MARY MAGDALENE TO CHRIST, CONCERNING THE ILLNESS OF HER BROTHER LAZARUS

The page that you, my life,[35] are reading, this bearer of bad news,
I am writing it in a great rush, with trembling hand. Perhaps,
if you stare at it a little while, you may well ask why my letter

[32]Mart. 8.21.8.
    [33]Cf. Ov. *Ep.* 20.241. Unlike Mary Magdalene, however, Acontius goes on to conclude his letter
to the ill Cydippe with an emphatic "vale!"
    [34]The word *titellum* is a variant of *titulus*. Magdalius uses it again in a liminary epigram for Jakob of
Hoogstraten's *Justificatorium principum Alamanie* [Cologne, 1508]: "titellum / Supplantatoris . . . habet."
    [35]Cf. John 14.6, where Jesus says: "I am the way, and the truth, and the life."

begins so abruptly. To put it all in a nutshell and stop you from wondering at the lack of a salutation: the wish for good health, I think, is not for me to offer, but for you. Without you there can be no salvation anywhere under the blazing sun. Besides (even assuming I were that blind) I would feel silly [10] if I wanted to tell you who wrote this letter, seeing you know every-thing. Certainly I can't imagine you'll fail to recognize the hand that repeatedly washed your feet with tears.[36] What is on my mind now, what is on my brother's or sister's, that is something my scrawly handwriting can show you. For the boundless grief, engraved deep in my heart, keeps turning the pen away from its intended path. Believe me, the sorrow that has taken hold of my tender frame is so great that the pen slips from my fingers again and again. The same reed that used to tremble at every breath of wind over the water [20] and learned to bend its head in all directions, now (perhaps from force of habit) makes its way where it shouldn't go, uprooted as it is from the soil. Drawn from the hollow chest, my panting sighs blow the reed's delicate tufts apart. Perhaps, wetted by my watery eyes, it dreams of standing in a swampy stream again.

If these words sound farfetched, my tear-stained letter will serve as witness. Look, if you don't mind comparing the blots with the words, [30] you'll scarcely find any characters that aren't smeared. Sleepless as I am night and day, incessantly gasping out groans, these marks, though mute, can speak a clear enough language. So I really don't need to weary the curved fingers, seeing that every single blot has the weight of words.

To keep the consuming fire from overwhelming me, how-ever, even as it rages with spreading flames around my smooth breast, and just to avoid having to endure the pain alone, I want to share it with you; and to make the burden of sorrow lighter I am dividing it in half.[37] As you know, power divided loses much of its force. [40] When boiling water is scattered, it cools off.

Fickle Fortune is looking at me with sinister eye and drawing back the hand she kindly offered me earlier. The stars that threaten dreadful diseases are all in the ascendant; the starry heavens are con-spiring to pierce my heart. Warlike Mars is growing savage in his horrid-sounding armor; and in his plodding course the old Sickle-bearer is raging with wrath.[38] Look at the years Lachesis once spun

[36]Mary Magdalene was traditionally identified with the sinful woman who washed Christ's feet with her tears and dried them with her hair. See n. 7 at *Her. Chr.* 3.118 (p. 187 below).

[37]In accordance with the proverbial thought, "A trouble shared is a trouble halved."

[38]Saturn, an ancient Italic god of agriculture identified with Kronos, was thought to bring on fevers and diseases.

out for me: her sister Fate is doing all she can to stand in the way and cut them short. Why do you aim your death-dealing arrows at small fry like us? [50] Let your weapons gleam with the blood of Hercules' sons! What is the point of waylaying green youths and hurling hard rocks at them with all your might? Spare those whose fair cheeks are just being overspread with down, and have old men and women die instead. Make someone like Aurora gouge her rosy limbs with her nails and sleep widowed in her cold bed.[39] Someone else can rule the great walls of turreted Troy — it's fine if a bereaved Hecuba weeps for her husband Priam.[40] But let the hour of premature death recede! [60] Let death be put to flight and driven far away from our home! The thread of life should be spun a little longer. Surely, dewy night can steal some twisted yarn from bright daytime!

It would have been more fitting if you had implored God.[41] Why then do you want to keep on talking about the Parcae, you learned Muse? Don't hesitate, I beg you, to return to the track you were on, before I saw you veer off for a moment.

Look, with all the tears I have shed before the Lord my God, it is to you, Christ, that I am offering these prayers, however unworthy. Grieving over my brother's illness, I fall down at your feet and [70] sorrowfully open the innermost doors of my heart. Since there is no hope for my brother in Colchian herbs, he has nothing to look forward to but to die. The drugs from Anticyra are of no avail; neither are the potions prepared by our physician. In fact, even when he feels like eating, he cannot hold down the food, and his bones lie just barely buried under his fragile skin. Warmed with much ivy-berried Bacchus, his tongue keeps asking for more draughts, but his lips will not cooperate. Even though a wine-soaked feather, [80] torn from the body of the winged flock, labors to relieve the fever, his rasping chest nevertheless (if I may say so) vomits up the wine and water he ingested earlier. As for me, I sit by his head, my blonde hair all disheveled. Martha stays by his virtually freezing feet. As we watch both eyes in his wasted face, we marvel at the silent marks that death is imprinting on his face. Once suffused with ruddy hue, his lips are as pale as the wax from a honeycomb. The tongue that so often held the eloquent spellbound [90] can do little more than stammer out barbarous sounds. His legs are stiff with cold; his drippy nostrils are withered; the sad eyes are sunken in their orbs.

---

[39]Aurora's husband Tithonus received the gift of immortality, but not of eternal youth. He eventually slipped into a decrepit old age.
[40]King Priam was already a very old man when he was killed during the destruction of Troy.
[41]Literally, "Jove."

Ah, how often I say to my sister Martha, "Beloved, tell me, what on earth could be keeping Christ so long?" How much longer are you going to stretch this delay? Be swayed by our tears and — for you can do that! — reach a healing hand out to us. It is you, yes, you that my sister and brother and I myself and our whole household are anxiously waiting for night and day, amid a flood of tears. I think you've arrived each time the guard dog [100] sends a terrific barking to the golden stars. Though a light slumber may be clasping me in its outspread wings, I wake up with a start and, sliding the bolt back, open the door wide. After I look around in every direction but fail to see you, I beat my naked breasts with my fists. Later, after I lay the weary limbs to bed again, sleep will not return to my doleful eyes. Wretched me, how often I throw myself down absentmindedly, only to find that my head is resting where the feet are supposed to lie! When Memnon's nurturing mother[42] illuminates the hilltops [110] and summons the day as she rides her crimson chariot, I immediately rise out of bed to see what kind of help the dying man requires. Often I clamber up to the smoky roof to get a good view of the road into town. Often I sadly stick my head out through the open windows, but the high hills block my view. Then, returning to the sickbed where I see the dangers coming to a crisis, I fall to my knees at the foot of the bed. With my hand I dry the eyes brimming with cold water [120] and join this silent language to these words of grief.

There is still much to sing of, but the letter-writing is wearying my body. Besides, this little sheet of paper has hardly space enough. For the same reason that my message lacks a wish for health at the start, it now cannot close with "farewell." May you grant what is missing in the conclusion and the heading, for it is to you alone that the end and the alpha[43] belong.

Despite its moments of pathos, Magdalius' experiment in the sacred heroic epistle can hardly be termed a success. The poet is far more interested in showing off his own cleverness and erudition than in reimagining his heroine's plight.[44] Indeed, it is not until the second half of the letter, after a long series of dark hints and mythological references, that he finally lets the Magdalene get to the point: her brother Lazarus is near death and desperately needs Christ's healing hand. Magdalius' achievement, accordingly, lies not so much in the poetic quality of his work as in the imaginative

[42]Aurora, goddess of the dawn.
[43]Magdalius alludes to Revelations 22.13: "I am the Alpha and the Omega, the first and the last, the beginning and the end."
[44]In this judgment I quite agree with Laurence Beck-Chauvard in "La déréliction: L'esthétique de la lamentation amoureuse de la latinité profane à la modernité chrétienne," 2 vols., doctoral thesis, Université de Paris IV–Sorbonne, 1999, 1:251, n. 1.

leap of translating the Ovidian genre into the world of Christianity. Ovid certainly retains a large presence throughout this letter, both as a model to be emulated and as a foil to be outdone. The opening imitates the start of Briseis' letter to Achilles, while the conclusion deliberately recalls the end of Acontius' letter to the ill Cydippe. But Briseis is a concubine, deserted by her lord and master; and the deceitful Acontius, who first caused Cydippe to fall deathly ill, now proposes with equal gall to cure her through marriage with him. To these pagan exempla Magdalius opposes the example of Mary Magdalene. Mary too writes to her Lord, who seems to have abandoned her. She too seeks a cure for a mortal illness. Her master, however, is the Christ who, in his own good time, will not only save humankind but also restore her brother to health. Thus *eros* is trumped by *agape*, carnal passion by divine love.

First published in the *Erarium aureum poetarum* of 1501, Magdalius' "Letter from Saint Mary Magdalene to Christ" appeared almost a decade before Eobanus began working on his own Christian *Heroides*. But though our poet never acknowledges him as a model or even so much as mentions his name, there can be no doubt that it was Magdalius who inspired his own essays in the genre.

We do well to remember that when Eobanus began his *Heroides* in 1510 Magdalius was still looked up to as a scholar of note, a humanist whom Hutten in that very year could wholeheartedly hail as the best poet of Cologne. His *Erarium*, reprinted in 1502, 1503, and 1506, was an indispensable handbook, offering advice on scansion (book 1), a thesaurus of poetic epithets (book 2), a dictionary of rare words and names (book 3), a discussion of accents, aspiration, dipthongs, and orthography (book 4), and a collection of periphrastic expressions (book 5). In short, it was a treatise no young poet could ignore — certainly not Eobanus, who boasts of having consulted the best authorities on prosody while writing his *Heroides* (ded. 16.2).

Let us assume, therefore, that Eobanus was familiar not only with the *Erarium* but also with the appended letter "Mary Magdalene to Christ." If so, we ought to be able to uncover at least some trace of Magdalius' influence on Eobanus as he wrestled with the possibilities and limitations of the new genre.

According to the dedicatory letter (7.3–5), Eobanus chose not to organize his heroic epistles according to some overriding principle, but kept them in the order in which he composed them: "As for the arrangement of these letters, I have left them in the same order in which each of them presented itself and came to mind during the writing. Indeed, when I cast about for suitable subjects, it quite often happened that minor saints were placed ahead of major ones. However, I do not think this makes any difference whatever, seeing that they all come together in a single book just the same, as if in an unbroken circle."

If taken at face value, this statement implies that the book's opening letters must also have been the earliest to be composed. Now, as we examine these poems, we notice at once that the first two are written by and to Emmanuel (Christ) and that the next two are both addressed to Christ. Even more significantly, of the latter two one is written by none other than Mary Magdalene. Barring a fortuitous coincidence, then, Eobanus must have started his *Heroides* in conscious imitation of Magdalius' letter "Saint Mary Magdalene to Christ." To be sure, Eobanus chose a different setting from the one treated by Magdalius. Nevertheless, the underlying situation that prompts the heroines' letters turns out to be exactly the same in each case. Both Marys have been expecting Christ for some time now. What could possibly be keeping him? Alarmed, the heroines feel compelled to unbosom themselves and plead with their Lord to tarry no longer. Upon setting pen to paper, however, neither finds herself able to send Christ the usual *salus* (salutation, health), since only he can offer health and salvation. As the letters progress, the writers' tears fall onto the page and smear the characters. The two women scan the horizon to see if the master is coming, but to no avail. And both appeal to his pity by reminding him of the loved ones who share their grief:

> Te soror et frater, te fletibus ipsa profusis,
>> Te domus omnis avens nocte dieque manet. (Magdalius, ll. 97–98)

> Te genitrix, te, noster amor, duodenaque turba,
>> Te bonus hoc anima supplice quisque rogat. (*Her. Chr.* 3.173–74)

Of course the reader knows all along that Christ will in each case arrive shortly to answer his beloved's appeal.

The parallels just uncovered suggest that Eobanus, while aiming to outdo his less-gifted rival, could at the same time not help but follow him step-for-step. In choosing the Lazarus story, however, Magdalius had clearly stolen a march on Eobanus and picked a far more tractable theme. In fact, the Gospel account specifically mentions that Mary and Martha sent to Christ to tell him about their brother's illness. Since Christ fails to arrive in good time, a follow-up appeal from Mary Magdalene a few days later is perfectly plausible, indeed, psychologically compelling. By contrast, the Easter story that Eobanus chose is not at all suited to the writing of a heroic letter to Christ. For why should Mary even think of writing Christ by his tomb? Where is the urgency? And even supposing she did write, what good would that do, given that she has no way of having the letter delivered? To keep up with Magdalius and, as it were, beat him at his own game, Eobanus had no choice but to reimagine the Gospel accounts of Easter morning and so to create his own fictional space. The key premise of this fiction is Mary's expectation that Christ will appear to her personally, right after the Resurrection. But alas! She has now waited until midday, and still Christ has not made good on his pledge. Why, she wonders in her grief, did he appear to his mother and the disciples, but not to her? Could it be because of her past life of sin?

Eobanus' letter is so full of pathos, so vividly imagined, that it is easy to overlook not only the artificiality of the situation in which the Magdalene writes but also the challenge it poses to the Gospel story. The Evangelists, after all, make it perfectly plain that Christ "appeared first to Mary Magdalene," well before such beloved disciples as Peter and John (Matthew 28.1–10; Mark 16.1–9; Luke 24.1–11; John 20.1–18). Nor is there any reference to some pledge on Christ's part that he would appear to the Magdalene on Easter morning. And, of course, the Gospels do not keep the angel on the scene for very long, or make him dictate a verse letter or serve as letter carrier.

The Easter story, in short, makes for such an unpromising situation for an experiment in the sacred heroic epistle that no author inventing the genre for himself could possibly have chosen it on his own. To put it differently: the very intractability of the theme proves how much Eobanus was under Magdalius' spell at this early stage. In truth, the poem looks for all the world like Eobanus' very first attempt in the genre. If so, Eobanus progressed from a close imitation of Magdalius to themes suggested by Baptista Mantuanus in his first two *Parthenicae* — the Annunciation to the Virgin (letters 1 and 2) and Catherine's letter to Christ (letter 4). It is only after he had finished these opening four letters that he could turn his full attention to Ovid. Tellingly, the fifth poem of the book — the letter "Elizabeth to Ludwig" — is also the one that most closely imitates Ovid's *Heroides*, for it parallels the letter "Laodamia to Protesilaus" (*Ep.* 13) right down to the smallest motifs.

Printing History

Despite its enthusiastic reception, the *Heroidum Chistianarum epistolae* was never reissued in its original form, though Eobanus does seem to have been planning a reprint in 1515. In the first part of that year he taught a quite successful course on the book.[45] Wishing to repeat his success, he posted a verse announcement in the autumn (*Sylv.* 4.13) that advertised the upcoming classes on the *Heroides*. But would there still be enough copies of the book on hand? If not, he had better arrange for a reprint in good time. Accordingly, he sketched out a brief preface to the reader, in which he not only acknowledges his debt to Ovid, but also alludes to the overwhelming praise he had received from such luminaries as Johann Reuchlin, Mutianus Rufus, Ulrich von Hutten, and Crotus Rubianus. The draft preface, written in a student's hand, has been preserved on the verso of the title page in the Münster copy:

> Eo. Hessus lectori salutem.
>   Ne mireris, candide lector, quod, cum permulta sunt quae citra factarum rerum usum a me describi potuissent, praecipue ad Christianas puellas tanquam rem levem stilum contulerim, scias velim nihil me magis unquam quam divinum Nasonis ingenium in elegiaco genere admiratum, idque solum semper quo ad potui sequi

---

[45]See *Orat.* 6.1–7.2, a lecture held on 23 May 1515: "Nuper autem . . . ex barbaris regionibus reversus Latinas Musas mecum attuli. . . . Bonam huius anni partem apud eas vobis quoque (ne solus haberem) insinuandas collocavi. Laudo vestrum studium, probo diligentiam, commendo consuetudinem. Amplexati estis et quasi ad animi societatem deosculati puellas castissimas — Heroidas scilicet Christianas, ut tandem nominemus nostrum illud novicium opus. Clam me non est fuisse multos, qui dicerent nunquam me istarum rerum prelectionem adeo festiviter institutam ad finem perducturum. Quorum opinioni quantum mea constantia detraxerim, vos ipsos testes appello, magis enim presentes habere non possum."

studuisse. Quod et consecutum me, nisi de me ipso gloriari puderet, doctissimorum virorum iudicio possem dicere Capnionis, Muciani, Hutteni, Croti, et aliorum etiam. Sed tibi, pie lector, liberum facimus iudicium ac estimatione⟨m⟩ in quantam altitudinem ac sublimitatem rem alioqui humilem erexerimus, futurum utique sperantes ut si nihil te stili gratia commoverit, ipsa certe delectet inventionis novitas.

Vale.

Eobanus Hessus to the reader, greetings.

Do not be surprised, kind reader, if, given the wealth of nonfictional topics I could have dealt with, I turned my pen instead to the — or so it might appear — trifling theme of Christian maidens. For I should like you to know that there is nothing I admire so much as Ovid's divine genius in elegiac verse; in fact, that I have always striven as best I could to follow him, and him alone. Were I not ashamed of boasting about myself, I could tell you that in the considered opinion of such eminent scholars as Reuchlin, Mutianus, Hutten, Crotus, and others besides, I have indeed had some success in emulating him. But you, gentle reader, are free to decide and judge for yourself to what height and sublim- ity I have raised this otherwise humble theme of mine. At any rate, I hope that if the charm of the style does nothing to move you, you will at least take delight in the novelty of invention.

Farewell.

To all appearances this letter was dictated by Eobanus himself, probably at the start of his second course on the *Heroides Christianae* in the autumn of 1515. However that may be, no reprint ever appeared. More ominously, the work would soon look dated. In the aftermath of the Lutheran Reformation, the legendary material on which so much of the book is based became the subject of passionate confessional disputes and, indeed, was largely rejected by the Protestants. Having himself become an enthusiastic advocate of Luther in 1521, Eobanus did labor hard to bring his masterpiece into line with the new thinking, without at the same time gutting it completely. But even with the help of Philip Melanchthon and Beatus Rhenanus he was unable to find a publisher for the revised version in either Wittenberg or Basel. It was not until 1532 that the work finally came out at Haguenau, under the title *Heroidum libri tres*. For this redaction Eobanus excised the too-outlandishly-legendary material, completely rewrote several poems, and arranged the resulting twenty-two letters into three books. The first book contains "historical" subjects based entirely on the New Testament. The second book brings a mix of the historical and the legendary, while the third offers only leg- endary subjects. With some minor stylistic revisions and the appending of his "Letter from the Afflicted Church to Luther" (1523), Eobanus reissued this redac- tion in the *Operum farragines duae* of 1539.

The editio princeps of the work was published by Melchior Lotter at Leipzig:

A (1514)

[*red, Fraktur:*] Helij Eobani Heſ | ſi Heroidū Chriſtianarum | Epiſtolae. opus Nouitium | nuper aeditum. Anno | M.D.xiiij. | [*roman:*] HESSI DE SE EVLOGIVM, | [*black, roman: 3 distichs*]

Colophon:	Impreſſum Lipczk, p̄ Melchiarem Lotter,
Collation:	4°: A–T⁶, V⁴, [$3 signed], 118 leaves, foliated as follows: *i*, ii–x, ²i, *ii*, iij–lxxiij, *lxiiij*, lxxv–lxxxij, lxxxij, lxxxiiij–cvi, *cvii–cviij*. Sig. O1ᵛ (= fol. 69ᵛ) bears the spurious folio number "Fo. lxx."
Contents:	A1ʳ title page; A1ᵛ blank; A2ʳ–B1ᵛ dedicatory letter; B2ʳ–B4ᵛ complimentary epigrams by Eobanus' friends; B4ᵛ table of contents; B5ʳ–V2ᵛ *Heroidum Christianarum liber*; V3ʳ–V4ʳ epigram to Veit Werler; V4ʳ *Candide lector, errata, quae apud quorundam characterum inversiones inter festinandum acciderunt sic emenda, precor,* followed by a list of errata; colophon; V4ᵛ blank.
Running titles:	No running titles for the dedicatory letter, the prefatory poems by Eobanus' friends, or the concluding epigram to Veit Werler. Each heroic epistle has its own running title — a complete or abbreviated form of the heading. Sig. C5ʳ has "Emmanuel Mariae" instead of "Maria Emmanueli"; sig. M6ʳ has "Maria Aegip." instead of "Pelagia Nonio"; and on sig. N5ᵛ the heading is "Pelagia Nonio" instead of "Maria Ioanni".
Copytext:	Munich, Universitätsbibliothek Call number: 4° P. lat. rec. 911/9

This copy (*A¹*) served as the copytext for the present edition. It contains copious manuscript notes on the title page and sigs. B5ʳ–D6ʳ. These notes evidently derive from one of Eobanus' courses on the book. I have checked *A¹* against the following copies:

A²	Aschaffenburg, Hofbibliothek (F 693/4). Leaves S3.S4 are lacking, being replaced by leaves R3.R4. Eobanus originally presented the copy to Ludwig Platz of Melsungen, for the title page bears the handwritten inscription, "Venerabili ac humanissimo viro, Domino Ludovico Platz Melsingensi, B. Arti⟨um⟩ Magistro, Sacrarum Litterarum Baccalaureo etc., domino suo colendo, Eobanus Hessus d⟨ono⟩ d⟨edit⟩."
A³	Leipzig, UB (Poet. lat. rec. 76). The copy contains numerous manuscript notes on the title page and sigs. D1ʳ–E3ʳ. It also has some notes in the margin of the dedicatory letter, but these are in a different hand.

A⁴ Münster, UB (Coll. Erh. 330). A comparison with other copies shows that sig. B3ᵛ and sig. B4ʳ in this copy were reset by the printer. The heading of poem A 4 on sig. B4ʳ is not in Fraktur and title case, but in roman type and capital letters throughout. On sig. B3ᵛ (poem A 3.48) "Suauiloqua" has been changed to "Suauiloquo"; on sig. B4ʳ (poem A 4.13) "Oenonen" has become "Oenonem". There are also numerous changes in punctuation on sig. B3ᵛ and sig. B4ʳ. The copy contains Eobanus' (unpublished) letter to the reader (see pp. 120–21 above) as well as numerous handwritten notes on the title page and sigs. B5ʳ–E6ʳ.

A⁵ Strasbourg, BNU (R 104197). Sigs. B3ᵛ and B4ʳ in this copy are reset, as in *A⁴*.

A⁶ Würzburg, UB (L. rr. q 33). In this copy the (connected) leaves V2.V3 are reversed (V V3.V2 V4). On the title page there is a personal inscription by Eobanus Hessus: "Nobili ac generoso Domino Erasm⟨o⟩ de Lympurgk Baroni etc., domino s⟨uo⟩ observando, Eobanus d⟨ono dedit⟩." The autograph has been trimmed slightly at the right.

A⁷ Zwickau, Ratsschulbibliothek (24.9.3/1). Sigs. B3ᵛ and B4ʳ in this copy are reset, as in *A⁴*.

There are further copies in Basel, UB; Cologne, UB (lacking sig. I3.I4); Dresden, Sächsische Landesbibliothek; Erfurt, Stadt- und Regionalbibliothek; Gießen/Lahn, UB; Jena, UB (two copies, of which one, Bud. Op. 43, lacks quire A); Leipzig, UB (a second copy); Nuremberg, Germanisches Museum; Vienna, ÖNB; Warsaw, Biblioteka Narodowa.

The *Heroidum Christianarum epistolae* was reissued, in thoroughly revised form, in 1532 and 1539:

B (1532)

[*Within a compartment cut from a single block:*] HELII | EOBANI HESSI | *Heroidum* Libri | *Tres.* | *Nuper ab* Authore *recogniti,* | *& ab æditionis prioris* | *iniuria uindicati.* | Haganoæ ex Officina | Seceriana. Anno | M.D.XXXII.

Colophon: *Haganoæ ex Officina Seceriana* | *Anno* M.D.XXXII. | [*printer's device*]

Collation: 8°: A–I⁸ [\$5 signed], K⁴ [3 signed], L⁸ [5 signed], (−L7, L8) = 84 (−2) leaves

Contents: A1ʳ title page; A1ᵛ blank; A2ʳ–A4ᵛ verse dedication to Paul von Schwarzenberg; A5ʳ–D2ᵛ *Heroidum epistolarum lib. I, qui historicas continet*; D2ᵛ–G3ᵛ *Heroidum epistolarum liber secundus, qui mixtas continet*; G3ᵛ–L6ʳ *Hero. epist. liber tertius, qui fabulosas continet*; L6ᵛ colophon. L7, L8 are lacking in this copy. From other copies it is evident that these leaves are blank.

Catchwords: Catchwords on versos only; lacking on A4^v and G1^v.

Running titles: Heroidum Epis. Liber I [II, III]. Sig. G2^r prints "Liber III." for "Liber II."

Location: Göttingen, Niedersächsische Staats- und Universitätsbibliothek Call number: an: 8° Hist. lit. biogr. IV, 1245

In addition to this copy I have consulted the ones in Bamberg, SB (L.r.r.o. 60); Chicago, University of Chicago Library (PA8527.H4H6 1532); Münster, UB (Coll. Erh. 331); and Tübingen, UB (D.K. II 309c). The Chicago copy lacks quire L; in the Tübingen copy sig. B3 is damaged, with some minor text loss. There are further copies in Aberdeen, University Library; Augsburg, SB; University of California at Berkeley, Bancroft Library; Dresden, Sächsische Landesbiblothek; Freiburg im Breisgau, UB; Stanford University Library; Strasbourg, BNU; Wrocław, University Library (two copies).

B was reprinted at Paris by Jacques Bogard in 1546.

O (1539)

Eobanus included a lightly revised edition of **B** in his *Operum farragines duae* (Schwäbisch Hall, 1539). For a bibliographical description see pp. 52–53 above. In **O** the *Heroidum libri tres* is printed on sig. g7^v (or g8^r)–t1^r of the first farrago. The title page (found on either sig. g7^v or g8^r, depending on the copy) reads: "Helii Eobani Hessi Heroidum libri tres. Iam novissime recogniti et correcti." Eobanus' "Ecclesiae afflictae epistola ad Lutherum. Captiva Luthero," which was first published in 1523, is appended on sig. s1^r–t1^r.

The third edition of the *Heroidum libri tres* was reprinted in Eobanus' *Operum farragines duae* (Frankfurt am Main: Peter Braubach, 1549 and 1564) and in *Delitiae poetarum Germanorum huius superiorisque aevi illustrium*, ed. A. F. G. G. (Frankfurt am Main, 1612), 2:1283–1409. The latter text omits the title page and dedicatory letter.

The *Heroidum libri tres* has been twice edited in its entirety. For a critical text based on **O** (with the variants of **A** and **B**, but excluding the appended "Ecclesiae afflictae epistola ad Lutherum"), see "Helii Eobani Hessi *Heroidum libri tres*," ed., with an introduction and commentary, Harry Vredeveld (PhD diss., Princeton, 1970). For a text based on **B**, see my *Helius Eobanus Hessus, Dichtungen: Lateinisch und Deutsch. Dritter Band: Dichtungen der Jahre 1528–1537* (Bern, 1990), 269–483. Since the latter edition was intended as a parallel text to the 1514 version, it contains a complete set of variants to **O**, but not to **A**. For editions of individual heroic epistles, see the supplementary notes.

The concluding epigram to Veit Werler (*Her. Chr.* B 1), omitted in **B** and **O**, is found in slightly different form in Eobanus' *Sylvarum libri VI* (Haguenau, 1535), sig. HH7^v–II1^r (= *Sylv.* 4.3). For a bibliographical description of this volume (**S**) see pp. 51–52 above. The *Sylvarum libri VI* was reprinted and augmented with three new books in the first farrago of *Operum farragines duae* (Schwäbisch Hall, 1539). Here the epigram appears on sig. ^{2}H1^r–H2^v.

CONCORDANCE

The Letters in the First Edition of 1514 and the Revised Editions of 1532/39

1514	1532/39	1532/39	1514
1	1.1	1.1	1
2	1.2	1.2	2
3	1.3	1.3	3
4	3.1	1.4	16
5	2.7	1.5	19
6	2.1	1.6	*Cf. 20*
7	3.5		
8	3.3	2.1	6
9	2.5	2.2	21
10	3.4	2.3	13
11	3.2	2.4	22
12	*Omitted*	2.5	9
13	2.3	2.6	18
14	3.7	2.7	5
15	3.6		
16	1.4	3.1	4
17	*Omitted*	3.2	11
18	2.6	3.3	8
19	1.5	3.4	10
20	*Replaced by 1.6*	3.5	7
21	2.2	3.6	15
22	2.4	3.7	14
23	3.8	3.8	23
24	3.9	3.9	24

SIGLA

A		*Heroidum Christianarum epistolae* (Leipzig, 1514)
	A^1	Copy of *A* in Munich
	A^2	Copy of *A* in Aschaffenburg
	A^3	Copy of *A* in Leipzig
	A^4	Copy of *A* in Münster
	A^5	Copy of *A* in Strasbourg
	A^6	Copy of *A* in Würzburg
	A^7	Copy of *A* in Zwickau
B		*Heroidum libri tres* (Haguenau, 1532)
S		*Sylvarum libri VI* (Haguenau, 1535)
O		*Operum farragines duae* (Schwäbisch Hall, 1539)

Helii Eobani Hessi
HEROIDUM CHRISTIANARUM EPISTOLAE
Opus novitium, nuper aeditum
anno M.D.XIIII

HESSI DE SE EULOGIUM

Sunt quibus omne iocis teritur iuvenilibus aevum
    Musaque servandos perdit inepta dies.
At mea, cui debet, Christo devota iuventa est.
    Huic ero devotus, si volet ipse, senex.
5   Cedite gentiles meritis, non arte poetae.
    Materia vates nos meliore sumus.

Tit. *A*: Helii Eobani Hessi Heroidum libri tres, nuper ab authore recogniti et ab aeditionis prioris iniuria vindicati. Haganoae ex officina Seceriana. anno M.D.XXXII. *B*, Helii Eobani Hessi Heroidum libri tres, iam novissime recogniti et correcti. *O*.
    Lim. *A*: *om. BO*.

Helius Eobanus Hessus
LETTERS OF CHRISTIAN
HEROINES
A novel kind of work, just recently completed
in the year 1514

HESSUS' TESTIMONIAL FOR HIMSELF

There are poets who fritter away their whole life in puerile trifles, while their fatuous Muse squanders the days that ought to be put to good use. As for me, my youth is devoted to Christ, to whom it belongs. To him, if he so wishes, I'll remain devoted in my old age. Give place, heathen poets, in merit, not art. We bards treat a nobler theme.

2 = A2ʳ

REVERENDISSIMO IN CHRISTO PATRI ET DOMINO, DOMINO IOBO DE DOBENECK, EPISCOPO POME-SANIENSI ETC., PRINCIPI PIO ET LIBERALI DOMINO SUO, UT GRATIOSO ITA PERPETUE OBSERVANDO, HELIUS EOBANUS HESSUS FOELICITATEM OPTAT.

1.1 Heroidas Christianas, opus novum toto fere triennio magnis a me, licet plaerumque intermissis vigiliis, elucubratum, tibi statim et a principio nuncupare statui, Iobe, pontifex optime. **2** Quod ut facerem, cum multas alias ob res, tum precipue tali quadam ratione sum inductus, quod videlicet res sacras non nisi sacrorum antistiti et reliquorum sacerdotum facile principi sub custodiam committendas esse putabam, ut vel sic aliquando sub tui sacri nominis tutela secundis ventis in prophanum vulgus abeuntes sacrae inscriptionis authoritate quodammodo reverentiores haberentur, tum etiam quia anno ab hinc tertio inter equitandum (ut recte memini) ipsum aliquando futurum bona tibi fide sum pollicitus.

2.1 Cuius instituti mei tantum abest ut me poeniteat, ut nuper ex aula tua pontificali ad otium litterarium dimissus quo maturius tibi gratificarer in hoc opere absolvendo, equis velisque usus esse videar et quasi Salaminia (ut aiunt) navi praevectus supremam illi manum addiderim. **2** Eram enim (ut scis) in hoc primum labore partim ita negligens ut plerumque duos, plerumque tres, nonnunquam quattuor integros menses non

A2ᵛ

perinde vehementer | occupatus intermitterem, partim vero vel epistolis cancellariorum tuorum (quibus me praefecisti) non sine ingenii mei occupatione intentus vel magnarum legationum tuarum itinera prosequtus, ita externis istis molestiis distractus ut institutum meum pene etiam oblitus vel contemnerem vel profecto non magnifacerem. **3** Quo factum ut serius etiam quam caetera mea solent absolveretur.

3.1 Quanquam futuros non dubito qui dicant — etiam si quid moramenti offenderint — praecipitanter aeditum, cum (ut suadet Horatius) in nonum usque annum premi debuerit

---

Dedicatio. *A. In* **BO** *substituitur dedicatio ad Paulum, baronem a Svartzenberg.*

---

[1]For Eobanus' patron, Bishop Job von Dobeneck, see Camerarius, *Nar.* 7.5, with n. 22 (1:25). The date 13 June 1514 given at the end of the dedicatory letter probably indicates the day the book went to the printer's. The letter was in fact written in the late summer of 1513, when Eobanus was still

TO HIS MOST REVEREND FATHER AND LORD IN CHRIST, LORD JOB VON DOBENECK, BISHOP OF POMESANIA ETC., HIS GRACIOUS PRINCE AND GENEROUS LORD, AS BELOVED AS HE IS DESERVING OF UNCEASING RESPECT, HELIUS EOBANUS HESSUS SENDS BEST WISHES.[1]

My *Christian Heroides* — the brand-new work over which I have been burning the midnight oil in great, if often interrupted, labors these past three-odd years — I immediately and from the very start resolved to dedicate to you, Job, best of bishops. Though I could cite many reasons why I should want to do so, one stands out in particular: in my opinion, things holy should be placed under the protection only of a bishop of the Holy Church, one whose primacy the other churchmen readily acknowledge. For if a volume of religious verse sets sail under the tutelage of your sacred name and so heads out with favoring winds to the profane crowd, the authority that the venerable dedicatee inspires will, to a certain extent at least, rub off on the book itself. Moreover, some three years ago while riding on horseback (if I remember correctly) I gave you my solemn word that I would indeed dedicate the book to you someday.

2 Do not believe for a moment that I regret this resolution of mine. For no sooner had you given me leave from your episcopal palace recently to devote myself wholly to literary pursuits, the quicker to oblige you with the completion of this work,[2] than it became quite obvious that I was going at it full tilt and was crowding all sails and (as they say) scudding along as if on a clipper ship from Salamis, so that before long I was putting the finishing touches to the book. For as you well know, at the start I used to be so casual about this undertaking that I would often let two or three or even four whole months go by without looking at it, though I was really not all that busy at the time. In large part, however, the initially slow pace may be blamed on my position as chief secretary, for either I had to concentrate, not without a great deal of mental effort, on the correspondence of your chancellery, or I was accompanying you on your great embassies abroad. As a result of those adventitious and troublesome distractions I sometimes half forgot my project or disregarded it or at the least did not make much of it. That is also the reason why this work has taken longer to complete than my other ones did.

3 All the same, I have no doubt that there will be some persons who — even if they are aware of the delay involved — will criticize me for having hurried the

---

studying law at Frankfurt an der Oder. At the start of the second paragraph Eobanus mentions that he left Prussia "recently." Equally telling are the phrases "three-odd years" and "some three years ago" in the first paragraph, both phrases referring to the start of work on the *Heroides* in 1510. (In the dedication to *Sylvae duae*, dated 1 January 1514, this reference becomes "the fourth year.")

[2]Eobanus withdrew from the episcopal court partly at the bishop's behest that he study law, partly to pursue his literary dreams. See the introduction to *Sylv. duae*, pp. 45–46 above. At *ded.* 8.4 below he does allude to his law studies at Frankfurt and concedes that poetic composition was really just a sideline, undertaken "in my spare time (for I did have other things to do)."

quod in publicum tandem diuturna lima cruciatum essem emissurus. **2** Quibus ego puto posse tam vere quam constanter responderi, esse etiamnum nimis sero aeditum quod omnino fere ea qua conceptum erat forma aedi debuit, neque ea me ingenii foelicitate praeditum, ut more Rhomani Homeri versus ursino more pariam, sed primo statim partu, licet infoeliciter alioqui et minus belle, qualitercunque tamen absolvam, admodumque rarenter mihi usu venire ut rudia quaedam atque indigesta quasi mortario conteram. **3** Aut, si hoc censorum diligentiae (ut futurum suspicor) neutiquam satisfecerit, dicam longe, aliam esse saeculi nostri a priscis illis temporibus rationem, puta quibus ita venerabilis erat illa litterarum maiestas ut expectatio etiam pulcherrimarum aeditionum multitudinis desyderia pasceret, spes foveret, animos erigeret, scriptoresque ipsos magis ac magis in admirationem poneret, et iam futuri beneficii gratiam gliscentis indies famae compendio aequipararet. **4** Qualis est illa de Vergiliana Aeneide tunc nondum aedita dulcissima titillatio:

> Cedite, Rhomani scriptores, cedite, Graii!
> Nescio quid maius nascitur Iliade.

4.1 Fuere et fortunatis illis temporibus principes non minus litterati quam litteratorum omnium patroni, sub quibus liberalibus ociis foti disciplinarum | proceres, si qui egestosiores essent, sine extrariarum rerum curis immortalitati tantum operabantur, habunde a principibus ipsis, si quid apte concinniterque blanditi fuissent, remunerati. **2** At nos, quibus est res angusta domi neque aes semper in arca, neque principes habemus vel doctos vel doctorum adsertores — preter admodum paucos, inter quos tu, ut non omnino primum, ita certe nec postremissimum locum occupas, Iobe, presul humanissime. **3** Non eatenus sumus foelices ut pro votis lucubratiunculas nostras, quando et qualitercunque libet, statim quoque nobis liceat publicare, dum privatis commodis inopiaeque nostrae illo ipso quo vobis immortalitatem comparamus consulere cogimur et quasi Copiae cornu offerentes operae precium videlicet furfuraceum (si diis placet) a vobis panem mendicare — tametsi tu in meis semper extitisti qui

3 = A3ʳ

---

[3]See Hor. *Ars* 386–89. Cf. *ded.* 5.2 below: "hide it at home until the ninth year."

book into print, when, as Horace recommends, I ought to have held it back until the ninth year and gotten it out to the public only after tormenting it with daily polishing.[3] To people of that stripe I believe I may respond no less frankly than firmly: Something that is bound to be published anyway in pretty much its original form is even now being published far too late. The fact is, I am not endowed with that felicity of mind that would let me create verses the way the Roman Homer did — by licking them into shape like a she-bear[4] — but prefer to let them stand exactly as I first wrote them down, be they ever so infelicitous or unsatisfactory otherwise, without regard to their quality; and only rarely do I find myself pounding down on some shapeless and disorderly mass, as if in a mortar. Or, if this explanation has in no wise satisfied those who insist on censuring my diligence (as I suspect will happen), I shall have to justify myself at some length. The present age has an outlook quite different from that of those olden days. To the ancients, for example, the grandeur of literature was something so awe-inspiring that the very anticipation of the most beautiful publications nourished the ardent desire of the masses, kept up their hopes, raised their spirits, and put the authors themselves more and more on a pedestal, and before long made the gratitude for the future blessing a shortcut to a reputation that would grow stronger by the day. This is how we may understand that most delightful titillation concerning Vergil's as-yet-unpublished *Aeneid*:

> Make way, ye Roman writers, make way, ye Greeks!
> Something greater than the *Iliad* is coming to birth.[5]

4 In those fortunate times, too, there were noble lords who were as much men of letters themselves as patrons of all men of letters. With their support the leading writers enjoyed ample leisure, so that they, if they happened to be rather poor, could devote themselves wholly to immortality, without having to worry about extraneous matters. And if they flattered their benefactors in some appropriate and striking way, they were richly rewarded by the princes themselves. We moderns of straitened means, by contrast, can boast neither coffers that are always chock-full of money nor noble lords who are either learned themselves or else backers of learned men — with very few exceptions, among whom you occupy, if not the very first place, then certainly not the last place either, Job, most humane of bishops. We are not in the happy position where we can publish our lucubrations as we see fit, whenever and however we please, or even as soon as we should like, so long as we are forced to look after our personal interests and our own indigence through the very means by which we secure immortality for you. Thus, while offering you a horn of plenty, so to speak, we ourselves are reduced to begging a loaf of bran bread[6] (supposing we're as lucky as that!) from you princes — though I must say

---

[4]When Vergil was writing his *Georgics* he reportedly said that he brought his progeny forth the way a she-bear does: by rapidly dictating a great number of verses and then laboriously licking the formless mass into shape. See Suetonius' life of Vergil (*Vita Donatiana*), par. 22; Gel. 17.10.2.

[5]Prop. 2.34.65–66 (trans. G. P. Goold), also quoted in Suetonius' life of Vergil, par. 30.

[6]Bran bread was considered fit only for the lowest classes. Cf. *Val.* 1.559–60.

promi quam condi officio sit propinquior. **4** Sed nos in eam temporum confusionem incidimus quae praeter divitias, voluptates, et ambitionem pene nihil pensi habeat, in qua, si velis prae caeteris excellere atque imperitae multitudini singulari quadam laude praestare, summa ope niti oportet, ut non tam multa promittas quam re ipsa exhibeas fiasque inter tot novorum operum authores propalatoresque non postremi nominis. **5** Admodum enim paucis nostro aevo contigit ut cum nullis litterarum monumentis celebrentur, sola tamen sed summae eruditionis fama habeantur celeberrimi, et haec quidem de quibusdam, non autem omnibus nostri ordinis affirmaverim.

5.1 Quod si haec quoque non procedent, dicam libere quod sentio. **2** Nemo mihi unquam persuadebit ut quod triennio elaboratum mihi sit in nonum usque annum domi, velut aulam auri Plautinus ille Euclio, sollicite reponam et cum tineis blattisque rixari sinam, quin potius aedam et partae multis sudoribus famae dulcissimo fructu interim vivens perfruar, ne quacunque causa praeven- | tus illud male audiam, "Corvum delusit hiantem," et, "Obsonium," ut dici solet, "quaerens, vestem amisit."

A3ᵛ

6.1 Quod si nec hac quidem ratione tutatus fuero, dicam fortasse etiam magis constanter. **2** Mihi sic videbatur: "Quot homines tot sententiae";

> Mille hominum speties et rerum discolor usus;
> Velle suum cuique est, nec voto vivitur uno;

et illud Euripidis:

> Cunctis idem si pulchrum et egregium foret,
> Nulla esset anceps hominibus contentio;

et, "Alia aliis placent deisque et hominibus"; et in hunc modum non parum multa. **3** Ego profecto in hiis rebus non tam praeceptorum meorum hortamenta quam mei ipsius animi iuvenilem quendam ardorem et (quod ingenue fateor) gloriae nominis fortasse immoderatam concupiscentiam sequi semper consuevi. **4** Qui affectus si vitio in me vertetur, ad Ciceronem eloquentiae et virtutum omnium communem patronum provocabo.

---

[7]Eobanus must have been thinking in particular of his friend and mentor Mutianus Rufus, who enjoyed great fame as a scholar, yet never published any of his writings. See Camerarius, *Nar.* 13.7–9; Eob. *Buc.* 6, with n. 49 (1:318–19). For Mutianus' life, see Camerarius, *Nar.* 12.12–13.10, with n. 36 (1:37–39).

[8]In Plautus' comedy *Aulularia* the miser Euclio jealously guards a pot of gold. Eobanus' reference to "the ninth year" does not apply to Euclio, but rather to Horace's recommendation that poets should keep polishing their work until the ninth year (*Ars* 386–89). Cf. *ded.* 3.1 above.

that in my experience you have always stood out as one who thinks it more blessed to give than to receive. The problem is that we live in a topsy-turvy world which cares about practically nothing but wealth, pleasure, and power and in which, if you want to surpass the rest and stand out from the unwashed multitude in some especially meritorious way, you have to struggle tooth and nail to be not just another promising author, but a proven one, and to earn a measure of fame among the myriad writers and editors of new works. As a matter of fact, in our day and age it has been given to just a few intellectuals to have no literary monuments to their name and yet be held in the highest esteem, solely by dint of their reputation for consummate learning;[7] and that, I should emphasize, holds true only for some, not however for all members of our profession.

5 But if this line of reasoning does not impress the critics either, I'll speak my mind freely. No one will ever persuade me that I ought to keep back what I have been working out for three years and anxiously hide it at home until the ninth year, much as Euclio did with his pot of gold in Plautus' comedy,[8] and let it fight a running battle with the moths and bookworms, rather than publish it and enjoy the sweetest fruit of hard-earned fame while I am still alive, lest, thwarted by something or other, I hear the taunting cry, "The gaping raven was duped,"[9] and, as they say, "Looking for a free lunch, he lost his shirt."[10]

6 But if even this reason fails to protect me, I may have to speak up more forcefully yet. I look at it this way: "Many men, many minds";[11]

> People come in a thousand types, each with a disparate outlook.
> All have desires of their own; no one shares the same aspiration;

and this from Euripides:

> If everyone agreed on what is fine and splendid,
> there would be no debating back and forth;

and, "Be they gods or men, each delights in different things"; and not a few other adages in this vein. In matters like this, indeed, I have always followed not so much the exhortations of my teachers as a certain youthful enthusiasm of mine and (to make a clean breast of it) a possibly immoderate craving for glory and renown. If this disposition of mine should be held against me, I shall appeal to Cicero, the patron not only of eloquence but of all the virtues.

---

[9]The expression (taken from Hor. *S.* 2.5.56) alludes to the well-known fable of the fox and the raven. A fox saw a raven sitting in a tree with a chunk of cheese in its beak. He complimented the bird on his good looks and wondered aloud if he had a voice to match. When the raven opened his beak to sing, he dropped the cheese. See Aesop 124 (Perry); Phaedr. 1.13; cf. Otto 448.

[10]Erasmus, *Adag.* 2.5.55. The adage is applied to people who try to gain some small advantage but end up losing something of far greater value.

[11]Ter. *Ph.* 454; Erasmus, *Adag.* 1.3.7. The immediately-following variations that Eobanus cites are also taken from *Adag.* 1.3.7, as found in the 1508 edition: (a) Pers. 5.52–53; (b) Euripides, *Ph.* 499–500; and (c) Euripides, *Hipp.* 104 (here Eobanus transposes the first two words in Erasmus' translation).

7.1 Ut igitur redeam unde digressus sum, Praesul optime: scripsi Heroidas has Christianas numero omnino vigintiquattuor, in quibus scribendis Ovidium Nasonem non tam imitatus quam admiratus sum. **2** Illud enim assequi, hoc praetermittere nunquam potui. **3** Neque alio ordine digessi quam quo quaeque scribendam sese obtulit atque in mentem venerat. **4** Dum enim argumenta quaero, saepius evenit ut minores maioribus praeponantur. **5** Neque hoc quicquam referre arbitror, quando nihilominus omnes uno in libro quasi circo conveniant.

8.1 Antea vero quam scribendarum heroidum provintiam (sane difficilem) assumerem, erat animus aliquandiu fastos Christianos condere. **2** Ad quam rem (multo etiam magis difficilem) cum animadverterem opus esse infinita pene lectione et optimorum librorum praecipue sacrorum multa supellectile, duxi id operae in multo oportunius otium reiiciendum periclitarique interim hiis liberioribus velut progymnasmatis quibusdam vires ingenii, ne nativa (si qua inesset) virtus per liberiorem istam aulicae consuetudinis | indulgentiam elanguesceret et negligentiae ignaviaeque situ obducta rerum voluptariarum luxu extingueretur. **3** Adieci igitur ad scribendas epistolas animum, quarum et maximam partem, puta priores quindecim, in Prussia, sed negligenter hoc (quod dixi) triennio absolvi. **4** Novem reliquas ad ripam Oderae Marchiaticae una aestate perfeci, et id quidem horis subcisivis (sunt enim et alia studia), sed tamen ad Aristophanis et Cleantis lucernam quodammodo. **5** Tum et priores quasdam, licet satis perfunctorie, repastinavi. **6** Quare candidum lectorem admonitum velim, si quid obelisco dignum inciderit (quid enim ex omni parte beatum?), condonet hanc properationi nostrae, non inscitiae veniam. **7** Quam tamen tantum abest ut velim defendere, ut etiam cum Socrate dicere soleam, unum id me scire quod nesciam. **8** Atque si quid est in me ingenii (quod sentio sane quam sit exiguum), perinde ac nebulam in pariete depictam existimem.

9.1 Causa scribendarum epistolarum ea potissimum fuit, quod videbam ea in re nullum hactenus poetarum admodum elaboravisse, indignum ratus omnem ingenii florem in prophanis quibusdam ac frivolis occupationibus desumere. **2** Nec enim eos probare soleo qui eousque antiquitatis sunt studiosi ut eius

4=A4ʳ

---

[12]In imitation of Ovid's *Fasti*, a work describing the ancient Roman calendar. Eobanus actually started writing such a work not long before his death. See the introduction, p. 103 above, with n. 1.

[13]In Frankfurt an der Oder, during the summer of 1513.

7 Well then, to return to the point from which I digressed, best of bishops: I have written twenty-four of these Christian heroides all told. In composing them I did not so much imitate Ovidius Naso as admire him. The former, certainly, is something I could do with some success; the latter is something I could never do enough of. As for the arrangement of these letters, I have left them in the same order in which each of them presented itself and came to mind during the writing. Indeed, when I cast about for suitable subjects, it quite often happened that minor saints were placed ahead of major ones. However, I do not think this makes any difference whatever, seeing that they all come together in a single book just the same, as if in an unbroken circle.

8 To tell you the truth, before I set myself the (decidedly difficult) task of writing heroic letters, I contemplated for quite some time describing the Christian calendar.[12] When it dawned on me that to tackle this theme — even more difficult by far — I would have to do a well-nigh endless amount of research and require a great supply of the very best books, especially on Church History, I thought it better to lay that work aside until a much more opportune time of leisure and in the meantime to test the strength of my talent with these, so to speak, freer preliminary exercises, lest my natural ability (assuming I have any to begin with) should grow flabby with disuse in that rather indulgent atmosphere of court life and, covered with the mold of negligence and idleness, be extinguished in the endless round of entertainments. This, then, is why I put my mind to the writing of these letters, the majority of which, specifically the first fifteen, I completed in Prussia, if rather carelessly, over a period (as I mentioned) of three years. The nine remaining ones I finished in a single summer on the banks of the Oder in the Mark Brandenburg,[13] and that in my spare time (for I did have other things to do), but nevertheless, in a manner of speaking, by the oil lamp of Aristophanes and Cleanthes.[14] At that time I also reworked some of the earlier letters, though in a rather perfunctory way. Hence I should like to urge the kind reader, if he runs into anything deserving an obelus[15] (after all, what is perfect in every respect?), to excuse this on account of my haste, not my ignorance. I am so far removed from wishing to defend my lack of knowledge, however, that with Socrates I too am in the habit of saying, "All I know is that I do not know." And if I possess any poetic talent (and I am keenly aware how slight it is), I esteem it about as highly as a shadow painted on a wall.

9 What moved me in particular to write heroic epistles was the realization that none of our poets thus far had bothered with this material to any extent. Frankly, I was shocked to see all the choicest talent squandered on certain profane and frivolous subjects. For I do not make it a practice to approve of those who are

[14]Erasmus, *Adag.* 1.7.72. The adage refers to the comic poet Aristophanes (late fifth century BCE) and the Stoic philosopher Cleanthes (d. 232/31 BCE), both of whom were proverbial for burning the midnight oil.

[15]Cf. Erasmus, *Adag.* 1.5.57, 1.8.14. Ever since the Homeric critic Aristarchus, scholars marked textual corruptions with an obelus (dagger). The expression thus figuratively indicates something worthy of a scholar's censure.

velut imaginem eo se expressius referre posse arbitrantur quo a
religione nostra magis sunt diversi, qui in omnibus suis poematis,
etiam levibus aliquando et futilibus, ita ethnica numina invocare
solent itaque spurcissimis istis veterum nominum illecebris, quasi
offa quadam Cerberea, inescari pessimeque affici ut Ioviani magis
quam Christiani videantur. **3** Quinetiam si quis bonus pro Iove
aut Phoebo Christum aut alium quempiam caelitum in carmen |

coegerit, hunc statim velut poeticae maiestatis reum calumniis
insectantur spurcissimi vitiligatores, tanquam divinum hoc
poeticae nomen in prophanis istis et aliquando impudicissimis
nugamentis, non secus ac limitibus quibusdam quos exire non
liceat, includatur ac prefinitum sit.

10.1 Quod mihi quoque, cum Cracoviae tecum, optime
Praesul, in legatione ista tua magnifica agerem nuptiasque divi
Sigismundi, regis Poloniae, heroico carmine aggressus Phoebum
Christo caedere coegissem, contigisse non ignoras. **2** Non enim
defuerunt qui Marsiam me appellitarent ineptissimisque quibusdam carminibus Phoebum contra Christum (o indignum facinus!)
ad decoriandum Marsiam alterum citare auderent. **3** Ipse vero
quam constanter pro Christo in acie steterim, te testem appello,
qui pulcherrimae meae victoriae dux et imperator extiteras unoque
milite et eo quidem rorario concitatissimam adversariorum multitudinem confregisti. **4** Quis enim tam iusta causa tamque bono
duce non vicerit? **5** Hoc vero de me periculum, quod omnino
non magnifecerim, si id tantum mihi et non etiam religioni contu-
meliosum esse ducerem.

11.1 Non desunt etiam qui prophanis diis omne suum
ingenium devovent ipsisque, dum "Naturales hymnos" conci-
nunt, quasi sacrificare videntur. **2** Non negaverim quosdam
naturae communis imaginem omnibus (ut aiunt) liniamentis
expressisse, sed ita ut pestem quandam in religionem seminasse
videantur, dum naturam ipsam solis deorum veterum
nominibus venerantur et quasi adorant, tanquam nisi dii vocen-
tur terra, aqua, aer, ignis et per et praeter haec existentia describi
non possint. **3** Quid enim Marullo, nostrae aetatis alioqui

---

10.1 Cracoviae *scripsi*: Cracovie *A*.   **11.2** liniamentis *A⁵–A⁷*: linea amentis *A¹–A⁴*.

---

[16]Cerberus was the three-headed dog that guarded the entrance to Tartarus. When the Sibyl
guiding Aeneas saw the monster bristling in his cavern, she pacified him by throwing him a honeyed
cake steeped in soporific drugs. See Verg. *A.* 6.417–23.

[17]In his *Encomium nuptiale* for King Sigismund I of Poland, written in February 1512, Eobanus
had invoked Christ and rejected Phoebus and the Muses. For the controversy that this invocation provoked see the introduction to that poem, pp. 6–9 above.

so immoderately fond of antiquity that they believe they can, as it were, reflect its image the more clearly, the further they distance themselves from our religion. In all their poems, sometimes even their trifling ditties, they are so eager to invoke the pagan gods, they act so enticed and bewitched by the nauseatingly disgusting charm of those ancient names — as irresistible to them as the honey-cake was to Cerberus[16] — that they come across more as Jovians than as Christians. Yes, and if some good Christian were to write a poem that called, not on Jove or Phoebus, but on Christ or some other celestial, the foul-mouthed quibblers would immediately charge him with *lèse majesté* against Poetry — as if that divine thing Poetry were, so to speak, confined within certain inviolable limits and cooped up in that profane and at times unspeakably obscene rubbish of theirs.

10 You yourself, best of bishops, are well aware that I myself was subjected to such attacks in Cracow when, working with you as part of that magnificent embassy of yours, I opened a heroic poem about the wedding of the godlike Sigismund, King of Poland, by compelling Phoebus to yield to Christ.[17] In point of fact, there were several people who kept calling me a Marsyas for this.[18] They even presumed in some unbelievably silly epigrams to summon Phoebus against Christ (oh, the shocking crime!) so he would be on hand to skin the second Marsyas. But I call on you to bear witness how resolutely I stood in the breach for Christ. It was you after all who directed and engineered my glorious victory; it was you who crushed the frenzied host of my adversaries — and with only one soldier, and a lightly armed one at that! Who indeed would not have emerged victorious in such a just cause and under such a fine general? That, at least, was my experience. And I would not have made a fuss about it at all, had I thought it an affront only to me personally and not also to our religion.

11 There is certainly no lack of poets who devote their whole talent to the pagan deities themselves and who, while singing their "Hymns to Nature," give the distinct impression that they are sacrificing to the gods.[19] I do not mean to deny that some of them have indeed managed to portray Mother Nature in all her lineaments, as the saying goes; but they do it in such a way as to seem, for all the world, to be spreading a kind of plague in our religion. For when they venerate Nature herself and, to all intents and purposes, worship her by using only the names of the ancient divinities, they make it appear as if earth, water, air, fire, and all that exists through them and beyond them, cannot be described unless they are referred to as gods. For where does Marullo, otherwise the most distinguished

[18]The satyr Marsyas challenged Apollo to a contest in flute playing. But the god defeated him and flayed him alive for his presumption. Cf. *Buc.* 5.50, with n. 45 (1:314).

[19]Eobanus alludes to the *Hymni naturales* (1497) by the Neo-Latin poet Michele Marullo (ca. 1453–1500). Though widely admired for his gifts as an epigrammatist and lyricist, Marullo had a bad reputation among the Christian humanists because each of his hymns to the forces of nature is addressed to one of the old pagan gods, starting with Jupiter. Erasmus condemns Marullo's paganism in *Ep.* 385, ll. 5–6; 1479, ll. 118–20; and *Ciceronianus, ASD* 1.2:666, l. 2. Beatus Rhenanus shared Erasmus' misgivings: see *Briefwechsel des Beatus Rhenanus*, ed. A. Horawitz and K. Hartfelder (1886; Nieuwkoop, 1966), nos. 12 and 432, first printed in Beatus' edition of Marullo's epigrams and hymns (Strasbourg, 1509); Erasmus, *Ep.* 1087, in which Beatus puts Thomas More's epigrams ahead of Marullo's. See further Walther Ludwig, *Antike Götter und christlicher Glaube: die "Hymni naturales" von Marullo* (Göttingen, 1992).

nobilissimo lyrico, ad summam ingenii foelicitatem nisi solus Christianae religionis fervor defuit? **4** Alios consulto praetereo, ne vel viventibus ex invidia derogare vel mortuorum cineres persequi | et (quod aiunt) cum larvis luctari videar, quandoquidem et de hac re plenissime simul et eruditissime scripsit quidam Macarius Mutius, eques Camers, vir non minus doctus quam verae, hoc est Christianae, religionis constantissimus adsertor.

12.1 Sed haec hactenus (ne ex epistola invectivam faciam) pro modestia mea consueta dicta sufficiant. **2** Sed eo quae dixi pertinent ut intelligant pii lectores ob hoc Christianas heroidas a me conscriptas, ut et religionem pro virili mea adiuvem et simul ostendam non deesse argumenta, si modo sacra tractare nobis plusquam prophana libeat. **3** Est in fide nostra argumentorum series pene infinita, exercendi ingenii campus immensus, exornandi inventiones nostras sylva multiplex, in quibus tamen veterum quoque nominum delitias immiscere possimus, ita tamen ut detestari, non adstruere videamur, si quid est Christianismo nostro contrarium.

13.1 Quod in epistolis meis quam facile praestiterim, aliorum sit iuditium. Hoc ausim testari, nihil me sacrae religioni scripsisse contrarium, immo vero multa ex sacris scriptoribus, evangelistis, et prophetis in versus meos transtulisse, ut videre licet in Emmanuele de Annunciatione, de incarnatione Verbi, in Catharina de Trinitate, in Barbara item de incarnatione Verbi, de simulachris deorum, in Maria Aegiptiaca de sacramento Eucharistiae, in Magdalena de resurrectione Christi, in Anna de conceptione Mariae, in Pelagia de contemptu mundi, in Maria de passione Christi, et in aliis in hunc modum alia multa. **2** Quot vero sacras hystorias graphice (non quidem in omnibus servato rerum ordine, quod nec poeta debet, sed pro decoro rei aliquando immutato) inseruerim, hii demum cognoscent qui has sanctissimas puellas diligenter aspexerint. **3** Neque enim ego hoc in loco singularum heroidum singula argumenta narrare constitui, quae profecto tam varia sunt quam pro rerum, quae scribuntur, diversitate | multiplicia. **4** Quod tametsi eadem res aliquando saepiuscule dicitur, fit tamen hoc et diversis in locis et stilo sibi ipsi semper dissimili, quem et fere ubique, quod Ovidium quoque observasse video, patheticum esse volui, maxime quod eum sic usurpatum huic materiae videbam esse accommodatissimum. **5** Schemata quoque, sine quibus arida et ieiuna est omnis oratio, congruentibus locis apposita nemo,

---

13.1 praestiterim *manus vetus in* A^1–A^4 A^6: praestaverim *A*.

lyricist of our time, fall short of true genius, except only in enthusiasm for the Christian religion? The others I deliberately pass over, for fear that I might seem either to be enviously disparaging the living or hounding the ashes of the dead and (as they say) wrestling with ghosts, all the more so as a certain Macario Muzio, a knight from Camerino, has written with admirable thoroughness and erudition on this subject too,[20] proving himself to be at once a man of learning and an unwavering champion of the true — that is, Christian — religion.

12 But this discussion will suffice for now, lest I forget my habitual restraint and turn this epistle into an invective. My aim, however, was to let the pious readers understand my motivation for writing Christian heroides — namely to uphold our religion to the best of my ability and, at the same time, to demonstrate that there are plenty of topics to choose from, if we really do wish to treat sacred subjects rather than profane ones. In our faith there is a practically infinite array of themes, an immense field for exercising the mind, a richly diverse forest for embellishing our arguments. These we may, to be sure, also season with the spice of antique names, provided we make it crystal-clear that we loathe them, not espouse them, should anything clash with our Christian faith.

13 How adroitly I have put this into practice in my own epistles, that is for others to judge. This I would venture to affirm: that I have written nothing at odds with our holy religion. On the contrary, I have put into my verses a great many themes from the sacred authors, evangelists, and prophets. In "Emmanuel," for instance, I deal with the Annunciation, with the incarnation of the Word, in "Catherine" with the Trinity, in "Barbara" likewise with the incarnation of the Word, with the images of the gods. In "Mary of Egypt" I deal with the sacrament of the Eucharist, in "Magdalene" with the Resurrection of Christ, in "Anna" with the conception of Mary, in "Pelagia" with disdain for the world, in "Mary" with the Passion of Christ, and much more in this vein in the other letters. How many sacred stories, in fact, I have artfully packed into this book is something readers will appreciate only after they have taken the time to study these most saintly maidens. Admittedly, I have not retained the order of events in all cases — no poet is obliged to do that — but have made changes here and there, as required by decorum. Readers will have to discern that for themselves, however. Certainly I myself have no intention of summarizing the storyline of each heroic epistle here. All I will say is that the stories and themes I take up are unquestionably as diverse as they are numerous. But even if the same topic occasionally does crop up a bit too often, this nevertheless occurs at widely separated places in the book, and invariably in a different manner from the earlier one. As regards style, I aim almost everywhere to excite pathos, partly because I also see Ovid doing that, but mostly because I feel such a style to be the one most suitable to this kind of material. The rhetorical figures too, without which all discourse is dry and jejune, will not, I daresay, be found wanting at the appropriate

---

[20]In two prefaces to his short epic on Christ's descent into hell, *De triumpho Christi*, first published at Venice in 1499. The poem was often reprinted and imitated. Many writers — including Erasmus (1499), Eobanus (1512/17), and Mathias Funck (1514) — followed with their own short epics on the harrowing of hell.

puto, desyderabit. **6** Erunt fortasse qui dicant nimium figuris usum, at hae (ut cum Policiano loquar) figurant epistolam. **7** Neque vero ita frequentes inserui ut ubique occurrant, nec tam antiquas aut obsoletas ut novitatem hanc obfuscare videantur, verum periphrases, paroemias, methaphoras, allegorias, emphases, scite dicta, sententias exquisitiores, et id genus alia multa sparsim ut decere visum est adieci.

14.1 Sed ne velut Peleum in machaera ipsi mihi placere aut cristas tollere quispiam me putet, tam de his breviter a me enarratis quam aliis omnibus quae in carmine spectari solent, erudito lectori iudicandum censeo, si hoc unum addidero, argumenta videlicet epistolarum omnino me ad sacrae historiae veritatem composuisse. **2** Qua in re Gregorium, Hieronymum, Augustinum, Eusebium, et alios quam plures Christianae veritatis verissimos adsertores imitatus sum, quibus non minorem fidem habere Christianum quemque decet quam Graecos Herodoto, Philostrato, Thucididi, et Latinos Livio, Salustio, Valerio, et aliis. **3** Quod si quis futurus est qui dicet in Halcione, Catharina, Elisabetha, et aliis quibusdam historiam intervertisse, meminerit is, queso, nihil tam esse alienum a bono poemate quam nudum historiae filum et rei gestae sine poeticis quibusdam velut parergis additis, contextum simplicem quod ipsum Lucano, non incelebri alioqui Civilium bellorum scriptori, pene poetici nominis palmam abstulisse quidam | adserunt.

6=A6ʳ

15.1 Quamvis, bone Deus, quid istac tanta excusatione in re tam excusata opus est, quandoquidem heroidas, non heroas scribimus? **2** In quibus tantum abest ut omnia ad historiae imaginem effigiari debeant, ut etiam eas sic, ut scriptae sunt, epistolas ultro citroque missitasse pulcherrima inventione excogitatum esse oporteat. **3** Quis hoc non videt? Quis non intelligit? **4** Sed tamen quod ad historiae veritatem pertinet per sibi dissimillimas introductiones ubique observavimus, neque transversum quidem unguem ab ipsa veritate sumus digressi. **5** Scripsit nostra aetate Parthenices (ut ipse appellat) heroidas doctissimus poeta Baptista Mantuanus, licet non eodem mecum stili genere. **6** Vide tamen, quaeso, quam diversissimo a sacrae historiae simplicitate argumento quot poeticas festivitates immisceat, quot fucos extraneos illinat! **7** Scripsit idem Georgium, stilo quidem heroico, sed tamen prorsus ab historia vulgari diverso, ex cuius statua ego

---

13.7 novitatem *scripsi*: novitantem *A*.   **15.2** epistolas *scripsi*: apostolos *A*.

---

[21]Erasmus, *Adag.* 2.8.26, alluding to the magic sword given as a reward by the gods to Achilles' father Peleus. The adage takes aim at people who are overly boastful of some possession.

places. Perhaps there will be critics who complain that I have used an excessive number of such figures; but these (to quote Poliziano) "adorn the letter." In truth, I have not inserted them so frequently that you run into them at every turn, nor are they so archaic or outmoded that they tend to overshadow their own novelty. But I did add paraphrases, proverbs, metaphors, allegories, allusions, witty sayings, choice maxims, and the like, scattered throughout the text, as I deemed fitting.

14 But lest anyone think that I am as pleased with myself as Peleus was with his sword[21] or that my head is swollen with pride, I suppose I can leave it to the learned reader to judge not only what I have briefly outlined above, but also all the other things that are commonly found in a poem, if I may add only this one point: namely, that in working out the storylines for these letters I have faithfully adhered to the truth of sacred history. In this matter I have followed the example of Gregory, Jerome, Augustine, Eusebius, and a great many other thoroughly reliable champions of Christian truth, in whom every Christian ought to place no less trust than the Greeks did in Herodotus, Philostratus, and Thucydides, and the Romans in Livy, Sallust, Valerius, among others. But if some future reader objects that in "Alcyone," "Catherine," "Elizabeth," and a few other letters I have embellished the story,[22] he should please remember that nothing is so alien to a good poem as the bare thread of historical events, without the addition, so to speak, of some poetic embroideries — a plain style of writing that in the opinion of certain critics is almost enough by itself to strip Lucan, the otherwise not undistinguished chronicler of the Civil Wars, of the honorable title of poet.

15 But, good Lord, why do I bother with such an elaborate justification in a matter that is so justified to begin with, seeing that I am writing heroides, not heroic epics? In this genre we are under no obligation whatsoever to fashion everything after the image of history. What is required, rather, is to make it appear, with all the ingenuity we can muster, that these letters were actually sent back and forth like this, just as they are written. Who doesn't see that? Who doesn't understand that? All the same I have closely adhered to the relevant historical situation in the highly diverse introductions to each of the letters and have not strayed one nail's breadth from the truth itself. In our own time the consummately learned poet Baptista Mantuanus has portrayed saintly heroines in a series of *Parthenicae*, as he himself called them, albeit in a different genre from mine.[23] But please notice how many liberties he takes with the simplicity of sacred history, how many charming inventions he weaves into his verse, how many extraneous colors he daubs on his canvas! The same poet composed an epic about St. George, cast in the heroic mold, to be sure, and yet far removed from the way he is traditionally presented.[24] It is after Mantuanus' image of

---

[22]Eobanus refers to the following three letters: "Alcyone to George" (12), "Catherine to Christ" (4), and "Elizabeth to Zechariah" (20).

[23]The Italian poet Baptista Mantuanus (1447–1516) wrote a series of short epic poems on virgin saints: the Virgin Mary, Catherine of Alexandria, Margaret, Agatha, Lucia, Apollonia, and Caecilia. Collectively entitled *Parthenicae*, the seven epyllia were published between 1481 and 1507.

[24]The epyllion about St. George was first published in 1507. As Eobanus notes, the work strongly influenced his own heroic epistle about the dragonslayer (*Her. Chr.* 12).

quoque simulachrum quodammodo effinxi, unde et nomen ipsum heroidis Halciones in meum usum transiit.

16.1 Hoc quoque pium lectorem admonitum volo, mirum nec esse nec videri debere, si prima et ultima epistolae non heroidum sed heroum potius denominationem sibi vendicare videntur, nihil iccirco principaliori heroidum appellationi officere, cum etiam (ut philosophi dicunt) a principaliori soleat fieri denominatio, et Ovidium idem in Paride, Leandro, et Acontio fecisse constet. **2** In quantitatibus autem syllabarum quibusdam in locis a neothericis dissentio rationibus, videlicet authoritatibus optimorum nominum animatus.

17.1 Sed ne tandem glossemata texere aut centones sarcire quispiam me dixerit, librum hunc (unicus enim esse debet) Heroidum mearum, qualisqualis est, tuo sacro nomini nuncupatum | dedicatumque publicae lectioni tradere, posteritati transmittere, immortalitatique consecrare non dubitavi, Iobe, pontifex optime, ut et avidissimae tuae expectationi et meae propensissimae erga te voluntati novo hoc poemate et quasi tuo tibi iure debito tandem satisfacerem. **2** Quid enim quod meum est tibi non debeatur, qui unicus es meorum studiorum liberalissimus Moecenas, qui et ipse per litterarum gradus ad tam sublime fastigium evectus litteras ipsas ita unice suspicis, ita diligis, ita veneraris, ut earum vindicatoribus, hoc est litteratis, omnibus faveas, adstruas, et patrocineris? **3** Cuius rei praesentissimum testimonium esse potest ludus ille litteratorius magnis impensis, maiori cura, summa vero prudentia apud Riseburgum tuum paucis ante annis a te erectus et fundatus, quo non solum tuae ditionis ingeniis, sed et toti Prussiae optime consuluisti. **4** Quam non contentus litterarum celebritatibus ornasse, animi quoque magnitudine mirifice illustras, ita ut post illustrissimum Principem Adalbertum, marchionem Brandeburgensem, Magnum Magistrum, Prussiae merito principem locum obtineas. **5** A subditis tuis fidelissima colaris observantia, ab extraneis ob virtutes admireris, praediceris, et in caelum usque laudibus extollaris, a bonis omnibus ameris, a malis mirum in modum timearis.

18.1 Verum ne encomium scribere videar et ultimam hanc meae praefationis partem in tuis (quod plerique solent) laudibus enumerandis occupem, taceo quot principibus ab ineunte fere aetate a consiliis fueris, quot respublicas summa prudentia et promoveris et aliquando erexeris, quot legationes magnificentissimas obieris, quanto in honore apud reges quoque eo usque sis habitus

A6ᵛ

16.2 videlicet *scripsi*: videlicet et **A**.   **17.1** dedicatumque *scripsi*: dedicatum **A**.

him that I too, in a manner of speaking, have modeled my own likeness of the saint. From him I have also borrowed the name of my heroine "Alcyone."

16 There is one last item to which I wish to draw the gentle reader's attention: namely, that it ought neither to be nor to seem strange if the opening and concluding letters do not appear to fit the category "letters from heroines" but rather "letters from heroes." But that is no reason to stop me from using the predominant designation "letters from heroines," since (as the philosophers say) denomination is customarily based on preponderance. Besides, it is common knowledge that Ovid did the same thing when he included letters by Paris, Leander, and Acontius.[25] As regards the metrical quantity of syllables, I have in certain instances departed from modern usage, being encouraged in this obviously by authorities of the highest reputation.

17 But lest in the end someone should accuse me of weaving glosses or telling a pack of lies: now that I have dedicated this book of my heroides to you — for it should be regarded as a single book — and have inscribed it, such as it is, with your sacred name, I do not hesitate to present it to the reading public, hand it down to posterity, and consecrate it to immortality, Job, best of bishops, in order to satisfy at long last not only your burning anticipation but also my own eager devotion to you with this new poem. Consider it yours, seeing that I rightly owe it to you. Indeed, is there anything of mine that I do not owe to you? You are the incomparable, most generous Maecenas of my studies. Having yourself climbed the steps of literary studies to so lofty a pinnacle, you evince such extraordinary respect, love, and reverence for literature that to all her champions — that is to say, to men of letters — you offer your favor, support, and patronage. The most telling evidence of this may well be that grammar school that you erected and established a few years ago in your Riesenburg, at great expense, with greater care, and certainly with the highest wisdom. By founding it you looked after the best interests not only of the young minds in your bishopric, but indeed of all Prussia. Not content with bringing in celebrated scholars to adorn this country, you have also lent it marvelous renown through your greatness of soul, so much so, that after the illustrious Prince Albert, margrave of Brandenburg and Grand Master,[26] you deservedly occupy the first place in Prussia. Your subjects honor you with the most faithful respect, and outsiders admire, laud, and extol you to the skies on account of your merits. You are loved by all good people, exceedingly feared by the bad.

18 So as not to give the impression, however, that I am writing an encomium and taking up this the concluding part of my preface (as is common practice) with an enumeration of your merits, I pass over in silence how many princes you have advised almost from your earliest manhood, how many states you have both supported and at times raised up with utmost wisdom, how many truly magnificent embassies you have undertaken, in what high esteem you are held even among kings, to such a degree that you have placed the royal diadem on some of them with your consecrated hands and

---

[25]See Ov. *Ep.* 16, 18, and 20.

[26]Albert, margrave of Brandenburg-Ansbach (1490–1568), was elected Grand Master of the Teutonic Order in 1511.

7=B1ʳ

ut sacris tuis manibus quibusdam regni diadema imposueris regiaque liberalitate non semel, sed sepenumero munificentissime sis donatus. **2** Taceo liberalitatem tuam, | taceo in subditos optime moderatam clementiam, taceo politicarum oeconomicarumque rerum miram experientiam. **3** Taceo denique eloquentiam tuam summam, quae tanta est ut nisi ab eloquentissimo aliquo exprimi non possit, qua et ego te saepenumero non orantem modo, sed fulminantem proque tuo arbitrio quascunque causas persuadentem et audivi et vehementer sum admiratus, quam et incredibili memoria fundatam omnibus pene reddis admirabilem. **4** Taceo miram futurarum rerum providentiam. **5** Militaris vero rei peritiam, quae in te (tametsi sacer es) est perfectissima, praestat ut sileam quam a superficie (quod aiunt) contingam. **6** Quid enim armamentarium illud tuum copiosissimum totaque Prussia celeberrimum referam? Quid tormenta? Quid machinas? Quid arces, quid oppida, quid propugnacula firmissimis a te munitionibus aedificata? **7** Ex quibus omnibus velut exemplar apparet arx tua Riseburgum (quae tibi sedes est), quam ita ingentibus vallis, altissimis fossis, turribusque et propugnaculis firmam inexpugnabilemque reddidisti, ut ab omni tormentorum vi expugnationumque insultu tutissimam fore tibi possis polliceri. **8** Nec arces modo, sed templa quoque et sacras aedes non restituis solum, sed ex ipsis fundamentis erigis. **9** Quid officinam istam ferraticam multiplici operariorum ordine Vulcanio artificio instructam, omnis generis ferramentorum largitricem, immensis vero a te sumptibus fundatam commemorem? **10** Pomesaniam vero tuam, diuturna bellorum difficultate pene desolatam, ita restituisti ut et renata sibi et in pristinam foelicitatem non multo post reditura videatur.

B1ᵛ

19.1 Cum igitur et genere (quod ruber ille pileus, pristinae libertatis indicium, quem tu fratresque germani et affines tui de Dobeneck genti- | litium signum habetis, vetustissimum testatur) et animo nobilis sis, merito te optimum, hoc est omnibus virtutibus cumulatissime ornatum, appellaverim. **2** Sed vereor ne laudum tuarum acervum vel summatim attingens inextricabilem labyrinthum ingressus eo me involvam unde exire facile non liceat. **3** Imitabor igitur (ut inquit ille) Timantem, et quod penicillo exprimere non possum, velo contegam. **4** Heroidas igitur hasce non prophanas, non ethnicas, non impudicas, sed sacras, sed Christianas, sed castissimas, opus utinam tam cultum quam pium, tam iucundum quam varium, sub tui clarissimi nominis sacrosanctam Reverentiam suscipe et adversum alienae virtutis osores fortiter (ut soles) defende. Vale.

5 Lypsi, Idibus Iunii M.D.XIIII.

---

²⁷The fire god Vulcan (Hephaestus) made thunderbolts for Jupiter and arms for such heroes as Achilles.

have been most generously rewarded with kingly munificence not just once, but on many occasions. I say nothing about your generosity, nothing about your well-tempered leniency towards your subjects, nothing about your amazing experience in political and economic affairs. Indeed, I say nothing about your perfect oratory, which is so great that it cannot be described except by the most forceful orator — an eloquence, with which you do not merely declaim, but hurl thunderbolts and carry your audience for every cause that you set your mind on, as I myself have often experienced and admired immensely, and which, anchored in your incredible memory, excites the admiration of virtually everyone. I say nothing about your astounding ability to plan for the future. Regarding your military expertise, which you (though you are consecrated) have brought to a high level of perfection, it is better to remain silent than (as they say) to scratch the surface. Why indeed should I mention that armory of yours, the best stocked and most famous in all of Prussia? Why mention the cannons and siege engines, why mention the castles, towns, and ramparts you have constructed, each of them protected with the strongest possible walls? Your own castle of Riesenburg, which serves as your residence, clearly serves as an exemplar for all the others. You have made it so strong and impregnable with huge earthworks, deep moats, and lofty towers and ramparts, that you can count on being absolutely safe from all artillery fire and capture by assault. You have restored not just castles, but also churches and sanctuaries, and even built them from the foundations up. What need is there to point to that iron factory, stocked with many different masters of Vulcan's craft,[27] that produces all kinds of iron implements, yet was established by you at enormous expense? Your Pomesania, practically desolated by the long ravages of war, you have revived so much that it feels reborn and about to be restored to its former prosperity in the very near future.

19 Since, therefore, you are noble by ancestry (the ancientness of which is attested by that emblem of antique liberty, the red cap that you and your full brothers and relations in the Von Dobeneck family have as a device in your coat of arms)[28] and are of noble character to boot, I have good reason to call you the best of men, that is, a man most bounteously adorned with every imaginable virtue. But I fear that even by just touching summarily on the great treasure heap of your virtues I have entered an inextricable labyrinth and am becoming so perplexed that I no longer see an easy way out. Accordingly, as a famed author put it, I shall imitate Timanthes by covering with a veil what I cannot express with the painter's brush.[29] Take these heroic epistles, therefore — not profane, not heathen, not unchaste, but sacred, Christian, and chaste to the core, a work I hope you will find as elegant as it is devout, as delightful as it is varied. Place them under the sacrosanct protection of your Reverence's illustrious name and shield them energetically (as you always do) against those who hate goodness in others. Farewell.

Leipzig, 13 June 1514.

---

[28]In Roman times manumitted slaves wore a felt cap (*pilleum*) to symbolize their liberty. See Erasmus, *Adag.* 2.1.27; cf. Eob. *Buc.* 8.90–94, with n. 71 (1:340).

[29]Eobanus alludes to Poliziano, *Ep.*, 1.6.1: "imitabor Timantem, quodque exprimere penicillo non possum, velo contegam." The painter Timanthes of Cythnos (late fifth century BCE) veiled Agamemnon's head at the sacrifice of Iphigenia because, in his view, the father's sorrow could not be portrayed with a brush. Cf. Cic. *Orat.* 74; V. Max. 8.11, ext. 6; Quint. *Inst.* 2.13.13; Plin. *Nat.* 35.73.

8=B2^r

**A 1 NOBILIS ET GENEROSUS DOMINUS CAROLUS
SCHENCK DE LYMPURGK BARO AD LECTOREM**

Augusto trifidum pacem moderante per orbem,
    Claruit imparibus Naso poeta modis.
Caesare Germano Latialia iura tenente,
    Helius arguta claret et ipse cheli.
5 Maxima Naso fuit Pelignae gloria terrae,
    Famaque Sulmoni maxima Naso fuit.
Helius Hessiacae decus insuperabile genti,
    Helius est patriae laus, honor, aura suae.
Carmina (quis nescit?) cultissima Naso reliquit.
10   Optima, ne dubites, Helius usque canit.
Ethnica commisit fluidus spectacula Naso,
    Enthea sed praestans Helius arte facit.
Dictat amatricum lascivas Naso tabellas,
    Mutua ut alternus pectora servet amor.
15 Hic est carminibus longe graviora sequutus
    Helius, aethereos nam movet inde viros.
Illius in verbis quam re meliora putantur,
    Huius et in verbis reque probata nitent.
Quid moror? In quantum superat res sacra profanam
20   Et sol flammivomi lucida signa poli,
Materia tantum (liceat modo vera fateri)
    Illius hic claro plectra nitore premit.
Quod si forte tibi res haec conficta videtur
    Nec sunt arbitrio verba recepta tuo,
25 Hoc, age, lector opus superum studiose sacrorum
    Tam tersum cupido non semel ore legas.
Tunc dices, reor: "Is nimium manifesta loquutus.
    Non potuit verbis verior esse suis."

A 1. *A: om.* ***BO****.*

A 1   THE HIGHBORN AND NOBLE-SPIRITED LORD, BARON KARL SCHENK VON LIMPURG, TO THE READER[1]

When Augustus maintained peace throughout the tripartite world,[2] Ovid enjoyed fame as a poet of elegiac verse. Now that a German emperor holds sway over the Roman Empire, it is Helius who is famed for his tuneful lyre. Ovid was the greatest glory of the Pelignian country; Ovid was the greatest pride of Sulmo. Helius is the unsurpassable ornament of the Hessian people; Helius is the glory, pride, and joy of his native land. Everybody knows that Ovid left us wonderfully elegant poems. [10] Don't doubt for a moment that Helius' poems are any less dazzling. The fluent Ovid put together heathen entertainments, but Helius in his masterful way produces poems inspired by God. Ovid composed wanton letters from mistresses, intended to keep mutual love burning in the other's heart. Our Helius pursues a far more serious goal in his poems, for they rouse saintly men to action. The poems of the former are considered better in style than morality; those of the latter are excellent both in style and moral tenor. What am I waiting for? As much as the sacred transcends the profane [20] and the sun outshines the bright stars in the flame-spewing sky, so much does the latter (if I may say the truth) overshadow the former in subject matter and brilliance of tone. But perhaps you think I'm making this up and won't take my word for it. Well then, studious reader, peruse this truly refined work for yourself. Read it with eager lips, and not just once either, for it deals with God and his saints. Then I'm sure you'll exclaim: "That fellow has obviously spoken the truth. His words couldn't be more on the mark."

---

[1] Baron Karl Sigismund Schenk von Limpurg (1498–1558), a canon at Würzburg since 1506, took up studies at Leipzig in the summer semester of 1511. In 1516 he matriculated at the University of Ingolstadt, where he was elected rector in the autumn of 1517. A supporter of Luther, he renounced his prebends in 1523 and was twice married.

[2] That is, in Europe, Africa, and Asia.

**A 2   NOBILIS ET GENEROSUS DOMINUS PAULUS
DE SCHWARTZENBERGK BARO AD LIBRUM**

> Exi frugifer, elegans, diserte
> Iamiam conspicuas liber per auras.
> Lima quum bene sis severiore
> Scabro et pumice naviter politus,
> 5   Non est qur metuas sagatiores
> In te qui cupiunt movere nasum,
> Nam te composuit bonus poeta,
> Hessus, blandiloquae comes Thaliae,
> Romanae decus elegantiaeque.
> 10   Cuius carmina, blandiore filo
> Contexta et sale delibuta casto,
> Pulchrarum chorus approbat sororum.
> Nec nugas etenim docet iocosve
> Nec tricas apinasve viliores,
> 15   Ut mos est veterum suus quibusdam.
> Sacra est materies bonusque vates,
> Cui Phoebus citharam dedit sonoram.
> Non barri, auriculae, ciconiaeque,
> Non osor malus improbusque Livor,
> 20   Non illi poterint nocere ronchi.
> Texerunt etenim decente lauro
> Musae doctiloqui caput poetae
> Immunemque odiis virum relinquunt.
> Quare nunc tenebris solute longis
> 25   Demum, quid dubitas? Favore magno
> Exi frugifer, elegans, diserte
> Iamiam conspicuas liber per auras,
> Ut solum ilia sic repente et ipsi
> Rumpantur misero nigella Codro.

A 2.   *A: om. BO.*

**A 2   THE HIGHBORN AND NOBLE-SPIRITED LORD, BARON
           PAUL VON SCHWARZENBERG, TO THE BOOK[3]**

Go forth, you fruitful, elegant, well-spoken book. Any minute
now you'll be blazing through the heavens. Since you've been
carefully smoothed with a sharp file and diligently polished with
abrasive pumice, you don't need to fear niggling critics who like
to turn up their noses at you. For a fine poet composed you:
Hessus, the companion of fair-spoken Thalia and ornament of
Roman elegance. [10] His songs are woven with charming thread
and steeped in chaste wit, which is why the choir of those lovely
Sisters[4] commends them. And indeed, he doesn't offer trifles
or jokes or bagatelles or cheap effects, as some of the ancients
were in the habit of doing. Here the theme is sacred, and the
poet a good one. Phoebus has given him the sonorous lyre. No
elephants, asses, and storks, no hateful devils and green-eyed
monsters, [20] no croaking frogs can ever hurt him. After all, the
Muses have crowned the head of this erudite poet with graceful
laurel, and have left him immune from the grudges of men.
Since you're now released at long last from obscurity, what is
holding you back? Go forth to great applause, you fruitful,
elegant, well-spoken book. Any minute now you'll be blazing
through the heavens. That ought to be enough to make the
wretched Codrus[5] burst his black guts on the spot!

[3]A canon at Bamberg since 1507, Baron Paul von Schwarzenberg (1498–1535) matriculated at
Leipzig in the summer semester of 1511. After studies at Ingolstadt from 1516 to 1522 he was named
a member of the cathedral chapter at Bamberg in 1523. Eobanus and Paul maintained their friendship
through visits, letters, and gifts. In 1532 Eobanus dedicated the revised *Heroidum libri tres* to him.
[4]The Muses.
[5]In Verg. *Ecl.* 7.26, the singer Thyrsis asks to be crowned with ivy, so his rival Codrus will burst with
envy. In his response to Veit Werler, Eobanus concludes with the same allusion. See *Her. Chr.* B 1.74.

9=B3ʳ   **A 3   VITUS VVERLERUS H. EOBANO HESSO SUO**

An quis non faveat tibi nec unquam
    Ardeat ingenti laudis amore tuae?
An non quisquis homo probet libenter
    Dotes quas lingua, mente, animoque refers?
5   Sive infirmus ero simulque febris,
    Hei, male defensam torquet acerba cutem,
Sive insit melior status virorum
    Et dicar voto dexteriore frui
Vel terras peragro vagus repostas
10   Sive ego sim vitreis, Hesse, futurus aquis,
Aut sit sors propriis iniqua rebus
    Aut mea regales archa refundat opes,
In summa, vicibus diem reducit
    Crinitus radiis donec Apollo suis,
15   Mellito mihi dulcior liquore,
    Crede, meo semper pectore fixus eris.
Hoc virtus merito facit decora,
    Si data iuditio sit tua vita meo.
Nam te tabifici movet nec ardor
20   Livoris, vultus sed sine nube geris.
Nulli detrahis, omnibus sed aequus
    Atque bonos tota sedulitate colis.
Non vires animi dolor quieti
    Frangit, nec sensus ira animosa premit.
25   Tu rectum sequeris, fugis mala, inde
    Cultor amicitiae sedulus esse soles.
Non te destituit fidele robur
    Corporis, et rutilum fundis ab ore iubar.
Vidisti varias peritus urbes,
B3ᵛ   30   Audisti claros, clarior ipse, viros.
O foelix nimium sacerque vates,
    Doctrina priscis aequiparande viris!
En Phoebus tibi dona subministrat,
    Nec negat auratam Calliopea lyram.
35   Qua fretus, bone Iuppiter, probatum
    Mira scripsisti nobilitate librum.
In quo Christicolas doces sorores
    Pulchra verecundo verba lepore loqui.
Non lusus Veneris libidinesque
40   Continet, at verum relligionis opus.

A 3.   *A: om. **BO**.*

A 3   VEIT WERLER TO HIS FRIEND H. EOBANUS HESSUS[6]

How can anyone not admire you or never burn with an over-whelming desire to sing your praises? Isn't everybody eager to commend the gifts that you demonstrate with tongue, mind, and soul? No matter what happens to me, Hessus, whether I fall sick as the pitiless fever racks my all too defenseless skin, or enjoy high status in life so that I'm said to have everything a man could desire, or roam faraway countries [10] or sail the glittering seas, whether fortune begrudges me her gifts or my coffers overflow with regal treasures: in brief, while long-haired Apollo still brings back the day each morning with his rays, you may be sure that you'll be sweeter to me than honey and always have a place in my heart.

That is what your shining virtue deserves, if I may pass judgment on the way you conduct your life. For you are untouched by the fire of all-consuming [20] Envy. As a matter of fact, there never is a cloud on your face. Instead of disparaging people, you treat everyone fairly and work hard to be friends with the good. Grief does not break the strength of your tranquil soul, nor does violent rage becloud your senses. You strive for what is right, you shun evil, and are hence an untiring wooer of friendship. Your robust physique never lets you down, and your ruddy cheeks are aglow with health. A well-traveled man, you have seen all kinds of cities; [30] you have listened to famous men, yourself more famous. O exceedingly blessed and sacred bard, in erudition a match for the ancients! Look, Phoebus grants you his gifts, and Calliope does not deny you her golden lyre. Relying on her, by Jove, you have written an excellent book of marvelous beauty. In it you teach sisters in Christ to speak lovely words with modest grace. There is not a word about amorous sport and wantonness here, [40] only the true works of faith.

---

[6]On Veit Werler of Sulzfeld see Camerarius, *Nar.* 11.4, with n. 33 (1:35–36).

Illo quid potuit magis disertum
    Esse? O ingenii gratia magna tui!
Naso sic loquitur, Tomos adire
    Non iussus nec adhuc Caesaris ira fuit.
45   Sic doctum video loqui Catullum,
    Sic est Rhomanus sermo, Tibulle, tuus.
Sic Ruffus nitidus Propertiusque
    Suaviloqua faciles voce dedere modos.
Talis Nestorei senis loquela
50   Dulcior Hybleo fluxit ab ore favo.
Et tales numeros dedit Pericles,
    In cuius labris Pitho canora fuit.
Tam clarus Siculo sonus profundo
    Continuit miseras in sua damna rates.
55   Sic tandem querulum lyra ciebat
    Murmur ad Ionias doctus Arion aquas.
Tam dulce Ismariis poeta in oris
    Cantat, quum subiit fata cruenta, melos.
Nec foenix aliud rogo propinquus,
60   Non aliud recinit funere carmen olor
Quam hoc quod iam Latiae nitore linguae
10=B4ʳ   Parturis, Hessiaci fama decusque soli.
Ergo perpetuum feres honorem,
    Et tua erit nullo Musa sepulta loco,
65   Namque inter nitidos tibi poetas
    Posteritas primum dat veneranda gradum
Necnon cuncta leget nimis frequenter
    Divite de vena quae tibi scripta fluunt.
Tu Viti interea memor sodalis,
70   Quo tibi non alter iunctior esse potest.
Sic comple Pyliam diu senectam
    Et capiant anni tempora longa tui.
Post vitae spacium Deus per aevum
    Det tantis meritis munera digna tuis.
75   Hoc pro te rogitant puer senexque.
    Haec etiam voti summa, Eobane, mei est.

48 Suaviloqua *A¹–A³ A⁶*: Suaviloquo *A⁴ A⁵ A⁷*.

What could be more fluent than this book of yours? Oh, the great charm of your mind! Had Ovid spoken like this, he would never have been exiled to Tomis or stirred the emperor's anger. This is the way I see the learned Catullus talk, this is the Roman speech of Tibullus. This is how delightfully and deftly the refined Rufus[7] and Propertius sang their verse. Such was the speech, [50] sweeter than the honey of Hybla, that flowed from the mouth of old Nestor. And such was the eloquence of Pericles, on whose lips melodious Peitho dwelt.[8] It was a harmony as enchanting as this that held poor sailors spellbound on the Sicilian deep and sent them to their doom.[9] Just as plaintive, finally, was the tune that learned Arion drew from his lyre beside the Ionian Sea. Equally sweet was the melody that the Thracian poet sang just before he died a bloody death.[10] Neither the phoenix as he approaches the funeral pyre [60] nor the dying swan sings a song different from the one that you now bring forth with all the brilliance of the Latin language, O you, Hesse's glory and pride.

Accordingly, you will win eternal renown, and your Muse will not pass into oblivion anywhere on earth. Among the refined poets, indeed, venerable Posterity will assign you the first rank and never stop reading all the writings that flow from your rich vein. Meanwhile do remember your comrade Veit, [70] the closest friend you could possibly have. Then may you attain Nestor's old age and go on living for many years to come. And when you have run the course of life, may God grant you the eternal reward you deserve for these great merits of yours. This is the prayer that young and old say for you. This, Eobanus, is also my dearest wish.

---

[7]The tragic and epic poet L. Varius Rufus. Horace mentions him in *Ars* 55 in the same breath with Vergil. Nothing of his work has survived.

[8]Peitho is the personification of eloquence and persuasion.

[9]Eobanus' poetry is more charming than the Sirens' song. Cf. *Ama.* 27.1–2, with notes.

[10]Orpheus was torn apart by the Bacchantes as he was lamenting the death of his wife Eurydice. See Ov. *Met.* 11.1–19.

A 4   GREGORIUS AUBANUS EOBANO HESSO SUO

Volvere quas tecum furtivo heroidas usu
   Non semel assuetus dissimulanter eram,
Ut mihi narrabas acri iam dedita limae
   Cuncta sub utrosvis mox abitura polos,
5   Mirandum est quam tunc praesenti pectore plenus
   Non cessaturae posteritatis eram!
Sic tuus est rebus dexter mihi visus Apollo,
   Materia rebus conveniente suis.
Crede mihi, vix qui Paridem lecturus adibit
10   Omnibus ex nobis unus et alter erit.
Non mihi Cydippe pomum nec Acontius illam
   Arguet, infandae scripta pudenda rei.
Non querar Oenonen, non me moritura movebit
   Dido, flagrantem iam subitura rogum.
15   Materiam nactus dignam nobisque Deoque,
   Illa perpetua commoditate fruar.
Tu modo, Germanae non ultima gloria famae,
   Hesse, velis votis addere vota meis
Nec desyderium contando incendere nostrum.
20   Saepe etiam cupidis vel mora parva nocet.

B4ᵛ

A 4.   *A*: *om. BO*.   **13** Oenonen *A¹–A³ A⁶*: Oenonem *A⁴ A⁵ A⁷*.

A 4   GREGOR AUBANUS TO HIS FRIEND EOBANUS HESSUS[11]

More than once I've discussed these heroides with you alone,
behind closed doors. So when you told me that you had now
smoothed them all with a sharp file and were planning to send
them off to the ends of the earth, it's amazing how my heart was
immediately filled with thoughts of never-ending posterity! For
that's how much Apollo, I think, has inspired you in this work,
a perfect marriage of content and form. Believe me, [10] there
will scarcely be one or two in all our number who will run off to
read Paris' letter.[12] I, for one, won't have Cydippe's blaming the
apple or Acontius' blaming her — shameful letters with a shocking theme! I won't be lamenting Oenone either, nor will the
doomed Dido tug at my heartstrings as she draws close to the
blazing pyre. In your book I have found a subject worthy of us
and of God. I am going to enjoy it to my everlasting profit. Now
you, Hessus, not the least ornament of German fame, be so kind
as to add your prayers to mine and don't inflame our desire with
further postponement. [20] Often even a short delay hurts the
longing heart.

---

[11]On Gregor (or Georg) Käl of Aub, see Camerarius, *Nar.* 11.4, with n. 33 (1:36).

[12]Letter 16 in Ovid's *Heroidum epistulae*. The following lines refer to other letters in the same
work. For Acontius' and Cydippe's letters, see Ov. *Ep.* 20 and 21; for Oenone's letter to Paris, see *Ep.* 5;
and for Dido's letter to Aeneas, see *Ep.* 7.

Scribunt in hoc opere epistolas

Emmanuel	Mariae,
Maria	Emmanueli,
Maria Magdalena	Iesu Christo,
Catharina Costis	Christo sponso,
Elisabeth	Ludovico,
Helena	Constantino,
Sabina	Alexio,
Kunegundis	Henrico,
Monica	Augustino,
Barbara	Origeni,
Thais	Paphnutio,
Alcione	Georgio,
Anna	Ioachimo,
Maria Aegiptia	Zozimae,
Pelagia	Nonio,
Maria	Ioanni,
Ursula	Aethereo,
Anastasia	Chrisogono,
Tecla	Paulo,
Elisabeth	Zachariae,
Paula	Hieronymo,
Martha	Maximino,
Dorothea	Theophilo,
Eobanus	Posteritati.

Index epistularum.   *A*: *om. **BO***.   Kunegundis *scripsi*: Kungundis *A*.

This work contains the following letters:

Emmanuel	to Mary
Mary	to Emmanuel
Mary Magdalene	to Jesus Christ
Catherine, Costus' daughter,	to her bridegroom Christ
Elizabeth	to Ludwig
Helen	to Constantine
Sabina	to Alexius
Cunegund	to Henry
Monica	to Augustine
Barbara	to Origen
Thais	to Paphnutius
Alcyone	to George
Anna	to Joachim
Mary of Egypt	to Zosimas
Pelagia	to Nonius
Mary	to John
Ursula	to Ethereus
Anastasia	to Chrysogonus
Thecla	to Paul
Elizabeth	to Zechariah
Paula	to Jerome
Martha	to Maximinus
Dorothy	to Theophilus
Eobanus	to Posterity

Helii Eobani Hessi
HEROIDUM CHRISTIANARUM
LIBER

1   EMMANUEL MARIAE

Quam legis, aeternam rebus paritura salutem,
  Non est mortali littera facta manu.
Pone metus, Virgo, superis gratissima. Non est
  Quem tremis infestus nuncius iste tibi.
5 Ales ab excelso iuvenis descendit Olympo,
  Qui tibi non falso pectore dicit, "Ave."
Sed tibi quod notae non venit epistola dextrae
  Forsan et ignotus palmifer ales erat,
Ergone te superum cuiquam dubitabis amari?
10 Et dices, "Istud quomodo fiet opus?"
Fiet, et ut lente dubites credasque futurum,
  Accipe de summa nuncia certa fide.
Qui super ingentis regnum tenet ardua mundi,
  Rex sine principio, Rex sine fine, Deus,
15 Concavitas vastae quem non capit ultima sphaerae,
  Cuius id immensum dextera claudit opus,

Tit. generalis. *A. Cf. titulum libri primi in* **BO**: Helii Eobani Hessi Heroidum epistolarum lib. I, qui historicas continet.

  Her. Chr. **1.** *Tit.* Emmanuel Mariae *A*: Deus Pater Mariae Virgini **BO**.   **10** Et — opus *A*: Mirarique voles quale sit illud opus **BO**.   **13** ingentis *A*: ingentes **BO**.   **14–15** Rex — sphaerae, *A*: *om.* **BO**.

[1]Emmanuel ("God with us") is the Son of God and future Messiah. The name, which comes from Isaiah 7.14, is first associated with Jesus in Matthew 1.23: "Behold, a virgin shall conceive and bear a son, and his name shall be called Emmanuel." In Eobanus' fiction, Emmanuel writes to announce that Mary will become his mother. He is eager to follow his Father's wish that he leave heaven in order to save the sin-sick world. Mary responds in *Her. Chr.* 2.

Helius Eobanus Hessus
A BOOK OF CHRISTIAN
HEROIDES

1   ## EMMANUEL TO MARY[1]

The letter you are reading, O you who are about to bring eternal
salvation into the world, this letter was not written by a mortal
hand. Do not be afraid, Virgin, favorite of Heaven. That messenger before whom you tremble is no menace to you. He has
descended from highest Olympus — the winged youth who
offers you his unpretending "Hail!" But just because the letter
you received was written by an unknown hand and the palm-
bearing angel was perhaps strange to you, is that reason enough
to doubt that someone in heaven loves you? [10] And will you
still say, "How shall this be accomplished?"[2] Let it be done; and
as you ponder these things and slowly trust to the future, hear
this indubitable message from the supreme authority.

The God who holds sway over the heights of the whole wide
world, King without beginning, King without end, he whom the
outermost sphere of the vast celestial globe cannot contain, he
who holds this immense creation in his right hand — I am that

---

Though Eobanus faithfully retells the Gospel story of the Annunciation and the birth of Jesus
(Matthew 1.18–2.16; Luke 1.26–2.20), he changes the angel's role from herald of God to letter carrier.
The idea of having God or Christ send a written message from heaven is, of course, by no means
unprecedented. In the Old Testament, for example, God himself writes the tablets of the Law (Exodus
20.1; 32.15–16; 34.1). Letters written by Christ were an especially popular genre in the Middle Ages
and beyond. See the article "'Himmelsbrief'" in *VL* 4, cols. 28–33. The idea is carried to its logical
conclusion in some late medieval German paintings that depict the Archangel Gabriel delivering a
sealed letter or letters from God to the Virgin. See Wolfgang Braunfels, *Die Verkündigung* (Düsseldorf,
1949), XIV; Louis Réau, *Iconographie de l'art chrétien*, vol. 2.2 (Paris, 1957), 184; *Lexikon der
christlichen Ikonographie*, ed. Engelbert Kirschbaum, vol. 4 (Rome, 1972), col. 431.

In the 1532/39 version this letter is *Her.* 1.1. In this redaction Eobanus changed "Emmanuel" to
"God the Father" and made the appropriate adjustments within the letter itself. The revised letter
evidently inspired François Habert, "La xx. Epistre de Dieu le Pere a la vierge Marie," in *Les epistres
heroides tressalutaires pour servir d'exemple à toute âme fidèle* (Paris, 1551. Habert would have known
Eobanus' *Heroidum libri tres* by way of the Paris reprint of 1546.) See Dörrie, 384.

[2]Cf. Luke 1.34.

Ille ego cui caeli, cui sydera cuncta moventur,
　　Cui miscent vires corpora prima suas,
B5ᵛ　Quem tremit inferni domus alta Deumque fatetur
20　　Quicquid ab inferna est conditione procul,
Cuius ab humanis non est effabile nomen
　　Vocibus, ignotum cui nihil esse potest,
Ille ego sum qui sceptra fero sublimia rerum,
　　Dignus in amplexus ire, Puella, tuos.
25　Ibimus et miserum tandem lustrabimus orbem
　　Quem velut exulibus iussimus esse domum.
Pande fores, Regina. Tua nascemur ab alvo,
　　Plena ubi iam nonae tempora mensis erunt.
At neque, noster amor, tactus patiere viriles,
30　　Nostra nec exuta virgine mater eris.
In te per teneram descendet Spiritus aurem,
　　Subque tuo Verbum pectore fiet homo.
Nec dubita. Qui cuncta potest, id posse necesse est,
　　Et facile est nasci virgine matre Deo.
35　Ut rata sint Solimi vulgata poemata vatis,
　　Excipe me casto, Virgo pudica, sinu.
Est amor afflictae tandem succurrere plebi
　　Quam cruciant multos Tartara clausa dies.
Insontes animae merita quo luce fruantur,
40　　Est mihi pro misero mors obeunda grege.
2=B6ʳ　Me Pater afflicto moriturum sufficit orbi;
　　Et libet et iustum est Patre iubente mori.
Ah, quoties aliquis superum mihi, "Vivito," dixit!
　　"Quod petis hoc nullo sanguine debet emi.
45　Liberet antiquos divina potentia manes,
　　Quaeque suum fecit dextera servet opus."
Ah, quoties alicui dicenti talia dixi:
　　"Iussa mihi aeterni sunt obeunda Patris.
Quae pater Adamus nostris deliquit in hortis
50　　Crimina sunt nostra persoluenda nece.
Quod licet exiguo divina potentia possit,
　　Ultima pro charo vult tolerare bono.

17–28 Ille — erunt *A*: Ille ego sum Deus et rerum suprema potestas, / Cuius habes manibus nunc data iussa tuis. / Pone metus. Iterum, nihil est hic, virgo, timendum; / Gaudia quin potius quae mediteris habes. / Num credis iam turpe nihil tibi posse parari, / Cum placeas casto casta puella Deo? / Et ne virgineas longis ambagibus aures / Detineam, de te quod meditemur habe. / Laeta tibi gratare: tua nascetur ab alvo / Subque tuo Verbum pectore fiet homo, [= *v. 32 in A*] / Verbum quo coelos terraeque creavimus orbem, / Quicquid et haec extra quicquid et intus habet *BO*.　　**32** Subque — homo *A*: Noster et haec uteri caussa tumentis erit *BO*.　　**35** Solimi — vatis *A*: veterum per te praesagia vatum *BO*.　　**36** me *A*: nos *BO*.　　**39–62** Insontes — homo." *A*: Amissam miseris iterum reparare salutem / Atque hominem nobis conciliare iuvat. *BO*.

God for whom the heavens and all the stars revolve, for whom the elements conjoin their powers, before whom the depths of hell tremble and whom [20] everything outside of hell confesses as Lord, the God whose name cannot be expressed in human words, to whom nothing can remain unknown. I am he who bears the sublime scepter of the universe, a God worthy of enjoying your embraces, Maiden. I am going to enjoy them and at long last redeem the wretched world that I commanded to be a home, as it were, to exiled humanity. Throw open the gates, Queen. It is from your womb that I shall be born as soon as the ninth month has run its course. But you, my beloved, will not experience physical contact with a male, [30] nor will you lose your virginity when you become my mother. The Spirit will descend into you through your tender ear,[3] and the Word will become man beneath your heart. Do not doubt it. With the Omnipotent all things are possible. For God it is easy to be born of a virgin mother.

In order that the celebrated prophecies of Jerusalem's seer[4] may be fulfilled, receive me, pure Virgin, in your chaste womb. It is my heartfelt desire to come at last to the aid of that afflicted people whom the prison of Tartarus has tormented for so long already.[5] So that guiltless souls may enjoy the life they deserve, [40] it is my duty to die for the unfortunate flock. The Father has appointed me to lay down my life for a world in distress; and because the Father has commanded it, it is both pleasing and just to die. Ah, how often has one of the celestials told me: "Live! What you seek should not to be bought with any blood. Let the power of God set those ancient shades free. And let the hand that created them also save its own handiwork." Ah, how often have I told someone who talks like that: "I must do the bidding of the eternal Father. The sins that father Adam committed in our gardens [50] can only be expiated by my death. Though the power of God could accomplish that in the twinkling of an eye, he wants to pay the ultimate price for the salvation he holds dear.

---

[3]According to an old tradition, the Virgin conceived the Word through her ear. See Salzer, 90–92; and, for example, Ennod., hymn to the Virgin (*CSEL* 6, 552–53), 10–11; Ven. Fort. "Hymnus Beatae Mariae," *AH* 50.72.3; Mant. *1. Parthen.* 2.665–67; Eob. *Hymn.* 37–38.

[4]The prophet Isaiah. Cf. Matthew 1.22–23, referring to Isaiah 7.14; Eob. *Her. Chr.* 2, ll. 36, 47–48.

[5]The souls of the righteous who died in Old Testament times will be liberated from Limbo when Christ descends into hell early on Easter morning. Cf. *Her. Chr.* 3.5–26, with notes.

Charius est multa quicquid mercede paratur,
    Magnaque vix partis gratia rebus inest.
55 Namque ego si nullo redimam certamine victor
    Hostili quondam perdita signa dolo,
Nemo meos toto laudabit in orbe triumphos
    Gratiaque est meriti parva futura mei.
Et quamvis maiora dedi quam credere possint,
60   Maius id exigui muneris instar erit,
Ni mihi devincam subiti quoque iure laboris
    Ut mihi deberi se sciat omnis homo."
Fecimus hunc primum patriisque locavimus hortis
B6ᵛ   Et facili dedimus iussa ferenda modo.
65 Excidit exiguo nostri reverentia tractu.
    Esse deos nobis se voluere pares!
Hac prius exciderat culpa caelumque reliquit,
    Qui miseris technae conditor huius erat.
Non tulimus patriam vacuam tot milibus arcem,
70   Quoque repleretur nec mora factus homo est.
Iamque ab eo cedunt annorum milia quinque
    Tempore, cum paucis quos numerare piget.
Sydera nemo hominum postquam super ardua venit,
    Dum Patris accessus ianua clausa negat.
75 Hanc veteri clausam delicto virginis Evae
    Tu facies partu virgo patere novo.
Currite foelici, properantia sydera, cursu!
    Natalem expectat quicquid ubique meum.
Iamdudum numerant captivi saecula vates
80   Et non praevisis cursibus ire timent.
Nobilis ante alios (Deus aspicit omnia) David
    Saepius in mediis patribus ista refert:
"Fidite, sperantes animae. Foelicia currunt
    Saecula, peccatum depositura vetus.
85 'Tollite,' ait, 'portas,' mihi vox praefertur ad aures,
3=C1ʳ   'Tollite Tartarei limina vestra duces!'
Atque ita dextra potens operabitur illa salutem,
    Cum rutilus nondum Lucifer ortus erit."
Saepius haec gravidum referentem verba prophetam
90   Laudat in obscura quaelibet umbra domo.

---

63 patriisque — hortis **A**: terrae de parte recentis. / Implerant totum foemina virque genus. / Inde frequentandos quos nos plantavimus hortos **BO**.   65 tractu **A**: lapsu **BO**.   67 caelumque **A**: coelosque **BO**.   68 technae **A**: noxae **BO**.   69 patriam **A**: coeli **BO**.   74 Dum — negat **A**: Dum stupet imposita ianua nostra sera **BO**.   77–90 Currite — domo. **A**: Nanque quid hoc hominum genus in mea regna creatum / Oppressum misere perfidus hostis habet? **BO**.

Whatever is obtained at high cost is bound to be dearer to us; and objects achieved with the utmost difficulty possess great charm. Indeed, if I did not put up a victorious struggle to redeem the banners lost to the Enemy's guile long ago, no one in the whole world would laud my triumphs, and my act of love would offer but small delight. And even if I gave more than anyone could possibly imagine, [60] such great blessings would count for little if my unexpected sacrifice did not also make people realize that, by rights, they owe their life to me."

We created them in the beginning and placed them in the Father's gardens and gave them commands that were easy to bear. All too soon they lost their awe of us. They wanted to be gods, our equals![6] The one who cunningly gave the wretches this idea had earlier succumbed to the same sin and fallen from heaven.[7] We could not bear to see the Father's citadel emptied of so many thousands, [70] and to make up for that loss we at once created humankind. Since that time five thousand years have passed, along with a few more that would be irksome to count.[8] Since then not a single soul has ascended above the stars of heaven, as long as the closed door blocks access to the Father. This door, shut long ago by the sin of the virgin Eve, you will cause to be opened when you miraculously give birth as a virgin.

Run swiftly, stars, on your blessed course! All creation looks forward to my birth. For a long time now the captive prophets have been counting up the centuries [80] and are afraid that the ages are taking an unforeseen course. David, noblest of them all (God sees everything), quite often exclaims amidst the other patriarchs: "Trust me, hopeful souls. The blessed age that will take away the ancient sin is hurrying near. A voice," he says, "is reaching my ears: 'Lift up your gates! Lift up your doors, you princes of hell!'[9] This is how that mighty right hand will work salvation, before the glittering morning star has risen."[10] As often as the venerable prophet proclaims these words, [90] someone or other among the shades praises him in their dark abode.

---

[6]Adam and Eve were commanded not to eat from the tree of the knowledge of good and evil that stood in the middle of the Garden of Eden. When the serpent persuaded them to eat of it nevertheless, he told them that they would then become like God, knowing the difference between good and evil. See Genesis 2–3.

[7]Cf. Isaiah 14.12 (where later interpreters identify the daystar Lucifer with the fallen angel, Satan); Luke 10.18; 2 Peter 2.4; Revelations 12.7–9.

[8]According to a calculation popular in the Middle Ages and Renaissance, Jesus was born at the end of the year 5199. See Oros. 1.1.5–6; and, for example, Petrus Comestor, *Historia scholastica*, "Historia evangelica" 5, *PL* 198, col. 1540 C; *Leg. aurea* 6.1; Eob. *Her. Chr.* 3.19–20; *Hymn.* 33–36; *Vict.* 59–60.

[9]Quoted from Psalm 24 (23 in the Vulgate), verses 7 and 9. These verses were traditionally interpreted as a prophecy of Christ's descent into hell. Cf. *Nicod.* 21; Eob. *Vict.* 206–07.

[10]That is, Christ will descend into hell during the night before Easter. See ll. 181–82 below.

Ergo graves dempto patiemur fine querelas?
    Ergone, saeve anguis, semper inultus eris?
Flammifer assiduis resonat clamoribus aether,
    "Solve salutifera vincula nostra manu!"
95 Vincor, et ex patrio terras deducor Olympo,
    Iamque ego sum ventris pars quota, Virgo, tui.
Sentis? Incluso an dubitas turgescere foetu
    Viscera, in hoc praestas quod nova miles opus?
Cornua, luna, cito se claude fugantia, donec
100   Ad decimum mensem ter tria clausa feras.
Tum Iudaea meo Bethleem laetabitur ortu,
    Quaeque Palestinus rura colonus arat.
Frigida stabit hyems, glacialibus alba pruinis,
    Illo quo primum tempore mater eris.
105 Nec mea Dalmaticum cunabula conteget aurum.
    Pauperies ortus maxima noster erit.
Sic tuus ille orbis Dominus, sub paupere tecto
    Aeditus, ignavum vagiet ante pecus.
In foeno et paleis proprio Deus aeditus orbi,
110   Exemplo cunctis regibus esse volo.
Nec taciti nascemur. Erunt nova gaudia, fient
    Omnia natalis lumine plena mei.
Quinetiam rudibus pecorum per rura ministris
    Cantabit natum caelica turba Deum.
115 Infantem populus venerabitur omnis Iesum;
    Hoc illo nobis tempore nomen erit.
Ortus ad auroram noster procedet, et ipsum
    In cunis oriens sentiet esse Deum.
Muneribus reges venient, Regemque puellum
120   Ducet adorantes praevia stella magos.
Solus et antiquo crudelior angue tyrannus,
    Rex Solymae, nato quaeret obesse tuo.
Quaeret in Hebraeo Iudaeum sanguine regem.
    Multus in immiti concidet ense puer.
125 Ipsa puerque tuus nobisque minister Ioseph

C1ᵛ

---

95 Vincor — Olympo *A*: Vincimur et supera terras e sede movemur ***BO***.   96 ego sum *A*:
sumus ***BO***.   97–102 Sentis — arat. *A*: *om*. ***BO***.   97 Incluso an *A* (*in erratis*): An incluso *A*
(*in textu*).   105 Nec — aurum. *A*: Atria nec statues regali splendida luxu. / Nulla tuo veniet
pompa puerperio. / Utque pares animum tibi non ignara futuri, ***BO***.   109 et *A*: est ***BO***.
110 Exemplo — volo *A*: Regibus exemplum quod vereantur erit ***BO***.   113–15 Quinetiam —
Iesum; *A*: Agresti populo natum cantabit Iesum / Coelitus infanti turba ministra Deo. / Nunquid
ut audisti dici miraris Iesum? ***BO***.   119 Muneribus — puellum *A*: Nam tibi laturos e Perside
munera meque ***BO***.   120 Ducet *AO*: Docet *B*.   122 Rex — obesse tuo *A*: Rex [Rex *om*. *O*]
Herodes regni nomine tristis erit. / Namque canent illo sapientes tempore nasci, / Qui regat Israel
sceptra superba domus ***BO***.   125 nobisque *A*: vobisque ***BO***.

Are we then to let the grievous laments continue without end? Will you, savage Serpent, then always go unpunished? The fiery ether resounds with the incessant cry, "Loosen our bonds with your salvific hand!"

Moved to pity, I am drawn down to earth from my Father's heaven, and already, Virgin, I am a small part of your body. Do you sense it? Or are you still in doubt that your womb can be swelling up with the fetus it conceals? You are, after all, a raw recruit, new to motherhood. Moon, be quick to join your crescent horns whenever they flee each other, until [100] by the tenth month they have closed up nine times in all. Then Bethlehem of Judea will rejoice in my birth, as will the country-side that the farmers of Palestine plow.

Cold winter, white with icy hoarfrost, will prevail at the time when you first become a mother. No Dalmatian gold will cover my cradle. My birth will take place in the most abject poverty. Thus that God of yours, the Lord of creation, will be born under a humble roof and wail before the idle beasts. A God brought into a world that is my very own, amid hay and straw, [110] I want to set an example for all kings. But I will not be born in secret. There will be unheard-of jubilation, and every-thing will be filled with the light of my birth. Yes, and an angelic host will appear to the rude shepherds in the fields and celebrate the birth of God in song. All the people will worship the infant Jesus: for this will be my name at that time.

The news of my birth will spread to the East, and the Orient will recognize that God himself is lying in a cradle. Kings will come bearing gifts. [120] Leading the way, a star will guide the Magi to the babe, whom they will adore as King. Only the King of Jerusalem, a tyrant more cruel than the ancient Serpent, will seek to harm your son. By spilling Hebrew blood, he will hunt for the King of the Jews. Many a boy will fall victim to the merciless sword. You yourself and your son and our mutual helper Joseph will flee to the country

Ibimus antiquae regna propinqua Pharo.
Scilicet ex illo nondum mea tempore virtus
    Cognita, sic poterit dissimulare Deum.
Nata Deo, paritura Deum, decus addita Divis,

4=C2^r   130   An ubi legisti triste quid aegra doles?
Ne doleas. Nulli ignorant sua gaudia luctus.
    Prudenter caelo vindice nemo dolet.
Non tamen ignoro quam sis animosa virago!
    Fortiter in casus quoslibet ire potes.

135   Scimus enim sacris nondum satis apta dicari
    Quanta frequentandam feceris ante domum.
Scimus et ad sacras quam sancte vixeris aras,
    O digna immensum claudere sola Deum!
Scimus; et ut credas, nunquam te, Virgo, reliqui.

140   Me sine pars vitae nulla peracta tuae est.
Sive dabas castis manibus pia thura ministris
    Seu nivea ferres lumina fota manu
Et modo seu tenui stares vittata mitella
    Seu tibi iam vestis sive revincta coma est,

145   Ipse aderam praesensque meo cupiebar amori
    Nesciaque es votis saepe potita tuis.
"Hic meus ardor erit," dixi, "meus ignis in illa.
    Haec est in thalamos digna venire meos."
Sed neque caelesti descendam tectus in auro

150   Nec mihi mentitus suscipietur olor.
Qualiter imprudens mentita est cunque vetustas

C2^v   Viderit, ingenio nos meliore sumus.
Nostrum virginea Verbum calefiet in alvo,
    Ut solet a Zephyris crescere planta recens.

155   Sum tecum tecumque fui puerilibus annis
    Adque tuos mores officiosus eram.
Nunc quoque cum legeres, "Virgo est paritura Tonantem,"
    Optasti posses illius esse comes.
Adstabam dextraque humerum complexus eburnum,

160   "Tune comes," dixi, "quae potes esse parens?"

126–28 Ibimus — Deum *A*: Ibitis igniferae proxima regna Pharo. / Nempe latens divina sui nec prodiga virtus / Praesentem poterit dissimulare Deum, / Donec ab humana solvatur luce tyrannus. / Natum ex Aegypto tunc revocabo meum *BO*.   **130** ubi *A*: quia *BO*.   **142** fota *A*: vota *BO*.
143–44 Et — est, *A*: *om. BO*.   **146** potita *A*: petita *BO*.   **149** caelesti *A*: nubigeno *BO*.

[11]Pharos was a small island near Alexandria with a world-famous lighthouse. Here, as often, Pharos stands for Egypt as a whole. Cf. *Her. Chr.* 20.148.
[12]According to the legends, Mary lived at the Temple until her fourteenth year, when she was betrothed to Joseph. For the stories about the young Mary in the Temple — including her climbing all

near the ancient lighthouse of Pharos.[11] Naturally, since my
power will not yet be recognized at that time, it will not be
hard to conceal my divinity.

Daughter of God, future Mother of God, splendor added to
the Godhead, [130] you were not aggrieved, were you, as you
read about those dismal events? Do not grieve. Every sorrow has
its own joys. It is not wise to grieve when Heaven watches over
you. But I am well aware what a courageous heroine you are! You
are bold enough to confront whatever may befall. For we know
how much you accomplished before the house of worship while
still too young to devote yourself to religion. We know also what
a saintly life you led at the holy altars, O you, alone worthy of
compassing the boundless God![12]

We know this; and believe me, Virgin, I have never once left
your side. [140] No part of your life has ever been spent without
me. Whether you were chastely offering sacred incense to the
priests or holding the lighted candles with snow-white hand,
whether you were standing there wearing a gauze headband or
girding your dress or binding up your hair, I was there and
straightway desired you as my love. Without your realizing it, I
often answered your prayers. "She will be my true flame," I said.
"My fire will burn in her. She is worthy of becoming my bride."

But when I come into the world, I will neither conceal
myself in a shower of gold [150] nor will I disguise myself in the
form of a swan.[13] For whatever it is that foolish antiquity may
have seen, it played fast and loose with the truth. We are better
minded. Our Word will be warmed in a virgin's womb, as a
young seedling grows in the breezes of spring. I am with you and
have been with you since your earliest childhood and have zeal-
ously watched over your morals. Even now, as you were reading,
"A virgin shall bear the Thunderer,"[14] you were wishing you
could be a companion of hers. Standing next to you, I put my
hand on your ivory shoulder [160] and said, "Do you want to be
a companion, when you could be the mother?"

---

fifteen steps of the Temple unassisted at age three, her speaking with the maturity of a thirty-year-old,
and her life of perfect holiness — see *Ps.-Matt.* 6. Cf. *Nativ. Mariae* 6–7; *Leg. aurea* 127; Eob. *Her.
Chr.* 13.81–82.

[13]Emmanuel will not follow the example of Jupiter, who entered Danaë's impregnable tower in a
shower of gold (cf. *Her. Chr.* 10.121–22) and seduced Leda in the guise of a swan. Cf. Prud. *c. Symm.*
1.62–68; Eob. *Nup.* 203–04. Mary too alludes to these and similar myths in *Her. Chr.* 2.49.

[14]Isaiah 7.14. In later medieval literature and art Mary is often shown reading this prophecy at the
Annunciation. See Gertrud Schiller, *Ikonographie der christlichen Kunst*, vol.1 (Gütersloh, 1981), 53.

Nec mora, de superis legatus Gabriel inquit,
  "Vive, parens Domino, Virgo, futura meo."
I nunc et dubita, quis nuncius iste, quis ales,
  Quid sine mortali sis paritura viro!
165 Vade tamen (quoniam nunc suspitione levata es),
  Accepta in tacito gaudia conde sinu.
Paulatim incipiet gravidus turgescere venter,
  Nec vulgo metuas illa vel ista loqui.
Tunc ubi me vitae primum donaveris isti
170 Et populis pacem temporibusque feres,
Imperium Augustus Rhomanum Caesar habebit,
  Foelici usurus tempore, sorte mala.
Quamvis ille etiam nostrum monstrante Sybilla
  Numen adorabit, se tamen ante feret.

5=C3ʳ

175 Saecula nascentur mecum, non qualia fama est
  Falciferum nato deseruisse senem,
Sed quae cum superis mortalia nomina iungant
  Et superas faciant sponte patere domos.
Alta dehiscentis patefiet ianua caeli;
180 Claudetur Stygii regia magna Iovis.
Ipse ego degeneris confringam claustra tyranni
  Nocte sacrum victor Paschatis ante diem.
O, quantos Mariae lux adferet una dolores!
  Una dies matri gaudia quanta dabit!
185 Quinetiam sanctae renovabitur ordo quietis.
  Cessabunt curvae bella sonare tubae.
Impia preteritos horrescet Rhoma triumphos
  Signaque et antiqua rapta trophaea manu.
Omnis odoratas populus conversus ad aras
190 Martia securo conteret arma pede.
Scuta virum et galeas mordax rubigo peruret;
  Contempto fiet gratior ense ligo.
Tuta locupletes proscindent arva coloni;
  Sponte sua pinguis luxuriabit humus.
195 Tum nova procedet rebus natura creatis;

C3ᵛ Ordo qui renovet saecula maior erit.
Ultima tunc veniet Cumaei carminis aetas,
  Verus ut incauto spiritus ore canit.

165–66 Vade — Accepta *A*: Certa tui, non hoc hominum vulgaveris ulli, / Ista sed *BO*.   169 me *A*: nos *BO*.   171–74 Imperium — feret. *A*: *om. BO*.   175 nascentur mecum *A*: nobiscum venient *BO*.   179 Alta — caeli *A*: Ianua placati reserabitur aurea coeli *BO*.   181–84 Ipse — dabit! *A*: *om. BO*.   187–88 Impia — manu *A*: Caerula non aliquae consternent aequora classes, / Nulla cruentata cede rubebit humus *BO*.   192 Contempto *A*: Abiecto *BO*.   195–202 Tum — cadet *A*: Omnia liberius producet munera tellus, / Quae vix agricolis ante coacta dabat *BO*.   198 canit *scripsi*: canet *A*.

In a moment, God's envoy Gabriel will say, "Good-bye, Virgin, Mother-to-be of my Lord!" Go now and wonder who that messenger, that winged angel might be, or how you are to give birth without a mortal husband! Still, since you are now rid of your feeling of mistrust, go, keep silent about the joys you have heard of and ponder them in your heart. Little by little your gravid womb will begin to swell; but do not be afraid what people might say behind your back.

Then, when you have bestowed me to human life [170] and brought peace to the peoples and ages, Caesar Augustus will rule the Roman Empire. He will make good use of his time,[15] bad use of his position. For even though he too, taught by the Sibyl, will adore my divine power, he will nevertheless put himself ahead of me.[16] Together with me a new age will dawn — not the Golden Age that the old Sickle-bearer is supposed to have left to his son,[17] but an age that will join mortal beings with the celestials and cause the mansions on high to open of their own accord. Heaven's lofty gate will open wide; [180] the great palace of Stygian Jove[18] will be closed. I myself will conquer that degenerate tyrant and shatter his dungeons in the night before the sacred day of Easter. Oh, how much grief will one single day bring you, Mary! How much joy will one single day give to you, Mother! And furthermore, the order of holy peace will be restored. The coiling trumpets will cease to sound wars. Impious Rome will shudder at her former triumphs and at her banners and at the trophies captured by ancient hands. All the people will turn to the sweet-smelling altars [190] and trample the implements of war with fearless foot. Biting rust will corrode the warriors' shields and helmets; the sword will be cast aside in favor of the hoe. The prosperous farmers will till their fields in safety; the fertile soil will spontaneously yield rich crops. Then a new nature will appear in creation; a greater order will arise and renew the eons. Then will arrive "the last era of Cumaean prophecy," as the inspired poet sings with more truth than he knows.[19] The world

[15]That is, he will end the civil wars and restore peace and tranquillity to the empire.

[16]On the day when Jesus was born, Augustus asked the Sibyl if the world would ever see a greater man than he. Thereupon the Sibyl, seeing a vision of a Virgin holding a child, told the emperor that this boy would someday be greater than he. See *Leg. aurea* 6.92–98.

[17]The "old Sickle-bearer" is Saturn, an ancient Italic god of agriculture identified with Kronos. After being dethroned by his son Jupiter, he presided over the Golden Age. See Verg. *A.* 8.319–25; Ov. *Met.* 1.89–114.

[18]The realm of hell, ruled by Satan.

[19]See Verg. *Ecl.* 4.4, alluding to the oracles of the Sibyl of Cumae. In this "Messianic" eclogue Vergil predicts the birth of a Child and a return of the Golden Age.

Se tibi, non Rhomae debere fatebitur orbis —
200   Ah, male Caesaribus, Rhoma, superba tuis!
Attamen hoc veniet tempus quo totus et omnis
    Ex Capitolina Iuppiter arce cadet.
Caetera quae restant, tecum, Regina, loquemur
    Cum Deus assumpto corpore tectus ero.
205   Interea parva pondus gestabis in alvo
    Quod non angelici sustinuere chori.
Iam, brevis ut solito claudatur epistola verbo,
    Accipe quod praestas omnibus ipsa "vale."

203–04 Caetera — ero *A*: Caetera, quem paries, tecum Deus ipse, loquetur. / Scribere nunc soli fas erat ista tibi *BO*.   **203** quae *scripsi*: que *A*.   **207** Iam — verbo *A*: Iam, quod nemo potest nisi nos tribuisse roganti *BO*.

will confess that it owes everything to you, not to Rome —
[200] ah, Rome, falsely proud of your Caesars! And yet the time
will come when each and every statue of Jupiter will fall from the
Capitoline Hill.

There is still much more for us to talk about, Queen, but that
can wait until I, your God, am clothed in the body that I have put
on. In your small womb, meanwhile, you will bear a burden that
the choirs of angels are unable to sustain.

And now, so my brief letter may close with the customary
word, receive the wish that you yourself fulfill for all humanity:
Farewell.

2 MARIA EMMANUELI

Quam sine te non est tellus habitura salutem,
    Ut partam per me possit habere, veni.
Littera quod sparsis non convenit ista lituris,
    Hoc breve mortalis dextera foecit opus,
5   Dextera, quae calamum vix nunc tenet aegra labantem.
    Heu, miserae quanti ponderis instat onus!
Ausa humilis magno rescribere virgo Tonanti,
    Quam ferat, aggredior, mens mea, maius opus.
Cor pavet, attonito rubor est confusus in ore,
10   Et secum pugnant hinc amor, inde timor.
Quamvis nota satis tua sit clementia nobis,
    Maiestas cui non illa stupenda tua est?
Nunc tamen, unanimi Princeps ter maxime regni,
    Da veniam si plus quam decet audet amans.
15   Et facis, et non est te uno mansuetior alter.
    Audaces venia cogimur esse tua.
Tu facis ut precibus suffultus navita iustis
    Audeat incerto credere vela mari.
Martius ipse tuo confisus numine miles
20   Non timet armatis obvius ire globis.
Denique cuncta tua pietate pericula temnit
    Quisquis gentiles non putat esse deos.
Iure igitur vasti servit tibi machina caeli,
    Quicquid et haec extra, quicquid et intus habet.
25   Iure capax regnum tibi terminat igneus orbis —
    Si posset regni terminus esse tui!
Iure tuum nomen mundus reverenter adorat,
    Te quando includit mitius ille nihil.
Ergo metus omnes posui. Sic ipse iubebas.
30   Fas homini non est spernere iussa Dei.
Sic etiam iuvenum pulcherrimus ille monebat,
    Qui mihi non falso pectore dixit, "Ave."

6=C4ʳ

C4ᵛ

Her. Chr. **2.** *Tit.* Maria Emmanueli *A*: Maria Virgo Deo Patri *BO*. **6** Heu, miserae . . . instat *A*: Hei, miseram . . . urget *BO*. **9–10** Cor — timor. *A*: *om. BO*. **12** illa *A*: ista *BO*. **16** esse *A*: ista *BO*. **18** incerto *A*: immenso *BO*. **23** vasti *A*: magni *BO*; machina *A*: fabrica *BO*. **29** omnes *scripsi*: omnis *A*, omneis *BO*.

2   MARY TO EMMANUEL[1]

So that I may bring into the world the salvation it cannot have without you, come!

If this brief note, with its blots and erasures, is no match for your letter, it is because it was written by a mortal hand, a hand so shaky that it is barely able now to hold the faltering pen. Alas, what an immense burden weighs upon me, poor soul! A humble virgin, I have presumed to reply to the mighty Thunderer and am undertaking a task too great for my mind to bear. My heart is aflutter with terror. I feel dazed as the blood flushes to my cheeks [10] and one emotion battles another, with love on the one side, fear on the other. No matter how well I know your clemency, who would not be overawed by that majesty of yours?

But now, thrice highest Ruler of a harmonious realm, grant forgiveness if she who loves you is bolder than she should.

You will do so, for no one is gentler than you. By your very forgiveness you compel us to be bold. It is your doing that the sailor, braced with righteous prayers, dares to entrust his sails to the unpredictable sea. Relying on your power, the valiant soldier [20] is unafraid to confront massed troops in battle. Thanks to your loving-kindness, in short, they scorn all danger who reject the pagan gods.

It is only right, therefore, that the machinery of the vast heavens is subject to you, as is everything beyond it and everything within. It is only right that your capacious realm is bounded by the sphere of fire[2] — if indeed your realm can have any bounds at all! It is only right that the world reverently adores your name, because it holds nothing more merciful than you. Accordingly, I have laid aside all fear. You yourself bade me do so. [30] Human beings must not spurn the commands of God. This is also what that most beautiful of youths advised me, the one who offered me his unpretending "Hail!"

---

[1]Because the Annunciation, as represented in *Her. Chr.* 1, was an epistolary event, Mary now responds to Emmanuel in a letter of her own: "Behold, I am the handmaid of the Lord; let it be to me according to your word" (Luke 1.38).

Eobanus often lauds the Virgin, especially in his earlier writings. See *Buc.* 5 and 11; *Hod.* B 7 (= *Sylv.* 3.8) and B 8; and *Sylv.* 2.27. She is also prominently featured in *Her. Chr.* 13 and 16. On the Mariology of the Renaissance humanists, see Hanna-Barbara Gerl, "Geschenk der Natur und des Himmels," in *Maria — für alle Frauen oder über allen Frauen?*, ed. E. Gössmann and D. R. Bauer (Freiburg i. Br., 1989), 116–45. See further Walter Delius, *Geschichte der Marienverehrung* (Munich, 1963), 191–95.

In the 1532/39 version this letter is *Her.* 1.2.

[2]According to medieval-Renaissance cosmology, the earth is surrounded by ten physical spheres. Beyond them lies the *caelum empyreum* (sphere of fire) where God and the angels reside. Cf. *Her. Chr.* 4.75; also l. 69 below.

Iam super Oceanum madido sol crine pependit;
    Flammiferae noctis nuncius ortus erat.
35 Sola fui thalamumque sera custode coegi.
    In manibus Solimi carmina vatis erant.
"Concipiet natum virgo paritura," legebam,
    Docta prius tanti mystica sacra viri.
"Nascere, magna parens. Foelix age fulgeat ortus!
40   Afflictis," dixi, "gentibus affer opem.
O mihi si liceat, quacunque in stirpe futura es,
    Aptarem famulas ad tua iussa manus!
Quae te digna manet genitrix, o filia maior?
    Nulla potest laudes lingua referre tuas.
45 O et foeminei, o et sine labe pudoris
    Gloria, spes in te nostra salusque manet.
Tu quoque, mundi Opifex, imple praesagia vatum.
    Pondere te foelix fiat onusta parens.
Fama Iovem falsum tot habet latuisse figuris
50   Et tot ficticios monstra fuisse deos.
Ante deos ostende Deum! De virgine nasci
    Da populis solum te potuisse fidem."

7=C5ʳ

Sic ego secreto mentis meditata recessu,
    Conticui — coram nuncius ales erat!
55 Qualis purpureum referens Aurora colorem,
    Qualis ab Oceana Lucifer exit aqua,
Talis erat niveo iuvenis velatus amictu.
    Mortalem credi non potuisse liquet.
Aurea caesaries humeros complexa comantes
60   Fulsit, et in dextra pacis oliva fuit.
Qui simul intravit tenebrasque removit obortas,
    Curvato missum poplite dixit "Ave."
Obstupui. Vocem timor abstulit. Unde quod ales
    Mirabar clausas transiit iste fores.
65 "Ne timeas, Maria," ille refert, "nam Spiritus in te
    Et tecum virtus Omnipotentis erit."
"Docta voluntatemque tuam iussumque Parentis,
    Pareo mandatis, Orbifer alme, tuis.
Labere perque alti, tua regna, voluminis orbes
70   Mitibus haec oculis inferiora vide.
En iacet et lachrymis moestus tibi supplicat orbis,
    'Sollicitas audi, Gloria nostra, preces.'"
Dum loquor, ecce levi velut auctior effluit alvus
    Pondere, nec laesi damna pudoris habet!

---

38 sacra *A*: scripta *BO*.   **46** manet *A*: manent *BO*.   **54** nuncius *A*: palmifer *BO*.   **57** velatus *A*: vestitus *BO*.   **67** iussumque Parentis *A*: meque ipsa resumens *BO*.   **71** moestus *A*: mersus *BO*. **73** effluit *A*: ebulit *BO*.

The sun, his locks already drenched, was hanging low above the ocean; the harbinger of star-studded night[3] had just appeared. Being alone, I locked the door of my chamber. In my hands were the prophecies of Jerusalem's seer. "A virgin shall conceive and bear a son,"[4] I read, well instructed as I was in the mystical writings of the great man.

"Be born, great mother," I exclaimed. "Let your blessed birth shine forth! [40] Give succor to the afflicted nations. Oh, if I had the chance, no matter from what stock you came, I would place myself at your every beck and call! What mother remains worthy of you, O greater daughter? No tongue can sing your praises. O immaculate Virgin, O ornament of feminine chastity, our hope for salvation rests on you. You too, Maker of the world, fulfill the prophecies of the seers. Let the blessed mother become heavy with you, the burden of her womb. It is said that the false Jove disguised himself in a multitude of forms [50] and that a great number of feigned gods are monstrosities. Before the gods reveal God! Prove to the peoples that you alone are able to be born of a virgin."

After I had pondered these things in the hidden recesses of my mind, I fell silent — in front of me there stood a winged messenger! Like the Dawn, when she restores her radiant blush to the sky, like the Morning Star, as he rises from the ocean wave, such was that youth, clad in raiment as white as snow. Obviously he could not be taken for a mortal. The golden locks that enveloped his shoulders [60] gleamed brightly, and in his right hand he held the olive branch of peace. As soon as he entered and dispelled the darkness that had fallen, he knelt down and offered the "Hail" he had been sent to say. I felt paralyzed, struck dumb with fear, bewildered at how this angel could have passed right through the closed door.

"Do not be afraid, Mary," he said, "for the Spirit will come over you and the power of the Almighty will be with you."

"Instructed in your will and the command of the Father, I obey your commands, O gracious Sustainer of the world. Glide down from heaven, and through the spheres of the celestial globe that is your realm [70] look upon these nether regions with merciful eyes. Behold, the sorrowful world lies prostrate before you and tearfully implores, 'You, our Glory, hear our anxious prayers.'"

As I speak, lo, my womb seems to grow fuller, as if with a slight burden, and yet suffers no loss or violation of its chastity!

---

[3] The evening star.
[4] Isaiah 7.14. Cf. Eob. *Her. Chr.* 1.157, with n. 14 (p. 167 above).

C5ᵛ   75 Ergo ego, quam toto cupiebam corde futuram,
                       Quam colui tantis laudibus, ipsa fui?
                   Ipsa mihi placui! Votis ignosce peractis.
                       Excidit in laudes inscia lingua suas.
                   Ergo ego digna fui mundo promissa iacenti
               80   Solvere et in terras ducere virgo Deum?
                   Digna fui; quis enim poterit te iudice falli?
                       Digna fui, quia te iudice digna fui.
                   Te mea virginitas, tua me claementia movit.
                       Non agitur forma praesule noster amor!
               85 Pulchra tibi mentis facie, pulcherrime rerum,
                       Quod placui, sed non qualibet arte, iuvat.
                   Est aliquid placuisse Deo, super omnia matrem
                       Esse Dei! Hoc meriti non leve pondus habet.
                   Scribis ut a primis mecum Deus egeris annis —
               90   O pietas terris non habitura locum!
                   Ipsa quoque ardentes seu te venerabar ad aras
                       Seu legerem clausa carmina sancta domo,
                   Seu tibi, non oculis hominum, gestamina sumpsi
                       Et nondum sacris apta sacerdos eram,
               95 Tu mihi tu praesens amor et meditatio dulcis,
                       Una tibi semper cura placere fuit.
8 = C6ʳ   Ah quoties, quaerente aliqua quid sola fuissem,
                       Fingebam effluxo cingula lapsa sinu!
                   Caelestes adii te contemplata recessus.
              100   Tu mihi tuta quies, tu mihi somnus eras.
                   Iusserat Anna parens, genitor Ioachime, monebas
                       Legitimo summum claudere fine decus.
                   Scilicet esse viro foecundam prole caduca
                       Quam non mortali semine maius erat?
              105 Quam bene constantem iuvisti in virgine mentem,
                       Quod non sum cupido nupta puella viro!
                   Ad tua confugi supplex altaria, crevi
                       Virgineos inter parva ministra choros.
                   Nunc tribus incipio quartum superaddere lustrum
              110   Et mea primaevo flore iuventa viret.
                   Eligor, Anna, tibi magnum paritura nepotem!
                       O quanti generi flos erit iste tuo!
                   Sed tibi quid refero, quae me prior omnia nosti?
                       Omne quod est usquam scitque videtque Deus.

---

88 leve *AO*: bene *B*.   **94** sacerdos eram *A*: ministra fui *BO*.   **98** effluxo *A*: fluxo *BO*.
104 Quam *A*: Qua *BO*.   **106** nupta puella *A*: tradita nupta *BO*.   *Post* **106** *add. BO*: Ille quidem caste, cui sum data nupta, sororem / Maluit et prior est virginitate mihi.

Was I myself then the one I yearned for with all my heart, the one I venerated with so much praise? I have been flattering myself! Forgive the wishes that have now come true. Without knowing it my tongue has lapsed into self-praise. Was I, then, worthy of fulfilling the promises made to the prostrate world [80] and, a virgin, of bringing God into the world? I was worthy of it; for who could be deceived with you as judge? I was worthy of it, because I was found worthy in your sight. You felt moved by my virginity, I by your merciful grace. It is not external beauty, first and foremost, that drives this love of ours! To you I am beautiful in the countenance of my soul, O most beautiful of beings. That I pleased you like this, and not by some artifice, is a profound joy. It is something to have pleased God, above all to be the mother of God! That is a merit of no mean distinction.

You write that you have been with me as God since my earliest childhood — [90] O loving-kindness without equal on earth! I too have never stopped thinking of you. Whether I was venerating you at the burning altars or reading the holy prophets behind closed doors at home, or put on ornaments for you, not for the eyes of men, and was your priestess when still too young to devote myself to religion, you, you were always present in my thoughts as my love, my sweet meditation. To please you was always my only concern. Ah, how often, when one of the girls asked me why I was keeping to myself, I pretended the girdle had slipped from my flowing dress! It was the heavenly abodes I was approaching, to contemplate you. [100] You were my safe repose, you my sleep.

My mother Anna bade me, my father Joachim urged me to crown the ultimate honor of chastity with holy wedlock. But come now, was it really nobler to be fruitful with the short-lived offspring of a man than with immortal seed? How well you supported my resolve to remain a virgin by not having me married to some lustful man! Humbly praying, I took refuge at your altars; I grew up a little acolyte among the choirs of virgins. To my three lusters I am now starting to add a fourth, [110] and my youth is blooming in its first flower. I have been chosen, Anna, to bear you a mighty grandson! Oh, how much will your family cherish that blossom!

But why am I telling you this, seeing that you knew everything long before I did? God knows and sees everything that happens on earth. Even though you are all-seeing, even though

115 Cuncta licet videas, semper licet omnia noris,
    Saepe tamen dici te tua facta iuvat.
Nam quid odoratas votis placaris ad aras
    Et facili iustas percipis aure preces?
C6ᵛ Si tamen ignotum quicquam tibi scribere coner,
120   Inde quod expectes nuda papyrus erit.
Finge loqui coramque rudes offerre tabellas;
    Mortalem non est posse docere Deum.
Clause sub hac lutea nostrae testudine carnis,
    Littera praesenti traditur ista tibi.
125 Attamen aedidimus scriptas utcunque lituras.
    Non erat in parva virgine grande sophos.
Non precor ut valeas, per quem valet omne quod usquam est.
    Illud idem verum possit ut esse, fave.

119–22 Si tamen — Deum. *A: om. BO.*   **123** Clause *A:* Clausa *BO*; nostrae *BO*: nostri *A* (*sed corr. manus vetus in A¹ et A⁴*).   **125–26** Attamen — sophos. *A: om. BO.*

you are all-knowing, you nevertheless delight in often having your deeds recounted. For why are you placated by offerings at the sweet-smelling altars? And why do you lend a willing ear to righteous prayers? If nevertheless I tried to write you something you did not know, [120] all you could expect from the effort is a blank sheet of paper. We may imagine that we are talking to God and presenting him with an awkward letter; to tell the Deity something new is beyond the power of us mortals.

Enclosed as you are beneath the clayey shelter of my flesh, you are getting this letter on the spot. Yet for all that, I have managed to write little more than blots and erasures. This little virgin does not pretend to great wisdom.

I am not going to close with a "Farewell." It is through you, after all, that everything in the world fares well. So that this may indeed come true, be gracious unto us.

3   MARIA MAGDALENA IESU CHRISTO

Mittere quam nequeo, largitus es ipse salutem,
    Nomen ut a victa morte "Redemptor" habes.
Regna iacent certe Stygio confusa profundo.
    Vix aliquis tanti qui peteretur erat.
5   Qualis apud manes fueris, quem viceris hostem,
    Audet apud superos garrula Fama loqui.
Vicisti, Mors victa iacet, redis, optime victor,
    Plurimaque est reditus turba sequta tuos.
Iamque aliquis, longa tecum de morte reversus,
10   Talia barbatos predicat ante patres:

9=D1ʳ

"Est locus, aeterna qua saeva voragine tellus
    Panditur et scaevo sulphure fumus olet.
Accipit hic sontes animas locus inque perhennes
    Exercet poenas perpetuasque cruces.
15   Vestibulum ante patet longo incomplebile tractu.
    Non est in Stygia crassior umbra domo.
Illuc nos serie saeclorum longa vetustas
    Clausit, et Adami noxa luenda patris.
Post duo fluxerunt decies iam saecula quinque
20   Victaque mortali bis tria lustra Deo.
Venit ad aeternae noctis loca luminis Author;
    Nubila divinum dispulit atra iubar.
Nec mora, disiectis patuerunt atria valvis,
    Unde vetus Dominum turba sequta sumus.
25   Pars habet aeterno viridantes germine colles.
    Corpora, quos secum surgere iussit, habent."
Praedicat haec aliquis. Sentit contraria vulgus,
    Sunt tamen et Solimae credula turba nurus.
Illae etiam, durae quum iam loca mortis adires,
30   Flebant impositam pondus habere crucem.

Her. Chr. 3.   **3** Stygio — profundo *A*: mortis, te, vita, perempto *BO*.   **7** redis — victor *A*: victorque redisti *BO*.   **11** saeva *A*: rupta *BO*.   **12** scaevo *A*: foedo *BO*.   **17** Illuc *A*: Illo *BO*.   **19** Post — quinque *A*: Post duo secla ierant decies quinque orbis ab ortu *BO*.   *Post* **22** *add. BO*: Tum nova degeneres lux aedita terruit umbras. / Victrices metuit plurima turba manus.

[1]Together with the other two Marys, Mary Magdalene has come to Christ's sepulcher early on Easter morning. She has found his tomb open and has heard the angel bring the good tidings. But Christ has not yet appeared to her, as he had promised her. Now, at midday, she sends him this urgent prayer of supplication. The reader knows from the Gospel stories that Jesus will not disappoint her. See Matthew 28.1–10, Mark 16.1–13, Luke 24.1–12, and, especially, John 20.1–18.

3   MARY MAGDALENE TO JESUS CHRIST[1]

The wish for salvation that I cannot send, you yourself have fulfilled, now that your victory over death has earned you the title "Redeemer." The Stygian realms, certainly, lie in ruins. Scarcely anyone was worthy of being rescued like this.

How you appeared among the shades, what enemy you vanquished, chattering Rumor ventures to report among the living. You have conquered, your conquest has left Death prostrate, you have returned, O best of conquerors, and a great throng has accompanied your return. And just now, someone who came back with you from long death [10] proclaims this story before the bearded fathers:[2] "There is a place where the wild earth opens into a bottomless pit and the fumes reek of noxious brimstone. This place receives the souls of evildoers and casts them into everlasting punishment and unremitting torments. In front of it extends an entrance hall, so vast that it can never be filled up. Nowhere in the house of Styx is the darkness thicker than here. It was there that we were confined throughout a series of ages, since time immemorial, to expiate the sin of our father Adam. Already fifty-two centuries had passed, [20] as well as the thirty-odd years that the mortal God lived through.[3] To the abodes of eternal night came the Author of light. His divine radiance dispelled the murky gloom. At once the doors were shattered, the great hall stood open, whence we, an aged throng, followed the Lord. Some now dwell on the hills verdant with eternal buds. Those whom he bade rise with him received bodies."

Someone or other is proclaiming these things. The people are of two minds, but there are also some women in Jerusalem eager to believe. When you were already approaching the place of your cruel death, [30] it was they who wept at the burden of the cross they had laid on you.

Mary Magdalene's letter arises out of her passionate longing to see the risen Christ, but is strongly colored by consciousness of her past sinfulness (see n. 7 below). Accordingly, the letter's structure is that of the forensic oration: introduction (ll. 1–8); narrative (9–94); argumentation, aiming chiefly to arouse sympathy for her plight (95–148); conclusion, with a final appeal to the emotions (149–74). For other letters with this type of structure, see *Her. Chr.* 8, 14, and 23.

In the 1532/39 version this letter is *Her.* 1.3. In that redaction, Mary Magdalene writes her letter after a full ten days have elapsed since the Resurrection.

[2]After Karinus and Leucius, the sons of Simeon, rose from the dead with Christ, they told the story of the Harrowing of Hell to the high priests Annas and Caiaphas as well as to Nicodemus, Joseph, and Gamaliel. See *Nicodem.* 17–26.

[3]By medieval reckoning Jesus was born 5,199 years after the creation of Adam. See *Her. Chr.* 1.71–72, with n. 8. Christ was about thirty when he began his three-year ministry: see Luke 3.23.

Iam subit illius tristissima lucis imago,
    Qua Iudaea tuo est sanguine facta nocens.

D1^v

Hei mihi, qualis eras! Quantum crudele luisti
    Supplicium, quod te non meruisse liquet!

35   Qualis erat quae te propere moestissima mater
    Est vinctum in mediis hostibus ausa sequi!

Flebat, et in terram quoties defecta cadebat,
    Vix qui semianimem tolleret unus erat.

Unus Ioannes custos fidissimus illi
40   Semper erat; nullo defuit ille loco.

Tunc mihi, si qua mori moerendo foemina posset,
    Trux potuit vitae terminus esse dolor.

Namque quis ista videns dirae nova nomina mortis
    Plorantes rigido non secet ungue genas?

45   Territa neglexit leges Natura suetas,
    Morte tua quando est nostra redempta salus.

Sol rubuit faciemque atro velavit amictu;
    Informis medio nox erat orta die.

Omnia non moto stupuerunt sydera mundo.
50   Vix etiam misere quassa resedit humus.

Per sua demissi ceciderunt culmina montes;
    Saxa procul querulo dissiluere sono.

Multaque quae trepidum sunt visa horrenda per orbem
    Non tulit imparibus littera nostra modis.

10=D2^r   55   Condoluit Natura tuae, Rex optime, morti,
    Et merito, quia tu Conditor huius eras.

Sola fuit rabies recutitae interrita gentis,
    Infula quam secta deside bina fovet.

Sed mihi quid moesti scripturae gaudia versus?
60   Tristia cum fuerint victa referre iuvat.

Tristia vicisti, victorem mundus adorat,
    Et solvit meritas terra redempta preces.

Victor, ubi es? Nec enim miserae te invenimus usquam,
    Quaesitum longo tempore. Victor, ubi es?

65   Et vacat iste locus quo te posuere sepultum,
    Et nusquam nobis conspiciendus abes.

Nondum Phoebaeos Aurora reduxerat ignes
    Vixque novum tremulo lumine mane fuit.

Nobilibus sumpsi preciosa alabastra venenis;
70   Exanimes artus ungere cura fuit.

---

33 Quantum *ABO*: Quam tum *Laurens*.   **41–42** mihi . . . / Trux — dolor *A*: ego . . . / Mortua funesto fracta dolore fui *BO*.   **49** non moto . . . mundo *A*: tunc stabili . . . coelo *BO*.   **57–58** Sola — fovet. *A*: *om. BO*.   **59** quid *A*: quo *BO*; moesti . . . versus *ABO*: maesta . . . versu *Laurens*.   **62** preces *A*: vices *BO*.   **63–66** Victor — abes. *A*: *om. BO*.   **67** Nondum Phoebaeos *A*: Non satis Eoos *BO*.

Now the heart-rending memory of that day steals upon me, the day Judea became guilty of shedding your blood. Oh, what a harrowing sight you were! What a brutal punishment you suffered, one you obviously did not deserve! What a figure of sorrow your mother was, as she unflinchingly dared to follow you, bound amid your enemies! She wept; but whenever she fell to the ground in a swoon, there was hardly anyone who would lift her up, though she was more dead than alive. John was the only one who always looked after her with the utmost devotion; [40] never once did he leave her side. If ever a woman could die of sheer anguish, the savage grief would certainly have been the end of me. For who could watch you die in that strange and horrible way without scratching her tearful cheeks with relentless nail?

Terrified, Nature ignored her customary laws when our salvation was ransomed with your death. The sun turned red and covered his face in a black mantle; hideous night had fallen at midday. In the unmoving sky all the stars stood still. [50] The pitifully shaken earth, too, could hardly stop trembling. Mountains came crashing down from their summits, and far in the distance rocks split asunder with a plaintive groan. Many other horrifying events were seen throughout the fearful world, but my letter in elegiac verse cannot bear to describe them. Nature mourned your death, best of kings, and rightly so, because you were her Creator. The only ones not terrified were the frenzied Jews, that circumcised race whom the two high priests encourage in their shiftlessness.[4]

But what are these sad verses to me, since I was intending to write about joyous things? [60] When we have put tribulations behind us, it is a joy to talk about them. You have conquered the tribulations, the world adores the conqueror, and the redeemed earth offers the prayers of thanks you deserve. Conqueror, where are you? For we wretched women cannot find you anywhere, though we have searched a long time. Conqueror, where are you? That place where they laid you to rest is empty. You have left us and are nowhere to be seen.

Aurora had not yet brought back Phoebus' fires, and day was just beginning to break with glimmering light. I took precious alabaster flasks of the finest balm [70], for I was anxious to anoint your lifeless limbs. By chance, two other women came

---

[4]Glosses in the Munich and Münster copies explain that the high priests Annas and Caiaphas encouraged the people in "their idle conspiracy" ("otiosa conspiratione").

Forte duae mecum — cognominis utraque nostra est —
    Quas non ex uno sustulit Anna viro.
Venimus ad clausi nuper loca visa sepulchri,
    Unde data est oculis littera nostra tuis.
75   Ecce sed ad dextram, dubitantibus omnia nobis,
    Ignoti visa est forma stupenda viri.

D2^v

Candidior nivibus vestis, coma purior auro,
    Plurimus in pulchro lumine fulgor erat.
Constitimus, subitaque retro formidine lapsas
80   Talibus impavidas vocibus esse iubet:
"Lugentes Mariae, nihil hic timeatis. Iesum
    Quaeritis. Est isto visus abire loco.
Rura prior Galilaea petet, nulli ante videndus.
    Dicite ut haec Petrus discipulique sciant."
85   Haec ita laetifico de te sermone loquto
    Tradita sunt manibus verba notata meis.
Illo namque breves elegos dictante notavi.
    Praebuerant dulcem frigida saxa thorum.
Ad tumulum comites, pro te tua signa rigantes
90   Fletibus, impresso procubuere genu.
Ipsa breves dextra feci famulante tabellas;
    Decidit in formas lachryma multa rudes.
Namque ut erant longo nova gaudia mista dolori,
    Laeticia hinc lachrymas aedidit, inde dolor.
95   Gratulor applaudoque tuae super omnia palmae;
    At dolor a vultu peior abesse tuo est.
Dum licuit, dulci obsequio te, Christe, colebam,
    Unaque te requies posse videre fuit.

11=D3^r

Testis Martha soror, quam te constanter amavi.
100   Illa meas flammas est quoque questa tibi.
Dicebas, "Nimium turbaris, Martha," recordor.
    "Electa foelix est tua parte soror."

---

71 nostra *ABO*: nostri **Laurens**.   72 Quas — viro *A*: Gaudebant comites illius esse viae *BO*.
73 visa *A*: nota *BO*.   74 Unde — tuis *A*: Deiectum grandi pondere marmor erat *BO*.   75 ad
dextram *A*: a dextris *BO*.   83 nulli — videndus *A*: sic ante monebat *BO*.   85–87 loquto —
notavi *A*: locutum / Nescio, sed stupidas deseruisse puto. / Ipsa quidem nimio confusa timore resedi
BO.   88 dulcem *A*: moestum *BO*.   89–92 Ad tumulum — rudes. *A*: *om. BO*.   **Post**
94 *add. BO*: Certe ibi dum comites fugientes assequor, aut te / Vidimus, aut oculos lusit imago tui. /
Vidimus at certe, nec enim tetigisse, nec ante, / Somnus erat, sacros procubuisse pedes.   **99** amavi
A: amarim *BO*.   100–01 Illa — recordor *A*: Quo se desertam tempore questa tibi. / Dicebas,
memini, "Nil te res ista moretur *BO*.   100 questa *BO*: quaesta *A*.

with me. Daughters of Anna by different husbands, they both bear the same name as I.[5] Together we arrived at the tomb that we had just recently seen being closed up. It is from there that my letter has been brought before your eyes. But behold, on our right we saw an astonishing figure — a man completely strange to us! We did not know what to make of him. His robe was whiter than snow, his hair purer than gold, and in his lovely eyes there was many a sparkle. We stood stock-still. But then, as we shrank back in sudden panic, [80] he told us in the following words to be unafraid: "Grieving Marys, you have nothing to be afraid of here. You seek Jesus. As you can see, he has left this place. He is going before you to Galilee and will not appear to anyone until then. Tell this to Peter and the disciples, so they will know."

The messenger who brought us the joyful news about you is also the one to whom I entrusted this letter, written with my own hand. Indeed, it is he who inspired me to commit these brief elegiacs to writing. The cool stones provided a pleasant couch. My companions fell to their knees by the graveside. Not having you to weep over, they drenched the place where you had lain [90] with a stream of tears. I myself composed this short letter with ministering hand; many a tear falls down upon the clumsy lines. For since my newfound joys are still mixed with long anguish, happiness provokes tears on the one side, grief on the other.

I rejoice with you and above all applaud your victory; but this only worsens my grief at being out of your sight.

While it was still possible, Christ, I devoted myself to you with sweet solicitude, and my one solace was being able to see you. My sister Martha can testify how faithfully I loved you. [100] Once she even complained to you about my ardent love. But you, as I remember, told her: "Martha, you worry too much. Your sister is blessed in the portion she has chosen." For your

[5]According to her legend, Anna had three husbands, Joachim, Cleophas, and Salome. By each she had a daughter named Mary, the first being the Virgin Mary. See, for example, *Leg. aurea* 127.19–26; Eob. *Her. Chr.* 13.131–34; cf. *Her. Chr.* 16.51–60; *Vict.* 468. The legend was already being criticized before the Reformation. After 1517 it could no longer be taken seriously. In the 1532/39 version, therefore, all references to the "trinubium" are carefully excised.

The Gospels agree that Mary Magdalene visited Christ's sepulcher on Easter morning, but offer somewhat conflicting versions about her companions. Matthew 28.1 says that she was accompanied by "the other Mary"; Mark 16.1 mentions "Mary the mother of James, and Salome"; Luke 24.10 refers to "Joanna and Mary the mother of James and the other women"; while John 20.1–18 speaks only about Mary Magdalene. Some medieval authors, however, give Salome's full name as "Maria Salome" (Mary, the daughter of Anna's third husband Salome). See, for example, Petrus Comestor, *Historia scholastica*, "Historia evangelica" 183, *PL* 198, col. 1635 C.

Nostra domus spreta est te propter Magdala nobis,
   Unde vetus claris nomen habemus avis.
105 Nuper et indigenas populos ubicunque docebas,
   Ipsa tibi famulae pars quota plebis eram.
Tunc quoque cum lachrymis supplex tua membra rigarem,
   "Quam bene," dicebas, "quam sapienter amat!"
Gaudia moverunt lachrymas concepta profusas,
110 Ut fluit a tepido nix liquefacta iugo.
Me miseram culpasse ferunt Simona dolentem,
   Hospitii per quem iure receptus eras.
Culparunt reliqui mea vota. Ego denique flebam,
   Quae deflenda magis quam prohibenda fui.
115 Hei mihi, quam certe mundi data praeda tyranno!
   Ne raperer, venia sum revocata tua.
Per mala Tartareo nupsi connubia regi —
   Quam bene apud manes fraus mea nomen habet!
Gratia, Christe, tibi! Tua me clementia salvam
120 Foecit et optato iussit amore frui.
Iesu, noster amor, iam non moriture Redemptor,
   Iam non mortali carne vidende, veni!
Langueo ut aestivis exustum solibus arvum;
   Areo ut in sicco quae sitit herba solo.
125 Perdita sim si non triduum hoc mihi longius anno est,
   Per quod fide tuo pro grege pastor abes.
Iamdudum incipio tempus numerare querique
   Tam longos tardis passibus ire dies.
Ibimus, est animus, Galilaeaque rura petemus,
130 Sed tamen hic nobis ante videndus eras.
Arva patent oculis vigilantibus obvia; caelum
   Metior, at nulla, spes mea, parte venis.
Iam medium aspirat mundi sol aureus axem,
   Vixque habet exiguum quaelibet umbra locum,
135 Nec tamen appares. Et iam vicinia tota
   Cantat ut inferni viceris arma ducis.

D3ᵛ

103–20 Nostra — frui. *A*: *om. BO*.   125–28 Perdita — dies *A*: Nunc mihi quot soles abeunt, tot metior annos; / Mensis habet spacium quaelibet hora mihi. / Nunc desyderio iustisque doloribus angi, / Nunc didici vero quid sit amore capi *BO*.   133–36 Iam — ducis *A*: Iamque abiere decem, tantum non saecula, luces, / Quas, quia sunt, potui dicere pene cruces. / Nec tamen appares, et nos te, Christe, volentes / Quaerere nemo viam quae sit eunda docet *BO*.

sake we gave up our house in Magdala, whence our illustrious family takes its ancient name.[6] No matter where you went to teach the local peoples in recent months, I myself was a small part of those who flocked to serve you. Then too, when I humbly moistened your limbs with my tears, you exclaimed, "How well, how wisely she loves!" The joy you gave me made the tears course down my cheeks, [110] as melted snow flows from a mountain in spring. They say that Simon the leper reproached me, poor woman, when you were a guest in his house. The others blamed me for my offering. Finally I began to weep, I, who was more to be pitied than restrained. Alas, how inexorably was I doomed to be a prey to the tyrant of this world! By your forgiveness I was snatched from his jaws. In sinful union I had wedded the king of Tartarus — how notorious is my crime among the shades in hell![7] Thanks be to you, Christ! Your mercy saved me [120] and bade me enjoy the love that I had yearned for.

Jesus, my beloved, now no longer destined to die, my Redeemer, no longer visible in mortal flesh, come! I languish like a field withering under the summer sun; I wilt like grass thirsting in parched soil. May I perish if these last three days have not seemed longer than a year, while you, faithful shepherd, have been gone for the sake of your flock.[8] For some time now I have begun counting the hours and lamenting that the long days are creeping by at such a slow pace.

We shall go — that is our intent — and make for Galilee. [130] All the same, you ought first to have appeared to us here. The fields stretch out before my watchful eyes; I look up and down the sky, but nowhere do I see you coming, my hope. Already the golden sun is nearing the midpoint of the sky and there is virtually no shadow anywhere; yet still there is no sign of you. And now the whole vicinity exults that you have conquered the prince of hell.

---

[6]According to *Leg. aurea* 92.16–19 and 101.1–3, Mary Magdalene, Martha, and Lazarus came from an ancient line of kings. Their father was governor of Syria and the coastal lands; Mary and her sister Martha were hereditary rulers of Magdala, Bethany, and part of Jerusalem. Cf. Eob. *Her. Chr.* 22.32.

[7]Eobanus identifies Mary Magdalene, out of whom Jesus had cast seven demons (Luke 8.2; Mark 16.9), with the Mary of Bethany who anointed Christ's feet and head (Matthew 26.6–7; Mark 14.3; John 11.2, 12.3) as well as with the sinful woman who washed Christ's feet with her tears and dried them with her hair (Luke 7.36–50, combined with Luke 8.2). Rejected by many of the Greek Fathers, this identification was popularized in the West by Gregory the Great, *Homiliae in Evangelia* 2.25 (*PL* 76, col. 1189–96) and 2.33.1 (*PL* 76, col. 1239). In the 1532 edition Eobanus excised ll. 105–18, partly for stylistic reasons, but mostly because the doctrine had by then been seriously questioned, particularly by Jacques Lefèvre d'Etaples in his *De Maria Magdalena et triduo Christi* (Paris, 1517) and *De tribus et unica Magdalena disceptatio* (Paris, 1519). He let the identification stand at some less-exposed places, however: see *Her.* 1.3.147–48 and 3.6.140 (Mary Magdalene as a sinful woman); 2.4, ll. 1 and 123 (Mary Magdalene as the sister of Martha and Lazarus).

[8]That is, ever since Christ was crucified on Good Friday.

Reddita testatur mundus tua signa renascens,
    Gaudet et in reditu quicquid ubique tuo.
Nunc iterum spondent Solimi sua balsama colles.
140   Reddit odoratas Hierichus alta rosas.
Verna cupressiferae praetexunt pallia sylvae.
    Ornat Idumaeum florida palma nemus.
Nubifer aestivos aperit Carmelus honores.
    Botrifera Engaddi vitis opacat humum.
145   Cuncta tibi redeunt, tecum simul omnia surgunt.
    Nos sine laetitia, nos sine honore sumus.
Author, ubi es, rerumque potens Reparator, Iesu?
    In melius versi temporis Author, ubi es?
Dum queror, ac mecum doleant, nisi falsa notavi,
150   Flexerunt tremulum lilia moesta caput.
Frigida pendentes commoverat aura capillos.
    Respitio; nullus post mea terga fuit.
Vidi aliquid, species amor obtulit. Inter eundum
    Constiteram et mixto laeta timore fui.
155   Aspitio quae tu loca frequentare solebas —
    Hei, loca non oculis dulcia, ut ante, meis,
Grata tamen, quia te referunt, quia grata fuerunt.
    Sic etiam ex ista parte dolere iuvat.
Nunc tua, quae possum pro te, vestigia tango,
160   Et lachrymas propior conbibit herba meas.
Aspicis hec oculis, sed non quibus ante solebas.
    Nec lachrymae nec te nostra querela movet.
An quia mortalis iam desinis esse, refugis
    Et mihi non unquam conspiciendus abes?
165   Corpora peccatrix non sum tua digna videre?
    Hei, qur ulla timet crimina noster amor?
Digna licet non sim, potui tamen esse videri.
    Da veniam, pietas nunc ubi tanta tua est?
Quid meruere alii, si te mihi, Christe, negabis,
170   Quid reliquus moesta cum genitrice chorus?
Restat ut accedat nostro tua gratia voto.
    Cura alias moestam nulla levare potest.
Te genitrix, te, noster amor, duodenaque turba,
    Te bonus hoc anima supplice quisque rogat.

---

140 Reddit — Hierichus *A*: Hierichus vernas exhibet *BO*.   144 Engaddi vitis *A*: Ergaddi vites *BO*.
Post 148 *add. BO*: Vicisti, Mors victa iacet victamque fatetur, / Iamque triumphatas porrigit illa manus. /
Victor, ubi es? Nec enim miserae te invenimus usquam. / Quaesitus longo tempore, victor, ubi es? [*cf. vv. 7*
et 63–64.]   155 Aspitio — solebas *A*: Aspicio loca nobiscum tibi culta frequenter *BO*.   156 Hei *A*:
Haec *B*, Heu *O*.   159 quae *BO*: que *A*.   160 propior *A*: proprior *BO*.   163 refugis *A*: recedis
BO.   164 unquam *A*: ultra *BO*.   165 Corpora . . . tua *A*: An quia . . . te *BO*.   166 Hei *A*: Heu
BO; ulla *AB*: illa *O*.   170 reliquus *BO*: reliqus *A*.   **Post 172** *add. BO*: Hoc te Martha soror, rogat
hoc qui lumine cassus / Lumina quae videat te duce frater habet.

The rebirth in nature affirms that the world is under your banner again and all creation rejoices at your return. Now the hills of Jerusalem are once more promising their balm. [140] Lofty Jericho is bringing back her sweet-scented roses. The cypress-bearing woods are putting on their vernal cloaks. The flowering palm adorns the groves of Edom. Wreathed in clouds, Mount Carmel displays the glories of summer. The grape-bearing vine shades the soil of Engedi. All nature is reviving for you; together with you all things are rising from the dead. But we, we feel joyless, unesteemed. Where are you, Creator and mighty Restorer of nature, Jesus? Creator of a regenerated age, where are you?

As I lamented, it seemed to me [150] that the mournful lilies bent their trembling heads, as if grieving with me. A cool breeze stirred my drooping hair. I looked over my shoulder; there was no one behind me. If I saw anything, it was because love put idle fancies in my head. Every so often, as I walked about, I would stop short, and my heart was filled with joy and fear at once. I go and see the places you used to visit so often — ah, places that no longer gladden my eyes the way they used to and yet are dear to me because they remind me of you, because they were once dear to me. In this respect too, grieving has its charms. Now I touch the footprints you left behind — that is all I can do in your stead — [160] and, as I bend my head low, the grass drinks up my tears.

You see all this, but with different eyes than before. Neither my tears nor my laments move you. Is it because you have ceased to be mortal that you turn your back on me and stay out of sight? Am I, poor sinner, unworthy of seeing you in the flesh? Oh, why is my love afraid of any such reproach?

Even though I am not worthy, you could still make it seem so. Forgive me! Where now is that vaunted loving-kindness of yours? What have the others done to deserve this, if you deny yourself to me, Christ? [170] What about the rest of the disciples along with your sorrowful mother?

All that remains is for you to be gracious to me and answer my prayer. Nothing else can relieve my sadness. This, my love, is what your mother and the twelve apostles ask for; this is what every decent person begs of you with suppliant heart.

4   CATHARINA COSTIS CHRISTO SPONSO

Quam legis, a sponsa tibi Costide littera venit.
　　Si liceat, nollet mittere, ferre volet!
Quisquis es, ex illo placuisti tempore nobis
　　Quo mihi legitime iunctus es, ipsa tibi.
5　Signa recognoscis quae pressit vincula gemmae —
　　Annulus in digitis heserat ille tuis.
Si qua potest igitur promissis credere amantum,
　　Pignore firmatam credimus esse fidem.
Nec, puto, tu velles tua pignora falsa putari.
10　Sis licet, es certe doctus amare, puer.
Nescio quae de te quidam mihi grandia narrat,
　　Esse Deum caeli, virgine matre satum.
Si Deus es, miserae quantum mihi restat amanti,
　　Quo mihi tu sponsus, quo tibi sponsa vocer!
15　Vel mihi fallaces dictastis inania somni,
　　Vel Deus indignam Costida summus amat.
Gratulor. At quoniam non sum de plebe lavata,
　　Incertam visis suspicor esse fidem.
Tu mihi, Christe (ferunt Christo tibi nomen Iesu),
20　Praestare antiquos diceris ante deos.

13=D5ʳ (line 10 marginal note)

Her. Chr. 4.   *Tit.* Catharina — sponso *A*: Catharina Christo **BO**.   6 ille *A*: iste **BO**.   13–14 amanti — vocer *A*: ut idem / Et Deus et sponsus conciliere mihi **BO**.

[1]According to her late medieval legend, Catherine of Alexandria was the only daughter of King Costus. One day, not long after her father's death, she and her companions were picking flowers in a field when she met a pious hermit. Converted by him, she received a dream vision of the Virgin and her Son and in a mystical marriage became the bride of Christ. After awakening she discovered a wedding ring on her finger. When Emperor Maxentius (306–12) began forcing everyone to offer sacrifice to the idols, the eighteen-year-old went to him and scolded him for his unbelief. Impressed with her beauty, erudition, and wisdom, he summoned fifty philosophers to debate her. With God's help she defeated and converted them. The philosophers were burned at the stake; Catherine was offered marriage to Maxentius. She refused and was herself taken to be martyred. But the wheel on which she was to be tortured broke apart and killed many of the spectators. Finally she was beheaded. Angels carried her body to Mount Sinai, where Emperor Justinian eventually founded a monastery dedicated to her.

4   CATHERINE, COSTUS' DAUGHTER, TO HER
     BRIDEGROOM CHRIST[1]

The letter you read comes to you from your bride, the daughter
of Costus. If she had an opportunity, she would refuse to send it,
and instead carry it herself!

Whoever you are, you have pleased me ever since we were
joined in marriage, you to me, I to you. You recognize the
imprint of my signet in the wax: it is the very ring you wore on
your finger. So if a girl can trust a lover's promises,[2] how much
more can I trust your vow, seeing that it is confirmed with a
pledge. But I don't suppose you would want your "pledges" misunderstood. [10] You may be a lad, but you certainly do know a
lot about love![3]

There is a man here who has told me some wonderful things
about you. You are supposed to be the God of heaven, born of a
virgin mother. If you are God, how much remains for me, poor loving girl, before you can be called my groom and I your bride! Either
deceitful dreams have put idle notions into my head or it is true
that the highest God loves Costus' unworthy daughter. That is
cause for rejoicing. But since I am not one of the baptized people,
I worry that my vision cannot be trusted.

Christ (besides *Christ* they give you the name *Jesus*), [20] I
am told that you are superior to the ancient gods. And indeed,

---

After the Virgin Mary, Catherine was one of the most popular saints in the late Middle Ages.
Hence, there are many literary treatments and versions of her life. For the tradition, with a special
focus on Germany, see *VL* 4, cols. 1055–73, with further literature. A collection of Latin verse and
prose texts on the saint, including Baptista Mantuanus' *Parthenice secunda*, can be found in A. P.
Orbán, ed., *Vitae Sanctae Katharinae*, CCCM 119 and 119A. See also *Leg. aurea* 168.

In Eobanus' refashioning of the legend, Catherine addresses Christ shortly after her conversion
and mystical wedding. She has returned to the palace, but put away all ostentation and pride. At the
beginning of her letter she is unsure of herself and her newfound faith. But as the writing progresses,
she meditates on the Trinity and Maxentius' idolatry and resolves to challenge the emperor in person.
By the end of the letter her early doubts have given way to unshakeable faith in Christ. She exults in
the martyrdom that is soon to follow.

In the 1532/39 version this letter is *Her.* 3.1.

[2]Lovers' oaths are proverbially made to be broken. See Otto 77.

[3]Catherine thinks of Christ as a lad, because that is how he appeared to her in the vision. See ll.
107, 121, and 129 below. His "pledge" is the wedding ring that he gave her: cf. ll. 121, 132, 140
below. It is, of course, not to be understood in the usual amatory sense, as a "pledge of love," or child
(cf., for example, l. 50 below).

Idque ego cum veterum scrutor sacra carmina vatum,
  Omnibus adstructum gratulor esse locis.
Te propter veterum mihi pagina multa relecta est
  Qui referunt uni sensa profunda Deo.
25 Legimus Haebraeos vates vatesque Sybillas
  Quosque habet Aegyptus relligiosa libros.
Legimus atque Arabum monumenta et carmina Thracum.
  Omnia sunt vultus lumine plena tui.
Quis foret ille Deus dubitabam, ignara quis esses,
30   Qui sine principio, qui sine fine manes,
Qui de confusa mundanam mole figuram
  Et tantum artifici mente crearit opus.

D5ᵛ

Interea genitor Costus fatalia solvit
  Munera. Defuncto regna parente vacant.
35 Urbis Alexandri sceptrum latura reservor,
  Infoelix aliqua prole futura parens.
Ipsa celebratas, muliebria nomina, laudes
  Servata mallem virginitate sequi.
Est aliquid claras heroidas inter haberi,
40   Quae potior stabili fama pudore venit.
Iamque ego sum certe maturo nubilis aevo.
  Plena quidem vitae sunt tria lustra meae.
Sollicitant regni proceres, nec me unus et alter,
  Turba, petunt, castis invidiosa, proci.
45 Et mihi dii patrii incipiunt sordescere, et istis
  Nescio quid nebulis mens mea maius avet.
Quid faciam? Stat celsa altis innixa columnis
  Regia; sunt regnis oppida multa meis.
Ibit in haec cultor falsorum quisque deorum,
50   Et feret e nostro pignora chara sinu.
Tu melius, tu nanque potes. Tibi nostra dicata est
  Virginitas, de te si modo vera fides.
Unde sit haec nostrae de te fiducia menti,

14=D6ʳ

  Quod non ignoras forte, referre iuvat.
55 Hic, ubi Pellaeo iacet urbs fundata tyranno
  Et piger illustri stat Mareotis aqua,
Est via declivi vallem complexa recessu.
  Intus heremicola stat casa facta manu.
Antra tenet senio quidam venerabilis albo,
60   Qui nobis de te sepe magister erat.

21–32 Idque — opus *A*: Idque ego dum studeo cognoscere clarius, alter / Fluxit et in cursu tertius annus
erat *BO*.   **30** manet *scripsi*: manes *A*.   **33** genitor Costus *A*: Costus genitor *BO*.   **34** vacant
AB: vocant *O*.   **38** Servata mallem *A*: Mallem servata *BO*.   **44** invidiosa *A*: insidiosa *BO*.
54 ignoras forte, [forte: *A*] referre *A*: ignoras, forte referre *BO*.   **60** Qui nobis *AB*: Ille mihi *O*.

as I search the holy prophecies of the old seers, I rejoice to find this affirmed wherever I look. To learn more about you, I have reread many a page of the ancients, who convey profound insights into the one God. I have read the Hebrew prophets and the Sibylline oracles as well as the books that devout Egypt has to offer. I have also read the writings of the Arabs and the songs of the Thracians.[4] All of them are filled with the light of your face. Knowing nothing about you, I pondered who that God could be [30] who exists without beginning and without end, one who created the ordered world out of Chaos and designed the vast universe with a craftsman's eye.

In the meantime, my father Costus paid the debt of nature. With my father deceased, his realms are without a king. I am destined to bear the scepter over Alexander's city[5] and become the unhappy mother of some child. In truth, I would prefer to seek glory and renown as a paragon of women by retaining my virginity. It is indeed something to be reckoned among the celebrated heroines; [40] but the fame that comes from perpetual chastity is more precious by far.

By now I'm certainly old enough to be married. In fact, I'm already over fifteen years old. The nobles of the realm are constantly pestering me. Suitors swarm around me asking for my hand — a detestable crowd for chaste women! Besides, the ancestral gods are starting to disgust me. My soul craves for something more substantial than these mists. What am I to do? The royal palace is a lofty structure resting on towering columns; my kingdom has many cities. Someday a worshiper of the false gods will go [50] and receive dear children from my bosom. May you grant me a better fate, for you can do that. My virginity is consecrated to you — at least, if the things I believe about you are true.

Though you probably know already where I found my trusting faith in you, still it is a pleasure to tell you. Here, just outside the city founded by the tyrant of Pella,[6] not far from the famed waters of sluggish Lake Mareotis, there is a road that winds down into a secluded valley. In it stands a hut built by a hermit's hand. A venerable graybeard lives in the hovel. [60] He is the one who has often taught me about you.

---

[4]By "Arabs" Eobanus presumably (if rather loosely) means the Babylonians and Chaldeans. The "songs of the Thracians" are the *Orphic Hymns*. These ancient poems were attributed to the Thracian singer Orpheus.

[5]Alexandria was founded by Alexander the Great in 332 BCE.

[6]Alexander the Great (356–323 BCE) was born at Pella in Macedonia.

Qua semel (ut soleo) nuper convalle resedi.
    Fons prope erat; dulcem prebuit umbra locum.
Venit et assedit longo vir callidus aevo.
    Florales comitum turba legebat opes.
65   Qui simul ut sedit, "Quid," ait, "tua tempora perdis?
    O immortali nubere digna Deo!
Tam tenerum incesta florem maculare iuventa
    Non decet. Est alio dignus honore frui!
Ah, fuge mortalis thalami commertia. Christus,
70   Quem docui, regnis plus valet ille tuis.
Non te regna tui moveant ditissima Nili.
    Sceptra geres alio divitiora loco.
Utque facis, falsosque Ioves Veneresque columnas,
    Linque deumque canem, linque deumque bovem.
75   Quaere Deum caeli Dominumque decemplicis orbis.
    Iam tibi divorum regia tota favet."
"Est amor, est," inquam, "laudato nubere Christo.
    Spes nova, mens alias nesciet ista faces!
At tua me miseram promissa ingentia terrent.
80   Heu, quantum est summo posse placere Deo!
Me quoque, quam laudas, Mater non passa maritum
    Forsitan indignam nolit habere nurum.
Denique quo studio Domino placuisse laborem?
    Tam longe absenti posse placere grave est.
85   Ut placeam, quis me vestro coniunget Iesu?"
    (Nescio dixissem quomodo pene, "meo"!)
"Quis dabit et placidas audire et reddere voces?
    Quis mihi coniugii sponsor et obses erit?
Ut cupiam iungi virgo cum virgine Christo,
90   Quis patrio tutam tollet ab orbe deus?"
Nil queror. Accipiet tutam Deus ipse deorum.
    Est Deus. Accenso sentio corde Deum,
Sentio! At haec non sunt tua spicula, false Cupido.
    Pectora divinus nostra subintrat amor.
95   Quam subito exangues caluerunt igne medullae!
    Non prius in nobis Spiritus ille fuit.
Quisquis es, o animae lux unica et ultima nostrae,
    Ne, rogo, te nobis, ut videare, nega.

D6ᵛ (line 65 margin)

15=E1ʳ (bottom margin)

---

61 nuper — resedi *AB*: cum nuper valle sederem *O*.   **62** Fons *BO*: Frons *A*.   **72** divitiora *A*: nobiliora *BO*.   **73** Veneresque *A*: mutasque *BO*.   **84** posse placere *A*: complacuisse *BO*. **85** vestro *A*: placito *BO*.   **86–87** (Nescio — voces? *A*: *om. BO*.   **91–94** Nil queror — amor *A*: Qualibus ille autem dictis incenderit et quot / Egerit hunc animum, dicere longa mora est. / Ipsa senem linquens meditabar sola quis esses, / Cuius flagraret pectus amore meum, / Ignotum potui quem sic vehementer [ardenter *O*] amare, / Quo fluit hic animus sicut ab igne chalybs *BO*.   **95** Quam *A*: Tam *BO*; caluerunt — medullae *A*: populata est flamma medullas *BO*.   **96** Spiritus — fuit *A*: tam gravis ardor erat *BO*.   **97** es *AB*: *om. O*.   **98** Ne *BO*: Nec *A*.

One day recently (as is my custom) I was visiting the glen. There was a spring nearby; the shade provided a delightful place to relax. A wise old man came by and sat down beside me. My companions were all busy gathering the riches of Flora. As soon as he was seated, he said: "Why are you wasting your time? Oh, you are worthy of wedding the immortal God! It is wrong to defile so tender a flower by an unchaste youth. You deserve better than that! Ah, shun the intercourse of human marriage. The Christ [70] I preach is worth more than all your realms. Don't let the wealthiest kingdom on the Nile sway you. You'll bear a richer scepter in another place. As you are doing already, turn your back on the false Jupiters and the stone Venuses; abandon the jackal god, abandon the bull god.[7] Seek the God of heaven, the Lord of the tenfold universe.[8] Even now all heaven is smiling on you."

"I would dearly love to wed the Christ you extol," I replied. "O new hope! My soul will know no other love. But your stupendous promises terrify me, poor girl. [80] Alas, what a daunting thing it is to please the supreme God! Also his virgin Mother, whom you praise so highly, may not want some undeserving girl like me as her daughter-in-law. And finally, what must I do to be pleasing to the Lord? It is hard to please someone so far away. But even supposing I please him, who will join me in wedlock to your Jesus?" (Somehow or other I nearly said, "my"!) "Who will give us the opportunity for a quiet conversation? Who will be sponsor and surety for the marriage? As much as I long to be joined as virgin with the virgin Christ, [90] what god will take me safely out of this world of ours?"

But I'm not complaining. The God of gods himself will take me up safely. For there is a God. In my blazing heart I feel God — yes, I feel him! But these are not *your* arrows, false Cupid. It is love divine that has stolen into my breast. How quickly has this fire kindled my marrow and utterly consumed it! Never before have I experienced that Spirit within me. Whoever you are, O sole and ultimate light of my soul, I beg you, do not deny yourself to me, as you appear to be doing.

---

[7]Anubis, the god of the dead in Egyptian mythology, was represented with the head of a jackal (or dog). Apis, closely associated with Osiris, was the sacred bull worshiped in Memphis.
[8]In medieval-Renaissance cosmology, the earth is surrounded by ten heavenly spheres.

Multa precaturam tenuis sine pondere somnus
100   Corpus in herbosa ponere iussit humo.
Utque sopor tremulos primum delusit ocellos,
        Talia sunt menti somnia visa meae.
Campus erat, viridi circumsitus undique sylva;
        Flore renidebat multicolore solum.
105   Illic odoratas errabam sola per herbas,
        Puniceis texens paucula serta rosis.
Hic ego te vidi puerum cum matre puella.
        Non mea veraci somnia teste carent!
Virgo erat alba, comas auro rutilante coactas,
110   Formosum nivea corpus amicta toga.
Sceptrum erat in dextra; te brachia laeva tenebant,
        Brachia Sithonia candidiora nive.
Hic neque Naiades neque sum causata Napeas
        De turpi matrem quamlibet esse deo.
115   Vidi aliquid maius sensique errore prophano,
        Nescio quem tacita mente professa Deum.
Iam prope constiterat, cum te ridente parumper
        Verba mihi mater visa erat ista loqui:
"Salve, flore alio mecum latura coronam.

120   Salve iterum, nato, Costis, amata meo.
Se tibi desponsat puer hic. Simul accipe pignus.
        Gemma sub articulo luceat ista tuo."
Dixerat. E digitis aurum quod forte gerebas
        Torsisti manibus in mea membra tuis.
125   "Accipe," dicebas. "Hoc te sibi pignore iungit,
        Imperium cuius cuncta creata manent."
Erubui. Vocem pudor abstulit, attamen ignem
        In vultu tacitum signa fatentis erant.
Lumina demisi cum tu, puer optime rerum,
130   Excipis e manibus lilia texta meis.
"Hoc mihi virgineum spondes, Catharina, pudorem,
        Pignus ut ardoris servet uterque sui."
Vix tantum, "Tua sum. Castos tibi dedimus annos.
        Sim tua," vix potui dicere, "sponsa, precor."

99 tenuis *A*: levis et *BO*.   **105** Illic odoratas *A*: Suavia spirantes *B*, Dulcia spirantes *O*.   **106** paucula
A: parvula *BO*.   **111** Sceptrum *A*: Virga *BO*; tenebant *A*: gerebant *BO*.   **113** Naiades — Napeas
A: Naiadum neque rebar Hamadryadarum *BO*.   **121** Se — pignus *A*: Accipe fine novum carituri pignus
amoris *BO*.   **124** manibus *A*: digitis *BO*.   **125–26** "Accipe — manent." *A*: Iam puero maior, iam
matre decentior ipsa, / Iam tua maiestas visa stupenda mihi est [stupenda fuit *O*]. *BO*.   **131** virgineum
A: devotum *BO*.

I still had so much to pray for, but a gentle, light drowsiness
[100] bade me lie down on the grassy ground. And as soon as
slumber deluded my trembling eyes, this was the vision I saw in
my mind.

There was a field girdled round with a green forest; the
meadow beamed with multicolored blooms. I was straying there
all alone amid the fragrant herbs, weaving a few garlands of crimson roses. Here it was that I saw you, a boy with your maidenly
mother. My dream did not lack a truthful witness![9] The Virgin
appeared all in white. A crown of glittering gold bound her hair
together. [110] Her lovely body was clad in a snow-white dress.
In her right hand she held a scepter; you she cradled in her left
arm, an arm whiter than Thracian snow. Here I was clearly not
dealing with some naiad or dell nymph who had become a
mother by the debauched god. I saw and sensed something
greater than the delusion of the heathens, and in my heart
I silently confessed a God I did not know. Now she was standing
next to me. And as you smiled at me for a little while, your
mother seemed to speak the following words to me: "Hail, daughter of Costus. Together with me you shall wear a garland of
different flowers.[10] [120] Once more, hail, beloved of my son.
This boy betroths himself to you. Take now the pledge of his love.
Let that gemstone sparkle on your finger."

She had finished speaking. From your fingers you twisted
the ring you happened to be wearing on your hand and put it on
mine. "Take it," you said. "With this pledge you become the
bride of him on whose bidding all creation waits." I blushed.
Shyness took away my voice; but on my cheeks were the signs
that pointed to a hidden fire. I cast down my eyes when you, best
of all lads, [130] accepted the lily wreath from my hands. "With
this, Catherine, you plight your virginity to me, so that each of
us may keep the other's pledge of love."

"I am yours," I stammered. "To you I devote the chaste
years of youth. Let me" — I could hardly utter the words — "let
me please be your bride."

---

[9]The Virgin Mary was witness to the wedding.
[10]The crown of perpetual virginity.

135 Lene videbaris subridens tangere dextram.
    E somno attactu sum relevata tuo.
    Ecce sed in digito gemmam qui proximus imo est.
    O non de patrio somnia visa deo!
    Serta prius collecta manu cecidisse putabam.
140   Sed, recolo, nostri pignus amoris erant.
    Caelesti impositam dum gemmam exosculor auro,

16=E2ʳ   Est etiam lachrymis humida facta meis.
    Quamque ego te vidi veracis imagine somni,
    Tam presens vigili pectore cura manes.
145 Laeticia expressit lachrymas in amore suetas.
    Iam primum didici quid fleat omnis amans.
    Non tamen hoc fletu incesti solantur amores.
    Nostra agit in lachrymas lumina castus amor.
    Vix longa revocata mora scrutabar ubi essem.
150   Nullus erat. Comites advoco: sola fui.
    Lumina ad aereum relevo vigilantia solem.
    Lumine sol nunquam lucidiore fuit.
    Quacunque aspicio, melior natura refulget.
    Est aliquid verum rebus adesse Deum!
155 Blanda susurrantes moverunt murmura sylvae.
    Moesta prius, vivo germine fragrat humus.
    Tam dulcis tenuem perflavit spiritus auram,
    Qualis in aetherea dicitur esse domo.
    Quae prius, aspicio vicini viscera fontis
160   Nobile caelestis ducere nectar aquae.
    Argutae viridi vernant in fronde volucres.
    Illo malueram posse manere loco.
    Tota Creatorem laudabat gratia coelo

E2ᵛ   Virginis ad lachrymas non renuisse trahi.
165 Consurgo comitesque voco clamore relictas.
    Crebra repercussum reddidit Echo sonum.
    Haec quoque desponsi revocanti nomen Iesu,
    Quam potuit, resona voce ferebat opem.
    Huc illucque vagor per opacae devia vallis,
170   Si loca te referant proxima forte mihi.
    Spes animum frustrata leves ubi cessit in auras,
    Hei mihi, quam tardo sydere tempus abit!
    Ille tamen, per quem nupsi tibi, cultor heremi,
    Ille levat sponsae tempora moesta tuae.

---

141 gemmam *A*: summam *BO*.   **142** Est *AB*: Et *O*.   **144** pectore *A*: pectora *BO*.   **147** Non —
amores *A*: Ite leves alio, miserorum crimen, amores *BO*.   **148** lachrymas *A*: fletus *BO*.
166 Crebra . . . Echo *A*: Crebra . . . aura *B*, Multa . . . aura *O*.   **167** revocanti *manus vetus in*
A³ et A⁴: revocantem *ABO*.   **171** cessit *A*: fugit *BO*.

Smiling, you seemed to touch my right hand ever so gently. It was this touch of yours that woke me from my sleep. But lo and behold, a ring on the next-to-last finger! Oh, this was no dream vision about the god of my fathers! The garland I had woven earlier must have slipped out of my hand, or so I thought. [140] But then it came back to me: that was the pledge of my love! While I fondly kissed the gemstone set in celestial gold, it was also moistened with my tears. And just as I saw you appear in my truthful dream, so you are always present in my waking thoughts. As is usual in love, joy elicited tears. Now for the first time I learned why every lover weeps. But these aren't the tears with which unchaste lovers assuage their amours. The love that drives these tears into my eyes is chaste.

No sooner had I awakened than I searched to see where I was. [150] Nobody was there. I called out to my companions: I was alone. I raised my watchful eyes to the sun high up in the sky. Never had the sun shone more brightly. Wherever I looked, the world gleamed with a nobler cheerfulness. It is something, when the true God is present in nature! The rustling woods raised pleasant whispers. Mournful before, the ground was now redolent of sprouting buds. The breeze passed through the thin air just as sweetly as it is said to do in the abode of heaven. Nearby, a well I had seen earlier [160] now seemed to be drawing exquisite nectar, celestial water. In the leafy boughs the birds were chirping a song of spring. How I wished I could have stayed in that place! All the beauty of heaven praised the Creator for letting himself be drawn to a virgin's tears. I rose and in a loud voice called the companions I had left. Each time the echo sent back the reverberating cry. It also supported me as much as it could with resounding voice, whenever I called out the name of my betrothed, Jesus.

Now I roam hither and yon through the remoter parts of that shady valley, [170] always hoping that the very next spot might bring you back to me. When I am disappointed and my hopes vanish into thin air, alas, how slowly the time creeps by! That hermit, however, the one through whom I was wedded to you, he helps your betrothed pass the melancholy hours. He is also the one who told me recently, as I was hesitating whether

175   Ille etiam nuper dubitanti scribere dixit:
           "Scribe. Feram Domino carmina scripta tuo."
       Gaudebam reperisse viam qua scribere possem,
           Protinus est manibus sumpta tabella meis;
       Et quae nunc patria cernis confusa papyro
180   Sunt mihi furtiva carmina facta mora.
       Saepe quidem repeto nostri loca conscia amoris.
           Mittitur ex illis littera nostra tibi.
       Aula vacat requie. Dolor est meus ista videre
           Quae patria fiunt relligione domi.
185   Sumebam calamum scriptura quid. Impia nutrix,
           "Quid facit haec? Facta est pallida!" dixit. "Amat!"
       Obstupui subitoque stilum cum voce repressi,
           Ne causam officii quaereret illa mei.
       Mirantur famulae solitos me spernere cultus,
190   Cur mihi non formae cura sit ulla meae.
       Si qua placere volet mundo, se vestibus ornet.
           Forma Creatori non placet ista Deo.
       Mens formosa Deum caeli se cogit amare.
           Haec manet; est ingens forma secunda malum.
195   Haec et cuncta quidem tu conspicis, et tua nunquam
           Maiestas falli qualibet arte potest.
       Rebus enim cunctis ut ines, potes omnia praesens.
           Foecit et hanc nobis pagina sancta fidem.
       Credo equidem venerorque libens tria nomina et unum,
200   Unum, non plures, omnia posse Deum.
       Non genitum factumve Patrem scio sive creatum,
           Sed Natum credo progenuisse Patrem.
       Tertius ingenitus, non factus sive creatus,
           Ex utroque sacer profluit ille vigor,
205   Et quae ferre elegi nequeunt maiora pedestres.
           Iam veteres divos novimus esse nihil.
       Heu, tamen errori caedunt haec regna vetusto;
           Concidit ad falsos victima multa Ioves.
       Impius instaurat veteres Maxentius aras,
210   Caesar enim Nili regna tyrannus habet.
       Sacra iubet fieri Caesar. Delubra frequentant
           Mactandosque trahunt, credula turba, boves.

17=E3ʳ

E3ᵛ

---

187 Obstupui *A* (*in erratis*) **BO**: Obstipui *A* (*in textu*).   **189** spernere *A*: ponere **BO**.   **190** non
A: nec **BO**.   **195** et cuncta *A*: ut cuncta **BO**.   **197–206** Rebus — nihil. *A*: *om.* **BO**.   **211** fieri
Caesar. Delubra *A*: fieri. Divum delubra **BO**.

to write you or not: "Go ahead and write. When you are finished, I'll take the verses to your Lord."

Happy to have found a way to write you, I immediately took
pen and paper in hand; and the hodgepodge you see before you on
the native papyrus [180] is the poem I furtively composed whenever I had the chance. Often, indeed, I go back to the places that
are privy to our love. It is from there that my letter is sent to you.

The palace affords me no rest. It pains me to see what is
being done here at home in the name of our ancestral religion.
I once picked up my pen to write a few lines. My nurse cried out
irreverently: "What is she up to? She's turned pale! She must be
in love!" Stupefied, I immediately stopped writing and talking,
for fear she might ask me the reason for this labor of mine.

The handmaidens are amazed to see me reject my usual
adornments, [190] and wonder why I no longer fuss about my
appearance. If I wanted to be like other girls and look attractive to
the world, I would adorn myself with finery. Beauty like that does
not please God the Creator. A beautiful soul feels compelled to
love the God of heaven. This kind of beauty endures; the other
kind is a great source of evil. You observe this and everything else
besides, and your majesty cannot be deceived by any wiles. For just
as you penetrate all things, so your omnipotence is everywhere
present. Holy Scripture has persuaded me of that truth, too.
Indeed, I do believe and willingly venerate three Persons in one.
[200] I believe that only the one God, not the many, can do all
things. I know that the Father is not begotten or made or created;
but I believe that the Son is begotten from the Father. The third
Person is not begotten, not made or created. His holy vigor proceeds from the other two.[11] There are even more sublime articles of
faith; but I cannot convey them in elegiacs as pedestrian as mine.
Now I know for sure that the old gods are nothing at all.

But alas, these realms of mine have yielded to ancient idolatry.
Many a victim is being offered as a sacrifice to the false Joves. The
ungodly Maxentius is restoring the old altars, [210] for that imperial tyrant lords it over our kingdom on the Nile. The emperor
commands us to worship the gods. Dutifully, the faithful frequent
the temples, dragging their sacrificial oxen along. The halls resound

---

[11]Catherine (anachronistically) paraphrases a portion of the Nicene Creed: "I believe in one God,
the Father almighty, maker of heaven and earth, of all things visible and invisible; and in one Lord
Jesus Christ, the only Son of God, begotten from the Father before all ages, Light from Light, true
God from true God, begotten, not made, of one substance with the Father, through whom all things
were made, who for us and for our salvation came down from heaven, and became incarnate by the
Holy Spirit and the Virgin Mary and was made human . . . and in the Holy Spirit, the Lord, the giver
of life, who proceeds from the Father [and the Son]." The phrase "and the Son" was not added to the
creed until the end of the sixth century, and then only in the Western Church: cf. *Her. Chr.* 10.67–68.

Atria mugitu resonant, ferit aethera clamor,
    Et tuba terribiles excitat unca sonos.
215   Omnia festivis lucent altaria flammis,
    Sordidaque effuso sanguine squallet humus.
Ipse genu flexo supplex procumbit ad aras;
    Hunc sequitur quisquis numina falsa colit.
Abnegat hoc aliquis doctus tua numina, Christe,
220   Ob rectam saevo concidit ense fidem.
Qualia crudelis cogat tormenta tyrannus,
    Turba docet miseram plurima passa necem.
Vidimus iniectas flammis ardere puellas
    Nudaque pinnata corpora fuste quati.
225   Vidimus et ferro teretes abscindere mammas,
    Affligi vinclis carceribusque premi.
Pascit inhumanus nostrum canis iste cruorem.
    Enormis saturum non sinit esse fames.
Aspicis hoc paciente oculo, sed lenta malignis

18=E4^r 230   Et sine iactura tardior ira tua est.
Quam pulchrum, Rex magne, tuo cecidisse sub hoste est!
    Munere emi caelum non meliore potest.
Ista triumphalem pariunt certamina palmam.
    Pars utinam tantae sim quota laudis ego!
235   Ire iuvat verbisque ferum terrere latronem.
    Quid furit in plebem perfidus iste tuam?
Ibimus, est animus! Non me tormenta movebunt
    Dira nec in poenae nomina mille cruces.
Devenerata deos lapides idola vocabo.
240   Ipse tuae praesens virginis ora move.
Traxerit in poenam, mors gloria nostra futura est,
    Et potero forsan fortiter ulta mori.
Est mihi sitque, precor, facundae gratia linguae,
    Artis et ingenii convenientis honor.
245   Argumenta, dolos, et frivola dicta refellam.
    Maior erit per me, te duce, recta fides.
Tunc mihi si dabitur pro te succumbere, restant
    Post quae coniungar tempora pauca tibi.
Tu dabis hoc aliqua corpus requiescere in urna.
250   Hoc tamen in posito marmore carmen erit:
E4^v "Costis in hoc tumulo sum condita. Viva Tonantis
    Nupta, sed aeterna virginitate fui.
Impius immeritam Maxentius ense peremit.
    Hic cinis est. Sponsae caetera sponsus habet."

---

219 tua — Christe *A*: te, Christe, fateri *BO*.   226 Affligi *BO*: Afflicti *A* (*sed corr. manus vetus in* *A*^{4}).
229 hoc *A*: haec *BO*.   *Post* 240 *add. BO*: Argumenta, dolos, et frivola dicta revellam [*pro* refellam]. /
Maior erit per me, te duce, recta fides [= *vv. 245–46*].   243–46 Est mihi — fides. *A*: *om. BO*.
245 refellam *scripsi*: revellam *A*.   249 corpus requiescere *A*: requiescere corpus *BO*.

with lowing, the clamor strikes the heavens, and the coiling trumpet sounds dreadful blasts. All the altars are alight with festal fires, and the filthy ground is squalid with spilled blood. He himself falls down on bended knee before the altars; his is the example that all the idolaters follow. If a believer in your divinity, Christ, rejects this, [220] he falls victim to the cruel sword because of his righteous faith.

What kind of torments the merciless tyrant can muster is demonstrated by the huge throng of those who have suffered a pitiable death at his hands. We have seen girls thrown into the flames and burned, their naked bodies beaten with winged cudgels. We have seen their rounded breasts cut off with the steel; we have seen maidens fettered and cast into dungeons. That inhuman dog feeds on our blood. His monstrous hunger can never be sated.

You watch all this with patient eye. But though you may be slow to anger, [230] your wrath is sure to strike the wicked with undiminished force. How beautiful it is, great King, to fall by your enemy's hand! Heaven cannot be purchased with a better sacrifice than this. Whoever fights this good fight will win the palm of victory. How I wish I could garner a small share of that stupendous renown!

It would be a pleasure to go and terrify the ruthless murderer with my words. Why does that scoundrel rage against your people? That's what I'll do. There's no holding me back! Neither excruciating torments nor the countless forms of martyrdom will deter me. The idols he worships I'll denounce as gods of stone. [240] Be with me, Christ, and guide the lips of your virgin bride. If he drags me off to be punished, death will be my glory. Perhaps I'll even be richly avenged when I die. At my command — and may this continue to be so, I pray! — I have graceful eloquence, rhetorical skill, and a temperament to match. Their arguments, sleights of hand, and frivolous sayings I'll tear apart. Through me the true faith will be made stronger, as long as you remain my guide.

Then, if I am given the chance to be martyred for you, it will not be long before I am joined to you. You will grant that my body may rest in some urn. [250] This, however, will be the inscription on the tombstone: "In this grave I, Costus' daughter, lie buried. Alive, I was the Thunderer's bride, but remained eternally chaste. The ungodly Maxentius killed the innocent girl with his sword. Here lie the ashes. Everything else of the bride is in the hands of her groom."

5   ELISABETH LUDOVICO MARITO

Si liceat, missam vellet transferre salutem
    Pannonis Hessiaco nupta puella viro.
Adriaco fama est vento tua vela morari.
    Heu nimium in curas ventus et unda meas!
5   Longa mora est postquam Solimas visurus abisti.
    At mihi, cum fugeres, ausus es ista loqui:
"Nona reformatum cum Cynthia clauserit orbem,
    Vir tibi, si vivam, redditus, uxor, ero."
Tertia noctivagae coierunt cornua Phoebes,
10   Nec tua de Veneto littore puppis abit.
Illud erat potius mecum tibi tempus agendum!
    Causa vetat: nulli scire futura datur.
Quid tamen, heu, spretis regno patriaque domoque,
    Tam longum infidum per mare carpis iter?
15   Regna petis siquidem Cancro subiecta perusto,
    Forsan et Orebi culmina celsa iugi,
Rura Philysteis quondam subiecta colonis,
    Mella ubi cum niveo dulcia lacte fluunt,
Inclyta praecipue Iudaeo maenia sceptro,
20   Sacra ubi victoris sunt monumenta Dei.
Relligio ista tua est, et opus laudabile. Qualem
    In superos animum semper habere soles.
Non ego te patrias cupio regnare per urbes,
    Quo minus hoc sanctum perficiatur opus.
25   In tua te doleo remorari damna tuisque
    Fortiter adversum navibus esse fretum.

19=E5^r appears in left margin beside line 17.

Her. Chr. 5. Tit. Elisabeth — marito *A*: Helisabetha [Elisabetha *O*] Ludovico *BO*.   **1** transferre *A*: perferre *BO*.   **3** Adriaco *A*: Tyrrheno *BO*.   **5** visurus *A*: petiturus *BO*.   **9** Tertia *A*: Altera *BO*.   **10** de Veneto *A*: Tyrrheno *BO*.   **12** Causa — datur *A*: Sed vetat heu sciri multa futura Deus *BO*.   **13** Quid *A*: Cur *BO*; heu *A*: ut *BO*.   **14–18** Tam — fluunt *A*: Iussa paras dubio credere vela mari? / Littora nempe petens scopulosa Typhoidos orae, / Qua nigra fumantes ructuat Aetna globos, / Inde per Aegaeum signantes Cycladas aequor / Ibis Aramaei [Amaraei *BO*] ditia regna Syri, / Quaeque Palaestini quondam tenuere coloni, / Arva nisi armata non [vix *O*] adeunda manu, / Nunc gentis populata armis et Marte prophanae — / Hei mihi, cur opibus restituenda tuis? / Mitteret armipotens opulentos Gallia reges. / His potius tellus ista tuenda fuit! / Itala venissent, patria Hungarus arma tulisset, / Totaque vicino Graecia Marte potens. / Solveret Hesperiis pugnax Hispanus ab oris. / Noster in hoc ducat Caesar iturus opus. / Forte tot ac tanti terrarum culmina reges / Auxilio poterant non eguisse tuo. / Misisses aliquos etiam, socia arma tulisses. / Quantum erat in patria te senuisse tua! / Nunc petis aestivo flammantia littora Cancro, / Lactis et aetherei nectare pasta favi *BO*.   *Post* **22** *add. BO*: Quod si certus amor, tam certus et ardor eundi est / Et nulla hunc animum res prohibere potest,   **23** cupio *A*: iubeo *BO*.

5   **ELIZABETH TO HER HUSBAND LUDWIG**[1]

If she could, the Hungarian girl would not have sent this greeting to her Hessian husband — she'd have carried it herself!

Rumor has it that your sails are being held up by the Adriatic
wind. Ah, I worry so much about the wind and the water! It has
been a long time since you left for Jerusalem. As you were speeding
away, however, you did venture to tell me this: "When the moon
has reshaped and closed her orb for the ninth time, then, if all goes
well, I, your husband, will be restored to you, my wife."

The horns of night-wandering Phoebe have joined for the
third time now, [10] and still your ship has not left the Venetian
coast. Those months could have been spent more profitably with
me! A good reason forbids it, though: no one can know what the
future holds. But alas, after spurning throne and country and
home, why are you undertaking such a long journey over the
treacherous sea? After all, you're making for the lands that lie
beneath torrid Cancer, perhaps also to the towering heights of
Mount Horeb, to the fields that were once subject to the
Philistines — a land flowing with snowy milk and sweet honey —
and especially to the famed capital of Judea [20] where are found
the holy monuments of our victorious Lord. You do this out of
religious fervor, for it is a laudable goal. But then you have always
shown the utmost devotion to God and his saints.

I do not desire that you rule over the cities of your homeland, seeing that this would keep you from accomplishing your
holy mission. What does grieve me is that the delays are hurting
you and that the sea is so intent on blocking your ships. You face

---

[1] In 1227 Ludwig IV (1200–27), landgrave of Thuringia and husband of St. Elizabeth of
Hungary (1207–31), volunteered to follow Emperor Frederick II on a crusade. He left his wife on
24 June 1227. Already sickened by a plague, he sailed from Brindisi in early September. He died on
board his ship in Otranto on September 11. Elizabeth heard the news in October, shortly after the
birth of their third child.

Elizabeth writes this letter in the third month after her husband's departure (ll. 9–10), that is to say,
in September. She praises his Christian dedication, but is concerned that the long delays in setting sail
from Italy will prevent him from keeping his promise to be back with her in nine months (ll. 7–8). She is
even more worried that he will be killed — she has just had a frightening dream about his death —
and therefore counsels him to avoid all unnecessary danger.

In structure and language the letter closely imitates Ov. *Ep.* 13. There the worried Laodamia
writes to her husband Protesilaus, who (as the reader already knows) will be the first to die in the
Trojan War. Both Laodamia and St. Elizabeth have heard a report that headwinds have kept their
husbands' fleets from sailing. Both go on to recall the sweet sorrow of their parting and describe their
own sadness at having to return to their now empty home; and both relate their dreams of ill omen to
warn their husbands to be careful at all costs.

In the 1532/39 version this letter is *Her.* 2.7.

Longa via est, pelagique immensa pericula vasti;
  Multa feres terra, taedia multa mari.
Idque ego, cum suprema mihi mandata dedisti,
30   Flebam posse tua te pietate capi.
"Quid fles," dicebas, "mea dulcis Elisabeth?" Ipsa
  Ad mea semianimis nomina pene fui.
Nescio quid timuit mea mens presaga futuri.
  O, ego sim reducis cuius euntis eram!
35 Oscula et amplexus qui te decuere dedisti;
  In tua non venit pectora turpis amor.
Terga meis oculis tua, qua potui usque, sequebar,
  Quod lachryma durum praepediente fuit.

E5ᵛ

Iamque oculis ereptus eras. "Super aequora," dixi,
40   "Sit tibi quem sequeris portus et aura Deus.
Christe, salus rerum, ventos da, frange procellas,
  Secura possit vir meus ire via.
Virgo, stella maris, lucem da, pelle tenebras,
  Ne cadat aequorea naufraga nocte ratis.
45 Et vos, o reliqui superum, date vester in alto
  Foelici stabiles remige sulcet aquas."
Obtestata deos, ut tu, Ludovice, valeres,
  Desertae redii tecta sub alta domus.
Quid famulae? Vir abest; solam iuvat esse. Sine illo —
50   Pene fuit vita coelibe! — dulce nihil.
Quid procerum collecta manus, vel quicquid in aula
  Spectatum tanti principis esse solet?
Ite, cruces animi vos non patientis, honores!
  More pii solam turturis esse iuvat.
55 Donec abest iuvenum flos pectora casta gerentum,
  Illi clausa mei gaudia cordis erunt.
Scilicet ipsa geram radians in vestibus aurum,
  Loricam nudis artubus ille ferat?
Assyrio noster satietur rore capillus,
60   Illius atque aestu flagret et imbre caput?

20=E6ʳ

Ipsa colar princeps tuta sublimis in aula,
  Vir meus in fracto gurgite speret opem?
Tu melius, qui fine cares, sine origine vivis,
  Tu famulae votis annue, Christe, tuae!

29–30 mihi — capi. *A*: dares mandata, querebar / Arma per et gladios ista trophaea peti. / Arma per et gladios, utinamque haec sola, nec usquam / Te veheret mediis pensile robur aquis! ***BO***.   33 timuit *A*: metuat ***BO***.   39 aequora *A*: aequore ***BO***.   43–46 Virgo — aquas. *A*: *om. **BO***.   51 vel *A*: quid ***BO***.   52 solet *A*: potest ***BO***.   58 ferat *A*: feret ***BO***.   59 rore *A*: odore ***BO***.   62 fracto *A*: medio ***BO***.

a long journey and immense dangers on the boundless deep;
you will endure much weariness on land, much weariness at sea.
Even as you were giving me your final instructions, [30] I wept
about this too, that your devoutness could have such a hold on
you. "Why are you weeping, my sweet Elizabeth?" you asked. At
the mention of my name, I felt ready to faint. My mind was
filled with foreboding. Oh, may I be as sure of your return as
I was of your departure!

You gave me kisses and embraces that became you; unseemly
love has never entered your heart. I kept my eyes on your back
for as long as I could, but a veil of tears made it hard for me to
see. And before long you vanished from my sight. [40] "May
God, whom you follow over the seas," I prayed, "be your harbor
and breeze. Christ, Savior of the world, grant him fair winds,
break the storms, so that my husband can go on his way in
safety. Virgin, star of the sea, grant him your light, dispel the
darkness, lest his ship be wrecked on the reefs at night. And you,
O you other saints, grant that your follower and his fortunate
crew may have smooth sailing on the deep."

Having beseeched Heaven to keep you, Ludwig, safe and
sound, I went back under the soaring roof of our deserted house.
What are the maidservants to me? With my husband gone, it
does my heart good to be alone. Without him [50] — almost it
seems a widow's life! — nothing is sweet. What have I to do with
the nobles who gather here? Or, for that matter, with anything
else of consequence at the court of so great a prince? Away with
you, honors — torments that my soul is no longer able to bear!
Like the faithful turtledove, I prefer to keep to myself.

As long as the flower of chaste-minded youths is gone, I will
shut my heart to all delights but him. Am I then to wear gowns
embroidered with glistering gold, while he wears a cuirass next to
his skin? Should my hair be steeped in Assyrian perfume,
[60] while his head burns in the heat and rain? Is it right that
I should receive homage in the safety of the palace, while my
husband hopes for help on the raging sea? Grant him a better
fate, O you who live without beginning and without end! Hear
the prayers of your handmaid, O Christ!

65   Quas dolor interea longus mihi crescet in horas,
        Dum vir, dum coniunx, dum mihi frater abes!
    Sive cibum capio seu pocula tradita sumo,
        Pocula te referunt, te cibus ipse mihi.
    Cura eadem vesper, dolor idem mane renascens;
70   Quamque die crucias, tam mihi nocte subis.
    Somnia te referunt variis nocturna figuris,
        Et sibi non unquam constat imago tui.
    Pallidus interdum occurris. Nunc laetior adstas,
        Nunc fugis et verso lumine terga refers.
75   Sive vident aliquae verum per somnia mentes
        Seu redit in vanos cura diurna metus,
    Praeteritae timidam faciunt spectacula noctis.
        Irrita cum ventis auferat ista Deus!
    Hic, ubi piscosus claram Lanus alluit urbem
80   Frivola quae falsi nomina Martis habet,
    Monte sub aereo turbam spectare videbar,
        Nec mihi de turba cognitus ullus erat;

E6ᵛ

    Et tamen intereram. Sed dum mirabar ubi essem,
        Respicio. Mecum non erat ulla comes!
85   Expavi voluique pedem revocare citatum,
        Ecce sed a longe es visus adesse mihi.
    Frigore constiterant artus — ita gaudia mentem
        Sustulerant! Mecum non satis ipsa fui.
    Dum propero, ex oculis raptum sum visa maritum
90   Quaerere, rorantes ungue secante genas.
    Huc illuc retroque errans et utroque cucurri,
        Sed quo te videam non locus ullus erat.
    Sic inter Danaos Aeneidos umbra Creusae
        Fertur anhelantem destituisse virum.
95   Tum primum indignos cepi laniare capillos,
        Et vox cum lachrymis tristibus aegra fuit.
    Hic mihi nescio quis, "Quid fles tua somnia?" dixit.
        "Est aliquid lachryma quod graviore fleas."
    Plura loquuturum somno fugiente reliqui,
100   Sumque fatigata reddita nocte mihi.
    Frigidus in toto manabat corpore sudor;
        Perfusae lachrymis immaduere genae.
    Aeger anhelabat sub pectore spiritus aegro.
        Vis animae multum fessa dolentis erat.

---

67 pocula tradita *A*: tradita pocula *BO*.   **76** redit *A*: cadit *BO*.   **77** noctis *A*: noctes *BO*.
79 piscosus . . . Lanus alluit *AB*: Lanus aquis . . . vagus abluit *O*.   **80** falsi *A*: prisci *BO*.   **83** dum
mirabar *A*: cum mirarer *BO*.   **85** pedem — citatum *A*: gradu rediisse citato *BO*.   **94** destituisse *A*:
deseruisse *BO*.   **97** Hic *A*: Hinc *BO*.   **103** Aeger *A*: Moestus *BO*.

In the meantime, how my lingering pain will grow hour by hour, as long as you remain far from me — my husband, my consort, my brother! Whether I eat the food or take the drink that is offered, the very drink, the very food reminds me of you. The same distress in the evening, the same grief reborn in the morning; [70] and as you afflict me by day, so you approach me by night. Nocturnal dreams bring you back in various guises, for your appearance is never the same. Now and again you run up to me looking deathly pale. Sometimes you stand there with a cheerier face; at other times you flee and, averting your gaze, turn your back on me. Whether people can actually see the future in dreams or whether the cares of the preceding day return to haunt us with baseless fears, the visions I had last night make me afraid. May God bring them to naught and scatter them to the winds!

Here where the fish-filled Lahn laps the illustrious city [80] that bears the frivolous name of the false god Mars,[2] I dreamt I saw a crowd of people at the foot of the airy mountain. I did not know anybody in this throng, however; and yet I was standing in its midst. But as I marveled at where I might be, I looked around. There was no companion in sight! This frightened me, and I was about to run the other way when, lo and behold, I saw you standing with me, but at some distance. I froze in my tracks — that is how ecstatically happy I was! I was beside myself with joy. When I rushed forward, you disappeared from sight, leaving me desperately searching for my husband, [90] my fingernails scratching the tear-dewed cheeks. I ran this way and that; I wandered back and forth, but you were nowhere to be seen. So among the Greeks, they say, the ghost of Creusa vanished from her panting husband Aeneas.[3]

Then for the first time I started to rend my hair, which did not deserve this, and my voice was choked with tears of grief. Hereupon somebody or other said to me: "Why weep at your dream? Save your tears for something worse." He was about to say more; but as the dream fled from me, I left him [100] and woke up from the exhausting night. My whole body was bathed in cold sweat; my cheeks were drenched with a flood of tears. The breath came in painful gasps from deep inside my heaving breast. The strength of my anguished soul was altogether spent.

---

[2]Marburg Castle did not in fact become the residence of the landgraves of Hesse until the second half of the thirteenth century. It still served that purpose in Eobanus' day: see Rener, 448. The derivation of the city's name from *Martis burgum* (*Mars-burg*) is a common humanistic conceit. The word actually comes from the older *Marbachburg*.

[3]The ghost of Creusa appeared to her husband Aeneas during the final hours of Troy: see Verg. *A.* 2.771–94. Since Ludwig disappears like her, he too must be dead: cf. ll. 98, 107–08, 111–12 below.

21=F1ʳ 105 Visa resumebam tristi perterrita monstro,
                 Sed nihil ex illis quod placuisset erat.
             Hem, qur ignotae mihi visus in agmine turbae
                 Effugis amplexus labilis umbra meos?
             Quid non militibus comitatus, ut ante, ministris
      110   Appares oculis moesta figura meis?
             Quid non visa fleam? Potiusne ego vera dolebo?
                 O superi, a nobis hoc prohibete malum!
             Omnia perpetiar duce te durissima, Christe,
                 Tutus ope ut possit vir meus esse tua.
      115 In patriam redeat tutus, patriaque sepultus,
                 Et non ignota dormiat exul humo.
             Hoc te tota rogat frequentibus Hessia votis,
                 Plurimaque accensas accipit ara faces.
             Per tua sancta quibus sanasti vulnera mundum
      120   Et per quam vita est nostra redempta necem,
             Per sacrae veneranda crucis signacula per quam
                 Et requies nobis venit et alma salus,
             Te precor, auxilium nostro fer, Christe, marito,
                 Ut quod agit foelix regrediatur iter.
      125 At tu, cuius amor castus mea pectora movit,
                 Ut facis, in superos spem cape, salvus eris.
F1ᵛ   Barbaricas etiam fraudes vitare memento.
                 Nescio quis miserae pendeat inde timor.
             Sancta Canopaeo servit Iudaea tyranno;
      130   Christicolas odit gens malefida viros.
             Si quis eo princeps ex nostro venerit orbe,
                 Vix hunc, ni lateat, posse redire putant.
             Improba gens, quia se, titulo quae servat iniquo,
                 Posse per insidias perdere regna timet.
      135 Tu quia vir princeps illo non solus abibis,
                 Virtutis noli prodigus esse tuae.
             Pocula non sumas, nisi qui tibi fuderit illa
                 Gustatim vero ter prius ore bibat.
             Barbara neve manus quod edas utcunque ministret,
      140   Talia sed praesens virus habere puta.
             Lurida nobilibus miscent aconita Phalernis;
                 Crede merum gemma quod datur esse nocens.

107 Hem *A*: Heu *BO*.   114 ut *BO*: *om. A*.   115 In — tutus *A*: Incolumis patriae redeat *BO*.
117 frequentibus *A*: solennibus *BO*.   121 signacula *A*: mysteria *BO*; quam *A*: quae *BO*.   124 Ut
quod — iter *A*: Possit ut hoc regredi quod modo coepit iter *BO*.   128 timor *A*: metus *BO*.
129–34 Sancta — timet. *A*: *om. BO*.   129 Canopaeo *A* (*in erratis*): Canapaeo *A* (*in textu*).
135 illo *A*: isto *BO*.   141 Phalernis *A*: venenis *BO*.   *Post* 142 *add. BO*: Victor adire voles Christi
loca morte sacrata, / Forsan et Orebi culmina celsa [cessa *B*] iugi.

Terrified by the dreadful portent, I went over all the things I had seen, but there was nothing about them I liked. Alas, why did you appear to me in that crowd of strangers only to escape my embrace like a fleeting shade? Why were you not, as earlier, accompanied by a retinue of soldiers? [110] Why did you present such a mournful, ghostly aspect to my eyes? And why should I not weep at the dream? Am I to grieve at the reality instead? O heaven, deliver us from this evil! Under your guidance, Christ, I would endure everything, even the hardest burdens, so that my husband can be safe with your help. Let him return safe and sound to his homeland. Let him be buried in his own country and not sleep as an exile in alien soil. For this all Hesse prays to you in frequent supplications, and untold altars receive the burning tapers. By your blessed wounds, through which you healed the world, [120] and by your death, through which our life was redeemed, by the venerable sign of the holy rood, through which solace and bountiful salvation came to us, I beseech you, Christ: help my husband so that he may happily return from the journey on which he has set out.

But you, whose chaste love touches my heart, place your hope in heaven, as you always do, and you will be safe. Also remember to be on your guard against the knavery of foreigners. Somehow a great fear of that hangs over me, poor woman. Holy Judea is subject to the Egyptian tyrant; [130] that treacherous race hates us Christians! If a prince comes there from our part of the world, it is thought that he can scarcely return unless he goes incognito. Those people are ruthless, because they are afraid of losing their ill-gotten kingdom to crafty plots. Since you, as one of the leaders, are not setting out unaccompanied for that place, do not be needlessly bold. Do not lift a goblet to your lips, unless your cupbearer tests it first by sipping it three times himself. Nor should you eat anything served up by a foreign hand. [140] Just assume such foods contain potent poison. Deadly aconite is readily mixed with vintage wines. Hence, take it for granted that any wine served in a jeweled cup is harmful.

Fida tibi comitum manus est, et lecta iuventus.
    Est aliquid docta fraude quod inde petas.
145 Ex illis aliquem dominum lege et esse saluta
    Teque fer exiguae sortis habere locum.
Non pudeat propriis dominum servire ministris
    Et famulo famulas exhibuisse manus.

22=F2^r

Foecit idem rerum Deus infinita potestas:
150   Immundos pueris laverat ille pedes.
Quod Christum decuit, quem non decet? Omnia vincet
    Qui bene fortunae congruus esse potest.
Saepe facit tempus rationem, saepe locorum
    Conditio et caecum quae dea lumen habet.
155 Invenies aliquem qui, si sic fata iuberent,
    Appositam pro te vellet obire necem.
Veste potes vili loca per non tuta latere.
    In corpus veniat purpura nulla tuum.
Tu tamen ingenio velut es praestante beatus,
160   Consilio potis es non eguisse meo.
Sed tamen in dubiis prudens timet omnia rebus.
    Convenit egregia cum ratione timor.
Omne quod audebis, vellem prius omne timeres.
    Audacem temere saepe fuisse nocet.
165 Ipsa Deum supplex, quamvis mora longa, precabor
    Contingas fausto regna beata pede.
Aspicies Solimos, Christi vestigia, colles —
    Heu, loca non oculis aspicienda meis.
Cum tamen attigeris nostrae monumenta salutis,
170   Me, rogo, non fias immemor esse tuam.

F2^v

"Coniugis," o utinam dicas, "miserere relictae,
    Qui tua salvifico sanguine membra rubes."
Ipse loco non est magis exorabilis ullo,
    Quam quo sanavit vulnera nostra, Deus.
175 Tu quoque non istic quicquam tibi crede negari,
    Si dederis fasso quas decet ore preces.
Desertae memor esto domus matrisque meique,
    Quoque ego sum tecum pignore facta parens.
Ipsa tuis etiam relevanda est Hessia votis
180   Ante flagellati vulnera rubra Dei.

---

152 bene . . . congruus esse *A*: se . . . composuisse **BO**.   156 Appositam *A*: Haud dubiam **BO**. 159–62 Tu tamen — timor. *A*: *om*. **BO**.   164 Audacem — nocet *A*: Convenit egregia cum ratione timor **BO** [= *v. 162*].   167–68 Aspicies — meis. *A*: *om*. **BO**.   170 non *A*: ne **BO**.   173–74 Ipse — Deus *A*: Audiat ex animo licet hic et ubique precantes, / Ista sit ad nullas ianua clausa preces, / Par tamen est credi quia non sit mitior ullo, / Quam quo sanavit vulnera nostra, loco **BO**. 175 istic *A*: illic **BO**.

You command a loyal band of comrades, all of them hand-picked warriors. There is a cunning deception you could draw from this. Choose one of them to be lord and address him as such, while you disguise yourself as a common soldier. It is no shame for a lord to obey his own subjects and lend his servants a serving hand. God, the boundless Lord of all creation, did that very thing: [150] he washed the filth from his disciples' feet. Who is too good for something that Christ thought fitting to do? If you can adapt yourself well to the circumstances, you will be able to overcome every obstacle. Often it is the hour that determines the tactics, often the type of terrain and blind Fortune herself. Surely you can find someone who, if fate should command it, would gladly lay down his life for you. In unsafe regions you can hide in a humble cloak. Under no circumstances should you wear the purple. Gifted as you are with a brilliant mind, however, [160] you are free to ignore my advice. Nevertheless, in risky situations a prudent man sees danger everywhere. Fear goes hand in hand with good sense. Because you will brave all danger, I would like you to fear all danger beforehand. It is the recklessly bold who often come to grief.

No matter how long it may take you, I myself will humbly pray to God that you may happily set foot in that blessed realm. You will walk in Christ's footsteps and see the hills of Jerusalem — places, alas, that I shall never see with my own eyes. But when you reach the monuments of our salvation, [170] please do not forget that I am yours. Oh, how I wish you would pray, "Have pity on the wife I left behind, O you whose limbs are red with your salvific blood." In no place on earth is God more easily entreated than there, where he healed our wounds. You, too, do not believe that anything will be denied you there, so long as you say your prayers, as you should, in a contrite voice. Remember the house you left behind, think of your mother and me and the child that I am expecting by you. In your prayers you should also lift Hesse up [180] before the ruddy wounds of the flagellated God.

Per mare sic habeant ventos tua vela secundos,
   Quando abis atque istinc quando redire voles.
Sic Rhodon et Cretam Cyprumque remensus aquosam,
   Concedas puppis unde soluta tua est.
185 Hoc precor, haec longo cura est mihi sedula voto.
   Dii faciant pondus possit habere! Vale.

Finis

---

182 Quando — quando *A*: Dumque iter hinc properas dumque *BO*.   183–84 Sic — puppis *A*: Sic
Cypron atque Rhodon Cretaeaque littora praeter, / Puppis, eo redeas *BO*.   185 precor *BO*: praecor
A; cura — sedula *A*: mihi cura est unica *BO*.   *Subscriptio* Finis *A*: *om. BO*.

So may your sails have favoring winds on the sea, both when you depart and when you're ready to return from there. So may you wend your way back past Rhodes and Crete and watery Cyprus and go to where your ship cast off. This is what I pray for; this is my sedulous concern, my lingering hope. May Heaven lend it weight! Farewell.

The End

6 HELENA CONSTANTINO

Littera, quae veram ferret tibi, nate, salutem,
    Quam merito matris debuit esse tuae!
Cum videas clausae signum venerabile chartae,
    Quid rectae dubitas esse salutis opus?
23=F3ʳ   5 Ista figura fuit caelo tibi visa sereno,
    Cum tibi Maxenti vis cohibenda foret.
In qua nostra salus, requies, et vita pependit,
    Per quam mortalis turba redempta sumus,
Quae mundi precium meruit portare redempti
    10 Cum Lux infernum solveret una cahos,
Arbor ab Eois longe dignissima sylvis,
    Nobilis humanae palma salutis opus,
Omnia quae passis ad se traxisse lacertis
    Creditur, immenso pondere facta gravis,
    15 Perdita Apelleae plus quam tria saecula genti,
    Crux opera matris, nate, reperta tuae est!
Ponimus hoc igitur caerata in fronte sigillum,
    Quod nullum signo principe maius erat.
Hoc gentilitiis decuit praeponere signis,
    20 Unde recens plena gloria laude venit.
Et maius meritum potioraque gaudia mundo
    Tempore in hoc credo non potuisse dari.

Her. Chr. **6.**   **4** rectae *A*: verae *BO*.   **6** Cum — foret *A*: Cum tua Maxenti cogeret arma furor *BO*.
7 requies *A*: requiesque *BO*.   **8** mortalis — redempta *A*: mortales libera turba *BO*.   **15** Apelleae *A*:
Niligenae *BO*.   **16** matris — reperta *A*: matris reddita, nate, *BO*.   **19** signis *A*: monstris *BO*.
21 mundo *AO*: mundi *B*.

[1]St. Helen (ca. 257–ca. 337), the mother of Emperor Constantine the Great (r. 306–37), recounts
how she discovered the true cross of Christ in Jerusalem and urges her son to remain strong in the
faith. The imperial eagles on his armies' standards, she insists, ought now to be replaced with the sign
of the cross.

    The legends on which Eobanus draws may be summarized as follows. In the night before his bat-
tle with Maxentius at the Milvian Bridge (312) Constantine saw a vision of a blazing cross inscribed
with the words "In hoc signo vinces" ("By this sign you shall conquer"). He therefore had a wooden
cross made and carried before his army into battle. After his victory, the emperor accepted the
Christian faith. In time he sent his mother, the Empress Helen, to Jerusalem to look for the true cross.
When the learned Jews told her that the only person who knew its location was a man named Judas,

6   HELEN TO CONSTANTINE[1]

How fitting it is, my son, that this letter, which sends you wishes
for true salvation, should come to you from your mother!

When you saw the venerable sign in the wax seal, why did
you doubt that it was the instrument of true salvation?[2] That was
the figure you saw in the cloudless sky, before you had to crush
Maxentius' might.

The tree, on which our salvation, solace, and life once hung,
the wood through which we mortals were redeemed, the rood
that deserved to bear the price for the redemption of this world
[10] when the one Light scattered the darkness of hell, by far the
worthiest tree from the Eastern forests,[3] the noble palm that
worked the salvation of humankind, the one that is believed to
have drawn everything to itself with outstretched arms, the very
one that was laden with an infinite burden, but was lost to the
Apellaean people[4] for more than three centuries — the cross, my
son, has been discovered through your mother's efforts! That is
why I stamped its image in the wax seal of my letter; for nothing
is more sublime than this our paramount emblem. It was only
right to prefer it to the heathen symbols, [20] now that it has
brought me so much acclaim and honor of late. And indeed,
I cannot imagine how in the present day anyone could bestow a
greater blessing and a nobler joy on the world.

Helen threatened to execute him unless he revealed its location. He refused; but after a week in prison
without food, he relented. The cross, he said, was buried beneath a temple of Venus erected by
Emperor Hadrian on Golgotha. Helen had the temple torn down at once. When Judas dug twenty
fathoms into the earth, he found three crosses. Christ's cross was soon identified, not only by the
inscription that Pilate had affixed to it but also because it alone was able to raise a young man from the
dead. Judas was converted to Christianity, given the name Quiriacus (Cyriacus), and appointed Bishop
of Jerusalem. See *Leg. aurea* 64.

In the 1532/39 version this letter is *Her.* 2.1.

[2]The seal bears an image of the newly-discovered cross. For the motif, cf. *Her. Chr.* 4.5, n.

[3]According to medieval legend, the cross was made from wood that originated in the tree of
Paradise: see *Leg. aurea* 64.4–10; *Marienlexikon*, ed. Remigius Bäumer and Leo Scheffczyk, vol. 3
(St. Ottilien, 1991), "Kreuzallegorie," 660–61. Cf. ll. 169–70 below, with n. 14.

[4]The epithet *Apellaean* (modeled on *Apellean*, which refers to the ancient Greek painter Apelles)
is formed from *Apella*, a credulous Jew mentioned in Hor. *S.* 1.5.100. Cf. Eob. *Hymn.* 78; *Vict.* 120.
However, as Porphyrio explains in his Horace commentary, *Apella* is actually a pun that applies a common name for a freedman to a man who, as a Jew, was "without a foreskin" (*a-*, "lacking" + *pelle*,
"skin"): that is to say, "circumcised." Cf. Calepino, *Dictionarium*, s.v. "Apella"; Eob. *Her. Chr.* 3.57 and
Vict. 472: "recutitae . . . gentis," "the circumcised people."

Maius erat certe tunc cum pateretur in illa,
    Per quem crux eadem sanctificata fuit.
25 Maius erat quando nostrae sub imagine carnis
    Virgine factus homo est parturiente Deus.
Sed tamen abiecto nasci quid profuit orbi,
    In cruce si natus non obiisset homo?
Vita magis morte est. Mors vita dignior illo,
30   Quod fuit haec nobis immediata salus.
Author morte Dei est nostrae crux alma salutis.
    Crux, mundi precio, sanguine rubra fuit.
Illa fuit putri — dolor est meminisse — latebra
    Clausa sub infami quo stetit ante loco.
35 Hic, ubi sub Cancro Solimas sol aspicit arces
    Ut non ex aliquo pene sit umbra loco,
Hic locus est nostra dictus "Calvaria" lingua.
    Accola Iudaea "Golgatha" voce vocat.
Hoc stetit illa rubens morientis sanguine Christi;
40   Hoc etiam nobis illa reperta loco est.
Sed neque qua celebres nostrum virtute laborem,
    Gloria nec mulier quam ferat ista fuit.
Hoc fecit qui cuncta facit miracula solus.
    Qui tulit, amissam reddidit ille crucem.
45 Magna quidem feci et longos abitura sub annos —
    Si qua brevis longum gloria nomen habet!
Compressi hostiles, et dux et foemina, terras
    Sumque Palestino quantus in orbe timor!
Non tamen hoc ausim nostris adscribere rebus
50   Nec titulum tantae laudis habere velim.
Scit Deus, hic animus per quem facit omne quod audet,
    Nullus in hoc unquam pectore fastus erat.
Ille dedit timidae certam sperare salutem;
    Quamque dedit, res est ipsa sequta fidem.
55 Venimus antiquam, notissima tecta, Siona,
    Qua posuit lyrico de duce templa satus.
Non populis regina iugum positura subactis,
    Non aliqua ex tota gente tributa tuli.
Longius haud potui Rhomanum extendere nomen,
60   Cui sol vix etiam finis uterque fuit.
Nec sequor aut Tomyrin magnisve Semiramin ausis.
    Nomina nemo Helenen talia velle putet!

F3ᵛ

24=F4ʳ

24 Per quem . . . sanctificata *A*: Cuius . . . sanguine rubra **BO**.   **29** morte *AB*: morti *O*.
30 Quod — salus *A*: Quod Phlegethontaeas proxima fregit opes **BO**.   **32** rubra *A*: tincta **BO**.
43 facit — solus *A*: potest et solus, et idem **BO**.   **48** orbe *A*: urbe **BO**.   **49** rebus *A*: factis
BO.   **61** Tomyrin *B*: Tomyrim *A*, Tomyrī *O*.

It was a greater blessing, to be sure, when he who hallowed
this cross was suffering on it. It was a greater blessing when God
took on our flesh and was made man, born of a virgin. All the
same, how could his birth have profited the downcast world, if
he had only been born and had not also died as a man on the
cross? Life is worth more than death. Death has more merit than
life in that [30] it was the means of our deliverance. Through
God's death the bountiful cross became the author of our salvation. The cross was red with the blood that ransomed the world.

It was locked up — the memory is painful — in a moldering
hiding place beneath the infamous spot where it once stood.
Here, where the midsummer sun looks directly down on the hills
of Jerusalem so that there is hardly any shade to be found, here is
the place we call *Calvary* in our language. The local people refer
to it with the Jewish word *Golgotha*. That is where the cross stood
when it was red with the blood of the dying Christ; [40] that is
also the spot where we found it again.

But there is no reason to attribute this achievement to any
excellence of mine, nor is it a woman who deserves that glory. The
one who made this possible is he who performs all miracles alone.
He, who bore the cross, also gave it back after it was lost. Still,
I have accomplished a great feat that will long be celebrated —
provided that brief glory can ever last long! A commander as well
as a woman, I subdued hostile countries, and what a terror I am in
the land of Palestine! Nevertheless, I would not venture to ascribe
this to my own exploits, [50] nor would I want to claim credit for
such praiseworthy deeds. If this spirit of mine accomplishes everything it dares undertake, it is only through God's grace. He knows
that there has never been a grain of pride in my breast. It is he who
enabled me, fearful woman, to be assured of deliverance; and the
confidence he gave me has been amply borne out by the fact.

We reached ancient Zion, the world-renowned city where the
poet-king's son[5] founded the Temple. I did not come as an
empress intent on imposing the yoke on a vanquished people, nor
did I exact any tribute from the country as a whole. I could not
extend the Roman Empire any further, [60] for even the rising
and the setting sun can scarcely encompass it all. I follow neither
Tomyris nor Semiramis in their grand ventures.[6] Let no one think
that Helen is looking for fame like that! While they achieved

[5]King Solomon, son of the Psalmist David.

[6]Tomyris was a legendary Scythian queen who defeated and killed Cyrus the Great. Semiramis,
a legendary Queen of Assyria, is said to have built Babylon and undertaken great wars of conquest.
Cf. *Ama.* 35.27; *Nup.* 186–87.

Si tamen est illis decori laus sanguine parta,
    Insignes titulo nos meliore sumus.
65 Regna et opes istae tantum terrena petebant;
    Nos alio petimus regna futura loco.
Sordibus his sequimur caelestia sola relictis.
    Da veniam. Timida talia mente loquor.

Illum ego, nate, sequor, quem tu quoque nuper ab istis
70   Egressus tenebris fassus es esse Deum.
Cuius in adversos hostes ut signa moverem,
    Multa tuli terris, multa pericla mari.
Nunc ego sublimi solio regina sedebam,
    Invita quatiens sceptra superba manu.
75 Contulit huc aliquam Rhomana potentia partem,
    Sub pedibus stabant milia multa meis.
Ad mea convenit populus mandata vocatus,
    Quando haec sedato pectore verba dedi:
"Dic, genus Israel, Pharii, dic, semen Ioseph,
80   Indice cui tellus contigit ista Deo,
Dic ubi, qur lateat? Qua crux est perdita culpa,
    Morte Creatoris facta beata tui?
Hoc tibi Rhomano Caesar qui praesidet orbi,
    Ut facias per nos hoc iubet ipse Deus.
85 Ante oculos vitamque vides mortemque paratam.
    Elige sive voles vivere sive mori."
Caesaris imperio concussum et nomine, vulgus
    In dubio faceret quidve negaret erat.
Cum tamen ad paucos ea res deducta fuisset,
90   Vix quoque qui verum noverat unus erat.

Hic erat a patribus qui se referebat Iudas
    Doctum quo lateat crux veneranda loco,
Sed qui nec precibus verbisve minacibus esset
    Ad mea speratam vota daturus opem.
95 Apposui mortem; mortem contempsit. Ab illa
    Vidit adhuc clausum carcere sexta dies.
Septima lux aderat, quum tristis inaedia verbum
    Iussit quod saturo noluit ore loqui.
Templa Cytheriaco stabant celeberrima scorto.
100   Vix locus in terris turpior ullus erat.
Quanta Dei nostri est patientia! Scilicet illa
    Improba pro Christo staret in aede Venus!

---

80 Indice *B*: Iudice *AO*.   85 paratam *BO*: parata *A*.   88 In — faceret *A*: Quid faceret dubium *BO*.   90 noverat *A*: diceret *BO*.   93 Sed *AO*: Si *B*.   94 opem *AB*: eram *O*.   95 Apposui *A*: Proposui *BO*; ab illa *BO*: ab illo *A*.   97 tristis — verbum *A*: vis famis improba dirae *BO*.   99 Cytheriaco *A*: Palaepaphio *BO*.   100 ullus *A*: alter *BO*.

renown through their glorious ancestry, we lay claim to a nobler title. Those women strove for nothing more than earthly kingdoms and riches; we strive for Kingdom Come in another world. Abandoning this temporal squalor of ours, we seek only the things of heaven. Forgive me! I say these things with a timid heart. Him I follow, my son, whom you too, [70] having left the pagan darkness, recently confessed as your God. To carry his banner against the enemy lines I have endured many dangers on land, many dangers at sea.

There I was, the empress, sitting on a majestic throne, waving the proud scepter with reluctant hand. Roman power had brought together a segment of the population. Beneath my feet stood many thousands. When they had assembled at my behest, I addressed them calmly in these words: "Tell me, people of Israel, tell me, seed of Egyptian Joseph,[7] [80] you to whom this land was given under God's guidance, tell me: Where and why is it hidden? By whose fault was it lost — the cross that the death of your Creator made blessed? The Caesar who governs the Roman Empire, indeed, God himself through me commands you to reveal this secret. Before your eyes you see life and death laid out. Choose whether you wish to live or die."

Shaken by the emperor's authority and prestige, the crowd was in doubt what to do or deny. But after we had traced this matter back to a few individuals, [90] there was just one who knew the truth. Judas, who belonged to the elders here, admitted that he had learned where the venerable cross was concealed; but neither entreaties nor threatening words could make him reveal the information I demanded and hoped for. I confronted him with death; he scorned death. The sixth day thereafter still saw him locked up in jail. On the seventh day, miserable starvation forced him to divulge the word he had refused to speak with sated lips.

There used to stand a much-frequented temple here, sacred to the harlot of Cythera.[8] [100] You would be hard pressed to find a more disgusting place anywhere on earth. How great is the forbearance of our God! For just imagine, in that shrine wanton Venus occupied the place of Christ! Often, when someone came

---

[7]Joseph, the son of Jacob (Israel), was sold into slavery in Egypt, but eventually became governor of the land. See Genesis 39–41.

[8]Venus, to whom the island of Cythera was sacred.

Illic sepe aliquis magnum veneratus Iesum
Visus Acidalias est coluisse faces.
105 Crimine de tanto dederat me vindice poenas.
Structa deae, nobis diruta templa iacent.
Ne scelerata etiam referat vestigia, iunctis
Eversam bobus sulcat arator humum.
Incultae vepres iuxta sentesque rigebant.
110 Nobilis est multis caedibus iste locus.
Ecce sed hic superos precibus cum rite vocaret,
Aura levis tactum est visa movere locum.

F5ᵛ Fodit et invenit terra tria signa regesta.
Ostendit veram scripta tabella crucem.
115 "Rex Iudaeorum, de Nazareth ortus Iesus" —
Talis in extrema littera fronte fuit.
Praeterea esse crucem Domini manifesta probarunt
Signa. Quibus certam quis neget esse fidem?
Putre ferebatur vicina ex morte cadaver.
120 Crux tetigit, tacto corpore vita data est.
Ille statim sacro petiit se fonte lavari,
Qui bona victoris reddidit arma Dei.
Nomina Cyriaco dedimus meliora renato.
Nunc pia sacrifici presulis arma gerit.
125 Vidit et indoluit doctor vetus ille malorum,
Terribili auditus taliter ore loqui:
"Quid facis heu, nobis ingrate, nequissime Iuda!
Heu mihi, quot mentes non sinis esse meas!
At non, cuius habes sine rebus nomina, noster
130 Talis, et in nobis noluit esse nocens.
Fraude mea mundo truncus fuit iste sepultus.
Ipse ego quam volui perdere, reddis opem.
At te digna manet pro tali paena reatu.
Gloria conveniens non erit ista tibi!"

26=F6ʳ 135 Ille crucem contra tollens, bona verba loquutus,
Ad Stygios hostem compulit ire lacus.
Gratia, Christe, tibi, nam tu de morte redemptos
In cruce nos propria vivere morte facis.
Tu quoque restituis mundo sua regna iacenti
140 Dux bonus et rectam pandis ad astra viam.

---

111 superos — cum *A*: precibus superos ubi *BO*. *Post* 111 *add. BO*: Qui Solima Macareus praesul in urbe fuit. / Cumque diu staret magnum veneratus Iesum, 112 tactum *A*: totum *BO*.
115–16 Rex — fuit. *A*: *om. BO*. 117 Domini manifesta *A*: Christi maiora *BO*. 122 bona *A*:
sacra *BO*. 127 heu *AO*: ita *B*. 128 Heu mihi *A*: Perfide *BO*; sinis *A* (*in erratis*) *BO*: suus *A* (*in
textu*). 131 Fraude *A*: Arte *BO*. 132 Ipse — volui *A*: Quam placuit nobis *BO*. 133 paena
scripsi: paenat *A*, poena *BO*. 137–38 redemptos — facis *A*: redemptis / Morte tua vitae de cruce
pandis iter *BO*. 140 rectam — viam *A*: saevi conteris hostis opes *BO*.

there to venerate Lord Jesus, it would look as if he had paid homage to the flames of lust. I could not let such a heinous crime go unpunished. Built for the goddess, the temple now lies in ruins at my command. So that not even a trace of that accursed structure should remain, a plowman turns and furrows the soil with a team of oxen. That place now bristles all round with a tangle of briers and thorns. [110] It is infamous for the many executions that once took place there.

But lo, as Judas was saying a solemn prayer to Heaven, a light breeze touched the place and visibly shook it. After digging deep into the ground, he discovered three crosses. An inscription on one of them identified it as the true cross. "The King of the Jews, Jesus of Nazareth" — that was the title placed at its head. Besides, several manifest signs proved that it was indeed the cross of our Lord. Who could deny their trustworthiness? The moldering corpse of a newly deceased person was brought near. [120] When the cross touched it, the body so touched was restored to life.

The man who gave back the potent armament of the victorious God immediately begged to be washed in the holy font. Born again, he received from us the more suitable name *Cyriacus*. Now he bears the pious insignia of a priestly bishop. That ancient teacher of evil, however, saw this and grieved. In a terrible voice he was heard to shriek: "What are you doing, ah, you ingrate, you base scoundrel, Judas! Alas, how many schemes of mine have you thwarted! That servant of mine whose name you bear without having his merit, [130] he never wanted to harm me like that. It was my stratagem to have that trunk lost to the world. The treasure I myself wanted to get rid of, you have restored. But for a crime like that you will get the punishment you deserve. *That* glory will not suit you so well!" But he, raising up the cross against him, spoke fair words and drove the Fiend back to the Stygian pools.

Thanks be to you, Christ: for through your own death on the cross you have delivered us from death and given us life. Like a good general, you have also liberated the fallen world from tyranny [140] and opened the right way to heaven. Thanks be to

Gratia, nate, tibi, nam tu Iove vera relicto
Et colis et toto pectore sacra iuvas.
Macte nova Caesar, nos, relligione, beatos
Efficis. Hac itur non meliore via.
145 Rhoma diu falsos coluit Mavortia divos
Et nunc, heu, plures quos veneretur habet.
Quod superest veterique iacet caligine mersum,
Ut videat, luci reddere, nate, stude.
Ut vetus expiret, tecum nova Rhoma revivat.
150   Quid dubitas orbem, quo cadat illa, trahi?
Caesar ut est unus terrae qui presidet uni,
Sic sciat haec unum Caesaris esse Deum.
Fiat ut hoc, Deus ipse tibi sua signa remittit;
His prius infernum vicerat ille Iovem.
155 Ibis in adversos cruce munitissimus hostes.
Christiferam fugiet turba prophana crucem.

F6ᵛ

Terribilem foecit qui cum pateretur in illa
Morte sua rerum terruit omne genus.
Hostibus incutiet trepidantibus illa timorem,
160   Non aliquo maior miles ab ense cadet.
Tu quoque, non aquilis Rhomana notantibus arma,
Caesaribus victor prae tribus unus eras.
Maximianaeum cruce te vicisse tyrannum
Scit Tybris, ultricem ducere visus aquam.
165 Qua virtute iacent ignobilis arma Licini?
Caetera qua finem laude tyrannis habet?
Heu fatuae mentes, quid nomina sola deorum?
Mentito numen crux Iove maius erat.
Sive sit hic Libani stipes de vertice sylvae
170   Seu paradisiaco creverit ille solo,
Est sacer ante decem praevisus saecula, quantum
Praecessit verum tanta Sybilla Deum.
Foelix quae potuit foelix cognoscere lignum,
Regina in Meroe digna potente coli.

---

151 Caesar *BO*: Coesar *A*.   **153** ipse *AB*: ecce *O*.   *Post* **154** *add. BO*: Nunc tu, sive bonis
pacatum legibus orbem / Sive regis forti tempora dura manu, / De cruce fac sola tua gloria pendeat
ista. / Christiferae cedat laurea victa cruci! / Nec tibi turpe puta signis infamibus uti. / Hinc tua, si
nescis, vita salusque venit. / Crux, ignominiae quondam nota, facta per illum, / Qui tulit, est nostrae
gloria militiae.   **159** timorem *AB*: pavorem *O*.   **165** Qua — Licini *A*: Qua Licini virtute
iacent ignobilis arma *BO*.   **167** quid *A*: quo *BO*.   **169–84** Sive — fores. *A*: *om. BO*.
173 quae *scripsi*: que *A*.

---

⁹Helen appeals to her son to found "a new Rome." Constantine did, in fact, found Constantinople
in 330 to serve as his "Second Rome" — the purely Christian capital of the empire.
¹⁰The old Roman emblem was the eagle. Constantine replaced this symbol with the cross.
¹¹Emperor Maxentius (r. 306–12) was the son of Emperor Maximian. He drowned in the Tiber
while fleeing from Constantine's army during the battle of the Milvian Bridge. Cf. ll. 5–6 above.

you, son: for now that you have abandoned Jove, you revere and
promote the true religion with heart and soul. Bless you,
Emperor, for your new faith, which makes us all blessed. You
could not travel on a better path than this.

The Rome of Mars has long worshiped the false gods and even
now, alas, she still venerates a great many. So that the rest of those
still buried in the old darkness may learn to see, you, my son, must
strive to lead them back into the light. In order that the old Rome
may perish, let a new Rome rise up together with you.[9] [150] Why
should you doubt that the world will follow him, to whom that city
is subject? Just as there is one Caesar who governs one single earth,
so the world should know that Caesar has but one God. To let you
accomplish that, God himself returns his ensign to you. With it he
earlier conquered the infernal Jove. Protected by the cross from all
harm, you will now charge fearlessly at the enemies ranged against
you. The impious host will flee from the Christ-bearing cross. He,
whose suffering and death on the cross terrified the entire world, has
made it a thing of terror. It will strike the enemy soldiers with fear
and trembling: [160] no Christian warrior will perish by the sword.

You, too, precisely because the Roman armies did not use eagles
on their standards,[10] emerged as the sole victor over three Caesars.
With the help of the cross you defeated the tyrant Maxentius, as the
Tiber well knows, for it seemed then to be running with a vengeful
current.[11] By whose aid did you crush the troops of lowborn
Licinius?[12] How ignominiously did the remaining tyranny end?[13]
Ah, the fools! What use are gods that are mere words without sub-
stance? The cross was mightier than the feigned Jupiter.

Whether it was the trunk of a tree on the crown of Mount
Lebanon [170] or grew in the soil of Paradise, the holy cross was
foreseen ten centuries ago — by that much did the exalted
prophetess precede the true God.[14] Blessed was she who was able
to recognize the blessed wood, a queen worthy of adulation in

---

[12]Emperor Licinius (r. 308–24), who came from peasant stock, was defeated by Constantine the
Great in 314 and 324, and was executed in 325.

[13]Maximian was emperor from 286 until his abdication in 305. Four years later he attempted to
regain the imperial crown, but his rebellion was suppressed by Constantine. Taken prisoner in Massilia
(Marseilles), he hanged himself (310).

[14]According to *Leg. aurea* 64.4–23, there were several stories in circulation concerning the origin
of the wood of the cross. According to one legend, the Archangel Michael gave Adam's son Seth a
branch of the tree of mercy in Paradise and told him to plant it on Mount Lebanon. Another version
says that the archangel gave him a branch from the tree of the knowledge of good and evil and told
him that the fruit of the new tree would someday bring Adam back to sound health. Planted on
Adam's grave, the branch grew into a great tree. Solomon had it cut down to use it to erect the Temple;
but since it could not be made to fit anywhere, he used it as a bridge across a pond. The Queen of
Sheba (Meroe) saw it there on her visit to King Solomon. Cf. also 1 Kings 10.1–10; 2 Chronicles
9.1–9; Peter Riga, *3. Reg.* 235–46.

175 Illa Deo mentem calidissima Pneumate fertur
    Talibus Hebraeum praemonuisse ducem:
    "Rex, ne temne. Vides" — lignum monstravit — "in illo
    Ille cadet cum quo vestra corona cadet."

27=G1ʳ   Ergo paludali mersum a Solomone profundo
180   Illesum Domino mansit (ut ante) suo.
    Interea optato saeclorum fine peracto
    Caeli iterum terris Rex abiturus erat.
    Protinus emersit laturum pondera quorum
    Infernae caderent sub gravitate fores.

185 Fortior et caelo, terra crux fortior ipsa,
    Et coelum et terras qui tulit, ipsa tulit.
    Christiferae similis qua sit ratione puellae,
    Si dubitas, ista parte videre datur.
    Si libet, esse puta lignum breve quale videtur;

190   Non tamen est longum qua ratione neges.
    Vertice nam caelos, radicibus infera pulsat,
    Brachia contingunt solis utramque domum.
    Vera loquor, sed quae multis non vera putantur.
    Vera tuum, Caesar, quo videantur erit.

195 Excute Rhomanas, gentilia signa, volucres.
    Conveniunt castris altera signa tuis.
    Arbor ab Eois longe dignissima sylvis
    Ut crescat, cura est amplificanda tua.
    Floreat et totum ramis vitalibus orbem

200   Contegat et ventos arceat atque nives.
G1ᵛ   Sed tamen Hesperidum ne quis ferus intret in hortos,
    Rite draco clausas excubet ante fores.
    Neu malus auratum vellus furetur Iason,
    Custodes armet noxia flamma boves.

205 Tu modo, si qua volet cedro succrescere taxus,
    Aemulaque immiti robora falce mete.
    Fallor, an haec paucis sunt eventura diebus?
    O sic cum nostro Caesare, Christe, velis!

---

188 datur *AB*: potes *O*.   193 putantur *A*: putentur *BO*.   200 Contegat *A*: Protegat *BO*. 201–04 Sed — boves. *A*: *om. BO*.   206 Aemulaque immiti *A*: Aemula, qua debes, *BO*.   207 sunt eventura *AB*: ita sunt ventura *O*.   208 sic *A*: ita *BO*.

powerful Meroe. Her mind all aglow with the Spirit of God, she
is said to have given the Hebrew king the following prediction:
"King, mark my words. Look," — here she pointed to the beam —
"on that wood a man will perish, and with him your crown."
Solomon therefore caused it to be buried in the depths of a
swamp, [180] where (as before) it waited unharmed for its Lord.
Meanwhile, the hoped-for end of an era arrived when the King
of heaven was preparing to leave the earth again. Forthwith the
wood rose up to the surface, ready to bear the burden under
whose weight the gates of hell would collapse. Stronger than
heaven, stronger than the earth itself, the cross bore him who
bears heaven and earth. In that respect, in case you were wondering, it evidently resembles the Christ-bearing Virgin. You could
look at it this way too, if you want. Outwardly it seems only a
short piece of wood. [190] Nevertheless, there is no reason why
you should not think of it as a towering tree. After all, it strikes
the heavens with its crown, the underworld with its roots, while
its branches reach both abodes of the sun.[15]

I speak the truth. But since many still do not believe the
truth, it will be your task, Caesar, to open their eyes to the truth.
Get rid of the Roman eagles, those heathen emblems. Your
armies should henceforth march under a different standard. If
this tree, by far the worthiest from the Eastern forests, is to continue growing, you must redouble your zeal. Let it blossom; let it
cover the whole world with its life-giving branches [200] and
ward off the winds and the snows. But lest some wild beast
should steal into the gardens of the Hesperides,[16] have a dragon
duly keep watch outside the locked gates. And to keep some
wicked Jason from stealing the Golden Fleece,[17] let fire-spewing
bulls stand guard. If a yew tree should try to grow up from under
that cedar,[18] cut the rival sapling down with a pitiless pruning
knife.

Am I mistaken, or are these events about to occur in the very
near future? Oh Christ, may that be your will with our Caesar!

---

[15]The Orient and the Occident.

[16]The Hesperides had a garden beyond the Atlas Mountains, on the western shore of the Ocean.
This garden contained a tree of golden apples that was guarded by the dragon Ladon. In the present
passage, the golden apples represent the treasure of the cross.

[17]Jason set out with the Argonauts to Colchis to bring back the Golden Fleece, which was
guarded by a dragon and fire-breathing bulls. Helen uses the myth here to symbolize the cross.

[18]With its dark-green leaves and poisonous needles, the yew was widely associated with the
underworld. The cedar, on the other hand, was a common image for the cross or for Christ himself:
see Salzer, 152. Cf. especially Sirach 24.13 (24.17 in the Vulgate), a text traditionally interpreted as
pointing to Christ on the cross. Also see Eob. *Her. Chr.* 18.141.

Tu quoque ne lateas aliqua, Palinure, sub unda,
210   Sed vigili rectam dirige mente ratem.
Sic te, nate, precor per nos inventa secundent
     Signa, maniplares non habitura notas.
Serviat Hebraeo Rhomana potentia Christo.
     Caetera sunt votis inferiora meis.

209–10 Tu — ratem. *A*: *om. BO*.

Do not become another Palinurus[19] and be buried somewhere beneath the waves, [210] but remain vigilant and steer a steady course. May the standard I discovered prosper you, my son — a standard that will not be mistaken for the old infantry emblem. May Roman power serve the Hebrew Christ. My other wishes are subordinate to these.[20]

[19]Aeneas' steersman Palinurus fell overboard after Somnus, the god of sleep, had touched him with his wand. Three days later he was washed ashore in Italy, only to be murdered by the inhabitants and left unburied. See Verg. *Aen.* 5.833–71; cf. Eob. *Her. Chr.* 15.171.

[20]Hence she does not end the letter with the usual wish, "Farewell."

7   SABINA ALEXIO

Sic, ubi perdiderit charum viduata sodalem,
  Turtur Acidalias concinit inter aves.
Non quia te nolim sacris gaudere professis,
  Sed mihi quod tecum non licet esse queror.
5 Tu quoque credentem potuisti fallere nuptam,
  Primaque de nobis fraus tua nomen habet.
Si mea non potuit ruditas meruisse favorem,
  Cur tua fit nostro crimine tarda fides?
Profuit hoc miserae tedas praeferre iugales?
10 Sic quoque Vestalis nubere virgo potest!
Quae mihi prima fuit, facta est nox ultima tecum,
  Quaeque dies nobis te dedit, illa tulit.
At mea virginitas bene tot servata per annos
  Moesticiae precium tristis et instar habet.
15 Hoc bene successit quod sum sine crimine nupta,
  Hoc male, quod cogi creditur ille pudor.
Vivere si lecto tecum licuisset eodem,
  Summa prior voti non fuit ulla mei.
Hoc tibi tuque mihi, qua sola nocte licebat,
20 Polliciti caelo testificante sumus.
Oscula non etiam plusquam fraterna dedisti,
  Sed tamen his peius lingua loquta tua est:
"Vive, soror, votum non demissura pudorem.
  Diversa exilio terra petenda mihi est.
25 Ut bona mutemus caelo peritura redempto,
  Ad loca quae superis sunt propiora feror.
Cum referet plenam ter septima messis aristam,
  Si vivam, reditu laeta ferere meo."

28=G2^r

Her. Chr. 7. **2** Turtur — aves *A*: Si canere hoc dicas, moesta columba canit *BO*.   **3** sacris *A*: rebus *BO*.   **8** fit *A*: sit *BO*.   **14** tristis *A*: pondus *BO*.   **17** si *BO*: sic *A*; eodem *A*: in uno *BO*.   **19** Hoc *A*: Hanc *BO*; qua *A*: quo *BO*.   **20** Polliciti — sumus *A*: Accepta dedimus conditione fidem *BO*.   **22** peius *A*: prius *BO*.   **23** demissura *A*: dimissura *BO*.   **25–26** Ut — feror. *A*: *om. BO*.

7   **SABINA TO ALEXIUS**[1]

Thus, when she has lost her dear mate, sings the widowed turtledove among the birds of Venus.[2] I lament, not because I want to keep you from enjoying your life of holiness, but because I don't have the chance to be by your side. You were also capable of misleading your trusting bride, and the first deceit between us was of your doing.

Even if I was too simpleminded to merit your favor then, why should that reproach keep you from coming back to me, as you promised? What good did it do me, poor girl, to get married? [10] On these terms even a Vestal Virgin could enter wedlock! My first night with you was also the last, and the same day that gave you to me also took you away. True, I have preserved my virginity intact for so many years now; but it has cost me no end of grief and sorrow. Things have turned out well in that I was married without losing my chastity. They have turned out badly in that my maiden-hood looks as if it were imposed on me.

If I could have shared a bed with you, I would have seen my dearest wish fulfilled. We did exchange vows to do just that, [20] as heaven is our witness; but it was granted to us for only one night. In fact, you gave me nothing more than brotherly kisses. Worse than that, you told me outright: "Good-bye, sister. You will never lose the virginity you plighted to me. I must go abroad into exile. To trade temporal goods for eternal redemption, I am drawn to the places that are closer to heaven. When the twenty-first harvest brings in the full ears of grain, then, God willing, you'll rejoice in my return."

[1]St. Alexius (fifth century) was the only son of the Roman nobleman Euphemius and his wife Aglaë. In accordance with his parents' wishes he married a wealthy girl. Wishing to live a life of utmost poverty and chastity, however, he left her on his wedding night, though not until he had instructed her in the faith and committed her to perpetual virginity. For seventeen years he lived as a beggar in Edessa, Syria. One day the servants, whom his father had sent to look for him, came to Edessa. They offered him alms, but failed to recognize him. After the Virgin Mary revealed his holiness, Alexius returned to Rome. There, unrecognized, he lived for another seventeen years as a servant in his father's house. His identity was not revealed until after his death. See *Leg. aurea* 90. None of the legends gives the name of Alexius' bride.

Sabina's letter — written on their twenty-first wedding anniversary — recalls the shocking events of their first and last night together. It goes on to describe her grief and that of her parents-in-law and assures Alexius that they intend to keep on looking for him. But how are they to recognize him now, after so many years? For all they know, he could be living in his parents' house right now. She therefore pleads with him to come back before she dies.

The lapse of a full twenty years between Alexius' departure and Sabina's letter is intended to remind us of Ovid's first heroic epistle. There the faithful Penelope writes Ulysses after his twenty-year absence and urges him to come back. Since neither heroine realizes that her husband is in fact already home, they intend to keep sending their letter to all corners of the world. The reader knows that both women will see their husbands again. But while Ulysses returns alive and well, Sabina will see her husband only in death.

In the 1532/39 version this letter is *Her.* 3.5.

[2]The turtledove, sacred to Venus, was a symbol of marital fidelity, even beyond the death of its mate. See *Her. Chr.* 5.54, n.

Non secus obstupui quam quae super Alpibus altis
30   Audiat immites pendula dama lupos.

"Scilicet accepto vivam sine coniuge coniux,
Quemque velim coram semper abesse querar?
Quid mihi Rhomulides meliori sydere nuptae,
Quid Latiae dicent, invida turba, nurus?
35   Omnia liberius credit mala vulgus iniquum.
Esse bonis semper fama maligna solet."
Qualiter incumbens adamantina robora ferrum,
Sic animum movit nostra querela tuum.
Et tibi iam Tyriae vestes, iam purpura fulgens
40   Excidit, est humeris mantica sumpta tuis.
Dextra tulit baculum, numeratos altera glandes.
Latus in obducta fronte galerus erat.
"Hei mihi, quid foeci? Quali sum nupta marito?
Huic forma nescit maxima Rhoma parem!"
45   Tempus erat, rebus nox abstulit atra colorem;
Per nigra non ullus nubila fulgor erat.
Oscula discedens lachrymis confusa dedisti,
Hoc repetens longo tempore: "Vive, soror."
"Ibis et heu miseram cui me, fugitive, relinquis?
50   Quam properas," dixi, "sim comes ipsa viae."
Et simul excideram. Vix tu solatus amantem,
"Tempore," dicebas, "sola fer esse brevi."

Hebdomas implevit ter septem tertia messes,
Nec tua promissa est verba sequta fides.
55   Durius invisas crescit mihi tempus in horas,
Quo sine te durum est vivere, dulce mori.
Aspiciunt aliae coram sua gaudia nuptae,
Seque laborantes qui tueantur habent.
Et vir abest nobis et sum sine fratre marito
60   Meque laborantem qui tueatur abest.
Ergo ego, turbato currentibus ordine fatis,
Quo sim nupta minus, sum data nupta viro!
Sola fui patiente animo. Sic esse iuvabat,
Quod volui vita virgine posse frui.
65   Cur tamen haec tecum non est concessa voluntas?
Hoc melior nobis palma petenda fuit.

---

31 accepto *A*: ipsa viro *BO*.   **37** Qualiter — ferrum *A*: Qualiter imbriferis tellus siccatur ab Austris *BO*.   **41–42** Dextra — erat. *A*: *om. BO*.   **50** Quam *AB*: Quum *O*.   **56** durum est *A*: miserum *BO*.   **59** Et vir — marito *A*: Absentem ipsa gemo, sine coniuge nupta, maritum *BO*. **66** Hoc *A*: Qua *BO*; petenda *A*: futura *BO*.

I was as stunned as [30] a cliff-hanging doe that hears the merciless wolves high up in the Alps. "You mean I'm now to live as wife without the husband I took? Am I now to lament that the man I wanted by my side will always keep far away? What will the happily married matrons of Rome say to me? And what about the young women of Rome, that spiteful crowd? The prejudiced masses would much rather believe anything bad. Gossip always hurts good people the most."

Like a hammer striking an anvil, so my lament moved your heart. And already you were taking off your Tyrian raiments,[3] already throwing aside the shimmering purple, [40] and were slinging a knapsack over your shoulders. Your right hand held a staff, the other a moneybag. A broad hat covered your forehead. "Alas, what have I done? What kind of husband am I married to? The whole great city of Rome has never seen the likes of him!"

It was the time when black night has robbed the world of its color. No flashes lit up the lowering clouds. As you left, you gave me kisses mingled with tears and kept saying this over and over: "Good-bye, sister."

"You are going. But ah, in whose hands, runaway, are you leaving me poor girl? [50] Let me," I appealed, "accompany you on the voyage you are rushing off to." And at the same time I fell into a faint. Scarcely trying to console your lover, you said, "Endure being alone for just a short time."

The twenty-first harvest has now concluded the third hebdomad,[4] and still you have not kept the promise you gave me. From hour to hateful hour the passing time is growing harder for me to bear: for without you it is hard to live, sweet to die. Other wives see their joy before their eyes and have someone to protect them when they're in distress. But my husband has left me; I live without my brotherly spouse; [60] and the one who should be protecting me when I'm in distress is far away. And so, with fate turning the normal course of events upside down, I am married to a man who is not married to me!

I have patiently stayed alone. That is the way I like it, because I always wanted to enjoy a life of chastity. But why couldn't this wish have been granted with you at my side? That way we both could have striven for a nobler prize. If you refuse to

---

[3]Expensive garments dyed with the purple produced in Tyre.
[4]In Hebrew usage, *hebdomad* means a group of seven years.

Laudatur qui cum possit peccare recusat.
   Quo careas facile est abstinuisse bono.
Innocui thalamo convenissemus in uno.
70   Maior ob hoc merces nostra futura fuit.
Sin ea coniugii tollat reverentia laudem,
   Noster in accepta prole stetisset amor.
Parvus in hac aliquis lusisset Alexius aula,
   Unde haec exiguum littera venit opus,

G3ᵛ   75   In qua, me miseram, quam tristibus obruta curis,
   Sufficio lachrymis non satis ipsa meis.
Ditibus ingredior triclinia strata tapetis;
   Mallem humilis tecum tecta subire casae!
Aula laborato preciosa renidet ab auro;
80   Quo videam nostrum talia lumen, abes.
Quaeque placent aliis, mihi sunt invisa, tedetque
   Qualescunque inter vivere delitias.
Anxius ipse pater multis Euphemius annis,
   Quod, nequit, ingratum est, dedoluisse semel.
85   Talis erat puerum quondam qui flevit ademptum
   Ad Pharon et glebam, Nile comose, tuam.
Mater et Aglae tua me solata dolentem
   Sepe aliquo visum nuper in orbe refert.
"Parce, nurus, lachrymis neque nos consume dolendo.
90   Magna tuum (fama est) vidit Edessa virum."
Multa igitur nobis te quaerere littera missa est,
   Littera sed semper reddita clausa mihi.
Misimus Hebraeas urbes veteremque Siona,
   Reddita nec fama est nominis ulla tui.
95   Non Hellesponti tetigisti littora, nec te
   Bosphorus angusto vexit uterque mari.

30=G4ʳ   Nec fera te, nobis consulta, Britannia vidit,
   Plenaque presenti Teutonis ora Deo.
Ad sacra non visum Zebedidae limina divi
100   Nemo sub Hispano vivere sole putat.
Misimus ad fortes aliquem te quaerere Gallos.
   Heu, nec apud Gallos quando videris, ubi es?
Ergo tuum nomen tibi convenit illud, Alexi!
   Littera responsu nulla onerata tuo est.
105   Forsan et agnosci non vis ubicumque locorum,
   Ex patria quenquam noris adesse domo.

---

67 Laudatur . . . possit . . . recusat *A*: Laudantur . . . liceat . . . recusant *BO*.   70 Maior — fuit *A*:
Castaque foedasset corpora nulla Venus *BO*.   75 obruta *A*: anxia *BO*.   79 preciosa *A*: speciosa
BO.   81 tedetque *A*: pigetque *BO*.   83–84 Anxius — semel. *A*: *om. BO*.   85–86 Talis —
tuam *A*: Talis erat puerum qui tot de fratribus unum / Deflevit senio iam subeunte pater. / Sic trabe de
querna luxit pendentia nati / Corpora Psalmographae duxque parensque lyrae *BO*.   92 sed *A*: quae
BO; mihi *A*: mihi est *BO*.   98 Plenaque *A*: Plenave *BO*.   104 responsu *A*: responso *BO*.

sin when you can, you win praise. It is easy to abstain from
a pleasure you don't have yourself. We could have gotten together
in the same bedroom, yet stayed perfectly blameless. [70] For this
we would have earned a much richer reward. But if our reverence
for matrimony had taken that merit away, our love would have
been fixed upon the child we conceived. Then there might well
have been a little Alexius playing in this hall, from where this
short letter has come to you and in which — overwhelmed with
heartache, poor me! — I have trouble restraining my tears.

I go into the dining room that is decked out with costly
rugs: I would rather live with you under the roof of some humble cottage! The sumptuous hall glitters with hammered gold;
[80] but you, the light by which I could see such splendors, are
absent. The things that other people find pleasing are hateful to
me, and it sickens me to live amidst luxuries of every kind. This
too is distressing: your father Euphemius, afflicted as he is with
anxious old age, is unable to put his anguish behind him once
and for all. He reminds me of that father who, long ago, wept for
the son he lost in Egypt, on the soil of longhaired Nile.[5]

Your mother Aglaë often assuages my grief by assuring me that
you have been spotted recently in some distant part of the world.
"Stop crying, daughter-in-law, and don't wear us out with your
grieving. [90] They say your husband has been seen in the great city
of Edessa." In search of you, therefore, we have sent off letter after
letter, but they have always been returned to me unopened. We sent
word to the Hebrew cities and to ancient Zion, but have received
no reports about you at all. You have not reached the shores of the
Hellespont, nor have the two Bosphoruses carried you on their narrow straits.[6] Barbaric Britain had not seen you when we asked there;
neither had Germany, so alive to God's presence. Since you have
not been seen at the shrine of St. James,[7] [100] nobody believes you
live under the skies of Spain. We sent someone to the valiant Gauls
to look for you. Alas, since you haven't been seen among the Gauls
either, where are you? So that name of yours fits you to a tee,
Alexius! For indeed, we have gotten no word from you in response.[8]
Perhaps you don't even want to be recognized, wherever you may
be, when you know somebody from your father's house is nearby.

---

[5]Jacob long mourned for his son Joseph, whom he believed dead, but who had in fact been sold
by his brothers into slavery in Egypt: see Genesis 37.12–36.

[6]The Thracian Bosphorus (between the Sea of Marmora and the Black Sea) and the Cimmerian
Bosphorus (between the Black Sea and the Sea of Azov).

[7]At Santiago de Compostela, the reputed burial site of St. James and a popular pilgrimage desti-
nation in the later Middle Ages. Since the tradition that James preached the gospel in Spain did not
become established until the eleventh century, Eobanus' reference is an anachronism. (The same, of
course, goes for Sabina's reference to a Christianized Germany.)

[8]In a pseudo-etymology, Sabina interprets *Alexius* to mean *a* ("without") + *lexis* ("a word"). The
name actually means "protector."

Hei mihi, sic etiam patria potes urbe latere
    Et sepe ex oculis tutus abire meis!
Multa ferunt anni fugienti incommoda formae,
110   Et nullo est unus semper in ore color.
Suspicor illius florem periisse iuventae,
    Legitima iuncti qua ratione sumus.
Quaeque abeuntis erant tenui vix pulvere sparsae,
    Fors tegit hirsutas improba barba genas.
115   Et quae cum patuit tabulas referebat eburnas,
    Ruga fatigata plurima fronte sedet.
Et pluviis madefacte et solibus uste diurnis,
    Hic etiam occultus si libet esse potes!

G4ᵛ

Qur tamen in misera crudelis coniuge dici,
120   Quod precor ut iam non esse, fuisse velis?
Illa tua hoc virtus, hoc nobilis ille requirit
    Qui tibi nunc tardo pectore sanguis hebet.
Sic ego debebam de te meruisse tot annis.
    Postulat hoc caelo teste relicta fides.
125   Aut illam reddas quae me male dextra fefellit,
    Aut tu qua fallis fraude ferere nocens.
Grata Deo non sunt fallentia pectora, nec te
    Fraude tua superis posse placere puta.
Qui nos coniunxit, coniunctos esse volebat.
130   Vita tua est illi dissona, crimen habet.
Finge dari veniamque tibi culpamque remitti.
    Quis dabit ut possis non nocuisse mihi?
At nocet utiliter qui quo nocet adiuvat idem.
    Nil queror. Est curis pars bona dempta meis.
135   Ferre decet patienter onus quod ferre necesse est.
    Qui iacet invitus, durius ille iacet.
Sors mea sunt lachrymae, tristes mea vita querelae.
    Unda sit o utinam sordibus illa meis!
Abluat et superum puram transmittat ad arces
140   Qua niveas ducit signifer Agnus oves.

31=G5ʳ

Illic, ut fueris nullo mihi in orbe repertus,
    Certe in caelitibus inveniere choris.
Membra sed ut possim prius hic tua tangere supplex,
    Castus in edomito pectore quaerit amor.
145   Deprecor, exaudi patriamque revertere in urbem,
    Si modo adhuc aliquo vivus in orbe lates.

---

110 unus *A*: idem *BO*.   **111** periisse *A*: cecidisse *BO*.   **118** occultus — potes *A* (*in erratis*): occultus si velis esse potes *A* (*in textu*), certe sic latuisse queas *BO*.   **123** annis *A*: annos *BO*. **133** At nocet *AB*: At vocet *O*.   **137** tristes *AB*: testes *O*.   **142** choris *A*: locis *BO*.

Ah me, for all I know, you could be hiding right here, in your own hometown, and move around fearlessly under my very nose!

The years inflict much damage on fleeting beauty, [110] and nobody's complexion stays fresh for long. I suspect that the bloom of your youth — a valid reason for our getting married — has wilted by now. Your cheeks, which at your departure were scarcely dusted with light down, are perhaps now covered with a heavy beard. And your forehead, which used to be as smooth as an ivory tablet, will now be deeply furrowed with fatigue. Drenched with rain and scorched by the heat of day, you could easily stay concealed right here, if you wished!

But why would you want people to say you've been heartless to your unhappy wife? [120] I beg you, stop being so cruel to me! That innate goodness of yours requires it; so does that noble blood which now runs sluggish in your aging breast. After all these years I ought to have deserved this from you. As heaven is our witness, that is what you promised to do when you left. Either give me back the hand that so badly deceived me, or be held accountable for the harm your faithlessness and deception have wreaked. False hearts are not pleasing to God. Don't think you can find favor with heaven by your deceit. He who joined us together wanted us to remain joined. [130] Your life is at odds with his command; hence it stands accused. Suppose you are forgiven and your guilt is remitted. Who will let you undo the suffering you have inflicted on me?

Nevertheless, the harm you caused has been a blessing in disguise. I don't complain. A large part of my cares has been taken from me by now. We should patiently bear the burden that we have to bear. If we don't lie down when we must, we lie down all the harder. Tears are my lot, sad laments my life. Oh, may they cleanse me of my sins! May they wash me and send me purehearted to the heights of heaven, [140] where the ensign-bearing Lamb leads his snow-white sheep. Even if I don't find you anywhere on earth, I shall certainly find you there, in the celestial choirs.

That I might humbly touch your limbs here beforehand, however, that is what the chaste love in my mortified breast desires. I entreat you, hear my prayer and return to your native city — if, at least, you are still alive and hiding someplace on

Prebueris vitamque mihi mortemque fugaris,
    In mea si dexter vota futurus eas.
Si minus, o curae, iam fine valete reperto.
150   Amplius in vobis spes mihi nulla manet.
Quod superest, uni tibi magne dicetur Iesu,
    Et tibi, quae nullo Mater es usa viro.
Tu quoque, ut occidero si forte redibis, Alexi,
    Quod doceat quo sim condita carmen habe:
155 "Dum gemit absentem sine crimine nupta maritum,
    Fessa malis, placida morte Sabina iacet."

149 iam — reperto *A*: tristes lachrymaeque, valete *BO*.

earth. You would give me life and drive away death, if you would grant me this wish. If not, O cares, you are at an end. Good-bye! [150] I'll no longer put my hopes in you. What remains of life will be devoted to you alone, Lord Jesus, and to you, Mother who had no relations with a man.

If perchance you come back when I am dead, Alexius, you too should know the inscription that will show where I lie buried: "Still grieving for her absent husband, a blameless wife worn out with anguish, here lies Sabina in peaceful death."

8 KUNEGUNDIS HENRICO

Quae tibi Teutonico non facta nomismate venit,
    Fungitur officio littera nostra novo.
"Quid tibi cum Latiis," ne quaeras, "barbara, Musis?"
    Tristia cum scribam, questibus apta lyra est,

5   Sive quod est numeris et vis et gratia maior,
    Vixque rudes animos barbara verba movent.
Nec, puto, tu nescis quia me Rhamnusia caeco
    Vel potius nullo lumine virgo videt.
Visa diu foelix et Caesare tuta marito,

10   Fluctibus heu quantis turbinibusque premor!
Cum bene sperarem, cecidi sine crimine meque
    Hostis ab excelso trusit ad ima loco.
Non tamen hanc sensi misere prostrata ruinam.
    O miseri qui non quo periere vident!

15   Ut modo conciderim, casum nescire dolendum est.
    Non venit ex causa nostra querela levi,
Nec meus est lachrymis dolor exaturabilis ullis.
    Qui sine peccato plectitur, ille dolet.
Ante mihi o utinam rupissent stamina Parcae,

20   Quam potui infoelix displicuisse tibi!
Aut ego confuso sum nata sub ordine fatum,
    Aut agit in poenas vindicis ira Dei.
Parce, Pater superum — merui graviora, sed illud
    Me nihil implicitam, quo rea dicor, habet.

25   Arguit immeritam violati fama pudoris;
    Inditium famae littera testis habet.
Quae simul ut venit notis mihi cognita signis,
    Verba modis uno plus tribus ista tulit:
"Prodiga pollicitis, verbis contraria rebus,

G5ᵛ   5

32=G6ʳ

Her. Chr. **8.**   4 questibus *BO*: quaestibus *A*.   8 virgo *A*: diva *BO*.   13 Non *A*: Nec *BO*.
27 ut *A*: ac *BO*.

8   CUNEGUND TO HENRY[1]

The letter you're receiving is not expressed in German coin, but then again it performs an extraordinary task. Don't ask, "Why are you, a German lady, belaboring the Latin Muses?" Since mine is a letter of sorrow, the lyre[2] suits my laments. Besides, verse has greater force and charm, and barbarian words scarcely affect rough-and-ready hearts.

You are not unaware, I think, that the Virgin of Rhamnus[3] has been looking on me with a blind — or, rather, no eye at all. I, who for so long seemed happy and secure as the emperor's consort, [10] am now buffeted, alas, by what violent floods and whirlwinds! Just when my hopes were highest, I fell from grace through no fault of my own; and from my exalted place the Fiend plunged me into the abyss. Prostrate with grief, I still cannot fathom this downfall. O, miserable are those who do not understand their ruin! If in fact I have fallen from grace, it pains me to know nothing about my misfortune. My lament is not brought on by some trivial reason, and no amount of tears can relieve my despair. Nothing is more painful than punishment undeserved.

Oh, how I wish the Fates had severed the thread of my life [20] before I, unhappy woman, could become displeasing to you! Either I was born under an evil star or God is punishing me in his righteous wrath. Forgive me, heavenly Father — I have deserved worse than this, but in the crime of which I stand accused I am not ensnared. Despite my innocence, rumor has charged me with violating my chastity; and a note from you testifies to my guilt.

As soon as it arrived, I recognized the familiar seal. The letter, all of four lines long, brought me this message: "Lavish

---

[1]St. Cunegund (d. 1033 or 1039?) was the wife of St. Henry, who as Henry II was Holy Roman Emperor from 1014 to 1024. According to legend, the couple made a vow of perpetual virginity on their wedding day. But after the devil impersonated a young man who was observed leaving her chamber early in the morning for three days on end, Cunegund was accused of adultery. The empress demanded a trial by fire and vindicated herself by walking barefoot over red-hot plowshares. It is this, the most famous part of her legend, that Eobanus treats in the present poem. Because it defends her innocence before a husband who is both accuser and judge, Cunegund's letter adopts the structure of a forensic oration: introduction (ll. 1–24); narrative (25–48); proof positive (49–70); rebuttal (71–108); and final appeal to the judge (109–46). For other letters with this type of rhetorical structure see nos. 3, 14, and 23.

In the 1532/39 version this letter is *Her.* 3.3.

[2]That is, poetry in a classical meter. Latin verse, Cunegund believes, touches the heart as their native ("barbarian") tongue cannot.

[3]The "Virgin of Rhamnus" (Nemesis) was often identified with the goddess Fortuna: see *Laud.* 503, with n. 77 (1:177).

30   Et tibi credentem fallere docta virum:
      Qui mihi devoto fruitur Kunegundis amore
      Saepius ex thalamo visus abire tuo est."
      Hec ubi legissem collapsis frigida membris,
      Vix etiam famula sum revocata manu.
35   Mane erat, et primo radiabant sole fenestrae,
      Iamque novum querulae concinuistis aves.
      Rursus ut exieram thalamo prostrata recumbo,
      Sicut agonales iam subitura rogos.
      Flebile ad exortum relevo caput anxia solem.
40   "Solne, iterum flammas laeta videbo tuas?
      Vocibus umbrifera vernate in fronde, volucres.
      Letitiae est prorsus causa peracta meae."
      Nunc iterum relego lachrymis tua scripta profusis,
      O vir, non precibus dexter, ut ante, meis!
45   Quis dabit unde querar pro re satis? aut ubi plorem?
      Tristitiae consors quis volet esse meae?
      Fama nocens nobis occlusit Caesaris aures;
      Offensum metuit curia tota ducem.
G6ᵛ   Ne tamen, ut taceam, scelus admisisse putemur,
50   Tristis ad invitum littera vade virum.
      Ut tamen ista legas oculis pacientibus oro.
      Dempseris a lachrymis milia multa meis!
      Ante ego, quae dicunt, peritura elementa putabam
      Et vacuum dempto corpore posse dari,
55   Quam tua me miseram mens dedignata fuisset.
      Ille sapit quisquis tuta timere potest.
      O vir et o frater, mihi nomine cedis utroque,
      Quis mihi ut odisses perfidus hostis erat?
      "Prodiga pollicitis" qur sum tibi dicta? Quid hoc est,
60   Me quod ais aliquem fallere posse virum?
      Cur tibi suspectus pudor est meus? An tibi adulter
      Saepius ex thalamo visus abire meo est?
      Adstruere ille potest solem non posse videri,
      Qui tibi commenti conditor huius erat.
65   Aut oculis daemon fallax illusit imago,
      Aut voluit mendax lingua nocere mihi.
      Et tibi devoti stat gloria salva pudoris,
      Nullaque adhuc novit crimina noster amor.

---

32 Saepius . . . tuo est *A*: Saepe est . . . tuo *BO*.   **45** re *A*: te *BO*.   **46** Tristitiae *A*: Moesticiae
BO.   **48** curia *AB*: regia *O*.   **53–54** putabam — dari *A*: putaram, / Mersuras orbem Daeucalionis
aquas *BO*.   **58** perfidus *A*: tam ferus *BO*.   **62** Saepius ex . . . meo est *A*: Saepe est e . . . meo *BO*.
63 Adstruere *A*: Adserere *BO*.   **65–66** Aut — Aut *A*: Vana vel incautis oculis illusit imago, / Vel *BO*.

with promises, saying one thing and doing another, [30] and clever at deceiving your trusting husband, Cunegund: the man enjoying the love that you once consecrated to me has often been observed stealing out of your chamber."

When I had read these words, my blood chilled and the limbs collapsed in shock. Only with the greatest difficulty did my servants revive me. It was morning. The windows gleamed with the first rays of sunshine, and already the querulous birds were warbling their matins. No sooner had I left my chamber than I fell prostrate again, as if about to be burned at the stake. Disconsolate, I raised my tearful head to the risen sun: [40] "Sun, will I ever be happy again to see your flames? Sing your vernal songs in the shady boughs, you birds. As for me, I have lost all reason to be glad." Then, as I reread your message, I once more burst into tears. O my husband, no longer sympathetic to my prayers! Who will give me strength enough to lament this tragedy? Or who will give me a place to weep? Who would want to be my companion in grief? Slanderous rumors about me have stopped the emperor's ears; the whole court is afraid of its exasperated lord. So that my silence will not be interpreted as an admission of guilt, however, [50] do you, sad letter, go up to my husband, loath though he may be.

All the same, do read these lines with patient eyes, I beseech you. You would save me untold tears! I always thought that the elements (as they say) would sooner be dissolved and turned into formless space than that your heart could ever scorn me, poor wretch. Only they are wise who mistrust what appears perfectly safe. O husband, O brother, grant me this in both those names: Who was the treacherous enemy who caused you to hate me so? Why do you call me "lavish with promises"? What do you mean [60] by saying that I am capable of deceiving my husband somehow? Why do you question my chastity? Was it you who often observed the adulterer stealing out of my bedroom? The fellow who concocted that story could just as well assert that the sun is invisible.

Either a demon has disguised himself to fool unsuspecting eyes, or a lying tongue has sought to do me harm. The glory of my chastity, which I devoted to you, continues to stand inviolate, and even now my love is conscious of no transgression. A witness

Teste opus est. Testem te, Christe, appello vocatum.
70   Pondera tu veri testis et instar habes.

33=H1ʳ

Forsitan ipse alios testes, Henrice, requiris.
   Anne putas ipsum fallere posse Deum?
Per superos, dices, facile est iurare prophanis
   Illis. Si qua volet fallere, tuta potest.
75 Ipsa velim potius multis periura videri,
   Quam super hoc uni displicuisse Deo.
At tibi servatum, quem nunc male credis, amorem,
   Da veniam, verbis aemula facta probent.
Ut male per superos tutum est iurare prophanis,
80   Sic vero gaudet testis adesse Deus.
Sanguine conveniant nobis ab utroque propinqui,
   Preterea quorum vita probata tibi est.
Regia ubi angusto protenditur aula recessu,
   Effigiem Mariae continet ara vetus.
85 Casta Dei Mater castis favet. Illa pudori
   Author ut est nostro, sic bona testis erit.
Barbaricum ignito pavimentum sternere ferro
   Quosque tibi fidos noris adesse iube.
Ipsa Deo fidens — aequum favet ille petenti —
90   Contingam nudo torrida strata pede.
Ardeat incestae teneras vis ignea plantas;
   Veridico castam servet ab igne Deus.

H1ᵛ

Qui solo potuit Verbo de virgine nasci,
   Te dabit ostendi virginis esse virum.
95 Quod precor hoc aliquis mihi te concedere forsan
   Non sinet et, "Fraudem callida," dicet, "agit."
Chare Deo, voces non audi, Caesar, iniquas!
   Iuditio livor tristis obesse solet.
Hunc animum fecit nobis mens conscia recti.
100   Consilii non est Phasias ulla mei.
Nescio, quae dicunt, magicae phantasmata sordis,
   Rustica qua semper simplicitate fui.
Si videor temere superos tentare, fatebor
   Quam quae deficiat spes mihi maior erat.
105 Adde quod aut ista volo suspitione levari,
   Aut tibi non vivae coniugis esse loco.
Non ego vana levis timeo ludibria vulgi,
   Sed tibi quod potui displicuisse dolet.

<hr/>

87 Barbaricum — pavimentum *A*: Grande pavimentum candenti *BO*.   91 teneras *BO*: temeras *A*. 92 Veridico castam *AO*: Veridicam casto *B*.   95 concedere *A*: permittere *BO*.   101 phantasmata *A*: ludibria *BO*.   104 deficiat *A*: deficeret *BO*.   107 ego . . . timeo ludibria *A*: quia . . . metuam convicia *BO*.

is required. I call on you, Christ, to be that witness. [70] You have the weight and credibility of a truthful witness.

As for you, Henry, perhaps you demand other witnesses. But do you really believe we can mislead God himself? To swear by heaven, you'll object, is easy for those impious women. If they want to cheat, they can do so with impunity. I myself would rather appear to all the world as a perjurer than to displease the one God on this account. With your leave, however, I will show you not just with words, but also with deeds that my love for you, though you distrust it now, remains intact. As dangerous as it is for the impious to swear by heaven, [80] so God rejoices in appearing as witness for the truth.

Let relatives from both sides of our family assemble here, also people whose life you approve of. In the spot where the royal courtyard narrows into a secluded corner, there is a venerable altar containing an image of Mary. The chaste Mother of God smiles on chaste women. As she is the model for my virginity, so she will be an unimpeachable witness. Command your men to cover the rude pavement with red-hot iron and order those to attend whom you know to be faithful to you. Trusting in God — for he graciously hears the prayers of the righteous — I myself [90] will walk barefoot on the scorching-hot strip. May the fiery heat burn my tender soles if I have been unchaste; but if I am chaste, may God preserve me from the truthtelling fire. He who was able to be born of a virgin through nothing but the Word will also prove that you are the husband of a virgin.

Perhaps someone will counsel you not to grant what I ask for and tell you, "The cunning lady has a trick up her sleeve." Emperor, beloved of God, do not listen to such prejudiced voices! It is typical of bitter envy to try to block justice. My sole motivation is a sense of innocence. [100] No Colchian princess is helping me out.[4] I know nothing about the phantasms of black magic that people talk about, for in such matters I have always been naive and simpleminded. If I seem to be recklessly putting heaven to the test, I must confess that my hope is too great to fail me. Let me add that I want either to be rid of this suspicion or cease to live as your wife. I am not afraid of the baseless derision of the fickle public. What does break my heart is that I displeased you. Therefore you

---

[4]Cunegund alludes to Medea of Colchis, the notorious sorceress who helped Jason win the Golden Fleece.

Ergo nec aspicies laetam, velut ante solebas,
110   Ni sim ignominiam fortiter ulta meam.
Ulcisci facile est: saltem concede quod opto.
    Materia audacem spes facit esse nova.
Longa mora est postquam doleo sine teste diesque
    Ingrato plures lumine tristis ago.

34=H2ʳ   115   Conscia mens animum stimulat de crimine falso
    Et male sub tanto pondere victa iacet.
Omnia quae potui Christo duce tristia ferre,
    Hoc uno videor mortua pene malo.
Quae mihi fors miserae si non inimica fuisset,
120   Staret adhuc animi gloria plena mei.
Frangor et heu quantis iactor confusa procellis!
    Quod videam est caelum preter aquasque nihil.
Sola quid immenso faciam et nova miles in alto?
    Ante ratis nunquam naufraga nostra fuit.
125   Christe, doce, nam tu solatia tristibus affers,
    Littora quae quassae sint propiora rati.
Tu potes et tuto dubitantem sistere portu
    Raptaque ab insanis vela referre Notis.
Rapta, precor, nostri bona nomina redde pudoris!
130   Immeritam videat vir meus ista pati.
Virgo viro data, virgo viro cum virgine vivo,
    Quamque ego nota mihi, tam vir et ipse fuit.
Vidit et indoluit vetus ille et perfidus anguis.
    Qua potius duci suspitione licet!
135   Simplicis heu pulchrum vitae turbavit honorem,
    Cui capto tantum nomine preda fui.

H2ᵛ   Corpora non potuit, famam incestavit adulter.
    Hoc nisi nil nostri, perdite Livor, habes!
Quem tibi promisi, Caesar, sine labe futurum,
140   Ius habet in nostro perfida lingua thoro.
Hanc preter non sunt in eo vestigia. Quamvis
    Sit proba, moechari quam volet illa potest.
At magis offensum ne reddat epistola forsan,
    Suprema hec animi summa rogantis erit:
145   Pondera coniugii nostris, precor, adde querelis
    Et da servatam posse docere fidem.

---

110 Ni *AO*: Ne *B*.   **111** concede *A*: permitte *BO*.   **126** sint *A*: sunt *BO*.   **131** virgo viro
cum *A*: virgo cum *BO*.   **133** anguis *A*: hostis *BO*.

will not see me happy again, as you used to, [110] unless I obtain full satisfaction for the loss of my good name. Obtaining satisfaction is easy: just grant me my wish. Hope gives the daring new mettle.

For a long time now I have been grieving all alone. And as the days come and go with their unwelcome light, I find no relief from sorrow. The consciousness that I am falsely accused never ceases to sting me; my spirit is crushed under so heavy a burden. Following Christ's example, I used to be able to endure all sadness. This one misfortune makes me feel all but dead. If fate had not been unkind to me, poor woman, [120] my spirits would still be as high as ever.

Alas, I am breaking up under the fearful pounding of these storms. I am being tossed to and fro in utter confusion. Besides the sky and the waves I can see nothing. What am I to do by myself, a raw recruit on the boundless deep? Our ship has never before suffered shipwreck. Christ (for you lend comfort to those in grief), show me the coast nearest the battered ship. You have the power to guide the imperiled vessel into a safe harbor and mend the sails torn by the furious gales. Restore my lost reputation for chastity, I beseech you! [130] Let my husband see that my suffering is undeserved.

Given as a virgin to my husband, I have lived as a virgin with my virgin husband; and as chaste as I know myself to be, so has my husband been too. That ancient, treacherous Serpent saw this and grieved. Be guided rather by that suspicion! Alas, the person to whom I fell victim — but only by his smearing my good name — has clouded the lovely dignity of my simple life. Unable to desecrate my body, the adulterer tarnished my fair name. Outside of that, depraved Envy, you have nothing whatsoever of me! Over our bed, which I promised to keep undefiled for you, Emperor, [140] a slanderous tongue now has power. This excepted, nobody has ever left a mark in our bed. No matter how virtuous a woman may be, slander can make an adulteress out of her.

But lest my letter should perchance give more offence, these final words will contain the crux of my plea: lend a husband's weight to my laments, I beg you, and allow me to prove that I have stayed faithful to you.

9   MONICA AUGUSTINO

Nec tua Phoenissae portu Carthaginis extant,
  Nec datur ignotum per mare vela sequi.
Causa duplex animum rapit in diversa dolentem.
  Non hoc debueras, nate, fuisse mihi!
5 Diceris Iliacam procul hinc concedere Rhomam
  Captaque Martigena Tybridis arva manu.
Ipse cito veheris Tyrrhena per aequora cursu.
  Me licet invitam Punica servat humus.
Nam quis amor patriae est sine te mihi, nate, futurus?
10   Maxima pars tecum cessit in alta mei.
Quam vellem tumidum in pelagus nova vela parantem
  Intempesta maris detinuisset hyems,
Aut Deus immani luctantes pondere ventos
  Aeris aut omnes precipitasset aquas!
15 Non tua de nostro solvisset littore puppis,
  Nec mater de te forsitan orba forem.
Non pudet, ut fugeres, cursus caelasse parentem?
  Qua licet invita quolibet ire tibi.
Scilicet hoc series studiorum immensa monebat,
20   Hoc septemgeminum picta Minerva caput.
Hoc vox admonuit vestri veneranda Platonis,
  Vos penes hoc omnes nomina tanta sophi.
Non decet obsequium praestare parentibus ergo.
  Ipsa cavillatrix philosophia tua est!
25 Turba pares estis doctorum semper in illo:
  Virtutem vobis est didicisse satis.
Ipsi negligitis quod pro mercede docetis.
  Ianua nunc etiam quaestibus illa patet.
Illa sed impugnet, si quem iuvat esse severum.
30   Nos humili tantum foemina mente sumus.

35=H3ʳ (margin, line 11)

Her. Chr. 9.   **6** Captaque *A*: Cultaque *BO*.   **8** licet *AB*: tamen *O*.   **20–21** Hoc — Platonis, *A*: *om. BO*.   **23–24** Non — est! *A*: *om. BO*.   **29** Illa — severum *A*: Ista sed impugnet, si quem iuvet esse severum *B*, Ista sed impugnent, si quos iuvet esse severos *O*.

[1]St. Monica writes to her son Augustine (Aurelius Augustinus, 354–430), who at the time of her writing is still a pagan — not the polytheist that Eobanus makes him out to be, but an adherent to Manicheism. She has just learned that he has left her behind in Carthage and secretly set sail for Rome to pursue his career as a teacher of rhetoric. The background is told in Augustine's *Confessions* 5.8.15: "Why I went from the one place and went to the other you knew, O God, but you did not reveal it to me or to my mother, who bitterly bewailed my journey and followed me even down to the seashore. But I deceived her, although she held onto me by force, so that she might either call me back or make the journey with me. I pretended that I had a friend whom I would not leave until a fair wind came and he could sail away. . . . Yet she refused to return without me, and I was hardly able to persuade her to spend the night in a place close by our ship, an oratory built in memory of Blessed Cyprian.

9   MONICA TO AUGUSTINE[1]

Your sails are nowhere to be seen in the harbor of Phoenician Carthage,[2] nor is it granted me to follow them over the unknown sea. These twin circumstances tear my grieving heart in different directions. That, my son, you ought not to have done to me!

I'm told that you have embarked for faraway Trojan Rome[3] and the fields along the Tiber, conquered by the sons of Mars.[4] But while you journey swiftly over the Tyrrhenian Sea, I have no choice but to stay behind on Punic soil. Indeed, as much as I love my country, what do I care about it now that you, my son, are gone? [10] The largest part of my soul departed with you on the deep. How I wished that, as you were preparing to set sail on the swollen main, an unseasonably stormy sea had detained you, or that God had hurled down brawling gales of enormous force or all the waters of the sky! Then your ship would not have cast off from our shore and I, your mother, would perhaps not have been bereaved of you.

Aren't you ashamed of yourself, not just for fleeing your mother, but for keeping her in the dark about it as well? Even against my wishes you are free to go wherever you please. Of course, what lured you away was the immense round of studies, [20] the seven-headed Minerva, as the artists depict her.[5] What beguiled you was the venerable voice of your master Plato,[6] not to mention all those other sages with their stellar reputations. So it is perfectly all right to snub your parents, is it? Your philosophy is pure sophistry! You men of learning are all the same in this respect: you think it is quite enough to have studied ethics. You yourselves disregard what you teach for pay. That door to riches now stands open for you too.

But I'll let others criticize this behavior, if it makes them feel good to be stern. [30] I am just a simple woman. May the lamenting

---

During the night I secretly set out; she did not, but remained behind, praying and weeping. What was it, my God, that she sought from you with so many tears, except that you would not let me sail away. But in your deepest counsels you heard the crux of her desire: you had no care for what she then sought, so that you might do for me what she forever sought. The wind blew and filled our sails, and the shore receded from our sight. On that shore in the morning she stood, wild with grief, and with complaints and groans she filled your ears." (Trans. John K. Ryan.)

In the present letter Eobanus subtly associates Monica not only with the poetess Sappho, abandoned by her lover Phaon, but also with Queen Dido, left behind in Carthage when her lover Aeneas secretly set sail for Italy. For Sappho, see Ov. *Ep.* 15. For Dido, see Verg. *A.* 4 and especially Ov. *Ep.* 7, where the heroine writes a desperate last appeal to Aeneas. But while her pagan counterparts commit suicide, Monica perseveres in her love and lives to see her son restored to her and become a Christian.

In the 1532/39 version this letter is *Her.* 2.5.

[2]Carthage was founded by Phoenicians from Tyre.

[3]Rome was supposedly founded by descendants of the Trojan hero Aeneas.

[4]Because Rome's founders, Romulus and Remus, were sons of Mars, all Romans were so called.

[5]As goddess of learning and culture, Minerva was the patroness of the seven liberal arts.

[6]In truth, Augustine did not study the Neoplatonists until well after his arrival in Italy.

Carmina lugentes dictent mihi moesta Camenae,
    A tibi contempta digna parente cani.
Illa quidem toto resonantia littore canto,
    Hic, ubi Elisaeam verberat aequor humum.

H3ᵛ

35   Audiit ex alto vicinus navita ponto.
    Qui simul in portu constitit illa refert:
"Filius hesterna tuus isthac luce per altum
    Venit in Ausoniam vela daturus humum."
Obstupuit subito commixtus frigore sanguis;
40   Vix gelidam ancillae sustinuere duae.
Tale quid, Aureli, de te restabat, ut essem
    Infoelix Poenas inter et orba nurus?
Ante quidem sensi, sed non abiisse putabam.
    Hic potior nostri causa doloris erat.
45   Non tua maternis amplecti membra lacertis,
    Non licuit summa voce dedisse vale.
An fuit hoc nimium matri dare? Finge fuisse,
    Nunquid eram cursus impeditura tuos?
Ante ego si qua tibi forsan mandata dedissem,
50   Debueras monitis fultus abire meis.
Certe ego non illo saltem contempta viderer.
    Nunc plena ex omni parte querela mea est.
Atque utinam quererer tantum fugisse, nec ullo
    Hoc praeter de te moesta dolore forem!
55   Non mea planxissem tortis praecordia palmis,

36=H4ʳ

    Nec, quo nunc, mordax unguis iturus erat.
Quique modo est vivo phoenix moriturus in igne,
    Forsan in hoc animus iam salamandra foret.
Non ego te volui Latio prohibere petito.
60   Ah, aliud quod te, nate, decebat erat.
Doctus ut es studiis nimiumque imbute prophanis
    Et factus curis cura molesta meis,
Aspicis ut toto cedentibus orbe deorum
    Numinibus Christum pro Iove quisque colat.
65   Spirat adhuc aliquo vix Cerberus ore trilinguis,
    Dum gemit Herculea guttura fracta manu.
Tot divos, tot monstra deum iam victa videmus.
    Quis vicit? Pietas solius alma Dei.

---

31 lugentes *AO*: legentes *B*.   **36** illa *A*: ista *BO*.   **37** altum *A*: aequor *BO*.   **39** commixtus *A*: concretus *BO*.   **54** Hoc *AB*: Hunc *O*.   **61** nimiumque *A*: multumque *B*, heu frustra *O*. **64** colat *A*: colit *BO*.   **66** guttura *O*: caetera *AB*.   **68** Pietas — alma *A*: Virtus unius alta *BO*.

Muses inspire me with songs of sorrow, worthy of being sung by the
mother you scorn. Indeed, those laments resound all along the coast,
here, where the surf lashes the Carthaginian shore.

A seaman heard me from nearby on the deep. As soon as he
had moored in the harbor, he told me, "Your son came that way
yesterday, intending to set sail for Italy over the open sea."
My blood congealed with a sudden chill. [40] Only with difficulty
were my two maids able to keep me from collapsing in shock.

Is this all I have left of you, Aurelius, that I am unhappy and
bereaved among the women of Carthage? Earlier, it is true, I knew
in my heart that you had gone away, but I could not believe it.
This made my grief all the harder to bear. I was not permitted to
clasp you in a mother's hug or give my farewell one last time. Was
that too much to give your mother? Supposing it was, do you
really think I would have blocked your voyage? If I could have
given you some warnings beforehand, perhaps, [50] you owed it
to yourself to leave with the benefit of my advice. Certainly I
would not feel as despised as I do, at least not in this regard. Now
my lament brims over with anguish.

And would that I had only your flight to lament, that
besides this pain I had no other cause to be distressed about you!
Then I would not be beating my breast and wringing my hands;
then my nails would not, as now, be scoring my cheeks. My soul,
which burns like a phoenix dying on the life-giving pyre, might
now perhaps be as cool as a salamander.[7]

It was never my intent to stop you from going to Rome.
[60] Ah, my son, there is something else that you ought to be
doing. Learned as you are and all too deeply imbued with secular
studies, you who worry me with endless worries: look about you!
You can see how the gods are losing their power all over the
world, how everyone is worshiping Christ instead of Jove.
Strangled by a Herculean hand, triple-tongued Cerberus can
barely breathe anymore through one of his mouths and now just
moans.[8] So many gods, so many monstrous idols we see brought
low these days. Who brought them low? The bountiful love of

[7]In other words: "If I had just your stealthy flight to bemoan, and not also your lack of Christian
faith, I would not be so devastated as I am now. Then I would not suffer like the phoenix shriveling to
ashes on the pyre, but, salamander-like, would remain cool in the flames of a mother's grief." The
phoenix was a fabulous bird that burned itself on a funeral pyre after 500 years and then rose from the
ashes for another long life. The rebirth theme, however, is secondary to Monica at this point: she
thinks only of the death by fire. But the choice of image does suggest that she has not given up hope;
cf. ll. 129–38 below. The salamander was popularly believed to live in fire.

[8]As part of his twelve labors Hercules dragged the three-headed guard dog Cerberus out of the
underworld. Recognizing the parallels to the harrowing of hell, patristic writers saw Hercules as a prefiguration of Christ. Eobanus follows this tradition also in *Vict.* 122–26.

Qur statuae, cur templa iacent, oracla fugantur?
70   Facta Creatori destituisse leve est.
Hactenus erratum est, nec adhuc errore caremus.
    Foelix errorem qui videt atque cavet.
Namque quid, o simplex plusquam vitiosa, vetustas
    Heu frustra plures credidit esse deos?
75   Cum sit et illa tuum scriptis reprobasse Platona
    Caelivaga quoties mente reliquit humum,
Quando haec virginibus sunt vaticinata Sybillis,
H4ᵛ   Et legis Hebraeis vatibus ista cani,
Cum sint quae colitis mortalia numina quaedam,
80   Caetera cum soli turba ministra Deo,
Fraudibus humanas mentes cepere, periti
    Naturae variis legibus ire rotam.
Quae modo daemonibus sublata potentia ab illo est
    Qui Deus ex Verbo virgine natus homo est.
85   Qui simul ut terras descendit ab arce paterna,
    Omnia sunt profugis templa relicta deis:
Craeta Iovi, Delos Phoebo, sua Rhoma Quirino,
    Vulcano Lemnos, India, Bacche, tibi.
Posthabuit Cytheraea Paphum, Samon improba Iuno,
90   Et quae praeterea vana referre pudet.
Arva papyriferi tetigit foelicia Nili;
    Orba figurato numine Memphis erat.
Caetera tu nosti, nisi nolis scire, potesque
    Addere in hoc maius quam mea scripta tibi.
95   Sollicitam modo pone fidem. Simul omnia nobis
    Reddideris quae te posthabuisse queror.
Catholicam modo sume fidem sopitaque pande
    Lumina. Tot noctes auferet una dies.
Ad vitam de morte redi. Quid vera relinquens
37=H5ʳ   100   Mavis, heu nimium perdite, falsa sequi?

---

69 oracla fugantur *A*: oracula cessant *BO*.   **73–74** Namque — deos? *A*: Nanque, sed heu simplex plus quam viciosa, vetustas / Tam multos frustra credidit esse deos. *BO*.   **77** virginibus — Sybillis *AB*: unanimes ita praedixere Sybillae *O*.   **79–80** Cum — Deo, *A*: *om. BO*.   **84** ex *A*: e *BO*. **95** Sollicitam *AB*: Infidam *O*.   **97** Catholicam *A*: Synceram *BO*.

[9]Monica here offers a brief history of the pagan gods. In classical antiquity, she explains, people still believed in polytheism. But after Plato attacked these beliefs and after the prophets and Sibyls proclaimed the one God, the old gods (in euhemeristic thinking) began to be regarded as merely deified mortals or (according to Stoic doctrine) as symbols of cosmic powers or natural laws. After the birth of Christ, Monica concludes, the old gods were dethroned and thrust into hell (ll. 83–92; cf. *Buc.* 5.102–04).

the one God. Why are their statues and temples lying in ruins? Why are the oracles dumb? [70] For the Creator it is easy to shatter what man has made.

Up to now there has been much confusion, and even today we are not free of error. Happy the person who sees the error and avoids it! For alas, why did antiquity (oh, more out of ignorance than depravity) vainly believe in many gods? Because your master Plato was able to reject this superstition too in his writings whenever he left the earth with heaven-wandering mind, because the virgin Sibyls predicted these things (and you've read that the Hebrew prophets also foretold them), because some of the gods you people worship are mortals [80] and the rest are spirits who serve the one God, the demons set about deceiving the hearts of men by spreading the doctrine that Nature's wheel turns according to manifold laws.[9]

This power was recently taken from the demons by the God who, through the Word, was born the son of a virgin. As soon as he came down to earth from his Father's heaven, the gods abandoned their temples, every one of them, and went into exile. Jupiter fled from Crete, Phoebus from Delos, Quirinus from his own city Rome. Vulcan forsook Lemnos, Bacchus India. The goddess of Cythera paid no attention to Paphos, implacable Juno to Samos.[10] [90] I am ashamed to mention any more of those empty names. He touched the fertile fields of the papyrus-bearing Nile: Memphis was bereft of her idol.[11] The rest you know yourself, unless you do not want to know; and you can add much more to what I have written you here.

Just give up your worrisome faith. You would immediately restore to me everything that you've lamentably neglected. Just take up the Catholic faith and open your slumbering eyes. That one day will dispel so many nights. Return from death to life. Why do you turn your back on the truth [100] and — alas, hopelessly lost — prefer to follow a fraud? You are going to your

---

[10]At the birth of Christ, the old gods abandon the centers of their cult and flee to the underworld. Jupiter deserts his homeland Crete, Apollo his birthplace Delos in the Aegean. Romulus, worshiped as Quirinus after his deification, flees Rome. Vulcan abandons his native island of Lemnos in the Aegean, Bacchus his birthplace India, Venus her cult center at Paphos in Cyprus. Juno ("implacable" because of her relentless hostility to Hercules, Troy, and Aeneas) forsakes her birthplace Samos.

[11]When Jesus arrived in Egypt, every idol in the country fell down from its pedestal. For this legend (inspired by a prophecy in Isaiah 19.1) see *Ps.-Matt.* 23, *Leg. aurea* 6.78 and 10.30, and, for example, Mant. *1. Parthen.* 3:397–411. Memphis was especially famed for its temple of the sacred bull Apis.

Vadis ad interitum, vita revocante, nec audis
 Clamantes, "Quam nunc pergis, iniqua via est!"
Floribus illa quidem variis peramena videtur
 In quibus Alcides forsitan ire volet.
105 At cito quae spondet negat interiore recessu.
 Prima rosam spirat, summa mephitin olet.
Accipit incautos spetie bonitatis. Ut autem
 Ceperit, in scopulos praecipitanter agit.
Quam bene per scopulos et saxa urentia primum
110 Itur ad aeternis cincta vireta rosis!
Arcta est ad superos paucis via trita, sed ampla est
 Quae fert ad Stygios milia multa lares.
Illa rudis, deserta, arens, super ardua ducit;
 Hec spatiosa, virens, inferiora petit.
115 Quas ferus Oechaliae raptor cum vidit Ioles,
 Arentem viridi praeposuisse ferunt.
Sed tamen hoc falsa dictum ratione molestum est.
 Exempla ex Christi dogmate plura feres.
Linque deos vanamque fidem. Sunt vana profecto
120 Quaecunque interiens gaudia mundus habet.
Aeternum cognosce Deum super omnia teque
 Perge Creatori conciliare tuo.

H5ᵛ

Reiice gentilem casto de corpore pallam.
 Spectandus niveis vestibus ire potes.
125 Talibus aetherea Christus redimitus in aula
 Praecedit niveas, signifer Agnus, oves.
Quod si falsa voles, ut debes velle, negare,
 Turpe salutaris diluat unda caput.
Et nisi me presaga boni mens fallat, ab ista
130 Sorde deum toto pectore noster eris.
Hoc tua promittit pietas mihi mensque fidesque,
 Precipue ingenii divitioris honos.
Saepe etiam de te mihi somnia longa videntur,
 Successu quorum pauca carere velim.
135 Nunc cruce signatus rubra mihi stare videris
 Proque fide stultis gentibus esse minax,
Nunc argumentis veteres confundere divos,
 Nunc sacra Christum primus in aede loqui.

104 forsitan *A*: forte quis *BO*. 105 spondet *AB*: spondent *O*. 112 lares *A*: lacus *BO*.
114 spatiosa *A*: nova, culta *BO*. 115 Oechaliae *AB*: Oechalidos *O*. 117 Sed — est. *A*: Cuius ut
interea haec, ceu somnia vana, refutes, *BO*. 118 ex *A*: e *BO*; dogmate *BO*: dogmata *A*.
119 deos *A*: nefas *BO*. 120 Quaecunque — habet *A*: Dogmata quae tecum milia multa tenent *BO*.
123 gentilem *A*: sordentem *BO*. 128 Turpe — diluat *A*: Signa animae lustrans abluat *BO*.
129 fallat *A*: fallit *BO*. 130 Sorde deum *A*: Perfidia *BO*. 131 promittit *A*: promittunt *BO*.
132 divitioris honos *A*: divitis altus honor *BO*. 137 confundere *AB*: convellere *O*.

doom, even as life calls on you to turn back, and refuse to heed those who are warning you, "The path you now follow is treacherous!" It certainly appears most delightful with its variegated flowers, among which a Hercules might well be tempted to stroll.[12] But what it promises early on, it denies further down. The beginning smells of roses; the end reeks of sulfurous fumes. It greets the unwary with a semblance of goodness. But once it has taken them in, it drives them headlong over the cliffs.

How much better it is to traverse boulders and scorching stones at the outset, [110] as we make our way up to the meadows ringed with unfading roses! Narrow is the way to heaven, and those who take it are few; but wide is the way that carries untold thousands down to the Stygian abodes. The former — rough, desolate, parched — leads you up to the heights. The latter — broad and verdant — takes you down to the depths. When the fierce abductor of Iole of Oechalia[13] saw these two paths, he is said to have preferred the parched road to the verdant one.

All the same, it bothers me to cite a mythological example like this. You can take many more examples from the teachings of Christ. Give up your vain belief in the gods. [120] Whatever the temporal world has to offer in the way of delights, they are assuredly empty. Above all get to know the eternal God and go on making yourself pleasing to your Creator. Throw off the heathen cloak from your chaste body. You could be a magnificent sight, as you walk in garments white as snow! Christ is clad like that as he goes about in the ethereal palace, an ensign-bearing Lamb leading the snow-white sheep.

But if you want to reject the false religion (as indeed you should want to), then let the salvific water wash your sinful head. And unless my high hopes deceive me, [130] you are going to cast off the filth of paganism and become one of us with heart and soul. Your loving heart gives me a promise of that, also your character and loyalty, above all your brilliant intellect. Moreover, I often have long dreams about you, the happy outcome of which I would not want to miss. Sometimes I see you standing there, emblazoned with a red cross and menacing the foolish heathens for the sake of the faith. Now you confute the old gods with your arguments, now you are a bishop preaching the Christ in church.[14]

---

[12]Monica alludes to the famous story of Hercules at the Crossroads. Forced to make a choice, Hercules eschewed the garden path of Pleasure and instead followed the arduous path of Virtue.

[13]After Hercules had killed Eurytus, King of Oechalia, he carried off his daughter Iole. Cf. *Ama.* 35.31–32, with n. 32 (1:245).

[14]Augustine became Bishop of Hippo in 395.

Ergo ego vel Christo famulum te, nate, videbo,
140   Aut requies vivae non erit ulla mihi.
Utque diu, superos quo tu salvere rogabo:
    Noster amat flecti voce rogante Deus.
Ad Styga detrusum pia flevit Otilia patrem;
    Ex Stygia superis redditus ille domo est.
145   Te quoque Tartarei subeuntem iura tyranni
    Exemplo mitem flebimus ante Deum.
Pectora vindicibus lassabimus anxia palmis,
    Conteret arentes plurima gutta genas.
Multa dies tristem, laetam non ulla videbit
150   Donec, ut es, misere perditus esse voles.
Liqueris erroremque tuum verumque probaris,
    Ex vetula iuvenis facta videbor anu.
O, illum superique diem sperataque fata
    Reddite! Sic vobis lex bona semper eat!
155   Nunc quoque, quam sequeris spatiosa per aequora, Rhomam
    Paulatim Christo subdere colla ferunt.
Hic aliquis, qui te longa de nocte redemptum
    Incipiat luci reddere, forsan erit.
Vel tu Caesaribus victis nova signa videbis
160   Et credes vanum numen habere deos,
Aut rapere indoctos spectans sine vindice caelum
    Triste feres doctos ad Phlegetonta trahi.
Questuram peiora veta morituraque serva
    Pectora, nec matrem desere, nate, tuam.
165   Sic tibi sint faciles Tyberina ad littora venti,
    Fataque succedant sed meliora. Vale.

38=H6ʳ

H6ᵛ

---

139 famulum *A*: fidum **BO**.   **140** Aut *A*: Vel **BO**.   **141** tu *AO*: te *B*; rogabo *A*: precabor **BO**. **143–46** Ad Styga — Deum. *A*: *om.* **BO**.   **147** lassabimus *A*: labassimus *B*, labascimus *O*. **149** non ulla *A*: me nulla **BO**.   **154** Reddite *A*: Ducite **BO**.   **159** Caesaribus *A*: pseudologis **BO**. **160** Et — deos *A*: Et Manii linques dogmata vana tui **BO**.   **162** trahi *AB*: rapi *O*. **163** Questuram *B*: Quaesturam *AO*.

Therefore, my son, either I'll see you as a servant of Christ [140] or I'll have no peace of mind while I remain alive. As I've done for so long already, I'll continue to pray to heaven that you may be saved. Our God loves to be moved by a prayerful voice. When her father was cast down to the Styx, Ottilia devoutly wept for him. He was delivered from the Stygian abode and taken up into heaven.[15] As long as you remain in the power of the tyrant of Tartarus, I too will follow her example and weep for you before the merciful God. With punishing hands I'll weary my anxious breast, and a torrent of tears will wear out my withered cheeks. Many a day will see me unhappy, none joyful, [150] as long as you choose to stay miserably lost, as indeed you are. But the moment you abandon your error and accept the truth, you will see me, old woman, rejuvenated. Grant me that day, O Heaven, O longed-for future! See to it that all may turn out well!

Even Rome, for which you are now making over the spacious seas, even Rome, they say, is gradually submitting her neck to Christ. Perhaps someone there will liberate you from the long night and begin restoring you to the light.[16] Either you will recognize the new ensigns that have conquered the Caesars [160] and believe that the gods' power is hollow, or you will be forced to watch helplessly as the unlearned take heaven by storm, while the learned are wretchedly dragged down to hell.

Keep me from lamenting the worst. Save my heart from death, son, and do not abandon your mother. So may you have fair winds to the banks of the Tiber, but may a happier future lie in store for us. Farewell.

---

[15]The Alsatian abbess St. Ottilia (Odilia), who lived from 660 to 720, was born of a noble family. According to the legend, her fervent prayers freed her father Adalric (Attich) from purgatory and caused him to be placed among the patriarchs in heaven. See *Leg. aurea* (Graesse) 190, p. 876. In the 1532/39 version Eobanus omitted this reference to her, not just to avoid the anachronism but also because, as a Protestant, he no longer believed either in purgatory or in the efficacy of prayers for the dead.

[16]It was Ambrose, the Bishop of Milan, who was to be instrumental in converting Augustine to Christianity: see August. *Confessiones* 5.13.

10   BARBARA ORIGENI

Si qua nephas Latiae sunt hic, ut plurima, linguae,
    Conveniens dominae littera nomen habet.
Nomine quae rebus sum conveniente vocata,
    Barbara me refero versibus ipsa meis.
5   Barbara, Migdoniae gentis sata, patre tyranno:
    Hac tibi sim lecta nota salute precor.
Esse velim quare ne sit tibi scire molestum.
    Magna est propositi causa decensque mei.
Magnus es, ut fama est, lota de gente sacerdos,
10   Diceris et verum posse docere Deum.
Gentiles nihil esse deos patriosque Penates
    Sollicitor multos, sed sine teste, dies.
Et quantum natura sinit rudis ire per altum,
    Tot membris unum suspicor esse caput.
15   Non tamen agnosco, patriis confusa tenebris,
    Quod velut ex nebula lumina nostra vident.
Ad te nostra igitur properavit epistola supplex.
    His rebus miserae quod potes esse velis.
Quoque modo id fiat, qua sim ratione docenda
20   (Si tamen, ut debes velle, docere voles),
Unus et hic animo mihi compatiente fidelis
    Ostendit per quem carmina nostra legis.
Sed ne forte putes de me tibi falsa referri —
    Quod de me nolles credere! — crede mihi.
25   Credenti facile est rescribere pauca puellae.
    Sum Latias, quamvis barbara, docta notas.
Me pater exactis tribus haec ad tempora lustris
    Sollicite ingenuas quaerere iussit opes.
Ergo, licet tenero vernet mea flore iuventus,
30   Non me, cui scribas, non satis esse puta.

39=11ʳ (margin)

Her. Chr. **10.** *Tit.* Origeni *A*: Eusebio *BO*.   **1** Latiae *A*: Graiae *BO*.   **3–4** Nomine — meis *A*: Quae tamen Eusebium nisi [mihi *B*] prima in fronte tulisset, / Nolles ignota scripta videre manu. / Aspice, si qua potes praegrandibus ocia curis / Furari; officio res eget ista brevi *BO*.   **5** Migdoniae — sata *A*: Bythino sata sanguine *BO*.   **8** Magna — mei *A*: Propositi non est caussa pudenda mei *BO*. **15** confusa *A*: infusa *BO*.   **16** Quod . . . ex *A*: Quae . . . e *BO*.   **22** Ostendit *A*: Ostendet *BO*. **26** Latias *A*: Graias *BO*.   **27** Me *AB*: Ne *O*.   **29** Ergo — iuventus *A*: Quamvis ergo mei vernent iuveniliter anni *BO*.

[1]The story of St. Barbara's correspondence with the famed theologian Origen of Alexandria (ca. 185–ca. 254) derives from her legend. See *Leg. aurea* (Graesse) 202. The well-educated daughter of Dioscorus, a rich man (or king) of Nicomedia in Bithynia, Barbara was confined by him in a high tower, lest her beauty should attract the attention of suitors. There she continued to study the liberal arts and meditate on things divine. Though she lacked knowledge of God, she nevertheless rejected her father's idols. One

10   BARBARA TO ORIGEN[1]

If there are errors in my Latin here (plenty, I'm sure!), my letter bears a name that suits the writer. Called by a name that fits the reality, I reveal myself as a barbarian in my verse. I, Barbara, am descended from a Bithynian family. My father is a tyrant. Now that I have introduced myself to you, please read on. You need have no concern about my motives, however. The reason I write you is important and seemly. You are reputed to be an eminent priest among the baptized people [10] and are said to be able to teach the true God. For many days now I have been secretly fretting that our heathen gods and ancestral Penates are in fact nothing at all. And insofar as untutored nature lets me reach this high, I suspect that so many limbs can have only one head. Nonetheless, confused in my native darkness, I cannot make out what my eyes are seeing, as if through a fog. That is the reason why my letter is humbly hastening to you. I hope you will be willing to help me, poor girl, in this matter, as much as you can.

How this might be carried out, by what means I can receive your instruction [20] — if, indeed, as you ought to do, you agree to instruct me — this you will learn from the one faithful soulmate I have, the man who brought you my letter. But lest you think I am perhaps not telling the truth about myself — do not believe that about me! — please have faith in me. It is easy to write a few lines back to the girl who has put her trust in you. Though a non-Roman, I know Latin well enough. At the present time I am just over fifteen years old, but my father always wanted me to pursue the treasures of the mind with utmost diligence. Hence, even though my youth is still in the tender bloom of its spring, [30] do not presume that I would not be adequately prepared for a letter of yours.

---

day she heard that the wise and eloquent Origen might be able to shed light on the true deity and provide her with arguments to confound the idolaters. She therefore wrote him a letter to say that she rejected the deaf and dumb idols and desired to know the true God. Origen promptly sent the priest Valentine to her with a letter and a collection of books. She was thereupon converted, instructed in the faith, and baptized. Unaware of her conversion, her father proposed that she marry one of her suitors, but she angrily refused. He then left on a journey abroad. Upon his return he discovered that she had rejected his idols and was now worshiping Christ. He had her imprisoned and tortured, but to no avail. In a rage, he took her to a mountain and beheaded her himself. As he returned home, fire from heaven struck him and utterly consumed him.

In the 1532/39 version this letter is *Her.* 3.4. There, in a departure from the legend, the addressee is Eusebius (ca. 260–ca. 340), Bishop of Caesarea in Palestine, who was not yet born when Origen died. After the Reformation, it appears, Eobanus no longer wished to give prominence to a theologian who, condemned by Jerome and others and anathematized by the Council of Constantinople in 553, was deeply distrusted by the Reformers. In the revision Eobanus also corrected the mistake of having Barbara write her letter in Latin, rather than in Greek.

Sunt equidem quae me suspensam sepe morantur
   Plurima de vestris scripta voluminibus;
Et quia tam firma niti ratione videntur,
   Plus etiam patria relligione placent.
35 Quae tamen ut vestri texerunt mystica vates,
   Mens mea quid claudant scire prophana nequit.
Scripseris ergo brevi quae nos nescire dolemus,
   Forte tuo poteris complacuisse Deo.
Quis Deus existens ante omnia saecula solus?
40   Quale apud hunc Verbum rere fuisse Deum?
Omnia quis foecit? Sine quo nihil? Aut quid in illo
   Vita est? Quam lucem nox capere ulla nequit?
Quis testis de luce fuit? Quae illuminat omnem
   Lux hominem? Quis non notus in orbe fuit?
45 Quem non excepere sui? Quod denique Verbum
   Fit caro? De Verbo quomodo facta caro est?
Arduiora quidem quam quae mediocria captent
   Ingenia. O hominem qui capere illa potest!
Vana per haec nostrae fiunt ludibria chartae.
50   Hei mihi, habet quales patria nostra deos!
Bella, doli, fraudes, et victa libidine regna
   Si faciunt divos, patria terra, sapis!
Sed, puto, de superis haec est sentire nephandum.
   Commendant vestrum sobria scripta Deum.
55 Praeterea, ingenti qui temperet omnia sceptro,
   Credibile est unum rebus inesse Deum.
Sicut enim plures male res capit una magistros,
   Sic bene qui multis praesidet unus erit.
Per multos reges regnum sibi dissidet unum.
60   Sume deos plures, munde, iacebis iners.
Unus et hic Trinus solo regit omnia nutu —
   Littera de vestra plurima lege docet!
Hunc Unum Trinumque animus cognoscere gestit.
   Fac nequeam per te non didicisse queri.
65 Hic quoque sunt nostrae quaedam sublimia menti.
   Quae nisi tu doceas, unde petemus opem?
Quis Pater et Natus? Quis Tertius exit ab illis?
   Dicere Tres Unum qua ratione potes?

31 equidem *A*: etenim *BO*.   **47** Arduiora quidem *A*: Ardua scripta magis *BO*.   **50–51** Hei — regna *A*: Heu mihi, quas larvas carmina nostra sonant! / Stupra, doli, fraudes, polluta libidine sacra *BO*.
54 Commendant *AB*: Commendent *O*; vestrum *AO*: nostrum *B*.   **55–56** Praeterea — Deum. *A*:
om. BO.   **58–59** Sic bene — unum *A*: Commodius plures qui regat unus erit. / Et gravis est uni divisa potentia regno *BO*.   **62** vestra *AO*: nostra *B*.   **67–68** Quis Pater — potes? *A*: Quis Pater ingenitus? quis Filius? et quis ab illis / Processit [Procedit *O*] patrio Spiritus igne potens? / Qui credam potuisse aliquem de virgine nasci, / Ni per te miserae luceat ista fides? *BO*.

As a matter of fact, in your scriptures there are a great many writings that often hold me in thrall; and because they appear to be so firmly grounded in sound doctrine, they actually appeal to me more than my ancestral religion. Since your bards, however, tend to cloak the meaning in enigmatic words, my uninitiated mind fails to penetrate the hidden sense. Thus, if you could briefly explain what, to my regret, I do not understand, you may perhaps be well pleasing to your God.

Who is the God who existed alone from all eternity? [40] What kind of Word, do you suppose, was with this God? Who made all things? Without whom was nothing made? Or why was the life in him? What light was the darkness unable to overcome? Who bore witness to the light? What light illumines every person? Who was not known in the world? Whom did his own people not receive? Finally, what Word became flesh? How was this Word made flesh?[2]

Such passages are really too sublime for ordinary minds to grasp. Oh, the man who can comprehend them! Next to them, our writings look like silly trifles. [50] Ah me, what sort of gods does my homeland have to offer! Wars, treachery, crime, kingdoms overthrown by lust — if such things make gods, then you, my native land, are an expert for sure!

But to think of the celestials in such terms, I believe, is an abomination. The sobriety of your scriptures speaks well for your God. It does indeed make sense that the universe has but one God who guides all things with his mighty scepter. For just as a state cannot thrive if it has many rulers, so it is best that the one governs the many. A kingdom with many kings is at odds with itself. [60] Embrace many gods, world, and you'll soon grind to a halt. One Trinity rules all things with a single will — a great many books have taught me about your doctrines! My soul craves to get to know this One and Three. Do not let me lament that I learned nothing from you.

Here too there are some doctrines that are too lofty for my mind. If you were not to instruct me, where could I go to find help? Who are the Father and the Son? Who is the third Person, who proceeds from those two?[3] How can you say that Three are One?

---

[2]Barbara paraphrases the opening verses of the Gospel of John (1.1–14).

[3]These articles of faith are (anachronistically) drawn from the Nicene Creed, as later revised in the Western Church. Cf. *Her. Chr.* 4.199–204, with n. 11 (p. 201 above).

Non haec Oleniae nutritum lacte capellae
70	De superis aliquem delituisse docent.
Ista nec in varias fugientem Prothea formas,
	Membra nec hic patrium parturit orba femur.
Nulla hic prolifico de vertice nata virago est,
	Non fert hic aliquam lubrica concha deam,
75	Non aliqua hic veterum deliramenta deorum.
	O sacram vera relligione fidem!
Quaeris ubi intuear legis mysteria vestrae?
	In patria (mirum) discimus ista domo.
Est vetus et multos prorsus neglecta per annos
80	Condita de vestra bibliotheca fide.
Hanc nisi deridens nemo conspexit, ab illo
	Quo primum in patrias tempore venit opes.
Quam prius, ut perhibent, rex Pontica sceptra gubernans
	Attulit affines depopulatus agros.
85	Hanc, quoties licuit, secura per ocia furtim
	Intrabam studiis officiosa novis.
12ᵛ	Utque sumus vetiti cupidissima turba puellae,
	Divinum rebar quo prohiberer opus.
Sed neque falsa fui, quamvis muliebriter egi,
90	Et iuvat a vetito non potuisse trahi.
Illic Hebraeos, divina poemata, vates
	Vidimus et famae nuperioris opus.
Vidimus antiquo congesta arcana Moisi,
	Vidimus et quicquid lex modo vestra probat.
95	Denique quicquid erat, sic nos vidisse fatemur
	Lumina ceu solem nostra videre solent.
Per nebulas ut tecta videt longinqua viator,
	Ut videt in tremula navita lumen aqua,
Sic ego, gentiles heu nondum exuta tenebras,
100	Quo videam miserae lumen abesse queror.
Qur aliena petam patriis exercita sacris,
	Nescio, si quaeris, sed tamen ista peto.
Nemo mihi est vestra de relligione magister,
	Ni mihi dicatur littera muta loqui.
105	Sic est, illa fuit mihi causa cupidinis huius,
	Prima mihi invisum foecerat illa Iovem.

---

71 fugientem *A*: labentem ***BO***.	75 Non — hic *A*: Nulla hic sunt ***BO***.	76 vera *A*: multa ***BO***.
79 et — prorsus *A*: hic omnes quibus est ***BO***.	83 Quam — perhibent *A*: Hanc paulo ante aliquis
BO.	91 Illic *A* (*in erratis*) ***BO***: Illic et *A* (*in textu*).	92 opus ***BO***: opes *A*.	93 congesta —
Moisi *A*: descripta oracula Mosi ***BO***.	99 Sic — tenebras *A*: Sic ego mortiferae nondum eruta
noctis ab umbra ***BO***.	102 quaeris *A*: quaeras ***BO***.

Your scriptures do not [70] teach that some god or other went into hiding and drank the milk of the Olenian goat.[4] They have nothing to say about Proteus' ability to change into all manner of shapes; they do not recount that a father's thigh was pregnant with a motherless fetus.[5] There you will find no myths about a warrior maiden springing from a childbearing head or about a slippery seashell that bears some kind of goddess to shore,[6] or other such nonsense about the ancient gods. O sacred faith! O religion grounded in truth!

You ask where I managed to peer into the mysteries of your doctrine? I learned about them — would you believe it? — in my father's house. For many years there has been an old and altogether neglected [80] library here, consisting of books about your faith. Except in derision, nobody has ever glanced at it since the time it came into my father's possession. The King of Pontus, they say, had earlier brought it here after plundering the adjoining territories. I secretly visited it as often as I could, at safe times of the day, and devoted myself to these new studies. And since we girls are by nature most attracted to what is forbidden, any prohibited work seemed to me divine. But I was not being willful, even if I acted like a typical woman, [90] and I am glad to say I can resist temptation.

That, then, is where I saw the divine poems of the Hebrew prophets as well as the work of more recent fame.[7] I saw the mysteries compiled by Moses of old; I also saw all the writings accepted by your church. In short, I confess that everything I saw appeared to me as bright as the sun. But like a wayfarer who espies a far-off town through the mists or like a sailor glimpsing a light on the rippling water, so I, unfortunate girl — still not freed, alas, from pagan darkness — [100] grieve to lack the light by which I might see. If you wonder why someone like me, trained in our native rites, is searching for a different faith, I really do not know, and yet I search for it anyway. There is no one here to teach me about your religion, unless you want to call books my silent teachers. And so they are. They created this desire within me; they first made Jupiter odious to me.

---

[4]Amalthea's goat (or, in another version, the goat Amalthea) suckled the young Jupiter in Crete, where he was hiding lest his father swallow him. See Ov. *Fast.* 5.111–28; cf. Eob. *Buc.* 7.98–100.

[5]When Semele died, Jupiter took his son Bacchus from the mother's womb and carried him to term in his hip. Cf. Ov. *Met.* 3.311–12.

[6]Pallas Athena sprang fully armed from the head of Jupiter. Venus was carried ashore at Cythera on a seashell.

[7]The New Testament.

Forsan et ille potest miserae favisse puellae,
    Quem Trinum nobis lectio multa refert.

41 = I3^r

Et nisi credentem vatum chorus ille fefellit,
110   Hoc est in toto mitius orbe nihil.

Adsit, et ut toties avida mihi mente vocatur,
    Sic se agnoscendum praebeat ipse mihi.

Tu quoque, cui nostrae dictant mandata Camenae,
    Pectora consiliis instrue nostra tuis.

115   Quid faciam per quod de sordibus eruar istis?
    Heu, quantum cultus displicet iste mihi!

Iamdudum libuit patrios exire penates,
    Sed timidam custos qui prohiberet erat.

Nunc tamen — o tenera crudelem in virgine patrem! —
120   Heu nimium duro carcere clausa premor.

Utque diu latuit quam fertur Abantius heros,
    Ne pareret, forti praepediisse sera,

Sic ego marmorea turri conclusa reservor,
    Ne studeam cupidis complacuisse procis.

125   Stulte parens! Non haec alicui debetur amanti.
    Virginitas uni nostra dicanda Deo est.

Rara comes mecum, sed quae fidissima certe est,
    Et vigil occlusas excubat ante fores.

Triste coarctatis caput effero saepe fenestris
130   Et iuga prospectu metior alta meo.

I3^v

Nunc aliquis volucres faceret mihi Dedalus alas,
    Nunc ego Triptolemi curribus ire velim!

Non me chara parens, non me pater anxius aevo,
    Non patrius plena messe movebit ager.

135   Protinus evadam gentis qua turba lavatae
    Veridico tantum praedicat ore Deum.

Sed vetor, et tristes meditor sine teste querelas,
    Ipsa animi testis conscia sola mei.

Quacunque aspicio, longo stant ordine circum,
140   Quos pater ut colerem iussit habere deos.

Heu dolor! Ista colam stulti ludibria saecli?
    Ah, pereat lapides qui putat esse deos!

Ipsa ego ut excessi primum puerilibus annis,
    Nunc quoque tot divos suspicor esse nihil.

145   Nec ratione caret qur sic ego credere malim:
    Est aliquid veteres evoluisse libros!

---

107 miserae *A*: timidae *BO*.   108 lectio *A*: littera *BO*.   110 toto *AB*: tot *O*.   123 turri *A*: in turri *BO*.   126 uni *A*: soli *BO*.   131 alas *BO*: ales *A*.

Perhaps he too can show me poor girl his favor — the one God whom much reading tells me is a Trinity. And unless that chorus of bards deceives the believer, [110] there is no one in the whole world more merciful than he. May he stand by me; and as I call on him again and again with eager mind, so may he reveal himself to me. You too, to whom my Muses send these requests, instruct my heart with your counsel. What must I do to escape this vile idolatry? Ah, how I detest this form of worship!

For a long time I have had a mind to leave home, but I have always been too timid to elude my guards. But now — oh, the cruelty of my father toward a tender virgin! — [120] now, alas, I am confined in a terribly hard prison. Like that maiden whom the heroic son of Abas, they say, long kept locked up in her room for fear she might bear a son,[8] so I am being kept locked up in a stone tower lest I try to win the affection of passionate wooers. Foolish father! My virginity is not reserved for some lover. It is to be dedicated to the one God.

Only rarely do I have a companion with me, but she is certainly a most faithful friend. Outside the barred doors a guard keeps constant watch. Every so often I sadly stretch my head out of the narrow windows [130] and scan the high mountains from my lookout. Now some Daedalus ought to make me fleet wings; now I wish I could ride off in Triptolemus' car! Not my dear mother, not my worried old father, not the grain-laden fields of home would hold me back. Immediately I'd fly to where the congregation of baptized people preaches the almighty God with truthtelling lips.

But that is impossible; and in my loneliness I think despondent thoughts. No one but I knows what is going on in my mind. Wherever I look, I see long rows of idols standing around — [140] the ones my father commands me to worship as gods. Oh the pain! So I am to worship these hallucinations of a stupid age? Away with people who maintain that stones are gods! As for me, just as I did when I emerged from childhood, I suspect even now that there simply cannot be so many gods. There is a good reason why I prefer to believe this: it is something to have perused old books!

---

[8]Danaë, the daughter of King Acrisius and granddaughter of Abas, was shut up in a tower by her father for fear that her son would kill him. But Jupiter descended on her in a shower of gold (cf. *Her. Chr.* 1.149) and fathered Perseus.

Praecipue hec animo nuper vigilante notavi
  Carmina, Iessaeo vaticinata seni:
"Quae diversa colunt gentes simulachra prophanae,
150   Ex aere humanae composuere manus.
Ora quibus nunquam vero sermone loquentur,
  Quo nequeant aliquid cernere lumen habent.

42=14^r

Nulla soni speties vacuas referetur ad aures;
  Nare sub ipsorum non erit ullus odor.
155 Organa deficient stupidas gustantia linguas,
  Et vacua humanae guttura vocis erunt.
In manibus nullum tactus erit instrumentum;
  Stant fulti, nequeunt quo tamen ire pede.
Noster at in caelo Deus est. Quaeque ipse volebat,
160   Omnia de veteri condidit orta caho."
Verius haud potuit tantus praedicere vates.
  Quis, nisi mentis inops, certa negare volet?
Eya igitur, dum laeta viret, dum pullulat aetas,
  Dum pudet ingrata relligione premi,
165 Eripe clamantem Stygia de nocte puellam,
  Caelestem populis aedere docte viam.
Si tua luminibus contingat epistola nostris,
  Non cupiam voto prosperiore frui —
Praecipue si quae mihi sint facienda docebit,
170   Quo valeam soli complacuisse Deo.
Tunc ego, vaticinor, totis accensa medullis,
  Clamabo veteres crimen habere deos.
Iam mihi per scopulos videor salebrosaque saxa
  Effugere irati iussa tremenda patris.

14^v   175 Ille quidem ferus est larvasque ita respicit istas,
  Cogitet ut vestram perdere saepe fidem.
Viderit aversam cultus sprevisse priores,
  Ipsius, certum est (tam furit!), ense cadam.
Nunc externa tamen longe est in regna profectus,
180   Et nunc absentem tertia luna videt.
Ignibus octavum postquam illa refecerit orbem,
  Longius a patria non erit ille domo.
Opportunus abest, nec tempore possumus unquam,
  Si libet, hoc ipso commodiore frui.
185 Non precor ut venias — longa est via — sed tamen oro
  Ut veniat pro te littera scripta mihi.

150 Ex aere … composuere *A*: Cuncta sibi … constituere *BO*.   **151** Ora *A*: Ore *BO*.
153 speties — ad *A*: venient vanas elementa per *BO*.   **156** Et — humanae *A*: Cassa loquuturae *BO*.
158 nequeunt *A*: nequeant *BO*.   **166** aedere *A*: pandere *BO*.   **170** valeam *A*: possim *BO*.
172 veteres *A*: patrios *BO*.   **178** certum est *A*: haud dubie *BO*.   **179** tamen *A*: quidem *BO*.
180 Et — absentem *A*: Absentemque domo *BO*.   **184** libet *BO*: velis *A* (*in textu*), velit *A* (*in erratis*).
185 precor *BO*: praecor *A*; longa *AO*: longe *B*.

Recently, as I was reading along with rapt attention, I was particularly struck by the following verses, sung long ago by Jesse's son:[9] "The various idols that the heathen nations adore [150] are made of bronze by human hands. They have mouths with which they will never speak a true word; eyes, with which they see nothing. No kind of sound will ever reach their deaf ears. No smell will ever affect their nose. Their unmoving tongue will lack the organs of taste. Their throat will be void of a human sound. Their hands will not have the sense of touch. They stand on feet, but cannot walk. But our God is in heaven. Whatever he wanted, he created himself, [160] everything that arose from primeval Chaos."

The great bard could scarcely have spoken more truly. Who but a mindless fool wants to deny the obvious?

So then, while my lusty youth is in full vigor and bloom, while I am still ashamed of being oppressed by a distasteful religion, deliver the wailing maiden from her Stygian darkness, O you, who are skilled at showing the nations the way to heaven. If a letter from you should reach my eyes, I could ask for nothing more — especially if it gives me instructions as to what I should do [170] to win the favor of the one and only God. Then, I prophesy, all my marrow will catch fire and I'll shout out that the ancient gods are a disgrace. Already I see myself fleeing over crags and rugged boulders to escape the terrible commands of my enraged father.[10] He is a ferocious man indeed; and he holds those idols in such high regard that he often makes plans to obliterate your faith. If he sees that I have rejected, no, scorned the cult I was raised in, it is certain (so crazed is he!) that I shall fall by his sword. At the moment, however, he is on a state visit to some remote countries [180] and has been gone for three months already. When the moon has repaired her orb with light for the eighth time, he will not be far from the ancestral home. He is absent at an opportune time. If you agree, we shall never have a more suitable opportunity than this. I do not ask you to come — it is a long journey — but I do beseech you to send me a letter in your stead.

[9]Jesse's son is King David. The passage that now follows paraphrases Psalm 115.3–7 (113.11–15 in the Vulgate).

[10]When Barbara's father first learned that she was a Christian, he tried to kill her right then and there; but she was whisked away and borne up to a mountaintop. See *Leg. aurea* (Graesse) 202, p. 900.

Hoc tamen ut peterem calamo dubitante, timebam.
  Ausuram vetuit grandius ipse pudor.
Iam satis inceptae numeramus taedia vitae.
190   O utinam placeat littera nostra tibi!
Ardeo quamprimum sacro de fonte lavari.
  Haec est propositi maxima causa mei.
Nunc te, si qua tibi est vestrae reverentia legis,
  Deprecor, hic miserae quam potes affer opem.
195 Nec me destituas dubiis, mitissime, rebus.
  Stat mala pro vobis qualiacunque pati.
43=15ʳ   Adde fidem famae de te mihi tanta loqutae,
  Et mihi si nequeas corpore, mente veni.

187 Hoc *A*: Quod *BO*.   188 grandius ipse *AB*: longius ire *O*.   189 inceptae *A*: ingratae *BO*.
193 vestrae *AO*: nostrae *B*.   195 Nec *AO*: Non *B*.

Even as I make this request with hesitant pen, I am afraid of offending you. I was going to make bold to ask you for something more momentous, but I am too shy to go ahead.[11] I have gone on long enough recounting the wearisome details of my youthful life. [190] Oh, how I hope that you will approve of my letter!

I am burning with desire to be washed as soon as possible in the sacred font. This is the main reason I decided to write you. Now then, if you have any reverence for your religion at all, I beg you to offer me, poor soul, whatever aid you can in this matter. Do not leave me a prey to doubts, most merciful father. I am firmly resolved to suffer all manner of torments for your faith. Confirm the rumor that has told me such marvelous things about you; and if you cannot come to me in body, do come to me in your thoughts.

[11]She is too shy to ask Origen to send a priest to baptize her.

11   THAIS PAPHNUCIO

Quam tibi debueram verbis mandare salutem,
  Hanc te pollicitum sis memor esse mihi.
Si qua liturarum tamen hic dispuncta notabis,
  Pars quota de lachrymis illa fuere meis.
5 Carcere, sancte pater, quo sum tibi iussa reponi —
  Sic merui, sic sum digna manere! — premor.
Quod legis, ex illo, Paphnuti, mittitur antro.
  Delitiae certe est nunc locus ille meae.
O utinam primis mea sic latuisset ab annis,
10 Quae nunc est misero crimine vita nocens,
Vel mihi Parcarum subeunti iura sororum
  Haesissent primo stamina rupta colo!
Non ego per vetitum commissae conscia culpae
  Flerem successu posse carere preces.
15 Tanta anima infoelix peccati mole gravatur,
  Ut dubitem offensum pene rogare Deum.
Namque quid esse putas Stygia semel obruta nocte
  Lumina nunc aliquam velle videre diem?
Sed tamen amissum per te sperare favorem
20 Praescriptoque Deum carmine iussa rogo.
Quod tamen indigno mihi non licet ore profari,
  Vix audet nomen littera picta loqui.
Antrum est, ut nosti, foedum squalore situque.
  Vix quota longinquae portio lucis adit.
25 Difficile exortum possis cognoscere solem,
  Tam capit admissum parva fenestra diem.
Hac supplex, seu mane rubet seu vesper anhelat,
  Emeditor iusso quas licet ore preces.
Prona caput, prostrata genu, dispassa lacertos,
30 Quem mihi fas non est ore referre, precor:
"Respice me miseram, qui me, qui cuncta creasti."
  Hoc nisi non audet lingua prophana loqui.
Nec mihi tu, memini, plus hoc audere dedisti,
  Nec mea spurcities plus meruisse potest.
35 Lingua Deum nescit vitiis maculata fateri;
  Sacra prophanato non decet ore loqui.
Atque utinam, ut fasso mihi non licet ore precari,
  Sic precibus faveat pectoris ipse mei!

I5ᵛ

Her. Chr. **11.** 3 hic *A*: huic *BO*; notabis *A*: videbis *BO*.   13 commissae *A*: patratae *BO*.
27 anhelat *BO*: anhelet *A*.   37 Atque *A*: At *BO*; fasso *AB*: falso *O*.

[1]St. Thais, who used to be a wealthy courtesan in an Egyptian city, writes this rueful letter to her confessor St. Paphnutius (d. ca. 360). She describes her present life of penitence in a dark cell and

11   THAIS TO PAPHNUTIUS[1]

The salvation I ought to have wished you by word of mouth, you — do not forget! — once promised to me.

Still, if you notice blots scattered here and there on the page, they are but a small fraction of my tears. Holy father, I am still confined in the cell where you commanded me to be kept. That is what I deserve. Here is where I deserve to stay! The words you are reading were sent from that cave, Paphnutius. This place is now certainly my delight. Oh, if only I could have stayed hidden like this from earliest childhood on! [10] Then my life would not have been stained with grievous crime, as it is now. How I wish the Fates had wielded their power at the moment I was born — that my life's thread had stuck fast on the Sisters' distaff and been broken before it was spun! Then the guilt I incurred for love of iniquity would not be tormenting my conscience now, nor would I be lamenting that prayers can remain unanswered. My unhappy soul is weighed down by such an enormous burden of sin that I almost hesitate to pray to the God I have offended. For what do you think it means when eyes once shrouded in Stygian darkness now want to see a glimmer of the light? All the same, at your behest, I go on hoping that I may regain the favor I lost [20] and keep calling on God with the prayer you taught me to say. His name, however, which I am not permitted to utter with unworthy lips, I scarcely dare mention even in the written word.

There is a cave, as you know, filthy with grime and mold. Only a few distant rays succeed in piercing the gloom. You can just barely make out the sun in the sky, so thoroughly does the tiny window block out the light of day. Here, whether dawn blushes or evening hurries near, I humbly repeat the prayer you told me to say. Head down, knees bent, arms spread wide,[2] [30] that is how I pray to him whose name is not to cross my lips: "Have pity on me poor wretch, O you who created me and the whole world." This is all my profane tongue dares say. You too, I remember, did not allow me to venture anything more. Indeed, my turpitude merits nothing else. A tongue defiled with vice is incapable of confessing God. It is not right for desecrated lips to utter sacred words. May he, whose name I am not permitted to entreat with confessing mouth, show favor to the prayers of my heart!

---

recalls how the abbot converted her from her former sinful state. The letter concludes with an appeal that he release her from her three-years' confinement. From her legend we know that Paphnutius will indeed take pity on her and grant her request. See *PL* 73, cols. 661–62; *Leg. aurea* 148; *Acta sanctorum*, October IV, Dies 8. The legend was dramatized by Hrotsvit von Gandersheim in *Pafnutius*, first edited by Konrad Celtis in 1501.

In the 1532/39 version this letter is *Her.* 3.2.

[2]Paphnutius had forbidden her to raise her hands to heaven in prayer.

Quod nisi tu dederis, venerando proxime caelo,
40   Nescio an heae poterint pondus habere preces.
Tu potes irati numen placare Tonantis,
    Neglectam miseris pandere docte viam.

44=16ʳ

Nunc mihi spes in te, pater, illa novissima restat.
    Qua si destituar, vivere crimen erit.
45   Non ego sufficio pro tot deformibus actis,
    Non, licet in poenas corpora mille feram.
Adde quod haec minor est quam me meruisse putarim.
    Istud adhuc poena vindice pectus eget.
Qur ego non proiecta feris, non obruta saxis,
50   Qur non sum turpi nuda revincta pyra?
In me desinitis crudeles esse, tyranni?
    In me tormenti deficit omne genus?
Foelices, quibus ante diem cecidisse, puellae,
    Et sancta licuit pro pietate mori!
55   Nunc ego Margaridos cuperem mihi fata velimque
    Per mala Niliacae Costidis esse comes!
Sed neque causa mihi est fidei suscepta tuendae
    Nec veteres dixi crimen habere deos.
Vota Deo sanctique undis lustrata lavacri,
60   Heu, duce sub proprio perfida miles eram.
Et Ducis alterius non sum data signa sequta,
    Et graviter laesi sub quibus ipsa fui.
Nunc dolor est hosti tantum favisse, nec illum,

16ᵛ

    Cum potui, celeri deseruisse fuga.
65   Filia lucis eram, sed lucem ingrata reliqui,
    Non intellectis mersa voraginibus.
Atque adeo longum per opacae devia noctis
    Processi, infernum iam prope limen eram.
Iam super infaustae puteum tollebar abyssi,
70   Infoelix Stygio praeda futura cani.
Actum erat, interii, cum tu, pater optime, victam
    Excipis et pulso fortiter hoste levas.
Et licet ingratum est sceleris meminisse pudendi,
    Causa in eo tamen est qur meminisse velis.
75   Plus solito vitiis virtus collata refulget,
    Qualis in obscoeno splendida gemma luto.
Me pudeat sceleris, quoniam scelus omne pudendum est;
    At sua virtuti gloria danda tuae est.
Tempus erat, medium tenuit sol aureus orbem,
80   Foecerat aequales utraque meta vias.

---

50 pyra *A* (*in erratis, metri gratia*): palo *A* (*in textu*) *BO*.   **54** sancta *A*: vera *BO*.   **55** fata *A*: facta *BO*.   *Post* **56** *add. BO*: Quis dabit ut saevo Bythinidos ense puellae / Aut quali cecidit Lucia morte cadam?   **73** sceleris *AO*: celeris *B*.   **74** velis *A*: voles *BO*.   **76** Qualis *A*: Sicut *BO*.
78 virtuti . . . tuae est *A*: virtuti est . . . tuae *BO*.

Unless you grant this, intimate of venerable heaven, [40] I do not know whether these prayers of mine can carry weight. You know how to placate the divine majesty of the wrathful Thunderer; you are expert at showing miserable sinners the road they missed. Now my last hope, father, is fixed on you. If I am deprived of that, life will be an endless reproach. I myself could never atone for so many abominable acts, no, not even if I had a thousand bodies to do penance. Moreover, I feel that my penance is less than I deserve. This breast of mine still needs the avenging punishment. Why was I not thrown to the wild beasts, why not stoned to death, [50] why not stripped naked and burned at the stake? Has your cruelty come to an end with me, tyrants? Are there no tortures of any kind left for me? Blessed the maidens who had the privilege to fall before their time and die for holy religion! Now I could crave the fate of Margaret and wish to share the martyrdom of that Egyptian girl, Costus' daughter![3]

But I have neither taken up the cause of defending the faith nor proclaimed that the ancient gods are a disgrace. Solemnly promised to God and cleansed with the water of the holy font, [60] alas, I deserted and struck out on my own. I did not follow the standards of that other Leader, though enrolled in his army, and did grave damage to the banners under which I had served. Now it grieves me that I gave the Enemy so much aid and comfort and did not run from him in swift flight, while I still could. I used to be a daughter of the light; but, ingrate that I was, I forsook the light and sank unawares into the quagmire. In fact, I had been wandering down the byways of murky night so long that I was already near the threshold of hell. Already teetering on the brink of the accursed abyss, [70] I was doomed to fall prey to the Stygian hound.[4] It was all over with me, I was done for, when you, best of fathers, caught me up as I fell and, boldly repulsing the Enemy, put me back on my feet. And though it is distressing to recall a shameful sin, there is nevertheless a good reason why you might want to remember it in this case. Virtue held side-by-side with vice shines more brilliantly than usual, much like a dazzling jewel in filthy mud. I should be ashamed of my sin, because every sin is shameful; but your virtue must be given the honor it deserves.

It was that time of day: the golden sun stood at the mid-point of his course, [80] equidistant from his rising and setting.

---

[3]St. Margaret of Antioch was tortured and beheaded. For the legend of "Costus' daughter," St. Catherine of Alexandria, see *Her. Chr.* 4.

[4]The three-headed watchdog Cerberus, who guards the entrance to the underworld.

Indixere sacri festiva silentia mystae,
    Tempore quo debent non nisi sacra coli.
Sola fui, formae studiis intenta colendae,
    Mirantes vultu fallere docta procos.
85   Cumque frui cuperem solito foedissima lucro
    Et fieret voti copia nulla mei,
Ecce venit senio quidam venerabilis albo.
    Hoc miserae nondum tempore notus eras.
Vestis erat non apta seni, quam forte gerebas,
90   Quam poterit credi non placuisse tibi.
Quae tum causa fuit tetricum posuisse cucullum?
    Quid loca philosopho non adeunda subis?
Errantes revocare animas doctissime, laus est
    Magna tuis quod sum foemina capta dolis.
95   Scis, pater, ut tanquam suspensus in oscula dixti
    Ut possim tecum quolibet esse loco —
Ah, pudet et dolor est meminisse! — petentibus illud
    Foemina me nunquam mollior ulla fuit.
Ad loca deductus rebus satis apta nefandis,
100   Ipse rogas furtis commodiora peti.
Interius conclave fuit; placuisse putabam.
    Plus nimio visum est lucis habere tibi.
Atria deduxi tacitae vix pervia luci.
    Non satis haec votis clausa fuere tuis.
105   "Quae tua nequitia est? Vel quis pudor, improbe adulter?
    Quis timor? Hic solus nos videt esse Deus!
Hic tu si quod ais verum est, quae tuta petemus?
    Hunc nihil est, inquam, quod latuisse potest."
"Ergo age," dicebas, "quam desipienter aberras!
110   Quod pudet ante homines, non pudet ante Deum?
Esse nocens superis, mundo sine labe videri —
    Sic misera es, sic te decipit hostis! — amas.
Non ego te veni turpi fruiturus amore,
    Sed tibi ut ostendam teque tuumque nefas.
115   Heu, misera, obscoeno maculata libidinis aestu
    Et nimium putri sordida facta luto,
Erras! Coelestem non haec via ducit in aulam!
    Quo ruis? Infernam corruis ante domum.
Siste referque pedem mortemque evade propinquam.
120   Me sequere ad vitam. Dux tibi fidus ero."

45=K1ʳ (line 86 margin)

K1ᵛ (line 108 margin)

---

90 poterit *A*: poterat *BO*.   **91** Quae *BO*: Que *A*.   **92** philosopho *A*: Christicolae *BO*.
94 Magna *AO*: Rara *B*.   **103** Atria — tacitae *A*: In loca deduxi minimae *BO*.   **104** Non *A*:
Nec *BO*.   **108** potest *scripsi*: putes *A*, queat *BO*.   **109** Ergo *AO*: Erga *B*.   **112** amas *AO*:
amans *B*.   **115** obscoeno *AO*: obscoena *B*.

The holy priests were imposing festal silence, this being the day when nothing but the sacred rites should be observed. I was by myself, engrossed in enhancing my beauty, for I was skilled at deceiving awestruck admirers with my good looks. And when I, loathsome creature, was eager to earn my accustomed income, but had no customers to fulfill my wish, lo and behold, in comes some venerable graybeard. At that time, fallen woman that I was, I did not know you yet. The garb you happened to be wearing did not suit an old man. [90] In fact, it seemed obvious that you did not care for it either.

What was your reason for taking off the gloomy cowl that day? Why did you visit a place no philosopher ought to go near? Expert at saving lost souls, you earned great renown by capturing a woman like me with your wiles! As you know, father, when you seemed intent on kisses and asked if you and I could get together someplace — ah, I'm embarrassed and pained to think back on it! — no woman was ever more tenderly inclined to such wishes than I. Taken to a place well-suited for the works of darkness, [100] you asked if we could go to a room more suitable for furtive love. There was an inner chamber that I thought would be acceptable. You thought it was still far too well-lit. I took you to a quiet room that admitted scarcely any light at all. Even this one was not sealed off enough to suit you.

"What kind of perversion is this? What is making you so bashful, dirty old man? What are you afraid of? The only one who can see us here is God! If what you tell me is true, what is the use of looking for a safe place? From him, I tell you, nothing can ever stay hidden."

"Well then," you replied, "how foolishly you have strayed! [110] What is shameful before men is not shameful before God? What you love doing is to sin against heaven and yet appear blameless to the world — that is how blind you are, that is how the Enemy has misled you! I did not come to you to enjoy squalid love, but to open your eyes to yourself and your wickedness. Alas, wretched sinner, polluted with the disgusting passions of lust and horribly sullied with putrid mud, you have gone astray! This is not the way that leads to the mansions of heaven! Where are you rushing to headlong? You have fallen at the gates of hell. Stop and turn back and escape imminent death. [120] Follow me to life. I shall be a faithful guide to you."

Finieras. Fassae insolitus pudor ora notavit,
    Factaque sum verum lumen avara sequi.
Non secus ac cupidus ruit in certamina miles,
    Cum vocat et rauca classica voce sonat.
125   Venit et abiecto reverentia nata pudori,
    Heu nimium sero lumine visa mihi.
Exciderat vitae mihi consuetudo prioris,
    Spretaque, sed nuper non odiosa Venus.
Hoc mihi tu poteras lingua praestare diserta!

46=K2^r   130   Credibile est verbis numen inesse tuis.
Quae mihi per longae tot devia noctis eunti
    Clausa erat, agnosci te duce cepta via est.
Et iam per tenebras nova lux apparuit. "Ite,
    Insidiae," dixi, "lucis abite novae!
135   Ite, leves animi vos dedignantis amores,
    Ite, voluptates illecebraeque breves!
Heu, male pro vobis iuvenile expendimus aevum.
    Nunc alia est nostra meta terenda rota."
Ipse aderas ignique dabas alimenta benigno,
140   Cum vindex nostras flamma peraedit opes.
Atque ut in igne novo mentem succensa calebam,
    Qur domina extarem rebus iniqua meis?
Quae mihi sepe duces in gaudia falsa fuerunt,
    Tristitiae comites fas erat esse meae.
145   In medio iam rubra foro pyra stabat, ut ipsa
    Orsa ita sum populo, testis es ipse, loqui:
"O quibus aut unquam placui aut quos nuper amavi,
    Causaque nequitiae turba comesque meae,
Aspicite haec nostrumque oculis haurite dolorem,
150   Discite et hac vestram Thaida parte sequi.
Vestra fui, vobis placui, vos ipsa colebam;

K2^v   Et placuisse grave est et coluisse nocet.
Quae superest igitur congesta libidine merces,
    Iam premitur vacua parva favilla manu.
155   Ipsa nocens veniam qualem docet iste precabor,
    Per quem de venia spes bona facta mihi est.
Munde, vale. Nimium tecum est, infide, moratum,
    Causaque nequiciae turba comesque meae."

---

124 vocat . . . sonat *A*: fragor . . . sonant *BO*.   134 Insidiae — novae *A*: Insidiatores, hostis abite doli
BO.   136 Ite — breves *A*: Supplicium, laquei, vincla, venena, cruces *BO*.   139–40 ignique — opes
A: tunc, cum Christi nova iura professa / Pauperibus miseras evacuarer opes *BO*.   141 Atque ut in *A*:
Quas ut ab *BO*.   142 Qur — meis? *A*: Ausa fui in medio pene cremare foro. *BO*.   143 mihi *A*:
quia *BO*; falsa *A*: vana *BO*.   145 In — ipsa *A*: Utque frequens spectatum aderat Thebaea iuventus,
BO.   154 Iam — manu *A*: Amplius hic curae debet habere nihil *BO*.

You were done. An unaccustomed blush stained my cheeks and confessed my crime. At once I hungered to follow the true light. No less eagerly does a warrior rush into the fray when the clarion blares its raucous call. Casting off my disgrace, I felt a sense of reverence being born in its stead, a godliness, alas, that my eye saw far too late. I abandoned my previous way of life and turned my back on the now scorned, but heretofore not odious, Venus. All this you were able to grant me with your eloquent tongue! [130] I am convinced that your words possess divine power. Under your guidance I began to see the road that had been closed to me when I was still roaming the many byways of unending night. And then a new light appeared in the darkness. "Begone!" I cried. "Away with you, pitfalls for the newfound light! Go, fleeting amours! I have nothing but contempt for you. Go, pleasures and brief allurements! Alas, it is for you that I misspent my youth. Henceforth I must race toward a different goal!"

You yourself were present and added fuel to the beneficial fire [140] when the avenging flame consumed my worldly riches. Being all aglow with a new fire myself, why should I cling to my ill-gotten goods? Since they had often steered me to false joys, it was only right that they should escort me also in my grief. The ruddy pyre was already blazing in the middle of the marketplace, when I began to address the people (you are my witness) as follows: "O you, to whom I seemed attractive at one time or other or whom I loved of late, you gallants who both caused and shared in my iniquity, look on this scene and gaze your fill on my anguish [150] and learn to follow your Thais in this respect too. I used to be yours, I pleased you, I courted you myself; but to have pleased you is wicked and to have courted you is a crime. What is left of the goods amassed by wanton behavior, therefore, is now a mere handful of ashes. I myself intend to ask pardon for my sins. That man there, he has taught me how — he is the one who has given me good hope for forgiveness. Farewell, faithless world! I have stayed with you too long. Oh, you gallants who both caused and shared in my iniquity."

Illic de populo quosdam movisse videbar,
160   Et multos sceleris poenituisse liquet.
Atque utinam ex illis aliquis sua crimina fassus
    Thaidos offensum sit memor ante Deum!
Forte erit ex multis cui faverit ille precanti,
    Et dicat miserans, "Haec quoque nostra fuit."
165   Tu quoque, cui nostrae commissa est cura salutis,
    Quam potes his miserae casibus affer opem.
Longa mora est postquam caecis inclusa latebris
    Non potui vultus, Phoebe, videre tuos.
Frugiferos aestas iam tertia colligit ignes.
170   An, rogo, adhuc nulla est gratia parta mihi?
An gravis offensi nondum cadit ira Tonantis?
    Heu, quantum est paucos emeruisse dies!
Spes tamen est maior vitae quam culpa peractae.
    Spes maneat, gravior nulla futura mora est.
175   Invisum tempus constans pacientia vincet,
    Donec erit moti mollior ira Dei.
Tu nostro veniam supplex pro crimine posce.
    Ipsa feram iusso quas licet ore preces.

47=K3ʳ

---

163 ex *A*: e *BO*; precanti *A*: roganti *BO*.   **167** caecis . . . latebris *A*: latebrosae . . . cavernae *BO*.
178 Ipsa *A*: Ipse *BO*.

To all appearances I did move some of the people there; [160] in fact, it is certain that many repented of their sin. How I wish that someone among them may confess his misdeeds and remember Thais before the offended Deity! Perhaps among the many there will be one to whose prayers God will incline his ear, and full of pity he'll say, "She too was once mine."

You too, to whom the care for my salvation is entrusted, bring me, poor soul, whatever aid you can in my plight. It has been a long time that I, shut up in this dark cell, have been unable to see the sun's face. Already the third summer is gathering the fruit-bearing heat. [170] Have I then, I ask you, still not merited any grace? Has the fierce anger of the offended Thunderer not subsided yet? Alas, how much has to be earned in a few days! Nevertheless, my hope is greater than the guilt of my past life. As long as hope remains, no delay will prove too burdensome. Steadfast patience will overcome hateful time, until the wrath of the indignant God grows softer.

Do ask him humbly for forgiveness of my sin. I myself will go on offering the prayer that you commanded me to say.

12 ALCIONE GEORGIO

Littera quod timidae non est tibi cognita dextrae,
De lachrymis fecit facta litura meis.
Cum tamen aspiceres primae signacula frontis,
Qur tibi non vincto nota dracone fuit?

5 Sic est ad patriam tibi bestia capta paludem,
Sic ego sum dextra virgo redempta tua.
Magne, triumphato, victor, metuende draconi,
Iamne quid aspitias quaeris et unde legas?
Fama est Rhomano graviter sub Caesare vinctum —

10 Heu nimium vera fama probata fide! —
Propterea quod sacra colas maiora, professus
Verum pro falsa relligione Deum.
Quinetiam poenas aiunt te morte daturum,
Esse sacra promptum pro pietate mori.

15 Vox nova quae nostras quo tempore contigit aures,
Frigidus in toto pectore sanguis erat.

K3ᵛ Fusa thoro, gelidis ut eram subnixa lacertis,
Sic iacui longa mortua pene mora.
Vix etiam, nutrix Hecale, vix, mater Agave,

20 Semianimem gelida restituistis aqua.

Her. Chr. 12. *A*: *om. BO.* **8** quaeris *A* (*in erratis*): nescis *A* (*in textu*).

[1]St. George (d. ca. 303) was a native of Cappadocia who served as tribune in the Roman army during the wars in Palestine. While in Libya, he found a girl sitting next to a large lake, not far from the town of Silena. Asked why she was weeping, the girl answered that she was the king's daughter, left as prey to a voracious dragon that otherwise would devastate the entire town. As they were talking, the dragon rose out of the water and hurtled toward them. Ignoring the girl's pleas to flee, George mounted his horse, armed himself with prayers and the sign of the cross, and killed the dragon. The elderly king, his family, and all the townspeople were baptized and instructed in the faith. The saint then departed. Learning that the prefect Dacian was violently persecuting the Christians, he publicly denounced the pagan gods. After all attempts to torture him to death failed through God's help, the prefect had George dragged through the city and beheaded. The prefect himself, however, was struck by lightning and consumed. See *Leg. aurea* 56.

The legend was retold in Baptista Mantuanus' short epic *Georgius* (1507). Eobanus explicitly mentions this work in *Her. Chr.*, ded. 15.7, as the source of the heroine's name *Alcione* (Mant. *Georgius*, fol. 206ᵛ–207ʳ). Why did Mantuanus pick this name for her? After her husband

12   ALCYONE TO GEORGE[1]

If you fail to recognize the timid hand that wrote this letter, it must be because the writing has been smudged with my tears. Still, when you studied the wax seal, why did you not recognize the dragon on a leash?[2] That is how you captured the monster beside the swamp in my homeland; that is how your right hand rescued me, young maiden. Mighty victor, a dreaded sight for the conquered dragon, do you still ask what it is you are reading and who might have sent it?

Rumor has it that you are languishing in jail under the Roman Emperor[3] — [10] alas, the rumor has proved all too well founded! — because you practice a greater religion and openly confessed your faith in the true God instead of idolatry. What is worse, they say that you are going to be executed, that you are prepared to die for the holy faith.

When the news reached my ears, all the blood in my breast turned cold. Stretched out on a couch, propped up as I was on chilled arms, this is how I lay for a long time, more dead than alive. Only with difficulty did my nurse Hecale and my mother Agave [20] manage to bring the half-dead girl back to life with ice-cold

---

Ceyx suffered shipwreck, the mythical Alcyone threw herself into the sea and, together with Ceyx, was changed into a halcyon. See Ov. *Met.* 11.379–748. Thus, as Josse Bade explains in his commentary to *Georgius* (*Opera B. Mantuani* [Paris, 1513], 1, fol. 226ʳ), "this name is well suited to one in grief." But while Mantuanus' Alcyone grieves because she is about to be devoured by a dragon, Eobanus' heroine grieves because she has fallen in love with a saint who prefers martyrdom to marriage. That is why she writes this letter, in a vain attempt to make him change his mind and return to her.

The idea that Alcyone might have fallen in love with her heroic rescuer, though not found in earlier treatments of the legend, is a natural consequence of Eobanus' humanistic habit of associating Christian heroes and heroines with their counterparts in ancient myth. For as both Mantuanus (fol. 206ᵛ) and Eobanus saw (cf. ll. 133–52 below, with the notes on pp. 551–52), the story of George the dragonslayer is strikingly similar to that of the Greek hero Perseus, who rescued the beautiful princess Andromeda from the clutches of a sea monster (Ov. *Met.* 4.663–739). Eobanus now pushes this parallel to its logical conclusion. For just as Perseus fell in love with Andromeda, so the king's daughter Alcyone now expects her hero to fall in love with her and become her husband.

With its amatory theme and legendary material, the letter was dropped entirely from the 1532/39 version. An allusion to the legend in *Her. Chr.* 22.81–82 was likewise excised in the revision, being replaced with a reference to the dragon of the apocalypse.

[2]Like *Leg. aurea* 56.57–75, Eobanus offers two variants of the dragon's death. According to the first version, which Eobanus follows here, George wounds the dragon with his lance. Thereupon the virgin binds the beast with her girdle and leads it into the city (cf. *Her. Chr.* 22.107–08, with the same motif). In the second version of the story George crosses himself and then rides out to kill the dragon. This is the version adopted in Mant. *Georg.*, fol. 207ʳ–207ᵛ as well as at ll. 187–90 below.

[3]Diocletian (r. 284–305) and Maximian (r. 286–305), according to *Leg. aurea* 56.15–17, 136. Mant. *Georg.*, fol. 211ᵛ, mentions only Maximian.

Reddita, conceptum verbis testata dolorem,
    Aptabam resides ad nova scripta manus.
Ergone crudeli mulctabere morte tyranno?
    Ergone supplicium pro pietate feres?
25   O utinam quae nunc per te est mihi vita superstes
    Danda sit, ut posses ipse valere, neci!
Non ego Rhomuleo metuendas fasce secures,
    Non metuam paenae quicquid ubique grave est.
Intrepida experiar teneros tormenta per artus —
30   Et mihi quod pectus vulnerer esse potest!
Hoc tibi debemus, hoc te meruisse fatemur
    Illo quo nobis tempore fortis eras.
Qui nunc dura subis sub iniquo iura tyranno,
    Quam multos fueras inclytus ante duces!
35   Primus ut ante omneis clarus pietate manuque
    Iura tribunitia publica lege dabas!
Hoc ego te memini nondum quoque tempore visum
    Non minus antiquis nomen habere deis.
48=K4^r Qur tua in obscurum compressa est gloria? Quare
40   Non gaudet titulis Caesar, ut ante, tuis?
Christicola vidit pro relligione molestum
    Et timuit lemures posse perire suas.
Nec frustra paulatim abeunt ceduntque per orbem
    Rhomanum vero numina falsa Deo.
45   Nostra tua grata est tibi pro pietate Silena,
    Quod tenebris pulsis te duce lumen habet.
Quam cito, per superos, totam delubra per urbem,
    Vana prius, cultu sunt decorata novo!
Concessit Christo venienti Iuppiter Ammon;
50   Cornua adhuc bibulo pulvere sparsa iacent.
Ante omneis prior ipse parens, iam tardior aevo,
    Excidit irata signa nefanda manu.
Excidit et dixit: "Fatui ludibria saecli,
    Ite! Deus vestro numine maior adest.
55   Ite Acheronteas, Christus iubet, ite sub undas,
    Deque fera Christi vindice victor eques."
Continuo cecidere altis innixa columnis
    Deturbatorum milia multa deum.
Tempore ab hoc, sacro per te de fonte renati,
60   Fortiter in Christum credula turba sumus.

water. Restored to consciousness, I gave vent to my grief in words and set my torpid hand to this letter — the first I have ever written you.

Are you then to suffer death at the command of a cruel tyrant? Are you then to be martyred for your faith? O, that I might die in your stead and give up the life you saved, so you yourself might go free! I would have no fear of the Roman fasces and their dreadful axes, no fear of punishment, no matter how severe. Undaunted I would let them torment my tender body — [30] I too have a breast they can wound as much as they want! This is what I owe you. This, I acknowledge, is what you have deserved ever since you proved your valor on my behalf.

You, who now endure a harsh sentence under the prejudiced tyrant, how renowned you used to be, more so than many other leaders! How you shone at the head of them all, illustrious through your piety and power, as you dispensed justice by virtue of your tribuneship! Even in those days when I had not yet laid eyes on you, I remember you were held in no less esteem than the old gods. Why is your glory thrust into obscurity? Why [40] doesn't the emperor rejoice in your achievements as in days past? He is outraged that you support the Christian religion and fears that his phantom deities may perish. And with good reason too, for everywhere in the Roman world the false gods are gradually disappearing and giving way to the true God. My hometown Silena is grateful to you for your devotion, because under your leadership it dispelled the darkness and saw the light. Good heavens, how quickly were the formerly pagan shrines throughout this city adorned with the new religion! As Christ advanced, Jupiter Ammon drew back. [50] Even now his horns lie scattered about in the thirsty sands.[4]

My father himself, though already slowed by old age, led all the people in tearing down the abominable idols with wrathful hand. And as he tore them down, he cried: "Hallucinations of a foolish age, away with you! A God mightier than you is here. Away with you! Begone beneath the waters of Acheron! Christ commands you, and so does this knight of Christ, the victor over the avenging beast." Instantly many thousands of gods fell from the high columns on which they stood and tumbled to the ground. Since that time, reborn through you in the holy font, [60] we have been a deeply Christian people.

---

[4]Ammon, identified with Jupiter as Jupiter Hammon, was an Egyptian god represented as a ram. Hence he lent his name to *ammonite*, the fossil shell of an extinct mollusk that resembles a ram's horn.

K4ᵛ

Nunc tamen in lachrymas patria, heu, conversa sine omni
    Laeticia et prisco squalida honore iacet.
Scilicet ipse aberis, nostrae spes prima salutis,
    Captivaque feres vincula dura manu,
65 Nos laeti praesente Deo festa otia agemus,
    Templa coronentur frondibus alta novis?
Quin potius luctu indecores lucemque perosi
    Flebimus. Est quare sic doluisse iuvet!
Ipsa tamen, quae plus aliis tibi debeo, nunquam
70   Donec abes laetos laeta videbo dies.
Nec, quamvis tentem, regales sumere cultus
    Me patitur, miserae causa dolenda, dolor.
Causa dolor certe solem quia cernere nolim,
    Seu cadat Oceana sive resurgat aqua.
75 Crescit et usque adeo miseros depascitur artus,
    Ut sit in hoc firmum corpore pene nihil.
Qui rubor ardenti quondam mihi fulsit in ore,
    Candorem qualem pallida buxus habet.
Demissi cecidere oculi, cecidere lacerti.
80   Nulla sub angusto pectore bulla tumet.
Pendula praeveniunt humiles velamina vultus;
    In toto circum corpore pulla toga est.
49=K5ʳ Talis eram, cum preda fero rapienda draconi
    Sum tua per meritum facta? Sed esse negas.
85 Qur etenim nobis tanquam rediturus abisti
    Nec tua promissa est verba sequta fides?
Quam bene servatae servasses virginis annos!
    Qur ego non tanto coniuge digna fui?
Ad genus addiderat titulos tibi gloria clarum;
90   Ipsa quidem magni filia regis eram.
Turpiter haud thalamo convenissemus eodem,
    Nec tibi dedecori nupta futura fui.
Uti etiam mecum potuisses virgine lecto,
    Qua tibi non unquam cedere laude velim.
95 Nam (nisi me fallam) vobis castissima vita est,
    Quorum militia est pro cruce posse mori.
Nos quoque servando iuvat indulsisse pudori,
    Nos quoque (si nescis) sub cruce turba sumus.
Quam bene coniungi poteras cum virgine virgo
100   Claraque militiae ponere signa tuae!
Non tua nunc dura manicas praebente cathena
    Vincta sub iniusto principe dextra foret.
Quae celebrem nuper victo tulit angue triumphum,
    Hei mihi, qur nostra tam procul illa domo est?

But now my fatherland, alas, is reduced to tears. Robbed of all its old gladness and high spirits, it feels crushed, disheartened. Knowing that you, our first hope of salvation, are gone, knowing that your captive hands are clapped in cruel irons, how can we go on happily celebrating the holy days in God's presence and decking the lofty churches with fresh garlands? No, dressed in mourning and loathing the light of day, we'll weep instead. We have good reason to seek consolation in grief! I myself, however, who am more indebted to you than all the others, will never [70] be happy or see happy days again for as long as you are absent. No matter how hard I try — a source of sorrow in itself for me, poor girl — grief does not allow me to put on any of my regal finery. Surely grief is the reason why I refuse to look at the sun, whether it sinks beneath the ocean waves or rises out of them again. It is the ever-deepening grief that makes my miserable limbs waste away so much that my body has hardly any firmness left. The blush that once shone on my glowing cheeks now has the whiteness of pallid boxwood. My eyes are downcast; my arms droop. [80] No locket swells beneath my straitlaced breast. Hanging veils cover my gaunt face; a dark cloak envelops my whole body.

Is that what I looked like when, a prey waiting to be carried off by the fierce dragon, I became yours through your merit? But you deny that I am. Why then did you leave us with the impression that you were going to return? And why did you not keep your promise? How well you would have preserved the youthfulness of her whom you preserved from death! Why was I not worthy of such a bridegroom? To your illustrious birth, glory had added noble titles. [90] Yes indeed, but I myself am the daughter of a great king. We could have shared the same bedroom without the least dishonor, nor would I have embarrassed you, had I become your bride. Even while married to me you could have kept your bed virginally pure. In that distinction I would never want to be inferior to you. For unless I'm mistaken, you people live a life of utmost chastity and your soldiering consists in being ready to die for the cross. But we too take pleasure in keeping our virginity. We too, in case you've forgotten, are a people under the cross.

How well might a virgin like you have joined in wedlock with a virgin [100] and laid down the glorious banners of your soldier's life! Then you wouldn't be fettered in cruel chains now, nor would the unjust emperor be keeping your right hand in irons. The hand that just recently won a famous triumph over the dragon, alas, why is it now so far from our house? Why is that

105   Illa venenosi victrix operosa draconis
                Qur iacet et nullo fulminat ense manus?
            Debuit illa truci rapuisse ex hoste trophaea
                Qui crucis obliquo lumine signa videt.
            Debuit hoc totum statuisse insigne per orbem
      110   Illa Deo in populos vindice dextra potens.
            Qualem Cappadoces rigidi videre tribunum
                Dura tot invicta conterere arma manu.
            Iura Palestinus subiit Rhomana coactus,
                Et tua turilegus signa timebat Arabs.
      115   Sive per Armenias seu per Syria arva ruebas
                Dux, populis solo nomine fulmen eras.
            Praecipue invictum Lybiae videre potentes,
                Hic ubi regna pater vasta Lycurgus habet.
            Hic, ubi claram urbem veteres posuere Sileni,
      120   De quibus aeternum nunc quoque nomen habet,
            Hic tua plus solito emicuit clarissima virtus.
                Putris adhuc fuso sanguine squallet humus.
            Tempus erat, medio iam sol altissimus orbe
                Acturus spatium quale peregit erat.
      125   Sorte mala patriae sic me cogente, resedi
                Ad mare letiferae preda relicta ferae.
Et iam certa mori vigilantia lumina movi,
                Aestuet in corpus si qua procella meum.
            Ecce, per adversum solem fulgentibus armis,
      130   Dum video, acceleras prepete vectus equo.
            Obstupui voluique amens fugisse, sed illud
                Ne facerem ferrum quod prohiberet erat.
            Iam prope constiteras, cum me fera vincla prementem
                Intrepidam verbis talibus esse iubes:
      135   "O non vulgares inter sata virgo puellas,
                Ne trepida, adventus ne vereare meos.
            Quin age dic, quis te ferus haec in vincla coegit?
                Crimine quo tantum demeruisse potes?"
            "Heu, fuge, nec nostri rationem quaere pericli!
      140   Me miseram," dixi, "sit satis ista pati.
            Non potes auxilium moriturae ferre puellae.
                Haec est non aliqua sors redimenda manu."
            Vix ea cum gemitu lachrymosa per ora loqutam
                Tristia constanter dicere fata iubes.
      145   Iussa recensebam crudelia fata simulque
                Ut fugeres suasi consiliumque dedi.

---

126 letiferae *scripsi*: laetiferae **A**.

hand, the powerful victor over the venomous dragon, now lying idle? Why isn't it flashing a sword? It ought to be snatching trophies from the savage Enemy who eyes the standards of the cross askance. [110] With God's help, your mighty right hand ought to be setting up this ensign over every nation in the world. That is how the rugged Cappadocians saw you in action as tribune, when you crushed so many battle-hardened armies with your invincible fist. You were the one who forced the Palestinians to submit to Roman rule; and the incense-gathering Arabs feared your troops. Whether you were leading the charge through the Armenias or through the fields of Syria, your very name was a thunderbolt that struck fear in everyone's heart. The powerful Libyans in particular can witness to your invincibility, here where my father Lycurgus rules his vast kingdom. Here, where the ancient Sileni founded the illustrious city [120] that to this day takes its immortal name from them, here your bravery flashed forth more brilliantly than usual. Even now the soil is gory with the blood you spilled.

It was the time of day when the sun is at its zenith, midway on its course, and still has the same distance to travel as it has just traversed. Forced there by the tragic fate of my homeland, I hunkered down by the sea, having been left behind as prey for the death-dealing beast. Convinced that I was doomed, I frantically looked about to see if an onslaught might already be swooping down on me. As I was watching — lo and behold! — your armor all aglint in the bright sunlight, [130] you galloped towards me on a swift steed. Stunned and frightened out of my wits, I wanted to run away, but my chains prevented me from doing so. Before long you stood before me. As I was still tugging at the cruel fetters, you told me to be unafraid: "O highborn maiden, have no fear! Do not be frightened at my arrival. Tell me rather: What brute put you in chains like this? What crime did you commit to deserve such heavy punishment?"

"Woe," I cried, "make your escape! Do not ask why I am in this danger! [140] It is bad enough that I, poor girl, have to suffer these things. There is no way you can help the doomed maiden. Nobody can save me from this fate!"

No sooner had I uttered these words with a groan, tears coursing down my cheeks, than you told me to stay calm and relate my misfortune. At your bidding I explained my cruel fate and at the same time urged and counseled you to escape. When

Ipse intellecto subeundae nomine poenae
    Talia cum risu verba decente dabas:

K6ᵛ

"Quanta fero parva de virgine praeda draconi!
150   Non potuit fortes forsitan esse viros.
Missus in auxilium, virgo, patriaeque tibique,
    Ostendam quo stet vindice vestra salus."
Et simul aptatis clipeo galeaque comanti,
    Inclinata ingens iam fuit hasta tibi.
155 Tum vero exultans animo iuveniliter alto
    Questus es absentem longius isse feram,
Sicut magnanimum deserta per alta leonem
    Exagitat longa praeda cupita mora.
Mirabar praestantem animum doluique quod esset
160   Arduus in poenam forsitan ille suam,
Questa simul: "Quo te lachrymarum gurgite plangam,
    O iuvenis, facilem non habiture deum!
Quis te participem nostri deus esse laboris?
    Quis voluit misera te quoque sorte mori?
165 Quae geris, arma manu tentabis Martia frustra.
    Frustra erit in dextra missilis hasta tibi.
Heu, fuge, tolle moras! Qur in tua damna moraris?
    O decus, o saecli gloria summa tui!"
Finieram. Procul ecce altis confusa procellis
170   Aequora sustulerant spemque animumque mihi.

51=L1ʳ

Ecce venit! Iamque egreditur littusque tenebat!
    Hic gelido potui pene timore mori.
Protinus ad praedam passis annititur alis,
    Tacturus spatio corpora nostra brevi,
175 Quum tu, quantum oculo potui dubitante notare,
    Signa facis certa qualiacunque manu.
Iamque ferocis equi celeri pede vectus in hostem
    Tentasti auspicio praelia prima bono.
Hesit in adversi iugulo gravis hasta draconis;
180   Ille putrem fosso gutture planxit humum.
Orbibus immensis tamen hic caudaque reflexa
    Implicitum spiris pene tulisset equum.
Spirabat tristi mixtas caligine flammas;
    Nigra venenata luce mephitis erat.
185 Ipsa deos, non docta Deum, venerabar ut essent
    Auxiliatores in tua facta mihi.
Interea eductum squamis in putribus ensem
    Abdideras, crebro vulnere pectus agens.
Ille iacens tandem morientes palpitat artus,
190   Et fugiunt una vita cruorque via.

---

157 magnanimum *A* (*in erratis*): magnanimi *A* (*in textu*).   **182** equum *scripsi*: aequum *A*.

you found out what kind of penalty I was to suffer, you answered me with a becoming laugh: "What a prey for a fierce dragon — a little maiden! [150] Perhaps he's had trouble chewing on valiant men. Sent to help your homeland and you, princess, I am here to show you by whose help you can be saved." Simultaneously you adjusted your shield and plumed helmet and tilted your enormous lance. Then indeed, exultant in the high spirits of youth, you complained that the absent beast was keeping you waiting too long, just as a long-stalked quarry excites the great-spirited lion in the high desert.

I marveled at your peerless courage, but grieved that [160] perhaps you might be overreaching yourself, to your own detriment, and at the same time lamented: "With what a flood of tears will I have to bewail you, O youth to whom no god will lend a ready hand! Which god wanted you to share in my distress? Who wanted you to die a miserable death with me? The weapons of war that you hold in your hands will be of no avail. The throwing spear in your right hand will be useless. Woe, make your escape! Do not delay! What are you waiting for? Do you want to be killed? O splendor, O highest glory of your age!"

I had finished. Look, far away the smooth expanse of the lake was stirred up with high-cresting waves — [170] they took away my hope and my courage! Look, it's approaching! It's already emerging from the water and coming ashore! Numb with fear, I nearly died then and there. Straight away it makes for its prey, its wings spread out. Another minute, and it will be upon me! But then, as far as I could tell in a doubtful glance, you made some kind of signs with unflinching hand.[5] And now, riding your high-mettled steed, you swiftly galloped at the enemy. The battle started auspiciously for you. The heavy lance stuck square in the dragon's throat. [180] Its gullet pierced, the beast fell heavily to the gory ground. Even so, writhing in huge coils and whipping its tail around, the monster came close to entwining your horse in its spirals and throwing him down. It breathed flames mixed with sooty smoke, and a pestilential stench filled the envenomed air. I myself, not knowing God, adored the gods for helping me by means of your exploits. In the meantime you had drawn your sword and buried it into the beast's slimy scales, covering its chest with many wounds. At last, lying in the agony of death, it was convulsed in every limb, [190] while life and gore escaped by one and the same path.

---

[5]As Alcyone will realize later, George is crossing himself. Cf. *Her. Chr.* 22.73, in similar context.

Acclamant miseri cives ex maenibus altis;
    Spectatrix populi multa corona fuit.

L1ᵛ   Et iam fama recens summam bacchatur ad arcem,
    Laeticiaque sonat regia tota nova.

195   Curritur ad muros speculisque videtur ab altis,
    Iamque omnis capitum plena fenestra fuit.

Vidit uterque parens traiectum in littore monstrum,
    "Nostraque, io Paean, filia vivit," ait.

Fulgentem nitidis populus conspexit in armis
200   Et te presentem credidit esse deum.

Caetera quae restant victo tibi gesta dracone
    Propositi non est enumerare mei,

Nec brevis historiam comprehendet epistola longam.
    Plus quoque quam virgo debuit illud erat.

205   Est mihi qui pictum paries te reddat ab illo
    Tempore quo nobis causa salutis eras.

A, quoties illum lachrymis contemplor obortis!
    Ah, illi quoties oscula longa dedi!

Contemplata diu, visa est mihi saepe moveri.
210   Visa etiam flere est nuper imago tui.

Heu mihi, qur solito facies tua tristior aut quid
    Pene videbatur muta figura loqui?

Hoc erat, hoc illud, quo te sub iniqua coactum
    Vincula nescio quae poena nefanda manet.

52=L2ʳ   215   At te per vestramque fidem Christumque potentem,
    Per sacrae obtestor signa tremenda crucis,

Plus nimio constantem animum fortemque remitte,
    Nec verbis odii saemina quaere tuis.

Cede, precor, lingua, firmo tibi pectore consta;
220   Et tibi si non vis vivere, vive mihi.

Rhomuleam verbis cedendo evade securim,
    Mente tamen caelo proximus esse potes.

Quam petis hinc, serva meliora in tempora laudem.
    Illa tuo nondum sanguine debet emi.

225   Qui sapit, in rebus lente festinat agendis.
    Plenius iste alia messe virebit ager.

Gentibus ante fidem caecis ostende beatam.
    Quid stat adhuc falso gloria multa Iovi?

Postmodo, cum Lybicas iterum conspexeris urbes
230   Et tuleris nostrae regia sceptra domus,

Cum tibi finitimas gentes adieceris et iam
    Cesserit imperiis Aphrica tota tuis,

---

201 quae *scripsi*: que *A*.   **217** nimio *A* (*in erratis*): minimo *A* (*in textu*).

From atop the high walls the careworn townsfolk cheered and applauded, for a great crowd of people had been watching. At once the latest news came rushing madly up to the lofty citadel, and the whole palace resounded with shouts of newfound joy. Everybody ran to the walls and looked down from the high battlements, and before long every window was full of heads. Both my parents saw the monster lying transfixed on the shore and shouted, "Hurrah, our daughter lives!" The people saw you refulgent in your shining armor [200] and believed you were a very present god in their midst.

It is not my intention to recount the other deeds you performed after you defeated the dragon, nor will my brief letter tell a long tale. Besides, I have already written more than a maiden should. I have a wall painting here that portrays you in the act of saving me. Ah, how often I gaze at it, with tears welling from my eyes! Ah, how often I give it lingering kisses! When I have contemplated it a long time, your likeness often appears to me to move about. [210] Recently I even saw it shed tears.

Alas, why has your face been looking sadder than usual? Or why did the mute figure almost seem to be talking? There can be only one reason: it is because you are unjustly kept in chains, awaiting some unspeakable punishment. But by your faith and by Christ the Lord, by the awe-inspiring banner of the sacred cross I implore you: give up your far too unyielding and resolute boldness and do not go out of your way to sow the seeds of hatred with your words. Yield with your tongue, I beg you, but remain true to yourself at heart; [220] and if you do not wish to live for yourself, live for me. Escape the Roman ax by being accommodating in your speech. You can still remain an intimate of heaven in spirit. The fame you seek from martyrdom, reserve it for a better occasion. It should not be purchased with your blood, at least not yet. When moved to action, the wise man makes haste slowly. Wait until that field of yours brings in another, far richer harvest. Before anything else, show the blind heathens the blessed faith. Why does the false Jove still retain so much of his glory? Later, when you have visited the cities of Libya again [230] and accepted the royal scepter of our house, when you have added the neighboring peoples to your realm and all of Africa has come under your sway, when you have extended

Cum vel ad imbelles tua signa extenderis Indos
   Quaque sub imposita mole laborat Atlas,
235 Ibis ad Aethrusci Mavortia Tybridis arva
   Et valida sternes aethnica castra manu.

L2ᵛ

Tum sine tum Caesar tibi vincla necemque minetur!
   Ah, quantum est laetos posse manere dies!
Tum sacra constitues summo Capitolia Christo,
240   Exuet antiquos impia Rhoma deos.
Occurret pulchrum esse mori pro nomine Christi,
   Cuius apud superos gloria merces erit.
Quis neget hoc pulchrum? Sed vivere pulchrius illis,
   Qui faciant multos vivere, turpe mori.
245 Indignum est, cum plura queas, consistere in uno.
   In multo virtus deficit aegra bono.
Sunt validae pulchro vires in corpore, necdum
   Chilias hebdomadum plena secunda tibi est.
Talibus ista premi fatis non debuit aetas!
250   Heu dolor! Heu, luctus quos, Datiane, facis!
Quid premis insontem? Nunquam Rhomana negavit
   Arma, sed ad partes addidit ille tuas.
Iura Palestinam retulit sub vestra rebellem,
   Quod te, quod multos non potuisse liquet.
255 Haec sunt pro meritis virtuti praemia tantis?
   Haec est militiae merces honesta piae?
Fidus erat nobis; fido tormenta parantur.
   Iustus erat; quare fingitur esse nocens?

53=L3ʳ

Quid tamen, ah, teneram iuvat exprobrare puellam,
260   Cuius erat niti, flere, dolere, queri?
Eia age, rumpe moras igitur, mea vita, molestas,
   Nostraque si non vis, in tua regna redi.
Nulla mihi de te reddatur epistola tristis,
   Non nisi quae dicat nuncia fama, "Venit!"
265 Quam simul attulerint nobis bona sydera vocem,
   Successu nolim prosperiore frui.
Mox sacra festivis adolescent atria flammis
   Et capiet fumos quaelibet ara novos.
Ipsa iterum positos cultus induta, videbor
270   Ne caperer multos delituisse dies.
Sin mea, quod nolim, vacuas spes ibit in auras,
   Quis dabit unde fleam? Quis dabit unde cadam?
Protinus ingrediar superantis inertia vitae
   Taedia, nec moestam qui revocabit erit.

---

240 deos *scripsi*: dies **A**.

your conquests to the unwarlike Indians and to where Atlas labors under the burden placed on him,[6] then you can march to the fields of Mars beside the Etruscan Tiber and overthrow the pagan camps with your mighty hand. Then, then let Caesar threaten you with imprisonment and death! Ah, how wonderful it would be, if we had those happy days to look forward to! Then you would consecrate the Capitol to Christ the Lord, [240] and impious Rome would shed her ancient gods.

To die for the sake of Christ must strike you as a noble goal, seeing that its reward will be glory in heaven. Who would deny that this is indeed a noble thing? But for someone who can save numerous lives, it is nobler to live, shameful to die. When you have the chance to achieve a great many goals, it is wrong to stick to just one. Only a weak man shrinks from doing all the good he can. Your handsome body possesses prodigious strength. You still have not completed the second season of life.[7] This is not the age to suffer such a death! [250] Alas, the pain! Alas, how much sorrow you cause, Dacian! Why are you persecuting an innocent man? Never once did he let the Roman army down; instead, he added to your territories. It was he who restored rebellious Palestine to your rule — an achievement that obviously neither you nor many others were capable of. Is that how you repay his courage, his marvelous feats? Is that an honorable reward for his devoted service? He was loyal to us; for his loyalty he is to be tortured. He was just; why is he being falsely accused?

But ah, what good does it do for a tender maiden to utter reproaches? [260] Her task is to bear up, to weep, grieve, lament. Come then, my life, stop delaying and making me worry! And if you don't want to come back to our country, then return to your own. Just don't let me receive a sad letter about you, only the good news, "He's on his way!"

As soon as my lucky stars bring me that report, all my prayers will be answered. Right away the sanctuaries will blaze with festal flames and every altar will fume with fresh incense. I myself will again don the finery I laid aside. I'll make it appear [270] as if I've long been in seclusion for fear of being wooed by someone else. But if — which I don't want to happen — my hope vanishes into thin air, who then will give me strength enough to weep and to collapse? At once I'll fall into a weary listlessness that will endure as long as I live, and no one will be able to lift me out of my depression.

---

[6]The Titan Atlas was condemned to hold up the sky. Later he was metamorphosed into the mountain in northwest Africa.

[7]Literally, "your second thousand weeks." The saint is still in his thirties and hence in the summer of life.

275   Parce tamen miseraeque, precor, miserere puellae,
      Quae grave nunc primum nomen amantis habet.
Tardior hoc aevo pater et iam frigida mater,
      Hoc te voce rogat supplice tota domus.
Tu modo quam tetri servasti a fauce draconis,
280   Servari ut possit longius ipsa, veni.
L3ᵛ   O, illum violisque diem cretaque notandum
      Quam primum niveo Cynthia portet equo!

275 precor *scripsi*: praecor *A*.

But spare me, I implore you. Take pity on the heartbroken girl who now, for the first time, has the weighty name "lover." This is what my elderly father and my now aged mother ask for. This is what my entire family humbly begs of you. So that she, whom you preserved from the jaws of the horrible dragon, [280] may continue to be preserved, come back! Oh, what a happy day that will be, worth marking with pale violets and chalk.[8] May the Moon bring it to me as soon as possible on her snow-white steed!

---

[8]The Thracians used to mark propitious days with white pebbles. For this proverbial practice, see Erasmus, *Adag.* 1.5.54; Otto 299; Eob. *Her. Chr.* 15.101.

13   ANNA IOACHIMO

Anna viro coniunx Ioachimo mitto salutem.
    Mitto simul fratri, si libet, Anna soror.
Illud enim potui nomen meruisse videri,
    Non ullo tecum pondere facta parens.
5 Legitimi solum tuleris commertia lecti,
    Iam soror ipsa tibi, iam mihi frater eris.
Scilicet, hinc sacris discedere iussus ab aris,
    Turpiter amisso moestus amore iaces.
Quinta fere Triviae coierunt cornua Lunae
10   Dum queror absentem sola relicta virum —
Ah, nimium vindex accepti poena pudoris!
    Quam premis est tanto culpa dolore minor.
Tu nemora et saltus et saxa horrentia lustras
    Et reliquo foetas cum grege pascis oves.
15 Ipsa gemens viduo iaceo sine luce cubili.
    Nox tamen est curis non satis ista meis.
An, quia te arguerit summus de lege sacerdos,
    Abiectum tota relligione putas?
An, quia desperes sterili de coniuge prolem,
20   Quod superest vita caelibe tempus ages?
Et mihi quod multa magis est ratione dolendum,
    Spernis in amplexus forte redire meos?
Spiritus ante leves, precor, hic exhalet in auras,
    Ne causam semper mortis abesse querar.
25 Quid mihi foecundae generoso semine matres,
    Quid reliquae dicent, libera turba, nurus?

54=L4ʳ (line 20)

Her. Chr. **13.**   **4** ullo . . . pondere *A*: aliquo . . . pignore *BO*.   **6** iam . . . eris *A*: tu . . . eras *BO*.
7–8 Scilicet — iaces. *A*: *om. BO*.   *Post* **10** *add. BO*: Nam quia sis sacris discedere iussus ab aris, /
Fama est ignotum constituisse mori.   **15** sine luce *A*: et sine luce *BO*.   **19** coniuge *BO*: coniunge
A.   **22** amplexus . . . meos *A*: abiectam . . . domum *BO*.   **24** semper *A*: sine te *BO*.   **25** generoso *A*: numeroso *BO*.

[1]Married for twenty years, Joachim of Nazareth and Anna of Bethlehem remained childless,
despite a vow that they would offer their offspring to God's service. One day, as Joachim went to
Jerusalem to offer his sacrifice at the Feast of Dedication, a priest chided him for being cursed with
childlessness and drove him from the altar. Too ashamed to return home to his wife, Joachim went to
live among the shepherds in the countryside. Five months later an angel appeared to him and told him
that Anna would conceive and bear him a daughter. She would be called Mary and be dedicated to God
from birth. And just as she herself was born in a miraculous way, so Mary in turn would give birth to
the Son of God. Joachim was to go to Jerusalem, where he would meet his wife at the Golden Gate. The
angel then appeared also to the grieving Anna in Nazareth and gave her the same message. After meeting
in Jerusalem, they joyously returned home. In due time Anna gave birth to the Virgin Mary.

13   ANNA TO JOACHIM[1]

This greeting, my husband Joachim, comes to you from your wife Anna. If you don't mind, I, Anna, send it as a sister to her brother. And indeed, for all anyone can tell, I deserve that term, seeing that I never did become the mother of a child by you. Just take away our marital relations, and I'd now be a sister to you, you'd now be a brother to me.

Of course, ordered to leave the sacred altars, you are mortified by the reproach of childlessness. The horns of Triform Luna[2] have grown together almost for the fifth time [10] since I, left behind alone, started lamenting my husband's absence — ah, too harsh a punishment for the rebuke you received! The sense of guilt you suppress is smaller than the great anguish it has caused.

You roam the woods and glades and rugged rocks as you pasture the gravid ewes along with the rest of the herd. I myself lie grieving in my dark, lonely bed. Even so, nights like these are still too short for my cares. Do you really think, just because the high priest reproved you, that you are an outcast of all religion? Or because you despair of offspring from your barren wife, [20] do you intend to spend the rest of your days as a bachelor? And, what is much more distressing to me, do you perhaps scorn to come back into my arms? May I breathe my last into the thin air, I pray, before I complain that the one who worries me to death is always gone!

What will the fertile mothers of good families tell me? What are the other women going to say, those prattling gossips?

Familiar from *Ps.-Matt.*, *Nativ. Mariae*, *Leg. aurea* 127, and many late medieval hymns, the story became extraordinarily popular among the Northern humanists in the decades preceding the Reformation. See in particular Rudolph Agricola, *Anna mater* (Deventer, [1484]); Mant. *1. Parthen.*, especially book 1 and the opening lines of book 2; Erasmus, *Carm.* 1 (1491?, but not published until 1518); Brant, *Var. carm.*, sig. H1ʳ–H4ᵛ (*Texte* 216–19), written in 1497–98 in response to Arnold Bostius' invitation to his friends to sing the praises of Sts. Joachim and Anna. Also cf. Eob. *Hod.* 301–12, on the famous relic of St. Anna in Düren. See further Angelika Dörfler-Dierken, *Die Verehrung der heiligen Anna in Spätmittelalter und früher Neuzeit* (Göttingen, 1992), with a discussion of Eobanus' poem on 186–89. Also see her article "Annenkult und humanistische Hagiographie," *Pirckheimer-Jahrbuch* 8 (1993), *Humanismus und Theologie in der frühen Neuzeit*, 57–89.

In the 1532/39 version this letter is *Her.* 2.3.

[2] Revered as Cynthia in heaven, as Diana on earth, and as Proserpina in Hades, the moon-goddess was called "Trivia" ("Triform") and worshiped at places where three roads meet.

Tota malum certe de me Galilea loquetur,
   Nec sat erit culpae Nazareth una meae.
Ipsa domo vacua perturbatos hymeneos,
30   Ipsa fleam sterilis damna pudenda thori.
Nec mihi continua lachrymarum mole gravatae
   Fas erit in vulgum quolibet ire loci.
Scilicet exierim nasutae fabula turbae,
   Saepe malis vultu, saepe notanda manu,
35   Atque aliquis miserae mihi dixerit impius osor,
   "Vir tuus, ut templis munera ponat, ubi est?"
Hei mihi, quid faciam tam grandibus anxia curis?
   Vulnera erunt cordi talia verba meo.
Tunc cuperem extremos, si qua est via, tollar ad Indos
40   Aut ubi stat vasto pondere nixus Atlas,
Seu qua Lycaoniam vis me iactaret ad Arcton,
   Qua ferus aeripedes Sarmata pascit equos.

L4ᵛ

Omnia dura prius quam duri opprobria vulgi
   Mens sibi demeriti conscia ferre potest.
45   Quamvis innocuum quid te meruisse putandum est?
   Causa nocens poenae vindicis ipsa fui.
Ipsa diu thalami vanos ignobilis usus
   Indicium culpae suspicor esse meae.
Atque ita dum vario curarum supprimor aestu
50   Et queror absenti displicuisse viro,
Spes nova de superis, nova consolatio venit —
   O bona et ex animo spes referenda mihi!
Esse quid hic reris, quod iam peiora querenti
   Tam cita laeticiae causa fuisse queat?
55   Non ego te longa suspensum ambage morabor.
   Si qua iuvant laus est dicere fine brevi.
Pronus anhelabat sub noctem condere Titan,
   Occeano radiis iam rutilante, diem.
Tristia difficilis flebam dispendia lecti,
60   Non tamen in vanas tota soluta preces.
Ecce per illunem iubar effulgere fenestram
   Totaque luce nova visa nitere domus.
Dum stupeo et tremulos gelidus timor occupat artus,

55=L5ʳ
   Ante meos oculos palmifer ales erat.

---

29 vacua *A*: vidua *BO*.   30 fleam *A*: feram *BO*.   32 erit *AB*: erat *O*; vulgum *A*: populum *BO*; loci *AB*: foras *O*.   33 turbae *A*: plebi *BO*.   37 Hei *A*: Heu *BO*.   39 cuperem *A*: cupiam *BO*. 41 iactaret *A*: iactarit *BO*.   42 aeripedes *A*: unguipedes *BO*.   48 Indicium *A*: Iam dudum *BO*. 52 bona et *BO*: non *A*.   56 iuvant *A*: placent *BO*.   *Post 64 add. BO*: Candida vestis erat, tenui pellucida filo; / Fallebant oculos attamen illa meos.

Certainly all Galilee will speak ill of me, and one Nazareth will not suffice to bruit my guilt. Home alone, I'll weep for our distressed marriage [30] and the shame of my infertility. Nor will I, burdened with an unending stream of tears, be able to go out in public wherever I please. You may depend on it: all the sharp tongues would start wagging against me the minute I stepped out. Malicious people would often single me out with a look, often point a finger at me. And some godforsaken hater would ask me disconsolate woman, "Where is that husband of yours, so he can bring his offering to the Temple?"

Dear me, what am I to do, worn out as I am with such great cares? Words like that would wound me to my heart. Then, if there were a way, I'd want to be whisked to remotest India [40] or where Mount Atlas stands leaning upon his vast bulk, or wish that some force could hurl me to the lands beneath the Lycaonian Bear, where the fierce Sarmatian grazes his bronze-shod steeds. A guilt-stricken conscience can sooner bear all hardships than the taunts of the cruel crowd.

But why should people think it is all your fault when in fact you are blameless? It is I who am to blame for this avenging punishment. I for one have long suspected that my inability to conceive is an indication of my guilt.

And as I was thus oppressed with various cares and worries [50] and lamented that my absent husband was displeased with me, fresh hope, fresh consolation came to me from heaven — O good hope that I must tell you straight from the heart! And what do you suppose happened to change my mood so quickly, from utter despair to joy? I won't keep you in suspense with a longwinded story. When there is good news to tell, it is a virtue to be brief.

The setting Titan[3] was hurrying to plunge the day beneath the night, his rays already tingeing the ocean with red. Though I was bewailing the sad sterility that has plagued our marriage bed, [60] I was nevertheless not lost in wholly futile prayers. For lo and behold, through the moonless window there streamed a brilliant radiance and the whole house seemed to sparkle in the miraculous light. As I watched transfixed and icy fear took hold of my shuddering limbs, a palm-bearing angel appeared before my eyes. From

[3]The sun god, offspring of the Titan Hyperion.

65 Quales saepe bonos primis heroas ab annis
    Vidisse et veteres credita fama nurus.
Nec qua meis fallax oculis illusit imago.
    Praebuerant certam verba sequta fidem:
"Quae nunc legitimi gemis ocia vana pudoris
70   Summaque pro danda numina prole moves,
Accipe, ne dubites neu sis ignara futuri,
    Ante Deum est precibus gratia parta tuis.
Vidit et ex alto visam exaudivit Olympo
    Immensi pietas officiosa Dei.
75 Visa diu sterilem mature ingressa senectam,
    Mox nova concepto pondere mater eris.
Atque ut mirifice clausa nascetur ab alvo,
    Sic quoque quam paries filia mater erit.
Nomen erit Mariae, primo (ut vovistis) ab aevo
80   Et sacra et ex utero Flamine plena Deo
Templa colet sacras stabitque iuvencula ad aras
    Nec vaga multiloquae fabula plebis erit.
Nec dubita tot te sterilem sine prole diebus
    Posse novis iterum foetibus esse gravem.
85 Sara novem decies sterilis permansit in annos,
    Qua tamen Isaac aeditus extat anu.
Israeliticis de fratribus orbus Ioseph
    Est infoecunda de genitrice satus.
Exiit obstricta Sanson robustus ab alvo;
90   Illud idem sacro de Samuele liquet.
Ergo diu remorata aegri solatia lecti
    Reddita, quo signo certificeris habe.
Est via, surgenti qua porta refulget Eoo;
    Sola inter Solimas 'Aurea' nomen habet.
95 Illac exieris, redeuntem amplexa maritum
    Excipies, quo post tempore mater eris.
I modo, virginei florem latura pudoris,
    Et plecti ex merito teque virumque puta."
Dixit et in tenues secus haud evanuit auras,
100   Quam cita consumpta fulgura nube solent.

L5ᵛ

65–67 Quales — imago. *A*: Tales saepe ferunt genios vidisse Deum, quas / Aetatum custos littera cantat anus. / Neve putes oculos lusos ab imagine falsa, ***BO***.   69 gemis *A*: genus ***BO***.   71 neu ***BO***: ne *A*.   73 alto *A*: ipso ***BO***.   74 Immensi *A*: Aeterni ***BO***.   78 quoque . . . mater *A*: te . . . maior ***BO***.   79 primo — aevo *A*: lucem quia gentibus edet, ***BO***.   80 utero *AO*: uero *B*. 82 Nec — erit *A*: Donec eam nasci qui iubet ipse volet ***BO***.   83 sterilem *A*: sterilem et ***BO***. 84 iterum — esse *A*: fieri foetibus, Anna, ***BO***.   86 extat *A*: exit ***BO***.   87 Israeliticis *A*: Israeligenis ***BO***.   89 obstricta *A*: occlusa ***BO***.   90 Illud — liquet *A*: Hoc nascente parens in Samuele fuit ***BO***.   92 certificeris *A*: confitearis ***BO***.   93 surgenti . . . refulget Eoo *A*: surgentem . . . salutat Eoum ***BO***.   97 modo *A*: nunc ***BO***.

the beginning of time, according to trustworthy tradition, virtuous heroes and old women have often seen angels like this.

This was no hallucination playing tricks on my eyes. That was proven by the words that followed: "You who lament the stigma of a childless marriage [70] and urge the supreme Deity to give you offspring, listen to my words so that you will neither doubt nor be ignorant of the future. Your prayers have found favor before God. From on high on Olympus the gracious love of the infinite God has seen and heard you. Though you have evidently long since entered barren old age, you will soon conceive and become a mother for the first time. And just as she will be born miraculously from a closed womb, so the daughter you bear will herself become mother. Her name will be called Mary. Consecrated to God from earliest childhood (as both of you vowed) [80] and filled with his Spirit from birth, she will dwell in the Temple and as a young girl stand at the holy altars[4] and never become the talk of the gossiping crowd. Do not doubt that a barren woman like you, childless for so long, can become pregnant again with new offspring. Sara remained sterile for ninety years, and yet bore Isaac in her old age. Forsaken by his Israelite brothers, Joseph was the son of an infertile mother. The stalwart Samson emerged from a closed womb; [90] that was obviously true also of the holy Samuel. Therefore, since you are to receive the long-delayed solace of your troubled marriage, here is a sign that will confirm my words. There is a road, the gate of which reflects the light of the rising morning star. Among the gates of Jerusalem it alone bears the name 'Golden.'[5] If you go out there and take your husband into your arms when he returns, you will become a mother thereafter. You, who will give birth to the flower of virginal modesty, go ahead and think that you and your husband still deserve to be blamed!"

With these words he vanished into thin air, [100] as quick as lightnings disappear from the clouds that they have consumed.

---

[4]Cf. *Her. Chr.* 1.135–42 and 2.107–08.
[5]The Golden Gate stood to the east of the Temple.

Ipsa ego qua potui fugientem voce sequebar,
Laeticiam lachryma testificante novam.
"Quisquis es, o superum comes et facunde minister,
Fac rata sint per te nuncia dicta mihi."
105 Nunc te, sive pari solatus numine (namque
Credere te nobis plus meruisse libet),
Sive manet tristi gravidus sub pectore torpor,
Ut tandem redeas in tua vota precor.
Ibis in amplexus pariturae coniugis olim —
110 Gaudia quanta tibi, gaudia quanta mihi!
O summi generosa Dei claementia, quam tu
Tempora gratifico lumine nostra vides!
Illa diu nostrae requies sperata senectae,
Viscera iucundum nostra gravabit onus.
115 Ecce maritalis quam digna repensio damni!
I nunc et sterilis taedia finge thori!
Quo, rogo, solennes pudefacto nuper ad aras,
Pulchrius amissus redditus esset honor?
Quanto igitur peius pressa est tua tempore ab illo,
120 Tanto nunc iterum gloria maior erit.
Aspiciet nostri quondam detrector honoris,
Et misero forsan quo crucietur erit.
Aspicient nobis qui condoluere, nec illis
Leticiae deerit copia grata novae.
125 Quam cito vicinas ea fama exibit in urbes
Quas Iudaea potens et Galilaea tenent!
Tunc tibi nec princeps volet exprobrare sacerdos,
Invida nec sacras claudere turba fores.
Dulcia desueto succrescent pondera ventri
130 Donec agat plenam Cynthia nona rotam.
Tum soror accedet cognominis illa duabus;
Unius ipse parens de tribus unus eris.
Tres enixa ferar Marias tribus ipsa maritis,
Extrema foelix prole futura parens.
135 Namque, quod haud credo, nisi fallat palmifer ales,
Magna erit haec certe filia, quicquid erit.

56=L6ʳ

L6ᵛ

---

103 Quisquis es *AO*: Nunc quisquis *B*.   **105** te *A*: tu *BO*.   **106** Credere . . . libet *A*: Credi . . . decet *BO*.   **107** torpor *A*: moeror *BO*.   **111–12** O summi — vides *A*: Iam dolor et curae valeant animique labores. / Membra voluptificum nostra gravabit onus *BO*.   **113** senectae *BO*: sanctae *A*.   **114** Viscera — onus *A*: Hoc venit uberior quo mage tarda venit *BO*.   **115** digna *A*: plena *BO*.   **120** iterum *A*: populis *BO*.   **121** detrector *A*: obtrectator *BO*.   **129** desueto *A*: inexperto *BO*.   **131–34** Tum — parens. *A*: *om. BO*.   **135** fallat *A*: fallit *BO*.

As he fled, I called after him as much as I could, while a tear gave proof of my newfound joy. "Whoever you are, O companion and eloquent messenger of heaven, see to it that the tidings you brought me are fulfilled."

Now then, whether you too have been consoled by an angel (for I like to think you deserve it more than I) or whether the torpor still weighs on your saddened breast, I beg you, return at last to make your prayers come true. You will go into the arms of a wife who'll bear you a child someday — [110] what a great joy for you, what a great joy for me! O generous mercy of the highest God, how kindly have you looked upon our times!

That long-hoped-for solace of our old age, that delightful burden will grow heavy in my womb. Look, what a fitting recompense for all your marital frustration! Go now and pretend that you're bored with your sterile wife! How, I ask, could your lost honor have been more beautifully restored to you, after you were shamed at the festal altars recently? The more you were humiliated since that time, therefore, [120] the higher you can now hold your head again. The miscreant who used to disparage our honor will see this, and maybe it will cut him to the quick. Those who commiserated with us will see this, and they will have plenty of good news to cheer about. How quickly this rumor will spread to the nearby cities of mighty Judea and Galilee! Then the high priest will not want to upbraid you, nor will the spiteful crowd try to close the Temple doors in your face.

In my womb, which is not accustomed to the feeling, the sweet burden will grow bigger [130] until the moon has filled her orb for the ninth time. Later on two sisters will join the first, each with the same name as she. Of these three, you yourself will father one. I shall be delivered of three Marys by three husbands, a happy mother-to-be in my old age![6] Indeed — which I do not believe for a moment — unless the palm-bearing angel deceived me, this daughter of ours will definitely be great, whatever may be. For why did he say

---

[6]For the legend of Anna's three marriages see *Her. Chr.* 3.71–72, with n. 5 (p. 185 above).

Nam quid mirifice? Quo semine? Quove marito?
    Quo merito? Quali pignore mater erit?
Quomodo plena Deo? Sacras qur stabit ad aras?
140   Qur populum fugiet syncharitesque nurus?
Certe ea virtutis certissima signa futurae
    Ille sacer vero nuncius ore docet.
Ergo nec immerito nostri penetralia ventris,
    Clausa diu, magnum parturiere decus!
145   Charius est quodcunque bonum spes longa morata est,
    Semper et in magnis rebus ubique mora est.
Et velut ex facili brevis addit gratia parto,
    Sic peregre quicquid venit habere iuvat.
Hinc decuit nostri remorari gaudia partus,
150   Maior ut ex tardo consequeretur honor.
Non fuit ergo aliqua culpa hoc venisse querendum.
    Consilium summi Principis illud erat,
Qui caelos terramque caho produxit inerti,
    Qui genus arbitrio temperat omne suo,
155   Quem nostri prima coluere ab origine patres,
    Cum puero genitor, cum genitore nepos,
Qui Rubro Pharium submersit in aequore regem
    Atque haec Israel duxit in arva genus,
Quique Philisteum David victore gygantem
160   Foecit ab imbelli procubuisse manu,
Solus in humanis qui mirabilia rebus
    Et facit et solus omnia solus habet.
Illi pro tanto referamus munere grates,
    Donec in hoc vivi corpore uterque sumus,
165   Ut, cum fugerimus praesentis taedia vitae
    Frigidaque impositus texerit ossa lapis,
Spiritus aethereis non exulet actus ab oris,
    Sed patrii foelix incolat arva soli.

57=M1ʳ

138–40 Quo — nurus? *A*: Quid, cuius lucis gentibus aedat opus? / Quid iam plena Deo? Sacras quid stabit ad aras, / Donec, eam nasci qui iubet, ipse volet? **BO**.   **141** Certe ea *A*: Haec sunt **BO**. **142** Ille sacer *A*: Quae bonus hic **BO**.   **148** peregre *A*: aegre **BO**.   **149** remorari *A* (*in erratis*) **BO**: remorati *A* (*in textu*).   **150** honor *A*: honos **BO**.   **152** Consilium — erat *A*: Consilii res haec Omnipotentis erat **BO**.   **153** caelos terramque *A*: coelum terrasque **BO**.   **154** Qui — suo *A*: Imperium cuius cuncta creata manent [= *Her. Chr. 4.126*] **BO**.   **157** submersit *A*: confudit **BO**.   **159–62** Quique — habet. *A*: *om.* **BO**.

"miraculously"? By whose seed? Or by what kind of husband? Through whose merit? Of what sort of child will she be the mother? How will she be filled with God? Why will she stand at the holy altars? [140] Why will she shun the people and the young women her own age? The predictions that the holy messenger offered me with truthful lips are the surest signs of her future excellence, that is for sure.

It was not without cause, therefore, that the long-closed recesses of my womb wanted to bring forth a great marvel! The longer a hope for something good is put off, the dearer it becomes. That is always the case when there is a delay in matters of consequence. And just as a goal easily attained holds only fleeting charm, so whatever was long in coming gives lasting delight. Hence it was fitting that the joy of my giving birth was postponed, [150] so that the delay might lead to greater honor.

We had no reason to lament, then, that these things came about through some fault of our own. This was the plan of the Most High, who made the heavens and the earth from inert Chaos, who rules all creatures at his pleasure, whom our ancestors worshiped from the very beginning, the father with his son, the grandson with his grandfather — the God who drowned the King of Egypt in the Red Sea and led the people of Israel to this land, who caused the Philistine giant [160] to fall by the unwarlike hand of victorious David, and who alone in the affairs of humankind produces all miracles alone and alone holds all things in his hands. To him we should give thanks for so great a blessing as long as we both remain alive in this body, so that, when we escape the weariness of our present life and a tombstone covers our cold bones, our soul may not be driven into exile from the ethereal shores, but joyfully dwell in the homeland of heaven.

## 14	MARIA AEGYPTIA ZOZIMAE

Accola fluctivagi rapidas ad Iordanis undas,
　　Cognita non ulli ter tria lustra vagor.
Proxima post nonam successit Olympias et iam
　　Alter in obliquo tramite Phoebus erat,

M1ᵛ　　5　Cum tot ab humanis positae congressibus annis
　　Missus es optatae ferre salutis opem.
Excidit? An memor es qua sis mihi parte monendus?
　　Aut etiam quae sim forsitan ipsa rogas?
Hoc te, sancte pater, non convenit esse putari.
　10　　Ex vultu probitas emicat ipsa tuo.
Non mea signatam quod habebat epistola frontem
　　Nec mihi qua premerem vincula gemma fuit,
Forte quis addubitet qui me non noverit unquam,
　　Sed tamen haud ratio convenit ista tibi.
　15　Nam mihi ut incoepta est titubanti littera dextra
　　Pro signo versus unus et alter erat.
Accola fluctivagi rapidas ad Iordanis undas,
　　Non tibi, si nescis, forte reperta fui.
Summa Dei pietas mihi te transmisit, ut esses
　20　　Communem populo testis inisse viam.
Et simul humanis abiturae rebus, eundum
　　Qua sit, opus verum praemonuisse fuit,
Neu tantae ieiuna viae commissa fatiger,
　　Ante hic caelestem participare cibum
　25　Quem nisi sacra nequit manus exhibuisse petenti
　　Et nisi purgata non decet esse gula.

58=M2ʳ　　Hunc ex te, monitore Deo, cum forte rogarem,
　　Polliciti (recolo) summa erat ista tui:
"Quaecunque es, tacitae cultrix insignis eremi,
　30　　Pars ego sim precibus quantulacunque tuis.
Non mihi sorte aliqua casuve reperta, sed ipso
　　Quem colis oblata es dispositore Deo,

Her. Chr. **14.**　**8** Aut *BO*: An *A*.　　**10** ipsa tuo *BO*: ipso tua *A*.　　**16** erat *A*: erant *BO*.
19 Summa — pietas *A*: Ipse Pater superum *BO*.　　**24–26** caelestem — gula *A*: coelesti me vegetare
cibo *BO*.　　**32** oblata — dispositore *A*: ut fieres nota volente *BO*.

[1]Mary of Alexandria in Egypt writes to Zosimas (Zosimus), a monk who had come across her at
Lent a year ago, living alone by the Jordan River. She reminds him of his promise to return the following Lent to give her communion and then tells the story of her life: her youth in Alexandria, where she
became a prostitute at age twelve; her decision, after seventeen years of prostitution, to join a band
of pilgrims traveling to Jerusalem for the Feast of the Holy Cross; her miraculous conversion there; her
life of penitence by the Jordan River for the past forty-seven years. Now she appeals to Zosimas to make

14   MARY OF EGYPT TO ZOSIMAS[1]

A dweller by the swift waters of the wave-wandering Jordan, I have been roaming here unbeknownst to anyone for over forty-five years.

The ninth Olympiad had passed, the next was in progress, and for the second time the sun was on his tilted path[2] — this is how many years I have been secluded from human society! — when you were sent to bring me the means of the salvation I had longed for. Did you forget? Or do you even remember what I am having to remind you of? Or worse, are you perhaps wondering who I might be? I can hardly believe that of you, holy father. [10] Your face fairly shines with probity.

That my letter bears no seal and I have no signet ring to press into the wax might raise the eyebrows of someone who never got to know me. But that kind of reasoning does not apply to you. For when I started this letter with faltering hand, the first two lines served as my signet.

In case you have forgotten, I am the one you found dwelling by the swift waters of the wave-wandering Jordan, and not by chance either. It was God's supreme love that sent you to me, so you might [20] bear witness to his people that I have entered on the way of all flesh. Since I am about to depart this life, I truly required someone to forewarn me about the road I must take. And lest I grow faint with hunger on so great a journey, I first needed to partake of the heavenly food that only a consecrated hand can offer the suppliant and only a throat purged of sin ought to eat.[3]

When, prompted by God, I happened to ask that favor of you, this (I recall) was the gist of your promise: "Whoever you are, remarkable inhabitant of the silent wilderness, [30] let me play a part, however small, in your prayers. It was not by mere chance or luck that I found you. Rather it was the will of God himself,

---

haste, for she desperately needs the viaticum — Holy Communion given to the dying to help them travel the road of death. The reader knows from the *vita* that Zosimas does not arrive until shortly after Mary's death. Next to her body the monk discovers her last will and testament, written in the sand, and learns that Mary died on the night following Good Friday, after receiving the mystic Banquet.

Like nos. 3, 8, and 23, this letter is rhetorically structured like a forensic oration: introduction (ll. 1–16); narrative (17–96); recapitulation of the narrative (97–100); argumentation (101–36); conclusion (137–66).

In the 1532/39 version this letter is *Her.* 3.7.

[2]The ninth Olympiad (a five-year period here, as often in poetry) is followed by two more years. The total number of years therefore is forty-seven. The sun's path is "tilted" because its annual course through the zodiac is at an angle to the earth's horizon.

[3]She longs for the viaticum, but only after confession and absolution.

Ut petis, integrum cum Phoebus obiverit orbem,
    Accipies iusto quem petis ore cibum."
35 Terribilis duodena rotae semel astra remensus,
    Sol stupet egressum iam rediturus iter,
Nostra nec interea tetigisti littora, necdum
    Addita pollicita est in tua verba fides.
Longa via est, et tu cumulato tardior aevo,
40   Nullaque forsan adhuc est via coepta tibi.
Hei mihi, quando feram languentis vota senectae —
    Spem veniae, vitae gaudia, mortis opem?
Ut sol occiduas fessus declinat in undas
    Nec iam cum superis amplius esse potest,
45 Sic mea praeteritos aetas dum respicit annos
    Vix se posse putat longius aegra trahi.
Iam mihi maturam faciunt ter quinque senectam
    Lustra; meas pulsat Mors remorata fores.
M2ᵛ Sat vitae fatisque datum! Quae deinde sequetur
50   Est alio melior vita futura loco.
Prima sed heu nimium iuveniliter acta iuventa est;
    Pars vitae brevior sola dicata Deo est.
Ah, pudet et veterem dolor est meminisse ruinam,
    Nam sua quis dici turpiter acta volet?
55 Sed tamen est ratio quae nos ea dicere cogat:
    Tu pondus merito praecipientis habes.
Prima suis lusit numeris improvida certe
    Quae tria vix aetas claudere lustra solet.
Hoc ego vulgares sum tempore tradita in usus,
60   Turpibus, heu, primum quaestibus ausa frui.
Nec me Cypriacis fuit unquam peior in armis —
    Tam bona pontigena sub duce miles eram!
Moenia Pellaeo iuveni fundata colebam,
    Quis nihil Aegyptus clarius alma tenet.
65 Iam nimia primam polluta libidine vitam,
    Perdita iam mundo vivere certa fui.
Fit peregrinantum Solimam concursus ad urbem.
    Causa novae populis crux pietatis erat.
Per mare sulcantes adii vada cerula nautas;
70   Non fuerant votis invida turba meis.

---

33 Ut — integrum *A*: Lucifer igniferum ***BO***.   34 iusto *A*: avido ***BO***.   40 forsan adhuc *A*: adhuc forsan ***BO***.   49 fatisque *A*: satisque ***BO***.   53 veterem . . . ruinam *A*: veteris . . . ruinae ***BO***. 55 Sed tamen *A*: Attamen ***BO***.   **Post 56** *add.* ***BO***: Et cur ante Deum pudeat malefacta fateri, / Ad veniam fassis qui pius esse solet?   59 tempore tradita *A*: tradita tempore ***BO***.   60 primum *A*: nimium ***BO***.   61 me *A*: *om.* ***BO***.   64 tenet *A*: videt ***BO***.   65 Iam *A*: Tam ***BO***.

whom you worship, that put you in my path. As you request,
when Phoebus has completed his annual round,[4] you will receive
the food you justly ask for."

Having traveled through the twelve signs of the terrifying circle
once already, the sun pauses to catch his breath before returning on
the course he has just completed. You, meanwhile, have not set foot
on the bank where I live and have yet to carry out your promise.
The journey is long, and you are getting slower as the years
advance. [40] For all I know, you have not even started out yet. Ah
me, when shall I receive the wishes of my frail old age — the hope
of forgiveness, the joy of life, the blessing of death? Just as the weary
sun sinks into the western waves and can no longer remain in the
upper world, so my ailing old age, looking back upon the bygone
years, believes it cannot drag itself much further. At seventy-five,[5]
I have reached a ripe old age. Long-delayed Death knocks at my
door. I have given enough to life and fate! The life that is to follow
hereafter [50] in another place will be better than this.

But alas, the first bloom of youth was spent in far too youthful a manner. Only the shorter part of my life has been dedicated
to God. Ah, I am ashamed and distressed to remember my old
downfall, for who wants to hear about one's own despicable
behavior? All the same, however, I have a compelling reason to
tell my story: I regard you by rights as my teacher.

Certainly the first portion of my life, the period that tends to
last fifteen years at most, went by in aimless dissipation. At that
time I became a public prostitute. [60] Initially, alas, I even dared
to take pleasure in that infamous occupation. Never was a woman
more wicked than I in Venus' army — so well did I soldier under
the command of that sea-born general!

I lived in the city founded by Alexander, the most famous
town in bountiful Egypt. Already I had defiled the first half of my
life with boundless lust; already I was resolved to live as a fallen
woman. One day a band of pilgrims flocked together to make for
the city of Jerusalem. What moved them to this extraordinary
outpouring of piety was the cross.[6] I turned to the sailors who
furrow the azure waves over the sea. [70] That crowd had never

[4]That is, next year at the vernal equinox. In the medieval calendar, the new year started at the
vernal equinox in March. Cf. Edmund Spenser, *The Shepheardes Calender* (1579), General Argument:
"For it is wel known . . . that the yeare beginneth in March. for then the sonne reneweth his finished
course, and the seasonable spring refresheth the earth." According to the *vita*, Zosimas returned with
the viaticum shortly after Good Friday.

[5]Eobanus arrives at this round number by the following calculation. Mary was twelve when she
came to Alexandria. After spending seventeen years there, she lived forty-seven more years in the
desert.

[6]The pilgrims wanted to celebrate the Feast of the Holy Cross in Jerusalem.

59=M3ʳ   Mercedem rigidus poscebat navita iustam;
                    Pro naulo miserum corpus habere dedi.
             Ventum erat ad sanctum, Solomonea templa, Sionem.
                    Illo constiterat crux veneranda loco.
75   Hic ego ter conata aedes intrare sacratas,
                    Ter iacui sacras ante repulsa fores.
             Dum queror (et merito!) ista pati sine teste, recordor,
                    Visa mihi a dextra est Matris imago Dei.
             Accessi supplexque Deam sic orsa precabar:
80   "O Mater, thalamo nullius usa viri,
             Aspice me qua corda soles pietate tuorum.
                    Vivam quod superest temporis omne tibi."
             Annuere oranti visa est mitissima Virgo;
                    Amplius haud ulla est passa repulsa mihi.
85   Hic mihi nescio quae stupidas vox fertur ad aures:
                    "Iordanis ad ripam vita petenda tibi est."
             Obstupeo vocemque sequor, iam certa prioris
                    Delitias vitae linquere, inire novam.
             Tempore ab hoc deserta colo, tot sola per annos.
90   Hic quam perdideram vita reperta mihi est,
             Hic mihi parta quies nullo mutabilis aevo.
                    Caelestem referunt hospita lustra domum!
M3ᵛ   Mobilis hic nostros derelinquat spiritus artus
                    Foedaque sub viridi cespite membra cubent.
95   Hic ego me vidisse aliquem tot euntibus annis
                    Non memini praeter teque trucesque feras.
             Tu mihi praesentis positurae munera vitae
                    Missus es ignotae lucifer esse viae.
             Ipsa viam ingredior, morti vicina propinquae.
100   Anne, precor, solam me, pater, ire iubes?
             Heu, timidam noctis terrent simulachra futurae
                    Suetaque ad extremos larva venire dies.
             Seu vigilant oculi caeca seu nocte premuntur,
                    Sollicitor variis hoste minante modis.
105   Tristia nunc stupidam turbant insomnia mentem,
                    Qualia lymphati sepe videre solent.
             Saepe mihi videor deserta per avia longam
                    Ignotamque egre carpere sola viam,
             Te, pater, interdum deserta quaerere terra,
110   Hostiles omni parte timere minas.
             Utque agit in somnis ferus ille et perfidus hostis,
                    Sic neque concessae tempore lucis abest.

---

73 Sionem *A*: Siona **BO**.   **84** passa *A*: facta **BO**.   **93–94** Mobilis — Foedaque *A*: Deserat hic fugiens morientes spiritus artus, / Hic mea **BO**.   **112** concessae *A*: concussae **BO**.

been ill-disposed to my wishes! The relentless captain demanded the regular fare. In lieu of cash I let him have my miserable body. We reached the Temple of Solomon in holy Zion. It was in that place that the cross had been set up for veneration. There I tried three times to enter the hallowed church; three times I lay repulsed before the sacred doors. As I lamented all alone that I had suffered this rebuff (and deservedly so!), I recall seeing to my right an icon of the Mother of God. I went up to it and humbly started to pray to the Goddess as follows: [80] "O Mother, you who never had relations with a man, look on me with the same loving-kindness with which you look on the hearts of your own people. What remains of life I shall live wholly for you."

The most merciful Virgin evidently granted my prayer, for I suffered no further rebuff. Then an unknown voice came to my stunned ears: "Go to the banks of the Jordan. There you will find life."

Dumbstruck, I obeyed the voice, for I was now determined to give up the wanton pleasures of my previous life and start afresh. Since that time I have been living in the wilderness, alone for so many years. [90] Here I have found the life that I had lost; here I have won the tranquillity that will remain untroubled for all eternity. These hospitable wilds offer me a foretaste of the heavenly abode. Here may the fleeing soul escape from my body and my vile limbs rest beneath the verdant sod!

In all the years that I have spent here, I cannot recall ever see-ing anyone besides you and the wild beasts. For as I was preparing to lay down the blessing of this present life, you were sent to be my lamp along that unknown path. Now I am entering that path and coming face-to-face with death. [100] I beseech you, father, you are not asking me to travel all alone, are you?

Alas, timid woman that I am, I am terrified of the ghosts of the coming night, the malevolent spirits that haunt the dying in their final days. Whether my eyes are wide awake or overwhelmed by blind night, I am being harassed by the Enemy, who threatens me in many different ways. Most recently, dreadful nightmares have been troubling my dazed mind, the kind of hallucinations that demented people tend to see. Often I dream that I am struggling through the remote wilderness on a long and unknown road, with no one to guide me. At times, father, I see myself searching for you in that desolate landscape [110] and fearing the Enemy's ubiquitous threats. And as that fierce and treacherous Fiend pursues me in my dreams, so he never leaves me alone by day. This is how

Haec ego te patior nostro tardante periclo.
   Spes tamen est animi fomes et aura mei.

60=M4^r 115   Spiritus infirmis vix artubus aeger adheret,
   Ut sitiens dura planta laborat humo.

Utque vagus liquidas cervus desyderat undas,
   Quando gravem poto pertulit angue sitim,

Omnibus impatiensque iugis et vallibus errat,
120   Arida ut invento pectora fonte riget,

Sic animus sitit hic vivum, sua gaudia, fontem,
   Sic panem mea mens esurit aegra Deum.

Quis dabit hoc miserae, ut corpus positura caducum
   Ex manibus capiam fercula sancta tuis?

125   Quando erit ut veniam et vultus ferar ante beatos,
   In quibus est superis gloria plena choris?

Credo equidem, nec vana fides, quia vivit et ipsum
   Vita redemptorem est nostra sequta Deum.

Quem propriis visura oculis in carne resurgam
130   Cum sub eo stabit iudice summa dies.

Hac spe laeta feram patiendae vulnera mortis,
   Haec est in tacito spes mihi clausa sinu.

Non tamen ante isto mortalis carcere vitae
   In se dissolvi spiritus iste potest,

135   Quam mihi promissae portanti dona salutis
   Ad sacros liceat procubuisse pedes.

M4^v Fiat ut hoc, praestare tuum est, idque esse memento.
   (Polliciti seriem diximus ante tui.)

Hoc est quod multis facit anxia pectora curis,
140   Hoc est quod requiem non sinit esse mihi.

Hoc ego tot lachrymis, hoc tot suspiro querelis,
   Haec voti series summaque summa mei.

Tardior ipse tamen nunquid spe ludis inani?
   Aut fortuna tuae non fuit aequa viae?

145   Ah, quoties rapidi remeavi ad Iordanis undam!
   Ah, quoties refero tristior inde pedem!

Spes tamen accessit nostris non frivola votis,
   Solatae caelo commiserante sumus.

Namque ita scribenti, tanquam spes omnis abisset,
150   Vox bona, "Ne dubita, iam properabit," ait.

---

116 Ut *A*: Et *BO*.   120 pectora *BO*: pectore *A*.   121 animus — hic *A*: sitit hic animus *BO*.
131 Hac spe *A*: Ergo *BO*.   133 Non *A*: Vix *BO*.   134 iste *A*: ipse *BO*.   142 mei *BO*: meae *A*.
143 ipse *BO*: ipsa *A*.   146 tristior *A*: tardior *BO*.   147 accessit . . . frivola *A*: adiecta est . . .
invida *BO*.

I suffer in my extremity while you take your time. Hope, however, is my soul's kindling and wind.

My ailing spirit just barely clings to the tottering body, much
as a thirsty seedling struggles in rocky soil. And as a wandering
hart longs for flowing streams, after he has devoured the snake,
and in his grievous thirst desperately roams all the mountains and
valleys [120] to find a source and drench his parching breast, so
my soul thirsts for the living Source, its true delight, so my ailing
soul hungers for the Bread, for God.[7]

Now that I am on the verge of laying down this fleeting
body, who will give me, poor woman, the opportunity to receive
holy communion from your hands? When shall I come and be
lifted up before the eyes of the blessed, before the heavenly hosts
in whom is the fullness of glory? I do believe, and it is no vain
belief, that the God I followed in my life, that my Redeemer
lives.[8] I shall behold him with my own eyes when I rise again in
the flesh, [130] when the Last Day stands beneath his judgment
seat. In this hope I shall gladly bear the wounds of death, as I
must. This is the hope I keep hidden within my silent breast.

Nevertheless, my spirit cannot set itself free from this prison
of mortal life until you bring me the promised gifts of salvation
and I can prostrate myself at your holy feet. Be as good as your
word, for that is your duty — do not forget! (I reminded you of
your promises earlier on.) This is what distresses my heart with
many worries; [140] this is what never allows me to have peace.
This is what I sigh for with so many tears, with so many laments;
this is the sum and substance of my prayer.

But you keep me waiting too long! You are not deluding me
with empty hope, are you? Or has fortune been unkind to your
journey? Ah, how often I go back to the water of the swift
Jordan! Ah, how often I return with a heavier heart!

In spite of this, I feel genuinely encouraged that my prayers
will be answered. Heaven has taken pity on me and given me
comfort. For when I was writing like this, as though bereft of all
hope, [150] a kindly voice told me: "Do not doubt it. He will
soon be hurrying near."

[7]Mary paraphrases the opening verses of Psalm 42 (41 in the Vulgate). She then links these verses
with the ancient notion that stags feed on snakes to renew their youth and thereupon desperately
search for a source of fresh water to quench their burning thirst. The linkage is common in Christian
literature. See Herbert Kolb, "Der Hirsch, der Schlangen frißt," in *Mediaevalia litteraria: Festschrift für
Helmut de Boor zum 80. Geburtstag*, ed. U. Hennig and H. Kolb (Munich, 1971), 583–610.
[8]Here and in the next sentence Mary paraphrases Job 19.25–27.

Sancte pater, propera promissaque debita firma.
　Causa est cur properes magna decensque tibi.
Non tibi nunc oneri neque tarda futura senecta est,
　Quemque feres tecum te feret ille mihi.
155　Ipse etiam rapidas sternet placidissimus undas,
　Qui sua de duplici nomina fonte tenet.
Utque olim placidum Christus superastitit aequor,
　Sic ibis sicco per vada summa pede.

61=M5ʳ　Ipsa frequentatum te prestolabor ad amnem.
160　Non via carpenda est longius ulla tibi.
Haec quoque verba loco partim nunc scribimus illo,
　Hei, male frigenti verba notata manu.
Cernis ut aerea liber est mihi raptus ab ulmo.
　Arida funebres fecit arundo notas.
165　Attamen hanc miserae satis est cecinisse querelam.
　Quod superest, unum te, pater, esse decet.

---

156 Qui — tenet *A*: Inclyta qui gemini nomina fontis habet *BO*.   160 Non . . . longius . . . tibi *A*:
Nec . . . longior . . . mihi *BO*.   162 notata *A*: novata *BO*.   163 liber est . . . ulmo *A*: cortex . . .
ulmo est *BO*.   165 Attamen *A*: Nunc tamen *BO*.

Holy father, make haste and fulfill your promise, as you should. You have a great and fitting reason to hurry. Now your old age will neither burden you nor slow you down; and he, whom you bring with you,[9] will also bring you to me. Even the river that takes his name after his twin source[10] will cause the raging floods to subside and turn perfectly placid for you. And just as Christ long ago treaded calmly on the sea, so you too will walk dry-shod upon the waves.

As for me, I shall be here waiting for you, beside the river that I come to so often. [160] You should not have to travel any further than necessary. It is in this very spot that I now write a good many of these words — words, alas, badly scribbled by my shaky hand. You see that I have stripped the bark from a towering elm. A dry reed scratched these funereal lines.

But it is enough for me poor woman to have sung this lament. The rest, father, is up to you alone.

---

[9]Christ, whose body Zosimas is bringing with him in the Eucharist.

[10]According to Hier. *In Matt.* 3 (*CCSL* 77:139, ll. 9–11) and, for example, Isid. *Orig.* 13.21.18, the Jordan is formed by the confluence of the two streams Jor and Dan.

15   PELAGIA NONIO

Tecta virum nigro mulier simulante cucullo,
    Ausa vir esse ipso nomine pene fui.
Et nisi tu nosses, etiam hoc mentita fuissem —
    Tanta sub hoc habitu cura latere mihi est!
5   Frons tamen exterior quod nomine scripta virili est,
    Cognita cum superis causa duobus erit.
Arte quidem misero qua sum bene perdita mundo
    Inveniam regni divitioris opes.
Si qualem decuit titulum professa fuissem,
10   Qur tegat exiguos penula longa pedes?
Iamque esset de quo gauderet perfidus hostis,
    Cognita si vulgo fabula facta forem.
Ergo vir et mulier scriptura decebat ut essem:
    Vir reliquis, uni foemina nota tibi.
15 Nec tibi, quae toties sum nomine dicta sororis,
    In prima fratrem fronte fuisse pudet.
Et soror et frater rogo te fratremque patremque. . . .
    Parce, erit in versu si qua litura meo.
Per scelus arma quidem multum desueta resumo.
20   Ingenio nocuit pristina vita meo.
Tunc quoque quae turpes ducebat saepe lituras
    Falleret ut multos officiosa manus,
Nunc stupet et nudam dubitat tetigisse papyrum,
    Tam pudet hoc sero posthabuisse nephas.
25 Conscia praeteriti sceleris, praesentia semper
    Mens timet et proprio tacta pudore rubet.
Et licet in melius mores abiere nefandi,
    Attamen et durum est et meminisse dolor.
Sicut enim quem nulla premit sentina malorum
30   Nulla sub erecta nubila fronte gerit,
Sic male quem tacito mens conscia fune flagellat
    Lucida vix audet tollere ad astra caput.
Tu nosti qua sorte prior mihi vita peracta est.
    Hei mihi, quam multos perdidit illa dies!
35 Formosa exterius, vultum depicta rubebam,
    Foeda sed interius tota mephytis eram.
Ancillis comitata tribus sublime ferebar,
    Dignior in putri sola iacere luto.

M5ᵛ (left margin, by line 14)

62=M6ʳ (left margin, by line 35)

Her. Chr. **15.**   **9** professa *A*: confessa *BO*.   **13** decebat ut essem *A*: docebat ut esse *BO*.   **22** multos
A: multas *BO*.   **26** tacta . . . rubet *A*: fracta . . . iacet *BO*.   **33** vita — est *A*: fluxerit aetas *BO*.

---

[1]St. Pelagia was a popular actress of Antioch, as beautiful as she was dissolute. Because of her
magnificent pearls she was often called Margaret ("pearl"). One day she was moved to attend church,

15   PELAGIA TO NONIUS[1]

Covered with a black cowl that allows me, a woman, to pass for a
man, I have ventured to be a man practically down to my name.
And if you were not in on the secret, I would have lied about this
too — that is how concerned I am to remain hidden in this
disguise! Why the outside of my letter nevertheless still bears a mas-
culine name, only heaven and we two will ever know. In truth, by
the same artifice through which I am rightly lost to this wretched
world, I shall inherit the wealth of a far richer kingdom.

Had I divulged my real name, [10] why should a long cloak
continue to cover up my tiny feet? That would also have given
the treacherous Enemy something to crow about, if people had
learned the truth and started to gossip about me. So it was
proper for me to write as both man and woman: to be known to
the rest as a man, only to you as a woman. And I, whom you
addressed so often by the name *sister*, am certainly not ashamed
to be your brother on the cover.

As both sister and brother I ask you, my brother and father. . . .
Forgive me if a tearstain mars my verse. Indeed, I am reaching back
to the long disused weapons of my sinful days. [20] My former way
of life still stabs me to the heart. Then too my solicitous hand would
often make disgraceful blots to deceive my many admirers. Now it
feels paralyzed and hesitates to touch the blank papyrus, so ashamed
is it of having renounced this depravity too late. Conscious of past
sinfulness, my mind is ever afraid of the present and blushes at the
thought of its own shame. And even though my wicked morals have
taken a turn for the better, nevertheless I find it hard and painful to
think back on those times. Just as people unburdened with the scum
of evil [30] can keep their head high and their brow unclouded, so
those whose guilty conscience flogs them with silent lash scarcely
dare raise their eyes to the glittering stars.

You know in what kind of condition I spent the earlier part
of my life. Ah me, how many days I squandered then! Outside I
looked beautiful, my face made up with rouge; but inside I was
all hideous stench. Accompanied by three maidservants, I was
extolled to the skies, though more deserving of lying by myself in

---

where the Bishop of Edessa, St. Nonius (Nonnus), happened to be preaching. She was so struck by his
sermon that she asked at once to be baptized. A week later, having given all her wealth to the poor, she
put on men's clothing and went to Jerusalem. There she lived in a small cell on the Mount of Olives,
revered by all as Brother Pelagius. A variant of this legend, however, relates that she entered a
monastery and was eventually elected abbot. Only after her death was her true sex discovered. For the
vita by Jacobus Diaconus, see *PL* 73, cols. 663–72; *Acta Sanctorum*, October IV, Dies 8. Cf. *Leg. aurea*
146 and 147.

In the 1532/39 version this letter is *Her.* 3.6.

Saepe aliquis spectans propere veneratus euntem
40   Nescius abscessit per mea facta nocens.
Saepe pudicarum numerus mihi cessit, et ibam
Matronas inter sordida scropha probas.
Extulit elatam damnosa superbia mentem.
Heu, quantum adiecit criminis illa mihi!
45   Quae fora, quae plateae, quae thermae quaeve dietae,
Quae non sunt fastu plena theatra meo?
Torta comas, fucata genas, discincta lacertos,
Cura iuventutis desipientis eram.
Immemor instantem tacite properare senectam,
50   In mediis vixi nata puella rosis.
Immemor esse malis positam pro crimine poenam,
Ipsa mihi tanquam non moritura fui.
Nec potui, si quis monuisset, ferre monentem —
Tam pectus saxo durius illud erat!
55   Ah, pudet ulterius veterum meminisse malorum.
Turpe quis ante homines facta pudenda refert?
Quam tamen haec vellem detur mihi nulla referri
M6ᵛ   Copia nec lapsam turpiter esse queri!
Namque ego non refero ut vulgo mea facta notentur,
60   Sed queror ut medicum tristis et aegra feram.
Quem precor, ut qualem primo te vulnere sensi,
Talis quae superant stigmata nigra leves.
Plura quidem superant quae quamvis oblita credas.
Est tamen haec saniem vulnera habere timor.
65   Attigeris medicante manu, pater inclyte Noni,
Nullus in hoc usquam corpore nevus erit.
Utque aliquo noster non est in corpore morbus,
Sic alia tanges vulnera nostra manu.
Antidotum veniens mihi portet epistola verum!
70   Credis? Habet longas littera scripta manus.
Namque quid absentem moveas ne forte timebis,
Cui tu praesenti fulminis instar eras?
Non etiam ut moneas opus est. Quis montibus umbras,
Quis gelidas vitreis fontibus addat aquas?
75   Moerentem solare animum quem, dive, ruentem
Ex Stygia revocas ne moreretur aqua.
Ille quidem per te sibi redditus ultima primis
Comparat et prudens haec odit, illa probat.

42 sordida scropha *A*: sus lutulenta *BO*.   43 damnosa *A*: ventosa *BO*.   47 discincta *A*: gemmata *BO*.   56 Turpe — refert? *A*: Turpe est ante viros facta pudenda loqui. *BO*.   57 referri *A*: referre *BO*.   59 non — vulgo *A*: nec refero vulgo ut *BO*.   61 Quem *A*: Quae *BO*.   64 vulnera *A*: multus *BO*.   71 moveas *BO*: moneas *A*.   72 eras *A*: eris *BO*.   76 Ex *A*: E *BO*.   78 odit *A*: fugit *BO*.

putrid mud. Often a man would pay homage to me as he watched me sweep by. [40] Unbeknown to himself, my deeds would leave him with a guilt-stained heart. Often a throng of modest women made way for me, and I would walk among the virtuous matrons like the sordid sow I was. Pernicious pride swelled up my overweening ego. Alas, how much did that add to my sin! What markets, streets, baths, or homes, what theaters were not filled with my conceit? Hair curled, cheeks painted, arms bared, I was the cynosure of foolish youth. Unmindful that looming old age was silently hurrying near, [50] I lived like a girl born amid roses. Unmindful that the wicked will be punished for their crimes, I felt as if I would never die. And if someone tried to admonish me, I could not brook his admonishments — so much harder than stone was my heart in those days!

Ah, I am ashamed to go on recounting my old sins. Who can be so shameless as to regale men with the tale of her abominations? How I wish, nonetheless, that I did not have such an abundance to tell of! If only I had no need to lament my despicable fall! For I am not telling my story so people will take note of my misdeeds; [60] I lament, rather, to secure a healer for my sorrow and sickness. I am asking you to be my physician. For just as you were the first to heal my wound, so you should now relieve the black stigmas that remain. Many of them are in fact still there, though you might have thought them completely erased. It is to be feared, however, that these wounds are still full of pus.

Once you have touched me with healing hand, renowned Father Nonius, not a single blemish will be left anywhere on my body. But just as my disease is not a physical one, so you must also treat my wounds with a different hand. The true antidote should come to me in a letter from you! [70] Do you believe it? A letter has far-reaching hands. Indeed, why are you afraid you might not touch a woman's heart in your absence, when you struck her like a thunderbolt in your presence? But you do not need to admonish me this time around. Who would add shade to the mountains? Who would pour icy water into crystal-clear springs? Comfort the grieving soul whom you, saintly man, stopped from plunging headlong into hell and saved from death eternal. Restored by you to its true self, my spirit compares the end with the beginning and wisely detests the latter, approves the

Et sua dum iusta trutinat commissa bilance,

63=N1ʳ   80   Non semel est fassus quod sapit esse tuum.

Ergo prius quem pulchra canunt mendacia vatum
 Solari exustam lampade tanget humum,
Ante mari volucres, pascentur in aere pisces,
 Ante oriens vesper, vesper Eous erit,

85   Quam mea mutatis languescant pectora votis.
 Devotam satis est me semel esse Deo.
Sicut enim assiduis decoctum solibus aurum
 Amplius exactum, quod fuit, esse nequit,
Sicut et aereo phoenix reparatus in igne

90   Non idem est iuvenis qui fuit ante senex,
Sic quem tota semel divini flamma caloris
 Hauserit, antiquum non remeabit iter.
O quam dulcis amor, quam delectabilis ardor,
 Quo tua nos pietas, maxime Christe, fovet!

95   Non ego quas toto cogit mercator ab orbe,
 Non ego quas totus continet orbis opes,
Denique non toto vellem prius orbe potiri
 Quam tua non toto pectore iussa sequi.
Gratia, dive, tibi! Tu me, pater, ista negantem

100   Duxisti ad rectae cognitionis iter.
Ah, quoties niveo subit illa notanda lapillo
N1ᵛ   Quae mihi te dederat prima videre dies!
Ut sacra celeber spectandus in aede sacerdos,
 Aeterni populo praeco Tonantis eras.

105   Iam tibi contempti mundi fallentis honores
 Materiam verbis exhibuere tuis,
Ut sit in hac vita brevis et fugitiva voluptas
 Cui paret aeternas altera vita cruces,
Utque sit in caelo cui sordeat ipsa futurus,

110   Ante triumphantes umbra beata choros.
Quamque incerta dies quae nos hoc corpore solvat,
 Quam certum cunctis debeat esse mori,
Denique quam sit homo facili mutabilis aura
 Dum memoras, verbis talibus usus eras:

115   "Bulla palustris homo, ventus, flos, pulvis, et umbra,
 Incipit et cessat, nascitur atque perit.
Umbrae somnium homo, flatus levis, umbraque fumi,
 Vix punctum unius temporis esse potest."

79 Et *A*: Qui *BO*.   86 Deo *A*: tibi *BO*.   91 Sic *A*: Si *BO*.   93–94 O quam — fovet *A*: O
dulces flammas, o grata incendia menti, / Quae tota in Christo liquitur atque fluit *BO*.   98 tua . . .
iussa *A*: te . . . , Christe, *BO*.   100 ad — cognitionis *A*: verae per pietatis *BO*.   101 illa *A*: ista
BO.   103 sacra celeber *A*: celebris sacra *BO*.   104 Aeterni *A*: Supremi *BO*.   109 ipsa *A*: ista
BO.   116 atque perit *A*: et moritur *BO*.   117–18 Umbrae — potest. *A*: *om. BO*.

former. And as it weighs its misdeeds on balanced scales, [80] it has confessed more than once that it owes this insight to you.

Sooner, therefore, will he, of whom the poets' lovely fictions sing, touch the scorched earth with the sun's lamp,[2] sooner will birds feed in the sea, fish in the air, sooner will east be west and west be east than I will change my mind or waver in the faith. I consecrated myself to God once, and that is enough. For just as gold melted down in constant heat cannot weigh more than it did earlier, and just as the phoenix, reborn on its airy pyre, [90] is not the same in youth as he was in his old age, so too a person who has once been totally consumed by the flame of God's love will never go back to his former ways. Oh, how sweet the love, how delightful the fire, Lord Christ, with which your loving-kindness warms our hearts! I would sooner give up all the wealth that the merchant gathers from around the globe, I would sooner renounce all the riches in the world, yes, even the whole wide world itself, than fail to follow your commands with heart and soul.

Thanks be to you, saint! For when I was still denying these truths, you, father, [100] guided me on the path to right understanding. Ah, how often do I think back to that day, worthy of being marked with a snow-white pearl,[3] the day that first brought you into my ken! A celebrated priest and respected bishop in the Holy Church, you rose up before the people as a herald of the eternal Thunderer. The contempt in which we should hold the goods of this deceitful world was the burden of your sermon that day. You preached that in this life all pleasure is brief and fleeting, in return for which the next life brings eternal torments, but that anyone who despises the world will go to heaven, [110] a blessed shade before the exultant choirs. And just as the day is uncertain that frees us from this body, so it is certain that everyone must die. Finally, when you mentioned how quickly we can be changed by even a light breeze, you expressed yourself in these words: "Like a swamp bubble, like wind, blossom, dust, and shadow, so man begins and ends, is born and perishes. Man is but the shadow of a dream, a breath of air, and the shadow of smoke; he can scarcely last longer than a single point of time."

[2]Phaeton tried to ride the sun's chariot. Unable to control the horses, however, he drove them too close to the earth. For the myth, see Lucr. 5.396–405; Ov. *Met.* 2.1–328.

[3]For the proverbial practice of marking propitious days with white stones, cf. *Her. Chr.* 12.281, with n. 8 (p. 295 above).

His mea movisti durissima pectora quondam.
120   Haec mihi tardanti non leve calcar erant.
Accessi et supplex populo spectante rogabam,
      Curvato nudum poplite flexa genu:
"Plene Deo linguaque potens, venerande sacerdos,

64 = N2ʳ

      Mole sua pressos docte movere animos,
125   En ego multiplicis tot molibus obruta culpae!
      Me miseram, fasso deprecor ore, iuva.
Poenitet indomitae nimis indulsisse iuventae.
      Ad Styga declivem paenitet isse viam.
O, mihi vel sero sit poenituisse saluti,
130   Ad veniam reditus si datur aede, precor."
Multa precaturam lachrymae vetuere, nec ipse
      Passus es aut frustra quaerere sive queri,
Atque ita: "Ne dubita, spera bene, siste querelas.
      Quam petis est facili res capienda manu.
135   Pondere multiplicis quantumlibet obruta culpae,
      Non est ad veniam ianua clausa tibi.
Tanta Dei pietas, tanta est clementia Christi,
      Ut miseros etiam vivere pene roget.
Quam misere et quoties cecidit peccator aberrans!
140   Ut citius surgat porrigit ille manum.
Venit enim salvare hominem, non perdere quenquam,
      Per quem Christicolae turba redempta sumus.
Magna habet haec aetas, maiora exempla vetustas.
      Tu quoque de multis pauca tenere potes.
145   Nil Maria Aegiptus, nil Thaide peius habebat.

N2ᵛ

      Peccatrix etiam Magdalis ipsa fuit.
Hiis tamen accessit repetiti gratia Christi,
      Nunc pascunt superas, turba beata, dapes.
Sperne igitur placidum mundi fallentis amorem.
150   Fide Deo. Maculas diluet ille tuas."
Sic breviter mecum populo spectante loquutus,
      Urebas quadam pectora nostra face.
O vox plena spei dulcis, vox plena salutis!
      Dulce melos nostris auribus illa fuit.
155   Vix gavisa magis praesentis voce Magistri est
      Magdalis, ex veteri surgere iussa caho.

---

119 durissima — quondam *A*: nuper durissima corda *BO*.   123 venerande sacerdos *A*: animose pia vi *BO*.   124 movere *A*: levare *BO*.   125–29 En ego — saluti *A*: Innumerabilium pressae gravitate malorum *BO*.   128 Styga *scripsi*: Stygia *A*.   131 lachrymae *BO*: lachryme *A*.   134 res — manu *A*: caussa tenenda modo *BO*.   135 quantumlibet *A*: quantumvis *BO*.   141 hominem *A*: omnes *BO*.   146 Peccatrix — fuit *A*: Improba Magdalidum de tribus una fuit *BO*.   151 spectante *A*: mirante *BO*.   153 spei dulcis, [dulcis: *A*] . . . salutis *A*: spei, dulcis . . . salutis *BO*.   156 Magdalis — caho *A*: Cui peperit veniam lachryma fassa nefas *BO*.

With these words you softened my formerly rock-hard breast. [120] It was they that spurred my sluggish soul into action. I went up to you. And as the people gaped, I threw myself down on my bare knees and humbly asked you: "Man of God and master of words, venerable priest skilled at rousing hearts crushed under the weight of guilt, behold, I am overwhelmed with so many burdens of manifold sin! Help me poor wretch, I beg you with confessing mouth. I repent that I allowed my unbridled youth all too free play. I repent that I walked the downhill path to hell. Oh, is it still possible to repent or is too late for me to be saved? [130] If there is a way to return to grace, do tell me, I beseech you."

Tears choked my voice, though there was much I still wanted to pray for. You did not suffer me to go on asking and lamenting in vain either, but answered: "Do not doubt, be of good cheer, stop your laments. What you ask for is easily within your grasp. Even though you are overwhelmed with the burden of manifold sin, the door to forgiveness is not closed to you. The loving-kindness of God is so great, the mercy of Christ so vast, that he virtually begs the unfortunates to live. How miserably and how often do straying sinners fall! [140] So that they may rise the sooner, he offers them his hand. For he, through whom we Christians are redeemed, came to save lives, not destroy them. The present age offers great examples, past ages even greater ones. Of the many instances you too may retain a few. Egypt had nobody worse than Mary, nobody worse than Thais. The Magdalene used to be a sinner too.[4] Yet each of them turned to Christ and received his grace. Now they feast among the blessed at the heavenly banquet. Therefore, spurn the alluring love of this deceitful world. [150] Trust in God. He will wash away your stains."

As you spoke with me briefly like this while the congregation looked on, you fired my heart as if with a torch. O voice full of sweet hope, voice full of salvation! Every word of yours was sweet music to my ears. The Magdalene could scarcely have rejoiced more than I when she heard the voice of the Master

---

[4]Eobanus devotes a heroic letter to each of these sinners who became great saints. See *Her. Chr.* 14 (Mary of Egypt), 11 (Thais), and 3 (Mary Magdalene). For Mary Magdalene as a sinner, see *Her. Chr.* 3.97–118, with n. 7 (p. 187 above); cf. ll. 155–56 below.

Laeticia quoque vix credo potiore fuisse
Quem solata Dei vox morientis erat.
Laetior inde abii, quamvis quoque tristis ut essem
160 Materies vitae causa prioris erat.
Tum mihi quot madido vigilatae lumine noctes,
Quam multa assiduis fletibus acta dies,
Donec, ut es miserum doctus miserescere, praesul,
Fulcita est manibus nostra ruina tuis!
165 Tu nimia obscurae mersam caligine noctis
Praebueras verum posse videre diem.
Per loca virosis erravi plena colubris;
65=N3ʳ Monstras quae rectam tendat ad astra viam.
Iactatam dubio pugnantibus aequore ventis
170 Duxisti in tutam, Typhi fidelis, humum.
Frigida somnifero quassatae tempora ramo
Mortua depulsa lumina nocte levas.
Denique iam tactae subeunti limen Averni,
"Non hac," dicebas, "itur ad astra via."
175 Protinus in tenebris apparuit error eunti,
Qui mihi delitiae nuper amorque fuit.
Tum primum agnovi quam me blandissima Syren
Pene sub infames praecipitasset aquas.
Sic quis in Ionio sulcans vada glauca profundo,
180 Ni caveat, dulci perditur exitio.
Hoc quendam cavisse ferunt duo lustra vagantem,
Dum spolia in patriam Troica portat humum.
Qui nisi sprevisset blandas audire querelas,
Subdisset miserae seque suosque neci.
185 Tu quoque vicina nisi me de morte tulisses,
Forte alerem infernos iam nova praeda canes
Umbraque Laethaeis latuissem nuda sub undis,
Heu quibus, heu quantis afficienda malis!

---

157 credo *A*: credam *BO*.   160 Materies — erat *A*: Facta prius vitae caussa fuere meae *BO*.
161 Tum *A*: Tunc *BO*.   163 praesul *A*: Noni *BO*.   166 Praebueras — diem *A*: Iussisti insolitae
lucis adire diem *BO*.   167 erravi *A*: errabam *BO*.   168 Monstras quae rectam [recta *A*] — viam
A: Tu poteras tutae restituisse viae *BO*.   173 Denique — tactae *A*: Iam quoque vicini *BO*.
179 glauca profundo *A*: caerula ponto *BO*.   183 querelas *BO*: quaerelas *A*.   186 Forte — nova
A: Infernos alerem iam quota *BO*.   187–88 Umbraque — malis! *A*: om. *BO*.

commanding her to rise from her old life of sin.[5] Even he, whom
the voice of the dying Lord gave comfort, can hardly, I believe,
have been more delirious with joy than I was then.[6] I went away
in great happiness, even though [160] the substance of my earlier
life also gave me reason to be sad. Thereafter, how many wakeful
nights spent with tearful eye, how many days spent incessantly
weeping, until — for you are expert in pitying piteous sinners,
bishop — until your hands propped up the wreckage of my life!

When I lay buried in the all too murky darkness of pitch-black
night, you opened my eyes to the true light of day. I wandered
through places teeming with venomous snakes; you showed me the
true way that leads toward the stars. As brawling winds drove me to
and fro on the perilous sea, [170] you, faithful Tiphys,[7] guided me
safely to land. The sleep-inducing branch had already touched my
cold temples.[8] You, however, dispelled the night and awakened my
dead eyes. In short, when I was already crossing the very threshold
of hell, you called out to me, "That is not the way to the stars!"
And I, who had been walking in darkness, forthwith woke up to
the error that until then had been my pleasure and passion. Then,
for the first time, I realized how very nearly that most enticing Siren
had succeeded in plunging me headlong beneath the infamous
waves. So some sailor furrowing the blue-gray waters of the Ionian
Sea [180] dies a sweet death, unless he takes his precautions. One
man at least, so they say, took the proper precautions, a man who
roamed far and wide for ten years as he carried the spoils of Troy
back to his fatherland. Had he not disdained to listen to the seduc-
tively melodious plaints, he would have exposed himself and his
crew to a wretched death.[9] Had you not saved me from imminent
death, I too might have fallen prey to the hellhounds by now.
A naked shade, I would now be lying hid beneath the waters of
Lethe, only to be afflicted, alas, by horrible torments of all kinds.

[5]One day, when Jesus was in the house of a Pharisee, a sinful woman came to him and washed
his feet with her tears, dried them with her hair, and anointed them with precious oil. Thereupon Jesus
told her that her sins were forgiven. See Luke 7.37–50. For the identification of this woman with Mary
Magdalene, see *Her. Chr.* 3.97–118, with n. 7 (p. 187 above); cf. l. 146 above.

[6]When the criminal asked Jesus on the cross to remember him after he came into his kingdom,
Jesus answered, "Today you will be with me in Paradise." See Luke 23.39–43.

[7]As helmsman of the Argonauts, Tiphys is the pilot par excellence.

[8]Having fallen asleep at the tiller, she nearly suffered the fate of Aeneas' steersman Palinurus, who
fell overboard after the god of sleep touched him with his magic wand. See Verg. *Aen.* 5.833–71; cf.
Eob. *Her. Chr.* 6. 209–10.

[9]Pelagia compares herself to Ulysses, who escaped the Sirens' alluring but deadly song. The story
is told in Hom. *Od.* 12.166–200. For the interpretation of the Sirens as prostitutes who sing the siren
song of erotic pleasures see Eob. *Ama.* 27.1–4, with notes. For the medieval-Renaissance commonplace
that Ulysses stopped his own ears with wax against the Sirens, see *Ama.* 27.2, with n. 20 (1:234–35).

N3ᵛ

At bene successit, quod gaudia falsa sequenti
190   Cognita te fuerant indice vera mihi.
Quae simul agnovi, "Valeat prius omne quod actum est!
Quae superant," dixi, "tempora lucis erunt."
Sic aliquis caeco forte enutritus in antro,
Lucis egens, tenebras omnia habere putat.
195   Qui simul invisae paulatim assueverit aurae,
Amplius in caeca non volet esse domo.
Miraturque novas formas et mille colores
Multaque inexpleto lumine monstra videt.
Sic aliquis, spectans fallacis inania somni,
200   Mente soporata gaudia vera putat.
Ut vero evigilat, blandae ludibria noctis
Damnat et ex animo non cecidisse dolet.
Sed ne forte tuas offendam pluribus aures,
Caetera sunt animo concipienda tuo.
205   Sponte sua nec enim decet addere calcar eunti;
Sic pietas nobis cognita saepe tua est.
Et nunc incipio canis albere capillis
Et prope supremum suspicor esse diem.
Quid faciam? Quo fine iubes hanc ire senectam?
210   Indicio certam da, pater, esse tuo.
Opprimor immodicis sub iniquo pondere curis

66=N4ʳ

Meque vocat primum subdita turba patrem.
An decet hoc caelare etiam et post fata latere?
Nunc ego sum vitae pene inimica meae.
215   Hac, pater, obtestor, me sollicitudine solvas,
Sive ego sim frater sive vocanda soror.
Iamque vale nostrisque favens accede querelis
Et lege placato carmina nostra Deo.

190 Cognita — indice *A*: Indice te fuerint cognita *BO*.   192 superant *A* (*in erratis*) *BO*: superat
A (*in textu*).   193 forte *A*: puer *BO*.   194 putat *A*: putet *BO*.   197 et mille *A*: rerumque
BO.   203 tuas *A*: pias *BO*.   205 decet *A*: licet *BO*.   216 sim *A*: sum *BO*.

My story has had a happy ending, however. For when I was pursuing false pleasures, [190] you acquainted me with true joys. As soon as I recognized this, I cried: "Begone, everything that has gone on before! My remaining days will belong to the light." So someone, who perchance was raised in a dark cave and is unaware of the light, believes that all things are enveloped in blackness. But after he has gradually gotten used to the odious daylight, he no longer wants to stay in his dark abode. He marvels at the new shapes and countless colors and gazes with insatiable eye at the many wonders around him. So someone seeing the idle images of an illusive dream [200] thinks in his somnolent mind that all these joys are real. No sooner has he woken up, however, than he rejects the mockeries of alluring night and is not sorry to find them vanished from his soul.

But lest perhaps I offend your ears with further ramblings, I leave the rest to your imagination. For I really must not spur a willing horse. Such indeed is the love you display, as I have often experienced it for myself.

And now my hair is beginning to turn white, and I suspect that my last day is fast approaching. What should I do? What goal do you want me to set for my old age? [210] Give me a clear sense of direction, father. The crushing burden of innumerable cares weighs heavy upon me, and the flock entrusted to me calls me its foremost father. Is it proper to hide the truth and keep it under wraps, even after my death? Now my life seems almost abhorrent to me. Father, I implore you, relieve me of this worry, whether I should let myself be addressed as father or as sister.

And now farewell. Graciously heed my laments and read my song aloud to the God I have placated.

16   MARIA IOANNI

Haec, dilecte Deo iuvenis, tibi venit ab illa
    Quae tibi, quo licuit tempore, mater erat.
Signa quid aspiciens gladium miraris utrumque?
    Hic mihi causa fuit vulneris, ille tibi.
5   Vidimus his laesi morientis vulnera Christi.
    Heu, quantum miseros est meminisse dies!
Nunc tamen hoc peius doleo, quo longius ipsum
    Me licet invitum deseruisse queror.
Missus ad Aegeam Rhomano a Caesare Pathmon,
10   Incolere ignotam diceris exul humum.
Quae simul ut nostras fama improba contigit aures,
    Sensibus excideram mortua pene meis.
Idque ego iamdudum vel tale quid aegra timebam,
    Docta satis casus posse timere graves.
15   Fortiter hic animus longoque induruit usu —
    Pectoris haec non sunt vulnera prima mei!
Ante per immensum pelagus iactata malorum,
    Ante in curarum gurgite mersa fui.
Tu quoque, non levibus mecum perculse periclis,
20   Scis bene quid casus sit tolerare graves.
Tu quoque, nostrarum comes et pars maxima rerum,
    Testis es afflictam sic potuisse queri.
Cum qua quicquid erat durum commune subisti,
    Adnumerans damnis nostra pericla tuis.
25   Qui mihi quod charae frater solet esse sorori,
    Cui fueram fratri quod solet esse soror,
Denique quem primum dilexi semper ab illo —
    Illo, qui nobis omnia solus erat,
Qui moriens, "Tuus hic mulier sit filius," inquit;
30   Inde tibi, "Hanc matrem tu quoque," dixit, "habe."

N4ᵛ *(line 15)*

Her. Chr. **16.**   7 peius *AO*: prius *B*.   7–8 ipsum — invitum *A*: has te / Meque simul terras *BO*.
9 Missus ad *A*: Pulsus in *BO*; Aegeam *BO*: Aegeum *A*.   19–20 Tu — graves. *A*: *om. BO*.
23 subisti *A*: tulisti *BO*.   24 nostra pericla *A*: vulnera nostra *BO*.   26 fratri *AB*: frater *O*.
29–30 Qui — habe." *A*: Qui moriens matrem tibi me mandavit, ut esses / Tu quoque desertae quod
fuit ille mihi. *BO*.

[1]This letter portrays the Virgin as Mother of Sorrows. Now sixty years old, Mary looks back on
a life that has given her not only great joys but also a surfeit of pain. Even John the Apostle — the
disciple whom Jesus entrusted to her as a son at the crucifixion — has not been the pillar of her old

16   MARY TO JOHN[1]

This letter, O youth beloved of God, comes to you from her
who, as long as she could, was a mother to you.

Why, as you ponder these symbols, are you taken aback by
the two swords? The one wounded me, the other one you. They
pierced through our hearts when we saw the wounds of the dying
Christ.[2] Alas, how painful it is to recall those days of woe! But
now I grieve the more, the longer I have to lament that you were
forced to leave me. Relegated by the Roman Emperor to Aegean
Patmos, [10] you are said to live as an exile in an alien land.

As soon as the appalling news reached my ears, I fell into a
faint and nearly died on the spot. For a long time I had been
nervously dreading this or something similar, for I know enough
to fear disaster. This soul of mine has been steeled by long
experience — this is not the first time I have been wounded in
the heart! Earlier already I was tossed about on a boundless sea of
troubles; earlier already I was engulfed by a flood of cares.

Battered alongside me by no mean dangers, [20] you too
know very well what it means to endure grievous disasters. You
too, companion and greatest part of my life, can testify that I,
afflicted woman, have a right to complain like this. It was you,
after all, who suffered every hardship alongside me and piled my
travails on top of your own. To me you were as a brother is to his
dear sister. To you I was as a sister is to her brother. In brief,
I have always loved you best, right after him — him, who alone
meant everything to us, whose dying words to me were,
"Woman, take him as your son," [30] and then to you, "You too,

---

age as she had hoped, now that he has been banished to the island of Patmos (Revelations 1.9; *Leg.
aurea* 9.17). It is to Patmos, then, that Mary sends this letter, in hopes of receiving a letter of consolation from John, along with news about his projects. But the real purpose of her letter is to recall her
sorrows — not to dwell on them for their own sake, but rather to overcome them and put them in per-
spective. That is why her letter, though full of the remembrance of grief, is ultimately not a lament.
The Virgin, in Eobanus' vision, remains a heroine of faith, at once *Mater Dolorosa* and *Mater Gloriosa*.

Since Mary was widely believed to have lived to age sixty (see *Leg. aurea* 115.5), this letter is,
after a manner of speaking, her swan song. Such letters are common in Ovid's *Heroides*: see *Ep.* 2, 7, 9,
11, 14, 15, and 18–19. They also recur in Eobanus' work: see *Her. Chr.* 4, 7, 14, 15, 17, 18, 23, and
Her. 1.6.

In the 1532/39 version this letter is *Her.* 1.4.

[2]In the opening sentence Mary has identified the addressee John as the "beloved of God" and
herself as his "mother." If John interprets these two "symbols" correctly, he (like Mary herself) will be
reminded of the crucifixion when Christ, seeing "his mother and the disciple whom he loved,"
enjoined Mary to be a mother to John and John to be her son: see John 19.26–27. Mary calls the
symbols "swords" in order to recall Simeon's prophecy in Luke 2.35. For when Joseph and Mary
brought Jesus to the Temple in Jerusalem, the old Simeon told Mary that a sword would pierce
through her soul also. This "sword" was traditionally associated with Mary's grief at the crucifixion.

Defeci terramque genu labente petebam,
    A terra officio sum relevata tuo.
Hoc pius aspitiens aliquis miseratus utrumque
    Dixerat, "Ah, quoties hec misera, ille miser!"
35 Flebant et Solimae tanquam sua viscera matres;
    Addidit immites impia turba minas.

67=N5ʳ Plura vetat meminisse dolor. Quis caetera fando
    Pallentes calido non riget imbre genas?
Omnibus intereras, mecum omnia dura tulisti —
40   O, nec adhuc aliquo fine quietus agens!
Qur igitur, tot passe animo famulante labores,
    Non mihi sollicito pectore flendus eras?
Qur non exciderim tam saeva exterrita fama?
    Non, si etiam saevo saevior angue forem!
45 Tunc ego vel potui crudelior esse videri
    Quam quibus est forti mamma resecta manu,
Nata feris, pavisse feras tigresque luposque,
    Non potui casto pascere lacte Deum;
Duricia potui superasse Lycaonis Arcton,
50   Ni te quae pateris non meruisse querar.
Namque quis agnato te sanguine iunctior uno?
    Quis mihi post natum charior alter erat?
Quis fidei maioris erat? Quis amantior alter?
    Charior hoc nobis nemo nepote fuit.
55 Ut taceam qua me toties pietate levaris,
    Quanta animi fuerim sarcina saepe tui!
Quinetiam hac debes charus mihi parte fuisse:
    Te peperit Salome nostra parente soror.

N5ᵛ Stirpe nepos, fili officio, pie frater amore,
60   Tres mihi, non unum, fas sit abesse queror.
Omnia solus eras soli mihi namque relictae,
    Postquam est in patriam redditus ille suam —
Ille decus nostrum, nostrae dator ille salutis.
    Hei mihi, cur nomen dicere triste fuit?
65 Nescio quae dulcedo meos renovare dolores
    Hic solet. In dicto nomine vulnus erat.

---

31 labente *O*: labante *AB*.   **32** officio . . . tuo *A*: manibus . . . tuis *BO*.   **33** utrumque *A*: utrunque
est *BO*.   **41** passe *A*: passae *BO*; famulante *A*: subeunte *BO*.   **44** Non — forem! *A*: Cur tua [tuo *B*]
non nostrum vulnera pectus agant? *BO*.   **46** forti *A*: propria *BO*.   **49–50** superasse — Ni te *A*:
superare adamanta videri, / Si non *BO*.   **51–54** Namque — fuit *A*: Quae quamvis placuisse queant tibi
forte per ipsum / Qui mala postremis deteriora tulit, / Te tamen indigne plecti dolet. O mihi saltem / Quis
dabit ut pro te tristia fata feram? / Cui quod non penitus cecidi, quod pene revixi / Mortua, cui quod sum
debeo quodque fui *BO*.   **57–60** Quinetiam — queror. *A*: *om. BO*.   **64** Hei *A*: Heu *BO*.
65 Nescio *AB*: Nescia *O*.

take her as your mother." Whenever I sank down exhausted,
knees buckling, you helped raise me from the ground. Some dear
soul watching the two of us would say in commiseration: "Ah,
how brokenhearted is she! How brokenhearted is he!" The mothers in Jerusalem wept over us too, as if we were their own flesh
and blood; the accursed mob heaped savage threats upon us.
Anguish keeps me from calling even more to mind. Who can tell
the rest of the story and not have hot tears coursing down his
ashen cheeks?

You accompanied me everywhere, you bore every ordeal
with me — [40] ah, even now you never stop to rest! Why then,
seeing that you have suffered so many tribulations to help me,
should I not weep for you with anxious heart? Why should I not
faint in horror at such cruel news? No, not even if I were more
savage than the savage snake! Then indeed I would have seemed
more inhuman than those women who with resolute hand cut
off their own breast.[3] Born to wild beasts, I could have given
suck to wild beasts, to tigers and wolves, not feed God with
virgin milk. In hardness I would have surpassed the Lycaonian
Arctic, [50] had I not lamented that all your sufferings are undeserved. For who has closer blood ties to me than you? Who, after
my son, was dearer to me? Who was more faithful, who more
loving to me? Nobody was dearer to me than this nephew of
mine.[4] I will not mention how often you consoled me with your
thoughtfulness, how heavy a burden I often was on your soul.
You have every right to be close to my heart for this reason too: it
was my half sister (her father being Salome) who bore you.
Nephew by blood, son by devotion, affectionate brother by love:
[60] with your absence I have not one, but three to lament. You
alone were the world to me, ever since I was left alone when he
returned to his fatherland[5] — he, our pride and joy, the giver of
our salvation.

Ah me, why does it hurt so much to say his name?
Whenever I do, some mysterious sweetness always brings back
my pain. Just mentioning his name wounds me to the quick.

---

[3]Mary alludes to the legendary Amazons.

[4]According to the legend of St. Anna's "trinubium" (see *Her. Chr.* 3.71–72, with n. 5, p. 185
above), Mary's mother Anna remarried after the death of her first two husbands. The third husband
was named Salome. Their daughter, having married Zebedee, became the mother of James the Great
and John the Apostle. Thus, John was the Virgin's half nephew.

[5]That is, after the Ascension: see Mark 16.19; Luke 24.50–51; Acts 1.9.

Maternum exanimant dilecta vocabula pectus,
  Et tamen est aliquid cur meminisse iuvet.
Sic quoque vicina iam lumina morte gravatus
70   Matris in indicto nomine mitis erat.
Tam miserae fractaeque malis passaeque dolores
  Dixisses quiddam blandius, interii.
Ecquae vel potuit gravius vel debuit unquam
  Quod peperit nostra mater amare fide?
75 Ecquae quid maius peperit? Cui deinde per omnem
  Cum partu vitam vivere peius erat?
Tempore ab hoc nostra quo terras venit ab alvo
  Humano Deitas corpore tecta latens,
Quot tulerim adversos non est numerare labores.
80   Tempore ab hoc paucis laeta diebus eram.
68=N6ʳ   Laeta fui tunc, cum mihi missus ab aethere dixit
  Pectore non falso nuncius ales, "Ave."
Tunc quoque, cum tantam peperi sine crimine prolem
  Cumque darent illi tres tria dona magi.
85 Laeta triumphata redeuntem morte videbam
  Calcantemque alacri nubila regna pede.
Spiritus a patria laetam quoque sede relabens
  Vidit; eras nostri pars quota et ipse chori.
Caetera dura tulit sortis tenor omnia iniquae.
90   Quod iuvet est praeter talia pauca nihil.
Quae si cuncta velim numero comprehendere certo,
  Palmiferas Libani dicere coner opes,
Quot cedros Carmelus alat, quot in alta Sionis
  Aereas Hermon mane refundat aquas.
95 Pauca tamen meminisse iuvat, quibus ipse notatis
  Tu quoque pacifico tristia corde feras.
Frigora pauperiemque pati leve posse videtur.
  Hoc nihil est; horum milia multa tuli.

---

67 exanimant *AB*: examinant *O*.   **68** aliquid — meminisse *A*: quare commeminisse *BO*.
75 quid *A*: vel *BO*.   **78** Deitas . . . latens *A*: soboles . . . Dei *BO*.   **79** Quot *BO*: Quod *A*;
adversos *A*: duros *BO*.   **81** fui *AB*: fuit *O*.   **90** praeter — pauca *A*: inter milia multa *BO*.
92 Palmiferas *A*: Frondiferas *BO*.   **93–94** in alta — aquas *A*: gignat odoras / Hierichus vernis
solibus usta rosas *BO*.   **97** leve posse *A*: res dura *BO*.   **98** Hoc *A*: At *BO*.

The beloved word throws the maternal breast into turmoil, and yet there is also a good reason why I like to call it to mind. In the same way, although his eyes were already heavy with impending death, he too [70] showed compassion for his mother by not mentioning my name.[6] Had you said something more personal to one so forlorn and brokenhearted and griefstricken, I would have died right there and then.

Has there ever been a mother who either could or should have loved the fruit of her womb more deeply and faithfully than I? Has anyone ever brought forth a greater child? And has anyone ever had a harder time with her son throughout her life? From the time when the Deity, concealed in human flesh, came into the world from my womb, the misfortunes I suffered are more than I can count. [80] Since that time there have been precious few days when I was joyful. I felt joyful then, when the winged messenger from heaven offered me his unpretending "Hail!" I rejoiced then too, when I blamelessly bore so great a son and when the three Magi gave him their three gifts. I was overjoyed to see him return from his triumph over death and briskly ascend above the realm of clouds. The Spirit too saw me rejoice when he glided down from the Father's house. You yourself were there, a small part of our group.[7]

For the rest, my cruel lot has brought me nothing but hardships throughout my life. [90] Apart from the few joys I just mentioned, I find nothing that delights. If I wanted to enumerate every one of my troubles, it would be like trying to count all the palm trees in Lebanon, determine how many cedars Mount Carmel supports, how many dewdrops Mount Hermon sprinkles at dawn on the heights of Zion. All the same, it will do me good to look back on a few of them. You too may listen with a tranquil heart as I recount my sorrows.

Being able to endure cold and poverty seems easy to me. That is nothing. I have borne countless hardships like those.

---

[6]When Jesus saw Mary and John standing beneath the cross, he addressed his mother as "woman": see John 19.26. Mary now offers a psychological explanation for this apparent heartlessness. Just as Mary cannot bear to say Jesus' name, so Jesus could not bear to address her as "Mary" or "mother." The explanation occurs also in Mant. *1. Parthen.* 3.672–73.

[7]Here Mary recounts five of the traditional "Joys of the Virgin": the Annunciation, the Nativity, the Adoration of the Magi, Christ's appearance to Mary at the Resurrection, his Ascension, and the outpouring of the Spirit at Pentecost. The New Testament is silent on the latter three joys. It was commonly assumed in the Middle Ages, however, that Mary was the first to see the resurrected Christ. See, for example, Ambros. *De virginitate* 3.14; Sedul. 5.361–62; *Leg. aurea* 52.146–58; Mant. *1. Parthen.* 3.685–712. The belief that Mary also witnessed the Ascension (Mark 16.19; Luke 24.51; Acts 1.9) and the outpouring of the Holy Spirit at Pentecost (Acts 2.1–4) was, among other considerations, inferred from Acts 1.14 and 2.1. See, for example, Mant. *1. Parthen.* 3.713–16.

Quem mihi tunc animum credis, dilecte, fuisse,
100　　Carmina fatidicus dum canit ista senex?
"Moeror et anxietas, dolor, inclementia fati
In puero hoc (video) sunt adeunda tibi."

N6ᵛ　Non secus obstupui quam si nil tale timenti
Hausissent medium taela cruenta latus.
105　Nondum convalui, nondum dolor ille resedit,
Ecce nova Herodes monstra tyrannus agit.
Audiit Hebraea venturum ab origine regem
Qui se de tanto pelleret imperio.
Extemplo edicto crudeli occidere mandat
110　　Quisquis adhuc linguae masculus esset inops.
Protinus immeritae plangunt sua viscera matres,
Saepius e medio viscera rapta sinu.
Gestiit innocuo crudelis sanguine miles.
Flebilius nihil hac caede fuisse liquet.
115　Ipsa, Deo monita, Aegiptum fugitiva petebam;
Dux mihi cum puero castus Ioseph erat.
Hic aliquot fatis sed tristibus egimus annos.
Praebuit angustum lana colusque cibum.
Ipse opera edoctus fabrilia semper agebat,
120　　Unde suis victum quaereret arte, senex.
Vix peregre patriam Galilaeaque rura reversi —
Instabat Solyma festus in urbe dies —
Venimus ad typici sacrum solenniter agni.
Dum timeo natum perdere, natus abest.

69=O1ʳ　125　Illum ego quaesitum tris soles anxia tandem
Inveni sacros disserere ante patres.
Vix isto annorum duo tempore lustra peregit,
Et potuit tantos ille docere viros!
Crevit et inde puer meliores induit annos;
130　　Me vacuam vidit nulla dolore dies.
Iamque vir egressus sexti confinia lustri
In sibi prescripta caeperat ire via.
Per nova mirantes tenuit miracula turbas
Et novus in tota gente propheta fuit.
135　Testis es ante alios, nec enim te charior illi
Alter erat, quo se gesserit ille modo.

---

99 tunc *AB*: nunc *O*.　　**100** fatidicus *A*: vaticinans *BO*.　　**101–02** fati — tibi *A*: fati, / Mater, in hoc puero sunt obeunda tibi *BO*.　　**103** tale *BO*: tabe *A*.　　**109** Extemplo *A*: Protinus *BO*. **111** Protinus immeritae *A*: Hic dolor, hic miserae *BO*.　　**113** Gestiit *A*: Saevit in *BO*.　　**114** liquet *A*: potest *BO*.　　**116** Dux — erat *A*: Duxit Iosepho nos comitante puer *BO*.　　**119–20** Ipse — senex. *A*: *om. BO*.　　**126** Inveni *A* (*in erratis*): Iuveni *A* (*in textu*), Invenio *BO*.　　**134** tota *AB*: toto *O*.

What, my beloved, do you think were my feelings then,
[100] when the oracular old man gave me the following prophecy? "Grief and anguish, pain, a harsh fate (as I foresee) await
you in this boy."[8] I was as stunned as one who, fearing nothing
of the sort, has just felt a bloody spear drive deep into his side.

I had not yet recovered, that pain had not yet subsided,
when — lo and behold — the tyrant Herod committed new
atrocities. He had heard that a king of Hebrew descent was coming to overthrow him. At once he gave the cruel order to kill
[110] every male that had not yet learned to speak. The mothers,
who had not deserved this, forthwith wept for their children,
their babies, often snatched straight from the bosom. The pitiless
soldiers reveled in the innocent blood. Clearly there has never
been anything so lamentable as this slaughter. Warned by God,
I fled to Egypt. The chaste Joseph led the way for me and the
boy. There we spent several depressing years. Wool and distaff
provided slender meals. The old man himself continued working
in the carpenter's trade [120] to help support his family.

Not long after returning from abroad to our hometown in
Galilee, we decided to go to Jerusalem to attend the annual feast
of the prefigurative paschal lamb. As I started to worry about
losing my son, my son was gone. After three days of anxious
searching I finally found him discoursing before the holy fathers.
At that time he had just barely completed one decade, and
already he was able to teach such learned men!

The boy grew and then entered the best years of his life.
[130] As for me, no day ever saw me free of pain. And now,
a man who had passed his third decade, he set out on the path
he had assigned himself. By unheard-of miracles he held the
crowds spellbound, and all the people looked up to him as
a new prophet. You, more so than the others (for you were
dearer to him than anyone else), can testify in what way
he conducted himself. How many sufferers, how many of the

---

[8]See Luke 2.25–35. With Simeon's prophecy Mary begins a recital of her Seven Sorrows: the
flight to Egypt (ll. 105–20); the disappearance of the twelve-year-old Jesus in Jerusalem (121–28);
Jesus' arrest, trial, and condemnation (129–202); the road to Golgotha (203–16); the crucifixion
(217–22); and the pietà scene (223–30).

Quot miseros, quot monstra hominum, quot lumine functos
    Reddiderit, per tot milia nemo rogat.
Scis quibus interea curis gemebunda tenebar,
140   Certa dolorificum non procul esse diem.
Saepe gemens dixi: "Cui me, moriture, relinquis?
    Quis dabit, heu, tecum me quoque posse mori?"
Ille quibus potuit verbis lenire dolorem!
    Saepe tibi dixit, "Vestra sit ista vide."
145 Te quoque saepe gravis flenti discrimina fati
    Non puduit madidas tergere veste genas,

O1ᵛ   Et mea saepe tuae lachrymae super ora cadebant,
    Exciderem manibus cum resupina tuis.
Et iam tempus erat fatalem solvere morsum.
150   Tristior effulsit quaelibet hora mihi.
Ascendit Solimam, palma sublimis, in urbem,
    Exceptus summi regis honore fuit.
Inde sacra vulgus deturbat ab aede prophanum;
    A populo saxis pene petitus erat.
155 Sex modo restabant quos vellet vivere soles —
    Heu nimis in curas area lata meas!
Hic mihi nec luces tacitae nec tempora noctis
    In lachrymas spacii sat habuere meas.
Anxia, sive aberat, quaerebam semper ubi esset;
160   Anxia, sive aderat, ne male abiret eram.
Omnia tu melius. Mecum tu semper agebas,
    Omnia tu memori mente tenere potes.
Quis ferat illius noctis meminisse cruentae,
    Quae typicum Paschae est prima sequuta cibum?
165 Vosne Cedroneae captum potuistis olivae
    Immeritum sicca fronde videre Deum?
Ipse rapax amnis lapsas de corpore guttas
    Sensit et attonita mollior ibat aqua.
70=O2ʳ Territa diffugit sub opacam Cynthia nubem,
170   Pene etiam caelo nox abitura fuit.
Mene quieturos posuisse cubilibus artus,
    Mene relaxata mente fuisse putas?
Quolibet usque illum tam longa nocte trahebant,
    Hac ego sum tacitis passibus ausa sequi.
175 Nunc ego per clausae rimas spectare fenestrae
    Dum cupio, indigne saepe repulsa fui.
Vidi ego vel probris lusum vel verbere caesum,
    Nullus in attonito pectore sanguis erat.

137 functos *A*: cassos *BO*.   150 effulsit *A*: affulsit *BO*.   152 summi *A*: veri *BO*.   154 populo
A: turba *BO*.   156 area lata *A*: tempora longa *BO*.   158 sat — meas *A*: sufficientis erant *BO*.
163 ferat *AB*: feret *O*.   164 Quae — cibum *A*: Quae coenam Paschae prima secuta fuit *BO*.
167 de *A*: a *BO*.

lame and halt, how many of the dead he restored to life and
health, no one asks because there are so many thousands of them.

You know the worries that kept me groaning all the while,
[140] convinced, as I was, that the day of woe was not far off.
Often I asked him with a groan: "In whose care will you leave me
after you die? Who, alas, will let me die together with you?" How
he could soothe my anguish with his words! Often he would tell
you, "Be sure to take good care of her." And indeed, as often as I
bewept the blows of grievous fate, you were not ashamed to wipe
my tearstained cheeks with your cloak. Often, in fact, your tears
would drop down on my face as I grew faint and sank back into
your arms.

And now the time had come for him to suffer the sting of
death. [150] To my mind, every hour shone forth with new
sadness. He himself, a palm exalted, rode up to the city of
Jerusalem and was hailed as the highest king. Thereupon he
drove the profane crowd from the holy Temple. The people
nearly stoned him to death.

Only six more days remained in which he wished to live —
a field, alas, too broad for my cares! Then neither the light of day
nor the hours of silent night gave me space enough for my tears.
If he was gone, I would anxiously keep on asking where he might
be; [160] and if he was with me, I would worry that he might be
going to his doom.

You know all this better than I. Though you and I went
through these times together, you can retain them all in your
memory. But who can bear to remember that gory night, the one
that immediately followed the prefigurative paschal meal? You
olives of Kidron, were you able to look on with dry boughs, as
God was undeservedly taken captive? Even the raging brook
sensed the drops that fell from his body and, thunderstruck,
began to flow with gentler current.[9] The moon fled in terror
behind a dark cloud. [170] Indeed, it almost seemed as if night
would never leave the sky.

Do you think I could lay down my limbs to rest? Do you
think I could put my mind at ease? Wherever they dragged him
that whole long night, there I dared follow with silent steps. And
after all this, when I wanted to peer through slits in a closed window, I was often rudely thrust away. Stunned, I saw how they
mocked him and flogged him, and all the blood drained from

---

[9]The brook Kidron flowed through the garden of Gethsemane, where Jesus was arrested: cf. John
18.1–12. Eobanus alludes to the Vulgate text, which here speaks of "the torrent Kidron" ("torrentem
Cedron").

Ah, quoties, ridente aliquo mea vulnera, flevi!
180   Ah, quoties supplex qualibus usque fui!
Hic quoque qua poteras miseram pietate iuvabas,
    Egressus dirae limina nota domus.
Quis meminisse queat dirae scelera omnia noctis?
    Non satis est tantis ulla querela malis.
185   Quot gelidae aestivis errant in montibus umbrae,
    Quot matutino gramina rore madent,
Tot mea presserunt lachrymosi corda dolores
    Illa, quae cladem nox mihi prima tulit,
Nox Acherontaeis intempestivior umbris,
190   Nox tamen in curas non satis ipsa meas.

O2ᵛ

Tristior in nostras lachrymas accessit Eous,
    Et peiora novum vulnera mane tulit.
Vix caput extulerat trepido sol territus orbi,
    Moestus in attonita perstrepit aure sonus:
195   "Quem data delusit Galilaei purpura regis,
    Quem pro lege iubet praesul uterque mori,
Rite coronatum preses Rhomanus Iesum
    Damnat ad extremam, iustior ipse, crucem."
"Parcitis immeritae, pubes Iudaea, parenti!"
200   Sic ego sic vestra voce levanda fui.
Hoc erat officium matri praestare relictae —
    O etiam veteri durius angue genus!
Et iam tota cohors portis erumpit apertis.
    Impositam collo baiulat ille crucem.
205   Qua licet usque sequor, te solo tuta ministro.
    In latebris comitum caetera turba fuit.
Attamen et Mariae mecum venere sorores,
    Sed novus has longe iusserat ire timor.
Non satis ipse oneri quoties cecidisset, amare
210   Vapulat, a tacta surgere iussus humo.
Tacta rubebat humus vestigiaque ipsa tenebat,
    Sanguine quae fuso fecit utrumque genu.

71=O3ʳ

Quid facerem? Tocies iacui iam frigida, flevi.
    (Nunc quoque, si quaeras, "Quid facit ipsa?", fleo,
215   Quasque legis toto frequentes carmine mendas,
    De lachrymis factas noveris esse meis).

191 accessit *A*: successit *BO*.   **194** attonita *BO*: attonito *A*.   **195** Quem — regis *A*: Qui nova credentem populum per signa fefellit, / Qui se praesentem dixit adesse Deum, / Qui sua praetulerit sanctae ludibria legi *BO*.   **207** Mariae mecum *A*: mecum quaedam *BO*.   **208** novus . . . iusserat ire *A*: gravis . . . iussit abesse *BO*.   **210** a tacta *A*: infecta *BO*.   **211** humus *A*: enim *BO*.   **214** ipsa *AB*: ista *O*.   **215** frequentes *A*: multas in *BO*.

my breast. Ah, how often I wept when someone laughed at my heartache! [180] Ah, how often I humbly pleaded for him — and to what sort of people! Here too you lovingly helped the sorrowful mother, as much as you could, after leaving the threshold of that dreadful house you know so well.

Who could possibly remember all the crimes of that terrible night? No one can ever lament those enormities enough. As many as the cool shadows that roam the mountains in summer, as many as the blades of grass that drip with morning dew, so many doleful sorrows pressed upon my heart that night, the night that first brought me disaster, a night more dismal than the shades of Acheron, [190] a night, all the same, too short to be the measure of my cares. The dawn added more misery to my tears, and the new morning brought even worse calamities. Scarcely had the terrified sun raised his head above the fearful world, when the sad cry resounded in my stupefied ears: "Behold the man, arrayed in purple to mock his claim of being King of the Jews — the man whom the two high priests commanded to die according to the Law, the duly-crowned Jesus! The Roman governor, himself more righteous, condemns him to death by crucifixion."[10]

"You men of Judea, spare the mother who does not deserve this!" [200] That, that is how they should have cried out to console me. That is the service they should have performed for the bereaved mother — oh that race, more hardhearted than the ancient Serpent himself!

And now the whole mob was tumbling headlong through the open gates. He bore the cross they had thrust upon his neck. As far as possible I followed behind, safe in the knowledge that you, at least, would help me. The rest of the disciples had gone into hiding. However, the other Marys, my half sisters,[11] came with me too, but a sudden panic forced them to keep their distance.

Whenever he sank down under the excessive burden, [210] he was grievously beaten and ordered to get up from the ground. The ground he touched turned red and kept the imprints of his bleeding knees.

What was I to do? Every time I fell down in shock, I wept. (Even now, if you should ask, "What is she doing these days?", I weep, and the blots you see scattered all over my letter you will now recognize as caused by my tears.)

---

[10] We may imagine these words coming from a herald announcing Pilate's sentence to the assembled crowd. Cf. John 19.1–16. The two high priests are Annas and Caiaphas: see John 18.12–24. That Pilate is less guilty of this miscarriage of justice goes back to Jesus' words to Pilate in John 19.11.

[11] For the legend, see *Her. Chr.* 3.71–72, with n. 5 (p. 185 above).

Ventum erat interea mortis loca ad alta statutae.
  Ecce sudes, clavos, arma, flagella, crucem!
Tunc ego vel nullos potui sensisse dolores,
220   Vel potui humani cordis habere nihil.
Sanguine iam roseo ligno sudante pependit,
  Transiit effossum militis hasta latus.
Iam mihi pendentes licuit tetigisse lacertos,
  Oscula iam nigro frigida ab ore tuli.
225 Dicite synchronae, foelicia nomina, matres,
  Dicite de vobis talia si qua tulit!
Nulla tulit, nulla est aevo latura sequenti.
  Curarum hoc pressit sarcina tota caput.
Tot mala, tot curas, tot iniquos passa dolores,
230   Conqueror extremum longius ire diem.
Quoque magis doleam, sine te, charissime, cogor
  Vivere, qui moestae dulce levamen eras.
Non ego te aspiciam vestri mandata Magistri
  Hystorica populis insinuare fide.
O3ᵛ   235 Non mihi sollicitae numeranti taedia vitae
  Artifici falles tempora longa mora.
Illaque quae mecum quondam monumenta solebas
  Visere, stant soli sola videnda mihi.
Illa ego, divitibus seu lucidus exit ab Indis
240   Seu cadat Hesperia Phosphorus ater aqua,
Flexa genu praesens fletu contemplor amaro.
  "Ille locus nostri signa doloris habet.
Illius apparent vestigia moesta perempti,
  Illius innocui cede cruenta viri.
245 Hic stetit, hic cecidit. Saxo defecit in illo.
  Hoc ego strata loco cum pateretur eram.
Haec illum crux alta crucem tulit inter utramque.
  Mortuus hic munda sindone tectus erat.
Hic me semianimem charissimus ille refecit,
250   Ille per Aegaeas nunc male pulsus aquas."
Talia dum meditor, mecum tua semper imago est,
  Tu procul hinc absis milia multa licet.
Ipsa quidem Solimis nunquam exeo corpore ab oris;
  Mens tamen et caelos et tua regna subit.
255 Mens spatio peregrina brevi quocunque volebat,
  Tollitur et nullo limite clausa volat.

---

217 statutae *A*: paratae *BO*.   225 synchronae *A*: prolificae *BO*.   229 iniquos *BO*: iniquas *A*.
232 moestae *A*: miserae *BO*.   237 Illaque quae mecum . . . solebas *A*: Nunc quoque quae tecum . . .
solebam *BO*.   240 Seu — aqua *A*: Seu niger Hesperiam Lucifer intrat aquam *BO*.

In the meantime they had reached the top of the hill where he was to be executed. Look — stakes, nails, weapons, scourges, the cross! Had I not felt any anguish then, [220] I would have been inhumanly heartless. Before long he hung on the cross that was dripping with his rose-red blood, and a soldier's lance pierced his opened side. Soon they let me touch his drooping arms. Soon I took cold kisses from his blackened lips.

Speak up, present-day mothers, you fortunate women! Speak up, if any of you has ever endured tribulations like these! No one has ever experienced the like; none ever will in all the ages to come. The whole burden of cares weighs on my head alone.

Having suffered so many woes, so many cares, so many dreadful sorrows, [230] I complain that my dying day is still tarrying so long. My distress is all the greater, now that I am forced to live without you, dearest, the one who used to afford sweet solace in my grief. I shall no longer watch you introduce your Master's teachings to the people and preach the gospel with a historian's eye for the truth. And when I enumerate the troubles of my anxious life, you are not there with me to beguile the long hours with your stories.

Those places, too, that remind us of him, the places you and I used to visit together, they can only be seen by my eyes now. Whether Lucifer rises bright from wealthy India [240] or sinks darkling into the western sea, I contemplate them by myself on bended knee, weeping bitter tears. "This place brings back memories of our pain. Here I can still see the sad traces of him who was killed, the bloody footprints of that innocent man. Here he stood; there he fell. There is the stone where his strength forsook him. Here is the spot where I was struck down as he was suffering. This is the high cross that bore him between the other two crosses. Here his dead body lay wrapped in a clean linen shroud. Here that dearest of men revived me from a swoon, [250] the man now unjustly exiled to the Aegean Sea."

As I meditate like this, your image is always with me, even though you are many miles distant from here. Of course I myself never leave the environs of Jerusalem in body. My mind, however, enters the heavens as well as the region where you live. In an instant my roving mind journeys to wherever it pleases and flies

72=O4ʳ   Haec igitur toties ad te spatiatur et errat
           Carceris haec extra testea claustra sui.
           Ipsa domo vidua, tacito secreta recessu,
260   Dum licet in iustas solvimus ora preces.
           Interdum repeto veterum presagia vatum,
           In curas quondam carmina scripta meas.
           Vix quantum natura cibi potusque requirit,
           Cruda tamen famula sumimus illa manu.
265   Frigidiora famem sedant sata pauperis horti,
           Pura fere siccam diluit unda sitim.
           Rara mihi est etiam reliqui frequentia vulgi,
           Quam quarum satis est vita probata tibi.
           Heae quoque sunt nostrae quod possunt esse senectae;
270   Flos prior aetatis decidit ille meae.
           Auferor inque dies venientibus opprimor annis.
           Plena quater vitae sunt tria lustra meae.
           Nec mihi scire licet quid agas, charissime rerum.
           Credentes etiam fallere fama solet.
275   Nullaque quae possit de te tot euntibus annis
           Dicere quantillum littera visa mihi est.
           Non tamen hoc miror, tot enim maria inter utrumque
           Forsitan ingratae causa fuere morae.
O4ᵛ   At tibi, qui nostro saepe est in amore minister,
280   Omnia mandatis fert mihi plena tuis.
           Hinc licet agnoscam quid agas, tamen omnia vellem
           Plenius et digitis scripta videre tuis.
           Ille etiam variis te nunc animalia formis
           Rettulit obscuro composuisse stilo,
285   Praetextu, dictante Deo, mysteria miro,
           Omnia supremos ante videnda dies.
           Talia non potuit melius praedicere quisquam.
           Cognita sunt soli tanta futura Deo.
           Tu vero, ex reliquis scribarum proximus illi,
290   Sydera sublimi vertice summa feris,
           Sicut ubi radios visu penetravit acuto
           Prima avium caelo proxima saepe volat.
           Scrinia vidisti cordis secreta profundi,
           Mystica quo nobis caena peracta loco est.

---

260 Dum — solvimus *A*: In meritas solvo dum licet *BO*; preces *BO*: praeces *A*.   262 quondam *A*: olim *BO*.   263–66 Vix — sitim. *A*: *om. BO*.   267 frequentia *A*: congressio *BO*.   268 tibi *A*: mihi *BO*.   276 Dicere — littera *A*: Littera vel minimum dicere *BO*.   277 Non *A*: Nec *BO*.   283–89 Ille etiam — illi, *A*: Interea loquitur pro te tua littera nobis, / Orbi, non soli littera scripta mihi, / Littera quae vestri testatur gesta Magistri / Usque sub extremum non peritura diem. / Quo sane mortale nihil meditare libello; *BO*.   293 Scrinia — profundi *A*: Abdita vidisti divinae scrinia mentis *BO*.

about untrammeled and free. This, then, is how it travels to you so often, as it roams outside the confines of its clayey prison.

I myself, hidden in a quiet recess of my lonesome house, [260] utter righteous prayers as long as I still can. From time to time I reread the prophecies of the old seers, songs written long ago in reference to my cares. Of food and drink I take barely as much as nature requires. I do force myself to eat raw vegetables and fruits, however. The colder plants in my poor garden serve to still my hunger;[12] pure water slakes my all but burning thirst. Only rarely do I associate with other people, those women excepted of whose life you approve. They also do everything they can for me in my old age, [270] the flower of my youth having long since wilted. I am being carried away and from day to day feel more oppressed by the onrushing years. After all, I have completed my sixth decade already.

What are you doing, dearest of men? I wish I knew for sure, seeing that rumor has a habit of deceiving even those who believe it. In all the passing years I have never yet received a letter that could tell me the least little bit about you. That is no wonder, of course. Indeed, the unwelcome delay may well have been due to the many seas that stretch out between us. But your messenger, through whom we often keep in touch, [280] does give me all your instructions. Although I know from him what you are doing, I should still like to see everything in more detail and written with your own hand.

Just now he told to me that you have composed a book in an obscure style with multifarious living beings, mysteries inspired by God and cloaked in wondrous images, revealing all the things that are to be seen before the Last Day. No one could predict such happenings better than you. Those tremendous events of the future are known only to God. Truly, since you are closer to him than any of the other evangelists, [290] you strike the topmost stars with your uplifted head, as when the king of birds, penetrating the sun's beams with acute vision, often flies next to heaven's gate.[13] For there, where the mystic supper was celebrated for us, you gazed into the secret shrine of his unfathomable heart.[14]

---

[12]Eating such "cold" vegetables as lettuce was thought to keep erotic desires in check and is thus appropriate to the Virgin. For this notion see *Buc.* 6.54–55, n.

[13]John is traditionally symbolized as the high-flying, keen-eyed eagle.

[14]At the Last Supper, John was closest to Jesus. It was to him that Jesus revealed his betrayer Judas: cf. John 13.23–26.

295   Illa utinam nobis non ultima caena fuisset,
        Aut esset propera morte sequta mihi!
    Sed tamen hoc melius cessit populoque redempto
        Et quibus est recto tramite cura sequi.
    Differri haud decuit quod opus restabat agendum.
300   Qua bona sit, causa nostra querela caret.

73=O5ʳ   Tu si quando potes moestam solabere matrem,
        Qur vacat officio dextera fida suo?
    Damna fer interea sortis patienter iniquae.
        Iam patria foelix divite civis eris.
305   Ipsa feram placide superantis taedia vitae,
        Quam precor ut paucis, qui dedit, ille ferat

---

296 sequta *AB*: peracta *O*.   **297** melius cessit *A*: cessit melius *BO*.   **299** Differri *BO*: Differre *A*; decuit *AB*: potuit *O*.   ***Post* 304** *add. BO*: Nec dubita post paulo Ephesum tua templa redibis, / Donec ab his curis vivus ad astra voles.   **305** placide *A*: placidae *BO*.

If only that had not been the last supper for us, or that I could have died soon after! All the same, it has turned out better this way, both for the redemption of humankind and for all those eager to follow on the right track. It would not have been right to defer the work that still needed to be done. [300] However good it may make me feel, my lament is ground-less. If ever you get a chance, do console the grief-worn mother. Why does your faithful hand shirk its duty?

In the meantime, patiently endure the strokes of bad for-tune. It will not be long before you are happily back in your prosperous hometown.[15] I myself shall quietly bear the weariness of my remaining days, but pray that he who gave me life may shortly take it away.

---

[15]In the same year that John was sent to Patmos, the emperor who had exiled him was killed on account of his excessive cruelty. Because all his edicts were revoked, John was allowed to return with honor to Ephesus. See *Leg. aurea* 9.18–20.

17   URSULA AETHEREO

Quod tibi non laeto mea venit epistola vultu,
  Exilio similis debuit esse meo.
Sera quidem venit, nec enim quo tempore primum
  Debuit, ut nunc es, verus amator eras.
5   Corpore tum vobis quod eram formosa petebar,
  Cura sed aeternae nulla salutis erat.
Nunc vetera exutus patrii contagia morbi,
  Quem petis, es nostro dignus amore frui.
Falsa deum linquens, Christi sacra vera professus,
10   Militiae debes signa movere novae.
Militia est servire Deo suprema triformi;
  Altera quos capiunt perdere castra solent.
Pessima liquisti, foeliciter optima tentas.
  Hec vitam pariunt arma, sed ista necem.
15   Patria nunc sequeris, nunc signa aliena refutas;
  Patria te decuit, non aliena sequi.
Et quia magnorum satus es de sanguine regum,
  Conveniunt armis regia signa tuis.
Non decet infami regem servire tyranno;
20   Hac quoque tu nuper labe notatus eras.
Addere rex debet partis nova signa tropheis.
  Hoc facis, hanc laudem tu quoque habere studes.
Formosum quoque te donis iuvenilibus aiunt.
  Nunc potes ex omni parte placere mihi!
25   Aevi flore decens, nunc mente decentior ipsa,
  Taliter in thalamos dignus es ire meos.
Tunc quoque dignus eras fortunae dotibus altae,
  Sed nocuit verum non coluisse Deum.
Par fortuna fuit, vitae professio dispar;
30   Phas erat hanc illi praeposuisse mihi.
Regis uterque genus, non legis uterque probatae.
  Hoc voluit, iungi non tulit illa duos.
At genus in sacram concessit nobile legem.
  Ille fuit verbis non simulatus amor!

O5ᵛ

Her. Chr. 17.   *A: om. BO.*

---

[1]Ursula was the daughter of a Christian king in Britain. Hoping to remain a virgin, she attempted to avoid marriage to the pagan Prince Ethereus of England by asking him for a delay of three years. Ethereus was furthermore to provide her with 11,000 virgins and a fleet of eleven ships. During their absence the prince was to be baptized and instructed in the faith. When the lovestruck young man consented to all these conditions, St. Ursula and her companions spent the next three years traversing the seven seas. At length the winds forced them to sail up the Rhine to Cologne and Basel.

17   URSULA TO ETHEREUS[1]

If my letter has an unhappy look about it when it reaches you,[2] it
is because it mirrors my exiled state, as it should. It has been long
in coming, I admit, for earlier on you were not, as you are now, a
lover in the true sense of the word. At that time you wooed me
because I appeared beautiful to you in body, but you had no concern for eternal salvation. Now that you are free from the old
contagion of your ancestral paganism, you are worthy of enjoying my love, which you seek. Having abandoned the false cults of
the gods and confessed the true religion of Christ, [10] you
should advance the banners of your new army. Your highest mission is to serve the triform God; the adversary's camp makes it a
practice to destroy those it ensnares. You have turned your back
on the worst and successfully seek the best. This kind of warfare
produces life; but the other one, death. Now you follow the banners of your fatherland and oppose the enemy's. You ought
indeed to be fighting for your fatherland, not against it. And
because you are sprung from the blood of great kings, your
troops deserve a royal ensign. It is not right for a king to be the
thrall of an infamous tyrant. [20] Not so long ago you were also
tainted with that stigma. A king ought to be adding new banners
to the trophies already won. You are doing that now; you are
striving to win this honor too.

   I am told you are also handsome and blessed with the gifts
of youth. Now you can please me in every way! Attractive in the
flower of youth, now even more attractive in spirit: like this you
are truly worthy of entering my chambers. You were worthy of it
then too by virtue of your high birth. What hurt you, however,
was that you did not worship the true God. We were equal in
fortune, unequal in our faith. [30] I was morally bound to prefer
the latter to the former. What we had in common was royal
birth, not the Law of God. The former wished, the latter did not
allow, us two to be joined in wedlock. But your noble stock has
since merged with holy religion. Your love was not just simulated
with words!

Thence they crossed the Alps and traveled to Rome. Returning to Cologne with Pope Cyriacus and
others, they were martyred by the Huns. Ethereus, who meanwhile had become king after the death
of his father, was told in a vision to join his bride in Cologne. There he too received the crown of
martyrdom. See *Leg. aurea* 154; *VL* 10, cols. 131–40.

   The letter was excised from the 1532/39 version, in part no doubt because the legend was too extravagant for Protestant tastes, in part also because of its discursive structure and rather patronizing tone.

   [2]Ursula's letter has an unhappy look about it because it is written in elegiacs, the verses of lament.
Cf. Hor. *Ars* 75; Ov. *Am.* 3.9.3–4; *Ep.* 15.5–8; Eob. *Her. Chr.* 20.89–92.

35 Iam mihi prisca suos aetas non iactet amantes.
    Ignibus his nostris fabula nulla subest.
Talem sponte mea potui petiisse maritum,
    Vix etiam tali coniuge digna fui.

74=O6ʳ

Seu mihi quis veterum fata improba narrat amantum,
40   Omnia sunt genii crimine plena mali.
Phyllidas, Hermionas, Bryseidas, Hypsyphylasque,
    Heu, solum miseras corpus amasse liquet.
Dumque uni placuisse student, fraudantur utroque.
    Error is est nulla parte probandus amor.
45 Aspice tot mortes stultique pericula amoris,
    Parsque sit ex illis si qua beata, vide.
Dulcibus hi flammis aegras caluere medullas,
    Et studium miseri corporis omne fuit.
Nunc miserae aeternos animae torquentur ad ignes;
50   Qui rogus hic illos torruit umbra fuit.
Credidit Elisium demens et stulta vetustas.
    Hei mihi, pro Elisio qualia prata ferunt?
Quae iuvat hic brevis est adeoque incerta voluptas;
    Quae nocet aeternum paena tenaxque manet.
55 Tempora diffugiunt, fugiunt simul omnia in illis,
    Nosque repercussi murmuris aura sumus.
Tam cito desinimus quam fulguris umbra chorusci.
    I nunc, regna tene, sceptra fer, arma move!
Omnia sunt ventis levibusque simillima plumis,

O6ᵛ
60   Quas quocunque volet quaelibet aura rapit.
Non est humanis tutum confidere rebus.
    Saepius ecce etiam maxima, prima cadunt.
Dic, ubi Troia potens Cadmaeaque maenia Thebae?
    Clausit in aeternos una favilla dies.
65 Vos quoque Cecropiae prorsus cecidistis Athenae
    Factaque presenti maenia sacra Deo.
Iam quoque, cunctarum caput et domina unica rerum,
    Relliquias numerat Martia Rhoma suas.
Quid tuti superesse potest ubi tanta premuntur
70   Magnaque tam parvo tempore regna cadunt?
Est quoque qui formae stultus confidit inani
    Et putat hunc florem posse virere diu.
Hic miser in sola tabescit imagine vultus.
    Heu heu, quam multos iste fefellit amor!
75 Omnia si numeres emensi saecula mundi,
    Invenies preter nomina pauca nihil.

---

60 quaelibet *scripsi*: quelibet **A**.   **65** Cecropiae *scripsi*: Crecopiae **A**.   **68** numerat **A** (*in erratis*):
munerat **A** (*in textu*).

Now I don't want to hear antiquity bragging about its lovers. There is nothing fictitious about this ardor of ours. It was only natural for me to seek a husband such as you. At the same time I was hardly worthy of such a bridegroom. Or if anyone were to tell me about the shameless way those ancient lovers lived and died, [40] I see them all filled with the crime of their evil genius. Heartbroken heroines like Phyllis, Hermione, Briseis, and Hypsipyle, alas, obviously loved nothing more than the body.[3] And as they strove to please the one, they cheated themselves out of both.[4] This kind of love is a delusion unworthy of respect. Look at all the deaths, all the perils brought on by foolish passion, and see if there is even a bit of happiness in lovers like them. They allowed their weary marrow to burn with the sweet flames of lust, and all their efforts went to satisfy the miserable body. Now their wretched souls are suffering torments in the eternal fires. [50] The pyre that burned them here was a mere shadow. Antiquity, in its madness, foolishly believed in an Elysium. Dear me, what kind of meadows did they propose as their Elysium? The pleasure that charms us here is fleeting and highly uncertain; the punishment inflicted on us will continue forever and ever. Time flies, all things fly away with time, and we are but a fast-fading echo. We end as quickly as the shadow from a flash of lightning. So go ahead, hold sway, bear a scepter, take up arms! All those things are best compared to the winds or the downy feathers [60] that a breeze carries off wherever it pleases. It is not safe to put our trust in things human. Very often even the greatest and finest fall into ruin. Tell me, where is mighty Troy? Where is the citadel of Thebes that Cadmus founded? One and the same ash has buried them for all eternity. Cecropian Athens, too, has totally collapsed, as has the city hallowed by God's presence.[5] Even the Rome of Mars — the head and sole mistress of the entire world — now counts up her relics. What can survive unscathed, when such mighty empires decline and [70] and fall in so little time?

No less foolish are they who put their trust in the vanity of outward beauty and think that this flower can go on blooming for long. Now there is a wretch, the man who pines away over good looks alone! Alas, alas, how many have been deceived by this kind of love! If you go back through all the epochs of world history, you will find nothing but a handful of famous names.

---

[3]The women mentioned by St. Ursula are all heroines in Ovid's *Epistulae heroidum*. For Phyllis, see Ov. *Ep.* 2; for Hermione, see *Ep.* 8; for Briseis, see *Ep.* 3; and for Hypsipyle, see *Ep.* 6.
[4]Both body and soul.
[5]Jerusalem.

Adde quod et quaedam celebrantur nomina quorum
    Perpes in infernis exulat umbra locis.
Te quoque falsus amor laqueo cepisset eodem,
80   Ni tibi favisset verus et alter amor.
Ille tuum nostro succendit pectus amore,
75=P1ʳ   Ut non desipias, sed sapienter ames.
Desipit omnis amans formam qui spectat inanem.
    Hanc aliquid preter qui petit, ille sapit.
85 Is tibi quae pateris dulcissima vulnera fecit,
    Is tua caelesti pectora fixit acu.
Questus eras, nondum lustrali ex fonte renatus,
    Quanta tibi Veneris moverit arma puer.
Verum est ille puer Veneris — non cuius ad aras
90   Idalii nemoris numen adorat amans,
Ille puer quem foeta Deo Spiramine mater
    Illaeso peperit casta pudore Venus.
Ille Cupido fuit qui te cupere optima fecit;
    Frivola gentilis taela Cupido iacit.
95 Nomine reque puer satus Oceanitide fertur,
    Noster at ex nullo tempore nomen habet.
Caeculus ille homines nullo discrimine laedit;
    Hic videt et vero lumine cuncta notat.
Sed quae stulta Deum dementia comparet umbrae? —
100   Quod nihil est dici si tamen umbra potest!
Ipsa Venus nihil est, nihil est puer ille Cupido,
    At Deus est aliquid, solus et ipse Deus.
Quis Deus ille, tenes iampridem. Dicere quid sit,
P1ᵛ   Non humiles elegi, lingua nec ulla potest.
105 Hunc cepta venerare fide. Sic omine fausto
    Ibis in amplexus, dignior ipse, meos.
Sic spatiosa tuis subiecta Britannia sceptris
    Innumerabilibus serviat aucta bonis;
Sic te conspiciat patria virtute potentem
110   Supremum in senium laetus uterque parens.
Eiice si qua tuo superant in pectore, quae te
    Errati veteris admonuisse queant.
Numinis antiqui plenos, tua damna, libellos
    Vindice peccati fortiter igne crema,
115 Aut ita conserva ne sis incautus in illis.
    Non legisse malum, sed didicisse nocet.
Cernis Arachne et apis florem scrutantur eundem.
    Haec dulces succos, illa venena bibit.
Sic qui blanda legunt saecli monumenta vetusti
120   Non omnes una conditione legunt.

86 pectora *scripsi*: pectore *A*.   **87** Questus *scripsi*: Quaestus *A*.

Add to this that some of these names are celebrated even though their shades are exiled forever in the underworld. False love would have caught you too in that very same snare, [80] had not the other, true love smiled on you. It was the latter that inflamed your breast with yearning for me, so that you would not lack understanding, but might love wisely. Foolish is every lover who looks only at transitory beauty. Wise is he who pursues something beyond that. This is the love that inflicted the sweetest wounds you bear. This is the love that pierced your breast with a celestial dart.

Before you were reborn in the baptismal font, you used to complain how much Venus' son was besetting you with his arrows. Yes, it was Venus' son — not the god whose [90] power the lover worships at the altars in the Idalian grove, but the boy whom his mother, chaste Venus pregnant with God the Spirit, brought into the world with her virginity unscathed. He was the Cupid who instilled in you a cupidity for the very best. Pagan Cupid only shoots frivolous arrows. In name and deed this boy is reputed to be the son of the ocean-born goddess. Ours, on the other hand, bears his name from all eternity. The former, being blind, wounds everybody indiscriminately. The latter, being clearsighted, observes all things with an unfailing eye.

But who in his right mind wants to compare God with a shadow? — [100] if indeed you can call something nonexistent a shadow! Venus herself is a nothing, and so is that son of hers, Cupid; but God is something, the one and only God. Who this God is, you have grasped long since. What he is, no humble elegiacs, no tongue can say. Continue to revere him faithfully. That will augur well for our marriage when you, yourself more worthy, come into my arms. So may spacious Britain, blessed with countless goods, be subject to your scepter and serve you. So may both your parents, watching you grow mighty with inborn virtue, [110] remain happy to the end of their days.

Purge your heart of anything that could remind you of the ancient error. Books that are full of the old paganism should be burned, for they are bound to harm your soul. Throw them resolutely into the sin-avenging fire, or keep them in such a way that you will not be caught off guard by their contents. What hurts is not the reading, but the learning of evil. You see the spider and the bee searching one and the same flower. The latter imbibes sweet juices, the former, poisons. Similarly, those who read the lovely writings of antiquity [120] do not all read them on the same terms.

Alter ut abiiciat quod non decet inspicit; alter,
　Quamvis non deceat quod iuvat, illud agat.
At sapiens aequa consyderat omnia lance
　Et bona mellificae colligit instar apis
125　Quae velut in Siculae consedit vallibus Hiblae,

　Inter odoratae milia multa rosae
Circuit et longo tot praeterit ordine flores
　Et nisi quae fuerint optima nulla legit.
Tu quoque, si quid amas molles tetigisse libellos,
130　Elige quaeque iuvant, eiice quaeque nocent.
Attigeris veterum mendacia turpia vatum,
　Utque leges praesens virus habere puta.
Nulla tibi hic lachrymas moveat Babilonia Thysbe,
　Non aliquo vates numine iussa mori.
135　Phyllida nec doleas aliquam periisse relictam,
　Non quam desertam barbara Naxos habet.
Nulla tibi placeat vetito quae fratris amore
　Arserit aut duro fregerit ense latus.
Non Paridem, non Aeaciden tibi finge, nec illum
140　Qui data Nessaea morte venena tulit.
Non aliquis pronas tibi ducat Acontius aures.
　Quisquis erit sine te Protesilaus amet.
Neu tibi sit mirum tumidis Leander in undis,
　Si natet et patrio Sesta puella freto.
145　Aspice nos toto iactatas aequore necdum
　In portu certam composuisse ratem.
Tertius aestivum Phoebus iam colligit ignem,

　Donec in his exul turba vagamur aquis.
Causa amor est, qui nos patria de sede quietas
150　Aegit et immensos iussit obire sinus.
Nec nos privato succendimur igne, sed auget
　Publica Christicolum commoda noster amor.
Ipsa nec immensum propero tibi sola per aequor;
　Mille quidem subsunt milia dena meo.
155　Ille puellarum numerus mea iussa sequentum
　Auspitio classis militat ista tuo.
I nunc et veteres nobis age confer amantes!
　I nunc et veri nomen amantis habe!

130 eiice *scripsi*: euce **A**.

The one examines books with a mind to reject the unseemly; the other, unseemly though it may be, acts out what he likes. But the wise man weighs all things on balanced scales and selects only the good, much like the honeybee that settles in the valleys of Sicilian Hybla, for example, and makes the rounds among innumerable fragrant roses and passes up so many flowers, one after the other, and chooses none but the very best. You too, if you have a hankering for love poetry, [130] pick out what is useful, throw out what is noxious. As you skim through the disgraceful lies of the old poets, keep telling yourself while you read that they contain potent venom. Don't let some Thisbe of Babylon move you to tears here, no poetess dying at the behest of some god.[6] Don't be grieved at the death of some abandoned Phyllis or at a girl left stranded in barbarous Naxos.[7] Don't sympathize with anyone who burns with forbidden love for her brother or plunges the cruel sword into her side.[8] Don't picture Paris or Achilles to yourself, nor the one [140] who was poisoned with Nessus' blood.[9] Don't let some Acontius incline your ears. Whoever he is, let Protesilaus love without you. Also don't marvel at Leander swimming in the swollen waves or at the girl from Sestos as she drifts in the strait near her home.[10]

Rather, keep your eyes on us, stormtossed as we are on all the seas, for even now we have not found a permanent harbor. The sun is gathering the heat of summer for the third time already since we exiled maidens began roaming these waters. The reason is love. Love drove us from the peace and quiet of our homeland [150] and commanded us to wander over the boundless deep. It is not some private flame that has set us on fire. This love of ours, rather, promotes the public weal of Christianity. As I eagerly hurry over the immense sea for your sake, I am by no means sailing alone. In fact, I have eleven thousand at my command. This throng of followers, this army of maidens is serving under your generalship. Go ahead, come on, compare us with the ancient lovers! Go ahead, live up to your reputation as a true lover! But

[6]The tragic tale of Pyramus and Thisbe is told in Ov. *Met.* 4.55–166. The poetess Sappho committed suicide after her lover Phaon deserted her: see Ov. *Ep.* 15.

[7]For the story of Phyllis' unhappy love for Demophoon, see Ov. *Ep.* 2. Ariadne was left behind by Theseus on the island of Naxos: see Ov. *Ep.* 10.

[8]Having borne a son by her own brother, Canace was forced by her father to commit suicide by the sword: see Ov. *Ep.* 11. Another of Ovid's heroines who committed suicide was Dido: see Ov. *Ep.* 7.

[9]Paris' passion for Helen is told in Ov. *Ep.* 16 and 17. For Achilles and Briseis, see Ov. *Ep.* 3. The hero "poisoned with Nessus' blood" is Hercules. Hoping to regain his love, Hercules' wife Deïanira sent him a cloak soaked in the poisoned blood of the centaur Nessus: see Ov. *Ep.* 9.

[10]Acontius assiduously wooed Cydippe: see Ov. *Ep.* 20 and 21. Laodamia worried about her husband Protesilaus as he set out for the Trojan War: see Ov. *Ep.* 13. And Leander drowned while swimming the Hellespont to see his lover Hero. Thereupon she too threw herself into the waves: see Ov. *Ep.* 18 and 19.

Et tu dum positis forsan teris ocia curis
160   Et nostro tandem fessus amore iaces,
Nos maria emensae Christi nova signa movemus;
    Ostendunt rubram candida vela crucem.
His immensa quidem sulcavimus aequora signis,
    Utraque ab immoto quae videt Ursa polo,
165 Qua iacet aeternis Hybernia foeta pruinis
    Vicina et patriae prospicit arva tuae.
Illis terdenas praevenimus Orchadas armis,
    Ultima qua Boreae flatibus unda stupet,
Regnaque ab immani quondam notissima Gottho
77 = P3ʳ   170   Iunctaque cum Codano Balthica stagna sinu
Et qua prata humiles tondent pecorosa Suedi
    Norvegamque frequens verberat aequor humum.
Ipsa etiam visa est celeri prevecta carina
    Quae modo non priscum Dacia nomen habet.
175 Vidimus et plures ignota per aequora terras,
    Dum natat incertis fluctibus acta ratis.
Non semel illustres circum, tua regna, Britannos
    Venimus et patrii non bene culta Scoti.
Sepe tuas alto speculata ex gurgite terras,
180   "Illa meum," dixi, "littora sydus habent!"
Saepe rates aliqua potuisti ex arce videre
    Quisque abeant terris quaerere quasve petant
Mirarique novas per linthea picta figuras.
    Salvatae his nostrae saepe fuere rates,
185 Seu mare turbabat pluviis niger ymbribus Auster
    Sive est horrisono quassa procella Noto
Seu nubes caelo contraxit caecias atro
    Seu Boream contra, Caure, malignus eras.
Denique quaecunque est cursu conspecta trienni,
190   Tempestas harum victa resedit ope.
Nec mirum, si vincat aquas! Quae Tartara vicit,
P3ᵛ   Crux quam perdidimus reddidit alma diem.
Iveris adversos hac tu signatus in hostes,
    Causa est quam timeas nulla futura tibi.
195 Hac igitur pelagique minas caelique maligni
    Vicimus et motus difficilesque vias.

while you, setting your cares aside, can perhaps take your ease
[160] and, worn out with love for me, lie down to sleep at last,
we sail the seas and carry the new banners of Christ, for our white
sails display a red cross.[11]

Under these ensigns, indeed, we have plowed the vast seas
on which the Great and Little Bear gaze down from the motion-
less pole, there where Hibernia lies teeming with eternal snows
and looks over at the nearby fields of your homeland. Armed
with these crosses we have sailed past the thirty Orkneys to
where the northernmost waters congeal under Boreas' blasts. We
have voyaged to the realms that in former times were best known
for the savage Goths[12] [170] and to where the Baltic Sea is joined
to the Kattegat, where the stocky Swedes mow their cattle-rich
meadows and the sea incessantly lashes the Norwegian coast.
Passing by in our swift ships, we also saw Dacia — not the
Roman province of that name, but the modern Denmark.[13] We
saw many other lands too, as our ships, driven by the ever-
changing currents, floated about over strange seas. We have
repeatedly rounded your famed kingdom of Britain and the ill-
cultivated lands of my native Scotland. Often, descrying your
lands from the high seas, [180] I would shout, "That shoreline
harbors my star!" Often you might see our ships from the top of
some castle and ask yourself what country they came from and
where they were making for and marvel at the new symbols
emblazoned on their sails.

It is these symbols that often saved our ships from disaster,
whether the black southwester stirred up the sea with torrents of
rain or the howling south whipped itself into a frenzy or the
northeaster piled up clouds in the murky sky or the northwester
brawled with the north wind. In short, every tempest that we saw
on our three-year voyage [190] settled down when confronted
with the power of the cross. No wonder it conquered the billows!
The life-giving cross, which conquered Tartarus, gave back the
light we had lost. If you carry this ensign against the enemy lines,
you will never have reason to fear defeat. With its help, therefore,
we overcame the threats of the malignant sea and sky, the storms
and difficult passages.

[11]The scarlet cross on a white background is the cross of St. George. Since George did not
become the patron saint of England until the later Middle Ages, Eobanus' allusion is an anachronism.
[12]The reputed homeland of the Goths was southern Scandinavia. See Jordanes, *De origine
actibusque Getarum* 3–4 (par. 16–25); Aen. Silv. *Europa* 29 (par. 96).
[13]In antiquity the name *Dacia* referred to a Roman province north of the Danube. In the later
Middle Ages it was regularly confused with *Dania* (Denmark). We are thus dealing here with another
anachronism.

Nunc, ita seu fatis acti seu numine divum,
    Nostra magis tuto est anchora fixa solo.
Eiectas fido suscepit Gallia portu;
200   Teutona succedens Rhenus in arva tulit.
Venimus Agrippae Zephyris melioribus urbem.
    Hic aliquis superum talia verba dabat:
"I, pete Rhomanas, Petreia limina, sedes,
    Ursula, virginea te comitante manu.
205   Credentes illic lustralibus abluet undis,
    Qui sacra Cyriacus maxima praesul habet.
En decet ut Christo duce te sub rege merentes
    Te duce sub Christo praemia digna ferant."
Plura quidem dixit, quae si volet ipse loquemur,
210   Cum simul herebunt brachia nostra tuis.
Inde igitur placido delatas flumine Rheni
    Accepit portu nos Basilaea suo.
Panthulus huic illo praesedit episcopus urbi

78=P4^r   Tempore, vir populis relligione pater.
215   Qui nunc Rhomulidum nobiscum venit ad arces;
    Egimus hoc totum turba pedestris iter.
Servat adhuc nostras pugnax Germania puppes,
    Regia qua Graecum moenia nomen habent.
Et iam clausa semel novat altera cornua Phoebe,
220   Advena dum sancta classis in urbe sumus.
Confluit externum diverso vulgus ab orbe,
    Nostraque non modicae castra sequuntur opes,
Ipse sed ante alios caelestis ianitor aulae
    (Multa suum sequitur tonsa corona ducem)
225   Ipsaque Trinacriae princeps Gerasina potentis
    Filia quam sequitur cum tribus hisque soror.
Sanguinis haec nostri pars est fideique sodalis;
    Ipse quoque est nostro presul ab orbe genus.
His ducibus sociisque viae tibi cepta subimus,
230   Cepta sub extremos usque ferenda dies.
Tu modo, noster amor, iuvenum decus, aethere dignus,
    Aethereo nomen sis memor esse tibi.
Ardorem referunt tua nomina. Scilicet ergo
    Ipse mei certe pectoris ardor eras!
235   Tam longe absentem potuisti exurere amantem,
P4^v   Dum solito arderes tu quoque ab igne magis.
Esse igitur praesta dignum cognomine caelo,
    Causaque sit potior nominis inde tui.
Fallentes pudeat divos coluisse tot annos,
240   Isse per aethereo Tartara cassa die.

Now, whether driven like this by fate or by the power of heaven, we have weighed anchor in the safety of a port. Gaul gave us outcasts shelter in a secure harborage. [200] Thereafter the Rhine bore us to the fields of Germany. With favoring breezes we reached Cologne, where one of the celestials instructed me: "Go, Ursula, and take your band of virgins to St. Peter's at Rome. There the head of Christendom, Pope Cyriacus, will wash the believers in baptismal water. Lo, it is fitting that those who serve under Christ's kingship and your command should, under your leadership and Christ's, obtain the reward they deserve." He had even more to say. God willing, I shall tell you about that myself, [210] as soon as my arms are entwined with yours.

Well then, from there the Rhine River bore us gently to Basel, where we found a welcome harbor. Panthulus, a saintly man who is a father to his people, was the city's bishop at that time. He now accompanied us to the hills of Rome, a journey we completed entirely on foot. Warlike Germany still watches over our ships in that "Queen City" with the Greek name.[14]

For the second time Phoebe has filled out her once-closed horns with light [220] since we foreign maidens arrived in the holy city. People have been converging on us from distant countries all over the world. Indeed, a huge army of them has joined our camp, above all the doorkeeper of the heavenly court (a great many tonsured priests are following their leader) as well as Gerasina, Queen of mighty Sicily, accompanied by her four daughters. Related to me by blood, she is also a companion in the faith. The pope himself also hails from our part of the world. With these people as my guides and wayfaring companions I am undertaking this enterprise for your sake, [230] an enterprise that will be celebrated to the end of time. You, my love, most handsome of youths, worthy of the ether, do remember to live up to your name *Ethereus*.

Your name rekindles my ardor. It is obvious, then, that you are indeed the one great fire in my heart! You were able to set your lover ablaze at such a great distance, while you too burn with a hotter flame than usual. So prove yourself worthy of your heavenly name, and let this henceforth be a better reason for bearing that name of yours. You should feel shame at having worshiped the false gods for so many years, [240] at having walked in Tartarean darkness, far from the ethereal light. You

---

[14]The name Basel comes from the fourth-century Roman fortification Basilia (Greek for "queen").

Ad veri placeat cultum venisse Tonantis.
Fulmina mentita non iacit ille manu.
Hic neque thure aliquo gaudet neque pinguibus extis;
Gratior huic animo est hostia nulla pio.
245 Hunc supplex accede, illum reverenter adora.
Hunc sequere, observa, dilige, quaere, cole.
Doctus es ille tibi qua sit ratione colendus.
Non labor est. Opta posse placere, places.
Hunc ubi supplicibus placasse videbere votis,
250 Mente tuae memori nomen amantis habe.
Atque utinam, "Errantis," dicas, "miserere puellae,
Maxime, nunc primum cognite, Dive, mihi.
Dive, ratem serva, ventos emitte faventeis,
Quam petit ut salvo remige tangat humum."
255 Sic ubi solenni fueris de more precatus,
Sacra vide mystae saepe precantis idem.
Ipsa quoque ut valeas pro te noctesque diesque
79=P5ʳ   Debita sollicito pectore vota fero.
Utque magis credas, sancta properamus ab urbe
260 Teutonicique iterum quaerimus arva soli.
Omnia tuta satis speramus ubique futura,
Tu modo, tu nobis, Rhene, fidelis eas.
Sanguine te gaudere ferunt quo saepius isse
Diceris et multos subrubuisse dies.
265 Parte tui vereor ne sis lesurus amantes:
Hunnus ad Agrippae maenia pugnat atrox.
Quicquid erit, tentanda via est. Non vulnera tanti,
Mors quoque non tanti est, segnis ut esse velim.
Ante ego sub bibula Rheni tumulabor arena,
270 Quam te non propter sit mihi velle mori.
Sed neque despera. Per tanta pericula salvas
Qui tulit, hac etiam sorte levare potest.
Sive igitur nos fata manent seu vita superstes,
Consulet ille mihi, consulet ille tibi.

should be pleased that you have come to worship the true
Thunderer. That God of ours does not hurl thunderbolts with
feigned hand. He delights neither in incense nor in fatty flesh.
No offering is so dear to him as a devout heart. Approach him
in a spirit of humility; adore him with reverence. Him you
should follow, honor, love, seek, worship. You know how he
likes to be worshiped. It is not difficult. Just wishing to please
will please him.

When you feel you have placated him with humble prayers,
[250] always keep the name of your beloved in mind. How I
wish you would say: "Have pity on the wandering maiden,
O Supreme Deity, whom I have just now gotten to know. God,
watch over her ship, send fair winds, so that she and her crew
may safely reach the land she is making for." After praying like
this with due solemnity, see to it that a priest keeps on reciting
the same prayer in church. I too offer a prayer for your welfare
night and day, with an anxious heart, for you deserve no less
from me. And to show you that I am as good as my word: we are
hastening away from the holy city [260] and are once more
headed for the fields of Germany. We expect our voyage to be
quite safe throughout, provided that you, Rhine, do not turn
against us. They say you revel in gore and quite often run red
with blood for days on end. There is one part of you where I fear
you may harm us lovers: the ferocious Huns are fighting before
the walls of Cologne.

Whatever is in store for us, I must brave the perils. Wounds
do not mean that much to me; death too does not weigh so
heavily with me that I would want to be idle. I would sooner lie
buried in the thirsty sands of the Rhine [270] than refuse to die
for your sake. But do not despair. He who brought us unharmed
through such great dangers can also save us from this fate.
Therefore, whether it is death or survival that awaits us, he will
look after me, he will look after you.

18   ANASTASIA CHRISOGONO

Mittit Anastasia cui debuit ipsa salutem,
    Ipsam Chrisogono se quoque debet amans,
Hinc ubi Tyrrhenos viridis Palmaria fluctus
    Proiicit in portus, Rhomule Tybri, tuos.

P5ᵛ   5   Primus ab hoc nuper qui solvit littore navim,
    Illi quae legeres scripta ferenda dedi.
Qui nunc oppressa vix tutus in urbe moraris,
    Exulis oblitus nunquid es anne memor?
Nanque nec ulla tuae visa est mihi littera dextrae
10   Postquam proscriptam luna secunda videt.
Et mihi Caesaribus qui lege fugantur eadem,
    Qum rogo num valeas, dicere posse negant.
Ergone es ignotus patria, vir tantus, in urbe?
    Quis patres etiam posse latere putet?
15   Nec puto quod lateas — nisi te quoque publica falso
    Flebilis edicti crimine iura notent.
Non tamen hac latebras, certum est, ratione subisti.
    Contemptricem animam tu quoque mortis habes.
Vidisti cecidisse viros pro nomine Christi,
20   Questus idem toties non licuisse tibi.
Quinetiam nimia grassantes caede tyrannos
    Ausus es in medio carpere saepe Foro,
Cum tua vix meruit veniam venerabilis aetas,
    Praeda cruentatis ne raperere lupis.
25   Nec dubito retineris adhuc vitalibus auris.
    Non posset tantum fama tacere nefas.

80 = P6ʳ   Sed timeo ne tu quoque forte ubicumque locorum
    A patriis longe finibus exul agas.
Hoc timeo, cura haec miseram sine fine molestat,
30   Mole sub hac graviter nocte dieque premor.
Quod si vera timor meus arguit, heu quibus unquam,
    Heu quibus invenient te mea scripta locis?
Clausa brevi teneor spatio terraeque marisque;
    Non mihi praescripto solvere ab orbe licet.

Her. Chr. **18.**   **1–2** Mittit — amans *A*: Quam dare non potuit, cui debuit ipsa salutem, / Chrysogono infoelix optat Anastasia *BO*.   **3** Hinc *BO*: Hunc *A*.   **10** luna secunda *A*: tertia luna *BO*. **12** Qum *A*: Dum *BO*.   **17** hac — est, *A*: hac, certum est, latebras *BO*.   **21–24** Quinetiam — lupis. *A*: *om. BO*.   **25** adhuc *BO*: ad huc *A*.   **29** Hoc — molestat *A*: Hic timor, illa animum sine fine molestia turbat *BO*.   **30** graviter *A*: gravius *BO*.   **31** timor meus *A*: animi metus *BO*.

18   ANASTASIA TO CHRYSOGONUS[1]

The loving Anastasia sends Chrysogonus a wish for the salvation she herself owes to him. Him, to whom she owes her very being, she greets from here where verdant Palmaria deflects the Tyrrhenian waves into the mouth of the Roman Tiber. The first sailor to cast off from shore this morning will take the letter you are reading and deliver it for me.

Now that you yourself live on the edge of danger in the oppressed city, you have not forgotten me, have you? Or do you still remember that I am an exile? The fact is, I haven't seen a letter from your hand [10] since I was proscribed two months ago. And when I ask people exiled by the same imperial decree if you're in good health, they say they have no way of telling.

Can so important a man like you, then, be an unknown in his own hometown? Who ever thought that even the fathers could go into hiding? But I don't believe you're in hiding — unless the state court has falsely condemned you too on the basis of that lamentable edict. But this cannot be the reason you have gone into hiding, that is for sure. You too have the courage to scorn death. Whenever you saw men go to their deaths for the name of Christ, [20] you complained that martyrdom was passing you by. Indeed, you often rose up in the middle of the Forum and boldly attacked the tyrants' penchant for bloody persecution, even though your venerable old age offered you scant protection from being carried off yourself as a prey for those bloodthirsty wolves.

I have no doubt that you still draw the breath of life. Rumor could not possibly keep silent about so heinous a crime. Still, I fear that you too might be living in exile someplace far from your native land. This is my fear, this is what constantly worries me, poor soul, [30] this is the burden that weighs on my mind night and day. But if my fear turns out to be well-founded, alas, where on earth and in what kind of place will my letter find you?

I myself am kept confined in a small corner of land and sea; I am not allowed to leave this place of banishment. There is no

---

[1]St. Anastasia, the daughter of the Roman nobleman Praetextatus and his Christian wife Fausta, was married to the pagan Publius. When her adviser St. Chrysogonus was imprisoned under Emperor Diocletian (r. 284–305), the two continued to exchange letters. Anastasia herself was arrested by the prefect Dulcitius. Brought to the island of Palmaria together with 200 other virgins, she was bound to a stake and burned alive. Her companions were also martyred in various ways. St. Apollonia recovered Anastasia's remains and buried them. Chrysogonus was beheaded around the same time. See *Leg. aurea* 7 and 167.

In the 1532/39 version this letter is *Her.* 2.6.

35   Non est quo fugiam. Clausit ferus omnia Caesar;
  Imperat hic terris, imperat ille mari.
Libera dimittar nec lege coercear ulla,
  Iam mihi difficilis nulla futura via est.
Chrisogonum longis quaeram peregrina sub oris.
40 Afficient teneros nulla pericla pedes.
Arida non calidis prohibebit solibus aestas,
  Non premet infesto morbifer ore Canis.
Non retrahet pluvius mixtis Aquilonibus Auster,
  Nullaque Riphaeo frigore tristis hyems.
45   Per iuga, per saltus vadam rupesque fragosas
  Saxaque calloso vix adeunda pede.
Neve quis errantem possit novisse puellam,
  Ipsa mei cultus forma virilis erit.

P6ᵛ   More virum tunicasque feram latosque galeros,
50 Neglectam dura forpice secta comam.
Foeminei facile est mutare vocabula sexus;
  Sordebit totum syllaba "fracta" genus!
His ego si liceat pro te maiora subirem,
  Nec meus est aliqua labe pudendus amor.
55   Ille quidem primis tibi me vincivit ab annis,
  Hunc neque Mors rapida finiet atra manu.
Ex manibus mihi vita tuis dulcissima venit;
  Ante datum per te mortua lumen eram.
Christicola genitor gentilem ex matre creavit;
60 At meritum de me tu, patre, maius habes.
Corporis ille artus, animi tu dona dedisti.
  Fecit uterque aliquid — tu magis, ille minus.
Ipsa etiam nunc cana parens ut nomine Fausta est,
  Sic ipso rerum pondere fausta fuit.
65   Illa mihi magno praelusit ad ubera Christo,
  Cumque ipso potui sugere lacte Deum.
Illa meam sacros linguam formavit in usus;
  Nullus in innocuo Iuppiter ore fuit.
Ne tamen interea durus pater ista notaret,
70 Saepius ingenio dicitur usa tuo.
81=Q1ʳ   Sacra deis quoties simulata Penatibus egi,
  Ipsa mihi dixit, "Sacra fac ista neges!"

39–46 Chrisogonum — pede *A*: Per loca Chrysogonum quaeram et sequar omnia, donec / Vel tecum vivam vel sine te moriar. / Dura nec ignitis prohibebit solibus aestas, / Trux licet infesto saeviat ore Canis. / Non rapidus Boreas pluviusve morabitur Auster, / Nec nive Riphaea sparsa tenebit hyems. / Per iuga, per saltus, per aquas, per iniqua viarum / Impedient teneros aspera nulla pedes *BO*. **50** forpice *A*: forfice *BO*. **52** Sordebit *BO*: Sorbebit *A*. **54** labe *A*: parte *BO*. **57** Ex *A*: E *BO*. **59** gentilem *BO*: gentilei *A*. **63** Fausta *A*: dicta *BO*. **69** interea *BO*: in tenera *A*. **71** egi *A*: agi *BO*.

way to escape. The ruthless emperor hems us in on all sides. He controls the land; he controls the sea. But if ever I am set free, when I am no longer constrained by some edict, no road will prove too difficult for me. I'll set off in search of Chrysogonus in far-distant lands. [40] No danger will slow down my tender feet. The parched summer won't stop me with its heat waves, nor will the pestilential Dog Star hold me up with its snapping jaws. The rainy south wind mixed with blasts from the north won't make me turn back, and gloomy winter won't deter me with its arctic frost. I'll press on through mountains and forests and rugged cliffs and rocks that are difficult to approach, even for calloused feet. And so that no one will be able to recognize the wayfarer as a girl, I'll dress in men's clothes. Like men, I'll wear tunics and broad-brimmed hats. [50] I'll neglect my hair and cut it with cruel shears. It is easy to change the epithet they apply to the feminine sex. Henceforth it won't do to label all of us women "weak"!

If I could, I would endure greater hardships for you than these. My love for you, however, is in no way tainted with shameful motives. As you know, it has bound me to you from earliest childhood, and even black Death will not end it with his violent hand. Life most sweet came to me from your hands. Before you bestowed the light on me I was dead. My father begot me as a heathen by a Christian mother; [60] but you, father, have a greater claim to my gratitude. He gave me the limbs of the body, you the gifts of the soul. Both of you accomplished something — you more, he less. The same is true for my now white-haired mother, a Fausta in name as well as in deed.[2] It was she who at her breast sang to me about Christ the Lord, and together with her milk I could also suck in God. She it was who shaped my tongue to holy usage. Never did the name *Jupiter* cross my innocent lips. But to keep my strict father from noticing these things in the meantime, [70] mother, I'm told, often put your ingenuity to good use. Whenever I pretended to worship the household gods, she would tell me, "Make sure you repudiate these rites!" And

---

[2]Fausta lived up to her name by being "fausta" (bringing good fortune).

Atque ita mentito genitor deceptus honore
Aetati indulsit libera frena rudi.
75   Nubilis interea venit sed iniquior aetas —
Detectrix animi prima erat illa mei.
Cur tamen accusem? Certe non aequa fuisset,
Si mea Laethaeis caepta dedisset aquis.
Sola ego de tanto latuissem ingloria vulgo,
80   Nullaque erat meriti fama futura mei.
Nec mihi forte fidem testari morte beatam
Quodque peto sacrum non licuisset opus.
O illum mihi fata diem sperata favete!
Eveniat capiti tanta corona meo!
85   Sanguine iam rubro rorantes undique venas,
Iam tremulas cerno per mea membra faces!
Iam furit ambusto flammis pyra fervida palo,
Iam feror angelicos inter et ante choros!
Omnia ut ipse volet magni Deus arbiter aevi,
90   Eius ad arbitrium cuncta ferenda feram.
Ergo nec innocuos aetas mea fleverit annos;
In lucem vultus protulit illa meos.
Q1ᵛ   Venimus ad thalamum non aequa lege iugalem:
Cui data sum, falso sub Iove miles erat.
95   Tunc Hymenaea fugax cecinit feralia bubo,
Iunctaque cum facibus moesta cupressus erat.
Non ultra simulare deos, non amplius ullum
Aversa potui fingere mente Iovem.
Fassa Deum primis coluisse, ut nunc quoque, ab annis,
100   "Quae colitis," dixi, "numina crimen habent!"
Scilicet erranti vixissem nupta marito
Quem potui rectae commonuisse viae?
Ante ego Caucasea diram sub rupe volucrem
Saepe renascenti pascere corde velim,
105   Ante ego (quam memorant) Cepheidos esse cathenis,
Perdita non ullo Gorgonis angue rapi,
Quam mea gentili desumere tempora lecto
Turpiter et vani crimen habere thori.
Tum me si qua suam fecissent pignora matrem,
110   Num potui misero perdita ferre patri?

---

81 Nec — beatam *A*: Nec mihi quem colimus sperata morte fateri *BO*.   82 peto sacrum *A*: sequor
tantum *BO*.   83 sperata *A*: superique *BO*.   85 rubro *A*: rubeo *BO*.   89–90 Omnia — feram
A: Viderit at de me magni Deus arbiter aevi, / Intrepide poenas quas volet ille feram *BO*.   103 diram
A: duram *BO*.   105 esse *A*: arcta *BO*.   106 Perdita — rapi *A*: In scopulos nunquam dissoluenda
mori *BO*.   107 gentili *A*: sic vetito *BO*.   109 me *BO*: mea *A*.

so my father, deceived by the feigned ceremony, gave free rein to my unripe youth.

Meanwhile I reached marriageable age — a more dangerous time for me, however, since it was destined to lay bare my soul. But why blame my youth? It certainly would not have been right, had this season of life buried my ambitions in the waters of Lethe.[3] I alone in such a huge throng would have remained unsung [80] and won no fame for any achievements of mine. Then perhaps I would not have had the chance to bear witness to the blessed faith through my death and accomplish the holy task that I seek.

O longed-for fate, bestow that day on me! Grant that my head may bear so glorious a crown![4] Already I see my veins everywhere dripping with the ruddy blood; already I see the torches flickering over my limbs! Already the stake is charred, the pyre roaring with blazing flames; already I am carried among and before the choirs of angels! Whatever torments God himself, the Lord of eternity, should require of me, [90] I shall gladly bear them all at his behest. My youthful age, therefore, should not have wept for its years of innocence. It was this time of life, after all, that revealed my true face to the world.

We did not enter wedlock on the same terms. The man to whom I was given in marriage was a pagan who served the false Jove. Then the elusive screech owl sang wedding songs that presaged death, and funereal cypress boughs were joined with the bridal torches. No longer could I feign belief in the gods, no longer go through the motions of revering some Jupiter. Confessing that I had worshiped God from my earliest youth and did so even now, I cried, [100] "The gods you adore are a disgrace!"

Think about it. Should I have gone on living as the wife of a straying husband to whom I could be showing the right way? I would rather be on some Caucasian cliff and feed that dreadful bird with ever-regenerating heart, I would rather be in Andromeda's chains, as the story goes, and not be rescued by Gorgon's snake-entwined head,[5] than disgracefully waste my time sharing a bed with a heathen and bear the reproach of an unchaste marriage. And then, supposing babies came along and made me a mother, [110] could I have borne the wretched father

---

[3]The waters of the Lethe River in the underworld were said to confer oblivion on those who drank of them: cf. Otto 943.

[4]Anastasia alludes to the martyr's crown: cf. 2 Timothy 4.8; James 1.12; 1 Peter 5.4; Revelations 2.10.

[5]Andromeda, the daughter of Cepheus, was left chained by the seashore as prey for a monster, but was rescued by Perseus (Ov. *Met.* 4.663–739). The hero had just killed the snake-haired Gorgon Medusa and cut off the head that turned all who looked on it to stone. However, he did not use it to rescue Andromeda, as Eobanus suggests.

Florida deformi foedassem tempora luctu
    Venissetque suos ante senecta dies,
Spiritus aut tenues meus hic exisset in auras
    Et potui nimio fracta dolore mori.

82=Q2ʳ   115   At melius nostris consultum est rebus ab illo,
    Immensum patria qui rotat arte globum.
Tuque, dator fideique bonae veraeque salutis,
    Maius Anastasia martyre nomen habes.
Nam nisi tu crescenti igni fomenta dedisses
    120   Et tibi ni virtus nostra agitata foret,
Forte ego, quae medios vulgavi signa per hostes,
    Percita non contra Caesaris ira foret,
Forte nec immeritas subiissem carceris umbras,
    Unde data a nobis littera multa tibi est.
    125   Sic tamen esse iuvat dulcissima vulnera passam.
    O, superet gravior poena obeunda mihi!
Omnium ut excutiant generum tormenta tyranni,
    Unius haec noster non facit assis amor.
Est leve pro certa mortem contemnere vita.
    130   Vita quidem longa est, mors quotacunque brevis.
Aspice dissectum lachrymoso vulnere Christum
    Et mala pro Christo tantula ferre nega!
Ipsa securigeros metuam tolerare maniplos,
    Huic lanient sanctam dira flagella cutem?
    135   Impositam collo mihi sit grave ferre cathenam?
    Immerito vinctus non semel ille fuit.
Q2ᵛ   Impia praesentis terrebor ad ora tyranni?
    Iudicium multo tristius ille tulit.
Ipsa comis dubitem caput exhibuisse trahendum?
    140   Ornatus sertis heu quibus ille fuit!
Ipse Deus moriens cedro pendebat ab alta.
    Haec anima ingratum tam male corpus amet?
Ipsa sequi dubitem castas animosa sorores?
    Flamma nocens Agapen Chyoniamque tulit.
    145   Tertia servatur vicinae in carcere morti —
    Heu, soror, aetatis crimine viva tuae.
Sufficit hoc etiam laesuros corpus in ignes,
    Sunt mihi quae tacto colla sub ense cadant!
Me quoque quin miserae revocatam redditis urbi?
    150   Est amor afflicta pro pietate mori.

---

113 meus *AO*: meas *B*; hic exisset *A*: exhalasset *BO*.   115 At *A*: Sed *BO*.   127 ut *A*: et *BO*.
132 mala *A*: male *BO*.   134 lanient *BO*: laniet *A*.   135 Impositam *A*: Iniectam *BO*.
144 Chyoniamque tulit *A*: sustulit et Chionem *BO*.   148 tacto *A*: stricto *BO*.

lost children? I would have disfigured my blooming youth with unsightly grief, and old age would have arrived before its time. My spirit would have breathed its last into the thin air and I might well have died of a broken heart. But he who revolves the immense sphere with fatherly skill has looked after me better than that.

And you, the man who gave me both sound faith and true salvation, you are going to enjoy greater fame, now that your Anastasia is a martyr. For had you not added kindling to the growing fire [120] and stirred up my virtue, I never would have raised the standard of the cross inside the enemy's camp and provoked the emperor's wrath, nor, perhaps, would I have experienced the undeserved gloom of prison, from where I used to send you so many letters.

But that is my delight, to go on suffering the sweetest wounds. Oh, may a still heavier punishment lie in store for me! Even if the tyrants afflict me with all manner of torments, my love wouldn't care a single penny. It is easy to scorn death when you are certain to live. [130] Life indeed is long; death, no matter how terrifying, is short.

Look at the lamentable gash where Christ was pierced, and then refuse to bear such slight tribulations for Christ! Should I fear to stand up to ax-wielding maniples when the frightful scourge lacerated his holy skin? Should I deem it hard to carry chains around my neck? He too was bound undeservedly more than once. Shall I be terrified of the tyrant's wicked face when I see him? Christ accepted a far grimmer sentence. Shall I hesitate to offer my head to be dragged along by the hair? [140] Alas, with what kind of crown was he adorned! God himself hung dying on a lofty cedar. Should my soul be so excessively enamored of its thankless body? Shall I think twice about bravely following those chaste sisters?[6] The baneful flames have already taken Agape and Chionia from us. The third is being held in jail, awaiting her death — alas, sister, alive only because of your youth, your only crime!

My body too has strength enough to face the consuming flames; I too have a neck that can fall by the executioner's sword! Why don't you also call me back to your miserable city? [150] I yearn to die for our persecuted religion. What are you waiting for?

---

[6]The three young sisters Agape, Chionia, and Irene were Anastasia's handmaids. The first two were burned alive. The youngest sister, Irene, was stripped naked and forced into a house of prostitution. But as God protected her there from all advances, she too was eventually executed.

Quae mora, quae pietas te nunc, prefecte, moratur? —
    O qui dulce nihil, nomina praeter, habes!
Adde meis comitem me, dure, sororibus illis,
    Laedere quas etiam te voluisse pudet.
155   Fer tamen impuram procul hoc a corpore dextram.
    Mens mea praesagit tristia fata tibi.
Non iterum gravibus lusus cedere flagellis.
    Ipse Deus vindex Caesare maior erit.

83=Q3ʳ

En tibi virginibus venio stipata ducentis.
160   Tu modo ut occidas ipse redire iube.
At te, seu lateas seu tutus in urbe moraris,
    Non pudeat famulae scribere pauca tuae.
Exercetne novas ignava potentia leges?
    Milia quot capitum pestis acerba fugat?
165   Quis bonus extrema certavit athleta palestra?
    Ah, ubi cum misera parvula matre soror?
An Praetextato subolevit nulla parenti
    Gratia? Quae dederam iussa vir anne facit?
Denique quae rerum speties sit in urbe novarum,
170   Quam cuperem scripto certior esse tuo!
Quod petimus ratio non est tibi iusta negandi:
    Advenit ex vestro littore nauta frequens.
Sed, puto, sic nolis miseram transire relictam
    Ut vel in hac minima parte iuvare neges.
175   Quod si sera tibi mea venit epistola, forsan
    Non potuit vultus ante videre tuos.
Illa tibi interea, quo sic iuvat esse coactam,
    Optima perpetui testis amoris erit.
Me si forte olim Deus ipse redire iubebit,
180   Omnia consilio sunt obeunda tuo.

Q3ᵛ

Si tamen exilium reliquos mihi finiet annos,
    Ossa precor patrios nostra fer in cineres.

---

159 venio *AO*: veni *B*.   **161** seu lateas *A*: sive lates *BO*.   **172** ex *A*: e *BO*; vestro *AO*: nostro *B*.
173–74 Sed — neges. *A*: *om. BO*.   **175** si — mea *A*: si sera meae tibi *B*, mea si sero tibi *O*.
175–76 forsan — tuos *A*: credes / Difficile exulibus cedere quicquid agant [agunt *O*] *BO*.   **177–78**
Illa — erit. *A*: *om. BO*.   **180** sunt obeunda *A*: prosequar acta *BO*.   **182** precor *BO*: praecor *A*.

What scruples are holding you back now, prefect? — O you, who apart from your name have nothing dulcet about you![7] Cruel man, add me as a companion to those sisters, the ones even you are ashamed of having wanted to harm. But keep your impure hand far from my body. My mind presages a dreadful fate for you. You will not get another chance to play your game with the heavy lashes. God himself, mightier than the emperor, will be my protector. Look, I am going to come to you with two hundred maidens in tow. [160] The only way you can make us go back is to slaughter us.

But you, whether you have gone into hiding or are keeping safe in the city, don't be ashamed to write your servant a few lines. Are the mean-spirited authorities still enforcing the new edicts? How many thousands of people has that pitiless plague driven away? Which athlete[8] has fought the good fight of martyrdom? Ah, where are my wretched mother and little sister? Has my father Praetextatus felt any stirrings of leniency? Has my husband carried out the instructions I gave him? In short, [170] how I would love to get a letter from you with the latest news in the city!

You really don't have a valid excuse for denying my request. In fact, there is a sailor who often arrives here from your shore. But I don't think you will forsake the poor girl like that and refuse to give me at least this little bit of comfort. If my letter doesn't find you until late, however, it probably had a hard time reaching your eyes. To you, meanwhile, to whom I have been writing with such pleasure, it will bear the best witness to my undying love.

If it turns out that God wants me to go back someday, [180] I shall let myself be guided in all things by your counsel. If, on the other hand, I am to end my remaining years in exile, pray bury my bones in the family vault.

---

[7] Anastasia alludes to the prefect's name. Despite being called *Dulcitius*, he is in fact anything but "dulcet." The name *Dulcitius* does not occur in *Leg. aurea*, but was familiar from the legend of Anastasia's handmaids Agape, Chionia, and Irene as presented, for example, in Hrotsvit von Gandersheim's play *Dulcitius*, first edited by Konrad Celtis in 1501. See also *Acta Sanctorum*, April I, Dies 3.

[8] The term *athlete* was used already in early Christianity to describe those Christians who contended for the prize of martyrdom. The metaphor goes back to 2 Timothy 2.5 and 4.7: cf. 1 Corinthians 9.24–25.

19   TECLA PAULO

Dum tibi sera venit, metitur epistola quantum
    Thuscus Oronthaeo littore Tybris abest.
Nam tenet evictis nunc me Seleucia curis.
    Nunc ego nec foelix Iconis esse velim.
5   At tu grata teris Galilaei limina Petri
    Duraque sub magno iura Nerone manes.
Quid tibi cum caeca, doctor clarissime, Rhoma?
    Assuescet monitis nunquid et illa tuis?
Quam timeo, magnum ne quando fatebere Christum,
10   Ipsa tibi poenas exiciumque paret!
Hoc cecidere modo tot milia temporis huius,
    Stultus ut imperium cum Iove Caesar habet.
Quam fuerat melius gentes docuisse minores!
    In tua plus Asiae nomina laudis erant.
15   Rhoma potens toti caput est et praesidet orbi
    Et nimium propria laude superba tumet.
Tam firmam heu quantus labor est impellere molem,
    Pondus precipue cuius et orbis idem!
Ipsa refert patria partos virtute triumphos
84=Q4ʳ   20   Et se presentes credit habere deos.
Ipse etiam superum socius pater urbis habetur,
    Cui locat ardentes quaelibet ara focos.

Her. Chr. **19.**   *Tit.* Tecla *A*: Lydia *BO*.   **1** Dum *AO*: Cum *B*.   **2** Thuscus — abest *A*: Tybridis a sacro fonte Caicus abest *BO*.   **3** me Seleucia *A*: pulchra Tyatira *BO*.   **4** Iconis *A*: Aematis *BO*.
5–6 At tu — magno *A*: Tu, dubium emensus Tyrrhena [Thyrrena *BO*] per aequora cursum, / Dura sub infami *BO*.   **9** timeo *A*: metuo *BO*.   **12** ut *AO*: et *B*.

19   THECLA TO PAUL[1]

If this letter takes a long time to reach you, it is because it has had to travel all the way from the banks of the Orontes to the Tuscan Tiber. For you should know that I have put my cares behind me and am now making my home in Seleucia. Now I would not want to live in Iconium anymore, no matter how happy I used to be there. You, on the other hand, often cross the dear threshold of Peter of Galilee while you await a harsh sentence under the mighty Nero.

Most celebrated of teachers, what have you to do with blind Rome? Do you really think this city too will start heeding your warnings? How I fear [10] that she is preparing to punish and kill you for preaching Christ the Lord! So many thousands have already fallen like this in recent years, just so the stupid emperor can share power with Jupiter. How much better it would have been, had you continued to teach the lesser peoples! Back here in Asia you could surely count on a lot more praise. As head and guardian of the entire world, mighty Rome has gotten far too swollen with pride at her own fame. What a huge labor it is, alas, to overthrow so immovable and gigantic a structure, especially when its mass and the world's are one and the same! She herself ascribes her triumphs to native valor [20] and believes the gods are bodily present with her. The people even revere the city's founder as a companion of the celestial beings, and every altar keeps a fire burning for him.[2]

---

[1]According to her legend, the virgin Thecla of Iconium was converted by the Apostle Paul to a life of perpetual chastity. She thereupon broke off her engagement to marry Thamyris. Condemned to the stake, she escaped unharmed with God's help and went to Antioch to be with Paul. Here too she was sentenced to die. But after one ordeal after another failed to kill her, she was released. Subsequently she lived in a cave at Seleucia on the Orontes River. Paul meanwhile had been arrested by the Roman authorities in ca. 60 CE and sent to Rome for trial. Later tradition holds that he died a martyr's death a few years later, under Emperor Nero (r. 54–68).

The Thecla legend was very popular in the Middle Ages. See Boninus Mombritius, *Sanctuarium seu Vitae Sanctorum*, ed. Monachi Solesmenses (1910; repr. Hildesheim, 1978), 2:559–64; *Acta Sanctorum*, September VI, Dies 23; Oscar von Gebhardt, *Passio S. Theclae virginis: Die lateinischen Übersetzungen der Acta Pauli et Theclae nebst Fragmenten, Auszügen und Beilagen*, Texte und Untersuchungen zur Geschichte der altchristlichen Literatur 22 (Leipzig, 1902).

In the 1532/39 version this letter is *Her.* 1.5. There the writer, however, is not Thecla, but the purple seller Lydia of Thyatira (Acts 16.13–15). The switch, which affected a relatively small number of verses, gave Eobanus the opportunity to kill two birds with one stone. It allowed him to eliminate an embarrassingly fabulous legend and at the same time increase the number of "historical" letters based entirely on the New Testament.

[2]Romulus, the city's founder and first king, was deified and worshiped under the name Quirinus.

Hanc tu posse putas tua per documenta moveri,
Quae sibi tot divos quot colit ipsa facit?
25   Et licet exuperes divinae lumine mentis
Et polyhistorico pectore cuncta feras
Blandaque florentis caedat tibi gratia linguae,
In labris sedeat Suada Minerva tuis,
Saxa prius scopulosque trahes sylvasque virenteis
30   Antraque linquentes per nemus omne feras,
Quam tu semideum possis mollire Neronem —
Si modo se totum non putat esse deum!
Sed pariunt magnam tam facta insignia laudem,
Tentatique satis fama decoris erit.
35   Quis neget? Hoc magno satis est voluisse Tonanti.
Res animo, non re ponderat ille animos.
Quis neget haec ipsis divis quoque magna videri,
Terrarum princeps sollicitare caput?
An potius fugiens operosae taedia vitae
40   Vis tandem senio posse quiete frui?
Idque ego propositi credam tibi, Paule, fuisse;
Hac libet, utcunque est, credulitate trahi.
Namque diu vasti iactatam errore profundi
In portum par est applicuisse ratem.
45   Arma per et varii raptum discrimina belli,
Militis emeriti nomen habere decet.
Hoc tibi tu poteras Rhomam sperare daturam?
Nil hac desperes conditione licet:
Flumina sic retro spera reditura lacusque
50   Ignibus arsuros, saxa futura feras!
Mortua, crede, loco pietas est omnis in illo.
Caesar ubi malus est, pax ibi nulla bonis.
Pars licet observet populi te multa tuisque
Audiat et verbis credat inesse fidem,
55   Pressa tamen trucibusque minis iraque tyranni
Dissimulat tacita quem colit arte Deum.
Ergo fuit melius gentes docuisse minores.
Qur tua nunc virtus languida facta iacet?
Sed tua nec languet virtus nec gloria marcet.
60   Da veniam si quid noster ineptit amor.
Ut tua me miseram nimiis absentia curis
Conficit, insana sic quoque mente loquor.

Q4v

---

24 quot *BO*: quos *A*.   27 florentis *A*: mellifluae *BO*.   28 Suada Minerva *A*: Suada canora *BO*.
29 virenteis *A*: sequaces *BO*.   34 decoris *A*: laboris *BO*.   40 senio *A*: vita *B*, placida *O*.
41–42 Idque — trahi. *A*: *om. BO*.   62 insana *A*: incauta *BO*.

Do you think you can move this city with your preaching, seeing that she herself creates the gods she worships? For though you shine with the light of God's mind and carry all knowledge within your polyhistoric breast and possess the winning charm of an eloquent tongue, and though Persuasive Minerva herself sits on your lips, you will sooner make rocks and crags and verdant trees follow you [30] and cause wild beasts to leave their dens all through the forest than you will manage to soften the demigod Nero's heart[3] — at least, if he does not regard himself an *entire* god!

No matter: such glorious deeds yield great renown, and the news of your attempt alone will bring you plenty of honor. Who would deny it? Just wanting to do this is enough for the mighty Thunderer. He weighs deeds according to their intention, not intentions according to their success. Who would deny that even the gods themselves consider it grand to discomfit the chief head of the world? Or would you rather escape the weariness of a toil-some life [40] and be able to enjoy a quiet retirement at last? I like to think you are of this mind yourself, Paul; indeed, I find some comfort in this belief, whatever it is worth. Your ship has certainly been tossed about long enough on the boundless deep. It is time to steer for the harbor. After all the battles, all the risks and uncertainties of war that you have been through, you have a right to an honorable discharge.

Can you hope that Rome will grant you this? Sure, hope for it as much as you want, on the following condition: trust like-wise that rivers will return to their source, lakes [50] blaze with fire, stones turn into beasts! In that place, trust me, all piety is dead. Where the emperor is evil, the virtuous have no peace. Though a large part of the people may respect you and mark your words and believe they are true, nevertheless, cowed by savage threats and the emperor's wrath, they pretend ignorance of the God they worship in private.

So it would have been better, had you continued to teach the lesser peoples. Why do you let your powers lie fallow? But your powers do not lie fallow, nor does your glory wither on the vine. [60] Forgive me if my love is making me talk gibberish. As my poor heart is cracked with relentless cares in your absence, so it was silly for me to utter thoughts like that. In our country at

---

[3]Even if Paul were a second Orpheus and could move rocks and trees, he would be unable to move Nero, a monster more hard-hearted than stone and deafer than the rocks on the sea shore. Cf. *Ama.* 33.7, n.

85=Q5^r

Candida floret adhuc nostras tua fama per oras,
    Gloria nec meriti est illa sepulta tui,
65 Quanta per innumeras urbes opera egeris, ex quo
    Factus es aeterni fortis athleta Dei,
Postquam clara nova vidit te luce Damascus
    Percussum patrios deseruisse deos.
Maenia adhuc illa rima stant pervia, per quam
70   Diceris occulta cautus abisse fuga.
Illa etiam quae tu nobis aliquando solebas
    Saepius in patria facta referre mea,
Illa vigent etiam nullis moritura diebus,
    O, sine non lachrymis enumeranda meis!
75 Immeritum poenis quibus affecere Philippi
    Flumina pene audent mutaque saxa loqui.
Hanc post fida tamen tua littera venit ad urbem,
    Quam dederas veram testificata fidem.
Qua virtute Ephesique feras Solimaeque tumultus
80   Viceris et Macedum Cappadocumque dolos!
Omnibus his tua scripta tamen transmissa leguntur —
    O bona pro meritis dona relata malis!
Praeterea Galatas quis nescit adisse feroces
    Et tua qui dives arva Corinthe tenet?
85 Te doctore tuo Rhodii famulantur Iesu,

Q5^v
    Qui sua de statua nomina Solis habent.
An nihil haec credas? An non ea gloria plena est?
    Rhoma, precor, titulis defuit una tuis?
Patria restabant Perseae moenia Tharsi.
90   Hei, quantum a vestro Tybride Cydnus abest!

---

64 illa *A*: ulla *BO*.   65–66 Quanta — Dei, *A*: *om. BO*.   68 patrios . . . deos *A*: leges . . . tuas
BO.   69 quam *A*: quae *BO*.   72 mea *A*: tua *BO*.   *Post* 78 *add. BO*: Saxa Lycaoniae scelus
indignantia Lystrae / Pene etiam mortis sunt [stant *O*] monumenta tuae. / Dicere Cecropios quo
fregeris ore magistros / Quam qui nil didicit dicere nemo nequit.   79 feras *A*: minas *BO*.
84 Et — tenet *A*: Teque tuas Christo fassa Corinthus [Chorinthus *B*] opes *BO*.   85–86 Te —
habent *A*: O electe Dei preco, decus orbis, ab ipsis / Quem tenebris luci est restituisse tuum, / O superum facunde comes fideique magister, / Fulmina sunt linguae singula verba tuae. / Fama est Ismarii
gelidas ad Strimonis undas / Omnia Threiciam monstra sequuta chelin. / Moverit Amphion lapides,
delphinas Arion, / Ogmius impositis traxerit ora iugis. / Tu potes eloquio coelos aperire potenti, / Tu
potes in terras ducere, Paule, Deum. / Cuncta tibi cedunt divinae munera virgae — / Tam fluit et linguae est aurea vena tuae. / Iamque renascentem membris vitalibus orbem / Totum divini munere lactis
alis, / Qualiter infantem tenui nutricula succo / Imbuit et firmis passibus ire docet *BO*.   87 credas
A: credes *BO*.   90 Hei *A*: Heu *BO*.

least your fame still shines with all its luster, and that glorious renown of yours is by no means buried here — the incredible wonders you worked in countless cities, ever since you became a sturdy athlete[4] of the eternal God, after famed Damascus saw how you, struck by that miraculous light, abandoned the faith of your fathers. The walls there still have the chink through which, [70] they say, you prudently stole out of the city.[5] Your other deeds, the ones you often used to tell me about while you were in my homeland, they too live on and will never perish. Oh, I cannot enumerate them without tears!

What kind of punishments the Philippians unjustly inflicted on you, the rivers and mute stones almost venture to cry out. Afterwards you nevertheless sent that city a faithful letter testifying to the genuine faith you gave her. With what bravery you overcame the wild beasts in Ephesus, the riots in Jerusalem, [80] the treachery of the Macedonians and the Cappadocians! And yet in all these places they have been reading the letters you sent them — oh, gracious gifts meted out for the evils they deserved! Besides, who does not know that you visited the fierce Galatians and the inhabitants of wealthy Corinth? The Rhodians, whose claim to fame is their statue of the sun god, now serve your Jesus, as you taught them to do. Do you think all that is nothing? Aren't you satisfied with that glory? Is Rome, I ask you, all you lack to crown your illustrious career?

You could always return to your hometown Tarsus, founded by Perseus. [90] Alas, what a great distance separates the Cydnus River from your Tiber! What a blessing it would be for your

---

[4]Cf. *Her. Chr.* 18.165, with n. 8 (p. 369 above).

[5]Paul (then still known as Saul) was on his way to Damascus to persecute the Christians when he was stopped in his tracks by a heavenly light and the voice of Jesus. Upon reaching the city he converted to Christianity. Learning that the Jews were plotting to kill him, he escaped by night through a window in the city wall. See Acts 9.1–25, 22.3–16, 26.4–18; 2 Corinthians 11.32–33; Galatians 1.13–17.

Quam fuit hoc nimium gravidae praestare senectae
 Rhomanis Cilicas praeposuisse tuos!
At tibi erat sacra pro relligione cadendum,
 Hanc prius hic aequum te docuisse fuit.
95 Grata senescentis quaerebas ocia vitae,
 In patria poteras consenuisse tua,
Dulcibus intentus studiis florentis Iesu
 (Non quae prisca tui Gammalielis habes!),
Aut certe ad gelidum nobiscum vivere Orontem.
100 Hic tua praecipuum gloria nomen habet.
Quod votis nisi saeva meis fortuna negasset,
 Nulla, reor, vitae pars foret atra meae,
Cresceret invisas nullum mihi tempus in horas,
 Deiiceret nullus pectora moesta dolor,
105 Nec me saepe cavo gemitus pulmone trahentem
 Tristitiae causam quaereret ulla meae.
Saepe meos blanda solatur voce dolores
86=Q6^r Per te surgenti fida Tryphena Deo.
Ah, quoties, illa referente quid egeris usquam,
110 Plurima luminibus liquitur unda meis!
(Nunc quoque perfusum lachrymis premit humida pectus
 Fascia, concepto pondere facta gravis.)
Praedita ut illa quidem facundae est munere linguae,
 De te quot verbis tot mihi taela refert.
115 Tempora tum subeunt nostrae quoque dulcia pugnae,
 O bene sub tanto pugna peracta duce!
Te duce crudeles victricia signa per hostes
 Sumptaque pro Christo fortiter arma tuli.
Aedita nobilium de sanguine Taecla parentum,
120 Infido sprevi nubere virgo viro.
Accusata tuli duras sine vulnere flammas.
 In tetro frustra carcere clausa fui.
Insanis obiecta feris illaesa manebam.
 Lingebat nudos dira leaena pedes;
125 Nil ursi nocuere truces saevique leones.
 Praebuerant mites amphitheatra feras.

93 tibi — sacra A: fuerat sancta BO. 94 aequum te docuisse A: fas te composuisse BO.
97 florentis A: crescentis BO. 99 nobiscum — Orontem A: melius vixisse Caicum BO.
102 Nulla — meae A: Improba pars vitae non foret ulla meae BO. 108 Per — Deo A: Iuncta
comes lateri fida Perilla meo BO. 115–33 Tempora — favoris. A: Tempora tum subeunt vitae
male cauta prioris, / Per quae quicquid erat vivere crimen erat. / Non ego nobilium sata Lydia stirpe
parentum, / Nupta viro moestas tota sequebar opes. / Praecipue gemmas Tyrios et avara colores /
Empta levi magno vendere docta fui. / Hos duce te quaestus, verissima damna, reliqui, / Nuda prius,
lucro facta beata novo. / Cuius et obstantes duce te nova signa per hostes / Sumptaque pro Christo
fortiter arma tuli. / Multa quidem vici nec vana pericula rerum, / Quae poterant ipsis pondus habere
viris. / Quae, quia nulla meis debetur gloria factis, BO. 126 amphitheatra scripsi: amphiteatra A.

much too burdened old age, if you could put your own Cilicians ahead of the Romans! But if you have to die for the holy faith, it seems fair that you should teach it here first. If you are looking forward to a pleasant retirement in your declining years, think of being able to grow old in your native land, intent on the sweet studies of flourishing Jesus (not those of your old teacher Gamaliel![6]), or, certainly, of coming to live with us by the frigid Orontes. [100] Here your name is held in particularly high esteem.

Had savage fortune not denied me my dearest wish, no portion of my life, I think, would seem black to me now. Then time would not be growing more hateful to me with every passing hour, no grief would depress my doleful heart, and no one who sees me heaving so many sighs from the depths of my lungs would inquire about the cause of my sadness. Tryphena, who through you is a believer in the risen Lord, often comforts my heartaches with her soothing voice.[7] Ah, how often, when she relates what you have done somewhere, [110] does a flood of tears well up in my eyes! (Even now the sodden breast-band, made heavy with the burden it has soaked up, is pressing on my tear-drenched chest.) Endowed as she is with the gift of eloquence, she stabs me to the quick with each word she speaks about you.

Then the sweet times of my own battle also come to mind — oh, a battle well fought under so brilliant a captain! Under your leadership I carried the victorious standards among the merciless enemies and boldly took up arms for Christ. Born into a noble family, I, Thecla, [120] wanted to remain a virgin and hence refused to marry an unbelieving husband. Condemned to death, I escaped the cruel flames unscathed. I was locked up in a foul dungeon, but to no avail. Thrown to the ravening beasts, I remained unharmed. The frightful lioness licked my bare feet; the ferocious bears and savage lions did me no harm at all. The amphitheater offered only tame beasts. Bullocks were ordered

---

[6]Gamaliel, a Pharisee (Acts 5.34), was Paul's teacher in the Law: see Acts 22.3.

[7]While in Antioch — not Seleucia, as Eobanus insinuates here — Thecla lived at the house of Queen Tryphena (a historical personage).

Tracta iubebantur discerpere membra iuvenci;
    Combussit tricas ferrea pruna graves.
Unde tot evasi? Qui tanta pericula vici?

Q6ᵛ   130   Callida non magica Phasias arte fui!
Illa est, illa apud oratum tua gratia Christum,
    Quam tibi, quam iustis omnibus ille favet.
Non ego me tantum fateor meruisse favoris.
    Tot mala quod vici muneris omne tui est.

135   Tu potes extremi penetrare volumina caeli
    Praesentemque alta mente videre Deum.
Ille tibi quaecunque voles largitur et addit
    Munera ad exiguas innumerata preces.
Illius exemplo miseros tibi cura iacentes

140   Tollere et ad superas est relevare domos.
Nec pateris, quo tu periisti pene, perire
    Vulnere, sed certa vivere lege facis.
Nemo quidem melius languenti consulit aegro
    Quam simili morbo qui prius aeger erat.

145   Hoc utinam videat qui se putat omnia Caesar
    Cernere, qui nec se nec sua facta videt,
Terribilisque sacra stupefactus imagine vultus
    Dicat, et hic tantus non putat esse deos.
Quod non ille putat tantus, prius ille putavit,

150   Ille quod est verum forte putare potest.
Viderit hoc Caesar — quid non sperare licebit? —

87=R1ʳ   In patriam reditus iam tibi certus erit.
Sed prius, heu, vereor, fluvios habitabit Oraeas
    Multaque per montes Oceanitis erit.

155   Ergone te miseris sine fine carere necesse est?
    Ergone non finem nostra querela feret?
Quinetiam nobis sperantibus optima forsan
    Adveniet mortis nuncia fama tuae.
Hei mihi, si nostras quicquam tale arguat aures,

160   Qur ego praeterito fortis agone fui?

---

134 quod *A*: quot *BO*; muneris *B*: numeris *A*, mumeris *O*.   **138** innumerata *AB*: non numeranda *O*. **140** relevare *A*: animare *BO*.   **142** vivere — facis *A*: conditione iuvas *BO*.   **143–44** aegro — erat *A*: unquam / Quam qui perniciem, quam levat, ipse tulit *BO*.   **146** nec se *AO*: neque se *B*.   **149** prius — putavit, *A*: quis credere possit? *BO*.   **151** quid . . . ? *A*: quod . . . , *BO*.   **153** vereor *A*: metuo *BO*; fluvios *A*: fluvius *BO*.   *Post* **154** *add. BO*: Quam sua destituant crudelem monstra Neronem — / Nominis o ipso vox metuenda sono!   **158** tuae *BO*: tui *A*.   **159** Hei *AB*: Heu *O*; arguat *O*: arguet *AB*.

to draw my limbs apart and tear my body to pieces, but red-hot
iron burned the heavy ropes.

By whose help did I escape? How did I survive such terrible
dangers? [130] I was no Medea cunningly working witchcraft! It
happened by the grace of Christ — by that grace which you
obtained through prayer and which he gladly bestows on you
and on all righteous persons. I confess I did not merit such a
great favor. That I survived all those torments is entirely owing to
you. You can penetrate the spheres of outermost heaven and with
sublime mind see God face-to-face. He grants you whatever you
wish and upon short prayers bestows gifts without number.
Following his example, you strive [140] to raise wretched sinners
from the ground and lift them up to their heavenly home. You
do not suffer them to die from the wound from which you yourself nearly perished, but restore them to life according to the
tried-and-true rule: no one looks after a sick patient better than
the physician who once was stricken with a similar disease.

How I wish the emperor could see that! He thinks he
observes everything, but in fact sees neither himself nor his own
deeds. But let his terrible visage be stupefied by the sacred icon,[8]
and he, great lord though he is, will stop believing in the gods. If
he, great lord though he is, can abandon his long-held beliefs,
[150] perhaps he can also believe the truth. And if the emperor
should see this — why not hope against hope? — you can count
on returning to your homeland. But alas, I fear, mountain
nymphs will sooner dwell in rivers and Oceanids throng the
mountains.

Is it inevitable, then, that we poor souls must do without
you forever? Will our lament, then, never come to an end? In
fact, even as we hope for the best, we may well get word of your
death. Woe is me! If news like this should ever reach my ears,
[160] why was I so brave in the amphitheater back then? What

---

[8]An icon of the crucified Christ.

In talem superesse diem quid profuit, in quo
   Hoc animi reliquum decidet omne mei?
Me timidam infaustae faciunt mala nomina Rhomae.
   Visa, precor, celeres somnia ferte Noti!
165 Nunc tu quicquid agis, seu dura negotia tractas,
   Ocia seu tuta dulcia mente legis,
Respice lugentem solita pietate puellam.
   Quam si vis aliqua parte valere, vale.

167 puellam *AB*: ministram *O*.

was the use of surviving to witness such a day, when all that remains of my courage will go to pieces? I am frightened by the evil reputation of accursed Rome. Swift winds, I beg you, whisk my nightmares away!

Now, whatever you may be doing, whether you continue to work hard or play it safe by choosing pleasant retirement, do show your customary concern for the grieving maid. As if you wish to fare well in some way — farewell!

20   ELISABETH ZACHARIAE

Sic mihi, Zacharia, sera iam prole gravatae,
    Dextera pro lingua saepe loquta tua est.
Nunc mihi non eadem ratio est quia fungar eodem
    Munere, nec dicor muta sed exul ego.

R1ᵛ   5   Exul ab Hebraei facie fugitiva tyranni,
    Quas habitem terras accipe quove loco.
Hic, ubi celsa petunt umbrosi sydera montes,
    Lambit Ioppaeam non procul aequor humum.
Apparent Solimae puro vix aere turres;
    10   Ipsa loco non est aeditiore Sion.
Huc simul ut veni, paucis comitata ministris,
    Regius in prima valle satelles erat.
Quo fugerem? Paret saevo vicinia regi,
    Persequor a multis foemina sola viris.
    15   Pene metu exanimata, genu labente resedi,
    Aut hoc aut certe tale quid orsa loqui:
"O qui me sera facis hac in prole parentem,
    Si quid adhuc miseros respicis, affer opem."
Dum loquor, ecce sua montis iuga sponte dehiscunt,
    20   Nec mora nativo fornice tecta fui.
Spirat et enato purissimus aer in antro
    Multaque secreta luce fenestra patet.
Iussa novas subito flores natura coegit,
    Dulcia precipuus balsama fragrat odor.
    25   Reptilibus frondent speciosa sedilia ramis,
    Fons prope manantem nectare fundit aquam.

88=R2ʳ   Huc aliqua Eoo species concessit ab horto —
    Tam lepide hunc ornat gratia verna locum!
Hic ego nunc absum bis quattuor anxia soles,
    30   Tuta licet magnae matris operta sinu.
Non ego respiro patrios remeare penates,
    Ipse sed ut valeas unica cura mihi est.
Hoc bene successit quod tute effugimus hostem;
    Hoc male quod peior te sine nostra fuga est.

Her. Chr. **20.**   *A*: *cf. Her.* 1.6 *in* **BO**.

[1]This letter, written by the mother of John the Baptist to her husband Zechariah, is only tangen-
tially based on the information given in Matthew 2 and Luke 1–2. King Herod has learned that the
Messiah has been born in Bethlehem. He has therefore ordered that all male babies in Bethlehem be
put to death. Forewarned in a dream, Mary, Joseph, and Jesus are already on their way to Egypt.
    Though Matthew has nothing to say about any danger to John the Baptist, Eobanus extrapolates
from Luke 1.39 ("a city of Judah") that his family lived in the Judean city of Bethlehem, and was hence

20   ELIZABETH TO ZECHARIAH[1]

It was in this way, Zechariah — with the right hand rather than the tongue — that you often spoke to me when I was heavy with the child of my old age.[2] My reason for writing, however, is not the same as yours was then. Rather than being mute, I myself am an exile. An exile fleeing from the face of the Hebrew tyrant, let me tell you in what land and place I live. Here, where the shade-filled mountains reach for the lofty stars, the nearby sea laps the shoreline of Joppa. When the air is clear, you can just barely make out the towers of Jerusalem. [10] Mount Zion itself is not this high.

At the very moment I arrived here, accompanied by a few servants, one of the king's henchmen blocked the entrance to the valley. Where could I flee? The region is subject to the savage king, and I, a woman all alone, am pursued by many men. Half dead with fear, I sank down on my knees and began saying this prayer, or certainly something like it: "O you, who made me a mother with this child of my old age, if you are still mindful of us poor souls, grant us your help."

Even as I speak, look, the mountainside opens up of its own accord! [20] Another moment, and I am sheltered by a natural vault. Within the new-formed cave there wafts the purest air imaginable, and the many windows let in light from some unseen source. At a command, nature suddenly conjures up fresh flowers. A marvelous fragrance, redolent of sweet balm, fills the air. Leafy branches intertwine to form attractive benches, while a nearby spring pours forth running water, sweet as nectar. Something of the beauty of that eastern garden[3] has come here — so agreeably is this place adorned with vernal charms!

Here I have now lived eight days in exile, still anxious, [30] though safely hidden in the bosom of the great Mother. It is not as if I pine to return home. My sole concern, rather, is for your welfare. This has turned out well in that we safely eluded the enemy, not so well in that our flight has been harder without you.

---

subject to Herod's decree. While Zechariah remains in Jerusalem as a priest in the Temple, Elizabeth has fled Bethlehem with her infant son John. Cornered by one of Herod's officers, they escape danger when (in a common legendary motif) the mountainside miraculously opens to receive them. It is from the safety of this paradisiacal grotto that she now writes to her husband.

　　With its fabulous elements, the letter could not remain in the post-Reformation version of 1532/39. Hence Eobanus replaced it with a more "historical" subject, by having Elizabeth write to John the Baptist, now preaching in the wilderness. See *Her.* 1.6.

　　[2]Because he refused to believe the angel's prophecy that Elizabeth would conceive a child in her old age, Zechariah was struck dumb for the duration of her pregnancy: see Luke 1.

　　[3]The Garden of Eden.

35 Tu mihi sicut eras rebus spes prima secundis,
      Debueras fatis tristibus esse comes.
    Exiguum aspiceres ludentem in pulvere natum,
      Saepeque cum risu vox tua mista foret.
    Ille ubi nunc vetulae blanditur ad ubera matri,
40   Lactenti lachrymas conbibit ore meas.
    Tristanti interea ceu solaturus adheret
      Quodque nequit lingua gestibus ille refert.
    Et tamen ipse suis puer est animosior annis.
      Aspiceres, aliquod numen habere putes.
45 Improba mentita est quendam Iove fabula natum
      In cunis angues enecuisse duos.
    Certe nulla meis insunt mendacia verbis:
      Hic aliquid maius quam puerile sapit.

R2^v Ac sacra concelebret veneratur sabbata, nec se
50   Sustinet assueto munere lactis ali.
    Nunc positas hausto perfundit fonte corollas
      Et moto quaedam pollice signa facit,
    Nunc mihi nescio quid digitis monstrare videtur,
      Tanquam praesaga mente futura videns.
55 Talia saepe mihi quaedam ventura canebas,
      Cum legerem digitis verba loquta tuis.
    An ita summa Dei certo prudentia fato
      Non alio quasdam pignore foetat anus?
    Hoc probat Isaac, Sanson, Iosephus, et ille
60   Qui tulit in regem chrismata prima novum.
    Sic mea foecunda est sero matertera partu,
      Anna, salutipara Virgine facta parens.
    Nunc tamen illa etiam patriis procul exulat oris,
      Heu, mihi perpetuo flenda dolore nurus!
65 Quo fugis, heu, nostri generis decus? Heu, ubi tandem
      Praesenti inveniam libera facta metu?
    Anne iterum dulces ego sum tactura lacertos?
      O decus, o nostrae gloria, Virgo, domus!
    Quo fugis? Heu, quae nam fecit te culpa nocentem?
70   Ah, tua (si nescis) crimine vita caret!
89=R3^r Sed neque me tutam quod sim sine crimine fecit.
      Virtus est nostrae maxima causa fugae.

---

50 munere **BO** (*Her. 1.6.134*): numere **A**.

Just as you were my foremost hope in prosperity, so you ought to have been my companion in adversity too. Then you could have watched our baby son playing in the sand, and your voice would often have joined in his laughter.

Now, as he fondly caresses his aged mother at the breast, [40] he drinks in my tears together with the milk. Meanwhile he clings to me, as if to console me in my sadness, and expresses in gestures what he cannot say with the tongue. But though he is just an infant, he nevertheless is spirited beyond his years. If you could see him, you would think a divinity stirs in him. A shameless myth says that some son of Jupiter[4] strangled two serpents in his cradle. Certainly I am not telling a falsehood: this boy is somehow far more discerning than is normal for his age. He honors the Sabbath and keeps it holy. Indeed, [50] he cannot abide my suckling him then, as on other days. Sometimes, after drinking from their fount, he pushes the nipples away, moistens them with milk, and makes certain signs over them with his thumb. At other times he seems to me to be pointing at something with his fingers, as if prophetically seeing events to come.[5]

That such things were about to happen, you yourself often predicted to me, as I read the words your fingers had spoken. Did not the supreme wisdom of God decree that other old women should become big with child, just as I was? This is demonstrated by Isaac, Samson, Joseph, and the one [60] who first anointed a new king.[6] So too my maternal aunt became fertile in her old age, Anna, the mother of the salvation-bearing Virgin.[7]

But she too is now living in exile, far from her homeland. Alas, cousin, that I must weep over you in constant grief! Where, alas, are you fleeing, pride and joy of our family? Alas, when shall I see you again and be freed at last of this nagging fear? Am I ever going to touch your sweet arms again? O Virgin, O ornament and glory of our house! Where are you fleeing? Alas, what have you done to deserve this? [70] Ah, your life (if you don't know) is beyond reproach! But then my innocence did not keep me safe either. Virtue is the chief reason for our flight. But why could we

---

[4]Hercules, Jupiter's son by Alcmene.

[5]Even as an infant, John already has visions of the future. He acts out his role as the Baptist (ll. 51–52) and points to the Lamb of God (53–54); cf. John 1.29–36. For John's precocious holiness cf. Luke 1.41, where the as yet unborn John leaps in the womb when the Virgin Mary greets his mother; Paul. Nol. *Carm.* 6.144–47.

[6]Samuel anointed Saul as the first King of Israel: see 1 Samuel 10.1. The same four exempla occur in Eob. *Her. Chr.* 13.85–90, where see notes.

[7]*Leg. Aurea* 127.16–17 indicates that Anna is Elizabeth's aunt. Cf. Luke 1.36, where we learn that Mary is Elizabeth's kinswoman. For the legend of Anna and Joachim, see Eob. *Her. Chr.* 13, with n. 1 (p. 296 above).

Sed qur non una licuit fugisse duabus?
  Tristibus haec requies una relicta fuit.
75 Qui mihi nunc frondet, thalamo frueremur eodem.
  Caelestem hunc faceret gratia vestra locum!
Demeret ut curas, et uterque alluderet infans
  Falleret et longum fabula multa diem.
Nunc ferus hoc prohibet patriaeque teterrimus hostis,
80 Per quem non una est tristis et orba parens.
O patria, o magnis domus inclyta patribus olim,
  Quo tua maiestas, quo tua fama ruit?
Quo tua relligio, virtus quo prisca fidesque?
  Quam deiecta, putri squallida sorde, iaces!
85 Aspice quid referant vatum monumenta tuorum,
  Praecipue qui te flet graviore lyra.
Ut canat ad Dominum convertere saepe videbis;
  Tu tamen aversa percipere aure negas.
Quid tamen exclament elegi lugubre professi?
90 Tristibus est tristis res peragenda modis.
Flebilis ut fortuna mea est, sic flebile carmen
  Fortunae debet vulnera flere meae,
Ut tibi, seu celebrem facias sacra praesul ad aram
  Seu lustres viduae limina moesta domus,
95 Reddita non nostris dispar sit epistola fatis
  Neve tui possis non meminisse queri,
Aut sic deliciis nobis famulantibus uti,
  Protinus ut possim dedoluisse putes,
Et simul admonitus natique meique tuorum
100 Ante Deum supplex servet utrumque roges.
Iam videor spectare oculis te nostra legentem
  Flentibus et sicca tergere scripta manu,
Iam canum patulis caput erectare fenestris
  Lataque vicini prospicere arva loci.
105 Ne fleto, venerande senex, ne cede dolori.
  Nunc ita nos istaec pondera ferre decet.
Neve tuis fragilem lachrymis corrumpe senectam.
  Secura currunt fata superba via.
Nemo datas fatis sapiens incessere leges
110 Tentat et ingentem sollicitare rotam.
Ipse tamen rerumque Pater mundique Monarcha,
  Cum libet, arbitrio temperat ista suo.
Sperandum est: nostrae requiem dabit ille senectae.
  Per mala spes animos ad meliora levat.

R3ᵛ

two not have fled together? At least we would have had that one
consolation left to us in our misery. Then we would have enjoyed
the same chamber that now puts forth its greenery for me. Your
charm would have made it a heaven on earth! To allay our
worries, the two infants would have played together and we
could have whiled away the long hours with much talking.

Now the cruel king makes this impossible — that monstrous enemy of our homeland [80] who has saddened and
bereaved so many mothers. O homeland, O house of Israel once
renowned for your great patriarchs, where has your majesty and
fame disappeared? Where your fear of God? Where the old virtue
and faith? How downcast you lie there, soiled with putrid dirt!
Look at what the writings of your prophets tell you, especially
the one who laments you in a graver strain.[8] You will see how
often he urges you to turn back to the Lord. Yet you keep turning a deaf ear and refuse to listen.

But why should my elegiacs cry out in doleful complaints?
[90] A plaintive theme must be treated in plaintive measures. As
my fate is mournful, so my mournful song must beweep the
strokes of my ill fortune. Whether you are offering sacrifices as a
priest at the celebrated altar or are treading the sad threshold of
our lonesome house, the letter you receive ought to match our
fate. I would not want you to complain that I have forgotten you
or have you think that I am enjoying the pleasures at my disposal
so heartily that I could end my grief just like that. At the same
time, I do want to remind you of your family, of your son and
me, [100] so you will pray humbly to God that he may keep
both of us safe.

In my mind's eye I can see you already, reading my letter
with weeping eyes and brushing off the tears with your dry hand.
Already I can imagine you stretching your white head out of the
wide-open windows and looking out over the broad fields of
the surrounding region. Do not weep, venerable old man.
Do not give in to your anguish. That is how we should bear these
burdens now. And do not undermine your fragile old age with
tears. The relentless fates must run their destined course.
Attempting to assail the laws ordained by fate [110] and to put
a spoke in that vast wheel is not wise. It is the Father of the
universe and Monarch of the world, however, who directs fate,
whenever he wishes and as he sees fit. We must remain hopeful:
in our declining years he will grant us peace. Hope can carry us
through these tribulations and raise our spirits toward a better
future.

---

[8] The prophet Jeremiah, to whom the Old Testament book of Lamentations is traditionally ascribed.

90=R4ʳ

115 At iuvat in dubiis etiam solertia rebus;
Spe sola mentem pascere decipere est.
Sit tibi certa tui custodia corporis isto
Quo non est hominum tempore certa fides.
Omnia sacrilegi vita convivia regis —
120 Insidias vitae praeparat ille tuae!
Baethica Sidoniis fundet tibi toxica vitris
Bebryciumque Arabo virus in aere dabit.
Hec ubi vitaris, timeas peiora necesse est.
Vix sacra tutatrix ara futura tibi est.
125 Tam furit et sacrum posuit virtutis amorem,
Sic metuit regni perdere sceptra sui!
Regius incautum perimat ne forte satelles,
E templo in populum quolibet ire time.
Forte sacras aliquid vel adhuc venerabitur aras
130 Nec sanctam diro polluet ense domum.
Sic mihi scribenti (quamvis nihil ominer unquam)
Nescio quis gelidus venit in ossa tremor.
Aspiciens me forte puer suspiria traxit,
Qualia desperans vota cupita solet.
135 Crassior et solito stupidam circumstetit aer;
Fluxit in excussum dextera lapsa sinum.

R4ᵛ

Ut redii, "Valeant," dixi, "quae talia curant!
Ominibus pereat credere si qua potest!
Certa Dei vis est certique potentia fati.
140 Ostentis fecit fabula vana fidem."
Tu quoque iamdudum, ut gravis es, levia ista refutas
Solaque sublimi caelica mente rotas.
Quare age, cum tanto stabis bene cautus ab hoste,
Placatum nostri sis memor ante Deum,
145 Servet ut incolumem puerum cum matre nec illos
Exilio miseros longius esse sinat,
Servet et incolumem puerum cum matre puella
Quae nunc marmoreae tendit ad arva Phari.
Heu lachrymae, heu gemitus, quoties mihi Virginis illud
150 Nomen et haec subiit pectora dulcis amor!
Quos nunc, Anna parens, non experiere dolores!
Heu, nunc illa tui gloria ventris ubi est?
Aeternum mea chara vale nurus. O tua saltem
Exilio doleant pectora casta brevi!
155 Tuque vale nostramque, senex, tueare salutem,
O mecum sero pignore facte pater!
Post, ubi grassantis desaeverit ira tyranni,
Forte erit in patrios posse redire lares.

But in these dangerous times we also need shrewdness. To rely on hope alone is to court disappointment. Be sure to look to your personal safety in this day and age when no one can be trusted anymore. Avoid all the banquets that the sacrilegious king might invite you to — [120] he is plotting an attempt on your life! He will pour Spanish venom into Sidonian crystal and offer you Bithynian poison in Arabian bronze. When you have stayed clear of that, you must brace yourself for worse. The sacred altar will scarcely protect you in the future.[9] That is how madly he has abandoned the holy love of virtue; that is how terrified he is of losing control of his kingdom! Lest perchance one of the king's henchmen should assassinate you when you are off your guard, take care not to leave the Temple and wander off into the crowd. With luck he may even now respect the sanctity of the altars enough [130] not to defile the house of God with his terrible sword.

As I was writing these words (though I really have no premonitions of disaster), a kind of cold shiver ran through my bones. The boy must have been eying me, for he heaved the sighs of one despairing of his fondest hopes. In my dazed state, the air seemed to surround me thicker than usual. My right hand sank down into my trembling lap. As soon as I became myself again, I said: "Away with anybody who cares about such things! Perish the woman who can believe in bad omens! God's might is immutable, as is the power of immutable fate. [140] Belief in portents is rooted in empty myth."

You too, serious-minded as you are, have long since rejected superstitions like this and revolve nothing but godly thoughts in your lofty mind. Come, then, since you will be careful to stay away from our archenemy, do remember us in your prayers to God. Placate him, so that he will keep mother and son safe and not let us unfortunates stay in exile any longer. May he also keep that maidenly mother and her son safe as they wend their way to the fields near the marble lighthouse of Pharos![10]

Alas the tears, alas the groans, whenever that Virgin [150] and her sweet love come into my mind! What griefs you must be suffering now, mother Anna! Alas, where now is that pride and joy of your womb? Farewell forever, my dear cousin! Oh, may *your* chaste heart, at least, suffer exile for just a brief time! You too, old man, good-bye and look after our wellbeing, O you, who became a father with me in our old age!

Later, when the crazed tyrant's fury abates, it may well be possible to return to home and family.

---

[9]In antiquity altars were an asylum. Anyone at an altar could not be dragged away for any reason.

[10]Pharos, a small island near Alexandria, Egypt, possessed a world-famous lighthouse: cf. *Her. Chr.* 1.126, with n. 11 (p. 166 above).

91 = R5ʳ   **21**   **PAULA HIERONIMO**

Si, pater, Haebraeos non est grave ponere vates,
    Perlege Rhomana pauca notata manu.
Sed quid et unde legas iamdudum, Hieronime, nosti,
    Notaque non posito nomine Paula fui.
5   Attamen unde loci tibi littera nostra feratur
    Quoque sit, ut noris, tempore scripta rogas?
Illa quidem veteris non venit ab urbe Quirini,
    Unde mihi vetus est praecipuumque genus.
Non Latii de parte data est quacunque feracis:
10   Itala iamdudum terra relicta mihi est.
Denique non de quacunque est regione profecta,
    Quodlibet a vestra quam secat aequor humo.
Iam, puto, me vestro sentiscis in orbe morari,
    Incertus quare, quomodo, quove loco.
15   Accipe, ne teneam doctas ambagibus aures,
    Sed solita tecum simplicitate loquar.
Flaminibus dextris Cyprium delata per aequor,
    Applicui in portus, Sidoni terra, tuos.
Extat adhuc Tyrio Rhomana in littore navis.
20   Ipsa per exiguum tempus in urbe moror.
Hic sumus, hunc nullus nos appulit error in orbem:
R5ᵛ   Certa fuit nostrae causa tenaxque viae.
Hanc quoque, si dubitas, de me fortasse requires —
    Si tamen ipse tui nescius esse potes!
25   Venimus et patriam te propter sprevimus, atque
    Quod magis est, viduae pignora chara domus.
At matrem natis de quattuor una sequta est,
    Eustochium, scriptis facta animosa tuis.
Illa tuos ut amat fidei studiosa libellos,
30   Non secus absentis flagrat amore tui.

Her. Chr. **21.** **4** non posito *A*: vel tacito *BO*.   **5–7** Attamen — veteris *A*: Si tamen addubitas per quem tibi littera nostra est [est *om. O*] / Reddita, quo data sit tempore quove loco, / Noveris haec prisci *BO*.   **8** mihi — praecipuumque *A*: vetus ducunt stemmata nostra *BO*.   **9** Latii de parte . . . quacunque feracis *A*: aliqua de parte . . . Oenotridos orae *BO*.   **12** Quodlibet — secat *A*: Quodquod ab Hebraea quam secet *BO*.   *Post* **12** *add. BO*: Si quo scripta rogas sit tempore, milia dic quot / Barbara Christipara distet ab urbe Tyrus. / Quo quia non potuit citius pedes ire minister, / A calamo parvi temporis egit iter.   **13** vestro — orbe *A*: sentis vestra in regione *BO*.   **14** quomodo *A*: quo duce *BO*.   **16–18** Sed — tuos *A*: Pene etiam puduit scribere pauca tibi. / Per mare delatas Cyprium foelicibus Euris / Excepit nostras Sidonis unda rates *BO*.   **21** appulit *A*: expulit *BO*.   **22–24** Certa — potes! *A*: Caussa fuit nostrae magna decensque viae. / Atque ea quae fuerit si tu fortasse requiris, / Incipis hic certe nescius esse tui. *BO*.   **25** sprevimus *AB*: liquimus *O*.   **30** Non secus *AB*: Sic etiam *O*.

21 PAULA TO JEROME[1]

If, father, it is not too much of a burden to lay the Hebrew bards
aside, peruse these few lines, written by a Roman hand.

But you have long since recognized, Jerome, what it is you
read and who wrote it. Even if I did not mention my name,
you would know it was Paula. Still, do you want to learn where my
letter was sent and when it was written? It certainly did not come
from the city of old Quirinus,[2] whence my ancient and preeminent
family traces its descent. Nor was it dispatched somewhere in fertile
Latium: [10] I left Italy some time ago. In fact, it did not set out
from any region that the sea cuts off from your soil.

Already, I think, it dawns on you that I must be staying in your
part of the world, though you are still unsure why, how, or where
exactly. So as not to keep your learned ears in suspense with circum-
locutions, let me tell you the facts with my customary simplicity.
After sailing across the Cyprian Sea with fair breezes, I landed in the
port of Sidon. The Roman ship still rides at anchor off the Tyrian
coast. [20] I myself plan on staying only a short time in the city.

This is where I am now. It was no errant course that
brought me to this part of the world: I had a firm and unwavering reason for my voyage. And if you are in doubt, you will
probably ask me about that too — but only if you're oblivious
of yourself! I came here because of you! It was to see you that
I spurned my homeland and, what is more, my dear children in
the motherless house. Of the four children, however, one has
followed her mother: Eustochium, made bold through your
writings. Just as she, ever zealous in the faith, loves reading
your books, [30] so she burns with love for you in your absence.

---

[1]St. Paula was a noble Roman lady (347–404), who traced her ancestry back to the Scipios and
other illustrious Romans. Married to the nobleman Toxotius, she bore him a son of the same name as
well as four daughters, Blesilla, Paulina, Eustochium, and Rufina. After her husband's death in 379, she
lived an austere life of charity in Rome. Through the Bishops Epiphanius of Salamis and Paulinus of
Antioch she not only became personally acquainted with Jerome (ca. 345–419/20) but also felt
inspired to follow a monastic life in Palestine. After Pope Damasus died in late 384, Jerome found
himself bitterly attacked by his enemies. He therefore departed for the Holy Land in August 385.
Paula, Eustochium, and other Roman women joined him at Antioch nine months later. After touring
the sacred sites of Palestine and Egypt for a year they settled into a life of work and prayer at
Bethlehem. See Hier. *Ep.* 108 (excerpted in *Leg. aurea* 29).

Since Jerome's account suppresses his own role in Paula's circuitous pilgrimage, Eobanus imagines
that Jerome is already living in Bethlehem. Accordingly he has Paula writing Jerome from the port of
Sidon, where she has just arrived from Rome via Cyprus. She explains her reasons for coming to see
him in the birthplace of Jesus. But first she and Eustochium plan to visit all the holy places in Palestine
and the Sinai Peninsula.

In the 1532/39 version this letter is *Her.* 2.2.

[2]Romulus, the founder of Rome, was worshiped under the name Quirinus.

O, quoties vita functae memor illa sororis
    Vestra super tristi funere scripta legit,
Atque ita, "Non levibus, foelix Blesilla, poetis,
    Sed cantata sacro carmine vivis!" ait
35   Moestaque in undantes exolvit lumina fletus,
    Saepe quod ut faciam me quoque cogit idem.
Nam quem tanta nihil moveat facundia, natum
    Bessagetas inter Sauromatasque putem.
Si tamen Odrysii traxerunt carmina vatis
40   Prata, homines, manes, flumina, saxa, feras,
Flectere barbaricas menteis animosque feroces
    Eloquii posset gratia viva tui.
Testis habet de te non unum Rhoma libellum,

92 = R6ʳ   Quem legat et laeto praedicet ore suum.
45   Ah, quoties aliquem de tot legisse iuvabat,
    Cum desyderio mens gemit aegra tui!
Nulla quidem rerum ratio nec temporis unquam
    Unum te nobis obliterasse potest.
Nostra tibi devota domus te semper adorat;
50   Acceptum referat quod tibi semper habet.
Sicut enim tota de relligione mereris,
    Sic bene nos titulo nobiliore novas.
Nam licet insignes veterum numeremus avorum
    Relliquias, fasces, arma, trophaea, duces,
55   Omnia gentili sordent squallore, nec ullum
    Elogium verae nobilitatis habent.
Nec tanto nobis decori fuit ille, subacto
    Qui Poeno clarum nomen ab hoste tulit.
Gloria terrenae parta est mihi laudis ab illo;
60   Tu facis immensi nos genus esse Dei.
Sanguine debemus tibi, Scipio magne, fatemur.
    Hinc sumus ex atavis regibus alta domus.
Altera sed nostri pars uni debet Iesu.
    Illa suo quiddam corpore maius habet.
65   Per te nobilior quae nunc, Hieronyme, facta est,

R6ᵛ   Corporis et vanum despicit alta genus —

---

31 vita functae *A*: olim charae *B*, olim chare *O*.   **34** Sed — carmine *A*: Ore sed aethereo prodita *BO*.
35–36 Moestaque — idem *A*: Et simul undantes in fletus lumina solvit, / Quae mihi res lachrymas saepe
movere solet. / Atque ita non flemus tam natam ego, nata sororem, / Quam querimur memores per tua
scripta tui *BO*.   **40** Prata . . . manes *A*: Monstra . . . naves *BO*.   **42** posset *A*: potuit *BO*.
47 unquam *AO*: ulla *B*.   **48** obliterasse *A*: eripuisse *BO*.   *Post* **48** *add. BO*: Quo minus
absentis nobiscum dulcis imago / Sit tua et his animis obvia semper eat.   **51** de relligione *A*: bene de
pietate *BO*.   **52** Sic — novas *A*: Illustres titulo nos meliore facis *BO*.   **53** licet insignes *A*: monumenta licet *BO*.   **60** immensi — Dei *A*: aetherei nominis esse genus *BO*.   **64** Illa *AB*: Ille *O*.
65 quae *BO*: que *A*; est *AB*: *om. O*.

Oh, how often, when she thinks back on her deceased sister,
does she read your letter about her tragic death and exclaim:
"Fortunate Blesilla! You live on, not in the praises of trivial
poets, but in a sacred song."[3] And as she does so, she lets a
stream of tears burst from her sorrowful eyes. Often this moves
me to do the same. For anyone who can remain untouched by
such powers of speech, must in my opinion have been born
among the Bessygitae and Sarmatians.[4] But if the songs of the
Thracian bard[5] could gather [40] meadows, men, shades, rivers,
stones, and wild beasts, the living charm of your eloquence
could move barbaric minds and savage hearts.

     Rome bears witness to that, for she possesses more than one
volume by you, which she reads and joyfully proclaims her own.
Ah, how often have people been blessed by reading those rich
pages, even as their anguished hearts sigh with longing for you!
Nothing in the world or in this age can ever efface you from
our mind.

     Our family, as devoted to you as ever, continues to revere
you. [50] Everything it has, it always attributes to you. Indeed,
just as you have earned the gratitude of all Christianity, so you
have thoroughly renewed us with a higher nobility. For though
we count the illustrious relics of ancient ancestors — fasces,
arms, trophies, generals — they are all soiled with the filth of
paganism and have none of the hallmarks of true nobility. Even
he, who won splendid fame by defeating the Carthaginian
enemy,[6] was not so great an ornament to us as you. From him I
inherited the glory of earthly renown. [60] You, by contrast,
make us part of the family of the boundless God. By blood we
are indebted to the great Scipio. We acknowledge that. On that
side we are an ancient family, descended from a long line of
kings. But the other side of our being is indebted to Jesus alone.
This part has greater value than its body. Now that it has become
nobler through you, Jerome, it scornfully looks down on the

---

[3]After Blesilla died in 384, Jerome wrote a letter of consolation to her mother Paula. See Hier.
Ep. 108, paragraphs 1 and 4. In keeping with the fiction of Eobanus' heroic epistle, Jerome's prose
letter is likewise said to have been a poem.

[4]According to Ambrogio Calepino's *Dictionarium*, first published in 1502 and well-known to
Eobanus, the Bessygitae were a cannibalistic people who lived by the Bessygas River in India. Cf. Eob.
Epic. 9.22: "inhumanos . . . Bessagetas." The Sarmatians were a nomadic people in eastern Europe.

[5]Orpheus.

[6]P. Cornelius Scipio Africanus (236–183 BCE), who defeated Hannibal in the Second Punic War.

Et merito, cum se partem de semine caeli
    Inclusam lutea sentiat esse domo.
Sentit, et ex isto patrias respirat ad arces
70   Exilio, carnis pondere fessa suae.
Talia multa tuis quis nescit scripta libellis?
    Pene fui tecum qualibus ausa loqui.
Omnia tu nosti, nihil est te doctius uno
    Inter caelivagi solis utrumque larem.
75   Quamque aliis praestas divinae lumine mentis,
    Tam sacra cunctis es pietate prior.
Saepe etenim, cum dulcis adhuc te Rhoma teneret
    Et premeret tonsum rubra tiara caput,
Sponte humiles etiam famulas dignatus adire
80   Sacraque mansueto pectore verba loqui,
Tum faciles nobis praebere rogantibus aures
    Atque rudes vivis saepe iuvare notis.
Ergone nos, tanto devinctos munere, credis
    Immemores unquam posse fuisse tui?
85   Nunquam, crede, tui dulcis praesentia nobis
    Excidit, Haebraeo donec in orbe manes.
Nulla tuos nostro exemit de pectore vultus,
    Nulla tuum nostro nomen ab ore dies.
93=S1ʳ
Aut ego sola domo vidua tua scripta relegi
90   Aut civi reliquas in mea vota nurus.
Illae, clavigeri seu forte ad principis aedem
    Sacrificae Christo pars quota plebis eram
Seu quaecunque patent totam delubra per urbem,
    Seu tererem lati publica strata Fori,
95   Saepe velut denso stipantes agmine circum
    De te quaerendi non habuere modum.

69 respirat *A*: aspirat *BO*.   75–76 Quamque — prior. *A*: *om. BO*.   77 etenim *A*: quidem *BO*. 78–82 Et premeret — notis. *A*: Doctrinae aedideras plurima signa tuae, / Ut taceam quoties dederis quae maxima, parvi / Ut facias, aequum nos petiisse fuit, / Quam fueris faciles praebere rogantibus aures, / Quam solitus nulla pectora mole premi! *BO*.   84 unquam posse *A*: aliqua parte *BO*. 85 Nunquam — nobis *A*: Illa tuae nunquam nobis pietatis imago *BO*.   86 Excidit *AO*: Excidet *B*; Haebraeo — manes *A*: Ausonia donec in urbe sumus *BO*.   90 vota *AB*: nota *O*.

body's sham nobility — and rightly so, since it recognizes that it is part of the seed of heaven, imprisoned in a house of clay. It recognizes this and, [70] weary of the burden of its flesh, it longs to leave this exile and return to its heavenly home.

Who does not know that your writings are replete with thoughts like these? I almost made bold to speak to you about them. You know everything. Nobody is more learned than you between the two abodes of the heaven-wandering sun. And as you outshine all others through the light of the divine mind, so you surpass all others in holy devotion. Indeed, when sweet Rome still held you fast and the red tiara covered your tonsured head,[7] you often deigned to visit your humble servants too [80] and speak sacred words to us that came straight from your gentle heart. In those days you would often lend us a ready ear, answer our questions, and delight us unversed women with lively letters.

Do you believe, then, that we, who are obliged to you for such marvelous kindness, can ever forget you? Your sweet presence, trust me, has never slipped our mind since you've been living in the Hebrew world. No day has ever taken your face from our hearts, no day taken your name from our lips. Either I would reread your writings alone in my widowed house [90] or urge other young women to follow my lead. In fact, whether I was a tiny part of the people who worship Christ in the church of the key-bearing bishop[8] or some of the other sanctuaries that are open throughout the city, or whether I walked up and down the public streets of the wide Forum, these women often thronged around me, so to speak, in serried ranks and never stopped asking about you.

[7]According to the early *vitas* (*PL* 22, cols. 202, 204, and 235) as well as *Leg. aurea* 142.33, Jerome was a cardinal before he left for the Holy Land. The legend was first debunked by Erasmus in his life of Jerome. See Wallace K. Ferguson, ed., *Erasmi opuscula: A Supplement to the Opera omnia* (The Hague, 1933), 155. Eobanus eliminated the legendary detail in the revision of 1532/39.

[8]St. Peter's in Rome.

Iamque aliquis populi de turba proximus illis
   (Sed cui nec mens est nec sua nota domus)
Nomen ut audivit, "Quis nam furor iste? Quis," inquit,
100   "Has igitur fatuas esse coegit anus?"
Hunc quidam, cui longa breves reverentia canos
   Sparserat, his toto iussit abire Foro:
"Vade, malum, sacra ne turbes consortia. Non sunt
   Incessenda odio nomina tanta tuo."
105   Sed tua nec virtus animo patietur iniquo,
   Si male quis loquitur qui bonus esse nequit.
Qui bonus est mala non loquitur, quia semper in ipso
   Virtutis vitio predominatur amor.
At qui nequitiam primo contraxit ab ortu,
110   Dum malus est, quenquam non putat esse bonum.
Qui placet ergo bonis, nihil huic nocet invidus osor,
   Hoc licet ignipotens ardeat Aethna minus.
Si multis tua fama bonis hic pura relicta est,
   Non mirum pauci si quid obesse student.
115   Invidus hos mores habet omnis, ut omnia semper
   Omnibus invideat quae minus ipse tenet.
Talia multa tuae meditata est cura Minervae.
   Quid referam multis aedita scripta locis?
Me magis apposito fas intendisse labori est
120   Et quae me nequeant dedecuisse loqui.
Ergo ubi multa diu suspiria ducta vicissim
   Nostraque patre suo languit orba domus,
Venerat Antiochi Praesul Paulinus ab urbe —
   O celebrem quanta relligione virum! —
125   Et Salaminaeis Epiphanius alter ab oris,
   Congrua qui propriis nomina rebus habet.
Horum ita summa meam movit constantia mentem,
   Sic memet virtus abstulit ista mihi,
Ut mihi quam primum rebus patriaque relictis
130   Venerit exilii commodioris amor.

S1ᵛ (margin at line 110)

97–112 Iamque — minus *A*: Est tamen ista malis probitas suspecta quibusdam, / Suetis metiri [Metiri solitis *O*] facta aliena suis. / Tu parvi facies animo nec habebis iniquo: / Invidiae virtus optima caussa subest *BO*.   114 pauci — student *A*: paucis displicuisse malis *BO*.   115–16 Invidus — tenet. *A*: *om. BO*.   117–19 Talia — est *A*: Quae tibi dum refero ceu soli lumina monstro / Et medium certae lucis egere diem. / Me fuerat satius praesenti intendere curae *BO*.   121 Ergo — vicissim *A*: Ergo ubi certa satis stabat sententia Romam / Linquere et exilii vertere amore solum, / Te procul a nobis tellus longinqua tenebat, *BO*.   126 Congrua *A*: Consona *BO*.   *Post* 126 *add. BO*: Is Romae nostras diverterat hospes in aedes, / Iunctus amicitia proximiore mihi. / Praesule quo Cyprus Galilaeo servit Iesu, / Sordibus Idalidos libera facta deae.   127 meam — mentem *A*: meum movit facundia pectus *BO*.

A lowbred fellow (but a mindless one, who wouldn't recognize his own house if you showed him) came up to them once. Hearing your name, he cried out: "What is all this ranting and raving? All right, who is the beau [100] that has swept these old wives off their feet?" But another man, whose short hair was sprinkled with the hoar of venerable old age, told him to leave the Forum: "Be off with you, evil brute! Do not disturb this sacred company or assail great names like his with your taunts!" But you in the goodness of your heart will take it in stride if someone unable to be good speaks ill of you. A good man does not speak ill, because the love of virtue in him always predominates over vice. But someone who has amassed depravity since he was born [110] cannot imagine that anyone is good, while he himself is evil. Whoever pleases the good, therefore, cannot be hurt by some malevolent hater, even if he burns hotter than fiery Etna itself. Considering that the many good people here continue to cherish your fame in all its purity, no wonder a few do their utmost to undermine it. Envious people have this habit in common: they always envy everybody for everything they do not have themselves.

Your mind has carefully pondered many such matters as this. Why am I telling you things that you have written about in many places yourself? It would be more appropriate for me to focus on the subject at hand [120] and to speak about topics that cannot discredit me.

Well then, after we had long heaved many a sigh to each other and our household was still faint with grief at losing its father, there came to us from the city of Antioch Bishop Paulinus — O, what a saintly man he is! — as well as another bishop from the shores of Salamis, Epiphanius, who bears a name that accords with his personal accomplishments.[9] Their exemplary steadfastness so moved my heart, their goodness so transported me, that I yearned to forsake my possessions and homeland as soon as possible [130] and seek a more desirable exile.[10]

---

[9]Epiphanius lives up to his name, because his life is an epiphany of God.

[10]Bethlehem will be a more agreeable exile than Rome. As the birthplace of Jesus, it is closer to the true homeland, heaven. Cf. ll. 69–70 above, l. 174 below.

94=S2^r

Et iam certa fui peregrinas visere terras,
    Iamque novus tota rumor in urbe fuit.
In luctum conversa domus sic flevit ut ipsae
    Vicinae cuperent me tenuisse nurus.

135 Praecipue Eustochium, pleno iam nubilis aevo,
    Talia cum lachrymis saepe loquta mihi est:
"O, quemcunque, parens charissima, pergis in orbem,
    Exilii comitem me velis esse tui.
Tene ego abire sinam solam? Mene ipsa relinquis?

140   Mors prius hoc opto syncopet atra caput."
His mihi saepe genas verbis madefecit, et ibant
    Cum lachrymis planctus illius atque mei.
Et iam tempus erat vento dare vela vocanti,
    Ultimaque in patria lux fuit orta mihi.

145 Egredior. Comes it iamiam Rufina trilustris
    Eustochiumque soror Theochiusque puer.
Haec mihi tunc aderant clausi iam pignora ventris.
    Caetera non eadem sors procul esse tulit.
Iamque egressa meis comitata affinibus urbem,

150   Iam prope conspecto littore portus erat.
Tum velut atra duae subiturae funera natae
    Fleverunt miserae, flevit et ipse puer.
Indoluisse graves scopulos et saxa querelas,

S2^v

    Audivisse etiam littora surda puto.

155 Et licet Adriaco non sit mansuetior aestu,
    Strata maris solito lenior unda fuit.
Oscula et amplexus postquam data multa vicissim
    Omnibus et summo diximus ore "Vale,"
Grandaevo (nam forte aderat) duo pignora fratri

160   Cum tota curae iussimus esse domo.
Tum comite Eustochio non magnam ingressa phaselum,
    "Quod bene sit," dixi, "navita, solve ratem."
Dum loquor et retro fugientia littora specto,
    Ni fallar, turbam me revocasse puto.

165 Iam clamosa manus versum mea vela tetendit,
    Triste quid indigno murmure visa queri.
"Rhoma, vale," dixi, "fidei domus inclyta sanctae,
    Iam verum Petro principe fassa Deum.

---

131 Et — terras *A*: Suffectura viae vestes atque aera parabam *BO*.   **132** tota *AO*: toti *B*; fuit *A*: fui *BO*.   **136** saepe *AB*: verba *O*.   **138** velis *A*: decet *BO*.   **139** relinquis *A*: relinquas *BO*.   **140** Mors — caput *A*: Ante meum rumpat de tribus una colum *BO*.   **144** fuit *A*: erat *BO*.   **145** iamiam *A*: iam tum *BO*.   **146** Theochiusque *A*: Toxotiusque *BO*.   **150** portus *A*: puppis *BO*.   **153** graves . . . querelas *A*: illis . . . querelis *BO*.   **156** maris solito *AB*: malis solis *O*.   **164** fallar *A*: fallor *BO*.   **165** Iam *A*: Tam *BO*; versum *AB*: versus *O*.   **166** indigno *A*: incerto *BO*.

Before long I had made up my mind to go abroad, and soon the whole city was abuzz with the news. The griefstricken family wept so bitterly that even the neighbor women wanted to hold me back. Especially Eustochium — she has reached womanhood now and is old enough to be married — often told me tearfully: "Oh, dearest mother, no matter to what part of the world you move to, you'll want me as your companion in exile, won't you? Do you think I can let you go by yourself? Can you bring yourself to leave me behind? [140] I would rather have black Death cut off my head." With these words she would often bring tears to my eyes, and the two of us would burst into weeping and wailing.

And then it was time to hoist our sails to the beckoning wind. The final day in my homeland had dawned. I went outside. The already fifteen-year-old Rufina accompanied me, along with her sister Eustochium and the boy Theochius. These were the children of my now-closed womb who were present with me then. A different fate had carried the others far from me.[11] Escorted by my relatives, I left the city behind in no time at all. [150] Before I knew it we were in sight of the coast and getting close to the port. Then the two daughters began weeping inconsolably, as if going to a melancholy funeral, and even the boy was crying. The very rocks and cliffs, I think, grieved at their heartrending laments. Even the deaf shores seemed to be listening to them. And though it is no gentler than the stormy Adriatic, the sea was stilled and its waves were calmer than normal.

After we had given each other many kisses and embraces and bidden everybody a final farewell, [160] I commended the two children along with the entire house to the care of my aged brother (for he happened to be there). Then, having boarded the small ship in the company of Eustochium, I said, "If all is in order, captain, set sail."

While I was talking and watching the coast recede, the crowd, unless I am mistaken, appeared to be calling me back. Now they were holding out their hands toward my clamorous sails and seemed to be indignantly murmuring some sad lament. "Rome, farewell," I cried, "glorious home of the holy faith, ever since you confessed the true God when Peter was bishop. Exalted

[11]Paula's eldest daughter Blesilla had died the previous year. Paulina had just married St. Pammachius, a Roman citizen who was a close friend of Jerome.

Aeternum, patria alta, vale, patriique nepotes,
170   Cumque tuis nuribus, terra Latina, vale!
Nunc ego supraema vos, littora, voce saluto,
    In quibus est patriae nobilis ora meae.
At tu, Rhoma, precor, tibi credita pignora serva.
    Ipsa colam patria dulcius exilium."
175   Dum loquor, aspectum turresque et terra relinquunt,

    Iamque patens oculis undique pontus erat.
Caetera quae tulimus superatum fata per aequor
    Ipsa tibi mecum filia testis erit.
Quae nunc nescio quid calamo quoque scribit anhelo,
180   Dum rogo, "Quid facias?" "Ipsane quaeris?" ait.
Gratulor. Ergo tibi reddetur epistola duplex.
    Quam bene sic pellex filia matris erit!
Quam bene et incolumes magni clementia Christi
    Reddidit optato constituitque solo!
185   Hic aliquot sacro precibus de more peractis,
    Ad Solimas arces pergere restat amor
Omniaque humano loca sanctificata Tonanti,
    Praecipue exangui pressa sepulchra Deo,
Costidis hinc etiam Sinaia templa puellae
190   Gestaque Mosaea signa videre manu.
Inde ubi me votis dabitur rediisse potitam
    Et fuerit mentis plena cupido meae,
Ad Bethleemiticos, caelo loca proxima, colles
    Ibimus optato, turba pusilla, gradu.
195   Hic, ubi tu studiis pulchrum caelestibus aevum
    Incomprehensibilis degis amore boni,
Hic etiam certo requies mea fine futura est,

    Nec locus in terris charior alter erit,
Et merito, quem sic nostri Reparator honoris
200   Natali clarum fecerit esse suo,
Qua stetit illa frequens et agrestibus horrida culmis,
    Quae casa nascentem vidit in orbe Deum.
Huic ego nec veteris celebrata palatia Rhomae
    Praetulerim et Latio templa superba Iove,
205   Non Ephesi delubra deae sacrata triformi
    Et magnum quicquid maximus orbis habet.

---

170 Cumque — vale *A*: Terrarum princeps, Romula terra, vale *BO*.   177 fata *AB*: vata *O*.
180 facias *AO*: facies *B*.   183–84 et [ut *A*] incolumes magni . . . Reddidit *A*: nos magni salvas . . . /
Praestitit *BO*.   185 Hic — peractis *A*: Hic actis aliquot vento [ventis *B*, ventos *O*] remorante
diebus *BO*.   191 potitam *AO*: petitam *B*.   193 Bethleemiticos *A*: Bethleemiacos *BO*.
194 turba *AO*: turbata *B*.   196 Incomprehensibilis — boni *A*: Degis et in terris cum superis
habitas *BO*.   197 etiam *A*: etenim *BO*.   198 charior *A*: gratior *BO*.   202 casa *AB*: casu *O*.
204 Praetulerim et *A*: Praetulero aut *BO*; Iove *AB*: Iovi *O*.   205–06 Non — habet. *A*: om. *BO*.

fatherland, farewell forever, and you, sons of your country!
[170] You too, land of Italy together with your women, farewell!
Now, for the last time, I salute you shores that fringe my celebrated homeland. But you, Rome, I beseech you, watch over the
children I entrusted to you. I myself will live in an exile sweeter
than my own native land." As I spoke, towers and land disappeared from view, and soon the sea stretched out before my eyes
on every side.

As for the other events on our sea voyage, you will find out
about them in a companion letter by my daughter. She too was
writing something just now with flying pen; [180] and when
I inquired, "What are you doing?" she answered, "And you are
asking me?" This gladdens my heart. So now you will get a dou-
ble letter. What a fine rival she'll make for her mother, if she goes
on like this!

How well has the mercy of Christ the Lord preserved us
and brought us safely to the longed-for land! After saying some
prayers of thanks here, in accordance with sacred custom, we are
eager to continue to the hills of Jerusalem and to all the places
sanctified by the human Thunderer, especially the sepulcher
where God's lifeless body lay. This done, we also want to visit
the church of Costus' daughter on Mount Sinai[12] [190] and see
where the hand of Moses worked miracles. Once these dreams
of mine have come true and I have looked around to my
heart's content, then we, little band of travelers, will return at
a comfortable pace to the hills of Bethlehem, the place closest to
heaven. There, where you are spending a beautiful life and
pursuing heavenly studies for love of the good that passes all
understanding, there I too will end my wanderings and find
peace. No spot on earth will be dearer to me, and rightly so,
considering that this is the place that the Restorer of our dignity
[200] made illustrious through his birth, where that crowded
hovel once stood, bristling with rustic thatch, the shed that saw
God being brought into the world. For this place I would not
trade the celebrated palace of ancient Rome and the temple
proud of Latium's Jove, not the shrine sacred to the triform goddess of Ephesus[13] or anything else of consequence in the whole

---

[12]The monastery of St. Catherine on Mount Sinai, where the saint's body was said to have been
carried by angels after her martyrdom, was in fact not constructed until the sixth century — well after
Paula's time. For St. Catherine of Alexandria, see *Her. Chr.* 4.

[13]Paula refers first to the imperial palace on the Palatine Hill and the Capitol on the Capitoline
Hill in Rome and then to Diana's celebrated temple in Ephesus. Diana (Artemis) is "triform" because
she was worshiped as Luna in heaven, Diana on earth, and Proserpina in the underworld.

Illa operosa fuit nascenti regia Christo,
    Aula fuit tanto tam speciosa Duci.
Istic angelici natum cecinere choraules,
210   Hic infans geminum vagiit ante pecus,
Hic tria donarunt sapientes munera Persae;
    Regibus aereum pro duce lumen erat.
Caelesti Bethleem domus inclyta pane vocatur;
    Omnis ibi saturo cedet ab ore fames.
215   O domus, hospitium fessae dare dulce senectae
    Non est quae possit te prior ulla mihi!
Te quoque, pertesum falsi ludibria mundi,
    Credibile est istic constituisse mori.
O mihi vel saltem placido sic fine quietae
96=S4ʳ   220   Contingat parvae condere tecta casae!
Pauperis ingrediar tuguri ducentia rimas
    Limina et insanis pervia septa Notis.
Scilicet exiguo pudeat me vivere in antro,
    Hic, ubi rara suum texit arundo Deum?
225   Quem, precor, hoc pudeat, cum tu quoque tantus eodem,
    Quamvis exiguo, legeris esse loco?
Non tamen exiguo, nam si virtutibus addas,
    Haec spatium caelo moenia maius habent.
Nam qui mole sua captus excesserat omnes,
230   Viderunt clausum parvula tecta Deum.
Totius haec igitur domus est clarissima mundi;
    Totius haec summum protulit orbis opus.
Non alio emeritam potuisti claudere vitam.
    Nos quoque non alio consenuisse decet.
235   Ipse tuae famulae redeant foeliciter ora.
    Longe aberit, si tu faveris, omne malum.
Utque facis, Christoque refer natam atque parentem,
    Tempore quo videas laetus utramque brevi.

---

209 Istic *A*: Illic *BO*.   **212** lumen *AB*: sydus *O*.   **218** istic *A*: illic *BO*.   **233–34** alio . . . alio *A*: alibi . . . alibi *BO*.   **237** Christoque — natam *A*: Christo natam trade *BO*.   **238** quo videas *A*: ut aspicias *BO*.

wide world. This was the ornate palace for the newborn Christ. It was the gorgeous residence for so mighty a Lord. There the choirs of angels sang of his birth; [210] there the babe wailed before the two beasts; there the Persian sages brought their three gifts. A light in the sky served those kings as guide.

Bethlehem is famed as the house of heavenly bread.[14] There all my hunger will be stilled. O house, nothing could offer my weary old age sweeter lodgings than you! I can well believe that you too, disgusted with the mockeries of this false world, are resolved to die nowhere else but there.

Oh, if I could at least [220] build a small cottage there and enjoy peace and rest at last! Then I would enter the poor hut with its cracking threshold, its walls open to the raging gales. Come now, should I be ashamed to live in a tiny shack here, where sparse reed once covered its God? Who, I ask, would be ashamed of this when even so great a man as you has chosen to live in the same place, small though it is? And yet it is by no means small. For if you also take the merits into account, these walls have more room than heaven itself. Indeed, [230] this little town has gazed on God bound in the flesh — on him, who in his infinity passes all bounds. This house, therefore, is the most illustrious in the whole world. It brought forth the supreme creation in the universe. You could not live out your leisure years anywhere else. For us too it would not be right to grow old in any other place.

Do pray that your handmaids may return safe and sound. If you favor us, we shall be spared all evil. And as you are doing already, commend daughter and mother to Christ, so that you may joyfully see the two of us in just a short time.

---

[14]The name *Bethlehem* was traditionally interpreted to mean "the house of bread." Cf. Hier. *Ep.* 108.10, where Paula exclaims (with an allusion to John 6.51), "Hail Bethlehem, house of bread, in which was born that bread which came down from heaven"; Isid. *Orig.* 15.1.23.

22 MARTHA MAXIMINO

Perlege, Magdalidos nisi sordet littera Marthae,
  Vix bene Iudaea facta Latina manu.
Quo magis erranti debes ignoscere dextrae,
  Hac patrias usae scripsimus ante notas,
5 Quaeque Haebraea prius didicit manus ire retrorsum,
  Rhomula directum nunc male tentat iter.
Ergo sua dispar si stat sine lege character,
  Haec ruditas veniam quo mereatur habet.
Non bene inexperti tentant iuga prima iuvenci,
10   Et male prima rudis praelia tyro movet.
At solet esse bonis pro munere grata voluntas,
  Quae virtus certa pro ratione tibi est.
Aspicies aliquas etiam fortasse lituras.
  Hoc flentes oculi scribere more solent —
15 Non quibus iratum Briseis flevit Achillem,
  Non quibus absentem Laodamia virum,
Sed quibus ipsa suum crudeli in funere natum
  Flevit inhumano semine facta parens.
Sic ego, longinquae cultrix velut exul eremi,
20   Multa diu sylvis et sine teste queror.
Hospitis ecce subit praesentia dulcis Iesu.
  Hic, precor, in lachrymas non ego tota fluam?
Externas abiit redivivus frater in oras;
  Nunc populis rectam predicat ille fidem.

S4ᵛ (margin, line 3)

Her. Chr. **22.** **1** littera *A*: epistola *BO*; Marthae *A*: Merthae *B*, Martha *O*.   **6** Rhomula . . . nunc male *A*: Nunc male . . . Romula *BO*.   **7** stat *A*: stet *BO*.   **9–12** Non — est. *A*: *om. BO*. **15** iratum — Achillem *A*: incesti lachrymis solantur amores *BO*.   **16** Laodamia *scripsi*: Laodomia *A*, deflet amica *BO*.   **18** inhumano *A*: in humano *BO*.   **19** velut *AB*: nunc *O*.

22   MARTHA TO MAXIMINUS[1]

Read over this letter from Martha of Magdala — provided you
don't find it too muddled! It is written in awkward Latin, I grant
you, but by a Jewish hand. To give you even more cause to
forgive my hand whenever it veers off course: before this I always
wrote using my native characters. The Hebrew hand, which
earlier learned to go backwards, now tries ineptly as a Roman to
plow straight ahead. Hence, if my penmanship looks uneven
and slovenly, pardon this clumsiness insofar as it deserves. Fresh-
broken steers don't take well to the yoke, [10] and the raw recruit
gets in his own way when fighting his first battle. To the kind-
hearted, however, good intentions count for much. That I meant
well is all the excuse you require of me.

You will probably also notice some blots here and there.
This is the way weeping eyes are apt to write — not the eyes, to
be sure, with which Briseis wept for the enraged Achilles or
Laodamia for her absent husband, but the eyes with which she
who became pregnant with superhuman seed wept at the cruel
death of her son.[2] Living as an exile here in the remote wilderness, I too [20] in my solitude have been lamenting long and
hard in these forests. And then, behold, the sweet presence of my
guest Jesus[3] comes over me. How, I ask you, could I keep myself
then from dissolving completely in tears?

The brother who was raised from the dead has gone away to
distant shores. Now he preaches the right faith to the heathens.[4]

---

[1]According to the Provençal legend that originated in the eleventh century and was embellished in
the thirteenth, the Christians in Jerusalem suffered persecution fourteen years after the Passion. The
Jews forced Martha, Mary Magdalene, Lazarus, Maximinus, and others into an oarless, rudderless ship
at Jaffa. With God's help, however, the party traversed the Mediterranean and eventually landed near
Marseilles. There they worked many miracles and converted the population to Christianity. Maximinus,
one of the original seventy-two disciples of Jesus, became Bishop of Aix. Lazarus was made Bishop of
Marseilles. The contemplative Mary Magdalene retired to a cavern in the wilderness. Martha — the
paragon of the active life (cf. Luke 10.38–42; John 11.20) — worked and preached in Avignon,
together with her servant Marcella. The most famous of her miracles is the one that she recounts in this
letter: the slaying of the dragon that had terrorized the area between Arles and Avignon.

See *Leg. aurea* 92 and 101. For the identification of Martha of Bethany, the sister of Lazarus and
Mary of Bethany (John 11.1–44), as the sister of Mary Magdalene, cf. Eob. *Her. Chr.* 3.97–118, with
n. 7 (p. 187 above); also cf. ll. 1 and 133–34 below.

In the 1532/39 version this letter is *Her.* 2.4.

[2]Unlike the two Ovidian heroines, who wept over mortal lovers, Martha will weep the kind of
tears that the Virgin Mary shed at Jesus' death. Martha alludes to Ov. *Ep.* 3 (Briseis' tearful letter to
Achilles, who is enraged at having to hand her over to Agamemnon) and to *Ep.* 13 (Laodamia's letter
to her husband Protesilaus, who, she fears, will be the first to die in the Trojan War).

[3]Jesus was once a guest in her house in Bethany: see Luke 10.38–42.

[4]Lazarus, whom Jesus had raised from the dead (John 11.1–44), is now preaching in another part
of southern Gaul: cf. ll. 46 and 134 below.

97=S5ʳ   25   Antra soror petiit longo deserta recessu,
                         Longius et forsan quam decuisset abest.
                     Te quoque saeva procul nobis fortuna coegit
                         Nec requiem passa est hanc superesse mihi.
                     Sola levat nostras Marcella pedissequa curas,
                30   Qua licet, et dominae est fida ministra suae.
                     Ipsa, domo exigua et parvo contenta sacello,
                         Pauperiem antiquis praefero divitiis,
                     Inter Arelatias et Avinia maenia turres,
                         Hic, ubi de braccis Gallia nomen habet.
                35   Venimus hunc tantis eiectae fluctibus orbem,
                         Hoc tandem nostra est anchora fixa loco.
                     Hic ego (quod nollem) iam non obscura frequentor,
                         Inque meos veniunt plebs numerosa lares.
                     Si tamen hec grata est victori gloria Christo,
                40   De toto ad nostras orbe venite fores.
                     "Qua tamen haec mota est novitate frequentia?" quaeris.
                         "Unde sit haec vulgo tam cito nota domus?"
                     Non tanti Iudaea feris erat advena Gallis;
                         Gloria virtutis non fuit ista meae.
                45   Ipse nova afflictae fecit spectacula genti
                         Qui fratri vitam reddidit ante meo.
S5ᵛ   Illius per me virtus operata salutem
                         Ut fuerit, brevibus commeminisse iuvat.
                     Est locus horrenti densissimus undique sylva;
                50   Rupe sub umbrosa stagnat opaca palus.
                     Innocuas prius infecit draco pestifer undas,
                         Iamque omnis circum noxius aer erat.
                     Lurida vicinas evasit pestis in urbes,
                         Rura nec agricolis tuta fuere suis.
                55   Strata iacent passim grassante cadavera morbo
                         Per fora, per plateas, compita, rura, vias.
                     Morbida quinetiam mediis animalia sylvis
                         Cum vita catulos deseruisse ferunt

---

30 Qua — suae *A*: Exilii cultrix haec quoque fida mei *BO*.   31 exigua *A*: vidua *BO*.
32 antiquis *A*: levibus *BO*.   *Post* 32 *add. BO*: Nam quibus in patria rebus praedives agebam, /
Gratulor hic certe quod caruisse licet. / Nam quibus ista semel venit sitis aemula Christi, / Diviciae
spinas et grave virus habent. / Libera ab his igitur curis Lernaque malorum, / Corpus in hoc regnum
non simulanter ago,   35 hunc — eiectae *A*: aequoreis hunc actae *BO*.   36 nostra *A*: nostro *BO*.
37 ego — obscura *A*: ego, quae virtus non est mea, nota *BO*.   38 Inque *A*: Adque *BO*.   39–42
Si — domus?" *A*: Grata sit o utinam victori ea gloria Christo! / Fumus ad hunc animum pertinet iste
nihil. / Quod si forte roges, "Unde ista frequentia?", caussam / Nec didicisse tibi est nec mihi turpe
loqui. *BO*.   44 Gloria virtutis . . . meae *A*: Ingenii merces . . . mei *BO*.   46 fratri vitam *A*:
vitam fratri *BO*.   47–48 Illius — iuvat. *A*: *om. BO*.   52 circum *A*: in ea *B*, iuxta *O*.
53 evasit *A*: invasit *BO*.   56 Per fora — vias *A*: Iratum populo dixeris esse Deum *BO*.

My sister has sought out a lonely cavern in some distant corner
and is perhaps too isolated for her own good. Ruthless fortune has
likewise driven you far from me and so denied me this comfort.
Only my handmaid Marcella is still with me. [30] Faithful servant
to her mistress that she is, she does everything in her power to
alleviate my cares. I myself, content with a tiny cottage and a little
chapel, have gladly exchanged the riches of yore[5] for a life of
poverty here between the towers of Arles and the walls of
Avignon, in the part of Gaul that is named for the breeches they
wear.[6] This is the part of the world where we came ashore, cast up
by the stormy waves; this is where we finally weighed anchor.
Here (though I did not desire it) I have since become a star
attraction, and people are coming to visit my house in droves.
But as long as this renown is pleasing to the victorious Christ,
[40] do come to my doors from all over the world!

"But what novelty," you ask, "has stirred these crowds to
visit you? How could the people have gotten to know your house
that quickly?" It was not as if the rough-and-ready Gauls thought
so highly of the Jewish newcomer. This celebrity status is no
achievement of mine. The one who performed the spectacular
miracle for the afflicted people was the very one who earlier
restored my brother to life.[7] How his power has worked salvation
through me is something I should like to describe in a few
words.

There is a place, hemmed in by dreadful woods and thickets.
[50] Beneath a shady cliff lies a murky swamp. A pestilential
dragon poisoned the formerly harmless water, and before long all
the air in the environs became noxious. The ghastly plague spread
to the nearby towns, and the fields were no longer safe for
their farmers. As the disease raged throughout the countryside,
corpses lay strewn where they had fallen, in the markets, streets,
crossways, fields, roads. Even in the deep forests, they say, the
infected animals abandoned their life and young; and often

---

[5]Cf. *Her. Chr.* 3.103–04, with n. 6 (p. 187 above).
[6]The Gauls in Provence wore breeches, while the Gauls in Northern Italy wore the Roman toga.
Hence Transalpine Gaul was known as "Gallia bracata," Cisalpine Gaul as "Gallia togata."
[7]Jesus raised Lazarus from the dead: see John 11.1–44.

Saepeque tabifico nubem cecidisse volucrum
60   Et vitam caelo non potuisse trahi.
Saepe latens etiam vicini in fluminis unda
Dicitur incautas precipitasse rates.
Interdum insidiis nactum loca tuta viarum
Innumeros homines dilaniasse ferunt.
65   Cladibus his igitur tristis vicinia, tandem
Fisa Deo, nostram sollicitavit opem.
Prebuimus facilem iustis hortatibus aurem.
Ad monstrata trucis venimus antra ferae.
98=S6ʳ   Multa timens longo plebs restitit intervallo,
70   Suspensa tacite mente futura manens.
Ipsa salutato Stigii victore draconis
Accessi audaci lustra inimica pede.
Ecce sed assuetis dum pectora munio signis,
Monstrosum iuxta conspicor esse pecus.
75   Exuvias hominis lambebat et ossa vorati.
Sanguine adhuc calido sparsa rubebat humus.
Dicere qua fuerit laetalis bestia forma
Nulla sine ingenti lingua tremore potest.
Ore tenus vasto Cadmaeo immanior angue
80   Quamque pyra vidit vindice Lerna mori.
Qualis erat cui vasta Lybis super arva Silenae
Armenis effossum transiit hasta latus.
Ampla venenivomis pandebat rictibus ora;
Vulnificis ingens dentibus ordo fuit.
85   Vibrabat tardis ingentes motibus alas,
Ore vorax, mordax dentibus, ungue rapax.
Turpiter immundum cauda desivit in anguem,
Multiplicem fecit lubrica spira rotam.
Hunc tamen immanem vita spoliavimus hostem —
90   Haec etiam victor gloria Christe tua est!
S6ᵛ   Non mea Amazoniam torquebat dextra securim,
Nec Lacedaemonio canduit ense manus.
Frons mea non galeam thoracave pectus habebat.
Arma quis in timida virgine sumpta probet?

---

64 homines — ferunt *A*: avida corripuisse manu [gula *O*] *BO*.   72 inimica *A*: timenda *BO*.   75
vorati *A*: perempti *BO*.   80 Quamque *A*: Quemque *BO*.   81–82 Qualis — latus *A*: Qualis erat
quem praecipitem de sede Michael / Aetherea Stygiae trusit ad antra domus *BO*.   83 Ampla
venenivomis *A*: Lata venenificis *BO*.

a cloud of birds, [60] unable to go on living in the tainted air, would drop out of the sky. The dragon, I am told, lurked in the nearby river too, and often sank unsuspecting boats. Sometimes it would reach safe places and lie in wait along the roads. There, they say, it tore countless people to pieces.

Well then, distressed by these calamities, the people of the region finally put their trust in God and urgently implored my help. I lent a willing ear to their well-founded pleas and had them show me the lair of the ferocious beast. Fearing all kinds of disaster, the crowd stayed a long way back [70] and anxiously waited in silence to see what would transpire. After I had hailed the victor over the Stygian dragon,[8] I boldly strode to the enemy's den. But as I was still fortifying my breast with the accustomed signs,[9] I suddenly caught sight of the monstrous creature close at hand. It was licking the clothes and bones of a man it had just devoured. The gory ground was red with his still-hot blood.

What the deadly beast looked like, no tongue can tell without enormous trembling. Right up to its immense maw it was more gigantic than Cadmus' serpent[10] [80] or the one that Lerna saw dying from the avenging flame.[11] It was as huge as the dragon whose flank was transfixed by the Armenian's lance on the vast fields of Silena in Libya.[12] Opening its gaping mouth with those venom-spewing jaws, it revealed a prodigious set of wound-inflicting teeth. With slow motions it flapped its enormous wings. The maw was ravenous, the teeth razor-sharp, the claws rapacious. Its tail ended in an ugly and disgusting snake that coiled itself into many slippery spirals.

Horrendous as this enemy was, I nevertheless despoiled it of life — [90] this glory too, victorious Christ, belongs entirely to you! My right hand did not swing the Amazon's broadax, nor did the Spartan's sword glint in my fist. I did not wear a helmet on my head or a cuirass over my chest. Who would approve of a timid virgin's taking up arms like that? Unswerving faith in

[8]Christ, as victor over the old Serpent, Satan.

[9]That is, as she is crossing herself. Cf. *Her. Chr.* 12.176, in similar context.

[10]Cadmus, son of King Agenor, killed the serpent of Mars, a huge monster with a golden crest and a triple row of teeth: see Ov. *Met.* 3.28–94.

[11]Each time Hercules cut off one of the heads of the Lernean Hydra, two heads immediately grew back. He finally killed the monster by burning out the stumps.

[12]Martha alludes to the dragon killed near the Libyan city of Silena by the Armenian hero St. George. For the story, see *Her. Chr.* 12.173–90. In the 1532/39 version Eobanus replaced the allusion with a reference to the dragon thrown down by the Archangel Michael (Revelations 12.7–9). He did so not only to replace the (by then embarrassingly legendary) tale, but also to get rid of the glaring anachronism.

95 Praebuit arma fides mihi praesentissima Christi.
    Relligio clipeus, crux mea signa fuit.
Mens devota Deo strictum sese obtulit ensem,
    In superos hastam non simulatus amor.
His instructa armis, hoc agmine tuta potensque,
100   Compressi immanem nuda puella feram.
Ille quidem, solito venienti blandior, omneis
    Sevitia posuit iam fugiente minas,
Sicut ubi irato vulpes blandita leoni
    Impresso supplex pectore reptat humi,
105 Sicut et imbellis coram tondentibus agnus
    Aut canis ad positas officiosa dapes.
Horrida iam vinctum muliebri guttura cesto
    Fortiter egressum traximus ante nemus.
Obruit hunc populus saxis, confodit et hastis,
110   Carmine testatus gaudia summa novo.
Sic cecidit victore Deo ferus ille potensque,
    Nuper Arelatii depopulator agri.
99=T1ʳ Gratia victori mox acta est debita Christo.
    Suscipiunt sacram milia multa fidem.
115 Ad nova conveniunt stupidae miracula gentes
    Lustralesque pia voce precantur aquas.
Chrismate Apostolico, venias, precor, uncte sacerdos.
    Praecipue sacrum te decet istud opus!
Credentis populi veteratas ablue sordes
120   Debitaque authori foenora redde Deo.
Pro pietate vacent Aquitanica templa parumper,
    Templa, pater, meritis facta beata tuis.
Frater in has merito partes quoque Lazarus isset,
    Sed procul hinc tellus Massiliensis abest.
125 Illum cura tenet commissae sedula plebis.
    Tu magis hic certe tutus abesse potes.
Tuque prior meritis cano et reverentior aevo,
    Praecipue sacrum te decet istud opus!
Et iam tota tuas miratur Gallia laudes,
130   Per te de veteri libera pene caho.

---

96 Relligio — fuit *A*: Spes rata pro clypeo, crux mihi cassis erat *BO*.   **100** nuda puella *A*: foemina nuda *BO*.   **104** Impresso *AO*: Impressa *B*.   **108** egressum *AB*: incultum *O*.   **118** istud *A*: illud *BO*.   **125** sedula *A*: strennua *BO*.   **128** istud *A*: illud *BO*.   **129** miratur *AB*: decantat *O*.

Christ served as my armor. Religion was my shield, the cross my banner. Devotion to God provided a drawn sword, unfeigned love of heaven a spear. Armed with these weapons, secure and mighty in this battle, [100] I, unarmed maiden, crushed the frightful beast.

The creature certainly put on its best behavior as soon as I drew near. Laying aside its savageness, it soon gave up all threats, just as when a fox, trying to ingratiate itself with an angry lion, grovels and cringes on the ground, or like a peaceful sheep before its shearers or like a dog eager to please at mealtime. Thereupon I bound its scaly throat with a woman's girdle and resolutely led it to the forest's rim. There the people overwhelmed it with stones and ran it through with spears, [110] all the while expressing the greatest joy in a new song of praise.

That is how God triumphed over the fierce and mighty beast that until recently had devastated the countryside of Arles. Before long we said the prayers of thanks that we owed to Christ, the victor. Thousands upon thousands accepted the holy faith. At the news of the miracle, the stunned heathens converged on me and with pious voice begged for the water of baptism.

As a priest anointed with the oil of the Apostles, come, I beseech you. That sacred task is especially fitting for you! Cleanse the believing people of their old filth [120] and render to God the Creator the interest he has earned. For piety's sake your church in Aix can do without you for a short time — a church, father, made blessed by your merits.

My brother Lazarus could by rights also come to these parts, but the land of Marseilles is far from here. Besides, the flock entrusted to his sedulous care holds him fast. Certainly it is safer for you to be gone awhile. You are superior to him in merits and more reverend in your hoary old age: that sacred task is especially fitting for you!

And already the whole of Gaul admires your achievements, [130] for you are the one who largely freed it from its ancient

Error adhuc paucis Dryidarum garrit in antris.
  Caetera virtute est fabula fracta tua.
Nam licet et Mariae gens debeat illa sorori,
  Quam tibi commissam, Lazare frater, habes,

T1ᵛ   135 Plus tamen acceptae per te stat gloria famae.
  Praecipue sacrum te decet istud opus!
De septem decies Christi viventis alumnis
  Additus es nostrae duxque comesque fugae.
Te duce nostra data est ventis sine remige navis;
        140   Te comite in portum non minus acta suum est.
Caerula tu fortes turbantes aequora ventos
  Iussisti celerem carpere saepe fugam.
Ad tua consedit Boreas mandata nivosus,
  Occuluit nigrum torva procella caput.

        145 Tu dux tuque comes, nobis tu rector et idem
  Navita tuque pater, tu quoque frater eras.
Omnia sicut eras et adhuc ut es omnia nobis,
  Praecipue sacrum te decet istud opus!
Ille etiam, Christi quem captum lumine virtus
        150   Donata iussit luce videre diem,
Ille etiam, pars exilii non ultima nostri,
  Longius hinc certe quam mihi constet abest.
Me lex foeminei sexus vetat addere cuiquam,
  Quae nisi de vestra non datur unda manu,

        155 Legitimus saltem si possit adesse minister.
  Non aliquam legem quicquid oportet habet.
100=T2ʳ   Ergo age, ne tardes. Populi te longa moratur
  Atque novum series discit avara Deum.
Officiosa quidem populo documenta ministro,
        160   Qua licet, et quantum virgo docere potest.
Nec male sic forsan Christi sudamus in agro.
  O utinam pietas grata sit ista Deo!
Sepius utque meas ire est dignatus in aedes,
  Hospes dignetur pectoris esse mei,

        165 Donec ab humanae resolutus alumine carnis
  Alta celer supra spiritus astra volet.
Plura vetant lachrymae per labra in verba cadentes,
  Quas amor ignavas non sinit esse. Vale.

---

131 Dryidarum *A*: Depudarum *B*, Dryudarum *O*; garrit *A*: spirat *BO*.   136 istud *A*: illud *BO*.
138 fugae *A*: viae *BO*.   140 suum est *A*: suam *BO*.   141 tu *AO*: te *B*.   143 nivosus *A*:
minosus *B*, nivalis *O*.   148 istud *A*: illud *BO*.   149–52 Ille — abest. *A*: *om. BO*.   154 non
datur *AO*: sumitur *B*.   157 Ergo *A*: Quare *BO*.   165 alumine carnis *A*: carcere vitae *BO*.

darkness. The error of the Druids chatters on in just a few grot-
tos. Thanks to you, the rest of their superstition has been
destroyed. For even though the people are also indebted to my
sister Mary, whom our brother Lazarus has taken under his wing,
the glory of the renown thus garnered is mostly yours. That
sacred task is especially fitting for you!

Of the seventy disciples of the living Christ[13] you were
assigned to be the guide and companion during our flight. Under
your guidance our oarless ship was given over to the winds;
[140] with you aboard it was driven into its harbor nonetheless.
The gales stirring up the cerulean seas you often ordered to take
swift flight. At your command the snowy north wind subsided,
the grim storm hid its lowering head. You were our guide and
companion, you our captain as well as our crew, our father and
also our brother. Just as you were everything to us and still mean
everything to us: that sacred task is especially fitting for you!

He too, that blind man to whom Christ's power [150] gave
sight so he might see the light of day, he too, by no means the
least among us exiles, is certainly farther away from here than
I know.[14] Church law does not allow a woman to sprinkle
anyone with the water that only your hand may give — at least,
if an ordained priest can be present. And indeed, whatever is
right and fitting should have the force of law. Come then, do not
tarry. A long line of people awaits you and is eagerly learning
about the new God. At all events I solicitously provide them
such instruction [160] as I am able to give and insofar as a virgin
may teach them. Perhaps I do not toil altogether unsuccessfully
like this in Christ's vineyard. O, if only my labor of love is pleasing to God! And as he often deigned to enter my home, may he
deign also to be a guest in my heart, until my soul, freed from
the clay of human flesh, flies swiftly over the stars on high.

The tears that fall over my lips at every word prevent me
from going on. Love will not let them be idle. Farewell.

---

[13]According to *Leg. aurea* 92.34, Maximinus was one of the seventy-two disciples whom Jesus
sent out in pairs to the places he intended to visit; cf. Luke 10.1.

[14]Cedonius, one of Martha's companions on the voyage across the Mediterranean, had been
cured of his blindness by Jesus: see *Leg. aurea* 92.35.

23   DOROTHEA THEOPHILO

Haec tibi de sponsi munuscula mittimus horto,
   Frigida quo nunquam tempore vernat humus.
Accipe, ne dubita. Non est rosa falsa, nec ipsa
   Inficit adiectus punica mala rubor.
5 Non tamen has Citheraea rosas Venus ulla colorat,
   Non has Idalio sub lare pavit Amor.
Rossidaque Hesperidum non legit ab arbore poma
   Qui tibi miranti tradidit ista puer.
Ipse suo sponsae transmisit Christus ab horto,

T2ᵛ   10   Gratia ubi aeternis vernat amaena rosis.
Ad loca ducebar patiendae proxima mortis,
   Ante meos oculos constitit iste puer.
"Has tibi, sponsa, rosas sponsus transmittit Iesus
   Hinc ubi nulla herbas bruma perurit," ait.
15 Mandati memor ipsa tui, "Puer optime," dixi,
   "An meus hinc aliquo nuncius esse voles?"
Annuit. "Ergo," inquam, "vade atque reversus in urbem
   Ardua Rhomani limina quaere ducis.
Protinus occurret tibi scriba Theophilus illic,
20   Cum tribus haec illi da tria mala rosis.
Si roget unde feras vernos in frigore odores,
   Hos tibi Dorotheam sic tribuisse refer."
Finieram. Iniectae reliquum vetuere cathenae
   Quassaque crudeli virga cruenta manu.
25 Constitit ille tamen, "Mandata" que "talia paucis
   Scribe," ait et tabulas protulit atque stilum.
Vix potui exiguo spacium exorare labori,
   Tam fera Fabricii consulis ira fuit.
Frigida adurentis consedi in tergore saxi,
30   Pallida iam virgis, frigore, fuste, metu.

Her. Chr. **23.** **3** ne *AO*: nec *B*.   **6** pavit *A*: ponit *BO*.   **14** Hinc *BO*: Huic *A*.   **15** ipsa
A: ipse *BO*.   **19** scriba — illic *A*: scribarum optimus illic, / Qui grave divini nomen amoris habet. /
Postquam constiterit, quae nunc mihi munera portas *BO*.   **21** roget *A*: rogat *BO*.   **27** exorare
A: exarare *BO*.   **29** Frigida adurentis *A*: Ipsa perurentis *BO*; tergore *A*: frigore *BO*.

[1]The daughter of a Roman senator, St. Dorothy was born and raised in Caesarea in Cappadocia.
There the pagan governor Fabricius fell in love with her. But when she, as a bride of Christ, refused to
marry him, he had her tortured and executed. As she was being led to her martyrdom on a bitterly cold
day in early February, the lawyer Theophilus mockingly asked her to send him some fruits from her
spouse's garden. She agreed to do just that. Shortly before reaching the place of execution she stopped
to pray. An angel appeared to her, bearing a basket with three apples and three roses. These she sent to
Theophilus, with the message that she would await him in the vernal garden from where these gifts

23   DOROTHY TO THEOPHILUS[1]

These small gifts that I am sending you come from my bridegroom's garden, in the season when the frosty soil is never verdant.
Go ahead, don't hesitate. The roses are not imitations, and the
crimson apples have not been artificially dyed. Venus of Cythera
did not color these roses either, nor did Amor nurture them in the
Idalian temple. And the youth who — to your astonishment —
handed you the dew-wet apples, did not pluck them from the
tree of the Hesperides.[2] It was Christ himself who sent his
bride these gifts from his garden, [10] the lovely beauty of which
blooms with ever-blowing roses.

I was being led to the nearby place of execution, when that
youth suddenly appeared before my eyes. "Bride," he said, "your
bridegroom Jesus sends you these roses from where no wintry
frost sears the plants."

Remembering your instructions, I replied, "Best of lads,
would you be willing to go on an errand for me?" He nodded.
"Well then," I continued, "go back to the city and look for the
lofty palace of the Roman governor. As soon as the notary
Theophilus rushes out to meet you there, [20] give him these
three apples along with the three roses. If he asks where you
obtained these vernal fragrances in the dead of winter, tell him
that Dorothy offered them to you in such-and-such a way."

This is all I could say. The chains that held me fast and the
bloodstained rod, brandished by a cruel hand, made it impossible
for me to go on. He stood stock-still, however. "Write these instructions down in a few words," he said, as he held out a writing tablet
and a stylus. Only after much entreaty was I permitted to take time
out for a brief letter, so fierce was Governor Fabricius' anger.
Chilled to the bone, I sat down on an icy cold rock, [30] I who was
already pale from the beatings, the frost, the clubbing, the fear.

---

had been sent. Converted to the Christian faith, Theophilus was himself martyred. See *Leg. aurea*
(Graesse) 210 — the only version of the legend that explicitly states that Dorothy's family originated in
Rome (cf. l. 111 below).

St. Dorothy's letter seeks to make an unassailable case to the lawyer Theophilus that the gifts she
is sending him have indeed come from heaven. Hence the letter, like nos. 3, 8, and 14 above, is structured in the manner of a forensic speech: introduction (ll. 1–10); narrative (11–42); argumentation
and rebuttal (43–98); conclusion (99–120).

In the 1532/39 version this letter is *Her.* 3.8.

[2]The Hesperides were sisters who watched over a garden with golden apples: cf. l. 73 below.

Multa minans lictor gladium vibrabat acutum.

101=T3ʳ
    Scribere tunc quicquam me potuisse putas?

Applicui tamen et digitos ad verba coegi.
    Ut glacies gelidae diriguere manus.

35   Afflabam calido torpentia membra vapore —
    Vivus adhuc nostri spiritus oris erat.

Parte manus liquefacta rudes utcunque lituras
    Edidit, exequias funeris ipsa sui,

Qualiter ad Phrygii Maeandri littora cygnus

40   Cantator mortis dicitur esse suae.

Mittimus ergo rosas quas et quae mala petisti,
    In paradisiacis utraque lecta iugis.

Hoc tam credideras fieri quam climate vestro
    Sole sub hyberno posse virere rosas.

45   At locus est Phoebi primo surgentis in ortu
    Aereae supra tertia regna plagae.

Culta ibi vivaci viridaria cincta smaragdo
    Caelesti florum fertilitate vigent.

Angelicis illic manibus sata semina fragrant.

50   Ver ibi perpetuum perpetuusque dies.

Flaminibus vivax agitur caelestibus aer.
    Nescit vitalem pestilis aura locum.

Denique non alicui locus ille obnoxius astro.

T3ᵛ
    Verna domus sponsi est delitiaeque mei.

55   Excipit hic puras terreno ex carcere mentes,
    Hic patet aethereae ianua prima domus.

Hunc vacuum fecit mortalibus Eva colonis,
    Heu nimis audaci noxia facta manu.

Hinc mihi vernantem puer attulit ille canistrum,

60   Quem tibi nunc idem, dona petita, tulit.

At tu si sapies, non tam mirabere dona
    Quam dare qui, quoties collibet, illa potest.

Februa sydereo quo luna in Pisce tenetur,
    Aestivas quis eo tempore quaerat opes?

65   Itala iam nullos mittit Lucania flores;
    Difficilis Poestum nobile clausit hyems.

Nullaque iam Siculae iactant violaria valles.
    Florida Riphaea spargitur Hybla nive.

Moeonis haud croceis floret nunc Lydia campis,

70   Nec nive, sed verno Tmolus odore vacat.

---

31 gladium . . . acutum *A*: virgas . . . et ensem *BO*.   33 ad *A*: in *BO*.   38 exequias *A*: inferias *BO*.
43 vestro *A*: nostro *BO*.   45 Phoebi primo *A*: primo Phoebi *BO*.   46 Aereae . . . plagae *A*: Aerei
[Aerea *BO*] . . . poli *BO*.   49 semina *A*: germina *BO*.   53 ille *A*: iste *BO*.   55 Excipit *A*: Accipit
BO.   59 vernantem *A*: florigerum *BO*.   62 illa *A*: ista *BO*.   66 Poestum *A*: pastum *BO*; clausit
A: claudit *BO*.   67 Nullaque — Siculae *A*: Nulla Syracusiae *BO*.   70 odore *A*: honore *BO*.

Uttering many a threat, the lictor waved his sharp sword. Do you think I was capable of writing anything then? Nevertheless, I set my fingers to the task and forced them to put down these words. My freezing hands became as stiff as ice. I blew steaming air on my numb fingers — at least my breath still had the heat of life in it. As best it could, the partly thawed hand has been scribbling clumsy smears, funeral obsequies for itself, just as the swan on the banks of Phrygian Meander [40] is said to be the minstrel of its own death.

Well then, I herewith send you the roses and apples you asked for, both plucked on the hills of Paradise. You had thought this as likely as roses' being able to bloom under the winter sun at your latitude. But in the Orient, where the sun first rises at dawn, there is a place that rises above the third realm, beyond the airy sky. Girdled with sparkling emeralds, cultivated flowerbeds flourish there with celestial fertility. There the seeds planted by angelic hands emit sweet fragrance. [50] Spring is eternal there and eternal the day. The vivifying air is stirred by heavenly breezes. Of pestilent effluence that lifegiving place knows nothing. In short, this spot is not exposed to any harmful star. My bridegroom's house is vernal and delightful. Here the pure souls are welcomed after leaving their earthly prison; here the original door to the etherial mansion stands open. This is the place that Eve emptied of its mortal inhabitants — a sin, alas, committed with an all too presumptuous hand. It is from there that this youth has brought me the spring basket, [60] the same one he now takes to you, as the gift you requested.

Now if you are wise, you will marvel not so much at the gifts as at him who can give them whenever he pleases. Who can expect the riches of summer during the season when the February moon is held in the sign of Pisces? Lucania in Italy does not export any flowers now. Hard winter holds famed Paestum in its grip.[3] Right now the valleys of Sicily do not boast any beds of violets. Flowery Hybla is covered with arctic snow. Maeonian Lydia does not bloom with its fields of saffron now; [70] and what Mount Tmolus lacks is not snow, but the aroma of spring.[4]

---

[3]Paestum in Lucania was famed for its roses.
[4]Mount Tmolus in Lydia was renowned for the saffron grown on its slopes.

Languit Assyrium florum genus omne per orbem.
  Moeret Hyperboreo Hierichus usta gelu.
Lugent Hesperidum pomaria nuda sororum.
  Perdidit aestivum Punica terra decus.
75 Omnia quae nostro sol despicit altus in orbe
  Nunc sine laeticia, nunc sine honore iacent.
Denique nunc vireantque rosae, nunc germinet arbor,
  Totaque florigeram gratia fingat humum,
Quis mihi propositae passurae vulnera mortis
80   Florea in extremo funere serta ferat?
Quisve sinat legisse manu per vincla retentam?
  Nullius hic causam suspitionis habes,
Nunc igitur praesens ratio te credere coget
  Haec nova de sponso dona venire meo.
85 Quoque magis credas, nunquam vigor iste peribit,
  Floridaque ut nunc est, sic rosa semper erit.
Ille idem superabit honor maloque rosaeque
  Illeque caelesti nectare pastus odor.
I nunc, Christicolae ride promissa puellae,
90   I nunc et Christum numen habere nega!
Quin potius per signa Deum cognosce potentem
  Et sequere hac qua me conspicis ire via.
Hac sequere. Ad superas haec proxima pertinet arces.
  Tartara desipiens hactenus ima petis.
95 Aspice preterea varias tot signa per urbes,
  Qualia vestrati sub Iove nemo facit,
Et vera cognosce Deum ratione potentem
  Et sequere. Hac iustis itur ad astra via.
Et nisi praesenti mens ebria fallat amore,
100   Mutato Christi pectore miles eris.
Tu quoque vivificae gustabis pocula mortis,
  Haec quoque victuro strata palestra tibi est.
Postmodo caelesti mihi respondebis in horto.
  Tunc reddes capiti florea serta meo.
105 Nunc ego sollicitor properatum imponere finem,
  Hei mihi, quam duram mox obitura necem!
Certa tibi interea fidei sint pignora nostrae,
  Addita purpureis punica mala rosis.

102=T4^r

T4^v

---

72 Moeret — gelu *A*: Hierichus Scythico moeret adusta gelu *BO*.   77 nunc germinet arbor *A*:
vernentque vireta *BO*.   78 fingat *A*: pingat *BO*.   80 Florea *A*: Florida *BO*.   83–88 Nunc —
odor. *A*: *om*. *BO*.   94 petis *A*: subis *BO*.   98 Et — via *A*: Et sequere hac qua me conspicis ire
via *BO*.   99 fallat *A*: fallit *BO*.   104 reddes — florea *A*: capiti reddes florida *BO*.   106 Hei *A*:
Heu *BO*.   107 Certa *A*: Certe *BO*.

Throughout the Eastern world every kind of flower has wilted. Seared with hyperborean frost, Jericho grieves.[5] The bare orchards of the Hesperian sisters are in mourning. Punic Carthage has lost its summer fruit.[6] Every region on which the lofty sun looks down in our hemisphere now languishes without gladness, without charm. Finally, even supposing the roses were now blowing, the trees were now in bud, and all manner of loveliness were adorning the blossoming ground, who would bring me [80] a garland of flowers — to me of all people, a maiden condemned to die, and so shortly before my execution too? Or who would let me pick them myself, considering that I am held fast in shackles? You have no grounds whatsoever for suspicion here.

Now then, this irrefutable argumentation will force you to believe that these miraculous gifts come from my bridegroom. And to bring it home to you: this freshness will never perish; and as flourishing as these roses are now, so they will always remain. Both the apples and the roses will always keep their beauty and their fragrance of heavenly nectar.

Go ahead, jeer at the promises of a Christian maiden! [90] Go ahead and deny that Christ has divine power! On the contrary, through these signs learn to know the almighty God and follow him on the path that you see me taking. Follow him on this path. It leads directly up to the heights of heaven. Hitherto you have foolishly made for the depths of Tartarus. Look too at the countless signs in cities large and small, at the miracles that no one under the Jupiter of your people can perform, and with true insight learn to know the almighty God and follow him. This is the way that leads the righteous to the stars.

And if my mind, intoxicated with zealous love, does not deceive me, [100] you yourself will have a change of heart and become a soldier of Christ. You too will taste the cup of lifegiving death; you too will fight the good fight and emerge victorious. Afterwards you will give me your answer in the heavenly garden. Then you will put the flowery garland back on my head.

Now they are pressing me to put a quick end to this letter. Woe, what a hard death I am soon to die! In the meantime, let the crimson apples and the scarlet roses serve as the sure pledges of the promise I gave you. If, however, posterity

---

[5] Jericho was known for its roses: cf. *Her. Chr.* 3.140, n.
[6] Pomegranates (*mala Punica*, or "Punic apples") were associated with the Phoenician colony Carthage.

Si tamen hoc aliqua corpus dignabitur urna
110   Posteritas, cineri sic, precor, adde meo:
"Rhoma genus dederat, genuit Moga, relligionem
     Christus. Dorotheam dixit uterque parens.
Numina spernenti veterum non vera deorum
     Fabricius vitam sustulit. Hospes, abi."
115   Caetera quae volui tecum puer iste loquetur.
     Sit licet, est superum numen ab arce, puer.
Frigida nunc avidae prebemus colla securi,
     Deque meo modicum carmine vulnus abest.
Christe, fer hanc animam promissi in gaudia caeli.
120   Ipsa tuo solvor carcere, terra! Vale.

111–14 Rhoma — abi *A*: Ultima Dorotheam pro Christo vulnera passam, / Hoc me idem tumulo condidit. Hospes, abi *BO*.

should deign to place my remains in some kind of urn, [110] pray add this epitaph to my ashes: "Rome gave me my lineage, Caesarea my birthplace, Christ my religion. Dorothy is what my parents named me. Because I rejected the false divinity of the ancient gods, Fabricius took my life. Stranger, depart."

Everything else that I wanted to say, this youth will discuss with you. He may look young, but he is an angel from heaven.

Now I offer my cold neck to the bloodthirsty ax. From my poem to the wound it is not far. Christ, carry my soul into the joys of heaven, as you promised. [120] I am about to be freed from your prison, earth! Farewell.

103=T5ʳ   **24   EOBANUS POSTERITATI**

Quam legis, hanc Hessus quondam tibi, diva, reliquit,
   Ipsa tuo ut legeres tempore, Posteritas.
Nam neque tunc fueras cum scriberet ipse, nec unquam
   Speravit vultus posse videre tuos,
5   Quam sibi praesentem nemo conspexerit unquam,
   Omnia quae sequeris ultima semper anus.
Quo magis appeteris, magis hoc fugis, improba, retro.
   Ludis amatores, lubrica diva, tuos!
Atque ut semper abes praesens viventibus aevum,
10   Sic, si respicias pristina, semper ades.
Sed neque praesentem nos te veneramur amantes.
   Nescio qua potius laude futura places.
Nata diu vivis, quae nondum nata futura es,
   Vatibus antiquis nata, futura mihi.
15   Nemo tuis potuit vivens amplexibus unquam,
   Nemo tuo praesens captus amore frui.
Lubrica decedens, veniens simul atque resistens,
   Non tua deprehendi mira figura potest.
Non mihi te Choi manus ingeniosa magistri,
20   Nemo Perinthiaca pinxerit arte senex.
Non vidit plures fingentem Prothea formas

T5ᵛ   Omnis in Oceano cognita turba mari.
Adde modo ut venias, vultu non semper eodem
   Constas, interdum nigra, aliquando nitens.
25   Saepe quidem multos qui te impacienter amarunt
   Reiicis et nulla laude superba iuvas.
Contra etiam multos ita diligis optima mater,
   Ut vita dignos perpete in astra leves.
Es tamen omnigenum iudex aequissima rerum,
30   Et iusta ex omni parte statera tua est.
Seu mihi dura igitur mater seu blanda futura es,
   Inter amatores fer, precor, esse tuos.

Her. Chr. **24.**   **1** hanc Hessus *A*: Hessus amans *BO*.   **3** ipse *A*: ille *BO*.   **20** Nemo — senex
A: Pinxerit aut Zeusis Parrhasiusve senex *BO*.   **22** Omnis *A*: Omnia *BO*.   **24** Constas
A: Constes *BO*.   **29** Es *A*: Et *BO*.

[1]The book concludes as it began: with a letter written by a man to his beloved. But while
Emmanuel's letter is immediately followed by Mary's response, Eobanus' wooing letter to Posterity cannot be answered within the book itself. It is we, the readers, who each in our own way must respond to
his appeal.

24   EOBANUS TO POSTERITY[1]

The letter you are reading, goddess Posterity, Hessus left it to you
in days past, so you could read it in your own good time. For
neither were you alive then, when he wrote it, nor could he ever
hope to see you face-to-face. No one has ever beheld you in person, because you, the ultimate dowager, always bring up the rear.
The more you find yourself courted, the more coyly you draw
back. You play hard-to-get with your lovers, slippery goddess!
But just as you always shrink from those who live at the present
time, [10] so, when you look at ages past, you are always here in
our midst. We lovers, however, don't adore you when you're
among us. Rather, in hopes of a bit of fame you please us only in
prospect. Once born, you live on forever; unborn, you belong to
the future. For the ancient bards you are born; for me you are
still to come. No one alive has ever managed to enjoy your
embraces; no present-day wooer has ever been able to enjoy your
love. Elusively slipping away, at once approaching and resisting,
your stunning figure cannot be pinned down. Neither the ingenious hand of the Coan master [20] nor the Perinthian artist of
old could have painted me a portrait of you.[2] No creature known
in the ocean waves has seen Proteus change into so many forms!
Moreover, even when you do arrive, you don't always keep the
same mien. Sometimes you glower, sometimes you beam with
delight. Often, indeed, you spurn many who loved you beyond
reason and haughtily deny them your praise. On the other hand,
like the wonderful mother you are, you also love many people so
much that you make them immortal and lift them on high to the
stars. Still, you are the fairest judge of all manner of endeavors,
[30] and your scales are balanced in every respect. So, whether
you'll turn out to be a stern mother to me or a caressing one,
pray accept me among your admirers, at least!

Like the book's dedication and the preceding eight letters, the present poem was written at
Frankfurt an der Oder in 1513. Cf. *Her. Chr.*, ded. 8.4, and ll. 129–30 below. At ll. 137–40 Eobanus
obviously still considers himself to be in the bishop's service; and at ll. 121–22 he alludes to
Maximilian's Venetian campaign, then ongoing (in September-October 1513). It is true that Leipzig is
mentioned as the place of publication (ll. 131–32); but those verses must have been inserted in the
spring of 1514.

In the 1532/39 version this letter is *Her.* 3.9.

[2]The great painter Apelles of Colophon (fourth century BCE) is sometimes called Coan because of
his celebrated portrait of Aphrodite Anadyomene on Cos. The "Perinthian artist" is the celebrated fifth-
century painter Zeuxis of Heraclea, probably the town in Lucania. Eobanus, however, opts for the city
of Heraclea in Thrace, as the epithet *Perinthian* indicates: Perinthus on the Thracian side of the Sea of
Marmora was later called Heraclea. In the 1532/39 revision he avoids the issue by referring instead to
Parrhasius of Ephesus (ca. 400 BCE).

Casta etiam patitur sese, ne peccet, amari.
    Peccatum est aliquem non sinere esse bonum.
35 Quisquis amat bonus est. Bonus est amor omnis honestus.
    Nequiter at Veneris suadet amare puer.
Ultima tu nostras heroidas inter haberis,
    Ultima nam cunctis rebus adesse soles.
Attamen, ut noris, primam te semper amavi,
40   O animae certe cura secunda meae!
Te prius ex animo finxi quam dicere possem
    Qua mihi praecipue parte sequenda fores.
Ingenium tibi pene puer iuvenile dicavi,
    Esse tuae cupiens pars quota militiae.
45 Prima tamen cessit magnis reverentia divis.
    Quem magis aeterna fama salute trahat?
Ergo utcunque leges olim mea carmina, quisquis
    Venturae socius Posteritatis eris,
Quae mihi terra parens, qui me genuere parentes,
50   Quae fuerint vitae tempora nosse voles.
Martia qua magnum cohibet Germania Rhenum
    Et velut in centrum Teutonis ora coit,
Terra viris colitur, Cattos dixere vetusti.
    Nunc aliud pugnax Hessia nomen habet.
55 Mons ibi Christiferae celeberrimus aede puellae;
    Radices vitreis Aedera lambit aquis.
Parva quidem, nostris sed Francoberga Camoenis
    Obscuras inter non habitura locum —
Si modo tu fama vatem dignaberis ulla,
60   Posteritas, qui te tam reverenter amat.
Hic igitur primum vitaleis carpsimus auras,
    Nascenti primam praebuit illa diem.
Iam ter quinque ierant post natum secula Christum;
    Annos inde tamen cum tribus abde decem.
65 Quaque ego nascebar fulsit Lyra nocte, fuitque
    Una ortus facies illius atque mei.
Non ego falsa loquor. Vertentem consule mundum.
    Sacra dies Iani Regibus illa fuit.

104 = T6ʳ (margin, line 44)

T6ᵛ (margin, line 66)

33–36 Casta — puer. *A*: *om. **BO**.*   **38** nam *AB*: non *O*.   **41** dicere *A*: discere **BO**.   **45–46** Prima — trahat? *A*: *om. **BO**.*   **47** leges *A*: legis **BO**.   **49** qui — parentes *A*: quae nostrae stirpis origo **BO**.   **51** Martia — cohibet *A*: Qua videt undantem fluvio **BO**.   **61** Hic — auras *A*: Illic vitales primum decerpsimus auras **BO**.   **63** post natum . . . Christum *A*: a nato . . . Christo **BO**.   **64** inde . . . abde decem *A*: deme . . . inde novem **BO**.

[3] As a Christian, Eobanus had to be primarily concerned for his eternal salvation: see ll. 45–46 below.

[4] The Chatti were a Germanic people in present-day Hesse: cf. Tac. *Germ.* 30–31. By the sixth century CE the name *Chatti* had evolved into *Hassi*, or *Hessi*.

Let me add that she lets herself be loved chastely, so as not
to fall into sin. It is sinful to keep someone from being good. All
those who love are good, for all good love is honorable. Venus'
son, however, urges us to engage in wanton love.

Among my heroines you occupy the last place, for you are
used to having the last word in all things. Nevertheless, just so
you know, it was you I always loved first — [40] O you, definitely the second love of my soul![3] I pictured you in my mind
well before I could say how best to court you. Barely a lad, I dedicated my youthful talent to you, for I longed to be a miniscule
part of your army. My highest reverence, however, was reserved
for almighty God. Who in his right mind would be drawn more
to fame than to eternal salvation? So when you read my poems
someday in the future, all you companions of Posterity to come,
you will want to know in what country I was born, what parents
brought me into being, [50] and in what times I lived.

There, where martial Germany keeps the mighty Rhine within
bounds and the German lands converge, as it were, in the center,
the soil is tilled by men whom the ancients called Chatti.[4]
Nowadays this warlike country bears the different name Hesse.
Here there is a mountain famed far and wide for the church of
the Christ-bearing Virgin.[5] With glittering water the Eder laps
against its base. Frankenberg is a small town, to be sure, but
thanks to my Muses she won't rank among the obscure ones —
provided, of course, that you deem her poet worthy of some fame,
[60] O Posterity, you whom he so reverently loves. Here, then, I
first breathed the vital air; that place offered the newborn his first
day of life.[6] Already fifteen centuries had passed since the birth of
Christ. From this number, however, take away thirteen years.[7] In
the night when I was born the Lyre shone brightly; indeed, its rising
coincided with mine.[8] I am not telling a falsehood. Consult an
almanac. That January day was sacred to the Kings.[9]

[5]The Church of Our Lady in Frankenberg.

[6]Eobanus was actually born in the little village of Halgehausen: cf. Camerarius, *Nar.* 5.7–10,
with n. 12 (1:20). But since that village is an obscure one, Eobanus preferred to give nearby
Frankenberg as his birthplace. Accordingly, he styled himself *Francobergius* in his earliest extant letters
and publications (1506–08).

[7]Though he was in fact born on 6 January 1488, Eobanus long believed that he had been born in
1487: see Camerarius, *Nar.* 5.15, with n. 13 (1:21). Cf. ll. 119–20 below.

[8]According to Ov. *Fast.* 1.315–16, Plin. *Nat.* 18.234, and Col. 11.2.97, the constellation
Lyra rises in the night preceding January 6. Hence Eobanus could lay claim to a distinction that the
much-admired poet Konrad Celtis could not. See Celtis, *Am.* 1.1.13, where the poet regrets that on his
birthday, February 1, "no one saw the Lyre in the sky." (Celtis goes on to say, however, that this handi-
cap did not stop him from becoming a poet.)

[9]The Feast of Epiphany, celebrated on January 6, commemorates the coming of the Three Kings
to Bethlehem.

Quae mihi signa domus, qui sint ne quaere parentes.
70   Pauper uterque fuit sed sine labe parens.
Non genus aut titulos numero nec stemmata avorum.
     Virtute o utinam nobilis esse ferar!
Prima quibus puero studiis accreverit aetas
     Nil moror et certe nemo rogare volet.
75   Protinus hinc primis quantumque recordor ab annis
     Nescio quo vatum numine raptus eram.
Nondum cognoram titulum nomenve poetae;
     Ipse mihi nondum Tytire lectus eras.
Dixerat incauto si quis tamen ore "poeta,"
80   Protinus impatiens et sine mente fui.
Nectebam numeros, ratus hoc utcunque decere;
     Lex mihi tum versus cognita nulla fuit.
Tam fuit ignotis fautrix natura poetis,
     (Da veniam!) superis hii mihi maius erant.
85   Vivere iam nullos, omnes vixisse putabam —
     Tam puer et nondum forte decennis eram.
Namque fere nuper Germania nostra solebat
105=V1ʳ   Non pueros studiis sed dare pene viros.
Quippe magis bello atque armis intenta gerendis,
90   Res tantum Latio protulit ore sacras.
Nunc vero Ausonias ita se convertit ad arteis
     Ut Latio fuerit pene Latina magis.
Atque ut eo redeam quo sum digressus: ut autem
     Nunc etiam vates vivere certus eram,
95   Sorduit humanas quicquid sibi subdere mentes,
     Displicuit posset quicquid amare puer.
Obtulit in triviis quendam fortuna magistrum
     Qui numeris certum diceret esse modum.
Hunc colui supplex, illi tantisper adhesi
100   Dum didici certis legibus ire pedes.
Sponte sua influxit brevibus mihi Musa diebus,
     Et mihi iam puero non leve nomen erat,
Ut non praecipuus dubitarit scribere vates,
     "Hesse puer, sacri gloria fontis eris."
105   Carmina cum primum populus mea lecta probaret,
     Clausa fere fuerant iam tria lustra mihi.
Illo me studiis Erphurdia magna fovebat
     Tempore et ingenii publica signa dedit.
Et iam quarta meis accessit Olympias annis,
V1ᵛ   110   Buccolicis lusit nostra iuventa modis

71 titulos — nec *A*: proavos numero, non *BO*.   76 numine *A*: nomine *BO*.   77 titulum nomenve *A*: nomen titulumve *BO*.   78 lectus *A*: notus *BO*.   79 Dixerat *A*: Dixerit *BO*. 81 hoc *A*: *om. BO*.   101 brevibus *A*: paucis *BO*.

Don't ask what my family crest was or who my parents might be. [70] Mother and father were poor, but blameless. Not being highborn, I cannot list titles or genealogical tables. Oh, that I might be thought noble by merit alone! As for my boyhood studies, I won't detain you with them, and surely no one will want to ask.[10] Shortly thereafter, as far as I remember those early years, I became spellbound by the bards' mysterious power. I still knew nothing about poets or what they were up to. I had not even read Vergil's eclogues yet. But if someone carelessly uttered the word *poet*, [80] I was immediately entranced and transported with joy. I wove verses myself, on the assumption that in poetry anything goes. In those days the laws of verse were still foreign to me. My temperament was so ardently disposed to the unknown poets that they (forgive me!) seemed to me greater than gods. I supposed that none was alive anymore, that all were dead — such a boy I was then, perhaps not yet ten years of age. Up to quite recently, you see, our Germany didn't let boys study until they were very nearly grown men. Why, more intent on warfare and feats of arms, [90] she used Latin only in church. But now she has turned with such zeal to the arts of Italy that she is practically more Latin than Latium itself.

But to return to my starting point: as soon as I found out that there were poets alive even today, I loathed everything that other people put their minds to and took a dislike to whatever boys might consider great fun. As luck would have it, I found a teacher in grammar school who, one day, remarked that verses display fixed rhythmical patterns.[11] Respectfully I besieged him with questions. I clung to him [100] for as long as it took to learn the science of metrical verse. Spontaneously the Muse streamed into me in just a few days, and even as a youth I enjoyed no mean fame, so much so in fact that a superb poet did not hesitate to write me, "Hessus, young man, you're bound to be Hippocrene's pride!"[12] When audiences first applauded my poems in recital, I had just passed my mid-teens.[13] At that time the great city of Erfurt was encouraging me in my studies and publishing the fruits of my talent. And when I was already in my early twenties, [110] my youthful age amused itself in bucolic

---

[10]For Eobanus' earliest schooling, see Camerarius, *Nar.* 6.1–4.

[11]In 1501 Eobanus enrolled in the grammar school at Frankenberg that was run by Magister Jakob Horle. It was Horle who initiated Eobanus into the world of poetry: see Camerarius, *Nar.* 6.5–9.

[12]The line is quoted from a verse letter of ca. 23 August 1506, in which Mutianus Rufus congratulates Eobanus on his just-finished, but still unpublished, poem *De pugna*: see Camerarius, *Nar.* 14.1, with notes.

[13]Deliberately drawing a parallel to his great model, Ovid (see Ov. *Tr.* 4.10.57–58), Eobanus asserts that he too began reciting his poems in public in his later teens, after matriculating at Erfurt in 1504. He was then sixteen (or, as he believed at the time, seventeen) years old.

Nostraque ad undecimum crevit rudis aegloga carmen,
Inque meo primus rure magister eram.
Plurima praeterea iuvenilia carmina lusi,
Quae, quia sunt etiam publica, nosse potes.
115 Multaque sub lima nondum vulgata supersunt,
Inque meo varia est condita sylva sinu.
Sunt etiam subito properata poemata versu,
Quae lyra diverso pectine nostra sonat.
Nunc mihi ab undecimo ter quintus vivitur annus.
120 Aetatis non est plusve minusve meae.
Tempore iam Caesar quo Maximus Aemilianus
In Venetos duri fulmina Martis agit,
Scribimus illustres heroidas ecce puellas.
Has tibi praecipue dedico, Posteritas.
125 Accipe, diva senex, gremio tua pignora amico,
Si potes, atque piae nomina matris habe.
Has partim absolvit sub iniquo Prussia caelo,
Qua vagus admissas Istula sorbet aquas,
Partim ubi flaventes niger Odera versat harenas
130 Absolvi vidit nobile gymnasium.
Edidit in lucem Musis celebrata Latinis
106=V2ʳ   Lypsis, Mysneae nobile gentis opus.
His mea Peligni mirari Musa poetae
Ingenium potius quam sapere ausa fuit.
135 Hactenus a studiis si non vera omnia scribo,
Ultima qua fallam causa sit ista precor.
Principibus quoque charus eram, sum tempore et isto.
Abstulit heu multos aula superba dies.
Quam fuerat melius parcae ieiunia Musae
140 Prandia magnorum quam coluisse ducum!

111–12 Nostraque — eram. *A*: *om.* *BO*.   **113** Plurima *A*: Plura *B*, Pluraque *O*.
115–18 Multaque — sonat. *A*: *om.* *BO*.   **120** plusve *AO*: plus *B*.   **121** iam . . . quo *A*: quo . . .
ter *BO*.   **126** habe *A*: habes *BO*.   **128** Istula *A*: Vistula *BO*.   **131–32** Edidit — opus. *A*: *om.*
BO.   **137–40** Principibus — ducum! *A*: *om.* *BO*.

strains. My rustic eclogue grew to eleven poems in all, and in my own country I was the first to shepherd a flock. Besides these bucolics I threw off various other poems in my youth. Since they have been printed, you can get to know them too.[14] A good many unpublished pieces still need more polishing. In fact, quite a miscellany of them is tucked away in my drawer.[15] There are also extemporaneous songs in a variety of lyrical meters. Right now I have lived fifteen years past the eleventh. [120] That is my age, no more and no less.[16]

Now, even as Emperor Maximus Aemilian[17] is hurling the thunderbolts of pitiless Mars against the Venetians, I am writing these heroic letters from illustrious maidens.[18] I dedicate them especially to you, Posterity. Take these children of yours, divine old lady. Hold them lovingly on your lap, if you can, and be an affectionate mother to them. They were completed in part under the inclement skies of Prussia, where the winding Vistula soaks up the inflooding waters. Another part [130] was finished at the renowned university where the black Oder churns up the golden sands.[19] Famed Leipzig in Meissen, a city celebrated by the Latin Muses,[20] has brought it before the public. In writing these letters, my Muse presumed more to admire the genius of the Pelignian poet[21] than to smack of it. If I haven't told you the whole truth about my literary activities thus far, may this, I pray, be the last time I ever tell a lie!

I was also a favorite of princes; indeed, I still am at present. Ah, the proud court has robbed me of many a day. How much better to starve with the frugal Muse [140] than to frequent the banquets of great lords!

[14]Eobanus studied at Erfurt from 1504 to 1509. It was there that he published his first poetic works, beginning with *De recessu* and *De pugna studentum* in 1506 and concluding with his *Bucolicon* in 1509. See vol. 1 of this edition.

[15]For this long-planned collection of occasional poems, entitled *Sylvae*, see the introduction to *Sylvae duae*, p. 55 above.

[16]At the time of writing (the late summer of 1513) Eobanus was in fact twenty-five years old, not twenty-six. For his mistaken belief that he was born in 1487 cf. ll. 63–68 above, with n. 7.

[17]The humanists liked to call Emperor Maximilian by this flattering name in order to associate him with two of Rome's greatest generals: Q. Fabius Maximus Cunctator, who outlasted Hannibal in the Second Punic War, and P. Cornelius Scipio Africanus Aemilianus, the hero of the Third Punic War.

[18]In September-October 1513 Maximilian and his Spanish allies waged a war of attrition against Venice, destroying and plundering everything they could on the Venetian mainland.

[19]Eobanus began the work at Riesenburg in Prussia and completed it at Frankfurt an der Oder: cf. *Her. Chr.*, ded. 8.3–5.

[20]In Hermann von dem Busche's *Lipsica*, published at Leipzig ca. 1504: cf. Eob. *Laud.* 542.

[21]Ovid was born in the Pelignian city of Sulmo in central Italy.

Quos tulerit nostro Germania tempore vates
    Ex multis aliquot dicere forte rogas.
Quisquis es, Hutteni, lector, percurre libellos.
    Quemque suo reddit nomine, quemque loco.
145 Inspice, Posteritas, Hutteni carmina vatis.
    Hunc recto poteris dicere iure tuum!
Hac igitur, forte atque alia ratione poetae
    Nullius in nostro carmine nomen erit.
Nomina transierim vatum non digna malorum,
150   Invidia dicar non caruisse malis.
Vatibus addidero doctis mala nomina forsan,
    Iudicium dicar non habuisse bonis.
Fortunae atque animi iamdudum munera nosti.
    Naturae superest dona referre meae.

V2ᵛ

155 Corpus erat membrisque decens patiensque laborum,
    Robore firma suo brachia, crura, latus.
Forma virum decuisse potest, sine labe decensque;
    Frons diversa, animi spiritus altus erat.
Hactenus haec iuvenem de se dixisse feretis,
160   O quibus aut lecta est aut mea Musa placet.
Lusimus haec certe properanti carmina plectro,
    Dum nimis ad metam noster anhelat equus.
Parcite, si qua minus iustum referuntur ad unguem:
    Haec sunt ingenii munera prima mei.
165 Tempora venturae tangam si forte senectae,
    Plura quidem primis et meliora dabo.
Tum quoque, Posteritas, tibi multa legenda relinquam.
    Primitias tanquam suscipere ista velis
Et me si mereor (nec enim est attingere primos)
170   Postremos inter temporis huius habe.

Τέλος

---

142 Ex *A*: E *BO*; rogas *A*: roges *BO*.   **143** Hutteni, lector, *A*: Hutteni lectos *BO*.
168 Primitias tanquam *A*: Tamquam primicias *BO*.   **Subscriptio** Τέλος *A*: Finis *B*, *om. O*.
Post ep. 24 additur in **O** *"Ecclesiae afflictae epistola ad Lutherum. Captiva Luthero," quae epistula in tomo quarto huius editionis invenietur.*

Perhaps you'll ask me to mention some of the many bards that Germany brought forth in our time. Whoever you are, reader, skim through that booklet of Hutten's where he refers to each one by name and by place.[22] Posterity, look into the songs of the poet Hutten. Him you'll be able to call your own by rights! For this reason, therefore, and maybe for another as well, no other poet's name will appear in my song. If I were to pass over the unworthy names of bad poets, [150] the bad ones would claim I wasn't free from envy. Were I perhaps to include bad names among the learned poets, the good ones would say I was lacking in taste.

For some time now you've become acquainted with my gifts of fortune and mind. It remains to tell you something about the favors I owe to nature. My body was good-looking in all its members and able to endure hard labor. Arms, legs, and trunk were strong and well built. My features were manly, unblemished, and handsome. Broad was my forehead, highminded my soul.

Don't take offense that the young man has been talking about himself all this time, [160] O you who read and enjoy my Muse! I have certainly played these songs at a very brisk tempo, while my horse was racing too fast to the post. Go easy on me if you find spots that haven't been smoothed to perfection. After all, these are my talent's first gifts to you. If perhaps I live to a ripe old age, I'll certainly give you more and better work than a firstling like this. Then too, Posterity, I'll leave you with much more to read. Take up these poems as a kind of first fruits and, if I deserve it (for I can't imagine reaching the headmost), [170] do count me among the hindmost of my own day and age.

The End

---

[22]Eobanus alludes to Ulrich von Hutten's elegy "To the Poets of Germany" (*Querelae* 2.10), published in 1510. There Hutten gives a survey of the German Neo-Latin poets of his day and lauds Eobanus as the greatest of them all (l. 86). Eobanus herewith returns the compliment. For Hutten's life, see n. 87 at *Laud.* B 3 (1:186–87).

V3ʳ

B 1 H. EOBANUS HESSUS VITO VVERLERO
SUO SALUTEM DICIT.

Dulcis amicitiae nostrae comes, unica verae
    Fidelitatis gloria,
Optima pars vitae melioris, denique vita,
    Beate Vite, candida,
5   Quem nemo bonus odit, amant, venerantur, honorant
    Quicunque non sunt pessimi:
Sub viridi nobis nuper spaciantibus umbra
    Propter susurranteis aquas
Multaque de studiis consueto more loqutis,
10   De livido sermo incidit.
Questus eras, memini, quam te sine crimine Livor
    Morsu insectetur perfido.
Ne doleas! Virtus haec praemia sola meretur
    Apud furentem Zoilum.
15   Vidit et indoluit summis te laudibus auctum
    Ille ille quisquis quisquis est.
Doctus es, et facilis floret tibi gratia linguae.
    Quis Livor hoc tantus ferat?
Comis et urbanus cum sis constansque piusque,
20   Venas miser depascitur.
Per fora, per plateas, per compita, templa, viasque
    Laudaris. Hoc Livor dolet.
Denique cuncta tibi pro voto cedere spectans,
    Pene eviratus concidit.
25   Nil miserabilius totum liquet esse per orbem
    Quam semper ardentem invidum.
Ardet et incluso miseras calet igne medullas.
    Cupido non tantum furit.
Saepe graves misero flammae minuuntur amanti;
30   Hic igne nunquam liber est.
Non graviora aliquis dederit tormenta Perillus,
V3ᵛ   Non impius Mezentius.
Et tantum (res mira!) sibi nocet et dumtaxat
    Se carnifex eviscerat.

B 1. *A*: *om. BO (Her.)*; *cf. Sylv.* 4.3 *in SO.*   **Tit.** H. Eobanus Hessus [Hes. *A*] — salutem dicit [sa. di. *A*] *A*, Ad Vitum Verlerum virtutem invidiae obnoxium esse *SO.*   7 Sub *A*: In *SO.*   12 insectetur perfido *A*: flagellet improbo *SO.*   16 ille quisquis *A*: ille cunque *SO.*   23 pro — cedere *A*: ad votum succedere *SO.*   25–26 totum — invidum *A*: rebus mortalibus ortum est, / Sic semper ardente invido *SO.*   27 incluso *A*: occulto *SO.*   31 graviora *A*: maiora *SO.*

**B 1   H. EOBANUS HESSUS TO HIS FRIEND
VEIT WERLER, GREETINGS[1]**

Comrade in this sweet friendship of ours, matchless ornament of
true fidelity, vital part of an upright life — indeed, the very soul
of unsullied vitality — blessed Veit, you, whom no decent person
hates, whom all but the worst villains love, revere, and honor:
The other day, when we were strolling in the green shade, hard
by a whispering brook, and were as usual going on about our
scholarly pursuits, [10] the topic fell upon jealousy. As I recall,
you complained how Envy, through no fault of your own, was
assailing you with his treacherous carping.

Don't let it bother you! In the eyes of frenzied Zoilus[2] this is
the only reward that virtue deserves. Whoever he is, whoever he
may be, he has watched you garner the highest honors, and that
cuts him to the quick. You are a man of learning, endowed with
graceful eloquence. How could self-important Envy put up
with that? And since you're cultured and sophisticated and steadfast
and loyal, [20] the miscreant eats his heart out. In marketplaces and
streets, at crossroads, in churches, on highways people praise you.
This rankles Envy. In fact, watching you succeed in everything
you undertake, he is virtually unmanned and collapses in a heap.

Obviously there is nothing in the whole world quite so
wretched as a man always burning with envy. He's all ablaze inside,
glowing with fire right down to his wretched marrow. Even Cupid
doesn't rage like that. For all his misery, the lover often finds his
grievous flames abating with time; [30] an envious person is never
free of fire. No Perillus, no godless Mezentius could inflict more
painful tortures.[3] Even so (a miracle!) he manages to harm and
eviscerate nobody but himself, self-tormentor that he is. Look how

---

[1]This poem to Veit Werler was also published (most probably from the original manuscript) as
Sylv. 4.3, "Ad Vitum Verlerum, virtutem invidiae obnoxiam esse" ("To Veit Werler, that Goodness is
Subject to Envy"). Eobanus sent it to thank his friend for the complimentary verses that he had con-
tributed to the *Heroides Christianae*: see *Her. Chr.* A 3, with notes.

[2]A sophist who poked fun at Homer's errors and inconsistencies, Zoilus became a byword for a
spiteful critic: see n. 16 at *Rec.* B 2.3 (1:115).

[3]Perillus was an Athenian sculptor who made a brazen bull for the tyrant Phalaris (ca. 570–554
BCE), in which to roast people alive. The Etruscan chieftain Mezentius, an ally of Turnus against
Aeneas, was notorious for his atheism and cruelty.

35 Aspice quam torvo distorquet lumina vultu
        Ut fictiles larvae solent!
   Quales ire ferunt Furias nocturna moventes
        Laetargicis insomnia.
   Aspectum metuit vitam sine crimine agentis,
40   Ut glauca solem noctua.
   Talem, crede mihi, cum tu patiare ferasque,
        Sum passus ipse et nunc fero.
   Quod si perstiterint non desinere esse molesti,
        Utrumque nominabimus.
45 Ardeat interea quantum volet — ardeat et se
        Livore inani torqueat!
   Nos alimenta igni dabimus virtutibus istis,
        Nos gratia quarum fugit.
   Cumque leget, si forte leget, quas scribimus unquam
50   Sacro puellas pectine,
   Aspiciet nostrae fidei documenta vicissim,
        Suspendet et se forsitan.
   Tu prior occurres illi stomachumque movebis
        Praeliminari pagina.
55 Huc quoque respiciet, nec enim leget omnia Livor,
        Vitumque rursus perleget,
   Eheu, quos gemitus dabis hic, moestissime Livor,
        Tam firmo amore territus!
   Quin age, ne garri contra neu, perfide, latres,
60   Ni perditum iri te voles.
   At tu, quicunque es, lector sine labe futurus,
        Ignosce Vito ac Helio.
   Est opus audaci muscas arcere flabello,
        Ne saepe pungant libere.
65 Irrequietum animal, rostro mordente timendum,
V4ʳ   Facessat in rem pessimam!
   At tu, nostrorum studii vitaeque sodalis,
        Quo vix magis quicquam placet,
   Ne doleas si te malus insectatur et audet
70   Livore dignum credere.
   Causa tua est virtus. Nunquam caret illa malignis
        Qui detrahant osoribus.
   Quin age deride caeptoque insiste labori.
        Codro crepabunt ilia.

Τέλος

49 quas *SO*: quae *A*.   55 leget *A*: legit *SO*.   63 flabello *A*: flagello *SO*.   ***Subscriptio*** Τέλος *A*: *deest SO*.

he rolls his eyes and twists his face, just like a gargoyle! That is how the Furies are said to stalk about when they foist nightmares on people in their sleep. He dreads the sight of a man leading a blameless life, [40] much as a bright-eyed owl fears the sun.

Believe me, even as you're putting up with and enduring him, I myself have had to put up with and am even now enduring just such an envier. But if those two persist and don't stop being a nuisance, we'll publicize their names. Meanwhile let him burn all he wants — let him burn and torment himself in helpless envy! We for our part will add fuel to the fire through the very virtues for which he shuns us. And someday when he reads — if he happens to read — the maidens' letters that I've written [50] in sacred verse, he'll spot the mutual testimonials to our staunch friendship[4] and maybe go hang himself. You'll catch his eye right at the start and turn his stomach on the preliminary page. He'll also look here, for Envy won't read everything, and thus will run into Veit a second time. Alas, chapfallen Envy, what groans you'll utter then, in your terror at such unfaltering love! All right then, scoundrel, don't jabber or bark at us, [60] unless you're bent on destroying yourself.

But you, whoever you are, blameless reader to come, forgive Veit and Helius. We have to make bold to swat at these flies, so they won't go on biting us at will. As for that tireless beast with its fearfully snapping jaws, let it go to hell! But you, my comrade in scholarship and life, pretty well the dearest friend I have, don't let it bother you if some scoundrel harries you and ventures [70] to believe that you're an enviable man. The reason is your all-around excellence. Merit like that has never lacked for hateful detractors. So just laugh them off and stick to your guns. That will make Codrus burst his sides.[5]

The End

---

[4]Veit Werler's complimentary poem to Eobanus (*Her. Chr.* A 3), printed at the head of the book, and this concluding response.

[5]Cf. *Her. Chr.* A 2.29, with n. 5.

SUPPLEMENTARY NOTES

Notes to
ENCOMIUM NUPTIALE

Liminary epigram

Meter: Elegiac distich.

1   **gelida . . . sub Arcto** = V. Fl. 6.140; cf. Luc. 1.252; Eob. *Nup.* 258; *Sylv.* 1.1.157; 4.5.1; cf. also *Nup.* 20, 310–11. Eobanus adopts the attitude of the ancient Romans, for whom the Sarmatians (the modern Poles and Russians) were indeed an arctic people. Cf., for example, Ov. *Pont.* 2.7.72; Sen. *Thy.* 127–28; Stat. *Silv.* 5.1.127–28.

2   **Non — legi** Cf. *Ama.*, lim. 6, n.

3   **Istula Rheno** ≈ *Sylv. duae* 1.59. For the form *Istula* (instead of *Vistula*, which would spoil the meter here), cf. Aen. Silv. *Europa* 29 (par. 96): "hunc fluvium alii Viscelam, . . . alii Iustulam, quidam Istulam vocavere"; Celtis, *Norimberga* 3, p. 117: "Istule"; p. 126: "Istulam"; Hutten. *Querel.* 2.10.20. Eobanus uses this form also at *Sylv. duae* 1.129; *Her. Chr.* 24.128; *Gen. ebrios.* 16.5; and *Sarmat.* 100.

4   **nostro pectore** = Prop. 2.13.2; Ov. *Tr.* 3.3.16; Eob. *Psalt.* 45.2: "Carmina, quae e nostro pectore dictat amor."
        pectore, verba = *Her. Chr.* 6.78, n.
        verba refer = Ov. *Ep.* 20.214.

6   **fere — scriptus** ≈ *Epic.*, app. 2.10: "Ista fere nullo tempore scripta dedit."
        nullo tempore = Ov. *Am.* 1.15.20; 2.19.8; 3.7.52; *Tr.* 3.2.24.

Dedicatory letter

3   **Quod non — deductum** Cf. Stella, *Boruss.*, praef., p. 285: "Ego autem hanc scribendi provinciam non tam mea sponte quam iussu venerandi antistitis Iobi Pomesaniensis a nullo antea tentatam accepi."
        "subito" — effluxerat In the preface to bk. 1 of his *Silvae*, Statius describes his poems as "libellos, qui mihi subito calore et quadam festinandi voluptate fluxerunt." Cf. Eob. *Buc.* 11.26; *Vict.*, app. 2.20: "Territa mi subitus fluxit in ossa calor"; *Sylv.* 1, ded.: "'subito,' ut ille inquit, 'calore' mihi effluxerant"; 1.7.23 (to Johannes Dantiscus in February 1512): "haec scribis subito fluxisse calore"; Dantiscus, *Carm.* 12.1.19 (introducing his epithalamium for King Sigismund, 12 February 1512): he had written the poem "subito . . . calore."
        invita . . . Minerva Erasmus, *Adag.* 1.1.42; Otto 1121.

4   **litteratioribus litteris** The phrase occurs also in Eobanus' letter to Georg Spalatin, dated 12 April 1512: "Parvo contentus ero, modo detur ad litteratiores literas reditus." See Mutian. *Ep.*, 2:368. Eobanus uses it again at the start of a letter to Joachim Vadianus (20 March 1514): "Quantae in literis literatioribus aestimationis . . . sis." See *Die Vadianische Briefsammlung der Stadtbibliothek St. Gallen*, ed. Emil Arbenz, vol. 1 (St. Gallen, 1890), no. 31.
        futurae posteritati — consecraretur Cf. *Ama.*, ded. 13, n.
        aeternitati consecraretur V. Max. 1.7, ext. 3: "aeternitati consecravit."

5   **nuptiarum scribendarum provinciam** Cf. *Her. Chr.*, ded. 8.1: "scribendarum heroidum provintiam." Eobanus must have remembered the expression from Stella, *Boruss.*, praef., p. 285: "hanc scribendi provinciam."

11   **quae istuc — misit** Erasmus, *Moriae encomium*, ded., *ASD* 4.3:67, ll. 10–11, first published at Paris in 1511: "Quae Pallas istuc tibi misit in mentem?"

12   **hoc quod — exiguum** Cf. Cic. *Arch.* 1: "Si quid est in me ingenii, . . . quod sentio quam sit exiguum"; Eob. *Laud.*, ded. 7; *Orat. Sylv.* 2; *Her. Chr.*, ded. 8.8; *Orat.* 4.8: "pro mei ingenii facultate (quae tamen sentio quam sit exigua)"; *Gen. ebrios.* 1.2: "meae si quid est eruditionis (quod tamen sentio quam sit exiguum) tenuitate."

15   **nuncupatum dedicatumque** Apul. *Met.* 11.16; Eob. *Her. Chr.*, ded. 17.1.

           libellum — tutela Cf. Celtis, *Am.*, praef. 42: "librosque quattuor sub tui nominis sacratissimi tutela et patrocinio edidisse"; Eob. *Her. Chr.*, ded. 1.2: "sub tui sacri nominis tutela"; *Dial.*, ded. 4: "sub tui nominis patrocinio"; *Idyl.*, ded. 1.20 (ded. 2.18): "Tuta patrocinio nominis . . . tui."

Encomium nuptiale

Meter: Hexameter.

1   **Regalis — iugales** Cf. *Sylv.* 1.1.29, addressed to King Sigismund in November 1512: "Regales cecini thalamos pompamque iugalem"; *Epic.*, app. 5.13, addressed to Johannes Dantiscus: "Regales celebrans thalamos pompamque iugalem, / Ausa est [mea Musa] semideis, te quoque teste, loqui."

           Regalis thalami ≈ Juvenc. 3.741: "Regales thalamos"; cf. Eob. *Nup.* 86, 336.

           taedasque iugales ≈ Sil. 17.73. Cf., for example, Catul. 64.302; Ov. *Ep.* 4.121; *Tr.* 4.5.33; Eob. *Nup.* 73, n.; *Her. Chr.* 7.9, n.

2   **Coniugiique — coronam** = l. 332 below.

3–4   **Canturo — vocare** Eobanus adopts the old Christian tradition of seeking the inspiration of the heavenly Muse, Christ. Like Paul. Nol. *Carm.* 15.30–33, he combines this invocation with a programmatic rejection of Phoebus and the Muses. For these traditions, see Curtius, *ELLMA*, chap. 13; Paul Klopsch, *Einführung in die Dichtungslehren des lateinischen Mittelalters* (Darmstadt, 1980), 21–27. In thus renewing tradition, Eobanus emphasizes that he is a Christian poet who takes his Christianity seriously. Implicitly, he also suggests that King Sigismund, the subject of his "Nuptial Encomium," embodies the ideal Christian ruler so perfectly that it would be offensive to present him with a pagan-style epithalamium, in which Venus, Cupid, and other gods and goddesses operate the machinery of love and marriage. Cf. further Eob. *Laud.* 13, n.; *Buc.* 11.16–22, n.; *Vict.* 1–7; *Val.* 1.1–2, with nn.

5   **per mille poemata** = Poliziano, *Silv.* 4.714.

8   **Latias . . . pascua Musas** = *Idyl.* 8.2 (likewise referring to his own pastorals).

           Latias . . . Musas ≈ Luc. 9.983.

9   **baculo . . . agresti** Ov. *Met.* 15.655; Eob. *Sylv. duae* 1.181.

           baculo pastor Ov. *Met.* 8.218.

           pastor contentus = Andrel. *Ecl.* 9.1: "Numquam sorte sua pastor contentus Iolas."

10   **Pectora — arundine** Cf. Ov. *Ep.* 9.161; Eob. *Buc.* 3.151, n.; *Sylv.* 1.6.16: "Non ego sum Paphia pectora laesus acu."

11   **Aoniis . . . fontibus** Locher, "Carmen ad S. Brant," *Stult.*, fol. 4ʳ: "Nil latet Aoniis fontibus huncce virum"; Eob. *Laud.* 241.

           extinguere — ignem Cf. Verg. *A.* 2.686.

12   **molli . . . versu** Prop. 1.7.19; Ov. *Tr.* 2.307; cf. Eob. *Laud.* 15, n.

           Flavia versu = *Sylv. duae* 2.33.

14   **florenti . . . aevo** Lucr. 3.1008; Stat. *Silv.* 4.6.93.

15   **Quicquid — ausa est** Cf. *Sylv.* 2, ded. (referring to his juvenilia): "quae prima aetas incautius effudit."

           Quicquid id est = Lucr. 3.135; 5.577, 1252; Verg. *A.* 2.49; Ov. *Ep.* 19.203; et al.; cf. Eob. *Buc.* 2.66.

           iuveniliter ausa est ≈ *Val.* 1.655: "me iuveniliter ausum."

16   **adhuc teneris . . . annis** = Gunther, *Lig.* 1.326; cf. Ov. *Ep.* 4.25; Stat. *Silv.* 2.7.54.

18   **grandia — moventur** ≈ *Sylv.* 6.3.15, likewise contrasting elegiacs with grander — that is, "heroic" — verse: "Sive elegos nobis seu grandia plectra moveret." Cf. ll. 360–61 below; *Hod.* 440; *Sylv.* 2.12.13: "maiora . . . plectra movemus"; *Idyl.* 16.164–65: "Tunc, ubi grandisono dignum pede nacta cothurnum / Liberiore manu sublimia plectra movebis." For the tag *plectra moventur*, see Ov. *Ep.* 3.113.

20   **Lycaoniam . . . sub Arcton** = *Sylv. duae* 1.21; cf. *Her. Chr.* 13.41, n.; 16.49, n.

21   **Sarmaticae . . . gentis** = Ov. *Tr.* 5.7.13; cf. Eob. *Laud.* 544.

22   **Quam — circum** = Verg. *A.* 5.250.

23   **Bella sonant** = Ov. *Tr.* 2.529.

24–25   **Tartarus . . . Epoto satiatus equo** Cf. Mart. *Sp.* 3.4; Eob. *Sylv. duae* 1.108, n.

26   **Fortibus . . . Polonis** *Sylv.* 1.2.38; *Tum.* 5.83; *Epic.*, app. 5.11.

        Fortibus arma = *Ilias Lat.* 127.

        diverso Marte Sid. *Carm.* 4.11.

27–28   **cognoscere — gens est** Cf. Flor. *Epit.* 2.29 (4.12.20): "tanta barbaria est, ut nec intellegant pacem"; Mart. *Sp.* 3.1.

30–31   **Martia — metallis** Cf. *Sylv.* 2.4.19–21 (of Saxony): "Inclyta divitiis tellus, operosa metallis, / Uberis insignis fertilitate soli, / Plena viris."

30   **terra viris** = Man. 4.686: "maxima terra viris et fecundissima doctis / artibus."

        Cerealibus — pratis Cf. Ov. *Tr.* 3.12.11: ". . . Cerealibus obruta sulcis."

31   **Dives — metallis** Cf. Verg. *A.* 10.174.

        Dives . . . pecoris Verg. *Ecl.* 2.20.

32   **Christiferae . . . crucis** *Sylv. duae* 1.33; *Her. Chr.* 6.156; *Sylv.* 1.1.66, 82.

33   **stravit — hostem** *Anthol. Lat.* 630.3 (Achilles): "stravi . . . armis victricibus hostes."

34   **Scythico . . . orbi** Ov. *Tr.* 3.12.51.

35–37   **Tempore — Galli** For this time reference, cf. Verg. *G.* 4.559–61; Eob. *Her. Chr.* 24.121–22; *Hod.* 26–30.

35   **Tempore iam Caesar** = Juv. 4.135.

        Caesar . . . Maximus Aemilianus *Epic.* 7.45–46. For the phrase *Maximus Aemilianus* at this metrical position see Celtis, *Rhapsodia*, app. E 1.11 (p. 27); Eob. *Nob.* 213; *Tum.* 3.143. Cf. Celtis, *Rhapsodia* 217; Eob. *Hymn.* 175–76; *Epp.* 4, sig. F7ʳ (25 May 1508): "Caesaris Aemyliani / Numine, cui duplex virtus dat maxima nomen"; sig. F8ʳ: "Caesar . . . / . . . fortissimus Aemylianus"; also cf. *Hod.* 27, n.: "Maximus Aemilius." To my knowledge, the first to suggest that the name *Maximilian* is a combination of *Maximus* and *Aemilianus* was Iason Maynus, "Ad serenissimum Maximilianum . . . epithalamium" (1494). I quote from the text printed in *Varia Philippi Beroaldi opuscula* (Basel, 1513), fol. 57ᵛ–58ʳ: "Tibi nomen Maximiliano parens indidit non sine quodam divino instinctu, ut Plato attestatur, quod duo significat Maximum et Aemilianum: ambo Rhomani militarium copiarum praestantissimi duces ac triumphales viri, Maximus enim Fabius Rhomanum imperium pene desolatum adversus Hannibalem Poenum cunctando restituit, Aemilianus vero Scipio Hannibale tandem devicto Carthaginensem triumphum egit."

36–37   **Fulminat — Galli** Cf. *Buc.* 10.130–33, with nn.; *Tum.* 3.139–40. For *fulminat*, cf. *Her. Chr.* 24.122, n.

36   **socia arma** = Verg. *A.* 8.120; 11.161.

37   **Rhomanas aquilas** = *Hod.* 324; cf. Ov. *Fast.* 5.586; Eob. *Hod.* 210; *Luth.* 2.28; *Sylv.* 1.1.173.

        fortis . . . Galli *Her. Chr.* 7.101.

38   **Sceptriger** = *Ilias Lat.* 8.

        Augusta . . . pace Ov. *Pont.* 2.5.18; Eob. *Hod.* 221.

        in pace regebat = Verg. *A.* 7.46; 8.325.

39   **Flore . . . iuvenili** For the image, cf. *Her. Chr.* 2.110, n.

        in regna vocatus ≈ Verg. *A.* 7.256.

40–41   **Maximus — secundus** Cf. *Sylv.* 8.23.5–6: "Eloquio veterum nulli florente secundus, / Maximus ingenio, maximus arte fuit."

40 **Maximus — armis** Cf. Ov. *Tr.* 2.424; Prud. *Apoth.* 450; Eob. *Ilias* 2.376: "Maximus ingenio est, bello fortissimus idem."

41 **nulli . . . virtute secundus** = Sil. 7.55; cf. Verg. *A.* 12.27; Eob. *Rec.* 156, n.
veterum virtute Verg. *A.* 11.441.

42–45 **Hannibal — regendis** For the pattern of praise — one man combines the virtues of several ancients — see *Laud.* 265–66, n.; ll. 56–58 below.

42 **Caesar in armis** = Prop. 2.7.5.

46 **virtutes agmine facto** = Bebel, "Amor Cymonis fatui," *Carm.*, sig. i6ᵛ. For the tag *agmine facto*, see Verg. *G.* 4.167; *A.* 1.82, 434; 8.595.

48 **Inque — residunt** Cf. Dantiscus, *Carm.* 12.2.84–85 (epithalamium for King Sigismund): "Omnes illius divo . . . / Corde deae resident."

49–51 **Sicut — hyacinthos** Cf. *Wirt.* 140–43.

49 **apum . . . examen** Liv. 21.46.1; 24.10.11; Eob. *Sylv. duae* 1.81.
Hybla Cf. *Laud.* 107, n.

50 **Nunc — illos** = Verg. *A.* 5.441.
florum — odores Cf. *Her. Chr.* 17.117.
scrutatur odores = Claud. *Rapt. Pros.* 2.148 (in some mss.).

51 **Pallentes — hyacinthos** = Man. 5.257; cf. Verg. *Ecl.* 2.47; Eob. *Buc.* 9.59.

52 **ubi praeteriit** = Ov. *Met.* 14.101.

53 **apiastri** *Buc.* 2.50, n.

55 **Virtutum — heroidum** Cf. *Epic.* 8.43: "chorus virtutum heroinarum." For *virtutum chorus*, see Cic. *Off.* 3.116; *Tusc.* 5.13.

55–56 **molestum — numeros** Cf. l. 168, n., below.

56 **Colligere in numeros** Cf. *Epp. fam.*, p. 19 (letter of 19 June 1519): "idyllion illud Theocryticum . . . Latinis numeris colligerem."

56–57 **gravitate — Achillem** Cf. *Laud.* 265–66, with nn.; ll. 42–45 above. The phrase "gravitate Catonem, / Relligione Numam" is also found in Balbi, *Opusc.* 56.7–8: "Religione Numam, priscum gravitate Catonem / Vicis." Cf. Paulus Crosnensis, *Carm.* 47.27–28, in a poem to Jan Lubrański published on 1 March 1512, together with his epithalamium for Sigismund I: "Qui sanctum pura vicit gravitate Catonem, / Pompeium fama, religione Numam." See Maria Cytowska, *Pauli Crosnensis Rutheni Carmina* (Warsaw, 1962), 163. In the epithalamium itself (*Carm.* 46.249–52) Paulus Crosnensis applies a whole catalogue of such phrases to the king himself: "Quo genio Fabius, vi Fulvius, arte Camillus, / Appius eloquio, religione Numa, / Sulla acie, Magnus fama, pietate Metellus, / Scipiadae bellis Atiliusque fide."

56 **gravitate Catonem** Cf. Cic. *Off.* 1.112; Otto 358; Häussler, 98, 146; Eob. *Epp. 4*, sig. F6ʳ (25 May 1508): "morum gravitate Cato."

57 **generoso pectore** Ov. *Met.* 12.234.
pectore Achillem = Stat. *Ach.* 1.228.

58 **omnes — virtutibus** Cf. *Nob.* 133.
virtutibus . . . aequat Ov. *Pont.* 2.3.1.

59 **superat virtute** = Ov. *Met.* 8.517.

60 **meritis — auctus** ≈ *Sylv.* 1.1.27 (addressed to King Sigismund); cf. *Tum.* 3.127–28.

61–62 **In principe rarum Sit** Plin. *Pan.* 60.6.

62 **Sit licet hoc** = Ov. *Met.* 13.18.

63 **Nobilis ex atavis** = *Rec.* 101, n.

64 **titulis . . . insignis avorum** Luc. 8.73.

65 **Quos — sedes** Cf. Verg. *A.* 10.143–44; ll. 102–03 below.
superas . . . sedes Verg. *A.* 11.532; Ov. *Fast.* 3.324.

66 **Talis hic et tantus** = Tifernate, "Hymnus in Trinitatem," *Carm.*, sig. A4ʳ; Eob. *Epic.* 9.75; l. 68 below.

67 **hominis — unguem** Cf. Hor. *S.* 1.5.32–33. For *ad unguem*, see Eob. *Buc.* 4.94, n.

68   **magnorum . . . regum** = Hor. *S.* 1.3.136; Ov. *Pont.* 4.2.1; cf. Eob. *Her. Chr.* 17.17, n.

70   **ut memini** See l. 39 above.

71   **exuit annos** = Tib. 1.4.35; Eob. *Epic.* 3.109; cf. *Buc.* 6.71, n.

72   **Regia . . . sceptra** *Her. Chr.* 12.230, n.
      celebs sine coniuge Ov. *Met.* 10.245.
      sceptra gerebat Verg. *A.* 12.206.

73   **Maturus . . . aevo** Ov. *Met.* 8.617.
      taedas . . . iugales = Ov. *Met.* 1.483; cf. l. 1, n., above.

74   **regni . . . insignia** = Verg. *A.* 11.334.

74–75 **prolem Sufficere** Verg. *G.* 3.65.

76   **procerum sententia** = Juvenc. 4.572.

77   **consortem thalami** Ov. *Met.* 10.246; Sen. *Ag.* 256; *Thy.* 235; Sil. 3.63.

79   **Legitimo . . . foedere lecti** Cf. *Venus* 2.119: "legitimi . . . foedere lecti"; *Epith.* 6: "legitimi . . . foedera lecti." Also cf. Ov. *Tr.* 2.536; *Ib.* 15; l. 313, n., below; *Nob.* 98.
      genialis . . . lecti *Buc.* 5.68, n.

80   **rudibus . . . lacertis** Claud. *IV. Cons. Hon.* 202.
      colla lacertis = *Rec.* 130, n.

81   **Quae — timent** Cf. Gunther, *Lig.* 1.26: "Te populi, te regna timent. . . ."

82   **Expertus metuit** = Hor. *Ep.* 1.18.87.

83   **Thanaim . . . nivalem** *Laud.* 209, n.

85–86 **dignissima . . . ire in thalamos** Cf. *Her. Chr.* 1.148, n.

86   **Regales . . . thalamos** l. 1, n., above.

87   **blanda — ridens** Cf. *Epith.* 188: "vos blanda Venus, vos Gratia ridens / Iunxit." For *blanda Venus*, see Ov. *Am.* 3.2.55; *Ars* 1.362; Stat. *Silv.* 2.7.84.

88   **facilis . . . Natura** *Lydia* 37, 77; Eob. *Sylv.* 9.4.25; cf. *Buc.* 10.64, n.
      ad unguem = l. 67 above; *Buc.* 4.94, n.

89–92 **Quam — Praelatam** Cf. *Buc.* B 2.39–42; Strozzi, *Eroticon* 1.2.49–51 (published in 1513): "Si Paris hanc faciem Phrygia vidisset in Ida, / Illo non isset iudice prima Venus. / Huic merito potuit Iuno invidisse figurae." The motif was inspired by Catul. 61.16–20 (the bride is just as lovely as Venus on Mount Ida).

89   **Phrygia . . . in Ida** *Buc.* B 2.41, n.

90   **Aurea . . . poma** Ov. *Met.* 10.650.

91   **Pallas glauca** Hermann von dem Busche, liminary poem to Magdal. *Erarium*, sig. A1ʳ: "glauce Pallados"; cf. Eob. *Pug.* 96, n.

92   **tantum — est** Cf. Ov. *Ep.* 18.73; Eob. *Buc.* 9.77.

93   **regibus aedita** Hor. *Carm.* 1.1.1.

94–99 **Paulatim — vetustas** Cf. Sen. *Dial.* 10.15.4: "Honores, monimenta, quidquid aut decretis ambitio iussit aut operibus extruxit, cito subruitur, nihil non longa demolitur vetustas et movet; at iis, quae consecravit sapientia, nocere non potest; nulla abolebit aetas, nulla deminuet."

94   **Paulatim . . . abolevit . . . vetustas** Cf. Verg. *A.* 1.720; l. 99, n., below.
      longa vetustas = Cic. *Arat.* 2.1; Ov. *Fast.* 5.131 (in many mss.); Luc. 8.867; Stat. *Silv.* 4.1.28; Eob. *Epp. 4*, sig. F5ʳ (25 May 1508); *Her. Chr.* 3.17.

96   **omnigenum rerum** *Her. Chr.* 24.29.
      rerum — ordo = Mant. *Dionys.*, fol. 167ᵛ; Eob. *Sylv.* 1.4.97; cf. *Sylv. duae* 1.165.

97–99 **Sola — vetustas** For the commonplace of true nobility, summed up in Sen. *Ep.* 44, Juv. 8.20, and Boeth. *Consol.* 3.m6, see Curtius, *ELLMA*, 179–80. See further Manfred Lentzen, introd. to Christoforo Landino, *De vera nobilitate*, Travaux d'Humanisme et Renaissance 109 (Geneva, 1970), 3–11; Albert Rabil, Jr., *Knowledge, Goodness, and Power: The Debate over Nobility among Quattrocento Italian Humanists* (Binghamton, NY, 1991). Eobanus devoted a lengthy elegy to the subject (*De vera nobilitate*, begun in 1513/14 but not published until ca. July 1515) and often touches on the topic elsewhere: see, for instance, *Laud.* 147, n.; *Her. Chr.* 6.63–64, with n.; 21.51–70, n.; 24.71–72; *Her.*, ded. 5–8.

97–98	**clara . . . Nomina** = Ov. *Am.* 2.1.35–36.
99	**abolere vetustas** = Ov. *Met.* 15.872; cf. l. 94 above.
100	**heroidas — haberi** = *Her. Chr.* 4.39; cf. Ov. *Tr.* 1.6.33; Eob. *Her. Chr.* 24.37.
101	**Nobilis ex atavis** = *Rec.* 101, n.
	transmisit habendam = Verg. *A.* 3.329.
102–03	**quem gloria . . . sublimem tollit** Verg. *A.* 10.143–44; cf. l. 65 above.
104	**nomine dicta** = Ov. *Met.* 8.235; Eob. *Her. Chr.* 15.15.
105	**Ergo . . . promissa dies** = Verg. *A.* 9.107.
	Ergo ubi iam = V. Fl. 4.433.
	foelicibus astris = Poliziano, *Silv.* 1.301: "heroes nati felicibus astris."
107	**tactura lacertos** = *Her. Chr.* 20.67.
108	**procerum — cohors** Cf. Paul. Nol. *Carm.* 21.77; Eob. *Laud.* 533; *Her. Chr.* 5.51.
109	**insignem . . . triumphum** Claud. *in Rufin.* 1.54.
	visura triumphum ≈ Mant. *Calam.* 2.365 (p. 62): "visura triumphos."
110	**Conveniunt . . . deducere** ≈ Verg. *G.* 1.255.
	deducere in urbem ≈ Ov. *Tr.* 4.2.61.
111	**Regibus . . . mos est** = Hor. *S.* 1.2.86.
112	**exultant animis** Verg. *A.* 2.386; 11.491; cf. Eob. *Her. Chr.* 12.155.
	animis ingentibus = Claud. *Bell. Get.* 584; cf. Verg. *G.* 3.207; 4.83.
114	**Fervet — frequentant** = l. 256 below.
115	**umbrosis . . . vallibus Idae** = Ov. *Ars* 1.289.
	Phrygiae — Idae = *Buc.* 7.150, n.
116	**Simoentis ad undam** = Verg. *A.* 1.618; 3.302.
117	**senior . . . Protheus** Cf. Ov. *Met.* 11.221.
	magnum . . . Achillem = Ov. *Met.* 12.163; *Ilias Lat.* 72 and 934.
118	**ruiturum — Troiae** ≈ l. 173 below. For *moenia Troiae*, see *Rec.* 27, n.
119	**Fit clamor** = *Pug.* 31, n.
119–20	**pulsatque — crepant** Cf. *Pug.* 27–28, where see nn.
119	**leves . . . auras** = Ov. *Met.* 3.43; cf. Lucr. 6.913; Verg. *G.* 3.274; *A.* 11.595; Ov. *Met.* 8.524; 14.432 (and elsewhere); Eob. *Her. Chr.* 4.171, n.; *Her. Chr.* 13.23.
120	**Concurritur — arcem** ≈ Petrarch, *Africa* 4.274: "concurrunt undique ad arcem."
120–21	**arcem Regalem** = ll. 288–89 below; cf. *Vict.* 134.
121	**Lectas . . . cohortes** = *Max.* 141; cf. Mutius, *Triumph.*, sig. c6ᵛ: ". . . lectasque cohortes"; Eob. *Idyl.* 13.13.
122	**praestantior armis** = *Epic.*, app. 5.19.
123	**induat aurum** ≈ Mant. *Votum*, fol. 54ʳ: "fulvum caput induit aurum."
124–28	**Sicut — iuventus** Cf. Verg. *A.* 4.402–07; Eob. *Nor.* 835–41.
125	**Sol pater** = Marul. *Hymn. nat.* 3.1.21, 281.
	agminibus . . . densis Lucr. 6.100; Verg. *A.* 2.450; 9.788; 12.442.
	agminibus fervent Sil. 8.619–20.
127	**assiduo . . . labori** = Stat. *Silv.* 4.4.29.
128	**consurgit in arma** Verg. *A.* 10.90; cf. Eob. *Pug.* 42, n.
	arma iuventus = Verg. *A.* 4.86; 11.453.
131	**Phrygios — penates** = *Laud.* B 3.29, n.
	fax For the play on the two senses of *fax* (the torch of love and the torch that will consume Troy), cf. Ov. *Ep.* 16.49–50.
132	**cohors** Verg. *A.* 11.500 likewise uses the word in the sense of "cavalry."
	fulgebat in armis = Verg. *A.* 11.769; Juv. 11.109; cf. l. 182 below.
133	**Rhomanus eques** = Luc. 7.19.
134	**milia multa** = Lucr. 3.724; cf. Eob. *Her. Chr.* 6.76, n.
135	**exercitus — hostes** = *Epp.* 4, sig. F3ᵛ (25 May 1508); cf. Verg. *A.* 9.25; Sil. 7.45.
136	**Magnanimum . . . Achillem** Ov. *Met.* 13.298.

137   **insignes auro** Verg. *A.* 4.134.
140   **diverso . . . confluxit ab orbe** Cf. Ov. *Met.* 9.741; *Tr.* 3.14.26; Poliziano, *Epigr.* 85.5:
        "Quae non diverso gens huc properabat ab orbe"; Eob. *Epp.* 4, sig. F3ᵛ (25 May 1508):
        "toto confluxit ab orbe"; *Her. Chr.* 17.221, n.; *Sylv.* 2.1.89: "omni circum confluxit ab
        orbe iuventus."
141   **Regales . . . opes** Man. 5.360; Phaed. 1.27.10; Eob. *Her. Chr.* A 3.12.
144   **duro . . . ense** *Ilias Lat.* 669, 965; Prud. *Perist.* 6.65; Eob. *Her. Chr.* 17.138.
        ferus ense = Stat. *Theb.* 9.267.
145   **Agmine . . . longo** = *Venus* 1.121; cf. Verg. *A.* 5.90; 10.769; Ov. *Met.* 7.624;
        Eob. *Nob.* 67.
        Agmine progreditur ≈ Sil. 14.180.
        sublimis . . . auro = Mant. *1. Parthen.* 3.363.
146   **sublimis equo** = *Ilias Lat.* 496; Sil. 4.219.
        sublimis . . . ostro = Ov. *Ep.* 12.179; *Tr.* 4.2.27.
148   **antiquum . . . honorem** = Sil. 6.460.
150   **Promptior — usus** Cf. *Sylv. duae* 1.113.
151   **Gemmiferas — harenas** Cf. [Tib.] 3.8.19–20; Otto 862.
        despumet harenas ≈ *Idyl.* 1.133: "Aedera, qui fulvas auro despumat harenas";
        cf. Claud. *Cons. Olyb. et Prob.* 54.
152   **vagus — auro** Cf. Verg. *A.* 10.142; Eob. *Sylv. duae* 1.144. For the epithet *vagus*, see
        Buc. 1.110, n. The Pactolus River in Lydia was proverbially rich in gold: see Otto 1320.
153   **gravibus . . . in armis** = *Her.* 1.6.143.
        cataphrattus . . . in armis *Max.* 257.
155   **nimium vicina** = Verg. *Ecl.* 9.28.
154–55 **Slesia tellus, Slesia** Cf. Celtis, *Am.* 2.4.34–35: "Slesia terra. . . . / Slesia."
157   **Magnanimi . . . duces** Verg. *G.* 4.4.
        unus et alter = Hor. *S.* 2.5.24; *Ep.* 2.1.74; *Ars* 15; Eob. *Her. Chr.* 4.43; *Nob.* 209;
        Hod. B 1.35; cf. *Her. Chr.* A 4.10, n.
158   **Numerare piget** *Her. Chr.* 1.72, n.
        forte necesse est = Hor. *Ars* 48.
159   **pugnax . . . Ungarus** *Max.* 277.
160   **patriis — oris** = l. 225 below.
        patriis . . . ab oris = Verg. *A.* 10.198; 11.281; cf. Eob. *Laud.* 314; *Her. Chr.* 20.63.
161   **Herciniae . . . sylvae** = Claud. *Bell. Get.* 330; *Cons. Stil.* 1.228.
162   **Teutonico . . . ritu** Verg. *A.* 7.741.
163   **Ora . . . squalentia** Ov. *Met.* 4.656; *Tr.* 3.10.9.
165   **Scythica . . . nive** *Sylv.* 1.5.17; *Accl.* 1.232.
166   **Bosphoreos** An incorrect genitive form. Eobanus may have remembered it from
        Brant, *Var. carm.*, sig. a7ᵛ (*Texte* 195.348): "Bosphoreosque mari." There, however,
        the intended phrase must be "Bosphoreoque mari," as in Ov. *Tr.* 2.298.
        qui vada . . . potat For the idiom, see *Buc.* 4.80, n.
        vada frigida = Mant. *5. Parthen.* 2, fol. 122ᵛ.
168   **numerare molestum est** *Max.* 157; cf. ll. 55–56 above; also cf. l. 158, n.
169   **Et iam — erat** = *Her. Chr.* 16.149; 21.143; *Hod.* 65; *Wirt.* 186; cf. Verg. *G.* 2.542.
        nix alta Verg. *G.* 1.310; Ov. *Met.* 1.50.
170   **Mariae . . . Februa** This phrase appears also in Jakob Micyllus, *Sylvarum libri
        quinque* (Frankfurt am Main, 1564), bk. 4, p. 308.
        celebrabant . . . mystae Sen. *Her. F.* 847; Aus. *Versus paschales* 2.
171   **Iamque — apertis** Cf. Verg. *A.* 8.585; 9.25; Eob. *Her. Chr.* 16.203, n.
173   **magnae . . . Troiae** = Stat. *Ach.* 2.32.
        ruiturus — Troiae ≈ l. 118, n., above.
174   **Cum subito ecce** = *Vict.* 425; cf. *Rec.* 98, n.
        ecce aderat Stat. *Theb.* 11.263; Sil. 4.493; 5.518; Eob. *Laud.* 285.
        tantum decus *Buc.* 9.49, n.

175   **digna . . . marito** *Buc.* 9.82, n.; Dantiscus, *Carm.* 12.2.14 (in an epithalamium for King Sigismund): ". . . Haec est te digna marito."

176   **Pulchra — parens** Verg. *A.* 1.75.

177   **Sarmatici — sceptri** = *Sylv.* 1.1.45; *Tum.* 3.103.

         moderator maxime = Petrarch, *Africa* 1.19; cf. Erasmus, *Carm.* 42.9.

180   **Barbara non — tantum** Cf. *Consol.* 11: "Barbara nec vitae meritis, sed nomine tantum"; *Her. Chr.* 10.1–4, with n.

181   **lecta manus** Verg. *A.* 10.294; Ov. *Met.* 8.300.

182   **longis . . . in armis** Luc. 1.423; cf. Luc. 6.259.

         effulsit in armis Cf. l. 132, n., above.

183   **sub gurgite vasto** = Verg. *A.* 6.741.

184   **Cyrenem** Verg. *G.* 4.321–44 represents her in the midst of the Nereids.

         glaucam Cymodocaeam For the epithet applied to the Nereids, see Stat. *Theb.* 9.351. The form "Cymodocaeam" comes from Verg. *A.* 10.225.

185   **agmine stipant** *Her. Chr.* 21.95; *Sylv.* 4.30.13; cf. Verg. *A.* 4.136.

187   **impexo . . . capillo** ≈ *Laud.* 571, n.

188   **Quid memorem** = *Laud.* 235, n.

189–90 **tot . . . monilia . . . bullas** Cricius, *Carm.* 2.2.20 (in his epithalamium for King Sigismund): "Tot torques, bullas, segmenta, monilia cerno / Quot nequit . . . lingua referre."

189   **preciosa monilia** = Ven. Fort. *Carminum spuriorum app.* 1.303.

190   **Quid loquar** = *Laud.* 56, n.

         in . . . pectore bullas Cf. *Her. Chr.* 12.80, n.

191   **labor est numerare** Mart. 8.55.22; Eob. *Nob.* 342; *Val.* 2.256.

192   **Quid memorem** = *Laud.* 235, n.

         auratos . . . currus *Culex* 43; Sen. *Oed.* 424.

193   **adultera coniunx** = Ov. *Am.* 3.4.37; Eob. *Epp. 4*, sig. F3ᵛ (25 May 1508), also referring to Helen of Troy; *Venus* 1.133.

195   **Iam — constiterant** = *Ilias* 6.165; cf. *Her. Chr.* 4.117; 12.133; *Vict.*, app. 2.15.

         Iam prope = Ov. *Ep.* 11.71; *Tr.* 1.3.5; *Pont.* 2.2.45; Eob. *Her. Chr.* 21.150.

195–96 **curru . . . inaurato** Prop. 1.16.3.

195   **Iam . . . cum regia virgo** = Mant. *2. Parthen.* 2.123; cf. Sil. 6.633. For *regia virgo*, see also Ov. *Met.* 2.570, 868; et al.; Eob. *Nup.* 260; cf. *Sylv. duae* 2.162.

197   **Virgineas . . . comas** = Stat. *Theb.* 2.255; cf. Ov. *Fast.* 2.560.

198   **Dii . . . quales vultus** *Epic.* 3.33, referring to Albrecht Dürer's artistry.

         Dii superi = *Ama.* 35.80, n.

         candida colla = Verg. *G.* 4.337.

199   **in ore rubor** = *Ciris* 180; Ov. *Am.* 3.3.6; *Ep.* 20.120; cf. Eob. *Her. Chr.* 2.9; 12.77, n.

201   **ardentes . . . viscera flammas** Cf. *Ama.* 33.11.1, n.

         iaculare . . . flammas Sen. *Thy.* 1086.

202   **exiguo . . . ore** Ov. *Met.* 7.625.

         pulvis . . . in ore Ov. *Ep.* 4.78: "et levis egregio pulvis in ore decet." Since *pulvis* is often associated with the dust raised by competions in the arena, Eobanus here uses the word by metonymy for the "strife" of lovemaking. For this image, cf., for example, Prop. 3.8.32; Ov. *Am.* 1.9.45; 2.10.29; *Ars* 3.3; Eob. *Val.* 1.494: "Veneris dulcia bella."

204   **quis superum** = Calp. *Ecl.* 4.143. Cf. Eob. *Ama.* 35.2, n.

205   **talis erat — ferebat** Modeled on Verg. *A.* 1.503, referring to Queen Dido.

206–07 **Qualis — colorem** Cf. *Hod.* 313–14.

207   **rebus — colorem** Cf. Verg. *A.* 6.272; Eob. *Her. Chr.* 7.45; *Nor.* 428.

         lux alma = *Rec.* 196, n.

208   **maiestate verendus** = *Buc.* 3.26, n.

209   **molli . . . lapsu** Luc. 10.315; V. Fl. 1.686.

         lubrica lapsu = Juvenc. 1.686.

210   **pleno . . . auro** = Verg. *A.* 1.739.

211   **parte ab utraque** Ov. *Met.* 4.666; 15.734.

212   **pleno . . . favore** = Claud. *Stil.* 1.1.

213   **Dicere — angustia** Cf. Hier. *Ep.* 133.11: "epistolaris angustia non patitur longi operis magnitudinem"; Eob. *Sarmat.* 83–84: "vix cupidum praesens angustia passa est / In tua degeneres ludere scripta modos"; *Sylv.* 9.30.17−18: "Nunc non passa fuit brevis haec angustia longum / Scribere."

214   **alicui . . . Maroni** *Wirt.* 513: "Si tibi forte aliquem pariant tua rura Maronem."

215   **sine numine vates** = *Nob.* B 1.17. For *sine numine* at this metrical position, see, for example, Lucr. 2.168; Verg. *A.* 1.133; 2.777.

216   **incoepto . . . labori** = Ov. *Met.* 13.297.

217   **ingentia facta** Hor. *Ep.* 2.1.6; Sil. 11.134; 15.411.

218   **facundus Ulysses** = Ov. *Ep.* 3.129, *Ars* 2.123, and *Met.* 13.92: "facundus Ulixes"; Eob. *Nob.* 139.

219   **sacra . . . ab urbe** Ov. *Fast.* 2.682.

221   **mandare salutem** = Ov. *Pont.* 4.6.13; Eob. *Her. Chr.* 11.1; *Sylv.* 8.7.17.

222   **Ianitor aethereae . . . aulae** Cf. *Her. Chr.* 17.223, n., also referring to the pope. For *aethereae aulae*, see *Her. Chr.* 9.125, n.

         pater optimus = Verg. *A.* 5.358; Hor. *S.* 1.4.105; cf. l. 226, n., below.

224   **clarum dat . . . nomen** Ov. *Fast.* 2.733; Sil. 5.567; cf. Eob. *Her. Chr.* 21.58, n.

225   **patriis — oris** = l. 160, n., above.

226   **pater optime** = Enn. *Ann.* 192; Verg. *A.* 1.555; 3.710; Ov. *Met.* 7.627; et al.; Eob. *Her. Chr.* 11.71; cf. l. 222, n., above.

227   **Pallia — candida** Cf. *Sylv. duae* 1.47, n.

         Presul Iobe ≈ *Sylv. duae* 1.155.

228   **celebres titulos** = *Ama.*, lim. 5.

229   **Teutonicae . . . militiai** = *Tum.* 3.83; cf. *Sylv.* 1.1.129: "Teutonicae princeps Albertus militiei"; *Sylv. duae* 1.161.

         ductor fortissime Verg. *A.* 8.513; 10.185.

231   **ante alios . . . primus** *Vict.* 233.

232   **consilio — annis** Cf. Verg. *A.* 9.246; Ov. *Met.* 8.617.

235   **Curarum . . . moles** *Sylv.* 1.1.5; *Accl.* 1.7; *Wirt.*, ded. 33; *Idyl.*, 2. ded. 87.

236   **utilibus . . . rebus** *Sarmat.* 57.

236–37 **negocia rebus Publica** = Mant. *Calam.* 1.592 (p. 34): "Publica privatis praeferre negotia rebus."

237   **pro nomine Christi** = Paul. Nol. *Carm.* 26.62; Juvenc. 3.383; Eob. *Her. Chr.* 12.241; 18.19.

238–39 **in omnes . . . casus** = Claud. *Bell. Gild.* 318–19.

240   **Christicola — molestum** = *Her. Chr.* 12.41.

241   **Qui simul — salute** Cf. Ov. *Met.* 14.11; Eob. *Nup.* 281.

242   **Sic fatur** = Verg. *A.* 6.1.

         vultus . . . in se convertit Cf. Ov. *Tr.* 4.3.9; *Ilias Lat.* 861; Mant. *2. Parthen.* 2.16: "Mox oculos in se populi convertit."

         in se — ora Cf. Lucr. 6.643: "finitimis ad se convertit gentibus ora"; Eob. *Sylv. duae*, ded. 5, n.: "in se et animos et oculos rapiunt."

244   **virgine flos . . . pudoris** ≈ *Her. Chr.* 13.97; cf. *Buc.* 2.73, n.

         virginei . . . pudoris = Stat. *Theb.* 12.205; *Ach.* 1.765; V. Fl. 5.356; cf. l. 261 below; *Buc.* 5.99, n.

246   **Magnanimo regi** ≈ Stat. *Theb.* 7.375; cf. *Theb.* 2.733; *Silv.* 5.3.10.

         nubere digna *Her. Chr.* 4.66.

         digna reperta es Ov. *Pont.* 3.1.118; cf. *Fast.* 1.650.

247   **regni . . . coronam** Verg. *A.* 8.505.

         latura coronam = Mant. *Georgius*, fol. 219ʳ; Eob. *Her. Chr.* 4.119.

248   **sibi promissam** ≈ Ov. *Met.* 14.818; *Fast.* 2.420.

         comitem . . . futuram Ov. *Am.* 2.16.43.

249 **faventibus astris** = Petrarch, *Ep.* 1.1.21; Eob. *Idyl.* 6.93; *Accl.* 2.219; *Sylv.* 2.8.27.

250 **populis — pater** Cf. *Her. Chr.* 17.214.

pietate pater Paul. Nol. *Carm.* 21.415.

251 **sola places** Ov. *Ars* 1.42: "elige cui dicas 'tu mihi sola places.'"

252–53 **Ingredere et . . . Ingredere adventuque tuo** = *Accl.* 1.113–15; cf. Verg. *G.* 1.42.

252 **fausto pede** Hor. *Ep.* 2.2.37; Eob. *Her. Chr.* 5.166.

255 **Venus aurea** = *Ama.* B 2.25, n.

256 **Fervet — frequentant** = l. 114 above.

258 **bono auspicio** = *Buc.* B 11.21, n.

gelidam . . . sub Arcton *Nup.*, lim. 1, n.

259 **adeas — secundo** Cf. Verg. *A.* 8.302; 10.255.

260 **Sic breviter fatus** Cf. Verg. *A.* 6.321; 10.621; Eob. *Sylv. duae* 2.161, n.

regia virgo = l. 195, n., above.

261 **virgineus . . . pudor** l. 244, n., above.

265 **magna . . . voce** = Verg. *A.* 10.873; Juv. 4.32.

266 **templa gubernat** ≈ Man. 3.126.

267 **tonsae . . . coronae** Literally, "the tonsured throng." Elsewhere Eobanus uses the phrase to mean "tonsured crown." See *Ama.* B 2.34, n.

Cracovia docta = l. 349 below; *Sylv.* 1.1.31; cf. *Pug.* 10, n. The city is "scholarly" because it boasts a university.

268 **sacris . . . aris** = *Her. Chr.* 13.7; *Nob.* 113; cf. *Laud.* 246, n.

decus addidit aris Cf. Luc. 3.762; Eob. *Her. Chr.* 1.129, n.

270 **Laude vir insignis** = *Epp.* 4, sig. F4ʳ (25 May 1508); cf. Tifernate, *Carm.*, sig. D1ᵛ: "vir et meritis et laude insignis equestri"; Eob. *Rec.* 76.

271 **virtus patitur** = Verg. *A.* 9.795.

271–72 **tu . . . Pontifices inter . . . gloria** Dantiscus, *Carm.* 1.3.363−64: "Tu . . . / Inter pontifices gloria magna sacros."

273 **sede tuetur** ≈ Stat. *Silv.* 1.1.77; Juvenc. 3.408.

275 **meritos . . . honores** = Verg. *A.* 3.118; 5.652; cf. Eob. *Buc.* 5.17, n.

278–80 **Ni se — undas** For these topoi, here used lightheartedly, see Curtius, *ELLMA*, 90–91, 487–94; cf. Eob. *Buc.* 1.124, n.

280 **in occiduas . . . undas** = Erasmus, *Carm.* 4.19; cf. Eob. *Her. Chr.* 14.43, n.; *Idyl.* 15.21: "sol occiduas . . . pronus in undas"; *Sylv.* 7.14.19. Cf. further Ov. *Fast.* 1.314; *Tr.* 4.3.4.

lucifer undas ≈ Verg. *A.* 8.589, referring to the Morning Star.

281 **dicta — reddita** Cf. l. 241, n., above.

282 **prono — iugales** *Theoc.* 32.158: "Flexerat ignivomos prono temone iugales."

prono temone = *Sylv.* 2.14.3; cf. *Buc.* 3.103, n.

temone iugales = Claud. *Cons. Olyb. et Prob.* 4.

284–85 **summa . . . Sydera** Prop. 1.8.43; Ov. *Fast.* 1.308; 3.34; et al.; Eob. *Her. Chr.* 16.290.

286 **stratoque . . . ostro** = Verg. *A.* 1.700.

287 **longo . . . ordine** = Luc. 6.146; Stat. *Theb.* 3.52; *Silv.* 5.3.129.

subit ordine = Stat. *Theb.* 10.274.

289–90 **regia — instruitur** Cf. Verg. *A.* 1.637–38.

290–91 **pictisque recumbunt . . . thoris** Cf. Verg. *A.* 1.708.

291 **pars multa** = Hor. *S.* 2.7.7.

ordine mensas = Mant. *1. Parthen.* 2.436.

291–93 **mensas — Baccho** Cf. Ov. *Met.* 8.571–73; Verg. *A.* 5.77.

292 **ordine longo** = Verg. *A.* 1.395.

294 **multifori . . . arundine** Cf. *Buc.* 10.6, n.

arundine Triton = Claud. *VI. Cons. Hon.* 378 (in the literal sense).

295 **sufflare monaulon** = *Buc.* 10.6, n.

296 **argutam . . . buxum** *Idyl.* 7.63.

297   **cythara . . . Iopas** = Verg. *A.* 1.740.

298   **chordas tangebat** Ov. *Rem.* 336; Eob. *Vict.* 293.

302   **plura brevi** = Magdal. *Ep.* 5: "Accipe plura brevi."

       omnibus omnis = *Buc.* 6.24, n.

303   **Gratia — ibat** Cf. *Epic.* 8.19: "Virtus comitata sororibus ibat."

306   **Iamque — umbras** Cf. Verg. *A.* 3.589; 4.7; *Ilias Lat.* 157: "postera lux tacitas ut primum dispulit umbras." The tag *dispulit umbras* occurs first in Verg. *A.* 5.839.

307   **rex et regina** = Pers. 2.37.

310   **Quod faustum foelixque . . . caedat** The phrase recalls an ancient formula of good omen. See, for example, Cic. *Div.* 1.102: "quod bonum, faustum, felix, fortunatumque esset"; Liv. 1.17.10: "quod bonum, faustum, felixque sit"; cf. Mutian. *Ep.* 450 (mid-October 1514), to Eobanus Hessus: "orabimus Deum, ut bonum tibi sit et felix et faustum matrimonium"; Eob. to Reuchlin (6 January 1515), in *Illustrium virorum epistolae . . . ad Ioannem Reuchlin Phorcensem* (Haguenau, 1519), sig. y3ᵛ (referring to his recent wedding): "quod faustum, foelix, fortunatumque sit."

311   **Lycaonis Ursae** Cf. Verg. *G.* 1.138; Eob. *Her. Chr.* 16.49.

313   **Foedere legitimo** = *Venus* 2.298; cf. l. 79, n., above.

       mentem — unam Cf. Mant. *1. Parthen.* 2.807: "vivent una duo pectora mente." For the commonplace, cf. Eob. *Laud.* B 6.2, n.

314   **Ite pares** = Ov. *Fast.* 6.99.

314–15 **nec brachia — columbis** Cf. Catul. 61.33–35, 102–05; Hor. *Carm.* 1.36.20; *Epod.* 15.5–6; *Anthol. Lat.* 711.2–3: "non murmura vestra columbae, / Brachia non hederae, non vincant oscula conchae"; Pontano, *Am.* 1.3.63–64: "Complexi, quales hederae sua brachia nectunt / Chaonis et qualis oscula iungit avis"; Fausto Andrelini, *Epithalamium de Claudia regia et Francesco Valesiorum duce* [Paris, 1506], sig. a3ᵛ: "Haud superent hederae tabulata per alta sequaces / Vestra simul molli corpora nexa thoro. / Blanda susurranti nec cedant verba columbae"; Eob. *Venus* 2.168: "Oscula coniugibus non cedant vestra columbis, / Brachia non hederis."

       sequaci . . . hederae Pers., prologus 6; Eob. *Sylv.* 4.31.10–11: "[Pierides] tuum sequaci / Intexant hedera caput."

315   **Paphiis . . . columbis** Mart. 8.28.13; Eob. *Sylv.* 1.11.3. Doves were sacred to Venus; cf. n. *Buc.* 7.130. Their affectionateness was proverbial. See Otto 414; Häussler, 19, 99, 149, 234, and 265.

316   **numerosa . . . prole** Celtis, *Am.* 2.6.67: "numerosa prole beatur."

318   **Prolifico** This late medieval word occurs also in *Her. Chr.* 10.73; *Her.* 1.4.221: "prolificae . . . matres."

319   **facilis . . . Lucina** Ov. *Fast.* 2.451.

       castae — Lucina Cf. Verg. *Ecl.* 4.10.

324   **Acclamat — favorem** Cf. *Ilias* 9.81: "plausu testante favorem / Acclament Danai."

325   **Dii . . . coeptis faveant** Dantiscus, *Carm.* 3.41.

       Dii faciles = Ov. *Am.* 2.14.43; Juv. 10.8; cf. Eob. *Laud.* 440, n.

       faveant — viroque Cf. l. 366, n., below. For *nuptaeque viroque*, see also l. 331, n.; *Venus* 2.181, 299; *Sylv.* 2.6.42.

326   **Rex bone** Verg. *A.* 11.344.

       optima coniunx = Ov. *Tr.* 3.3.55; Stat. *Theb.* 3.378.

327   **strepitus clamorque virum** Mant. *Calam.* 2.540 (p. 67): "strepitus clamorque virorum."

327–28 **clamorque — Exoritur** = Verg. *A.* 2.313; cf. *A.* 11.192.

328   **nova gaudia** = *Buc.* B 8.1, n.

329   **aulaea diaetas** ≈ *Nob.* 317.

330–31 **Discumbuntque . . . thoris** Verg. *A.* 1.708.

       altis . . . thoris Verg. *A.* 6.603–04.

330   **stipante corona** = Stat. *Theb.* 1.612.

331   **Nuptaque virque thoris** ≈ Ov. *Ep.* 6.164; cf. l. 325, n., above.

	rite peractam ≈ Juv. 12.86.
332	**Coniugiique — coronam** = l. 2 above.
333	**Tempus erat quo** = Verg. *A.* 2.268; Ov. *Met.* 6.587; 10.446; *Fast.* 5.497; cf. Eob. *Rec.* 1, n.
334	**primo . . . cursu** = Luc. 2.653.
334–35	**frigida cursu Nox** Mant. *Calam.* 2.430−31 (p. 64): "medio dum frigida cursu / Suspiceret Cancrum nox"; cf. Eob. *Buc.* 4.117, n.; *Vict.* 87, n.
335	**Nox erat** = Verg. *A.* 3.147; 4.522; 8.26.
336	**Regalem . . . thalamum** l. 1, n., above.
	castoque . . . cubili = Prud. *Amart.* 786; cf. Catul. 66.83; Verg. *A.* 8.412; Eob. *Ama.* 22.7.1.
337	**incensis . . . taedis** ≈ Prop. 2.32.9.
338	**plena omnia** = *Buc.* 1.84, n.
339	**Nox ea** = Stat. *Theb.* 2.89.
340	**aestivum — ignem** Cf. *Rec.* 216, n.
341–43	**Postquam — recessit** Being chaste themselves, the Muses cannot enter the bridal chamber. For the motif, cf. Ov. *Ars* 2.703–04; Eob. *Venus* 2.240–41, 304–06.
342–43	**pudicos — vultus** Cf. Paul. Nol. *Carm.* 6.114: "vultus demissa pudicos"; Ov. *Met.* 10.367: "demisit vultus."
344	**longo . . . carmine** = Man. 2.928; cf. Ov. *Am.* 1.8.18.
345	**multis . . . diebus** = Ov. *Fast.* 4.505.
	celebrata diebus = Sil. 8.200.
346	**Caesareo . . . triumpho** ≈ Ov. *Pont.* 2.1.1; Luc. 8.430.
349	**Cracovia docta** = l. 267, n., above.
351	**Hystoriam . . . ab origine** = Mant. *Ecl.* 1.10: "historiam prima repetens ab origine pandam."
352–53	**Vos — Apollo** Cf. *Hod.* 508–09: "Plura canent alii, quibus et sunt ocia forsan / Liberiora domi meliorque aspirat Apollo."
352	**tranquilla quies** = *Buc.* 6.70, n.
353	**Divitis ingenii** = Ov. *Tr.* 2.335; Eob. *Hod.* 63; *Epic.*, app. 5.27; cf. *Epic.* 5.68: "Divitis aeternis dotibus ingenii"; *Her.* 2.5.126; *Sylv.* 5.29.40–41.
	meliorque — Apollo = *Hod.* 509; cf. *Buc.* 4.75, n.; *Ilias Lat.* 165–66.
355	**Certatim . . . celebrate** Sil. 11.493.
356–57	**nobis — ignoscite** For this modesty formula, cf. *Laud.* 54–55, 588–90; *Her. Chr.* 24.163–64.
356	**versu . . . inepto** = Nor. 930; *Sylv.* 2.23.3; cf. *Luth.* 7.9.
357	**Non ego vobis** = Calp. *Ecl.* 6.89.
358	**deos testor** Ter. *Hec.* 476; Verg. *A.* 4.492.
360–61	**grandia . . . Plectra movet** l. 18, n., above.
361–62	**me . . . Sublimem rapit** Cf. Mutian. *Ep.* 45 (letter of 1 October 1506 to Eobanus): "Deus . . . te . . . per sacrosancta carmina sublimem rapit"; Ov. *Met.* 4.363; 7.222.
363	**elegos . . . molles** *Laud.* 15, n.
	commendat gratia = Stat. *Theb.* 8.558; Mart. 13.33.1; Eob. *Laud.* 460.
365	**Nostra . . . Germania** = Max. 159; *Sylv.* 2.5.29; cf. *Her. Chr.* 24.87, n.; *Hod.* 459.
366	**Iam satis est** = Hor. *S.* 1.1.120; 1.5.13; *Ep.* 1.7.16.
	fave — viroque = *Epith.* 185; cf. l. 325, n., above.
367	**subitis — Camaenis** = *Hod.* 507; cf. *Idyl.* 5.83: "subitis ego respondebo Camoenis."
368	**Nunc age, qui nuper . . . solebas** = *Luth.* 7.1; cf. *Laud.* 577, n.
369	**Nos — nihil** Cf. Mart. 13.2.8; Eob. *Her. Chr.* 4.206; 10.144; *Sylv.* 1.4.96: "nos illam novimus esse nihil."
Postscript	**Conscientia — testes** For this proverb see *Buc.* 10.88, n.

Notes to
SYLVAE DUAE

Title   **nuper aeditae** Cf. the subtitle of *Her. Chr.*: "nuper aeditum"; subtitle of *Dial.*: "nuper aediti"; *Hod.* B 1.23: "aedita nuper." Elsewhere Eobanus uses the phrase only in the sense of "newly published."

Liminary epigram

Meter: Elegiac distich.

1–6   **Quamvis — suis** Myricius makes the same point, with a similar play on the author's name, in his liminary epigram for Stella, *Boruss.*, p. 282: "Borussia dotibus beata / Quamvis innumeris sit . . . / [. . .], / Lethaeis tamen hactenus latebris / Haec mersa indigenis modo patebant. / Ad lucem retulit sagax supernam / Cuncta haec omnibus offerens legenda / Parvo hoc Stella libro haud ineleganter."

5   **cunctis . . . oris** = Verg. *A.* 3.97.

6   **Carminibus . . . celebrando** Verg. *A.* 8.303.

7–8   **Nunc — cani** Cf. Ov. *Pont.* 3.5.15–16; 4.10.76.

Dedicatory letter

1–4   **Quartus — invenirem** Cf. *Orat. Sylv.* 30–31.

1   **Quartus — aggressus** Cf. *Her. Chr.*, ded. 1.1.

2–3   **Quas cum — polliceri** Cf. *Her. Chr.*, ded. 8.3–4.

4   **minutulo** Cf. *Orat. Sylv.* 29: "his minutulis."

         velut praemetio Cf. *Val.* 1.265–66: "ista futurae / Praemetium messi carmina pauca damus"; *Sylv.* 1, ded. (conclusion): "Interim hunc Sylvarum mearum librum primum velut praemetium futurae messis mittere ad te volui."

5   **gladiatores — rapiunt** Cf. *Praef.*, sig. C1ʳ: "palestritae gladiatores . . . in arenam descendentes in progymnasmatis quidem istis mire gestiunt spectatoribusque sic impense placent."

         in se — rapiunt Cf. Verg. *A.* 11.800; Liv. 45.19.1: "convertit in se omnium oculos animosque"; Gel. 5.14.9: "animos oculosque omnium in sese converterat"; Eob. *Nup.* 242, n.

7   **ex aliqua — parte** Cf. *Laud.*, ded. 8, n.

8   **Es enim tu** Eobanus uses the same phrase in *Laud.*, ded. 4.

1. Generalis Prussiae descriptio

Title   **Generalis — descriptio** By choosing this title Eobanus deliberately links his topography of Prussia to Konrad Celtis' poetic description of Germany as a whole. First published as *De situ et moribus Germanie additiones* in an edition of Cornelius Tacitus' *De origine et situ Germanorum* (Vienna, between 1498 and 1500), the work was later appended to Celtis' *Quatuor libri amorum* (Nuremberg, 1502). It is to this much better known version that Eobanus alludes here. For on sig. a8ʳ of the 1502 version Celtis' topographical poem is announced as "Generalis Germaniae descriptio carmine heroico." At the head of the poem itself the title is given as "Germania generalis." For an annotated edition, see Gernot M. Müller, *Die "Germania generalis" des Conrad Celtis: Studien mit Edition, Übersetzung und Kommentar*, Frühe Neuzeit 67 (Tübingen, 2001).

1	**Quam — salutem** The model is Ov. *Pont.* 3.2.1; cf. Eob. *Her. Chr.* 24.1.
	Quam legis . . . salutem = *Her. Chr.* 1.1, n. The phrase *quam legis* also begins the letter in Ov. *Ep.* 3.1; *Tr.* 5.7.1; *Pont.* 3.5.1; 4.6.1; Eob. *Her. Chr.* 4.1. Cf. *Her. Chr.* 11.7, n. For *quam salutem*, see also Ov. *Ep.* 4.1; 19.1; and Eob. *Her. Chr.* 2.1; 11.1.
	hanc . . . mittit tibi . . . salutem Ov. *Met.* 9.530–31; *Tr.* 5.13.1; *Pont.* 1.3.1; 4.9.1–2; cf. *Pont.* 2.2.3.
1–2	**mittit . . . salutem Hinc ubi** *Her. Chr.* 18.1–3.
2	**Hinc — aquas** Cf. Ov. *Pont.* 3.5.2; *Ib.* 462; Eob. *Her. Chr.* 18.3; *Epic.*, app. 5.10: "In mare qua . . . Vistula fertur aquis."
3–16	**Qui licet — libet** There is a very similar discussion in *Her. Chr.* 16.251–58. Cf. further Lucr. 1.72–74; Cic. *N. D.* 2.153; Ov. *Tr.* 4.2.57–64; *Met.* 15.62–64; Mant. *1. Parthen.* 2.539–54; Eob. *Vict.* 263–69; *Sylv.* 4.12.21–24: "Ut ora praesens non videam tua, / Mentem videbo, mente ero proximus. / Mens quolibet tuto vagatur, / Legibus impeditata nullis"; 7.28.7–12: "Quis neget humanum . . . / Ingenium . . . / . . . nunc sidereas arces transire supraque / Moenia flammantis scandere celsa poli, / Nunc animo Stygiis innare paludibus aut se / Tollere momento per freta longa brevi?"
3–4	**Qui licet — tibi** Cf. Ov. *Tr.* 3.4.73–74; *Pont.* 2.11.3–4.
3	**licet . . . regionibus absit** Cf. Ov. *Ep.* 15.125; *Met.* 12.41.
4	**contiguus . . . tibi** Ov. *Ars* 3.410.
6	**vinclo — ligat** Cf. Ov. *Met.* 9.550; Eob. *Sylv.* 6.8.15: "quia nos ratio vinclo propiore ligarit / Et sit amicitiae nostra probata fides"; also cf. *Sylv.* 1.11.32: "quod amas vinclo proximiore."
8	**vincula nulla** = Ov. *Ep.* 21.138; *Fast.* 1.410; 5.432.
9	**partes . . . in omnes** = Verg. *A.* 4.630: "partis animum versabat in omnis."
10	**Mobiliusque — habet** Cf. Erasmus, *Carm.* 95.24, referring to youth: "Qua nil mobilius maximus orbis habet"; Celtis, *Am.* 4.9.60: "mobilius . . . muliere nihil."
	maximus — habet = Ov. *Fast.* 1.600; Eob. *Her. Chr.* 21.206; *Eccles.* 184; *Val.* 1.338; 2.20; *Venus* 3.48; cf. *Buc.* B 2.26.
11	**mare . . . terrae** = Petr. 119.2: "qua mare, qua terrae, qua sidus currit utrumque."
	igneus aether = [Tib.] 3.7.22; V. Fl. 1.616; Sil. 1.135.
12	**numen habet** = Ov. *Am.* 3.3.12; *Ep.* 21.150; *Fast.* 1.90; 5.674; cf. *Fast.* 6.241: "Mens quoque numen habet."
13	**Numen habet** = *Laud.* B 2.2, n.
13–14	**si se partem — domo** Cf. Mant. *Mort.*, fol. 122ᵛ: "Ignea cum tibi sit vis et coelestis origo, / Quid cupis hac lutea degere clausa domo?"
13–15	**se partem — arenis** Closely paralleled in *Her. Chr.* 21.67–70. Cf. *Sylv.* 1.4.61–64: "Mens generosa polos ultra volat, ultima mundi / Transilit, ex ista dicitur orta domo. / Semine coelesti sata mens coelestia quaerit / Semina, terrenum cogitat illa nihil."
13	**semine caeli** ≈ Ov. *Met.* 1.81: "natus homo est, sive hunc divino semine fecit / ille opifex rerum, mundi melioris origo, / sive recens tellus seductaque nuper ab alto / aethere cognati retinebat semina caeli." Cf. Lucr. 2.991; Verg. *A.* 6.730–31; Eob. *Sylv.* 4.19.33: "alto semen ab aethere."
14	**Inclusam** For the body as prison of the soul, see *Her. Chr.* 14.133, n.
	lutea . . . domo Cf. Vulg. *Job* 4.19; Eob. *Her. Chr.* 2.123, n.
	sentiat esse = Ov. *Am.* 2.15.28; *Ep.* 21.18; *Fast.* 4.930.
15	**spatiatur arenis** ≈ Verg. *G.* 1.389. Cf. Ov. *Tr.* 4.2.59, in similar context (see n. to ll. 3–16, above).
16	**Pars . . . nostri maxima** = *Luth.* 6.28, addressing Ulrich von Hutten: "Pars . . . tu nostri maxima nuper eras"; cf. *Her. Chr.* 9.10, n.
17	**animo non deficiente** = *Ilias* 9.467: "labores / Erumnasque animo non deficiente tulissem"; cf. Cic. *S. Rosc.* 10: "animo non deficiam."
18	**Fortunae — credidimus** Cf. Ov. *Met.* 2.140; Hor. *Carm.* 1.9.9; Eob. *Sylv.* 2.8.27: "Caetera quae restant permitte faventibus astris"; 9.26.14: "Caetera permittens . . . Deo."
	Fortunae dominae Cic. *Marc.* 7; *Fin.* 2.89; *Tusc.* 5.25.

20	**quove loco** = *Her. Chr.* 20.6; 21.14.
21	**Lycaoniam . . . sub Arcton** = *Nup.* 20, n.
22	**despicit Ursa** = Celtis, *Am.* 3.7.2: "Utraque quam gelido despicit Ursa polo."
23	**occupat orbem** = *Ama.* 35.3, n.
24	**de Germanis . . . nomen habet** Cf. *Her. Chr.* 22.34, n. For the tag *nomen habet*, see also Ov. *Ep.* 16.144; *Ars* 1.72; 3.536; *Fast.* 1.336; et al.; Eob. *Sylv. duae* 1.140; 2.200; *Her. Chr.* 3.118; 6.46; 7.6; 10.2; et al.; cf. *Her. Chr.* 17.218, n.
	nunc quoque — habet = Ov. *Fast.* 5.128; Eob. *Her. Chr.* 12.120; *Tum.* 5.90: "Anglia Germanum nunc quoque nomen habet"; cf. Ov. *Pont.* 3.2.96.
25	**quem — probabas** *Dicta Catonis* 4.28: " . . . quem tu saepe probaris."
26	**Ludere — chelim** Eobanus alludes to Mutian. *Ep.* 79, l. 28 (Mutianus' first letter to him, written on ca. 23 August 1506): "Hesse puer, sacri gloria fontis eris. / Me nisi fama globi vatum vulgata fefellit, / Ludis ad auratam verba canora chelyn." Cf. Celtis, *Am.* 1.1.36: "Lusit et ad citharam verba canora suam."
27	**non retroeuntibus astris** More literally, "since the stars are not turning back": that is, "you can't turn the clock back." A ms. note in the Zwickau copy glosses *astris* with "fatis."
28	**te . . . posse carere** Tib. 1.2.64.
29	**Omnia praestiterit** ≈ Ov. *Met.* 12.203.
	si te fortuna = Sil. 4.730.
30	**Barbara . . . terra** *Hod.* B 1.70, n.
	terra Latina = *Her. Chr.* 21.170.
32	**Rhodon et Cretam** = *Her. Chr.* 5.183.
	Lydia regna = *Sylv.* 8.25.30.
33–38	**Haec est — cruci** Cf. Aen. Silv. *Europa* 28 (par. 95): "Livonia . . . , Christianarum ultima provinciarum, ad septentrionem Ruthenis iungitur. Tartari eam sepe incurrunt, in qua nostra etate magnas acceperunt strages. Fratres Theotonici, qui Beate Marie vocantur, hanc armis quesivere et Christi sacra suscipere coegerunt, cum esset antea gentilis et idola coleret."
33	**Christiferae . . . crucis** *Nup.* 32, n.
35	**Regna . . . proxima** Ov. *Met.* 8.595–96; V. Fl. 4.589; Eob. *Nob.* 50, n.
	pharetrati . . . Rhussi = *Sylv.* 1.1.153; cf. Dantiscus, *Carm.* 12.2.109 (in an epithalamium for King Sigismund): "pharetrati . . . Mosci."
36	**Gens fera** = Mant. *2. Parthen.* 2.595.
37–38	**Prussia — cruci** Cf. *Tum.* 5.87–88.
37	**magno . . . Christo** = *Hod.* 389; *Accl.* 1.131; *Her.* 1.6.157; cf. *Buc.* 6.87, n.
38	**Teutonicae . . . cruci** ≈ *Sylv.* 1.1.126; cf. l. 52 below; *Sylv.* 1.1.72.
	subdita regna = Hutten, *Querel.* 1.7.10: "subdita regna duci."
39–44	**Parte — tenent** Eobanus later adapted this passage in *Nor.* 124–33. The source is Aen. Silv. *Europa* 29 (par. 96), following a brief description of Livonia in chap. 28: "Quod ultra fluvium [Viscelam] est, Sarmatici iuris fuit; quod citra, Germanici. Ad orientem ac meridiem Masovite Polonique rura colunt, occidentem Saxones occupant, aquilonem Balthei maris excipit littus."
39	**vergit in Eurum** = *Nor.* 106; cf. Stat. *Theb.* 2.379.
42	**rura — arat** = *Max.* 278; cf. Mart. 10.15.6.
44	**Hirsutus Boreas** Cf. Ov. *Met.* 2.30: "Hiems . . . hirsuta"; Eob. *Buc.* 2.27.
	Balthica stagna = *Her. Chr.* 17.170; cf. *Sylv.* 5.29.30: "Baltica stagna colentes."
45	**Tam late — patet** Cf. *Sylv.* 2.1.87: "Quam late, quam longa patet Germania."
46	**Inclyta — manu** The pattern, in which each of the first three words is completed, in order, by the last three words of the line, recalls the *versus rapportati* that were so popular in the Middle Ages.
47–64	**Hanc — vadis** Cf. *Sylv.* 1.1.67–80, addressed to King Sigismund in late 1512:

> Sanguine Teutonico . . . postquam fortiter empta est,
>   Exuit antiquos Prussia tota deos.

Romana imperii Friderichus sceptra tenebat;
  Illius hic certe nominis alter erat.
Cum Mahometigenae capta Ptolomaide Turcae
  Teutonicam Syria destituere crucem,
Tum, quod erat gentilis adhuc atque impia cultu,
  Haec a Teutonicis terra petita fuit.
Annuit atque armis permittit quaerere Caesar,
  Si forte obtineant iura petita loci.
Quaesitam obtinuit terram gens inclyta bello,
  Teutonicum subiit protinus illa iugum.
Hinc urbes positaeque altae victoribus arces
  Firmaque ductilibus oppida cincta vadis.

47   **Hanc — signatus** ≈ Brant, *Var. carm.*, sig. e7ʳ (*Texte* 79.17): "Hinc cruce signatus";
         Eob. *Her. Chr.* 9.135.
         cruce — nivali Cf. *Nup.* 227.
         palla . . . nivali *Hymn.* 62.
48   **partam sanguine** *Her. Chr.* 6.63, n.
         sanguine miles = Prop. 2.7.14; Ov. *Am.* 3.8.54.
49–58   **Caesarea — iugum** Eobanus' source is Aen. Silv. *Europa* 29 (par. 97): "Barbara hec
         gens et idolorum cultrix usque ad Fridericum imperatorem eius nominis secundum
         fuit. Sub eius vero imperio cum amisissent Christiani Tholomaidem, Syrie civitatem,
         Fratres Theutones, quos Sancte Marie diximus appellari, inde fugati in Germaniam
         rediere, viri nobiles et rei militaris periti qui, ne per ocium marcerent, Fridericum
         accedentes Prussiam Germanie conterminam Christi cultum spernere dixerunt; sepe
         illius gentis homines in Saxones ceterosque vicinos excurrere. . . . Esse in animo sibi
         compescere barbaram gentem. Annuat tantum imperator provinciamque Fratribus
         perpetuo iure possidendam tradat, si eam armis acquirant. . . . Illi sumptis armis
         brevi tempore quidquid Prutenici iuris citra Viscelam fuit occupavere. . . . Bellum
         pluribus annis productum est. Ad extremum fortuna Fratrum imperio arridens
         omnem eis Prussiam subiecit. Victe barbare nationes iugum subiere."
50   **Stygia nocte** Ov. *Met.* 3.695; Luc. 7.817; Eob. *Her. Chr.* 10.165; 11.17.
         nocte sepulta = *Sylv.* 3.9.18; cf. Avit. *Carm.* 2.290: "infernali . . . nocte sepultis";
         Locher, *Stult.* 3, fol. 13ᵛ: "inferna nocte sepultus"; Eob. *Luth.* 1.80; *Epic.* 3.114; *Val.*
         3.25: "obscura . . . nocte sepultam."
52   **Teutonicam . . . crucem** l. 38, n., above.
54   **terra petita fuit** = Celtis, *Am.* 3.5.40; cf. Ov. *Ep.* 7.148; 16.30; *Fast.* 4.822.
55   **summus . . . sacerdos** = *Her. Chr.* 13.17; cf. Luc. 8.850; Prud. *Perist.* 10.1011.
56   **optati . . . soli** = Arator, *Ep. ad Vigilium* 12.
         iussit habere = *Pug.* 46, n.
57   **cruce munitissimus** = *Her. Chr.* 6.155; *Sylv.* 1.1.147.
59–60   **Scit vagus — ferunt** Cf. *Her. Chr.* 17.263–64, n.; *Tum.* 4.179; *Wirt.* 68.
59   **vagus . . . Vistula** = Celtis, *Am.* 1.12.87; 1.15.43; cf. Eob. *Sylv. duae* 1.144; *Her.*
         3.9.116; cf. *Her. Chr.* 24.128. For the epithet, see *Buc.* 1.110, n.
         magno — Rheno Cf. Celtis, *Germania* 157: "quantum Rhenus sic Vistula distat ab
         ortu"; Eob. *Nup.*, lim. 3.
60   **Sanguine — ferunt** Cf. *Sylv.* 3.18.6: "Littora ut effuso sanguine tota rubent."
61–62   **Vistula — vago** Cf. Aen. Silv. *Europa* 29 (par. 96): "[Viscela] exoriens in montibus
         qui Poloniam Hungariamque dirimunt, partem Polonie irrigat; Prussiam vero, quam
         longa est, percurrit ab oppido Torni usque Gedanum, quo in loco Baltheum influit.
         Hunc fluvium alii Viscelam, ut diximus, quibus etatis nostre sermo congruit, alii
         Iustulam, quidam Istulam vocavere."
61   **oriens e montibus** = *Laud.* 40.
62   **Quam longa est** = Sil. 13.243; cf. Verg. *A.* 8.86; Eob. *Eccles.* 365.

perluit amne = Petr. 120.97.

63   **Hinc — arces** Cf. Celtis, *Am.* 1.15.37, recounting the work of the Teutonic Order in Prussia: "Hic multas urbes validas construxit et arces."
victoribus arces = Stat. *Theb.* 6.114.

64   **Firmaque — vadis** Cf. *Nob.* 185: "firma cavae cingebant oppida fossae."
ductilibus Cf. *Epic.* 3.89: "Fortia ductilibus circundare moenia vallis."
oppida — vadis = *Sylv.* 7.4.10.

65–112 **Hic etiam — eras** Eobanus amplifies Aen. Silv. *Europa* 29 (par. 96): "Frumenti ferax regio est, aquis irrigua et plena colonis. Multa ambiciosa oppida, multi maris sinuosi reflexus amenam efficiunt. Pecorum ingens vis, multa venatio, piscatio dives." Cf. also Stella, *Boruss.* 1, pp. 288–92; Sebastian Myricius, liminary poem to Stella, *Boruss.*, p. 282: "Borussia dotibus beata / Quamvis innumeris sit omnibusque / Certet fertilibus locis, amoenis / Dives fluminibus, genus refertis / Multis piscibus omne, divaganteis / Gignat saltibus inviis ferosque / Felix alipedes." Stella goes on to mention elk, aurochs, and amber.

65   **ut noris** = *Her. Chr.* 24.39; *Hod.* B 1.17; cf. *Her. Chr.* 21.6, n.
fine quietus ≈ *Her. Chr.* 21.219; *Tum.* 4.3; cf. *Her. Chr.* 16.40.

66   **Omnibus — rebus** Cf. Cic. *Parad.* 4.27.

67   **Dum — annus** = *Nor.* 318.
melior . . . annus Stat. *Theb.* 9.406: "melior venit annus in agros."

69   **plenis . . . messibus . . . agros** *Buc.* 11.59, n.

70   **Ut queat — loco** Cf. letter to Camerarius (1527?) in *Nar.*, sig. G6ʳ: "tam praesentes habeant haec moenia divos, / Ut queat his credi nata Minerva locis."

71   **suo — colono** Cf. *Nor.* 217: ". . . nec ipsa suis satis est urbs ampla colonis."

72   **Lataque . . . arva** = *Her. Chr.* 20.104; cf. Verg. *A.* 8.605; Ov. *Am.* 1.7.8; *Ep.* 12.46; *Fast.* 1.546; 2.210.
frugibus arva Man. 1.86; 4.824.
arva patent *Her. Chr.* 3.131.

73–76   **Est mare — aqua** Cf. Plin. *Nat.* 4.103; 37.42–43; Tac. *Ger.* 45.4; Celtis, *Germania* 118–20: "Codonea . . . equora . . . / Que glesum eiiciunt, quod succinus ore Latino / Dicitur et nostris tantum reperitur in oris"; Stella, *Boruss.* 1, p. 288: "succinum, quod abundantius barbari illic inter maris eiecticia soli omnium gentium excepere."

73   **nobilibus . . . lapillis** Erasmus, *Carm.* 50.22.

74   **primae — habet** Cf. *Sylv.* 8.7.16: "Prima . . . nomina laudis habet"; Eob. to Mutianus Rufus (April 1516), in Mutian. *Ep.* 556: "aeternae nomina laudis habes"; *Laud.* 303, n.; *Her. Chr.* 5.80, n.; 19.14; *Ilias* 2.1019: "Primae laudis equae."

75   **puerique — puellae** Combining Ov. *Tr.* 3.12.5 with *Am.* 3.13.23 and *Rem.* 33.

76   **prima — aqua** Cf. Ov. *Ep.* 18.100.

77–78   **Est mare — Pharos** Cf. Stella, *Boruss.* 1, p. 292: "Piscationes quoque diversis in locis non incommodas exhibet. Nam pisces omnis generis tum ex lacubus tum ex aestuanti mari illic prendunt, ceu psittas, soleas, lingulas, rumbos, trossulos, mullos, asellos, salmones, marinos canes et id genus alios. Anguillas praeter caeteros numerosiores. . . ."

77–78   **sunt fluvii — Pharos** Cf. Celtis, *Germania* 269–70: "Ingentesque lacus varias vastasque paludes / Et fluvios varios, sapido qui pisce redundant."

77   **stagna — lacusque** = Ov. *Met.* 1.38.

78   **Non — Pharos** Mela 1.52 says that the Nile teems with fish; Plin. *Nat.* 5.51 lists three species of fish that live there.

80   **venit** Wrongly with a short first syllable.

81–88   **Sunt et apum — favos** The passage offers a poetic paraphrase of Stella, *Boruss.* 1, p. 292: "Habent et sylvae praeter id suas divitias, unde quasi sponte compendium non modicum provenit. Apum scilicet ingentem multitudinem, quarum alveos ceu nativos intra arbores ad hoc cavas cernere est, ex quibus tanta mellis et cerae copia provenit, ut

Germaniae Britanniaeque ac caeteris adiacentibus insulis commode harum rerum usum suppeditet. Nec apiarii arte vel industria examina illic curant, nullis enim satorum floribus aut herbis ipsa invitant, nec si longius evolant, revocant; e frondibus et sylvestribus floribus succum contrahunt, quo opera conficiunt sua, quae compendii ingentis argumento sunt."

81 **apum . . . examina** *Nup.* 49, n.

82 **Qualia non unquam** = l. 111 below.

Sicelis Hybla = *Luth.* 3.18; cf. *Buc.* 6.26, n., and n. at *Laud.* 107.

83 **res mira** = *Buc.* 11.46, n.

84 **dulces . . . favos** Mart. 1.43.4; Locher, "Hecatostichon in proludium," *Stult.*, fol. 9ᵛ: "Turba apium dulces perstrepat . . . favos."

85 **molli . . . herba** = Verg. *Ecl.* 3.55; Eob. *Buc.* 7.75.

graminis herba = *Buc.* 4.110; cf. Verg. *Ecl.* 5.26; Ov. *Met.* 10.87.

86 **Flava . . . mella** Ov. *Met.* 1.112; Mart. 1.55.10.

poplite mella = Ven. Fort. *Carm.* 3.9.26; cf. Eob. *Laud.* 108, n.

87 **Panchaeaque rura** = Ov. *Met.* 10.478. Eobanus confuses Panchaia, an imaginary island in the Indian Ocean, with Pangaea, a mountain in Macedonia.

rura Lyaeus = Stat. *Silv.* 4.2.37.

88 **Nesciet** The London and Zwickau copies add the ms. gloss "oblivisceret."

inventos — favos Bacchus was the first to discover honey: see Ov. *Fast.* 3.735–62 (noted in ms. glosses in both the London and Zwickau copies).

89 **pando — asello** = Ov. *Ars* 1.543; *Fast.* 1.399.

90 **Crabronum — feret** Cf. Ov. *Fast.* 3.753.

92 **avido . . . devoret ore cibum** Cf. Ov. *Rem.* 209; Hutten, *Nemo* (I) 78 (*Opera*, 3:117): "Quod superest rapido [avido *1518*] devorat ore cibi"; Eob. *Her.* 3.7.32. For the tag *ore cibum*, see also Ov. *Ars* 1.94; Eob. *Her. Chr.* 14.34.

93 **Sunt — sylvae** Cf. *Nor.* 515–16: "Sunt tamen et nemora et saltus, est plurima sylvae / Copia, venantum studiis accommoda."

nemora et saltus = Celtis, *Am.* 2.9.34: "Per nemora et saltus"; Eob. *Her. Chr.* 13.13; *Sylv.* 5.22.21; cf. Verg. *Ecl.* 10.9.

gloria sylvae Sen. *Phaed.* 27.

95 **alta — stabula** Cf. Verg. *A.* 6.179; Stella, *Boruss.*, concluding elegy, p. 297: "Terra nutrit sylvas, sunt haec stabula alta ferarum."

96 **Maenalon — suum** See Ov. *Met.* 2.415–16, 441–42.

98 **claudere — dies** = Maxim. 1.290: "et laeto stabiles claudere fine dies"; cf. Eob. *Her. Chr.* 2.102; *Her.* 1.6.188: ". . . optato claudere fine velit."

99–108 **Hic damae — pastus equo** Cf. Stella, *Boruss.* 1, pp. 290–91: "Generat et terra haec feras multiiugas eas etiam nec alibi cognitas. Praeter enim ursos, apros, cervos, quibus abundant, uros excellenti vi et velocitate profert, qui vastitate corporis parum infra elephantum sunt eaque ferocitate, ut neque homini neque ferae, si quam conspicati fuerint, parcant. Cornutumque id animal est, eius cornuum magnitudo tanta visa est, ut urnas binas unius capitis cornua, ut Plinius testatur [*Nat.* 11.126], impleverint. . . . Gignit haec terra et bizontes iubatos, qui e boum sylvestrium genere sunt, sed nostra aetate admodum infrequentes. . . . Gignit et alces . . . , magnitudine inter camelum et cervum." Stella was the first to associate the three large mammals with Prussia. Caes. *Gal.* 6.25–28 says only that the Hercynian Forest teems with bison (*wisent*), aurochs, and elk (cf. l. 104 below). Konrad Celtis adds that bison (*visontes*) and aurochs (*uri*) still flourish in the Hercynian Forest east of the Vistula, but only in Mazovia (in East-Central Poland). See Celtis, *Norimberga* 3, p. 126; *Am.* 1.15.7–10; *Germania* 255.

99 **damae — fugaces** Cf. Verg. *G.* 3.539; Ov. *Met.* 1.442; Pontano, *Ecl.* 1.5.47: "et damae capreaeque et aper."

100 **cadit — aper** ≈ Ov. *Ep.* 4.172; *Rem.* 204.

101–04 **Hic sua — nemus** According to Mutian. *Ep.* 484, Eobanus told his friends in March 1515 that the bison, elk, and aurochs that used to roam in the Hercynian Forest were not extinct, for he had seen them himself in Prussia: "Nolite . . . dubitare, in Prewssen lawffen die thire und hab das wilprat gesehen." In *Val.* 1.329–30 he claims to have eaten their flesh: "Quas ego non alces, immania monstra, comedi? / Quos ego non uros semiferasque boves?"

101–03 **Hic sua — cornibus uri** Cf. Sen. *Phaed.* 63–65: "Tibi dant . . . / . . . villosi terga bisontes / latisque feri cornibus uri."

102–03 **Hic plenum — uri** Cf. *Nor.* 506–07: "immensis horrendos cornibus uros, / . . . stupidas gignit praelongis cruribus alces."

102 **omne nemus** = Ov. *Fast.* 1.436; cf. Eob. *Buc.* 5.45, n.

104 **Hercinium . . . nemus** Celtis, *Germania* 164; *Od.* 2.18.10.

 contigit ista = *Her. Chr.* 6.80.

105 **Hyrcani . . . saltus** Sen. *Phaed.* 70.

 novere cubilia = *Nob.* 161.

106 **leporosus Athos** Cf. Ov. *Ars* 2.517.

107 **non decolor Indus** = Prud. *Amart.* 497; cf. Prop. 4.3.10; Ov. *Ars* 3.130; *Tr.* 5.3.24.

108 **Sarmata — equo** = Mart. *Sp.* 3.4; cf. Eob. *Nup.* 24–25; *Her. Chr.* 13.42.

109 **Quid loquar** = *Laud.* 56, n.

 ingentem pecorum vim Aen. Silv. *Europa* 29 (par. 96): "pecorum ingens vis."

 Qualia nunquam = Ov. *Met.* 14.658.

111 **Qualia — Lycaei** Cf. Verg. *G.* 4.538–39.

 Qualia non unquam = l. 82 above.

 colles . . . Lycaei Cf. Ov. *Met.* 1.698: "colle Lycaeo"; Stat. *Theb.* 9.895: "colle Lycaei"; Eob. *Theoc.* 1.178: "dumeta Lycaei."

113 **Maior — usus** Cf. *Nup.* 150.

114 **patria nostra** = Locher, "Carmen ad S. Brant," *Stult.*, fol. 3ᵛ: "Crassiloquas voces patria nostra tulit"; Eob. *Her. Chr.* 10.50; *Luth.* 6.72; *Idyl.*, 2. ded. 96. The London and Zwickau copies add the ms. gloss "Hessia."

117 **Vestibus . . . vulgaribus** *Sylv.* 3.4.63: "Nobilis obfuscat vulgares purpura vestes."

119–24 **Pocula — cadis** Cf. *Gen. ebrios.* 16.

119 **Pocula — aristis** Cf. Verg. *G.* 1.8–9; Eob. *Sylv.* 7.19.15–16: "pro Baccho nobis Acheloia constent / Pocula."

 crassa Ceres Cf. *Epp. fam.*, p. 41 (24 March 1525), referring to beer: "Cerere illa nostrate crassa"; also cf. *Gen. ebrios.* 18.3: "cerevisia — crassus ille . . . humor"; *Val.* 1.647–48: "Qui docuit crasso Cererem confundere succo, / Huic iratus erat Bacchus, et ipsa Ceres."

121 **Vina . . . non inferiora** = *Idyl.* 1.88: "Vinaque . . . non inferiora Phalerno."

 Teraphnaeis A ms. note in the Zwickau copy explains that the name *Teraphne* (that is, *Therapne*), while normally reserved for the town near Sparta where Helen was born, is also used for the island of Corsica, "unde vinum Cursicum optimum." The London copy has a similar gloss. Cf. Niccolò Perotti, *Cornu copiae* 1.6.322, in *Cornu copiae seu linguae Latinae commentarii*, vol. 4, ed. Marianne Pade and Johann RammJnger (Sassoferrato, 1994), 237–38: "Cyrnum, a quo insula in mari Lygustico Cyrnos appellata, qum antea Teraphne diceretur, nostri Corsicam vocant"; Calepino, *Dictionarium*, s.v. "Terapne." In Eobanus' time Corsican wines were highly prized. See, for example, Pontano, *Hendec.* 1.17.18–19; Bartolomeo Platina, *De honesta voluptate et valetudine* 10.69, in *Platina, On Right Pleasure and Good Health*, ed. and trans. Mary E. Milham (Tempe, AZ, 1998), 466; *Epistolae obscurorum virorum* 2.5: "optimum vinum Cursicum."

123 **peregrinis . . . ab oris** Petrarch, *Ecl.* 1.20; Mant. *2. Parthen.* 3.166.

124 **Per mare — cadis** Cf. Mant. *Sylv.* 1, fol. 252ʳ: "vina Phalerni / Creticaque Idaeis trans mare vecta cadis"; Mart. 1.18.2.

125 **ad humanos . . . usus** Man. 5.644; cf. Hor. *Carm.* 3.3.51.

127 **Sunt — urbes** Cf. *Rec.* 176; *Epp. fam.*, 11, written on 18 February 1510, not long after Eobanus' arrival in Prussia: "Mirum quam praeclarae in hac regione urbes." The now-following description of Prussian cities is found neither in Aen. Silv. *Europa* nor

in Volaterranus' *Commentaria*. Celtis, *Am.* 1.15.41–52 describes Thorn, Marienburg, and Danzig.

opibusque superbae ≈ Verg. *A.* 5.268; Sil. 17.620.

128   **mirum** = *Her. Chr.* 10.78; cf. Ov. *Met.* 7.790; 11.51; *Fast.* 2.413.

Teutonis ora = Celtis, *Am.* 2.3.24; 3.2.42; Eob. *Her. Chr.* 7.98; 24.52; *Luth.* 5.24; *Sylv.* 2.2.86; et al.; cf. *Buc.* B 9.21, n. A gloss in the London and Zwickau copies explains that the phrase means "exterior Germania": that is, the rest of Germany. A further note in both copies adds that the term *Germania* includes many nations that do not speak German, while *Teutonia* includes only the German-speaking areas.

129   **Istula** For this form, here required by the meter, see *Nup.*, lim. 3, n.

130   **littora prima** = *Val.* 2.382: "littora prima petam"; *Sylv.* 6.10.68: "Moeni littora prima colunt"; cf. V. Fl. 5.117; Eob. *Sarmat.* 53 (of Danzig): "Littora contigerant Codoneae prima lacunae"; *Hod.* 278: "littora prima tenemus."

131–34   **Urbs dominis — crucem** These lines, evidently added in December 1513, show Eobanus in his role as propagandist of the Teutonic Order regarding the cities lost to Poland in the previous century. In a private letter letter of 18 February 1510 he expresses a much more realistic view: "Mirum quam praeclarae in hac regione urbes sub eius dominio, quae olim, cum nimiam superbiam et insolentiam Teutonicorum dominorum ferre non possent, ad regem defecerunt." See *Epp. fam.*, 11.

131   **nisi forte fuisset** = *Eras.* 97; cf. *Buc.* 7.14.

134   **Excisa . . . arce** l. 143 below.

135   **mercibus inclyta** = *Idyl.* 6.43: "navigeri vada mercibus inclyta Moeni."

136   **Et minor est** = *Buc.* B 4.4.

140   **nomen habet** = l. 24, n., above.

142   **Pulchra quidem** = Mart. 1.108.2.

ut ante fuit = Ov. *Ep.* 8.22; Eob. *Eras.* 118.

143   **excisae . . . arcis** l. 134 above.

144   **vagus . . . Vistula** l. 59, n., above.

vagus undanti = *Nup.* 152.

lambit aqua ≈ *Her. Chr.* 24.56, n.; cf. Hor. *Carm.* 1.22.7–8; Stat. *Theb.* 4.51–52; Eob. *Her. Chr.* 20.8; *Sylv.* 2.4.40; 7.29.4.

145   **imitata ruinas** = l. 169 below; *Sylv.* 1.1.89.

147   **quondam — inclyta** *Tum.* 3.83: "Teutonicae quondam domus inclyta militiai."

domus inclyta = Mant. *1. Parthen.* 1.852; Eob. *Sylv.* 3.1.35; cf. *Her. Chr.* 20.81, n.

148   **nullo crimine . . . nocens** = *Sylv.* 6.6.16: "Me iuvat opprobriis lacerari saepe malorum, / Dum mea sit nullo crimine vita nocens." Cf. Prop. 2.6.34.

crimine facta nocens = Pico, *Deprecatoria*, p. 378, l. 33: "Quae mens . . . / . . . non proprio crimine facta nocens?"; Eob. *Val.* 2.368; *Sylv.* 6.4.4; cf. Mart. 9.30.2: Eob. *Her. Chr.* 3.32; 11.10; and 15.40.

149   **data serva** = *Luth.* 5.43.

150   **sed sine labe** = Ov. *Tr.* 2.110; Eob. *Her. Chr.* 24.70; cf. *Her. Chr.* 2.45, n.

151   **Noganum — amaenum** Cf. Lucr. 4.1024; Verg. *A.* 9.680; Eob. *Sylv.* 8.4.9: "fluvium sita propter amoenum."

153   **Non procul inde** Cf. Verg. *A.* 8.642.

nobile Musis = *Hod.* 236; *Sylv.* 7.1.9: "nostris Martburgum nobile Musis." A gloss in the Zwickau copy, quoting from one of Eobanus' lectures, explains: "notum, celebratum meis carminibus." The London copy has a similar note.

154   **Pinguia . . . arva** = Marul. *Epigr.* 2.47.4; cf. [Tib.] 3.3.12.

foecundi . . . soli Ov. *Met.* 7.417.

possidet — soli = *Nor.* 473.

155–58   **Moenia parva — lacu** Cf. *Her. Chr.*, ded. 18.6–9.

155–56   **Moenia — facit** For the thought, cf. *Laud.* 124–25, n.

155   **parva quidem, sed quae** = Ov. *Met.* 2.855; cf. Eob. *Her. Chr.* 24.57, n.

Presul Iobus ≈ *Nup.* 227.

156 **aeternum nomen** *Buc.* B 2.19, n.

nomen habere = Prop. 1.4.8; 3.16.30; Ov. *Am.* 2.17.28; et al.; Eob. *Her. Chr.* 12.38; 19.46, n.; *Nob.* 268; *Sylv.* 2.29.10; et al.

159 **Hactenus, unde legas** = Ov. *Ars* 1.263; cf. Eob. *Her. Chr.* 12.8, n.; 21.3; *Hod.* B 1.13; *Sylv.* 8.4.1.

properatam . . . salutem = *Sylv. duae* 2.7; *Hod.* B 1.21.

161–78 **Prussia — locum** These verses appear in virtually the same form in *Sylv.* 1.1.81–98 (addressed to King Sigismund in November 1512). Since the passage looks like an afterthought here and, besides, is missing in *Sylv.* 1.2, it must have been taken from the as yet unpublished elegy to Sigismund and added here for publication in 1514. The same goes for ll. 49–58, 63–64 above: see n. at ll. 47–64 above.

161 **Teutonicae . . . militiei** *Nup.* 229, n.

162 **Christiferae Virginis** *Hod.* 305; cf. *Her. Chr.* 6.187, n.

163 **plures . . . dominata per annos** Cf. Verg. *A.* 2.363.

late dominata ≈ Prud. *Amart.* 243; cf. Stat. *Theb.* 2.162; Eob. *Tum.* 3.65.

165–78 **Atque — locum** The mutability of all things terrestrial was proverbial: see Otto 1292; Häussler, 195; Eob. *Her. Chr.* 17.59–70; *Luth.* 5.47–50; *Idyl.* 17.121–23; *Sylv.* 2.1.9–12: "Ipsa suas et regna vices, et tempora mutant. / Quis vetet hac urbes conditione trahi? / Rebus in humanis ludit, lascivit, et errat / Nixa volubilibus lubrica diva rotis."

165 **rerum — ordo** Cf. *Nup.* 96, n.; *Sylv.* 1.4.97: ". . . est rerum mutabilis ordo." For *rerum ordo* at this metrical position, see Verg. *A.* 7.44.

166 **Fortunae — rotam** Fortune's fickleness, symbolized by her wheel, was proverbial: see Otto 695; cf. Otto 698; Eob. *Sylv.* 1.4.31: "Insidet instabili Fortuna volubilis orbi"; *Max.* 331–32. See further Boeth. *Consol.*, bk. 2; Eob. *Ama.* 5.2–6, with nn.

instabilem . . . rotam = Celtis, *Am.* 2.12.4, referring to Fortune: "Vertens instabilem mobilitate rotam."

167 **polleret honore** = Suet. *Vita Terentii* 7 (in a verse attributed to Julius Caesar): "comica ut aequato virtus polleret honore."

169 **veteres rerum . . . ruinas** = *Sylv.* 2.1.45; cf. Ov. *Met.* 15.424.

rerum . . . ruinas = Lucr. 1.740; 1.1107; Man. 1.904.

imitata ruinas = l. 145, n., above.

171 **Martia . . . Rhoma** *Her. Chr.* 17.68, n.

173 **Sic Thebae, sic Troia** = Hieronymus Emser, "Hodoeporicon" 11, in Busch. *Lips.*, sig. A1ᵛ (ed. Neff, p. 75): "Sic Thebae, sic Troia iacet, sic Pallados arces, / Sic Solymae fato templa superba suo"; Eob. *Idyl.* 13.96; cf. Ov. *Am.* 3.12.15.

sic Troia — Corinthus Cf. Giovannantonio Campano, *Carm.* 1.9.217, in *Poeti Latini del Quattrocento*, ed. F. Arnaldi et al. (Milan, 1964), 804: "cuncta ruent. Sic Troia stetit, sic alta Corinthus: / pascit sulcantes utraque terra boves."

174 **Tyria . . . manu** Stat. *Theb.* 9.160.

moenia — manu = *Sylv.* 1.5.50 (referring to Rome): "Celsaque Martigena moenia structa manu."

177–78 **omnia mutat . . . dea** Cf. *Tum.* 6.63: "sors omnia mutat."

178 **habere locum** = *Buc.*, lim. 4, n.

179 **Omnia quis referat** = *Eccles.* 129; *Val.* 2.69.

180 **minima parte** = Ov. *Am.* 3.10.30; Eob. *Her. Chr.* 18.174.

181–82 **baculo — gregem** Cf. *Buc.*, lim. 5, n.

181 **baculo . . . agresti** *Nup.* 9, n.

182 **Teutona — gregem** Cf. *Nob.* 279: "Teutona Romulidas quis duxit in arva Camaenas."

Teutona . . . in arva = *Her. Chr.* 17.200; *Sylv.* 2.2.32; cf. *Nob.* 279; *Sylv.* 1.11.8.

duxit in arva = Ov. *Pont.* 4.16.18; Eob. *Her. Chr.* 13.158.

183 **At . . . noster amor** = *Her. Chr.* 1.29, n.

consors — lyraeque = Ov. *Ep.* 15.29; cf. Eob. *Sylv.* 1.11.5–6: "patriaeque lyraeque / Consortem"; 1.11.45: "nostrarum patriaeque lyraeque sodalis"; 2.5.36: "Consortem patrii nominis atque lyrae"; 2.7.1: "Musarum patriaeque comes . . . mearum"; *Hod.*, app. 1: "Consors et patriae et studii . . . meorum"; *Wirt.* B 2.7.

184 **tubam** For the image, cf., for example, Mart. 8.3.22; 10.64.4; 11.3.8; Eob. *Nob.* 138, n., all referring to epic. Here the emphasis is on Mutianus' eloquence and mastery of the Latin language, as glosses in the London and Zwickau copies confirm: "eloquentiam. Latini sermonis edocte."

185–86 **Quid — lupos** Imitated in Cordus, *Eleg. duae* 1.9–10, referring to his students, who were left without a teacher during his illness in 1516: "Quam timeo, absenti ne grex pastore vagetur, / ne ferus incurrat vos lanietque lupus."

185 **amisso . . . magistro** = Verg. *A.* 5.867.

186 **saevos . . . lupos** ≈ Tib. 1.5.54.

187 **Quid facit is . . . cui** ≈ Catul. 88.1, 3.

 pagina nostra Cf. Mart. 5.2.2. A ms. note in the Zwickau copy adds the gloss: "liber noster. bucolicum nostrum."

 nostra dicata est = *Her. Chr.* 4.51.

188 **Hei mihi, quam** = Tib. 2.1.70; Ov. *Am.* 1.6.52; *Ep.* 13.48; et al.; Eob. *Buc.* 3.75; *Her. Chr.* 3.115; 4.172; 15.34; 23.106; *Nob.* 280.

 nostra carina = Ov. *Ep.* 15.72. For the nautical metaphor, cf. Eob. *Laud.* 477–78, n. Here the reference is to Eobanus' impetuous departure from Erfurt. Cf. the gloss in the Zwickau copy: "in abitu. navis nostra. i. quam festinanter oportuit me abire" (the London copy glosses: "in abitu. navis").

189 **mentito . . . nomine** Ov. *Met.* 10.439; Stat. *Theb.* 7.303.

 nomine dictus = Ov. *Fast.* 5.427.

191 **Vivite, deliciae nostrae** = *Sylv.* 2.5.39.

192 **Longius — abest** Cf. *Her. Chr.* 22.26. For *longius abest*, see Ov. *Tr.* 2.188.

193–94 **vultis — vivere** Notice the heavy alliteration.

195 **solita . . . virtute** = Ov. *Met.* 9.163.

196 **sub hoc — erit** Cf. *Hod.*, app. 12: "Sub quocunque etiam sidere noster eris."

2. Illiciti amoris antidotarium

Meter: Elegiac distich.

1 **patria . . . eadem** = Hutten, *Querel.* 2.10.33: "Hic mihi non patria tantum sociatur eadem."

2 **carmina — cheli** = *Sylv.* 5.20.22; cf. Ov. *Rem.* 392.

3–4 **Quae — abis** In *Sylv.* 1.5.63–64 Eobanus had concluded his farewell poem to Temonius with the wish, "Quaeque iterum referent nobis te fata precabor, / Sic referant illo tempore, sicut abis."

3 **clavigeri** *Her. Chr.* 21.91, n.

6 **audet adire** Verg. *A.* 5.379.

7 **Quid velit** = Hor. *Ep.* 1.12.19; Ov. *Met.* 9.526.

 properatam . . . salutem = *Sylv. duae* 1.159; *Hod.* B 1.21.

 inopina salutem = Verg. *A.* 8.476.

9 **crine soluto** = Ov. *Met.* 13.584; Luc. 2.23; 7.38.

10 **Esse — potest** Cf. Ov. *Tr.* 1.1.61; Eob. *Epic.*, app. 5.8: "Est [Musa] . . . ex ipso nota colore tibi"; *Sylv.* 9.13.10: "Non opus ergo meas tibi depinxisse Camoenas, / Quas satis ex ipso nosse colore potes."

11 **residem . . . Thaliam** Cf. *Sylv.* 6.1.45, to Willibald Pirckheimer: "Adsere nunc ergo residem, vir docte, Camoenam."

12 **vacua . . . aure** Lucr. 1.50; Hor. *Ep.* 1.16.26; Ov. *Am.* 3.1.62; *Met.* 4.41; 12.56; cf. Eob. *Her. Chr.* 10.153 (in a different sense).

13 **Tyrium . . . ostrum** Verg. *G.* 3.17; Ov. *Ep.* 12.179; *Met.* 10.211.

14   **in ore color** = Ov. *Am.* 2.11.28; *Med.* 98; Eob. *Her. Chr.* 7.110; *Epic.* 3.34.

15–18   **Nulla — placet** Cf. *Sylv.* 3.5.15–17, where Eobanus tells his Muse: "Non calamistra tuos crispent nec sulphura crines. / Neglecta poteris pulchrior esse coma. / Unio nec collum nec tempora contegat aurum."

15   **niveo . . . collo** = Ven. Fort. *Carminum spuriorum app.* 1.303: "adnectens niveo pretiosa monilia collo"; cf. *Ciris* 170.

16   **Nulla — tumet** Cf. *Her. Chr.* 12.80, n.

17   **Plus — videri** Cf. *Eleg.* 3.21: "bona . . . plus quam formosa videri."

20   **Claudicet . . . pede** Ov. *Am.* 2.17.20.

21   **tamen in dextra** = Ov. *Fast.* 3.172.

         fronte solebat = Juv. 5.44.

22   **gerit — comis** Cf. Tib. 1.3.66; Ov. *Ars* 2.734.

         effusis . . . comis = Tib. 1.3.8; Ov. *Am.* 1.9.38; *Ep.* 7.70; *Ars* 3.784; et al.

23   **comitata — venit** Ov. *Fast.* 2.463; cf. *Ep.* 16.115.

24   **Veste . . . posita** Ov. *Am.* 1.6.19; *Fast.* 2.284.

25   **Quid sit amor** = *Ama.* B 2.22, n.; cf. l. 28, n., below.

         charum . . . sodalem Hor. *Carm.* 1.36.5; Ov. *Ars* 1.753; *Tr.* 4.8.11; Eob. *Sylv. duae* 2.67; *Her. Chr.* 7.1.

26   **Qui sedet — malum** A gloss in the Zwickau copy (alluding to *Ama.* 35.43–44) here adds: "Hessus: 'Gaudet amans primum, quia non intelligit ignes. / Incautus laqueos non videt ante pedes.'" The verses are also quoted in the London copy. For the paradoxes of love, cf. ll. 81–82, n., and 121–24 below.

         igne malum = *Eleg.* 3.42: "Nutris Idalio saevius igne malum."

27   **Quid tibi cum** = *Her. Chr.* 8.3, n.; 19.7, n.

28   **dicere — amor** = *Buc.* 3.58, n.; cf. l. 25, n., above.

29   **virgine Musa** *Ama.* 25.6 (where see n. at 25.2–7); l. 152 below; *Idyl.* 13.123.

32   **Ignibus . . . mediis** = Prud. *Apoth.* 154.

         mite levamen erat ≈ Ov. *Ep.* 3.62; cf. Eob. *Her. Chr.* 16.232.

33   **Flavia versu** = *Nup.* 12.

35   **tacitum . . . ignem** Cf. *Buc.* 3.132, n.

36   **Per mala — fui** Cf. *Calum.* 182: "Per mala tot Christo principe victor eris."

37   **Illa meas flammas** = *Her. Chr.* 3.100; *Sylv.* 1.6.18, referring to Flavia: "Illa meas flammas abstulit, illa tenet."

38   **Quid dubitas . . . posse loqui** = *Hymn.* B 2.2; cf. *Her. Chr.* 6.150, n.

         posse loqui = Ov. *Ep.* 17.90; *Ars* 2.626; *Trist.* 5.2.46; *Pont.* 2.8.10.

39   **Quis pudor est** = *Sylv.* 3.18.13; cf. Juv. 14.178.

42   **fune trahit** ≈ Ov. *Ars* 1.764; cf. Eob. *Sylv.* 2.22.5: "Anne iterum veteri te Fulvia fune retraxit?"

43   **Oportuna . . . tempora** = Gunther, *Lig.* 9.498. For the spelling "oportuna," see n. at Eob. *Ama.*, ded. 2.

44   **sine teste** = Ov. *Ep.* 20.182; Mart. 1.33.4; 7.62.6; Eob. *Her. Chr.* 10.12; 22.20; cf. *Buc.* 1.13; *Her. Chr.* 8.113, n.

45   **medicas . . . artes** = Ov. *Met.* 2.618; cf. *Ep.* 5.145.

46   **Dii — queas** Cf. *Hypocr.* 58: "Dii faciant nequeat stare, stetisse queat"; *Eleg.* 3.46.

         Dii faciant = Prop. 2.9.24; 3.16.25; Ov. *Ep.* 2.66; 13.96; Eob. *Her. Chr.* 5.186.

48   **Palles — amas** Pallor is a conventional symptom of lovesickness: see *Laud.* 237, n. For the phrasing, cf. *Her. Chr.* 4.186; 12.213; *Psalt.* 70.8: ". . . hoc erat illud, habet."

50   **palleat — amans** = Ov. *Ars* 1.729; cf. Eob. *Ama.* B 2.52, n.

51   **peste** For the image, see *Ama.* 35.7, n.

53–70   **Sanus — sedent** Eobanus amplifies Aen. Silv. *Medela*, 608: "Equidem qui amat in alium mutatur virum, nec loquitur nec facit quae ante solebat."

53–54   **Sanus — tibi** Cf. *Ama.* 35.55.

54 **quolibet ire tibi** = l. 66 below; *Her. Chr.* 9.18; cf. Prop. 1.8.4; Ov. *Tr.* 3.8.22; *Pont.* 3.5.48; Eob. *Her. Chr.* 13.32; 20.128.

56 **Laeticia . . . potiore** *Her. Chr.* 15.157.

57 **invictam . . . mentem** = Aus. *Ephem.* 3.31.

58 **desinis esse tui** = *Sylv.* 9.19.18; cf. Catul. 76.12.

59 **Vincula — langues** For the commonplace *slaves of love*, see Rüdiger Schnell, *Causa amoris. Liebeskonzeption und Liebesdarstellung in der mittelalterlichen Literatur* (Bern, 1985), 476–90.

61 **color est mutatus in** = Ov. *Met.* 15.46.

62 **tenuis . . . spiritus** Hor. *Carm.* 2.16.38.

63 **Non tamen — in illo** Cf. Pl. *Cist.* 211–12; Aen. Silv. *Medela,* 608: "cum mulierem diligis, non in te sed in illa vivis."

64 **posse videre** = Prop. 4.2.6; Ov. *Pont.* 1.3.34; [Tib.] 3.4.48; Eob. *Her. Chr.* 3.98; 24.4.

65 **durae . . . legis** = Stat. *Theb.* 8.60.

66 **quolibet ire tibi** = l. 54, n., above.

67 **charos . . . sodales** l. 25, n., above.

69 **Lumina demittis** ≈ Ov. *Ep.* 16.227; Eob. *Her. Chr.* 4.129, n.
    suspiria longa = Prud. *Psych.* 35.

70 **Multa — sedent** Cf. *Her. Chr.* 15.30; Ov. *Met.* 5.512; Stat. *Silv.* 3.5.11; Mart. 2.11.1.
    fronte sedent = Mart. 8.33.22; 11.84.14; cf. Eob. *Her. Chr.* 7.116.

71 **expertum . . . amorem** *Ciris* 325.
    necquicquam This medieval spelling recurs in Renaissance authors. Eobanus uses it also at *Vict.* 368, 381, 418; *Venus* 1.173.

72 **prebet amor** = Prop. 3.21.4.

75 **totis . . . ossibus ignem** = Stat. *Ach.* 1.303; cf. Verg. *G.* 3.258.

76 **Alta . . . vulnera** Stat. *Theb.* 3.130, 327; et al.

77 **possint consurgere** ≈ Lucr. 6.1021.

78 **Auxiliatrices . . . manus** = *Psalt.* 7.8; *Epp. fam.,* 163 (letter of 18 October 1537).
    applicuisse manus = [Tib.] 3.10.4: "medicas applicuisse manus."

80 **sumpta nocent** = *Val.* 1.638.

81 **Flamma — venenum** Cf. Mant. *Calam.* 1.1138 (p. 48): "Flamma latens venis Venus est, furor ossibus haerens." For the tag *per ossa venenum,* see Prud. *Psych.* 329.

81–82 **sapidum — placens** For these paradoxes of love — a conventional feature in late medieval descriptions of love — cf. Petrarch, *Rem.* 1.69 (p. 76): "est . . . amor latens ignis, gratum vulnus, sapidum venenum, dulcis amaritudo, delectabilis morbus, iucundum supplicium, blanda mors"; Eob. *Ama.* 29.1–2, n.; *Buc.* 3.164, n.; *Sylv. duae* 2.121–24.

83 **icta . . . corda** Boeth. *Consol.* 3.m7.6.
    levi . . . sagitta = Stat. *Silv.* 1.2.62.
    corda sagitta = *Buc.* 7.134; cf. Ov. *Am.* 1.2.7; *Met.* 6.266.

84 **non sinit esse** = Prop. 2.22.38; Ov. *Fast.* 1.414; et al.; Eob. *Her. Chr.* 4.228; 14.140; 22.168; cf. l. 240, n., below; *Her. Chr.* 6.128, n.

85 **proprii . . . honoris** = Claud. *Cons. Stil.* 3.26.

88 **intentatum nil sinit esse** Cf. Hor. *Ars* 285; Erasmus, *Adag.* 1.4.30, *ASD* 2.1:429, l. 543: "nihil . . . intentatum relinque."

89–90 **Gargaricae — amor** Cf. Ov. *Ars* 2.517–19; *Tr.* 4.1.57–60; *Pont.* 2.7.25–30. For the type of comparison, cf. also Eob. *Her. Chr.* 16.91–94.

90 **turpis amor** = Ov. *Am.* 3.11.2; Eob. *Her. Chr.* 5.36; cf. *Her. Chr.* 11.113, n.

91–95 **Cura — noctes** For this catalogue of the ills of love, cf. Pl. *Mer.* 24–31; Eob. *Ama.* 29.5–8.

93 **Iusticiae fuga** Mant. *1. Parthen.* 1.203.
    dispendia rerum = Avit. *Carm.* 3.334.

95–96 **Multaque — modis** Cf. *Her. Chr.* 3.53–54, with n. at l. 54.

95 **turbant — noctes** = *Buc.* 7.121, n.

96   **brevibus — modis** = *Val.* 1.566. Cf. Balbi, *Opusc.* 62.2: "I, pete laurigeros celeri pede, Musa, penates / Baptiste et brevibus ora resolve modis."

98   **sollicita . . . via** ≈ Ov. *Tr.* 1.11.2 (in some mss. and early eds.); cf. Eob. *Venus* 3.46: "Sollicitae virtus est tibi causa viae."

      longius ire = Ov. *Fast.* 5.650; Eob. *Her. Chr.* 16.230; cf. *Her. Chr.* 12.156, n.

      ire via = Prop. 2.25.38; 3.16.12; Eob. *Her. Chr.* 5.42; 23.92.

99   **puerum . . . Amorem** Prop. 2.12.1. For *puer*, see also Eob. *Ama.* 32.37, n.

100   **decus — habet** Cf. *Sylv.* 3.22.12: "decus victis Hercule maius habes."

      Hercule maius = Tifernate, "Triumphus Cupidinis," *Carm.*, sig. A7ᵛ: "Nil . . . in terris Hercule maius erat."

101   **Naemaeum . . . leonem** Cf. Sen. *Oed.* 40; *Ag.* 829–30; Luc. 1.655. Notice the long first syllable of "Naemaeum," as in Stat. *Theb.* 1.575 (in many mss.); Poliziano, *Sylv.* 3.52 (ed. Del Lungo): "Nemaei vellera monstri."

102   **Aetolum . . . suem** Mart. 13.41.2, alluding to the boar killed by Meleager. Cf. Pl. *Per.* 3: "apro Aetolico," referring (as here) to the boar killed by Hercules.

103   **Infernum . . . canem** = Mant. *2. Parthen.* 1.550: "Infernum domuisse canem"; cf. Sen. *Her. O.* 460; Eob. *Her. Chr.* 15.186, n.

104   **Stymphalis unda** Ov. *Met.* 9.187; *Fast.* 2.273.

105   **vastae . . . pericula terrae** = Verg. *A.* 10.57.

106   **vicit Amor** ≈ Ov. *Ep.* 9.26 (of Hercules).

107   **ludibria sortis** = Walter, *Alex.* 2.534: "ludibria sortis / Humanae"; 6.265: "durae ludibria sortis"; Andrel. *Livia* 1.3.41: "dubiae ludibria sortis"; Locher, *Stult.* 23, fol. 34ᵛ: "vanae ludibria sortis"; Eob. *Sylv.* 1.4.59; 3.2.37.

108   **Turpiter . . . iaces** = *Her. Chr.* 13.8.

      victus Amore = Ov. *Ep.* 15.176; cf. Verg. *A.* 12.29; Ov. *Am.* 3.10.29.

109   **delapsus ab alto** = Ov. *Tr.* 3.4.19.

110   **excelso — loco** Cf. Mant. *Epigr.*, fol. 117ʳ: "Trudet ab excelso vos mora parva loco"; Hutten, *Querel.* 1.4.4: "Et male sublimi trusus ad ima loco"; Eob. *Her.* 8.12, n.

111   **summo — caelo** Cf. Ov. *Met.* 11.365; Luc. 9.351; Man. 3.604; Eob. *Buc.* 10.146; *Her. Chr.* 11.39; 12.222, n.; 16.292, n.; 21.193.

112   **infernae . . . domus** = *Hod.* B 7.4; cf. Verg. *A.* 5.732; Luc. 5.628; Eob. *Her. Chr.* 11.118; *Vict.* 1.

113   **dubia . . . nocte** Ov. *Met.* 4.401.

      nocte viator = Ov. *Fast.* 4.167.

114   **Antra . . . subit** Ov. *Met.* 12.417; *Fast.* 2.315; 5.661–62.

      die claro Catul. 61.85; Hor. *Saec.* 23.

      non adeunda subit ≈ *Her. Chr.* 11.92. Cf. Tib. 1.6.22 (3.5.2; Ov. *Fast.* 4.496; et al.): "non adeunda."

115   **per . . . discrimina noctis euntem** Cf. *Her. Chr.* 11.131.

116   **duxit in antra** = Claud. *Epith.*, praef. 10.

117   **Venus aurea** = *Ama.* B 2.25, n.

118   **nox . . . sedet** Sen. *Her. F.* 704–05: "pigro sedet / nox atra mundo."

120   **posse dolere** = Ov. *Tr.* 3.11.60.

121–24   **Iste dolor — iuvat** For these paradoxes of love, cf. ll. 26 and 81–82, n., above.

121   **Iste dolor** = Verg. *A.* 9.139.

      blanda voluptas = Lucr. 2.966; 4.1263; 5.178; Ov. *Fast.* 4.99.

122   **ista pati** = Ov. *Am.* 3.11.28; Eob. *Her. Chr.* 8.130; 12.140.

123   **mentibus adsit** = Paul. Nol. *Carm.* 26.7.

124   **perire iuvat** = Prop. 1.4.12; Ov. *Ep.* 2.140.

125   **sunt — pusilli** For the phrasing, cf. Ov. *Ars* 2.519; Tifernate, *Carm.*, sig. A8ʳ (quoted in Eob. *Ama.* 29.3): "Gaudia si spectes, ea sunt in amore pusilla"; Eob. *Ama.* 35.18, n.

126   **Ludus — viros** Cf. *Buc.* 3.40, n.; l. 226 below.

      fortes . . . viros = Ven. Fort. *Carm.* 2.14.6; Mant. *Mort.*, fol. 122ʳ; Locher, *Stult.* 93, fol. 108ʳ; Eob. *Her. Chr.* 12.150.

127	**Fortis — peruri** For the image, cf. *Buc.* 7.132–33, n.
128	**igne chalybs** = *Her.* 3.1.84: "Quo fluit hic animus sicut ab igne chalybs"; cf. Mant. *Mort.*, fol. 123ʳ: "curvabitur . . . / Igne chalybs."
129	**pectora morsu** = Stat. *Silv.* 5.2.3.
130	**rodere dente** = Balbi, *Epigr.* 80.8; Eob. *Buc.* B 1.6, n.
131–70	**Quoque — dei** The story is also told in *Ama.* 25.7, where see nn.
131	**Quoque magis credas** = Ov. *Met.* 3.290; Eob. *Her. Chr.* 23.85; cf. Hor. *S.* 2.2.112; Eob. *Her. Chr.* 17.259.
132	**multa . . . fide** = [Tib.] 3.4.64 (in one ms. tradition).
	fabula — fide Cf. Mart. *Sp.* 6.2: ". . . accepit fabula prisca fidem"; Ov. *Fast.* 2.304: "antiqui fabula plena ioci"; Eob. *Sylv.* 8.24.28: "Non est hic aliqua fabula cassa fide."
133	**volucri . . . puello** ≈ *Venus* 1.225, also referring to Cupid.
134	**venit in arva** = *Sylv.* 2.2.32.
135	**Constitit — montis** Cf. Ov. *Met.* 1.467; Eob. *Buc.* 4.77, n.; *Coluth.*, sig. A4ᵛ: "Venit ab aerio Parnassi culmine montis."
	aereo . . . vertice montis ≈ Catul. 68.57; cf. Verg. *A.* 5.35; 11.526; Ov. *Met.* 11.503.
136	**in viridi — chorea** Cf. *Epith.* 19, referring to the Muses: "In viridi faciles ducebant valle choreas"; l. 146 below.
137	**Movit . . . pharetram** Ov. *Pont.* 4.13.35.
	taela Cupido = Ov. *Met.* 5.366; Eob. *Sylv.* 1.3.165.
138	**ille refert** = Ov. *Ep.* 16.48; *Fast.* 6.354; Eob. *Her. Chr.* 20.42.
139	**totum . . . orbem** = *Laud.* 96, n.
	subegimus orbem ≈ Luc. 1.285.
140	**in superos — deos** ≈ Ov. *Ep.* 4.12 (as quoted in Eob. *Ama.* 8.5).
141	**Movimus . . . manes** Verg. *G.* 4.505; Eob. *Epic.* 1.73, 75.
142	**nova furta** Luc. 4.416.
143	**aequoreo . . . profundo** Prud. *Amart.* 471.
	regna profundo = Sil. 7.418.
144	**aereum . . . genus** Nemes. *Ecl.* 4.28.
146	**in viridi . . . valle** l. 136, n., above.
147	**steriles . . . Musae** Andrel. *Ecl.* 7.33: "O ego vixissem patrio contentus agello / . . . / Et steriles Musae desertaque plectra fuissent!"; Eob. *Val.* 2.313.
149	**ex alto — ducens** Cf. Ov. *Met.* 1.656; Mant. *Georg.*, fol. 207ᵛ: ". . . extrema trahens suspiria pectore anhelo"; Eob. *Ama.* 1.2: "ex imo pectore crebra suspiria ducens"; *Sylv.* 1.3.149.
151	**aereo de culmine** Cf. *Buc.* 8.48, n.
	de culmine lapsa Luc. 8.8; Eob. *Luth.* 5.44.
	lapsa resedit = Verg. *A.* 2.739 (in one ms. tradition).
152	**Virginibus Musis** l. 29, n., above.
	orsa loqui = Verg. *A.* 6.125, 562; Ov. *Met.* 4.320; et al.; Eob. *Her. Chr.* 20.16.
153	**Quid iuvat usque adeo** = Locher, *Stult.* 82, fol. 96ᵛ: "O male fidentes, vitam sic ferre nocentem / Quid iuvat usque adeo?"
	sterilem . . . vitam Pontano, *Urania* 1.501: "virgo, absenti cum sola marito / Suspirat sterilem lecto traducere vitam."
	deducere vitam = Erasmus, *Carm.* 64.93: "in longumque . . . deducere vitam."
154	**Contemptrix . . . turba** Sil. 17.410; Eob. *Hod.* B 1.83.
	turba novena = Poliziano, *Eleg.* 3.14: "Sic faveat semper turba novena tibi."
155	**consumpta iuventus** = Juv. 2.155; cf. Ov. *Met.* 4.17.
157	**Ocia . . . vitae** *Her. Chr.* 19.95, n.
	miserae . . . vitae = Ov. *Pont.* 4.15.5; V. Fl. 4.86.
158	**Castalio . . . liquore** Cf. *Laud.* 254, n.
159	**piae . . . sorores** = Poliziano, *Silv.* 4.136: "alternumque piae cecinere sorores."
160	**inferet arma** = Ov. *Rem.* 246: "inferet arma tibi saeva rebellis Amor."
	arma puer = Mart. 1.22.6; Eob. *Her. Chr.* 17.88.

161   **Contra — fata est** Cf. Verg. *A.* 6.398; Eob. *Nup.* 260, n.
       cui nomen Amantis Cf. Ov. *Ars* 2.16. For *nomen Amantis*, see *Met.* 1.474; Eob. *Her. Chr.* 17.158, n.

162   **sacri . . . chori** = Ov. *Fast.* 2.156.
       regia virgo *Nup.* 195, n.

165   **Pierides castae** = *Laud.* 161, n.
       numina vatum = *Buc.* 11.19, n.

166   **in tua regna** = *Her. Chr.* 12.262.

168   **Venus . . . alma** *Buc.* 3.147, n.

171   **sepe puellas** = Mart. 4.42.13.

172   **Nec solum — tibi** Cf. *Sylv.* 8.25.26: "Nec tantum sudet Pieris una tibi."

173   **Ardua . . . culmina Cyrrhae** = Funck, *Primitie*, sig. A4ʳ: "Ardua Phoebeae scanden-
       tem culmina Cyrre"; cf. Stat. *Theb.* 10.840. As a ms. gloss in the London and
       Zwickau copies indicates, Cirrha (Cyrrha) was the port of Delphi, at the foot of
       Mount Parnassus. The name was also given to one of Parnassus' two peaks: see n. at
       Eob. *Buc.* 2.31.
       culmina Cyrrhae = Busch. *Lips.* 13; cf. Eob. *Hod.* 238.

174   **factus eques** = Ov. *Am.* 3.15.6; *Tr.* 4.10.8.

175   **Ecquid — igitur** ≈ Ov. *Pont.* 4.8.65.
       exercite sacris = *Her.*, ded. 133: "Musarum exercite sacris"; *Epith.* 36, where the
       Muse addresses Eobanus: "nostris iamdudum exercite sacris."

178   **degeneri . . . timore** *Ilias* 13.65; cf. *Sylv.* 3.2.13: "degeneri . . . pavore"; Verg. *A.*
       4.13.

179   **ostensi . . . flagelli** ≈ Claud. *in Eutr.* 1.511.
       terrore flagelli = Paul. Nol. *Carm.* 20.230: "sacri monitus terrore flagelli."

180   **iurat adesse** = Ov. *Fast.* 4.236.
       adesse necem = Ov. *Tr.* 1.2.40.

181   **Quo ruis** = Prop. 4.1.71; Ov. *Ep.* 16.123; Eob. *Her. Chr.* 11.118; *Luth.* 3.95;
       Idyl. 16.160.
       duris . . . laboribus Hor. *Epod.* 5.30–31; Ov. *Tr.* 4.10.115.

183   **clauserunt . . . catasta** *Vict.* 374.

184   **ficta . . . voce** Ov. *Met.* 9.55.

187   **Ah — nefandum** Cf. *Her. Chr.* 11.97, n.; 14.53; 15.55.
       Ah, pudet et = Tib. 1.5.42; Ov. *Pont.* 4.13.19.
       scelus . . . nefandum = *Ciris* 323.

188   **Sydera . . . alta** Verg. *A.* 3.619–20; Ov. *Met.* 1.153; 2.71.

189–94 **Heu — "Ave"** Cf. Lotario dei Segni (Pope Innocent III), *De miseria condicionis
       humane*, ed. Robert E. Lewis (Athens, GA, 1978), 2.22: "Invadit [luxuries] . . . ad
       extremum etiam sacerdotes, qui nocte Venerem amplexantur, mane Virginem vene-
       rantur. Turpe dictu, set turpissimum actu, dici liceat ut agi non libeat: nocte filium
       Veneris agitant in cubili, mane Filium Virginis offerunt in altari."

189   **pollice . . . tangis** Ov. *Am.* 1.4.22.

190   **Oscula . . . sumis** ≈ Ov. *Ars* 1.669.

192   **Vade — habe** Cf. *Ama.* 35.36; *Her. Chr.* 17.158, n.
       piae . . . relligionis = *Hypocr.* 72; cf. Sedul. 5.183.

193   **Atria . . . limina** = Stat. *Silv.* 1.2.48.
       dominae . . . fores *Ama.* A 3.4, n.
       fores et limina serva ≈ Gunther, *Lig.* 4.47: "templique fores et limina servat"; cf.
       Stat. *Theb.* 9.723.

194   **profer "Ave"** = Eobanus' letter of 20 March 1514 to Joachim Vadianus, in *Die
       Vadianische Briefsammlung der Stadtbibliothek St. Gallen*, ed. Emil Arbenz, vol. 1
       (St. Gallen, 1890), no. 31: "Mandatum flexo poplite profer 'Ave.'"

195   **Pura — mystae** Cf. *Gen. ebrios.* 21.6.7–8 (inspired by Tib. 2.1.11–14): "Pura Deo
       castus persolvat liba sacerdos, / Cui neque sit Bacchus nec mala nota Venus."
       libamina mystae = *Accl.* 2.205; cf. *Buc.* 11.83.

196 **Sancta — manus** = *Gen. ebrios.* 21.6.4.
 Sancta . . . ara Ov. *Met.* 3.733.
 Sancta prophanatas ≈ *Tum.* 5.105: "Sancta prophanatos reparet concordia mores."
 ara manus = Ov. *Tr.* 5.2.44.

197 **niveo . . . vestitus amictu** = *Her.* 1.2.55; cf. Ov. *Fast.* 3.363; Stat. *Silv.* 3.3.3; Arator
 2.98: ". . . carnis vestitus amictu"; Balbi, *Opusc.* 52.27: "Parrhasio . . . vestitus
 amictu"; Eob. *Her. Chr.* 2.57, n.

198 **praesentem . . . ante Deum** = *Psalt.* 106.16; cf. Ov. *Tr.* 2.54; Eob. *Her. Chr.* 7.98,
 n.; 12.200; *Luth.* 3.56.

199 **epoto . . . sanguine** = Sil. 13.706.
 consumpti The London and Zwickau copies add the gloss "assumpti proprie, non
 consumpti."
 sanguine Christi = Paul. Nol. *Carm.* 19.191; Sedul. 1.119; 5.48, 291; Eob. *Her.*
 Chr. 6.39.

200 **Sub memori — habes** *Sylv.* 2.9.24: "Subque tuo nostrum pectore nomen habe";
 cf. Ov. *Ep.* 13.66; Mant. *1. Parthen.* 3.315: "cunctaque sub memori servabat pectore Virgo"; *Ecl.* 9.132: ". . . quae moneo memori sub pectore serva"; Eob. *Orat.*,
 lim. 6: "Hoc memori clausum pectore carmen habe"; also cf. *Buc.* B 7.22, n.; *Her.*
 Chr. 16.162, n.
 dominae . . . nomen habes ≈ Ov. *Fast.* 5.128; Eob. *Her. Chr.* 10.2.

201 **tacita . . . mente precaris** Ov. *Ars* 1.602; cf. Eob. *Her. Chr.* 4.116, n.

202 **Christophago** *Gen. ebrios.* 21.6.3: "Ebria Christophagi vitent convivia mystae."

205 **debuit aetas** = *Her. Chr.* 12.249.

206 **tonsa corona** = *Ama.* B 2.34, n.

207 **erranti populo** Vulg. *Psa.* 94.10.
 de lege sacerdos = Juvenc. 2.574: "panes, / Sumere quos solus poterat de lege sacerdos"; Eob. *Her. Chr.* 13.17. The London and Zwickau copies gloss *lege* with "religione."

209 **Veneris . . . libido** *Ciris* 69.

210 **sacro pectore** Luc. 9.255; Stat. *Theb.* 8.183; Mart. 7.1.4; 7.2.5.

212 **grave . . . opus** Verg. *A.* 8.516; Tib. 2.1.6; Ov. *Tr.* 4.1.6.
 relligionis opus = *Laud.* 346, n.

213 **Multa — vetustas** Cf. *Her. Chr.* 15.143, n.
 Iudaea vetustas = Mant. *2. Parthen.* 2.281.

214 **nequeunt — breves** Cf. *Her. Chr.* 3.54, n.; 4.205; 17.104; *Sylv.* 1.1.122: "Dicere
 non elegi sustinuere breves." For *elegi breves*, see also *Her. Chr.* 3.87.

215 **Doctus — cognoscere, in** = *Sylv.* 3.5.39; cf. *Her. Chr.* 9.61.

217 **Aspice praeterea** = *Her. Chr.* 23.95.
 veterum — vatum *Her. Chr.* 4.21; cf. Claud. *Carm. minora* 30.146; Eob. *Buc.* 11.34,
 n.; *Her. Chr.* 17.131, n.

218 **Non est propositi . . . mei** *Her. Chr.* 12.202; *Her.* 3.4.10: "Propositi non est caussa
 pudenda mei"; cf. *Her. Chr.* 10.8, n.; *Nob.* 226.
 cuncta referre Ov. *Pont.* 4.16.37; Eob. *Max.* 191.

219 **ubicunque libellos** = Mart. 1.2.1; Eob. *Orat.*, lim. 5: "At quicumque legis nostros
 ubicumque libellos."

223 **Ad propiora vocor** = Ov. *Ars* 2.511; *Fast.* 6.83.

224 **Paphias . . . fores** = *Ama.* 35.50.

226 **Vincitum — virum** Cf. l. 126, n., above. The unusual form *vincitum* (for *vinctum*)
 may well derive from the opening sentence of Aen. Silv. *Medela*, as printed in the
 Nuremberg editions of 1486 and 1496 (also in the Basel edition of 1571, p. 607):
 "Querebaris mecum . . . quod amori operam dares nec delibutum ac vincitum animum solvere posses." (The Louvain edition of 1483 reads "vinctum.")

227 **Quid . . . adhuc . . . non** = *Buc.* 4.6, n.

228 **fortes . . . manus** = Ov. *Fast.* 4.302.
 experiare manus ≈ Prop. 2.15.18.

229–42   **Surge — iuvet** For the thought that erotic passion reduces us to the level of beasts, see *Ama.* 19.15, n.

229–30   **olentes . . . hyrcos** Petrarch, *Ecl.* 6.115; Mant. *7. Parthen.*, fol. 149ʳ: "olentibus hircis"; Eob. *Val.* 1.306.

230   **aesopa** See *Buc.* B 6.9, n. A ms. gloss in the Zwickau copy observes: "Cale. de littera O legit Oesopa." The reference is to Ambrogio Calepino's oft-reprinted Latin dictionary, first published in 1502.

231   **Quod amas — abibit** Cf. Aen. Silv. *Medela*, 609: "Non est in muliere stabilitas. Quae nunc te amat, cras alium amabit."

232   **posse dolore mori** *Her. Chr.* 18.114.

233   **Absentem . . . amicam** Hor. *S.* 1.5.15.

237   **Non amplius ista** = *Max.* 67.

239   **Exue . . . indue** Cf. *Sylv.* 5.28.3: "Abiice quicquid habes quod mordeat, indue quicquid / Laeticiae moveat gaudia plena novae."

    quod non decet = *Her. Chr.* 17.121.

240   **non sinat esse** = Prop. 2.19.4; Ov. *Ep.* 1.78; cf. l. 84, n., above.

241   **Cum brutis — voluptas** A ms. note in the London and Zwickau copies ("ut scribit Macro.") indicates that Eobanus was thinking especially of Macr. 2.8.12: "Istas autem voluptates duas, gustus atque tactus, id est cibi et Veneris, solas hominibus communes videmus esse cum beluis, et idcirco in pecudum ferorumque animalium numero habetur quisquis est his ferarum voluptatibus occupatus"; and Macr. 2.8.15: "quis igitur habens aliquid humani pudoris voluptatibus istis duabus, coeundi atque comedendi, quae homini cum sue atque asino communes sunt, gratuletur?" Eobanus quotes both passages in *Gen. ebrios.* 2.2, 6. Cf. also Verg. *G.* 3.242–44 (partly quoted in Eob. *Buc.* 3.54–55).

    illa voluptas = Ov. *Met.* 9.485; Juv. 6.368.

242   **Quae — iuvet** Cf. *Her. Chr.* 7.120.

243   **Carmina — ibunt** Cf. *Buc.* 6.93.

244   **carmina — probas** = Balbi, *Epigr.* 53.1; Eob. *Sylv.* 1.7.28; cf. Ov. *Ars* 3.792; *Fast.* 2.568; *Tr.* 3.1.82; 4.1.102; *Pont.* 3.6.6.

245–46   **Iam tibi — tuo** Cf. Aen. Silv. *Medela*, 607–08: "Rogasti . . . me magnisque precibus efflagitasti egritudini tuae ut aliquam afferrem medelam ac iter ostenderem tibi quo posses ardentis amoris flammas effugere. Parebo desiderio tuo. Salubria praebebo tibi remedia si ea amplecti volueris."

247   **Quod si — calenti** Cf. *Ama.* 36.6.

    sub pectore flamma Andrel. *Livia* 2.10.40: "Nulla sub ingenuo pectore flamma latet."

248   **iacebit iners** = Ov. *Ars* 2.706; Eob. *Her.*, ded. 104; cf. *Her. Chr.* 10.60.

249   **castae . . . sorores** = Pontano, *Urania* 1.10, referring to the Muses.

251   **solitae . . . vires** = Celtis, *Am.* 4.6.25.

    in carmine vires ≈ Ov. *Ep.* 15.197; *Fast.* 1.17.

252   **Fertis — deo** Cf. Ov. *Ep.* 9.104.

    rapta trophea = *Her. Chr.* 1.188, n.

253   **triumphali . . . fronde** *Epic. Drus.* 334.

254   **timidus . . . Amor** Ov. *Ep.* 19.172.

255   **nimio . . . aestu** = Claud. *Rapt. Pros.* 1.165.

    perditus aestu = *Theoc.* 1.119: "iniquo perditus aestu."

256   **displicet omne** = Celtis, *Am.* 1.2.4: "mihi Pierium displicet omne nemus."

257   **Vive — tuorum** Cf. *Wirt.* B 2.23: "Vive memor vatisque tui laudisque tuorum"; *Luth.* 6.107: "Vive, decus gentisque tuae fideique labantis"; *Epic.*, app. 5.59: "Vive, decus gentisque tuae regisque Poloni"; *Sylv.* 6.1.57: "Vive, decus patriaeque tuae praesentis et aevi."

    fratrumque tuorum = Ov. *Ep.* 16.327.

258   **gravi . . . amore** Hor. *Epod.* 11.2; Prop. 3.8.10; 3.21.2.

Notes to
HEROIDUM CHRISTIANARUM EPISTOLAE

Title   **Opus novitium** Eobanus repeats this phrase in *Orat.* 6.4: "Heroidas . . . Christianas, ut tandem nominemus nostrum illud novicium opus."

              nuper aeditum Cf. the subtitle of *Sylv. duae* (where see n.): "nuper aeditae."

Liminary epigram

Meter: Elegiac distich.

1   **Sunt quibus** = Verg. *G.* 4.165; Hor. *Carm.* 1.7.5; *S.* 2.1.1; Ov. *Ars* 2.435; et al.

              omne . . . teritur . . . aevum Verg. *A.* 9.609.

3–4   **At mea — senex** Reused in the verse paraphrase of Psalm 104 (Vulg. *Psa.* 103.33), ll. 89–90, in *Hypocr.*, sig. 7ʳ: "Huic mea, quem laudat, Domino devota iuventa est. / Hunc ego cantabo, si volet ipse, senex."

4   **si volet ipse** *Her. Chr.* 17.209; cf. Ov. *Ars* 1.356; *Tr.* 1.2.68.

5–6   **Cedite — sumus** Christian poets are superior to their pagan counterparts, not in technical skill, but in subject matter. For this commonplace, see Paul Klopsch, *Einführung in die Dichtungslehren des lateinischen Mittelalters* (Darmstadt, 1980), 9–18; Eob. *Her. Chr.* A 1.11–18.

5   **Cedite . . . poetae** Cf. Prop. 2.34.65, quoted in Eob. *Her. Chr.*, ded. 3.4.

              gentiles . . . poetae = Sedul. 1.17

6   **Materia . . . meliore** Ov. *Ep.* 8.51; Eob. *Nob.* 22; "De fructu et utilitate lectionis Psalmorum," l. 77, *Psalt.*, fol. 6ʳ: "materia fieri meliore poetam / Iuvit."

              vates nos . . . sumus *Ama.* B 2.74, n.

              nos — sumus = *Her. Chr.* 1.152; 6.64.

Dedicatory letter

1.1   **Heroidas — optime** Cf. Celtis, *Am.*, praef., opening sentence: "Libros amorum nostrorum . . . a me conscriptos cui merito (tamquam primitias agrestis et rudis mei ingenii) dedicare et offerre debeo, rex serenissime . . ."; Eob. *Ama.*, ded. 8.

1.2   **Quod ut facerem** Ter. *Ph.* 733.

              sub tui — nominis tutela Cf. *Nup.*, ded. 15, n.

              prophanum vulgus *Laud.* 384, n.

2.1   **instituti mei . . . poeniteat** Cic. *N.D.* 1.8.

              tantum abest ut me poeniteat Liv. 44.38.4.

              equis velisque Erasmus, *Adag.* 1.4.17 (a pseudo-adage created by Erasmus). In the present letter Eobanus shows himself a keen student of Erasmus' *Adagiorum chiliades*, first printed at Venice in 1508 and reprinted (without Erasmus' permission) at Basel in August 1513.

              Salaminia . . . navi The expression refers to a very fast ship: see Erasmus, *Adag.* 3.3.4.

3.1   **Quanquam — aeditum** Cf. *Ama.*, ded. 10.

              lima For this familiar image see, for example, Hor. *Ars* 291; Ov. *Tr.* 1.7.30; *Pont.* 1.5.19; Erasmus, *Adag.* 1.5.58, *ASD* 2.1:534, ll. 379–80; Eob. *Her. Chr.* A 2.3; A 4.3; 24.115.

3.2   **neque ea — conteram** For Eobanus' habit of writing down whatever popped into his head, cf. Camerarius, *Nar.* 4.1; 7.9; and 22.7–10.

[469]

Rhomani Homeri Aus. *Precationes variae* 1.17; cf. Macr. 1.16.43: "Homerus vester Mantuanus"; Erasmus, *Adag.* 3.8, praef., *ASD* 2.6:482, l. 19: "Latinum Homerum."
rudia . . . atque indigesta Cf. Ov. *Met.* 1.7, of Chaos.

3.3   **futurum suspicor** Cf. Cic. *Fin.* 1.1, to his critics: "Postremo aliquos futuros suspicor qui. . . ."
gliscentis indies famae Cf. Tac. *Hist.* 2.8.

3.4   **Qualis — Iliade** Cf. Suetonius' Vergil biography (*Vita Donatiana*), par. 30: "Aeneidos vixdum coeptae tanta extitit fama, ut Sextus Propertius [2.34.65–66] non dubitaverit sic praedicare: 'Cedite, Romani scriptores, cedite, Grai: / nescio quid maius nascitur Iliade.'"

4.2   **nos, quibus — domi** Cf. Mant. *Ecl.* 5.6, to miserly patrons: "Vos quibus est res ampla domo, quibus. . . ."; Juv. 3.165, 6.357: "res angusta domi."
quibus est . . . aes semper in arca *Anthol. Lat.* 499 (traditionally ascribed to Vergil): "Ludite securi, quibus aes est semper in arca."
neque principes — humanissime These sardonic comments on the abysmal ignorance of modern noblemen (the dedicatee excepted) are modeled on Erasmus, *Ep.* 104, ll. 32–48, first published at the head of *Carm.* 4 in 1500 and often thereafter.

4.3   **vobis immortalitatem comparamus** See *Laud.* 61–64, n.
furfuraceum . . . panem Cf. Gell. 11.7.3: "furfureum panem."
promi — propinquior Cf. Vulg. *Act.* 20.35, also alluded to by Erasmus in *Ep.* 104, ll. 4–5, as a quality to be expected of high nobility.

4.4   **nos in — incidimus quae** Cf. *Hod.*, ded. 1: "in eam nos aetatem incidisse quae. . . ."
temporum confusionem Cic. *Off.* 2.65.

5.2   **in nonum usque annum** As recommended by Horace in *Ars* 386–90. Cf. Eob. *Her. Chr.*, ded. 3.1.
cum tineis blattisque rixari Poliziano, *Ep.* 1.1.1: "exempla [epistolarum] . . . quae diu iam cum blattis et tineis rixabantur." For *tineis blattisque*, see also Hor. *S.* 2.3.119; Mart. 6.61.7; 14.37.2.
ne . . . male audiam *Orat.* 5.3: "ne fortasse cuipiam ex re non perinde magna cristas tollere videar atque illud, quod dici solet, male audiam, 'Suum cuique pulchrum.' "

6.3   **Ego — consuevi** Cf. *Orat.* 7.5, referring to his *Heroides*: "Inerat autem . . . in isto opere invulgando quidam gloriae vermiculus, cuius plerumque corruptione sic extimulamur ut popularis aure cupiditate fiamus prorsus ebrii." Eobanus' thirst for fame, which comes out not only in the earlier works but also in the letter to Posterity (*Her. Chr.* 24), is similarly highlighted in *Hod.* 38–42.

6.4   **ad Ciceronem . . . provocabo** See, for example, Cic. *Arch.* 26.
Ciceronem — patronum Cf. *Orat.* 4.6: "Cicero, Latinae eloquentiae vindex."

7.1   **Ut . . . redeam unde digressus sum** Oros. 2.12.1; Hier. *Vita Sancti Pauli* 7; cf. Hor. *S.* 1.1.108; Quint. *Inst.* 2.4.15; Eob. *Her. Chr.* 24.93.
in quibus — admiratus sum Cf. *Her. Chr.* 24.133–34. Also compare Eobanus' draft preface to the reader, edited in the introduction, pp. 120–21 above: "scias velim nihil me magis unquam quam divinum Nasonis ingenium in elegiaco genere admiratum, idque solum semper quo ad potui sequi studuisse." Eobanus is more deprecating in a letter of 12 April 1512. See Mutian. *Ep.*, 2:368: "Iam tres anni sunt, dum in scribendis Epistolis heroidibus, videlicet Christianis, occupatus sum, simiam, puto, Ovidii referens."

7.2   **assequi** Cf. Stat. *Theb.* 12.816–17, telling his book to follow Vergil's *Aeneid* at a respectful distance.

7.5   **uno in libro** Cf. ded. 17.1 below: "librum hunc (unicus enim esse debet) Heroidum mearum."

8.1   **scribendarum heroidum provintiam** Cf. *Nup.*, ded. 5, n.: "nuptiarum scribendarum provinciam."

8.2   **id operae in multo oportunius otium reiiciendum** Cf. *Ama.* A 1.4, in a letter that Peter (Petrejus) Eberbach sent Eobanus in 1508: "nisi ad ociosum tempus id operae reiiciamus, actum erit de studiis nostris et evanescet virtus omnis."

periclitarique — extingueretur Cf. *Ama.*, ded. 5, where Eobanus offers similarly high-minded motives for writing. Also cf. *Orat. Sylv.* 2–3.

periclitari . . . vires ingenii Cic. *de Orat.* 1.157.

8.3–4   **Adieci — aestate perfeci** Cf. *Sylv. duae*, ded. 2; *Her. Chr.* 24.127–30; *Sylv.* 7.18.11–12; "Cum mihi Christicolas Heroidas ore canentem / Imberbi stupida Vistula vidit aqua."

8.4   **horis subcisivis** For the phrase, see *Ama.* B 3.1, n.

8.6   **quid enim — beatum?** Cf. *Buc.* B 11.20, n.

condonet — veniam Cf. *Eleg.* 3, postscr.: "ob nimiam festinationem . . . nulla prorsus ignorantia, sed sola incuria nos esse lapsos."

8.7   **cum Socrate — nesciam** See, for example, Cic. *Ac.* 2.74; Hier. *Ep.* 53.9; 57.12.

8.8   **si quid est — quam sit exiguum** Taken from Cic. *Arch.* 1. Cf. Eob. *Nup.*, ded. 12, n.

nebulam — depictam Erasmus, *Adag.* 2.4.38, quoting the preface to Aus. *Cupido cruciatus.*

9.2   **offa . . . Cerberea** Cf. Verg. *A.* 6.420; Mutian. *Ep.* 130, p. 187, letter to Eobanus (early 1509): "tales offae Cerbero sufficient"; Eob. *Orat.* 8.5: "velut offa Cerbero."

Ioviani magis quam Christiani Cf. Hier. *Ep.* 22.30: "Ciceronianus es, non Christianus."

9.3   **pro Iove . . . Christum** *Buc.* 2.16; *Her. Chr.* 9.64.

vitiligatores The word comes from Plin. *Nat.*, praef. 32, where it occurs as a variant reading in some mss. and early eds. for "vitilitigatores"; it occurs in this form also in Calepino, *Dictionarium*, s.v. "vitiligo." Pliny adds that the word was coined by Cato from *vitium* and *litigator*. Erasmus reintroduces the expression as *Adag.* 2.6.19 and uses it in his preface to *Moriae encomium*, *ASD* 4.3:68, l. 22: "non deerunt fortasse vitilitigatores, qui calumnientur."

10.2   **Non enim — auderent** Cf. *Sylv.* 1.10.43–44, where Eobanus ironically quotes his anonymous Polish antagonist (Johannes Dantiscus): "Phoebe magister, ades: te Marsia provocat alter. / Ecce tibi haec etiam dilanianda cutis!"

o indignum facinus Ter. *Ad.* 173.

11.2   **omnibus — expressisse** Cf. Mutian. *Ep.* 555, where Petrejus Eberbach writes (1516): "Capnionis caussam omnibus, ut dicitur, lineamentis tibi exprimam."

11.4   **cum larvis luctari** Erasmus, *Adag.* 1.2.53; Otto 1147.

12.2   **Christianas heroidas a me conscriptas** Cf. Celtis, *Am.*, praef., opening sentence: "Libros amorum nostrorum . . . a me conscriptos."

pro virili mea Elliptically for "pro virili mea parte." For the expression, see, for example, Erasmus, *Adagia* 3.8.92: "Pro mea virili."

12.3   **campus immensus** Cic. *de Orat.* 3.70, 124.

in quibus — nostro contrarium Eobanus makes the same point in his verse letter to Johannes Dantiscus of February 1512. See *Sylv.* 1.10.23–30 (quoted in the note to *Buc.* 8.119–21).

13.1   **praestiterim** Eobanus had first written "praestaverim," a late Latin form. The change to the more classical form was made by hand in many copies, no doubt still in the printing shop.

aliorum sit iuditium Cic. *Off.* 1.3.

13.2   **non quidem — poeta debet** Following the precepts of Hor. *Ars* 140–52.

13.5   **sine quibus — omnis oratio** See Quint. *Inst.* 2.4.3.

13.6   **figurant epistolam** See Poliziano, *Ep.* 1.1.2: "Figuras habebit: hos ergo ipsos quasi gestus amat epistola sermoni propior. Carebit figuris: at hoc ipsum carere figuris figurat epistolam."

13.7   **methaphoras — exquisitiores** Cf. Erasmus, *Ep.* 211, ll. 20–22 (preface to the *Adagiorum chiliades* of 1508; repr. in August 1513): "metaphoras insignes, scite dicta, sententias eximias, allusiones venustiores, allegorias poeticas." In rhetorical terminology, *emphasis* is a way of conveying meaning through implication: see Quint. *Inst.* 8.3.83–86.

14.1   **ne velut Peleum — putet** Cf. *Epp. fam.*, 93 (letter of 6 July 1524): "ne velut Peleus aliquis in machaera ipse mihi placere et cristas tollere videar." For *cristas tollere*, see Erasmus, *Adag.* 1.8.69.
    erudito lectori — censeo Cf. *Ama.*, ded. 12.
    si hoc unum addidero Apul. *Apol.* 87: "Sed iam de epistulis satis dictum habebo, si hoc unum addidero."

14.2   **Qua in re — et aliis** Cf. Aen. Silv. *Germania* 3.16: "Credunt Greci Herodoto, Tuchididi, Diodoro, Xenophonti, credunt Romani Tito Livio, Crispo Salustio, Trogo Pompeio, Lucio Floro. . . . Cur non credamus nos scriptoribus nostris?" Enea Silvio refers to the writers of the Old and New Testament, Eobanus to the Church Fathers.

14.3   **nihil tam esse — adserunt** Cf. *Orat. Sylv.* 5–7. This judgment of Lucan's epic has a long tradition behind it: see Quint. *Inst.* 10.1.90; Mart. 14.194; Serv. *A.* 1.382; Isid. *Orig.* 8.7.10.

15.2   **epistolas ultro — missitasse** Cf. Aen. Silv. *Hist.*, 105, l. 8: "ultro citroque litteras missitandi."

15.4   **transversum . . . unguem . . . sumus digressi** Cf. Cic. *Att.* 13.20.4: "a recta conscientia traversum unguem non oportet discedere"; Erasmus, *Adag.* 1.5.6; Otto 1825.

16.1   **a principaliori — denominatio** For this axiom of medieval logic, see, for example, [Bede?], *Sententiae, sive axiomata philosophica* 1 ("Sententiae ex Aristotele collectae"), C (*PL* 90, col. 985 C): "a principaliori fiat denominatio"; and, for example, Marsilius of Padua, *Auctoritates Aristotelis*, a widely-used and oft-printed handbook. For the latter, see Jacqueline Hamesse, *Les Auctoritates Aristotelis. Un florilège médiéval. Etude historique et édition critique*, Philosophes médiévaux 17 (Louvain, 1974), 12, sententia 186: "omnis denominatio debet fieri a principaliori"; 12, sententia 214: "denominatio fit a principaliori."

17.1   **centones sarcire** Pl. *Epid.* 455; Erasmus, *Adag.* 2.4.58 (where "Farcire centones"); Eob. *Orat.* 10.2: "ne ex aliorum laciniis centones mihi sarcire videar."
    librum hunc — immortalitatique consecrare Cf. *Ama.*, ded. 13, n.
    unicus enim esse debet Cf. ded. 7.5 above.
    nuncupatum dedicatumque *Nup.*, ded. 15, n.

17.2   **liberalissimus Moecenas** In a letter to Georg Spalatin of 12 April 1512 Eobanus complains that the bishop, though kind, was hardly a generous patron: "Princeps mihi est . . . bonus, per Deum, sed non satis liberalis, puta apud quem nunc pene triennium non amplius triginta nummum auri signati stipendio annuatim mereo." See Mutian, *Ep.*, 2:367. Cf. the introduction to *Sylv. duae*, pp. 45–46, with n. 3, above.

18.1   **quod plerique solent** Cf. Hor. *S.* 1.6.5.

18.3   **fulminantem** For the metaphor, cf. *Laud.* 120, n.

18.6–9   **Quid enim — commemorem?** Cf. *Sylv. duae* 1.155–58, a passage added in December 1513.

19.1   **pileus, pristinae libertatis indicium** Cf. Celtis, *Norimberga* 6, p. 153: "pileoque suae libertatis indice capita tecti"; Eob., *Epp. 4*, sig. F4ʳ (1508): "Pileolus tegit, indicium qui tempore prisco / Libertatis erat."
    gentilitium signum *Nob.* 313; *Epp. 3*, sig. C8ᵛ: "Quod gentilitiis posset praeponere signis / Huttenus, Musis Gratia iuncta fuit." Cf. *Her. Chr.* 6.19 (in a different sense).

19.2   **inextricabilem labyrinthum** *Ama.* 12.11, n.; *Orat. Sylv.* 12.

A 1

Meter: Elegiac distich.

2   **imparibus . . . modis** = Ov. *Pont.* 4.16.36; Eob. *Her. Chr.* 3.54; cf. Ov. *Tr.* 2.220.
    Naso poeta = Ov. *Am.* 2.1.2; *Tr.* 3.3.74; *Pont.* 3.5.4.

5–6   **Maxima — fuit** For the epanalepsis, so popular in medieval verse, cf. *Rec.* B 2.3–4, n.

5	**Maxima — terrae** Cf. Ov. *Am.* 3.15.8.
9	**Naso reliquit** ≈ Ov. *Pont.* 3.1.3.
11–18	**Ethnica — nitent** For the theme, see *Her. Chr.*, lim. 5–6, n.
13	**Dictat — tabellas** Cf. Poliziano, *Silv.* 4.443, alluding to Ovid's *Heroides*: ". . . dat amatricum dictatas ore tabellas."
14	**Mutua — amor** Adapted from Poliziano, *Eleg.* 6.34: "meque tuum memori sub mente reconde / Mutuaque alternus pectora servet amor."
19	**Quid moror** = [Tib.] 3.7.147; Verg. *A.* 4.325; 6.528.
	sacra profanam ≈ *Laud.* 378, n.
20	**lucida signa poli** = Mart. 9.71.8.
21	**liceat — fateri** = Gunther, *Lig.* 8.123; 10.581.
25	**lector . . . studiose** Mart. 1.1.4.
26	**ore legas** = Ov. *Ars* 3.344.
27	**nimium manifesta** Ov. *Ars* 3.599; *Tr.* 4.3.11 (in many mss.).

A 2

Meter: Hendecasyllable.

1–2	**Exi — auras** = ll. 26–27 below.
1	**frugifer, elegans, diserte** Taken from Veit Werler's liminary epigram for his edition of Plautus' *Amphitryon* (Leipzig, 1511; repr. 1513), l. 8: "Salsus, frugifer, elegans, disertus." See Friedrich Ritschl, "Veit Werler als Leipziger Docent und die Leipziger Plautusstudien im Anfang des sechzehnten Jahrhunderts," in his *Kleine philologische Schriften*, ed. Curt Wachsmuth, vol. 5 (Leipzig, 1879), 72.
3	**Lima . . . severiore** Celtis, *Am.* 3.7.30; cf. Eob. *Her. Chr.*, ded. 3.1, n.
4	**pumice . . . politus** Ov. *Tr.* 1.1.11.
6	**movere nasum** Cf. Erasmus, *Adag.* 1.8.22; Otto 1198; Eob. *Rec.* B 2.6, n.
7	**bona poeta** = Mart. 12.63.8.
10–11	**filo Contexta** Cf. Mutian. *Ep.* 149, l. 48 (1:221): ". . . gracili contexta poemata filo" (modeled on Col. 10.227: ". . . gracili conectere carmina filo"). For the old image of poetry as weaving, see also Eob. *Buc.* B 6.4; *Hod.* 488: ". . . levi nectentem carmina filo"; *Nor.* 48–50; *Sylv.* 7.27.9: "facili texunt filo tua carmina Musae."
10–12	**carmina — sororum** Imitating Herc. Strozzi, *Epigr.*, fol. 85ʳ: "casto sale delibuta sensa, / Quae non dissimulet, sed aure blanda / Sanctarum chorus hauriat sororum."
14	**tricas apinasve viliores** Cf. Mart. 14.1.7; Erasmus, *Adag.* 1.2.43; Otto 127.
17	**citharam . . . sonoram** [Tib.] 3.4.69.
18–20	**Non barri — ronchi** Cf. Poliziano, *Epigr.* 50.6–12 (responding to a critic who had taunted him about his nose): "Nam quis te, rogo, sic inelegantem, / Insulsum, illepidum videns, ineptum, / Versus scribere prorsus infacetos, / Non centum cupiat sibi esse nasos? / Centum rhinocerotas atque barros, / Ronchos, auriculas, ciconiasque / Cum splene et petulantibus cachinnis?"
25	**Favore magno** Ov. *Fast.* 5.291; *Tr.* 2.506.
26–27	**Exi — auras** = ll. 1–2 above.

A 3

Meter: Hendecasyllable followed by a dactylic pentameter — a combination modeled on Boeth. *Consol.* 4.m4. For Eobanus' answer see *Her. Chr.* B 1.

The poem was first edited in: Friedrich Ritschl, *Kleine philologische Schriften*, ed. Curt Wachsmuth, vol. 5 (Leipzig, 1879), 81–82.

2	**ingenti . . . amore** Verg. *G.* 2.476.
	laudis amore = Ov. *Pont.* 4.7.40.

4   **lingua — refers** = Poliziano, *Epigr.* 41.4: "coelum lingua, mente, animoque refers."

6   **male defensam** ≈ Ov. *Met.* 15.770; *Fast.* 6.81.

9   **terras . . . repostas** Verg. *A.* 3.364.

10   **vitreis . . . aquis** = Celtis, *Am.* 4.13.4; Eob. *Her. Chr.* 24.56; cf. Stat. *Silv.* 1.3.73–74.

12   **regales . . . opes** *Nup.* 141, n.

14   **Crinitus . . . Apollo** *Rec.* 50, n.

15   **Mellito — liquore** Proverbial: see Otto 1081; Häussler, 110, 185, 240, 279; l. 50 below.

19–70   **Nam te — esse potest** Lines 19–28 and 61–70 imitate Strozzi, *Eroticon* 6.6.17–34:

> Cui magis est Latiae nitor et facundia linguae
>   Cognita? quis Graio doctior eloquio?
> Quis iuvenum tanto moderari examine menteis
>   Novit? et ingenuis artibus imbuere?
> Tu rectum sequeris, vitium fugis, optima suades:
>   Tu sanctae constans cultor amicitiae.
> Non tibi tabificus carpit praecordia livor,
>   Non te spes vana credulitate regit;
> Non animi vireis frangit dolor, improba non te
>   Transversum attonitis sensibus ira trahit.
> Te iuvat alterius benefacta audire nec ulli
>   Detrahis, atque bonos officiosus amas;
> Te fors non potuit male sana per ocia talem
>   Fingere, sed virtus et labor et ratio.
> Ergo tibi meritas certant impendere laudes
>   Ad quos fama tui pervenit ingenii:
> Horum ipse in numero, tenui licet ore susurrem,
>   Conor idem; tu, qui te veneratur, ama.

20   **nube** For the image, cf. *Sylv. duae* 2.70, n.

28   **rutilum — iubar** Cf. Mart. 8.65.4.

29   **Vidisti — urbes** Cf. Hor. *Ars* 142, referring to Ulysses.

30   **claros, clarior ipse** Cf. Verg. *Ecl.* 5.44.

31–34   **O foelix — lyram** Imitating Strozzi, *Eroticon* 1.8.15–18: "O nimium felix, o fortunate poeta, / Ingenio priscis aequiparande viris: / Ecce tibi faciles donant sua carmina Musae, / Nec negat Aoniam pulcher Apollo lyram."

31   **sacer . . . vates** Hor. *Carm.* 4.9.28; Ov. *Am.* 3.9.41.

34   **auratam — lyram** ≈ Poliziano, *Eleg.* 6.24: "Cederet aurata Calliopea lyra."

39   **lusus — libidinesque** Cf. Herc. Strozzi, *Epigr.*, fol. 85ʳ: "Ni lusus, Veneres, facetiasque / Narret."

40   **relligionis opus** = *Laud.* 346, n.

41–46   **Illo quid — Tibulle, tuus** Werler adapts Strozzi, *Eroticon* 4.22.5–8: "Illis quid potuit numeris ornatius esse? / Quae vis, ingenii gratia quanta tui? / Sic ego Nasonem, sic te, iucunde Properti, / Sic ego te video, culte Tibulle, loqui."

42   **ingenii — tui** Cf. Prop. 2.20.26.

44   **Caesaris ira** = Ov. *Tr.* 2.124; 3.11.18; 3.11.72; et al.

45   **doctum . . . Catullum** [Tib.] 3.6.41; Ov. *Am.* 3.9.62.

46   **est Rhomanus sermo** Poliziano, *Prologus in Plauti Menaechmos* 15: "Romanus est hic sermo."

49–62   **Talis — Parturis** Here Werler imitates Herc. Strozzi, *Epigr.*, fol. 84ᵛ: "Quale Pericleo manabat nectar ab ore, / Quale suo recinit funere carmen olor, / Quale melos Siculo tenuit cita vela profundo, / Tale refers, sed et hoc, Borgia, dulce magis."

49–50	**Talis — favo** Nestor's "honeyed eloquence" was proverbial: see Erasmus, *Adag.* 1.2.56; Otto 1224. For the phrase *sweeter than honey*, see n. to l. 15, above.
50	**Dulcior — favo** Cf. Dantiscus, *Carm.* 1.3.276: "Dulcior Hyblaeis vox erat illa favis."
	Hybleo . . . favo Stat. *Silv.* 2.1.48; cf. Eob. *Laud.* 107, n.
	fluxit ab ore Prud. *Apoth.* 820.
51–52	**Pericles — fuit** Cf. Cic. *Brut.* 59; Filippo Beroaldo, "Oratio habita in enarratione rhetoricorum, continens laudationem eloquentiae atque Ciceronis," in *Varia Philippi Beroaldi opuscula* (Basel, 1513), fol. 10ᵛ, comparing Cicero to Pericles: "in cuius labris illam persuadendi deam sessitavisse credimus, quae a Graecis Pitho, a Latinis Suada sive Suadela nominatur"; Erasmus, *Adag.* 3.4.73.
54	**in sua damna** = Andrel. *Livia* 1.9.54; Locher, *Stult.* 61, fol. 72ᵛ.
56	**Ionias . . . aquas** = Prop. 4.6.58.
	doctus Arion Andrel. *Livia* 4.11.39.
58	**fata cruenta** = Ov. *Ars* 2.130.
59	**foenix** At sunrise the phoenix sings a song more beautiful than even that of the dying swan: see Lact. *Phoenix* 43–50.
60	**recinit — olor** = Herc. Strozzi, *Epigr.*, fol. 84ᵛ; cf. Eob. *Buc.* 10.31, n.
61	**Latiae . . . linguae** *Laud.* 115, n.
62	**fama decusque** = Mart. 8.28.2.
64	**nullo . . . loco** = Prop. 2.22.44; Ov. *Tr.* 5.8.16; *Pont.* 1.3.66; 4.1.10.
68	**Divite . . . vena** Hor. *Ars* 409; Erasmus, *Adag.* 2.6.76.
70	**Quo — iunctior** Cf. Ov. *Pont.* 4.4.17.
71	**Pyliam . . . senectam** = Mart. 8.2.7; 10.38.14. King Nestor of Pylos was proverbial for his longevity: see n. at Eob. *Laud.* B 5.5.
72	**tempora longa** = Ov. *Ep.* 7.142; 19.10; et al.
73	**vitae spacium** Catul. 63.90; Ov. *Met.* 3.124.
74	**tantis meritis** *Her. Chr.* 12.255, n.
	munera digna = Ov. *Am.* 1.14.54.
76	**voti summa . . . mei est** Cf. *Her. Chr.* 7.18; 14.142.

A 4

Meter: Elegiac distich.

1	**furtivo . . . usu** Tib. 1.9.55.
3	**limae** For the image see n. at *Her. Chr.*, ded. 3.1.
7	**rebus dexter** = Verg. *A.* 4.294.
	dexter . . . Apollo *Ama.* B 2.75, n.
8	**Materia — suis** Cf. Ov. *Am.* 1.1.2; *Tr.* 5.1.6.
9	**Crede mihi** = Prop. 1.2.7; 2.5.29; et al.
10	**unus — erit** ≈ Ov. *Am.* 2.5.22; *Ep.* 15.182; *Tr.* 1.3.16; Eob. *Her. Chr.* 14.16; cf. *Nup.* 157, n.
14	**iam subitura rogum** ≈ *Her. Chr.* 8.38; cf. Ov. *Rem.* 38.
16	**commoditate fruar** ≈ Ov. *Ep.* 16.312.
17	**Germanae — famae** Cf. *Hod.* B 1.95. For the tag *gloria famae*, see *Laud.* 481, n.
18	**velis votis — meis** Cf. Ov. *Pont.* 4.9.72; *Tr.* 2.60.
19–20	**Nec — nocet** For the thought that time passes all too slowly for those who long for someone, cf. Ov. *Ep.* 19.3; *Met.* 6.501; 11.451; Erasmus, *Adag.* 3.3.86, *ASD* 2.5:232, l. 598: "Desiderantibus omne tempus longum est"; Eob. *Her. Chr.* 3.125–28; *Max.* 23: "Quantulacumque nocet cupidis mora."
20	**Saepe etiam cupidis** = Avit. *Carm.* 2.66.
	mora . . . nocet = Locher, "Latina navis seu barca socialis," *Stult.*, fol. 135ᵛ: "mora cuncta nocet."

Heroidum Christianarum epistolae

1

Meter: Elegiac distich.

1–2 **Quam legis, . . . salutem, . . . littera** Ov. *Pont.* 1.7.1–2; cf. Ov. *Ep.* 3.1; Eob. *Sylv. duae* 1.1, n.; *Her. Chr.* 2.1; 4.1; 24.1; *Epic.*, app. 5.1–2. For the play on *salutem*, see *Her. Chr.* 3.1, n.

1 **aeternam . . . salutem** Vulg. *Isa.* 45.17; *Hebr.* 5.9; Eob. *Her. Chr.* 17.6; 24.46.
 paritura salutem = Paul. Nol. *Carm.* 6.111, of Mary: "mundi paritura salutem."

2 **Non — manu** Cf. Ov. *Ep.* 5.1–2; *Pont.* 2.10.4; Eob. *Her. Chr.* 22.1–2.
 mortali . . . manu = Prop. 2.32.50.

3–4 **Pone — tibi** Cf. Mant. *1. Parthen.* 2.592–93: "'Pone metus,' inquit. 'Superis gratissima Virgo: / laetus ab aetheria venio tibi nuntius arce'"; Vulg. *Luc.* 1.30; Eob. *Her. Chr.* 2.63–66.

4 **Quem tremis** = Sil. 10.443; cf. l. 19, n., below.
 nuncius iste = Ven. Fort. *Carm.* 10.10.6, referring to Gabriel: "quando aeternalem concepit virgo salutem, / dona redemptoris nuntius iste ferens." In Christian poetry Gabriel is often called *nuncius* (translating the Greek for "angel," "messenger"): see Juvenc. 1.12, 31, 57, 67, et al.; Mant. *1. Parthen.* 2.173, 586; Eob. *Her. Chr.* 1.163; 2.54; 13.142; 16.82. Ancient Roman poets use the term for Mercury, the messenger of the gods: see, for example, Verg. *A.* 4.237.

5–6 **Ales — "Ave"** Cf. *Her. Chr.* 16.81–82.

5 **Ales — Olympo** ≈ *Psalt.* 35.21: "Ales ab excelso iuvenis delapsus Olympo"; cf. Man. 1.609; Mant. *1. Parthen.* 2.584–86 (of Gabriel): "Olympo / labitur et veniens fulgentes explicat alas / nuntius." Cf. Eob. *Her. Chr.* 1.8; 2.54, n.: "nuncius ales."

6 **Qui — "Ave"** ≈ *Her. Chr.* 2.32.
 non falso pectore Andreas Manovius Pomeranus, commendatory poem in Trebelius, *Carm.*, sig. a1ᵛ: "Si quis amat sacras non falso pectore Musas"; cf. Eob. *Her.*, ded. 7: ". . . quod amas non ficto pectore Musas."
 dicit, "Ave" ≈ Ov. *Rem.* 640.

7 **tibi — dextrae** Cf. *Her. Chr.* 17.1, n.; *Sylv.* 2.7.9: "Multa . . . Hessiacae tibi venit epistola dextrae."
 epistola dextrae ≈ Ov. *Tr.* 4.7.9.

8 **palmifer ales erat** = *Her. Chr.* 13.64; cf. *Her. Chr.* 13.135; *Her.* 1.2.52. The palm branch is a traditional attribute of angels and saints: cf. Vulg. *Apoc.* 7.9; Salzer, 180–83. It was not until the late Middle Ages, however, that Gabriel at the Annunciation began to be depicted in literature and art as bearing a palm branch, symbolic of the peace and reconciliation offered by the incarnation: see Dante, *Paradiso* 32.112; Gertrud Schiller, *Ikonographie der christlichen Kunst*, vol. 1 (Gütersloh, 1981), 62. That *palmifer* is to be understood symbolically rather than literally can be seen from Eob. *Her. Chr.* 2.60, n., where Gabriel is said to be holding an olive branch at the Annunciation.

10 **quomodo fiet opus** = Alan. *Parab.* 5, col. 590 C: "Quomodo fiet opus, nisi primitus incipiatur?"

12 **Accipe — fide** Cf. Brant, *Var. carm.*, sig. C1ʳ (*Texte* 95.2), referring to Mary: "Et capis a summo nuncia laeta Deo."
 Accipe . . . nuncia certa fide = *Sylv.* 2.8.10.

13 **super . . . ardua mundi** Mant. *Calam.* 3.299–300 (p. 78): "super ardua mundi / Culmina"; 3.795 (p. 90): "super ardua culmina mundi / Aeternum regnare Patrem sceptrumque tenere." Cf. also Prud. *c. Symm.* 1.148.
 ingentis . . . mundi Luc. 8.290.
 regnum tenet Ov. *Met.* 11.270 (in some mss.); Eob. *Eccles.* 310.

14   **sine principio . . . sine fine** For this patristic formula, based on Vulg. *Hebr.* 7.3, see, for example, Prud. *Cath.* 4.8; *c. Symm.* 2.95; *Ecl. Theoduli* 187–88: "tu sine fine, / tu sine principio"; cf. Eob. *Her. Chr.* 4.30, n.; 5.63, n.

16   **Cuius — opus** = Verse paraphrase of Psalm 104 (Vulg. *Psa.* 103), l. 6, in *Hypocr.*, sig. 5ᵛ. Cf. Pico, *Deprecatoria*, p. 378, ll. 20–21: "Cuius et immensum hoc . . . / Omnipotens quondam dextra creavit opus"; Eob. *Psalt.* 51.2: "Summe Pater . . . / Cuius . . . hoc tantum dextera claudit opus." Cf. further Vulg. *Isa.* 40.12; 48.13.

        immensum . . . opus Cf. *Her. Chr.* 18.116.

17–23 **Ille ego . . . Ille ego sum qui** = Ov. *Pont.* 4.3.13–17; cf. *Pont.* 1.2.129, 131.

17   **Ille ego cui** ≈ Verg. *A.* 1.1a; Ov. *Tr.* 4.10.1; *Pont.* 1.2.33; Eob. *Hod.* 23.

        sydera cuncta = *Culex* 351: "sidera cuncta minantur"; cf. Eob. *Buc.* 10.156, n.

        cuncta moventur = Man. 1.289.

18   **Cui — suas** When he created the world out of Chaos, God caused the four elements — fire, water, earth, and air — to stop warring and join their forces. For this idea, cf. Plato, *Tim.* 32b–c; Boeth. *Consol.* 3.m9.1–12; 4.m6.19–24; Eob. *Hymn.* 141–44; *Vict.* 8–18.

        vires corpora = Mant. *Mort.*, fol. 119ᵛ: "quae vires corpora tanta movent?"; Celtis, *Am.* 4.11.4: "Ut caperent vires corpora fessa novas."

        corpora prima suas = Celtis, *Am.* 2.2.18: "renovent species corpora prima suas." For *corpora prima*, see also, for example, Lucr. 1.61, 171, 510, 538.

19   **Quem — domus** Cf. Verg. *A.* 8.296; August. *C. D.* 19.23: "Deum . . . , quem tremit et caelum et terra atque mare et infernorum abdita"; Eob. *Vict.* 183, 322.

        domus alta *Rec.* 45, n.

20   **ab . . . conditione procul** = Tifernate, *Carm.*, fol. C4ᵛ: "foelicius aevum / Ducis ab humana conditione procul."

21–22 **Cuius — Vocibus** = *Psalt.* 31.1–2.

22   **ignotum — potest** Cf. *Val.* 2.60: ". . . occultum cui nihil esse potest"; Ov. *Tr.* 5.8.2.

23   **sceptra . . . sublimia** *Nob.* 19.

24   **Dignus — tuos** Cf. Ov. *Ep.* 16.86; 17.94; *Met.* 11.228; *Fast.* 2.180; 6.554; Eob. *Her. Chr.* 17.106; cf. further *Her. Chr.* 13.22; 13.109, n. In Ovid's poetry, the phrase *in amplexus ire* is invariably a euphemism for lovemaking. But, Emmanuel hastens to reassure the Virgin, he will not descend to earth like Jupiter, to ravish another young maiden.

25   **Ibimus et . . . lustrabimus orbem** = Mant. *Bapt.*, fol. 230ʳ: "Ibimus et caecum simul illustrabimus orbem."

        miserum . . . orbem Luc. 8, 340; Stat. *Theb.* 7.25.

27   **Pande fores** = Stat. *Silv.* 1.2.17; 4.8.1.

        Regina Mary is traditionally lauded as "Queen of Heaven": see Salzer, 458–67.

28   **tempora mensis** Ov. *Fast.* 3.883.

29   **At . . . noster amor** = *Sylv. duae* 1.183; cf. *Buc.* 2.15, n.; *Her. Chr.* 3.121, 173; 17.231. For *noster amor*, see also *Her. Chr.* 2.84, n.

        tactus . . . viriles Ov. *Met.* 10.434; Mant. *1. Parthen.* 2.597 (at the Annunciation): ". . . tactus non passa viriles."

30   **virgine mater** ≈ l. 34, n., below.

31   **In te — aurem** Cf. Vulg. *Luc.* 1.35; Mart. 5.61.3; Eob. *Hymn.* 37.

32   **Subque — homo** Vulg. *Joan.* 1.14.

        fiet homo = Brant, *Var. carm.*, sig. A6ʳ (*Texte* 106.20), where Gabriel tells Mary, "In tua delapsus viscera fiet homo."

33   **Nec dubita** = Ov. *Ars* 2.211; *Met.* 9.698; Eob. *Her. Chr.* 13.83; cf. *Her. Chr.* 14.150; 15.133; 23.3, n.

        Qui cuncta — est Cf. Vulg. *Matt.* 19.26; *Marc.* 10.27; *Luc.* 1.37.

        Qui cuncta potest = Arator 1.1073.

34   **virgine matre** = Paul. Nol. *Carm.* 25.160: "quo deus adsumpsit virgine matre hominem"; Eob. *Ama.* 25.8, n.; *Her. Chr.* 4.12; cf. l. 30 above.

35	**Ut rata sint** Paul. Nol. *Carm.* 32.227; Erasmus, *Carm.* 2.243. **Solimi . . . poemata vatis** Cf. *Her. Chr.* 2.36, n. **vulgata poemata** = *Sylv.* 2.29.7: "Scripsimus exiguo vulgata poemata versu." **poemata vatis** = *Sylv.* 5.31.13; "De fructu et utilitate lectionis Psalmorum," ll. 5 and 33, *Psalt.*, fol. 4ᵛ and 5ʳ: "psalmographi divina poemata vatis." In Christian poetry the term *vates* often refers to the Old Testament prophets: see, for instance, Prud. *Cath.* 9.25; *Apoth.* 234; Eob. *Her. Chr.* 1.79; 2.36, 47.
36	**Virgo pudica** = Pontano, *Laud.* 5.8, addressing the Virgin Mary. Cf. Salzer, 363–64.
37	**Est amor** = *Her. Chr.* 4.77; 18.150 (in both cases followed by an infinitive). **afflictae tandem . . . plebi** = *Vict.* 300.
38	**multos . . . dies** = [Tib.] 3.6.32; Ov. *Ars* 2.170; Eob. *Her. Chr.* 10.12; 12.270; 15.34; 17.264; 24.138. **Tartara** This term for hell is also used in Vulg. *2. Petr.* 2.4.
39	**Insontes animae** ≈ Sil. 9.46; cf. Stat. *Silv.* 2.1.229. **luce fruantur** ≈ Verg. *A.* 4.619.
40	**mors obeunda** = Tifernate, *Carm.*, sig. B1ʳ: "mors obeunda mihi est."
41	**Me Pater** = Ov. *Ep.* 1.81; Eob. *Her. Chr.* 10.27.
43	**Ah, quoties** = Prop. 1.18.21; 2.33.11; et al.; Eob. *Her. Chr.* 1.47; 2.97; 12.207; 14.145–46, n.; 15.101; 16.179–80; 19.109; 21.45. **aliquis superum** = *Buc.* 8.110, n.
44	**sanguine debet emi** = *Her. Chr.* 12.224; cf. Ov. *Am.* 2.10.32; Eob. *Her. Chr.* 4.232, n.
45	**divina potentia** = Ov. *Pont.* 4.3.49; l. 51 below.
47	**Ah, quoties** = l. 43, n., above. **dicenti talia** ≈ Stat. *Theb.* 3.720.
48	**aeterni . . . Patris** Paul. Nol. *Carm.* 10.298; Juvenc. 3.203; et al.
49	**pater Adamus** *Vict.* 233–34. **Adamus . . . in hortis** Mant. *Calam.* 1.83 (p. 21): ". . . cultis Adamus in hortis."
51	**divina potentia** = l. 45, n., above.
53–54	**Charius — inest** Cf. Walther 2367: "Carius est, quidquid magna mercede paratur"; Juv. 11.16; Eob. *Her. Chr.* 13.145–48, n.
53	**multa . . . mercede** Verg. *G.* 2.62.
54	**gratia rebus inest** = Maxim. 1.82: "maior enim mediis gratia rebus inest."
55	**certamine victor** = Verg. *A.* 5.493.
56	**Hostili . . . dolo** Marul. *Epigr.* 2.5.2.
57	**toto . . . orbe** *Ama.* 35.7, n. **orbe triumphos** = Luc. 3.310; Man. 4.52.
58	**Gratia . . . meriti . . . mei** Cf. Ov. *Pont.* 4.5.44. **parva futura** = Ov. *Ep.* 2.144.
59	**quamvis maiora dedi** Prop. 1.8.37. **credere possint** = Lucr. 4.402; Ov. *Met.* 9.203.
60	**exigui — erit** = Ov. *Ars* 2.286.
61	**subiti . . . laboris** *Luth.* 5.15; *Epic.* 3A.44; *Sylv.* 4.13.23.
62	**Ut — homo** Cf. l. 199 below. **omnis homo** = Ven. Fort. *Carm.* 3.14.12; 5.3.4; et al. The phrase is very common in the Vulgate: see, for example, *Lev.* 18.6; 22.3; *Joan.* 2.10; *Jac.* 1.19.
63–68	**Fecimus — erat** See Vulg. *Gen.* 1–3; cf. Eob. *Her. Chr.* 23.57–58; *Hymn.* 25–32; *Vict.* 30–38.
64	**facili — modo** Cf. Brant, *Var. carm.*, sig. bc2ᵛ (*Texte* 195.553): ". . . facili sunt solvenda modo"; Eob. *Her.* 3.6.128: "est facili . . . tenenda modo."
65	**exiguo . . . tractu** Luc. 7.241. **nostri reverentia** = Mant. *2. Parthen.* 1.105.
67	**prius** According to patristic belief, Satan's fall took place before the creation of the material world: see Jeffrey B. Russell, *Satan: The Early Christian Tradition* (Ithaca, 1981), 130–32. **caelumque reliquit** ≈ Juvenc. 4.151.

68 **conditor — erat** = *Her. Chr.* 8.64, n.

69–70 **Non tulimus — est** The doctrine that humankind was created to replenish the ranks of heaven is patristic: see, for example, August. *Enchiridion* 9.29, *CCSL* 46:65; 16.61, *CCSL* 46:82; and *C. D.* 22.1. From the twelfth century on this belief was increasingly being questioned: see M.-D. Chenu, "Cur homo? Le sous-sol d'une controverse," in *La théologie au douzième siècle* (Paris, 1957), 52–61. Renaissance poets, however, continued citing the doctrine: see, for instance, Mant. *1. Parthen.* 1.546–49; Brant, *Var. carm.*, sig. a2ʳ (*Texte* 195.44–45); Erasmus, *Carm.* 110.110–12; Eob. *Vict.* 332–34, 343–45.

69 **patriam . . . arcem** *Her. Chr.* 21.69, n.

71 **Iam . . . annorum milia quinque** *Vict.* 59; cf. Hor. *Ep.* 1.6.43.

72 **cum — piget** Cf. Bebel, "De miseria humanae conditionis," *Carm.*, sig. l5ᵛ: ". . . et multis quos numerare piget"; Man. 1.513: "saecula dinumerare piget . . ."; Eob. *Nup.* 158, 168; *Nob.* 147; *Venus* 1.97: "referre piget numero"; *Nor.* 298; *Sylv.* 1.5.59: "Enumerare piget. . . ."

73–74 **Sydera — negat** Cf. *Vict.* 45–46, 351–53.

73 **Sydera . . . ardua** *Buc.* 3.16, n.

   super ardua venit = Verg. *A.* 6.515.

74 **accessus . . . negat** = Ov. *Ep.* 10.64.

   ianua clausa = Prop. 2.23.12; 4.9.62; Ov. *Rem.* 506; *Pont.* 2.7.38; et al.; Eob. *Her. Chr.* 15.136.

75–76 **Hanc — novo** Cf. Sedul. 2.30–31: "Evae . . . / Virginis antiquae facinus nova virgo piaret." Since Eve is traditionally a type of Mary, the Virgin is frequently called the second Eve: see Salzer, 476–87; Jaroslav Pelikan, *Mary Through the Centuries: Her Place in the History of Culture* (New Haven, 1996), 39–52.

76 **Tu — novo** Cf. Salzer, 541–45 (Mary as gateway to heaven); Ven. Fort. *Carminum spuriorum app.* 1.123: "[O virgo,] mundatura novo partu de crimine mundum"; Mant. *1. Parthen.* 2.780: "Sidera tu mundo reseras: tu Tartara claudis"; Eob. *Hod.* B 7.2.

77 **Currite foelici . . . cursu** Locher, "Ad Iohannem Bergmannum de Olpe . . . decatostichon," *Stult.*, fol. 5ᵛ: "Tempora foelici currunt praesentia cursu"; cf. Ov. *Met.* 15.13.

78 **quicquid ubique** = Prop. 3.22.18; Eob. *Her. Chr.* 3.138; 12.28; cf. *Buc.* 9.55, n.

79–90 **Iamdudum — domo** The story is taken from *Nicodem.* 21. Cf. Eob. *Vict.* 297–307.

79 **numerant . . . saecula** ≈ *Her. Chr.* 17.75.

81 **ante alios . . . David** Mant. *1. Parthen.* 3.832: "Ante alios David et murice clarus et auro."

   aspicit omnia = Ov. *Met.* 2.32.

83–84 **Foelicia — Saecula** Mant. *1. Parthen.* 3.147, at Jesus' birth; cf. Juv. 3.312–13.

84 **peccatum . . . vetus** Prud. *Cath.* 1.99.

85 **vox — aures** Cf. *Her. Chr.* 14.85, n.

87 **dextra — salutem** Cf. Vulg. *Phil.* 2.12; Eob. *Psalt.* 118.49: "Dextra Dei virtute potens operata salutem est"; *Her. Chr.* 22.47.

   dextra potens = *Psalt.* 89.53: "Ut mea dextra potens ipsum tueatur"; cf. Verg. *A.* 7.234; Eob. *Her. Chr.* 12.110; *Vict.* 282–83, 331.

88 **Lucifer ortus erit** ≈ Ov. *Ep.* 18.112; *Met.* 4.665; *Tr.* 1.3.72; Eob. *Nob.* B 1.24.

90 **in obscura — domo** = *Sylv.* 3.10.12; cf. *Her. Chr.* 3.16, n.; 3.134.

91 **graves . . . querelas** Marul. *Epigr.* 3.31.15; Eob. *Her. Chr.* 21.153.

   dempto . . . fine querelas Cf. *Ama.* 29.5: "sine fine querelae." For *dempto fine*, see *Ama.* 32.40, n. For the tag *fine querelas*, see Paul. Nol. *Carm.* 23.35.

92 **saeve anguis** Sedul. 2.1, referring to the serpent of Vulg. *Gen.* 3. Cf. also Vulg. *Apoc.* 12.9; 20.2; Eob. *Her. Chr.* 1.121, n.; 8.133; 22.71.

   inultus eris ≈ Ov. *Ep.* 12.182.

93 **resonat — aether** = Ov. *Ars* 3.375.

94 **salutifera . . . manu** = Andrel. *Livia* 4.5.2; Eob. *Sylv.* 1.1.112; cf. Magdal. *Ep.* 96.

95 **patrio . . . Olympo** = Mant. *4. Parthen.*, fol. 116ʳ: "patrio soboles descendit Olympo / Sancta Patris summi"; cf. [Sen.] *Oct.* 209.

96   **Iamque ego sum** = *Her. Chr.* 4.41.

           pars quota = Ov. *Am.* 2.12.10; *Ep.* 13.60; *Pont.* 3.6.30; Eob. *Her. Chr.* 3.106;
           16.88; 21.92; 24.44; *Nob.* 28; *Luth.* 3.60; 8.12; cf. *Buc.* 2.92, n.

97   **Sentis . . . an dubitas** *Sylv.* 1.3.109.

97–98   **Incluso . . . foetu Viscera** Ven. Fort. *Carm.* 8.3.325.

98   **nova miles** = Ov. *Ep.* 11.48; cf. Eob. *Her. Chr.* 8.123. For *miles* as a feminine noun,
           see also Ov. *Met.* 2.415; Eob. *Her. Chr.* 11.60; 14.62.

101–16   **Tum — erit** Vulg. *Luc.* 2.1–21.

102   **rura — arat** ≈ Mart. 10.15.6; cf. Eob. *Sylv. duae* 1.42.

103–04   **Frigida — eris** Though the Gospels make no mention of the season of Christ's birth,
           later tradition placed it on December 25. For the wintry scene imagined here, cf.
           Mant. *1. Parthen.* 3.68–80; Eob. *Buc.* 11.47–48.

103   **Frigida . . . hyems** Sen. *Her. F.* 950.

           glacialibus — pruinis = Mant. *Nebul.*, fol. 135ᵛ.

104   **Illo — eris** ≈ Hermann von dem Busche, *De saluberrimo fructuossimoque dive virginis
           Marie psalterio triplex hecatostichon* 1 (Leipzig, 1509), sig. A3ᵛ: "Illo quo primum tem-
           pore mater eras"; cf. [Ov.] *Nux* 16: "nullaque non illo tempore mater erat"; Eob. *Her.
           Chr.* 13.96; 16.2.

105   **Nec . . . conteget aurum** *Sylv.* 3.5.17.

           Dalmaticum . . . aurum Bebel, "De miseria humanae conditionis," *Carm.*, sig. l5ʳ;
           cf. Stat. *Silv.* 1.2.153; 3.3.89–90.

107–08   **Sic — pecus** The paradox of the Almighty as a squalling infant in the crib recurs in
           medieval poetry: see, for example, Sedul. 2.55–62; Ven. Fort. *Carm.* 2.2.11–13; *AH*
           7.23.4b; 53.17.7; Erasmus, *Carm.* 42.7–8: "Hic cuius tonitru tellusque tremiscit et
           aether / Teneris crepat vagitibus"; Eob. *Buc.* 11.47. Cf. also l. 138, n., below.

107   **sub paupere tecto** = Hor. *Ep.* 1.10.32; Mant. *1. Parthen.* 3.437.

108   **ignavum . . . pecus** *Pug.* B 1.10, n., in a different sense. Here Eobanus refers to the
           ox and ass, traditionally said to have witnessed Jesus' birth: see *Buc.* 11.49–50, n.

           vagiet — pecus ≈ *Her. Chr.* 21.210.

109   **foeno et paleis** Cf. Vulg. *Gen.* 24.32; Mant. *Ecl.* 6.75: "faeno sepelet paleisque recon-
           dit." For *paleis* in the (unclassical) sense of "straw," see also Vulg. *Exod.* 5.7, 10, 12;
           Isa. 11.7; Mant. *Ecl.* 10.137; Eob. *Nob.* 132.

110   **Exemplo — volo** According to Mant. *1. Parthen.* 3.116–19, Christ's birth in a lowly
           stable ought to teach the great lords of this world to be humble. The same reflection
           appears in Gerald. *Ecl.* 2.47–48 and Erasmus, *Carm.* 42.25–27.

           regibus esse = Ov. *Ep.* 17.166.

111   **nova gaudia** = *Buc.* B 8.1, n.; Mant. *1. Parthen.* 3.144 (at Jesus' birth): "nova gaudia
           mundus / accipit."

111–12   **fient Omnia . . . lumine plena** *Psalt.* 68.35–36: "omnia fient / Regna Evangelii
           lumine plena novi"; cf. *Her. Chr.* 4.28, n.

113   **per rura ministris** ≈ Juvenc. 3.10: "Messores patrii venient per rura ministri"; Mant.
           2. Parthen. 1.407: "mittuntur docti per rura ministri."

115   **populus . . . omnis** Ov. *Tr.* 4.2.19; Sen. *Phoen.* 551; Luc. 7.841; l. 189 below.

116   **tempore — erit** = *Nob.* B 1.30; cf. Ov. *Am.* 1.15.20.

117–26   **Ortus — Pharo** Ms. glosses in the Munich and Münster copies suggest that Eobanus
           here follows the liturgy by combining Vulg. *Psa.* 71.10–11 with *Matt.* 2.1–18. Cf.
           Eob. *Her. Chr.* 16.83–84, 105–20; 21.211–12.

118   **sentiet esse** = Tib. 1.2.40; Ov. *Tr.* 1.1.14.

120   **praevia stella** *AH* 53.30.3: "adorandus / monstratur stella praevia"; 54.239.5; et al.;
           Poliziano, *Hymn.* 2.21.

121–24   **Solus — puer** King Herod ordered all the male infants of Bethlehem to be put to
           death: see Vulg. *Matt.* 2.1–18; Eob. *Her. Chr.* 16.105–14; 20.79–80.

121   **antiquo — angue** Cf. l. 92, n., above; 16.202 below. The phrase *antiquo angue* is
           based on Vulg. *Apoc.* 12.9 and 20.2. For *crudelior angue*, cf. Eob. *Ama.* 32.3, n.

           crudelior . . . tyrannus Cf. *Ama.* 35.47, n.

123   **Hebraeo . . . sanguine** Prud. *Cath.* 5.71.

124   **concidet ense** ≈ *Her. Chr.* 4.220.

126   **Ibimus — Pharo** Cf. Mant. *1. Parthen.* 3.340–41: "[Ioseph] vicina petivit / regna Phari"; Eob. *Her. Chr.* 20.148, referring to the Virgin Mary.
        Ibimus . . . regna For the idiom, see n. at *Buc.*, ded. 7.

127   **Scilicet ex illo** = Ov. *Ep.* 14.85; *Ars* 1.133.
        ex illo . . . tempore = Paul. Nol. *Carm.* 18.159; Eob. *Her. Chr.* 4.3, n.; cf. Verg. *A.* 1.623; Ov. *Fast.* 4.154; 5.44.

128   **dissimulare Deum** Ov. *Ep.* 4.56; *Fast.* 5.504; 6.507; Eob. *Her. Chr.* 19.56.

129   **Nata — Deum** In a traditional paradox, Mary is both the daughter and mother of God: see Salzer, 109–10.
        Nata Deo Glosses in the Munich and Münster copies show that Eobanus alludes to Vulg. *Eccli.* 24.14 (a praise of Wisdom, here identified with Mary): "ab initio ante saeculum creata sum." Cf. also *Eccli.* 24.12.
        paritura Deum = Arator 1.66; cf. Paul. Nol. *Carm.* 6.153; l. 1 above.
        decus addita divis ≈ Verg. *A.* 8.301. For *decus* as a term of praise for the Virgin, see Eob. *Buc.* 11.54, n.

130   **An ubi legisti** = *Hod.* B 1.1.

131   **Nulli — luctus** Cf. *Her. Chr.* 3.158, n.
        gaudia luctus = Mant. *1. Parthen.* 3.814: "mutetque suos in gaudia luctus"; *2. Parthen.* 3.703: "inter gaudia luctus."

132   **Prudenter — dolet** Cf. *Accl.* 2.198: "Prudenter coelo vindice nemo timet."

133   **Non tamen ignoro** ≈ Hor. *Ep.* 1.7.23; 1.12.25; Ov. *Ep.* 20.129, 213; 21.231; et al.
        animosa virago = Mant. *1. Parthen.* 2.783 (Deborah); *3. Parthen.*, fol. 111ᵛ (St. Margaret); *4. Parthen.*, fol. 117ᵛ (St. Agatha); Eob. *Sylv.* 1.4.93 (Fortuna). Erasmus uses the phrase to describe the Virgin in *Paean Virgini Matri, LB* 5, col. 1231 A. Since Vulg. *Gen.* 2.23 uses "virago" for Eve, we may take the word here as a reminder that Mary is the second Eve. See n. at ll. 75–76, above.

134   **in casus . . . ire** Cf. Verg. *A.* 9.291–92.

135   **Scimus enim** = Calp. *Ecl.* 4.72.
        satis apta = Ov. *Tr.* 1.3.7; Eob. *Her. Chr.* 11.99.

137   **Scimus et ad** = Ov. *Fast.* 1.23.
        ad sacras . . . aras *Laud.* 246, n.

138   **immensum — Deum** Cf. Vulg. *Jer.* 31.22: "Femina circumdabit virum," generally interpreted as a prophecy of Christ's birth. The paradox of "Immensity cloysterd in thy deare wombe" (John Donne, "Annunciation") is traditional. See, for example, Claud. *Carm. minora* 32.12–15; *AH* 11.83.1; 11.85.1; 11.90.5; 50.72.1–4; Brant, *Var. carm.*, sig. I3ᵛ (omitted in *Texte*): "conclusus Virginis alvo, / Claudere quem caeli sphaeraque nulla potest"; Eob. *Her. Chr.* 1.205–06; 21.229–30. Cf. also n. at ll. 107–08, above; *Her. Chr.* 6.185–88 below. For *immensum Deum*, cf. *Buc.* 11.47.

139   **nunquam . . . reliqui** = Ov. *Am.* 2.9.3.

140   **pars — tuae** Cf. Mant. *2. Parthen.* 3.626–27: "pars . . . vitae / Ulla tuae." For *pars vitae*, see Verg. *Ecl.* 4.53; Ov. *Tr.* 4.8.34; 5.5.22; Eob. *Her. Chr.* 14.52; 19.102, n.; B 1.3.

141   **castis manibus** Ov. *Ep.* 20.10.
        pia thura = Ov. *Ep.* 21.7; *Met.* 11.577.
        ministris Glossed as "sacerdotibus" in both the Munich and the Münster copies.

142   **nivea** A common epithet of the Virgin: see *Buc.* 11.43, n.
        lumina fota manu Cf. Ov. *Fast.* 3.427. The students' notes in the Munich and Münster copies gloss *lumina fota* as "candelas accensas" (lighted candles).

145   **Ipse — praesensque** Cf. Ov. *Met.* 14.727.
        Ipse aderam ≈ Mant. *1. Parthen.* 2.198 (Gabriel to Mary): "Ipse adero"; Eob. *Her. Chr.* 11.139.

146   **votis — tuis** Cf. Ov. *Am.* 3.7.2: ". . . votis saepe petita meis." For *votis potita*, see *Met.* 9.313; Eob. *Her. Chr.* 21.191.

147   **Hic meus ardor erit** = Ov. *Fast.* 2.308.

       meus ignis in illa ≈ Ov. *Ep.* 18.85; cf. Eob. *Laud.* 182.

148   **Haec — meos** Cf. *Nup.* 85–86; *Her. Chr.* 17.26; Ov. *Fast.* 2.794.

149   **caelesti . . . auro** *Her. Chr.* 4.141; cf. Ov. *Met.* 4.611.

151–52 **Qualiter — Viderit** Cf. *Ama.* B 2.27.

151   **imprudens . . . vetustas** Cf. *Ama.* B 2.31.

       mentita est . . . vetustas Cic. *N. D.* 2.15.

152   **nos meliore sumus** = *Her. Chr.*, lim. 6; *Her. Chr.* 6.64.

153–54 **Nostrum — recens** Cf. Mant. *1. Parthen.* 1.87–102: "infuso caluerunt viscera fetu. / Coepit et humanos paulatim sumere vultus / semen, et in nostram sensim transire figuram. / Ut, cum vere novo tepefacta rosario multae / vestit frondis honor . . . , / [9 *lines*] / sic nova progenies utero congesta parentis / emersit, non tota simul." For the botanical imagery, cf. Eob. *Buc.* 5.78–79, and the Messianic prophecy of Vulg. *Isa.* 11.1 (to which Mary alludes at Eob. *Her. Chr.* 2.112).

153   **virginea . . . in alvo** = Pontano, *Laud.* 5.13: "hunc tu virginea conceptum, mater, in alvo / fovisti"; cf. Eob. *Rec.* 12, n.

154   **Ut — recens** Cf. *Theoc.* 31.133: "ut planta recens adolescit in agro / Ubere, . . . / Crescebat."

155   **Sum — annis** The model is Ov. *Ep.* 5.157.

       puerilibus annis = *Rec.* 104, n.

157–58 **Nunc — comes** Cf. *Her. Chr.* 2.35–46.

157   **cum legeres** ≈ Ov. *Ep.* 15.41.

       Virgo — Tonantem For the phrasing, cf. Sedul. 2.40: "Virgo . . . paritura parentem"; Agricola, *Anna*, 301: "summum paritura Tonantem."

       Tonantem See *Buc.* 11.41, n.

159   **dextraque — eburnum** Cf. Mant. *2. Parthen.* 3.577: ". . . capulum dextra complexus eburnum."

       humerum . . . eburnum Verg. *G.* 3.7 (in a different sense). For the epithet *eburnum*, see Eob. *Buc.* 11.44, n.

       humerum complexus ≈ *Her. Chr.* 2.59.

161–62 **Nec mora — meo** Cf. Vulg. *Luc.* 1.26–31. Since Gabriel's role in Eobanus' fiction is reduced to that of a letter carrier, he speaks only the greeting "Ave, Maria," along with some general words of prophecy and comfort: see *Her. Chr.* 1.6; 2.62, 65–66; 16.81–82.

161   **Nec mora** = *Pug.* 85, n.

162   **Vive — meo** Cf. *AH* 7.107.4a (Gabriel at the Annunciation): "Ave, Maria, / Domini mei mater alma"; Erasmus, *Carm.* 50.125–26.

       parens . . . futura *Her. Chr.* 4.36, n.; 13.134.

163   **I nunc et dubita** = Ov. *Ars* 2.222; Mart. 8.63.3; Juv. 6.306; cf. Eob. *Buc.* 4.63, n.

       nuncius . . . ales Cf. *Her. Chr.* 2.54, n.; also cf. l. 4, n., above.

164   **Quid — viro** Cf. Vulg. *Luc.* 1.34.

       mortali . . . viro = Marul. *Epigr.* 1.48.60; Balbi. *Epigr.* 98.4.

166   **Accepta — sinu** Cf. Vulg. *Luc.* 2.19. For the phrasing, cf. Prop. 2.25.30; 3.21.32; [Tib.] 3.19.8; Erasmus, *Adag.* 1.3.13 (adduced in a ms. gloss in the Munich and Münster copies); Eob. *Her. Chr.* 14.132; *Hod.* B 1.34.

167   **gravidus . . . venter** = Ov. *Met.* 10.505; cf. *Ep.* 16.44.

169–98 **Tunc — canit** The birth of the Child will bring back the Golden Age. The promise is based not only on such prophecies as Vulg. *Isa.* 11, *Ezech.* 34, *Mich.* 5.2–4, and *Zach.* 9, but also on Vergil's "Messianic" eclogue (*Ecl.* 4). This eclogue, which prophesies the birth of the Child and the coming of a new Golden Age, was traditionally interpreted as foretelling the birth of Christ. Accordingly, it was often imitated by Christian poets describing the birth of Christ: see, for example, Prud. *Cath.* 11.53–80; Mant. *1. Parthen.* 3.144–49.

       The idea of inserting an evocation of the future Golden Age into the Annunciation itself goes back to Mant. *1. Parthen.* 2.643–48. There Gabriel prophesies: "Felices annos et quae tua protulit aetas / aurea non Caesar renovavit saecula, verum / tuque puerque tuus: nam primi dulcia mundi / tempora converso coeperunt currere gressu. / Laeta quies oritur: niveis Pax aurea pennis / descensura leves humeris circumligat alas."

For some ancient descriptions of the Golden Age, see, for example, Hes. *Op.* 109–20; Verg. *G.* 1.125–28; 2.538–40; Tib. 1.3.35–48; Hor. *Epod.* 16.41–62; Ov. *Met.* 1.89–112; 15.96–110.

170	**populis — feres** Cf. *Luth.* 3.10, referring to Low Sunday: "Festa dies aderat qua Christus carne resumpta / Discipulis pacem temporibusque dedit"; *Epic.* 1.10: "Qui vobis requiem temporibusque dedit." The thought that the Messianic Age will restore peace goes back to Vulg. *Psa.* 71.7 (quoted in a ms. gloss in the Munich and Münster copies). It is repeated in the angels' message to the shepherds at Jesus' birth (*Luc.* 2.14).
171	**Imperium — habebit** Cf. Verg. *A.* 9.449.
172	**sorte mala** Ov. *Met.* 13.485; Eob. *Her. Chr.* 12.125.
173	**Sybilla** See *Her. Chr.* 4.25, n.
176	**Falciferum . . . senem** Ov. *Fast.* 5.627; *Ib.* 214; Mart. 11.6.1.
177	**cum superis — iungant** Cf. *Vict.* 442 (of the Resurrection): "terras caelo coniunxit."
178	**Et superas — domos** Cf. ll. 75–76 above.
	superas . . . domos *Laud.* B 1.8, n.
	sponte patere *Rec.* 186; *Psalt.* 78.68: "Iussit et aetherias sponte patere fores."
179	**ianua caeli** = Alan. *Parab.* 5, col. 590 D; cf. Catul. 68.115.
180	**Stygii regia . . . Iovis** = Ov. *Fast.* 5.448; cf. Eob. *Buc.* B 11.8, n.: "Stygio . . . Iovi."
	regia magna Iovis = *Epic. Drusi* 214.
181	**Ipse — tyranni** For this prediction of Christ's descent into hell, cf. Vulg. *Psa.* 106.16, a verse traditionally applied to the *descensus*. See especially *Nicod.* 21.1–3.
	degeneris . . . tyranni = *Eccles.* 405, referring to the pope.
	claustra tyranni = Andrel. *Livia* 1.4.35; cf. Juv. 8.261.
184	**gaudia quanta** = *Her. Chr.* 13.110, n.
185	**renovabitur — quietis** Cf. Verg. *Ecl.* 4.5; Mant. *1. Parthen.* 2.643–47 (quoted in n. to ll. 169–98 above); 3.144–45: "nova gaudia mundus / accipit et rerum melior contexitur ordo"; l. 196 below.
186	**Cessabunt — tubae** For the motif, cf. Ov. *Met.* 1.98; Calp. *Ecl.* 1.67–68; Boeth. *Consol.* 2.m5.16.
	curvae . . . tubae Prud. *Apoth.* 386: "tuba curva"; Eob. *Her. Chr.* 4.214: "tuba . . . unca"; cf. *Pug.* 27, n.: "tuba ductilis." However, the ancient Roman *tuba*, or war trumpet, had a straight tube; it was the *cornu*, or bugle, that was coiled: cf. Ov. *Met.* 1.98.
	bella sonare tubae ≈ Mart. 8.56.4.
187	**Impia . . . Rhoma** Sil. 5.601; Eob. *Her. Chr.* 12.240.
	preteritos . . . triumphos = Sid. *Carm.* 5.1.
	Rhoma triumphos = Mart. 7.6.7; 8.15.5.
188	**rapta — manu** Cf. Verg. *G.* 3.32; Eob. *Sylv. duae* 2.252.
189	**Omnis . . . populus** l. 115, n., above.
	odoratas . . . ad aras = *Her. Chr.* 2.117. The altars are sweet-smelling because of the burning incense. Cf. Hor. *Carm.* 3.18.7–8; Ov. *Met.* 15.574; *Pont.* 3.3.90 (with similar verse beginning); Vulg. *Exod.* 30.1–9.
190	**Martia . . . arma** = *Max.* 114; cf. *Her. Chr.* 12.165; *Luth.* 6.69. Cf. also *Pug.* 20, n.
191	**Scuta — peruret** For the sentiment, cf. Hor. *S.* 2.1.43; Ov. *Fast.* 4.925–26.
	Scuta — galeas Cf. Verg. *A.* 1.101; 8.539.
	mordax For the image, cf. Luc. 1.243.
192	**Contempto — ligo** Cf. Vulg. *Mich.* 4.3; also *Isa.* 2.4.
193	**arva coloni** = Verg. *G.* 1.125; Ov. *Met.* 11.33.
194	**Sponte sua** = Lucr. 2.1158; Verg. *Ecl.* 4.45; Ov. *Met.* 1.90 (all referring to the Golden Age, past or future); also Verg. *Ecl.* 8.106; *G.* 2.11, 47. The curse that rested on fields and farmers since the fall of Adam and Eve (Vulg. *Gen.* 3.17–19) will be lifted after the birth of the new Adam, Christ.

pinguis luxuriabit humus Cf. Ov. *Ep.* 1.54; *Ars* 1.360.

195   **rebus natura creatis** = Paul. Nol. *Carm.* 19.140.

196   **Ordo — erit** Cf. l. 185, n., above.

198   **incauto . . . ore** *Her. Chr.* 24.79.

        ore canit = Poliziano, *Eleg.* 6.20; cf. Ov. *Pont.* 4.10.76; Eob. *Sylv. duae*, lim. 8.

199   **Se tibi — orbis** *Ilias*, praef. 99: "Se tibi Romanus debere fatebitur orbis"; cf. *Her. Chr.* 1.62; 21.61, n.

201–02   **Attamen — cadet** Cf. *Leg. aurea* 6.49, 77.

201   **veniet tempus quo** = Sil. 3.584.

        tempus — omnis = *Wirt.* 514.

203   **Caetera — loquemur** Cf. Ov. *Ep.* 17.267; Eob. *Her. Chr.* 12.201–02; 15.203–04; 17.209–10; 21.177–78; 23.115; *Max.* 339; *Hod.* B 1.103.

        Caetera quae restant = *Her. Chr.* 12.201; *Sylv.* 2.8.27; *Venus* 2.306.

204   **corpore tectus** *Her. Chr.* 16.78.

205–06   **Interea — chori** Cf. ll. 107–08, n., above; also l. 138, n.

205   **pondus** For the sense of "unborn child," see *Laud.* B 3.11, n.

206   **angelici . . . chori** ≈ *Her. Chr.* 18.88, n.

207–08   **Iam — vale** Cf. *Tr.* 5.13.33–34; Ov. *Ep.* 20.242. For the play on the meaning of *vale*, cf. also Ov. *Ep.* 16.1–2: "salutem, / quae tribui sola te mihi dante potest." Here, of course, it has Christian implications; cf. Mary's response, Eob. *Her. Chr.* 2.127–28, n. For the similar play on *salus* in the salutation, see n. at *Her. Chr.* 3.1, below.

207   **brevis . . . epistola** = *Her. Chr.* 12.203.

        claudatur epistola ≈ Ov. *Ep.* 13.165.

208   **vale** The word also concludes Ov. *Ep.* 9.168; 20.242; 21.248; *Tr.* 3.3.88; 5.13.34; Eob. *Her. Chr.* 5.186; 9.166; 19.168; 22.168; 23.120; cf. *Her. Chr.* 15.217; 20.155. For the motif, cf. also Magdal. *Ep.* 125–26.

2

Meter: Elegiac distich.

1–2   **Quam — veni** Cf. Ov. *Ep.* 19.1–2; for l. 1, cf. also *Ep.* 4.1; *Met.* 9.530.

1   **Quam . . . salutem** *Her. Chr.* 1.1, n.; cf. *Her. Chr.* 3.1, n.

2   **Ut . . . possit . . . veni** *Her. Chr.* 12.280.

        possit habere = Ov. *Ars* 3.438; Eob. *Her. Chr.* 5.186.

3–4   **Littera — opus** Cf. Ov. *Tr.* 3.1.15–16.

3   **non convenit ista** ≈ *Sylv. duae* 2.203.

        lituris For the motif of the tearstained love letter, see Prop. 4.3.3–4; Ov. *Ep.* 3.3–4 (imitated in Magdal. *Ep.* 29–34); 15.97–98; cf. Eob. *Her. Chr.* 2.125; 3.92; 11.3–4; 12.1–2; 15.18; 16.215–16; 22.13–18. Ovid uses the motif also in his letters from exile: *Tr.* 1.1.13–14; 3.1.15–16; 4.1.95–96; 5.4.5–6. Cf. Eob. *Max.* 322.

4   **Hoc breve — opus** The verse contrasts with *Her. Chr.* 1.2.

        Hoc breve . . . opus = Ov. *Ep.* 15.4. Cf. Eob. *Her. Chr.* 7.74; *Sylv.* 1.1.4.

5–8   **Dextera — opus** For the sentiment, cf. Vulg. *Job* 9.14: "Quantus ergo sum ego ut respondeam [Deo], et loquar verbis meis cum eo?"

5   **Dextera . . . calamum . . . tenet** Ov. *Ep.* 11.3.

        calamum . . . labantem Petrarch, *Africa* 1.68: "calamumque labantem / Firmabis."

7   **humilis . . . virgo** Mant. *1. Parthen.* 2.655.

        magno . . . Tonanti = Stat. *Theb.* 11.496; V. Fl. 4.119; Eob. *Her. Chr.* 19.35; cf. Ov. *Met.* 1.170; 2.466.

        virgo Tonanti ≈ Mart. 6.10.9; Eob. *Hod.* B 7.33.

8   **Quam — opus** Cf. *Psalt.*, ded. 34: "Aggressus maius quam decuisset opus."

        mens mea, maius = Ov. *Ep.* 12.212; Eob. *Her. Chr.* 4.46; cf. *Buc.* 3.136, n.

        maius opus = Ov. *Am.* 3.1.24; *Fast.* 5.568.

9–10   **Cor — timor** Cf. *Buc.* 7.154–58, describing the symptoms of timid love.
9   **Cor pavet** = Ov. *Ep.* 14.17.
     attonito . . . in ore Ov. *Tr.* 3.9.18 (in one ms. tradition): "pallor in attonito virginis ore sedet."
     rubor . . . in ore *Nup.* 199, n.
10   **hinc amor, inde timor** Cf. Ov. *Ep.* 12.61; Eob. *Her. Chr.* 5.128.
12   **Maiestas — est** Cf. Ov. *Tr.* 2.512; *Pont.* 2.8.30; Eob. *Her.* 3.1.116, of the Christ child: "Iam tua maiestas visa stupenda mihi est."
13   **Princeps ter maxime** *Hod.* 125 (addressing a cardinal). Cf. Brant, *Var. carm.*, sig. D1ᵛ (*Texte* 96.5), of St. Sebastian: "ter maxime martyr"; Gianfrancesco Pico della Mirandola, "Staurostichon," in his *Opera omnia* (1557; repr. Hildesheim, 1969), 355: "ter maxime Caesar"; Eob. *Eccles.* 89 (the pope); *Accl.* 1.27: "ter maxime Caesar"; *Her.* 3.9.109: "Caesar ter maximus Aemilianus."
14   **Da veniam si** = *Her. Chr.* 19.60; cf. Ov. *Ep.* 4.156; 7.105; 17.225; and often; Eob. *Her. Chr.* 3.168; 6.68; 8.78; 24.84.
     audet amans = Celtis, *Am.* 3.5.12; 4.8.38.
15   **Et facis — alter** Cf. Ov. *Tr.* 2.41, addressing Caesar Augustus; Eob. *Sylv.* 1.1.115, to King Sigismund: "Et potes, et non est regum te fortior alter." For the idiom, cf. *Buc.* 2.105–06, n.
16   **Audaces — tua** Modeled on Ov. *Ep.* 20.54.
17   **Tu facis ut** = Ov. *Met.* 7.819; *Tr.* 1.6.7.
     precibus . . . iustis = Ov. *Met.* 1.377; cf. *Met.* 3.406; Eob. *Her. Chr.* 2.118; 16.260; *Hymn.* 146.
18   **incerto — mari** Cf. Hor. *Epod.* 9.32; Claud. *Carm. minora* 23.4: "Ionio credam turgida vela mari"; Eob. *Her.* 2.7.14: "Iussa paras dubio credere vela mari; *Accl.* 1.74: ". . . dubio credita vela mari."
19   **Martius . . . miles** Ov. *Met.* 14.798–99.
20   **Non — globis** Cf. Marul. *Epigr.* 3.37.34: "[miles] . . . adversum non timet ire globos." **armatis . . . globis** Sil. 15.370.
21   **cuncta . . . pericula** = Luc. 5.577.
22   **gentiles . . . deos** *Her. Chr.* 10.11.
     non — deos = Prop. 2.29.12; Ov. *Rem.* 784; Eob. *Her. Chr.* 19.148; cf. *Her. Chr.* 10.142; 19.32, n.; 21.110; *Hymn.* B 6.2.
23–28   **Iure — nihil** Modeled on Ov. *Tr.* 2.37–38.
23   **machina caeli** = Stat. *Theb.* 7.812; 8.310; *Silv.* 3.1.181.
24   **Quicquid — habet** = *Val.* 2.68; cf. Ov. *Tr.* 3.4.54; *Pont.* 4.8.54; Mart. 10.80.6.
25   **regnum — orbis** Cf. Mant. *Calam.* 1.6 (p. 19): "Summe Deum, decimus regnum cui terminat orbis."
     regnum — terminat Cf. *Buc.* 1.72–73, n.
26   **Si posset — tui** Cf. Vulg. *Bar.* 3.25; Arator 1.185: "Deus omnipotens, cui numquam terminus instat."
27   **mundus . . . adorat** *Her. Chr.* 3.61, n.
     reverenter adorat = *Vict.* 286; cf. *Her. Chr.* 17.245; Mant. *Calam.* 3.454 (p. 82): "Patrem . . . reverenter adoret"; *Georg.*, fol. 208ʳ: ". . . reverenter adorant."
28   **Te — nihil** Cf. Ov. *Tr.* 4.8.38; 5.2.38; 5.8.25–26; Eob. *Her. Chr.* 10.110; *Hod.* B 1.64.
29   **Sic ipse iubebas** Mary alludes to Emmanuel's words of comfort in *Her. Chr.* 1.3.
     ipse iubebas = Prud. *Perist.* 9.73.
30   **Fas homini . . . est** Ov. *Tr.* 5.2.46.
31–32   **Sic — Ave** Cf. *Her. Chr.* 1.5–6, with nn.; 16.81–82.
31   **Sic . . . ille monebat** *Buc.* 7.172, n.
     iuvenum — ille Stat. *Silv.* 2.6.71; cf. Ov. *Met.* 4.55.
32   **falso pectore** = Locher, *Stult.* 99, fol. 116ᵛ: "Qui Christi falso pectore sacra colunt."
33–74   **Iam — habet** Eobanus closely follows Mant. *1. Parthen.* 2.466–667, in phrasing and motifs: After sunset Mary locks her room and meditates on Isaiah's prophecy. She

now bursts out in a praise of the blessed Virgin. Gabriel suddenly appears and tells her not to be afraid. After the Annunciation, Mary humbly accepts her role as Mother of God. She miraculously conceives, and her womb begins to swell.

33–34   **Iam — erat** The Annunciation traditionally took place at dusk: cf. Hrabanus Maurus, *Allegoriae in universam sacram scripturam, PL* 112, col. 1076 C: "*Vespere* est tempus incarnationis"; Stephan Beissel, *Geschichte der Verehrung Marias im 16. und 17. Jahrhundert* (1910; repr. Nieuwkoop, 1970), 31–32. In *Her. Chr.* 13.57–58, Eobanus extends this tradition to Gabriel's appearance to Mary's mother Anna.

33   **Iam super Oceanum** = Ov. *Am.* 1.13.1.

     madido . . . crine The sun god is now so low above the horizon that his locks are already touching the ocean waves: for the image, cf. Stat. *Theb.* 3.407–09; also cf. Ov. *Met.* 5.440.

34   **Flammiferae noctis** Luc. 5.402.

     noctis nuncius Sen. *Phaed.* 750.

35   **Sola fui** = *Her. Chr.* 7.63; 11.83; cf. *Her. Chr.* 4.150.

     thalamumque — coegi The locked room, paralleling the *hortus conclusus* of Vulg. *Cant.* 4.12, is symbolic of Mary's virginity: cf. Eob. *Buc.* 11.31, n.; also cf. l. 64, n., and l. 92 below. For the motif, see, for example, *AH* 26.14, In 1. Vesperis 5: "Intrat clausum vultu claro / Virginale thalamum, / Ave dicit verbo caro / Super omne balsamum"; 26.16, In 2. Nocturno, Antiphonae 3: "Conclusus est thalamus / . . . / Ubi archangelus Gabriel / Descendebat de caelo."

36   **Solimi carmina vatis** *Calum.* 7; cf. *Her. Chr.* 1.35.

     carmina vatis = "In poema Davidis elegiaca commendatio" 16, in *Thomae Vvolphii Iunioris In Psalmum tercium et trigesimum expositio* (Erfurt, 1507), sig. a2ᵛ: "Quicquid Iessaei carmina vatis habent"; cf. *Her. Chr.* 21.39, n.

38   **Docta — viri** Mant. *1. Parthen.* 1.618–31 describes how Mary studies the prophets Isaiah and Jeremiah and the rest of the Old Testament.

     mystica sacra = Ov. *Ep.* 2.42 (of mystical rites); Mant. *2. Parthen.* 3.847.

39   **Nascere . . . age** = Verg. *Ecl.* 8.17.

     Nascere — parens Cf. Mart. 6.3.2.

     magna parens = Verg. *G.* 2.173.

     Foelix — ortus = *Theoc.* 17.101: "Euge, beate puer, foelix age fulgeat ortus." For the play on the two senses of *ortus* ("birth" and "rising of a star"), cf. Mant. *Bapt.*, fol. 229ᵛ: "Vade prior, praecede meos, nove Lucifer, ortus"; Eob. *Her. Chr.* 24.65–66. Underlying the wordplay are some traditional images likening Mary to a star, the sun, or "the light of the world." For Mary as a star, see Salzer, 399–418; Eob. *Buc.* 11.55, nn.; for Mary as a sun, see Salzer, 391–99; Eob. *Hod.* B 7.26.

40   **Afflictibus — opem** Cf. *Her. Chr.* 1.37; *Theoc.* 27.8: "Gentibus afflictis requiem pacemque dedisti."

     affer opem = *Her. Chr.* 10.194, n.; 11.166, n.

41   **O mihi si liceat** = Claud. *IV. Cons. Hon.* 650; cf. Mant. *1. Parthen.* 2.575–76: "Oh, mihi, si tantum non est audere superbum, / conceptus liceatque tuos vultusque tueri!"

     quacunque — es Cf. Mant. *1. Parthen.* 2.563, where Mary exclaims in praise of the future Mother of God: "O felix nimium, . . . quaecumque futura es."

42   **Aptaram — manus** Cf. Ov. *Am.* 1.13.14; *Ep.* 20.78; Eob. *Her. Chr.* 12.22, n.; *Sylv.* 1.1.168: "Et feret auctrices ad tua facta manus."

     famulas . . . manus = *Her. Chr.* 5.148; cf. Sil. 10.646; Eob. *Her. Chr.* 8.34; 16.264.

     ad tua — manus = Maxim. 5.130; cf. Mant. *Votum*, fol. 54ᵛ, in praise of Mary: "Caelestes volitant ad tua iussa chori."

43   **Quae — maior** Cf. Hor. *Carm.* 1.16.1; Eob. *Her.* 2.3.80 (the angel announces the birth of Mary): "Sic te quam paries filia maior erit."

     te digna manet = Verg. *G.* 1.168; Eob. *Her. Chr.* 6.133.

44   **Nulla — tuas** It is a commonplace in the praises of Mary that she can never be praised enough: see Salzer, 437–43.

	laudes . . . tuas = Ov. *Fast.* 5.188; *Tr.* 5.3.4.
	lingua referre = Ov. *Ep.* 13.122.
45–46	**O et — Gloria** Cf. Ov. *Met.* 14.832–33.
45	**foeminei . . . pudoris** *Rec.* 157.

sine labe pudoris = *Epp. 4*, sig. F4ʳ (25 May 1508); cf. l. 74, n., below.
sine labe = Ov. *Ep.* 17.69; *Met.* 2.537; *Fast.* 4.335; et al.; Eob. *Her. Chr.* 8.139; 11.111; 24.157; B 1.61; cf. *Sylv. duae* 1.150, n.
labe pudoris Sen. *Phaed.* 893; V. Fl. 7.386.

46 **spes** *Buc.* 11.54, n.
manet For the incongruity of the single verb and plural subjects, cf. *Her. Chr.* 9.131.

47 **mundi Opifex** Cic. *N. D.* 1.18; Prud. *Amart.* 116. The idea of God as craftsman-maker, or Demiurge, is ancient: see Curtius, *ELLMA*, 544–46; Eob. *Her. Chr.* 4.31–32; *Nob.* 25, n.
imple — vatum Cf. *Her. Chr.* 1.35, n.
praesagia vatum = Ov. *Pont.* 3.4.89; Eob. *Her. Chr.* 16.261.

48 **Pondere . . . fiat . . . parens** Cf. *Her. Chr.* 13.4. For *pondus* in the sense of "unborn child," see *Laud.* B 3.11, n.
foelix . . . parens = Ov. *Fast.* 6.560.

49–50 **Fama — deos** Cf. *Her. Chr.* 1.149–50 (with n. 13).

49 **Iovem falsum** ≈ Mant. *1. Parthen.* 1.575; cf. Erasmus, *Carm.* 42.17; Eob. *Her. Chr.* 4.73, 208; 12.228; 18.94; cf. also *Her. Chr.* 6.168.

50 **tot — deos** Cf. Prud. *c. Symm.* 1.452: "credere monstra deos"; *Perist.* 1.69: "vobis monstra divos fingitis"; Eob. *Her. Chr.* 9.67; *Sylv.* 1.10.15–16: "Prisca deos coluit lapides et ligna vetustas / Et tot fictitios, nil nisi monstra, Ioves."

51 **De virgine nasci** = Gunther, *Lig.* 5.157; Eob. *Her. Chr.* 8.93.

53 **mentis . . . recessu** Pers. 2.73–74.

54 **nuncius ales** = Ov. *Ep.* 16.68; Eob. *Her. Chr.* 16.82. Cf. *Her. Chr.* 1.4, n.; 1.5, n.; 1.163.

55–60 **Qualis — Fulsit** Cf. Mant. *7. Parthen.*, fol. 151ʳ: "alis / Angelus explicitis discussa apparuit aura, / Ore refulgenti, qualem Latonida Lunam / Cernimus, opposito cum fulget Apolline tota, / Qualis et ipse novus roseo cum surgit ab ortu / Phoebus, in extremo visum qui terminat orbe. / Diffusae per colla comae (fila aurea dicas) / Applaudunt humeris, auro toga lucida plantas / Influit. Hoc habitu venit paranymphus et ore." Cf. also Eob. *Her. Chr.* 3.75–78; 13.61–66.

55 **purpureum . . . colorem** = Ov. *Met.* 3.485.
Aurora colorem = Mant. *Calam.* 3.300 (p. 78): "roseum surgens aurora colorem / Explicat."

56 **Qualis — aqua** Cf. Ov. *Fast.* 6.474; *Pont.* 2.5.50; Ven. Fort. *Carm.* 3.9.4: "qui vagus Oceanas exit . . . aquas."
Oceana . . . aqua = *Her. Chr.* 12.74; cf. *Her. Chr.* 24.22.

57 **Talis erat** = Verg. *A.* 1.503; 6.208; Ov. *Am.* 1.2.47; *Ars* 2.7; et al.; Eob. *Her. Chr.* 7.85.
niveo . . . velatus amictu ≈ Paul. Nol. *Carm.* 18.19: "niveo tellus velatur amictu"; cf. Ov. *Fast.* 3.363; Eob. *Sylv. duae* 2.197, n.; *Her. Chr.* 3.77–78. For the scriptural basis of this description, see Vulg. *Matt.* 28.3.

58 **non potuisse liquet** = *Her. Chr.* 12.254.

59 **Aurea caesaries** = Verg. *A.* 8.659.
caesaries — complexa Cf. Sen. *Phaed.* 801–02 (of Phoebus): "caesaries . . . / perfundens umeros ornat et integit"; Eob. *Buc.* 7.112, n.
humeros . . . comantes Cf. Stat. *Silv.* 1.2.2.

60 **pacis oliva** = Brant, "Pacis in Germanicum Martem nenia," *Texte* 266.28: "Serta mihi texit, pacis oliva comes." Cf. AH 27.203.10 (after Noah's Flood): "Ramum missa ferens ore columba, / Ramum paciferae munus olivae." Just as the second dove brought a leafy olive branch to Noah to show that the flood was over and a new age of the world was at hand (Vulg. *Gen.* 8.10–11), so now the Archangel Gabriel carries an olive branch to Mary to signal that a new era of salvation is dawning. The olive branch, of course, is

also an old symbol of peace: see, for example, Verg. *A.* 8.116; Stat. *Ach.* 1.727. The idea of having Gabriel bear an olive branch at the Annunciation recurs in late medieval paintings. Eobanus' immediate model, however, was Erasmus, *Carm.* 50.153–56, in praise of Gabriel: "Noster, o salve, bone pacifer, qui / Surculum adportans oleae virentem / Nuncias primus meliora mersis / Saecula terris."

61–66 **Qui simul — erit** Cf. Vulg. *Luc.* 1.28–30.

61 **Qui simul — obortas** Cf. *Nativ. Mariae* 9.2: "ingressus [angelus] ad eam cubiculum quidem ubi manebat ingenti lumine perfudit." Cf. Ov. *Met.* 3.177; 11.616: "Quo simul intravit . . . / . . . , vestis fulgore reluxit / sacra domus."

 tenebrasque . . . obortas ≈ Ov. *Ep.* 13.23 (in a figurative sense).

 tenebras . . . removit Prud. *Apoth.* 678.

62 **Curvato — "Ave"** Cf. Eobanus' letter to Joachim Vadianus (20 March 1514) in *Die Vadianische Briefsammlung der Stadtbibliothek St. Gallen*, ed. Emil Arbenz, vol. 1 (St. Gallen, 1890), no. 31: "Mandatum flexo poplite profer 'Ave.'"

 Curvato . . . poplite = *Her. Chr.* 15.122; cf. Mant. *1. Parthen.* 1.468.

63 **Obstupui — abstulit** Cf. Ov. *Ep.* 16.67–68; Verg. *A.* 2.774; 3.48; Eob. *Her. Chr.* 4.127. For *obstupui* at the hexameter opening, see *Buc.* 4.104, n.

 Vocem — abstulit Cf. Ov. *Met.* 14.177–78; [Sen.] *Oct.* 736: "continet vocem timor."

64 **clausas — fores** The angel's passing through a closed door is intended to remind the reader of Vulg. *Ezech.* 44.1–4, where God passes through the closed door of the Temple — traditionally interpreted as foreshadowing the incarnation: see Salzer, 26–28 and 117 (with n. 7). Cf. l. 35, n., above.

 clausas . . . fores = Tib. 1.9.44; Ov. *Ars* 2.704; *Fast.* 4.110; *Tr.* 2.460; 3.2.30; Eob. *Her. Chr.* 6.202, n.

67–70 **Docta — vide** Cf. Vulg. *Luc.* 1.38; Mant. *1. Parthen.* 2.655–57: "humilis firmato pectore Virgo, / 'Imperio,' dixit, 'magni parere Tonantis / cogimur'; et miti curvans caput annuit ore."

68 **Pareo mandatis . . . tuis** = *Epp. 1*, sig. O2ᵛ: "Pareo mandatis, dulcis amice, tuis." The term *mandata* occurs in this context also in Mant. *1. Parthen.* 2.594 (Gabriel speaking): "venio tibi . . . / aeterni iucunda ferens mandata Tonantis."

 Orbifer In this sense the word is a neologism.

69 **tua regna** Cf. Verg. *Ecl.* 1.69; Eob. *Her. Chr.* 17.177.

 voluminis orbes Cf. Busch. *Lips.* 398: ". . . super octavae flammata volumina sphaerae"; Eob. *Her. Chr.* 19.135, n.

70 **Mitibus . . . oculis** V. Max. 1.8.2.

72 **Sollicitas . . . preces** Ov. *Pont.* 3.1.148.

 Gloria nostra = Ov. *Rem.* 466; *Pont.* 1.7.20.

73–74 **Dum — Pondere** Cf. Mant. *1. Parthen.* 2.661–62: "Tum divina gravem subitis conceptibus alvum / extulit atque sinus soboles extendit onustos."

73 **Dum loquor, ecce** = Mart. 10.37.17; Eob. *Her. Chr.* 20.19; cf. Ov. *Am.* 1.11.15; 3.2.41; 3.6.85; and often: "dum loquor . . ."; Eob. *Her. Chr.* 21.163, 175.

74 **laesi — habet** Cf. Ov. *Ars* 1.100; Celtis, *Am.* 3.6.6: ". . . facies laesi signa pudoris habet"; also cf. l. 45 above.

 laesi . . . pudoris Ov. *Ep.* 7.97; *Met.* 2.450; 7.751.

75–76 **Ergo ego, quam . . . ipsa fui?** Cf. Ov. *Met.* 9.513–14.

75 **toto . . . corde** Ov. *Ep.* 19.156.

77 **Ipsa — placui** ≈ Ov. *Pont.* 4.1.13.

 Votis . . . peractis Juv. 10.6.

78 **Excidit — suas** The model is Mant. *1. Parthen.* 2.584 (after Mary meditates on the future Mother of God): "in laudes ignara suas prorumpit."

 in laudes . . . suas = Ov. *Pont.* 3.2.34.

 inscia lingua = Ov. *Ep.* 21.2.

79 **mundo . . . iacenti** = *Her. Chr.* 6.139.

80 **in terras ducere . . . Deum** = *Her.* 1.5.94; cf. *Buc.* 11.45–46, n.

82 **te iudice — fui** Cf. Ov. *Tr.* 4.4.30.

83   **Te mea — movit** Cf. Ov. *Ep.* 17.180: ". . . tua me, te mea forma capit." Mary's sub-
      stitution of *claementia* for *forma* in Ovid's verse is deliberate, for in the next line she
      assures God that physical beauty (*forma*) can have no place in their love.
      Te mea virginitas Cf. Mant. *1. Parthen.* 1.806: "Me mea virginitas. . . ." Also cf. Ov.
      Ep. 2.115; 17.104; *Met.* 6.536; 14.133; Eob. *Her. Chr.* 7.13.

84–86 **Non — iuvat** Cf. *Her. Chr.* 4.191–94. For Mary's beauty, cf. *Buc.* 11.41–44, nn.

84   **Non . . . noster amor** = Ov. *Ep.* 18.156.
      Non agitur = Ov. *Ep.* 15.72.
      forma . . . amor = Ov. *Ep.* 6.94.
      noster amor = Ov. *Ep.* 17.246; 18.150; Eob. *Her. Chr.* 3.166; 8.68; 17.152; cf. *Her.
      Chr.* 1.29, n.

85   **pulcherrime rerum** = Ov. *Ep.* 4.125; *Ars* 1.213; *Met.* 8.49 (in some mss.). God is
      often addressed as "the most beautiful one": see, for example, August. *Confessiones*
      1.4.4: "pulcherrime"; 1.7.12: "formosissime"; Boeth. *Consol.* 3.m9.7: "pulcherrimus";
      Erasmus, *Carm.* 43.11 (Christ). Cf. Vulg. *Psa.* 44.3, traditionally applied to Christ:
      "speciosus forma prae filiis hominum."
      mentis facie Paul. Nol. *Carm.* 27.600; *Ep.* 23.10.

86   **qualibet arte** = Ov. *Ars* 1.612; *Rem.* 34; Eob. *Her. Chr.* 4.196, n.
      arte, iuvat = Ov. *Pont.* 1.5.36.

87   **Est — Deo** Cf. Ov. *Fast.* 6.27.
      Est aliquid = *Buc.* 10.56, n.
      super omnia matrem ≈ Ven. Fort. *Carminum spuriorum app.* 1.203 (referring to Mary):
      "O virgo excellens, vincens super omnia matres." The thought is based on Vulg. *Luc.* 1.42.
      super omnia = Verg. *A.* 8.303; 9.283; Ov. *Met.* 6.526; 8.677; Eob. *Her. Chr.* 3.95;
      9.121.

88   **Hoc meriti . . . pondus habet** Cf. Ov. *Ep.* 2.30.
      non leve — habet Cf. Ov. *Fast.* 3.230; *Pont.* 1.7.50; 2.8.54; Eob. *Her. Chr.* 5.186.

89–96 **Scribis — fuit** Cf. *Her. Chr.* 1.139–46.

89   **Scribis ut** = Ov. *Ep.* 21.207; *Tr.* 5.12.1.
      a primis . . . annis = *Idyl.* 1.46; cf. *Laud.* 557, n.: "primis . . . ab annis."
      mecum Deus Cf. *Her. Chr.* 1.155.

90   **non habitura locum** = *Her. Chr.* 24.58, n.

91   **ardentes . . . ad aras** = *Buc.* 11.60, n.

91–92 **venerabar . . . legerem** Note the shift from the indicative to the subjunctive, for
      metrical reasons.

92   **Seu — domo** Cf. ll. 35–36 above.

93   **oculis hominum** = Ov. *Ep.* 17.125.

96   **cura placere** = Ov. *Ars* 3.380.

97   **Ah — aliqua** Cf. *Her. Chr.* 16.179.
      Ah quoties = *Her. Chr.* 1.43, n.

98   **effluxo . . . sinu** Cf. Verg. *A.* 1.320.
      lapsa sinu = Mart. 1.15.10.

99   **Caelestes adii . . . recessus** Cf. Ov. *Met.* 15.63; Mant. *1. Parthen.* 2.539–54; Eob.
      Vict. 264, 485. For the commonplace, see *Sylv. duae* 1.3–16, n.; *Her. Chr.* 16.253–54.

100   **Tu mihi . . . tu mihi** = Ov. *Ep.* 13.104.
      tuta quies = Sabell. *In natal.* 13, sig. C3ᵛ, addressing the Virgin: "Per te tuta quies,
      per te sunt ocia terris."
      tu mihi . . . eras = Ov. *Ep.* 3.52; *Rem.* 464; *Pont.* 1.7.22.

101–02 **Iusserat — decus** Cf. Mant. *1. Parthen.* 1.690–780.

101   **Anna parens** = *Her. Chr.* 20.151; cf. *AH* 43.119.1: "Salve, parens Anna";
      Agricola, *Anna,* 297 (opening verse): "Anna parens, summae genitrix veneranda
      parentis."

102   **Legitimo . . . fine** Ov. *Ars* 1.282 (in a different sense).
      summum . . . decus = Mant. *c. Am.,* fol. 178ʳ.
      claudere fine = *Sylv. duae* 1.98, n.

103   **foecundam prole** = Mant. *1. Parthen.* 2.724: "sera fecundam prole parentem."
104   **non — semine** Cf. *Buc.* 5.69; *Her. Chr.* 22.18.
       mortali semine Ov. *Met.* 15.760.
105–06   **Quam — viro** For the legends about Mary's marriage to the old, but chaste, Joseph, see *Nativ. Mariae* 7–8; *Ps.-Matt.* 7–8; *Leg. aurea* 127.
       Quam bene . . . Quod non sum Cf. Ov. *Tr.* 1.2.41.
105   **Quam bene** = *Buc.* B 2.25, n.
       virgine mentem = Sil. 2.168.
106   **cupido — viro** Cf. [Tib.] 3.4.52; Eob. *Her. Chr.* 5.2.
107–08   **Ad tua — choros** Cf. *Her. Chr.* 1.135–37, with n. 12.
107   **Ad tua — altaria** Cf. Verg. *A.* 1.666; Mant. *Votum,* fol. 54ʳ: "Ad tua confugio supplex altaria, Virgo."
108   **Virgineos inter . . . choros** = Tifernate, *Carm.,* sig. D2ʳ: "Virgineos inter virgo recepte choros"; cf. Mant. *1. Parthen.* 1.679: "virgineos inter coetus comitesque puellas."
       parva ministra = Sabell. *In natal.* 7, sig. b2ᵛ: "Constitit ante ipsum parva ministra tholum"; 8, sig. b3ᵛ: "Placabatque suos parva ministra lares."
109   **Nunc — lustrum** According to tradition, Mary was fourteen when she was betrothed to Joseph: see *Nativ. Mariae* 7.3; *Ps.-Matt.* 8.1; *Leg. aurea* 127.68. The Annunciation occurred not long thereafter.
110   **primaevo — iuventa** Cf. Verg. *A.* 7.162; Sil. 1.376; Eob. *Her. Chr.* 10.29; 16.270.
111   **paritura nepotem** ≈ Stat. *Ach.* 1.656.
112   **flos** Cf. Vulg. *Isa.* 11.1, traditionally associated with Mary and Jesus.
113   **Sed — nosti** Cf. Ov. *Ep.* 9.143; Calp. *Ecl.* 3.65. For the motif, cf. also *Magdal. Ep.* 9–10; ll. 119–20 below.
114   **Omne — usquam** = *Val.* 1.580; cf. Ov. *Met.* 12.41; l. 127, n., below.
115   **licet videas** = Ov. *Fast.* 3.837.
       omnia noris ≈ Ov. *Pont.* 1.2.71.
116   **dici — iuvat** Cf. Ov. *Tr.* 2.69–70; Eob. *Her. Chr.* 3.60, n.
       dici . . . tua facta Cf. Verg. *Ecl.* 4.54; 8.8.
117   **odoratas . . . ad aras** = *Her. Chr.* 1.189, n.
118   **facili — preces** Cf. Mant. *Mort.,* fol. 123ʳ: "Quam facili nostras audiat aure preces"; Eob. *Psalt.* 1.26: ". . . avida iustas percipit aure preces"; 28.14: ". . . facili nostras accipis aure preces."
       iustas . . . preces = *Her. Chr.* 16.260; cf. l. 17, n., above.
119–20   **Si tamen — erit** For the motif, cf. l. 113, n., above.
120   **nuda papyrus** *Her. Chr.* 15.23.
122   **posse docere Deum** = *Her. Chr.* 10.10; cf. *Her. Chr.* 8.146.
123   **Clause — carnis** Cf. *Her. Chr.* 6.25, n.; *Vict.* 53; *Hod.* 441–42.
       lutea Cf. Vulg. *Gen.* 2.7; *Job* 4.19; 10.9; 33.6; *Rom.* 9.21; Prud. *Cath.* 3.138; *Apoth.* 1022; Eob. *Sylv. duae* 1.14 (with n. to ll. 13–14); *Her. Chr.* 21.68.
       testudine carnis August. *Quaestiones XVI in Matthaeum* 12. The image goes back to Plato, *Phdr.* 250c.
125   **scriptas . . . lituras** *Sylv.* 2.7.19 (spring 1514?): "Et scriptas forsan misisti saepe lituras." In that poem Eobanus uses *lituras* to mean "letters" — a medievalism.
       utcunque lituras = *Her. Chr.* 23.37.
126   **parva — sophos** The Munich and Münster copies offer the ms. gloss: "in humili puella. magna sapientia."
       parva virgine = Catul. 66.26; cf. Eob. *Her. Chr.* 12.149.
       grande sophos Mart. 1.3.7 and 6.48.1, where the phrase means "a mighty 'bravo.'" Here Eobanus uses *sophos* in the Greek sense of "wisdom." Cf. Locher, *Katherina* 104: "Omne sophos quondam claris quod fulsit Athenis"; Brant, *Var. carm.,* sig. k5ᵛ (*Texte* 189.55): "Cuius ab ingenio sophos et prudentia fluxit."
127–28   **Non precor — fave** Mary alludes to and varies the conclusion of Emmanuel's letter. Cf. *Magdal. Ep.* 125–26, with a similar request for the *vale* that the writer herself cannot send.

127   **Non precor ut** = Ov. *Tr.* 2.183; Eob. *Her. Chr.* 10.185.
             omne — est = Juv. 8.122; cf. l. 114, n., above.
128   **possit ut esse** = Ov. *Pont.* 1.10.18.

3

For the history of the Mary Magdalene theme, see Hans Hansel, *Die Maria-Magdalena-Legende: Eine Quellenuntersuchung* (Greifswald, 1937); Helen M. Garth, *Saint Mary Magdalene in Mediaeval Literature* (Baltimore, 1950); Victor Saxer, *Le culte de Marie Madeleine en occident des origines à la fin du moyen âge,* 2 vols. (Auxerre, 1959); Susan Haskins, *Mary Magdalen: Myth and Metaphor* (New York, 1993); Madeleine Boxler, *"ich bin ein predigerin und appostlorin": Die deutschen Maria Magdalena-Legenden des Mittelalters (1300–1550), Untersuchungen und Texte* (Bern, 1996); *VL* 5, cols. 1258–64; and Laurence Beck-Chauvard, "La déréliction: L'esthétique de la lamentation amoureuse de la latinité profane à la modernité chrétienne," 2 vols., doctoral thesis, Université de Paris IV-Sorbonne, 1999 — a dissertation inspired by a reading of the present poem.

Eobanus' immediate model was Jacobus Magdalius Gaudensis' heroic epistle, "Epistola Dive Marie Magdalene ad Christum in infirmitate Lazari fratris," *Erarium aureum poetarum* (Cologne, 1501), sig. H2ʳ–H3ʳ. See the introduction, pp. 110–20 above.

A critical text of the 1539 redaction, with introduction, translation, and commentary, appeared in Harry Vredeveld, "Der heroische Brief 'Maria Magdalena Iesu Christo' aus den 'Heroidum libri tres' des Helius Eobanus Hessus (1488–1540)," *Daphnis* 6 (1977), 65–90; partially reprinted in *Deutsche Literatur des 16. Jahrhunderts,* ed. A. Elschenbroich (Munich, 1981), 1:246–55; 2:1129–33. A somewhat abbreviated text of the letter, with an introduction and translation, was printed according to the 1539 version in *Musae reduces: Anthologie de la poésie latine dans l'Europe de la Renaissance,* ed. and trans. Pierre Laurens (Leiden, 1975), 1:399–409; that text was reprinted in Laurence Beck-Chauvard, "La déréliction," 2:141–44. A much more truncated text appeared in *Anthologie de la poésie lyrique latine de la Renaissance,* ed. and trans. Pierre Laurens ([Paris], 2004), 184–89. Beck-Chauvard's previously-mentioned dissertation discusses this "magnifique poème" in 1:248–52, 366–71. The analysis is based solely on the 1539 redaction, as abbreviated in *Musae reduces.* On 368–69 the author notes the poem's unmistakable influence on Pierre Campson's *Comoedia tragica, quae inscribitur Magdalena evangelica* (Antwerp, 1546).

Meter: Elegiac distich.

1   **largitus es . . . salutem** Cf. Juvenc. 2.560, where Jesus says: "humili dulcem largitur
             corde salutem."
             salutem For the play on the two meanings of *salus* ("greetings" and "welfare"), cf. Ov.
             Ep. 4.1–2; 16.1–2; *Met.* 9.530–31; *Tr.* 5.13.1–2; *Pont.* 1.10.1–2. In borrowing the
             wordplay from Ovid, Eobanus invests it with Christian meaning, so that *salus* also means
             "salvation": cf. *Her. Chr.* 1.1; 2.1; 6.1; 11.1; 18.1. In this he follows Magdal. *Ep.* 6–8.
3–4   **Regna — erat** The model is Ov. *Ep.* 1.3–4.
3   **Stygio . . . profundo** ≈ Mant. *Calam.* 1.359 (p. 28): "Stygii faex ima profundi"; cf.
             Calam. 1.220 (p. 24): ". . . Stygio rabies egressa profundo."
4   **aliquis** A ms. gloss in the Munich and Münster copies adds the word "patrum."
5   **apud manes** = Ov. *Met.* 1.586.
             quem — hostem Cf. Ov. *Tr.* 2.49; Sil. 7.510; 8.15.
6   **apud superos** = Luc. 7.113; Sil. 13.665, 777.
             garrula Fama = Celtis, *Am.* 1.10.14; 1.13.10; cf. Sen. *Her. F.* 193–94.
7   **Vicisti . . . victa . . . victor** For the play on the root of *vincere,* cf., for example, Ov.
             Ep. 9.2, 70; *Met.* 3.95; 8.56–57; 12.608–09; Eob. *Laud.* 223–24; *Her. Chr.* 3.60–64;
             Hymn. 11–12, 150.
8   **Plurimaque — tuos** See Vulg. *Matt.* 27.52–53.
             Plurima . . . turba Verg. *A.* 6.667; Eob. *Her. Chr.* 4.222.
             turba sequta tuos = Ov. *Tr.* 2.88; cf. Prop. 3.1.12; Ov. *Am.* 1.2.36; l. 24 below.

9   **longa . . . morte** Verg. *A.* 8.488.
            de morte reversus ≈ Stat. *Silv.* 5.1.172.
11–26   **Est — habent** The doctrine of Christ's descent into hell goes back to several New
            Testament passages, particularly Vulg. *Act.* 2.31; *Rom.* 10.7; *Eph.* 4.9; *1. Petr.* 3.19
            and 4.6. Patristic authors speculated that Christ went down to hell to preach to the
            spirits of the damned and to release the souls of the Old Testament saints from their
            prison, the limbus patrum (cf. Eob. *Her. Chr.* 1.37–38, 79–90). The fullest and most
            influential telling of the Harrowing of Hell is the one given in the apocryphal *Gospel
            of Nicodemus*, retold, for example, in *Leg. aurea* 52. See *The Medieval* Gospel of
            Nicodemus: *Texts, Intertexts, and Contexts in Western Europe,* ed. Zbigniew Izydorczyk
            (Tempe, AZ, 1997). For the development of the doctrine, see J. A. MacCulloch, *The
            Harrowing of Hell* (Edinburgh, 1930); Josef Kroll, *Gott und Hölle: Der Mythos vom
            Descensuskampfe* (Leipzig, 1932); Heinz-Jürgen Vogels, *Christi Abstieg ins Totenreich
            und das Läuterungsgericht an den Toten* (Freiburg, 1976).
                 The first Neo-Latin retelling of the story was Macario Muzio's *De triumpho
            Christi,* an epyllion first published at Venice in 1499 and frequently reprinted.
            (Eobanus alludes to the book's preface at *Her. Chr.,* ded. 11.4.) Erasmus imitated the
            poem in *Carm.* 112, written in 1499, but not published until 1706. Other imitations
            followed: Paulus Crosnensis with a sapphic *De inferorum vastatione et triumpho
            Christi* (*Carm.* 53), published at Cracow in 1513; Mathias Funck with his short epic
            Triumphus Christianus, which appeared at Frankfurt an der Oder in 1514; and
            Tilmann Conradi (Thiloninus Philymnus) with *Triumphus Christi* (Wittenberg,
            1516), likewise in hexameters. In 1517 Eobanus himself brought out a *Victoria
            Christi ab inferis, carmine heroico.* Though published later than the works by Paulus
            Crosnensis, Mathias Funck, and Tilmann Conradi, Eobanus' epyllion was in fact
            written some time earlier, in a poetic competition with Johannes Dantiscus at
            Cracow in February 1512. See Harry Vredeveld, "Eobanus Hessus in Krakau,"
            Humanismus in Erfurt, Akademie gemeinnütziger Wissenschaften zu Erfurt. Acta
            Academiae Scientiarum 7, Humanismusstudien 1, ed. Gerlinde Huber-Rebenich
            and Walther Ludwig (Rudolstadt and Jena, 2002), 161–76; introduction to *Nup.,*
            pp. 6–9 above. Eobanus' *Victoria Christi* was later plagiarized in *Triumphus Christi
            heroicus* (reprinted as an appendix to Juvencus in *PL* 19:385–88). This poem has
            been variously ascribed to Juvencus or some late medieval or humanistic author. In
            fact (as I have just discovered) it was composed by the Lutheran preacher Johann
            Spangenberg (1484–1550). Earlier I had suspected the opposite scenario. See Harry
            Vredeveld, "The Unsuspected Source of Eobanus Hessus's *Victoria Christi ab Inferis,*"
            in *Acta Conventus Neo-Latini Sanctandreani,* ed. I. D. McFarlane (Binghamton,
            1986), 293–97.
11–22   **Est — iubar** Cf. *Vict.* 223–32.
11–12   **Est — olet** Cf. Verg. *A.* 6.237–41 (the entrance to Hades); also *A.* 7.569–70.
11   **Est locus . . . qua** = Ov. *Fast.* 4.337; cf. Eob. *Her. Chr.* 22.49, n.
            saeva . . . tellus Luc. 8.827.
12   **sulphure . . . olet** Cf. Ov. *Met.* 5.405; Vulg. *Apoc.* 14.10.
13   **Accipit — locus** Cf. Ov. *Met.* 4.441; Eob. *Her. Chr.* 23.55.
            sontes animas = Mant. *1. Parthen.* 2.305, referring to the souls in purgatory. Cf.
            Verg. *A.* 10.854; Ov. *Met.* 6.618; Stat. *Theb.* 1.56; Walter, *Alex.* 10.60: "Est locus
            extremum baratri devexus in antrum, / Perpetua fornace calens ubi crimina punit / Et
            sontes animas ultricis flamma Iehennae"; 10.112.
14   **Exercet poenas** = Verg. *A.* 6.543; Sedul. 2.297.
15   **Vestibulum ante** = Verg. *A.* 2.469; 6.273 (in the underworld).
            longo . . . tractu = Luc. 10.257.
            incomplebile Cf. Vulg. *Prov.* 27.20; 30.15–16; Erasmus, *Adag.* 1.10.33, *ASD*
            2.2:440, ll. 532–33: "Zenodotus et Tartarum ipsum recte accipi inexplebile dolium
            putat, quod tot milibus defunctorum nunquam expleatur."

16	**Non — domo** Cf. Mart. 12.52.12; Eob. *Her. Chr.* 1.90, n.; 9.144. For the proverbial darkness of the underworld, see, for example, Vulg. *Job* 10.21–22; *Matt.* 8.12; Verg. *A.* 4.25–26; 6.461–62, 534; l. 21 below; *Vict.* 60, 152.
17	**serie saeclorum** = *Epic.* 3.17; cf. Juvenc. 1.308; Eob. *Tum.* 2.84.
	longa vetustas = *Nup.* 94, n.
19	**Post . . . iam saecula quinque** = Ov. *Fast.* 4.255.
	fluxerunt . . . saecula Stat. *Silv.* 3.3.146.
20	**Victa** Not the past participle of *vinco*, but of *vivo*. This unusual derivation is confirmed by ms. glosses in the Leipzig, Munich, and Münster copies.
	mortali . . . Deo Christ. For the phrase, see Cic. *Fin.* 2.40; Quint. *Inst.* 1.10.5.
	bis tria lustra Cf. *Her. Chr.* 4.42, n.; 14.2.
21–22	**Venit — iubar** For Christ's entering the underworld in a blaze of light, see *Nicodem.* 18.1; 21.3; Prud. *Cath.* 9.76–77; Eob. *Vict.* 150–55.
21	**aeternae noctis loca** Cf. Sen. *Her. O.* 1949; Eob. *Vict.* 152. For *aeternae noctis*, see Lucr. 5.980–81; Verg. *G.* 1.468; *A.* 10.746; et al.
	luminis Author = Mant. *Calam.* 1.1146 (p. 48); cf. Prud. *Perist.* 10.318.
22	**Nubila — iubar** Cf. Stat. *Theb.* 2.56–57.
	Nubila . . . atra Verg. *A.* 5.512 (in many mss.); Sen. *Phaed.* 955.
23	**Nec — valvis** Cf. Vulg. *Psa.* 106.16, traditionally applied to the *descensus*; Eob. *Vict.* 219.
	Nec mora, disiectis ≈ Sil. 7.523. Cf. Eob. *Pug.* 85, n.
	disiectis — valvis Cf. Ov. *Met.* 4.762–63.
24	**vetus . . . turba** Ov. *Fast.* 3.434; Sen. *Thy.* 671–72 (the dead rising from their tombs).
	turba sequta = l. 8, n., above.
25–26	**Pars — habent** While some of the righteous return to earth with Christ, most ascend to the earthly Paradise: see *Nicodem.* 25–26; Eob. *Vict.* 392–409; cf. *Her. Chr.* 23.45–58, with nn.
27	**contraria vulgus** = Verg. *A.* 2.39.
28	**Sunt tamen et . . . turba** Ov. *Ars* 2.281.
	credula turba = Ov. *Rem.* 686; *Fast.* 2.716; 4.312; [Tib.] 3.10.18; Eob. *Her. Chr.* 4.212; 12.60. In Christian authors, *credula* is often used in a positive sense: see, for example, Sedul. 5.314; Prud. *Apoth.* 580.
	turba nurus = Ov. *Ep.* 8.12.
29–30	**Illae — crucem** See Vulg. *Matt.* 27.55–56; *Marc.* 15.40; *Luc.* 23.27; *Joan.* 19.25.
29	**durae . . . mortis** Verg. *G.* 3.68; *A.* 10.791; Eob. *Vict.* 483, n.
	loca — adires ≈ Ov. *Met.* 14.125; cf. Eob. *Her. Chr.* 16.217; 23.11.
30	**impositam . . . crucem** *Her. Chr.* 16.204.
	pondus habere = Prop. 3.7.44; Ov. *Am.* 2.7.14; *Ars* 3.806; *Rem.* 688; Eob. *Her. Chr.* 11.40.
31–32	**Iam — nocens** The model is Ov. *Tr.* 1.3.1–2.
31	**lucis imago** = Stat. *Theb.* 4.424.
32	**Iudaea — nocens** Cf. Paul. Nol. *Carm.* 6.163–64: "Iudaea nocens et sanguine regis / conmaculata tui"; Arator 2.958: "O Iudaea nocens! Auctorem perdere vitae / Cum cuperes. . . ."
	facta nocens = *Sylv. duae* 1.148, n.
33	**Hei — Quantum** ≈ Verg. *A.* 2.274.
33–34	**Quantum — Supplicium** Cf. Verg. *A.* 11.841–42; Vulg. *Isa.* 53.5, 9; *1. Petr.* 2.21–24.
35–56	**Qualis — eras** Christ's passion is described indirectly, through its effect on the Virgin Mary (ll. 35–40), the writer herself (41–44), and all nature (45–56).
35	**moestissima mater** = Ov. *Ep.* 15.153.
36	**in mediis hostibus** Ov. *Ep.* 1.106; *Pont.* 1.2.13.
38	**Vix — erat** Cf. Ov. *Tr.* 3.1.22; Eob. *Her. Chr.* 6.90.
39–40	**Unus — loco** Cf. Vulg. *Joan.* 19.26–27; Eob. *Her. Chr.* 16.19–32.
39	**custos fidissimus** Cf. Ov. *Met.* 1.562 and *Fast.* 5.45: "fidissima custos."
40	**nullo . . . loco** = Prop. 2.22.44; Ov. *Tr.* 5.8.16; *Pont.* 1.3.66; 4.1.10.

41   **mori moerendo** Cf. Ov. *Ep.* 19.117.
42   **vitae terminus** Lucr. 2.1087.
43   **videns** Mary Magdalene was among the women who witnessed the crucifixion. The
            Gospels describe her as either watching from afar (Vulg. *Matt.* 27.55–56; *Marc.*
            15.40) or standing next to the cross (*Joan.* 19.25).
            dirae . . . mortis Tib. 1.10.4; Sen. *Her. F.* 56; *Her. O.* 928.
            nova nomina = Luc. 5.5; Sil. 7.20; Mart. 12.29.5.
            nomina mortis Cf. *Her. Chr.* 12.147, n.
44   **Plorantes . . . genas** = *Ama.* 32.18.
            rigido — genas Cf. Ov. *Am.* 2.6.4; *Fast.* 6.148. The motif is a commonplace in
            ancient poetry: cf. Eob. *Her. Chr.* 5.90, n.; 9.56, with n.
45–56   **Territa — eras** Eobanus combines Vulg. *Matt.* 27.45–51, *Marc.* 15.33, and *Luc.*
            23.44–45 with *Apoc.* 6.12–14 (the last-mentioned text is quoted in a student's note
            in the Munich copy and is alluded to in the Münster copy, along with a reference to
            the Gospel texts). Cf. Prud. *Cath.* 9.79–81; Sedul. 5.234–36: "sol nube coruscos /
            Abscondens radios, tetro velatus amictu, / Delituit, tristemque infecit luctibus
            orbem"; Eob. *Her. Chr.* 6.157–58; *Vict.* 64–76. For the commonplace — Nature's
            grief at Christ's death and her joy at his resurrection — cf. Curtius, *ELLMA*, 96; Eob.
            Her. Chr. 16.165–70.
45   **Territa . . . Natura** Arator 1.8–9: "cruce territa Christi / Vult pariter natura pati."
            neglexit leges *Epic.* 2.89: "Neglexisse putem solitas vaga sydera leges."
46   **Morte . . . redempta salus** Andrel. *Livia* 4.3.36: ". . . alterna morte redempta salus."
            nostra — salus = *Psalt.* 130.16; cf. *Her. Chr.* 5.120.
47   **faciem . . . velavit amictu** Prud. *Apoth.* 333; cf. Catul. 64.266; [Tib.] 3.4.55;
            Ciris 250.
            atro . . . amictu V. Fl. 6.745; Sil. 15.284.
48   **Informis — die** Cf. Ov. *Ep.* 16.320; *Fast.* 6.472.
49   **Omnia — mundo** Cf. Vulg. *Matt.* 24.29; *Nicodem.* 22.1: "in tua morte . . . universa
            commota sunt sydera."
            Omnia . . . sydera mundo = Man. 1.276.
            moto . . . mundo = Sil. 15.145: "moto strepuere tonitrua mundo."
50–52   **Vix etiam — sono** See Vulg. *Matt.* 27.51.
51   **culmina montes** Cf. Sen. *Apoc.* 15.1; V. Fl. 4.260; Stat. *Theb.* 3.633; 11.319; *Silv.* 1.1.59.
52   **Saxa . . . dissiluere** Lucr. 1.491; cf. Juvenc. 4.706 (at the crucifixion): "Dissiliuntque
            suo ruptae de corpore cautes."
            querulo . . . sono = Prop. 3.6.18.
53–54   **Multaque — modis** Cf. *Sylv. duae* 2.95–96.
53   **Multa . . . horrenda** Verg. *A.* 3.712.
            trepidum . . . orbem Luc. 5.160; Stat. *Theb.* 11.120; Eob. *Her. Chr.* 16.193.
54   **Non — modis** For the "inexpressibility topos," see Curtius, *ELLMA*, 159–62.
            Eobanus, however, was also aware that elegiacs are unsuited to expressing grand
            themes. Cf. Ov. *Pont.* 3.4.85–86; *Fast.* 2.125–26; Eob. *Sylv. duae* 2.214, n. Though
            none of them was ever a poetess in life, Eobanus' heroines are often quite conscious
            that they are writing in verse: see n. to *Her. Chr.* 4.176.
            Non . . . littera nostra = Ov. *Tr.* 4.4.22. Cf. *Ep.* 12.114; 16.340; 17.144; et al.;
            Eob. *Her. Chr.* 3.74; 4.182; 8.2; 10.190; also cf. *Her. Chr.* 21.5.
            imparibus . . . modis = *Her. Chr.* A 1.2, n., referring (as here) to elegiacs.
55   **Rex optime** = Verg. *A.* 11.294.
56   **Et merito** = *Laud.* 483, n.
            Conditor — eras ≈ *Her. Chr.* 8.64, n.
57   **Sola — gentis** Cf. *Vict.* 472. For *rabies gentis* see Filippo Beroaldo, "Carmen de die
            dominicae passionis" (1481), in his *Varia opuscula* (Basel, 1513), fol. 62ᵛ, referring to
            the Jews: "O gentis rabies."
            recutitae . . . gentis = Mant. *2. Parthen.* 1.141.
59   **Sed mihi quid** = Ov. *Ep.* 1.47.

60   **Tristia — iuvat** "The memory of past sorrows is sweet." See Erasmus, *Adag.* 2.3.43; 4.9.27; Otto 889; cf. Eob. *Pug.* 5, n. Mary Magdalene, of course, realizes that Christ already knows the story she is about to recount. Hence she inserts a brief justification for her doing so: it will give her (and Jesus) pleasure. Cf. *Her. Chr.* 4.53–54; 16.95–96. For a related justification see *Her. Chr.* 2.116, n.

60–64   **victa — Victor** For the play on the root of *vincere*, see l. 7, n., above.

60   **referre iuvat** = Ov. *Fast.* 2.620; Eob. *Her. Chr.* 4.54.

61   **mundus adorat** = Paul. Nol. *Carm.* 27.58; cf. Luc. 7.708; Eob. *Her. Chr.* 2.27; *Hymn.* 84: "surgentem . . . renascens / Mundus adorat."

64   **longo tempore** = Ov. *Ars* 1.38; *Fast.* 3.682; *Tr.* 3.1.76; Eob. *Her. Chr.* 7.48.

66   **conspiciendus abes** = l. 164 below.

67–68   **Nondum — fuit** See Vulg. *Joan.* 20.1; cf. *Matt.* 28.1; *Marc.* 16.2; *Luc.* 24.1.

67   **Phoebaeos — ignes** Cf. Verg. *G.* 1.249; Ov. *Met.* 3.149–50; 4.81; 15.665.
         Phoebaeos . . . ignes = Germ. *fr.* 4.25: "At cum Phoebeos Mavors effugerit ignes"; cf. Ov. *Met.* 5.389; Luc. 2.415.
         reduxerat ignes = *Buc.* 8.36.

68   **novum . . . mane** Verg. *G.* 3.325; Eob. *Her. Chr.* 16.192.
         tremulo lumine Verg. *A.* 7.9; 8.22; Ov. *Ep.* 18.59.
         lumine mane fuit = *Epic.* 3A.42.

69–71   **Nobilibus — est** See Vulg. *Marc.* 16.1; *Luc.* 23.55–56.

69   **alabastra** Cf. Vulg. *Matt.* 26.7; *Marc.* 14.3; *Luc.* 7.37.
         venenis For the sense of "balm" or "ointments," cf. Luc. 8.691; Eob. *Theoc.* 23.106, at the death of Adonis: "preciosis unge venenis."

70   **Exanimes artus** = Ov. *Am.* 1.7.53 (in a different sense); Luc. 6.721; cf. Ov. *Met.* 2.336.

71   **cognominis** A genitive of specification with *nostra*.

73–84   **Venimus — sciant** See Vulg. *Marc.* 16.2–8.

73   **Venimus ad** = Hor. *Ep.* 2.1.32; Ov. *Fast.* 4.13, 39; Eob. *Her. Chr.* 16.123; 18.93.
         clausi . . . sepulchri = Sedul. 5.244; cf. Ov. *Met.* 15.389.

74   **Unde — tuis** Cf. *Her. Chr.* 4.182; 7.74; 11.7; 14.161.
         Unde data est = Ov. *Fast.* 4.754.
         oculis littera = Ov. *Pont.* 1.9.4.
         littera nostra = l. 54, n., above.

75   **Ecce sed** = Juvenc. 1.733; 2.9, 44, 361; et al.; Eob. *Laud.* 178, n.

76   **Ignoti — viri** Cf. Verg. *A.* 3.591; Mant. *1. Parthen.* 2.589 (the Virgin marvels at the sight of the Archangel Gabriel): "formam mirata viri."

77–78   **Candidior — erat** Cf. Vulg. *Matt.* 28.3. For the description, cf. also Eob. *Her. Chr.* 2.57.

77   **Candidior nivibus** = Ov. *Am.* 3.5.11.
         coma purior auro Cf. Stat. *Ach.* 1.162: ". . . coma gratior auro."

78   **Plurimus — erat** Cf. Ov. *Ep.* 15.50.
         in . . . lumine fulgor Cf. Ov. *Ars* 2.721; Eob. *Her. Chr.* 7.46.
         pulchro lumine Cf. *Buc.* 11.94, of the Virgin Mary.

79   **subita . . . formidine** = Verg. *A.* 3.259; 6.290.

80   **Talibus — iubet** Cf. *Her. Chr.* 12.134.

81   **Lugentes Mariae** *Hymn.* 61.

83   **Rura . . . Galilaea** l. 129, n., below.

85   **sermone loquto** ≈ Juvenc. 1.220; Arator 2.923; Eob. *Her. Chr.* 10.151.

86   **Tradita — manibus** = *Sylv.* 1.1.30: "Tradita sunt manibus carmina nostra tuis."
         manibus — meis Cf. *Sylv.* 5.47.10 (9.1.8): ". . . digitis verba notata tuis"; *Her. Chr.* 14.162, n.; 21.2, n.

87   **breves elegos** *Sylv. duae* 2.214, n.

88   **Praebuerant — thorum** Cf. Ov. *Ep.* 5.14.
         frigida saxa = Prop. 4.7.66.

89   **pro te tua signa** Cf. l. 159, n., below.

89–90   **rigantes Fletibus** Ov. *Met.* 11.419; cf. Verg. *A.* 6.699.

90   **impresso . . . genu** Verg. *A.* 12.303.

        procubuere genu = Ov. *Fast.* 2.438; 3.220.

92   **Decidit — rudes** For the motif, cf. *Her. Chr.* 2.3, n.

93   **longo . . . dolori** Verg. *A.* 4.693; Ov. *Met.* 14.716; Eob. *Her. Chr.* 5.65.

        nova gaudia *Buc.* B 8.1, n.

        gaudia — dolori Cf. Ov. *Met.* 9.527; Juvenc. 1.94: ". . . gaudia mixta pudore."

94   **Laeticia — aedidit** Cf. l. 109, n., below.

95   **Gratulor — palmae** Cf. *Sylv.* 2.28.3; 5.47.17; 9.17.29: "Gratulor applaudoque tuae super omnia famae."

        super omnia = *Her. Chr.* 2.87, n.

96   **At dolor — est** Modeled on Ov. *Ep.* 16.236.

97   **Dum licuit** = Mart. 1.73.3.

        dulci obsequio Ennod. *Carm.* 1.6.8.

98   **posse videre** = *Sylv. duae* 2.64, n.

99–102   **Testis — soror** The story is told in Vulg. *Luc.* 10.38–42.

100   **Illa meas flammas** = *Sylv. duae* 2.37, n.

104   **vetus . . . nomen** Verg. *A.* 12.823; Ov. *Tr.* 3.9.5.

105   **indigenas populos** = Mant. *1. Parthen.* 1.387: "indigenas populos abigebat Iesus."

106   **pars — eram** = *Her. Chr.* 21.92; cf. *Her. Chr.* 1.96, n.

107   **Tunc quoque cum** = Ov. *Ars* 2.621; *Ib.* 139 (in some mss.); Eob. *Her. Chr.* 16.83.

        lachrymis . . . membra rigarim *Epic.* 5.106; cf. Verg. *A.* 9.251; Vulg. *Luc.* 7.38; Magdal. *Ep.* 11.

        supplex tua membra *Her. Chr.* 7.143.

108   **sapienter amat** ≈ Mant. *Nat. Am.*, fol. 178ᵛ: "sapienter ama." Cf. Ov. *Ep.* 2.27; 21.57; *Ars* 2.501, 511; 3.565; *Rem.* 745; Eob. *Her. Chr.* 17.82.

109   **Gaudia — concepta** Cf. Prud. *Apoth.* 600; Eob. *Her. Chr.* 3.94; 4.145; 13.102.

        Gaudia . . . concepta = Mant. *3. Parthen.*, fol. 113ᵛ.

        lachrymas . . . profusas ≈ *Her. Chr.* 8.43, n.

110   **Ut — iugo** Cf. Ov. *Ep.* 13.52.

111   **Me miseram** = Prop. 1.3.40; Ov. *Am.* 1.8.26; 2.18.8; *Ep.* 5.149; and often; Eob. *Her. Chr.* 15.126.

112   **Hospitii . . . iure** Celtis, *Am.* 2.4.19.

115   **Hei mihi, quam** = *Sylv. duae* 1.188, n.

        data praeda = Verg. *A.* 9.485.

117   **Tartareo nupsi . . . regi** ≈ Claud. *Rapt. Pros.* 1.217.

118   **fraus — habet** Cf. *Her. Chr.* 7.6.

        nomen habet = *Sylv. duae* 1.24, n.

119   **Gratia — tibi** = *Her. Chr.* 6.137, n.

120   **optato . . . amore** Catul. 64.372.

        amore frui = Ven. Fort. *Carm.* 7.4.32; Mantuan. *c. Am.*, fol. 176ʳ; Celtis, *Am.* 3.12.6; Eob. *Her. Chr.* 17.8; 24.16; cf. *Her. Chr.* 8.31; 11.113.

121   **noster amor** = *Her. Chr.* 1.29, n.

122   **carne vidende** ≈ Ven. Fort. *Carminum spuriorum app.* 1.36; cf. Prud. *Apoth.* 71; Eob. *Hymn.* 72.

123   **aestivis . . . solibus** Verg. *G.* 4.28; Sen. *Her. F.* 235.

        exustum — arvum Cf. Stat. *Theb.* 3.259; Mant. *2. Parthen.* 1.395–96: "solumque / Solibus exustum assiduis."

124   **Areo — solo** For the image, cf. *Her. Chr.* 14.116.

        in . . . herba solo = Ov. *Am.* 2.16.6.

        sitit herba Verg. *Ecl.* 7.57.

125   **triduum — est** For this hyperbole, cf. Verg. *Ecl.* 7.43; Ov. *Ep.* 18.25. For the thought that time passes all too slowly for those who eagerly long for someone, cf. Eob. *Her. Chr.* A 4.19–20, n.

128   **longos . . . dies** [Tib.] 3.6.54; Eob. *Buc.* 6.72–73, n.

        tardis passibus Sil. 13.614.

        ire dies = Ov. *Tr.* 2.142; [Tib.] 3.4.54.

129–30	**Ibimus — eras** Cf. Vulg. *Matt.* 28.7; *Marc.* 16.7; l. 83 above.
129	**Ibimus . . . petemus** = Ov. *Ep.* 15.175.
	Ibimus, est animus = *Her. Chr.* 4.237.
	est animus = Verg. *A.* 4.639; 10.715; Ov. *Ep.* 7.181; *Met.* 5.150; et al.
	Galilaeaque rura = Mant. *Ecl.* 10.2; Eob. *Her. Chr.* 16.121; cf. *Her. Chr.* 3.83; *Vict.* 470.
	rura petemus ≈ Hor. *Ep.* 1.14.14; Ov. *Fast.* 4.685.
131–32	**Arva patent — venis** For the motif, cf. Magdal. *Ep.* 113–16.
131	**Arva patent** *Sylv. duae* 1.72.
	patent oculis = Ov. *Ep.* 2.122; cf. Eob. *Her. Chr.* 21.176.
	oculis . . . obvia = Ov. *Pont.* 1.2.35; cf. Verg. *Ecl.* 6.57.
	oculis vigilantibus Verg. *A.* 5.438; Stat. *Theb.* 5.212; cf. Eob. *Her. Chr.* 4.151, n.; 14.103.
132	**spes mea** = Ov. *Ep.* 18.186; 19.150; *Tr.* 4.3.12.
133–34	**Iam — locum** Cf. *Her. Chr.* 6.35–36; *Sylv.* 1.9.9–10: "medium cum sol ascenderit orbem / Et brevis ex omni facta erit umbra loco."
133	**Iam — axem** Cf. Verg. *A.* 6.536; Luc. 3.423; Eob. *Her. Chr.* 11.79, n.
	mundi sol aureus = Verg. *G.* 1.232; cf. *G.* 4.51.
134	**Vixque habet . . . locum** = Ov. *Pont.* 2.7.42.
	quaelibet umbra = *Her. Chr.* 1.90, n.
135	**Nec — appares** ≈ Calp. *Ecl.* 3.4.
	vicinia tota = Hor. *Ep.* 1.16.44; cf. Eob. *Buc.* 4.76, n.
137–45	**Reddita — surgunt** Medieval writers often describe nature's joy at Christ's return and link the resurrection with the rebirth of nature in springtime: see, for example, August. *Serm. supposititii* 164.2, *PL* 39, col. 2067; Ven. Fort. *Carm.* 3.9.1–46; *AH* 1.62.1; 53.36.18–19; 54.148.1–4. See further Eob. *Hymn.* 83–128; *Vict.*, ded. 1–16, with nn.
137–38	**Reddita — tuo** Cf. Ven. Fort. *Carm.* 3.9.31–34: "ecce renascentis testatur gratia mundi, / omnia cum domino dona redisse suo. / namque triumphanti post tristia Tartara Christo / undique fronde nemus, gramina flore favent."
138	**quicquid ubique** = *Her. Chr.* 1.78, n.
139	**Solimi . . . colles** Mant. *Calam.* 2.292 (p. 60); *Ecl.* 10.2; Eob. *Her. Chr.* 5.167.
140	**Reddit — rosas** For the *roses of Jericho*, cf. Vulg. *Eccli.* 24.18; Eob. *Her. Chr.* 23.72; *Her.* 1.4.89–90.
	odoratas . . . rosas ≈ Tib. 1.3.62; *Eleg. Maec.* 1.94; Eob. *Her. Chr.* 17.126.
	alta Jericho lies in the Dead Sea valley, but *alta* is a common epithet of ancient cities — whether on account of their elevation, their high walls, or their lofty reputation.
141	**cupressiferae** Ov. *Ep.* 9.87; *Fast.* 5.87.
	praetexunt . . . sylvae *Nor.* 353.
142	**Idumaeum** Idumea (Edom), south of Judea, was famed for its palm groves: cf. Verg. *G.* 3.12; Luc. 3.216; Sil. 7.456; Mart. 10.50.1.
143	**Carmelus honores** = Mant. *1. Parthen.* 3.291; cf. Vulg. *Isa.* 35.2.
144	**Botrifera — humum** Cf. Vulg. *Cant.* 1.13; Peter Riga, *3. Reg.* 234: "inter / Engaddi vites."
	Botrifera . . . vitis *Psalt.* 78.129; 107.182.
	opacat humum = Ven. Fort. *Carm.* 1.20.16: "palmes opacat humum"; cf. Verg. *A.* 6.195–96; Stat. *Theb.* 5.153.
145	**omnia surgunt** = Lucr. 6.788.
146	**Nos — sumus** Cf. *Her. Chr.* 23.76, n.
	sine honore Verg. *A.* 5.272; Ov. *Met.* 2.387; 11.216; 13.447; et al.
147	**rerum . . . potens** Claud. *Carm. minora* 32.1; Paul. Nol. *Carm.* 17.41; Prud. *Amart.* 699 (all referring to Christ).
	Reparator = *Her. Chr.* 21.199.
148	**In melius versi** [Tib.] 3.4.95.
	temporis Author Prop. 4.6.53.
149	**Dum — notavi** ≈ *Epic.* 2.95.

           Dum queror = *Laud.* 285, n.

           ac For *ac* in the sense of "ac si" (with following subjunctive), see *Her. Chr.* 20.49.

150   **tremulum . . . caput** Juv. 6.622.

           lilia The lilies are singled out because of their symbolic connection to Easter.

151   **Frigida . . . aura** *Buc.* 4.68–69, n.

           commoverat — capillos Cf. Ov. *Met.* 1.529; 4.673–74; 6.303; *Fast.* 5.609; Hor. *Epod.* 15.9. In these examples, the motif tends to occur in an erotic context.

152   **Respitio — fuit** Cf. *Her. Chr.* 5.84.

153   **Vidi aliquid** = *Her. Chr.* 4.115.

           species — obtulit For the thought, cf. Verg. *Ecl.* 8.108; Pub. *Sent.* A 16: "Amans quod suspicatur vigilans somniat"; Mant. *1. Parthen.* 3.732: "[amor] se . . . reperturum credit quae ardentius optat."

154   **mixto — fui** Cf. Vulg. *Matt.* 28.8; Ov. *Ep.* 16.6; Verg. *A.* 1.513–14; 11.807.

155–60 **Aspitio — meas** The motif — a woman haunts the places where she and her beloved used to be together — comes from Ov. *Ep.* 10.51–53 and 15.137–50, as the close verbal parallels show. Cf. further Ov. *Rem.* 725–28. Eobanus uses the motif also at *Her. Chr.* 4.169–70, 181; 16.237–50, n.: cf. *Epic.* 4.19–22.

156   **loca — meis** Cf. Ov. *Ep.* 15.18; *Dirae* 24: "dulcia non oculis . . . ferantur"; Eob. *Her. Chr.* 8.44.

158   **parte dolere** = Ov. *Ep.* 20.4.

           dolere iuvat Cf. *Her. Chr.* 1.131; 12.68.

159   **tua — tango** = Ov. *Ep.* 10.53.

160   **lachrymas — meas** Cf. Ov. *Ep.* 15.150; Eob. *Her. Chr.* 20.40.

161   **Aspicis hec oculis** Cf. Verg. *A.* 4.208, 372; 9.209; Eob. *Her. Chr.* 4.229.

           quibus ante solebas ≈ Ov. *Fast.* 6.171; cf. Eob. *Her. Chr.* 8.109, n.

162   **Nec — movet** Cf. Ov. *Met.* 8.111–12; Stat. *Theb.* 10.719.

           nostra querela = Ov. *Ep.* 2.8; 17.12; Eob. *Her. Chr.* 7.38; 8.16; 16.300; 19.156.

164   **conspiciendus abes** = l. 66 above.

165   **peccatrix** Cf. ll. 115–18 above, with n. 7; *Her. Chr.* 15.146.

166   **crimina noster amor** = *Her. Chr.* 8.68; cf. *Her. Chr.* 2.84, n.

167   **esse videri** = Ov. *Tr.* 4.1.37; Eob. *Her. Chr.* 16.45.

168   **Da veniam** = *Her. Chr.* 2.14, n.

           pietas . . . tanta *Her. Chr.* 15.137; cf. *Her. Chr.* 14.19, n.

169   **Quid meruere** = Ov. *Met.* 15.120; Stat. *Theb.* 1.651.

171   **Restat ut** = Hor. *Ep.* 1.1.27; Ov. *Ep.* 21.248 (end of letter); *Fast.* 3.771.

172   **levare potest** = Mart. 14.22.2; Eob. *Her. Chr.* 17.272.

173–74 **Te — rogat** Cf. Magdal. *Ep.* 97–98; Eob. *Her. Chr.* 12.277–78, n.

173   **noster amor** *Her. Chr.* 1.29, n.

4

Meter: Elegiac distich.

1   **Quam — venit** The verse adapts Ov. *Ep.* 3.1. Cf. Eob. *Her. Chr.* 1.1, n.

           Costide *Laud.* 487, n.

2   **Si — volet** Cf. Ov. *Ep.* 18.1; *Pont.* 3.5.5–6; Eob. *Her. Chr.* 5.1.

3   **Quisquis es, ex illo** = Ov. *Rem.* 366.

           ex illo . . . tempore nobis Verg. *Ecl.* 7.70; cf. Eob. *Her. Chr.* 1.127, n.

5   **Signa recognoscis** = *Hod.* B 1.25; cf. Ov. *Pont.* 2.10.1–2. The image in the wax seal is also mentioned in Eob. *Her. Chr.* 6.3–4, 17–18; 12.3–4.

           vincula gemmae Cf. *Her. Chr.* 14.12. For *vincula* meaning "seal," see Ov. *Tr.* 4.7.7 and *Pont.* 3.7.6; for *gemma* in the sense of "signet," see, for example, Tib. 1.6.25; Ov. *Am.* 2.15.16; *Tr.* 2.451; 5.4.6.

6   **Annulus — tuis** See ll. 123–24 below.

           Annulus in digitis = Ov. *Ars* 3.446.

7   **Si qua potest . . . credere** *Her. Chr.* 20.138.

       promissis — amantum For the phrasing, cf. Prop. 2.17.1.

8   **Pignore firmatam** Verg. *A.* 3.611.

       firmatam . . . fidem Pl. *Mil.* 453; Ter. *An.* 462.

9   **Nec, puto, tu** = *Her. Chr.* 8.7.

10   **Sis — puer** Cf. *Her. Chr.* 23.116. For *sis licet*, see *Buc.* 10.55.

12   **Deum caeli** For this biblical phrase, see, for example, Vulg. *Gen.* 24.7; *2. Par.* 36.23; *1. Esdr.* 1.2; l. 75, n., and l. 193, below.

       virgine — satum ≈ Arator 1.47; Eob. *Ama.* 25.8, n.; cf. *Her. Chr.* 1.34, n.

13   **miserae . . . amanti** = V. Fl. 7.107; cf. Verg. *A.* 4.429.

       restat amanti = Prop. 2.23.23.

15   **fallaces . . . inania somni** Cf. Catul. 64.56; Ov. *Ep.* 9.39; Poliziano, *Epigr.* 109.1: "O mihi quanta datis fallaces gaudia somni"; Eob. *Her. Chr.* 15.199.

16   **Deus . . . summus** Vulg. *Tob.* 3.24; 4.12; *Marc.* 5.7; *Heb.* 7.1; Ov. *Fast.* 2.592; *Pont.* 4.3.56; Eob. *Her. Chr.* 4.80; 13.111.

17   **de plebe lavata** Cf. *Her. Chr.* 10.9, 135. For *lavare* in the common Christian sense of "baptize," see also *Her. Chr.* 6.121, n.; 10.191.

18   **suspicor esse** = Prop. 2.6.14; Ov. *Ep.* 1.74; 17.146; et al.; Eob. *Her. Chr.* 10.14, 144; 13.48; 15.208.

20   **antiquos . . . deos** = *Her. Chr.* 12.240; *Sylv.* 1.1.68.

21   **veterum . . . sacra carmina vatum** *Sylv. duae* 2.217, n.

23   **veterum . . . pagina** *Vict.* 396: "veterum . . . pagina vatum."

24   **uni . . . Deo** = *Her. Chr.* 8.76; 10.126; *Nob.* B 1.10; *Sylv.* 1.10.28.

       sensa profunda = *Psalt.* 119.338: "Fac sapiam verbi sensa profunda tui."

25–27 **Haebraeos vates — Arabum monumenta** Cf. Mant. *2. Parthen.* 2.281–82, where St. Catherine argues that all sacred literature points to Christ: "Sic Arabum libri, sic vult Iudaea vetustas; / Sic . . . cecinere Sibyllae." In *1. Parthen.* 1.631–32, Mantuanus mentions that the Virgin Mary studied not only the Old Testament but also "quicquid inest Arabum libris."

25   **Haebraeos — Sybillas** Cf. Mant. *2. Parthen.* 3.110: "Solymi vates . . . vestraeque Sibyllae." For *Haebraeos vates*, see Eob. *Laud.* 98, n.

       Sybillas Originally there was only one Sibyl, but different authors placed her in different locations. Later the number of Sibyls grew: Lactantius lists ten of them in *Inst.* 1.6.8–12. Their prophecies were collected in the Sibylline books. Fairly early in the Christian era, however, forgeries made their way into these collections, prophesying Mary and the virgin birth of Christ. These interpolations, along with the prophecy of the Cumaean Sibyl in Vergil's fourth eclogue, gave the Sibyls an extraordinary reputation throughout the Middle Ages and the early Renaissance, almost on a par with the Old Testament prophets. Cf. Eob. *Her. Chr.* 1.173; 9.77–78.

28   **Omnia — tui** Cf. *Her. Chr.* 1.112; *Psalt.* 45.32: "Lumine sunt vultus omnia laeta tui."

30   **Qui — manes** = *Psalt.* 6.2; 44.2. Cf. Peter Riga, *Gen.* 8: "Qui sine principio, qui sine fine manet"; Eob. *Her. Chr.* 1.14, n.; *Psalt.* 93.8.

31   **confusa . . . mole** Ov. *Ars* 2.467.

32   **Et tantum — opus** Reused in the verse paraphrase of Psalm 104 (Vulg. *Psa.* 103.5), l. 14, printed at the end of *Hypocr.*, sig. 5ᵛ: "Et tantum artifici mente crearet opus." For the idea of God as craftsman-maker, see n. to *Her. Chr.* 2.47.

33   **Interea genitor** = Verg. *A.* 10.833.

       genitor Costus Cf. Mant. *2. Parthen.* 2.233: "Costus genitor."

33–34 **fatalia — Munera** = *Rec.* 116–17.

35   **Urbis Alexandri** = *Laud.*, lim. 5, n.

36   **Infoelix — parens** Cf. *Her. Chr.* 13.134, n.

       futura parens = Ov. *Am.* 3.6.34.

37   **muliebria nomina** = *Salom.* 7, sig. C1ʳ: "Iudice contuleram muliebria nomina fama."

38   **Servata . . . virginitate** *Her. Chr.* 7.13.

39   **Est aliquid** = *Buc.* 10.56, n.
      heroidas inter haberi = *Nup.* 100, n.
41   **Iamque ego sum** = *Her. Chr.* 1.96.
      maturo — aevo Cf. Verg. *A.* 7.53; Eob. *Buc.* 3.73; *Her. Chr.* 21.135, n.
42   **Plena — meae** Cf. Poliziano, *Eleg.* 7.46: "Exigeres vitae cum tria lustra tuae"; Eob. *Her. Chr.* 3.20; 16.272; 24.106. According to her legend, Catherine was then eighteen years old.
43   **unus et alter** = *Nup.* 157, n.
44   **Turba . . . proci** = Ov. *Ep.* 1.88: "Turba ruunt in me luxuriosa proci."
45   **dii patrii** = Sil. 4.819; cf. Verg. *G.* 1.498; *A.* 2.702; Eob. *Her. Chr.* 19.68, n.
      incipiunt sordescere = Mant. *3. Parthen.*, fol. 112ᵛ: "templa incipiunt sordescere."
46   **Nescio — avet** Imitating Ov. *Ep.* 12.212.
      mens mea maius = *Her. Chr.* 2.8, n.
47   **Quid faciam** = Tib. 1.9.39; Ov. *Ep.* 10.59; Eob. *Her. Chr.* 10.115; 15.209.
47–48 **Stat — Regia** Cf. Ov. *Ep.* 1.34; *Met.* 2.1.
47   **altis — columnis** = *Her. Chr.* 12.57; cf. Ov. *Pont.* 3.2.49; [Tib.] 3.3.13; Stat. *Silv.* 4.2.38.
48   **sunt — meis** Cf. Ov. *Ep.* 16.34.
      oppida multa = Ov. *Fast.* 6.642.
50   **pignora chara** = Ov. *Fast.* 3.218; *Tr.* 1.3.60; Eob. *Her. Chr.* 21.26; cf. *Buc.* 7.63, n.
51   **Tu melius — potes** Cf. Verg. *A.* 10.632.
      Tu melius = Mart. 4.75.7; Eob. *Her. Chr.* 5.63.
      nostra dicata est = *Sylv. duae* 1.187.
52   **si . . . vera fides** *Buc.* B 2.13, n.
53   **Unde — menti** Cf. Walter, *Alex.* 1.500: "Unde hec tanta meae surgat fiducia menti"; Eob. *Sylv.* 1.1.37: "Hinc . . . timidae venit fiducia menti." For the tag, see *Sil.* 1.191.
54   **referre iuvat** = Ov. *Fast.* 2.620; Eob. *Her. Chr.* 3.60.
55   **Pellaeo . . . tyranno** Mart 9.43.7; cf. Eob. *Her. Chr.* 14.63, n.
56   **piger . . . Mareotis** Luc. 9.154.
      illustri In both the Munich and Münster copies this epithet is glossed as "nobili."
57   **Est via declivi** ≈ Ov. *Met.* 4.432; 7.410.
      vallem — recessu = *Nor.* 115; cf. *Buc.* 2.5, n.
58   **heremicola** For this spelling see n. to l. 173 below.
      facta manu = Ov. *Ep.* 5.2; 12.70; *Pont.* 2.10.4; Eob. *Her. Chr.* 1.2.
59   **senio — albo** = *Her. Chr.* 11.87; cf. *Her. Chr.* 22.127; *Ilias* 2.462: ". . . senio venerabilis albo."
60   **sepe magister erat** ≈ Ov. *Tr.* 3.7.24.
61   **convalle resedi** Cf. Verg. *A.* 8.232.
62   **Fons — locum** For the "locus amoenus," see *Ama.* 1.1, n.
      Fons prope = *Her. Chr.* 20.26.
63   **longo — aevo** Cf. Ov. *Am.* 1.13.37.
64   **Florales . . . opes** Cf. *Buc.* 4.38–39.
      comitum turba Ov. *Met.* 3.186; 6.165; Eob. *Her. Chr.* 16.206.
65   **Quid — perdis** Cf. Mant. *4. Parthen.*, fol. 117ʳ: "'Quid tempora perditis,' inquit"; *6. Parthen.*, fol. 141ʳ: "'quid perdimus,' aiunt, / 'Tempora?'"; cf. Eob. *Buc.* 1.17, n.
66   **immortali . . . Deo** = Tifernate, "In Beatam Mariam Virginem," *Carm.*, sig. A4ᵛ: "Per te nostra caro . . . / Est immortali conciliata Deo."
      nubere digna *Nup.* 246.
68   **dignus — frui** = Andrel. *Livia* 4.2.34.
69   **thalami commertia** Cf. *Her. Chr.* 13.5.
71   **regna . . . Nili** l. 210 below.
72   **Sceptra — loco** Cf. *Her. Chr.* 6.66, n.
      alio . . . loco = Ov. *Am.* 3.2.84.
73   **Utque facis** = Ov. *Ep.* 3.141; *Rem.* 704; *Met.* 7.815; *Tr.* 4.5.19; Eob. *Her. Chr.* 21.237; cf. *Her. Chr.* 5.126, n.

falsos . . . Ioves *Her. Chr.* 2.49, n. For the plural form, see Cic. *N. D.* 3.42; l. 208 below.

74 **Linque — bovem** For this type of verse, in which only the last word of each hemistich is varied, see, for example, Ov. *Ep.* 15.184; Eob. *Her. Chr.* 13.110; 17.274.

75 **Deum — orbis** Cf. *AH* 2.28.2: "deum coeli dominumque terrae." For *Deum caeli*, cf. also l. 12, n., above.

 decemplicis orbis Cf. Mant. *c. Poet.* 119: ". . . coelique decemplicis astra"; Eob. *Her. Chr.* 2.25, n.

76 **Iam — favet** = *Sylv.* 2.8.28.

 regia tota = Ov. *Ep.* 4.164; Eob. *Her. Chr.* 12.194.

77 **Est amor** = *Her. Chr.* 1.37; 18.150 (in both cases followed by an infinitive).

 inquam A ms. note in the Münster copy adds the gloss "dixi."

78 **Spes nova** = *Her. Chr.* 13.51; *Luth.* 6.108.

 alias . . . faces = Ov. *Fast.* 2.562.

79 **tua me miseram** = *Her. Chr.* 8.55; 19.61.

80 **Heu — Deo** The line became proverbial: see Walther 10772; cf. Eob. *Her. Chr.* 2.87.

 Heu, quantum est = *Her. Chr.* 11.172; *Her.* 1.6.192.

 summo . . . Deo l. 16 above, n.

 posse — Deo = Ven. Fort. *Carm.* 7.12.34: "trino posse placere deo"; cf. Ov. *Ep.* 11.6; 14.88; 15.92; *Ars* 3.430; *Pont.* 2.5.24; l. 84 below.

81 **passa maritum** = *Theoc.* 1.152: "Venus . . . pastorem est passa maritum"; cf. Ov. *Fast.* 5.156.

82 **Forsitan indignam** ≈ Nemes. *Ecl.* 2.70.

 nurum In Mant. *2. Parthen.* 2.165 the Virgin tells Catherine that Christ will be her bridegroom and adds, "nurus es mea."

83 **placuisse laborem** = Ov. *Ep.* 15.77.

84 **Tam — grave est** Cf. *Her. Chr.* 17.235.

 posse placere = l. 80, n., above.

85 **Ut . . . quis** Cf. ll. 89–90, n., below.

87 **Quis dabit** = *Her. Chr.* 7.132; 8.45; 12.272; 14.123; 16.142.

 dabit . . . audire et reddere voces Cf. Verg. *A.* 1.409; 6.688–89.

88 **Quis — erit** ≈ Ov. *Ep.* 2.34.

89–90 **Ut . . . Quis** = Ov. *Ep.* 7.15–16; cf. ll. 85–86 above.

89 **virgo cum virgine** Cf. *Her. Chr.* 8.131; 12.99, n.

90 **Quis . . . deus** Verg. *G.* 4.315; *A.* 9.77; et al.; Eob. *Her. Chr.* 12.163.

 patrio . . . orbe = *Hymn.*, lim. 2.2.

 orbe deus = Ov. *Fast.* 1.234.

91 **Nil queror** = Poliziano, *Epigr.* 9.3; Eob. *Her. Chr.* 7.134.

 Deus ipse deorum = *Psalt.* 50.19; cf. Vulg. *Deut.* 10.17; *Psa.* 49.1; Ov. *Met.* 3.291.

92 **Accenso — Deum** Cf. Ov. *Ep.* 11.26. In Ovid the line refers to Cupid. That is why Catherine immediately follows up with a clarification in ll. 93–94.

94 **Pectora . . . amor** = Ov. *Ep.* 13.30.

 divinus . . . amor = Pontano, *Laud.* 4.24: "tua divinus corda replevit amor"; cf. Verg. *A.* 8.373.

95 **Quam subito** = *Rec.* 96, n.

 caluerunt — medullae Cf. Ov. *Ep.* 4.15; Eob. *Laud.* 203; *Her. Chr.* 17.47; B 1.27.

96 **prius in nobis** = Ov. *Pont.* 4.2.26.

97 **Quisquis es, o** = Ov. *Met.* 3.613; 12.80; Eob. *Her. Chr.* 13.103; cf. Prop. 1.9.30; Eob. *Rec.* B 2.1, n.

 o animae — nostrae Cf. *Psalt.* 22.1: "Mi Deus, o animae spes unica et ultima nostrae."

99 **Multa precaturam** = *Her. Chr.* 15.131; cf. Verg. *A.* 11.697; Sil. 7.749.

 tenuis — pondere Cf. Verg. *A.* 6.292.

 tenuis . . . somnus Stat. *Theb.* 7.463; cf. Magdal. *Ep.* 101: "tenuis sopor."

 sine pondere = Lucr. 1.363; Ov. *Ep.* 5.109; *Met.* 1.26.

100	**Corpus — humo** Cf. Prop. 3.15.16; Ov. *Am.* 3.11.10; *Ep.* 4.44; *Ars* 2.524; *Met.* 10.128; *Tr.* 1.2.54.
	herbosa . . . humo = Maxim. 4.38.
101–02	**Utque — meae** Cf. Ov. *Am.* 3.5.1–2, introducing a dream vision.
101	**Utque — ocellos** Cf. Prop. 1.10.7; 2.1.11; Ov. *Fast.* 3.19.
102	**somnia visa** Walter, *Alex.* 1, arg. 10; Petrarch, *Ep.* 3.30.14: "somnia visa renarrat"; Eob. *Her. Chr.* 4.138; 19.164.
103	**Campus erat** = Ov. *Ars* 2.135; *Fast.* 2.215.
	viridi . . . sylva Ov. *Met.* 3.324.
	undique sylva = *Her. Chr.* 22.49.
104	**Flore renidebat** Prud. *Perist.* 12.54: "prata vernis floribus renident"; Andrel. *Livia* 3.2.2: "Pictaque purpureo flore renidet humus."
	Flore . . . multicolore Hrotsv. *Gongolf.* 161: "flores . . . multicolores"; Erasmus, *Carm.* 95.43: "Multicolore . . . flore."
105–06	**Illic — rosis** Cf. *Buc.* 5.87–88, referring to the Virgin Mary. Both Catherine and Mary symbolically weave their own bridal garlands.
105	**odoratas . . . herbas** ≈ Ov. *Fast.* 2.703; cf. Eob. *Hymn.* 111–12.
	errabam . . . per herbas Ov. *Met.* 4.635–36; 15.14.
106	**Puniceis . . . rosis** ≈ Pontano, *Am.* 2.7.50: "Puniceasque . . . rosas"; cf. Hor. *Carm.* 4.10.4; Andrel. *Livia* 3.3.38: "puniceis lilia mixta rosis." The idea of weaving roses and lilies together seems to have been in Eobanus' mind too, because at l. 130 below he has Catherine offer Christ a garland of lilies. As roses are a symbol of love and martyrdom, so lilies are a symbol of virginity: cf. August. *Serm.* 304.2, *PL* 38, col. 1396: "rosas martyrum . . . et lilia virginum"; Honorius Augustodunensis, *Sigillum Beatae Mariae* 8, *PL* 172, col. 517 D: "Per rosas martyres, per lilia intelligimus virgines."
107	**ego te vidi** = Verg. *Ecl.* 3.17; Ov. *Ep.* 12.31; Eob. *Her. Chr.* 4.143; *Sylv.* 1.1.21.
	te vidi . . . cum matre Verg. *Ecl.* 8.37–38.
	puerum — puella = *Her. Chr.* 20.147; cf. *Her. Chr.* 20.145.
108	**teste carent** ≈ *Buc.* B 2.12, n.
109	**Virgo — comas** = Mant. *Ecl.* 2.95 (of a shepherdess): "virgo erat, alba comas." The Virgin Mary is dressed in white, partly to symbolize her virginity (cf. Eob. *Buc.* 11.43, with n.), partly because she has come down from heaven where all the saints are so appareled: cf. Vulg. *Apoc.* 3.4–5; 4.4; Eob. *Her. Chr.* 9.124–26; Mant. *2. Parthen.* 2.154, of the Virgin appearing to Catherine: "gradiens in vestibus albis"; *Votum,* fol. 54ʳ: "Albicat intactum niveo velamine corpus."
	comas — coactas For Mary's golden crown, see *Buc.* 11.91, with n.
110	**Formosum** Cf. *Buc.* 11.41, n.
	corpus amicta = Ov. *Fast.* 2.298.
111	**Sceptrum — dextra** Cf. Verg. *A.* 12.206. For Mary's holding a scepter, see Eob. *Buc.* 11.28, n.; Mant. *Votum,* fol. 54ʳ: "Signa tenes regni, fulvum caput induit aurum [cf. l. 109 above], / Virgineam decorat regia virga manum"; Mant. *1. Parthen.* 3.701, 812, 955.
	laeva Mary is nearly always depicted holding the Christ child on her left arm, close to her heart.
112	**Brachia — nive** = Ov. *Am.* 3.7.8, in a decidedly racy context. For the emphasis on luminous whiteness, cf. Eob. *Buc.* 11.44, n.
113–14	**Hic — deo** Cf. Mant. *Ecl.* 8.78, where a shepherd describes the Virgin as follows: "Non erat illa Dryas neque Libethris nec Oreas." The newly converted Catherine still thinks in terms of pagan mythology.
114	**De — deo** Cf. Ov. *Ep.* 9.48, addressing Hercules. Catherine refers to Jupiter, notorious for his countless amours. Cf. Eob. *Her. Chr.* 1.149–50; l. 138 below.
	turpi . . . deo Prud. *Perist.* 2.498.
115	**Vidi aliquid maius** Cf. *Her. Chr.* 3.153; 20.48.
	errore prophano = Locher, *Stult.* 27, fol. 38ᵛ.
116	**Nescio quem . . . Deum** = Ov. *Ep.* 11.26 (also used in l. 92 above); *Fast.* 2.398.

	tacita mente = Ov. *Ars* 1.602; cf. Catul. 62.37; [Tib.] 3.12.16; Ov. *Am.* 1.4.23; 3.7.63; et al.; Eob. *Sylv. duae* 2.201.
117	**Iam prope constiterat** ≈ *Nup.* 195, n.
119	**flore** Cf. *Buc.* 2.73, n., of the flower of chastity.
	latura coronam = *Nup.* 247, n.
122	**Gemma — tuo** Cf. Ov. *Ep.* 15.74.
123	**quod — gerebas** ≈ Verg. *A.* 11.552; cf. Eob. *Her. Chr.* 11.89.
124	**in mea membra** = Prop. 3.16.6.
126	**Imperium — manent** = *Her.* 2.3.152. Eobanus imitates Anon. *Vita Katherine* 296, where St. Catherine says: "o conditor orbis, / Cuius ad imperium cuncta creata manent." **cuncta creata** = Ven. Fort. *Carm.* 3.9.38.
127–29	**Erubui — demisi** The model is Ov. *Ep.* 11.35–36, referring to Canace, after the nurse has discovered her guilty secret. Catherine's blushing and speechlessness, by contrast, are the result of love divine.
128	**In vultu tacitum** ≈ Ov. *Am.* 2.7.6.
129	**Lumina — cum tu** ≈ Ov. *Ep.* 16.227; cf. Eob. *Sylv. duae* 2.69; *Her. Chr.* 12.79. **puer optime** = Stat. *Silv.* 5.2.82; Eob. *Her. Chr.* 23.15. **optime rerum** = Mant. *Bapt.*, fol. 230ᵛ: "Deus optime rerum"; Marul. *Hymn. nat.* 1.1.99, to Jove: "pater optime rerum"; Eob. *Epic.* 5.41.
130	**Excipis . . . lilia** Stat. *Silv.* 1.2.22–23. **lilia** Cf. l. 106 above, n.
131	**virgineum . . . pudorem** *Buc.* 5.99, n.
134	**vix — dicere** Ov. *Ep.* 13.14.
136	**sum relevata tuo** = *Her. Chr.* 16.32.
137	**Ecce sed** = *Her. Chr.* 3.75, n.
138	**patrio . . . deo** Jupiter, as in l. 114 above. For the phrase, cf. *Her. Chr.* 19.68, n. **somnia visa** = l. 102 above, n.
139	**Serta — cecidisse** Cf. Ov. *Met.* 14.350. **cecidisse putabam** ≈ Ov. *Met.* 7.378.
140	**nostri pignus amoris** Stat. *Silv.* 3.2.81. **pignus — erant** ≈ Ov. *Ars* 2.248; cf. *Ep.* 4.100. The phrase (an allusion to ll. 131–32 above) occurs also in Mant. *2. Parthen.* 2.168, where it refers to the ring that Jesus gives to St. Catherine: "Immortale . . . divini pignus amoris."
141	**Caelesti . . . auro** *Her. Chr.* 1.149.
142	**Est — meis** Cf. Ov. *Pont.* 1.9.2.
143	**ego te vidi** = l. 107, n., above. **imagine somni** = Ov. *Ep.* 16.45; *Met.* 7.649; 8.824; et al.
144	**vigili pectore** Ven. Fort. *Carm.* 7.16.3; Marul. *Hymn. nat.* 4.2.34. **pectore cura** = Ov. *Pont.* 1.2.74.
145	**Laeticia — lachrymas** Cf. *Her. Chr.* 3.94; 3.109, n.
146	**fleat omnis amans** = Balbi, *Epigr.* 25.1: "Iam fleat omnis amans"; cf. Eob. *Ama.* B 2.52, n.
147	**Non — amores** Cf. *Her.* 2.4.11: "Non quibus incesti lachrymis solantur amores." For *incesti amores*, see Hor. *Carm.* 3.6.23. **solantur** This deponent verb is used here in the passive voice.
148	**castus amor** *Laud.* 240, n.
149–50	**scrutabar — fui** Cf. *Her. Chr.* 5.83–84.
150	**Nullus erat** = Ov. *Ep.* 10.11.
151–62	**Lumina — loco** For the effect of an epiphany on nature, cf. *Buc.* 11.24–27, with nn. Cf. further Lucr. 1.6–9; Ov. *Fast.* 6.251–52; Calp. *Ecl.* 4.109–16; Eob. *Her. Chr.* 3.137–45, n.
151	**Lumina . . . vigilantia** = Ov. *Ep.* 18.31 (in a different sense); cf. *Ep.* 19.35; Claud. *VI. Cons. Hon.* 234; Eob. *Her. Chr.* 3.131, n.; 12.127, n. **aereum . . . solem** Prud. *Amart.* 503.

153   **Quacunque aspicio** = Pontano, *Eridanus* 1.7.25; Eob. *Her. Chr.* 10.139; cf. Ov. *Tr.* 1.2.23.

melior natura = Ov. *Met.* 15.194; cf. *Met.* 1.21; Eob. *Ruf.* 107: "melior viridis natura renascitur anni"; *Hymn.* 83–84.

154   **Est aliquid** = *Buc.* 10.56, n.

verum . . . Deum = *Her. Chr.* 6.172; 10.10; 17.28; cf. *Her. Chr.* 12.12, 44; 21.168. The phrase is biblical: see, for example, Vulg. *Sap.* 12.27; *Joan.* 17.3.

rebus adesse = Ov. *Tr.* 2.216; Eob. *Her. Chr.* 24.38.

155   **Blanda . . . murmura** Prud. *Perist.* 6.155.

156   **Moesta . . . humus** = Mart. 9.70.4.

vivo — humus Cf. *Epic.* 6.40: "Luxuriat vivo germine dives humus"; *Val.* 2.406: ". . . vario germine floret humus"; Poliziano, *Eleg.* 7.74: ". . . florifero germine vernat humus."

157–58   **Tam — domo** Cf. *Her. Chr.* 20.21; *Vict.* 401–02 (in Paradise): "tenuissimus aer / Spirat."

157   **tenuem . . . auram** = Verg. *A.* 4.278; 9.658.

perflavit — auram ≈ *Buc.* 5.88, n.

158   **in aetherea . . . domo** = Mant. *Bapt.*, fol. 229ᵛ: "Omnis in aetherea sancta caterva domo"; cf. Prop. 2.16.50; Eob. *Her. Chr.* 23.56, n.; *Hod.* 43–44.

dicitur esse = Ov. *Fast.* 2.748; Mart. 5.3.4; Eob. *Her. Chr.* 23.40.

159   **Quae prius** A ms. gloss in the Münster copy indicates that the verb *aspexi* is understood.

159–60   **vicini — aquae** Cf. *Her. Chr.* 20.26, of a paradisiacal landscape.

159   **vicini . . . fontis** Ov. *Met.* 4.98.

160   **Nobile . . . nectar** Mart. 13.104.2.

caelestis . . . aquae ≈ Ov. *Ars* 2.352; *Fast.* 4.386.

161   **Argutae — volucres** Cf. *Her. Chr.* 8.41; *Nor.* 426: "Vernant argutae volucres"; Ov. *Tr.* 3.12.8. For *argutae volucres*, cf. Prop. 1.18.30; *Eleg. Maec.* 1.36.

viridi . . . fronde = V. Fl. 1.137; cf. Tib. 2.1.40; Verg. *Ecl.* 1.80; *Culex* 390.

163   **Tota . . . gratia** *Ama.* 32.54, n.

gratia caelo = Sedul. 2.48, at Jesus' birth: "Quae nova lux mundo, quae toto gratia caelo?"

165   **comitesque voco** = Ov. *Met.* 3.604.

166   **Crebra — sonum** Cf. *Epic.* 2.96: "Mota repercussum reddidit aura sonum"; *Buc.* 3.3, n.; *Her. Chr.* 17.56; *Vict.*, app. 2.6. For *repercussum reddidit*, cf. Ov. *Met.* 2.110.

Echo Notice the short second syllable.

167–69   **Haec — vagor** Cf. Ov. *Ep.* 10.19–24.

168   **resona voce** Ov. *Met.* 3.496.

voce . . . opem = Ov. *Pont.* 4.3.42.

ferebat opem = Ov. *Fast.* 3.674; 5.62; *Tr.* 1.5.76.

169–70   **Huc — mihi** For the motif, cf. l. 181 below; *Her. Chr.* 3.155–60, n.

169   **Huc illuc** = Verg. *G.* 2.297; 4.363; 5.408; et al.; Eob. *Her. Chr.* 5.91.

per opacae devia = *Her. Chr.* 11.67.

opacae . . . vallis Hor. *Ep.* 1.16.5–6; Ov. *Met.* 11.277; Sen. *Phoen.* 16.

170   **loca . . . proxima** Verg. *A.* 6.434; Ov. *Met.* 11.365.

171   **Spes — auras** Cf. *Rec.* 98, n.

leves . . . in auras = Ov. *Met.* 3.43; cf. Eob. *Nup.* 119, n.

cessit in auras = Ov. *Met.* 14.848; Sil. 6.39.

172   **Hei mihi, quam** = *Sylv. duae* 1.188, n.

tardo sydere = Celtis, *Am.* 2.8.54.

173   **cultor heremi** Cf. *Her. Chr.* 14.29 and 22.19: "cultrix . . . eremi." A ms. gloss in the Leipzig and Münster copies corrects the medieval spelling "heremi" to "eremi." The unclassical spelling occurs also at l. 58 above, but nowhere else in Eobanus' works.

174   **tempora moesta** = Celtis, *Am.* 1.11.28; 3.14.10; 4.3.66.

175–76   **Ille — Scribe** Modeled on Ov. *Ep.* 4.13.

176   **Domino carmina** = Mart. 8.82.2.

carmina scripta = *Her. Chr.* 16.262; *Her.* 1.6.160. For *carmina* in the sense of "letter in verse," see, for example, Catul. 65.16; Ov. *Pont.* 2.4.13; 3.6.2; 4.1.1; Eob. *Her. Chr.* 24.148. Catullus, Ovid, and Eobanus, of course, were all poets and could rightfully point to their letters as poetic productions. The same is true for Ov. *Ep.* 15, where Sappho self-consciously explains her use of the elegiac meter in this her last letter (ll. 5–8). The other heroines and heroes of Ovid's *Heroides*, not being poetesses and poets, are quite unconscious of the form in which Ovid couches the letters. One might expect that Eobanus would have wanted to follow suit, seeing that none of his heroines was a poetess in life. Nevertheless he often has them mention or comment on the poetic form of their letters. In most cases they simply call their letter "carmen," as Catherine does here and at l. 180. See *Her. Chr.* 9.31; 10.22; 15.218; 16.215; 20.91; 23.118. Some writers, however, specifically mention that they are writing verses (3.59, 87; 10.4; 14.16). They explain why they are using elegiacs (8.1–6; 17.1–2; 20.89–92) and point to the expressive limits of elegiac verse (3.54; 4.205; 17.103–04). Others compare writing to singing (7.1–2; 14.165; 23.39–40) and acknowledge the Muses' inspiration (9.31–32; 10.113).

177   **reperisse viam** ≈ Verg. *A.* 5.807.
    scribere possem = Hor. *S.* 1.10.47.
178   **sumpta tabella** Ov. *Fast.* 1.93; *Tr.* 5.12.33; *Pont.* 4.2.27.
    tabella Here used in the sense of "paper," as the next line makes plain: cf. Mart. 14.186.2.
179   **patria . . . papyro** = Juv. 4.24.
180   **carmina — mora** = Val. 1.16; *Sylv.* 3.8.24; cf. Ov. *Tr.* 2.220; *Pont.* 1.8.10.
181   **Saepe — amoris** For the motif, see *Her. Chr.* 3.155–60, n.
    Saepe . . . repeto = Ov. *Ep.* 10.51.
    Saepe quidem = Luc. 9.930; Stat. *Theb.* 3.179.
    loca — amoris Cf. Ov. *Rem.* 725–26.
182   **Mittitur — tibi** Cf. *Her. Chr.* 3.74, n.
    littera — tibi = *Her. Chr.* 10.190; *Sylv.* 1.7.32; 6.4.16; cf. *Her. Chr.* 3.54, n.
183   **Dolor — videre** Slightly changed from Ov. *Ep.* 16.235.
184   **patria . . . relligione** *Her. Chr.* 10.34, n.
185–87 **Impia — repressi** The model is Ov. *Ep.* 11.33–35. Mant. *2. Parthen.* 2.4 also mentions St. Catherine's old nurse ("sedula nutrix").
186   **Quid . . . haec** = Ov. *Ep.* 15.120.
    pallida Pallor is a conventional symptom of lovesickness: see n. to *Laud.* 237.
187   **Obstupui — repressi** Cf. Verg. *A.* 2.378.
188   **Ne causam . . . quaereret illa mei** ≈ Ov. *Ep.* 16.242.
    caussam officii Ov. *Pont.* 1.7.66; Juv. 2.134.
189–90 **Mirantur — meae** For the motif, cf. Ov. *Ep.* 13.35–36; Eob. *Her. Chr.* 5.57–62, n.
189   **solitos . . . cultus** Claud. *Carm. minora* 30.222: ". . . non solitos gemmarum sumere cultus."
190   **formae cura** Ov. *Met.* 13.764.
191   **Si qua — volet** = *Sylv.* 1.6.33.
    vestibus ornet Ov. *Met.* 10.263.
193–96 **Mens — potest** Cf. *Her. Chr.* 2.84–86.
193   **Mens formosa** *Buc.* 10.65, n.
    Deum caeli See l. 12 above, n.
    cogit amare = Ov. *Ep.* 19.171.
194   **Haec manet** = *Epic. Drusi* 266.
    forma secunda = Prop. 2.3.32, Ov. *Am.* 1.8.25 and 1.13.44, but in a different sense.
    forma . . . malum For the brevity of youthful beauty, see *Buc.* 7.168–70, with nn.
195–96 **Haec — potest** Cf. Boeth. *Consol.* 5.3.4: "cuncta prospicit deus neque falli ullo modo potest"; Eob. *Hypocr.* 40: "Cuncta videns nulla fallitur arte Deus."
196   **qualibet — potest** = *Sylv.* 2.1.76; *Calum.* 148; cf. *Her. Chr.* 2.86, n.
198   **Foecit . . . pagina . . . fidem** Locher, "Carmen ad S. Brant," *Stult.*, fol. 4ʳ: ". . . facit emeritam pagina scripta fidem."

pagina sancta = Brant, *Varia carm.*, sig. B7ᵗ (*Texte* 115.56), sig. B7ʳ: "mille figurae, / Plena quibus tota est pagina sancta patrum"; Eob. *Val.* 2.192.

199   **Credo equidem** = *Buc.* 4.21, n.

      tria — unum Cf. Paul. Nol. *Carm.* 19.136: "haec tria sunt deus unus nomina semper."

200   **omnia posse Deum** = Paul. Nol. *Carm.* 6.51.

205   **quae — pedestres** Cf. *Her. Chr.* 3.54, n.

206   **veteres divos** Cf. *Buc.* 3.19, n.

      divos — nihil Cf. *Her. Chr.* 10.144; *Nup.* 369, n.

208   **Concidit . . . victima** Ov. *Met.* 8.763–64.

      Concidit ad . . . Ioves Cf. Tib. 1.2.62.

      falsos . . . Ioves l. 73 above, n.

209–18   **Impius — colit** Cf. Mant. *2. Parthen.* 1.40–42: "Maxentius artes / Vertitur ad magicas veterumque ad sacra deorum / Instaurat delubra"; 1.381–84: "rex iam squallida multo / Templa situ iubet ornari veteresque per aras / Purpureos spargi flores et rite parari, / Danda ecatumbaeo quae sunt animalia sacro" (whereupon all but the Christians follow Maxentius' example); 1.411–22: "Adducant delecta boum qui corpora centum. / [. . . .] / Iamque dies solemnis adest, mugitibus aurae / Per fora perque vias, urbis per compita clamant. / Aera crepant, clangore tubae complentur acuto. / Consequitur vulgi strepitus turbaeque frequentis / Murmur, et inflato resonat cava tibia buxo. / Clarus ad illustres graditur Maxentius aras / Et circum Pellea micat Romanaque pubes." Now Catherine knows that her martyrdom is not far off (2.11–14): "Iam delubra subit [*sc.* Catharina], lucent ardoribus arae, / Mugitu cava tecta sonant, strepit undique murmur / Plaebis et astantum. Solio Maxentius alto / Gestit." She stands before his throne and publicly confesses her faith in Christ.

209   **Impius . . . Maxentius** = Mant. *2. Parthen.* 1.188: "Impius ad magicas rediit Maxentius artes"; cf. l. 253 below.

      veteres . . . aras = Mant. *Georgius*, fol. 212ᵛ: "Christi dogma novum veteres . . . dispulit aras."

      Maxentius aras = Mant. *2. Parthen.* 1.155, 421.

210   **Nili regna** l. 71 above.

211   **Sacra iubet fieri** Cf. Ov. *Fast.* 1.627–28; 2.682; 3.381; 4.159. Cf. further Hor. *Epod.* 5.52; Ov. *Fast.* 3.809; 6.307; Eob. *Buc.* 11.68.

212   **credula turba** = *Her. Chr.* 3.28, n.

213   **mugitu resonant** Prud. *c. Symm.* 1.218; Eob. *Buc.* 3.3, n.

      ferit — clamor = Verg. *A.* 5.140.

214   **Et tuba terribiles** Cf. Verg. *A.* 9.503.

      tuba . . . unca Cf. *Her. Chr.* 1.186, n.

215   **festivis . . . flammis** = *Her. Chr.* 12.267; cf. *Hymn.* 131–32.

      lucent — flammis = Man. 1.20; cf. Verg. *Ecl.* 8.105; Mant. *3. Parthen.*, fol. 105ʳ: ". . . lucent rapidis altaria flammis."

216   **Sordidaque — humus** Cf. *Her. Chr.* 12.122, n.

      effuso sanguine = Ov. *Ars* 1.650 (in many mss.); Eob. *Sylv.* 3.18.6; cf. Eob. *Buc.* 9.32, n.

      sanguine . . . humus = Verg. *Cat.* 9.32; Ov. *Ep.* 1.54.

217   **genu flexo** = Cic. *Arat.* 290; Mant. *c. Poet.* 101; cf. Ov. *Tr.* 4.2.2.

      supplex — aras = *Buc.* 11.60, n.

218   **Hunc sequitur** = *Ilias Lat.* 233.

      numina — colit ≈ Peter Riga, *3. Reg.* 256: "numina falsa colens"; cf. Mant. *2. Parthen.* 1.3: ". . . numina falsa deorum"; 3.179: ". . . numina falsa, valete"; Eob. *Ama.* B 2.28; *Her. Chr.* 12.44; 23.113.

220   **rectam . . . fidem** Prud. *Apoth.*, praef. 2.2; and often in patristic writings; Eob. *Her. Chr.* 4.246; 22.24, n.; *Vict.* 58.

      saevo . . . ense = Ov. *Ib.* 294; cf. *Tr.* 3.7.49; *Ib.* 545.

      concidit ense ≈ *Her. Chr.* 1.124.

221   **crudelis . . . tyrannus** *Ama.* 35.47, n.

      tormenta tyrannus ≈ Celtis, *Am.* 1.13.7; Eob. *Her. Chr.* 18.127.

222   **Turba ... plurima** *Her. Chr.* 3.8, n.
        miseram . . . necem Luc. 7.416; Prud. *Cath.* 3.183.
        passa necem Ov. *Met.* 10.627; *Ib.* 517.
223–25 **Vidimus . . . Vidimus et** Cf. *Her. Chr.* 10.92–94.
224   **Nuda ... corpora** = Ov. *Fast.* 2.284.
        fuste quati = *Luth.* 1.58 (where *fuste* is also feminine, rather than masculine): "aerata cymbala fuste quati."
225   **ferro — mammas** This detail may have been suggested by the martyrdom of St. Agatha (recounted, for example, in Mant. *4. Parthen.*).
        teretes ... mammas ≈ *Sylv.* 1.7.11; 3.5.19; cf. Celtis, *Am.* 2.9.49; Eob. *Buc.* 3.71, n.
227   **nostrum . . . cruorem** *Sylv.* 4.28.23: "Qui nostrum penitus bibunt cruorem."
        canis For this insult cf. Otto 315 and 316.
228   **non sinit esse** = *Sylv. duae* 2.84, n.
229–30 **Aspicis — est** Though not always swift, God's punishment will inexorably strike the guilty: cf. Vulg. *Eccli.* 5.3–4; Erasmus, *Adag.* 4.4.82; Otto 520 and 521; Häussler, 100–01, 153, 268; Stat. *Theb.* 5.688–89; Eob. *Max.* 325–26; *Eccles.* 331–32; *Idyl.* 17.49–50.
        lenta . . . ira tua est Cf. Ov. *Ep.* 3.22; Juv. 13.100.
229   **Aspicis — oculo** Cf. *Her. Chr.* 3.161, n.; *Psalt.* 37, arg. 1: "patiente oculo videas florere malignos."
230   **tardior ira** = *Accl.* 2.166: "Cur tua Turcarum tardior ira venit?"
231   **Quam — est** Cf. Vulg. *Phil.* 1.21; Eob. *Her. Chr.* 12.241; *Hod.* 263.
        Rex magne = V. Fl. 4.63; 5.624; Mart. 12.62.1; cf. Verg. *A.* 1.241.
232   **Munere — potest** Cf. Paul. Nol. *Carm.* 27.304: "vendere terram, / caelum emere"; Mant. *1. Parthen.* 3.280: "Mercibus his emitur caelum"; *2. Parthen.* 2.530: "sic emitur coelum." Cf. further Eob. *Her. Chr.* 1.44, n.
233   **triumphalem . . . palmam** ≈ *Laud.* 405.
        certamina palmam ≈ *Buc.* 10.101, n. The image is biblical: see Vulg. *1. Cor.* 9.24–25; *2. Tim.* 2.5; 4.7. Cf. further Eob. *Her. Chr.* 18.165, n.
234   **Pars . . . quota laudis** Ov. *Am.* 2.12.10; Eob. *Sylv.* 7.7.16. For *pars quota*, see *Buc.* 2.92, n.
        utinam — sim = *Sylv.* 1.5.2: "O utinam tantae sim comes ipse viae."
236   **Quid — tuam** Cf. *Accl.* 2.200: "Quid lacerat gentes perfidus iste tuas?"
237   **Ibimus, est animus** = *Her. Chr.* 3.129, n.
237–38 **tormenta . . . Dira** Ov. *Met.* 3.694–95.
238   **nomina mille** = *Sylv.* 2.1.60; 7.9.26; cf. Verg. *A.* 7.337.
239   **Devenerata** For this sense see Ov. *Ep.* 2.18 (in some mss and early eds.): "deos . . . / sum prece turicremis devenerata sacris"; Eob. *Sylv.* 1.11.42: "te vatem / . . . deveneratus eram."
        deos lapides Aus. *Ephem.* 3.44; Eob. *Her. Chr.* 10.142; *Sylv.* 1.10.15.
240   **ora move** Ov. *Met.* 15.143.
242   **fortiter ulta** = Ov. *Ep.* 8.120; *Ars* 1.284; Eob. *Her. Chr.* 8.110.
        ulta mori = Ov. *Fast.* 3.638.
243   **Est mihi — precor** = Ov. *Fast.* 6.219; *Tr.* 1.10.1; Mart. 9.18.1; cf. Ov. *Ep.* 1.111.
        facundae — linguae = Concluding epigram in *Heus lector, hic habentur Campani de miseria poetarum Sapphicum . . . et quaedam alia lectu digna ad eandem rem facientia,* ed. Eobanus Hessus [Erfurt, 1515]: "Si tibi succrescet facundae gratia linguae"; *Sylv.* 6.4.45; 7.35.5; 9.23.3; cf. Aus. *Urb.* 89; Locher, *Katherina* 88: ". . . facundae gloria linguae"; Eob. *Laud.* 460, n.; *Her. Chr.* 19.113.
244   **Artis et ingenii** = *Idyl.* 10.14; *Epic.* 3C.2.1.
        ingenii . . . honor *Her. Chr.* 9.132.
245   **frivola — refellam** = *Val.* 2.149, where the early eds. read "revellam" (corrected in *Operum farr.*); cf. Verg. *A.* 4.380; 12.644; Eob. *Ilias* 9.97: ". . . mea dicta refellat" (where the original text reads "revellat"). The verbs *refello* and *revello* are likewise confused in Locher, *Stult.* 105, fol. 124ʳ: "Nec tamen audacter mea scripta revellere possunt / Nec temere haec contra verba proterva loqui."

246   **recta fides** l. 220 above, n.
248   **tempora pauca** = Ov. *Pont.* 2.4.10.
249   **hoc — urna** Cf. *Her. Chr.* 23.109.
        requiescere in urna ≈ *Rec.* 133, n.
250   **Hoc — erit** The model is Ov. *Ep.* 7.194. Cf. Eob. *Rec.* 136, n.
251–54 **Costis — habet** Epitaphs recur in ancient elegiac poetry: see, for example, Ov. *Ep.* 2.147–48; 7.195–96. See further Tib. 1.3.55–56; 3.2.29–30; Prop. 2.13.35–36; 4.7.85–86; Ov. *Am.* 2.6.61–62; *Tr.* 3.3.73–76. They are also common in Eobanus' elegiacs. See *Her. Chr.* 7.155–56; 23.111–14; *Epic.* 1.111–14; 2.137–42; 7.101–02; 9.117–20; *Eras.* 155–58; *Sylv.* 3.3.87–88.
251   **in — condita** Cf. Ov. *Fast.* 5.451; Aus. *Epit.* 5.1; Eob. *Rec.* 156, n.; *Her.* 3.8.108: "Hoc me . . . tumulo condidit."
251–52 **Tonantis Nupta** Apul. *Met.* 6.3.
253   **Impius . . . Maxentius** l. 209 above, n.
254   **caetera . . . habet** = Ov. *Fast.* 5.382; *Tr.* 3.4.46.

5

The 1514 version of this poem was first edited, with an introduction, translation, and notes, in Monika Rener, "Helius Eobanus Hessus, Heroides IV: 'Elisabeth Ludovico marito suo' oder: Die wundersame Einbürgerung des thüringischen Landgrafen in Hessen," in *Hundert Jahre Historische Kommission für Hessen 1897–1997*, Veröffentlichungen der Historischen Kommission für Hessen 61 (Marburg, 1997), ed. W. Heinemeyer, 437–61.
    Meter: Elegiac distich.

1–2   **Si — viro** Cf. Ov. *Ep.* 13.1–2, combined with *Ep.* 4.2.
1   **Si — salutem** Cf. *Her. Chr.* 4.2, n.
        missam . . . salutem *Laud.* 17, n.
2   **Hessiaco . . . viro** Though not a Hessian in the modern sense of the term, Ludwig was landgrave of Thuringia and lord of Hesse. A ms. note in the Münster copy of the book, taken down during one of Eobanus' classes, therefore quite rightly refers to him as "Prince of Thuringia and Hesse" ("Turingorum atque Hessorum principi"). As a native Hessian himself, however, Eobanus took special pride in Ludwig and Elizabeth, who had long since become closely associated with his homeland. For after Ludwig's death Elizabeth left the family seat at the Wartburg and spent the last years of her life in Marburg. Her burial place there became a shrine that attracted pilgrims from all over Germany and beyond until 1539, when Landgrave Philip of Hesse removed her relics. By 1514 she had become so thoroughly identified with Hesse that Eobanus had no difficulty presenting her and her husband as Hessians who had their residence in Marburg (ll. 79–80 below): see Rener, 445–51. Rener suggests that Eobanus altered the historical facts quite consciously, given that our humanist remarks at *Her. Chr.*, ded. 14.3: "Quod si quis futurus est qui dicet in Halcione, Catharina, Elisabetha, et aliis quibusdam historiam intervertisse, meminerit is, queso, nihil tam esse alienum a bono poemate quam nudum historiae filum et rei gestae sine poeticis quibusdam velut parergis additis." The reference there, however, is not to the present letter "Elisabeth Ludovico" but rather to "Elisabeth Zachariae" (*Her. Chr.* 20), where Eobanus did indeed embellish the story significantly.
        nupta — viro = *Her. Chr.* 2.106, n.; cf. also Ov. *Ars* 1.54, 682.
3   **Adriaco — morari** Cf. Ov. *Ep.* 13.3.
4   **Heu — meas** Laodamia likewise expresses fear of the storms at sea: see Ov. *Ep.* 13.123–24; cf. ll. 41–46 below.
        Heu nimium = Verg. *A.* 6.189; Ov. *Tr.* 2.180; et al.; Eob. *Her. Chr.* 10.120; 11.126; 12.10.
        in curas . . . meas = Ov. *Ep.* 1.72.

	ventus et unda = Prop. 2.28.8; Ov. *Am.* 2.16.46; *Ep.* 7.44.
5	**Longa — postquam** = *Her. Chr.* 8.113; 11.167. Cf. Ov. *Ep.* 19.3; *Met.* 1.214.
	visurus abisti = Ov. *Ep.* 2.99.
6	**At — fugeres** Cf. Ov. *Ep.* 13.4.
7–10	**Nona — abit** Cf. Ov. *Ep.* 2.3–6; Eob. *Her. Chr.* 7.53–54; 14.35–38.
7	**Nona — orbem** For the time expression, cf., for example, Ov. *Met.* 8.11; Luc. 2.577; Eob. *Her. Chr.* 1.99; 5.9; 10.180–81; 13.9; 17.219.
8	**Vir tibi . . . ero** Ov. *Ep.* 6.60.
	si vivam = *Buc.* 2.98, n.
9	**Tertia — Phoebes** Cf. Verg. *A.* 3.645.
	noctivagae . . . Phoebes Sen. *Oed.* 254; cf. Verg. *A.* 10.216.
	cornua Phoebes = V. Fl. 4.361; cf. Eob. *Her. Chr.* 17.219, n.
10	**tua — puppis** *Sylv.* 2.5.33: "Ut cito de Veneto solvat tua littore puppis." For *littore puppis* at this metrical position, see Ov. *Tr.* 3.12.32; Mart. 9.35.8; cf. Eob. *Her. Chr.* 9.15, n.
11	**Illud erat . . . tempus** Ov. *Ep.* 13.6.
12	**nulli — datur** *Ruf.* 41–42: "nulli / Scire futura datur"; cf. Ov. *Met.* 3.338. A ms. gloss in the Münster copy indicates that Eobanus was thinking especially of Vulg. *Act.* 1.7. The gloss goes on to quote two aphorisms by Menander (nos. 608 and 479 Jaekel): "Nullus de futuro tuta deliberat"; and "Imminet autem unicuique hoc quod debet pati." For the commonplace, see also, for example, Verg. *A.* 10.501; Hor. *Carm.* 3.29.29–30; Stat. *Theb.* 3.562–63.
	scire futura = Ov. *Am.* 1.11.18.
13	**regno — domoque** = Ov. *Ep.* 12.161.
14	**longum . . . iter** = Ov. *Tr.* 1.10.16.
	infidum . . . mare Lucr. 2.557; Plin. *Pan.* 66.3; cf. Verg. *G.* 1.254.
	per mare . . . iter = Ov. *Ep.* 19.92.
	carpis iter = Ov. *Fast.* 5.666.
15	**Cancro — perusto** Cf. Sen. *Phaed.* 287; Eob. *Buc.*, ded. 2, with n. 5; *Her. Chr.* 6.35.
16	**culmina . . . iugi** = *Venus* 3.36: "Alta Pyrenaei culmina scande iugi."
	culmina celsa = Ven. Fort. *Carm.* 7.16.16; Poliziano, *Eleg.* 7.72.
18	**Mella — fluunt** Palestine was "a land flowing with milk and honey": see, for example, Vulg. *Exod.* 3.8, 17; 13.5; Eob. *Vict.* 252.
	Mella . . . dulcia . . . fluunt Ven. Fort. *Carm.* 1.15.102; 11.12.4; Eob. *Sylv.* 2.29.28; cf. Verg. *G.* 4.101.
	Mella — lacte Cf. Ov. *Met.* 14.274; *Fast.* 4.151; [Tib.] 3.2.20; Eob. *Buc.* 10.17, n.
19	**Inclyta . . . maenia** Verg. *A.* 2.241–42.
20	**victoris . . . Dei** = *Her. Chr.* 6.122; *Luth.* 4.36; cf. Mart. 8.26.6; Eob. *Her. Chr.* 22.39, 90, 113.
	monumenta Cf. l. 169 below; also *Her. Chr.* 16.237.
21–22	**Qualem . . . semper habere** Prop. 1.3.40.
23	**Non ego te** = Catul. 64.221; Verg. *Ecl.* 3.17; *G.* 2.101; *A.* 10.185; Ov. *Ep.* 10.67; et al.; Eob. *Her. Chr.* 9.59; 11.113; 13.55; 16.233.
	patrias . . . regnare per urbes Cf. Verg. *A.* 3.295; Mant. *Sylv.* 2, fol. 266ʳ: ". . . patrias regnare per urbes." For *patrias urbes*, see Eob. *Rec.* 102, n.
25	**In tua . . . remorari damna** Cf. *Her. Chr.* 12.167; Ov. *Am.* 3.11.22; *Ep.* 1.96; 5.58; *Pont.* 1.2.44.
26	**adversum — fretum** Cf. Ov. *Ep.* 17.236.
27	**Longa via est** = Ov. *Tr.* 1.1.127; *Pont.* 4.5.3; Eob. *Her. Chr.* 14.39; cf. Ov. *Fast.* 5.501; Eob. *Her. Chr.* 10.185, n.
	pelagique . . . pericula vasti Cf. Verg. *A.* 6.83; 10.57.
28	**Multa — mari** Cf. *Her. Chr.* 6.72, n.
	Multa . . . multa = Ov. *Ep.* 13.120; *Ars* 1.262; *Pont.* 4.7.50.
29	**mandata dedisti** Cf. *Her. Chr.* 9.49, n.
30	**Flebam posse** Ov. *Ep.* 1.18.

31	**Quid fles** = Prop. 2.20.1; Ov. *Am.* 3.6.57; *Ep.* 3.24.
32	**semianimis . . . fui** Ov. *Ep.* 10.32.
	semianimis . . . pene Cf. *Her. Chr.* 8.118, n. For the motif — fainting at the husband's departure — cf. Ov. *Ep.* 13.23–26.
33	**Nescio quid . . . mea mens** Ov. *Ep.* 12.212.
	mea mens *Buc.* 3.136, n.
	mens — futuri = Balbi, *Opusc.* 59.5; cf. Ov. *Met.* 11.457; Luc. 6.414–15; Eob. *Eleg.* 1.131; *Sylv.* 3.7.9. Cf. further *Her. Chr.* 9.129, n.; 20.54, n.
34	**sim reducis — eram** Cf. Ov. *Ep.* 6.112.
35–46	**Oscula — aquas** For the farewell scene, cf. especially Ov. *Ep.* 13.7–24. Such scenes recur in Ovid's *Epistulae heroidum*: see *Ep.* 2.91–98; 3.13–24; 5.41–58; 6.57–74; 8.75–80; 10.3–58. Cf. Eob. *Her. Chr.* 7.21–52; 21.145–76. In Ov. *Ep.* 15.99–116, and Eob. *Her. Chr.* 9.35–52, n., the heroines lament that they have been denied a proper farewell.
35	**Oscula . . . dedisti** = Ov. *Ep.* 5.51; Eob. *Her. Chr.* 7.21, 47; cf. Ov. *Ep.* 13.7.
	Oscula et amplexus = Aus. *Pater ad filium* 6; Celtis, *Am.* 4.8.38; 4.11.2; Eob. *Her. Chr.* 21.157 (also in a farewell scene); *Eleg.* 3.43: "Oscula et amplexus miseros solantur amantes."
36	**turpis amor** = *Sylv. duae* 2.90, n.
37–38	**Terga — fuit** Cf. Ov. *Ep.* 5.55–56; 13.17–18.
38	**lachryma . . . praepediente** Cf. *Buc.* 3.162, n.
39	**Iamque oculis — eras** = Ov. *Ep.* 10.43; cf. *Met.* 7.776.
	Super aequora = Lucr. 5.1227; 6.108; Ov. *Met.* 4.752; 8.849; et al.; Eob. *Vict.* 222.
40	**portus et aura** = Ov. *Ep.* 1.110 (in mss. and older eds.); Poliziano, *Eleg.* 5.30: "o animi portus et aura mei"; Brant, *Var. carm.*, sig. E4ʳ (*Texte* 193.40 and Eob. *Hod.* B 7.28): "portus et aura rati"; sig. bc2ᵛ (*Texte* 195.527). Cf. Eob. *Laud.* 514, with n.; *Her. Chr.* 14.114.
41	**Christe, salus rerum** = Ven. Fort. *Carm.* 3.9.47.
42	**Secura . . . via** = *Her. Chr.* 20.108.
	vir meus = Ov. *Ep.* 13.50; Eob. *Her. Chr.* 5.114; 8.130; cf. l. 62 below.
	ire via = *Sylv. duae* 2.98, n.
43	**stella maris** *Buc.* 11.55, where see nn.
	pelle tenebras Ov. *Met.* 7.703; Sen. *Phaed.* 751; Luc. 2.326.
44	**Ne . . . aequorea naufraga** ≈ Ov. *Ep.* 7.62.
	naufraga . . . ratis = Ov. *Ars* 1.412 (different); cf. Eob. *Her. Chr.* 8.124.
46	**remige sulcet aquas** ≈ Jakob Locher, "Epiodion de morte Plutonis et reliquorum daemonum," *Poematia* (n.p., after 16 October 1512), sig. a3ʳ: "[Charon] . . . nullo remige sulcat aquas."
47	**Obtestata — valeres** The line both imitates and inverts Ov. *Ep.* 2.17.
48	**Desertae . . . domus** l. 177 below, n.
	tecta . . . alta Verg. *A.* 4.343.
49	**Quid . . . ? Vir abest** = Ov. *Ars* 2.369.
	solam iuvat esse l. 54 below.
49–50	**Sine illo . . . dulce nihil** Cf. Verg. *A.* 12.882–83; Claud. *in Rufin.* 2.268; Prud. *Cath.* 3.11; Eob. *Buc.* 7.119–21, n.
50	**vita coelibe** = *Her. Chr.* 13.20; cf. Hor. *Ep.* 1.1.88; Ov. *Tr.* 2.163.
51	**procerum — manus** Cf. Ov. *Met.* 13.382; Eob. *Nup.* 108, n.
51–52	**in aula . . . principis** *Buc.* B 2.15, n.
52	**tanti principis** ≈ Ov. *Tr.* 2.242; cf. Claud. *Epith.* 307–08; Eob. *Buc.* B 2.25, 47.
53	**cruces animi** *Psalt.* 102.3: "Audi verba, cruces animi testantia. . . ."
	animi . . . patientis = Ov. *Pont.* 4.10.9.
54	**More pii . . . turturis** The turtledove was said to remain true to its mate, even after its death, and so became a stock emblem of marital love and fidelity: see T. Peach,

"Sources et fortunes d'une image: 'sur l'arbre sec la veufve tourterelle,'" *BHR* 48 (1986), 735–45; Prop. 2.15.27; Plin. *Nat.* 10.104; Eob. *Buc.* 7.130; *Her. Chr.* 7.1–2, n.

solam . . . esse iuvat l. 49 above.

55   **iuvenum — gerentum** Cf. *Epith.* 174–75: "Ille decus iuvenum Studaeus casta gerentum / Pectora." For *iuvenum flos*, see Catul. 100.2; for *pectora casta*, see Ov. *Ep.* 13.30; Eob. *Her. Chr.* 20.154.

56   **clausa . . . gaudia** Prop. 2.25.30; Eob. *Hod.* B 1.34.

57–62   **Scilicet — opem** The model is Ov. *Ep.* 13.37–42. Cf. *Ep.* 15.73–78; Eob. *Her. Chr.* 12.63–66; 12.71–72; 18.131–44. For ll. 57–58, cf. also Stat. *Theb.* 4.204–06.

57   **Scilicet ipsa** ≈ *Her. Chr.* 12.63.

radians — aurum = *Nob.* 157. For the tag *vestibus aurum*, see Ov. *Met.* 3.556.

59   **Assyrio . . . rore capillus** Cf. [Tib.] 3.4.28; Ov. *Ep.* 15.76; *Met.* 11.57; Pontano, *Parthen.* 2.14.4: "Assyrio tingere rore comam"; Eob. *Nob.* 73.

61   **sublimis in aula** = Juvenc. 4.34; cf. Ov. *Ep.* 12.179.

62   **Vir meus** Cf. l. 42 above, n.

fracto gurgite Petr. 123.241.

63   **Tu melius** = *Her. Chr.* 4.51, n.

qui fine — vivis Cf. *Her. Chr.* 1.14, n.; 4.30, n.

qui fine cares ≈ Prud. *c. Symm.* 1.326, referring to God.

64   **votis annue** Ov. *Pont.* 2.8.51.

65   **dolor — horas** Cf. Verg. *Ecl.* 10.73; Eob. *Her. Chr.* 7.55; 19.103.

dolor . . . longus *Her. Chr.* 3.93, n.

66   **Dum vir — abes** Cf. Ov. *Ep.* 3.52; Eob. *Her. Chr.* 13.6.

67   **pocula . . . sumo** Ov. *Am.* 1.4.31; *Ep.* 16.226; 17.79–80; et al.; l. 137 below.

69–118   **Cura — faces** In these verses Eobanus amplifies Ov. *Ep.* 13.103–12 (partly used also in Eob. *Ama.* 9.1–8, where see n.).

69–70   **Cura — subis** Cf. *Buc.* 7.119–21, n.

69   **Cura eadem** = *Buc.* 6.79.

mane renascens = *Nor.* 427 (of the sun).

71   **Somnia . . . variis . . . figuris** = Claud. *Rapt. Pros.* 3.124; cf. Eob. *Ama.* 9.1, n.

Somnia . . . nocturna Hor. *Carm.* 4.1.37.

73   **Pallidus** As if he were already dead. So Laodamia sees her husband in a dream as "pallens imago" (Ov. *Ep.* 13.109).

75–77   **Sive — noctis** Cf. [Tib.] 3.4.11–13.

76   **redit — metus** For the proverbial thought that dreams reflect the things that occupy us by day, see, for example, Cic. *Div.* 1.45; *Dicta Catonis* 2.31; Claud. *VI. Cons. Hon.*, praef. 1–2.

in vanos . . . metus = *Sylv.* 1.4.60: "Non cadit in vanos mens generosa metus"; cf. Ov. *Ep.* 16.344.

77   **Praeteritae . . . noctis** Prop. 2.14.9; Juv. 10.235; Eob. *Buc.* 8.25.

timidam — noctis Cf. Prop. 3.8.15.

78   **Irrita — Deus** Cf. [Tib.] 3.4.95–96; Ov. *Ep.* 13.92; *Rem.* 286; Otto 1864; Eob. *Her. Chr.* 19.164, n.; *Idyl.* 17.195.

79–80   **Hic — habet** ≈ *Psalt.*, ded. 55–56: "Hic, ubi monticolam Lanus tuus alluit urbem, / Inclyta quae prisci nomina Martis habet"; *Epith.* 1–3: "Hic, ubi prisca feri cognomina Martis habentem / Lanus arenosa praetextus arundine ripas / Praeterit atque imis radicibus alluit urbem"; cf. *Eras.* 101–02: "Hic, ubi belligeri Martis cognomine Burgum / Ardua praecelsae culmina rupis habet." For the phrasing, cf. also *Her. Chr.* 12.119–20; *Epic.* 7.95–96.

79   **Hic — urbem** Cf. *Laud.* 250; *Buc.* 3.1; 9.56–57, n.

piscosus For the epithet, see, for example, Verg. *A.* 11.457; 12.518; Hor. *S.* 1.5.97; Ov. *Fast.* 3.581; Eob. *Hod.* 94.

claram . . . urbem = Ov. *Tr.* 1.2.79; cf. Eob. *Her. Chr.* 12.119.

80   **nomina . . . habet** = Prop. 4.2.50; Ov. *Fast.* 3.4, 118, 150, 246; et al.; Eob. *Sylv. duae* 1.74, n.; *Her. Chr.* 21.126.

81   **Monte sub aereo** = Verg. *A.* 6.234 (the mountain where Aeneas buried Misenus). Here the reference is to the hill on which Marburg and its castle are built. Cf. Eob. *Eras.* 101–02 (quoted in n. at ll. 79–80 above); *Sylv.* 7.1.7–8: "monte sitam celso . . . urbem."

83–84   **dum — comes** Cf. *Her. Chr.* 4.149–50; also cf. *Her. Chr.* 3.152.

85   **pedem . . . citatum** Catul. 63.2.
        pedem revocare Verg. *A.* 9.125.

86   **Ecce sed** = *Her. Chr.* 3.75, n.
        a longe This late Latin expression recurs in the Vulgate: see, for example, *Tob.* 11.6; *Matt.* 26.58.
        visus — mihi = Verg. *A.* 2.271; Dantiscus, *Carm.* 1.3.208.

87   **Frigore constiterant** Ov. *Met.* 9.662; *Tr.* 5.10.1; *Pont.* 1.2.79.
        gaudia mentem = Petr. 128.6: "mox ubi fugerunt elusam gaudia mentem"; cf. Catul. 64.236; Ov. *Am.* 3.7.63; *Tr.* 5.8.21.

88   **Mecum — fui** Cf. Ov. *Ars* 3.664 (different); Eob. *Hod.* B 1.66: ". . . mecum non satis ipse fui"; *Epp. fam.*, 77 (23 June 1527): "In tanta amicorum . . . discordia mecum non satis eram."

90   **rorantes — genas** Cf. Lucr. 3.469; Ov. *Am.* 2.6.4; *Ep.* 5.72; Eob. *Her. Chr.* 3.44, n.

91   **Huc — cucurri** Cf. Ov. *Ep.* 10.19 (quoted in Eob. *Ama.* 10.1).
        Huc illuc = *Her. Chr.* 4.169, n.

93   **umbra Creusae** = Verg. *A.* 2.772.

94   **anhelantem . . . virum** ≈ *Luth.* 3.6; cf. Prud. *c. Symm.* 2.34.

95   **indignos . . . capillos** = Ov. *Am.* 3.9.3.
        laniare capillos = Ov. *Am.* 1.7.11; 2.5.45; *Met.* 9.354; cf. Eob. *Buc.* 9.81, n.

96   **vox . . . aegra** *Vict.* 458.
        lachrymis tristibus Tib. 1.1.62.

97   **Hic — dixit** Cf. Verg. *A.* 2.735; Ov. *Ep.* 15.109; Eob. *Her. Chr.* 14.85.

99   **Plura — reliqui** Cf. Verg. *A.* 2.790–91; Ov. *Rem.* 575–76; *Met.* 13.966.
        Plura loquturum = Ov. *Met.* 1.525; cf. *Met.* 7.348; *Fast.* 4.385.
        somno — reliqui ≈ Paul. Nol. *Carm.* 23.185: "stratum somno fugiente relinquens."

100   **fatigata . . . nocte** Cf. Prop. 4.11.81; Verg. *A.* 8.94. That the dream takes place after midnight indicates that it is truthful: cf. Eob. *Buc.* 8.97, n.

101   **Frigidus — sudor** = *Epic.* 3A.39 (after a dream); cf. Verg. *A.* 3.175; Ov. *Met.* 5.632. Also cf. Eob. *Her. Chr.* 12.16, n.; 12.82, n.: "In toto . . . corpore."

102   **Perfusae lachrymis . . . genae** Verg. *A.* 12.64–65; cf. Ov. *Ep.* 14.127; *Fast.* 5.407; Eob. *Her. Chr.* 19.111.
        lachrymis — genae ≈ Ov. *Tr.* 1.9.34.

103   **Aeger — aegro** Cf. *Psalt.* 77.11: "Spiritus exangui sub pectore deficit aeger."
        Aeger . . . spiritus Juvenc. 1.743; Eob. *Her. Chr.* 14.115.
        Aeger anhelabat = Paul. Nol. *Carm.* 16.29.

104   **Vis animae** = Lucr. 4.917; Man. 1.250; cf. Lucr. 5.560; Eob. *Hod.* B 7.54.

105   **tristi — monstro** Cf. Verg. *A.* 3.307; Stat. *Ach.* 1.662; Sil. 8.185.

107   **agmine turbae** = Tib. 1.5.63.

108   **Effugis . . . umbra** Ov. *Fast.* 5.476.
        amplexus . . . umbra meos Cf. Prop. 4.7.96.
        labilis umbra Pontano, *Tum.* 1.7.7: "Seu tantum cinis es . . . seu labilis umbra."

109   **militibus comitatus** Ov. *Am.* 1.6.33.

110   **moesta figura** = Ov. *Ep.* 10.134. For *figura* in the sense of "ghost," see Verg. *A.* 10.641.

112   **O superi — malum** Cf. Verg. *A.* 3.265; Tifernate, *Carm.*, sig. C2ᵛ: ". . . a nobis hoc prohibete nefas."
        O superi = Ov. *Met.* 9.244; Luc. 2.296; 7.869.

113   **Omnia perpetiar** = Prop. 2.26.35; Ov. *Ep.* 20.83.
114   **Tutus ope** Ov. *Rem.* 473.
        vir meus = l. 42, n., above.
116   **ignota . . . exul humo** ≈ *Her. Chr.* 16.10, n.; cf. Ov. *Ep.* 16.276; *Fast.* 1.490;
        2.444.
117   **Hoc — votis** Cf. *Sylv.* 1.1.125: "Hoc te tota rogat communi Prussia voto."
        Hessia votis = l. 179 below.
118   **Plurimaque — faces** Cf. Mant. *Ecl.* 6.187: ". . . plures faculas accendimus aris." For
        faces in the sense of "candles," cf. also Eob. *Buc.* 11.81; *Hymn.* 131–37.
        accensas . . . faces = Prop. 3.16.16; Ov. *Am.* 1.1.8.
        accipit ara = Ov. *Am.* 3.13.9.
119   **Per — mundum** Cf. *AH* 51.107.3: "Per illa sancta / te rogamus vulnera, / Quae
        mundi cuncta / diluerunt crimina."
        sanasti vulnera Cf. l. 174 below.
120   **nostra redempta** = *Her. Chr.* 3.46.
121   **Per sacrae . . . crucis signacula** Cf. *Her. Chr.* 12.216.
122   **alma salus** Stat. *Theb.* 10.611.
123   **Te precor** = *Buc.* B 11.28, n.
124   **foelix . . . iter** = Ov. *Ep.* 21.74.
125–64 **At tu — nocet** The motif — the worried wife offers advice to her husband — is
        taken from Ov. *Ep.* 13.65–78. Cf. Eob. *Her. Chr.* 20.115–30.
125   **amor castus** *Laud.* 240, n.
        mea — movit = Ov. *Met.* 7.28.
126   **Ut facis** = Ov. *Pont.* 2.3.48; Mart. 10.33.7; cf. Eob. *Her. Chr.* 4.73, n.
        salvus eris ≈ Ov. *Ep.* 20.178.
127   **vitare memento** = Ov. *Ep.* 13.67 (Laodamia's advice to Protesilaus); Juv. 6.572.
128   **inde timor** = *Her. Chr.* 2.10.
129   **Sancta . . . Iudaea** Paul. Nol. *Carm.* 26.37.
132   **posse redire** = Ov. *Ep.* 13.78; *Tr.* 5.12.30; Eob. *Her. Chr.* 20.158.
135   **solus abibis** ≈ Ov. *Ars* 2.361; Eob. *Buc.* 7.22.
137   **Pocula . . . sumas** l. 67, n., above.
138   **vero . . . ore** = [Tib.] 3.4.50; Eob. *Her. Chr.* 13.142.
        ore bibat = Ov. *Am.* 2.10.34.
140   **praesens — puta** = *Her. Chr.* 17.132, n.
141–42 **Lurida — nocens** Cf. *Ama.* 35.99–100, n. For l. 141, cf. Ov. *Met.* 1.147. Eobanus
        appears to allude to the old Hessian tradition according to which Ludwig's premature
        death was due to poisoning: see Rener, 449, with n. 42.
141   **nobilibus . . . Phalernis** Prud. *Cath.* 9.28.
142   **merum gemma** Cf. Ov. *Met.* 8.573.
143   **comitum manus** Stat. *Silv.* 5.3.262; Sil. 6.334.
        lecta iuventus = Verg. *A.* 8.606.
144   **Est — petas** Cf. Ov. *Ars* 1.230; Eob. *Hod.* B 1.98.
        docta fraude Erasmus, *Carm.* 4.114, referring to the judgment of Solomon.
145–58 **Ex — tuum** For this survival trick, see Vulg. *3. Reg.* 22.30 (*2. Par.* 18.29).
145   **dominum . . . saluta** ≈ Juv. 8.161; Mart. 4.83.5.
146   **exiguae sortis** *Hod.* 511.
        sortis — locum = *Psalt.* 37.66; 105.56; cf. *Buc.*, lim. 4, n.
148   **famulas . . . manus** = *Her. Chr.* 2.42, n.
149–50 **Foecit — pedes** See Vulg. *Joan.* 13.5–17.
149   **rerum — potestas** Cf. Verg. *A.* 10.18, 100; Prud. *Amart.* 20: "deus . . . rerum cui
        summa potestas"; Eob. *Her.* 1.1.15: "Deus et rerum suprema potestas."
150   **Immundos . . . pedes** Prop. 4.4.78.
151   **Quod . . . decuit, quem non decet?** = Ov. *Ars* 2.241.
        Omnia vincet = V. Fl. 1.236; cf. Verg. *G.* 1.145.

153–54 **Saepe — habet** Cf. Ov. *Am.* 1.4.54; *Tr.* 1.1.92.
    locorum Conditio Quint. *Inst.* 12.10.2; Fron. *Str.* 1.6.3; 2.6.6.

154 **caecum — habet** Fortuna was proverbially blind: see Otto 694; Häussler, 103, 164, 236; Eob. *Her. Chr.* 8.7–8; *Sylv.* 1.1.98: ". . . dea quae tectum sindone lumen habet"; 1.4.32; 3.7.10. For the phrasing, cf. Ov. *Ep.* 18.74.

155 **Invenies aliquem qui** = Ov. *Tr.* 1.1.27.
    sic fata iuberent ≈ *Rec.* 94, n.

157 **Veste . . . vili** = Ov. *Ep.* 15.75.
    loca . . . tuta *Her. Chr.* 22.63, n.

158 **purpura nulla** = *Epic. Drusi* 186.

159 **ingenio . . . beatus** = *Sylv.* 1.2.127: "Crotus, ingenio plus quam florente beatus."
    ingenio . . . praestante Mant. *1. Parthen.* 1.249.

160 **Consilio — meo** ≈ *Ama.* 35.118, n.

161 **in dubiis . . . rebus** = Mant. *1. Parthen.* 2.135; Eob. *Her. Chr.* 20.115; cf. *Her. Chr.* 10.195, n.

164 **Audacem — nocet** Cf. *Buc.* 7.24, n.

165 **Ipsa Deum supplex** ≈ Andrel. *Ecl.* 4.85: "Ipse Deum supplex . . . rogavit."
    supplex . . . precabor Ov. *Ep.* 4.149; *Tr.* 2.201; Eob. *Her. Chr.* 14.79.
    mora longa = Hor. *Carm.* 1.28.35; Ov. *Am.* 2.2.23; *Met.* 6.215; et al.

166 **Contingas . . . pede** ≈ Ov. *Tr.* 1.1.16.
    fausto . . . pede = Guarino, *Carm.* 3, sig. g6ᵛ: "tetigi fausto regia tecta pede"; cf. Hor. *Ep.* 2.2.37; Eob. *Nup.* 252.
    regna beata = Ov. *Ep.* 12.24.

167 **Solimos . . . colles** *Her. Chr.* 3.139, n.

168 **oculis aspicienda** = Ov. *Ep.* 9.124.

169 **nostrae — salutis** = verse in an Easter Mass, *PL* 78, col. 241 A: "Digna manus nostras Christi custodia servet, / Ut tractare queant nostrae monumenta salutis." For *monumenta*, cf. l. 20, n., above.

170 **immemor esse tuam** ≈ Ov. *Am.* 1.14.38; cf. *Ep.* 15.106.

172 **sanguine . . . rubes** ≈ Ov. *Tr.* 4.6.34.

173 **magis exorabilis** ≈ *Buc.* 11.62.

174 **sanavit vulnera** Cf. l. 119 above.
    vulnera nostra = Prop. 3.21.32; Ov. *Ep.* 11.10; *Pont.* 1.6.22; 2.3.94; Eob. *Her. Chr.* 15.68.

176 **fasso . . . ore** = Ov. *Ars* 2.556; Eob. *Her. Chr.* 15.126; cf. *Her. Chr.* 11.37.
    quas . . . ore preces = Ov. *Pont.* 4.9.130; Eob. *Her. Chr.* 11.28, 178.

177 **Desertae . . . domus** = Mant. *2. Parthen.* 2.707: "Desertae miserere domus"; cf. Ov. *Tr.* 3.8.9; l. 48 above.
    memor esto Cf. Verg. *A.* 10.280–81; Mant. *1. Parthen.* 3.597: "esto mei saltem memor et miserere tuorum."

178 **tecum — parens** ≈ *Her. Chr.* 13.4; cf. *Her. Chr.* 18.109; 20.156; Ov. *Ep.* 12.198. Elizabeth is expecting her third child.
    facta parens = Ov. *Am.* 2.19.28; *Ib.* 564; Eob. *Her. Chr.* 13.4; 20.62; 22.18.

179 **Hessia votis** = l. 117 above.

180 **Ante — Dei** Modeled on Mant. *c. Poet.* 100: "Ante flagellati vulnera quinque Dei."

181 **ventos — secundos** Cf. Verg. *A.* 3.683; 7.23.

182 **redire voles** = Ov. *Rem.* 238.

183 **Rhodon et Cretam** = *Sylv. duae* 1.32.

185 **longo . . . voto** = Stat. *Theb.* 1.323.
    cura . . . sedula Aus. *Prof.*, praef. 3; Paul. Nol. *Carm.* 14.121; 21.664; Eob. *Her. Chr.* 22.125; *Nor.* 439.

186 **Dii faciant** = *Sylv. duae* 2.46, n.
    pondus — habere Cf. *Her. Chr.* 2.88, with nn.
    possit habere = Ov. *Ars* 3.438; Eob. *Her. Chr.* 2.2.

6

Meter: Elegiac distich.

1   **veram . . . salutem** Avit. 4.639; Eob. *Her. Chr.* 18.117; cf. also l. 4 below: "rectae . . . salutis." For the play on the two meanings of *salus*, see *Her. Chr.* 3.1, n.

2   **debuit esse** = Prop. 3.5.10; Ov. *Ep.* 21.106; Eob. *Her. Chr.* 17.2.

3   **signum venerabile** Sebastian Brant, poem for Hrabanus Maurus' *De laudibus sanctae crucis* (Pforzheim, 1503), in *Texte* 269.27: ". . . pedibus calcant venerabile signum."

4   **salutis opus** = Ven. Fort. *Carm.* 3.26.2; 6.10.70; et al.; Eob. *Her. Chr.* 6.12.

5   **caelo . . . sereno** = Verg. *G.* 1.260; *A.* 3.518; Ov. *Met.* 1.168.

7   **In qua nostra salus . . . pependit** *Missale mixtum secundum Regulam B. Isidori dictum Mozarabes, PL* 85, col. 421 B: "O Sancta Crux, in qua salus nostra pependit"; Jakob Wimpfeling, afterword to Hrabanus Maurus' *De laudibus sanctae crucis* (Pforzheim, 1503), in his *Briefwechsel,* ed. Otto Herding and Dieter Mertens, vol. 1 (Munich, 1990), 355: "sanctae Crucis, 'in qua salus nostra pependit.'" Cf. Rufin. *Eusebii Caesariensis Historia ecclesiastica: continuatio* 10.8: "lignum beatum, in quo salus nostra pependit."
     vita pependit = Paul. Nol. *Carm.* 27.289: "ligno mea vita pependit."

8   **Per — sumus** Cf. *Her. Chr.* 15.142; *Tum.* 5.118: "Verbo / Per quod mortalis turba redempta sumus"; *Nob.* 23: "mortalis turba."

9   **mundi precium . . . redempti** Liminary epigram by Eobanus for *Philippi Beroaldi de die dominice passionis carmen* (Leipzig, 1518), l. 1: "Nate Deo, mundi pretium non vile redempti"; cf. Ven. Fort. *Carm.* 2.10.10; 3.9.68; *AH* 50.386.1; cf. l. 32 below. The concept is based on Vulg. *1. Cor.* 6.20; cf. also *1. Cor.* 7.23.

10   **infernum . . . cahos** This patristic phrase occurs also in Marul. *Hymn. nat.* 1.1.78. The spelling "cahos" for "chaos" is common in the Renaissance. For *chaos* in the sense of "underworld," see, for example, Ov. *Met.* 10.30; 14.404; *Fast.* 4.600; for the sense of "hellish darkness," cf. Eob. *Her. Chr.* 22.130; *Vict.* 72.

11–12   **Arbor — opus** Cf. Ven. Fort. *Carm.* 2.2.22–23 (*AH* 50.66.8): "Crux fidelis, inter omnes arbor una nobilis / (nulla talem silva profert flore fronde germine)."

11   **Arbor — sylvis** = l. 197 below.
     Arbor ab Eois . . . sylvis Cf. Mant. *2. Parthen.* 1.14–16 (referring to the Tree of Life in Paradise): "fronde . . . / Arboris Aeoae, medio quam legimus horto / Spargere felicem ramis vitalibus umbram"; Eob. *Her. Chr.* 6.169–70, with n. 14.
     longe dignissima Mant. *1. Parthen.* 2.564: "longe . . . dignissima Virgo."

12   **palma** The symbol of victory and peace, the palm also became a symbol of the cross in patristic literature. Gregory the Great, for example, interprets the palm in Vulg. *Cant.* 7.7–8 as referring allegorically to the cross: see *Super Cantica canticorum expositio, PL* 79, col. 536 B–C. See further Salzer, 181–82.
     salutis opus = l. 4 above, n.

13–14   **Omnia — Creditur** Cf. Ambros., *De Abraham* 1.8.78: "virgultum illud patibulum crucis [est], et in hoc ligno praestantissimus ductor gregis exaltatus omnia traxit ad se, ut ab omnibus cognosceretur"; Paul. Nol. *Ep.* 5.16: "exaltatus omnia traxit ad se"; and, for example, *AH* 54.120.6: "Haec [*sc.* crux] est scala peccatorum, / Per quam Christus, rex caelorum, / Ad se traxit omnia." The idea is based on Vulg. *Joan.* 12.32, where Jesus alludes to his crucifixion: "et ego si exaltatus fuero, a terra omnia traham ad me ipsum."

13   **passis . . . lacertis** *Buc.* 8.67.

14   **immenso pondere** Cf. ll. 185–88 below, n.
     pondere — gravis = *Her. Chr.* 19.112; cf. Mart. 7.53.8.

15   **Apelleae . . . genti** Mutian. *Ep.* 251 (written in August 1513): "quota portio gentis Apelleae."

17   **fronte** Cf. *Her. Chr.* 14.11; 15.16.

19   **gentilitiis . . . signis** = *Nob.* 313; *Epp. 3,* sig. C8ᵛ: "gentilitiis posset praeponere signis / Huttenus"; cf. *Her. Chr.,* ded. 19.1. The parallels just mentioned all refer to family crests. Here *gentilitiis* is used in the sense of "pagan." Cf. l. 195 below.

21	**potiora . . . gaudia** Prud. *c. Symm.* 2.163–64.
	gaudia mundo = *Buc.* 9.97, n.
23	**cum — illa** = l. 157 below; cf. *Her. Chr.* 16.246.
25–26	**nostrae — Deus** Cf. *Vict.* 53–54. For *nostrae sub imagine carnis,* cf. Ov. *Met.* 1.213; Brant, *Var. carm.*, sig. I3ᵛ (omitted in *Texte* 215): "Filius humana lustrans sub imagine mundum"; Eob. *Her. Chr.* 2.123. For the patristic phrase *virgine factus homo,* see, for example, August. *In Johannis evangelium tractatus* 19.15: "ex virgine Maria homo factus, filius hominis est"; cf. Eob. *Her. Chr.* 9.84, n. Also cf. *Her. Chr.* 1.70.
27	**abiecto . . . profuit orbi** *Hod.* 307.
29–30	**Vita magis — salus** Cf. Prud. *Cath.* 10.89–92.
29	**vita dignior** = Verg. *A.* 9.212.
31	**Author . . . nostrae . . . salutis** *Hod.* B 7.35 (the Virgin Mary); cf. Luc. 4.399–400; Prud. *Cath.* 4.12.
	crux alma Ven. Fort. *Carm.* 2.3.18; Eob. *Her. Chr.* 17.192.
32	**mundi precio** l. 9 above, n.
33	**dolor est meminisse** = Petrarch, *Africa* 7.392; Eob. *Her. Chr.* 14.53; cf. *Her. Chr.* 11.97; 15.28; *Nor.* 215.
34	**infami . . . loco** Ov. *Ep.* 18.141.
35–36	**Hic — loco** Cf. *Her. Chr.* 3.133–34, n., where the time paraphrase refers to noon. Here it refers to the summer solstice, when the sun enters the Crab. Cf. *Buc.*, ded. 2, with n. 5.
35	**ubi . . . sol aspicit** = Man. 1.242: "hanc ubi ad occasus nostros sol aspicit ortus"; cf. Verg. *A.* 7.100–01; Hor. *Epod.* 9.16.
	Solimas . . . arces Mant. *1. Parthen.* 1.690; 3.231; Eob. *Her. Chr.* 21.186, n.
36	**aliquo . . . loco** = Ov. *Tr.* 2.524.
	umbra loco = *Sylv.* 1.9.10, at noon: "brevis ex omni facta erit umbra loco."
37–38	**Hic locus — vocat** Cf. Vulg. *Matt.* 27.33; *Marc.* 15.22; *Joan.* 19.17.
37	**Hic locus est** = Verg. *A.* 6.540; Ov. *Met.* 1.175; *Tr.* 3.1.29.
38	**Iudaea — vocat** Cf. Mant. *2. Parthen.* 3.769–70: "'polyandrion' Hellas / Voce vocat patria."
39	**Hoc stetit — Christi** Cf. *Sylv.* 2.27.3: "Sic stetit illa videns morientis vulnera Christi"; *Her. Chr.* 16.5.
	sanguine Christi = *Sylv. duae* 2.199, n.
41	**virtute laborem** = Sil. 12.511.
43	**qui — solus** Cf. Vulg. *Psa.* 71.18; 135.4; Eob. *Her. Chr.* 13.161–62; *Psalt.* 77.35: "Tu Deus es qui summa facis miracula solus"; 136.9: "Qui toties tot, tanta facit miracula solus."
45	**Magna — feci** Combining Ov. *Ep.* 16.141 et al. ("magna quidem . . .") with Ov. *Met.* 13.160 ("plura quidem feci . . .").
	longos — annos = *Ilias* 7.105; cf. *Luth.* 2.3; *Nor.* 1383.
	longos . . . annos = Verg. *A.* 10.549; cf. Ov. *Am.* 2.19.23.
46	**gloria — habet** = *Her. Chr.* 19.100; *Val.* 3.4: "Omnibus haec maius gloria nomen habet"; cf. Prop. 2.7.17. For *nomen habet,* see Eob. *Sylv. duae* 1.24, n.
48	**quantus . . . timor** = *Luth.* 6.64: "Sic Troiae fueras quantus, Achille, timor."
50	**titulum — velim** Cf. Ov. *Tr.* 1.11.30; Eob. *Luth.* 6.24: ". . . titulum laudis habere volet."
51	**omne quod audet** = Paul. Nol. *Carm.* 26.231.
52	**Nullus — erat** Cf. *Psalt.* 27.14: "Nullus in hoc gelidus pectore sanguis erit"; *Her. Chr.* 15.66, n.
53	**certam — salutem** Cf. Verg. *G.* 4.294; Mart. 12.90.5; Eob. *Rec.* 22, n.
54	**Quamque dedit** = Ov. *Tr.* 1.2.61.
	res est — fidem Cf. Ov. *Met.* 4.550; Eob. *Her. Chr.* 7.54, n.
55	**Venimus — Siona** Cf. *Her. Chr.* 14.73; also *Her. Chr.* 7.93.
	notissima — Siona Cf. Sil. 1.27.
56	**posuit . . . templa** Verg. *A.* 6.19; Mant. *1. Parthen.* 1.849.
	lyrico . . . duce Cf. *Ama.* 26.4: "lyrici Davidis."

58   **ex tota — tributa** = Ov. *Ep.* 4.54, where the phrase refers to Venus.
59   **Rhomanum — nomen** Cf. Ov. *Met.* 1.201.
60   **Cui — fuit** For the commonplace that the Roman Empire is bounded only by the rising and setting sun, see, for example, Verg. *A.* 7.99–101; Hor. *Carm.* 4.15.13–16; Tib. 2.5.57–60; Ov. *Fast.* 2.136; Claud. *Bell. Gild.* 48 (the Roman Empire): "ad solem victrix utrumque cucurri."
61   **Nec sequor — ausis** Cf. Ov. *Ep.* 18.149.
       magnis . . . ausis = Ov. *Met.* 2.328.
63   **sanguine parta** = Walter, *Alex.* 4.245; Petrarch, *Africa* 2.350: "sanguine parta / Gloria." Cf. Ov. *Ep.* 1.94; Sil. 15.255; Eob. *Sylv. duae* 1.48.
64   **Insignes — sumus** Cf. *Her. Chr.* 21.52. For the commonplace of true nobility, see *Nup.* 97–99, n. That the person being praised is noble by birth *and* accomplishments is a panegyric commonplace: see *Laud.* 147, n. For the Christian use of the theme, cf., for example, Erasmus, *Enchiridion, LB* 5, col. 41 D: "Vera nobilitas est inanem contemnere nobilitatem; vera nobilitas est servum esse Christi. Hos tibi maiores esse puta, quorum virtutes aemularis."
       nos — sumus = *Her. Chr.*, lim. 6, n.
66   **Nos — loco** Cf. Mant. *Bapt.*, fol. 229^v: "Regna manent alio nos meliora loco"; Eob. *Her. Chr.* 4.72, n.; 14.50; *Epic.* 5.108: "Quae nunc est alio vita futura loco."
       alio . . . loco = Ov. *Fast.* 5.724.
67   **sequimur caelestia** Arator 1.880–81: "Petrum caelestia semper, / Non terrena sequi."
68   **Da veniam** = *Her. Chr.* 2.14, n.
       Timida — mente Cf. Ov. *Tr.* 1.1.87; *Pont.* 2.8.75; Eob. *Epic.* 3A.28.
       mente loquor = *Her. Chr.* 19.62.
71   **Cuius — moverem** For the commonplace of spiritual warfare, see Vulg. *Job* 7.1; *1. Tim.* 1.18; *2. Tim.* 2.5; Sen. *Dial.* 7.15.5–7; Erasmus, *Enchiridion*, especially *LB* 5, col. 1 A–10 F. See further Andreas Wang, *Der "miles christianus" im 16. und 17. Jahrhundert und seine mittelalterliche Tradition* (Bern, 1975); Eob. *Her. Chr.* 11.123–24; 12.96; 17.9–22; 18.94, 121; 19.115–18; 22.95–100; 23.100; cf. also *Her. Chr.* 14.61–62; 18.94.
       in adversos hostes = Ov. *Rem.* 377; cf. l. 155, n., below.
       signa moverem ≈ *Her. Chr.* 17.161, n.
72   **Multa — mari** Cf. Tifernate, *Carm.*, sig. B3^r: "Multa patent terra, multa pericla mari"; cf. also Ov. *Ep.* 10.94; *Tr.* 3.2.7; Eob. *Her. Chr.* 5.28; 18.36.
73   **sublimi solio** *Orat.* 24.2, n.: "in sublimi solio residens."
74   **Invita . . . manu** = Ov. *Pont.* 3.2.66.
       sceptra superba manu Sen. *Ag.* 10; cf. Lucr. 5.1137; Ov. *Rem.* 480; *Pont.* 1.8.22.
75   **Rhomana potentia** = Verg. *A.* 8.99; Ov. *Met.* 15.877; *Fast.* 2.483; *Tr.* 5.2.35; l. 213 below.
76   **Sub pedibus** = *Buc.* 6.27, n.
       stabant — multa = *Luth.* 3.24.
       milia multa = Ov. *Am.* 1.8.58; Eob. *Her. Chr.* 8.52; 9.112; 12.58; 16.98; 16.252 (referring to Roman miles); 17.126; 22.114; *Nob.* 84; cf. *Nup.* 134, n.
78   **haec — dedi** Cf. Avianus, *Fabulae* 24.10: ". . . rabido pectore verba dedit"; Eob. *Luth.* 2.38. Cf. further Verg. *A.* 9.740; Ov. *Am.* 2.2.58; *Ep.* 18.98. For *pectore verba* at this metrical position, see also Eob. *Nup.*, lim. 4; *Her. Chr.* 21.80.
79   **genus Israel** Vulg. *Lev.* 23.42; *Phil.* 3.5; Eob. *Her. Chr.* 13.158; *Vict.* 251.
80   **contigit ista** = *Sylv. duae* 1.104.
81   **Dic ubi** = *Buc.* 3.54, n.
82   **Morte Creatoris** = *Vict.* 67.
       facta beata tui ≈ Prop. 2.28.26 (in some mss.): "facta beata tuae"; Eob. *Her. Chr.* 22.122; cf. Prop. 2.6.6; 2.15.2.
83   **Rhomano Caesar . . . orbi** ≈ *Nob.* 201. For *Rhomano orbi*, see *Her. Chr.* 12.43–44, n.
       qui praesidet orbi = Mant. *Bapt.*, fol. 229^v: "toti qui praesidet orbi"; cf. Prop. 3.11.57; Eob. *Her. Chr.* 19.15; l. 151 below.

84	**iubet ipse Deus** Tib. 1.6.43.
85	**Ante oculos** = Lucr. 2.113; 3.185; 4.979; Tib. 2.5.49; Verg. *A.* 11.311.
	vitamque . . . mortemque Ov. *Ep.* 12.74.
86	**vivere sive mori** = *Luth.* 2.64; cf. Ov. *Ep.* 3.140; V. Fl. 7.351–52; Eob. *Her. Chr.* 7.56, n.; 12.244.
87	**Caesaris imperio** = Ov. *Pont.* 4.13.38.
92	**crux veneranda loco** = *Her. Chr.* 14.74; cf. Paul. Nol. *Carm.* 25.192.
93–94	**nec precibus — opem** Cf. Ov. *Am.* 1.6.61–62.
93	**verbis . . . minacibus** Ov. *Met.* 5.669.
97	**Septima lux aderat** = Claud. *Epith.*, praef. 15; cf. Sedul. 3.258 (Mant. *1. Parthen.* 2.233; 3.510; Eob. *Hod.* 152): "Tertia lux aderat. . . ."; cf. also Ov. *Am.* 2.6.45.
98	**Iussit . . . loqui** = Tib. 1.9.28.
	saturo . . . ore = *Her. Chr.* 21.214.
	ore loqui = Ov. *Ep.* 12.72; *Fast.* 2.614; Eob. *Her. Chr.* 6.126; 11.36; *Nob.* 286.
99	**Templa . . . celeberrima** = Mant. *1. Parthen.* 1.589.
	Cytheriaco . . . scorto Venus; cf. *Her. Chr.* 9.89, n. In euhemeristic tradition Venus was originally a prostitute: see n. to *Ama.* 27.4.
100	**locus in terris** = *Laud.* 215, n.
101	**Quanta — patientia** Cf. Ov. *Tr.* 5.4.19; Paul. Nol. *Carm.* 6.103: "quanta dei pietas! . . ."; Eob. *Ama.* B 2.39.
102	**Improba . . . Venus** *Laud.* 239, n.
103	**magnum . . . Iesum** = *Nor.* 978; cf. *Her. Chr.* 7.151; *Buc.* 6.87, n.
	veneratus Iesum For the tag, cf. *Buc.* 11.78.
104	**Acidalias** Cf. *Buc.* 6.67, n.
105	**Crimine . . . tanto . . . poenas** Mart. *Sp.* 12.3; cf. Eob. *Pug.* 94, n.
	dederat . . . poenas Ov. *Fast.* 1.353.
	vindice poenas = Juvenc. 1.498; cf. Catul. 64.192.
106	**nobis diruta** = Ov. *Ep.* 8.104.
	diruta — iacent = Brant, *Var. carm.*, sig. d6ʳ (*Texte* 147.293); cf. Eob. *Sylv.* 1.5.20: "diruta templa Iovis."
107	**referat vestigia** ≈ Mant. *1. Parthen.* 2.501: "ne volitent verso referant vestigia gressu."
107–08	**iunctis — humum** Cf. *Hymn.* 95–96.
108	**sulcat . . . humum** Ov. *Tr.* 3.10.68.
110	**Nobilis . . . locus** Sedul. 5.296 (referring to Christ's sepulcher).
111	**Ecce sed** = *Her. Chr.* 3.75, n.
	precibus . . . vocaret Verg. *A.* 7.133.
	rite vocaret Hor. *Carm.* 1.32.16; Luc. 7.168. For the subjunctive with *ubi*, see Eob. *Buc.* 11.23, n.
112	**Aura levis** = Ov. *Ep.* 5.53; cf. Eob. *Buc.* 4.78, n.
	est — locum Cf. Ov. *Ep.* 16.59.
113	**Fodit et** = Ov. *Am.* 3.5.24; *Met.* 7.315.
	signa For *signa* in the sense of "crosses," cf. ll. 3, 18 above; ll. 153, 212 below; *Her. Chr.* 12.108.
114	**scripta tabella** = *Max.* 28; cf. Ov. *Ars* 3.621. The true cross is identified by the inscription that Pilate put on it: see Vulg. *Luc.* 23.38; *Joan.* 19.19–20.
115	**Rex Iudaeorum** Sedul. 5.196, quoting the inscription on the cross.
117–18	**manifesta . . . Signa** Ov. *Met.* 5.468.
117	**manifesta probarunt** ≈ Ov. *Am.* 2.2.55.
118	**certam . . . fidem** = *Her. Chr.* 13.68; *Ebn.* 6; cf. *Buc.* 8.26, n.
	quis neget esse = Prop. 4.2.24.
119	**Putre . . . cadaver** Paul. Nol. *Carm.* 32.125; Mant. *c. Poet.* 28; Brant, *Var. carm.*, sig. I1ʳ (*Texte* 221.50); Erasmus, *Enchiridion, LB* 5, col. 4 E; Eob. *Epic.* 3.152.
	vicina . . . morte Luc. 7.50; Paul Nol. *Carm.* 31.125; Eob. *Her. Chr.* 15.185; 16.69; 18.145.
	morte cadaver = Sedul. 3.138; Arator 2.797: "surgit de morte cadaver."

120   **tacto corpore** = Ov. *Ars* 2.634.
        vita data est = Ov. *Tr.* 3.3.36.
121   **sacro . . . se fonte lavari** Cf. *Her. Chr.* 10.191; cf. further *Her. Chr.* 12.59, n.
        fonte lavari = Ov. *Ep.* 21.177; Prud. *Apoth.* 687; *Tit. hist.* 33.132; Sedul. 5.421;
        cf. Eob. *Buc.* 2.98, n. For *lavare* in the sense of "baptize," see also *Her. Chr.* 4.17, n.
122   **victoris . . . Dei** = *Her. Chr.* 5.20, n.
        arma Dei The cross, spear, sponge, and nails are the "weapons" with which Christ
        conquered Satan at the Passion. See *Lexikon für Theologie und Kirche*, vol. 10
        (Freiburg, 1965), cols. 907–08; cf. Eob. *Her. Chr.* 16.218. Judas uncovered not only
        the cross itself, but also the nails used in the crucifixion: see *Leg. aurea* 64.130–31.
123   **renato** He is "born again" in the holy font of baptism: cf. Vulg. *Joan.* 3.3–5; Eob.
        Her. Chr. 12.59, n.: "sacro . . . de fonte renati."
124   **pia — gerit** Cf. *Laud.* 522.
125   **Vidit — malorum** Cf. *Her. Chr.* 8.133; *Hymn.* 25–26; *Hod.* B 7.13. For *vidit
        et indoluit*, see also *Her. Chr.* B 1.15; *Praef.*, lim. 3; *Tum.* 7.91; cf. Ov. *Fast.* 2.377;
        Eob. *Buc.* 5.77, n.
126   **Terribili . . . ore** Avit. *Carm.* 3.74: "Tum sic terribili . . . deus increpat ore"; 6.323:
        "Illum terribili dominus tunc increpat ore."
        ore loqui = l. 98 above, n.
128   **non sinis esse meas** ≈ Hutten, *Querel.* 2.5.62: "requiem studiis non sinis esse meis";
        cf. Eob. *Sylv. duae* 2.84, n.
129–30 **At non — nocens** The devil compares him to the Judas who betrayed Jesus: cf. *Leg.
        aurea* 64.119–22: "Dyabolus . . . in aera vociferabatur dicens: 'O Iuda, quid hoc
        fecisti? Iude meo contraria operatus es. Nam ille me suadente fecit proditionem et tu
        me renuente Ihesu invenisti crucem.'"
        At non — Talis Cf. Verg. *A.* 2.540–41.
129   **sine rebus nomina** Cf. Ov. *Am.* 3.3.23.
130   **noluit esse** = Prop. 2.6.30; Ov. *Ib.* 24.
133   **At te — reatu** Cf. Tib. 1.8.77; Eob. *Her. Chr.* 2.43, n.; 12.213–14; *Tum.* 4.99; *Psalt.*
        50.55: "Sed te iusta manet pro tali poena reatu."
        paena reatu = Prosper Aquitanus, *Epigr.* 47.5: "Crescit enim occulte cum longo
        poena reatu."
134   **Gloria — tibi** Cf. Ov. *Rem.* 312; *Pont.* 4.9.103.
135   **bona verba** *Buc.* 6.58, n.
        verba loquutus = Verg. *A.* 8.404; Stat. *Silv.* 2.1.74.
136   **Ad Stygios . . . ire lacus** = Hermann Trebelius, l. 6 of a poem at the end of Hutten,
        Querel.: "Foelices, quibus innocuis sine crimine fama / Ad Stygios olim contigit ire
        lacus"; cf. Verg. *A.* 6.134; Mart. 5.25.6; Eob. *Her.* 2.5.106.
137–38 **Gratia — facis** Cf. *Her. Chr.* 15.99–100; *Hod.* B 7.17–18.
137   **Gratia — nam tu** Cf. Ov. *Tr.* 4.10.117; *Pont.* 2.1.19; Eob. *Her. Chr.* 3.119; 6.141, n.
        de morte redemptos = *Eccles.* 339; cf. Verg. *A.* 6.121; Arator 2.779: ". . . propria de
        morte redemptum"; Eob. *Vict.* 360.
138   **propria . . . morte** Arator 2.779 (quoted above).
139   **mundo . . . iacenti** = *Her. Chr.* 2.79.
140   **Dux bonus** = Ov. *Ars* 3.527.
        rectam . . . ad astra viam = *Her. Chr.* 15.168.
        pandis — viam ≈ Ven. Fort. *Carm.* 8.3.54: "pandit ad astra viam." Cf. Eob. *Her.
        Chr.* 23.98; *Nob.* 64. Cf. further Ov. *Ep.* 16.72; *Pont.* 2.9.62; Sen. *Her. F.* 437; Eob.
        Her. Chr. 15.174, n.; 24.28, n.; *Val.* 2.408: "Haec . . . proxima ad astra via est."
141   **Gratia — tibi** = *Eccles.* 253. Cf. *Her. Chr.* 6.137, n.
142   **et toto — sacra** = *Sylv.* 6.5.26: "toto pectore sacra foves."
        toto pectore = [Tib.] 3.1.20; Ov. *Ep.* 12.142; 19.208; *Ars* 2.536; et al.; Eob. *Her.
        Chr.* 9.130; 12.16; 15.98. The expression was proverbial: see Erasmus, *Adag.* 1.4.26;
        Otto 1368; Häussler, 78, 198–99, 242, 283.
143–44 **Macte — via** Cf. Verg. *A.* 9.641.

144   **Hac itur — via** Cf. *Her. Chr.* 15.174, n.; *Sylv.* 1.11.28: "ista / Ad superos itur non potiore via." For *meliore via*, see Luc. 9.394; Stat. *Silv.* 5.1.71.

145   **Rhoma . . . Mavortia** Mant. *Georg.*, fol. 210ᵛ; cf. Verg. *A.* 1.276–77; Eob. *Her. Chr.* 17.68, n.

147   **Quod superest** = Lucr. 1.50; 2.39, 491; et al.; Verg. *G.* 2.346; et al.; Eob. *Her. Chr.* 7.151; 13.20; 14.166.
        veteri . . . caligine Paul. Nol. *Carm.* 19.16.
        caligine mersum = Stat. *Theb.* 6.510; cf. Verg. *A.* 6.267; Eob. *Her. Chr.* 15.165, n.

148   **luci reddere** = *Her. Chr.* 9.158.

149–50 **Ut vetus — trahi** = *Accl.* 2.227–28; cf. *Accl.* 1.221–22.

149   **nova Rhoma** = Mart. 5.7.3.

150   **Quid — trahi** = *Luth.* 4.50.
        Quid dubitas = Verg. *A.* 9.12; Ov. *Her.* 7.125; 20.234; *Trist.* 5.2.37; Eob. *Sylv. duae* 2.38, n.
        orbem The *orbis terrarum* is often identified with the Roman Empire: see, for example, Verg. *A.* 4.231; Ov. *Am.* 1.15.26; *Fast.* 1.85–86; Eob. *Her. Chr.* 17.67–68; 19.15–18. Cf. also ll. 60 and 83 above.

151   **Caesar — uni** Cf. l. 83 above, n.
        Caesar ut est = Ov. *Pont.* 4.9.128.

153   **Fiat ut hoc** = *Her. Chr.* 14.137.
        signa remittit ≈ Ov. *Met.* 3.460; *Fast.* 6.467.

154   **infernum . . . Iovem** = Celtis, *Am.* 2.8.12; cf. Eob. *Buc.* B 11.8, n.: "Stygio . . . Iovi."

155–60 **Ibis — cadet** Closely paralleled in *Sylv.* 1.1.145–50, referring to the cross worn by the Teutonic Knights of Prussia: "Hostibus incutiet trepidantibus illa timorem, / Non aliquo maior miles ab ense cadet. / Ibis in adversos cruce munitissimus hostes, / Invicta sternes impia castra manu. / Terribilem fecit qui cum moreretur in illa, / Morte sua rerum terruit omne genus."

155   **Ibis in adversos . . . hostes** = *Accl.* 2.229; cf. Ov. *Am.* 1.9.11; *Met.* 8.403; Verg. *A.* 12.266, 456, 461; Eob. *Her. Chr.* 6.71, n.; 17.193, n.
        cruce munitissimus = *Sylv. duae* 1.57.

156   **Christiferam . . . crucem** *Nup.* 32, n.
        turba prophana = *Pug.* 80, n.

157   **cum — illa** = l. 23 above; cf. *Her. Chr.* 16.246.

158   **Morte — genus** Cf. *Her. Chr.* 3.45–56, n.
        omne genus = *Ama.* B 2.18, n.

159   **incutiet . . . timorem** ≈ Mant. *1. Parthen.* 3.910: "horrorem incutiunt mortis gelidumque timorem."

160   **maior miles** I take this phrase to mean "miles Christi." For this commonplace, see n. to l. 71 above.
        ense cadet ≈ Ov. *Pont.* 3.2.58; Eob. *Her. Chr.* 10.178; 18.148.

161   **Tu quoque, non** = Ov. *Ars* 3.254; *Tr.* 4.1.105.
        Rhomana . . . arma Luc. 10.4: Eob. *Her. Chr.* 12.251–52.

162   **tribus unus eras** ≈ *Her. Chr.* 13.132, n.

164   **Scit Tybris** Cf. *Buc.* B 2.29, n.: "Scit . . . Rhenus."
        ultricem . . . aquam Cf. Ov. *Met.* 3.190.

167   **Heu — mentes** Cf. Verg. *A.* 4.65; Sil. 2.28; Eob. *Vict.* 77; *Luth.* 3.67.
        nomina . . . deorum = Paul. Nol. *Carm.* 19.159; cf. Vulg. *3. Reg.* 18.24–25.

168   **Mentito . . . Iove** Sil. 1.417 (of Jupiter as deceiver); Andrel. *Livia* 2.5.8: "mentitum . . . Iovem."
        numen — erat Cf. *Her. Chr.* 12.54.
        Iove maius erat = Ov. *Fast.* 5.126.

169   **Libani . . . de vertice** Mant. *3. Parthen.*, fol. 108ᵛ.
        vertice sylvae = Verg. *G.* 2.440; Ov. *Met.* 12.412.

173   **Foelix quae potuit . . . cognoscere** ≈ Verg. *G.* 2.490.

174   **Meroe** According to Josephus, *A.J.* 2.249, the Ethiopian capital Meroe was originally
          called Saba (Sheba). Cf. Boccaccio, *De mulieribus claris* 43, in *Tutte le opere di
          Giovanni Boccaccio*, vol. 10, ed. Vittorio Zaccaria (Milan, 1967), 182, speaking of the
          Queen of Sheba: "in Meroe, insula Nyli permaxima, habuisse regiam."
          digna potente coli = Ov. *Fast.* 1.88.

175   **mentem — Pneumate** Cf. *Buc.* 3.13, n.

181   **optato . . . fine** Aus. *Parent.* 30.10.

184   **Infernae . . . fores** Sedul. 5.229.

185–88   **Fortior et — datur** Cf. Petrus Chrysologus, *Collectio sermonum* 143, referring to the
          Virgin Mary: "Vere benedicta, quae fuit maior caelo, fortior terra, orbe latior, nam
          deum, quem mundus non capit, sola cepit; portavit eum, qui portat orbem." Cf. also
          Eob. *Her. Chr.* 1.138, n.; 1.205–06; 6.14.

186   **tulit, ipsa tulit** Cf. Ov. *Ep.* 14.130.

187   **Christiferae . . . puellae** *Her. Chr.* 24.55; cf. Brant, *Var. carm.*, sig. B7ᵛ (*Texte*
          115.92): "Christifera o genitrix"; sig. E4ᵛ (*Texte* 98.2): "Christiferae . . . virginis";
          Eob. *Buc.* 5.67–68: "Virginis . . . Christophorae"; *Sylv. duae* 1.162, n.

188   **Si dubitas** = Ov. *Am.* 3.14.36; *Ep.* 18.74; *Pont.* 1.1.29.

189   **lignum** This term was frequently used for the cross: see, for example, Vulg. *Psa.*
          95.10 (in a spurious, but widely quoted addition): "Dominus regnavit *a ligno*"; *Apoc.*
          22.2 ("lignum vitae"), commonly interpreted as referring to the cross; [Tert.] *De ligno
          vitae, PL* 2, cols. 1113–14; Prud. *Psych.* 408; Eob. *Her. Chr.* 16.221.

190   **Non — ratione** Cf. Ov. *Ep.* 10.144.

191–92   **Vertice nam — domum** Following Vulg. *Eph.* 3.18 ("quae sit latitudo et longitudo et
          sublimitas et profundum"), patristic writers often gave the cross a cosmic dimension.
          See in particular [August.] *Sermo de symbolo* 4, *PL* 40, col. 1192: "et ipsa crux mag-
          num in se mysterium continet. Cuius positio talis est, ut superior pars coelos petat,
          inferior terrae inhaereat, fixa in infernorum ima contingat, latitudo autem eius partes
          mundi appetat"; Cassiodorus, *Expositio Psalmorum* 21.17, *CCSL* 97:198: "crucis ipsa
          positio talis est, ut pars eius superior caelos petat, inferior terras non deserat, fixa
          infernorum ima contingat, et velut quibusdam brachiis extensis, latitudo eius totius
          partes appetat mundi, iacens vero quatuor cardines orbis designat."

191   **Vertice — pulsat** Cf. Verg. *G.* 2.291–92; *A.* 4.445–46.
          Vertice . . . caelos . . . pulsat Cf. *Buc.* 8.79, n.

192   **solis utramque domum** = Ov. *Ep.* 9.16; cf. Eob. *Her. Chr.* 21.74.

193   **Vera loquor** = Juvenc. 1.486; 3.314; cf. Ov. *Ep.* 16.60.

195   **Rhomanas — volucres** Cf. l. 161 above; *Tum.* 2.85: "Romanas . . . , victricia signa,
          volucres."
          gentilia signa Cf. l. 19 above.

197   **Arbor — sylvis** = l. 11 above, where see nn.

199–200   **Floreat — nives** For the image of the cross as a cosmic Tree of Life, cf. Vulg. *Apoc.*
          22.1–2; [Tert.] *De ligno vitae, PL* 2, cols. 1113–14. Cf. also Ov. *Fast.* 3.33, of the
          cosmic tree symbolizing the Roman Empire.

199   **ramis vitalibus** = Mant. *2. Parthen.* 1.16 (quoted in n. to l. 11 above), of the Tree of
          Life.

201   **Hesperidum . . . hortos** ≈ *Epic.* 6.37; cf. Luc. 9.358; Mart. 4.64.2.

202   **clausas — fores** Cf. *Nob.* 60. Also cf. *Her. Chr.* 2.64, n.; 10.128, n.

204   **noxia flamma** Poliziano, *Silv.* 4.259; Celtis, *Am.* 3.11.27.

205   **Tu modo** = *Buc.* 6.87, n.

206   **falce mete** ≈ Ov. *Ep.* 6.84; *Ars* 2.322.

207   **Fallor, an** = *Buc.* B 11.19, n.
          paucis . . . diebus = [Aus.] *De rosis nascentibus* 47; Mant. *1. Parthen.* 3.218.

209   **Palinure, sub unda** Cf. Verg. *A.* 3.202; Ov. *Rem.* 577.

210   **vigili . . . mente** Sedul. 5.158.

212	**non habitura** = *Her. Chr.* 24.58, n.
213	**Rhomana potentia** = l. 75 above, n.
214	**Caetera — meis** Cf. Ov. *Fast.* 4.862.

7

Meter: Elegiac distich.

1–4	**Sic — queror** The verses imitate Ov. *Ep.* 7.1–6.
1–2	**Sic — aves** Cf. *Leg. aurea* 90.21–22: "Sponsa vero ad socrum suam dixit: 'Donec audiam de sponso meo dulcissimo, instar turturis solitaria tecum manebo.'"
1	**charum . . . sodalem** *Sylv. duae* 2.25, n.
4	**quod — esse** Cf. *Sylv.* 3.4.26: "Quod solito tecum non licet esse, dolet." For *non licet esse* at this metrical position, see Prop. 2.9.46; Ov. *Ep.* 14.64; 15.134.
5	**credentem — nuptam** Cf. *Her. Chr.* 8.30.
	fallere nuptam ≈ Ov. *Pont.* 3.3.53.
6	**fraus — habet** ≈ *Her. Chr.* 3.118, n.; cf. Ov. *Ep.* 20.31.
7	**mea . . . ruditas** Cf. *Her. Chr.* 22.8; *Luth.* 3.40: "ruditas . . . nostra."
	meruisse favorem = Paul. Nol. *Carm.* 6.88; cf. Eob. *Her. Chr.* 19.133.
8	**nostro crimine** ≈ Ov. *Tr.* 3.5.52; cf. *Met.* 2.590; 8.129; 13.46; Eob. *Her. Chr.* 11.177.
	tarda fides Ov. *Ep.* 17.130; *Fast.* 3.350.
9	**tedas . . . iugales** = Ov. *Met.* 1.483; cf. Eob. *Nup.* 1, n.
10	**nubere virgo** = Mart. 12.42.2; Eob. *Her. Chr.* 19.120.
11–12	**Quae — tulit** Cf. Verg. *A.* 10.508; Ov. *Ep.* 11.114.
11	**Quae — fuit** Cf. Mart. 11.65.2.
12	**Quaeque — tulit** Cf. Ov. *Ib.* 218; *Anthol. Lat.* 38.2: "prima dies, bello quae dedit, ipsa tulit."
13	**At mea virginitas** Cf. *Her. Chr.* 2.83, n.
	virginitas . . . servata *Her. Chr.* 4.38.
	servata per annos = Lucr. 1.1029; Verg. *A.* 2.715; 7.60.
14	**precium . . . et instar habet** Cf. Mart. Cap. *De nuptiis Philologiae et Mercurii* 5.436: "immortalitatis instar ac pretium"; Eob. *Her. Chr.* 8.70, n.
15–16	**Hoc — male, quod** Cf. *Her. Chr.* 20.33–34.
15	**Hoc bene successit** Ter. *Ad.* 287; cf. Ov. *Ep.* 4.33; Eob. *Her. Chr.* 15.189.
	sine crimine nupta l. 155 below.
	sine crimine = Verg. *A.* 4.550; Hor. *Ep.* 1.7.56; Prop. 4.11.45; Ov. *Am.* 1.3.13; et al.; Eob. *Her. Chr.* 8.11; 16.83; 20.71; B 1.11, 39; cf. l. 155 below.
17	**Vivere . . . lecto** Prop. 2.2.1.
18	**Summa — mei** *Her. Chr.* A 3.76; 14.142.
21–52	**Oscula — brevi** For the farewell scene, cf. *Her. Chr.* 5.35–46, n.
21	**Oscula . . . dedisti** = *Her. Chr.* 5.35, n.; l. 47 below.
21–23	**fraterna . . . soror** Cf. *Her. Chr.* 8.57, n.
22	**lingua — est** Cf. Ov. *Tr.* 3.5.47 (in many mss.): ". . . lingua locuta est."
23	**Vive, soror** Ov. *Ep.* 11.59; l. 48 below.
24	**exilio — mihi est** Cf. Ov. *Ep.* 15.164; *Fast.* 3.576.
27	**Cum — aristam** Cf. *Sylv.* 1.4.19: ". . . mihi stat plenis ter septima messibus aestas"; *Laud.* 1, n. For the tag, cf. Ov. *Fast.* 5.357; *Met.* 11.614.
28	**Si vivam** *Buc.* 2.98, n.
29–30	**Non — lupos** Cf. Magdal. *Erarium*, ded., sig. A2ʳ: "Non secus ac vivax nemorum per inhospita tesqua / Cerva cruentatis expetat acta lupis, / Obstupui."
29	**Non — quam** = *Her. Chr.* 16.103; *Tum.* 7.123; cf. Ov. *Tr.* 1.3.11.
	Alpibus altis = Sil. 1.370.
30	**Audiat — lupos** Cf. Ov. *Fast.* 3.646.
	immites . . . lupos ≈ *Sylv.* 1.6.32: "Non tenet immitem parva capella lupum."

31	**sine — coniux** = Erasmus, *Carm.* 13.7; cf. Ov. *Met.* 7.589.
32	**abesse querar** ≈ Ov. *Ep.* 2.2.
33–36	**Quid — solet** Cf. Ov. *Ep.* 17.209–12; Eob. *Her. Chr.* 13.25–28.
33	**meliori — nuptae** Cf. *Sylv.* 4.1.9: ". . . meliori sydere natos"; Ov. *Ep.* 11.105; Stat. *Theb.* 11.700: "meliora . . . sidera."
34	**Latiae . . . nurus** Ov. *Met.* 15.486; *Fast.* 4.133.
	invida turba = *Her. Chr.* 14.70; cf. Prop. 3.1.21; Eob. *Her. Chr.* 13.128.
	turba nurus = Ov. *Ep.* 8.12.
35	**Omnia liberius** = Verg. *G.* 1.128.
36	**Esse — solet** Cf. *Epic.* 7.16: "Fama quidem vivis esse maligna solet."
	fama maligna = Ov. *Tr.* 4.10.126; cf. *Ep.* 16.146.
37–38	**Qualiter — Sic** For the ironic comparison, cf. *Buc.* 10.122–23, n.
38	**animum movit** *Buc.* 8.24, n.
	nostra querela = *Her. Chr.* 3.162, n.
39	**tibi iam . . . vestes, . . . purpura fulgens** Lucr. 2.500–01.
	Tyriae vestes Tib. 1.7.47; Prop. 3.14.27.
	purpura fulgens ≈ Ov. *Fast.* 1.81; cf. *Pont.* 3.8.7.
40	**humeris . . . tuis** Cf. Ov. *Ars* 2.50; *Ep.* 21.90.
41	**numeratos . . . glandes** The sense of "ready money" (*numerata pecunia*) is unparalleled, but is clear from the context and the legend itself. For according to *Leg. aurea* 90.11, Alexius took along money, which he later distributed among the poor in Edessa. *Glandes* is a masculine (rather than feminine) noun also in Eob. *Vict.* 215 (written in early 1512).
42	**Latus . . . galerus** *Her. Chr.* 18.49.
	obducta fronte Hor. *Epod.* 13.5.
43	**Hei — foeci** = Ov. *Ep.* 9.145; cf. Eob. *Her. Chr.* 13.37, n.
	nupta marito = Catul. 64.374; Ov. *Ep.* 5.107; 13.139; *Pont.* 2.8.43; Eob. *Her. Chr.* 18.101; cf. l. 155 below.
44	**maxima Rhoma** = Mart. 7.96.2; 10.58.6; cf. Verg. *A.* 5.600–01; 7.602–03.
45	**Tempus erat** = *Rec.* 1, n., also with ellipsis of *quo*.
	rebus — colorem = Verg. *A.* 6.272; cf. Eob. *Nup.* 207; *Nor.* 428.
46	**fulgor erat** = *Her. Chr.* 3.78.
47–48	**Oscula — soror** Cf. Verg. *Ecl.* 3.78–79.
47	**Oscula — dedisti** Cf. Tib. 1.1.62; Ov. *Ep.* 3.14; *Tr.* 1.3.58.
	Oscula . . . dedisti = *Her. Chr.* 5.35, n.; 7.21.
	lachrymis confusa Mant. *1. Parthen.* 3.671: "confusus lacrimis cruor."
48	**longo tempore** = *Her. Chr.* 3.64, n.
	Vive, soror Ov. *Ep.* 11.59; l. 23 above.
49	**Ibis — relinquis** Cf. Ov. *Ep.* 3.61; Eob. *Her. Chr.* 16.141.
50	**sim — viae** ≈ *Sylv.* 1.5.2: "O utinam tantae sim comes ipse viae."
51	**excideram** For the motif — fainting upon receiving bad news — cf. Ov. *Ep.* 3.59–60; *Ars* 2.449–50; Eob. *Her. Chr.* 8.33–34; 9.39–40; 12.15–20; 16.11–12. Cf. further Verg. *A.* 4.391; Ov. *Ep.* 13.23–26; Luc. 8.58–61.
	solatus amantem = V. Fl. 7.412.
53–54	**Hebdomas — fides** Cf. *Her. Chr.* 5.7–10, n.; ll. 27–28 above. For the sentiment, cf. Ov. *Ep.* 2.2.
53	**Hebdomas** For this Hebrew usage, cf., for example, Hier. *In Dan.* 3, commenting on Vulg. *Dan.* 9.24: "septuaginta annorum hebdomadas dicit esse completas, id est annos quadringentos nonaginta"; Isid. *De natura rerum* 3.1: "Hebdomada apud Graecos et Romanos septem dierum cursu peragitur. Apud Hebraeos autem septem anni sunt"; Celtis, *Am.* 4.6.1–2, at age forty-three: "Iam mihi sexta fluit collectis viribus aetas, / Septenam hebdomaden . . . spero meam."
54	**Nec — fides** = *Her. Chr.* 12.86; cf. *Her. Chr.* 13.68; 14.37–38.
	promissa . . . fides Verg. *A.* 4.552; 6.346; Ov. *Fast.* 6.549.

verba — fides Cf. Ov. *Met.* 3.527; *Fast.* 1.359; Eob. *Vict.* 308: "certa fides . . . mea dicta sequta est." For the pentameter close, cf. *Her. Chr.* 6.54, n.

55 **Durius — horas** Cf. *Her. Chr.* 19.103; *Sylv.* 6.3.9–10: "degeneres mihi tempus in horas / Crescit"; also *Her. Chr.* 5.65, n.

56 **Quo — mori** Cf. Ov. *Ep.* 3.140; Poliziano, *Epigr.* 69.2 and *Eleg.* 7.160: "cum dulce est vivere, dulce mori est"; cf. further Hor. *Carm.* 3.2.13; Eob. *Ama.* 32.16, n.; *Her. Chr.* 6.86, n.

57 **sua gaudia** = Verg. *A.* 10.652; *Lydia* 45.
gaudia nuptae = V. Fl. 4.164.

58 **qui — habent** ≈ *Buc.* B 8.2, n.

59 **Et vir abest nobis et . . . sine** = Ov. *Ep.* 17.179.
fratre marito = Luc. 10.138.

61 **Ergo — fatis** Cf. *Her. Chr.* 8.21; *Sylv.* 2.9.1 (*Epic.* 2.29): ". . . non aequo curren-tibus ordine fatis"; Ov. *Ep.* 1.101. For *currentibus fatis*, see also Sil. 7.307; Eob. *Her. Chr.* 20.108.
turbato . . . ordine = Mant. *Calam.* 1.1010 (p. 45); cf. *Calam.* 3.291 (p. 77).

62 **data nupta** = Ov. *Pont.* 1.2.136.
nupta viro = Ov. *Tr.* 2.500.

63 **Sola fui** = *Her. Chr.* 2.35, n.
patiente animo Sen. *Med.* 152.

64 **posse frui** = Ov. *Ep.* 20.72; *Tr.* 5.9.14; [Tib.] 3.3.32.

65–70 **Cur — fuit** Cf. *Her. Chr.* 12.91–94.

65 **concessa voluntas** ≈ Stat. *Theb.* 5.568.

66 **melior . . . palma** *Laud.* 494.
palma petenda = Ov. *Am.* 3.2.82.

68 **abstinuisse bono** ≈ Ov. *Ep.* 17.98.

69 **thalamo . . . in uno** Ov. *Ep.* 6.95; cf. Eob. *Her. Chr.* 12.91, n.

70 **nostra futura fuit** = *Pug.* 102.

72 **Noster — amor** Cf. Verg. *A.* 1.646.

73 **Parvus — aula** Modeled on Verg. *A.* 4.328–29; cf. Eob. *Her. Chr.* 20.37.

74 **Unde — opus** Cf. *Her. Chr.* 3.74, n.
exiguum . . . opus Ov. *Fast.* 2.4; *Pont.* 3.4.5; Eob. *Vict.* 5; *Her.*, ded. 134.

75 **tristibus . . . curis** = Mant. *Calam.* 2.311 (p. 61); cf. Verg. *G.* 4.531; *A.* 12.801–02.
obruta curis = Claud. *Bell. Get.* 226.

78 **humilis . . . casae** Verg. *Ecl.* 2.29; Tib. 2.5.26; Ov. *Ep.* 5.16.
tecta — casae Cf. Ov. *Fast.* 4.526; Andrel. *Ecl.* 7, motto: "Splendida sunt magno laudanda palatia luxu, / Parva sed exilis tecta colenda casae." Cf. further Ov. *Fast.* 4.516; Eob. *Her. Chr.* 21.220.
tecta subire = Mart. 2.53.8.

79 **renidet ab auro** Cf. Lucr. 2.27; Hor. *Carm.* 2.18.1–2.

80 **Quo — abes** Cf. *Her. Chr.* 10.100.

83 **Anxius — annis** Cf. *Her. Chr.* 10.133.
Anxius . . . pater Stat. *Theb.* 10.621–22; V. Fl. 1.401; 2.413.
multis . . . annis = Ov. *Fast.* 2.435; *Tr.* 1.5.59.

84 **Quod — est** Cf. Ov. *Am.* 2.19.3; Eob. *Her. Chr.* 11.73.
dedoluisse semel = Ov. *Fast.* 3.480; cf. *Rem.* 294.

86 **Ad Pharon — tuam** Cf. Juv. 6.83.
comose Like all river gods, the Nile has long hair.

87 **solata dolentem** = Ov. *Fast.* 1.365.

88 **aliquo . . . in orbe** Ov. *Ep.* 1.58; l. 146 below.

89 **Parce . . . lachrymis** = Stat. *Silv.* 5.1.179.
neque — dolendo Cf. Mant. *1. Parthen.* 3.690: ". . . quid te fletu consumis acerbo?"

91–102	**Multa — ubi es** The motif comes from the *vita*, but the language is taken, in part, from Ov. *Ep.* 1.63–66 (Penelope to Ulysses).
93	**veterem . . . Siona** Cf. *Her. Chr.* 6.55.
95	**tetigisti littora** = *Her. Chr.* 14.37; cf. Catul. 64.172; V. Fl. 8.432.
98	**presenti . . . Deo** = *Her. Chr.* 17.66; cf. Prud. *Cath.* 11.90 and Erasmus, *Carm.* 42.36 (referring to Jesus in the crib); Eob. *Sylv. duae* 2.198, n.; *Her. Chr.* 12.65; 19.136.
	Teutonis ora = *Sylv. duae* 1.128, n.
101	**fortes . . . Gallos** *Nup.* 37.
103–04	**Ergo — est** Late versions of *Leg. aurea* 90 offer a different explanation: "Alexius dicitur ab a, quod est valde, et lexis, quod est sermo: inde Alexius quasi valde in verbo Dei robustus." See *Leg. aurea* 90.1, apparatus criticus on p. 621; *Leg. aurea* (Graesse) 94, p. 403. For the play on proper names, see also Eob. *Her. Chr.* 10.1–4; 17.231–32; 18.63–64, 152; 21.125–26.
104	**Littera — est** Cf. Aus. *Ep.* 21.35: "multiplici . . . oneret sermone tabellas."
105	**ubicumque locorum** = Hor. *Ep.* 1.3.34; Eob. *Her. Chr.* 18.27.
106	**patria . . . domo** = *Her. Chr.* 10.78; cf. Pl. *Merc.* 831; Ov. *Met.* 11.269; Eob. *Her. Chr.* 10.182, n.
	noris adesse = *Her. Chr.* 8.88.
107	**patria . . . urbe** = *Her. Chr.* 18.13; cf. *Her. Chr.* 7.145, n.
109	**Multa — formae** Cf. Hor. *Ars* 169, 175. The brevity of youthful beauty was proverbial: see Eob. *Buc.* 7.168–70, n.
	fugienti . . . formae *Val.* 2.145: ". . . fugientis gaudia formae."
110	**in ore color** = *Sylv. duae* 2.14, n.
111	**florem — iuventae** = *Sylv.* 2.1.37; cf. *Buc.* 7.170, n.
113	**tenui . . . pulvere** Juv. 7.48. For *pulvere* meaning "facial down," cf. Ov. *Ep.* 4.78.
114	**hirsutas . . . genas** = Mart. 6.52.4.
	barba genas = *Priap.* 3.4; Mart. 9.76.4.
116	**Ruga — sedet** Cf. Ov. *Tr.* 3.7.34.
	fronte sedet ≈ *Sylv. duae* 2.70, n.
117	**pluviis — uste** Cf. Lucr. 6.1102; Hor. *Epod.* 2.41; Ov. *Ep.* 5.112.
	et solibus — diurnis ≈ *Epic.*, app. 5.7.
119	**misera . . . coniuge** Ov. *Met.* 11.655.
120	**precor . . . esse . . . velis** Ov. *Rem.* 274; *Pont.* 3.3.108.
121–22	**Illa — hebet** Cf. *Luth.* 6.95–96.
121	**ille requirit** = *Laud.* 319.
122	**Qui — hebet** Cf. Verg. *A.* 5.395–96; Ov. *Ep.* 3.146; Eob. *Her. Chr.* 12.16.
123	**de te meruisse** Cf. Verg. *A.* 4.317 (Dido, abandoned by Aeneas); Ov. *Met.* 7.854.
	tot annis = Ov. *Tr.* 5.10.3; cf. Eob. *Laud.* 62, n.
124	**caelo teste** Luc. 9.836; Sen. *Phaed.* 525.
	relicta fides = Ov. *Ars.* 3.460.
125	**dextra fefellit** = Luc. 4.559.
125–26	**fefellit — ferere** Notice the alliteration.
127–28	**Grata . . . posse placere puta** ≈ Ov. *Pont.* 2.5.23–24; cf. Mart. 6.44.4.
127	**Grata — sunt** = Mant. *Mort.*, fol. 123ʳ: "Grata Deo non sunt fumantia thura."
129	**Qui — volebat** Cf. Vulg. *Matt.* 19.6.
130	**crimen habet** = Ov. *Ep.* 18.142; *Ars* 1.586; 2.634; *Fast.* 2.162; cf. Eob. *Her. Chr.* 18.100, n.
131	**Finge dari** = Ov. *Ep.* 10.63 (with similar verse structure).
	culpamque remitti ≈ V. Fl. 3.407.
132	**Quis . . . non nocuisse** = Ov. *Fast.* 2.414.
	Quis dabit ut = *Eccles.* 97; *Tum.* 7.172; cf. Brant, *Varia carm.*, sig. a7ʳ (*Texte* 195.340–41): "Quis mihi, quis lachrymas dabit ut deflere ruinam / Communem possim?"; Eob. *Her. Chr.* 4.87, n.

134   **Nil queror** = *Her. Chr.* 4.91, n.
       Est — meis Cf. Ov. *Pont.* 1.8.74.
135–36   **Ferre — iacet** The distich became proverbial. See Walther 9343. Cf. Eob. *Buc.* 7.16, n.
135   **Ferre — onus** Cf. *Dicta Catonis* 1.21: "Paupertatis onus patienter ferre memento"; Eob. *Her. Chr.* 11.175, n.
136   **Qui iacet — ille iacet** For the thought, cf. Erasmus, *Adag.* 1.3.46.
137   **tristes . . . querelae** = *Vict.* 164; cf. *Her. Chr.* 10.137, n.
138   **Unda — meis** Cf. Vulg. *Act.* 22.16, of baptism.
139–40   **superum — oves** Cf. *Her. Chr.* 9.125–26.
140   **Qua — oves** = *Epic.* 6.114.
       signifer Agnus Medieval and Renaissance artists often depict Christ as a lamb bearing the royal ensign.
       Agnus oves = Ven. Fort. *Carm.* 3.9.84.
143   **Membra . . . tua . . . supplex** *Her. Chr.* 3.107.
       Membra . . . tangere Ov. *Ep.* 8.112.
144   **Castus . . . amor** *Laud.* 240, n.
       quaerit amor = Prop. 1.9.12.
145   **patriamque — urbem** Cf. Sil. 6.529; l. 107, n., above.
146   **aliquo . . . in orbe** Ov. *Ep.* 1.58; l. 88 above.
       in orbe lates ≈ Ov. *Tr.* 3.1.50; *Pont.* 4.9.126.
147   **Prebueris — fugaris** Cf. *Her. Chr.* 9.151 (with similar sentiment and line structure).
       mortemque fugaris ≈ Claud. *Carm. minora* 32.17.
150   **spes mihi nulla** = Ov. *Tr.* 5.8.22.
151   **Quod superest** = *Her. Chr.* 6.147, n.
       magne . . . Iesu *Her. Chr.* 6.103, n.
152   **quae — viro** The Virgin Mary. Cf. *Her. Chr.* 14.80; *Vict.*, ded. 20; *Luth.* 5.18.
154   **carmen habe** ≈ Ov. *Ep.* 5.28, introducing an epitaph. For *carmen* in the sense of "epitaph," see Eob. *Rec.* 136, n. For the epitaph in elegiac poetry, see n. to *Her. Chr.* 4.251–54.
155   **absentem . . . maritum** ≈ Ov. *Ep.* 16.305.
       sine crimine nupta l. 15, n., above.
       nupta maritum = Ov. *Ep.* 3.69; cf. l. 43, n., above.
156   **Fessa malis** = Ov. *Met.* 9.293; cf. Eob. *Eccles.* 19.
       placida morte Verg. *A.* 9.445; Eob. *Buc.* 3.165.

8

St. Cunegund's *vita* can be found in *Acta Sanctorum*, March III, and *PL* 140, cols. 205–20. See also *Leg. aurea* 113.180–86 and R. Klauser, *Der Heinrichs- und Kunigundenkult im mittelalterlichen Bistum Bamberg* (Bamberg, 1957).
       Eobanus' poem was first edited (according to the 1539 version) by Hans Rupprich in: *Humanismus und Renaissance in den deutschen Städten und an den Universitäten*, vol. 2 of *Deutsche Literatur: Reihe Humanismus und Renaissance* (1935; repr. Darmstadt, 1964), 205–09.
       Meter: Elegiac distich.

1   **nomismate** For the image, cf. Juv. 7.54–55: "qui / communi feriat carmen triviale moneta"; Locher, *Stult.*, opening verse of the introductory epigram, fol. 1ᵛ: "Carmina sint quamvis triviali sculpta moneta."
2   **Fungitur — novo** = Ov. *Ep.* 17.144.
       littera nostra = *Her. Chr.* 3.54, n.
3–4   **Quid — est** Cf. Ov. *Ep.* 15.5–8, written by the poetess Sappho. For Cunegund's awareness that she is writing verse, cf. Eob. *Her. Chr.* 4.176, n.

3   **Quid tibi cum . . . Musis?** Petrarch, *Ep.* 2.17.6, 9, 13, et al.: "Quid tibi cum
         Musis? . . ."; Mant. *Epigr.*, fol. 103ᵛ: "Quid tibi cum Musis qui tanta negocia trac-
         tas?"; cf. Eob. *Sylv. duae* 2.27; *Her. Chr.* 19.7, n.
         Latiis . . . Musis = Germ. *Arat.* 15; Luc. 9.983; Eob. *Hod.* 483.

5   **est — maior** Cf. *Val.* 1.9–10: "Adde quod et numeros facile est meminisse, nec ullis /
         Dotibus ingenii gratia maior inest"; 2.39–40: "Quod quia non potuit fieri sermone
         pedestri, / Forsitan in versu gratia maior erit."
         et gratia maior = Mart. 12.62.13; Mant. *1. Parthen.* 3.855.

6   **rudes animos** = Prop. 3.15.5; Ov. *Fast.* 4.97; Eob. *Epp. 3*, sig. C7ᵛ (letter of 9 July
         1536): "Docte rudes animos studiis formare, Mathesi."
         animos . . . verba movent Mant. *c. Poet.* 23 (quoted in Eob. *Orat.* 8.11): "Verba
         movent animos."
         barbara verba = *Laud.* B 3.28, n.

7   **Nec, puto, tu** = *Her. Chr.* 4.9.

7–8   **me Rhamnusia — videt** Cf. Magdal. *Ep.* 41; Walther 16676 (of love): "videt omnia
         lumine ceco." Fortuna was proverbially blind: see Eob. *Her. Chr.* 5.154, n. For
         lumine videt, see *Ama.* B 2.40, n.
         nullo lumine = *Sylv.* 3.7.10, of Fortuna: "nullo lumine diva potens."

9   **Visa diu foelix** = *Epic. Drusi* 1; cf. Eob. *Her. Chr.* 13.75.
         Caesare . . . marito = Mant. *2. Parthen.* 3.737: "Caesare digna marito."

11   **bene sperarem** ≈ *Rec.* 97, n.
         sine crimine = *Her. Chr.* 7.15, n.

12   **ab excelso — loco** Cf. *Sylv. duae* 2.110, n.; Dantiscus, *Carm.* 1.3.254, of Fortuna: ". . .
         lubrica quos trusit ad ima dea."

13   **prostrata ruinam** ≈ Paul. Nol. *Carm.* 15.137.

15   **Ut modo conciderim** = *Eleg.* 3.87.

16   **Non — levi** Cf. Ov. *Ep.* 2.8; Eob. *Her. Chr.* 3.162, n.; 16.300.
         ex causa . . . levi Locher, *Stult.* 35, tit., fol. 46ʳ: "De iracundia ex levi causa."

17   **exaturabilis** Verg. *A.* 5.781.

18   **Qui — dolet** Cf. Ov. *Ep.* 5.7–8. For the wording, cf. also Mart. 1.33.4.
         plectitur, ille = Ov. *Ep.* 11.110, of undeserved punishment.

19–20   **Ante — Quam** Cf. [Sen.] *Oct.* 14–16; cf. also Luc. 3.19; Stat. *Theb.* 8.13; Eob. *Her.
         Chr.* 11.11–12.

19   **rupissent — Parcae** = Gunther, *Lig.* 5.348.

20   **Quam potui infoelix** Cf. Verg. *A.* 7.309.
         displicuisse tibi = Mart. 1.23.4.

21   **confuso — fatum** Cf. *Her. Chr.* 7.61, n.; *Vict.* 362.

22   **vindicis ira** ≈ Ov. *Pont.* 3.3.76 (in some mss. and eds.). Cf. *Pont.* 2.9.77; 3.6.49.
         ira Dei = [Tib.] 3.6.26; Ov. *Tr.* 1.5.84; 1.10.42; 5.12.14; Eob. *Her. Chr.* 11.176.

23   **Parce, Pater** = Tib. 1.3.51; Ov. *Tr.* 2.181.
         Pater superum Verg. *A.* 6.780; Mart. 9.20.9.
         merui graviora Cf. [Sen.] *Oct.* 826.

26   **littera testis habet** = *Eleg.* 1.8; *Her.*, ded. 54; *Sylv.* 1.4.18; cf. Magdal. *Ep.* 28.
         testis habet = Ov. *Tr.* 1.6.18; *Pont.* 3.9.50.

27   **Quae — venit** Cf. Ov. *Fast.* 4.497; Eob. *Vict.* 231.

29   **verbis — rebus** Cf. Ov. *Met.* 14.301.

30   **credentem — virum** Cf. *Her. Chr.* 7.5.
         fallere . . . virum = [Tib.] 3.4.62.
         fallere docta = *Her. Chr.* 11.84; cf. Tib. 1.9.37.

31   **mihi devoto . . . amore** Cf. l. 67 below.
         fruitur . . . amore = Tib. 1.5.17; cf. Eob. *Her. Chr.* 3.120, n.

33–34   **Hec — manu** Cf. Verg. *A.* 4.391; Eob. *Her. Chr.* 7.51, n.; 9.39–40; 12.15–20.

33   **frigida membris** = Paul. Nol. *Carm.* 18.350.

34   **Vix — manu** Cf. Ov. *Ep.* 13.26.

	famula . . . manu = *Her. Chr.* 16.264; cf. *Her. Chr.* 2.42, n.
35–36	**Mane — aves** Cf. Aus. *Ephem.* 1.1–2.
35	**Mane erat, et** = Prop. 2.29.23; Ov. *Ep.* 12.62; 14.79.
	et primo . . . sole Ov. *Met.* 9.93.
36	**querulae . . . aves** Sen. *Phaed.* 508; Eob. *Buc.* B 7.24.
	concinuistis aves = Ov. *Am.* 3.12.2.
37	**exieram thalamo** Ov. *Ep.* 11.91.
38	**iam subitura rogos** ≈ *Her. Chr.* A 4.14.
39	**exortum . . . solem** = *Her. Chr.* 11.25.
	relevo caput Luc. 8.268.
40	**iterum . . . videbo** Verg. *A.* 10.671.
	laeta videbo = *Her. Chr.* 12.70.
41	**vernate — volucres** Cf. *Her. Chr.* 4.161, n.
42	**causa peracta meae** ≈ Ov. *Ep.* 21.152.
43	**lachrymis . . . profusis** = Ov. *Met.* 7.91; *Fast.* 6.605; cf. Eob. *Her. Chr.* 3.109.
44	**O vir, non** = Ov. *Tr.* 5.2.50.
	non — meis Cf. *Her. Chr.* 3.156, n.
45–46	**Quis — meae** Cf. *Eccles.* 97–98. For l. 45, cf. also *Her. Chr.* 12.272.
45	**Quis dabit** = *Her. Chr.* 4.87, n.
46	**Tristitiae consors . . . meae** Maxim. 5.94; cf. Eob. *Her. Chr.* 11.144.
47	**Fama nocens** Sedul. 4.66.
	Caesaris aures = Ov. *Pont.* 4.9.125; Luc. 2.273; 6.163; 10.104.
49	**Ne — putemur** Cf. Vulg. *4. Reg.* 7.9: "Si tacuerimus . . . sceleris arguemur"; Eob. *Pod.* 17–18: "Ut ne, si taceam nec me defendere pergam, / Obiecti credar criminis esse nocens." The thought was proverbial: see Otto 1734; Häussler, 64–65, 80, 216, 289.
50	**Tristis . . . littera** Ov. *Am.* 2.18.33; *Ars* 1.483; Eob. *Her. Chr.* 12.263.
52	**milia multa** = *Her. Chr.* 6.76, n.
53–54	**Ante — dari** For the adynata, see n. to *Buc.* 10.98–101. For the cosmic catastrophe imagined by Cunegund, cf. Vulg. *2. Petr.* 3.10; Mant. *Ecl.* 6.250: "si terra (ut perhibent) flammis abolebitur umquam."
54	**posse dari** = Ov. *Pont.* 1.2.60; 2.7.20.
55	**tua me miseram** = *Her. Chr.* 4.79; 19.61.
56	**Ille sapit quisquis** = Mart. 5.58.8.
	tuta timere Cf. Verg. *A.* 4.298; Ov. *Met.* 7.47; *Tr.* 5.2.37; *Pont.* 3.6.15.
57	**vir et . . . frater** Cunegund calls Henry "husband and brother" because (according to the legend) the couple has never made love: cf. *Her. Chr.* 7.21–23; 13.1–2.
58	**perfidus hostis** Hor. *Carm.* 3.5.33; Eob. *Her. Chr.* 14.111, n., referring to the devil.
59–62	**Prodiga — est** Cf. ll. 29–32 above.
60	**fallere posse** = l. 72, n., below.
63	**solem — videri** Cf. Otto 1663.
	non posse videri = Prud. *Apoth.* 44.
64	**Qui — erat** ≈ *Sylv.* 3.2.94: "Qui tibi fortunae conditor huius erat"; cf. *Her. Chr.* 1.68; 3.56.
65	**oculis — imago** Cf. Claud. *VI. Cons. Hon.*, praef. 21; Vegius, *Aen.* 418: ". . . haud vera illusit imago"; Eob. *Her. Chr.* 13.67.
	fallax . . . imago = Stat. *Silv.* 1.3.18.
66	**mendax lingua** Vulg. *Prov.* 6.17; Prud. *Cath.* 2.102.
	lingua nocere ≈ Ov. *Am.* 1.8.20; cf. Verg. *Ecl.* 7.28; Prop. 2.28.14.
67	**tibi devoti . . . pudoris** Cf. l. 31 above.
	stat — pudoris Cf. *Buc.* 2.73.
68	**crimina noster amor** = *Her. Chr.* 3.166; cf. *Her. Chr.* 2.84, n.
69	**Teste opus est** *Idyl.* 11.138; cf. *Laud.* 507.
70	**Pondera . . . et instar habes** Cf. Ov. *Ep.* 2.30; Eob. *Her. Chr.* 7.14.
71	**Forsitan . . . requiris** = Ov. *Ep.* 15.5 (different); cf. Eob. *Her. Chr.* 21.23, n.

	alios testes . . . requiris *Wirt.* 235.
72	fallere — Deum ≈ Tib. 1.8.56; Ov. *Ep.* 20.196; cf. l. 60 above.
74	Si qua . . . fallere [Tib.] 3.4.62.
77	male credis Ov. *Ep.* 7.54.
78	Da veniam = *Her. Chr.* 2.14, n.

verbis . . . facta probent = Balbi, *Epigr.* 26.8: "Hoc non fit verbis, . . . facta probent."
aemula facta Sil. 4.4; 13.463.

79	per superos = *Buc.* 7.30, n.
81	Sanguine . . . ab utroque Cf. Stat. *Ach.* 1.899.
82	quorum — tibi est Cf. Erasmus, *Carm.* 12.5: "est mea vita tibi . . . probata"; Dantiscus, *Carm.* 1.3.352: "sacerdotum . . . , / . . . quorum vita probata nitet"; Eob. *Ruf.* 110: "Vita probata tua est"; *Her. Chr.* 16.268.
84	ara vetus Hor. *Carm.* 3.18.7; Ov. *Met.* 6.326; 11.198; 12.12.
85	Casta — Mater Cf. Mant. *c. Poet.* 35: "Casta Dei genitrix . . ."; Eob. *Buc.* 11.33, n.

pavimentum Notice the short second syllable.

87	sternere ferro = Verg. *A.* 7.692.
88	noris adesse = *Her. Chr.* 7.106.
89	favet For *faveo* as a transitive verb, see n. to *Her. Chr.* 18.83.
90	Contingam . . . pede = Ov. *Tr.* 1.1.16.

nudo . . . pede = Ov. *Am.* 3.6.50; *Fast.* 4.426; *Tr.* 4.6.20.

91	teneras . . . plantas = Col. 10.276; cf. Verg. *Ecl.* 10.49.

vis ignea Ov. *Met.* 1.26.

ignea plantas ≈ Verg. *A.* 11.718.

92	Veridico . . . igne Deus Cf. *Her. Chr.* 10.136, n.
93	de virgine nasci = Gunther, *Lig.* 5.157; Eob. *Her. Chr.* 2.51.
98	obesse solet = Ov. *Am.* 1.8.36.
99	animum — nobis Cf. Prop. 2.1.4.

mens — recti = Sedul. 4.152; Eob. *Epic.* 5.43; cf. *Buc.* 10.88, n.; l. 115, n., below.

100	Phasias Ov. *Ars* 2.103; *Met.* 7.298; Eob. *Her. Chr.* 19.130.
102	Rustica . . . simplicitate Pontano, *Eridanus* 2.13.11 (Eob. *Idyl.* 14.140): "Rustica simplicitas. . . ."
103	temere — tentare Cf. Vulg. *Deut.* 6.16; *Matt.* 4.7; *Luc.* 4.12.
104	Quam quae . . . maior erat Cf. Ov. *Ep.* 9.108.
105	Adde quod = *Buc.* B 2.21, n.
106	coniugis esse = Ov. *Tr.* 1.6.26; *Pont.* 2.11.16.
107	vana levis . . . ludibria vulgi = *Tum.*, ded. 11; cf. *Laud.* 264; *Nob.* 331; *Sylv.* 6.6.7–8: "Nam sibi quae constat, quae mens sibi conscia recti est, / Nulla levis vulgi murmura vana timet." Cf. also *Her. Chr.* 13.43.

vana . . . ludibria = Mart. 10.4.7; cf. Eob. *Vict.*, app. 2.21, n.

levis . . . ludibria vulgi Cf. Erasmus, *Carm.* 36.1: "Nil moror . . . levis . . . convicia vulgi."

109	velut ante solebas = Mant. *2. Parthen.* 1.454; cf. Eob. *Her. Chr.* 3.161, n.
110	fortiter ulta = *Her. Chr.* 4.242, n.
112	Materia — nova Cf. *Pug.* 45–46, n.
113	Longa — postquam = *Her. Chr.* 5.5, n.

sine teste = Ov. *Met.* 4.225; 15.37; Eob. *Her. Chr.* 10.137; 14.77; cf. *Sylv. duae* 2.44, n.

115	Conscia mens = Ov. *Fast.* 1.485; 4.311; cf. l. 99 above, n.

crimine falso = Ov. *Ib.* 617 (in some mss. and eds.); Eob. *Vict.* 248.

116	sub tanto pondere Mart. 6.64.14.

pondere victa = Prop. 3.2.24.

117	Christo duce = Paul. Nol. *Carm.* 12.29; Eob. *Eccles.* 39; cf. *Her. Chr.* 17.207.

tristia ferre = Sil. 13.309.

118	mortua pene = Pontano, *Am.* 1.10.34; Eob. *Her. Chr.* 12.18; 16.12; cf. *Her. Chr.* 5.32.

119	**fors . . . inimica** Andrel. *Livia* 3.6.38.
120	**gloria plena** = *Her. Chr.* 14.126; *Epic.* 6.76; cf. *Her. Chr.* 19.87.
121–28	**Frangor — Notis** Cf. *Her. Chr.* 8.10; 15.169–70.
121	**confusa procellis** = *Her. Chr.* 12.169.
122	**Quod — nihil** Cf. Verg. *A.* 3.193; Ov. *Tr.* 1.2.23.
123	**nova miles** *Her. Chr.* 1.98, n.
124	**ratis . . . naufraga** *Her. Chr.* 5.44.
125	**nam tu solatia . . . affers** Cf. Ov. *Tr.* 4.10.117.
126	**Littora — rati** Cf. Ov. *Tr.* 1.5.36. For *littora propiora*, see Ov. *Ep.* 18.91.
	quassae . . . rati ≈ Ov. *Pont.* 2.3.58; cf. Hor. *Carm.* 1.1.17–18; 4.8.32; Eob. *Sylv.* 1.4.8: "Volvor, ut in medio gurgite quassa ratis."
127	**tuto . . . portu** Verg. *A.* 3.78.
	sistere portu Cf. Paul. Nol. *Carm.* 13.34: ". . . placido consistere portu."
128	**Rapta . . . vela . . . Notis** V. Fl. 1.645–46.
	insanis . . . Notis = *Her. Chr.* 21.222; cf. Tib. 2.4.9: "insanis . . . ventis."
	vela referre Notis ≈ Ov. *Ep.* 2.12.
130	**vir meus** = *Her. Chr.* 5.42, n.
	ista pati = *Sylv. duae* 2.122, n.
131	**virgo . . . cum virgine** *Her. Chr.* 12.99, n.
132	**vir — fuit** = *Her.* 1.6.72: "Aevo debilior iam vir et ipse fuit."
133	**Vidit — anguis** Cf. *Her. Chr.* 6.125, n.; 14.111, n. For *vetus anguis*, cf. *Her. Chr.* 1.121, n.
135	**pulchrum . . . honorem** Stat. *Theb.* 2.704.
	vitae . . . honorem = Verg. *G.* 4.326; cf. Eob. *Buc.* 7.141, n.
136	**tantum nomine** = *Val.* 2.360: "qui tantum nomine sunt medici."
137	**Corpora — adulter** Cf. Ov. *Ars* 2.633–34. The thought occurs also in the *vita* (par. 2): "Invidus enim omnium bonorum diabolus, ubi thorum immaculatum sauciare non potuit, zelotypiae livore foedare cogitavit et eius saltem famam laedere, cui vulnus corruptionis infligere non valuit."
139	**sine labe futurum** ≈ *Her. Chr.* B 1.61; cf. *Her. Chr.* 2.45, n.
140	**perfida lingua** = *Buc.* B 1.4, n.
141	**vestigia** For this word in an erotic context, see, for example, Tib. 1.9.57; Prop. 2.9.45; 2.29.35; Ov. *Am.* 1.8.97.
142	**volet illa potest** = *Sylv.* 1.1.178.
145	**Pondera — querelis** Cf. Hutten, *Querel.* 1.6.27: "Adde meis pondus quovis sermone querelis."
146	**posse docere** = *Her. Chr.* 2.122; 10.10.

9

The letter (in the 1539 version) has been edited and translated by Wilhelm Kühlmann, Robert Seidel, and Hermann Wiegand in *Humanistische Lyrik des 16. Jahrhunderts, Lateinisch und deutsch*, Bibliothek der Frühen Neuzeit 1.5 (Frankfurt am Main, 1997), 318–27, with introduction and notes on 1134–39.

Meter: Elegiac distich.

1	**Phoenissae . . . Carthaginis** *Theoc.* 16.128: "Phoenissa . . . Carthago." For the epithet, cf. Sil. 7.409; 17.631.
3	**Causa duplex** = Ov. *Fast.* 6.43.
	animum . . . dolentem Luc. 7.190.
	animum — diversa *Pod.* 452: "In diversa animum cura molesta rapit"; cf. Vulg. *Job* 20.2; Ter. *An.* 260.

5	**Iliacam . . . Rhomam** Cf. Prop. 4.1.87.
	procul hinc . . . Rhomam Verg. *A.* 8.635.
6	**Captaque — manu** Cf. *Sylv.* 1.5.50 (referring to Rome): "Celsaque Martigena moenia structa manu"; cf. Bebel, "Amor Cymonis fatui," *Carm.*, sig. k4ᵛ: "Martigena . . . manu."
	Capta . . . arva manu Prud. *Psych.* 214; cf. Ov. *Ep.* 12.46; *Ib.* 444.
	Tybridis arva Verg. *A.* 3.500; Eob. *Her. Chr.* 12.235.
7	**Tyrrhena per aequora** = Ov. *Met.* 14.8.
8	**Me — invitam** ≈ *Her. Chr.* 16.8; cf. l. 18 below.
	Punica . . . humus Ov. *Ep.* 7.140.
	servat humus = *Sylv.* 1.5.8: "moenia . . . / Quae Thyringa sinu divite servat humus."
9	**amor patriae** = Verg. *A.* 6.823; Ov. *Pont.* 1.3.29.
	sine te mihi = Mart. 6.85.1.
10	**Maxima pars . . . mei** Cf. Ov. *Tr.* 3.6.20; Eob. *Sylv. duae* 1.16, n.; *Sylv.* 2.7.2: "Maxima pars animi . . . mei"; *Epic.* 4.220; 5.20. For the image, cf. further *Laud.* B 4.4, n.
	Maxima pars = Hor. *S.* 2.3.121; Ov. *Pont.* 1.2.81.
11–14	**Quam — aquas** Cf. Ov. *Ep.* 13.4–6.
11–12	**vellem . . . detinuisset hyems** For the wish, cf. Ov. *Ep.* 4.68.
11	**vela parantem** ≈ Prop. 1.17.13; Ov. *Ep.* 8.23; *Met.* 13.224.
13	**immani . . . pondere** Verg. *A.* 5.401.
	luctantes . . . ventos Verg. *A.* 1.53; cf. Eob. *Buc.* 9.35, n.
14	**omnes . . . aquas** Ov. *Met.* 11.207–08.
	precipitasset aquas = *Her. Chr.* 15.178; cf. Ov. *Fast.* 4.164; *Ib.* 324, 462.
15	**solvisset — puppis** Cf. Luc. 2.649; V. Fl. 1.628–29; Eob. *Her. Chr.* 5.10, n. For the tag *littore puppis*, see, for example, Verg. *A.* 3.135, 277.
16	**Nec mater . . . orba** = Ov. *Ep.* 11.120.
	mater de te = Ov. *Ep.* 9.48.
18	**licet invita** ≈ l. 8 above.
	quolibet — tibi = *Sylv. duae* 2.54, n.
19	**Scilicet . . . studiorum** = Ov. *Pont.* 1.5.35.
	series — immensa Cf. *Laud.* 114, n.
22	**nomina tanta** = Ov. *Am.* 3.6.102; *Fast.* 1.592; *Tr.* 2.442; Eob. *Her. Chr.* 21.104.
23–28	**Non decet — patet** For the theme, cf. Sen. *Ep.* 108.36.
25	**Turba . . . doctorum** Ov. *Tr.* 2.119.
29	**Illa sed impugnet** Cf. Hor. *Ep.* 2.1.89.
30	**humili . . . mente** Paul. Nol. *Carm.* 25.146.
31	**Carmina — Camenae** Cf. Ov. *Ep.* 15.27; Boeth. *Consol.* 1.m1.3: "mihi lacerae dictant scribenda Camenae"; Eob. *Her. Chr.* 10.113; *Max.* 25; *Vict.* 281.
	lugentes . . . Camenae = *Epic.* 2.65; cf. *Ebn.*, lim. 1.
32	**digna parente** = Ov. *Tr.* 4.2.40; *Pont.* 2.9.38.
33	**toto . . . littore** = Verg. *A.* 4.416 and Ov. *Ep.* 10.21 (in both instances associated with the furtive departure of a loved one).
34	**Elisaeam** The epithet is derived from *Elissa*, another name for Dido. Hence it recalls the fate of Dido, who, left behind on Carthage's shore by Aeneas, desperately writes him a letter (Ov. *Ep.* 7).
	verberat — humum = *Her. Chr.* 17.172; cf. Verg. *A.* 9.669; Ov. *Fast.* 3.568; *Tr.* 1.4.8; Eob. *Her. Chr.* 20.8.
35–52	**Audiit — mea est** Cf. Ov. *Ep.* 15.99–116, with similar context and motifs. Just as Phaon has deserted Sappho without giving her the proper farewell scene (see n. to Eob. *Her. Chr.* 5.35–46), so Augustine has stolen away from his mother. When the two heroines discover their abandonment, their blood runs cold (*Ep.* 15.107–12/ *Her. Chr.* 9.35–40). Each reproaches the beloved for his stealthy departure

(*Ep.* 15.99–106/*Her. Chr.* 9.41–52): there were no last goodbyes, no embraces or parting kisses, no last-minute admonishments (*mandata*). Nothing remains of the beloved but grief.

35   **navita ponto** = Verg. *G.* 1.372.

37   **hesterna . . . luce** = Mart. 1.68.5; Eob. *Sylv.* 1.8.1; cf. *Buc.* 4.16, n.

38   **Ausoniam . . . humum** ≈ Ov. *Fast.* 5.658.

       vela daturus = Andrel. *Livia* 4.5.34: "Ulla nec in patriam vela daturus eras."

39–40   **Obstupuit — duae** Cf. *Her. Chr.* 7.51, n.; 8.33–34, n.

39   **Obstupuit — sanguis** Cf. Verg. *A.* 3.259–60; 12.905; Ov. *Fast.* 1.98.

       Obstupuit ≈ *Buc.* 4.104, n.

40   **Vix — duae** Cf. Ov. *Ep.* 2.130; 13.25–26.

44   **potior . . . causa** Paul. Nol. *Carm.* 15.115; Mant. *2. Parthen.* 3.583; Eob. *Her. Chr.* 17.238.

       causa doloris erat ≈ Ov. *Am.* 1.14.14.

45   **amplecti membra lacertis** Cf. Ov. *Met.* 10.407.

46   **Non — vale** Cf. *Rec.* 131; *Her. Chr.* 21.158.

       Non licuit = Verg. *A.* 4.550; 5.82; Ov. *Met.* 11.572.

       voce dedisse = Ov. 1.4.70.

47   **fuit hoc nimium** = *Her. Chr.* 19.91.

48   **cursus . . . tuos** = Ov. *Ep.* 2.14; *Ars* 2.726.

49   **mandata dedissem** = Tib. 1.3.15; Ov. *Ep.* 15.105; cf. Eob. *Her. Chr.* 5.29.

50   **monitis . . . meis** = Ov. *Am.* 2.19.34; *Ep.* 19.188; *Rem.* 296, 804.

51   **Certe — viderer** Cf. Verg. *A.* 4.330 (if Dido had had a child by Aeneas): "non equidem omnino capta ac deserta viderer."

       Certe ego non = Ov. *Met.* 8.99.

52   **Nunc — mea est** Cf. *Max.* 122; *Epic.* 2.126; *Sylv.* 2.10.22: "Iustior ex quadam parte querela tua est." For *ex omni parte*, see *Ama.* 35.8, n.

53   **Atque utinam** = *Buc.* 1.36, n.

55–56   **Non mea — erat** For these conventional gestures of sorrow, cf. Verg. *A.* 4.673; Ov. *Am.* 2.6.3–4; *Ep.* 11.91–92; 12.153–54. Cf. also Eob. *Her. Chr.* 3.44, n.; 5.90, n.; ll. 147–48 below.

55   **praecordia palmis** = *Ciris* 346.

57   **phoenix . . . in igne** Cf. *Her. Chr.* 15.89, n.

59   **Non ego te** = *Her. Chr.* 5.23, n.

60   **aliud quod te** = Ov. *Pont.* 3.3.72.

61   **Doctus — studiis** = *Sylv. duae* 2.215; *Sylv.* 3.5.39.

       studiis . . . imbute Cic. *Deiot.* 28; Gunther, *Lig.* 1.65: "studiis imbutus honestis"; 8.498; cf. Hor. *Ep.* 2.2.7.

62   **Et . . . cura molesta** = Ov. *Ars* 3.602; cf. Prop. 3.14.28; Ov. *Am.* 2.2.8; Eob. *Sylv.* 1.7.34.

63–64   **Aspicis — colat** Cf. *Her. Chr.* 12.43–44.

63   **Aspicis ut** = *Buc.* 7.54, n.

64   **Christum pro Iove** *Buc.* 2.16; *Her. Chr.*, ded. 9.3.

65   **Spirat adhuc** = Stat. *Theb.* 7.546.

       Cerberus — trilinguis Cf. Hor. *Carm.* 2.19.29–32; 3.11.17–20; Eob. *Vict.* 93, n.

66   **Herculea . . . fracta manu** Cf. Ov. *Am.* 3.6.36. For *Herculea manu*, see Hor. *Carm.* 2.12.6; Sen. *Her. F.* 882; *Med.* 701; Luc. 6.348. For *fracta manu*, see Prop. 3.25.10.

       guttura — manu Cf. Hor. *Epod.* 3.1–2; Luc. 2.154.

67   **monstra deum** Verg. *A.* 3.59 and 8.698 (in a different sense); Eob. *Her. Chr.* 2.50, n.

68   **Pietas . . . Dei** *Her. Chr.* 14.19, n.

69–92   **Qur — Memphis erat** The passage is largely based on Mant. *2. Parthen.* 3.78–111.

69   **Qur — fugantur** Cf. Prud. *Apoth.* 442–46 (after the birth of Jesus).

72   **Foelix — cavet** For the inverse, cf. *Ama.* 19.20.

73   **simplex . . . vetustas** Prud. *c. Symm.* 1.99.

74   **frustra — deos** Cf. Mant. *Ecl.* 8.115: "numina quae veteres frustra coluisse feruntur."

        credidit — deos = Ov. *Met.* 8.220; cf. Eob. *Her. Chr.* 12.200.

75–80 **Cum — Deo** Cf. Lact. *Inst.* 7.7.8: "Factum esse a deo mundum dixit Plato. Idem prophetae locuntur, idemque ex Sibyllae carminibus apparet."

76   **Caelivaga** This word appears to occur first in Mant. *Georgius*, fol. 211ᵛ: "coelivagis . . . astris." Eobanus uses it also at *Her. Chr.* 21.74; *Val.* 2.340: "caelivagi solis"; *Venus* 1.255: "coelivagos . . . Amores"; *Psalt.* 79.9: "Coelivagas volucres"; *Sylv.* 5.31.2: "coelivagus . . . Phoebus."

        reliquit humum = Ov. *Fast.* 1.250.

77–78 **Quando — cani** Cf. *Her. Chr.* 4.25, with nn.

80   **turba — Deo** = *Her.* 1.1.76 (angels); cf. *Psalt.* 148.4: "Laudet in excelsis turba ministra Deum"; *Luth.* 3.80.

81   **Fraudibus** Cf. Lact. *Inst.* 4.14.17: "Deus enim cum videret malitiam et falsorum deorum cultus per orbem terrae ita invaluisse, ut iam nomen eius ex hominum memoria fuisset paene sublatum — siquidem Iudaei quoque, quibus solis arcanum Dei creditum fuerat, relicto Deo vivo ad colenda figmenta inretiti daemonum fraudibus aberrassent nec increpiti per prophetas reverti ad Deum vellent — filium suum principem angelorum legavit ad homines, ut eos converteret ab inpiis et vanis cultibus ad cognoscendum et colendum Deum verum"; *Epit.* 23(28).9: "Sic fraudibus suis obduxerunt [daemones] humano generi tenebras, ut, oppressa veritate, summi ac singularis Dei nomen in oblivionem veniret." By *fraudibus* Lactantius means such black sciences as astrology, augury, and necromancy. Cf. also Mant. *2. Parthen.* 3.101–02: "istorum fraudem detexit [Christus] et artes / Spirituum."

        humanas — cepere Cf. Mant. *1. Parthen.* 1.513–14: "nam quaedam hostiles . . . umbrae / humanas ambire solent et fallere mentes."

        humanas mentes = Mant. *1. Parthen.* 2.549; cf. Eob. *Her. Chr.* 24.95, n.

        periti For the sense of "demons," cf. Lact. *Inst.* 2.14.6: "daemonas autem grammatici dictos aiunt quasi δαήμονας, id est peritos ac rerum scios; hos enim putant deos esse."

83   **daemonibus** In the following verses they are identified with the ancient gods. Cf. Vulg. *Psa.* 95.5: "omnes dii gentium daemonia."

84   **virgine — est** = Paul. Nol. *Carm. app.* 1.80 ([Prosper], *Poema coniugis ad uxorem* 80); cf. Paul. Nol. *Carm.* 31.56; Ov. *Met.* 1.78; Mart. 4.83.4; Eob. *Her. Chr.* 6.26; *Vict.* 54.

85–92 **Qui simul — erat** Cf. *Buc.* 5.102–04.

85   **descendit — paterna** Cf. Hrotsv. *Theoph.* 449: "Qui miserans hominis descendit ab arce parentis."

87–89 **Craeta — Iuno** Cf. Lact. *Inst.* 1.15.8: "Romani Quirinum, . . . Athenae Minervam, Samos Iunonem, Paphos Venerem, Vulcanum Lemnos, Liberum Naxos, Apollinem Delos"; Polydore Vergil, *De inventoribus rerum* 1.6, ed. and trans. Brian P. Copenhaver (Cambridge, MA, 2002), 32: "Romani Quirinum, Athenae Minervam, Samos Iunonem, Paphos Venerem, Delphos Apollinem, Lemnos Vulcanum, Naxos Liberum, Cretenses Iovem."

87   **Craeta Iovi** ≈ Verg. *A.* 3.104.

89   **Posthabuit . . . Samon** Cf. Verg. *A.* 1.16 (of Juno).

        Cytheraea Paphum Notice the ironic playfulness: it is as goddess of the Aegean island Cythera that Venus deserts Paphos in Cyprus.

        improba Iuno = Sil. 11.390.

90   **Et quae praeterea** = Ov. *Am.* 3.7.12; *Ep.* 21.101; *Met.* 4.16; *Pont.* 3.4.111; [Tib.] 3.3.19; cf. Eob. *Vict.* 180.

        referre pudet = Ov. *Ep.* 19.64.

91   **papyriferi . . . Nili** = Ov. *Met.* 15.753.

95	**Sollicitam — fidem** Cf. Ven. Fort. *Carm.* 3.9.65: "Pollicitam sed redde fidem . . ." (where some early eds. read "Sollicitam . . . fidem").
97	**Catholicam . . . fidem** In the post-Reformation versions (*BO*), this time-honored phrase is changed to "Synceram . . . fidem."
98	**auferet una dies** = Prop. 2.20.18; cf. Ov. *Ep.* 7.138; *Pont.* 1.2.4.
99	**Ad vitam — redi** Cf. *Ama.* 35.116.
99–108	**Quid — agit** Cf. Mant. *Ecl.* 7.88–119, where the shepherd Pollux reclines under a poplar — the tree sacred to Hercules — and has a vision of the Virgin Mary. The Virgin then shows him that he (like Hercules of old) is at a crossroads and must choose between the broad and easy path that leads to perdition or the narrow, hard path that leads to heaven.
101–06	**Vadis — olet** The lines are quoted and explained in *Adnot.*, sig. N1ᵛ–N2ʳ. After quoting Hes. *Op.* 289–92 in the original Greek, Eobanus adds his own translation: "Difficilis labor est virtutem attingere. Divi / Illius ante thronum duros posuere labores. / Aspera ad hanc et longa via est quae ducit. Ut autem / Ardua contigeris facilis fit quae ante rigebat." He then continues: "Hanc sententiam nos olim in Heroidibus nostris παραφραστικῶς expressimus, ubi filium ethnicum mater Christiana sic admonet: 'Vadis ad interitum . . . [*etc.*].'" In quoting the passage, Eobanus follows the text of *A* (1514), but changes *scopulos* in l. 108 to "scrupulos," and *lares* in l. 112 to "lacus."
101	**Vadis ad interitum** *Ama.* 19.24.
103	**Floribus . . . variis** = Verg. *A.* 6.708.
104	**Alcides** In *Adnot.*, sig. N2ʳ, Eobanus remarks that Monica alludes to the story of Hercules at the Crossroads, as told in Cic. *Off.* 1.118.
106	**mephitin olet** = *Ama.* 35.98; cf. *Her. Chr.* 15.36.
107–08	**Accipit — agit** Cf. *Psalt.* 10.33–34: "Excipit incautos specie bonitatis. Ut autem / Coeperit, in laqueos et loca mortis agit."
108	**praecipitanter agit** = *Ama.* 35.10.
109–10	**Quam — rosis** For the thought, see Otto 161; Häussler, 43, 261–62.
109	**per scopulos et saxa** Mant. *2. Parthen.* 1.442: "Per scopulos et saxa. . . ."; cf. Verg. *G.* 3.276; Ov. *Fast.* 6.742; Eob. *Her. Chr.* 10.173; 19.29; 21.153.
110	**aeternis . . . rosis** = *Her. Chr.* 23.10; cf. Prud. *Amart.* 857; Eob. *Vict.* 402: "aeternos florum . . . honores"; *Epic.* 6.39: "aeterna rosaria."
	vireta Taken from Vergil's description of Elysium in *A.* 6.638 ("amoena virecta"), this word became popular in Christian descriptions of Paradise: see, for example, Paul. Nol. *Carm.* 31.605; Prud. *Cath.* 3.101; Sedul. 1.53.
111–12	**Arcta — lares** Cf. Vulg. *Matt.* 7.13–14.
111	**ad superos . . . via** *Sylv.* 1.11.28: "Ad superos itur non potiore via"; *Hypocr.* 74: "ad superos . . . reperisse viam."
	via trita [Tib.] 3.19.10.
112	**ad Stygios . . . lares** = Brant, *Var. carm.*, sig. I1ʳ (*Texte* 221.68).
	milia multa = *Her. Chr.* 6.76, n.
113	**super ardua ducit** = Luc. 4.739.
114	**inferiora petit** = *Calum.* 122; cf. Sedul. 2.214: "Inferiora petens. . . ."
115	**Oechaliae . . . Ioles** *Venus* 1.58.
116	**praeposuisse ferunt** Cf. Ov. *Ep.* 2.82.
117	**falsa . . . ratione . . . est** = Lucr. 1.377.
119–20	**Sunt vana — habet** Cf. *Rec.* 143.
120	**mundus habet** = Ov. *Pont.* 3.1.128; 4.14.12.
121	**Aeternum — Deum** Cf. Mant. *Calam.* 3.270 (p. 77): "Et facilem cognosce Deum . . ."; Eob. *Her. Chr.* 23.97.
	super omnia = *Her. Chr.* 2.87, n.
123–26	**Reiice — oves** Cf. Vulg. *Apoc.* 3.4–5.
123	**Reiice — pallam** Cf. Celtis, *Am.* 4.13.21: "Abice, quaeso, tuam niveo de corpore pallam"; Ov. *Met.* 9.32.

125   **aetherea . . . aula** = Arator 1.119; cf. Mart. 13.4.1; Sen. *Thy.* 1077–78; Juvenc. 2.195; Eob. *Nup.* 222.
126   **Praecedit — oves** Cf. *Her. Chr.* 7.140, n.
127   **Quod — negare** Cf. *Sylv.* 2.13.19: "Quod si vera voles, ut debes velle, fateri"; *Her. Chr.* 10.20.
128   **Turpe . . . caput** Verg. *G.* 3.52.
        diluat unda ≈ Mart. 8.33.4.
        unda caput = Prop. 3.7.58; Ov. *Tr.* 1.2.106.
129–30 **Et nisi — eris** Cf. *Her. Chr.* 23.99–100; *Sylv.* 5.20.11–12: "Et nisi me fallunt animi praesagia, in isto / Tu quoque . . . victor eris"; *Her.*, ded. 135–36: "Quod nisi me fallant animi praesagia, toto / Pectore laetatus iam mea scripta legis."
129   **nisi me — fallat** Cf. Calp. *Ecl.* 3.96: ". . . nisi me praesagia fallunt."
        presaga boni mens Cf. Verg. *A.* 10.843; Eob. *Her. Chr.* 5.33, n.
130   **toto pectore** = *Her. Chr.* 6.142, n.
131   **Hoc tua promittit** ≈ *Sylv.* 3.14.5 (7.27.33; *Her.* 2.5.125): "Hoc tua promittunt. . . ." For the incongruity of verb and subjects, cf. *Her. Chr.* 2.46.
        mensque fidesque Paul. Nol. *Carm.* 14.11.
132   **ingenii . . . honos** *Her. Chr.* 4.244.
        ingenii divitioris = *Sylv.* 7.28.26: "ingenii divitioris opes"; cf. *Nup.* 353, n.
133   **somnia** For Monica's dreams about her son's conversion, see August. *Confessiones* 3.11.
134   **Successu . . . carere** *Her. Chr.* 11.14, n.
135   **cruce signatus** = *Sylv. duae* 1.47, n.
        cruce . . . rubra *Her. Chr.* 17.162.
136   **stultis gentibus** Prud. *Perist.* 10.268.
137   **veteres . . . divos** *Her. Chr.* 4.206; cf. *Buc.* 3.19, n.
138   **sacra . . . in aede** *Buc.* 10.78, n.
        Christum . . . loqui Prud. *Perist.* 10.563, 928.
141   **Utque diu** = Ov. *Pont.* 1.2.99.
142   **flecti voce — Deus** Ov. *Ars* 1.442.
144   **Stygia . . . domo** *Her. Chr.* 3.16, n.
147   **Pectora . . . palmis** Catul. 64.351; Ov. *Ep.* 10.15; *Ars* 1.535; *Met.* 2.584; et al. For the gesture, cf. l. 55, n., above.
        Pectora . . . anxia Ov. *Ep.* 20.198; *Met.* 11.411; Eob. *Her. Chr.* 14.139.
        Pectora . . . lassabimus Ov. *Met.* 13.614.
148   **arentes . . . genas** = *Sylv.* 6.5.88; cf. Sen. *Phaed.* 1263.
149   **Multa dies** = Verg. *A.* 11.425; Hor. *Ars* 293.
        dies — videbit Cf. Ov. *Ep.* 18.184; Stat. *Theb.* 4.611–12; Eob. *Buc.* 6.72.
150   **misere perditus** Plaut. *Aul.* 731.
        esse voles ≈ *Her. Chr.* 10.18, n.
151–52 **Liqueris — anu** Cf. *Her. Chr.* 7.147–48.
152   **vetula . . . anu** *Her.* 1.6.182.
        facta videbor anu ≈ Ov. *Ep.* 1.116.
153–54 **O illum — Reddite** Cf. *Her. Chr.* 12.281–82; 18.83.
154   **Sic . . . semper eat** Ov. *Tr.* 1.9.66.
155   **spatiosa per aequora** = Aus. *Epigr.* 7.1; Mant. *c. Am.*, fol. 176ᵛ.
156   **Paulatim — ferunt** Cf. Tib. 1.4.16.
        subdere colla = Tib. 1.2.90.
158   **luci reddere** = *Her. Chr.* 6.148.
159   **nova signa** = Luc. 2.115; 7.203; Eob. *Her. Chr.* 17.21, 161.
160   **vanum numen** Ov. *Met.* 3.559–60.
        numen — deos = *Tum.* 7.66: "Quos male credidimus numen habere deos"; cf. *Her. Chr.* 20.44, n.; 23.90, n.
        habere deos = Prop. 1.1.8; Ov. *Rem.* 688; *Fast.* 1.174; et al.; Eob. *Her. Chr.* 10.140, 172; 11.58; 19.20.

161–62   **rapere — trahi** Here Monica predicts an episode recounted in August. *Confessiones* 8.8, where Augustine exclaims, "surgunt indocti et caelum rapiunt, et nos cum doctrinis nostris sine corde ecce ubi volutamur in carne et sanguine!" The form in which she paraphrases her son's dictum, however, does not come from the *Confessions* directly, but from a late medieval and Renaissance tradition: see *Leg. aurea* 120.74: "Surgunt indocti et celum rapiunt et nos cum doctrinis nostris in infernum demergimur"; J. Trapman, "*Surgunt indocti*: Augustine's Dictum (*Confessiones* VIII, 8) in the 16th and 17th Centuries," *BHR* 59 (1997), 51–56.

161   **sine vindice** = Ov. *Ep.* 8.7; *Met.* 1.93; *Fast.* 3.551.

163   **Questuram — veta** Cf. *Eccles.* 425.

165   **Sic tibi sint faciles** Aus. *Ep.* 8.17: "sic tibi sint Musae faciles. . . ."
       Tyberina . . . littora Stat. *Silv.* 5.2.113.
       littora venti = Verg. *A.* 12.455.

166   **Fata . . . meliora** Verg. *A.* 6.546; Ov. *Pont.* 4.9.9; Sil. 1.572; Eob. *Rec.* 229, n.

10

Meter: Elegiac distich.

1–2   **Si qua — habet** Cf. Ov. *Tr.* 3.1.17–18; 4.1.1–2; Eob. *Her. Chr.* 22.1–8. For the exordial topic of affected modesty, see Curtius, *ELLMA*, 83–85.

1   **Latiae . . . linguae** = Aus. *Mosella* 379, 383; cf. Eob. *Laud.* 115, n.

2   **Conveniens — habet** For the play on *Barbara*, continued in the next distich, cf. *AH* 51.144.3: "De barbara propagine, / Ad hoc vocata 'Barbara'"; Eob. *Nup.* 180; *Consol.* 11–12: "Barbara nec vitae meritis, sed nomine tantum. / Hei, quam barbaries hinc procul omnis erat!"
       dominae . . . nomen habet = Ov. *Fast.* 5.128; cf. Eob. *Sylv. duae* 1.24, n.

4   **refero versibus** = Ov. *Tr.* 2.10.
       versibus . . . meis = Ov. *Am.* 3.1.38; *Pont.* 2.2.8.

7   **ne sit tibi . . . molestum** = Mant. *Ecl.* 7.158.

8   **Magna — mei** Cf. *Her. Chr.* 10.192; 14.152, n.; *Sylv. duae* 2.218, n.

9   **ut fama est** = Lucr. 3.981; 5.395; Verg. *A.* 6.14; Prop. 2.6.15; Ov. *Ep.* 13.57.
       lota de gente Cf. *Her. Chr.* 4.17, n.
       de gente sacerdos = Verg. *A.* 7.750.

10   **verum . . . Deum** = *Her. Chr.* 4.154, n.
       posse docere Deum = *Her. Chr.* 2.122; cf. *Her. Chr.* 8.146.

11   **Gentiles . . . deos** *Her. Chr.* 2.22.

11–12 **nihil esse — Sollicitor** Cf. Ov. *Am.* 3.9.36; Mart. 4.21.1; Eob. *Her. Chr.* 10.144; 17.101.

11   **patriosque Penates** = *Rec.* 66, n.

12   **multos . . . dies** = *Her. Chr.* 1.38, n.
       sine teste = *Sylv. duae* 2.44, n.

13   **Et quantum — sinit** Cf. Walter, *Alex.* 7.45: "In quantum natura sinit . . ."; Ov. *Met.* 6.167; Eob. *Her. Chr.* 16.263.
       ire per altum = Camerarius, *Nar.* 6.11, n., quoting an early verse by Eobanus.

14   **suspicor esse** = *Her. Chr.* 4.18, n.

15–16 **Non — vident** For the light-and-darkness metaphors, cf. ll. 95–100, 165 below.

15   **confusa tenebris** *Luth.* 1.71.

16   **velut ex nebula** Cf. Otto 1210; Häussler, 61, 76, 112, 281; l. 97 below.
       lumina nostra vident = Ov. *Ep.* 6.72.

18   **His — velis** Cf. *Her. Chr.* 10.194; 11.166; *Eccles.* 420.
       quod potes esse = Ov. *Ep.* 12.206.
       esse velis = Prop. 2.17.10; 2.28.48; Ov. *Ep.* 13.96; *Rem.* 750; et al.

19	**Quoque — fiat** = *Sylv.* 2.1.131.
20	**Si tamen — voles** Cf. *Her. Chr.* 9.127, n.
21–22	**Unus — legis** Cf. Ov. *Ep.* 18.9–10. For the motif of the faithful messenger, cf. Eob. *Her. Chr.* 16.279–80.
22	**carmina — legis** ≈ Mart. 1.4.6.
23	**Sed ne forte putes** = Lucr. 2.718, 842; 4.129; Hor. *Ep.* 2.1.208; Ov. *Rem.* 465.
24	**Quod de me** = Ov. *Ep.* 20.94.
25	**Credenti . . . puellae** Ov. *Ep.* 2.63.
27	**Me pater** = Ov. *Ep.* 1.81; Eob. *Her. Chr.* 1.41.
	exactis tribus Verg. *G.* 3.190.
28	**ingenuas . . . opes** = Locher, *Stult.* 34, fol. 45ᵛ: "Graias concessit ad oras, / Quo tandem ingenuas concumularet opes"; cf. Eob. *Rec.* 87, n.: "ingenuas . . . artes."
	quaerere . . . opes = *Nob.* 330: "Mansuras animi quaerere debet opes."
29	**tenero . . . flore** Ov. *Fast.* 3.254; Prud. *Perist.* 3.109: "flore . . . occidis in tenero."
	vernet — iuventus Cf. Celtis, *Rhapsodia* 101: "Cum tibi primaevo vernaret flore iuventus"; Prud. *c. Symm.* 2.7: ". . . vernantes flore iuventae"; Eob. *Idyl.* 1.125: ". . . dum primo vernat tua flore iuventa"; *Sylv.* 7.1.17: ". . . licet in primo vernet tua flore iuventus."
	flore iuventus = Verg. *A.* 7.162; cf. Eob. *Her. Chr.* 2.110, n.
30	**non satis esse** = *Eleg. Maec.* 1.138; Mart. 9.30.4; 9.59.10.
31	**quae me suspensam** = Verg. *A.* 4.9.
33	**niti — videntur** = Q. Serenus, *Liber medicinalis* 17.2: "vera niti ratione videntur."
34	**patria relligione** = Celtis, *Am.* 2.9.142; cf. Eob. *Her. Chr.* 4.184.
35	**Quae tamen ut** = Ov. *Met.* 3.494; 6.352.
36	**Mens . . . prophana** Ov. *Met.* 2.833.
	Mens mea = *Buc.* 3.136, n.
38	**complacuisse Deo** = l. 170 below; cf. Ov. *Fast.* 2.612.
39	**Quis Deus** = Verg. *G.* 4.315; *A.* 9.77; et al.; Eob. *Her. Chr.* 17.103.
	ante omnia saecula = Tifernate, *Carm.*, sig. A2ʳ (in a hymn to the Trinity): "Germen ab aeterno atque ante omnia saecula natum." Cf. Ov. *Met.* 6.208; 15.878.
41	**Sine quo nihil** = Paul. Nol. *Carm.* 22.56: "hoc verbum est, sine quo nihil, omnia per quod / facta vigent."
44	**notus in orbe** Mart. 1.1.2.
	in orbe fuit = Ov. *Ars* 1.56; *Fast.* 1.284.
49	**Vana . . . ludibria chartae** Mart. 10.4.7; cf. Eob. *Her. Chr.* 8.107.
50	**patria nostra** = *Sylv. duae* 1.114, n.
51–52	**Bella — sapis** Cf. Mant. *2. Parthen.* 3.46–47: "Furta, arma, rapinae, / Stupra, doli, fraudes: opera haec preclara deorum"; cf. further Eob. *Laud.* 431–35, n.
51	**victa libidine** = Ov. *Met.* 9.625; Eob. *Vict.* 247; *Tum.* 2.151.
52	**faciunt divos** = *Buc.* B 2.50.
	patria terra = Celtis, *Am.* 4.2.12; Eob. *Sylv.* 1.2.28.
53	**de superis — nephandum** Cf. Mant. *Ecl.* 3.38: "Heu nescis male de superis sentire nefandum?"
55	**qui temperet omnia** ≈ Ov. *Met.* 4.169.
56	**Credibile est . . . inesse** = Ov. *Am.* 3.1.2.
	rebus inesse = Ov. *Ep.* 17.130.
57	**plures — magistros** The thought comes from Hom. *Il.* 2.204–05, translated by Lorenzo Valla as: "Neque probandus est plurium principatus. Unus sit rex, unus sit princeps." Cf. also Sen. *Thy.* 444: "Non capit regnum duos"; Andrel. *Livia* 4.6.33: "Nulla duos unquam coeperunt regna tyrannos"; Erasmus, *Adag.* 2.2.24.
60	**iacebis iners** ≈ *Sylv. duae* 2.248, n.
61	**Unus et hic** = Ov. *Ep.* 18.9.

solo — nutu Cf. Prosper Aquitanus, *Epigr.* 41.1: ". . . regit omnia nutu"; Tifernate, *Carm.*, sig. A4ʳ (in a hymn to the Trinity) and Mant. *Calam.* 3.455 (p. 82): ". . . solo movet omnia nutu"; Mant. *1. Parthen.* 1.38: ". . . Dei, solo qui temperat omnia nutu"; Eob. *Idyl.* 4.107: ". . . solo qui dirigis omnia nutu."

63   **Unum Trinumque** = Andrel. *Ecl.* 4.92 (of the Trinity).

65   **Hic quoque sunt** = Ov. *Tr.* 3.9.1.

66   **unde . . . opem** = Ov. *Ep.* 17.228.
   petemus opem ≈ Ov. *Rem.* 436.

67   **Pater et Natus** = Sedul. 2.173.
   exit ab illis = *Rec.* 42.

69   **Oleniae . . . capellae** = Ov. *Met.* 3.594; *Fast.* 5.113; Eob. *Vict.* 56; cf. Mant. *1. Parthen.* 3.162–63 (after the birth of Christ): "Non erat Oleniam fama haec nutrire capellam / Cretaea sub rupe Iovem"; cf. Eob. *Buc.* 7.100, n.; B 10.1.

71   **nec in — formas** Cf. *Her. Chr.* 24.21.
   in varias . . . formas = Man. 1.533.
   Prothea formas = Poliziano, *Silv.* 4.229: "innumeras variantem Protea formas."

72   **patrium . . . femur** Sid. *Carm.* 22.29.

73   **prolifico** *Nup.* 318, n.
   de vertice nata . . . est *Priap.* 1.4: ". . . de patrio vertice nata dea est"; cf. Luc. 9.350.

74   **lubrica concha** = *Anthol. Lat.* 476.6.

75   **veterum — deorum** = *Vict.* 6; cf. Verg. *A.* 8.187; Ov. *Met.* 10.694; Eob. *Buc.* 3.19, n.; *Her. Chr.* 23.113.

76   **sacram . . . fidem** Prud. *Perist.* 14.14; Eob. *Her. Chr.* 22.114.

77   **legis — vestrae** ≈ Mant. *Calam.* 1.1152 (p. 48): "legis mysteriae nostrae."

78   **patria . . . domo** = *Her. Chr.* 7.106, n.
   mirum = *Sylv. duae* 1.128, n.

79   **vetus et multos . . . per annos** = Ov. *Am.* 3.1.1; cf. Eob. *Rec.* 68, n.

81   **nemo conspexit** = Celtis, *Am.* 1.1.13.

82   **patrias . . . opes** = Ov. *Am.* 3.13.32; *Tr.* 4.5.8.

83   **ut perhibent** = *Laud.* B 5.4, n.
   rex . . . sceptra gubernans Locher, "In commendationem philosophiae," *Stult.* 109, fol. 130ʳ: "Hac sine non princeps, non rex sua sceptra gubernant."

84   **depopulatus agros** = Gunther, *Lig.* 8.340; Eob. *Eccles.* 378; cf. *Her. Chr.* 22.112.

85   **secura . . . ocia** = Ov. *Tr.* 3.2.9; cf. Verg. *G.* 3.376–77; Ov. *Fast.* 1.67–68.

87   **vetiti cupidissima** Cf. Ov. *Am.* 3.4.17.
   turba puellae = Ov. *Am.* 2.9.53; *Ars* 2.281; 3.417, 811.

90   **non potuisse trahi** = *Her. Chr.* 22.60.

91   **Hebraeos . . . vates** = *Her. Chr.* 21.1; cf. *Laud.* 98, n.
   divina — vates ≈ "De fructu et utilitate lectionis Psalmorum," ll. 5 and 33, *Psalt.*, fol. 4ᵛ and 5ʳ: "psalmographi divina poemata vatis."
   divina poemata = Ven. Fort. *Carm.* 2.9.19; 8.3.7; Poliziano, *Silv.* 1.306.

92–94   **Vidimus et . . . Vidimus . . . Vidimus et** Cf. *Her. Chr.* 4.223–25.

95   **Denique — erat** ≈ Ov. *Ep.* 1.21.

97   **Per nebulas** Cf. l. 16, n., above.

98   **tremula . . . aqua** ≈ Ven. Fort. *Carm.* 10.9.4; Celtis, *Am.* 4.13.24.
   lumen aqua = *Epic. Drusi* 410.

99   **exuta tenebras** = Claud. *Bell. Get.* 36.

100   **Quo — queror** Cf. *Her. Chr.* 7.80.
   lumen abesse = Ov. *Tr.* 1.9.56.
   abesse queror = Ov. *Ep.* 2.2; Eob. *Her. Chr.* 16.60; cf. *Her. Chr.* 13.24.

101–02   **Qur — peto** Cf. Catul. 85.1–2.

101   **patriis . . . sacris** = Pontano, *Laud.* 6.1: "Annua iam redeunt patriis solemnia sacris."

103–04	**Nemo — loqui** Cf. *Leg. aurea* (Graesse) 202, p. 899: "Amplius, quae Dei erant, quaesivit et quae sursum sunt, capiens libros, quos ei Origenes miserat, diligenter legit et valde crevit in scientia divinorum etiam sine magistro et in sapientia divina." For the thought that books are silent teachers, see Erasmus, *Adag.* 1.2.18, "Muti magistri."
103	**Nemo mihi est** = Ov. *Met.* 15.600.
104	**littera . . . loqui** = *Her. Chr.* 11.22.
	littera muta *Sylv.* 7.3.8: "Si modo muta aliquid littera vocis habet."
107	**miserae . . . puellae** Prop. 2.8.23; Ov. *Ars* 3.45.
110	**Hoc est — nihil** Cf. *Her. Chr.* 2.28, n.
111	**avida . . . mente** *Culex* 61; Ov. *Ep.* 7.153; Luc. 6.29.
113	**Tu — Camenae** Cf. *Her. Chr.* 9.31, n.
	Tu quoque, cui = Ov. *Ars* 3.785, 797.
	nostrae . . . Camenae ≈ Calp. *Ecl.* 4.46; Eob. *Buc.* 10.23, n.
115	**Quid faciam** = *Her. Chr.* 4.47, n.
	de sordibus — istis ≈ *Luth.* 1.9.
117	**patrios . . . penates** = Tib. 1.3.33; Ov. *Fast.* 6.603; Eob. *Her. Chr.* 20.31; cf. *Rec.* 66, n.
118	**qui — erat** = *Tum.* 5.28; cf. *Her. Chr.* 12.132, n.
119	**tenera . . . virgine** Catul. 61.3–4; Hor. *Carm.* 1.21.1; 4.1.26.
120	**Heu nimium** = *Her. Chr.* 5.4, n.
	duro — clausa Gunther, *Lig.* 4.241: "duro servabat carcere clausum"; cf. Man. 1.924; 2.93; Eob. *Her. Chr.* 19.122.
	carcere . . . premor *Her. Chr.* 11.5–6.
121	**Utque diu latuit** Cf. Ov. *Fast.* 3.239.
	Abantius heros = Pontano, *Urania* 4.303.
123	**marmorea turri** Poliziano, *Epigr.* 89.2.
	ego . . . reservor = Ov. *Ep.* 14.119.
125	**Stulte parens** = Locher, *Stult.* 6, fol. 16ᵛ; 86, fol. 100ᵛ.
127	**Rara comes** = Stat. *Theb.* 10.385.
128	**excubat ante fores** = Tib. 1.3.72; cf. Eob. *Her. Chr.* 6.202, n.
129–30	**Triste — meo** The motif and wording come from Magdal. *Ep.* 115–16. Cf. Eob. *Her. Chr.* 20.103–04, n.
129	**Triste . . . caput** Ov. *Tr.* 3.12.48.
130	**prospectu — meo** = Ov. *Ep.* 10.28.
131–36	**Nunc — Deum** The model is Ov. *Tr.* 3.8.1–10, especially ll. 1–2, 5–6. Cf. *Am.* 3.6.13–16; Eob. *Buc.* 2.30–33, n.; *Hod.* 90–91; *Psalt.* 55.15–18: "O mihi nunc volucres aliquis connecteret alas, / Qualibus in ventos ire columba solet. / Protinus evadam qua me non ulla sequentes / Deferat humano semita trita pede."
133	**me chara parens** *Buc.* 4.37; cf. *Rec.* 152, n.
	pater anxius aevo Cf. *Her. Chr.* 7.83, n.
134	**patrius . . . ager** *Buc.* 1.122, n.; *Nob.* 183.
	plena messe Man. 3.152; Eob. *Buc.* 11.59, n.; *Wirt.* 459.
	messe . . . ager = *Buc.*, ded. 6, n.
135	**Protinus evadam** = *Hod.* B 1.45.
	gentis . . . lavatae Cf. *Her. Chr.* 4.17, n.; l. 9 above.
136	**Veridico . . . ore Deum** Cf. Lucr. 6.6; Mart. 10.37.2; Pontano, *Laud.* 3.18: ". . . tibi veridico praestitit ore Deus"; Eob. *Her. Chr.* 8.92.
	praedicat ore Deum = Peter Riga, *Gen.* 258: "Et verum vero predicat ore Deum"; cf. Alan. *Nat.* 5.44: "Ut proprio proprium predicet ore deum"; Eob. *Her. Chr.* 21.44.
137	**tristes . . . querelas** = *Ciris* 174; cf. Eob. *Her. Chr.* 7.137, n.
	meditor . . . querelas Ov. *Pont.* 3.4.45 (different).
	sine teste = *Her. Chr.* 8.113, n.

138   **conscia sola** Ov. *Met.* 13.15.
139   **Quacunque aspicio** = *Her. Chr.* 4.153, n.
        longo — circum Cf. Verg. *A.* 2.766–67; Eob. *Her. Chr.* 17.127, n.
140   **iussit habere** = *Pug.* 46, n.
        habere deos = *Her. Chr.* 9.160, n.
141   **Heu dolor** = *Ama.* 35.1, n.
        stulti ludibria saecli Cf. Andrel. *Livia* 3.6.31: ". . . nostri ludibria saecli"; Eob. *Her. Chr.* 12.53, n.; 21.217, n.
142   **Ah, pereat — deos** Cf. Prop. 2.29.12.
        Ah, pereat = Prop. 1.6.12; 1.17.13; 2.33.27; [Tib.] 3.4.62; Eob. *Nob.* 191.
        lapides . . . deos *Her. Chr.* 4.239.
        qui — deos Cf. *Her. Chr.* 2.22, n.
143   **excessi — annis** Cf. *Psalt.* 71.45: "Doctior excessi per te iuuenilibus annis."
        puerilibus annis = *Rec.* 104, n.
144   **divos — nihil** Cf. *Her. Chr.* 4.206; *Nup.* 369, n.
        suspicor esse = *Her. Chr.* 4.18, n.
146   **Est aliquid** = *Buc.* 10.56, n.
147   **animo . . . vigilante** = Lucr. 5.1170.
148   **Iessaeo . . . seni** = *Psalt.* 29, arg. 2; cf. Mant. *c. Poet.* 16: ". . . Iessei regia Musa senis"; Eob. *Buc.* 6.90, n.
149–60 **Quae — caho** These lines versify Vulg. *Psa.* 113.11–15, with some transpositions for poetic effect. The sense of taste (l. 155) is not mentioned in the biblical text. Cf. Eobanus' paraphrase of these verses in *Psalt.* 115.7–18:

> At Deus astriferi noster tenet aurea coeli
>   Moenia et arbitrio cuncta agit ipse suo.
> Verum illi simulacra colunt argentea, vel quae
>   Ex auro humanae composuere manus,
> Ora quibus nunquam vero sermone loquentur,
>   Quo nequeant aliquid cernere lumen habent.
> Nulla soni veniunt vanas elementa per aures,
>   Nare sub ipsorum non erit ullus odor.
> Organa deficiunt stupidas gustantia linguas,
>   Cassa locuturae guttura vocis habent.
> Quid quod inutilibus nil possunt tangere palmis?
>   Quodque pedes nunquam qui moveantur habent?

Eobanus' use of the Psalm text in Barbara's letter was suggested by the *vita* itself. See *Leg. aurea* (Graesse) 202, p. 900: "praeses autem videns miram pulchritudinem eius dixit ei: quid vis? parce tibi ipsi et sacrifica diis, aut acerrimis tormentis traderis. Cui illa: ego habeo sacrificare Deo meo Iesu Christo, qui fecit coelum et terram et omnia, quae in iis sunt. De daemonibus tuis dicit propheta, Psalm. CXIII: os habent et non loquuntur, oculos habent et non videbunt."

149–50 **Quae — manus** Cf. *Psalt.* 135.41–42: "Quae gentes idola colunt ex quolibet aere, / Pro diis humanae composuere manus."
149   **Quae — simulachra** Cf. *Psalt.* 115.1: "Quae gentes simulacra colunt sunt vana. . . ."
        diversa . . . simulachra Ov. *Met.* 5.211.
        gentes . . . prophanae Prud. *Psych.*, praef. 9; Eob. *Her.* 2.7.21.
150   **humanae . . . manus** ≈ Prop. 3.7.30.
151   **sermone loquentur** ≈ *Her. Chr.* 3.85, n.
153   **vacuas — aures** ≈ Ov. *Met.* 4.41 (in a different sense).
156   **humanae . . . vocis** Ov. *Am.* 2.6.37.
158   **Stant fulti** Stat. *Theb.* 3.326.

159   **Noster at** = *Her. Chr.* 17.96; *Max.* 269.
       ipse volebat = Ov. *Met.* 12.360.
160   **Omnia — caho** Cf. Mant. *Epigr.*, fol. 111ᵛ: "Cunctaque de veteri . . . orta chao";
       Eob. *Her. Chr.* 13.153; 15.156; 22.130; *Vict.* 17.
161   **Verius — vates** Cf. *Psalt.* 14, arg. 1: "Verius haud potuit praesaga mente prophetes /
       Dicere."
162   **Quis, nisi mentis inops** = Ov. *Ars* 1.465; cf. *Rem.* 127.
163–64 **dum . . . dum . . . Dum** For this anaphora, cf. *Buc.* 7.72–73, n.
163   **dum laeta viret . . . aetas** Cf. Verg. *G.* 3.63; Hor. *Epod.* 13.4; Eob. *Her. Chr.* 2.110,
       n.; also cf. l. 29, n., above.
       dum . . . dum = Verg. *G.* 3.325; Calp. *Ecl.* 5.86.
       dum pullulat aetas = *Ruf.* 43; cf. *Buc.* 1.103, n.
164   **ingrata relligione** = Aus. *Prof.* 16.20.
165   **Eripe — puellam** Cf. Verg. *A.* 6.365: "eripe me his, invicte, malis. . . ."
       Stygia . . . nocte *Sylv. duae* 1.50, n.
166   **Caelestem — viam** Cf. *Her. Chr.* 11.42.
167   **luminibus contingat** Cf. Ov. *Ars* 1.156.
168   **voto — frui** Cf. *Her. Chr.* A 3.8; Ov. *Ep.* 6.75.
       prosperiore frui = Ov. *Pont.* 3.7.30; Eob. *Her. Chr.* 12.266.
169   **Praecipue si** = Ov. *Ars* 2.665; 3.681.
       quae mihi sint facienda Cf. Ov. *Am.* 1.4.11.
170   **complacuisse Deo** = l. 38 above; cf. Ov. *Fast.* 2.612.
171   **ego, vaticinor** = Ov. *Tr.* 1.8.9.
       totis — medullis Cf. Ov. *Met.* 9.484; 14.351.
172   **veteres — deos** Cf. *Her. Chr.* 11.58; also cf. *Her. Chr.* 9.160, n.; 18.100, n. For
       veteres deos, see *Buc.* 3.19, n.
       crimen habere = Ov. *Rem.* 328; Eob. *Her. Chr.* 11.58; 18.108.
173–74 **Iam — Effugere** Cf. Verg. *Ecl.* 10.58.
173   **per scopulos . . . saxa** *Her. Chr.* 9.109, n.
       salebrosaque saxa Ov. *Ep.* 4.103–04 (in some mss. and early eds.); cf. Eob. *Buc.* 6.33, n.
174   **iussa tremenda** = Dantiscus, *Carm.* 1.3.214.
175   **Ille quidem ferus est** = Ov. *Ars* 1.9.
       ita respicit istas = *Sylv.* 1.4.71.
177   **cultus . . . priores** = Luc. 2.28; Paul. Nol. *Carm.* 28.275: "cultus oblita priores";
       Prud. *c. Symm.* 2.442: "servit Roma Deo cultus exosa priores."
178   **ense cadam** ≈ *Her. Chr.* 6.160, n.
179–84 **Nunc — frui** The motif — the fortunate absence of a hindering person — does not
       occur in the *vita*, but comes from Ov. *Ep.* 4.109–10 and 17.155.
180–81 **Et — orbem** For the time indication, cf. *Her. Chr.* 5.7, n.
180   **tertia luna videt** = *Her.* 2.6.10; cf. *Her. Chr.* 18.10; *Sylv.* 3.4.54: "nunc me /
       Postquam missa fui luna secunda videt."
182   **patria . . . domo** = Ov. *Rem.* 262, 474; cf. Eob. *Her. Chr.* 7.106, n.; l. 78 above.
185   **Non precor ut** = Ov. *Tr.* 2.183; Eob. *Her. Chr.* 2.127.
       longa est via = Ov. *Am.* 1.9.9; Eob. *Hod.* 71; cf. *Her. Chr.* 5.27, n.
       tamen oro = V. Fl. 6.733.
186   **littera scripta** = Ov. *Ep.* 5.24; Eob. *Her. Chr.* 15.70.
189   **numeramus — vitae** ≈ *Her. Chr.* 16.235. For *taedia vitae*, see *Laud.* 320, n.
190   **littera nostra tibi** = *Her. Chr.* 4.182. For *littera nostra*, see *Her. Chr.* 3.54, n.
191   **sacro — lavari** Cf. *Her. Chr.* 6.121, n.
192   **Haec — mei** Cf. l. 8 above; *Sylv. duae* 2.218, n.
       Haec . . . maxima causa mei ≈ Ov. *Rem.* 322; cf. Eob. *Eccles.* 166.
194   **hic miserae — opem** Cf. Ov. *Pont.* 2.3.48; Eob. *Her. Chr.* 2.40; 11.166; 20.18.
       miserae . . . opem = Ov. *Ep.* 10.24.

195	**dubiis . . . rebus** = Verg. *A.* 6.196; cf. *A.* 11.445; Eob. *Her. Chr.* 5.161, n.
197	**Adde — loqutae** Cf. *Sylv.* 3.2.105: "Adde fidem famae de te non falsa loquutae."
	Adde fidem = Ov. *Ep.* 7.110; 12.194.
	de te mihi = Prop. 4.4.65.
198	**Et mihi — veni** Cf. Ov. *Ep.* 18.30.

11

Meter: Elegiac distich.

1–2	**Quam . . . salutem, Hanc** = Ov. *Met.* 9.530–31.
1	**Quam — salutem** Cf. Ov. *Ep.* 19.1; Eob. *Sylv.* 2.24.1: "Quam tibi debueram toties misisse salutem."
	mandare salutem = *Nup.* 221, n. For the play on the two meanings of *salus*, see *Her. Chr.* 3.1, n.
2	**Hanc — mihi** Cf. *Psalt.* 119.152: "Sisque ea pollicitum te memor esse mihi"; 119.214: "Et te hoc pollicitum sis memor esse mihi"; Mant. *Bapt.*, fol. 229ʳ: "Auxilio generi sis memor esse tuo"; Eob. *Her. Chr.* 17.232; *Sylv.* 1.1.132.
3–4	**Si qua — meis** Cf. Prop. 4.3.3–4; Ov. *Ep.* 11.1. For the motif of the tear-stained letter, see Eob. *Her. Chr.* 2.3, n.
3	**Si qua — notabis** Cf. *Sylv.* 3.5.7: "Si qua liturarum forsan dispuncta videbis."
4	**Pars quota de** = Ov. *Pont.* 3.4.41; cf. Eob. *Buc.* 2.92, n.
	illa fuere meis = Ov. *Ep.* 15.138.
5–6	**Carcere . . . premor** *Her. Chr.* 10.120.
5	**sancte pater** = Mart. 10.28.7; Eob. *Her. Chr.* 14.9; cf. *Her. Chr.* 14.151, n.
6	**Sic merui, sic** = Stat. *Silv.* 5.5.35; cf. Ov. *Pont.* 1.5.70.
7	**Quod legis — antro** Cf. Ov. *Ep.* 10.3; *Pont.* 4.2.1–2; Eob. *Her. Chr.* 3.74, n.
9	**O utinam primis** = Ov. *Met.* 8.501.
	utinam . . . latuisset Ov. *Tr.* 1.9.55.
	primis . . . ab annis = *Buc.* 3.65, n.
10	**crimine — nocens** = *Sylv.* 6.6.16; cf. *Ama.* A 3.2, n.; *Sylv. duae* 1.148, n.
11–12	**Vel — colo** Cf. Prop. 2.13.43–44; Eob. *Her. Chr.* 8.19, n.
11	**iura sororum** = *Sylv.* 3.3.11: "heu ferrea iura sororum."
12	**stamina rupta** = *Eleg. Maec.* 1.76.
13	**conscia culpae** = Ov. *Ep.* 7.191; *Met.* 2.593; cf. Eob. *Her. Chr.* 15.25–26, n.
14	**Flerem — carere** = Ov. *Ep.* 1.18; cf. Eob. *Her. Chr.* 9.134.
	carere preces = Ov. *Pont.* 3.7.2.
15	**peccati — gravatur** Cf., for example, August. *In Iohannis evangelium tractatus* 49.19: "cum tanta mole peccati gravaris"; Eob. *Psalt.* 51.5: "Respice me nimia peccati mole gravatum."
16	**offensum . . . Deum** = l. 162 below; cf. Ov. *Tr.* 1.10.42; *Fast.* 1.482; l. 171 below.
17	**Stygia . . . nocte** *Sylv. duae* 1.50, n.
19	**sperare favorem** = Luc. 8.117.
20	**Praescripto . . . carmine** See l. 31 below.
21	**ore profari** = Poliziano, *Silv.* 4.718: "non ore profari / evaleam."
22	**littera . . . loqui** = *Her. Chr.* 10.104.
23–24	**Antrum — adit** Cf. *Buc.* 8.17.
23	**foeda . . . situ** Luc. 6.516; Eob. *Val.* 1.7.
	squalore situque = Calp. *Ecl.* 1.43.
24	**quota . . . portio** Juv. 3.61; Eob. *Vict.* 32; also cf. *Buc.* 2.92, n.
	portio lucis Juvenc. 3.564; Prud. *Cath.* 8.12.
25	**exortum . . . solem** = *Her. Chr.* 8.39.
	possis cognoscere = Verg. *G.* 2.226.

26   **admissum . . . diem** ≈ Ov. *Rem.* 412.
      parva fenestra = Ov. *Fast.* 6.166; cf. *Fast.* 6.577.
27   **mane rubet** ≈ *Buc.* 7.169; cf. Ov. *Met.* 15.193; Mant. *1. Parthen.* 1.536: "nondum mane rubens. . . ."
      anhelat *Her. Chr.* 13.57.
28   **iusso — preces** = l. 178 below; cf. *Her. Chr.* 5.176, n.
29   **Prona — lacertos** Cf. Mant. *Ecl.* 1.73: "Nuda pedem, discincta sinum, spoliata lacertos"; 8.25.
      dispassa Cf. Gel. 15.15.4: "Itaque Plautus in Milite glorioso [360] 'a' littera in 'e' mutata per compositi vocabuli morem 'dispessis' dicit pro eo, quod est 'dispassis.'"
30   **ore referre** Verg. *A.* 7.436; Ov. *Pont.* 4.5.33.
31   **Respice — creasti** ≈ *Psalt.* 13.11: "Respice me miserum, qui me, qui cuncta creasti"; cf. Vulg. *Psa.* 21.2: "Deus Deus meus, respice me"; 68.17: "Domine, . . . respice me."
33   **Nec mihi tu** = Ov. *Ep.* 7.75.
36   **Sacra prophanato** = Gianfrancesco Pico della Mirandola, "Staurostichon," in his *Opera omnia* (1557; repr. Hildesheim, 1969), 355: "Sacra prophanato diffudit lumina mundo"; cf. Mant. *2. Parthen.* 3.185: "Sacra profanantes . . ."; Eob. *Tum.* 7.155: "Sacra prophanatas . . . per aras." Cf. further *Laud.* 378, n.
      ore loqui = *Her. Chr.* 6.98, n.
37   **Atque utinam** = *Buc.* 1.36, n.
      fasso . . . ore *Her. Chr.* 5.176, n.
39   **Quod nisi tu dederis** ≈ Ov. *Ep.* 4.1; *Met.* 9.530.
      proxime caelo ≈ *Sylv. duae* 2.111, n.
40   **heae** This medieval spelling occurs also in an autograph letter of 12 April 1512 to Georg Spalatin: "heae Prussiaticae nebulae." See Mutian. *Ep.*, 2:367 (where *heae* is misspelled as "haec"). The form occurs also in Eob. *Her. Chr.* 16.269; *Orat.* 12.3 and 24.1; *Dial.* 2, sig. C2ᵛ; and *Theoc.* 4.17. Cf. *Nor.* 817: "eae [= heae] . . . partes."
      pondus habere preces = Ov. *Ars* 3.806.
41   **irati . . . Tonantis** Sil. 13.20; Eob. *Hod.* B 7.33.
      numen . . . Tonantis = Mant. *1. Parthen.* 3.394.
      numen placare = Stat. *Theb.* 12.486.
42   **Neglectam — viam** Cf. *Her. Chr.* 10.166.
      pandere — viam = *Her.* 3.4.168; cf. Verg. *A.* 12.626; Luc. 3.467.
43–44 **Nunc — erit** Cf. Ov. *Ep.* 3.142–43; ll. 173–74 below.
43   **novissima restat** = Ov. *Met.* 10.373.
44   **vivere — erit** ≈ *Her.* 1.5.130; cf. Prop. 2.28.2 (Ov. *Ep.* 20.38; *Ars* 1.34; et al.): ". . . crimen erit."
45   **deformibus actis** = *Psalt.* 5.37.
47   **Adde quod** = *Buc.* B 2.21, n.
      haec — meruisse Cf. Ov. *Pont.* 1.1.62.
48   **poena vindice** Catul. 64.192; Paul. Nol. *Carm.* 20.239–40; Prud. *Apoth.* 930; Eob. *Her. Chr.* 13.11, 46.
49   **obruta saxis** Cf. *Her. Chr.* 22.109.
52   **tormenti . . . genus** Verg. *A.* 8.487.
      omne genus = *Ama.* B 2.18, n.
53   **ante diem cecidisse** *Laud.* 501–02, n.
54   **sancta . . . pietate** Mart. 8.15.7.
      pro pietate mori = *Her. Chr.* 12.14; 18.150.
55–58 **Nunc — deos** Cf. Mant. *2. Parthen.* 1.340–41, where St. Catherine resolves to die a martyr's death: "Cur non, quae pertulit Agnes, / Ipsa feram? Cur non Agathes imitabile fatum?"
55   **Nunc ego . . . cuperem** = Ov. *Tr.* 3.8.1.

56	**Costidis** *Laud.* 487, n.
57	**mihi — tuendae** *Nor.* 1118–19: "fidei non est suscepta tuendae / Ulla mihi ratio."
58	**veteres . . . crimen habere deos** *Her. Chr.* 10.172, n.
59	**Vota — lavacri** The *vita* does not say expressly that she was baptized as a child. Her baptism, however, may be inferred from her knowledge of God (ll. 106–08). Cf. l. 65 below.
	sancti . . . undis . . . lavacri *Ebn.* 63: "sancti quos unda lavacri / Abluit."
60	**duce sub . . . miles eram** *Her. Chr.* 14.62.
	duce sub proprio *Tum.* 7.104.
	miles eram = Ov. *Ep.* 11.48: "nova miles eram." Cf. Eob. *Her. Chr.* 1.98, n.
61	**signa sequta** ≈ Verg. *A.* 8.52; Luc. 2.531; 9.281; 10.10.
64	**celeri . . . fuga** = Ov. *Fast.* 5.706; *Tr.* 4.2.60; cf. Eob. *Her. Chr.* 22.142, n.
65	**Filia lucis** Cf. Vulg. *Luc.* 16.8; *Joan.* 12.36; *Ephes.* 5.8; *1. Thess.* 5.5.
	ingrata reliqui ≈ Calp. *Ecl.* 3.8.
66	**Non intellectis** ≈ Ov. *Fast.* 2.716; *Met.* 10.365.
67	**per opacae devia** = *Her. Chr.* 4.169.
	opacae . . . noctis Verg. *A.* 4.123; 8.658; 10.161–62; Ov. *Ep.* 16.47; Eob. *Vict.* 287.
	devia noctis l. 131 below.
68	**iam prope limen eram** ≈ Ov. *Ep.* 11.71; cf. Eob. *Buc.* 8.63.
69	**Iam super** = Ov. *Am.* 1.13.1; *Met.* 5.648; Luc. 8.1.
	puteum . . . abyssi = *Ama.* 35.45, n.
70	**Stygio — cani** Cf. *Her. Chr.* 15.186.
	Stygio . . . cani ≈ Claud. *Rapt. Pros.* 2, praef. 34; cf. Sen. *Her. F.* 783; *Phaed.* 223; *Her. O.* 1257.
71	**Actum erat** Erasmus, *Adag.* 1.3.39.
	pater optime = *Nup.* 226, n.
73–78	**Et licet — tuae est** Cf. *Her. Chr.* 14.53–56 and 15.55–60.
73	**licet ingratum est** = Ov. *Am.* 2.19.3 (different); cf. Eob. *Her. Chr.* 7.84.
	sceleris In Christian poetic usage, *scelus* often means "sin": see, for example, *AH* 32.10.8: "Oppressum mole scelerum"; Brant, *Varia carm.*, sig. B8ʳ (*Texte* 116.15): "Ipse ego peccator, scelerum quoque mole gravatus"; Eob. *Her. Chr.* 11.77, 160; 15.19, 25.
77	**scelus omne** = Verg. *A.* 1.356.
79–80	**Tempus — vias** Cf. *Her. Chr.* 12.123–24, n.
79	**Tempus — orbem** Cf. Verg. *G.* 4.426; *A.* 8.97; Stat. *Theb.* 4.680–81; Pontano, *Eridanus* 1.7.21: ". . . per medium rapitur sol aureus orbem"; Eob. *Buc.* 3.102, n.
	Tempus erat For the construction, with its elision of *quo*, see *Rec.* 1, n.
80	**Foecerat — vias** Cf. Ov. *Met.* 3.145.
81–82	**Indixere — coli** Cf. *Buc.* 11.68.
81	**Indixere . . . silentia** ≈ Gunther, *Lig.* 10.500: "Indixitque manu placidoque silentia vultu."
82	**Tempore quo** = Lucr. 2.164; Catul. 68.15, 113; Verg. *A.* 9.80; Prop. 4.10.7; Ov. *Ep.* 4.67; et al.; Eob. *Her. Chr.* 12.206; 21.238.
	sacra coli = Ov. *Fast.* 3.280.
83	**formae . . . colendae** Cf. Ov. *Met.* 10.534.
	studiis intenta = Prosper Aquitanus, *Epigr.* 26.3: "mens . . . piis studiis intenta"; cf. Eob. *Buc.* 5.6; *Her. Chr.* 19.97.
84	**fallere . . . procos** = Ov. *Pont.* 3.1.108.
	fallere docta = *Her. Chr.* 8.30; cf. Tib. 1.9.37.
86	**copia nulla** = Ov. *Pont.* 1.10.32.
87	**Ecce venit** = Ov. *Met.* 2.635; 6.165, 451; Eob. *Her. Chr.* 12.171.
	senio — albo = *Her. Chr.* 4.59, n.
88	**Hoc . . . nondum tempore** *Her. Chr.* 12.37.
	nondum tempore . . . eras ≈ *Priap.* 68.38.

89	**quam forte gerebas** ≈ *Her. Chr.* 4.123, n.
90	**poterit credi** = Ov. *Pont.* 3.1.78.
91	**tetricum . . . cucullum** *Ama.* B 2.38, n.
92	**loca . . . non adeunda** = Ov. *Tr.* 1.4.18; 3.10.76.
	non adeunda subis ≈ *Sylv. duae* 2.114, n.
93	**Errantes — doctissime** Cf. *Ama.* 12.6.
	revocare animas ≈ Prud. *c. Symm.* 1.91: "extinctas . . . / in lucem revocasse animas."
94	**sum . . . capta dolis** Ov. *Ep.* 21.122.
	foemina — dolis ≈ Peter Riga, *Gen.* 343 (of Eve): "Femina capta dolo."
95	**suspensus — dixti** ≈ Dantiscus, *Carm.* 12.2.143 (in an epithalamium published in February 1512): "suspensus in oscula, dixit." Cf. Claud. *Epith.* 116–17.
96	**quolibet . . . loco** = Ov. *Ars* 3.608; *Pont.* 1.1.4.
97	**Ah — meminisse** Cf. *Sylv. duae* 2.187, n.; *Her. Chr.* 6.33, n.
98	**Foemina — fuit** Cf. Ov. *Pont.* 4.6.40.
99	**rebus — nefandis** Cf. Ov. *Ars* 1.415; *Tr.* 1.3.7; Eob. *Her. Chr.* 1.135.
101	**placuisse putabam** = Ov. *Pont.* 2.4.15.
102	**Plus nimio — tibi** Cf. Ov. *Fast.* 6.115.
105	**Quae tua — est** = Ov. *Ep.* 17.29.
106	**Quis timor** = Luc. 6.666; Stat. *Theb.* 2.548.
107	**tuta petemus** ≈ Ov. *Met.* 10.714; cf. Verg. *A.* 11.871.
108	**Hunc — potest** Cf. Ov. *Pont.* 4.9.126; Locher, *Stult.* 28, fol. 39ᵛ: "[Deus] omnia noscit / Cordaque scrutatur, hunc latet atque nihil."
109	**Ergo age** = *Buc.* 1.103, n.
111	**sine labe** = *Her. Chr.* 2.45, n.
113	**Non ego te** = *Her. Chr.* 5.23, n.
	turpi . . . amore = Hor. *S.* 1.4.111 (for a prostitute); cf. Prop. 2.16.36; 3.21.33; Ov. *Am.* 3.11.2; et al.; Eob. *Sylv. duae* 2.90, n.
	fruiturus amore *Her. Chr.* 3.120, n.
114	**teque tuumque** = Catul. 66.40.
115	**libidinis aestu** August. *C. D.* 14.16; et al.
116	**putri . . . luto** = *Ama.* 35.92; *Her. Chr.* 15.38.
	sordida facta luto = *Luth.* 1.42.
117	**Coelestem . . . aulam** Juvenc. 3.496; Prud. *Perist.* 14.62; Eob. *Her. Chr.* 17.223, n.
118	**Quo ruis** = *Sylv. duae* 2.181, n.
	Infernam . . . domum ≈ *Sylv. duae* 2.112, n.
119	**referque pedem** = Ov. *Ars* 1.716.
	mortem . . . propinquam Lucr. 6.1218; Eob. *Her. Chr.* 14.99.
121	**pudor — notavit** = Dantiscus, *Carm.* 12.2.262 (in an epithalamium published in February 1512); cf. Ov. *Am.* 3.6.78; *Met.* 4.329; 9.515.
123–24	**Non secus — sonat** Cf. Ov. *Pont.* 3.4.31–32. For the commonplace of spiritual warfare, see Eob. *Her. Chr.* 6.71, n.
123	**Non secus ac** = *Laud.* 106, n.
	ruit in certamina = Sil. 5.383.
	certamina miles = Sil. 5.671.
124	**rauca . . . voce** Mart. 8.3.15; cf. Prop. 3.3.41; Verg. *G.* 4.71; *A.* 8.2.
	classica . . . sonat Cf. Verg. *A.* 7.637: "classica iamque sonant."
	classica voce = *Luth.* 6.97: "Meque fer haec alacri ceu classica voce canentem."
	voce sonat = Ov. *Ep.* 11.74.
126	**Heu nimium sero** = Ov. *Tr.* 3.1.8.
127	**vitae . . . prioris** Lucr. 5.169, 1105; Ov. *Pont.* 2.7.49; Eob. *Her. Chr.* 14.87–88; 15.33, 160.
	vitae . . . consuetudo Ter. *Hau.* 283.
129	**lingua . . . diserta** *Buc.* B 8.4, n.

130   **Credibile — tuis** Cf. Ov. *Am.* 3.1.2.

131   **per . . . devia noctis eunti** Cf. *Sylv. duae* 2.115. For *devia noctis*, see l. 67 above.

133   **nova lux** = V. Fl. 3.188; 5.466; cf. Verg. *A.* 9.110, 731; Ov. *Met.* 13.592; Eob. *Her. Chr.* 13.62; 19.67.

135   **Ite — amores** Cf. *Her.* 3.1.137: "Ite leves alio, miserorum crimen, amores."
        Ite, leves = Ov. *Pont.* 4.5.1.

137   **iuvenile . . . aevum** = Mant. *Calam.* 1.23 (p.19): "iuvenile peregimus aevum."

138   **meta — rota** = Ov. *Ars* 1.40 (in some mss.); Eob. *Eras.* 146, referring to death: "Omnibus haec certa est meta terenda rota"; cf. Prop. 3.3.18; Ov. *Ars* 2.426.

139   **Ipse aderas** ≈ *Her. Chr.* 1.145, n.
        igni . . . benigno Aus. *Ecl.* 23.2.
        ignique — alimenta *Her. Chr.* B 1.47.

140   **vindex . . . flamma** Prud. *Perist.* 10.824.

141   **igne novo . . . succensa** *Sylv.* 5.37.4: ". . . succensa novo pruriat igne Venus."
        igne novo = Ov. *Met.* 4.195.
        mentem succensa = Avit. *Carm.* 6.573: "Femina praeclaro mentem succensa pudore"; Mant. *1. Parthen.* 2.583: "caelesti mentem succensa calore."

142   **domina extarem** Hor. *S.* 1.5.55.

143   **gaudia falsa** = *Her. Chr.* 15.189; cf. Ov. *Ep.* 13.108; [Tib.] 3.6.33; Eob. *Ama.* 9.6.

144   **Tristitiae — meae** Cf. *Her. Chr.* 8.46, n.

145   **In medio . . . foro** = *Nor.* 831; cf. *Her. Chr.* 18.22, n.

146   **testis es ipse** = *Sarmat.* 128; cf. *Max.* 60.

148   **Causa . . . comesque** Ov. *Met.* 4.152.
        nequitiae . . . meae = Ov. *Am.* 2.1.2; cf. *Ars* 2.392.

149   **oculis haurite** Verg. *A.* 4.661; 12.945–46.

152   **et coluisse nocet** Cf. Ov. *Ep.* 21.34; *Met.* 15.131.

154   **vacua . . . manu** Luc. 2.113; Mart. 6.72.5.
        parva favilla = Ov. *Tr.* 5.12.62.

156   **spes bona** = Ov. *Ep.* 17.234.

157   **Munde . . . infide** Prud. *c. Symm.* 2.1002.
        Munde, vale Cf. *Rec.* 144, n.; *Her. Chr.* 23.120.

161   **Atque — aliquis** Cf. Verg. *Ecl.* 10.35; Ov. *Met.* 8.128. For *atque utinam*, see Eob. *Buc.* 1.36, n.

162   **offensum . . . Deum** = l. 16, n., above.
        sit — Deum ≈ *Her. Chr.* 20.144.

163   **Forte — multis** Cf. Ov. *Ars* 1.344; 3.422.
        cui faverit ille Cf. Ov. *Ars* 1.146.

164   **Et dicat — fuit** Cf. Ov. *Ep.* 3.80; *Ars* 2.628.

165   **cura salutis** = Nemes. *Ecl.* 2.40; *Dicta Catonis* 2.30.1; cf. Eob. *Her. Chr.* 17.6.

166   **Quam — opem** Cf. *Her. Chr.* 10.18; 10.194, n.
        casibus affer opem = Aen. Silv. *Carm.* 119.18, addressing the Virgin Mary: "nunc etiam nostris casibus affer opem"; cf. Sen. *Phaed.* 123.

167   **Longa — postquam** = *Her. Chr.* 5.5, n.
        caecis . . . latebris = Ov. *Met.* 1.388; cf. Lucr. 1.408; Verg. *A.* 3.232, 424.

168   **vultus . . . videre tuos** = Ov. *Pont.* 2.4.8; Eob. *Her. Chr.* 18.176; 24.4.
        Phoebe, videre = Prop. 2.32.28.

169   **Frugiferos — ignes** Cf. *Rec.* 216, n.
        aestas iam tertia Sen. *Her. O.* 596–97; cf. Verg. *A.* 1.755–56; 5.626.

170   **gratia parta** = *Her. Chr.* 13.72.

171   **gravis offensi . . . ira Tonantis** Cf. Ov. *Pont.* 1.4.44; V. Fl. 4.428, 474; Eob. *Her. Chr.* 11.16, n.; *Eccles.* 29, 331.

172   **Heu, quantum est** = *Her. Chr.* 4.80, n.
        paucos . . . dies = [Tib.] 3.18.2; Mart. 1.15.4.

173   **Spes — peractae** Cf. ll. 43–44 above.
        vitae . . . peractae = Locher, *Stult.* 31, fol. 42ʳ: "vitae et delicta peractae / Emendet."
174   **futura mora est** = Ov. *Ep.* 2.144.
175   **Invisum — vincet** For the thought, cf. Hor. *Carm.* 1.24.19–20; Eob. *Her. Chr.* 7.135, n.
        constans — vincet Cf. Hutten, *Querel.* 1.2.69: "Vicerit insanos constans patientia morbos."
176   **Donec — Dei** Cf. Ov. *Tr.* 1.5.84.
177   **nostro . . . crimine** *Her. Chr.* 7.8, n.
        veniam — posce Cf. Mant. *c. Poetas* 99: ". . . veniam superos pro crimine posce."
        supplex . . . posce = Verg. *A.* 1.666.
178   **iusso — preces** = l. 28 above; cf. *Her. Chr.* 5.176, n.

12

Meter: Elegiac distich.

1–2   **Littera — meis** Cf. Prop. 4.3.3–4; Ov. *Ep.* 15.1–2. For the motif of the tear-stained letter, see Eob. *Her. Chr.* 2.3, n.
2   **De lachrymis — meis** Cf. *Her. Chr.* 16.216, n.
3   **tamen aspiceres** = Ov. *Ep.* 21.227.
        primae — frontis For the motif of the signet, see *Her. Chr.* 4.5, n.; Ov. *Pont.* 2.10.1–4.
8   **Iamne — legas** Cf. Ov. *Ep.* 2.106; *Pont.* 3.5.1; Eob. *Her. Chr.* 21.3, n.
        et unde legas = *Sylv.* 2.24.4: "Scriptane iam sentis et unde legas?"; cf. *Sylv. duae* 1.159, n.
9–20   **Fama — aqua** Cf. *Her. Chr.* 16.9–12.
9   **Fama est** = Verg. *A.* 3.578; 12.735.
        Rhomano . . . Caesare *Her. Chr.* 16.9, n.
10   **Heu nimium** = *Her. Chr.* 5.4, n.
        vera . . . fide = Ov. *Ep.* 16.42; 19.68; *Pont.* 3.7.24.
        probata fide = Andrel. *Liv.* 3.6.46: "hystorica dicta probata fide."
12   **Verum . . . Deum** *Her. Chr.* 4.154, n.
        falsa relligione Mant. *3. Parthen.*, fol. 104ʳ.
13   **poenas . . . morte daturum** Gunther, *Lig.* 9.555: ". . . penas sibi morte daturum"; Mant. *Georg.*, fol. 215ʳ: ". . . poenas iam morte daturum"; cf. *Epic. Drusi* 272.
14   **sacra . . . pietate** *Her. Chr.* 21.76.
        pro pietate mori = *Her. Chr.* 11.54; 18.150.
15–20   **Vox — aqua** Cf. *Her. Chr.* 8.33–34, n.
15–16   **Vox — erat** Cf. Ov. *Ep.* 3.59–60; *Ars* 2.449–50. For the motif, cf. Eob. *Her. Chr.* 7.51, n.
16   **Frigidus . . . sanguis** Verg. *G.* 2.484; *A.* 10.452.
        Frigidus in toto = *Her. Chr.* 5.101, n.
        in toto pectore . . . erat = Ov. *Ep.* 12.142.
        pectore — erat = *Her. Chr.* 16.178, n.; cf. Ov. *Ep.* 3.146; Eob. *Her. Chr.* 7.122.
17   **Fusa thoro** Ov. *Ars* 3.782; *Pont.* 3.3.8.
18   **longa . . . mora** = Prop. 1.10.6; Ov. *Ars* 3.650; *Fast.* 3.204; et al.; l. 158 below.
        mortua pene = *Her. Chr.* 8.118, n.
19–20   **Vix etiam — aqua** The model is Ov. *Ep.* 13.25–26. For the motif, cf. also Eob. *Her. Chr.* 8.33–34, n.; 9.40.
21   **conceptum . . . dolorem** Vulg. *Psa.* 7.15; Sedul. 3.135.
        testata dolorem ≈ Ov. *Met.* 2.486.

22	**Aptabam — manus** = *Vict.*, app. 2.10, probably written in the late winter of 1512; cf. *Her. Chr.* 2.42, n.
23	**crudeli . . . tyranno** = Mant. *2. Parthen.* 3.633; cf. Eob. *Ama.* 35.47, n.
25	**vita superstes** = *Rec.* 64, n.
28	**quicquid ubique** = *Her. Chr.* 1.78, n.
29	**teneros . . . artus** = Mant. *1. Parthen.* 3.418; cf. Ov. *Ep.* 20.117; *Med.* 51.
30	**Et — potest** Cf. *Her. Chr.* 18.148, n.
31	**meruisse fatemur** = Ov. *Met.* 8.492.
33	**dura . . . iura** *Her. Chr.* 19.6.
35	**Primus . . . ante omneis** = Verg. *A.* 2.40; cf. l. 51 below.
37	**Hoc . . . nondum . . . tempore** *Her. Chr.* 11.88.
	Hoc ego . . . memini = Calp. *Ecl.* 4.105.
	tempore visum = Verg. *A.* 6.409; Ov. *Met.* 7.494.
38	**nomen habere** = *Sylv. duae* 1.156, n.
40	**titulis . . . tuis** = Ov. *Ep.* 10.130; *Fast.* 4.44; Eob. *Her. Chr.* 19.88.
41	**Christicola — molestum** = *Nup.* 240.
42	**posse perire** = Mart. 5.64.6.
43–44	**Nec — Deo** Cf. *Her. Chr.* 9.63–64.
43	**Nec frustra** = Verg. *G.* 1.257; Prop. 3.12.37; Ov. *Rem.* 779; *Met.* 7.218.
43–44	**orbem Rhomanum** = Luc. 8.441–42; cf. Luc. 10.456; Eob. *Her. Chr.* 6.83, n.; *Venus* 3.23; *Tum.* 3.17.
44	**vero . . . Deo** *Her. Chr.* 4.154, n.
	numina falsa = *Her. Chr.* 4.218, n.
46	**tenebris pulsis** Ov. *Met.* 7.703; cf. Eob. *Buc.* 8.2: "pulsa . . . nocte."
47	**Quam cito** = *Buc.* 7.170, n.; *Her. Chr.* 13.125.
	per superos = *Buc.* 7.30, n.
	totam — urbem = Verg. *A.* 8.716; Eob. *Her. Chr.* 21.93.
48	**cultu . . . novo** Ov. *Fast.* 6.691.
49	**Iuppiter Ammon** = Luc. 9.518.
50	**bibulo pulvere** Mant. *Calam.* 1.380 (p. 29); Eob. *Psalt.* 107.74; cf. *Her. Chr.* 17.269, n.
	pulvere sparsa = *Ebn.* 34 (*Sylv.* 2.1.38): "pulvere sparsa caput"; cf. Ov. *Am.* 3.2.41; Eob. *Buc.* B 3.2.
51–58	**Ante — deum** This story was invented by Eobanus.
51	**Ante omneis** = Verg. *A.* 5.406; Stat. *Theb.* 2.300; cf. l. 35, n., above.
	parens . . . tardior aevo Cf. Ov. *Met.* 6.321–22; Eob. *Her. Chr.* 12.277; 14.39.
52	**Excidit — manu** Cf. *Pug.* 20, n. As in l. 53 below, the transitive verb *excidit* is scanned incorrectly with a short second syllable.
53	**Fatui — saecli** = *Vict.* 180; cf. *Her. Chr.* 10.141, n.
54	**Deus — adest** Cf. *Her. Chr.* 6.168.
55	**Acheronteas . . . undas** ≈ Locher, *Stult.* 20, fol. 31ᵛ: "Hic Acherontaeis animam demerget in undis"; cf. Claud. *Rapt. Pros.* 2.351; Eob. *Her. Chr.* 16.189.
	Christus — ite Cf. Prud. *Apoth.* 411, addressing a demon: "pulsus abi . . . ; Christus iubet, exi."
	ite sub undas = Ov. *Fast.* 2.403.
57	**altis — columnis** = *Her. Chr.* 4.47, n.
58	**milia — deum** Cf. Prud. *Amart.* 95–96: "multa deorum / milia."
	milia multa = *Her. Chr.* 6.76, n.
59	**Tempore ab hoc** = Ov. *Met.* 13.236; Eob. *Her. Chr.* 14.89; 16.77, 80; *Vict.* 351.
	sacro . . . de fonte renati Cf. Juvenc. 2.193: "Liquido . . . de fonte renatus"; Hrabanus, *Carm.* 97.3: ". . . sacro fonte renatus"; Eob. *Her. Chr.* 6.121; 10.191; 17.87. The image is based on Vulg. *Tit.* 3.5.
60	**credula — sumus** = Ov. *Rem.* 686; *Fast.* 4.312; cf. Eob. *Buc.* 11.95, n.
61–62	**sine omni — iacet** Cf. *Her. Chr.* 23.76, n.

62   **prisco . . . honore** Verg. *A.* 8.339; Sil. 15.416; Eob. *Laud.* 210, n.
            squalida . . . iacet ≈ *Her. Chr.* 20.84.
63–66   **Scilicet — novis** For the motif, cf. *Her. Chr.* 5.57–62, n.; ll. 71–72, 80–82
            below.
63   **Scilicet ipse** = Luc. 7.449; Calp. *Ecl.* 1.84; cf. Eob. *Her. Chr.* 5.57.
            nostrae — salutis Cf. Alcuin. *Carm.* 124.1: ". . . nostrae spes sola salutis"; Eob.
            Rec. 60, n.
            spes prima = *Her. Chr.* 20.35; cf. Poliziano, *Epigr.* 5.8: "Spes hominum prima es . . .";
            8.8: "Spes sibi tu prima es. . . ."
            prima salutis = Verg. *A.* 6.96.
64   **Captivaque — manu** Cf. Ov. *Pont.* 1.2.46; *Epic. Drusi* 274.
65   **praesente Deo** *Her. Chr.* 7.98, n.
            festa otia agemus *Buc.* B 6.3.
66   **Templa — novis** ≈ Brant, *Var. carm.*, sig. bc4ᵛ (*Texte* 65.6): "Templa coronantur
            frondibus ampla novis"; cf. Ov. *Met.* 8.264.
            Templa . . . alta Verg. *A.* 6.41.
67   **lucemque perosi** = Verg. *A.* 6.435.
68   **Est quare . . . iuvet** = *Her.* 1.4.64: "est quare commeminisse iuvet."
            doluisse iuvet Cf. *Her. Chr.* 1.131; 3.157–58.
70   **laetos . . . dies** = l. 238 below; cf. Hor. *Carm.* 4.2.41.
            laeta videbo = *Her. Chr.* 8.40.
71–72   **Nec — dolor** For the motif, cf. *Her. Chr.* 5.57–62, n.; ll. 63–66 above.
71   **regales . . . cultus** Hor. *Carm.* 4.9.15.
            sumere cultus = Claud. *Carm. minora* 30.222.
72   **patitur . . . dolor** = Hutten, *Querel.* 1.2.50: "Non patitur durus commeminisse
            dolor"; cf. Ov. *Ep.* 10.33.
            miserae causa = Ov. *Pont.* 4.13.42.
            causa dolenda = Ov. *Tr.* 5.4.14.
73   **Causa . . . quia** = Ov. *Fast.* 2.329.
74   **Seu cadat** = *Her. Chr.* 16.240.
            Oceana . . . aqua = *Her. Chr.* 2.56, n.
            resurgat aqua ≈ Ov. *Pont.* 4.8.28.
75–82   **Crescit — toga est** Pining away and turning wan are conventional symptoms of
            lovesickness. Cf., for example, Ov. *Ep.* 3.141: "abiit corpusque colorque"; 11.27–28. For
            pallor as a symptom of lovesickness, see Eob. *Laud.* 237, n.
75   **miseros — artus** Verg. *A.* 2.215; cf. *G.* 3.458.
            miseros . . . artus = *Buc.* 6.81, n.
76   **in hoc — nihil** Cf. *Eccles.* 18.
77   **rubor . . . fulsit in ore** Dantiscus, *Carm.* 1.3.350: ". . . fulsit in ore rubor"; cf. Eob.
            Nup. 199, n.
78   **pallida buxus** Cf. Ov. *Met.* 4.134–35; 11.417–18; Mart. 12.32.8.
79   **Demissi . . . oculi** Cf. Ov. *Met.* 15.612; Eob. *Her. Chr.* 4.129, n.
            cecidere lacerti = Ov. *Am.* 2.5.47.
80   **Nulla — tumet** = *Sylv.* 1.3.16; cf. *Nup.* 190. For the motif in this context,
            cf. Ov. *Ep.* 15.74.
            sub angusto pectore Mant. *Calam.* 1.1216 (p. 50): ". . . levat angusto sub pectore
            ventrem."
81–82   **Pendula — toga est** For the motif, cf. Ov. *Ep.* 15.75; ll. 63–66, n., above.
81   **Pendula . . . velamina** = Mant. *1. Parthen.* 1.406.
            velamina vultus = Stat. *Theb.* 12.368.
82   **In toto . . . corpore** = Ov. *Am.* 1.5.18; cf. Eob. *Her. Chr.* 5.101, n.
            pulla toga *Hypocr.* 42. Cf. Ov. *Ars* 3.189–90: "pulla decent niveas [cf. ll. 77–78
            above]: Briseida pulla decebant; / cum rapta est, pulla tum quoque veste fuit."
83   **preda — draconi** Cf. Ov. *Met.* 7.31; also cf. l. 149 below.

84	**Sum — facta** Cf. Ov. *Ep.* 12.82.
	per meritum Ov. *Ep.* 10.141.
85	**rediturus abisti** Cf. Ov. *Ep.* 5.59; 17.158.
86	**Nec tua — fides** = *Her. Chr.* 7.54, n.
87	**Quam — annos** Cf. Ov. *Ep.* 3.149 (of Briseis).
	Quam bene = *Buc.* B 2.25, n.
	servatae servasses Cf. ll. 279–80 below.
	virginis annos = V. Fl. 8.409; cf. Ov. *Ep.* 21.11; *Tr.* 3.7.17.
88	**Qur ego non** = Ov. *Am.* 2.11.54.
	tanto coniuge Verg. *A.* 3.317.
	coniuge digna fui = *Her. Chr.* 17.38; cf. Ov. *Tr.* 2.162.
89	**genus . . . clarum** Hor. *S.* 1.5.54; Sen. *Med.* 210; Sil. 3.106; 6.627.
90	**magni filia regis** Ov. *Met.* 2.844.
	filia regis eram ≈ Ov. *Fast.* 3.468.
91–94	**Turpiter — velim** Cf. *Her. Chr.* 7.65–71.
91	**thalamo . . . eodem** = Ov. *Ars* 1.697; cf. Eob. *Her. Chr.* 20.75, n.
92	**Nec tibi — fui** Cf. Ov. *Am.* 2.15.21; Claud. *Carm. minora* 40.24.
	nupta futura = Prop. 2.3.54; Ov. *Ep.* 16.370.
94	**cedere laude** Ov. *Met.* 6.6.
96	**Quorum militia** ≈ Ov. *Fast.* 3.244. For the commonplace of spiritual warfare, see Eob. *Her. Chr.* 6.71, n.
	posse mori = Ov. *Ars* 2.28; *Tr.* 1.1.34; Eob. *Her. Chr.* 16.142.
97	**iuvat — pudori** Cf. Verg. *A.* 2.776.
98	**Nos . . . (si nescis) . . . turba sumus** = Tifernate, "Ad Pium Pontificem Maximum," *Carm.*, sig. B2ʳ: "Nos tua, si nescis, nos tua turba sumus." For *si nescis*, see also Ov. *Ep.* 16.246; 17.198; et al.; Eob. *Her. Chr.* 14.18, n.; 20.70. For *turba sumus*, see Eob. *Buc.* 11.95, n.
99	**bene coniungi** = Mant. *1. Parthen.* 2.373: "non bene coniungi."
	cum virgine virgo *Her. Chr.* 4.89; 8.131; cf. Ov. *Met.* 2.579; 9.725.
100	**militiae . . . signa tuae** = Locher, *Katherina* 93; cf. Hor. *Carm.* 4.1.16; Ov. *Am.* 1.11.12; 2.12.28; Eob. *Her. Chr.* 17.10.
101	**dura . . . cathena** Prop. 3.15.20; Ov. *Am.* 1.6.1, 47; *Ep.* 10.89.
103	**celebrem . . . triumphum** *Buc.* 4.52, n.
106	**iacet . . . manus** = Ov. *Ep.* 9.136.
	fulminat ense manus = Ov. *Am.* 2.2.64; cf. Eob. *Her. Chr.* 22.92.
107	**rapuisse — trophaea** Cf. Verg. *G.* 3.32.
108	**crucis . . . signa** l. 216 below.
	obliquo lumine Ov. *Met.* 2.787; cf. Eob. *Buc.* 10.67, n.
109	**totum . . . per orbem** = Hor. *Ep.* 2.1.254; Luc. 4.574.
110	**Deo . . . vindice** = *Luth.* 4.12; cf. *Eccles.* 4; *Psalt.* 54, arg. 2; 24, arg. 3.
	dextra potens *Her. Chr.* 1.87, n.
111	**Cappadoces** A native of Cappadocia, St. George became a tribune there: cf. l. 36 above.
112	**Dura . . . arma** Ov. *Ep.* 13.40; Eob. *Nob.* 165; *Max.* 257.
	invicta . . . manu = Ov. *Am.* 3.3.28.
	arma manu = *Pug.* 42, n.
113–16	**Iura — eras** Mant. *Georgius*, fol. 210ʳ–210ᵛ, reports that after his victory over the dragon St. George continued his heroic exploits in Egypt, Syria, Palestine, and Persia. *Leg. aurea* 56.84 says only that he conquered Palestine with Christ's help: cf. l. 253 below.
113	**Iura . . . Rhomana** Luc. 10.11–12; Mant. *1. Parthen.* 3.2.
114	**turilegus . . . Arabs** Ov. *Fast.* 4.569.
116	**Dux — eras** Cf. Ov. *Met.* 9.442.

fulmen eras = *Luth.* 6.80. For the image, cf. Lucr. 3.1034, of P. Cornelius Scipio, the Elder Africanus: "Scipiadas, belli fulmen"; Verg. *A.* 6.842, of the two Scipios: "duo fulmina belli"; Brant, *Var. carm.*, sig. h1ᵛ (*Texte* 175.113–14): "Maxmilianus, / Qui fulmen belli est"; Eob. *Hod.* 222 (William II of Hesse); *Luth.* 6.25 (Ulrich von Hutten and Franz von Sickingen): "Vos duo . . . Rhomanae fulmina pesti." Cf. *Her. Chr.* 24.122, n.

118   **regna . . . vasta** Luc. 10.475.
         Lycurgus The name (after the ancient Greek statesman) is Eobanus' invention.

119–20 **Hic, ubi — habet** This eponymic explanation comes from Mant. *Georgius*, fol. 204ʳ: "Hanc veteres urbem fama est posuisse Silenos / Huc duce Nysaeis Baccho de finibus actos / Hisque locis nomen, muros, gentemque dedisse." For the wording, cf. Eob. *Her. Chr.* 5.79–80, n.

120   **De quibus — habet** For the idiom, cf. *Her. Chr.* 22.34, n.
         aeternum . . . nomen = Ov. *Am.* 2.10.32; cf. Eob. *Buc.* B 2.19, n.
         nunc quoque — habet = *Sylv. duae* 1.24, n.

121   **clarissima virtus** = *Wirt.* 127.

122   **Putris — humus** Cf. *Her. Chr.* 4.216, n.; *Psalt.* 79.16: "Putris adhuc multa caede madescit humus." For *putris humus*, see l. 180 below; cf. Verg. *A.* 8.596; 11.875.
         fuso sanguine Verg. *A.* 12.690–91; *Culex* 323; Ov. *Tr.* 2.75; Eob. *Her. Chr.* 16.212; cf. *Buc.* 9.32, n.

123–24 **Tempus — erat** Cf. Ov. *Met.* 11.353–54; Celtis, *Am.* 3.1.1–2: "Tempus erat, mediam dum Phoebus fecerat umbram / Et parili steterant noxque diesque mora"; Eob. *Her. Chr.* 11.79–80. *Leg. aurea* 56 does not mention the time of day at which the battle takes place; Mant. *Georgius*, fol. 205ᵛ, places it at dawn.

123   **Tempus — orbe** ≈ *Idyl.* 10.1: "Tempus erat, medio iam sol altissimus aestu / Ussit agros." For the elision of *quo*, see *Rec.* 1, n.

125   **Sorte mala** *Her. Chr.* 1.172.
         sic me cogente Cf. Ov. *Ep.* 17.155.

126   **mare** Cf. l. 5, where the body of water is called a swamp ("paludem").
         letiferae . . . ferae Notice the internal rhyme.
         preda — ferae ≈ Ov. *Ep.* 4.116.

127   **certa mori** Verg. *A.* 4.564; Ov. *Met.* 10.428.
         vigilantia lumina = Ov. *Ep.* 19.35 (different); Claud. *VI. Cons. Hon.* 234; cf. Eob. *Her. Chr.* 4.151, n.

129   **Ecce — armis** Suggested by Mant. *Georgius*, fol. 207ᵛ: "eximit ensem / Sole repercusso iaculantem in moenia flammas."
         Ecce, per adversum = Sil. 4.622.
         per adversum solem Cf. Verg. *A.* 4.701; 5.89; Ov. *Met.* 3.183.
         fulgentibus armis = Verg. *A.* 2.749; 6.217, 861; et al.

130   **vectus equo** = Sil. 12.67.

131   **Obstupui** = *Buc.* 4.104, n.

131–32 **sed — erat** Cf. *Theoc.*, ded. 66: "Ne tamen hoc facerem qui prohiberet erat"; *Her. Chr.* 10.118, n.

133–52 **Iam — salus** This conversation is found in *Leg. aurea* 56.43–56, but not in Mant. *Georgius.* Cf. Ov. *Met.* 4.678–88, with a similar conversation between Perseus and Andromeda.

133   **Iam prope constiteras** ≈ *Nup.* 195, n.
         fera vincla Ov. *Pont.* 1.2.46. In the *Legenda aurea* there is no mention of the girl's being chained. That detail comes from Ov. *Met.* 4.672–81 (Andromeda), by way of Mant. *Georgius*, fol. 206ᵛ — a passage explicitly comparing Alcyone to Andromeda: "mox colla catenis / Innodant famuli tristes solamque relinquunt. / . . . / Stabat ut Andromede monstris exposta marinis."

134   **Intrepidam — iubes** Cf. *Her. Chr.* 3.80.
         verbis talibus = *Her. Chr.* 15.114; cf. *Her. Chr.* 13.38, n.

135–38   **O non — potes** Cf. Ov. *Met.* 4.678–81 (where Perseus addresses Andromeda).
135   **vulgares . . . puellas** ≈ Ov. *Fast.* 4.865.
         sata virgo = Stat. *Theb.* 11.136; cf. Verg. *A.* 7.331.
136   **Ne trepida** = Stat. *Theb.* 4.642; Juv. 9.130.
137   **in vincla coegit** = Petrarch, *Africa* 7.211.
138   **Crimine — potes** Cf. Ov. *Ep.* 2.28.
139   **Heu, fuge** = *Buc.* 4.13, n.; l. 167 below
140   **Me miseram," dixi** = Ov. *Ep.* 15.204.
141   **potes auxilium . . . ferre** Ov. *Ep.* 5.154.
         moriturae . . . puellae Verg. *G.* 4.458.
142   **aliqua . . . manu** = *Max.* 190; *Sylv.* 3.6.34.
143   **cum gemitu** = Verg. *A.* 11.831; 12.952.
144   **Tristia . . . fata** = Ov. *Tr.* 4.10.112; cf. Eob. *Laud.* B 3.20, n.
         dicere fata = Prop. 4.1.71.
145   **crudelia fata** = Petrarch, *Africa* 3.766; Andrel. *Livia* 2.8.73.
147   **nomine poenae** Cf. Verg. *A.* 6.627; Eob. *Her. Chr.* 3.43.
149   **fero . . . praeda draconi** Cf. Ov. *Met.* 7.31; l. 83 above.
         parva . . . virgine *Her. Chr.* 2.126, n.
150   **fortes . . . viros** = *Sylv. duae* 2.126, n.
151   **patriaeque tibique** = Luc. 7.30.
153–54   **Et simul — tibi** Cf. Verg. *A.* 2.391–93.
153   **clipeo galeaque** ≈ Ov. *Ep.* 13.147.
         galeaque comanti ≈ Sil. 16.167.
154   **ingens . . . hasta** Verg. *A.* 2.50; 10.553, 579; 12.398.
155   **Tum vero** = *Buc.* 4.102, n.
         exultans — alto Cf. Mant. *Ecl.* 4.58: ". . . exsultantem risu iuveniliter alto."
         exultans animo *Nup.* 112, n.
156   **longius isse** = Ov. *Ars* 2.404.
157–58   **Sicut — mora** For the image, cf. Verg. *A.* 10.454–56.
157   **magnanimum . . . leonem** = *Buc.* 1.51; cf. *Laud.* 286, n.
         deserta — leonem Cf. Sedul. 1.356: ". . . ut alta fremit vox per deserta leonis";
         Mant. *Dionys.* 2, fol. 187ᵛ: ". . . iratum loca per deserta leonem."
158   **longa . . . mora** = l. 18, n., above.
         praeda cupita = Brant, *Var. carm.* sig. h2ᵛ (*Texte* 192.38); also sig. l1ʳ (*Texte* 24.35),
         but misprinted as "praeda capita."
160   **forsitan ille** = Ov. *Ep.* 2.14; cf. *Fast.* 2.498.
161   **Quo — plangam** Maxim. 5.89.
162   **facilem — deum** Cf. *Luth.* 5.22: ". . . facilem vos habuisse Deum"; *Epic.* 2.140: ". . .
         faciles non habiture deos"; 4.134: ". . . faciles non habuisse deos." For *facilem deum*, cf.
         Ov. *Ep.* 12.84; *Met.* 5.559; *Pont.* 4.4.30; Eob. *Sylv.* 1.5.32: ". . . deos faciles non habet
         iste locus."
         non habiture Cf. *Her. Chr.* 24.58, n.
163   **Quis . . . deus** *Her. Chr.* 4.90, n.
         te participem . . . esse laboris Sil. 15.350–51.
164   **misera . . . sorte mori** Cf. Gunther, *Lig.* 10.375: "misera perituram sorte."
165   **Quae geris, arma** = Ov. *Ep.* 14.98.
         arma . . . Martia *Her. Chr.* 1.190, n.
         arma manu = Stat. *Theb.* 3.643; 12.618; *Ach.* 2.106.
166   **in dextra — hasta** = Ov. *Fast.* 3.172. The term *throwing spear* does not match the
         earlier and later references to the knightly lance.
167   **Heu, fuge** = *Buc.* 4.13, n.; l. 139 above.
         fuge, tolle moras Mant. *Ecl.* 7.123: "tolle moras igitur, . . . fuge."
         in tua — moraris Cf. *Her. Chr.* 5.25, n.

168	**O decus — tui** Cf. Ov. *Ep.* 15.94; 16.273; Marul. *Epigr.* 2.32.89: "O decus, o nostri rarissima gloria saecli"; Eob. *Buc.* 11.105, n.; *Her. Chr.* 20.68, n.
	gloria summa = *Epic. Drusi* 366; Mart. 8.30.2.
169	**Finieram** = *Laud.* 255, n.
169–71	**Procul — tenebat** Cf. Verg. *A.* 2.203–09.
169	**Procul ecce** = Luc. 6.214; *Aetna* 506; cf. Eob. *Vict.* 100, n.
169–70	**confusa . . . Aequora** Cf. Ov. *Ep.* 18.129.
169	**confusa procellis** = *Her. Chr.* 8.121.
169–70	**procellis Aequora** = Luc. 5.612–13.
171	**Ecce venit** = *Her. Chr.* 11.87, n.
172	**gelido . . . timore** Ov. *Tr.* 1.4.11.
	potui . . . mori = Ov. *Ep.* 2.60.
173	**Protinus ad praedam** = Gunther, *Lig.* 4.307; 10.467.
	ad praedam — alis Cf. Mant. *Georgius,* fol. 207ʳ: ". . . passisque ad praedam annititur alis" (at which point St. George rushes to Alcyone's aid).
174	**corpora nostra** = Ov. *Am.* 2.10.24; *Rem.* 800, 802.
176–80	**Signa — humum** Cf. Mant. *Georg.,* fol. 207ʳ: "Infremit ac miserans cruce pectora signat equumque / Concitat et pressa monstro volat obvius hasta. / [2 lines] / . . . intima mucro / Guttura perfodiens latam penetravit in alvum."
176	**certa . . . manu** = Ov. *Am.* 3.10.26; Mart. 6.32.4.
	qualiacunque manu = Ov. *Tr.* 1.11.18; Eob. *Sylv.* 1.1.164.
177	**ferocis equi** = Ov. *Ep.* 4.79; Stat. *Silv.* 5.2.116.
	celeri pede = Ov. *Met.* 10.653.
178	**Tentasti . . . praelia** Verg. *A.* 2.334; 3.240; 11.912.
	auspicio . . . bono = *Max.* 218; cf. *Buc.* B 11.21, n.
	praelia prima Verg. *G.* 4.314; *A.* 5.375; 12.103; Ov. *Fast.* 1.569.
179	**Hesit — draconis** Modeled on Ov. *Met.* 15.162.
	gravis hasta = Ov. *Met.* 12.82.
180	**putrem . . . humum** l. 122, n., above.
	fosso gutture Cf. Ov. *Met.* 7.314–15.
	planxit humum = Ov. *Ep.* 10.106.
181–84	**Orbibus — erat** Cf. *Vict.* 376–78, describing a Libyan dragon caught in a trap.
181	**Orbibus immensis** Verg. *G.* 2.153; *A.* 2.204; cf. Ov. *Met.* 3.41–42, 77; Eob. *Her. Chr.* 22.88; *Vict.* 377.
182	**Implicitum spiris** Cf. Verg. *A.* 2.214–17.
183–84	**Spirabat — erat** The monster breathes fire and smoke. For the motif, cf. Lucr. 2.705; Verg. *A.* 8.198–99, 252–59; Ov. *Met.* 3.76; 8.356; Eob. *Vict.* 377–78.
183	**tristi . . . caligine** *Tum.* 6.7.
	mixtas caligine Ov. *Met.* 11.595; Stat. *Theb.* 5.197.
184	**mephitis erat** ≈ *Her. Chr.* 15.36.
185–86	**Ipsa — mihi** Mant. *Georgius,* fol. 206ᵛ–207ʳ, shows Alcyone praying to the gods of heaven, the sea, and the underworld.
187–90	**Interea — via** The dragon's death is recounted according to a variant of the legend that is mentioned just briefly in *Leg. aurea* 56.75: "Georgius se cruce munivit et draconem aggrediens interfecit." This is also the version followed in Mant. *Georgius,* fol. 207ʳ–207ᵛ. When he started writing this letter, however, Eobanus was still thinking in terms of the more popular version, told in *Leg. aurea* 56.57–61: St. George wounds the dragon with his lance and knocks it to the ground; he thereupon has the girl bind the monster with her girdle and lead it into the city. See l. 4 above: "vincto . . . dracone."
187–88	**Interea — agens** St. George finishes the monster off with his sword, as in *Leg. aurea* 56.67, 75, and Mant. *Georgius,* fol. 207ᵛ. Cf. Ov. *Met.* 4.734 (Perseus frees Andromeda).
187	**eductum . . . ensem** Sil. 13.442.

187–88   **squamis — Abdideras** Cf. Ov. *Met.* 4.719–20, of Perseus; Verg. *A.* 2.553.

188   **crebro vulnere** Sil. 9.575–76.

189   **morientes . . . artus** = Ov. *Met.* 12.423.

    palpitat artus = Luc. 6.754; Eob. *Vict.* 371.

190   **Et fugiunt — via** Here Eobanus varies a familiar epic formula. Cf. Verg. *A.* 2.532 (Ov. *Met.* 2.610): "vitam cum sanguine fudit"; 10.487; Ov. *Met.* 6.253; 11.327.

191   **Acclamant — altis** Cf. Ov. *Met.* 4.735–36, after Perseus' victory over the monster; Mant. *Georgius,* fol. 207ᵛ, after St. George kills the dragon: "Continuo exurgunt plausus a moenibus altis."

    miseri cives Verg. *Ecl.* 1.71–72; Luc. 6.102; Eob. *Nor.* 734.

    maenibus altis = Lucr. 5.232; Verg. *A.* 1.95; 3.322; 9.805; 10.469.

192   **populi . . . corona** Cf. Ov. *Met.* 13.1: "vulgi . . . corona."

    multa corona = Ov. *Rem.* 32 and *Fast.* 6.792 (in a different sense).

193   **Et iam — arcem** Cf. Verg. *A.* 4.665–66; cf. Eob. *Rec.* 147–48; 159, n.

    fama recens = Mart. 9.43.5.

    summam . . . arcem = Ov. *Met.* 2.306 (different).

194   **Laeticia . . . nova** ≈ Mart. 8.11.4; cf. Eob. *Pug.* 18, n.

    regia tota = Ov. *Ep.* 4.164; Eob. *Her. Chr.* 4.76.

195   **Curritur ad** = Juv. 7.82.

    speculis . . . altis = Mant. *Mort.* fol. 122ᵛ.

196   **Iamque omnis** = Verg. *A.* 9.25; Eob. *Nup.* 171.

197   **uterque parens** = Ov. *Met.* 4.387; *Fast.* 5.181; cf. Eob. *Laud.* 152; *Her. Chr.* 17.110, n.; 23.112; 24.70.

198   **io Paean** = Ov. *Ars* 2.1.

    filia — ait = Ov. *Ep.* 15.120.

199   **Fulgentem . . . conspexit in armis** Cf. Verg. *A.* 6.826.

    nitidis . . . conspexit in armis ≈ Avianus, *Fabulae* 10.3: "nitidis . . . conspectus in armis." Cf. Ov. *Tr.* 4.6.33.

200   **Et te — deum** Cf. *Her. Chr.* 9.74, n.; 19.20, n.; *Her.* 1.4.190: ". . . se praesentem dixit adesse Deum"; Ov. *Ep.* 16.334. In Mant. *Georgius,* fol. 208ʳ, some people look upon St. George as a god or demigod: "Sunt quoque qui credant equitis sub imagine tectum / Esse vel Alciden vel Castora belligeramve / Pallada vel Martem."

    te presentem . . . deum = Ov. *Tr.* 2.54; cf. Eob. *Sylv. duae* 2.198, n.

201–02   **Caetera — mei** Cf. *Her. Chr.* 1.203–04, n.

202   **Propositi non est . . . mei** = *Her.* 3.4.10; cf. *Sylv. duae* 2.218, n.

203   **brevis . . . epistola** *Her. Chr.* 1.207.

204   **Plus quoque quam** = Ov. *Ep.* 19.18.

205–12   **Est mihi — loqui** For the motif, cf. Ov. *Ep.* 13.151–58 (Laodamia has a lifelike wax bust of Protesilaus that she embraces and talks to).

205   **Est mihi qui** = Ov. *Ep.* 3.146.

    paries Cf. *Buc.* 11.31–32, n.: "pictus . . . paries."

206   **Tempore quo** = *Her. Chr.* 11.82, n.

    causa salutis eras ≈ Ov. *Tr.* 3.9.24.

207   **A, quoties** *Her. Chr.* 1.43, n.

    lachrymis . . . obortis = *Laud.* 289, n.

208   **oscula longa dedi** Tib. 1.8.25–26; cf. Ov. *Ep.* 3.14; *Tr.* 1.3.58; *Pont.* 2.3.72.

209   **Contemplata diu** = Mant. *1. Parthen.* 3.528.

    visa est mihi . . . moveri = Ov. *Ep.* 16.59; cf. Eob. *Her. Chr.* 18.9, n.

211   **qur — tristior** Cf. Vulg. *Gen.* 40.7: "cur tristior est hodie solito facies vestra?"; Eob. *Ama.* B 2.3, n.

213   **Hoc erat . . . illud** *Sylv. duae* 2.48, n.

    Hoc erat, hoc = *Buc.* 6.31, n.

213–14   **te . . . poena . . . manet** *Her. Chr.* 6.133, n.

215   **fidem — potentem** = Andrel. *Ecl.* 11.16: "sprevisse fidem Christumque potentem."

216   **Per sacrae . . . signa . . . crucis** Cf. *Her. Chr.* 5.121; 12.108.
       signa tremenda = Claud. *Cons. Stil.* 3, praef. 10.
217   **animum fortem** Pl. *Am.* 646; Hor. *S.* 2.5.20.
218   **odii saemina quaere** = Ov. *Rem.* 308; cf. *Ars* 3.512.
219   **firmo . . . pectore consta** *Psalt.* 91, arg. 4: "Si constet firmo pectore, salvus erit"; cf.
       Pl. *As.* 944; Verg. *A.* 6.261.
220   **Et tibi — mihi** Cf. Ov. *Ep.* 4.162; 19.205.
       vis vivere, vive = Hutten, *Vir bonus* 32: "Disce frui, et si vis vivere, vive diu."
221   **cedendo** = Ov. *Ars* 2.197: "cede repugnanti: cedendo victor abibis."
222   **caelo proximus** ≈ *Her. Chr.* 16.292, n.
223   **Quam petis hinc** ≈ Ov. *Met.* 15.637.
       serva — tempora Hutten, *Querel.* 2.6.13: "Dii tibi tantum animum meliora in
       tempora servent"; cf. Mant. *Ecl.* 5.184: ". . . meliora in tempora vive."
224   **sanguine debet emi** = *Her. Chr.* 1.44, n.
225   **Qui sapit** = Ov. *Ars* 1.760; [Tib.] 3.19.8.
       in rebus . . . agendis Lucr. 2.290; Eob. *Nor.* 496.
       lente festinat Erasmus, *Adag.* 2.1.1.
226   **messe . . . ager** = *Buc.*, ded. 6, n.
227   **fidem . . . beatam** = *Her. Chr.* 18.81; cf. Locher, *Stult.* 95, fol. 112ʳ: ". . . fidemque
       beatam"; Eob. *Hymn.* 155.
228   **falso . . . Iovi** *Her. Chr.* 2.49, n.
229   **Lybicas . . . urbes** = Mart. 9.56.1; cf. Verg. *A.* 4.348; Mant. *Georgius*, fol. 206ʳ:
       "Libycas . . . per urbes."
230   **regia sceptra** = Brant, *Varia carm.*, sig. a5ʳ (*Texte* 195.226); Eob. *Sylv.* 2.29.46; et al.;
       cf. *Nup.* 72; *Nob.* 264.
232   **Aphrica tota** = Prop. 3.20.4.
233   **imbelles . . . Indos** = Mant. *2. Parthen.* 2.572; cf. Verg. *G.* 2.172; Eob.
       Max. 295.
233–34 **Indos . . . Atlas** The eastern and western ends of the ancient world. Cf. *Her.*
       Chr. 13.39–40, n.
234   **laborat Atlas** Ov. *Met.* 2.296.
235–36 **Ibis — manu** Cf. *Sylv.* 1.1.147–48: "Ibis in . . . hostes, / Invicta sternes impia castra
       manu." Also cf. *Eccles.* 405–06.
235   **Aethrusci . . . Tybridis** Cf. *Her. Chr.* 19.2, n.
       Tybridis arva = Verg. *A.* 3.500; cf. Eob. *Her. Chr.* 9.6.
236   **valida . . . manu** Verg. *A.* 11.552; 12.98; Ov. *Am.* 3.2.72; *Rem.* 480.
       castra manu = Ov. *Ep.* 6.52.
238   **laetos . . . dies** = l. 70, n., above.
239   **sacra . . . Capitolia** Sil. 12.741; Eob. *Tum.* 6.17.
       summo . . . Christo Paul. Nol. *Carm.* 15.192; 17.79–80.
240   **Exuet — deos** Cf. *Sylv.* 1.1.68: "Exuit antiquos Prussia tota deos"; *Her. Chr.* 4.20.
       impia Rhoma Sil. 5.601; Eob. *Her. Chr.* 1.187.
       Rhoma deos = Ov. *Fast.* 1.210.
241   **Occurret — Christi** Cf. *Her. Chr.* 4.231, n.; *Hod.* 263; *Luth.* 5.6; *Ebn.* 68.
       pulchrum . . . mori = Verg. *A.* 2.317.
       pro nomine Christi = *Nup.* 237, n.
243   **Quis neget** = Stat. *Silv.* 1.4.5; *Theb.* 2.110.
244   **vivere . . . mori** = *Her. Chr.* 6.86, n.; 7.56, n.
       vivere, turpe = Ov. *Tr.* 5.10.16: "vivere turpe putant."
245   **Indignum est** = Verg. *A.* 10.74.
247   **validae . . . vires** Lucr. 5.886; Verg. *A.* 2.50; 6.833.
       pulchro — corpore Cf. Verg. *A.* 5.344, 396, 475; Prop. 3.15.23.
249   **debuit aetas** = *Sylv. duae* 2.205.
250   **Heu dolor! Heu** = Stat. *Theb.* 11.616; Sil. 5.190; 10.222; cf. Eob. *Ama.* 35.1, n.

251–58   **Quid — nocens** Cf. Mant. *Georgius*, fol. 213ᵛ: "Tribunum / Victorem toties, toties felicibus armis / In varios casus Romano a Caesare missum / Fune ligant, facibus torrent, ac viscera sulcant / Unguibus."
251   **premis insontem** Sen. *Her. O.* 748.
251–52   **Rhomana . . . Arma** Luc. 10.4; Eob. *Her. Chr.* 6.161.
252   **ad partes . . . tuas** = Ov. *Pont.* 3.1.42.
253   **Iura — rebellem** Cf. l. 113 above (with n. to ll. 113–16); Mant. *Georgius*, fol. 210ʳ: "Palaestinam regi tum forte rebellem / Caesareo gravibus bellis Romana coegit / Iura pati."
254   **non potuisse liquet** = *Her. Chr.* 2.58.
255   **Haec — tantis** For the reproach, cf. Verg. *A.* 1.253: "hic pietatis honos?"; Ov. *Ep.* 14.84; *Met.* 5.14–15; Mant. *1. Parthen.* 3.568–69: "virtuti honor hic, haec praemia dantur / moribus innocuis?"
     pro meritis . . . praemia Juvenc. 3.558; Prud. *c. Symm.* 2.750.
     meritis . . . tantis = Ov. *Pont.* 4.1.21; cf. *Met.* 5.14; Eob. *Her. Chr.* A 3.74.
256   **militiae . . . piae** Ov. *Met.* 7.482–83.
257   **tormenta parantur** ≈ Prud. *c. Symm.* 1.532.
259   **teneram . . . puellam** *Buc.* 9.84, n.
     exprobrare puellam ≈ Ov. *Ars* 2.641.
260   **flere — queri** = Peter Riga, *Gen.* 1044; Eob. *Eccles.* 144; *Tum.* 7.162; *Accl.* 2.104; *Ebn.* 144; *Eras.* 48; *Pod.* 352; *Consol.* 6; cf. *Hymn.* B 1.2.
261   **Eia — moras** = Verg. *A.* 4.569; Mart. 2.64.9.
     mea vita = Prop. 2.3.23; 2.20.11; 2.26.1; Ov. *Am.* 2.15.21.
262   **in tua regna** = *Sylv. duae* 2.166.
263–64   **Nulla — Venit** Cf. *Sylv.* 3.6.31–32: "Postquam nulla mihi quae possit epistola venit / Dicere de Iona, 'Quem colis, Hesse, valet.'"
263   **reddatur epistola** = Tifernate, *Carm.*, sig. B4ᵛ; cf. Ov. *Ep.* 18.9–10.
     epistola tristis Cf. *Her. Chr.* 8.50, n.
264   **nuncia fama** = Ov. *Ep.* 16.38; Eob. *Her. Chr.* 19.158.
266   **prosperiore frui** = Ov. *Pont.* 3.7.30; Eob. *Her. Chr.* 10.168.
267   **sacra — flammis** Cf. *Accl.* 1.85: "sacra turicremis adoleverit atria flammis"; cf. Verg. *G.* 4.379; Paul. Nol. *Carm.* 20.113: "sacra . . . atria."
     festivis . . . flammis = *Her. Chr.* 4.215; cf. *Hymn.* 131–32.
268   **Et capiet — novos** Cf. Ov. *Ep.* 13.112.
     quaelibet ara = *Her. Chr.* 19.22.
270   **multos . . . dies** = *Her. Chr.* 1.38, n.
271   **mea — in auras** Cf. *Rec.* 98, n.
     quod nolim = Ov. *Ep.* 20.100; *Ib.* 143.
     vacuas . . . in auras = Ov. *Met.* 6.398; 12.469; 15.220; et al.
     ibit in auras = Ov. *Ep.* 10.121.
272   **Quis — fleam? Quis — cadam** Cf. *Her. Chr.* 8.45, nn.
273–74   **superantis . . . vitae Taedia** *Her. Chr.* 16.305; cf. *Laud.* 320, n.
273   **inertia vitae** = *Culex* 385; Eob. *Laud.* 512.
275   **miserae . . . puellae** = Prop. 2.8.23; Ov. *Ars* 3.45.
     miserae . . . miserere For this wordplay see, for example, *AH* 50.170.1 (repeated at the beginning of each of the following strophes): "O Deus, miseri / miserere servi"; 54.250.10: "Miserere miseris"; Hutten, *Querel.* 1.5.87: "Si te quid miseret, miseri miserere poetae"; Eob. *Her. Chr.* 15.163.
     precor, miserere Verg. *A.* 6.117; 12.777; Ov. *Met.* 11.133; 14.12.
     miserere puellae = Prop. 2.28.1; Ov. *Ep.* 5.155; Eob. *Her. Chr.* 17.251.
276   **grave . . . nomen amantis** Marul. *Epigr.* 2.32.97: ". . . grave nomen amantis."
     nomen amantis habet ≈ *Her. Chr.* 17.158, n.
277–78   **Tardior hoc — domus** Cf. Ov. *Pont.* 2.2.97–101; Eob. *Her. Chr.* 3.173–74, n.

277	**Tardior . . . aevo pater** Cf. l. 51, n., above.
	frigida mater = *Buc.* 3.47, n.
278	**te . . . tota domus** Cf. Magdal. *Ep.* 98: "Te domus omnis."
	voce — supplice Ov. *Met.* 2.396; 6.33.
279	**tetri . . . draconis** = Arator 2.1149.
279–80	**servasti . . . Servari** Cf. l. 87 above.
280	**ut possit . . . veni** *Her. Chr.* 2.2.
281	**O, illum . . . diem** = *Her. Chr.* 9.153; 18.83.
	violis That is, *violis albis*, since the context demands white.
	diem — notandum Cf. Hor. *Carm.* 1.36.10.
282	**Quam — equo** Cf. Ov. *Am.* 2.11.55–56; Eob. *Laud.* B 1.4, n.

13

Meter: Elegiac distich.

1	**Anna — salutem** Cf. Ov. *Ep.* 4.1–2; 13.1–2; 16.1; Eob. *Sylv.* 1.4.5: ". . . mitto salutem"; 3.5.1: "Hanc tibi . . . mitto . . . salutem."
1–2	**viro coniunx . . . fratri . . . soror** Cf. *Her. Chr.* 8.57, n.
4	**tecum — parens** ≈ *Her. Chr.* 5.178, n.; cf. *Her. Chr.* 2.48, n.
5	**Legitimi . . . lecti** = Andrel. *Ecl.* 4.84: "Legitimi . . . vincula lecti"; Eob. *Idyl.* 16.122; cf. Sen. *Tro.* 877; Celtis, *Am.* 2.8.87: "legitimi . . . gaudia lecti"; Eob. *Venus* 2.119: "Vivite legitimi sociati foedere lecti."
	commertia lecti Cf. *Her. Chr.* 4.69.
6	**Iam soror — eris** Cf. Ov. *Ep.* 3.52; 8.28.
7	**sacris . . . ab aris** = *Nob.* 113; cf. *Laud.* 246, n.
8	**Turpiter . . . iaces** = *Sylv. duae* 2.108.
	amisso . . . amore *Ilias Lat.* 71.
9	**Quinta — Lunae** Cf. Ov. *Met.* 8.11. For the time expression, cf. Eob. *Her. Chr.* 5.7, n. *Ps.-Matt.* 2.1–2 says that Joachim has been gone five months by this time. *Nativ. Mariae* 3.1 and *Leg. aurea* 127.43, are more vague, stating only that "some time" ("aliquamdiu") has elapsed since his departure from Jerusalem. Mant. *1. Parthen.* 1.42 proposes several years.
	Triviae . . . Lunae Cf. *Laud.* 380, nn.
	cornua Lunae = Ov. *Am.* 2.1.23; *Met.* 3.682; 8.11; 10.479; 12.264.
10	**Dum queror** = *Laud.* 285, n.
	absentem . . . virum = *Her. Chr.* 22.16; *Sylv.* 5.23.6: "Si qua sit absentem questa puella virum"; cf. l. 50 below.
	sola relicta virum ≈ Prop. 2.24.46; Ov. *Ep.* 7.84.
11	**vindex . . . poena** *Her. Chr* 11.48, n.
12	**est . . . culpa dolore minor** Cf. Ov. *Ep.* 7.86.
13	**Tu nemora — lustras** Cf. *Sylv.* 5.22.21: "Tu nemora et saltus praeruptaque saxa peragras"; *Buc.* 3.124; *Sylv. duae* 1.93, n.
	saxa horrentia Ov. *Met.* 4.778; Sil. 9.467.
15	**Ipsa — cubili** Cf. Ov. *Am.* 2.10.17; *Ep.* 16.317.
16	**Nox — meis** Cf. *Her. Chr.* 16.190, n.
17	**summus . . . sacerdos** = *Sylv. duae* 1.55, n. In *Ps.-Matt.* 2.1 the high priest is called Ruben; in *Nativ. Mariae* 2.2 his name is Isachar.
	de lege sacerdos = *Sylv. duae* 2.207, n.
18	**tota relligione** *Her. Chr.* 21.51.
19	**quia desperes** = Hor. *Ep.* 1.1.30.
	sterili . . . coniuge = Peter Riga, *Gen.* 895 (Rebecca): "Isaac vota sterili pro coniuge fundit."

20 **Quod superest** = *Her. Chr.* 6.147, n.
vita caelibe = *Her. Chr.* 5.50, n.

21 **quod — dolendum** Cf. *Eccles.* 67: "Quod tamen in primis multa ratione dolendum est"; *Eras.* 41: ". . . hac nobis non sit ratione dolendum."

22 **in amplexus . . . meos** = *Her. Chr.* 17.106, n.; cf. l. 109, n., below.

23 **Spiritus — auras** Cf. Ov. *Ep.* 12.85; *Tr.* 1.5.11–12; also cf. *Ep.* 10.121; *Met.* 8.524; Eob. *Her. Chr.* 18.113, n.
exhalet in auras ≈ *Rec.* 118, n.

24 **causam . . . mortis** Ov. *Ep.* 7.195; 18.200; *Ars* 3.40; *Fast.* 3.549; et al.
abesse querar ≈ *Her. Chr.* 10.100, n.

25–28 **Quid mihi — meae** Cf. Ov. *Ep.* 17.209–12; Eob. *Her. Chr.* 7.33–34.

25 **foecundae — matres** Cf. *Sylv.* 2.27.5 (in an epigram on the Mother of Sorrows): "Dicite, mortali foecundae semine matres"; also cf. *Her. Chr.* 16.225.
generoso semine = Ov. *Met.* 9.280.

25–26 **matres . . . nurus** Ov. *Ep.* 15.54; *Fast.* 4.295; *Tr.* 2.23.

29–31 **Ipsa — gravatae** Cf. Mant. *1. Parthen.* 1.29–30 (quoted below at l. 47).

29 **Ipsa — hymeneos** Cf. *Buc.* 9.80–81, n.
Ipsa domo vacua Cf. Verg. *A.* 4.82; Mant. *Calam.* 1.246 (p. 25): "Sola domo vacua"; Eob. *Her. Chr.* 16.259, n.

30 **sterilis . . . thori** = l. 116 below.
damna pudenda = Andrel. *Livia* 2.6.42; 2.10.12; Eob. *Eccles.* 212; *Sylv.* 2.1.34.

31 **mole gravatae** ≈ Juvenc. 2.786: "curarum mole gravatis"; cf. Eob. *Her. Chr.* 11.15, n.

32 **in vulgum — ire** Cf. *Sylv. duae* 2.54, n.; *Her. Chr.* 20.128.

33–36 **Scilicet — ubi est** Cf. Ov. *Am.* 3.1.19–22.

34 **Saepe . . . saepe** = Prop. 2.4.2; Ov. *Am.* 2.9.46; 2.19.20; et al.
saepe . . . manu = Prop. 1.8.16.

35 **Atque aliquis . . . dixerit** Cf. *Buc.* 2.109, n.

36 **templis munera** Verg. *A.* 4.217; Ov. *Met.* 9.791, 792; Erasmus, *Carm.* 1.29 (referring to St. Joachim): "Templis ferentem munera / Procax sacerdos reppulit."

37 **Hei — faciam** = Ov. *Pont.* 1.2.7; cf. Eob. *Her. Chr.* 7.43, n.
anxia curis = Ov. *Met.* 9.275; Stat. *Silv.* 3.4.71; V. Fl. 2.113; 4.7.

38 **talia verba** = Ov. *Ep.* 6.58; 14.52; *Fast.* 2.590; et al.; Eob. *Her. Chr.* 17.202.

39 **extremos . . . ad Indos** = Hor. *Ep.* 1.1.45; cf. Catul. 11.2; Sen. *Oed.* 114.
si qua est via Verg. *A.* 6.194, 367.

39–41 **Indos . . . Atlas . . . Arcton** Conventionally, the ends of the world. Cf. *Ama.* 32.65–72, n.; *Her. Chr.* 12.233–34.

40 **ubi . . . Atlas** Verg. *A.* 4.481; 6.796.
vasto pondere = Ov. *Ep.* 9.88.

41 **Lycaoniam . . . ad Arcton** = Ov. *Fast.* 3.793; cf. Eob. *Nup.* 20, n.

42 **aeripedes — equos** Cf. *Sylv. duae* 1.108, n.; *Eras.* 78: ". . . aeripedi Sarmata pastus equo"; cf. *Nup.* 24–25. For the epithet *aeripedes*, cf. Verg. *A.* 6.802; Ov. *Ep.* 6.32; 12.93; *Met.* 7.105.

43 **Omnia dura** Hor. *Carm.* 1.18.3; Sil. 7.577–78; Eob. *Her. Chr.* 16.39.

44 **Mens — conscia** Cf. *Her. Chr.* 15.25–26, n.

46 **Causa nocens** = Ov. *Met.* 7.526.
poenae vindicis *Her. Chr.* 11.48, n.

47 **Ipsa — usus** Cf. Mant. *1. Parthen.* 1.29–30: "Anna diu vanos secum ploraverat usus / conubi sterilemque torum tristemque hymenaeum." For *usus*, cf. also Eob. *Her. Chr.* 14.59, n.

48 **culpae — esse** = Ov. *Ep.* 17.146; cf. Eob. *Her. Chr.* 4.18, n.

49 **vario — aestu** Cf. Verg. *A.* 4.564; 8.19; 12.486.

50 **absenti . . . viro** ≈ l. 10, n., above.
displicuisse viro = Ov. *Tr.* 2.140.

51	**Spes nova** = *Her. Chr.* 4.78, n.
	nova consolatio = *Pod.* 331; *Psalt.* 1, arg. 1; *Consol.* 1.
54	**causa fuisse** = Ov. *Ep.* 14.4; *Ars* 1.600; *Tr.* 1.1.124.
55–56	**Non — brevi** Cf. Andrel. *Eleg.* 1, sig. b5ᵛ: "Non ego vos longa fessos ambage morabor. / Arctanda est spacio queque loquela brevi."
55	**Non — morabor** Cf. Verg. *A.* 6.722; Hor. *Ep.* 1.7.82–83; Ov. *Met.* 7.520; Eob. *Laud.* 45–46, n.
	Non ego te = *Her. Chr.* 5.23, n.
56	**dicere fine brevi** = *Tum.* 4.5.
57–58	**Pronus — diem** For the time of day at which the angel appears, cf. *Her. Chr.* 2.33–34, n. In Anna's case, the sources either do not mention the time of day or place it at noon, as in *Ps.-Matt.* 3.4.
57	**Pronus . . . Titan** Ov. *Met.* 11.257; Luc. 3.40.
	anhelabat *Her. Chr.* 11.27.
57–58	**condere . . . diem** Verg. *G.* 1.458; Sen. *Her. F.* 243.
58	**Occeano — rutilante** Cf. Verg. *A.* 7.25.
59	**Tristia — lecti** Cf. *Her.* 1.6.67, where Elizabeth tells her son John the Baptist: ". . . cum difficilis flerem dispendia lecti."
60	**vanas . . . preces** = Ov. *Pont.* 2.9.16; 3.7.2. For Anna's prayers, see *Ps.-Matt.* 2.2; Mant. *1. Parthen.* 1.29–85.
62	**luce nova** *Her. Chr.* 11.133, n.
63	**Dum — artus** Cf. Magdal. *Erarium*, ded., sig. A2ᵛ: ". . . tremulos gelidus timor anxerat artus"; Eob. *Theoc.* 36.94: "Obstupeo atque omnes gelidus timor occupat artus." Cf. further Verg. *A.* 7.446; 11.424; Ov. *Met.* 3.40; Luc. 1.246.
	Dum stupeo = Ov. *Ep.* 16.253; Eob. *Laud.* 191.
	gelidus timor Ov. *Tr.* 1.4.11.
	occupat artus = Magdal. *Ep.* 17; Eob. *Buc.* 7.65; cf. *Vict.* 457.
64	**Ante meos oculos** = Ov. *Ep.* 9.121; 12.60; *Pont.* 1.9.7; Eob. *Her. Chr.* 23.12.
	palmifer ales erat = *Her. Chr.* 1.8, n.
65	**primis — annis** = *Sylv.* 3.1.39; cf. *Idyl.* 1.101: ". . . primisque heroas ab annis"; *Theoc.* 17.7: ". . . primis heroes ab annis"; *Sylv.* 3.1.17: ". . . primis claros heroas ab annis"; *Nob.* 135. For *primis ab annis* at this metrical position, see *Laud.* 557, n.
67	**Nec — imago** Cf. *Her. Chr.* 8.65, n.
68	**Praebuerant — fidem** Cf. *Her. Chr.* 7.54, n.
	certam . . . fidem = *Her. Chr.* 6.118, n.
	sequta fidem = *Her. Chr.* 6.54; cf. *Her. Chr.* 7.54, n.
69	**legitimi . . . pudoris** = *Consol.* 33: "legitimi specimen fuit illa pudoris."
	ocia vana = *Luth.* 1.29; cf. *Ruf.* 74.
71	**Accipe, ne dubites** = Calp. *Ecl.* 3.75; cf. Eob. *Her. Chr.* 23.3, n.
	neu sis — futuri Cf. Ov. *Met.* 15.815.
72	**Ante — tuis** ≈ *Her.* 1.6.78. For *gratia parta*, see also *Her. Chr.* 11.170.
73	**et ex alto . . . Olympo** = Mant. *1. Parthen.* 3.259; cf. Tib. 1.6.83.
74	**Immensi . . . Dei** *Her. Chr.* 21.60.
	pietas — Dei = *Psalt.* 38, arg. 4; *Consol.* 160; cf. *Her. Chr.* 14.19, n.; Strozzi, *Eroticon* 4.13.4: ". . . Borsii pietas officiosa ducis."
75	**Visa diu sterilem** ≈ *Her.* 1.6.68: "Visa diu steriles inter habenda nurus." For *visa diu*, see *Her. Chr.* 8.9, n.
	sterilem . . . senectam = Paul. Nol. *Carm.* 6.34: "prole carens sterilem ducebat maesta senectam"; Erasmus, *Carm.* 2.203.
76	**concepto — eris** ≈ *Her.* 1.6.80; cf. *Her. Chr.* 19.112 (different).
77	**clausa . . . alvo** = Mant. *1. Parthen.* 3.93. Cf. Eob. *Her. Chr.* 13.89, 143–44; 21.147.
	nascetur ab alvo = *Her.* 1.1.23.

79–80   **Nomen — Deo** Cf. *Nativ. Mariae* 3.8: "vocabis nomen eius Mariam. Haec erit, ut vovistis, ab infantia statim sua domino consecrata et spiritu sancto replebitur adhuc ex utero matris suae."

79   **primo . . . ab aevo** = Ov. *Pont.* 2.2.97; cf. Eob. *Laud.* 510, n.

80   **Flamine plena Deo** Cf. *Her.* 1.6.84: "Flamine sacra Deo pectora plenus erit"; cf. Peter Riga, *Lev.* 474: ". . . Flamine plena Sacro."

81   **Templa colet** ≈ Stat. *Theb.* 8.207; cf. Ov. *Ep.* 20.180; *Met.* 11.578.
       sacras . . . aras *Laud.* 246, n.

83   **Nec dubita** = *Her. Chr.* 1.33, n.

85–90   **Sara — liquet** These exempla are also given in *Nativ. Mariae* 3.5–6; Mant. *1. Parthen.* 1.81–83; cf. Eob. *Her. Chr.* 20.59–60.

85–86   **Sara — anu** See Vulg. *Gen.* 17.15–19; 18.10–14; 21.1–7.

85   **permansit in annos** = Ov. *Fast.* 5.33; *Tr.* 4.10.73.

87   **Israeliticis — Ioseph** Joseph and his brothers were the sons of Jacob, also known as Israel. See Vulg. *Gen.* 32.28; 35.10.
       orbus Joseph was sold into slavery by his brothers. See Vulg. *Gen.* 37.12–28.

88   **Est — satus** The long-sterile Rachel finally had her prayers answered and bore Joseph: see Vulg. *Gen.* 29.31; 30.1, 22–24.

89   **Exiit — alvo** See Vulg. *Judic.* 13.

90   **Illud — liquet** See Vulg. *1. Sam.* 1.1–20.

93   **surgenti . . . Eoo** Sil. 11.515

94   **nomen habet** = *Sylv. duae* 1.24, n.

95   **Illac exieris** Anna is still in Nazareth; cf. ll. 27–28 above.
       redeuntem . . . maritum Mant. *1. Parthen.* 2.36: "[Anna] . . . offendit redeuntem rure maritum."
       amplexa maritum = Luc. 2.366.

96   **quo post — eris** Cf. *Her. Chr.* 1.104, n.

97–98   **I modo . . . Et** Cf. l. 116 below, n.

97   **virginei florem . . . pudoris** ≈ *Nup.* 244, n.
       florem . . . pudoris Cf. *Buc.* 2.73, n.

99–100   **Dixit — solent** Cf. Agricola, *Anna*, 300, where the angel has just spoken to Joachim: "Dixit et in tenues sublatus protinus auras / Fulminis ut rapidi stridula flamma fugit"; Eob. *Hymn.* 73–76.

99   **Dixit — auras** Cf. Celtis, *Am.* 3.14.93 (Eob. *Vict.*, app. 2.19): "Dixit et in tenues fugiens evanuit auras." Both Celtis and Eobanus follow classical models: see Verg. *A.* 4.278; 5.740; 9.658; Ov. *Met.* 14.432; *Fast.* 2.509; *Pont.* 3.3.93.

100   **Quam — solent** ≈ *Psalt.* 30.18: "Ipsius ira brevis cito praeterit, exit in ictu, / Quam cito consumpta fulgura nube solent."
       consumpta . . . nube For the image, cf. *Buc.* 5.73, n.

101   **Ipsa — sequebar** Cf. Verg. *A.* 1.406; 9.17.

102   **Laeticiam — novam** Cf. *Vict.* 240; *Her. Chr.* 22.110, n. For *laeticiam novam*, see *Pug.* 18, n., and l. 124, n., below.

103   **Quisquis es, o** = *Her. Chr.* 4.97, n.
       o superum — minister Cf. Mart. 7.74.1, of Mercury as messenger of the gods: "Cyllenes caelique decus, facunde minister"; Eob. *Her.* 1.5.87, of the Apostle Paul: "O superum facunde comes fideique magister." For the association of Gabriel with Mercury, cf. *Her. Chr.* 1.4, n. For *minister* applied to an angel, cf. Vulg. *Hebr.* 1.14; Lact. *Inst.* 1.7.4–8; Juvenc. 1.52.

104   **Fac rata sint** Cf. Ov. *Am.* 3.2.80.

107   **tristi . . . pectore** = Stat. *Theb.* 7.148.

108   **in tua vota** = Ov. *Ep.* 16.282; 21.240; *Pont.* 2.8.28; 4.4.30.

109   **Ibis in amplexus** = Celtis, *Am.* 3.4.53; Eob. *Her. Chr.* 17.106; cf. Ov. *Ep.* 16.86; *Fast.* 6.554; Eob. *Her. Chr.* 1.24, n.; 13.22.

110	**Gaudia — mihi** For the pentameter structure, cf. *Her. Chr.* 4.74, n.
	Gaudia quanta = Ov. *Met.* 9.483; Eob. *Her. Chr.* 1.184.
111	**summi . . . Dei** *Her. Chr.* 4.16, n.
	Dei claementia = Ov. *Tr.* 5.4.19.
113	**nostrae requies . . . senectae** = Mart. 4.25.7; Mant. *1. Parthen.* 1.712, where Anna tells Mary: "tu nostrae requies, tu sola senectae / gloria"; cf. Verg. *A.* 9.481–82; Stat. *Silv.* 2.1.70; Eob. *Her. Chr.* 20.113; *Her.* 1.6.155: "Nate, meae requies et honor supreme senectae."
114	**gravabit onus** ≈ Ov. *Ep.* 11.38.
115	**repensio** For this rare patristic word, see, for example, Ennod. *Ep.* 9.30.
116	**I nunc et** = *Buc.* 4.63, n.; *Her. Chr.* 1.163, n.
	sterilis . . . thori = l. 30 above; cf. Mant. *1. Parthen.* 1.30.
	taedia . . . thori = *Val.* 1.478 (of an aphrodisiac): "Illa levat fessi tedia longa thori"; cf. Ov. *Met.* 7.572.
117	**solennes . . . ad aras** Verg. *A.* 2.202; cf. Eob. *Hymn.* 147–48.
119	**tempore ab illo** = *Buc.* 10.107, n.
120	**gloria maior erit** ≈ Ov. *Ep.* 12.76; *Fast.* 1.714.
121	**Aspiciet nostri** ≈ *Her. Chr.* B 1.51.
124	**Leticiae . . . novae** = Mart. 8.11.4; cf. l. 102, n., above.
	copia grata = Ov. *Fast.* 3.672.
125–26	**Quam — tenent** Cf. Vulg. *Luc.* 1.65: "super omnia montana Iudaeae divulgabantur omnia verba haec."
125	**Quam — urbes** Cf. Verg. *A.* 4.173–74; Eob. *Her. Chr.* 12.47, n.
	vicinas . . . in urbes = *Her. Chr.* 22.53; cf. Verg. *G.* 1.510; Hor. *Ars* 66.
128	**Invida . . . turba** *Her. Chr.* 7.34, n.
	sacras . . . fores = *Her. Chr.* 14.76, n.
129	**Dulcia — ventri** Cf. Mart. 14.151; Eob. *Buc.* 5.97.
	pondera ventri = Mant. *1. Parthen.* 1.692, where Anna addresses Mary: "Nata, meo quondam suavissima pondera ventri"; cf. Eob. *Buc.* 11.63, n.
130	**Donec — rotam** Cf. *Her. Chr.* 5.7. For the time expression with reference to childbirth, cf. Ov. *Met.* 2.453; Mant. *1. Parthen.* 1.310–11 (the birth of Mary). Cf. further l. 9, n., above.
132	**de tribus — eris** Cf. Ov. *Ep.* 9.92; *Tr.* 2.246; Eob. *Her. Chr.* 6.162.
133	**Tres — maritis** Modeled on Mant. *1. Parthen.* 1.861–62: "Tres triplici partu Marias: tribus Anna maritis / progenuit sanctum et summo genus aethere dignum."
134	**foelix — parens** Cf. Ov. *Am.* 3.6.34; V. Fl. 5.383; Eob. *Her. Chr.* 4.36.
135	**palmifer ales** *Her. Chr.* 1.8, n.
137–40	**Nam quid — nurus** Anna alludes to the angel's message in ll. 77–82 above.
141	**virtutis . . . signa futurae** Cf. *Buc.* 9.92–93, n.
	certissima signa = Verg. *G.* 1.439.
142	**Ille sacer . . . nuncius** Ven. Fort. *Carminum spuriorum app.* 1.186: "Gabrihel, nuntius ille sacer."
	vero . . . ore = [Tib.] 3.4.50; Eob. *Her. Chr.* 5.138.
	nuncius ore = Ov. *Fast.* 6.674. For the term *nuncius*, see Eob. *Her. Chr.* 1.4, n.
	ore docet = Ov. *Fast.* 6.386: "sacro . . . ore docet."
143	**Ergo nec immerito** = *Buc.* B 2.47, n.
	penetralia ventris = Juvenc. 3.394.
144	**magnum . . . decus** Verg. *A.* 10.507; *Cat.* 9.3; [Tib.] 3.7.49.
145–48	**Charius — iuvat** Cf. *Nativ. Mariae* 3.7: "crede dilatos diu conceptus et steriles partus mirabiliores esse solere"; Agricola, *Anna*, 298: "Quod venit ex facili, faciles segnesque tenemus; / Quod spe quodque metu torsit, habere iuvat." Cf. further Eob. *Her. Chr.* 1.53–54, n.
145	**spes longa — est** Cf. Stat. *Theb.* 11.671; Eob. *Laud.* 551, n.

146	**magnis rebus** = Ov. *Ep.* 17.130.
147	**ex facili** = Ov. *Ars* 3.579; *Pont.* 1.5.59.
	brevis . . . gratia [Aus.] *De rosis nascentibus* 41; Juvenc. 2.782.
149	**gaudia partus** = Mutius, *Triumph.*, sig. c5ʳ, referring to Sara: "sua gaudia partus / Attulit."
153	**Qui caelos — inerti** Cf. *Her. Chr.* 10.160, n.
	caelos terramque ≈ Verg. *A.* 1.133.
154	**arbitrio — suo** Cf. Mant. *Mort.*, fol. 120ʳ: ". . . imperio temperat omne suo"; Eob. *Her. Chr.* 20.112. For *arbitrio suo* at this metrical position, see Ov. *Rem.* 380.
155	**Quem — patres** Cf. Mant. *7. Parthen.*, fol. 176ʳ: "Numina, quae nostri coluere ab origine patres."
	prima . . . ab origine = Lucr. 5.548; Verg. *G.* 3.48; 4.286; *A.* 1.372; Ov. *Tr.* 2.559.
157	**Qui — regem** See Vulg. *Exod.* 14.21–31.
	Rubro . . . aequore Verg. *G.* 3.359; Prop. 1.14.12.
	Pharium . . . regem Luc. 2.636; 6.308; Stat. *Silv.* 3.1.31.
	in aequore regem ≈ V. Fl. 1.342.
158	**haec — genus** Cf. *Her. Chr.* 6.79, n.; *Vict.* 250–51.
	duxit in arva = *Sylv. duae* 1.182, n.
160	**imbelli . . . manu** ≈ Prop. 4.3.24.
161–62	**Solus . . . qui mirabilia . . . facit** Vulg. *Psa.* 71.18; 135.4; cf. Eob. *Her. Chr.* 6.43, n.
161	**in humanis . . . rebus** = Ov. *Pont.* 4.3.49.
162	**omnia solus habet** ≈ Mart. 3.26.5; Aus. *Mosella* 31.
163	**Illi pro — grates** Cf. Mart. 12.9.3.
165	**praesentis . . . vitae** = Prud. *c. Symm.* 2.908: "praesentis gaudia vitae"; cf. Eob. *Buc.* 11.103, n.
	taedia vitae = *Laud.* 320, n.
166	**Frigida . . . ossa** Mant. *1. Parthen.* 1.367.
	texerit ossa lapis Cf. Tib. 1.4.60; 3.7.204.
167	**aethereis — oris** Cf. Mant. *Ecl.* 9.1: ". . . patriis procul actus ab oris"; Eob. *Her. Chr.* 17.78; 20.63.
	aethereis . . . oris = Sil. 3.137; cf. Lucr. 4.411; 5.85; 6.61.
168	**arva soli** = *Buc.* B 10.4, n.

14

For the background and history of this legend, see Konrad Kunze, *Studien zur Legende der heiligen Maria Aegyptiaca im deutschen Sprachgebiet*, Philologische Studien und Quellen 49 (Berlin, 1969), with a discussion of Eobanus' poem on 129–33; Kunze, *Die Legende der heiligen Maria Aegyptiaca: Ein Beispiel hagiographischer Überlieferung in 16 unveröffentlichten deutschen, niederländischen und lateinischen Fassungen*, Texte des späten Mittelaters und der frühen Neuzeit 28 (Berlin, 1978), with an edition of the text according to the 1532 version on 143–48; and Kunze's article in *VL* 5, cols. 1251–55. See further Harry Vredeveld, "Mittelalterliche Legende in ovidischer Form: Wege der Worte in den *Heroidum Christianarum epistolae* des Helius Eobanus Hessus, am Beispiel des Briefes 'Maria Aegyptia Zozimae,' " in *Wege der Worte: Festschrift für Wolfgang Fleischhauer*, ed. Donald C. Riechel (Cologne, 1978), 237–62, with an annotated edition of the 1539 redaction.

According to Kunze, *Studien*, 131, and *Die Legende*, 143, Eobanus' source for this letter is the Latin translation of the Greek *vita* by Paulus Diaconus, reprinted in *PL* 73, cols. 671–90. As the many extant manuscripts attest, this translation was particularly popular in Northern Europe (Kunze, *Studien*, 27). Cf. *Leg. aurea* 54. For dramatic effect Eobanus streamlines the legend slightly by suppressing Zosimas' intermediate visit.

Meter: Elegiac distich.

1	**Accola — undas** = l. 17 below; *Her.* 1.6.9. **fluctivagi** Stat. *Theb.* 1.271; 9.305, 360; *Silv.* 2.1.95; 3.1.84. **rapidas — undas** Herc. Strozzi, *Eleg.*, fol. 57ᵛ: "ad rapidas . . . Iordanis undas." Cf. Sedul. 2.141, as given in one ms. and in the errata of the Aldus edition (Venice, 1502): ". . . placidas ad Iordanis undas" (for "placidam Iordanis ad undam"); see *PL* 19, col. 611, n. to l. 141. Also cf. l. 145 below. The scansion of *Iordanis* with a short second syllable occurs also in Brant, *Varia carm.*, sig. B2ᵛ (*Texte* 93.46): "Iordanis donec petiit fluenta"; Eob. *Vict.* 337; *Psalt.* 42.29; 72.23; 114.6, 10. **rapidas ad . . . undas** Ov. *Met.* 9.104; cf. l. 155 below, n.
2	**ter tria lustra** Cf. *Her. Chr.* 3.20; 4.42, n.
3–4	**Proxima — erat** Cf. *PL* 73, col. 683 C–D: "Zosimas dixit ad eam: Quot anni sunt, o domina, ex quo hanc inhabitas solitudinem? Respondit mulier: Quadraginta septem anni sunt . . . ex quo de sancta civitate egressa sum."
3	**Proxima post nonam** = Ov. *Met.* 14.228. **Olympias** An *Olympiad* is normally a period of four years, but in poetry the term often means a period of five years: see, for instance, Ov. *Pont.* 4.6.5; Mart. 7.40.6; Eob. *Her. Chr.* 24.109; *Sylv.* 1.4.19–20.
4	**obliquo tramite Phoebus** Sen. *Apoc.* 2.4; cf. *Thy.* 845.
6	**optatae — opem** = *Accl.* 1.186; cf. Gunther, *Lig.* 10.252: "Ferre salutis opem . . ."; Andrel. *Livia* 3.5.42: "Et feret optatae quanque salutis opem"; Eob. *Eccles.* 400. For the tag *salutis opem,* see, for example, Ven. Fort. *Carm.* 3.9.60.
7	**Excidit — memor es** Cf. Ov. *Ep.* 12.71.
8	**Aut etiam — rogas** Cf. Ov. *Ep.* 2.106; *Fast.* 3.3.
9	**sancte pater** = *Her. Chr.* 11.5, n.
10	**Ex vultu — tuo** Cf. Vulg. *Eccl.* 8.1; Eob. *Sylv.* 6.5.33: "Simplicis in vultu fidei pudor emicat ipso."
11–12	**Non mea — fuit** For the motif, cf. *Her. Chr.* 4.5–6, nn.
11	**frontem** Cf. *Her. Chr.* 6.17; 15.16.
14	**Sed tamen haud** = Lucr. 4.689. **ratio — ista** = *Sylv.* 6.5.24.
15	**titubanti . . . dextra** = *Theoc.* 32.36: "Rustica fingebat titubanti pocula dextra"; cf. Avit. *Carm.* 2.218: ". . . titubans sub pondere dextra." Also cf. l. 162 below. **littera dextra** ≈ *Her. Chr.* 18.9, n.
16	**versus — erat** ≈ Ov. *Ep.* 15.182.
18	**tibi, si nescis** = *Max.* 290; *Sylv.* 3.5.1; cf. *Her. Chr.* 12.98, n.
19	**Summa — transmisit** Cf. the *vita* (*PL* 73, col. 678 C): "te gratia Spiritus sancti direxit, ut aliquod ministerium exhibeas meae exiguitatis corpori congruum." **Summa Dei pietas** = *Psalt.* 59.29; cf. Paul. Nol. *Carm.* 6.103; *Ep.* 32.5: "Mira dei pietas . . ."; Eob. *Her. Chr.* 9.68; 13.74; 15.137.
20	**Communem . . . viam** = Mant. *c. Am.*, fol. 175ᵛ, opening distich: "te . . . monerem, / Communem iuvenum ne sequerere viam." **inisse viam** ≈ Prop. 2.33.8; Ov. *Rem.* 578. For the image, see, for example, Vulg. *3. Reg.* 2.2; Hor. *Carm.* 1.28.16; Prop. 3.7.2; 3.18.22; ll. 98–99, 108 below.
21–22	**Et simul — fuit** Cf. ll. 97–100 below.
21	**humanis — rebus** Cf. Sen. *Ben.* 4.22.1: "abire e rebus humanis."
21–22	**eundum Qua sit** Ov. *Tr.* 3.1.19.
24	**caelestem . . . cibum** The Eucharist.
26	**purgata** The final syllable is lengthened before the caesura. **decet** The modal sense of "should" is unusual.
27	**monitore Deo** Sil. 4.723. **cum forte rogarem** Mart. 6.10.1.

28   **Polliciti — tui** Cf. Ov. *Ep.* 2.66.

29   **tacitae . . . eremi** Cf. *Her.* 1.6.183: "taciturnam . . . eremum."
          cultrix . . . eremi = *Her. Chr.* 22.19; cf. *Her. Chr.* 4.173.

30   **Pars ego — tuis** Modeled on Ov. *Pont.* 4.15.14.

33–38   **integrum — fides** Cf. *Her. Chr.* 5.7–10, n.

34   **ore cibum** = Ov. *Ars* 1.94; Eob. *Sylv. duae* 1.92.

35   **Terribilis . . . rotae . . . astra** Cf. *Val.* 1.58, in the 1524 edition, also referring to the
          zodiac: "Signaque terribilis saepe timenda rotae." Cf. further Prop. 4.1.82; Eob. *Val.*
          1.58, in the 1531 redaction: "obliquae signa timenda rotae."
          duodena . . . astra Cf. Verg. *G.* 1.232; Ov. *Met.* 13.618–19.

37   **tetigisti littora** = *Her. Chr.* 7.95, n.

38   **Addita — fides** Cf. Ov. *Ep.* 12.194; 21.136; *Fast.* 3.366; Eob. *Her. Chr.* 7.54, n.
          pollicita . . . fides *Wirt.*, ded. 2: "En tibi pollicita carmina iussa fide."
          in tua verba = Ov. *Pont.* 2.5.70; 3.5.24.

39   **Longa via est** = *Her. Chr.* 5.27, n. According to the *vita* (*PL* 73, col. 688 C) the
          journey took some twenty days.
          cumulato — aevo Cf. l. 153, n., below.
          tardior aevo = *Her. Chr.* 12.51, n.

42   **Spem veniae** = Hor. *Ars* 267; cf. Eob. *Vict.* 178.
          vitae gaudia = *Ebn.* 128 (of eternal life): "Invenit vitae gaudia vera novae"; *Consol.*
          170 (of eternal life): "Versa est in vitae gaudia poena gravis." Cf. Verg. *A.* 11.180;
          [Tib.] 3.3.7.

43   **sol . . . fessus** Erasmus, *Carm.* 64.54: "Invitis sol fessus equis"; Celtis, *Od.* 1.2.63; cf.
          Sil. 1.209: "atque ubi fessus equos Titan immersit anhelos"; *Ilias Lat.* 616–17.
          occiduas . . . in undas = Hutten, *Querel.* 2.4.15: "Dum ruit occiduas Germanus
          Rhenus in undas"; cf. Eob. *Nup.* 280, n.
          declinat in undas = Mant. *1. Parthen.* 2.607: "Hesperias . . . declinat in undas."

44   **Nec iam . . . amplius** Verg. *A.* 3.192, 260; 5.8; 11.807.

45   **mea — annos** Cf. Tifernate, *Carm.*, sig. C1ʳ: "Mens mea praeteritos quam longe
          respicit annos"; Andrel. *Ecl.* 6.25: "Cur tua venturos aetas non respicit annos?"; Mart.
          10.23.3; Eob. *Her. Chr.* 18.91.
          praeteritos . . . annos = *Buc.* 6.71, n.

46   **longius . . . trahi** Boeth. *Consol.* 2.m7.23: "longius vitam trahi"; Eob. *Epic.* 3.162:
          "Longius hanc [vitam] querimur non potuisse trahi."
          longius aegra = Ov. *Ep.* 21.246.

47   **maturam . . . senectam** ≈ Ov. *Met.* 3.347.

48   **meas — fores** Cf. Ov. *Ep.* 21.46; Hor. *Carm.* 1.4.13–14; Eob. *Her.* 1.6.34: "Et vicina
          meas Mors cubat ante fores."

49   **Sat — datum** Cf. Verg. *A.* 2.291; 9.135.
          Quae deinde sequetur ≈ Verg. *A.* 3.327; 6.756.

50   **Est alio — loco** Cf. *Her. Chr.* 6.66, n.
          Est alio . . . loco = Ov. *Fast.* 5.724.
          vita futura = Ov. *Ib.* 160.

51   **Prima . . . iuventa** Prop. 3.5.19; Verg. *A.* 7.51; 8.160; 9.181; Ov. *Am.* 3.1.28;
          Ep. 16.365; et al.
          nimium iuveniliter Ov. *Tr.* 2.117; Eob. *Her.*, ded. 67.

52   **Pars vitae — est** Cf. Erasmus, *Carm.* 2.221: "Huic [Christo] saltem pars [vitae] dete-
          rior breviorque dicetur."
          Pars vitae = Ov. *Tr.* 5.5.22; cf. Eob. *Her. Chr.* 1.140, n.

53–56   **Ah, pudet — habes** Cf. *Her. Chr.* 11.73–78; 15.55–60. In the *vita* (*PL* 73, col. 679
          D) Mary justifies the narrative of her sinful life as follows: "Vere erubesco, ignosce,
          abba meus, dicere tibi turpitudinem meorum actuum; tamen quia vidisti nudum
          corpus meum, denudabo tibi et opera meorum actuum, ut cognoscas quam turpis
          luxuriae et opprobrio confusionis repleta est anima mea."

53   **Ah, pudet — ruinam** Cf. *Her. Chr.* 11.97, n.
       veterem . . . ruinam Sedul. 4.73: "Si nos poeniteat veterem quaesisse ruinam";
       cf. Ov. *Met.* 15.424.
54   **Nam sua — volet** Cf. Ov. *Met.* 9.4–5.
       turpiter acta = Prop. 4.6.22 (different).
55   **Sed tamen — quae** Cf. Ov. *Fast.* 1.31; Eob. *Sylv.* 1.10.23: "Sed tamen est ratio
       cur . . ."; *Sylv.* 1.6.19: "Non tamen est ratio cur . . ."; 6.10.31: "Non tamen est ratio
       quae. . . ."
57   **suis . . . numeris** For the idiom, cf. Ov. *Am.* 3.7.18; *Tr.* 1.8.48. For the phrasing, cf.
       Ov. *Fast.* 2.6: "cum lusit numeris prima iuventa suis."
       improvida certe = Mant. *Ecl.* 6.19: "improvida certe / turba sumus iuvenes."
58   **Quae — solet** Cf. Hor. *Carm.* 2.4.23–24; Eob. *Her. Chr.* 24.106.
59–60 **vulgares . . . quaestibus** = Ov. *Fast.* 4.865–66.
59   **usus** For the sense of "usus Veneris," see, for example, Tib. 1.9.55; Ov. *Am.* 3.7.3;
       Rem. 357; Eob. *Her. Chr.* 13.47, n.
61–62 **Nec me — eram** The association of love and warfare is a commonplace in erotic
       poetry: see, for example, Prop. 1.6.30; 4.1.137; Hor. *Carm.* 4.1.16; Ov. *Am.* 1.9; *Ars*
       2.233. Cf. Eob. *Her. Chr.* 24.44.
62   **pontigena** Brant, *Texte* 39.2–3 (unknown to Eobanus): "Pontigenam . . . deam. /
       Venus . . . Pontigena"; Eob. *Sylv.* 9.9.1: "pontigenam Venerem." Cf. Calepino,
       Dictionarium, s.v. "Pontigonus"; Catul. 36.11, of Venus: "creata ponto"; Ov. *Met.*
       4.537–38; *Fast.* 4.61–62; Sen. *Phaed.* 274: "Diva . . . generata ponto"; Mart. Cap. *De
       nuptiis Philologiae et Mercurii* 9.915: "spumigenae"; Eob. *Her. Chr.* 17.95: "Oceanitide."
       sub duce miles eram *Her. Chr.* 11.60.
63   **Pellaeo iuveni** = Juv. 10.168; cf. Eob. *Her. Chr.* 4.55, n. Alexander the Great,
       a native of Pella, founded Alexandria in 332 BCE.
64   **Quis — tenet** Cf. Ov. *Ars* 3.338.
65   **polluta libidine** = *Her.* 3.4.53; cf. Mant. *Epigr.*, fol. 110ᵛ: "Forma . . . polluta libidinis
       usu."
66   **Perdita . . . mundo** *Her. Chr.* 15.7.
       mundo vivere Paul. Nol. *Epist.* 8.5: "vive deo; nam vivere mundo / mortis opus."
69   **Per mare sulcantes . . . nautas** Cf. *Ruf.* 21–22: "navita . . . / Per mare
       sulcat iter."
       sulcantes . . . vada cerula Hod. 273; *Her.* 3.6.173; *Psalt.* 48.15: "vada sulcantes . . .
       caerula naves"; cf. *Buc.* 11.69, n.; *Her. Chr.* 15.179, n.; 17.163.
       vada cerula = Verg. *A.* 7.198.
70   **votis invida . . . meis** = *Sylv.* 8.20.30. For *votis meis* at this metrical position, see
       Prop. 1.10.4; Ov. *Am.* 2.19.16; 3.7.2; *Ep.* 6.152; *Pont.* 4.9.72.
       invida turba = *Her. Chr.* 7.34, n.
72   **Pro — dedi** Cf. the *vita* (*PL* 73, col. 680 C): "corpus enim meum in potestate
       habentes, pro naulo accipient"; cf. *Leg. aurea* 54.22: "pro naulo habeatis corpus
       meum."
       miserum corpus = *Sylv.* 9.18.24; cf. Ov. *Met.* 9.368; Calp. *Ecl.* 5.76; Eob. *Her.
       Chr.* 17.48.
       corpus habere = Ov. *Tr.* 1.3.98; *Pont.* 2.7.76.
73   **Ventum erat — Sionem** Cf. *Her. Chr.* 6.55.
       Ventum erat ad = Verg. *A.* 6.45; Hor. *S.* 1.9.35; Ov. *Fast.* 3.13, 651; cf. Eob.
       Her. Chr. 16.217.
       Solomonea templa = Erasmus, *Carm.* 42.13; cf. Mant. *1. Parthen.* 3.233.
74   **crux veneranda loco** = *Her. Chr.* 6.92; cf. Paul. Nol. *Carm.* 25.192.
75–76 **ter conata . . . Ter** For this formula, see Verg. *A.* 2.792–93; 10.685; Ov. *Ep.* 4.7;
       Met. 11.419; *Fast.* 2.823. In the *vita* (*PL* 73, col. 681 D) the wording is similar:
       "Hoc ter et quater passa et facere conans."
75   **aedes . . . sacratas** *Laud.* 170.

76   **sacras ante . . . fores** Tib. 1.3.30; Ov. *Met.* 15.407; cf. Eob. *Her. Chr.* 13.128.
77   **Dum queror** = *Laud.* 285, n.
       queror . . . sine teste *Her. Chr.* 22.20; cf. *Her. Chr.* 8.113, n.
79   **Accessi supplexque . . . precabar** Cf. *Her. Chr.* 5.165, n.; 15.121; *Hod.* B 7.11.
       Accessi . . . -que = Verg. *A.* 3.24; Ov. *Met.* 5.592.
       Deam For this title, see *Buc.* 11.37, n.
       sic orsa = Verg. *A.* 7.435.
80   **Mater — viri** Cf. *Her. Chr.* 7.152, n.
81   **Aspice me** Cf. *Buc.* 11.95, n., addressing the Virgin.
82   **Vivam — tibi** Cf. Hor. *Ep.* 1.18.107–08; Ov. *Ep.* 5.158.
83   **Annuere oranti** Verg. *A.* 11.797; Ov. *Met.* 4.539; *Fast.* 3.337.
       mitissima Virgo = Alcuin. *Carm.* 99.12.9. Cf. Salzer, 361.
85–86 **Hic mihi — est** Cf. the *vita* (*PL* 73, col. 683 A): "audivi vocem alicuius a longe
       clamantis: Iordanem si transieris, bonam invenies requiem."
85   **Hic mihi — aures** Cf. Verg. *A.* 3.93; Eob. *Her. Chr.* 1.85; 5.97, n.; *Luth.* 1.65.
       stupidas . . . aures = *Laud.* 299.
86   **petenda tibi est** = Ov. *Tr.* 5.14.42.
87   **Obstupeo** ≈ *Buc.* 4.104, n.
87–88 **prioris . . . vitae** *Her. Chr.* 11.127, n.
89   **Tempore ab hoc** = *Her. Chr.* 12.59, n.
       tot . . . per annos = Verg. *G.* 3.47; Eob. *Max.* 99.
91   **Hic mihi parta quies** = *Buc.* 3.6, n.
       nullo — aevo = Tifernate, *Carm.*, sig. A2^r.
92   **Caelestem . . . domum** Prud. *Perist.* 2.42.
       hospita lustra Cf. Sil. 16.103: "inhospita lustra."
93   **nostros — artus** Cf. Lucr. 3.129; Ov. *Ib.* 123–24, in most mss.: "spiritus artus /
       deserat"; Sil. 6.126; Celtis, *Am.* 1.3.89: "fessos prope linquat spiritus artus." For the
       tag *spiritus artus*, see also Luc. 1.456; 4.643.
94   **viridi cespite** = Ov. *Ars* 3.688; cf. Eob. *Ama.* 9.5, n.
       cespite membra = Andrel. *Livia* 2.5.30: "Tectaque non ullo cespite membra."
95–96 **Hic — feras** Cf. the *vita* (*PL* 73, col. 685 B): "Crede mihi, non vidi hominem
       ex quo Iordanem transivi, nisi te hodie: sed neque feram aut aliud animal quale-
       cunque, ex quo in hanc deveni solitudinem."
95   **tot euntibus annis** = *Her. Chr.* 16.275; *Hod.* 471; *Epic.*, app. 5.15; *Wirt.* 304;
       cf. Hor. *Ep.* 2.2.55; Claud. *in Eutr.* 1.488; Eob. *Laud.* 62, n.; *Max.* 193.
96   **trucesque feras** = *Eccles.* 58; cf. Tib. 1.9.76; [Sen.] *Oct.* 569; Eob. *Her. Chr.* 22.68.
97   **praesentis . . . vitae** *Buc.* 11.103, n.
       munera vitae = Mart. 3.6.5; Sil. 14.177; cf. Eob. *Buc.* 10.7, n.; *Vict.* 62.
98   **ignotae . . . viae** Vulg. *Sap.* 18.3; Verg. *A.* 8.113; Ov. *Rem.* 578 (at this metrical posi-
       tion); l. 108 below. For the image, see l. 20, n., above.
99   **Ipsa viam ingredior** Cf. Vulg. *3. Reg.* 2.2: "ego ingredior viam universae terrae";
       Mant. *7. Parthen.*, fol. 144^v: "Iamque viam ingredior. . . ."
       morti . . . propinquae Lucr. 6.1218; Eob. *Her. Chr.* 11.119.
101   **Heu — futurae** Cf. Prop. 3.8.15; Celtis, *Am.* 4.3.59: "Venturae mortis terrent simu-
       lacra sopitum."
       noctis . . . simulachra Ov. *Ep.* 13.111. The *simulachra* are the malevolent ghosts of
       the dead, known as *lemures* or *larvae*. Cf. George Thaniel, "*Lemures* and *Larvae*," *The
       American Journal of Philology* 94 (1973), 182–87.
       simulachra futurae = Sil. 7.119.
102   **extremos . . . dies** = *Her. Chr.* 17.230, n.
103   **Seu — premuntur** Cf. Ov. *Ep.* 16.101.
       vigilant oculi Cf. *Her. Chr.* 3.131, n.
       caeca . . . nocte = *Ciris* 523; cf. Eob. *Buc.* 8.36, n.
       nocte premuntur = Verg. *A.* 6.827.

104 **variis . . . modis** = Ov. *Tr.* 2.432 (different); Maxim. 4.14.

   hoste minante = Alan. *Parab.* 3, col. 587 A.

105 **turbant insomnia mentem** = Damasus, *Epigr.*, ed. Maximilian Ihm (Leipzig, 1895), 27.9: "nocte soporifera turbant insomnia mentem"; cf. Eob. *Buc.* 7.121, n. The term *insomnia* often denotes frightening dreams: see, for instance, Verg. *A.* 4.9, of Dido; Eob. *Her. Chr.* B 1.38.

107–09 **Saepe — terra** Mary's symbolic dream is closely modeled on Verg. *A.* 4.465–68, describing Dido's nightmares just before her death.

107 **deserta per avia** = Lact. *Phoenix* 67.

108 **carpere . . . viam** = Celtis, *Am.* 2.13.42; cf. Ov. *Ars* 2.44; *Rem.* 214.

110 **Hostiles . . . timere minas** Cf. Mart. 6.76.4.

   omni parte = *Ama.* 35.8, n.

111 **agit — ille** Cf. Verg. *A.* 4.465–66.

   ferus ille — hostis = *Hod.* B 7.27 (the devil); cf. *Her. Chr.* 8.58, n.; 8.133; 15.11; 20.79.

112 **concessae . . . lucis** Mutius, *Triumph.*, sig. C2ʳ: ". . . aetheria concessa in luce quiete."

   tempore lucis *Her. Chr.* 15.192, n.

113 **te . . . tardante** Cf. the *vita* (*PL* 73, col. 686 C): "Beatissima autem illa tardante muliere, Zosimas non dormitavit, sed sollicite attendebat solitudinem, sustinens quod videre desiderabat." For this motif shifting, cf. l. 158, n., below.

   nostro . . . periclo = Prop. 1.15.27.

114 **Spes — mei** Mary's hope for the viaticum fans the dying embers of her life.

   Spes tamen est = Ov. *Ep.* 19.207; cf. *Ep.* 3.142: "sustinet hoc animae spes tamen una tui."

   animi — mei Cf. Poliziano, *Eleg.* 5.30: ". . . o animi portus et aura mei"; Eob. *Her. Chr.* 5.40, n.

115 **Spiritus . . . aeger** *Her. Chr.* 5.103, n.

   infirmis . . . artubus Lucr. 1.260; Ov. *Met.* 6.27.

116 **Ut — humo** For the image, cf. *Her. Chr.* 3.124.

   dura . . . laborat humo ≈ Ov. *Fast.* 4.416.

117–26 **Utque vagus — choris** Mary paraphrases Vulg. *Psa.* 41.2–3, according to the version often found in mss. and early printed eds.: "Quemadmodum desiderat cervus ad fontes aquarum, ita desiderat anima mea ad te, Deus. Sitivit anima mea ad Deum fontem vivum [for "fortem vivum"]. Quando veniam et apparebo ante faciem Dei?" Cf. Eobanus' paraphrase of these verses in *Psalt.* 42.1–8:

> Ut vagus absentes aspirat cervus ad undas
> Ut cursu nimio languida membra levet
> Omnibus impatiensque iugis et vallibus errat
> Arida ut invento pectora fonte riget:
> Sic sitit hic animus vivum, sua gaudia, fontem,
> Sic mea viventem mens sitit aegra Deum.
> Quando erit ut veniam et vultus ferar ante beatos,
> Ante creatoris numina sancta Dei?

117 **Utque vagus . . . cervus** Cf. Ov. *Tr.* 3.11.11.

   liquidas . . . undas = Catul. 64.2; Ov. *Met.* 1.95; 4.380.

118 **gravem . . . sitim** = Andrel. *Livia* 4.1.16.

   poto . . . angue For the wording, cf. Mart. *Sp.* 3.4; Eob. *Nup.* 25.

119 **iugis et vallibus** Cf. Ov. *Met.* 14.425. Cf. also Verg. *A.* 4.72, referring to Dido.

   vallibus errat = Stat. *Theb.* 5.523; cf. Eob. *Buc.* 1.45, n.

120 **Arida . . . pectora** V. Fl. 4.699–700.

121–22 **Sic animus — Deum** Cf. Vulg. *Luc.* 22.19–20; *Joan.* 6.35; *1. Cor.* 11.23–25.

121   **sua gaudia** = Verg. *A.* 10.652; Ov. *Ars* 2.419, 481; et al.
122   **mens . . . aegra** [Tib.] 3.4.19; Ov. *Tr.* 3.8.25; 5.2.7; et al.; Eob. *Her. Chr.* 21.46, n.
123   **Quis dabit** = *Her. Chr.* 4.87, n.
       corpus . . . caducum Cic. *N. D.* 1.98; Aus. *Prof.* 2.31; Paul. Nol. *Carm.* 23.225.
125–26 **Quando — choris** Cf. *Psalt.* 13.3–4: "Quando erit ut videam et vultus ferar ante beatos, / In quibus est miseris spesque salusque tuis?"
125   **Quando erit ut** = Ov. *Ep.* 7.19; 13.117.
126   **superis . . . choris** = Locher, "Hecatostichon in proludium," *Stult.*, fol. 9ʳ; Dantiscus, *Carm.* 1.3.396.
       gloria plena = *Her. Chr.* 8.120, n.
127   **Credo — fides** = Verg. *A.* 4.12; cf. Eob. *Buc.* 4.21, n.
129   **carne resurgam** *Vict.* 433.
130   **summa dies** Verg. *A.* 2.324; Ov. *Am.* 3.9.27; et al. Christian writers often use the phrase to refer to Judgment Day: see, for example, Juvenc. 1.706.
131   **patiendae . . . mortis** = *Her. Chr.* 23.11.
       vulnera mortis = Alcuin. *Carm.* 70.3.2; Eob. *Her. Chr.* 23.79.
132   **Haec est — sinu** ≈ *Psalt.* 27.16; cf. *Her. Chr.* 1.166, n.
133   **Non tamen ante** = Catul. 64.188; Ov. *Met.* 14.724.
       isto — carcere vitae Cf. *Her.* 2.4.161: ". . . ab humanae resolutus carcere vitae." For the old idea that the body is the soul's prison, see, for example, Plato, *Phd.* 82e–83d; *Phdr.* 250c; *Cratylus* 400c; Cic. *Rep.* 6.14; *Tusc.* 1.74; *Scaur.* 4: "corpore animus tamquam carcere saeptus teneretur"; Verg. *A.* 6.734. It is also a commonplace in Christian writers. See, for example, Tert. *Apol.* 17: "[anima] carcere corporis pressa"; August. *Enarrationes in Psa.* 141.18: "posset dici et corpus nostrum carcer, non quia carcer est quod fecit Deus, sed quia poenale et mortale"; Juvenc. 1.192; Prud. *Perist.* 13.62–64. Cf. Eob. *Sylv. duae* 1.13–14; *Her. Chr.* 16.258; 23.55, 120; *Nob.* 47; *Vict.* 265–66; *Ebn.* 163–64.
       mortalis . . . vitae = Sen. *Apoc.* 4.1; cf. Verg. *G.* 4.326.
134   **spiritus iste** = Prop. 1.9.32; Ov. *Am.* 3.1.30.
135   **dona salutis** = V. Fl. 2.488; Juvenc. 2.66, 334; Eob. *Her.* 1.6.45.
136   **liceat — pedes** = Sabell. *In natal.* 8, sig. b4ᵛ: "Ante tuos liceat procubuisse pedes"; cf. Tib. 1.9.30; Ov. *Ep.* 12.186; Eob. *Her.* 1.3.90.
137   **Fiat ut hoc** = *Her. Chr.* 6.153.
       esse memento = Tib. 1.8.27; Ov. *Tr.* 3.11.29; Eob. *Vict.* 329.
139   **anxia pectora** *Her. Chr.* 9.147, n.
       pectora curis = Ov. *Pont.* 1.2.55; 1.8.53.
140   **requiem — mihi** Cf. Locher, *Stult.* 42, fol. 53ʳ: "fatuae . . . turba cohortis, / Quae requiem satyrae non sinit esse meae"; Eob. *Sylv. duae* 2.84, n.
142   **Haec — mei** Cf. *Her. Chr.* A 3.76; 7.18.
143   **spe ludis inani** = *Idyl.* 7.149; cf. Gunther, *Lig.* 1.457: ". . . veniae spe lusus inani"; Erasmus, *Carm.* 96.1: ". . . spe lusus inani"; Eob. *Buc.* 3.161, n.
145–46 **Ah, quoties . . . Ah, quoties** = Prop. 3.15.13–15; Ov. *Am.* 2.19.11–13; *Ep.* 16.241–43; et al.; Eob. *Her. Chr.* 16.179–80.
145   **rapidi . . . ad Iordanis undam** Cf. l. 1, n., above.
146   **refero . . . pedem** = Ov. *Tr.* 2.16.
149   **spes — abisset** Luc. 5.455.
150   **Ne dubita** = *Her. Chr.* 23.3, n.
151   **Sancte pater** = Prop. 4.9.71; Ov. *Fast.* 2.127; cf. Eob. *Her. Chr.* 11.5, n.
       promissaque . . . firma ≈ Ov. *Met.* 10.430.
       promissaque debita = Arator 1.141.
152   **Causa . . . magna decensque** = *Her.* 2.2.26; cf. Ov. *Ep.* 17.156; Eob. *Her. Chr.* 10.8.

153   **Non tibi — est** Cf. the *vita* (*PL* 73, col. 677 B), referring to the first time that Zosimas saw Mary: "Zosimas autem, aetatis senectam obliviscens et laborem non reputans itineris, tetendit rapidissimo cursu."
       tibi . . . oneri = Ov. *Ars* 2.586.
       tarda . . . senecta Ov. *Tr.* 4.8.23; Sen. *Her. F.* 849.

155   **rapidas . . . undas** = Lucr. 4.421; Ov. *Met.* 7.6. Cf. l. 1, n. above.
       placidissimus undas ≈ Petrarch, *Ep.* 3.1.5: "Sorgia surgit ibi, querulis placidissimus undis."

156   **Qui — tenet** Cf. *Her. Chr.* 22.34, n.
       nomina . . . tenet = Ov. *Ars* 1.288; *Fast.* 4.160; 6.578; *Pont.* 3.2.70.

157   **olim — aequor** See Vulg. *Matt.* 14.25; *Marc.* 6.48; *Joan.* 6.19.
       placidum . . . aequor Verg. *A.* 8.96; 10.103.

158   **ibis — pede** For the phrasing, cf. Ov. *Met.* 14.50; *Tr.* 3.10.40. The motif comes from the *vita* (*PL* 73, col. 687 D). There, however, it is Mary who walks on the Jordan, not the monk. For a similar motif shifting, see l. 113, n., above.
       sicco . . . pede Calp. *Ecl.* 2.14; Prud. *Apoth.* 666; *Psych.* 652–53.

161   **Haec — illo** Cf. *Her. Chr.* 3.74, n.

162   **male — manu** Cf. Prop. 4.3.5–6.
       frigenti Cf. *Buc.* 3.47, n.
       verba — manu = Ov. *Ars* 2.596; cf. Eob. *Her. Chr.* 3.86, n.

163   **Cernis ut** = *Buc.* 4.50, n.
       aerea . . . ab ulmo = Verg. *Ecl.* 1.58.

165   **Attamen . . . satis est** Cf. Ov. *Met.* 3.283.
       hanc . . . cecinisse querelam = *Idyl.* 17.234; cf. *Nob.* 225: ". . . cecinisse querelam"; Verg. *G.* 1.378, of frogs.
       satis est cecinisse = Strozzi, *Eroticon* 1.2.65: "At mihi formosam satis est cecinisse puellam"; cf. Verg. *Ecl.* 10.70.

166   **Quod superest** = *Her. Chr.* 6.147, n.

15

Meter: Elegiac distich.

1   **nigro . . . cucullo** *Rec.* 59.

3   **Et nisi tu nosses** According to the *vita*, St. Nonius remained unaware of Pelagia's pious deceit.

6   **causa duobus erit** ≈ Ov. *Am.* 1.10.2.

7   **perdita mundo** *Her. Chr.* 14.66.

8   **regni divitioris** ≈ Ov. *Ep.* 16.34.

10   **Qur — pedes** Cf. Ov. *Am.* 3.13.26; *Ars* 1.32; *Tr.* 2.248.
       exiguos . . . pedes Ov. *Am.* 3.3.7; *Ars* 1.622.

11   **perfidus hostis** = *Her. Chr.* 14.111, n.

12   **vulgo fabula facta** Cf. Mant. *Ecl.* 3.53: "populo iam fabula factus"; Tib. 1.4.83; Hor. *Ep.* 1.13.9.

13   **vir et mulier** = Ov. *Rem.* 659.

14   **Vir reliquis — tibi** Cf. Mart. 4.42.14.

15   **nomine dicta** = Ov. *Met.* 8.235; Eob. *Nup.* 104.

16   **In prima . . . fronte** Lucr. 1.879; 4.97; Ov. *Tr.* 1.7.33.

17   **soror et frater** = Magdal. *Ep.* 97.
       fratremque patremque = Man. 5.465; cf. Ov. *Met.* 7.51.

18   **erit — meo** Cf. Prop. 4.3.4. For the motif, see Eob. *Her. Chr.* 2.3, n.

19   **arma . . . desueta** Verg. *A.* 2.509.

20   **Ingenio . . . meo** = Prop. 4.1.66; Ov. *Am.* 2.17.34.
      pristina vita = Locher, *Stult.* 78, fol. 90ᵛ.

22   **officiosa manus** = *Epic.* 3.148.

23   **nudam . . . papyrum** *Her. Chr.* 2.120.

25–26 **Conscia . . . sceleris . . . Mens** Mant. *2. Parthen.* 3.374; cf. Eob. *Buc.* 10.88, n.; *Her. Chr.* 11.13, n.; 13.44; *Her.* 1.6.22.

27   **in . . . mores abiere** Ov. *Ep.* 15.83.

28   **meminisse dolor** *Her. Chr.* 6.33, n.

29   **sentina malorum** = Petrarch, *Ep.* 3.33.6; Eob. *Sylv.* 2.1.43; *Tum.* 4.17; *Psalt.* 130.1. Cf. the proverbial *Lerna malorum* (Erasmus, *Adag.* 1.3.27).

30   **erecta . . . fronte** Mant. *1. Parthen.* 2.721.
      nubila — gerit Cf. *Sylv. duae* 2.70, n.; *Her. Chr.* A 3.20, n.

31   **male — flagellat** For the image, cf. Lucr. 3.1018–19; Juv. 13.192–95; Bebel, *Prov.* 15.

32   **Lucida — caput** Cf. *Psalt.* 30.4: "Lucida iussisti tollere ad astra caput." Cf. further Eobanus' verse letter in Trebelius, *Epigr.*, sig. F1ᵛ: ". . . tollit ad astra caput." For the motif, cf. Ov. *Fast.* 2.75; *Met.* 1.86; Sil. 15.84–85.
      Lucida . . . astra = Ov. *Pont.* 2.9.62; cf. Eob. *Buc.* 5.63, n.

33   **prior . . . vita** *Her. Chr.* 11.127, n.

34   **Hei mihi — dies** The line is modeled on Ov. *Ars* 2.170.
      Hei mihi, quam = *Sylv. duae* 1.188, n.
      multos . . . dies = *Her. Chr.* 1.38, n.

35–36 **Formosa — eram** Cf. *Ama.* 35.97–98 (of a prostitute); *Her. Chr.* 9.105–06.

36   **mephytis eram** ≈ *Her. Chr.* 12.184.

37   **sublime ferebar** = *Buc.* 8.60; cf. Lucr. 4.133; Verg. *Ecl.* 9.29; Nemes. *Ecl.* 1.18.

38   **putri . . . luto** = *Ama.* 35.92; *Her. Chr.* 11.116. For the insinuation that Pelagia lived like a sow, see l. 42 below.

39   **Saepe aliquis . . . euntem** = Ov. *Am.* 3.1.19.
      aliquis spectans = Ov. *Am.* 3.15.11.

40   **facta nocens** = *Sylv. duae* 1.148, n.

43   **Extulit . . . superbia mentem** Cf. Vulg. *Abd.* 3: "superbia cordis tui extulit te"; Claud. *Cons. Mall. Theod.* 244 (Prud. *Psych.* 203): ". . . superbia mentem."
      elatam . . . mentem = Mant. *c. Am.*, fol. 177ᵛ: "amor elatam studuit subvertere mentem."
      damnosa superbia = Ov. *Ars* 3.509.

45   **Quae fora, quae plateae** Cf. *Her. Chr.* 22.56, n.

46   **plena theatra** = *Her.*, ded. 52; cf. Prop. 3.18.13; Ov. *Tr.* 5.7.25.

47   **Torta — lacertos** Modeled on Mant. *Ecl.* 1.73: "nuda pedem, discincta sinum, spoliata lacertos."
      fucata genas = Claud. *Cons. Stil.* 2.136; cf. Eob. *Nob.* 65, 83.

48   **Cura iuventutis** Cf. Hor. *Carm.* 2.8.7–8.

49   **instantem — senectam** For the thought that old age steals upon us unawares, see, for example, Cic. *Sen.* 2.4; Ov. *Ars* 2.670; *Tr.* 3.7.35–36; Juv. 9.128–29; Erasmus, *Carm.* 2.110–11.
      instantem . . . senectam ≈ Marul. *Epigr.* 1.21.3: "Lilia [mitto], ut instantis monearis virgo senectae"; cf. Hor. *Carm.* 2.14.3.

50   **nata puella** = Ov. *Am.* 2.5.4; *Ep.* 16.198.
      rosis Sacred to Venus, the rose often symbolizes spring and youth: cf. *Buc.* 7.168–70, nn.

51   **pro crimine poenam** = Luc. 8.781.

52   **non moritura** = Prop. 4.6.64.

53   **Nec — monentem** The inability to accept criticism is a sure sign of folly. Cf. Vulg. *Prov.* 1.7; *Eccl.* 1.15; Locher, *Stult.* 51, fol. 62ʳ–62ᵛ, especially fol. 62ᵛ: "Nec sinit [fatuus] ut quisquam sibi dogmata sana ministret, / Nec patitur quenquam qui corrigit aut monet ipsum."
      monuisset . . . monentem Cf. Ov. *Ars* 2.509.

54   **pectus saxo durius** *Psalt.* 22, arg. 4; cf. Otto 1593; Häussler, 79, 116, 209; Ov. *Ep.* 21.229.
55–60   **Ah, pudet — feram** Cf. *Her. Chr.* 11.73–78; 14.53–56.
55   **Ah, pudet ulterius** = *Eccles.* 143.
            veterum — malorum Verg. *A.* 11.280; cf. *A.* 6.527; Ov. *Met.* 12.542.
60   **Sed queror** = Ov. *Ep.* 7.30.
            tristis et aegra Tifernate, "Triumphus Cupidinis," *Carm.*, sig. A8ʳ, quoted in Eob. *Ama.* 29.1.
61   **primo . . . vulnere** Luc. 8.72; Man. 5.182; Stat. *Silv.* 3.5.24; 5.1.18.
62   **stigmata nigra** = Locher, "Socialis navis mechanicorum," *Stult.*, fol. 139ᵛ: "culpas et stygmata nigra merentur."
65   **pater inclyte** = Avit. *Carm.* 3.420; cf. Stat. *Silv.* 1.4.95; 3.4.48.
66   **Nullus — erit** Cf. Ov. *Tr.* 5.13.14; Eob. *Her. Chr.* 6.52, n.
68   **vulnera nostra** = *Her. Chr.* 5.174, n.
70   **longas . . . manus** = Ov. *Ep.* 17.166.
            littera scripta = Ov. *Ep.* 5.24; Eob. *Her. Chr.* 10.186.
72   **fulminis instar** = Ov. *Ars* 3.490. For the metaphor, see Eob. *Laud.* 120, n.
73–74   **Quis montibus — aquas** Cf. Ov. *Am.* 2.10.13–14.
73   **montibus umbras** ≈ Verg. *Ecl.* 1.83; *G.* 1.342; *A.* 1.607; Eob. *Her. Chr.* 16.185.
74   **gelidas . . . aquas** Tib. 1.1.47; Mart. 14.33.2.
            vitreis fontibus = Andrel. *Livia* 3.2.12; cf. Eob. *Ama.* 32.33, n.
75   **Moerentem . . . animum** Paul. Nol. *Carm.* 31.382: "Maerentes animos."
76   **Ex Stygia revocas . . . aqua** Cf. Ov. *Tr.* 5.9.19.
            Stygia . . . aqua = Ov. *Pont.* 2.3.44.
77   **ultima primis** = Hor. *S.* 1.4.59; Ov. *Ep.* 9.23.
79   **iusta trutinat . . . bilance** *Laud.* 457, n.
81–85   **Ergo — votis** For the adynata, cf. *Buc.* 10.98–101, n. For ll. 83–84, cf. especially Verg. *Ecl.* 1.59–62; for l. 84, cf. Eob. *Sylv.* 1.11.36: "Sydera conversis prius omnia legibus ibunt, / Quique modo est oriens, hic modo vesper erit"; Ov. *Ib.* 38: "[prius] eadem regio vesper et ortus erit."
81   **mendacia vatum** = Ov. *Am.* 3.6.17; *Fast.* 6.253; cf. Eob. *Her. Chr.* 17.131; also cf. *Her. Chr.* 1.151.
82   **Solari . . . lampade** Cf. Verg. *A.* 4.6; Sil. 10.111; Eob. *Buc.* 9.95, n.
85   **pectora votis** = Paul. Nol. *Carm.* 19.433; 26.9.
86   **Devotam — Deo** Cf. Ov. *Ep.* 20.2; 21.4; Eob. *Rec.* 165, n.
87   **assiduis . . . solibus** = Poliziano, *Epigr.* 6.3; cf. Lucr. 5.252; Ov. *Ep.* 5.112.
88   **quod fuit, esse** = Ov. *Ep.* 1.48.
89   **Sicut . . . phoenix . . . igne** = Mant. *Lud. Morb.*, fol. 227ʳ: "Sicut in ardenti phoenix se collocat igne, / Ut reparet vitae tempora longa suae."
            phoenix — igne ≈ Brant, *Var. carm.*, sig. A7ʳ (*Texte* 103.35): "Unica semper avis foenix reparatur in igne"; Eob. *Ruf.* 63: "Nobilis aereo foenix reparatur in igne"; cf. *Her. Chr.* 9.57, with n. 7.
90   **iuvenis — senex** Cf. Ov. *Fast.* 6.88.
93   **dulcis amor** *Buc.* 3.46, n.
94   **maxime Christe** = Pontano, *Laud.* 6.10; 7.10; Eob. *Sylv.* 1.10.12.
95   **quas toto — orbe** Cf. *Buc.* 2.37, n.
            toto . . . ab orbe = *Nob.* 231; cf. *Ama.* 35.7, n.
96   **quas totus — opes** Cf. Ov. *Ars* 3.114; *Met.* 7.59; [Tib.] 3.3.30; Eob. *Psalt.* 19.50: "Quascunque immensus continet orbis opes."
98   **toto pectore** = *Her. Chr.* 6.142, n.
99–100   **Gratia — iter** Cf. *Her. Chr.* 6.137–38, n.
101   **Ah, quoties** = *Her. Chr.* 1.43, n.
101–02   **niveo . . . notanda lapillo . . . dies** Cf. Plin. *Ep.* 6.11.3; Mant. *Sylv.* 1, fol. 259ʳ: "luxit niveo signanda lapillo / . . . dies."

103   **sacra . . . in aede sacerdos** *Buc.* 10.78, n.
104   **Aeterni . . . Tonantis** Mant. *1. Parthen.* 2.594.
       praeco Tonantis Cf. Prud. *c. Symm.* 1, praef. 1: "Paulus, praeco Dei"; Eob. *Her.* 1.5.85: "Dei preco."
105   **mundi — honores** = *Eccles.* 295; cf. Paul. Nol. *Carm.* 21.505: ". . . mundi fallentis imago"; Eob. *Her. Chr.* 15.149, n.
106   **verbis . . . tuis** = Ov. *Am.* 3.14.46; *Ep.* 13.110 (in the mss. and early eds.); 19.22.
107–08 **sit in hac — cruces** Cf. *Her. Chr.* 17.53–54; *Luth.* 3.69–70.
107   **brevis et . . . voluptas** = Ov. *Pont.* 1.2.51; cf. Eob. *Ama.* 35.101, n.
       brevis et fugitiva Mart. 12.96.4: "brevis . . . et fugitiva Venus."
110   **Ante — choros** Cf. *Her. Chr.* 18.88, n.
       umbra beata = Andrel. *Livia* 4.3.48: "Haelysiis umbra beata plagis."
111–12 **Quamque — mori** These verses are based on the proverbial saying *Mors certa, hora incerta.* Cf., for example, Anselm, *Meditationes* 7, *PL* 158, col. 741 A: "Nihil certius morte, nihil hora mortis incertius. Cogitemus ergo quam brevis sit vita nostra, quam lubrica via, quam certa mors, et hora mortis incerta"; Bernard of Clairvaux, *Ep.* 105, in *S. Bernardi opera,* vol. 7, ed. J. Leclercq and H. Rochais (Rome, 1974), 264: "Nil mortalibus vel morte certius, vel incertius hora mortis"; Petrarch, *Secretum* 1, in *Opere latine di Francesco Petrarca,* ed. Antonietta Bufano (Turin, 1975), 1:82: "nil morte certius, nil hora mortis incertius"; Walther 15117: "Mors certa est, incerta dies"; 15123; 15133; 15134. For the thought, cf. also Cic. *Sen.* 74: "Moriendum enim certe est, et incertum an hoc ipso diem."
111   **nos — solvat** Cf. Verg. *A.* 4.703.
113   **facili — aura** = *Theoc.* 2.8 (referring to inconstant love); cf. *Epic.* 2.24. For *facili aura,* see Ov. *Ep.* 18.45; Eob. *Ama.* 35.83.
114   **verbis . . . usus eras** ≈ Ov. *Fast.* 6.120.
       verbis talibus = *Her. Chr.* 12.134, n.
115   **Bulla . . . homo** A proverbial expression. See *Buc.* 7.170, n.
       ventus Vulg. *Job* 7.7.
       flos . . . et umbra Vulg. *Job* 14.2.
       pulvis, et umbra = Paul. Nol. *Carm.* 10.289; cf. Hor. *Carm.* 4.7.16.
116   **Incipit — perit** Cf. *Epic.* 2.112.
117–18 **Umbrae   somnium . . . , umbraque   fumi, . . . punctum . . . temporis** These images are taken from Erasmus, *Adag.* 2.3.48, "Homo bulla," *ASD* 2.3:260, ll. 958–74.
121   **Accessi — rogabam** Cf. *Her. Chr.* 14.79, n.
       supplex . . . rogabam Ov. *Am.* 2.5.49; Stat. *Theb.* 10.422–23; *Ach.* 1.50.
       populo spectante = Hor. *Ep.* 1.6.60; Mart. 7.82.5; Eob. *Vict.* 485; l. 151 below.
122   **Curvato . . . poplite** Cf. *Her. Chr.* 2.62, n.
       flexa genu *Her. Chr.* 16.241.
123   **lingua . . . potens** Vulg. *Eccli.* 21.8; Aus. *Ep.* 9(b).10; Eob. *Luth.* 3.4.
       venerande sacerdos = Prud. *Perist.* 11.179.
125   **multiplicis . . . obruta culpae** = l. 135 below; cf. *Her.* 1.6.23: "multiplicis . . . piacula noxae."
126   **Me miseram** = *Her. Chr.* 3.111, n.
       fasso . . . ore = *Her. Chr.* 5.176, n.
127   **nimis indulsisse** = *Epic.* 2.59: "Sed quid opus iusto nimis indulsisse dolori."
128   **declivem . . . viam** Ov. *Met.* 4.432; 7.410 (in both cases referring to the road down to Hades).
       isse viam = Prop. 1.20.18.
130   **Ad veniam reditus si** = liminary epigram, l.4, in Judocus Textor, *Forma recte penitendi et confitendi* (Erfurt, 1515); cf. *Psalt.* 51, arg. 3.
131   **Multa — vetuere** Cf. *Her. Chr.* 22.167, n.
       Multa precaturam = *Her. Chr.* 4.99, n.

132   **quaerere . . . queri** Sen. *Ben.* 6.32.3: "maluit queri quam quaerere"; Eob. *Idyl.* 17.12.
133   **Ne dubita** = *Her. Chr.* 23.3, n.
        spera bene = *Max.* 133; cf. *Rec.* 97, n.
        siste querelas Ov. *Met.* 7.711.
134   **facili . . . manu** = Tib. 1.1.8; Ov. *Ars* 1.160.
135   **multiplicis . . . obruta culpae** = l. 125, n., above.
136   **Non est — tibi** = *Sylv.* 2.7.14; 9.10.10.
        ianua clausa = *Her. Chr.* 1.74, n.
137   **Tanta Dei pietas** ≈ Paul. Nol. *Carm.* 6.103: "quanta Dei pietas!"; cf. Eob. *Her. Chr.*
        14.19, n.
        clementia Christi = Paul. Nol. *Carm.* 23.316; Eob. *Her. Chr.* 21.183.
139–40 **Quam misere — manum** Cf. August. *Enarrationes in Psa.* 95.7: "descendit enim ad
        te ille qui non cadit: tu cecideras, ille descendit, porrexit tibi manum."
140   **porrigit ille manum** ≈ Ov. *Pont.* 4.5.28. Cf. Erasmus, *Adag.* 4.9.8: "Porrigere manus."
141   **Venit — quenquam** Cf. Vulg. *Luc.* 9.55 (in many mss. and eds.): "filius hominis non
        venit animas perdere, sed salvare"; Eob. *Tum.* 2.187: "Qui venit servare omnes, non
        perdere quenquam."
        perdere quenquam = Juvenc. 3.417.
142   **Per quem — sumus** Cf. *Her. Chr.* 6.8, n.
143   **Magna — vetustas** Cf. Cic. *Arch.* 14: "plena exemplorum vetustas"; Boeth. *Consol.*
        3.5.2: "plena est exemplorum vetustas, plena etiam praesens aetas"; Eob. *Ama.* 24.2:
        "Exemplis plena est omnis vetustas"; *Sylv. duae* 2.213.
144   **de multis pauca** = *Epic.*, app. 5.50; *Sylv.* 6.1.48; cf. *Nor.* 818; Lact. *Inst.* 5.9.18: "de
        multis pauca collegi"; Hier. *Ep.* 127.10: "vix de multis pauca dicere"; Magdal. *Erarium*,
        ded., sig. A2ᵛ (at this metrical position): "e multis pauca."
146   **Magdalis** This form first appears in late medieval patristic literature: see *PL* 202, cols.
        834 A, 834 D, and 837 C: "Maria Magdalis"; col. 838 A: "Magdalis." Eobanus uses
        the form again at l. 156 below.
147   **accessit . . . gratia Christi** ≈ *Her.* 1.6.157: "Non temere accessit magno tua gratia
        Christo." For the tag *gratia Christi*, see, for example, Paul. Nol. *Carm.* 16.283;
        18.166, 182; 21.832; Juvenc. 4.803.
148   **turba beata** = Mant. *Bapt.*, fol. 229ᵛ.
149   **placidum . . . amorem** = *Venus* 1.259; cf. Tib. 2.1.80.
        mundi — amorem ≈ Paul. Nol. *Carm.* 19.40: "mundi fallentis amores"; cf. l. 105,
        n., above.
150   **Fide — tuas** Cf. *Eccles.* 36; *Psalt.* 37, arg. 4: "Fide Deo. Sordes eluet ille tuas."
        Maculas diluet ≈ Prud. *Perist.* 8.6: "veteres maculas diluit amne novo."
151   **populo spectante** = l. 121, n., above.
152   **pectora nostra** = Ov. *Ep.* 11.58; 15.212; 17.92, 178; et al.
154   **Dulce melos** = Alcuin. *Carm.* 61.9; Eob. *Vict.* 317.
        nostris auribus = Mart. 4.41.2.
156   **veteri . . . caho** *Her. Chr.* 10.160, n.
        surgere iussa = Plin. *Nat.* 31.7, quoting an epigram by M. Tullius Laurea; cf. Eob.
        Her. Chr. 16.210.
157   **Laeticia . . . potiore** *Sylv. duae* 2.56.
160   **vitae . . . prioris** *Her. Chr.* 11.127, n.
161   **vigilatae . . . noctes** = Ov. *Ars* 1.735.
162   **assiduis fletibus** Catul. 64.242.
163   **miserum . . . miserescere** For the wordplay, cf. *Her. Chr.* 12.275, n.
164   **Fulcita — ruina** Cf. Ov. *Tr.* 1.6.5; 5.13.8; *Pont.* 2.3.60; Luc. 8.528.
        nostra ruina = Ov. *Pont.* 3.1.56; Mart. 13.25.2.
165   **obscurae . . . noctis** = Aus. *Ephem.* 3.15; cf. Tib. 1.2.24; Verg. *A.* 2.420; 4.461.
        mersam caligine ≈ Stat. *Theb.* 10.735; cf. Eob. *Her. Chr.* 6.147, n.
        caligine noctis = Sil. 11.513; Eob. *Vict.* 60, 201, 421.

166 **verum — diem** *Consol.* 98; cf. Prop. 4.2.6; Ov. *Pont.* 1.3.34; [Tib.] 3.4.48.

168 **Monstras — viam** Cf. Ov. *Pont.* 2.9.62; Eob. *Her. Chr.* 6.140, n.; *Nob.* 64, n.

169–72 **Iactatam — levas** Cf. *Sylv.* 7.2.5–6: "Ac mea si Stygio quassarit tempora ramo, / Exicio venit qui, Palinure, tibi"; also cf. *Her. Chr.* 8.121–28, n.

169 **Iactatam dubio . . . aequore** Cf. Verg. *A.* 1.29; Ov. *Pont.* 4.10.10; Eob. *Her. Chr.* 16.17; 17.145; 19.43; *Vict.* 40–41.

  dubio — ventis Cf. Lucr. 2.1.

  dubio . . . aequore = *Sylv.* 3.11.9: "dubio deprensus in aequore nauta."

  pugnantibus . . . ventis Lucr. 6.98; cf. Eob. *Buc.* 9.35, n.

170 **Typhi** Ov. *Ep.* 6.48; *Tr.* 4.3.77.

171 **somnifero . . . ramo** Cf. Ov. *Met.* 1.671–72, of Mercury's caduceus.

  tempora ramo = Verg. *A.* 7.135.

172 **lumina nocte** = Tib. 1.9.42; Ov. *Ars* 3.648.

174 **Non hac — via** Cf. Verg. *A.* 9.641; Eob. *Her. Chr.* 6.144; 23.98; 24.28, n.

  ad astra via = Celtis, *Am.* 4.1.54; cf. Eob. *Her. Chr.* 6.140, n.

178 **infames . . . aquas** = Mant. *c. Poet.* 52: "stringit ubi infames sulfuris ardor aquas."

  praecipitasset aquas = *Her. Chr.* 9.14, n.

179 **Ionio . . . profundo** = Sil. 11.22; 14.73.

  sulcans vada glauca Cf. *Her. Chr.* 14.69, n.

  sulcans vada = Mant. *Calam.* 1.62 (p. 20); cf. Verg. *A.* 5.158.

  vada glauca Prud. *Apoth.* 664.

180 **dulci . . . exitio** Sil. 12.35–36 (brought about by one of the Sirens); Eob. *Sylv.* 6.6.38 (caused by the Sirens): "Ne dulce incautos perderet exitium."

181 **duo lustra vagantem** Cf. Ov. *Pont.* 4.10.10; 4.16.14; Eob. *Hod.* 1.

182 **in patriam . . . humum** = Andrel. *Livia* 3.5.18; cf. Eob. *Accl.* 1.122; Ov. *Tr.* 3.3.32.

183 **blandas . . . querelas** = [Tib.] 3.4.75.

  audire querelas ≈ Catul. 64.195; Ov. *Fast.* 3.471.

184 **seque suosque** = Aus. *Parent.* 5.8; cf. Catul. 64.201.

185 **vicina . . . morte** *Her. Chr.* 6.119, n.

186 **Forte — canes** Cf. *Her. Chr.* 11.70.

  infernos . . . canes Cf. Hor. *S.* 1.8.35; Luc. 6.733; Eob. *Sylv. duae* 2.103, n.

  nova praeda Ov. *Am.* 1.2.19; *Ep.* 15.51.

  praeda canes = Mart. 10.37.14.

187 **Umbra . . . nuda** Stat. *Theb.* 9.298.

  Laethaeis . . . undis ≈ *Culex* 215; Mart. 7.96.7.

188 **quantis . . . malis** = Prop. 2.16.30.

189 **At bene — quod** Ov. *Ep.* 4.33; cf. Eob. *Her. Chr.* 7.15.

  gaudia falsa = *Her. Chr.* 11.143, n.

191 **Quae simul agnovi** ≈ Ov. *Met.* 5.471; 11.94.

192 **tempora lucis** = Ov. *Fast.* 3.404; cf. Eob. *Her. Chr.* 14.112.

193–98 **Sic — videt** The image may have been inspired by the cave myth in Plato, *R.* 7.514a–516b.

193 **Sic aliquis** = *Ama.* 35.99, n.; l. 199 below.

  caeco . . . in antro Maxim. 1.141; cf. Luc. 4.458.

  enutritus in antro Cf. Ov. *Met.* 4.289; Sil. 8.514; 14.527.

194 **Lucis egens** = Ov. *Met.* 1.17.

195 **Qui simul invisae** ≈ Sil. 2.526.

196 **caeca . . . domo** Ov. *Ib.* 372; cf. Eob. *Vict.* 225.

197 **formas . . . colores** = Lucr. 2.1005.

  mille colores = Ov. *Rem.* 353; *Met.* 6.65.

198 **inexpleto lumine** Ov. *Met.* 3.439 (of Narcissus gazing at his own image).

199–202 **Sic — dolet** For the image, cf. Vulg. *Psa.* 72.20; Eob. *Ebn.* 149–50; *Consol.* 87–100.

199	**Sic aliquis** = *Ama.* 35.99, n.; l. 193 above.
	aliquis, spectans = Ov. *Am.* 3.15.11.
	fallacis inania somni Cf. *Her. Chr.* 4.15, n.
200	**Mente soporata** Mant. *Calam.* 3.910 (p. 93): "Clara soporatas illustrent lumina mentes."
	gaudia vera = Mart. 7.5.2.
201–02	**Ut — Damnat** Cf. Ov. *Met.* 7.643: "Somnus abit; damno vigilans mea visa."
202	**et ex animo** = Ov. *Am.* 2.5.51.
	ex animo . . . cecidisse = Hutten, *Querel.* 2.2.4: "Non decet ex animo me cecidisse tuo"; cf. *Querel.* 2.2.10: "Quid cadit ex animo Fagina Musa tuo?"; Celtis, *Am.* 2.11.44: "Nec cadet ex animo Norica terra tuo"; Eob. *Luth.* 7.14.
	non cecidisse = Ov. *Tr.* 1.11.10.
203	**ne . . . tuas offendam . . . aures** Cic. *Lig.* 24.
204	**Caetera — tuo** Cf. Ov. *Tr.* 3.4.56; Mart. 9.41.4.
205	**Sponte — eunti** For this proverbial expression, cf. Plin. *Ep.* 1.8.1; Erasmus, *Adag.* 1.2.47; Otto 486.
	Sponte sua = *Buc.* 1.6, n.
207	**canis albere capillis** = Ov. *Ep.* 13.161.
208	**Et prope — diem** Cf. Mant. *Votum*, fol. 55ʳ: "Non procul extremum suspicor esse diem."
	suspicor esse = *Her. Chr.* 4.18, n.
209–10	**Quid — tuo** Cf. Verg. *A.* 3.88–89.
209	**Quid faciam** = *Her. Chr.* 4.47, n.
211	**iniquo pondere** = Verg. *G.* 1.164.
212	**subdita turba** = Hutten. *Querel.* 2.8.80, addressed to Eobanus Hessus: "Cogitur a domino subdita turba suo." Eobanus here follows the closely related legend of St. Margaret. Having left her husband on her wedding night, she dressed as a man, entered a monastery as Brother Pelagius, and eventually became abbot: see *Leg. aurea* 147.
213	**post fata** = Verg. *A.* 4.20; Prop. 4.11.63; Ov. *Am.* 1.15.39; *Met.* 13.180.
216	**Sive . . . sive . . . soror** = [Tib.] 3.1.26.
217	**Iamque vale** = Verg. *G.* 4.497; *A.* 2.789; 5.738; 11.827; Ov. *Ep.* 9.165; *Met.* 2.363.
	nostris . . . querelis = Ov. *Ep.* 15.71: "Ultima tu nostris accedis causa querelis."
218	**placato . . . Deo** Ov. *Tr.* 1.3.40; 4.4.88; Eob. *Her. Chr.* 20.144.
	carmina — Deo = *Sylv.* 1.10.18; cf. *Sylv. duae* 2.244, n.

16

Meter: Elegiac distich.

1	**dilecte Deo** = Ven. Fort. *Carm.* 9.14.3; cf. Claud. *III. Cons. Hon.* 96; Eob. *Buc.* 11.41, n.
2	**Quae — erat** Cf. *Sylv.* 3.5.48: "Qui tibi, quo licuit tempore, frater eram."
	tempore, mater erat = *Nux* 17.
3	**Signa** Cf. Ov. *Tr.* 1.5.7; 4.4.7.
4	**Hic mihi causa** = Ov. *Fast.* 2.259.
5	**morientis — Christi** = *Sylv.* 2.27.3: "Sic stetit illa videns morientis vulnera Christi"; cf. *Her. Chr.* 6.39; Prud. *Perist.* 8.17: ". . . vulnera Christi."
6	**miseros . . . dies** Sen. *Her. O.* 642.
9–12	**Missus — meis** Cf. *Her. Chr.* 12.9–20.
9	**Rhomano a Caesare** = Mant. *Georgius*, fol. 213ᵛ; cf. Eob. *Her. Chr.* 12.9.
10	**ignotam . . . exul humum** = Marul. *Epigr.* 3.37.20: "Cum semel ignotam presseris exul humum." Cf. Ov. *Tr.* 3.8.2; Eob. *Her. Chr.* 5.116.

11–12	**Quae — meis** For the motif — fainting upon hearing bad news — see n. to *Her. Chr.* 7.51.
11	**fama improba** V. Fl. 5.82.
	contigit aures = Ov. *Ep.* 3.59; *Met.* 15.497; Eob. *Her. Chr.* 12.15.
12	**mortua pene** = *Her. Chr.* 8.118, n.
14	**graves . . . casus** = l. 20 below; cf. *Val.* 1.230; *Venus* 2.218.
15	**longoque — usu** = *Vict.* 119; cf. Ov. *Tr.* 5.2.5; Eob. *Buc.* 7.52, n.
16	**Pectoris — mei** Cf. Ov. *Ep.* 7.189.
	vulnera prima = Mart. 11.78.6.
17	**per . . . pelagus iactata malorum** Cf. *Vict.* 40–41; *Her. Chr.* 15.169, n.
	immensum pelagus = *Laud.* 153, n.
	pelagus . . . malorum Erasmus, *Adag.* 1.3.28 ("mare malorum"), translating Euripides, *Hipp.* 822–23: "Tantum malorum pelagus aspicio miser, / Unde enatandi nulla spes alluceat."
18	**gurgite mersa** ≈ Ov. *Fast.* 4.48.
19–40	**Tu quoque — agens** Cf. *Her. Chr.* 3.37–40, nn.
20	**graves . . . casus** = l. 14, n., above.
21	**Tu quoque, nostrarum . . . rerum** = Ov. *Tr.* 5.6.1.
	pars maxima rerum = Ov. *Ars* 3.229.
25	**Qui — sorori** Cf. Ov. *Ep.* 8.41; *Ars* 1.130.
	frater . . . sorori = Ov. *Ep.* 8.29.
27	**primum . . . ab illo** Cf. Ov. *Ep.* 20.157.
28	**qui nobis — erat** = Ov. *Ep.* 12.162; cf. Eob. *Her. Chr.* 16.61; 22.147.
31	**terramque genu . . . petebam** Cf. Lucr. 1.92.
	genu labente = *Her. Chr.* 20.15; *Ilias* 16.457; cf. *Ilias* 5.425; 14.548.
32	**officio . . . tuo** = Ov. *Am.* 1.10.46; 2.2.54; *Ep.* 8.30; et al.
	sum relevata tuo = *Her. Chr.* 4.136.
35	**sua viscera matres** = l. 111 below; cf. Ov. *Rem.* 59.
36	**impia turba** = Tib. 1.3.70; cf. Ov. *Met.* 3.629.
	turba minas = Ov. *Tr.* 1.2.60.
37	**Plura vetat** ≈ *Her. Chr.* 22.167.
	vetat — dolor Cf. Hutten, *Querel.* 1.2.50: "Non patitur durus commeminisse dolor"; Eob. *Idyl.* 7.90: "Nec patitur meminisse dolor. . . ."
37–38	**Quis caetera — genas** Cf. Verg. *A.* 2.6–8, 361–62.
38	**Pallentes . . . genas** Sen. *Ag.* 762; Stat. *Theb.* 2.506; V. Fl. 3.287.
	riget imbre genas Ov. *Ars* 1.532.
39	**omnia dura** *Her. Chr.* 13.43, n.
40	**fine quietus** Cf. *Sylv. duae* 1.65, n.
42	**sollicito pectore** = *Her. Chr.* 17.258; cf. Ov. *Met.* 2.125.
43	**exterrita fama** Cf. Ov. *Met.* 9.141: ". . . perterrita fama."
44	**saevo saevior angue** = Mant. *c. Am.*, fol. 177ʳ; cf. Eob. *Ama.* 32.3; *Her. Chr.* 1.121.
45	**Tunc — videri** Cf. Ov. *Am.* 1.7.5.
	esse videri = Ov. *Tr.* 4.1.37; Eob. *Her. Chr.* 3.167.
46	**resecta manu** = Ov. *Ars* 1.518; *Tr.* 5.7.18.
47	**Nata feris** If she were that cruel, she would be the offspring of wild beasts: cf. Catul. 60.1–3; Ov. *Ep.* 7.38; *Met.* 7.32; 8.121–22; 9.613.
	pavisse feras To prepare for l. 48, Eobanus varies the normal form of the ancient motif ("a wild animal suckled you"): cf. Verg. *A.* 4.367; Ov. *Met.* 9.615; *Tr.* 1.8.43–44; 3.11.3; *Ib.* 227–30.
	tigresque luposque = Erasmus, *Carm.* 6.47.
48	**potui — Deum** Cf. *Her. Chr.* 18.66.
49	**Duricia — Arcton** Cf. Ov. *Ep.* 2.137; Otto 17.
	Lycaonis Arcton = Verg. *G.* 1.138; cf. Eob. *Nup.* 20, n.
50	**non meruisse querar** = Ven. Fort. *Carm.*, app. 21.2.

51   **quis . . . sanguine iunctior** *Accl.* 1.35.
       agnato . . . sanguine *Tum.* 4.179.
52   **charior alter erat** ≈ Prop. 2.9.2; Eob. *Her. Chr.* 21.198.
55   **Ut taceam** = Ov. *Am.* 2.4.31; *Ep.* 3.134; *Tr.* 5.2.30.
56   **animi . . . sarcina** Cf. Ov. *Ep.* 4.24; l. 228 below, n.
58   **parente soror** = Ov. *Ep.* 4.64.
60   **abesse queror** = *Her. Chr.* 10.100, n.
61   **Omnia solus eras** Cf. l. 28, n., above.
63   **decus nostrum** Verg. *A.* 6.546.
       nostrae — salutis = *Psalt.* 18.117.
64   **cur nomen — fuit** To refer to her son by name would mean tearing open old
       wounds. Hence Mary mentions the name Jesus only once in this letter, in l. 197
       below, and then only in a quotation. Elsewhere she consistently paraphrases his
       name. Cf. Verg. *A.* 4.479, 495–498, where Dido refuses to utter the name *Aeneas.*
       dicere triste = Ov. *Ep.* 13.14.
65   **Nescio quae dulcedo** Verg. *G.* 1.412; 4.55; Ov. *Pont.* 1.3.35.
       renovare dolores ≈ Verg. *A.* 2.3.
67   **Maternum . . . pectus** Ov. *Am.* 1.13.32; Sen. *Phoen.* 469–70.
68   **tamen est aliquid** = Ov. *Met.* 15.408; *Tr.* 3.13.25.
       meminisse iuvet Cf. *Pug.* 5 and 6, nn.
69   **vicina — gravatus** Cf. Ov. *Met.* 4.145; Eob. *Psalt.* 123.3: ". . . oculos vicina
       morte gravatos." For *vicina morte,* see *Her. Chr.* 6.119, n.
71   **fractae . . . malis** *Max.* 329, n.
       passae . . . dolores [Sen.] *Oct.* 201; l. 229 below.
72   **interii** For the indicative in a vividly imagined unreal condition, see also l. 45 above
       ("potui").
73–74 **potuit . . . amare fide** Prop. 1.12.8; cf. Ov. *Am.* 1.3.6; *Ars* 3.544.
77   **Tempore ab hoc** = *Her. Chr.* 12.59, n.
78   **corpore tecta** *Her. Chr.* 1.204.
79   **Quot tulerim . . . non est numerare** *Buc.* 5.24; cf. Ov. *Tr.* 3.12.25.
80   **Tempore ab hoc** = *Her. Chr.* 12.59, n.
81–82 **cum mihi — "Ave"** Cf. *Her. Chr.* 1.5–6, nn.
       cum mihi . . . dixit . . . nuncius ales Cf. Ov. *Ep.* 16.68. Ovid's Mercury is here
       replaced with the Archangel Gabriel. Cf. n. at Eob. *Her. Chr.* 1.4.
81   **missus ab aethere** = Ov. *Met.* 7.219: "demissus ab aethere currus"; cf. Verg. *A.*
       4.574, of Mercury; Eob. *Buc.* 9.111, n.
82   **nuncius ales** = *Her. Chr.* 2.54, n.
83–84 **Tunc — magi** See Vulg. *Matt.* 2.1–12; cf. Eob. *Her. Chr.* 1.117–20.
83   **Tunc quoque cum** = *Her. Chr.* 3.107, n.
       sine crimine = *Her. Chr.* 7.15, n.
84   **tres tria dona** = Peter Riga, *Evangelium* 444: "puero cum simplice voto / Aurum,
       thus, myrram — tres tria dona — ferunt"; 949: "Post ortum Christi cum tres tria
       dona tulerunt."
85   **Laeta triumphata** ≈ Ov. *Am.* 1.2.39.
86   **Calcantemque — pede** Cf. Verg. *Ecl.* 5.57; Eob. *Vict.* 484, referring to the
       Ascension; *Epic.* 2.124, of a blessed soul in heaven: ". . . pedibus nubila regna
       premit." For *calcantem pede,* see Sen. *Phaed.* 234.
87   **patria . . . sede** Verg. *A.* 7.192–93; Ov. *Pont.* 4.14.59.
88   **nostri pars . . . chori** = Ov. *Tr.* 5.3.52.
       nostri pars quota Mart. *Sp.* 34.3; cf. Eob. *Her. Chr.* 1.96, n.
89   **sortis . . . iniquae** = l. 303 below; cf. Verg. *A.* 6.332; 12.243.
       sortis tenor Cf. Ov. *Ep.* 7.112; Stat. *Silv.* 5.1.165.
91–94 **Quae si — aquas** For this type of expression see Ov. *Ars* 2.517–19; *Tr.* 4.1.57–60;
       4.10.107–08; 5.2.27–28; *Pont.* 2.7.25–30; Eob. *Sylv. duae* 2.89–90; *Her. Chr.*
       16.185–88; *Nob.* 342; *Eccles.* 167–70.

91–92   **Quae si — opes** Modeled on Ov. *Tr.* 5.2.27–28. Cf. Eob. *Psalt.* 139.51–52: "Illa ego si numero certo comprehendere coner, / Omnis inexhausti cedet arena maris."

91   **numero — certo** = Gunther, *Lig.* 10.105; Eob. *Idyl.* 4.29; cf. Verg. *G.* 2.104; Ov. *Ars* 2.447; 3.151.

93–94   **quot in — aquas** See Vulg. *Psa.* 132.3.

94   **refundat aquas** ≈ Hutten, *Querel.* 1.7.14: "Qua celer ulvosas Fulda refundit aquas."

95   **Pauca tamen** = Verg. *Ecl.* 4.31; Ov. *Tr.* 1.8.20.

    meminisse iuvat = Stat. *Ach.* 2.167; cf. Eob. *Pug.* 5, n.

96   **tristia corde feras** Cf. Ov. *Tr.* 3.11.58.

97   **pauperiem . . . pati** Hor. *Carm.* 1.1.18; 3.2.1; 4.9.49. Poverty was proverbially among the greatest of burdens: see Cic. *Sen.* 14; Bebel, *Prov.* 132.

98   **Hoc nihil est** = Mart. 4.5.10.

    milia multa = *Her. Chr.* 6.76, n.

99   **Quem — fuisse** Cf. Ov. *Ep.* 11.87; *Met.* 5.626; 7.582; 14.177; *Tr.* 3.3.5–6.

100   **fatidicus . . . senex** Sabell. *In natal.* 9, sig. b5ᵛ, likewise referring to Simeon; Eob. *Eccles.* 24.

101   **inclementia fati** = Stat. *Silv.* 1.4.50; Eob. *Hod.* B 1.69.

102   **sunt adeunda** = Mart. 1.70.12.

103   **Non — quam si** = *Tum.* 7.123; cf. Ov. *Tr.* 1.3.11; Eob. *Her. Chr.* 7.29.

103–04   **nil tale — latus** Cf. Ov. *Met.* 8.439–40; *Tr.* 3.9.25–26.

103   **nil tale timenti** = Stat. *Ach.* 1.567.

104   **Hausissent . . . latus** Ov. *Met.* 9.412.

    taela cruenta = Ov. *Tr.* 5.7.34; Eob. *Eccles.* 318.

105–21   **Nondum — reversi** See Vulg. *Matt.* 2.1–23; cf. Eob. *Her. Chr.* 1.121–28; 20.79–80.

105   **Nondum convalui** = Hutten, *Querel.* 2.8.97 (addressed to Eobanus Hessus).

    convalui, nondum = Ov. *Ep.* 21.211.

106   **nova . . . monstra** Hor. *Carm.* 1.2.6; Ov. *Met.* 1.437; 11.391; Eob. *Vict.* 153; *Eccles.* 336.

110   **linguae . . . inops** That is, "infans" (incapable of speech).

111   **sua viscera matres** = l. 35 above; cf. Ov. *Rem.* 59.

112   **e medio — sinu** Cf. Ov. *Met.* 4.516–17; 13.450; Mant. *1. Parthen.* 3.336–37: "de matrum sinibus sua pignora miles / auferet"; *Calam.* 1.431–33 (p. 30): "per rura furens Galilaea satelles / De trepidis matrum sinibus lactentia vulsit / Pignora."

113   **innocuo . . . sanguine** = Prud. *Psych.* 501; cf. Mant. *1. Parthen.* 3.325: "innocuo Bethlemica rura cruore / tinxit"; Eob. *Buc.* 4.25–26.

    sanguine miles = Luc. 4.181; Sil. 8.511.

114   **caede fuisse** = Ov. *Tr.* 3.9.6.

115   **Ipsa, Deo monita** In Eobanus' fiction, Mary was forewarned in Emmanuel's letter (*Her. Chr.* 1.121–28). According to Vulg. *Matt.* 2.13, only Joseph was warned.

    fugitiva petebam ≈ Maxim. 1.67.

117   **aliquot . . . annos** Traditionally seven years: see *Leg. aurea* 10.29; Mant. *1. Parthen.* 3.481.

    fatis . . . tristibus Eob. *Buc.* 9.17, n.

    egimus annos = Ov. *Met.* 8.708.

118   **Praebuit — cibum** Cf. Ter. *An.* 75.

    angustum lana = Celtis, *Am.* 2.9.50: "Nec tenera angustum lana foramen habet."

    lana colusque = Ov. *Ep.* 14.66.

119   **opera . . . fabrilia** Verg. *A.* 8.415.

120   **victum quaereret** *Buc.* 8.87, n.

    arte, senex = Ov. *Ib.* 262.

121–28   **Vix peregre — viros** The story is told in Vulg. *Luc.* 2.41–48.

121   **Galilaeaque rura** = *Her. Chr.* 3.129, n.

123   **Venimus — agni** Cf. Mant. *1. Parthen.* 3.490–92, referring to the Holy Family: "ad primi maxima veris / orgia, cum typico faciunt solemniter agno, / convenere."

Venimus ad = *Her. Chr.* 3.73, n.

typici . . . agni *AH* 50.387.3. The paschal lamb (cf. Vulg. *Lev.* 23.12; *Matt.* 26.17; etc.) is a prefiguration, or type, of Christ, the Lamb of God. Cf. *Joan.* 1.29; *1. Cor.* 5.7; *1. Petr.* 1.19. For *typicus* in this theological sense, see also Eob. *Buc.* 11.34; l. 164 below.

125   **Illum — anxia** Cf. Mant. *1. Parthen.* 3.496–98 (of Mary's searching for Jesus): "Tres illum gemebunda dies, tres anxia noctes / . . . / . . . Parens quaesivit."

       tris soles anxia Cf. *Her. Chr.* 20.29.

129   **Crevit — annos** Cf. Vulg. *Luc.* 2.40, 52.

       Crevit et inde puer Stat. *Silv.* 5.3.180.

       meliores — annos Cf. *Laud.* 509, n.; Claud. *Cons. Stil.* 3.121: ". . . teneros sic moribus induit annos."

131–32   **Iamque — via** Cf. Vulg. *Luc.* 3.23.

131   **sexti — lustri** = *Epic.* 2.27; *Sylv.* 9.27.3; cf. Mant. *Somn.*, fol. 216ʳ: "aetas / Nostra quater decimi transit confinia lustri."

132   **caeperat ire via** = Ov. *Fast.* 1.432.

133–34   **Per nova — fuit** Cf., for example, Vulg. *Matt.* 21.11 and *Luc.* 24.19.

133   **Per nova . . . miracula** Paul. Nol. *Carm.* 6.10; cf. Avit. *Carm.* 2.296 and Mant. *1. Parthen.* 1.504 (at this metrical position): "nova . . . miracula"; Eob. *Her. Chr.* 22.115.

       mirantes . . . turbas Paul. Nol. *Carm.* 20.113.

134   **tota gente** = Catul. 79.2; Ov. *Ep.* 4.54; Eob. *Her. Chr.* 6.58.

135–36   **nec enim — erat** Cf. ll. 1–2 above, with n. 2. For the phrasing, cf. Verg. *A.* 12.639; Ov. *Tr.* 3.6.3; *Pont.* 4.4.17; Eob. *Buc.* 2.105–06, n.

137   **monstra hominum** Ter. *Eu.* 696; Gel. 17.1.1.

       lumine functos ≈ Mant. *2. Parthen.* 2.31: "vitae . . . lumine functus."

138   **nemo rogat** = *Nob.* 232; *Max.* 194; *Epic.* 4.150; cf. *Luth.* 3.80.

140   **non procul esse** = Hutten, *Querel.* 2.8.104 (addressed to Eobanus Hessus).

141   **Saepe . . . dixi, "Cui** = Ov. *Tr.* 4.1.93.

       Cui — relinquis Cf. *Her. Chr.* 7.49, n.

142   **me quoque posse** = Ov. *Ep.* 16.14; 17.44; *Tr.* 5.8.34; *Ib.* 204.

       posse mori = *Her. Chr.* 12.96, n.

143   **quibus — dolorem** Cf. Hor. *Ep.* 1.1.34–35; Marul. *Epigr.* 2.32.171: "potes . . . verbis lenire dolorem."

145   **gravis . . . fati** Sen. *Oed.* 75; Stat. *Silv.* 1.4.50.

       discrimina fati = Claud. *in Rufin.* 2.474.

146   **madidas — genas** Cf. Tib. 1.9.38.

       madidas . . . genas = Ov. *Ep.* 5.72; *Tr.* 5.4.6.

147   **tuae lachrymae — cadebant** Cf. Ov. *Tr.* 3.4.39.

149   **Et iam tempus erat** = *Nup.* 169, n.

150   **quaelibet hora mihi** = *Her.* 1.3.104; cf. Sen. *Ag.* 85; Celtis, *Am.* 3.12.4: "Dum partem vitae quaelibet hora rapit."

151–52   **Ascendit — fuit** For Jesus' entry into Jerusalem on Palm Sunday, before the Passover feast, see Vulg. *Matt.* 21.1–9; *Marc.* 11.1–10; *Luc.* 19.29–38; *Joan.* 12.12–13.

151   **palma sublimis** Lact. *Phoenix* 69.

153   **Inde — prophanum** See Vulg. *Matt.* 21.12–13; *Marc.* 11.15; *Luc.* 19.45–46; cf. *Joan.* 2.13–16.

       sacra . . . aede *Buc.* 10.78, n.

       vulgus . . . prophanum *Laud.* 384, n.

154   **A populo — erat** Cf. Vulg. *Joan.* 8.59; 10.31. For the phrasing, cf. [Ov.] *Nux* 2: "a populo saxis praetereunte petor."

155   **Sex . . . soles** Jesus entered Jerusalem five days before the Passover feast and was crucified the day after Passover: cf. Vulg. *Joan.* 12.1, 12.

156   **in curas — meas** = Ov. *Ep.* 1.72.

157	**tacitae — noctis** Cf. Ov. *Fast.* 2.552; V. Fl. 5.231. For the tag *tempora noctis,* see Prop. 1.3.37; 3.20.13; Ov. *Am.* 2.10.27; Luc. 6.120.
161	**Omnia tu melius** Cic. *Att.* 13.7: "Haec omnia tu melius."
162	**memori mente tenere** Lucr. 2.582; Mant. *1. Parthen.* 1.831–32; cf. Eob. *Buc.* B 7.22, n.; *Her. Chr.* 17.250.
163–224	**Quis — tuli** See Vulg. *Matt.* 26–27; *Marc.* 14–15; *Luc.* 22–23; *Joan.* 18–19.
163	**Quis — cruentae** Cf. l. 183 below.
	Quis — meminisse Cf. Verg. *A.* 2.361–62. The phrase *illius noctis* also recalls Ov. *Tr.* 1.3.1.
165–70	**Vosne — fuit** For the commonplace — Nature's grief at Christ's death and her joy at his resurrection — see *Her. Chr.* 3.45–56, nn.
167	**de corpore guttas** = Andrel. *Ecl.* 4.27: "toto fluxas de corpore guttas"; cf. Ov. *Met.* 5.633. For the story, see Vulg. *Luc.* 22.44.
168	**mollior ibat aqua** Cf. Verg. *A.* 8.726; Eob. *Wirt.* 194.
169	**opacam . . . nubem** = Cic. *Arat.* 201; cf. Ov. *Ars* 2.619.
	Cynthia nubem ≈ Ov. *Met.* 15.537; Luc. 8.721.
173	**tam longa nocte** = Ov. *Ep.* 16.317.
177	**probris . . . verbere** = Mant. *2. Parthen.* 3.510: "probris et multo verbere."
178	**Nullus — erat** Modeled on Ov. *Ars* 1.540; cf. Eob. *Her. Chr.* 12.16, n.
	in attonito pectore = Marul. *Epigr.* 2.32.20; cf. Stat. *Silv.* 5.1.29.
179–80	**Ah, quoties . . . Ah, quoties** = *Her. Chr.* 14.145–46, n.
179	**Ah — aliquo** Cf. *Her. Chr.* 2.97.
182	**Egressus — domus** Cf. Vulg. *Joan.* 18.15–16: Peter and "another disciple" (John) follow Jesus into the high priest's palace ("dirae limina . . . domus"). Cf. *Matt.* 26.57–58; *Marc.* 14.53; *Luc.* 22.54.
	limina . . . domus = Mant. *Epigr.,* fol. 106ʳ: "sacrae limina clausa domus"; Eob. *Her. Chr.* 20.94. Cf. Ov. *Tr.* 3.5.8; 5.4.34.
	limina nota Verg. *A.* 7.491; Mant. *1. Parthen.* 1.694. John was acquainted with the high priest: see Vulg. *Joan.* 18.15.
183–84	**Quis — malis** Cf. Verg. *A.* 2.361–62. Cf. also l. 163 above.
183	**dirae scelera omnia** = *Eccles.* 401.
184	**tantis . . . malis** = Catul. 65.4; Ov. *Tr.* 1.1.48; 4.1.88; *Ib.* 194.
185–87	**Quot gelidae — dolores** For comparisons such as these, cf. Ov. *Tr.* 1.5.47–48; 4.1.55–56; 5.1.31–33; 5.2.23–27; cf. also *Tr.* 5.6.37–41; ll. 91–94, n., above.
185	**gelidae . . . umbrae** *Buc.,* ded. 5, n.
	errant in montibus = Verg. *Ecl.* 2.21; Ov. *Met.* 12.416.
	in montibus umbrae = Verg. *G.* 1.342; cf. Eob. *Her. Chr.* 15.73, n.
186	**matutino . . . rore madent** *Anthol. Lat.* 584.2, in an epigram traditionally attributed to Vergil: "matutino rore madebat humus."
187	**corda dolores** ≈ Verg. *A.* 1.209.
189	**Nox . . . intempestivior** Cf. Enn. *Ann.* 102 (167; Verg. *G.* 1.247; *A.* 12.846): "nox intempesta." Eobanus confuses *intempestivus* ("unseasonable") with *intempestus* ("dismal," "pitch-black").
	Acherontaeis *Her. Chr.* 12.55, n.
190	**Nox — meas** Cf. *Her. Chr.* 13.16; Ov. *Am.* 2.10.12; *Ep.* 2.44.
192	**novum . . . mane** Verg. *G.* 3.325; Eob. *Her. Chr.* 3.68.
193	**Vix caput extulerat . . . sol** Cf. Ov. *Met.* 15.30–31; [Tib.] 3.7.123; Sil. 6.17.
	trepido . . . orbi *Her. Chr.* 3.53.
	sol territus Cf. *Her. Chr.* 3.45, n.
194	**attonita . . . aure** Sen. *Her. O.* 1129; Stat. *Theb.* 1.590; 4.669; 7.227.
196	**pro lege** See Vulg. *Joan.* 19.7.
197	**Rite coronatum** For Jesus' crown of thorns, see Vulg. *Matt.* 27.29; *Marc.* 15.17–18; *Joan.* 19.2–3.
198	**iustior ipse** For the idiom, cf. *Her. Chr.* A 3.30, n.; *Her. Chr.* 17.106.

199   **Parcitis** The present indicative is here used in place of an imperative.
        immeritae . . . parenti ≈ Stat. *Theb.* 1.234.
200   **Sic ego — fui** Cf. Ov. *Ep.* 12.116. For the rhetorical doubling of *sic*, see, for exam-
        ple, Verg. *Aen.* 4.660; Sen. *Her. F.* 1218; Eob. *Buc.* 7.141, n.
201   **Hoc erat officium** = *Eleg.* 3.103.
202   **veteri . . . angue** Cf. *Her. Chr.* 1.121, n.; Vulg. *Matt.* 23.33.
        durius angue = *Epic.* 6.80.
203   **tota cohors** = Juv. 13.173.
        portis — apertis Cf. Verg. *G.* 4.78; *A.* 8.585; Eob. *Nup.* 171.
204   **Impositam — crucem** Cf. Vulg. *Joan.* 19.17.
        Impositam . . . crucem *Her. Chr.* 3.30.
        Impositam collo = *Her. Chr.* 18.135.
205   **Qua licet usque** = Claud. *Rapt. Pros.* 3.335.
206   **In latebris — fuit** Of the disciples, only John stood by the three Marys at the cross:
        see Vulg. *Joan.* 19.26–27. For the disciples' fear of the Jews, see *Joan.* 20.19.
        comitum . . . turba Ov. *Met.* 3.186; 6.165; Eob. *Her. Chr.* 4.64.
        caetera turba = Prop. 4.1.136; Ov. *Ep.* 15.16; *Fast.* 3.628; *Pont.* 1.8.8.
207–08 **Attamen — timor** See Vulg. *Matt.* 27.55–56; *Marc.* 15.40; *Luc.* 23.49.
208   **novus . . . timor** Ov. *Ep.* 19.89.
        iusserat . . . timor Sen. *Phaed.* 1089; Eob. *Pug.* 58.
210   **tacta surgere . . . humo** = Ov. *Tr.* 3.4.18.
        surgere iussus ≈ *Her. Chr.* 15.156, n.
211–12 **Tacta — genu** Cf. Ov. *Met.* 10.210; Sil. 4.205; Eob. *Her. Chr.* 22.76.
211   **vestigiaque — tenebat** Cf. Mant. *1. Parthen.* 2.728–29, referring to the Virgin's foot-
        prints: "tellus . . . / . . . servavit presso vestigia dorso."
212   **Sanguine . . . fuso** *Her. Chr.* 12.122, n.
213   **Quid facerem** = Verg. *Ecl.* 1.40; 7.14; Ov. *Fast.* 5.313; *Tr.* 1.3.49.
        iacui . . . frigida Ov. *Ep.* 1.7; 14.38.
        iam frigida = Verg. *G.* 4.506.
        flevi Cf. *Her. Chr.* 3.37.
214   **Nunc — fleo** Cf. Ov. *Rem.* 8.
215–16 **Quasque — meis** For the motif, see *Her. Chr.* 2.3–4, nn.
215   **carmine** See *Her. Chr.* 4.176, n.
216   **De lachrymis — meis** Cf. Prop. 4.3.4; Ov. *Tr.* 1.1.14; Eob. *Her. Chr.* 12.2.
217   **Ventum erat . . . ad** *Her. Chr.* 14.73, n.
        mortis loca *Her. Chr.* 3.29, n.
218   **sudes — crucem** Cf. n. to *Her. Chr.* 6.122. For the asyndetic listing of the *arma
        Christi,* cf. Venantius Fortunatus' famous hymn "Pange lingua gloriosi," *Carm.*
        2.2.19: "Hic acetum, fel, harundo, sputa, clavi, lancea."
219–20 **Tunc ego vel . . . potui . . . Vel** Ov. *Am.* 1.7.5–6.
220   **humani — nihil** *Gen. ebrios.* A 1.10; cf. Mart. 2.8.6.
221   **Sanguine . . . ligno sudante** Cf. Lucr. 6.1147–48; Verg. *A.* 2.582.
        Sanguine iam roseo Cf. *Her. Chr.* 18.85. For *sanguine roseo,* see Apul. *Met.* 5.23.
        ligno . . . pependit = Paul. Nol. *Carm.* 27.289: "ligno mea vita pependit." On
        lignum as a term for the cross, see Eob. *Her. Chr.* 6.189, n.
222   **Transiit — latus** See Vulg. *Joan.* 19.33–34. For the phrasing, cf. Ov. *Ep.* 3.126;
        Ib. 46; Eob. *Her. Chr.* 22.82, n.
224   **Oscula . . . ab ore tuli** Ov. *Ep.* 16.255–56.
        Oscula . . . frigida Ov. *Ep.* 11.117; *Met.* 11.738.
225–28 **Dicite — caput** Cf. *Sylv.* 2.27.5–8, in an epigram on the Mother of Sorrows:
        "Dicite, mortali foecundae semine matres, / Dicite de vobis talia siqua tulit. / Nulla
        tulit, nulla est aevo latura sequenti, / Illa sed humani summa doloris erat."
225–26 **Dicite . . . Dicite** = Ov. *Fast.* 3.255–56.
225   **Dicite — matres** Cf. *Buc.* 9.22, n.; *Her. Chr.* 13.25.

227   **aevo . . . sequenti** Verg. *Ecl.* 8.27.
228   **Curarum . . . sarcina** August. *Ep.* 101.3: "curarum ecclesiasticarum sarcina"; 127.5: "curarum noxiarum sarcinis"; et al.; Eob. *Vict.* 120; cf. l. 56, n., above.
        hoc pressit . . . caput Ov. *Tr.* 2.102.
229   **Tot — dolores** Cf. *Ciris* 291; [Sen.] *Oct.* 201; l. 71 above.
230   **Conqueror . . . ire diem** Cf. Ov. *Ep.* 1.8.
        extremum . . . diem = Poliziano, *Eleg.* 7.174: "extremum sentit adesse diem"; Mant. *Votum,* fol. 55ʳ: "Non procul extremum suspicor esse diem"; cf. Ov. *Ep.* 1.114.
        longius ire diem = Stat. *Theb.* 4.3; cf. Eob. *Sylv. duae* 2.98, n.
231   **Quoque magis doleam** = Ov. *Met.* 3.448.
232   **dulce levamen eras** = Tifernate, *Carm.*, sig. D2ʳ: "Quique patri quondam dulce levamen eras"; and in another epigram on the same page: "Dulce patri studium dulce levamen eras." Cf. Catul. 68.61; Eob. *Sylv. duae* 2.32, n.
233   **Non ego te aspiciam** Ov. *Ep.* 10.67–68; cf. Eob. *Her. Chr.* 5.23, n.
        mandata Magistri ≈ Juvenc. 2.526. In the Gospels Jesus is often addressed as "Master."
234   **Hystorica . . . fide** Ov. *Am.* 3.12.42; Paul. Nol. *Carm.* 20.29: "historica narrabo fide sine fraude poetae." Mary is thinking here of John as a biographer of Jesus.
        populis insinuare Juvenc. 1.436: "sancta serebat / Insinuans populis regni praeconia Christus."
235   **sollicitae . . . vitae** = Hor. *S.* 2.6.62; Prop. 3.7.1.
        numeranti taedia vitae ≈ *Her. Chr.* 10.189, n.
236   **falles tempora longa** Cf. *Her. Chr.* 20.78, n.
        tempora longa mora = Ov. *Ep.* 19.10; Eob. *Her.* 1.6.38.
237–50 **Illaque — aquas** Cf. *Leg. aurea* 115.2: "virgo beata in domo iuxta montem Syon posita dicitur remansisse omniaque loca filii sui, scilicet locum baptismi, ieiunii, passionis, sepulture, resurrectionis et ascensionis quoad vixit devotione sedula visitabat"; Mant. *1. Parthen.* 3.727–32; Erasmus, *Obsecratio ad Virginem Matrem Mariam, LB* 5, col. 1238 C–D. For the motif, see also Eob. *Her. Chr.* 3.155–60 (imitating Ovid).
237   **mecum quondam . . . solebas** = *Buc.* 4.1, n.
        quondam monumenta = Man. 5.253; Locher, "Obiectio Voluptatis," *Stult.*, fol. 132ʳ: "Qui mea spreverunt quondam monumenta"; cf. Eob. *Her. Chr.* 5.20, 169.
239   **divitibus . . . Indis** Prop. 3.4.1; Eob. *Nob.* 327. The wealth of India was proverbial: see *Ama.* 32.66, n.: "divitis Indiae."
240   **Seu cadat** = *Her. Chr.* 12.74.
        Hesperia . . . aqua = Prop. 4.1.86.
241   **Flexa genu** *Her. Chr.* 15.122, n.
        fletu . . . amaro August. *De consensu evangelistarum* 3.2.7: "amaro fletu et cordis dolore"; Mant. *Calam.* 1.1099 (p. 47): "amaros . . . fletus."
242   **Ille — habet** Cf. Ov. *Ep.* 7.190.
        signa doloris = Ov. *Tr.* 4.3.28; cf. *Ep.* 19.107.
243   **apparent vestigia** = *Hod.* 234; *Idyl.* 17.140; cf. Prop. 2.29.35; Sil. 17.599.
244   **cede cruenta** = Ov. *Ep.* 6.162.
        viri For the avoidance of the name *Jesus*, see n. to l. 64 above.
245–48 **Hic stetit — erat** Cf. Erasmus, *Obsecratio ad Virginem Matrem Mariam, LB* 5, col. 1238 D, imagining the Virgin's inner monologue as she ponders the events in her life with Jesus: "Hic stabat, cum caecum illuminaret. Ad hunc puteum, itinere fessus, quievit. Hic mihi uni haec atque illa dixit. Hic ductus est, hic pependit. Hoc in tumulo situs est." Cf. also Ov. *Rem.* 727–28, counseling avoidance of former trysting places lest the memory arouse sorrow.
246   **cum pateretur** = *Her. Chr.* 6.23, 157.
247   **crux alta** *Hymn.* 41; *Eccles.* 93.
        crucem . . . inter utramque Vulg. *Matt.* 27.38; *Marc.* 15.27; *Luc.* 23.33; *Joan.* 19.18.

248   **Mortuus — erat** See Vulg. *Matt.* 27.59–60; *Marc.* 15.46; *Luc.* 23.53; *Joan.* 19.40.
        sindone tectus *Sylv.* 1.1.98; 1.4.32.
249   **Hic — refecit** Cf. *Her. Chr.* 3.37–40, with n. to ll. 39–40.
250   **Aegaeas . . . aquas** ≈ Prop. 3.24.12; cf. Ov. *Met.* 9.448.
251–58 **Talia dum — sui** For a very similar discussion, see *Sylv. duae* 1.3–16, nn.
251   **Talia dum — est** Cf. Ov. *Tr.* 3.4.59; *Pont.* 1.9.7–8; 2.4.7–8.
252   **Tu procul hinc absis** = Tib. 1.9.51.
        milia multa = *Her. Chr.* 6.76, n., in a different sense.
253   **Solimis . . . oris** = Juvenc. 2.281.
255   **Mens . . . peregrina** Erasmus, *Adag.* 3.6.47 (referring to absentmindedness).
        spatio . . . brevi = Ov. *Fast.* 6.495.
256   **nullo limite** = Ov. *Am.* 3.8.42.
        volat Mant. *Bapt.*, fol. 230ᵛ: ". . . polos ultra mens animosa volat"; Eob. *Sylv.*
        1.4.61–62: "Mens generosa polos ultra volat, ultima mundi / Transilit." The idea that
        the winged soul traverses the universe goes back to Plato, *Phdr.* 246b–c.
258   **Carceris . . . claustra sui** Cf. Luc. 6.721–22; Paul. Nol. *Carm.* 24.749–50. For the
        concept of the body as prison of the soul, see Eob. *Her. Chr.* 14.133, n.
        testea Macr. 7.15.15: "testeis terrenisque corporibus"; *Somn. Scip.* 1.11.12: "huius
        indumenti testei."
259   **Ipsa domo vidua** = Ov. *Ep.* 9.35; Eob. *Her.* 2.3.29; 2.4.27; cf. *Buc.* 9.80, nn.; *Her.*
        Chr. 13.29, n.; 22.31.
        tacito . . . recessu = Stat. *Silv.* 1.2.271 (the womb).
        secreta recessu = *Buc.* 2.5, n.
260   **iustas . . . preces** = *Her. Chr.* 2.118; cf. *Her. Chr.* 2.17, n.
        solvimus ora = [Tib.] 3.5.14.
261   **veterum — vatum** Accl. 2.133; *Her.* 1.1.33; cf. *Her. Chr.* 2.47, n.; *Sylv. duae* 2.217, n.
262   **carmina scripta** = *Her. Chr.* 4.176; *Her.* 1.6.160.
263   **Vis — requirit** Mary avoids the sin of gluttony and, at the same time, follows sound
        medical advice: cf. [Sen.] *Formula vitae honestae* 4 (= *Martini episcopi Bracarensis*
        opera omnia, ed. Claude W. Barlow [New Haven, 1950], 242): "Considera tecum
        quantum natura poscat, non quantum cupiditas expetat. . . . Ede citra cruditatem,
        bibe citra ebrietatem"; *Flos medicinae* 313: "Non bibe ni sitias, et non comedas satu-
        ratus"; Ficino, *De vita* 1.11, ll. 5–6: "Famem (si commode fieri potest) cibus, sitim
        potus expectet"; Eob. *Val.* 1.163: "Vina sitim, comedenda famem spectare decebit";
        1.168: "Sic pota ut sitias, sic ede ut esurias."
        natura . . . requirit Lucr. 2.23
264   **famula . . . manu** = *Her. Chr.* 8.34; cf. *Her. Chr.* 2.42, n.
265   **pauperis horti** = Verg. *Ecl.* 7.34.
266   **Pura . . . unda** = *Vict.*, app. 2.6; cf. Verg. *A.* 6.229.
        siccam — sitim Cf. Ov. *Tr.* 4.8.26; Mant. *c. Poetas* 86: ". . . vitreo siccam diluit
        amne sitim"; Eob. *Val.* 1.516; *Hypocr.* 42: ". . . levent siccam dulcia vina sitim."
268   **quarum — tibi** Cf. *Her. Chr.* 8.82, n.
269   **Heae** For this spelling, see *Her. Chr.* 11.40, n.
270   **Flos . . . ille** Cf. *Her. Chr.* 2.110, n.
        Flos . . . aetatis decidit Cf. *Buc.* 7.170, nn. For *flos aetatis*, see Lucr. 3.770;
        4.1105–06; 5.847; Eob. *Venus* 2.204, 248.
271   **Auferor** = Ov. *Am.* 2.4.8; *Fast.* 4.448.
        venientibus . . . annis Poliziano, *Silv.* 3.169.
        opprimor annis = *Her.* 1.6.33: "gravibus nunc opprimor annis."
272   **Plena — meae** Cf. *Her. Chr.* 4.42, n.
273   **Nec . . . scire . . . quid agas** ≈ Ov. *Rem.* 641.
        charissime rerum ≈ Ov. *Pont.* 3.4.51.
275–76 **Nullaque — est** For the complaint, cf. Ov. *Tr.* 4.7.3–4; 5.13.11; Paul. Nol. *Carm.*
        10.1–4; Eob. *Her. Chr.* 18.9–10.

275   **Nullaque quae possit** = Ov. *Ib.* 3.
       tot euntibus annis = *Her. Chr.* 14.95, n.
277–78 **Non tamen — morae** Cf. Ov. *Tr.* 4.7.21–24; Eob. *Sylv.* 2.7.15–16.
278   **causa fuere morae** Cf. Ov. *Ep.* 1.74.
279   **At tibi, qui nostro** = Prop. 3.8.37.
       in amore minister ≈ Ov. *Fast.* 2.5, of elegiac distichs. For the motif of the faithful
       messenger, cf. Eob. *Her. Chr.* 10.21–22.
282   **digitis scripta** = Prop. 3.8.26; Ov. *Tr.* 3.3.2.
283–86 **Ille etiam — dies** The messenger has evidently told her that John is working on the
       book of Revelations: cf. Vulg. *Apoc.* 1.9.
283   **variis . . . animalia formis** = Poliziano, *Silv.* 3.571: "variisque horrenda animalia
       formis." Cf. Ov. *Met.* 1.416.
289   **proximus illi** = Man. 1.593; 2.11; Calp. *Ecl.* 6.11.
290   **Sydera — feris** Cf. *Psalt.* 110.30: "Sydera sublimi vertice summa petet." The model
       is Hor. *Carm.* 1.1.36.
       Sydera . . . summa *Nup.* 284–85, n.
291   **visu — acuto** ≈ Mant. *2. Parthen.* 1.234, speaking about St. Catherine of
       Alexandria: "Mysteria miris / Invelata modis visu penetrabat acuto."
292   **caelo proxima** = Ov. *Fast.* 6.32; Mart. 10.51.14; cf. Eob. *Sylv. duae* 2.111, n.; *Her.
       Chr.* 12.222.
293   **Scrinia . . . cordis** This medieval phrase occurs, for example, in the correspondence
       of Anselm of Canterbury. See his *Opera omnia,* ed. F. S. Schmitt, vols. 3–5
       (Edinburgh, 1946–51), *Ep.* 100: "in scrinio cordis . . . servare"; *Ep.* 178: "in cordis
       scrinio servare."
       cordis secreta = Juvenc. 1.304; 2.488; 3.146.
       secreta profundi = Claud. *Rapt. Pros.* 2.117.
296   **properata morte** Aus. *De herediolo* 3; Juvenc. 4.16.
298   **recto tramite** Paul. Nol. *Carm.* 20.376; Boeth. *Consol.* 1.m7.23.
299   **Differri . . . opus** Ov. *Ars* 1.409; *Fast.* 1.74.
300   **causa — querela** = *Her. Chr.* 8.16, n.
       nostra querela caret = *Eccles.* 224.
302   **vacat officio . . . suo** = Celtis, *Am.* 3.1.24: "Dum vacat officio Suevica lingua suo."
303   **Damna — iniquae** Cf. *Buc.* 7.16, n.; *Sylv.* 6.6.23: "fer . . . sortem patienter iniquam."
       sortis . . . iniquae = l. 89, n., above.
305–06 **Ipsa feram — ferat** Cf. Ov. *Tr.* 1.2.61–62, 68.
305   **superantis — vitae** *Her. Chr.* 12.273–74. For *taedia vitae,* see *Laud.* 320, n.
306   **Quam precor ut** = Ov. *Ep.* 18.218, at the end of the letter.

17

Meter: Elegiac distich.

1–2   **Quod — meo** Cf. Ov. *Tr.* 1.1.3–4; 5.1.3–6; Eob. *Her. Chr.* 20.89–92.
1   **Quod — vultu** Cf. *Sylv.* 3.3.7: ". . . moesto tibi venit epistola vultu"; 6.4.1: "Altera
       iam grato mihi venit epistola vultu." For the heroine's consciousness of writing
       elegiac verse, see n. to *Her. Chr.* 4.176.
       tibi . . . venit epistola Ov. *Tr.* 5.7.1; *Pont.* 4.6.1; Eob. *Her. Chr.* 1.7, n.; 18.175, n.;
       19.1.
       laeto . . . vultu = Ov. *Ib.* 409; cf. Eob. *Buc.* B 8.1, n.
2   **debuit esse** = *Her. Chr.* 6.2, n.
3   **Sera — venit** Cf. Ov. *Pont.* 4.8.1–2; Eob. *Her. Chr.* 18.175; 19.1.
       Sera quidem = Stat. *Theb.* 5.689; 11.155; *Silv.* 5.1.16.
       quo tempore primum = Verg. *G.* 1.61.

4	**ut nunc es** ≈ Ov. *Ep.* 16.50; 17.169.
	verus amator eras ≈ Ov. *Ep.* 16.246.
6	**Cura . . . salutis** *Her. Chr.* 11.165, n.
	aeternae . . . salutis *Her. Chr.* 1.1, n.
	nulla salutis erat = Ov. *Fast.* 4.538.
7	**contagia morbi** = Lucr. 3.471; 6.1236.
8	**dignus amore** = Mart. 6.29.2; 10.13.6.
	amore frui = *Her. Chr.* 3.120, n.
9–22	**Falsa — studes** For the commonplace of spiritual warfare, see n. to *Her. Chr* 6.71.
9	**Falsa deum** = *Ama.* B 2.28.
	Christi — professus Cf. *Eccles.* 171 (*Hypocr.* 79): ". . . Christi pia sacra professum"; *Ama.* B 2.35.
10	**Militiae — novae** Cf. Ov. *Am.* 2.12.28; Eob. *Her. Chr.* 12.100, n.
11	**servire Deo . . . triformi** Mant. *1. Parthen.* 1.559.
17	**magnorum — regum** Cf. Hor. *S.* 1.3.136; Prop. 3.9.1; Ov. *Pont.* 4.2.1; Stat. *Theb.* 5.636; Mant. *2. Parthen.* 2.699: "sata sanguine regum"; Eob. *Nup.* 68, n.; *Sylv.* 3.2.77: "Aedite magnorum regum de sanguine."
19	**servire tyranno** = Prop. 2.25.11; Mart. 9.65.5.
21	**partis . . . tropheis** Ov. *Ep.* 17.242.
	nova signa = *Her. Chr.* 9.159, n.
24	**ex omni — placere** = *Buc.* B 11.20, n.
25	**Aevi flore** Lucr. 1.564; Ov. *Met.* 9.436; cf. Eob. *Her. Chr.* 2.110, n.
26	**Taliter — meos** Cf. *Her. Chr.* 1.148, n.
27	**fortunae dotibus** Plin. *Ep.* 3.3.4; Strozzi, *Eroticon* 4.29.64; Eob. *Tum.*, ded. 15; *Sylv.* 2.6.28; cf. *Her. Chr.* 24.153, n.
28	**verum . . . Deum** = *Her. Chr.* 4.154, n.
29	**Par fortuna** Ov. *Ars* 2.559.
31	**Regis . . . genus** *Eleg. Maec.* 1.13.
	uterque genus Ov. *Fast.* 4.66.
34	**non simulatus amor** = Gibertus Barbetta, poem in Konrad Celtis, *Libri odarum quatuor* (Strasbourg, May 1513), sig. 24^r; Eob. *Her. Chr.* 22.98; cf. Ov. *Am.* 1.8.71; *Ep.* 16.238; 17.36.
35–44	**Iam mihi — amor** Cf. *Laud.* 235–39.
35	**prisca . . . aetas** Sid. *Carm.* 2.183; Pontano, *Hort.* 2.197; Eob. *Buc.* B 9.9.
36	**nostris — nulla** = Ov. *Tr.* 1.5.80.
	fabula . . . subest = Ov. *Fast.* 5.604.
37	**Talem . . . maritum** Ov. *Ep.* 20.227.
38	**tali coniuge** Catul. 62.59.
	coniuge digna fui = *Her. Chr.* 12.88; cf. Ov. *Tr.* 2.162.
39	**veterum . . . amantum** l. 157 below; cf. *Laud.* 235; *Ama.* 35.105.
	fata improba *Sylv.* 4.9.19.
41–50	**Phyllidas — fuit** Cf. ll. 131–41, nn., below.
41–42	**Phyllidas — liquet** Cf. Nikolas Marschalk, "De moribus amatoris," *Enchiridion poetarum clarissimorum* (Erfurt, 1502), bk. 4, sig. Q3^r: "Hypsiphilen, Helenen, Briseida, Phyllida, Phaedram, / Hermionem, vivas quid nisi amare iuvat?"
42	**corpus amasse** Ov. *Am.* 3.11.38; Eob. *Her. Chr.* 18.142.
44	**Error . . . amor** For the wordplay, see *Laud.* 236, n.
	nulla parte = Ov. *Ep.* 7.110; 18.48; *Pont.* 2.6.20; 3.1.100.
	probandus amor = Mart. 4.75.8.
45	**stulti . . . amoris** For passionate love as a form of insanity, see *Ama.* 20.10, n.
47	**Dulcibus . . . flammis** *Buc.* 2.42, n.
	flammis — medullas Cf. Catul. 35.15; 100.7; Verg. *A.* 4.66; Eob. *Her. Chr.* 4.95, n.
48	**miseri corporis** = *Epic.* 7.66; cf. *Her. Chr.* 14.72, n.
49	**aeternos . . . ignes** = Paul. Nol. *Carm.* 21.525, of hell. For the phrase, see also Verg. *A.* 2.154 (the stars); Ov. *Fast.* 3.421 (an eternal flame).

51   **demens . . . vetustas** = *Ama.* B 2.31.

52   **prata** Cf. *Her. Chr.* 9.110, n.: "vireta."

53–54   **Quae — manet** Cf. *Her. Chr.* 15.107–08; *Luth.* 3.69–70.

53   **brevis est . . . voluptas** = Ov. *Ep.* 19.65, of a dream; cf. *Met.* 9.485; Eob. *Ama.* 35.101, n.

55   **Tempora . . . in illis** = Walther 31206: "Tempora mutantur, nos et mutamur in illis." For the proverbial thought that time flies, see Otto 530; Häussler, 101, 154, 235, 268; cf. Ov. *Fast.* 6.771–72; Eob. *Laud.* 62, n.

          Tempora diffugiunt = Ven. Fort. *Carm.* 1.15.19; Petrarch, *Africa* 2.348: "Tempora diffugiunt; ad mortem curritis; umbra, / Umbra estis pulvisque levis vel in ethere fumus / Exiguus, quem ventus agat." Cf. Ov. *Met.* 15.183; Col. 10.159–60.

56   **repercussi — aura** Cf. *Her. Chr.* 4.166 (changed in *Her.* 3.1.156 to "Crebra repercussum reddidit aura sonum").

          repercussi murmuris ≈ Ven. Fort. *Carm.* 6.5.130.

          murmuris aura Verg. *Ecl.* 9.58.

57   **Tam — desinimus** = *Psalt.* 90.33: "Tam cito desinimus, tam sors haec nostra caduca est."

          fulguris . . . chorusci ≈ Petr. 122.122.

58   **I nunc** = *Buc.* 4.63, n.

59–70   **Omnia — cadunt** Cf. *Sylv. duae* 1.165–78, nn.

59   **ventis . . . -que simillima** = Verg. *A.* 2.794; 6.702.

          levibus . . . plumis Ov. *Met.* 15.357; Eob. *Am.* 35.83, n.

60–61   **Quas — rebus** Cf. *Epic.* 2.23–24: "Quid iuvat humanis etiam nunc fidere rebus, / Quas tam non stabiles quaelibet aura movet?"

60   **Quas — rapit** = *Psalt.* 1.20 (referring to chaff). For *quaelibet aura* at this metrical position, see Ov. *Ars* 2.650.

61   **Non est — rebus** Cf. Eob. *Sylv.* 3.3.23: "Quid iuvat humanis etiam nunc fidere rebus"; *Pod.* 353: "Cum doceam nihil humanis confidere rebus"; *Psalt.* 62, arg. 3–4: "Fallitur, humanis si quis confidere rebus / Nititur"; Verg. *A.* 10.152.

          Non est . . . tutum Ov. *Ep.* 4.11.

          confidere rebus = Verg. *A.* 1.452.

63–68   **Dic, ubi — suas** Cf. Ov. *Met.* 15.418–35.

63   **Dic, ubi** = *Buc.* 3.54, n.

          Cadmaeaque — Thebae Cf. Prop. 1.7.1; Stat. *Theb.* 12.635. The citadel of Thebes in Boeotia was supposedly founded by Cadmus, the son of Agenor.

64   **in aeternos . . . dies** = *Epic.* 6.120; *Sylv.* 7.35.10; *Psalt.* 121.16; et al. Cf. Paul. Nol. *Carm.* 16.16: "aeternosque dies"; Mant. *Mort.*, fol. 119ʳ: ". . . aeternos sunt habitura dies"; *Dionys.* 1, fol. 169ʳ: "volumina . . . / Quae legat aeternis aetas ventura diebus"; Eob. *Hod.* B 1.28.

65   **Cecropiae . . . Athenae** = *Aetna* 582; cf. Eob. *Laud.*, lim. 3, n.

          prorsus — Athenae = *Sylv.* 6.14.9: "Nondum Palladiae prorsus cecidistis Athenae."

66   **presenti . . . Deo** = *Her. Chr.* 7.98, n.

          maenia sacra Deo ≈ Ov. *Fast.* 6.62.

67   **quoque, cunctarum . . . rerum** = Ov. *Pont.* 3.4.51.

67–68   **caput . . . rerum, . . . Rhoma** Aus. *Mosella* 409; Claud. *Bell. Gild.* 1.459–60; cf. Ov. *Met.* 15.736. Rome is often called "caput orbis": see, for example, Ov. *Am.* 1.15.26; *Met.* 15.435; *Fast.* 5.93; Eob. *Her. Chr.* 19.15.

67   **domina . . . rerum** Ov. *Met.* 15.447 (Rome).

          domina unica = *Hod.* 318, of the Virgin Mary.

68   **Relliquias — suas** Cf. *Hod.* 258–59, of Trier.

          Martia Rhoma = Ov. *Tr.* 3.7.52; *Epic. Drusi* 246; cf. Ov. *Pont.* 1.8.24; 4.9.65–66; Eob. *Sylv. duae* 1.171; *Sylv.* 1.1.91; also cf. *Her. Chr.* 6.145.

69   **Quid tuti superesse** ≈ Ov. *Ars* 2.637; *Fast.* 1.383.

70   **parvo tempore** = Ov. *Ep.* 3.24.

71–74   **Est quoque — amor** Cf. *Buc.* 7.168–71, nn.

71   **Est quoque — inani** Cf. *Buc.* 3.127, n.; l. 83 below.

72   **posse virere** = *Her. Chr.* 23.44; *Sarmat.* 4.

73   **imagine vultus** = Ov. *Tr.* 1.7.1; *Pont.* 2.8.21; Eob. *Her. Chr.* 19.147.

74   **Heu — amor** Cf. *Sylv.* 9.4.14: "Hei mihi, quam multos iste fefellit amor!"
       Heu heu, quam = Verg. *Ecl.* 3.100.
       fefellit amor = Prop. 2.2.2; Ov. *Am.* 3.4.20; *Rem.* 42.

75   **Omnia . . . saecula** Ov. *Met.* 6.208; 15.878.
       numeres . . . saecula ≈ *Her. Chr.* 1.79.
       saecula mundi = Germ. *Arat.* 103; Ven. Fort. *Carm.* 4.24.3.

76   **Invenies — nihil** Cf. Ov. *Tr.* 5.1.4; Eob. *Salom.* 1, sig. A5ʳ, paraphrasing Vulg. *Eccl.*
       1.14: "Omnia scrutatus quaecunque sub aethere fiunt, / Inveni praeter nomina vana
       nihil."
       nomina pauca = Ov. *Tr.* 3.4.50. Cf. Prop. 2.1.72; Ov. *Met.* 15.429–30; Boeth.
       Consol. 2.m7.17–18; Mant. *Ecl.* 9.199–201: "Luna, Hadria, Troia / . . . / nomine sunt
       solo, delevit cetera tempus."

77   **Adde quod** = *Buc.* B 2.21, n.

78   **infernis — locis** Cf. *Epic.* 4.222: "Nec tua Tartareis exulet umbra plagis"; *Her. Chr.*
       13.167, n.
       umbra locis = Ov. *Tr.* 5.7.24.

79–98 **Te quoque — notat** To the terrestrial love embodied in the pagan Cupid, Ursula
       now opposes the divine love of Christ, the true Cupid: cf. *Her. Chr.* 4.92–94. The
       idea of the two kinds of Love, profane and heavenly, originates in Plato, *Symposium*
       180c–187e. This concept, much discussed by the Italian humanists, was extended by
       Erasmus to include not just two Venuses, but also two Cupids: see, for example,
       Enchiridion, LB 5, col. 58 B, and *Ep.* 173, ll. 10–13. From there it is only a small
       step to associate the heavenly Cupid with Jesus himself, as Eobanus does here. I do
       not know if Eobanus was the first to take this step. In any case, the association
       Cupid-Jesus became quite popular in seventeenth-century poetry and emblem books:
       see Eric Jacobsen, *Die Metamorphosen der Liebe und Friedrich Spees "Trutznachtigall":
       Studien zum Fortleben der Antike I* (Copenhagen, 1954), with many illustrations.

79   **falsus amor** Ov. *Ars* 1.618; *Tr.* 2.340.
       laqueo For the image, cf. Ov. *Ars* 3.591; *Rem.* 502; Vulg. *Eccl.* 7.27.

80   **verus . . . amor** Verg. *A.* 11.892; Prop. 2.15.30; Ov. *Ars* 1.618 (opposed to false
       love); *Tr.* 1.5.21; 4.4.71.
       alter amor = Prop. 2.3.46; Ov. *Rem.* 444; cf. *Ep.* 7.17.

81   **succendit — amore** ≈ *Buc.* 8.46, n.

82   **sapienter ames** ≈ *Her. Chr.* 3.108, n.

83   **Desipit — inanem** Cf. l. 71, n., above.
       Desipit omnis amans = *Buc.* 7.171, n.

84   **ille sapit** ≈ Mart. 9.10.2; 13.32.2; 14.210.2.

85   **dulcissima vulnera** = *Her. Chr.* 18.125; cf. *Buc.* 3.39, n.
       vulnera fecit = Ov. *Met.* 3.232; 12.443; *Tr.* 1.1.99.

86   **pectora . . . acu** = *Sylv.* 1.6.16: "Non ego sum Paphia pectora laesus acu."
       fixit acu ≈ Ov. *Ars* 3.240; cf. Eob. *Buc.* 3.91, n.

87   **Questus eras** = *Her. Chr.* B 1.11, n.
       lustrali . . . fonte Cf. l. 205, n., below.
       ex fonte renatus ≈ Arator 1.960; cf. Eob. *Her. Chr.* 12.59, n.

88   **Veneris . . . puer** Ov. *Am.* 1.10.17; 3.9.7; *Ars* 1.165; 3.762; Eob. *Her. Chr.* 17.89;
       24.36. Cupid is often called "puer": see *Ama.* 32.37, n.
       moverit arma ≈ Ov. *Tr.* 4.1.72; *Pont.* 2.2.12.
       arma puer = Mart. 1.22.6; Eob. *Sylv. duae* 2.160.

89   **ille puer** *Buc.* 3.36, n.
       puer Veneris = Ov. *Ars* 1.165; cf. l. 88, n., above.

90   **numen adorat** Verg. *A.* 1.48; 3.437; Ov. *Met.* 11.540.

91   **Ille puer** *Buc.* 3.36, n.
93   **Cupido . . . cupere** Notice the wordplay (*annominatio*).
94   **taela Cupido** = Mart. 9.56.2.
95   **Nomine reque** *Eleg.* 1.84; *Sylv.* 2.29.14.
          Oceanitide The foam-born Aphrodite (Venus). Cf. *Her. Chr.* 14.62, n.
96   **Noster at** = *Her. Chr.* 10.159; *Max.* 269.
          nullo — habet ≈ Ov. *Am.* 1.15.20; cf. Eob. *Nob.* 336.
97–98   **Caeculus — notat** In the Renaissance, sensual love was often symbolized with a
          blind Cupid, spiritual love with a keen-sighted Cupid: see Erwin Panofsky, *Studies in
          Iconology: Humanistic Themes in the Art of the Renaissance* (1939; New York, 1967),
          95–128, especially 125–28.
97   **nullo — laedit** ≈ *Ama.* 35.117; cf. *Laud.* 83, n.
99   **quae . . . dementia** Verg. *Ecl.* 2.69; 6.47; *A.* 5.465; 9.601; Ov. *Met.* 13.225; Eob. *Ama.*
          35.15.
          comparet umbrae ≈ *Sylv.* 1.4.65: "[Mens] res humanas pereunti comparat
          umbrae."
101   **Ipsa Venus — Cupido** Cf. Prud. *Perist.* 3.76: "Isis, Apollo, Venus nihil est"; Eob.
          Her. Chr. 10.11–12, n.
          puer ille Cupido = *Buc.* 3.36, n.
102   **solus et ipse** = Ov. *Ep.* 16.318.
103   **Quis Deus** = *Her. Chr.* 10.39, n.
103–04   **Dicere quid — potest** Cf. Aus. *Ephem.* 3.4–5 (Paul. Nol. *Carm.* 5.4–5):
          "[Omnipotens] cuius formamque modumque / nec mens complecti poterit nec
          lingua profari"; Eob. *Buc.* 3.58–59, nn.; *Her. Chr.* 22.77–78. See further n. to *Her.
          Chr.* 3.54.
104   **humiles elegi** For the heroine's consciousness of writing elegiacs, see n. to *Her.
          Chr.* 4.176.
105   **omine fausto** = Sil. 3.217; cf. Ov. *Met.* 6.448; *Tr.* 2.6.
106   **Ibis in — meos** Modeled on Ov. *Ep.* 16.86. Cf. Eob. *Her. Chr.* 13.22; 13.109, n.
          dignior ipse For the idiom, cf. *Her. Chr.* A 3.30, n.; 16.198.
108   **Innumerabilibus . . . aucta bonis** *Pod.* 268; cf. Sedul. 5.435: "Innumerabilium . . .
          bonorum"; Eob. *Laud.* 326, n.: "Aucta bonis."
109   **patria virtute** = Juvenc. 2.601; cf. Prud. *Psych.* 2; Eob. *Her. Chr.* 19.19, n.
110   **uterque parens** = Ov. *Am.* 1.3.10; *Ep.* 6.62; *Ib.* 260; Eob. *Her. Chr.* 23.112; *Nob.*
          308; cf. *Her. Chr.* 12.197, n.
111–32   **Eiice — puta** The problem of how a Christian should approach the pagan classics was
          hotly debated throughout the Middle Ages and beyond. The Renaissance humanists
          agreed that there was indeed much that was morally offensive in the classics; but with the
          good far outweighing the bad, they advised Christians to read such works with careful
          discrimination: see, for example, Erasmus, *Enchiridion*, *LB* 5, cols. 7 D–8 C. The stan-
          dard authority for the humanists' argument was St. Basil, whose letter *Ad adolescentes*
          concludes that Christians may read the pagan authors, provided they follow the example
          of the honeybee by selecting from their reading what is good and rejecting what is
          unwholesome. See further Luzi Schucan, *Das Nachleben von Basilius Magnus "ad adoles-
          centes": Ein Beitrag zur Geschichte des christlichen Humanismus*, Travaux d'Humanisme et
          Renaissance 133 (Geneva, 1973). For the reception of Basil's treatise at the German
          universities in the late fifteenth and early sixteenth century, most notably at Leipzig,
          see Götz-Rüdiger Tewes, "Die Erfurter Nominalisten und ihre thomistischen
          Widersacher in Köln, Leipzig und Wittenberg. Ein Beitrag zum deutschen
          Humanismus am Vorabend der Reformation," *Die Bibliotheca Amploniana: Ihre
          Bedeutung im Spannungsfeld von Aristotelismus, Nominalismus und Humanismus*,
          Miscellanea Mediaevalia 23, ed. Andreas Speer (Berlin, 1995), 447–88, especially
          462–69.
113   **tua damna** = Ov. *Fast.* 1.367.

114   **Vindice . . . igne** = *Sylv.* 6.6.56: "Vindice sic culpae puniet igne malos"; *Psalt.* 140.26: "Vindice mendaces obruat igne viros"; cf. *Her. Chr.* 22.80, n.
        igne crema ≈ Ov. *Ep.* 3.64.
117–18 **Cernis Arachne — bibit** The image was proverbial in the late Middle Ages and the Renaissance. See, for example, Walther 8353: "Ex uno flore trahitur bene melque venenum"; Brant, *NS* 111.40–43; Celtis, *Am.*, praef. 35: "ex eodem . . . flore favum apis et aranea venenum sugit et colligit"; Erasmus, *Enchiridion, LB* 5, col. 50 B; Morris P. Tilley, *A Dictionary of the Proverbs in England in the Sixteenth and Seventeenth Centuries* (Ann Arbor, 1950), 38, no. B208: "Where the Bee sucks honey the spider sucks poison."
117   **Arachne** A Lydian girl who challenged Pallas to a weaving contest, Arachne was changed into a spider: see Ov. *Met.* 6.5–145.
        florem scrutantur Cf. *Nup.* 50.
118   **dulces succos** Ov. *Fast.* 3.735.
119   **saecli — vetusti** = *Sylv.* 1.5.55. For *saecli vetusti* at this metrical position, see Mant. *1. Parthen.* 3.129. For the tag *monumenta vetusti*, see Sedul. 2.240.
120   **una conditione** = *Nob.* 30; *Sylv.* 8.20.14.
121   **quod non decet** = *Sylv. duae* 2.239.
123   **aequa — lance** Cf. Mant. *Calam.* 2.191 (p. 57): ". . . iusta librat Deus omnia lance"; 3.901 (p. 93): "Corda pius Pater aequali regat omnia lance"; Eob. *Psalt.* 33.11: "Iudicat et iusta consyderat omnia lance"; *Laud.* 457, n. For *aequa lance*, see, for example, Plin. *Nat.* 7.44; Celtis, *Am.* 4.9.2.
124   **instar apis** = Bebel, "De laude et utilitate poetices et saecularium litterarum," *Carm.*, sig. q3ʳ (in similar context): "Optima carpemus dulcia et instar apis." For the image, cf. ll. 117–18, n., above. Baptista Mantuanus uses the honeybee image in *1. Parthen.* 1.653–55 to describe the Virgin's studies of ancient Greek and Roman literature: "Quicquid in his tumidum, quicquid crudele procaxque / et quaecumque pios non attestantia mores / offendit, damnabat, apes imitata legendo."
125   **Siculae . . . Hiblae** *Buc.* 6.26, n.
126   **odoratae . . . rosae** ≈ *Her. Chr.* 3.140, n.
        milia multa = *Her. Chr.* 6.76, n.
127   **et longo . . . ordine** = Verg. *A.* 11.79; cf. Eob. *Her. Chr.* 10.139, n.
128   **nisi quae — nulla** = *Psalt.* 38.56: "nisi quae fuerint optima, nulla sequar."
129   **molles — libellos** Cf. Ov. *Rem.* 757; Magdal. *Erarium,* ded., sig. A2ᵛ: ". . . tetigisse libellum." For *molles libellos,* see Mart. 12.43.4; cf. Eob. *Laud.* 15, n.
130   **Elige — nocent** Cf. *Her.* 1.6.24: "Ponite quaeque nocent, sumite quaeque iuvant."
131–44 **Attigeris — freto** Cf. Mant. *2. Parthen.* 2.448–56: "Sed nihil est sine fraude. Latent sub melle venena: / Quae postquam imprudens biberis, fugit illa repente / Laeta dolis, manet infixum sub pectore virus. / Dic, ubi nunc illae, quarum vulgata theatris / Crimina conculcant probitatem humanaque corda / Mortiferis adigunt studiis: Briseis, Elisa, / Phyllis et Oenone, Sappho, Chryseis et Helle, / Tyndaris et mater, Medeaque Pasiphaeque / Atque meae Cleopatra domus grave dedecus?" For the catalogue of unfortunate lovers, all of whom are portrayed in Ovid's *Heroides* or *Metamorphoses,* cf. Eob. *Ama.* 10.9–10; 35.17–40; ll. 41–50 above.
131   **veterum mendacia . . . vatum** Ov. *Am.* 3.6.17; cf. Eob. *Sylv. duae* 2.217, n.; *Her. Chr.* 15.81, n.
        mendacia turpia Ov. *Am.* 3.11.21.
132   **praesens — puta** = *Her. Chr.* 5.140; cf. Jakob Dornberg in Jakob Wimpfeling, *Adolescentia,* ed. Otto Herding (Munich, 1965), 352: "Verba impura cave cantus et respue turpes; / lascivum carmen virus habere puta"; Eob. *Ama.* 35.68: "virus habere"; *Val.* 1.488, 538.
133   **tibi . . . lachrymas moveat** Cf. Ov. *Ep.* 18.180.
        Babilonia Thysbe = Ov. *Met.* 4.99.
134   **numine iussa mori** ≈ *Epic.* 4.112; cf. Ov. *Ep.* 3.144.

135	**Phyllida . . . relictam** Ov. *Am.* 2.18.22.
137–38	**vetito quae — Arserit** ≈ Ov. *Ars* 1.283–84.
138	**duro . . . ense** *Nup.* 144, n.
	ense latus = Prop. 2.8.22; Ov. *Tr.* 3.9.26: "rigido perforat ense latus."
140	**Qui — tulit** Cf. Ov. *Ib.* 489; Eob. *Laud.* 225, n.
141	**pronas . . . aures** = Claud. *Bell. Gild.* 426.
142	**Protesilaus amet** = Ov. *Ep.* 13.84.
143–44	**Neu tibi — freto** Cf. Andrel. *Livia* 1.9.107–08 (in *A*): "Mergitur infoelix caeca Leander in unda, / Dum natat in vestros, Sesta puella, sinus."
143	**Neu tibi — undis** Cf. Ov. *Ib.* 273; Mart. 14.181.1; also cf. Ov. *Tr.* 1.5.77.
144	**Si . . . Sesta puella** = Ov. *Ep.* 18.2.
145	**Aspice nos** = *Buc.* 11.95, n.
	toto — aequore Verg. *A.* 1.29; cf. Eob. *Her. Chr.* 15.169, n.
146	**In portu . . . ratem** ≈ *Her. Chr.* 19.44.
147	**Tertius — ignem** Cf. *Rec.* 216, n.
148	**turba vagamur** = Ov. *Ep.* 14.62.
149	**patria de sede** = Stat. *Theb.* 4.76; Prud. *Apoth.* 542; cf. Verg. *A.* 7.192–93; Eob. *Her. Chr.* 16.87.
	sede quietas ≈ Ov. *Ib.* 156; Eob. *Vict.* 105.
150	**immensos . . . sinus** *Aetna* 137.
152	**Publica . . . commoda** Hor. *Ep.* 2.1.3; Ov. *Met.* 13.188.
	noster amor = *Her. Chr.* 2.84, n.
153	**immensum . . . aequor** = Verg. *G.* 2.541; cf. l. 163 below.
155	**iussa sequentum** ≈ Verg. *A.* 3.114.
156	**classis** Cf. l. 220 below.
157–58	**I nunc et** = *Buc.* 4.63, n.
157	**I nunc . . . confer** Ov. *Ep.* 12.204.
	veteres . . . amantes l. 39 above; cf. *Laud.* 235; *Ama.* 35.105.
158	**I nunc — habe** The verse pointedly inverts Ov. *Ep.* 3.26: "i nunc et cupidi nomen amantis habe!" Cf. Eob. *Sylv. duae* 2.192; *Her. Chr.* 12.276; l. 250 below.
159	**positis . . . ocia curis** *Ilias* 13.340: ". . . positisque agere ocia curis."
	teris ocia = Verg. *A.* 4.271.
	ocia curis = Claud. *in Rufin.* 2, praef. 13; Mant. *Calam.* 2.311 (p. 61): "tristibus otia curis / Libera"; Eob. *Vict.*, app. 1.29; *Idyl.* 16.82; *Her.* 1.6.37; 3.4.5.
161	**Nos — movemus** Cf. *Sylv.* 1.10.49: ". . . nos Christi signa feremus."
	nova signa = *Her. Chr.* 9.159, n.
	signa movemus = Sil. 11.517; cf. Eob. *Her. Chr.* 6.71.
162	**rubram . . . crucem** *Her. Chr.* 9.135.
	candida vela = Locher, "Epigramma in Narragoniam," *Stult.*, fol. 5ᵛ; "Hecatostichon in proludium," *Stult.*, fol. 9ᵛ; cf. Eob. *Rec.* 220, n.
163	**immensa . . . sulcavimus aequora** Cf. Ov. *Pont.* 1.4.35; Eob. *Her. Chr.* 14.69, n. For *immensa aequora*, see Verg. *A.* 6.355; l. 153, n., above.
	aequora signis = Luc. 3.24.
164	**Utraque . . . videt Ursa polo** Cf. Ov. *Ep.* 18.152; Celtis, *Am.* 3.7.2: "axem, / Utraque quam gelido despicit Ursa polo"; Eob. *Val.* 1.604: "Quosque . . . Parrhasis Ursa videt"; *Epp. 3*, sig. C7ᵛ, letter of 9 July 1536: "Vidit ab Arctoo Parrhasis Ursa polo"; *Sylv.* 8.20.34: "loca quae propior Parrhasis Ursa videt."
165	**aeternis . . . pruinis** = Stat. *Theb.* 4.393.
	Hybernia The notion that Ireland is a land of eternal snow is derived from a pseudo-etymological explanation of the name (*hibernus* = "wintry").
	foeta pruinis = Mant. *2. Parthen.* 1.23: "rura novis effoeta pruinis."
166	**prospicit arva** = Tib. 2.5.58; cf. Ov. *Met.* 8.330; Eob. *Her. Chr.* 20.104.
167	**terdenas . . . Orchadas** Cf. Mela 3.54: "triginta sunt Orcades." Plin. *Nat.* 4.103 speaks of forty islands. There are actually some ninety in all.

168   **Boreae flatibus** = *Sylv.* 6.12.2; cf. Verg. *A.* 4.442.
170   **Codano . . . sinu** = Celtis, *Am.* 1.3.42.
        Balthica stagna = *Sylv. duae* 1.44, n.
171   **prata . . . tondent** Verg. *G.* 1.289–90; *Ilias Lat.* 888.
172   **verberat — humum** = *Her. Chr.* 9.34, n.
173   **celeri . . . carina** = Ov. *Ep.* 17.103; cf. *Met.* 9.447.
174   **priscum . . . nomen** Ov. *Met.* 14.850.
        nomen habet = *Sylv. duae* 1.24, n.
175   **ignota — terras** ≈ V. Fl. 2.592; cf. Mant. *1. Parthen.* 3.920: ". . . sparsasque per aequora terras."
176   **incertis fluctibus** Cf. Ov. *Met.* 8.166; Sen. *Her. F.* 683–84.
        fluctibus — ratis = Locher, "Latina navis seu barca socialis," *Stult.*, fol. 135ᵛ.
178   **non bene culta** = Locher, "Carmen ad S. Brant," *Stult.*, fol. 3ᵛ; Eob. *Sylv.* 7.1.4: "Moenia Thuringi non bene culta soli." Cf. Ov. *Am.* 3.7.1.
179–81 **Sepe . . . dixi . . . Saepe** ≈ Ov. *Ep.* 2.17–20.
179   **alto . . . ex gurgite** Lucr. 5.387. Cf. Verg. *Ecl.* 6.76; *A.* 6.310; 7.704; 12.114.
        gurgite terras = Sil. 12.356.
180   **Illa — habent** Cf. Ov. *Ep.* 18.86, where Leander writes: "'illa meum,' dixi, 'litora lumen habent!'"
181   **rates . . . ex arce videre** Cf. Ov. *Rem.* 57–58.
183   **novas . . . figuras** Cf. ll. 161–62 above.
185   **pluviis . . . ymbribus** Ov. *Fast.* 6.282.
        niger — Auster = Luc. 9.320; Stat. *Theb.* 5.705. For the Auster as a rain-bearing wind, see Eob. *Buc.* 7.178, n.
187   **nubes — Caecias** Cf. Hor. *Epod.* 13.1; Gel. 2.22.24; Erasmus, *Adag.* 1.5.62.
188   **Seu — eras** For the motif of the brawling winds, see *Buc.* 9.35, n.
191   **Nec mirum** = *Buc.* 2.44, n.
        Tartara vicit = Ven. Fort. *Carm.* 8.7.3.
192   **Crux . . . alma** *Her. Chr.* 6.31, n.
193   **Iveris — hostes** Cf. Ov. *Ep.* 13.73; Eob. *Her. Chr.* 6.155, n.
195   **pelagique minas caelique** = Verg. *A.* 6.113.
196   **difficilesque vias** = Mant. *Nat. Am.*, fol. 178ᵛ.
197   **seu — divum** Cf. Stat. *Theb.* 12.420: "seu forte . . . seu numine divum."
        fatis acti Verg. *A.* 1.32; Ov. *Met.* 13.260.
198   **Nostra — solo** Cf. *Her. Chr.* 22.35.
199   **Eiectas** *Her. Chr.* 22.35, n.
        fido . . . portu Cf. Ov. *Tr.* 4.5.5.
        suscepit . . . portu Cf. l. 212, n., below.
        Gallia The mouth of the Rhine, in northern Gaul.
200   **Teutona . . . in arva** = *Sylv. duae* 1.182, n.
201   **Agrippae . . . urbem** Hermann von dem Busche, *Flora* 19, in Hans Rupprich, ed., *Humanismus und Renaissance in den deutschen Städten und an den Universitäten* (1935; Darmstadt, 1964), 140: "Urbis . . . Agrippae." Cf. Celtis, *Od.* 3.21.1: "Agrippe moenibus"; l. 266 below. According to one tradition, Cologne was founded by the Roman general M. Vipsanius Agrippa (64/63–12 BCE): see *Die cronica van der hilliger stat van Coellen 1499* (*Koelhoffsche Chronik*), ed. Hermann Cardauns in *Die Chroniken der deutschen Städte vom 14. bis ins 16. Jahrhundert*, vol. 13 (Leipzig, 1876), 280–84. Cf. Eob. *Laud.* 539, n.
        Zephyris melioribus Claud. *Rapt. Pros.* 2.288.
202   **aliquis superum** = *Luth.* 2.44; cf. *Buc.* 8.110, n.
        talia verba dabat = V. Fl. 7.251; cf. Eob. *Her. Chr.* 13.38, n.
203   **I, pete** = Ov. *Met.* 15.23 (in some ms. traditions); *Fast.* 4.731; Eob. *Luth.* 4.3; 7.85; *Val.* 2.339, 340.
        limina, sedes ≈ Verg. *A.* 2.634.

204   **virginea . . . manu** = Ov. *Ep.* 12.130 and Mart. 11.8.6 (both referring to a hand).

205   **lustralibus — undis** ≈ Mant. *1. Parthen.* 2.340: "ad Iordanis aquam lustralibus abluit undis"; *Consol.*, fol. 134ʳ: "maculas lustralibus abluat undis"; cf. Eob. *Her.* 1.6.185–86: "lustralibus undis / Abluis." Cf. further Vulg. *Act.* 22.16; Eob. *Her. Chr.* 7.139; 17.87; 22.116; 22.119, n.

207   **Christo duce** *Her. Chr.* 8.117, n.

208   **praemia digna ferant** = Verg. *A.* 1.605; cf. Ov. *Ars* 2.702; Eob. *Eccles.* 40.

209–10   **Plura — tuis** For the motif, cf. *Her. Chr.* 1.203–04, n.

209   **Plura quidem dixit** Ov. *Met.* 13.493.
        si volet ipse *Her. Chr.*, lim. 4, n.

210   **brachia nostra tuis** = Ov. *Ep.* 18.96.

211   **placido — flumine** ≈ *Hod.* 104. For *placido flumine*, see also *Nor.* 72, 330.
        flumine Rheni = *Buc.* 10.2, n.

212   **Accepit — suo** Cf. Ov. *Ep.* 17.6; l. 199 above.

214   **populis relligione pater** Cf. *Nup.* 250.

216   **Egimus . . . iter** Ov. *Ars* 2.84; *Met.* 2.714–15; 8.225.
        turba pedestris Sedul. 1.138.

217   **Servat adhuc** = Ov. *Met.* 14.760.
        pugnax Germania = Gunther, *Lig.* 1.204; 5.82; Locher, *Stult.* 4, fol. 14ᵛ.

218   **Graecum . . . nomen** Ov. *Fast.* 4.63.
        moenia nomen habent = Ov. *Fast.* 4.80; cf. *Am.* 1.15.20; *Ars* 2.96; *Pont.* 3.2.96; Eob. *Sylv. duae* 1.24, nn.

219   **novat — Phoebe** Cf. Ov. *Met.* 1.11. For the time expression, cf. Eob. *Her. Chr.* 5.7, n.

220   **sancta . . . urbe** Vulg. *Dan.* 9.24; Paul. Nol. *Carm.* 31.336; l. 259 below.
        classis Cf. l. 156 above.
        in urbe sumus = *Her.* 2.2.92; *Sylv.* 6.3.8; 6.5.56.

221   **Confluit — orbe** Cf. *Buc.* 11.76, n.; *Accl.* 1.49: "Contrahit immensum diverso vulgus ab orbe"; *Nup.* 140, n.
        diverso . . . orbe = Ov. *Ep.* 13.151; *Ars* 1.685; *Met.* 2.323.

222   **castra sequuntur** = *Nob.* 88; cf. Luc. 4.676; 10.407.

223   **Ipse . . . ante alios** Verg. *A.* 4.141.
        caelestis — aulae = Ov. *Fast.* 1.139 (Janus); cf. Eob. *Nup.* 222 (Julius II); *Max.* 107 (Leo X): ". . . superorum ianitor aulae"; *Nor.* 1026: "Petre, . . . caelestis claviger aulae."

224   **tonsa corona** = *Ama.* B 2.34, n.

225–27   **Ipsaque — sodalis** Cf. *Leg. aurea* 154.14: "Sancta quoque Gerasina regina Sicilie . . . cum quatuor filiabus suis, Babilla, Iuliana, Victoria et Aurea et parvulo suo Adriano . . . relicto regno in manu unius filii sui usque in Britanniam navigavit." Gerasina was Ursula's aunt on the maternal side. See *Leg. aurea* 154.14: "Gerasina, . . . soror . . . Darie matris sancte Ursule."

228   **Ipse — genus** Cf. *Leg. aurea* 154.21: "papa Cyriacus . . . ipse de Britannia oriundus esset et multas inter eas consanguineas haberet."

230   **Cepta — dies** Cf. *Her.* 1.4.278: "Usque sub extremum non peritura diem."
        extremos . . . dies = *Her. Chr.* 14.102.

231   **Tu modo** = *Buc.* 6.87, n.
        noster amor = *Her. Chr.* 1.29, n.
        iuvenum decus = *Hod.* 139; *Venus* 3.45.

231–32   **aethere — tibi** For the play on Ethereus' name cf. *Her. Chr.* 7.103–04, n.

231   **aethere dignus** ≈ Mant. *1. Parthen.* 1.862 and 3.752: "summo genus aethere dignum"; *Calam.* 3.879 (p. 92): "aethere digna."

232   **sis memor esse** = *Her. Chr.* 11.2, n.

234   **pectoris ardor eras** ≈ Ov. *Ars* 3.714.

235   **Tam longe — amantem** Cf. *Her. Chr.* 4.84.

237	**dignum cognomine** = Juvenc. 1.422; cf. Ov. *Pont.* 2.5.49.
238	**Causaque — tui** Cf. Ov. *Ep.* 16.360.
	Causa . . . potior *Her. Chr.* 9.44, n.
	nominis inde tui = *Sylv.* 2.29.12: "Rex es et est ratio nominis inde tui."
239	**pudeat — annos** Cf. *Her.* 1.6.5: "pudeat vixisse tot annis / Non intellectae sub regione viae."
	coluisse tot annos ≈ *Vict.* 114; cf. Verg. *A.* 1.47.
241	**veri . . . Tonantis** Prud. *Amart.* 376; Mant. *1. Parthen.* 2.931.
242	**Fulmina . . . iacit . . . manu** Ov. *Pont.* 1.2.126; Eob. *Max.* 50.
243–44	**Hic neque — pio** Cf. Vulg. *Psa.* 50.18–19; Ov. *Ep.* 20.181–82.
243	**pinguibus extis** Verg. *G.* 2.396.
245	**reverenter adora** ≈ *Her. Chr.* 2.27, n.
247	**qua sit ratione** = Ov. *Met.* 1.688.
248	**Non labor est** Cf. Ov. *Ep.* 4.137.
	posse placere = Ov. *Ep.* 11.6; 14.88; 15.92; et al.
249	**supplicibus . . . votis** Verg. *A.* 8.61.
250	**Mente — habe** Cf. Ov. *Ep.* 13.66. For *mente memori*, see Eob. *Her. Chr.* 16.162, n.
	nomen amantis habe = l. 158, n., above.
251	**Atque utinam** = *Buc.* 1.36, n.
	miserere puellae = *Her. Chr.* 12.275, n.
253	**ventos . . . faventeis** Ov. *Ep.* 2.19; *Met.* 15.49.
	ventos emitte Cf. Ov. *Met.* 1.264; 11.433; *Tr.* 1.4.17; *Ib.* 33.
254	**tangat humum** = Ov. *Ep.* 13.94.
255	**de more precatus** Cf. Ov. *Met.* 15.593.
257	**Ipsa — valeas** = *Val.* 2.282; cf. *Her. Chr.* 20.32.
	noctesque diesque = *Rec.* 204, n.
258	**Debita . . . vota** = Mart. 9.31.4.
	sollicito pectore = *Her. Chr.* 16.42; cf. Ov. *Met.* 2.125.
	pectore vota = Mart. 6.25.4.
	vota fero = *Hod.* B 7.6; *Psalt.* 86.10. Cf. V. Fl. 3.415.
259	**Utque magis credas** Cf. *Sylv. duae* 2.131, n.
	sancta . . . urbe l. 220, n., above.
260	**Teutonici . . . arva soli** Cf. *Buc.* B 10.4, n.: "Germani . . . ad arva soli." For *Teutonici soli*, see Celtis, *Am.* 4.9.46; Eob. *Nob.* 150.
261	**Omnia tuta satis** *Luth.* 3.32; cf. Verg. *A.* 1.583; 4.298.
262	**Tu modo** = *Buc.* 6.87, n.
263–64	**Sanguine — dies** Cf. Prop. 3.3.45–46; Ov. *Tr.* 4.2.42; *Pont.* 3.4.108. For the phrasing, cf. also Eob. *Sylv. duae* 1.59–60, nn.
263	**Sanguine . . . gaudere** Verg. *G.* 2.510; Ov. *Met.* 1.235; 15.87; *Fast.* 6.176.
264	**multos . . . dies** = *Her. Chr.* 1.38, n.
265	**lesurus amantes** Ov. *Ars* 2.515.
266	**Agrippae maenia** Celtis, *Od.* 3.21.1; cf. l. 201, n., above.
267	**Quicquid erit** = Verg. *A.* 5.710.
	tentanda via est = Verg. *G.* 3.8; cf. Eob. *Rec.* 172.
269	**bibula . . . arena** = Ov. *Met.* 13.901; cf. Lucr. 2.376; Verg. *G.* 1.114; Ov. *Ep.* 19.201; Eob. *Her. Chr.* 12.50, n.
	tumulabor arena ≈ *Ciris* 442; Ov. *Met.* 7.361; *Pont.* 1.6.49.
271	**Per tanta pericula** = Verg. *A.* 1.615; Ov. *Met.* 10.576; cf. Verg. *A.* 9.200, 483; Ov. *Met.* 7.97; Eob. *Her. Chr.* 19.129.
273	**nos fata manent** = Pontano, *Am.* 2.3.43: "Ista senes nos fata manent"; cf. Verg. *A.* 10.438; Eob. *Ruf.* 29: "Quae nos fata manent . . . ?"
	vita superstes = *Rec.* 64, n.
274	**Consulet — tibi** Cf. Ov. *Ep.* 15.184. For the parallelism, cf. also *Ep.* 13.166 (at the end of the letter); and, for example, Eob. *Buc.*, lim. 6.

18

Meter: Elegiac distich.

1–3   **Mittit . . . salutem . . . Hinc ubi** *Sylv. duae* 1.1–2.

1   **Mittit . . . salutem** = Ov. *Ep.* 18.1; *Pont.* 2.2.3. For the play on *salus*, see Eob. *Her. Chr.* 3.1, n.

3   **Hinc — fluctus** Cf. *Sylv. duae* 1.2, n.
      Tyrrhenos . . . fluctus Juv. 6.92.

4   **in portus — tuos** Cf. *Sylv.* 9.6.6: "Venerit in sylvas, Romule Tybri, tuas"; cf. Ov. *Ep.* 18.198; *Fast.* 4.502; *Tr.* 1.10.18; Eob. *Her. Chr.* 21.18.

5–6   **Primus — dedi** For the maritime postal delivery, cf. Ov. *Ep.* 18.9–10; see also l. 172 below.

5   **littore navim** Hor. *Carm.* 1.32.8; cf. Eob. *Her. Chr.* 21.19, n.

7   **tutus — moraris** = l. 161 below; cf. *Her. Chr.* 21.13, n.; 21.20, n.

9   **nec ulla — dextrae** Cf. *Her. Chr.* 16.275–76, n.
      visa est mihi = Ov. *Ep.* 16.59; *Fast.* 3.541; *Met.* 4.514; Eob. *Her. Chr.* 12.209.
      littera dextrae = Ov. *Ep.* 15.1; Eob. *Her. Chr.* 12.1.

10   **luna — videt** = *Sylv.* 3.4.54; cf. *Her. Chr.* 10.180, n.

12   **dicere posse** = Prop. 2.34.28, 62; Ov. *Tr.* 4.5.12; *Pont.* 4.13.8.
      posse negant = Ov. *Fast.* 6.182.

13   **patria . . . urbe** = *Her. Chr.* 7.107, n.
      vir tantus Ov. *Ep.* 16.150; *Met.* 5.192; et al.; cf. Eob. *Ama.* B 2.46, n.

14   **posse — putet** = *Sylv.* 6.6.58; cf. *Luth.* 2.34, n.; Ov. *Pont.* 2.3.92.

19   **cecidisse — Christi** Cf. *Nup.* 237, n.; *Her. Chr.* 12.241, n.

21   **nimia . . . caede** Verg. *A.* 9.354.
      caede tyrannos ≈ Luc. 9.1088.

22   **in medio . . . Foro** = Ov. *Fast.* 6.684; *Tr.* 5.10.44; cf. Eob. *Her. Chr.* 11.145.

24   **cruentatis . . . lupis** = Magdal. *Erarium*, ded., sig. A2ʳ: "Cerva cruentatis expetat acta lupis."

25   **Nec dubito** = Ov. *Ep.* 17.11, 245; 20.62; *Ars* 1.316; et al.
      vitalibus auris = Lucr. 3.577; 5.857; cf. Eob. *Her. Chr.* 24.61, n.

26   **Non — nefas** Cf. *Sylv.* 6.14.32: "Non potuit totum fama tacere decus."
      tantum . . . nefas = *Ama.* 35.110, n.

27   **Sed timeo ne tu** Cf. Ov. *Tr.* 3.7.21.
      ubicumque locorum = *Her. Chr.* 7.105, n.

28   **patriis . . . finibus** Lucr. 6.909; Ov. *Pont.* 2.7.65.
      exul agas Ov. *Ep.* 7.115; *Met.* 15.589.

30   **nocte dieque** = Ov. *Pont.* 3.1.40; Mart. 2.43.2; et al.

31   **timor . . . arguit** Verg. *A.* 4.13.

33   **Clausa . . . teneor** = Ov. *Ep.* 14.3.
      brevi . . . spatio Lucr. 2.78; 4.159, 161; Ov. *Met.* 1.411; et al.
      terraeque marisque = Verg. *A.* 1.598; Ov. *Met.* 2.96; cf. Eob. *Buc.* 11.37, n.

35   **omnia Caesar** = Ov. *Tr.* 2.323; *Pont.* 1.7.43.

36   **terris . . . mari** = *Her. Chr.* 6.72, n.

37–50 **Libera — comam** Cf. *Her.* 1.6.35–46; *Laud.* 209, n.

39   **longis . . . oris** = Sil. 6.628; Mart. *Sp.* 27.1.

40   **Afficient — pedes** Cf. Ov. *Fast.* 1.410. For *teneros pedes* at this metrical position, see also Tib. 1.7.46; 1.9.30; Ov. *Ep.* 16.66; *Ars* 2.534.

41–44 **Arida — hyems** Cf. Ov. *Ars* 2.231–32; Mant. *1. Parthen.* 3.314: "non . . . hyems, non ignea solibus aestas"; Eob. *Sylv.* 8.20.23–28.

41   **solibus aestas** = Verg. *G.* 1.66.

42   **premet — Canis** Cf. *Pug.* 1, n.

43   **pluvius . . . Auster** Ov. *Met.* 1.66. For the Auster as a rain-bearing wind, see Eob. *Buc.* 7.178, n.
       Aquilonibus Auster = Mant. *Calam.* 3.611 (p. 86): "pulsus claris Aquilonibus Auster."

44   **Riphaeo frigore** Claud. *Rapt. Pros.* 3.321–22; cf. Eob. *Her. Chr.* 23.68, n.
       tristis hyems Verg. *Georg.* 4.135; Ov. *Ep.* 16.29; *Ars* 1.409; et al.

45   **Per iuga, per saltus** Cf. *Buc.* 10.169, n.
       rupesque fragosas ≈ Aus. *Cupido cruciatus* 69; Eob. *Hod.* 202.

46   **vix adeunda pede** Cf. Ov. *Ep.* 18.8; *Tr.* 1.8.38; *Pont.* 1.8.12.

48   **forma virilis** = Ov. *Ep.* 4.76.

49   **More virum** = Aus. *Parent.* 6.6.
       latos . . . galeros *Her. Chr.* 7.42.

50   **Neglectam . . . comam** ≈ *Sylv.* 3.5.16; cf. Ov. *Ars* 3.153.

51   **mutare vocabula** ≈ Sil. 14.38.

53   **His — subirem** Cf. *Buc.* 7.145–46.
       maiora subirem ≈ Hor. *S.* 1.3.120.

54   **pudendus amor** = Ov. *Ep.* 5.44; *Fast.* 3.500.

55   **primis . . . ab annis** = *Buc.* 3.65, n.

56   **Hunc — manu** Cf. Tib. 1.3.4; Eob. *Epic.* 2.70: "Quam nulli placidas Mors habet atra manus"; 4.206: ". . . Mors avida traxit acerba manu"; *Her. Chr.* 21.140.
       rapida . . . manu = Poliziano, *Eleg.* 7.54: "Parca tamen rapida te trahet inde manu"; Eob. *Pug.* 42, n.

58   **mortua** For the concept of being dead in sin, see Vulg. *Ephes.* 2.1, 5; *Col.* 2.13.

59   **ex matre creavit** Cf. Verg. *A.* 7.283; Ov. *Met.* 2.553; *Tr.* 3.14.13.

61   **Corporis . . . artus** *Ciris* 198; Hor. *Carm. saec.* 64; Ov. *Met.* 7.317.
       dona dedisti = Ov. *Met.* 9.213.

62   **Fecit . . . ille minus** Cf. Mart. 1.21.8.

63–64 **Ipsa — fuit** Cf. Paul. Nol. *Carm.* 12.1: ". . . meritis et nomine Felix"; 13.1.

64   **rerum pondere** = Hutten. *Querel.* 1.4.2: "Et titulo et rerum pondere nomen habens"; cf. Ov. *Tr.* 2.237; *Ib.* 247.

65   **magno . . . Christo** = *Buc.* 6.87, n.

66   **Cumque — Deum** Cf. Cic. *Tusc.* 3.2: "ut paene cum lacte nutricis errorem suxisse videamur"; Prud. *c. Symm.* 1.201–02; *Perist.* 10.684–85; Eob. *Nob.* 275–76.
       potui — Deum Cf. *Her. Chr.* 16.48.

67   **sacros . . . in usus** Mant. *1. Parthen.* 1.658.

69   **durus pater** = Ov. *Am.* 1.15.17; 3.8.31.

74   **libera frena** For the image, cf. *Buc.* 10.140, n.

75   **Nubilis interea . . . aetas** = Claud. *Cons. Stil.* 1.69.

76   **animi prima . . . mei** Cf. Ov. *Ep.* 12.32.

78   **Si mea — aquis** Cf. Ov. *Ars* 3.340; *Tr.* 1.8.36; 4.9.2.

81   **fidem . . . beatam** = *Her. Chr.* 12.227, n.

82   **sacrum . . . opus** = *Her. Chr.* 22.118 (refrain); cf. Mant. *Ecl.* 6.153.

83   **O illum — favete** Cf. V. Fl. 6.733–34; Eob. *Her. Chr.* 9.153–54; 12.281.
       favete Eobanus often uses this verb with an accusative object: see *Her. Chr.* 8.89; 19.132, and, for example, *Hymn.* 181; *Venus* 1.4, 259; 2.211; 3.13; *Idyl.* 13.43–44; 15.11. For this usage, see also Celtis, *Am.* 2.10.73: "Mercurius citharam, faveat tibi carmina Phoebus."

84   **Eveniat capiti . . . meo** Cf. Ov. *Ib.* 446.
       capiti . . . corona meo = Prop. 3.1.20; cf. Ov. *Ars* 1.582; Eob. *Her. Chr.* 23.104, n.

85   **Sanguine . . . rorantes** Verg. *A.* 11.8; Stat. *Theb.* 3.536; 9.596.
       Sanguine . . . rubro Cf. *Her. Chr.* 16.221. For *sanguine rubro*, see Verg. *Cat.* 9.32; Hor. *Carm.* 3.13.7.
       undique venas = *Aetna* 121, 176.

86   **tremulas . . . faces** Cf. Lucr. 4.404; Verg. *Ecl.* 8.105.

88   **angelicos — choros** ≈ Trebelius, *Epigr.*, sig. C2ʳ: "angelicos inter et esse choros." For *angelicos choros* at this metrical position, see Ven. Fort. *Carm.* 2.9.50; 4.14.16: "inter et angelicos . . . choros"; cf. Paul. Nol. *Carm.* 18.141; Prud. *Perist.* 3.48; Eob. *Her. Chr.* 1.206; 15.110.

       inter et ante = *Sylv.* 6.1.56; *Psalt.* 8.24; 9.44; 122.4.

89   **magni Deus — aevi** = *Psalt.* 44.1: "Conditor omnipotens magni Deus arbiter aevi"; cf. *Psalt.* 38.3: ". . . magni Deus autor et arbiter orbis"; Aus. *Ecl.* 22.10: ". . . Deus arbiter aevi."

90   **Eius ad arbitrium** Cf. Lucr. 2.281 and Prud. *Apoth.* 210: "cuius ad arbitrium. . . ."

91   **aetas mea . . . annos** *Her. Chr.* 14.45, n.

93   **Venimus ad** = *Her. Chr.* 3.73, n.

       thalamum . . . iugalem ≈ Pontano, *Ecl.* 1.4.26: "nulli conubia amantes, / Nulli etiam thalamos nymphae petiere iugales"; *Am.* 2.4.55: "torum thalamique faces violare iugalis."

       aequa lege Hor. *Carm.* 3.1.14.

94   **falso . . . Iove** *Her. Chr.* 2.49, n.

       miles For the image of spiritual warfare, see *Her. Chr.* 6.71, n.

95–96   **Tunc — erat** For the motif of the ill-omened wedding, cf. Verg. *A.* 4.166–72; Ov. *Ep.* 2.117–20; also *Ep.* 6.43–46; 7.93–96; *Met.* 6.428–32.

95   **feralia bubo** = Stat. *Theb.* 3.511. The owl was traditionally a bird of ill omen: see, for example, Verg. *A.* 4.462; Ov. *Ep.* 2.118 (at a wedding); *Met.* 5.549–50; 6.431–32 (at a wedding).

96   **Iunctaque — erat** Cypresses were associated with death and mourning: see *Buc.* B 3.5, n. Thus the wedding torches have turned into funeral torches. Cf. Prop. 4.3.13–14; Ov. *Ep.* 2.120; 6.41–42, 45–46; 21.172.

       moesta cupressus Sil. 10.534.

98   **Aversa . . . mente** Ov. *Pont.* 1.2.8; Sil. 2.618; Eob. *Nor.* 1376.

       fingere mente = [Tib.] 3.6.34.

99   **primis . . . ab annis** = *Buc.* 3.65, n.

       ut nunc quoque = Paul. Nol. *Carm.* 10.160; cf. Ov. *Tr.* 5.12.33.

100   **numina — habent** Cf. Prop. 2.32.2; Ov. *Am.* 2.5.6; *Ars* 2.272; Eob. *Her. Chr.* 7.130, n.

101   **nupta marito** = *Her. Chr.* 7.43, n.

103–04   **Caucasea — corde** Cf. *Pug.* B 1.23–24, with n. 12.

103   **Caucasea . . . sub rupe** = Andrel. *Livia* 2.9.39; cf. Prop. 2.1.69; Ov. *Ars* 3.195; Aus. *Ecl.* 19.21: ". . . Caucasea sub rupe Prometheus."

       diram . . . volucrem V. Fl. 4.79.

105   **Cepheidos** Man. 1.436.

108   **crimen habere** = Ov. *Rem.* 328; Eob. *Her. Chr.* 10.172; 11.58.

109   **fecissent — matrem** Cf. *Her. Chr.* 5.178, n.

110   **misero . . . patri** Verg. *A.* 11.63.

111–12   **Florida — dies** The thought that grief makes one grow old before one's time is proverbial: see, for example, Vulg. *Prov.* 17.22; *Eccli.* 30.22–26; Ov. *Tr.* 3.8.24–34; 4.6.39–50; *Pont.* 1.4.1–20; Boeth. *Consol.* 1.m1.9–12; *Flos medicinae* 14–16: "Triste cor, ira frequens, . . . labor ingens / Vitam consumunt haec tria fine brevi: / Haec namque ad mortis cogunt te currere metas"; Walther 31596; Erasmus, *Adag.* 3.10.62. Cf. also Eob. *Buc.* 7.141–43, n.

111   **Florida . . . tempora** *Buc.* 1.17, n.

113   **Spiritus . . . exisset in auras** = Ov. *Tr.* 4.3.41; cf. Eob. *Her. Chr.* 13.23, n.

       tenues . . . in auras = *Her. Chr.* 13.99, n.

114   **potui — mori** Cf. *Sylv. duae* 2.232; *Her.* 1.3.44.

       nimio . . . dolore = Pontano, *Tum.* 1.32.8: "nimio muta dolore tacent."

115   **melius . . . consultum est** Pl. *Capt.* 719; *Cist.* 97; Ov. *Met.* 2.141; et al.

116	**Immensum . . . globum** Cf. *Her. Chr.* 1.16.
	rotat . . . globum Cf. Verg. *A.* 4.269; Sen. *Phaed.* 961–63; Boeth. *Consol.* 1.m5.3, addressing God: "rapido caelum turbine versas."
	patria . . . arte Stat. *Theb.* 6.770; cf. Prop. 3.5.26.
117	**verae . . . salutis** Cf. *Her. Chr.* 6.1.
118	**Maius . . . nomen** Prop. 3.1.24; Ov. *Fast.* 3.187.
	nomen habes = *Pug.* 84, n.
119	**igni fomenta** *Idyl.* 15.79; *Sylv.* 2.1.74.
121–24	**ego — est** Cf. *Leg. aurea* 7.4-6: "[Vir eius] audiens eam . . . in vili habitu Christianorum carceres circumire et eis necessaria ministrare, fecit eam arctissime custodiri. . . . Putans . . . se mori dolorosas litteras Grisogono mittebat et ille consolatorias remittebat."
121	**ego** The pronoun is in the nominative case, partly because of grammatical attraction to the following relative clause, partly because Eobanus is already looking ahead to l. 123.
	quae — hostes Cf. *Her. Chr.* 19.117–18. For the commonplace of spiritual warfare, see *Her. Chr.* 6.71, n.
	medios . . . per hostes = Verg. *A.* 3.283.
122	**Caesaris ira** = *Her. Chr.* A 3.44, n.
123	**carceris umbras** = Ven. Fort. *Carm.* 3.9.73; Mant. *2. Parthen.* 2.388, 403; cf. Juvenc. 1.409; 2.510.
124	**littera multa** = *Her.* 3.4.110.
125	**dulcissima vulnera** = *Her. Chr.* 17.85; cf. *Buc.* 3.39, n.
	vulnera passam = *Her.* 3.8.107; cf. Verg. *A.* 6.660; 7.182; Ov. *Met.* 6.297; 13.391.
127	**tormenta tyranni** = Celtis, *Am.* 1.13.7; Eob. *Her.* 1.6.191; cf. *Her. Chr.* 4.221.
128	**Unius . . . non facit assis** Cf. Catul. 5.3; 42.13; Otto 175.
131–44	**Aspice — tulit** Cf. *Her. Chr.* 5.57–62, n.
135	**Impositam collo** = *Her. Chr.* 16.204.
137	**Impia . . . ora** = Celtis, *Am.* 1.14.126; cf. [Tib.] 3.5.14.
	ora tyranni = Stat. *Theb.* 3.82; V. Fl. 5.387.
140	**sertis** The crown of thorns. Cf. *Her. Chr.* 16.197, n.
	heu quibus ille Verg. *A.* 4.13.
141	**cedro** *Her. Chr.* 6.205, with n. 18.
142	**corpus amet** ≈ Ov. *Am.* 3.11.38; cf. Eob. *Her. Chr.* 17.42.
145	**vicinae . . . morti** *Her. Chr.* 6.119, n.
	carcere morti ≈ Prud. *Psych.* 595; Ven. Fort. *Carm.* 3.9.81.
147	**Sufficit . . . in ignes** Ov. *Met.* 7.613.
	corpus in ignes = Paul. Nol. *Carm.* 27.294.
148	**Sunt — cadant** Cf. Ov. *Ep.* 3.146; 5.86; Eob. *Her. Chr.* 12.30.
	ense cadant ≈ *Her. Chr.* 6.160, n.
150	**Est amor** = *Her. Chr.* 1.37; 4.77 (in both cases followed by an infinitive).
	pro pietate mori = *Her. Chr.* 11.54; 12.14.
152	**qui dulce — habes** Cf. *Val.* 1.332: "Qui nihil humani, nomina praeter, habet."
	dulce nihil *Her. Chr.* 5.50, n.
153	**Adde . . . comitem me** Sen. *Her. O.* 952; cf. Verg. *A.* 6.777.
155	**Fer — dextram** Cf. Sen. *Phaed.* 704–05.
156	**Mens mea** = *Buc.* 3.136, n.
	tristia fata = *Laud.* B 3.20, n.
157	**gravibus . . . flagellis** Mant. *1. Parthen.* 2.870.
159	**virginibus . . . ducentis** = Walter, *Alex.* 8.10: "virginibus . . . comitata ducentis."
161	**tutus — moraris** = l. 7 above, n.
164	**pestis acerba** = Verg. *G.* 3.419.
165	**Quis — palestra** For the image of the martyr as an athlete who contends for the eternal crown, cf. *Her. Chr.* 4.233, n.; 19.66; 23.102. Cf. further Brant, *Var. carm.*, sig.

F6ᵛ (*Texte* 92.166–68) "utinam misello / Spes sit athletam fore me palestra / Carthusianae"; sig. F7ʳ (*Texte* 109.1–2) "De numero aethereae quisquis cupis esse palestrae / Principe sub Christo et miliciae esse comes."
athleta palestra ≈ *Buc.* 10.96.

166   **cum misera . . . matre** Ov. *Am.* 3.9.51.

170   **scripto — tuo** = Ov. *Ep.* 6.4.

172   **Advenit — frequens** Cf. ll. 5–6, n., above.

174   **minima parte** = Ov. *Am.* 3.10.30; Eob. *Sylv. duae* 1.180.

175   **Quod — epistola** Cf. *Her. Chr.* 17.1–3, nn.; 19.1; *Eccles.* 9: "Sera sed haec forsan si littera visa venire est."

176   **vultus . . . videre tuos** = Ov. *Pont.* 2.4.8; Eob. *Her. Chr.* 11.168; 24.4.

181–82   **Si — cineres** Cf. *Leg. aurea* 7.38–39: "Apollonia autem corpus sancte Anastasie in viridario, facta ibi ecclesia, honorifice sepelivit. Passa est autem sub Diocletiano."

181   **mihi finiet** = Ov. *Ib.* 137; cf. Eob. *Buc.* 3.93, n.

182   **patrios . . . in cineres** Hor. *Ars* 471.

19

Meter: Elegiac distich.

1   **sera venit . . . epistola** *Her. Chr.* 18.175, n.

1–2   **quantum — abest** Cf. l. 90 below.

2   **Thuscus . . . Tybris** Verg. *G.* 1.499; Ov. *Ib.* 136; cf. Eob. *Her. Chr.* 12.235.

3   **Nam — curis** Cf. Tib. 1.3.3; Eob. *Buc.* 4.4, n.
Seleucia = Ven. Fort. *Carm.* 8.3.171, also with a long first syllable: "Seleucia Theclam."

5–6   **At tu — manes** According to tradition, Peter and Paul were at Rome together and were martyred on the very same day. See Hier. *De viris inlustribus* 5; *Leg. aurea* 84. 291–300; 85.31. By 1523 Eobanus (following Luther) was questioning the tradition: see *Eccles.* 79–80. Though Peter's stay at Rome is excised in the revision of the present letter (*BO*), Eobanus overlooked the motif at *Her.* 2.2.166 (= *Her. Chr.* 21.168).

5   **teris . . . limina** Mart. 10.10.2.
Galilaei . . . Petri = *Eccles.* 77.
limina Petri = Claud. *Carm. minora* 50.1.

6   **Dura . . . iura** *Her. Chr.* 12.33.

7   **Quid tibi cum . . . Rhoma** Cf. Ov. *Ep.* 15.52; Eob. *Her. Chr.* 8.3, n.
doctor clarissime = Brant, *Texte* 194.29.

8   **monitis . . . tuis** = Ov. *Ars* 3.48.

9   **magnum . . . Christum** *Buc.* 6.87, n.

10   **poenas exiciumque** = *Ama.* 35.100; *Pod.* 60.

11   **Hoc — huius** Cf. *Calum.* 159: "Hoc periere modo tot milia tempore nostro."
temporis huius = Ov. *Fast.* 6.69.

12   **cum Iove Caesar** = Ov. *Pont.* 4.4.34. Roman emperors were conventionally deified: cf. ll. 20, 31–32 below. Thus, as Jupiter reigned in heaven, so the emperor reigned on earth: see Hor. *Carm.* 3.5.1–3.

13   **Quam — minores** Cf. l. 57 below.
Quam fuerat melius = *Her. Chr.* 24.139; *Idyl.* 14.49; 15.112; cf. Ov. *Ep.* 21.125: "At fuerat melius, si . . ."; Mant. *Ecl.* 2.87 (Celtis, *Am.* 1.5.17; 3.14.61): "quam melius fuerat. . . ."
gentes . . . minores = Claud. *Bell. Get.* 393. Paul preached especially in Asia Minor and Greece.

14   **nomina laudis** = *Sylv. duae* 1.74, n.

15	**Rhoma potens** = Gunther, *Lig.* 3.370; Petrarch, *Africa* 1.536; Mant. *6. Parthen.*, fol. 130ʳ; Eob. *Tum.* 6.66; cf. Hor. *Ep.* 2.1.61; Ov. *Fast.* 4.255; Stat. *Silv.* 4.1.28.
	toti . . . praesidet orbi Prop. 3.11.57 and Mant. *Bapt.*, fol. 229ᵛ: ". . . toti qui praesidet orbi"; cf. Eob. *Her. Chr.* 6.150.
	caput A common title for Rome in the heyday of the Roman Empire: see n. to *Her. Chr.* 17.67–68.
16	**laude superba** = Hutten, *Querel.* 1.7.60; Eob. *Her. Chr.* 24.26.
18	**Pondus — idem** Cf. Ov. *Fast.* 2.684; Eob. *Her. Chr.* 6.150, n.; *Psalt.* 87, arg. 4: "Regni sit spacium cuius et orbis idem."
19	**patria — triumphos** Cf. Mant. *Calam.* 1.595 (p. 34): ". . . tot egregia partos virtute triumphos"; Eob. *Tum.* 2.59–60.
	patria . . . virtute = *Idyl.* 13.10; cf. *Her. Chr.* 17.109, n.
20	**Et se — deos** Cf. *Her. Chr.* 12.200, n.
	presentes . . . deos = *Accl.* 1.40; *Epic.* 2.48; *Venus* 3.22 (all referring to temporal rulers, including the emperor); *Sylv.* 1.5.40 (poets like Vergil and Baptista Mantuanus); cf. Ov. *Tr.* 2.54; *Pont.* 2.8.52. From the Augustan period on, Roman emperors were regularly referred to as gods.
	credit habere = Ov. *Fast.* 1.324.
	habere deos = *Her. Chr.* 9.160, n.
21	**pater urbis** = Verg. *A.* 8.134; cf. Ov. *Fast.* 3.72 and Juv. 2.126.
22	**quaelibet ara** = *Her. Chr.* 12.268.
23	**documenta** Cf. Mant. *2. Parthen.* 2.32–33: "Sed neque post Petri vocem documentaque Pauli / Roma Deum nescire potest."
25	**Et licet exuperes** = *Nob.* 133; cf. Ov. *Ars* 3.399.
	divinae — mentis = *Her. Chr.* 21.75; cf. *Buc.* 11.18, n.; *Her.* 1.4.283.
26	**pectore cuncta** = Balbi, *Opusc.* 51.22: "Iura quidem memori pectore cuncta tenes"; Eob. *Buc.* B 7.22; cf. Hor. *S.* 2.4.90.
27	**Blanda . . . gratia** = Ven. Fort. *Carm.* 6.2.103; Eob. *Sylv.* 5.20.33; cf. Ov. *Pont.* 2.2.96.
	florentis . . . gratia linguae = *Laud.* 460, n.
28	**In — tuis** For this proverbial expression, cf. Cic. *Brut.* 59; Quint. *Inst.* 10.1.82: "in labris eius sedisse quandam persuadendi deam"; Poliziano, *Silv.* 1.307: "cui blandis insidet Suada labellis"; Erasmus, *Adag.* 3.4.73, *ASD* 2.5:277, ll. 849–50.
29	**Saxa . . . trahes sylvasque** Cf. Ov. *Tr.* 4.1.17–18; Man. 1.329.
	Saxa . . . scopulosque = Stat. *Theb.* 10.97.
	sylvasque virenteis = *Culex* 22.
30	**per nemus omne** = Ov. *Fast.* 3.746; 4.460, 760.
32	**non — deum** = Prud. *Apoth.* 188; Eob. *Sylv.* 1.4.90; *Psalt.* 14.2; cf. *Her. Chr.* 2.22, n.; l. 148 below.
33–34	**Sed pariunt — erit** For the thought, cf. Prop. 2.10.5–6; Ov. *Pont.* 3.4.79; Erasmus, *Adag.* 2.8.55.
33	**facta insignia** Ov. *Ep.* 3.121.
34	**Tentatique — erit** Cf. Verg. *A.* 9.194–95.
35	**magno . . . Tonanti** = *Her. Chr.* 2.7, n.
36	**Res animo** = *Hymn.*, lim. 1.4.
38	**Terrarum princeps** = *Her.* 2.2.168 (Rome).
39	**taedia vitae** = *Laud.* 320, n.
43–46	**Namque — decet** Cf. Ov. *Tr.* 4.8.17–24.
43	**vasti . . . profundi** V. Fl. 8.314.
44	**In portum . . . ratem** ≈ *Her. Chr.* 17.146.
	applicuisse ratem = Prop. 1.20.20.
45–46	**Arma — decet** For the commonplace of spiritual warfare, see *Her. Chr.* 6.71, n.
45	**discrimina belli** = Luc. 8.389.
46	**nomen — decet** = *Luth.* 1.2; *Epic.* 1.2; cf. *Sylv. duae* 1.156, n.

49–50   **Flumina — feras** For the adynata, see *Buc.* 10.98–101, n.; ll. 153–54 below.
49   **Flumina . . . retro . . . reditura** Cf. Prop. 3.19.6; Ov. *Tr.* 1.8.1–2; *Pont.* 4.5.43. For this proverbial impossibility, see Erasmus, *Adag.* 1.3.15; Otto 678; Häussler, 57, 73, 163, 236, 271; Eob. *Sylv.* 6.10.56.
        retro . . . reditura Lucr. 4.310; Verg. *A.* 9.794; Ov. *Met.* 15.249.
49–50   **lacusque — arsuros** Cf. Ov. *Tr.* 1.8.4; Eob. *Buc.* 10.157.
51   **Mortua, crede** = Ov. *Ep.* 11.63.
53   **Pars . . . populi** Ov. *Fast.* 2.531; Luc. 2.236.
        licet observet ≈ Ov. *Ars* 3.617.
54   **verbis — fidem** Cf. *Sylv.* 7.19.16: ". . . si verbis credis inesse fidem." For *inesse fidem*, see Ov. *Ep.* 17.130.
55   **trucibus . . . minis** Aus. *Cupido cruciatus* 93.
56   **Dissimulat . . . Deum** Cf. *Her. Chr.* 1.128, n.
        tacita . . . arte = *Calum.* 30: "Insontem tacita circuit arte virum"; cf. Stat. *Silv.* 3.4.69; Mant. *1. Parthen.* 2.211, where God says: "Tacita nos arte movemus / corda hominum."
57   **Ergo — minores** Cf. l. 13 above, n.
58   **Qur tua — iacet** Cf. *Accl.* 2.165: "Cur tua lenta iacet virtus . . . ?"
        virtus languida = *Sylv.* 6.6.18: "hoc virtus languida calcar habet." Cf. Mant. *Calam.* 2.190 (p. 57): ". . . quondam florens, modo languida virtus."
        languida facta iacet Ov. *Ep.* 9.136; cf. *Fast.* 3.20; 5.318.
59   **tua . . . gloria marcet** *Idyl.* 17.91.
        languet virtus *Ama.* B 2.41.
60   **Da veniam si quid** = Luc. 8.749; cf. Eob. *Her. Chr.* 2.14, n.
        ineptit amor For the pentameter close, cf. *Ama.* B 2.78, n.: "ineptus amor."
61   **tua me miseram** = *Her. Chr.* 4.79; 8.55.
62   **insana . . . mente** Tib. 2.6.18.
        mente loquor = *Her. Chr.* 6.68.
63   **Candida . . . fama** Celtis, *Am.* 2.11.60; 3.7.32.
        tua fama per oras = Celtis, *Am.* 1.8.29.
64   **Gloria . . . sepulta** = *Epic.* 6.92.
65   **innumeras urbes** Ov. *Ep.* 16.179.
66   **fortis — Dei** Quodvultdeus (Ps. Prosper), *Liber promissionum et praedictorum Dei* 1.22: "Iob ille fortissimus athleta dei." The expression *fortis athleta Dei* recurs in late medieval hagiographic literature. See also Eob. *Her. Chr.* 18.165, n.
67   **Postquam clara** = Luc. 7.787.
        clara . . . Damascus Q. Serenus, *Liber medicinalis* 27.5.
        nova . . . luce For the phrase in this sense, see *Her. Chr.* 11.133, n.
68   **patrios . . . deos** = Ov. *Ep.* 1.26; 12.128; *Rem.* 158; *Fast.* 2.728; Eob. *Her.* 3.4.174; cf. *Her. Chr.* 4.45, n. The phrase is odd in this context, given the Jews' monotheism. In the revised edition (*BO*) Eobanus changes it to "leges . . . tuas."
70   **occulta . . . fuga** Sil. 7.331.
        cautus — fuga ≈ Celtis, *Am.* 2.11.38: "Ille solet tacita cautus abire fuga."
72   **facta referre** = Tib. 1.10.44; Ov. *Am.* 3.14.8; *Ep.* 19.64; et al.
74   **sine non lachrymis** Hor. *Carm.* 3.7.7–8.
75   **Immeritum — Philippi** In Philippi he was severely beaten and thrown into jail: see Vulg. *Act.* 16.19–24.
76   **Flumina — loqui** = *Epic.* 6.108; cf. Vulg. *Luc.* 19.40; Eob. *Her. Chr.* 21.153–54, n.; *Hymn.* B 2.2, 4; *Ebn.* 80.
77   **littera** Paul's letter to the Philippians in the New Testament.
78   **veram . . . fidem** = *Eccles.* 130; cf. Paul. Nol. *Carm.* 19.265; Prud. *Apoth.* 638; *Perist.* 9.20.
79   **Ephesique feras** See Vulg. *1. Cor.* 15.32.
        Solimaeque tumultus See Vulg. *Act.* 21.27–36.

80   **Macedum — dolos** For Paul's treatment at the hands of the Macedonians, see Vulg. *Act.* 16.19–40. The book of Acts makes no mention of any troubles with the Cappadocians; but cf. *Act.* 14.19, where Paul is said to have been stoned at Lystra, in neighboring Galatia, by the Jews of Antioch and Iconium.

82   **bona . . . dona** Paul. Nol. *Carm.* 26.382.

83–84   **Praeterea — tenet** See Vulg. *Act.* 18.1–23.

85–86   **Te doctore — habent** Cf. Vulg. *Act.* 21.1. On the Colossus of Rhodes, see Eob. *Laud.*, lim. 4, with n. 2.

87   **gloria plena** *Her. Chr.* 8.120, n.

88   **titulis . . . tuis** = *Her. Chr.* 12.40, n.

89   **Patria — Tharsi** Paul was a native of Tarsus in Cilicia: see Vulg. *Act.* 22.3.
       Perseae . . . Tharsi Luc. 3.225. According to legend, the city's founder was Perseus.

90   **quantum — abest** Cf. ll. 1–2 above. Tarsus lies on the Cydnus River.

91   **fuit hoc nimium** = *Her. Chr.* 9.47.

93   **At tibi — cadendum** Cf. Ov. *Met.* 12.610; Mant. *Somn.*, fol. 218ᵛ: ". . . Christi pro relligione cadentes."

95   **ocia vitae** = Ov. *Tr.* 4.10.105; Stat. *Silv.* 3.5.85; 4.4.49; Eob. *Nob.* 181; cf. *Sylv. duae* 2.157.

96   **In patria — tua** Cf. Ov. *Tr.* 4.8.12; Eob. *Her.* 2.7.32: "Quantum erat in patria te senuisse tua"; *Sylv.* 2.6.16: "In patria poterat delituisse sua."

97   **intentus studiis** Cf. *Her. Chr.* 11.83, n.

98   **Gammalielis** For this medieval spelling, see, for example, *Nicodem.* 1.1.

100   **gloria nomen habet** = *Her. Chr.* 6.46, n.

101   **saeva . . . fortuna** = Andrel. *Livia* 3.10.45; cf. Eob. *Her. Chr.* 22.27, n.
        fortuna negasset ≈ Verg. *A.* 10.435; Luc. 6.159.

102   **vitae pars . . . meae** Ov. *Pont.* 1.2.144; 4.10.20; cf. Eob. *Her. Chr.* 1.140, n.

103   **Cresceret — horas** Cf. *Her. Chr.* 7.55, n.

104   **pectora — dolor** = Dantiscus, *Carm.* 1.3.186: "pressit pectora maesta dolor."

105   **gemitus . . . trahentem** = V. Fl. 4.135.

106   **Tristitiae — quaereret** Ov. *Tr.* 5.4.7.

107   **blanda — voce** = Avit. *Carm.* 3.379.
        solatur — dolores ≈ Claud. *Rapt. Pros.* 2.276.

109   **Ah, quoties** = *Her. Chr.* 1.43, n.

111   **perfusum lachrymis** *Her. Chr.* 5.102, n.
        lachrymis . . . humida Prop. 1.16.4; Ov. *Tr.* 3.3.82; *Pont.* 1.9.2; Eob. *Her. Chr.* 4.142.

111–12   **premit . . . pectus Fascia** Cf. Prop. 4.9.49.

112   **concepto pondere** = *Her. Chr.* 13.76, n., in a different sense. Cf. Ov. *Met.* 6.396–97: "madefactaque terra . . . / concepit lacrimas."
        pondere — gravis = *Her. Chr.* 6.14; cf. Mart. 7.53.8.

113   **facundae . . . linguae** = *Her. Chr.* 4.243, n.
        munere linguae = Mart. 7.88.9; Paul. Nol. *Carm.* 18.46.

114   **taela** For the image, cf. Ov. *Pont.* 4.6.36: "linguae tela . . . tuae."

117   **victricia signa** = Sil. 6.599; 14.179.
        signa per hostes = *Her. Chr.* 18.121.

118   **Sumptaque — tuli** Cf. *Sylv.* 1.10.46: "Sume age pro Phoebo fortiter arma tuo."
        Sumptaque . . . arma = Ov. *Pont.* 1.3.28.
        fortiter arma = Tib. 2.6.2.

119   **nobilium de sanguine . . . parentum** Cf. Hor. *Carm.* 2.20.5–6; Mant. *5. Parthen.*, fol. 122ᵛ: "Lucia, nobilium soboles generosa parentum"; Eob. *Her.*, ded. 99.

120   **nubere virgo** = Mart. 12.42.2: "hac qua lege viro nubere virgo solet"; Eob. *Her. Chr.* 7.10.

122   **tetro . . . carcere** Paul. Nol. *Carm.* 16.23; Eob. *Vict.* 2.
        carcere clausa = *Her. Chr.* 10.120, n.

123   **illaesa manebam** ≈ Juvenc. 1.718; Mant. *1. Parthen.* 2.969.
124   **nudos . . . pedes** = Prop. 3.17.32; Ov. *Am.* 3.7.82; *Ars* 2.698.
       dira leaena = Locher, *Stult.* 61, fol. 73ʳ: "Saevitiam superat, dira leaena, tuam."
125   **ursi . . . truces** V. Fl. 2.73.
       saevique leones = *Buc.* 6.41; cf. Lucr. 3.306; Claud. *Rapt. Pros.* 2.243.
129   **tanta pericula** = *Her. Chr.* 17.271, n.
130   **Callida — fui** Cf. *Her. Chr.* 8.100, n.
       magica . . . arte = Alan. *Nat.* 1.6; cf. Verg. *A.* 4.493; Ov. *Am.* 3.7.35; et al.
132   **favet** For *faveo* with an accusative object, see *Her. Chr.* 18.83, n.
133   **Non . . . fateor meruisse** = Ov. *Tr.* 5.5.63.
       tantum . . . meruisse favoris Cf. Paul. Nol. *Carm.* 6.88; Eob. *Her. Chr.* 7.7.
134   **muneris omne tui est** = Ov. *Tr.* 1.6.6; cf. Hor. *Carm.* 4.3.21.
135–36   **Tu potes — Deum** Cf. *Vict.* 264–69.
135   **extremi . . . volumina caeli** For the cosmology, cf. *Her. Chr.* 2.25, with n. 2. Also cf. *Her. Chr.* 2.69, n.
       extremi . . . caeli = Stat. *Theb.* 5.485.
       penetrare — caeli Cf. Vulg. *Eccli.* 35.21.
       volumina caeli = *Vict.* 341: "Multiplicis . . . volumina caeli"; *Psalt.* 8.13 (19.5): "ingentis spaciosa volumina coeli"; 57.17, 33: "super alta volumina coeli"; 104.7: "spaciosa volumina coeli"; Erasmus, *Carm.* 49.3 (first published in September 1514): "stelligeri spaciosa volumina caeli"; cf. Eob. *Eleg.* 1.105 (*Sylv.* 7.34.9): "multiplicis . . . volumina sphaerae."
136   **Praesentem . . . Deum** = *Her.* 1.1.92; cf. *Sylv. duae* 2.198, n.
       alta mente Verg. *A.* 1.26.
137   **Ille — largitur** Cf. Brant, *Var. carm.*, sig. F7ᵛ (*Texte* 111.5–6), addressed to St. Apollinaris: "Nempe tuis meritis magnus concessit Olympi / Rector, ut exores, quicquid ubique voles."
138   **exiguas . . . preces** = Ov. *Ars* 1.440.
139   **Illius exemplo** = Ov. *Ib.* 615.
139–40   **miseros — domos** Cf. *Hod.* 54–55, referring to Erasmus of Rotterdam.
140   **ad superas . . . domos** = *Laud.* B 1.8, n.
142   **Vulnere** The deadly wound of sin. For the image, cf. *Her. Chr.* 15.61–68.
       certa — facis ≈ *Val.* 2.116.
143–44   **Nemo — erat** Cf. Vulg. *Hebr.* 2.18; Verg. *A.* 1.630.
145–46   **Hoc — videt** Cf. Ov. *Pont.* 1.7.43; Eob. *Sylv.* 6.6.51–52: "Fallitur humanas ratio ingeniosa per artes / Et caeca est cum se cuncta videre putat."
145   **se putat omnia** = *Dicta Catonis* 1.17.
146   **nec sua facta videt** = Locher, *Stult.* 29, fol. 40ᵛ: "Quicquid delirant alii, mox carpit iniquo / Dente Theonino, nec sua facta videt."
147   **Terribilis . . . vultus** Ov. *Met.* 1.265.
       sacra . . . imagine = Luc. 7.357.
       imagine vultus = *Her. Chr.* 17.73, n.
148   **non — deos** = *Her. Chr.* 2.22, n.
151   **quid non — licebit** *Anthol. Lat.* 413.49: ". . . quid non homini sperare licebit?"
152   **In patriam reditus** = Verg. *A.* 10.436.
153–54   **prius — erit** For the adynata, cf. Ov. *Met.* 14.37–38; ll. 49–50, n., above.
156   **nostra querela** = *Her. Chr.* 3.162, n.
158   **nuncia fama tuae** ≈ Ov. *Ep.* 16.38; cf. Eob. *Her. Chr.* 12.264.
160   **Qur ego — fui** For the sentiment, cf. Ov. *Tr.* 3.2.25.
163   **mala nomina** = Ov. *Ars* 3.453; Eob. *Her. Chr.* 24.151; *Vict.*, ded. 33.
164   **Visa — Noti** Cf. Strozzi, *Eroticon* 2.4.24: "In celeres abeant somnia dira Notos"; Eob. *Her. Chr.* 5.78, n.
       Visa . . . somnia *Her. Chr.* 4.102, n.
       celeres . . . Noti = Ov. *Fast.* 5.686; Mart. 9.38.6.

166   **Ocia . . . dulcia** *Ama.* 35.79, n.
167   **Respice . . . solita pietate** Alcuin. *Carm.* 99.12.8: "Tu quoque respiceres solita pietate precantes."
        pietate puellam = Mant. *5. Parthen.*, fol. 126ʳ; *Georgius*, fol. 207ᵛ.

20

Meter: Elegiac distich.

1–4   **Sic mihi — ego** Cf. *Her.* 1.6.1–4.
1   **sera . . . prole** Mant. *1. Parthen.* 2.724, referring to Elizabeth: "sera fecundam prole parentem"; l. 17 below; cf. also l. 61, n., and l. 156 below.
2   **Dextera . . . loquta tua est** Cf. Ov. *Ep.* 18.20; l. 56 below.
3   **non eadem — est** = *Max.* 13; cf. Ov. *Pont.* 3.9.15; Eob. *Hod.* 16; *Val.* 1.401.
3–4   **fungar . . . Munere** = Verg. *A.* 6.885–86; Ov. *Rem.* 795–96.
4   **dicor . . . exul** Ov. *Tr.* 2.137.
6   **Quas — terras** ≈ Ov. *Ep.* 1.66.
        quove loco = *Sylv. duae* 1.20, n.
7   **celsa petunt . . . sydera** Mart. 9.61.10; Eob. *Nor.* 278; cf. Ov. *Met.* 1.316. For *celsa sydera*, see also Stat. *Theb.* 7.3–4; 8.61.
        umbrosi . . . montes [Tib.] 3.9.2.
        sydera montes = Ov. *Met.* 1.153.
8   **Lambit . . . aequor humum** Cf. *Sylv. duae* 1.144, n.; *Her. Chr.* 9.34, n.
9   **puro . . . aere** Ov. *Tr.* 2.36; Stat. *Silv.* 1.1.32; l. 21 below.
11   **paucis . . . ministris** = *Her.* 1.6.51.
        paucis comitata ≈ Verg. *A.* 10.186.
        comitata ministris = Verg. *A.* 2.580.
12   **Regius . . . satelles** Luc. 10.468–69; l. 127 below.
        satelles erat = Ov. *Fast.* 5.538.
13   **saevo . . . regi** ≈ Verg. *A.* 12.849.
14   **multis . . . viris** = Prop. 2.6.6; Ov. *Am.* 1.5.12.
        foemina sola viris ≈ Mart. 12.96.6.
15   **Pene metu exanimata** Mant. *Georgius*, fol. 207ᵛ: ". . . gelidamque metu, pene exanimatam"; cf. Ter. *Ph.* 564: "exanimatam metu"; Eob. *Nob.* 61: "pene exanimata."
        genu labente = *Her. Chr.* 16.31, n.
16   **Aut hoc — tale quid** Cf. Ov. *Ep.* 2.146.
        tale — loqui Cf. *Sylv. duae* 2.152, n.; *Luth.* 1.66: ". . . tale quid ausa loqui."
17   **me . . . facis . . . prole parentem** Cf. Verg. *A.* 1.75; Eob. *Sylv.* 2.8.25: ". . . faciet te prole parentem"; also cf. *Buc.*, ded. 36, n.
        sera . . . prole parentem = Mant. *1. Parthen.* 2.724; cf. l. 1, n., above.
18   **affer opem** = *Her. Chr.* 10.194, n.
19   **Dum loquor, ecce** = *Her. Chr.* 2.73, n.
        montis iuga = *Culex* 46; Luc. 8.372; cf. Verg. *Ecl.* 5.76; Ov. *Met.* 10.172.
        sponte dehiscunt Prud. *Perist.* 7.50.
20   **Nec mora** = *Pug.* 85, n.
        nativo fornice tecta Cf. Ov. *Met.* 10.692.
21–28   **Spirat et — locum** For this paradisiacal landscape cf. *Buc.* 2.16–19, n.; *Her. Chr.* 4.153–62; 23.45–56, nn.
21   **purissimus aer** l. 9, n., above. Pure, untroubled air was one of the hallmarks of the earthly Paradise (believed to be situated on top of a mountain in the East, high above the earth's contagion). Cf. *Vict.* 395.
        aer Notice the short second syllable. Eobanus uses this scansion also at *Her. Chr.* 22.52; *Val.* 1.38; *Psalt.* 11.24; 18.32; and elsewhere. In this he follows Mant. *5. Parthen.*,

fol. 124ᵛ: "cum sibilat aer et armos / Sudat anhelantes"; Celtis, *Am.* 4.9.24: ". . . quam vehit aer avis."

23   **natura coegit** = Lucr. 4.846; 5.1354.

24   **balsama fragrat** Apul. *Met.* 6.11: "fragrans balsama Venus."
        fragrat odor V. Fl. 4.493; Prud. *Cath.* 3.22.

26   **Fons prope** = *Her. Chr.* 4.62.
        nectare fundit aquam ≈ Ov. *Fast.* 2.146.

28   **gratia verna** = *Sylv.* 1.4.12; cf. *Ruf.* 14.

29   **bis quattuor — soles** Cf. *Her. Chr.* 16.125.

30   **magnae — sinu** Cf. *Hod.* 265; *Dial.* 1, sig. B2ʳ: "In sinu magnae matris." For the old idea that the earth is the mother of all living beings, see, for example, Lucr. 1.250–51; 2.598–99; Verg. *G.* 2.325–26; Ov. *Met.* 1.393; Plin. *Nat.* 2.154; Eob. *Buc.* 1.1–2, n.; *Hymn.* 30; *Nob.* 15, 23; *Vict.* 22.
        matris . . . sinu Ov. *Met.* 4.516; 13.450.

31   **patrios . . . penates** = *Her. Chr.* 10.117, n.
        remeare penates = Stat. *Silv.* 3.5.12.

32   **Ipse . . . ut valeas** *Her. Chr.* 17.257, n.
        sed ut valeas = Ov. *Rem.* 226.
        unica cura = Marul. *Epigr.* 2.32.90; Celtis, *Am.* 3.4.8.

33–34   **Hoc bene — quod** Cf. *Her. Chr.* 7.15–16, n.

35   **rebus . . . secundis** = Verg. *A.* 1.207; 10.502; Ov. *Ars* 2.437.
        spes prima = *Her. Chr.* 12.63, n.
        prima secundis ≈ Hor. *S.* 2.5.53 (different).

36   **fatis tristibus** = Strozzi, *Eroticon* 2.2.12; cf. Eob. *Buc.* 9.17, n.

37   **Exiguum — natum** Cf. *Her. Chr.* 7.73, n.

39   **ad ubera matri** ≈ Mant. *Ecl.* 9.161 and *1. Parthen.* 3.143: "ad ubera matris"; cf. also Verg. *G.* 3.187; Stat. *Theb.* 10.695.

40   **Lactenti . . . ore** Paul. Nol. *Carm.* 24.514: "in aula parvulus ludit dei / et ore lactenti canit."
        lachrymas — meas Cf. Ov. *Ars* 2.326; *Ep.* 15.150; Eob. *Her. Chr.* 3.160.

42   **ille refert** = *Sylv. duae* 2.138, n.

43–54   **Et tamen — videns** Cf. *Her.* 1.6.127–38.

43   **suis . . . animosior annis** = *Idyl.* 13.9; cf. *Max.* 91.

44   **numen — putes** = Mant. *2. Parthen.* 2.696; Eob. *Sylv.* 1.10.26; cf. Ov. *Am.* 3.9.18; *Ep.* 15.158; Eob. *Her. Chr.* 9.160, n.

45–46   **Improba — duos** See, for example, Ov. *Ep.* 9.21–22; *Ars* 1.187–88.

45   **mentita est . . . fabula** = *Sylv.* 8.25.13; cf. Stat. *Theb.* 10.875.
        Iove . . . natum Ov. *Met.* 4.645, 697; 9.104; et al.; Eob. *Hymn.* 50 (Tantalus); B 11.1 (Hercules).

47   **mendacia verbis** = Juvenc. 4.472.

48   **aliquid — quam** = *Max.* 40; cf. *Her. Chr.* 4.115.
        puerile sapit = Balbi, *Epigr.* 27.6: "Ingenium pueri nil puerile sapit."

49   **Ac** For the sense of "ac si" (with following subjunctive), see *Her. Chr.* 3.149.

50   **munere — ali** = Val. 1.612; cf. Ven. Fort. *Carm.* 8.3.104: ". . . munere lactis alit"; Eob. *Her.* 1.5.134: ". . . munere lactis alis." For *munere lactis*, see Stat. *Theb.* 4.452–53.

51   **hausto . . . fonte** Stat. *Theb.* 4.38.

54   **praesaga — videns** Cf. Luc. 6.414–15; Eob. *Her. Chr.* 5.33, n.; *Vict.* 302.

56   **Cum legerem — tuis** Cf. Ov. *Am.* 1.4.20; l. 2 above; *Sylv.* 5.47.10 (9.1.8): ". . . digitis verba notata tuis."

59–60   **Hoc probat — novum** Cf. Mant. *1. Parthen.* 1.81–83: "Sic alacer Sanson, sic et formosus Ioseph, / sic puer Isaacus satus est et filius Annae, / Qui primum liquido regem perfudit olivo"; Eob. *Her. Chr.* 13.85–90, n.

61–62   **Sic mea — parens** The story is told in *Her. Chr.* 13.

61	**mea — partu** The model is Mant. *1. Parthen.* 2.769, where Elizabeth asks Mary: "Tune illa propago / . . . / . . . / quam mea iam sero genuit matertera partu?" For *sero partu*, cf. l. 1, n., above.
62	**facta parens** = *Her. Chr.* 5.178, n.
63	**patriis — oris** Cf. Stat. *Theb.* 1.312; Mant. *Ecl.* 9.1: ". . . patriis procul actus ab oris"; Eob. *Her. Chr.* 13.167.
	exulat oris = Verg. *G.* 3.225.
64	**nurus** That is, "cousin," as in l. 153 below. Cf. Mant. *1. Parthen.* 2.725, where Elizabeth is termed Mary's "cognatam nurum."
65	**Quo fugis** = Verg. *A.* 10.649; Prop. 2.30.1; Ov. *Ep.* 7.41; 10.35; et al.; Eob. *Buc.* 3.157, n.; l. 69 below.
	generis decus Sil. 8.227.
66	**Praesenti . . . metu** [Sen.] *Oct.* 724.
	libera facta = Prop. 3.13.4.
67	**tactura lacertos** = *Nup.* 107.
68	**O decus — domus** Cf. Ov. *Fast.* 6.810; Eob. *Her. Chr.* 12.168, n.
69	**Quo fugis** = l. 65, n., above.
70	**si nescis** = *Her. Chr.* 12.98, n.
	crimine vita *Ama.* A 3.2, n.
71	**sim sine crimine** = *Nux* 1; cf. Eob. *Her. Chr.* 7.15, n.
72	**nostrae — fugae** = Ov. *Tr.* 5.12.46.
75	**thalamo . . . eodem** ≈ Ov. *Met.* 4.328; cf. Eob. *Her. Chr.* 12.91, n.
76	**gratia vestra** = Ov. *Am.* 2.1.36.
77	**Demeret . . . curas** Verg. *A.* 2.775.
78	**Falleret — diem** Cf. Ov. *Ep.* 1.9; *Met.* 8.651; *Tr.* 3.3.11–12; Eob. *Her. Chr.* 16.236.
79	**ferus . . . hostis** = Ov. *Tr.* 2.77; cf. Eob. *Her. Chr.* 14.111 (n).
80	**orba parens** = Ov. *Rem.* 30; *Ib.* 266.
81–82	**O patria — Quo tua** Cf. Verg. *A.* 2.241; Sil. 1.598: "o patria, o Fidei domus inclita, quo tua nunc sunt / fata loco?"; Eob. *Luth.* 5.47.
81	**domus inclyta** = *Her. Chr.* 21.213; cf. *Sylv. duae* 1.147, n.
84	**squallida . . . iaces** ≈ *Her. Chr.* 12.62.
86	**qui te — lyra** Cf. Mant. *1. Parthen.* 1.620–21, likewise referring to Jeremiah: "maestisque virum qui versibus urbem / plorat."
88	**aversa . . . aure** = [Tib.] 3.3.28.
89–92	**Quid tamen — meae** Cf. *Her. Chr.* 17.1–2, nn.
90	**Tristibus . . . modis** Cf. *Ama.* 32.78, n.: "flebilibus modis."
	res peragenda = *Luth.* 1.6.
91	**Flebilis — carmen** Cf. Ov. *Tr.* 5.1.5; also cf. *Ep.* 15.7. For the heroine's awareness that she is writing in elegiac verse, see n. to Eob. *Her. Chr.* 4.176.
92	**Fortunae . . . vulnera** Marul. *Hymn. nat.* 3.1.246; Pontano, *Eridanus* 2.31.74.
94	**lustres . . . limina** Ov. *Ib.* 111.
	viduae . . . domus = *Her. Chr.* 21.26; cf. *Buc.* 9.80, n.
	limina . . . domus = *Her. Chr.* 16.182, n.
98	**possim dedoluisse** ≈ Ov. *Fast.* 3.480.
100	**Ante — supplex** = *Psalt.* 77.1: "Ante Deum supplex . . . precabor."
101	**videor spectare** Ov. *Ep.* 19.59; Eob. *Max.* 27.
	spectare oculis = Paul. Nol. *Carm.* 28.141.
101–02	**oculis . . . Flentibus** *Her. Chr.* 22.14, n.
102	**tergere . . . manu** Ov. *Met.* 13.132.
103–04	**Iam canum — loci** Cf. *Her. Chr.* 10.129–30, n.
103	**patulis . . . fenestris** *Pug.* 51, n.
	caput erectare ≈ Magdal. *Erarium*, ded., sig. A2^r: "caput erecturus ad auras / Aethereas"; Eob. *Val.* 1.151: "Mane relucentes caput erecturus ad auras."

104	**Lataque . . . arva** = *Sylv. duae* 1.72, n.
	prospicere arva *Her. Chr.* 17.166, n.
105	**venerande senex** = Gerald. *Ecl.* 3.50; cf. Ven. Fort. *Carm.* 3.18.17.
	ne cede dolori = *Idyl.* 17.225.
106	**pondera ferre** = Ov. *Am.* 2.14.14; *Pont.* 2.5.30; Eob. *Sylv.* 1.4.100; *Val.* 1.660.
107	**fragilem . . . senectam** = Mant. *Somn.*, fol. 209ʳ.
	lachrymis corrumpe ≈ Ov. *Am.* 3.6.57; *Ars* 1.129.
108	**Secura . . . via** = *Her. Chr.* 5.42.
	currunt fata *Her. Chr.* 7.61, n.
	fata superba = Bebel, "De miseria humanae conditionis," *Carm.*, sig. l2ᵛ: "Orbe sub hoc nihil est ex omni parte beatum, / Nec cuiquam semper fata superba favent."
109	**Nemo — leges** Cf. *Eras.* 145.
	datas fatis ≈ Ov. *Ep.* 16.281.
111	**rerum . . . Pater** Sen. *Her. F.* 1072; *Her. O.* 1587; Paul. Nol. *Carm.* 6.1.
	Monarcha Erasmus, *Carm.* 43.19: ". . . caelique solique monarcha"; Eob. *Vict.* 19.
112	**arbitrio — suo** Cf. *Her. Chr.* 13.154, n.
113	**Sperandum est** = Ov. *Pont.* 3.3.92; Eob. *Sylv.* 1.4.89.
	nostrae requiem . . . senectae ≈ *Her. Chr.* 13.113, n.
114	**Per mala — levat** = *Sylv.* 1.4.88; *Salom.* 9, sig. C3ʳ.
115–30	**At iuvat — domum** The motif — the worried wife offers advice to her husband — comes from Ov. *Ep.* 13.65–78. Cf. Eob. *Her. Chr.* 5.125–64.
115	**in dubiis . . . rebus** = *Her. Chr.* 5.161, n.
	solertia rebus = Ov. *Met.* 6.575.
116	**Spe sola — est** For the proverbial thought that hope is deceptive, see Otto 1684.
118	**certa fides** = Ov. *Tr.* 4.3.14; cf. Eob. *Buc.* 8.26, n.
119	**convivia regis** = Ov. *Met.* 4.764.
120	**Insidias — tuae** ≈ Strozzi, *Eroticon* 1.6.52: "Insidias vitae praeparet ille tuae."
121–22	**Baethica — dabit** Cf. *Her. Chr.* 5.141–42, n.
124	**sacra . . . ara** *Laud.* 246, n.
125	**sacrum . . . amorem** Poliziano, *Silv.* 1.313.
	virtutis amorem = Stat. *Theb.* 4.128; 12.177; Sil. 10.194.
126	**regni . . . sceptra** Mant. *2. Parthen.* 2.176; Eob. *Nob.* 19; *Tum.* 3.123.
127	**Regius . . . satelles** l. 12, n., above.
128	**in populum — ire** Cf. *Sylv. duae* 2.54, n.; *Her. Chr.* 13.32.
129	**sacras . . . aras** *Laud.* 246, n.
130	**sanctam . . . domum** Prud. *Perist.* 10.102.
	diro . . . ense Luc. 8.677.
132	**gelidus — tremor** Cf. Ov. *Ep.* 5.37–38; Verg. *A.* 2.120–21; 6.54–55; 12.447–48; Eob. *Epic.* 3A.26: "Attonita exanguis venit in ossa tremor."
133	**suspiria traxit** = Prud. *c. Symm.* 1.480; cf. Ov. *Met.* 2.753.
135	**Crassior . . . aer** Lucr. 5.696; Hor. *Ep.* 2.1.244; Eob. *Vict.* 227.
136	**Fluxit — sinum** Cf. Ov. *Ars* 3.212.
137	**quae — curant** ≈ Verg. *A.* 2.536.
138	**pereat — potest** Cf. Prop. 1.6.12. For *pereat*, cf. also Eob. *Her. Chr.* 10.142, n.
	credere — potest *Her. Chr.* 4.7.
139	**potentia fati** = Stat. *Theb.* 9.180; Juv. 7.200.
140	**fecit . . . fidem** ≈ Ov. *Am.* 2.8.18.
	fabula vana = Ov. *Ep.* 19.132; cf. Eob. *Buc.* 8.119.
141	**levia ista** = *Vict.*, ded. 11; *Idyl.* 8.8.
142	**sublimi . . . mente** Ov. *Pont.* 3.3.103; Celtis, *Od.* 1.8.14: "latentes / Mente sublimi reperire causas."
	mente rotas Petrarch, *Africa* 5.490: "singula secum / Ancipiti cum mente rotat."
143	**Quare age** = Verg. *A.* 7.429; Stat. *Silv.* 1.4.31.
	bene cautus Ov. *Ep.* 1.44.

144   **Placatum . . . Deum** *Her. Chr.* 15.218, n.
          sis memor — Deum ≈ *Her. Chr.* 11.162, n.

145   **puerum cum matre** = *Her. Chr.* 4.107; l. 147 below.

147   **puerum — puella** = *Her. Chr.* 4.107; cf. l. 145 above.

149   **Heu . . . heu** = Verg. *A.* 6.878.

150   **dulcis amor** *Buc.* 3.46, n.

151   **Anna parens** = *Her. Chr.* 2.101, n.

153   **Aeternum . . . vale** = *Her. Chr.* 21.169; cf. Verg. *A.* 11.98 and Mart. 5.66.2.
          nurus That is, "cousin," as in l. 64, n., above.

154   **pectora casta** = Marul. *Epigr.* 1.41.2; cf. Ov. *Ep.* 13.30; Eob. *Her. Chr.* 5.55.

156   **mecum — pater** Cf. *Her. Chr.* 5.178, n.
          sero pignore Cf. l. 1, n., above: "sera . . . prole."

157   **desaeverit ira** Luc. 5.303.
          ira tyranni Ov. *Met.* 6.549.

158   **patrios . . . lares** = Prop. 2.30.22 (household gods); Mart. 5.42.2.
          posse redire = *Her. Chr.* 5.132, n.

21

Meter: Elegiac distich.

1   **Si . . . non est grave** Mart. 5.6.1.
          Haebraeos . . . vates = *Her. Chr.* 10.91; cf. *Laud.* 98, n.

2   **Perlege** = Ov. *Ep.* 4.3; 20.3; et al.; Eob. *Her. Chr.* 22.1.
          notata manu = Ov. *Am.* 1.11.14; *Ep.* 3.2; *Ars* 2.596; Eob. *Her. Chr.* 14.162.

3   **quid et unde legas** = *Hod.* B 1.13; cf. Ov. *Ars* 1.263; Eob. *Her. Chr.* 12.8, n.

4   **posito nomine** *Epic. Drusi* 6.

5–6   **unde loci — scripta** Cf. Ov. *Tr.* 3.14.28.

5   **tibi littera nostra** Ov. *Ep.* 18.9; cf. Eob. *Her. Chr.* 3.54, n.

6   **ut noris** = Ov. *Fast.* 1.116; *Tr.* 4.10.2; cf. Eob. *Sylv. duae* 1.65, n.

7   **urbe Quirini** = Ov. *Tr.* 1.8.37; *Pont.* 1.5.73.

10   **Itala — est** Cf. *Sylv.* 2.23.4: "Itala . . . terra relicta tibi est." For *Itala terra*, see also
          Verg. *A.* 7.643–44.
          terra relicta = Ov. *Tr.* 3.10.70.

13   **in orbe morari** Cf. Ov. *Met.* 12.97; Eob. *Her. Chr.* 18.7, n.

14   **quove loco** = *Sylv. duae* 1.20, n.

15   **ne teneam — aures** Cf. Ov. *Met.* 3.692; Eob. *Eleg.* 1.17: "Ne teneam cupidas longis
          ambagimus aures"; *Accl.* 2.25; *Her.* 1.1.21–22. Also cf. *Laud.* 45–46, n.
          doctas . . . aures = Ov. *Pont.* 4.5.1.

16   **simplicitate loquar** ≈ Mart. 11.20.10.

18   **in portus . . . tuos** = *Her. Chr.* 18.4, n.

19   **in littore navis** ≈ Celtis, *Am.* 4.13.63: "stant tutae in litore naves"; cf. Hor. *S.*
          2.3.205; Eob. *Her. Chr.* 18.5, n.

20   **exiguum tempus** Lucr. 1.1016; Prop. 1.12.12; Ov. *Am.* 2.2.40; 3.1.67; et al.
          tempus in urbe = Ov. *Tr.* 1.3.2.
          in urbe moror = Ov. *Pont.* 2.8.12; cf. Eob. *Her. Chr.* 18.7, 161.

21   **Hic sumus — orbem** Cf. Ov. *Ep.* 16.28–29.

22   **Certa — viae** Cf. Ov. *Ep.* 17.156.
          Certa . . . tenaxque Ov. *Tr.* 5.8.16.

23   **fortasse requires** ≈ Catul. 85.1; Ov. *Pont.* 4.5.29; Eob. *Her. Chr.* 8.71.

24   **Si tamen ipse** = Ov. *Met.* 9.511; *Tr.* 5.13.7.
          nescius esse = Ov. *Am.* 3.11.40; *Ars* 1.64; *Fast.* 3.874.

25   **Venimus et** = Verg. *A.* 6.671; Ov. *Met.* 7.766.

26   **viduae . . . domus** = *Her. Chr.* 20.94; cf. *Buc.* 9.80, n.; l. 89 below.

       pignora — domus = Prud. *Amart.* 726; cf. Eob. *Buc.* 7.63, n.; *Her. Chr.* 4.50, n.

30   **flagrat amore** = Mart. 12.52.4.

32   **tristi funere** Lucr. 3.72; *Aetna* 19; Eob. *Vict.* 465.

33–34 **Non levibus . . . poetis . . . vivis** For the commonplace that poets confer immortal-
       ity on those they celebrate, see *Laud.* 61–64, n.

33   **levibus . . . poetis** = Mant. *2. Parthen.* 3.63: "Scaenica sunt levibus vulgo recitanda
       poetis."

34   **sacro carmine** = Ov. *Rem.* 252.

35   **Moesta . . . lumina fletus** ≈ Catul. 68.55; cf. Eob. *Rec.* 224, n.

37–38 **Nam — putem** Only a barbarian could remain unmoved by such eloquence. Cf.
       Her. Chr. 19.25–32; *Hod.* B 1.77–78, n.; *Sylv.* 2.12.23–24.

37   **moveat facundia** Arator 2.748: "cuius facundia movit / Hos animos"; Eob. *Luth.*
       3.41.

38   **Bessagetas — putem** Cf. Ov. *Tr.* 3.3.6; 3.10.5.

39–42 **Si tamen — tui** Cf. *Ama.* 33.7, n.

39   **Odrysii . . . vatis** Stat. *Silv.* 5.1.203.

       carmina vatis = Prop. 4.1.51; Luc. 1.564; Eob. *Her. Chr.* 24.145; *Hod.* 11; cf.
       Her. Chr. 2.36; 4.21.

40   **Prata, . . . flumina, saxa, feras** ≈ *Luth.* 1.48; cf. Ov. *Ars* 3.321–22; Guarino, *Carm.*
       1, sig. a5ʳ: "Orphea . . . / Ducentem silvas, flumina, saxa, feras"; 3, sig. h6ʳ: "Per . . .
       silvas, flumina, saxa, feras"; Eob. *Accl.* 2.4.

41   **barbaricas menteis** ≈ Sil. 5.648.

       menteis animosque = Luc. 1.354.

       animos . . . feroces Sen. *Ag.* 619; Sil. 15.496–97.

42   **gratia viva** Paul. Nol. *Carm.* 21.633; Eob. *Epic.* 3.39.

43   **Testis — unum** Cf. *Nob.* 287.

43–44 **libellum, Quem legat** ≈ Prop. 3.3.19–20.

44   **laeto . . . ore** Ov. *Met.* 9.242.

       praedicet ore ≈ *Her. Chr.* 10.136, n.

45   **Ah, quoties** = *Her. Chr.* 1.43, n.

46   **desyderio . . . gemit . . . tui** Cf. Cic. *Pis.* 25: "nemo . . . qui non gemeret desiderio
       mei."

       mens — aegra Celtis, *Am.* 1.8.47. Cf. Eob. *Her. Chr.* 14.122, n.

50   **Acceptum referat** ≈ Ov. *Tr.* 2.10.

51–70 **Sicut — suae** Paula is noble by birth and through her accomplishments. For this
       commonplace, see *Laud.* 147, n.; cf. *Nup.* 97–99, n. The theme is prefigured in
       Hier. *Ep.* 108.1, praising Paula who has exchanged a palace in Rome for a hovel in
       Bethlehem: "Nobilis genere, sed multo nobilior sanctitate; potens quondam
       divitiis, sed nunc Christi paupertate insignior; Graccorum stirps, suboles
       Scipionum."

51   **tota . . . relligione** *Her. Chr.* 13.18.

52   **titulo nobiliore** *Laud.* B 4.6.

53–54 **insignes — Relliquias** Cf. *Her. Chr.* 24.71.

53   **veterum . . . avorum** = Prud. *c. Symm.* 1.39; cf. Verg. *A.* 7.177; Ov. *Fast.* 6.657. In
       Ep. 108.3 Jerome says that Paula was of noble descent on both sides of her family:
       "[mater] Scipionum Gracchorumque progenies est, [pater] per omnes Graecias usque
       hodie et stemmatibus et divitiis ac nobilitate Agamemnonis fertur sanguinem trahere,
       qui decennali Troiam obsidione delevit."

54   **fasces — duces** Cf. *Accl.* 1.160: ". . . fasces, sceptra, tropaea, duces."

56   **Elogium — habent** Cf. *Salom.* 1, sig. A5ᵛ: "studia ista . . . / Elogium veri quae sapi-
       entis habent."

       verae nobilitatis = *Nob.* 228, 300; *Sylv.* 6.4.26.

       nobilitatis habent = Ov. *Pont.* 3.2.104; Eob. *Nob.* 126.

58   **clarum — tulit** Cf. Mart. 9.101.20; Strozzi, *Eroticon* 4.30.4: "clarum egregia nomen ab arte ferat"; Eob. *Epic.* 3.30. For *clarum nomen*, see Verg. *A.* 12.225–26; Ov. *Met.* 6.425; 11.285–86; et al.; Eob. *Nup.* 224, n.; *Nob.* 124.
     ab hoste tulit = Ov. *Pont.* 4.3.38; *Epic. Drusi* 338.

59   **Gloria terrenae . . . laudis** Juvenc. 2.681.

60   **immensi . . . Dei** *Her. Chr.* 13.74.

61   **debemus tibi . . . fatemur** Cf. Ov. *Met.* 4.76; *Pont.* 4.5.31; Eob. *Laud.* 456; *Her. Chr.* 1.199, n.; *Max.* 117.
     tibi, Scipio magne Ov. *Ars* 3.410.

62   **atavis regibus** = Mart. 12.3.2; cf. Hor. *Carm.* 1.1.1; Verg. *A.* 7.474.
     alta domus = Sil. 11.280; Prud. *Psych.* 834.

64   **quiddam — habet** = *Epic.* 7.22; *Sylv.* 6.10.84; cf. Ov. *Am.* 3.4.30; *Rem.* 232; Eob. *Epic.* 7.32.

65–70   **Per te — suae** The passage closely parallels *Sylv. duae* 1.13–15, where see nn.

65   **Per te nobilior . . . facta est** *Epic.* 4.204.

67   **Et merito** = *Laud.* 483, n.

69–70   **ex isto — Exilio** Paula espouses the Neoplatonic notion that the soul longs to escape its exile on earth and return to its true homeland. Cf. *Epic.* 9.105–08.

69   **patrias . . . arces** = Ov. *Met.* 8.54; cf. *Met.* 1.673; Eob. *Hymn.* 150 (heaven); *Her. Chr.* 1.69.

70   **carnis pondere** Cf. *Buc.* 6.76, n.
     pondere fessa ≈ Luc. 5.354; V. Fl. 1.831.

71–72   **Talia — loqui** Cf. ll. 117–18 below.

71   **Talia multa** = Ov. *Met.* 14.435.
     tuis . . . scripta libellis = *Eccles.* 329.

72   **ausa loqui** = Ov. *Fast.* 3.206.

73   **Omnia tu nosti** = Anon. *Vita Katherine* 874.
     nihil . . . doctius Pl. *Mos.* 279; Plin. *Ep.* 1.22.1; Hier. *Ep.* 58.9; Eob. *Buc.* B 2.14.

74   **caelivagi — larem** = *Val.* 2.340; cf. *Tum.* 3.10; *Her. Chr.* 6.192, n.
     solis utrumque = Ov. *Fast.* 2.136: "solis utrumque latus."

75   **divinae — mentis** = *Her. Chr.* 19.25, n.

76   **sacra . . . pietate** *Her. Chr.* 12.14.
     pietate prior = Mart. 12.44.4; cf. Verg. *A.* 11.292.

77   **cum — teneret** Cf. *Epic.* 4.161: ". . . cum dulcis adhuc te vita teneret." Cf. further Ov. *Ep.* 16.295; Eob. *Buc.* 4.4, n.

79   **humiles . . . famulas** Ov. *Ep.* 3.75.
     dignatus adire = Arator 2.513; cf. Paul. Nol. *Carm.* 19.194.

80   **mansueto pectore** = Ov. *Ib.* 26.
     pectore — loqui Cf. *Her. Chr.* 6.78, n.

81   **faciles . . . praebere . . . aures** Juv. 5.107; Eob. *Her. Chr.* 22.67.

85   **dulcis praesentia** = Alcuin. *Carm.* 13.5: "dulcis praesentia Christi."

86   **in orbe manes** ≈ Ov. *Fast.* 1.712.

87   **pectore vultus** = Verg. *Ecl.* 1.63; *A.* 4.4.

89   **sola domo vidua** Cf. Verg. *A.* 4.82; Eob. *Buc.* 9.80, n.; l. 26 above.

90   **in mea vota** = Ov. *Ep.* 4.16; cf. *Ep.* 21.240.

91   **clavigeri** Assigned to Janus in Ov. *Fast.* 1.228, this epithet was transferred to Peter by Christian authors because Christ gave him the keys of the kingdom of heaven (Vulg. *Matt.* 16.19). See, for instance, Arator 1.899; Alcuin. *Carm.* 45.38; 109.3.1; Eob. *Nor.* 1026. Cf. *Sylv. duae* 2.3, referring to Peter's successor, Pope Julius II.
     ad principis aedem ≈ Celtis, *Am.* 2.8.77.

92   **pars — eram** = *Her. Chr.* 3.106; cf. *Her. Chr.* 1.96, n.

93   **totam — urbem** = Verg. *A.* 8.716; Eob. *Her. Chr.* 12.47.

95   **denso . . . agmine** = [Tib.] 3.7.186; Ov. *Ep.* 16.185.
     stipantes agmine *Nup.* 185, n.

96   **non — modum** = *Nob.* 252, n.; cf. Andrel. *Livia* 1.6.42: ". . . non habitura modum."

97   **proximus illis** ≈ *Her. Chr.* 16.289, n.

98   **nec sua nota domus** Cf. the proverbial *sicut sua domus nota.* See Otto 575.

99   **Quis . . . furor iste** Verg. *A.* 5.670.

102   **toto . . . Foro** Prop. 2.24.2; Ov. *Ars* 3.450; *Ib.* 14, 230.
        iussit abire = Ov. *Am.* 2.19.12; *Tr.* 3.1.68.

103   **Vade, malum** = *Theoc.* 24.4: "Vade, malum, procul hinc."

104   **nomina tanta** = *Her. Chr.* 9.22, n.

105   **animo patietur iniquo** Ter. *Eu.* 212.

106   **Si — nequit** Cf. *Dicta Catonis, ex Columbano* 3: "Vir bonus esse nequit nisi qui siet omnibus aequus"; Eob. *Sylv.* 6.6.12: "Quid tibi, qui malus est, quod bonus esse nequit?"

107   **Qui — loquitur** Cf. *Buc.* 10.84.

108   **predominatur amor** = *Ama.* 35.114, n.

109   **primo . . . ab ortu** = Germ. *Arat.* 340; Mant. *1. Parthen.* 1.535; Eob. *Nob.* B 1.19; *Vict.* 392; cf. *Hymn.* 13.

110   **non putat esse** = *Her. Chr.* 2.22, n.

111   **invidus osor** = Trebelius, *Epigr.*, sig. C4ᵛ, in a poem to Eobanus written in 1508: "Es pius et facilis, placidus, non invidus osor."

112   **Aethna** Mount Etna was proverbial for its searing heat. See Otto 34; Häussler, 21, 52, 258. Cf. Eob. *Buc.* 7.173.

114   **Non mirum . . . si** = Ov. *Ars.* 3.24; cf. Eob. *Buc.* 2.44, n.; *Nor.* 482.

116   **Omnibus invideat** ≈ Mart. 1.40.2.

117–18 **Talia — locis** Cf. ll. 71–72 above.

117   **cura Minervae** = Ov. *Met.* 14.475.

118   **Quid referam** = Ov. *Am.* 2.6.43; *Ep.* 12.129; 19.31; *Met.* 7.734; et al.

121–76 **Ergo — erat** Based on Hier. *Ep.* 108.6.

123   **Antiochi . . . urbe** ≈ Gunther, *Lig.* 1.731; cf. Arator 2.40; Locher, *Stult.* 95, fol. 112ʳ: "urbs . . . Antiochi." Antioch was founded in 300 BCE by Seleucus I in honor of his father Antiochus.

125   **Salaminaeis** Instead of *Salaminiis* or *Salaminiacis,* neither of which fit the meter.

126   **Congrua — habet** Cf. *Calum.* 26: "Consona quae propriis nomina rebus habent"; *Sylv.* 2.8.14: "Et merita ex ipsis nomina rebus habes." For the play on proper names, see n. to *Her. Chr.* 7.103–04.

127   **constantia mentem** = Juvenc. 3.108.

129   **rebus patriaque** = *Sylv.* 6.3.43: "rebus patriaque potitos."

130   **exilii commodioris** = Ov. *Pont.* 2.8.72; cf. l. 174 below.

131   **peregrinas — terras** Celtis, *Am.* 1.3.11; cf. Ov. *Met.* 3.24.

132   **tota — fuit** = Mart. 2.72.6.

133–48 **In luctum — tulit** Paula's account of her departure from Rome is in part modeled on Ov. *Tr.* 1.3, the celebrated description of Ovid's departure from Rome into exile. For ll. 133–45, cf. especially *Tr.* 1.3.77–89.

133   **In luctum conversa** Vulg. *Macc.* 1.41–42; 9.41.

135   **pleno — aevo** = Mant. *Georgius,* fol. 205ʳ; cf. Verg. *A.* 7.53; Eob. *Buc.* 3.73; *Her. Chr.* 4.41. Eustochium is a few years older than her fifteen-year-old sister Rufina (l. 145 below), whom Jerome characterizes as "iam nubilis" in *Ep.* 108.6.

137–38 **O, quemcunque — tui** For the motif of following a beloved person to the ends of the world, see *Laud.* 209, n.

137   **quemcunque . . . in orbem** = *Her.,* ded. 37.

138   **Exilii comitem** = Mart. 12.25.6 (in one ms. tradition).

140   **Mors . . . atra** *Her. Chr.* 18.56, n.

142   **illius atque mei** = *Her. Chr.* 24.66.

143–76 **Et iam — pontus erat** For the farewell scene, cf. *Her. Chr.* 5.35–46, n.

143   **Et iam tempus erat** = *Nup.* 169, n.
        vento . . . vocanti Cf. Ov. *Ep.* 13.9–10.
        vento dare vela = Ov. *Ars* 1.51; cf. Eob. *Rec.* 220, n.
144   **Ultima . . . lux** Verg. *A.* 2.668.
145   **trilustris** Petrarch, *Africa* 8.143: "bello . . . trilustri"; Celtis, *Am.* 3.12.43:
        "Aetatemque tuam . . . trilustrem." Girls were considered ready for marriage by age
        fifteen: cf., for example, Ov. *Met.* 11.301–02; Eob. *Her. Chr.* 2.29, n.; 4.41–42;
        21.135, n.
147   **clausi . . . ventris** Cf. *Her. Chr.* 13.77, n.
        pignora ventris = Mart. *Sp.* 16.1.
150   **Iam prope** = *Nup.* 195, n.
        littore . . . erat = Celtis, *Am.* 2.11.80; cf. Ov. *Tr.* 3.12.32.
151   **velut — funera** For the image, cf. Ov. *Tr.* 1.3.97–98.
        funera natae ≈ Catul. 64.401; Ov. *Rem.* 127; Eob. *Her. Chr.* 22.17.
152   **flevit et ipse** = Prop. 2.16.54.
153–54 **Indoluisse — puto** Their laments could move reefs and stones and cause the deaf sea
        to pay heed. For the motif, cf. Cic. *de Orat.* 1.245; Ov. *Met.* 9.303–04; Eob. *Her.
        Chr.* 19.76, n.
153   **graves . . . querelas** *Her. Chr.* 1.91, n.
        scopulos et saxa *Her. Chr.* 9.109, n.
154   **littora surda** = Prop. 4.11.6.
155   **Adriaco . . . aestu** The Adriatic was notorious for its storms: see, for example, Hor.
        Carm. 1.3.14–16; 1.33.15; 3.9.23.
156   **Strata . . . unda** Ov. *Ep.* 7.49.
        lenior unda Sen. *Her. O.* 651.
157–58 **Oscula . . . "Vale"** = Ov. *Ep.* 5.51–52 (as the beloved is about to set sail).
157   **Oscula et amplexus** = *Her. Chr.* 5.35, n.
158   **summo — "Vale"** Cf. Ov. *Met.* 11.460; Eob. *Rec.* 131; *Her. Chr.* 9.46.
159   **nam forte aderat** Ov. *Met.* 11.162.
162   **navita, solve ratem** = Balbi, *Opusc.* 7.1, 2, repeated as a refrain. Cf. Ov. *Ep.* 15.214.
163   **Dum loquor et** = Ov. *Tr.* 1.3.71; 1.4.23; cf. Eob. *Her. Chr.* 2.73, n.
        retro — littora = *Hod.* 159; cf. Lucr. 4.389.
164   **Ni fallar** *Buc.* 2.65.
165   **vela tetendit** = Ov. *Ep.* 13.15.
167   **fidei — inclyta** Sil. 1.598; cf. Eob. *Sylv. duae* 1.147, n.
168   **verum . . . Deum** *Her. Chr.* 4.154, n.
        Petro principe Ven. Fort. *Carm.* 6.5.358. For the tradition of Peter's stay at Rome,
        see n. to Eob. *Her. Chr.* 19.5–6.
169   **Aeternum . . . vale** = *Her. Chr.* 20.153, n.
        patria alta Verg. *A.* 10.374; 11.797.
        patrii . . . nepotes *Laud.*, postscr.
170   **terra Latina** = *Sylv. duae* 1.30.
171   **Nunc ego — saluto** Cf. Theoc. 1.172: ". . . vos extrema nunc voce saluto"; 28.41:
        "Et nunc extrema tua limina voce saluto."
        supraema . . . voce Ov. *Ep.* 2.97.
        voce saluto = Mart. 14.76.1.
172   **In quibus — meae** Cf. *Sylv.* 6.5.58: ". . . Herciniae nobilis ora plagae"; 7.9.22:
        "Epicedia . . . / In quibus est patriae nobilis huius honor."
        patriae . . . ora meae = *Sylv.* 2.4.18: "Vicina est patriae Saxonis ora meae"; cf. Prop.
        4.1.122.
174   **patria — exilium** Cf. l. 130 above; *Sylv.* 9.18.14: "Exilium patria dulcius esse facis."
        patria . . . exilium = Verg. *Cat.* 3.8.
175   **Dum loquor** = *Her. Chr.* 2.73, n.
175–76 **aspectum — erat** Cf. Verg. *A.* 3.192–93.

175	**aspectum . . . reliquunt** Verg. *A.* 9.657.
176	**Iamque patens oculis** Cf. Ov. *Ep.* 2.122; Eob. *Her. Chr.* 3.131.
182	**pellex . . . matris** Ov. *Met.* 10.347.
183	**magni . . . Christi** *Buc.* 6.87, n.
	clementia Christi = *Her. Chr.* 15.137, n.
185	**de more peractis** = Ov. *Fast.* 6.629.
186	**Ad Solimas arces** = *Vict.* 413; cf. Mant. *1. Parthen.* 3.231; Eob. *Her. Chr.* 6.35, n. For Paula's desire to visit Jerusalem, see Hier. *Ep.* 108.7.
189	**Costidis** See *Laud.* 487, n.
191	**votis . . . potitam** *Her. Chr.* 1.146, n.
193	**caelo loca proxima** *Sylv. duae* 2.111, n.
195–96	**pulchrum . . . aevum . . . degis** Cf. Lucr. 5.172.
197–200	**Hic etiam — suo** Cf. Hier. *Ep.* 108.10, where Paula says: "Haec requies mea, quia Domini mei patria est. Hic habitabo, quoniam Salvator elegit eam."
198	**locus in terris** = *Laud.* 215, n.
	charior alter erit = Prop. 2.9.2; cf. Eob. *Her. Chr.* 16.52.
199	**Et merito** = *Laud.* 483, n.
	Reparator = *Her. Chr.* 3.147.
201–02	**Qua stetit — Deum** These lines are modeled on Erasmus, *Carm.* 42.2–3.
202	**nascentem . . . Deum** *Buc.* 11.49–50; cf. l. 207, n., below.
	vidit in orbe = *Epic. Drusi* 314.
203–12	**Huic ego — erat** Cf. *Her. Chr.* 1.105–20, nn.
203–04	**Huic ego — superba Iove** Modeled on Erasmus, *Carm.* 42.11–18.
	palatia Rhomae . . . templa superba = *Tum.* 6.23–24.
203	**palatia Rhomae** = Erasmus, *Carm.* 42.11; Mutian. *Ep.* 56, in similar context: "Ipse etenim genitor rerum, moderator Olympi, / dum peteret terras, non alta palatia Romae, / ast adiit servile genus stabulumque pudicum"; Eob. *Max.* 229.
204	**Latio . . . Iove** Stat. *Silv.* 5.3.292.
	templa superba = Mant. *Sylv.* 3, fol. 286ʳ: "Et Capitolini templa superba Dei"; *Epigr.*, fol. 110ʳ: "et Solymi templa superba Dei."
	superba Iove = Ov. *Am.* 3.10.20.
205	**Non — triformi** Cf. *Hod.* 115. Cf. also Hor. *Carm.* 3.22.4 and Ov. *Met.* 7.177: "diva triformis"; Ov. *Met.* 7.94–95: "triformis / . . . deae."
206	**maximus — habet** = *Sylv. duae* 1.10, n.
207	**operosa** = Erasmus, *Carm.* 42.13.
	nascenti . . . Christo Mant. *1. Parthen.* 1.852–53; 3.785; Erasmus, *Carm.* 42.25.
208	**Aula . . . speciosa** *Her.* 3.5.75.
209	**choraules** For this plural form (instead of "choraulae") see Sid. *Carm.* 23.300 (in the mss. and early eds.); Locher, "Obiectio Voluptatis," *Stult.*, fol. 132ʳ: ". . . blandique choraules"; Eob. *Hymn.* 5.
210	**vagiit — pecus** ≈ *Her. Chr.* 1.108.
211–12	**Hic tria — erat** Cf. *Her. Chr.* 1.117–26, n.
212	**pro duce** = Ov. *Ep.* 10.72.
213	**Caelesti . . . pane** Vulg. *Psa.* 104.40; Sedul. 1.148.
	domus inclyta = *Her. Chr.* 20.81, n.; cf. Mant. *1. Parthen.* 1.852 (of Bethlehem): "triticea Cereris domus incluta Christo / conscia nascenti."
214	**saturo . . . ore** = *Her. Chr.* 6.98.
215	**O domus** = V. Fl. 1.721; Eob. *Laud.* 91.
	fessae . . . senectae = Vegius, *Aen.* 257; cf. Luc. 2.128.
216	**Non est . . . prior ulla** Ov. *Ep.* 18.69.
217–18	**Te quoque . . . Credibile est** Ov. *Am.* 3.6.83.
217	**falsi ludibria mundi** Cf. Mant. *Consol.*, fol. 128ᵛ: "miserae vana . . . ludibria terrae"; Locher, *Stult.* 40, fol. 51ᵛ: ". . . vani ludibria mundi"; Eob. *Her.* 1.6.57 (following Ov. *Met.* 15.155): "falsi . . . pericula mundi"; *Her. Chr.* 10.141, n.; *Hod.* 439.

218   **Credibile est . . . mori** = Mart. 4.32.4: "credibile est ipsam sic voluisse mori."

219–24 **O mihi — Deum** Paula lived for three years in a hovel in Bethlehem. See Hier. *Ep.* 108.1: "Romae praetulit Bethlem, et auro tecta fulgentia informis luti vilitate mutavit"; *Ep.* 108.14: "in sancta Bethleem mansura perpetuo angusto per triennium mansit hospitio, donec extrueret cellulas ac monasteria et diversorium peregrinorum iuxta viam conderet, quia Maria et Ioseph hospitium non invenerant."

219   **fine quietae** ≈ *Sylv. duae* 1.65, n.

220   **parvae . . . tecta casae** Cf. Ov. *Fast.* 4.526; Eob. *Her. Chr.* 7.78, n.

221   **Pauperis . . . tuguri** Verg. *Ecl.* 1.68; *Priap.* 3.6.

221–22 **tuguri — Notis** Cf. Erasmus, *Carm.* 42.21–22. Paula's hut is to be no better than the one in which Jesus was born. For the wording, cf. also Ov. *Met.* 15.301–02.

221   **ducentia rimas** Ov. *Met.* 4.65.

222   **insanis . . . Notis** = *Her. Chr.* 8.128; cf. Tib. 2.4.9: "insanis . . . ventis."
        pervia . . . Notis Cf. Ov. *Met.* 2.762; 15.302.

227–30 **Non tamen — Deum** Cf. Vulg. *Matt.* 2.6 (following *Mich.* 5.2).

227   **virtutibus addas** = Hor. *Ep.* 1.20.22.

229–30 **Nam qui — Deum** Cf. *Her. Chr.* 1.138, n.

230   **parvula tecta** = Balbi, *Epigr.* 8.2.

231–32 **Totius — opus** Cf. Erasmus, *Carm.* 42.15–16; Prud. *Cath.* 12.77–80; *Tit. hist.* 101–02.

231   **domus** Bethlehem; cf. l. 213, n., above.
        clarissima mundi = Verg. *G.* 1.5.

233   **emeritam . . . vitam** = Claud. *in Rufin.* 2.473; cf. Nemes. *Ecl.* 1.19.

237   **Utque facis** = *Her. Chr.* 4.73, n.

22

Meter: Elegiac distich.

1–2   **Perlege — manu** The opening imitates Ov. *Ep.* 5.1–2. Cf. also Eob. *Her. Chr.* 10.1–2.

1   **Perlege** = *Her. Chr.* 21.2, n.
        nisi sordet Cf. *Buc.*, ded. 38; *Val.* 1.340: "Si modo non sordent haec elementa tibi."

2   **Vix — manu** Cf. Ov. *Ep.* 3.2. In Ovid's poem, the motif makes good sense: the non-Greek Briseis has no choice but to use Greek in addressing Achilles. But why should Martha write in labored Latin to a friend and countryman, when Hebrew would come so much more naturally to both of them? To Eobanus' mind, however, setting up an associative link between Martha and her Ovidian counterpart was paramount. A few lines later (ll. 13–18) he will exploit this association to bring out the superiority of Christian love over the love demonstrated by the ancient heroines.

3   **Quo magis — dextrae** Cf. Ov. *Tr.* 1.11.35; *Pont.* 3.4.43.
        erranti . . . dextrae Verg. *A.* 7.498.

8   **mereatur habet** = Ov. *Ep.* 21.202.

9   **Non — iuvenci** Cf. Ov. *Am.* 1.2.13–14; *Ep.* 4.21; *Rem.* 235.

10   **prima . . . praelia . . . movet** Ov. *Fast.* 1.569; cf. Verg. *A.* 7.603.
        rudis . . . tyro Luc. 5.363.

11   **grata voluntas** = *Culex* 230.

13–14   **Aspicies — solent** Cf. Ov. *Ep.* 3.3 (Briseis). For the motif of the tear-stained letter, see Eob. *Her. Chr.* 2.3, n.

14   **flentes oculi** ≈ Boeth. *Consol.* 1.m1.16; cf. Eob. *Her. Chr.* 20.101–02.

15   **iratum . . . Achillem** = Ov. *Am.* 2.18.1.

16   **absentem . . . virum** = *Her. Chr.* 13.10, n.

17   **crudeli . . . funere** = Verg. *Ecl.* 5.20; *G.* 3.263; *A.* 4.308; cf. Eob. *Rec.* 31–32, n.
        funere natum ≈ *Her. Chr.* 21.151, n.

18   **inhumano semine** Cf. *Buc.* 5.69; *Her. Chr.* 2.104. For *inhumano,* cf. also *Epic.* 6.74, of heaven: "inhumanae tertia regna plagae."
       facta parens = *Her. Chr.* 5.178, n.
19   **cultrix . . . eremi** = *Her. Chr.* 14.29; cf. *Her. Chr.* 4.173.
20   **et sine teste** = *Epic.* 9.64; cf. *Sylv. duae* 2.44, n.
       sine teste queror *Her. Chr.* 14.77.
21   **Hospitis** Cf. l. 164 below.
       praesentia — Iesu Cf. Alcuin. *Carm.* 13.5: "O mihi dulcis amor, dulcis praesentia Christi"; Eob., poem in Trebelius, *Epigr.,* sig. F2ʳ: "Tua . . . praesentia dulcis."
22   **in lachrymas . . . fluam** Locher, *Stult.* 28, motto, fol. 39ʳ: "In lachrymas fluerent maestas"; Eob. *Epic.* 4.80: "Omnis . . . in lachrymas unda soluta fluit."
23   **Externas . . . oras** *Rec.* 139, n.
24   **rectam . . . fidem** = Locher, concluding line of "Responsio Virtutis," *Stult.,* fol. 134ᵛ: "Ut sapiant rectam pectora vestra fidem"; cf. Eob. *Her. Chr.* 4.220, n.
25   **Antra . . . longo . . . recessu** Cf. Verg. *A.* 8.193; Ov. *Met.* 11.592; Mant. *Calam.* 1.462 (p. 31): "Antra . . . grandi laterum sinuata recessu."
26   **Longius — abest** Cf. *Sylv. duae* 1.192. For *longius abest,* see also Ov. *Tr.* 2.188; l. 152 below.
27   **saeva . . . fortuna** = Mart. 4.18.7; cf. Eob. *Her. Chr.* 19.101, n.
       fortuna coegit = Luc. 5.522.
29   **Marcella pedissequa** Cf. *Leg. aurea* 92.35: "Marcilla pedissequa Marthe."
30   **fida ministra** = Ov. *Tr.* 3.7.2.
31   **Ipsa, domo** = *Her. Chr.* 16.259, n.
       et parvo — sacello Cf. Ov. *Fast.* 1.275; Eob. *Buc.* 3.41, n.
33   **Inter — turres** Cf. *Leg. aurea* 101.10, referring to the dragon's lair: "inter Arelatem et Avinionem."
       maenia turres = Luc. 3.456.
34   **Hic — habet** Cf. Ov. *Fast.* 1.582; 3.412; 6.478; Eob. *Sylv. duae* 1.24, n.; *Her. Chr.* 12.120; 14.156.
35   **eiectae fluctibus** Ov. *Ep.* 7.89; cf. Eob. *Her. Chr.* 17.199.
36   **nostra — loco** Cf. *Her. Chr.* 17.198.
39   **victori . . . Christo** ll. 90, 113 below; cf. *Her. Chr.* 5.20; 6.122.
       gloria Christo = *Luth.* 2.63; *Accl.* 1.131.
45   **nova . . . spectacula** Calp. *Ecl.* 7.5; Eob. *Hod.* 268.
       fecit spectacula = Mant. *Calam.* 1.631 (p. 35): "Tristia Niliacae fecit spectacula plebi."
46   **vitam reddidit** = Poliziano, *Epigr.* 65.2.
47   **operata salutem** *Her. Chr.* 1.87, n.
48   **commeminisse iuvat** = *Pug.* 6, n.
49   **Est locus** = Verg. *A.* 1.530; 3.163; 7.563; Ov. *Met.* 2.195; 8.788; et al.; Eob. *Her. Chr.* 3.11, n.
       undique sylva = *Her. Chr.* 4.103.
50   **Rupe sub** = Verg. *G.* 4.508.
       opaca palus Cf. Verg. *A.* 6.107, of the infernal river Acheron: "tenebrosa palus"; 7.801; [Tib.] 3.3.37; Sen. *Thy.* 665–66.
51–60 **Innocuas — trahi** For this description of the plague brought on by a dragon, cf. Mant. *Georgius,* fol. 204ᵛ. Cf. further Eob. *Rec.* 11–60, n.
51   **Innocuas prius** Prud. *Amart.* 233.
       infecit Ov. *Met.* 3.76, referring to the dragon slain by Cadmus.
       draco pestifer *Leg. aurea* 56.19, retelling the legend of St. George: "Iuxta quam civitatem erat stagnum instar maris in quo draco pestifer latitabat."
52   **Iamque omnis** = Verg. *A.* 9.25; Eob. *Nup.* 171.
       aer For the scansion (maintained in the later redactions), see n. to *Her. Chr.* 20.21.
53   **Lurida . . . pestis** Brant, *Var. carm.,* sig. C8ᵛ (*Texte* 125.104).
       vicinas . . . in urbes = *Her. Chr.* 13.125, n.

54   **tuta fuere suis** = Ov. *Fast.* 6.174.
55   **Strata — morbo** Ever since Thuc. 2.47–52, accounts of the plague typically report that the survivors are too few to bury the dead: see, for example, Lucr. 6.1215–16; Ov. *Met.* 7.584–86; Luc. 6.100–02; Celtis, *Am.* 3.14.57–58.
        Strata . . . cadavera Celtis, *Rhapsodia* 86.
        Strata iacent passim = Verg. *Ecl.* 7.54.
        grassante . . . morbo Sil. 14.625; Eob. *Sylv.* 1.1.111.
56   **Per fora, per plateas** = Locher, *Stult.*, praef., fol. 9ʳ: "Per fora, per plateas, vicos, madidasque tabernas"; Eob. *Her. Chr.* B 1.21; cf. *Her. Chr.* 15.45; *Buc.* 4.92–93 (with n. at ll. 85–96).
        compita . . . vias = Ov. *Fast.* 1.142.
57–60   **Morbida — trahi** That the wild animals and birds fall victim to the plague is also mentioned in Lucr. 6.1219–22; Verg. *G.* 3.480, 546–47; Ov. *Met.* 7.536–37.
57   **mediis . . . sylvis** = Ov. *Met.* 6.453.
59   **nubem — volucrum** Cf. Stat. *Silv.* 1.6.75–76; also cf. Verg. *A.* 7.705.
60   **vitam . . . trahi** Verg. *A.* 2.92; Boeth. *Consol.* 2.m7.23: "longius vitam trahi."
        non potuisse trahi = *Her. Chr.* 10.90.
61   **vicini . . . fluminis unda** Sil. 9.615; Eob. *Nor.* 360.
62   **incautas — rates** *Sylv.* 6.6.36, referring to the Sirens.
63   **loca tuta** = *Buc.* 10.48; cf. Cic. *Att.* 5.18.2; Liv. 22.11.3; 22.60.10; et al.; Locher, *Stult.*, introductory epigram, l. 8, fol. 1ᵛ: "salubres portus et loca tuta"; *Stult.* 58, fol. 69ᵛ: ". . . templi vix loca tuta manent"; Eob. *Her. Chr.* 5.157.
64   **Innumeros homines** Juvenc., praef. 6.
        dilaniasse ferunt = *Sylv.* 2.10.2.
67   **Prebuimus facilem . . . aurem** Juv. 5.107; Eob. *Her. Chr.* 21.81.
68   **trucis . . . ferae** *Her. Chr.* 14.96, n.
        antra ferae Cf. Ov. *Pont.* 1.6.52; Stat. *Theb.* 9.719.
69   **Multa timens** Ov. *Met.* 14.739 (in most mss.); Sil. 8.73.
        longo . . . intervallo = Verg. *A.* 5.320; cf. Eob. *Buc.* 6.2.
70   **Suspensa . . . mente** Verg. *A.* 5.827–28.
72   **audaci . . . pede** *Idyl.* 3.23.
75   **Exuvias — vorati** Cf. Ov. *Met.* 3.55–57, of Cadmus' dragon.
76   **Sanguine — humus** Cf. Verg. *A.* 8.195–96; Eob. *Her. Chr.* 16.211.
        Sanguine . . . calido Verg. *A.* 9.422; Ov. *Met.* 6.238; Ov. *Fast.* 1.321.
77–78   **Dicere — potest** Cf. *Her. Chr.* 17.103–04, n.
80   **pyra . . . vindice** Cf. Ov. *Met.* 1.230; Sen. *Med.* 532; Eob. *Her. Chr.* 17.114, n. For *pyra* in the sense of "fire," see Vulg. *Act.* 28.2.
82   **transiit — latus** = *Nor.* 897; cf. Ov. *Ep.* 3.126; Eob. *Her. Chr.* 16.222.
83   **Ampla . . . ora** Mart. 1.60.1.
        rictibus ora = Celtis, *Am.* 2.5.3: "Torrida vulnificis aperit Leo rictibus ora."
84   **Vulnificis . . . dentibus** Sen. *Phaed.* 346.
87   **cauda — anguem** Cf. Ov. *Met.* 4.726–27, of the sea monster slain by Perseus; Hor. *Ars* 3–4.
88   **Multiplicem — rotam** Cf. *Her. Chr.* 12.181–82, nn.; Ov. *Met.* 3.77.
89   **vita spoliavimus** Verg. *A.* 6.168; Ov. *Ib.* 619.
90   **victor . . . Christe** l. 39, n., above.
91–93   **Non — habebat** Cf. Ov. *Ep.* 21.116–20.
91   **Amazoniam . . . securim** Hor. *Carm.* 4.4.20; Ov. *Pont.* 3.1.95.
92   **ense manus** = Ov. *Am.* 2.2.64; *Ep.* 14.46; Eob. *Her. Chr.* 12.106.
94   **quis . . . probet** Ov. *Am.* 1.1.9; Mart. 2.72.2.
95–98   **Praebuit — amor** Martha has "put on the whole armor of God" to withstand "the wiles of the devil" (Vulg. *Eph.* 6.11). For this "armor of God," cf. Vulg. *Sap.* 5.18–21; *Eph.* 6.14–17; *1. Thess.* 5.8. For the commonplace of spiritual warfare, see Eob. *Her. Chr.* 6.71, n.

97   **Mens devota Deo** = Ven. Fort. *Carm.* 6.4.1; cf. Prud. *c. Symm.* 2.1130.
      strictum . . . ensem = Ov. *Ep.* 7.185; *Met.* 8.207.

98   **non simulatus amor** = *Her. Chr.* 17.34, n.

100   **nuda puella** = Prop. 3.14.4; Mart. 11.104.8.

101   **solito . . . blandior** Ov. *Ars* 2.411.

103   **irato — leoni** The lion and the fox are often paired in Aesop's fables: see, in particular, fable 154 (Hausrath); cf. Hor. *Ep.* 1.1.73.

105   **Sicut — agnus** Cf. Vulg. *Isa.* 53.7; *Act.* 8.32; Lact. *Inst.* 4.18.16: "sicut agnus coram tondentibus." The image is prefigured in the legend. See *Leg. aurea* 101.13: "Qui protinus victus ut ovis stans a sancta Martha proprio cingulo alligatur et illico a populo lanceis et lapidibus perimitur."
      imbellis . . . agnus ≈ *Buc.* 10.122; cf. *Buc.* 1.108–09, n.

109   **Obruit . . . saxis** Cf. *Her. Chr.* 11.49.

110   **Carmine . . . novo** Cf. Vulg. *Psa.* 32.3 (39.4; and elsewhere): "canticum novum."
      Carmine — gaudia Cf. Ov. *Met.* 8.238. For *testatus gaudia*, see also *Met.* 6.660; 8.420; Eob. *Luth.* 2.55; cf. *Her. Chr.* 13.102, n.
      gaudia summa = Ven. Fort. *Carm.* 7.1.42; Eob. *Eccles.* 238.

112   **depopulator agri** Cf. *Her. Chr.* 10.84, n.

113   **victori . . . Christo** l. 39, n., above.

114   **sacram . . . fidem** Prud. *Perist.* 14.14; Eob. *Her. Chr.* 10.76.
      milia multa = *Her. Chr.* 6.76, n.

115   **nova . . . miracula** = *Her. Chr.* 16.133, n.

116   **Lustrales . . . aquas** Cf. *Her. Chr.* 17.205, n.; Ov. *Pont.* 3.2.73.
      pia voce = Ov. *Ep.* 16.120.
      voce precantur ≈ *Nob.* 62; cf. Verg. *A.* 9.403; 11.784; Eob. *Vict.* 235.

118   **Praecipue — opus** The verse is repeated as a refrain at ll. 128, 136, 148. Cf. Ov. *Ep.* 9.146, reprised at ll. 152, 158, 164. Also cf. Eob. *Buc.* 2.15, n. For the phrasing, cf. Ov. *Ep.* 15.210; Eob. *Accl.* 1.132.
      Praecipue . . . decet Ov. *Ars* 3.309; *Fast.* 3.252.
      sacrum . . . opus = *Her. Chr.* 18.82; cf. Mant. *Ecl.* 6.153.

119   **ablue sordes** = Pico, *Deprecatoria*, p. 378, l. 24: "nostras precor ablue sordes"; cf. Vulg. *Isa.* 4.4; Eob. *Her. Chr.* 17.205, n.

121   **Aquitanica** Wrongly for *Aquensia*, which, however, does not fit the meter. Aix-en-Provence was originally called "Aquae Sextiae."

122   **facta beata tuis** ≈ *Her. Chr.* 6.82, n.

125   **cura . . . sedula** *Her. Chr.* 5.185, n.
      commissae . . . plebis *Sylv.* 3.2.53: "Tu tibi commissae curares commoda plebis."

127   **cano . . . aevo** = Strozzi, *Eroticon* 1.8.329: "pater cano venerabilis aevo." For the epithet, cf. Catul. 108.1; Mant. *1. Parthen.* 2.352: "cana senectus"; Eob. *Her. Chr.* 4.59, n.

129   **miratur Gallia** = Claud. *Cons. Stil.* 1.20.

130   **de veteri . . . caho** = *Her. Chr.* 10.160, n.

131   **Dryidarum** For this spelling, see, for example, Bebel, "Satyricum carmen," *Carm.*, sig. m4ᵛ: "Teutonici Dryides"; "Epicoedion in funere doctoris Galtheri de Vernia," *Carm.*, sig. p6ʳ: "Philosophos, vates, dryides." Elsewhere Eobanus spells the name as "Dryudae." See *Hymn.* B 12.6, n.; *Her.* 2.4.131.

135   **gloria famae** = *Laud.* 481, n.

138   **duxque — fugae** = Ov. *Tr.* 1.10.10; cf. *Tr.* 3.7.18; *Pont.* 4.12.23; l. 145, n., below.

139   **sine remige navis** Cf. Sil. 12.448; Claud. *IV. Cons. Hon.* 223.

140   **in portum . . . acta . . . est** Mant. *Ecl.* 1.158.
      portum . . . suum = Celtis, *Am.* 4.14.58: "Ut capiat portum nostra carina suum."

141   **Caerula . . . aequora** = Catul. 64.7; Eob. *Her.* 1.1.143.
        fortes . . . ventos Ov. *Met.* 11.431–32.
        turbantes — ventos Cf. Lucr. 2.1.
142   **Iussisti — fugam** Cf. Mart. 8.55.10; Eob. *Her. Chr.* 11.64.
        carpere . . . fugam Sil. 10.62.
143   **Boreas . . . nivosus** Mant. *1. Parthen.* 1.727.
144   **Occuluit . . . caput** Tib. 1.7.24; Ov. *Met.* 2.255.
        procella caput = Ov. *Tr.* 3.2.26; *Pont.* 2.7.54.
145   **Tu dux tuque comes** Cf. Ov. *Tr.* 4.10.119; l. 138, n., above.
145–46 **tu rector et idem Navita . . . eras** Cf. Ov. *Ep.* 18.148.
146   **tu . . . frater eras** = Ov. *Ep.* 3.52.
147   **Omnia . . . eras . . . nobis** *Her. Chr.* 16.28, n.
149   **captum lumine** = *Idyl.* 3.113; cf. Ov. *Fast.* 6.204.
150   **luce — diem** = *Luth.* 7.26.
152   **Longius . . . abest** = l. 26, n., above.
153   **lex . . . vetat** Prop. 3.14.21.
157   **Ergo age** = *Buc.* 1.103, n.
157–58 **longa . . . series** Stat. *Theb.* 1.7; 2.267.
160   **Qua licet, et quantum** = Ov. *Pont.* 2.4.34.
        quantum — potest Cf. Ov. *Met.* 2.434; *Rem.* 52; *Tr.* 2.348.
161   **Christi — agro** For the image, cf., for example, Vulg. *Matt.* 9.37–38; *Luc.* 10.2; Eob. *Luth.* 1.18.
        sudamus in = Ov. *Ep.* 20.41.
162   **pietas grata . . . Deo** = Ov. *Fast.* 3.78.
163   **Sepius — aedes** See Vulg. *Luc.* 10.38–42; *Joan.* 12.1–3.
164   **Hospes . . . pectoris** Prosper Aquitanus, *Epigr.* 93.6: "[sapientia] pectoris hospes erit"; Petrarch, *Africa* 1.483: "Pietas sit pectoris hospes / Sancta tui." Cf. l. 21 above.
165–66 **Donec — volet** Cf. *Her. Chr.* 16.258, n.; 21.67–70, nn.
165   **humanae — carnis** Cf. Sedul. 5.173: ". . . humanae positurus tegmina carnis"; Eob. *Vict.* 53 and *Hod.* 441: ". . . humanae lutea testudine carnis."
166   **Alta . . . astra** = Prop. 2.32.50; cf. Ov. *Met.* 15.147–48, 875–76.
        spiritus astra = Ven. Fort. *Carm.* 1.10.2; 4.5.6; 4.8.6; Poliziano, *Epigr.* 67.2: "Fama etenim terras, spiritus astra colit."
167–68 **Plura — Vale** Cf. Ov. *Ep.* 14.131–32; *Tr.* 3.3.85–88.
167   **Plura — cadentes** ≈ *Idyl.* 17.224; cf. *Her. Chr.* 15.131; 16.37; Ov. *Tr.* 3.5.13; Stat. *Silv.* 2.1.17–18; Mant. *2. Parthen.* 3.332: "lachrymae . . . inter verba cadentes." For the motif, cf. also l. 13, n., above.
168   **ignavas — esse** Cf. Andrel. *Livia* 3.8.52: "Qui sapit, ignavos non sinit ire dies"; Eob. *Sylv. duae* 2.84, n.

23

Meter: Elegiac distich.

1   **Haec — horto** Cf. Mart. 7.49.1; 9.54.11. For the letter opening, cf. also Ov. *Ep.* 1.1; 16.1; *Pont.* 1.3.1; 3.4.1–2.
2   **Frigida — humus** That is, from the earthly Paradise: cf. ll. 45–58 below.
        vernat humus = Poliziano, *Eleg.* 7.74: "florifero germine vernat humus"; Eob. *Sylv.* 2.4.32; 2.18.4; cf. *Buc.* 1.3, n.
3   **Accipe, ne dubita** = Calp. *Ecl.* 3.75 (in some mss.); cf. *Ecl.* 4.78; Eob. *Her. Chr.* 1.33, n.; 13.71, n. For *ne dubita* at this metrical position, see also, for example, Prop. 2.20.14; Ov. *Am.* 1.7.63; *Ars* 1.343; Eob. *Her. Chr.* 14.150; 15.133; *Max.* 121, n.
4   **Inficit . . . rubor** = Pontano, *Am.* 2.1.88: "inficit . . . non sua labra rubor"; cf. Luc. 5.214.

5	**Citheraea . . . Venus** Hor. *Carm.* 1.4.5; for the epithet, cf. Eob. *Her. Chr.* 9.89, n. The rose was sacred to Venus: see Mart. 7.89.1–4; Maxim. 1.91–92; Erasmus, *Carm.* 4.74–75.
6	**Non — Amor** Cf. Poliziano, *Eleg.* 5.6: "Vosne in Acidaliis aluit Venus aurea campis? / Vosne sub Idalio pavit Amor nemore?" Idalium on Cyprus was sacred to Venus.
	sub lare = Ov. *Pont.* 1.7.58.
7	**Rossida . . . poma** Prop. 1.20.36; cf. Verg. *Ecl.* 8.37.
	arbore poma = Verg. *Ecl.* 1.37; 7.54.
8	**tibi miranti** = [Tib.] 3.8.4.
	tradidit — puer = Mant. *Bapt.*, fol. 230ʳ: "puero tradidit ista puer."
10	**aeternis . . . rosis** = *Her. Chr.* 9.110, n.
11	**loca . . . proxima mortis** *Ilias* 16.94; cf. Ov. *Met.* 14.126; Eob. *Her. Chr.* 3.29, n.
	patiendae . . . mortis = *Her. Chr.* 14.131.
12	**Ante — puer** Cf. Ov. *Am.* 3.5.10; *Ep.* 15.162; 16.61; *Ars* 3.44; Eob. *Her. Chr.* 13.64, n.
15	**Puer optime** = *Her. Chr.* 4.129, n.
16	**nuncius esse voles** Ov. *Ep.* 12.146.
18	**Rhomani . . . ducis** Ov. *Met.* 15.826.
19	**Protinus occurret** ≈ Ov. *Ep.* 7.67.
21	**vernos . . . odores** Cf. l. 70 below. For *odores* in the sense of "flowers," see Verg. *G.* 1.56; Balbi, *Epigr.* 63.81: "Cymodoce violas, roseos dat Phyllis odores."
23	**Finieram** = *Laud.* 255, n.
	Iniectae — cathenae Cf. Ov. *Ep.* 14.131–32; Eob. *Eccles.* 425. For the phrasing, cf. also Sil. 4.359.
24	**crudeli . . . manu** = Ov. *Am.* 2.14.24.
27	**exiguo . . . labori** Ov. *Tr.* 5.3.20.
28	**fera . . . ira** Ov. *Tr.* 3.11.17.
31	**Multa minans** = Strozzi, *Eroticon* 2.12.51.
33	**Applicui — coegi** Cf. *Epic.* 3A.43: "Quassabam calamos digitosque in verba coegi."
34	**gelidae . . . manus** ≈ Ov. *Ib.* 152.
35	**Afflabam — vapore** Cf. Lucr. 5.567, 593, 798.
	torpentia membra = Sil. 3.637; 4.69; 12.19; cf. Sil. 2.136.
36	**spiritus oris** Verg. *G.* 4.300; Ov. *Met.* 15.303.
37	**utcunque lituras** = *Her. Chr.* 2.125.
38	**exequias — sui** Cf. *Epic. Drusi* 460; Mart. 13.77.2 (also used at l. 40 below).
39–40	**Qualiter — suae** Dorothy's letter is, in effect, her swan song. The belief that swans sing a melancholy, but marvelously beautiful song just before their death was proverbial. See n. to *Buc.* 10.31. The motif occurs also in Ov. *Ep.* 7.1–2.
39	**Phrygii Maeandri** Ov. *Met.* 8.162.
40	**Cantator — suae** Cf. Mart. 13.77.2.
	dicitur esse = *Her. Chr.* 4.158, n.
41	**Mittimus ergo** = Mart. 9.54.11.
43–44	**Hoc tam — rosas** Eobanus reuses this distich in *Sarmat.* 3–4.
44	**Sole sub hyberno** Cf. Verg. *G.* 3.302; Eob. *Rec.* 2, n.
45–58	**At locus — manu** For this description of the earthly Paradise, traditionally believed to be situated on an eastern mountain that reaches up to the lunar sphere, cf. *Buc.* 2.16–19, n.; *Vict.* 392–409; Lact. *Phoenix* 1–30; Sedul. 5.222–26; Prud. *Cath.* 3.101–10; Bocc. *Ecl.* 14.170–92; Mant. *2. Parthen.* 3.264–77:

> Est locus Aeoos Phoebi nascentis ad ortus
> Arduus attollens vicina cacumina coelo:
> Thraicia maior Rhodope, sublimior Ossa [. . . .]
> Illic perpetuo vernantia gramine rura,

Perpetui fructus aeternaque gratia florum
Vernaque temperies semper, sine nubibus aer
Lympidus. Auster abest, Boreas non sibilat, Eurus
Exulat, occidua Zephyrus non murmurat aura.
Hic primaeva quies homini, ieiuna priusquam
Infelix vetita viciasset guttura fruge.
In medio fons est lato pulcherrimus orbe,
Quattuor unde fluunt occulto flumina cursu.

45–46	**At locus — plagae** Cf. *Epic.* 6.35–36.
45	**At locus — ortu** Cf. Lact. *Phoenix* 1: "Est locus in primo felix oriente remotus"; 41: ". . . Phoebi nascentis ad ortus"; Eob. *Vict.* 392; *Idyl.* 16.29; *Psalt.* 113.5: ". . . primo Phoebi surgentis ab ortu." For *Phoebi surgentis,* see Luc. 8.228; V. Fl. 3.437.
46	**Aereae . . . plagae** Cf. Verg. *A.* 1.394; 9.638; Eob. *Eccles.* 304: ". . . aethereae regna beata plagae."
	tertia regna plagae = *Epic.* 6.74, referring to the "third realm," or heaven (the other two realms being earth and sea). For *tertia regna* in this sense and at this metrical position, see Ov. *Am.* 3.8.50; *Fast.* 4.584; [Tib.] 3.5.22; cf. Eob. *Epic.* 6.113: "Regna . . . melioris tertia mundi."
	regna plagae = Claud. *Carm. minora* 26.18.
47	**smaragdo** Cf., for example, Vulg. *Tob.* 13.21; *Ezech.* 28.13; *Apoc.* 21.19; Prud. *Psych.* 862.
49	**Angelicis . . . manibus** Avit. *Carm.* 3.267: "Angelicis manibus . . . in sublime levatus."
50	**Ver ibi — dies** Cf. Tifernate, *Carm.*, sig. D2ʳ, referring to Paradise: "Ver ubi perpetuum perpetuusque dies"; Bocc. *Ecl.* 14.190, referring to Paradise: "Ver ibi perpetuum . . ."; cf. also Ov. *Met.* 5.391. Eternal spring was a standard feature in descriptions of the Golden Age: see, for example, Verg. *G.* 2.149; Ov. *Met.* 1.107; Prud. *Cath.* 3.103: "ver ubi perpetuum redolet"; Eob. *Vict.* 35 (in Paradise), 403 (in heaven).
52–53	**Nescit — astro** Cf. Hor. *Epod.* 16.61–62, referring to the Isles of the Blessed.
52	**Nescit — locum** Cf. *Epic.* 6.42, of heaven: "Nulla est in tali pestilis aura loco."
	pestilis aura = Trebelius, *Epigr.*, sig. B4ᵛ; Eob. *Val.* 1.116; *Tum.*, ded. 38.
55	**Excipit — mentes** Cf. *Her. Chr.* 3.13, n.
	Excipit hic = Sil. 9.535.
	puras . . . mentes = Paul. Nol. *Carm.* 6.304; cf. *Carm.* 19.233.
	terreno . . . carcere Boeth. *Consol.* 2.7.23: "mens conscia terreno carcere resoluta caelum libera petit." For the concept of the body as prison of the soul, see Eob. *Her. Chr.* 14.133, n.
	carcere mentes = Avit. *Carm.* 2.190.
56	**Hic — domus** Cf. Lact. *Phoenix* 2: "Est locus . . . / qua patet aeterni maxima porta poli"; Eob. *Vict.* 395–96, referring to the earthly Paradise.
	aethereae . . . domus = Balbi, *Epigr.* 76.10; 99.50; *Opusc.* 45.8; cf. Eob. *Her. Chr.* 4.158, n.
57–58	**Hunc — manu** Cf. *Her. Chr.* 1.63–76, nn.
58	**audaci . . . manu** = Ov. *Ep.* 11.40.
61	**At tu si sapies** Cf. Ov. *Met.* 14.675: "Sed tu si sapies. . . ."
63	**Februa — tenetur** Cf. *Leg. aurea* (Graesse) 210, p. 911: "Tunc Theophilus prorupit in voces laudando et glorificando Christum Deum Dorotheae, qui mense Februario, dum magna frigora terram cogebant nec aliquod virgultum frondibus vestitur, rosas et poma, quibus vult, mittere potens est."
	sydereo . . . Pisce Cf. Ov. *Fast.* 4.941.
66	**clausit hyems** Verg. *G.* 2.317.
68	**Florida . . . Hybla** Ov. *Tr.* 5.6.38; Mart. 2.46.1. Hybla in Sicily was famed for its honey and flowering herbs: see Eob. *Laud.* 107, n.

Riphaea . . . nive = Sabell. *In natal.* 2, sig. a3ᵛ (7, sig. b2ᵛ): "Limina Rhyphea can-didiora nive"; Strozzi, *Eroticon* 2.3.10: "Collaque Riphoea non minus alba nive." Cf. Luc. 4.118; Sen. *Phaed.* 8; Eob. *Her. Chr.* 18.44, n.

69   **Moeonis — campis** Lydia in Asia Minor was renowned for its saffron. Since Maeonia was a region in Lydia, *Moeonis* is an *epitheton ornans.*

70   **verno — vacet** Cf. Verg. *G.* 1.56. For *verno odore,* see l. 21 above.

71   **Assyrium . . . orbem** Juv. 2.108.

72   **Hyperboreo — gelu** Cf. *Sylv.* 1.2.4: "Prussia, Hyperboreo semiperusta gelu"; 9.1.46: "Hyperboreo regna perusta gelu." For *usta gelu,* see *Hod.* B 1.4; cf. Ov. *Fast.* 4.918; *Tr.* 3.4.48; 5.2.66.

73   **Hesperidum . . . sororum** Cf. l. 7 above, with n. 2.

74   **aestivum . . . decus** *Nor.* 394.
     Punica terra = Pontano, *Laud.* 13.2; Dantiscus, *Carm.* 12.3.12; cf. Prud. *Perist.* 13.1.

75   **Omnia — orbe** Cf. Ov. *Met.* 13.852–53; Prud. *Amart.* 504; Eob. *Vict.* 25. Cf. further *Buc.* 7.140, n.: "sub sole."
     sol . . . altus Ov. *Met.* 2.417.

76   **Nunc — iacent** Cf. Ov. *Ars* 3.411; Eob. *Her. Chr.* 3.146; 12.61–62.

77   **germinet arbor** ≈ Balbi, *Opusc.* 44.97: "germinat arbos"; Pontano, *Urania* 1.268: "quando omnis germinat arbos"; cf. Eob. *Buc.* 6.18, n.

78   **Totaque — humum** Cf. Poliziano, *Eleg.* 7.74: "Pictaque florifero germine vernat humus." For *tota gratia,* see Eob. *Ama.* 32.54, n.; for *florigeram humum,* see *Luth.* 2.8.

79   **passurae vulnera** = Ov. *Met.* 12.386.
     vulnera mortis = *Her. Chr.* 14.131, n.

80   **Florea . . . serta** l. 104, n., below.
     extremo funere ≈ Prop. 2.11.4.

82   **Nullius — habes** Cf. Trebelius, *Epigr.,* sig. F2ʳ: "Immeritae causam suspitionis habes."

83   **praesens ratio** = Man. 1.483; Prud. *Psych.* 18.

85   **Quoque magis credas** = *Sylv. duae* 2.131, n.

88   **caelesti nectare** Ov. *Met.* 4.252.
     nectare pastus ≈ *Her.* 2.7.34.

89–90 **I nunc . . . I nunc et** Cf. *Buc.* 4.63, n.

90   **numen — nega** ≈ Mant. *2. Parthen.* 3.25: "Numen habere nego"; cf. Eob. *Her. Chr.* 9.160, n.; 20.44, n.

91–92 **Quin — via** Cf. ll. 97–98 below.

91   **Deum — potentem** Cf. *Ama.* 35.89; *Buc.* 11.50; *Her. Chr.* 9.121; l. 97, n., below.
     Deum . . . potentem Ov. *Ep.* 9.43.

92   **ire via** = *Sylv. duae* 2.98, n.

93   **Hac sequere** = Stat. *Theb.* 5.246.
     superas . . . arces = V. Fl. 2.94; 4.73.
     proxima pertinet = *Vict.* 185.

94   **Tartara . . . ima** = Strozzi, *Eroticon* 2.8.58; cf. Ov. *Ib.* 571–72; Sen. *Oed.* 869.

95   **Aspice preterea** = *Sylv. duae* 2.217.
     varias . . . per urbes = Stat. *Ach.* 2.66.

97–98 **Et vera — via** Cf. ll. 91–92, nn., above.

97   **Et vera — potentem** Cf. Mant. *Calam.* 3.270 (p. 77): "Et facilem cognosce Deum . . . faventem"; l. 91, n., above.

98   **Hac . . . itur ad astra via** *Her. Chr.* 15.174, n.

99–100 **Et nisi — eris** Cf. *Her. Chr.* 9.129–30, n.

99   **mens ebria** Mant. *Ecl.* 3.52–53, referring to passionate love; *Dionys.* 3, fol. 196ᵛ: "dulcedine tanta / Ebria mens"; *Consol.,* fol. 126ʳ.

100 **Mutato . . . pectore** Walter, *Alex.* 6.307: "mutato pectore mutans / Consilium."
     Christi . . . miles For the commonplace, see *Her. Chr.* 6.71, n.

101   **gustabis — mortis** Cf. Vulg. *Joan.* 8.52; *Hebr.* 2.9.

        pocula mortis = *Ecl. Theoduli* 43; Brant, *Var. carm.*, sig. h4ʳ (*Texte* 200.25); cf. Cic. *Clu.* 31: "poculo mortis."

102   **palestra** For the image, cf. *Her. Chr.* 18.165, n.

103   **caelesti . . . horto** = *Nob.* 27.

104   **capiti — meo** Cf. Pontano, *Parthen.* 1.18.14: "hinc veniant capiti laurea serta meo"; Celtis, *Ludus* 157: "Imponas capiti laurea serta meo"; Eob. *Her. Chr.* 18.84, n.

        florea serta = Tib. 1.1.12 and 1.2.14 (in mss. and older eds.); Mart. 8.77.4; Eob. *Eleg.* 1.86; *Sylv.* 2.15.6; cf. l. 80 above.

105   **imponere finem** = Luc. 8.785; Calp. *Ecl.* 6.92; Claud. *In Rufin.* 2.192.

106   **Hei mihi, quam** = *Sylv. duae* 1.188, n.

        duram . . . necem V. Fl. 2.455–56.

108   **purpureis . . . rosis** = Mant. *Epigr.*, fol. 110ʳ; Andrel. *Livia* 3.4.32; cf. *Copa* 14.

109   **hoc — urna** Cf. *Her. Chr.* 4.249.

110   **precor, adde meo** ≈ Ov. *Fast.* 6.536.

111–14 **Rhoma — abi** For the epitaph, cf. n. to *Her. Chr.* 4.251–54.

111   **Moga** A corruption of *Mazaca*, an earlier name for Caesarea. Cf. Freculphus, *Chronicorum tomi duo*, 1.27, *PL* 106, col. 933 C (repeated in Calepino, *Dictionarium*, s.v. "Moga"): "Moga vero primum dicebatur, quae postea Cappadocia, nunc autem Caesarea a Romanis hoc vocabulum sortitur, id est, a Caesare." Cf. further Plin. *Nat.* 6.8; Hier. *De viris inlustribus* 116: "Caesareae Cappadociae, quae prius Mazaca vocabatur."

112   **uterque parens** = *Her. Chr.* 17.110, n.

113   **Numina . . . non vera deorum** Cf. *Psalt.* 96.11: "statuae, non vera deum sunt numina"; *Her. Chr.* 4.218, n.: "numina falsa."

        veterum . . . deorum = *Her. Chr.* 10.75, n.

114   **Hospes, abi** = Pontano, *Tum.* 1.20.22 (concluding an epitaph).

115   **Caetera — loquetur** Cf. *Her. Chr.* 1.203, n.

116   **Sit licet . . . puer** ≈ *Her. Chr.* 4.10.

        ab arce, puer = Ov. *Ib.* 494, 562.

117   **prebemus — securi** Ov. *Tr.* 4.2.45; *Pont.* 4.4.31; cf. *Met.* 12.249; 15.126.

119   **gaudia caeli** = Paul. Nol. *Carm.* 21.839.

120   **carcere** Cf. *Her. Chr.* 14.133, n.

        terra! Vale = *Rec.* 144, n.

24

In this concluding poem, a wooing letter to the goddess Posterity, Eobanus introduces himself to his future readers. Such a self-presentation at the end of a collection of poems is a regular feature in ancient poetry: see Verg. *G.* 4.559–66; Hor. *Ep.* 1.20; *Carm.* 3.30; Prop. 1.22; Ov. *Am.* 3.15; and — of special importance as a model for Eobanus' letter — *Tr.* 4.10, addressed explicitly to posterity. Cf. also Aus. *Praef.* 1. But Eobanus was also inspired by Petrarch's influential prose letter to posterity, written in 1371/72 and first published in 1496 in the Basel edition of his *Opera*, at the end of *Senilium rerum libri*. In that autobiographical letter, entitled "Franciscus Petrarca Posteritati," the great Italian humanist not only recounts the story of his life and aspirations but also describes his character and physical appearance, just as Eobanus does in the present poem. Unlike Petrarch, however, who neither personalizes nor deifies posterity, Eobanus turns Posterity into a goddess and expresses his undying love for her. For a penetrating study of Petrarch's letter, see Karl Enenkel, "Modelling the Humanist: Petrarch's *Letter to Posterity* and Boccacio's Biography of the Poet Laureate," in *Modelling the Individual: Biography and Portrait in the Renaissance*, ed. K. Enenkel, B. de Jong-Crane, and P. Liebregts (Amsterdam, 1998), 11–49, with a brief discussion of Petrarch's influence on Eobanus' autobiographical elegy on 35, 41–42. For a text and translation see Enenkel's article, "A Critical Edition of Petrarch's *Epistola Posteritati*," in *Modelling the Individual*, 243–81.

On the genre, see Jozef IJsewijn, "Humanistic Autobiography," in *Studia Humanitatis: Ernesto Grassi zum 70. Geburtstag* (Munich, 1973), 209–19; and Hans R. Velten, *Das selbst geschriebene Leben: Eine Studie zur deutschen Autobiographie im 16. Jahrhundert*, Frankfurter Beiträge zur Germanistik 29 (Heidelberg, 1995). For detailed interpretations of Eobanus' autobiographical poem, see Rener, 440–45; Karl Enenkel, "Autobiographisches Ethos und Ovid-Überbietung: Die Dichterautobiographie des Eobanus Hessus," *Neulateinisches Jahrbuch* 2 (2000), 25–38, with a brief bibliography; and Enenkel, "In Search of Fame: Self-Representation in Neo-Latin Humanism," in *Medieval and Renaissance Humanism: Rhetoric, Representation and Reform*, ed. S. Gersh and B. Roest (Leiden, 2003), 93–113 (104–09 in particular).

Eobanus' autobiographical poem strongly influenced the concluding elegy "To the Reader" in bk. 4 of Johannes Gigas' *Sylvarum libri IIII* (Wittenberg, 1540), sig. G1ʳ–G3ʳ, as well as Klemens Janicki's elegy "De se ipso ad posteritatem" (1541), *Tristia* 7. For the latter, see *Klemens Janicki, Carmina: dzieła wszystkie*, ed., trans., and annotated J. Krókowski, E. Jedrkiewicz, and J. Mosdorf (Wrozław, 1966), 48–59, 351–53; cf. Andrzej Budzisz, "Ad Posteritatem — adresat w autobiograficznych elegiach Klemensa Janickiego, Eobana Hessa i Owidiusza," *Roczniki Humanistyczne* 46 (1998), 127–36. Another humanist who used Eobanus' elegy extensively was the poet's student and friend Jakob Micyllus (1503–58). Micyllus mined it for the biographical details that he wove into his *epicedion* for the poet, first published in *Epicedia scripta a Iacobo Micyllo in mortem Eobani Hessi poetae et Simonis Grynaei* (Wittenberg, 1542) and reprinted at the head of Johann Drach's edition of *Helii Eobani Hessi . . . epistolarum familiarium libri XII* (Marburg, 1543), sig. *3ʳ–*7ᵛ, and in bk. 1 of Micyllus' *Sylvarum libri quinque* (Frankfurt am Main, 1564), 41–56.

The present poem to Posterity was first edited (in the redaction of 1539) by Johann T. Kreyssig in *Ioachimi Camerarii narratio de Helio Eobano Hesso. Accesserunt Christ. Theoph. Kuinoelii oratio de Helii Eobani Hessi in bonas literas meritis et Helii Eobani Hessi carmina . . . iterum edita* (Meissen, 1843), app. 3, 86–90, with numerous philological notes. Since then it has proved popular with anthologizers (in each case according to the 1539 version). See Harry C. Schnur, ed. and trans., *Lateinische Gedichte deutscher Humanisten* (Stuttgart, 1967), 210–19, with introd. and nn. on 447–48; Alessandro Perosa and John Sparrow, eds., *Renaissance Latin Verse* (London, 1979), 434–36 (extracts); and Wilhelm Kühlmann, Robert Seidel, and Hermann Wiegand, eds. and trans., *Humanistische Lyrik des 16. Jahrhunderts, Lateinisch und deutsch*, Bibliothek der Frühen Neuzeit 1.5 (Frankfurt am Main, 1997), 328–37, with introd. and nn. on 1140–43.

Meter: Elegiac distich.

1–2	**Quam — Posteritas** Cf. Ov. *Tr.* 4.10.1–2, introducing an autobiography in verse.
1	**Quam — reliquit** Cf. *Sylv. duae* 1.1, n.
	quondam . . . reliquit = Verg. *A.* 11.819.
4	**vultus . . . videre tuos** = Ov. *Pont.* 2.4.8; Eob. *Her. Chr.* 11.168; 18.176.
	posse videre = *Sylv. duae* 2.64, n.
5	**sequeris** The final syllable is lengthened before the caesura.
7	**Quo magis . . . magis hoc** = Ov. *Met.* 14.302.
	fugis . . . retro Verg. *A.* 11.405; Hor. *Carm.* 2.11.5.
8	**lubrica diva** = *Sylv.* 2.1.12; 3.17.4; and 6.7.38 (all referring to Fortuna). Cf. ll. 17–18 below. For the epithet *lubrica* applied to Lady Luck, see also Boeth. *Consol.* 1.m5.28–29; Hutten, *Querel.* 1.10.70; Dantiscus, *Carm.* 1.3.254: "lubrica . . . dea"; 1.3.485: "dea lubrica"; Eob. *Max.* 133–34, 167.
11	**veneramur amantes** = Prop. 3.5.1.
13–14	**Nata — mihi** Cf. *Idyl.*, 1. ded. 55–56 (2. ded. 53–54): "Sicut enim illorum, quondam nova, sera sequuta est, / Sic mea posteritas me quoque sera manet."
14	**Vatibus antiquis** = Ennod. *Carm.* 1.9.1; cf. Man. 1.446.
16	**captus amore** = Ov. *Ep.* 1.76.
	amore frui = *Her. Chr.* 3.120, n.
17	**Lubrica** See n. to l. 8 above.

19	**Non . . . Choi . . . magistri** Mant. *Calam.* 1.553 (p. 33), referring to Hippocrates: "non Coi sancta magistri / Pharmaca sufficiant"; cf. Ov. *Pont.* 4.1.29; Eob. *Laud.* 364, n.
	manus ingeniosa Erasmus, *Carm.* 11.6; *Adag.* 1.7.70, *ASD* 2.2:198, l. 536.
20	**arte senex** = Ov. *Ib.* 262.
21	**plures — formas** Cf. *Her. Chr.* 10.71, nn.
22	**Omnis — mari** Cf. *Ama.* 35.72, n.
	Oceano . . . mari = Aen. Silv. *Carm.* 103.6; cf. Eob. *Her. Chr.* 2.56, n.
23–24	**modo — nitens** Cf. Ov. *Tr.* 5.8.17–18, referring to Fortuna.
	vultu — Constas Cf. Walter, *Alex.* 1.495 (of Fortuna): ". . . numquam vultu persistit eodem."
23	**vultu . . . eodem** = Verg. *A.* 4.556; Ov. *Met.* 3.418.
	non semper eodem = Ov. *Ars* 2.429.
25	**impacienter amarunt** ≈ Mant. *Ecl.* 7.65; Eob. *Buc.* 3.158, n.
26	**laude superba** = Hutten, *Querel.* 1.7.60; Eob. *Her. Chr.* 19.16.
27	**optima mater** = Verg. *A.* 10.557; *Epic. Drusi* 341; Sil. 5.596.
28	**vita . . . perpete** Juvenc. 2.508.
	in astra leves ≈ Celtis, *Am.* 4.14.34: "in astra levat"; Eob. *Idyl.*, 1. ded. 12 (2. ded. 10): "Quae victura tuum nomen in astra levet." The stars are a proverbial symbol of immortality, in the secular as well as religious sense: see Otto 197; Häussler, 233, 262; and, for example, Hor. *Carm.* 4.2.23; Ov. *Met.* 9.272; Eob. *Her. Chr.* 6.140, n.
29	**omnigenum . . . rerum** *Nup.* 96.
30	**ex omni parte** = *Ama.* 35.8, n.
31	**dura . . . mater** Mart. 4.31.6.
32	**Inter . . . fer . . . esse** *Nob.* 293; *Sylv.* 7.35.13–14: "tot Aonidum cultores inter et Hessum / Praeconem laudis fer, precor, esse tuae."
	fer — tuos ≈ *Epic.*, app. 5.16; cf. Ov. *Pont.* 3.3.108.
35–36	**Quisquis — puer** For these thoughts, cf. *Orat. Sylv.* 22–24.
35	**Quisquis amat** = *Laud.* 321, n.
36	**Veneris . . . puer** *Her. Chr.* 17.88, n.
	suadet amare = Ov. *Tr.* 2.314.
37	**Ultima tu nostras** ≈ Ov. *Ep.* 15.71.
	heroidas — haberis ≈ *Nup.* 100, n.
38	**rebus adesse** = Ov. *Tr.* 2.216; Eob. *Her. Chr.* 4.154.
39	**Attamen, ut noris** Cf. *Hod.* B 1.17. For *ut noris*, see Ov. *Tr.* 4.10.2 (addressing posterity); Eob. *Her. Chr.* 21.6, n.
	semper amavi = Verg. *Cat.* 8.3; Ov. *Rem.* 7.
40	**O animae — meae** Cf. *Sylv.* 2.7.4: "Pectoris est certe cura secunda mei"; 2.25.2: "O et adhuc animi maxima cura mei"; 6.10.66: "Semper eris Musae cura secunda meae." For *cura secunda* at this metrical position, see also Prop. 2.1.26; Mart. 9.79.4.
41	**Te — possem** Cf. Ov. *Ep.* 16.36–37; Eob., verse letter to Hermann Trebelius, in Trebelius, *Epigr.*, sig. F2ʳ: "Te prius optabam coram quam cernere possem."
	quam — possem ≈ Ov. *Fast.* 6.649.
43	**pene puer** Ov. *Ep.* 16.359, 361; *Met.* 9.398; *Pont.* 4.3.12; 4.12.20.
44	**pars — militiae** = *Luth.* 8.12; *Eras.* 126; cf. Prop. 1.21.4; Ov. *Ep.* 8.46; *Met.* 7.483; 11.216; Eob. *Eccles.* 200. For the image of love as warfare, cf. *Her. Chr.* 14.61–62, n.
	pars quota = *Her. Chr.* 1.96, n.
45	**magnis . . . divis** = Verg. *A.* 12.296; Ov. *Met.* 6.526.
46	**aeterna . . . salute** *Her. Chr.* 1.1, n.
	fama salute = Ov. *Pont.* 3.9.46: "vilior est operis fama salute mea."
47–50	**Ergo — voles** Cf. Aus. *Praef.* 1.1–4: "Ausonius genitor nobis, ego nomine eodem; / qui sim, qua secta stirpe lare et patria, / ascripsi ut nosses, bone vir, quicumque fuisses, / et notum memori me coleres animo"; Petrarch, *Posteritati* 1, opening

sentence: "Fuerit tibi forsan de me aliquid auditum . . . , et illud forsitan optabis nosse, quid hominis fuerim aut quis operum exitus meorum"; Janicki, *Tr.* 7.1–3, imitating Eobanus: "Si quis eris olim nostri studiosus, ob idque / Nosse voles vitae fata peracta meae, / Perlege, quae propere dictavi carmina."

48   **Venturae . . . Posteritatis eris** = *Laud.* B 1.2, n.

49   **Quae mihi — parentes** Cf. *Ilias Lat.* 621. Cf. further Verg. *A.* 1.606; 10.597.

50   **vitae tempora** = Ov. *Tr.* 5.10.12; *Pont.* 2.5.74.

        tempora nosse = Celtis, *Ama.* 4.1.26.

51–52   **Martia — coit** Cf. *Nor.* 76–77; *Sylv.* 7.9.7–8: "Qua . . . fertur in aequora Rhenus, / Qua velut in centrum Teutonis ora coit."

51   **Germania Rhenum** = *Buc.* 9.4; cf. Mart. 2.2.3.

52   **Teutonis ora** = *Sylv. duae* 1.128, n.

53   **viris colitur** Cf. Verg. *A.* 1.532; 3.165.

        Cattos dixere vetusti Cf. Verg. *A.* 3.693; Ov. *Met.* 15.332; *Fast.* 2.491; 6.107; *Pont.* 3.2.45.

54   **pugnax Hessia** Cf. *Buc.* B 3.1, n.

        nomen habet = *Sylv. duae* 1.24, n.

55–60   **Mons — amat** Cf. *Wirt.* 475–78. Eobanus describes Frankenberg more fully in *Rec.* 174–83.

55   **Christiferae . . . puellae** *Her. Chr.* 6.187, n.

56   **Radices . . . lambit** Aen. Silv. *Germania* 1.21: "in monte Frisingensi, cuius radices fluvius lambit Ysera."

        vitreis . . . aquis = *Her. Chr.* A 3.10; cf. Stat. *Silv.* 1.3.73–74.

        lambit aquis = *Sylv. duae* 1.144, n.

57–58   **Parva — locum** For the thought, cf. *Laud.* 124–25, n.; also cf. *Wirt.* 477–78: "Francoberga, meis non ignoranda Camenis, / Si qua manet me fama et si mea carmina vivent."

57   **Parva quidem** = Ov. *Met.* 8.630; *Tr.* 2.110; *Pont.* 4.8.35; cf. Eob. *Sylv. duae* 1.155, n.

        nostris . . . Camoenis = *Buc.* 10.23, n.

58   **Obscuras — locum** = *Luth.* 2.32 (referring to Wittenberg); cf. *Sylv.* 5.20.18.

        non habitura locum = *Her. Chr.* 2.90; cf. Ov. *Ep.* 16.6; *Tr.* 1.5.50; *Pont.* 4.5.42; Eob. *Her. Chr.* 6.212; 12.162.

61   **vitaleis — auras** Cf. Verg. *A.* 1.387–88; Eob. *Her. Chr.* 18.25, n.

63–68   **Iam — fuit** Closely paralleled in *Sylv.* 1.12.21–26; cf. *Nob.* B 1.19–24.

63   **Iam — Christum** ≈ *Epic.* 3A.3; *Wirt.* 146; *Sylv.* 1.12.23.

        ter quinque Ov. *Met.* 2.497; 8.749; *Tr.* 1.1.117; 3.14.19.

        quinque . . . secula = Ov. *Met.* 15.395.

65   **fulsit Lyra** Ov. *Fast.* 2.76.

66   **illius atque mei** = *Her. Chr.* 21.142.

67   **Non — loquor** = Ov. *Ep.* 14.45 (in one ms. tradition).

        Vertentem . . . mundum Hyg. *Astr.* 2.10; 4.10, 11. Eobanus refers to the calendars and astronomical tables printed in the almanacs.

68   **Sacra — fuit** Cf. *Pug.* 8, n.

        dies Iani Ov. *Pont.* 4.9.60, referring to January 1. For *Ianus* in the sense of "January," see Ov. *Fast.* 2.1; Stat. *Silv.* 1.6.3.

69–71   **Quae mihi — avorum** Cf. Petrarch, *Posteritati* 2: "Honestis parentibus . . . fortuna mediocri et — ut verum fatear — ad inopiam vergente . . . natus sum."

69   **mihi — domus** = *Nob.* 311.

70   **Pauper — fuit** = Claud. *Carm. minora* 23.16.

        uterque . . . parens *Her. Chr.* 12.197, n.

        sed sine labe = *Sylv. duae* 1.150, n.

71   **titulos . . . stemmata avorum** ≈ *Her.*, ded. 5; cf. *Laud.* 492, n.

72   **Virtute — ferar** Cf. *Nob.* 343–44. For the commonplace, see *Nup.* 97–99, n.

73   **studiis — aetas** = *Her.* 1.6.125.

74   **Nil moror** = Verg. *A.* 11.365; Hor. *Ep.* 2.1.264.

75–84   **Protinus — erant** Cf. Ov. *Tr.* 4.10.41–42; Eob. *Sylv.* 1.11.33–34: "Semper enim sacros colui ceu numina vates — / Tantus in hoc vatum pectore flagrat amor"; Dantiscus, *Carm.* 7.5: "sacrorum . . . numina vatum"; Janicki, *Tr.* 7.31–38, after taking up studies in grammar school: "Hic quendam invenio magna cum laude docentem, / Quicquid habet Latium, Graecia quicquid habet [cf. ll. 97–98 below], / Qui nostri curam laetus suscepit agelli, / Illum sincera percoluitque fide. / Tum primum nomen magni immortale Maronis / Audivi et nomen, Naso beate, tuum. / Audivi, colere incepi dixique poetis / Post divos terras maius habere nihil."

75–76   **Protinus — eram** Cf. *Epic.* 5.47–48, where Hutten says of himself: "Parvus adhuc primaque notans lanugine malas / Musarum certo numine plenus eram."

75   **primis . . . ab annis** = *Buc.* 3.65, n.

        quantumque recordor Ov. *Met.* 15.436; Eob. *Epic.* 5.50.

76   **numine raptus** *Buc.* 3.15.

77   **titulum — poetae** Cf. Hor. *Ars* 299; Ov. *Rem.* 1; Celtis, *Am.* 2.8.63: "Primus ego titulum gessi nomenque poetae"; 3.10.19: ". . . titulum vatis nomenque poetae."

78   **Tytire** For this medieval and Renaissance spelling (retained in the 1532/39 version) see, for instance, Bocc. *Ecl.* 1.83; 3.95, 103; Erasmus, *Opus de conscribendis epistolis* (Basel, 1522), 241 (not recorded in the critical apparatus at *ASD* 1.2:435, l. 13). Vergil's first eclogue, which opens with the name *Tityre,* was standard reading in medieval and Renaissance grammar schools. But the primary school in Gemünden, where Eobanus began to learn Latin, evidently did not teach Vergil. In a poem written in late 1516 Euricius Cordus makes the same complaint about his early schooling in Hesse. See Cordus, *Eleg. duae* 2.99–102: "Hic pater ignaris vicina per oppida ludis / me dedit, hic praeter barbara nil didici. / His male neglecti ter quattuor egimus annos / nec tuum adhuc notum, Tityre, nomen erat."

79   **incauto . . . ore** *Her. Chr.* 1.198.

80   **sine mente** = Ov. *Ars* 1.122.

81   **Nectebam numeros** Pontano, *Lyra* 5.17, to the sun god Phoebus: "Tu choros primus numerosque nectis"; cf. Ov. *Pont.* 4.2.30.

84   **Da veniam** = *Her. Chr.* 2.14, n.

87–92   **Namque — magis** Cf. *Laud.* 32–37, n.; *Nob.* 277–88, n.; *Idyl.* 14.62–82.

87   **Germania nostra** = Brant. *Var. carm.*, sig. a8ᵛ (*Texte* 195.412); cf. Eob. *Nup.* 365, n.

89   **bello atque armis** = Mant. *Calam.* 3.556 (p. 84): "Apta prius bello atque armis"; cf. Verg. *A.* 1.545.

90   **Latio . . . ore** = *Nob.* 286.

        protulit ore = Pontano, *Am.* 2.7.62: "hos . . . Acidalio protulit ore sonos."

91–92   **Nunc — magis** Eobanus proudly insinuates that Rudolph Agricola's prediction, made in 1470 and first published ca. 1475, has now at length been fulfilled. See *Rudolph Agricola, Letters*, Medieval and Renaissance Texts and Studies 216, ed., trans., and annotated Adrie van der Laan and Fokke Akkerman (Tempe, AZ, 2002), *Ep.* 3.5, p. 68, where Agricola prophesies to Rudolf von Langen: "ingentem de te concipio fiduciam summamque in spem adducor fore aliquando, ut priscam insolenti Italiae et propemodum occupatam bene dicendi gloriam extorqueamus, vindicemusque nos et ab ignominia, qua nos barbaros indoctosque et elingues et si quid est his incultius esse nos iactitant, exolvamus, futuramque tam doctam atque literatam Germaniam nostram, ut non Latinius vel ipsum sit Latium." (I owe this note to Monika Rener, "Eine Krise der Latein-Studien in der Reformation? Philipp Melanchthon und Helius Eobanus Hessus," *Jahrbuch für Internationale Germanistik* 32.2 [2002], 64.)

93   **Atque — digressus** Cf. *Her. Chr.*, ded. 7.1, n.: "Ut igitur redeam unde digressus sum."

95–96   **Sorduit — puer** Cf. *Buc.* 2.43–44.

95   **humanas . . . mentes** = Ov. *Met.* 1.55; cf. Eob. *Laud.* 344; *Her. Chr.* 9.81, n.

97   **Obtulit . . . fortuna** Lucr. 5.960; Locher, *Stult.* 20, fol. 31ᵛ: "Quod fortuna levis obtulit"; Eob. *Sylv.* 6.3.11: "Obtulit arridens unum fortuna sodalem.
            in triviis . . . magistrum *Buc.* 11.72, n.

100   **certis legibus** = Strozzi, *Eroticon* 6.10.94; Eob. *Eccles.* 258; cf. Ov. *Fast.* 5.65–66; Eob. *Nob.* 77, n. For the phrase referring to metrical scansion, see Cic. *Orat.* 198: "in . . . [versibus] certa quaedam et definita lex est."
            ire pedes = Prop. 2.12.24.

101–04   **Sponte — eris** Mutianus Rufus quotes these lines in *Ep.* 416, p. 76 (letter to Eobanus of August 1514). He thereupon rewards Eobanus with further lines of praise and once more quotes the verse, "Hesse puer, sacri gloria fontis eris."

101   **Sponte — diebus** Cf. Ov. *Tr.* 4.10.25–26, quoted in Eob. *Ama.* 34.2.
            Sponte sua = *Buc.* 1.6, n.

102   **Et mihi iam puero** Cf. Ov. *Tr.* 4.10.19.
            non leve nomen = Marul. *Epigr.* 3.52.2.

103   **Ut non — vates** Cf. Suetonius' Vergil biography (*Vita Donatiana*) 30: "Aeneidos vix-dum coeptae tanta extitit fama, ut Sextus Propertius non dubitaverit sic praedicare: 'Cedit, . . .'"; Eob. *Ama.* 34.1: "ita ut . . . in Tristibus scribere non dubitarit."
            praecipuus . . . vates Macr. 5.3.16: "duos praecipuos vates."

104   **sacri gloria fontis** Mant. *Epigr.*, fol. 117ᵛ.
            gloria fontis eris = Balbi, *Epigr.* 72.16: "Bellerophontei gloria fontis eris."

105–06   **Carmina — mihi** Cf. *Buc.* 2.1–3. In thus highlighting his precociousness, Eobanus invites the reader to associate the modern Ovid with his ancient counterpart. For in *Tr.* 4.10.57–58, Ovid declares that he first recited his poetry in public shortly after he began shaving — that is, when he had just passed his mid-teens. Johannes Dantiscus draws exactly the same parallel in 1510. See *Carm.* 7.27–28, in a poem that Eobanus knew very well: "Excessi vixdum raptus tria lustra puellis / Sum puer Aoniis militi-aeque datus." Klemens Janicki follows suit in *Tr.* 7.49–50: "Carmina cum pleno recitavi prima theatro, / Addideram menses ad tria lustra novem."

105   **Carmina . . . lecta probaret** *Epic.* 1.24; cf. *Idyl.* 13–17, praef. 3: "Quae [carmina] . . . lecta probabis."

106   **Clausa — mihi** Cf. *Her. Chr.* 14.58, n.
            tria lustra = *Her. Chr.* 4.42, n.

107–23   **Illo — puellas** The model is Verg. *G.* 4.559–66.

107   **me studiis — fovebat** Cf. *Rec.* 52–53, n.
            Erphurdia magna Locher, *Stult.* 27, fol. 38ᵛ: "Hic volat ad Wiennam, tenet hunc Erfordia magna." In the early sixteenth century Erfurt ranked among Germany's most populous cities, right after Cologne, Lübeck, Ulm, and Straßburg: see Rener, 443, n. 26. But the epithet *magna* also suggests Erfurt's importance as one of Germany's most distinguished centers of learning: cf. Eob. *Rec.* 230; the encomiastic poem *De laudibus et praeconiis incliti gymnasii apud Erphordiam* (1507); *Ama.* B 4.5.

108   **ingenii . . . signa** Janicki, *Tr.* 7.128.
            publica — dedit = *Accl.* 1.80; cf. *Epic.* 3.96, of Dürer's books: "Praesentem faciunt publica signa fidem"; *Her.* 2.2.84, of the books that Jerome published at Rome: "Doctrinae aedideras plurima signa tuae."
            publica signa Luc. 2.319; 7.164.

109–10   **Et iam — modis** Cf. *Idyl.*, 1. ded. 27–28 (2. ded. 25–26): "Bis duo lustra, duas messes, mea vita peregit, / Quo toga sylvestris tempore sumpta mihi est."

109   **Olympias** A span of five years, as at *Her. Chr.* 14.3, n. When he published his *Bucolicon* in late September 1509, Eobanus was twenty-one years old (or, as he him-self believed at the time, twenty-two).

110   **Buccolicis — modis** Cf. Ov. *Tr.* 2.538: "bucolicis iuvenis luserat ante modis"; Eob. *Epp. 3*, sig. C7ᵛ (letter of 9 July 1536) "Bucolicis lusit numeris iuvenilior aetas." For the spelling "buccolicis," see, for example, the title of Boccaccio's *Buccolicum carmen*; Erasmus, *Carm.* 102, entitled "Carmen buccolicum."

111	**aegloga** For this form, see introductory note to *Buc.* 1 (1:455).
112	**magister eram** = Ov. *Tr.* 3.7.24.
113	**Plurima praeterea** = Hutten, *Querel.* 2.10.215: "Plurima praeterea iuvenum consortia vatum."
	iuvenilia . . . lusi Ov. *Tr.* 5.1.7.
	iuvenilia carmina = Ov. *Tr.* 2.339; *Pont.* 3.3.29; cf. Eob. *Buc.* 11.107, n.
	carmina lusi Verg. *G.* 4.565.
114	**nosse potes** = Ov. *Am.* 2.3.2; *Fast.* 5.346, 636.
115	**lima** For the image, see n. to *Her. Chr.*, ded. 3.1.
	nondum vulgata = Ov. *Met.* 1.164; Mart. 10.93.3.
117	**poemata versu** Ven. Fort. *Carm.* 7.12.111; Eob. *Sylv.* 2.29.7, referring to his *Heroides*: "Scripsimus exiguo vulgata poemata versu."
119	**ab undecimo . . . annus** = Verg. *Ecl.* 8.39; cf. Eob. *Buc.* 9.10.
120	**Aetatis . . . meae** = Ov. *Pont.* 1.4.6.
	plusve minusve = Ov. *Rem.* 560; *Fast.* 5.110; 6.274; Mart. 8.71.4; cf. Eob. *Luth.* 2.23.
121–23	**Tempore — puellas** Cf. *Nup.* 35–36, nn.
121	**Tempore iam Caesar** = Juv. 4.135.
122	**duri . . . Martis** Verg. *Ecl.* 10.44; *A.* 12.73.
	fulmina Martis Amm. 31.3.8; Petrarch, *Africa* 7.1068; Eob. *Tum.* 5.102; *Nor.* 663; cf. Sil. 8.222; Eob. *Nob.* 189, n. The image is also used to describe Maximilian's attacks on the Venetians in *Max.* 50 and 96; *Tum.* 3.139–40: "in Venetos . . . / Fulmina praeduri Martis iacit." Cf. further *Her. Chr.* 12.116, n.
123	**puellas** Eobanus call his heroic epistles "puellas" also in *Her. Chr.* B 1.50; *Her.*, ded. 47, 51, 75, 85, 107, 115, 131.
125	**Accipe . . . gremio** Verg. *A.* 1.685.
	gremio . . . amico Claud. *III. Cons. Hon.* 128–29.
126	**atque — habe** Cf. *Hod.* B 7.66, addressing the Virgin Mary: "Et nunc ista piae nomina matris habe"; Hutten, *Querel.* 1.2.44: "I nunc et magni nomina vatis habe." For *piae matris*, see also Ov. *Ep.* 15.115; 19.123; *Met.* 13.301; *Fast.* 4.555; 6.559; Eob. *Nob.*, lim. 8.
127–28	**Has — aquas** Cf. *Sylv.* 7.18.11–12: "Cum mihi Christicolas Heroidas ore canentem / Imberbi stupida Vistula vidit aqua."
127	**iniquo . . . caelo** Luc. 10.230–31.
128	**Qua — aquas** Cf. Ov. *Am.* 3.6.86; *Ep.* 2.114; cf. Eob. *Sylv. duae* 1.2, n.
	Qua . . . aquas = Ov. *Fast.* 2.68.
	vagus . . . Istula Cf. *Sylv. duae* 1.59, 144. For the epithet *vagus*, see *Buc.* 1.110, n. For the form "Istula," see *Nup.*, lim. 3, n.
	sorbet aquas = Ov. *Ars* 2.352.
129	**ubi — harenas** Cf. Verg. *G.* 3.350; Eob. *Eleg.* 1.19: "Hic ubi flaventes viridis Pegnesus arenas / Aestuat"; *Idyl.* 16.24–25: "Hic ubi flaventes pulcher Pegnesus arenas / Volvit"; *Epic.* 1.107: "Hic ubi flaventes exaestuat Albis arenas."
	niger Odera Cf. Celtis, *Am.* 3.12.72: "Oderae nigras . . . aquas." According to Celtis, *Germania* 242, the Oder was called "Nigra" in antiquity. For the epithet, cf. Eob. *Sarmat.* 54, of another Polish river: "niger . . . Mottila."
	versat harenas Ov. *Met.* 2.456.
131	**Edidit in lucem** ≈ Ov. *Met.* 15.221.
132	**nobile — opus** = Ov. *Tr.* 1.10.30; Mart. 9.93.6; cf. Eob. *Buc.* B 2.26, n.
133–34	**His — fuit** Eobanus expresses the same thought in *Her. Chr.*, ded. 7.1–2 (where see n.).
133	**Peligni . . . poetae** Mart. 2.41.2; Andrel. *Livia* 2.10.3.
	Musa poetae = *Buc.*, lim. 1, n.
135–36	**si non — precor** Cf. Ov. *Fast.* 4.227–28; Eob. *Epic.* 3A.9–10.
136	**Ultima . . . causa** Ov. *Ep.* 15.71; *Fast.* 1.332.
	causa sit ista = Ov. *Am.* 2.10.30.

137   **Principibus — eram** = *Epic.* 5.99 (of Hutten); cf. *Sylv.* 8.23.9: "Principibus quoque charus erat"; *Nob.* 339, n. The model is Petrarch, *Posteritati* 8: "Principum ac regum familiaritatibus et nobilium amicitiis usque ad invidiam fortunatus fui. Maximi regum et mee etatis et amarunt et coluerunt me."

138   **Abstulit . . . multos . . . dies** Ov. *Ars* 2.170; cf. Eob. *Her. Chr.* 1.38, n.
        aula superba = *Sylv.* 3.4.64.

139   **Quam fuerat melius** = *Her. Chr.* 19.13, n.

140   **magnorum . . . ducum** = Ov. *Pont.* 3.3.32.

141   **Quos — vates** Cf. Ov. *Tr.* 4.10.125; Eob. *Buc.* 1.43–44, n.
        nostro . . . tempore = Lucr. 1.26; Prop. 2.32.43; Eob. *Nob.* 3.

143   **Quisquis es, . . . lector** *Eleg.* 3, postscr.: "Quisquis es, lector. . . ."
        Quisquis es = Tib. 1.4.60; Prop. 1.9.30; Verg. *A.* 1.387; 4.577; et al.

144   **Quemque — loco** Cf. Hutten, *Querel.* 2.10.9–11: "[Elegia,] pete Germanos ex ordine quemque poetas, / Patria vel quos hoc nomine terra colit, / Ut quemque invenies, pro condicione saluta." Cf. further Ov. *Ars* 2.253; 3.530; *Tr.* 3.4.64.

145   **carmina vatis** = *Her. Chr.* 21.39, n.

146   **recto . . . dicere iure** = *Eras.* 152.

147   **forte . . . alia ratione** Lucr. 1.665.

148   **Nullius — erit** Cf. *Sylv.* 1.1.40 (imitating Ov. *Ars* 1.34 and *Tr.* 2.250): "Inque meo nullum carmine foenus erit."
        in nostro carmine . . . erit = Mart. 7.84.6; cf. Ov. *Tr.* 4.4.14; Eob. *Her.*, ded. 110.
        carmine nomen = Ov. *Pont.* 4.16.12.

150   **Invidia . . . caruisse** Ov. *Met.* 13.139.

151   **mala nomina** = *Her. Chr.* 19.163, n.

153   **Fortunae . . . munera** Verg. *A.* 7.243–44; Ov. *Ars* 2.256; cf. Eob. *Her. Chr.* 17.27, n.
        Fortunae — animi = *Sylv.* 8.2.1.

155–58 **Corpus — erat** Cf. Camerarius' description of Eobanus' appearance in *Nar.* 31.3–4. For the motif of poetic self-description, cf. Hor. *Ep.* 1.20.24–25, and, especially, Petrarch, *Posteritati* 4: "Corpus iuveni non magnarum virium, sed multe dexteritatis obtigerat. Forma non glorior excellenti, sed que placere viridioribus annis posset; colore vivido inter candidum et subnigrum, vivacibus oculis. . . ."

155   **Corpus — laborum** Cf. Ov. *Tr.* 1.5.71; 4.10.37.

156   **Robore firma** *Nob.* 163.

157   **sine labe** = *Her. Chr.* 2.45, n.

161   **Lusimus haec . . . carmina** = *Culex* 3. Cf. Dantiscus, *Carm.* 8.3: "Lusimus haec teneris nondum matura sub annis."
        properanti . . . plectro = Alcuin. *Carm.* 1.378; 3.2.13.3.
        carmina plectro = *Buc.* 3.92, n.

162   **ad metam — equus** The image of the poet as charioteer is ancient. See Prop. 2.10.2; 3.3.18; 3.9.58; 4.1.70: "has meus ad metas sudet oportet equus"; Ov. *Am.* 3.15.18; *Rem.* 394: ". . . noster anhelat equus"; *Fast.* 2.360; 4.10; 6.586. Cf. further Eob. *Val.* 1.28, 360, with nn.

163–64 **Parcite — mei** For this modesty formula, cf. *Laud.* 54–55, 588–90; *Nup.* 356–57; Dantiscus, *Carm.* 8.11–12: "Quare si quidquam fuerit non rite politum / Aut minus argutum, consule, quaeso, boni!"; Gigas, *Sylv.* 2, sig. D5ᵛ: "Parce mihi, veniam iuvenilia scripta merentur: / Haec sunt ingenii pignora prima mei."

163   **ad unguem** = *Buc.* 4.94, n.

164   **Haec sunt ingenii** ≈ Andrel. *Livia* 3.6.10: "Haec sunt ingeniis praemia digna novis."
        ingenii munera . . . mei = Poliziano, *Eleg.* 6.32; cf. Eob. *Accl.* 1.140.
        munera prima = Poliziano, *Eleg.* 8.16: "Virtutis referens munera prima suae"; Locher, *Stult.* 79, fol. 91ᵛ: "Divitibus solis munera prima patent."

165–68 **Tempora — velis** Cf. Lact. *De opificio Dei* 20.1: "plura et meliora lecturus, si nobis indulgentia caelitus venerit"; Poliziano, *Silv.* 4, arg.: "Deinceps autem plura melioraque forsitan accipies, modo hunc primum quasi gustum non asperneris"; Eob. *Laud.*, ded. 11, n.; *Guil.*, at the end of the dedicatory letter: "multo deinceps et plura et meliora sim daturus"; *Val.* 1.21–26: "Has igitur tibi primitias ignobilis agri / Parvaque de sterili munera rure damus. / Accipe ferque libens inopis mediocria Musae. / Saepe etiam divis vilia dona placent. / Tunc, ubi me studiis maior melioribus usus / Induet, his parvis splendidiora dabo"; *Idyl.*, 1. ded. 37 (2. ded. 35): "His plura adii-ciam, faveant modo tempora Parcae"; *Idyl.* 9.95: "plura et meliora canemus, / Crastina Phoebaeos ubi lux reparaverit ignes."

165   **Tempora — senectae** Cf. Prop. 4.11.93; Ov. *Ars* 3.59; *Met.* 3.347; Eob. *Epic.* 2.85: "Tempora venturae tetigisses prima senectae."

168   **Primitias — velis** Cf. Celtis, *Am.*, praef. 1: "tamquam primitias agrestis et rudis mei ingenii"; Dantiscus, *Carm.* 8.26: "Primitias grata suscipe fronte meas"; 12.3.2: "Primitias scribae suscipe, quaeso, tui." For the image of the first fruits, cf. Curtius, *ELLMA*, 87.

169–70 **Et me — habe** Cf. *Wirt.* 530–31.

170   **temporis huius habe** = Ov. *Tr.* 1.1.4; cf. *Fast.* 5.266; *Ib.* 426.

B 1

The epigram answers Veit Werler's poem to Eobanus (*Her. Chr.* A 3). It was first edited in Friedrich Ritschl, *Kleine philologische Schriften*, ed. Curt Wachsmuth, vol. 5 (Leipzig, 1879), 82–84. For the theme — envy as the inescapable companion of virtue and excellence — see the introductory note to Eob. *Pug.* B 1 (1:407).

    Meter: First Pythiambic, as in Hor. *Epod.* 14 and 15.

1   **Dulcis — comes** = *Epp. fam.*, 244, to Antonius Corvinus; cf. *Sylv.* 5.48.1: ". . . amici-tiae nostrae comes unice, Luca"; 7.5.1: ". . . amicitiae comes unice nostrae"; 7.13.9: "amicitiae . . . comes unice nostrae."
     Dulcis amicitiae = Pontano, *Urania* 2.1318; Eob. *Epic.* 4.166; *Wirt.* B 2.2; cf. Paul. Nol. *Carm.* 11.42: "Dulcis amicitia. . . ."

3   **Optima pars vitae** = Marul. *Epigr.* 1.48.55; cf. Eob. *Her. Chr.* 1.140, n.
     vitae melioris Sil. 12.316; Eob. *Buc.* 7.141.

7   **viridi . . . umbra** *Buc.* 4.37, n.
     nobis . . . spaciantibus *Nor.* 1241.
     spaciantibus umbra ≈ Ov. *Rem.* 85.

9   **consueto more** = Hrotsv. *Agn.* 437; Eob. *Pug.* 9.

11   **Questus — memini** = Luth. 6.9; cf. Ov. *Ars* 3.659; Eob. *Her. Chr.* 17.87.
     sine crimine = *Her. Chr.* 7.15, n.

12   **Morsu** For the image, see *Pug.* B 1.1, n.

15   **Vidit et indoluit** = *Her. Chr.* 6.125, n.

17   **floret — linguae** Cf. *Laud.* 460, n.; *Epic.*, app. 5.27: "Divitis ingenii floret tibi gratia. . . ."

19   **Comis et urbanus** = Hor. *S.* 1.10.65; Celtis, *Am.* 1.4.21.

21   **Per fora, per plateas** = *Her. Chr.* 22.56, n.
     compita, templa, viasque Cf. Mant. *Ecl.* 4.238: "compita, templa, vias."

25–27 **Nil — medullas** Cf. Luth. 2.59–60; 3.75–76.

25   **Nil miserabilius** = Mart. 6.33.1.
     totum . . . per orbem = *Laud.* 96, n.

27–34 **Ardet — eviscerat** Cf. Luth. 5.61–62; *Eleg.* 3.39–44.

27   **Ardet — medullas** Cf. Andrel. *Livia* 3.4.69 (imitating Ov. *Ep.* 4.15): ". . . miseras fovet igne medullas"; Eob. *Psalt.* 38, arg. 1: "Ardet et incensas magno calet igne medullas"; *Her. Chr.* 4.95, n.

29   **misero . . . amanti** *Buc.* 7.129, n.

32	**impius Mezentius** Cf. Verg. *A.* 7.648; 8.7.
33	**res mira** = *Buc.* 11.46, n.
34	**Se — eviscerat** ≈ *In Ed. Leeum* 21.14: "Te carnifex eviscerat."
35	**Aspice quam** = *Buc.* 6.29, n.
	torvo . . . vultu *Laud.* 503, n.
	distorquet lumina Cf. Hor. *S.* 1.9.65.
	lumina vultu = Verg. *A.* 6.156, 862; Ov. *Met.* 13.456; 14.840.
39–40	**Aspectum — noctua** Cf. *Luth.* 5.63–64.
39	**vitam — agentis** Cf. Verg. *A.* 4.550–51. For *sine crimine* at this metrical position, see Eob. *Her. Chr.* 7.15, n.
40	**glauca** Eobanus plays on the Greek word for the little owl (*glaux, glaukos*), so called becaused of its gleaming eyes. But *glauca* is also a standard epithet of Pallas Athena, to whom the owl was sacred: see *Pug.* 96, n.
43	**desinere — molesti** ≈ *Eleg.* 3.123: "nisi desinis esse molestus."
45	**Ardeat — et se** Cf. *Luth.* 3.75.
47	**alimenta — dabimus** *Her. Chr.* 11.139.
	virtutibus istis = Ov. *Pont.* 3.1.63.
49	**Cumque — leget** Cf. *Epic.*, app. 1.1: "Qui legis haec, si quis tamen haec legis. . . ."
50	**Sacro . . . pectine** Balbi, *Epigr.* 63.48: "Facundum . . . sacro pectine tanget ebur."
	puellas *Her. Chr.* 24.123, n.
51	**Aspiciet nostrae** ≈ *Her. Chr.* 13.121.
52	**Suspendet . . . se** Cf. *Luth.* 2.57–58.
54	**Praeliminari pagina** Cf. *Hymn.*, ded. 6: "in anteliminari pagina."
57	**Eheu, quos gemitus** = Stat. *Ach.* 1.68.
	quos gemitus dabis Verg. *A.* 4.409.
	moestissime Livor = *Eleg.* 3.35.
58	**firmo amore** Ov. *Ep.* 20.86.
59	**latres** *Pug.* B 1.1, nn.
61	**At tu — lector** = Aus. *Parent.*, praef. (B) 15; cf. Hor. *Epod.* 15.17; Ov. *Rem.* 371.
	sine labe = *Her. Chr.* 2.45, n.
65	**Irrequietum animal** = Mant. *Ecl.* 2.67; cf. Eob. *Buc.* 4.95.
67	**nostrorum — sodalis** = *Val.* 2.1, of Martin Hune.

LIST OF ABBREVIATIONS

INDEX OF MEDIEVAL AND NEO-LATIN WORDS

GLOSSARIAL INDEX

GENERAL INDEX

LIST OF ABBREVIATIONS

Abbreviations of ancient and patristic works as well as books of the Vulgate follow the ones given in P. G. W. Glare, ed., *Oxford Latin Dictionary* (Oxford, 1983); Charlton T. Lewis and Charles Short, *A Latin Dictionary* (1879; Oxford, 1966); and Henry G. Liddell and Robert Scott, *A Greek-English Lexicon*, revised by Henry S. Jones (1968; Oxford, 1985). To distinguish *Baebi Italici Ilias* from Eobanus Hessus' translation of Homer's *Iliad*, the ancient abridgment is referred to as *Ilias Lat.* As for *Anthologia Latina* (Shackleton Bailey, fasc. 1; Riese, fasc. 2), it is cited as *Anthol. Lat.* Other works cited in abbreviated form are given below.

A. Patristic, Medieval, and Renaissance Authors and Works

Aen. Silv. *Carm.*	*Enee Silvii Piccolominei postea Pii PP. II carmina*, Studi e testi 364, ed. Adriaan van Heck (Vatican City, 1994).
Aen. Silv. *Europa*	*Enee Silvii Piccolominei postea Pii PP. II de Europa*, Studi e testi 398, ed. Adriaan van Heck (Vatican City, 2001).
Aen. Silv. *Germania*	*Aeneas Silvius: "Germania" und Jakob Wimpfeling: "Responsa et replicae ad Eneam Silvium"*, ed. Adolf Schmidt (Cologne, 1962).
Aen. Silv. *Hist.*	Aeneas Silvius, *Historia de duobus amantibus*. In *Aeneas Silvius Piccolomini (Pius II) and Niklas von Wyle, The Tale of Two Lovers, Eurialus and Lucretia*, ed. Eric J. Morrall (Amsterdam, 1988).
Aen. Silv. *Medela*	Aeneas Silvius, *Ep.* 106, "Amoris illiciti medela." In *Aeneae Sylvii Piccolominei . . . opera quae extant omnia* (1571; repr., Frankfurt am Main, 1967), 607–10.
Agricola, *Anna*	Rodolphus Agricola, *Anna mater* (1484). In *Lucubrationes aliquot lectu dignissimae*, ed. Alaard of Amsterdam (Cologne [1539]), 297–306. Cited by page number.
AH	*Analecta hymnica medii aevi*, ed. Guido M. Dreves, Clemens Blume, and Henry M. Bannister (1886–1922; repr., New York, 1961). 55 vols. Cited by volume, poem, and strophe numbers.
Alan. *Nat.*	Alan of Lille, *De planctu Naturae*, ed. Nikolaus M. Häring. In *Studi Medievali* 19 (1978), 797–879.
Alan. *Parab.*	Alan of Lille, *Liber parabolarum*. In *PL* 210, col. 581–94.
Alcuin. *Carm.*	Alcuinus, *Carmina*, ed. Ernst Dümmler. In *MGH, Poetae Latini aevi Carolini*, 1:169–351.
Andrel. *Ecl.*	Fausto Andrelini, *Eclogae*. In *The Eclogues of Faustus Andrelinus and Ioannes Arnolletus*, ed. Wilfred P. Mustard (Baltimore, 1918).
Andrel. *Eleg.*	Fausto Andrelini, *Elegiae* (Paris, [1496]).
Andrel. *Livia*	Fausto Andrelini, *Livia*. In *Publi Fausti Andrelini "Amores" sive "Livia"*, ed. Godelieve Tournoy-Thoen (Brussels, 1982).
Anon. *Vita Katherine*	Anonymous, *Vita beate Katherine metrica "Floruit insignis."* In *Vitae Sanctae Katharinae, Pars prima*, ed. A. P. Orbán, *CCCM* 119 (Turnhout, 1992), 1–53.
Arator	Arator, *De actibus apostolorum*, ed. Arthur P. McKinlay. In *CSEL* 72.
Avit. *Carm.*	Alcimus Ecdicius Avitus, *Carmina*, ed. Rudolf Peiper. In *MGH, Auctores antiquissimi*, 6.2:203–94.
Balbi, *Epigr.*	Girolamo Balbi, *Epigrammata* (Paris, 1487; repr. Leipzig, 1493). In *Hieronymus Balbus: Poet, Humanist, Diplomat, Bischof: Opera omnia quae supersunt*, Editiones Neolatinae 5/1, ed. Anton. F. W. Sommer (Vienna, 1991), 1:60–103.

Balbi, *Opusc.* Girolamo Balbi, *Opusculum epigrammaton* (Vienna, 1494). In *Hieronymus Balbus: Poet, Humanist, Diplomat, Bischof: Opera omnia quae supersunt,* Editiones Neolatinae 5/1, ed. Anton. F. W. Sommer (Vienna, 1991), 1:126–69.

Bebel, *Carm.* Heinrich Bebel, *Carmina.* In *Oratio ad regem Maximilianum de laudibus atque amplitudine Germaniae* (Pforzheim, 1504).

Bebel, *Prov.* Heinrich Bebel, *Proverbia Germanica,* ed. Willem H. D. Suringar (1879; repr. Hildesheim 1969).

Bocc. *Ecl.* Giovanni Boccaccio, *Buccolicum carmen.* In *Opere latine minori,* ed. Aldo F. Massèra (Bari, 1928), 3–85.

Brant, *NS* Sebastian Brant, *Das Narrenschiff,* ed. Friedrich Zarncke (1854; repr. Hildesheim, 1961).

Brant, *Texte* *Sebastian Brant, Kleine Texte,* ed. Thomas Wilhelmi (Stuttgart, 1998). 2 vols. in 3.

Brant, *Var. carm.* Sebastian Brant, *Varia carmina* (Basel, September 1498).

Busch. *Lips.* Hermann von dem Busche, *Lipsica* [Leipzig, 1504?]. In *Helius Eobanus Hessus, Noriberga illustrata und andere Städtegedichte,* ed. Joseph Neff (Berlin, 1896), 73–91.

Calepino, *Dictionarium* Ambrogio Calepino, *Dictionarium* (1502); reprinted as *Vocabularius, thesaurus copiosissimus, ex Nicolai Perotti Cornucopie . . . doctorum denique omnium Grecorum pariter ac Latinorum voluminibus accurate decerptus ac summa vigilantia castigatus* (Toscolano, 1522).

Camerarius, *Nar.* *Narratio de H. Eobano Hesso, comprehendens mentionem de compluribus illius aetatis doctis et eruditis viris, composita a Ioachimo Camerario Pabebergensi* (Nuremberg, 1553); Eob. *Poetic Works,* 1:10–91.

Celtis, *Am.* Konrad Celtis, *Amores,* ed. Felicitas Pindter (Leipzig, 1934).

Celtis, *Germania* Konrad Celtis, *De situ et moribus Germanie additiones.* In Gernot M. Müller, ed., *Die "Germania generalis" des Conrad Celtis: Studien mit Edition, Übersetzung und Kommentar* (Tübingen, 2001), 89–109.

Celtis, *Ludus* Konrad Celtis, *Ludus Dianae.* In Conrad Celtis, *Ludi scaenici,* ed. Felicitas Pindter (Budapest, 1945), 1–6.

Celtis, *Norimberga* Konrad Celtis, *De origine, situ, moribus et institutis Norimbergae libellus.* In Albert Werminghoff, *Conrad Celtis und sein Buch über Nürnberg* (Freiburg i. B., 1921). Cited by chapter and (where required) page number.

Celtis, *Od.* Konrad Celtis, *Libri odarum quattuor,* ed. Felicitas Pindter (Leipzig, 1937).

Celtis, *Rhapsodia* Konrad Celtis, *Rhapsodia.* In Conrad Celtis, *Ludi scaenici,* ed. Felicitas Pindter (Budapest, 1945), 7–13.

Cordus, *Eleg. duae* Euricius Cordus, *Ex Nosematostichis elegiae duae, altera ad discipulos, altera ad filios, ut addiscant.* In Carl Krause, "Zwei neue Gedichte des Euricius Cordus (1486–1535)," *Hessenland* 9 (1891), 114–19.

Cricius, *Carm.* *Andreae Cricii carmina,* ed. Kazimierz Morawski (Cracow, 1888).

Dantiscus, *Carm.* *Ioannis Dantisci poetae laureati carmina,* ed. Stanislaw Skimina (Cracow, 1950).

Ecl. Theoduli *Ecloga Theoduli.* In *Seven Versions of Carolingian Pastoral,* ed. R. P. H. Green (Reading, 1980), 111–49.

Eob. Eobanus Hessus.

Eob. *Dichtungen* Helius Eobanus Hessus, *Dichtungen: Lateinisch und Deutsch. Dritter Band: Dichtungen der Jahre 1528–1537,* ed. and trans. Harry Vredeveld (Bern, 1990).

Eob. *Poetic Works* *The Poetic Works of Helius Eobanus Hessus,* ed., trans., and annotated Harry Vredeveld (Tempe, AZ, 2004–).

Erasmus, *Adag.*	Desiderius Erasmus, *Adagia*. In *ASD* 2.1–9.
Erasmus, *Carm.*	Desiderius Erasmus, *Carmina*, ed. Harry Vredeveld. In *ASD* 1.7.
Erasmus, *Ep.*	Desiderius Erasmus, *Opus epistolarum*, ed. P. S. Allen, H. M. Allen, and H. W. Garrod (Oxford, 1906–58). 11 vols.
Flos medicinae	*Flos medicinae scholae Salerni*, ed. Salvatore de Renzi (2nd ed., Naples, 1859).
Funck, *Primitie*	Mathias Funck Haynoviensis, *Primitie carminum . . . In Genethlium salutifere virginis Marie, quibus hystoriam nativitatis graphice prosequitur* [Frankfurt an der Oder, 1513].
Gerald. *Ecl.*	Antonio Geraldini, *Eclogues*, ed. Wilfred P. Mustard (Baltimore, 1924).
Gigas, *Sylv.*	Johannes Gigas (Heune), *Sylvarum libri IIII* (Wittenberg, 1540).
Guarino, *Carm.*	Battista Guarino, *Carmina* (Modena, 1496).
Gunther, *Lig.*	Gunther der Dichter, *Ligurinus*, ed. Erwin Assmann. In *MGH, Scriptores rerum Germanicarum in usum scholarum separatim editi*, vol. 63 (Hannover, 1987).
Herc. Strozzi, *Am.*	Hercules Strozzi, *Amores*. In *Strozii poetae pater et filius* (Venice, 1513), fol. 62^r–82^r.
Herc. Strozzi, *Eleg.*	Hercules Strozzi, *Elegiae*. In *Strozii poetae pater et filius* (Venice, 1513), fol. 51^r–62^r.
Herc. Strozzi, *Epigr.*	Hercules Strozzi, *Epigrammata*. In *Strozii poetae pater et filius* (Venice, 1513), fol. 82^v–95^r.
Herc. Strozzi, *Pros.*	Hercules Strozzi, *Proseuchon liber*. In *Strozii poetae pater et filius* (Venice, 1513), fol. 6^r–13^v.
Hrotsv. *Agn.*	Hrotsvit von Gandersheim, *Passio Sanctae Agnetis virginis et martiris*. In *Hrotsvit, Opera omnia*, ed. Walter Berschin (Munich, 2001), 114–30.
Hrotsv. *Gongolf.*	Hrotsvit von Gandersheim, *Passio Sancti Gongolfi martiris*. In *Hrotsvit, Opera omnia*, ed. Walter Berschin (Munich, 2001), 42–62.
Hrotsv. *Theoph.*	Hrotsvit von Gandersheim, *Lapsus et conversio Theophili vicedomni*. In *Hrotsvit, Opera omnia*, ed. Walter Berschin (Munich, 2001), 78–93.
Hutten, *Opera*	*Ulrichi Hutteni opera quae reperiri potuerunt omnia*, ed. Eduard Böcking (1859–70; repr., Aalen, 1963). 5 vols. and 2 supplementary vols.
Hutten, *Querel.*	Ulrich von Hutten, *Querelarum libri duo*. In Hutten, *Opera*, 3:19–83.
Hutten, *Vir bonus*	Ulrich von Hutten, *Vir bonus*. In Hutten, *Opera*, 3:11–18.
Janicki, *Tr.*	Klemens Janicki, *Tristia*. In *Klemens Janicki, Carmina: dzieła wszystkie*, ed., trans., and annotated J. Krókowski, E. Jedrkiewicz, and J. Mosdorf (Wrozław, 1966), 16–81.
Leg. aurea	Iacopo da Varazze, *Legenda aurea*, ed. Giovanni Paolo Maggioni (2nd ed., Tavarnuzze, 1998). 2 vols.
Leg. aurea (Graesse)	Jacobus a Voragine, *Legenda aurea*, ed. Th. Graesse (3rd ed., 1890; repr., Osnabrück, 1969).
Locher, *Katherina*	Jakob Locher Philomusus, *Carmen de sancta Katherina*. In *Vitae Sanctae Katharinae, Pars secunda*, ed. A. P. Orbán, *CCCM* 119 A (Turnhout, 1992), 341–49.
Locher, *Stult.*	Jakob Locher Philomusus, *Stultifera navis* (Basel: Johan Bergmann, 1497).
Magdal. *Ep.*	Jacobus Magdalius Gaudensis, "Epistola Dive Marie Magdalene ad Christum in infirmitate Lazari fratris," in Magdal. *Erarium*, sig. H2^r–H3^r; Eob. *Poetic Works*, 2:111–17 (introduction to *Her. Chr.*).
Magdal. *Erarium*	Jacobus Magdalius Gaudensis, *Erarium aureum poetarum, omnibus Latinae linguae, cuiuscunque etiam facultatis fuerint, professoribus accommodum, immo et omnium poetarum sine ipsis commentariis elucidativum* (Cologne, 1501).
Mant. *Bapt.*	Baptista Mantuanus, *In laudibus Ioannis Baptistae*. In *Opera omnia* (Antwerp, 1576), vol. 2, fol. 229^r–231^r.

Mant. *Calam.*	Baptista Mantuanus, *De calamitatibus temporum*, ed. Gabriele Wessels (Rome, 1916).
Mant. *c. Am.*	Baptista Mantuanus, *Elegia contra Amorem*. In *Opera omnia* (Antwerp, 1576), vol. 1, fol. 175^v–178^r.
Mant. *Consol.*	Baptista Mantuanus, *Consolatio in morte Collae Asculani*. In *Opera omnia* (Antwerp, 1576), vol. 1, fol. 124^r–134^r.
Mant. *c. Poet.*	Baptista Mantuanus, *Contra poetas impudice loquentes, cum Sebastiani Murrhonis interpraetacione*, ed. Mariano Madrid Castro. In *HL* 45 (1996), 93–133.
Mant. *Dionys.*	Baptista Mantuanus, *De Dionysii Areopagitae conversione, vita et agone*. In *Opera omnia* (Antwerp, 1576), vol. 2, fol. 159^r–200^v.
Mant. *Ecl.*	Baptista Mantuanus, *Eclogae*, In *Adulescentia: The Eclogues of Mantuan*, ed. and trans. Lee Piepho (New York, 1989).
Mant. *Epigr.*	Baptista Mantuanus, *Epigrammata ad Falconem*. In *Opera omnia* (Antwerp, 1576), vol. 1, fol. 100^r–118^r.
Mant. *Georgius*	Baptista Mantuanus, *De vita et agone D. Georgii martyris*. In *Opera omnia* (Antwerp, 1576), vol. 2, fol. 201^r–219^v.
Mant. *Lud. Morb.*	Baptista Mantuanus, *De vita D. Ludovici Morbioli Bononiensis*. In *Opera omnia* (Antwerp, 1576), vol. 2, fol. 220^r–229^r.
Mant. *Mort.*	Baptista Mantuanus, *De contemnenda morte*. In *Opera omnia* (Antwerp, 1576), vol. 1, fol. 118^v–123^v.
Mant. *Nat. Am.*	Baptista Mantuanus, *De natura Amoris ad iuvenes, carmen iuvenile*. In *Opera omnia* (Antwerp, 1576), vol. 1, fol. 178^r–178^v.
Mant. *Nebul.*	*In obitu Petri Nebularii declamatoris eximii threnos*. In *Opera omnia* (Antwerp, 1576), vol. 1, fol. 134^v–139^r.
Mant. *1. Parthen.*	Baptista Mantuanus, *Parthenice prima sive Mariana*, ed. and trans. Ettore Bolisani (Padua, [1957]).
Mant. *2. Parthen.*	Baptista Mantuanus, *Parthenice secunda (Catharinaria)*. In *Vitae Sanctae Katharinae, Pars secunda*, ed. A.P. Orbán, *CCCM* 119 A (Turnhout, 1992), 351–435.
Mant. *3. Parthen.*	Baptista Mantuanus, *Parthenice tertia*. In *Opera omnia* (Antwerp, 1576), vol. 2, fol. 101^r–114^r.
Mant. *4. Parthen.*	Baptista Mantuanus, *Parthenice quarta*. In *Opera omnia* (Antwerp, 1576), vol. 2, fol. 114^v–121^r.
Mant. *5. Parthen.*	Baptista Mantuanus, *Parthenice quinta*. In *Opera omnia* (Antwerp, 1576), vol. 2, fol. 121^v–128^r.
Mant. *6. Parthen.*	Baptista Mantuanus, *Parthenice sexta*. In *Opera omnia* (Antwerp, 1576), vol. 2, fol. 129^v–141^v.
Mant. *7. Parthen.*	Baptista Mantuanus, *Parthenice septima*. In *Opera omnia* (Antwerp, 1576), vol. 2, fol. 142^r–158^v.
Mant. *Somn.*	Baptista Mantuanus, *Somnium Romanum*. In *Opera omnia* (Antwerp, 1576), vol. 3, fol. 208^v–220^v.
Mant. *Sylv.*	Baptista Mantuanus, *Sylvae*. In *Opera omnia* (Antwerp, 1576), vol. 3, fol. 242^v–317^v.
Mant. *Votum*	Baptista Mantuanus, *Votum ad divam Virginem*. In *Opera omnia* (Antwerp, 1576), vol. 2, fol. 54^r–55^r.
Marul. *Epigr.*	Michael Marullus, *Epigrammaton*. In *Michaelis Marulli carmina*, ed. Alessandro Perosa (Zürich, 1951), 1–102.
Marul. *Hymn. nat.*	Michael Marullus, *Hymni naturales*. In *Michaelis Marulli carmina*, ed. Alessandro Perosa (Zürich, 1951), 105–65.
Mutian. *Ep.*	Konrad Mutianus Rufus, *Epistulae*. In *Der Briefwechsel des Conradus Mutianus*, Geschichtsquellen der Provinz Sachsen 18, ed. Karl Gillert (Halle, 1890). 2 vols.
Mutius, *Triumph.*	Macarius Mutius, *De triumpho Christi* (Venice, 1499).

Nar.	See Camerarius, *Nar.*
Nativ. Mariae	*Libellus de nativitate Sanctae Mariae*, ed. Rita Beyers. In *Libri de nativitate Mariae*, Corpus Christianorum. Series Apocryphorum 10 (Turnhout, 1997).
Nicodem.	*The Gospel of Nicodemus: Gesta Salvatoris*, ed. H. C. Kim (Toronto, 1973).
Peter Riga	*Aurora: Petri Rigae Biblia versificata*, ed. Paul E. Beichner (Notre Dame, 1965). 2 vols.
Petrarch, *Africa*	Francesco Petrarca, *Africa*, ed. Nicola Festa (Florence, [1926]).
Petrarch, *Ecl.*	Francesco Petrarca, *Bucolicum carmen*, ed. Marcel François; Paul Bachmann (Paris, 2001).
Petrarch, *Ep.*	*Epistolae metricae*. In Francesco Petrarca, *Epistulae metricae. Briefe in Versen*, ed., trans., and annotated Otto und Eva Schönberger (Würzburg, 2004).
Petrarch, *Posteritati*	*Franciscus Petrarca Posteritati*. In Karl Enenkel, "A Critical Edition of Petrarch's *Epistola Posteritati*," in *Modelling the Individual: Biography and Portrait in the Renaissance*, ed. K. Enenkel, B. de Jong-Crane, and P. Liebregts (Amsterdam, 1998), 243–81.
Petrarch, *Rem.*	Francesco Petrarca, *De remediis utriusque fortunae*. In *Francisci Petrarchae opera quae extant omnia* (1554; repr., Ridgewood, NJ, 1965), 1:7–254.
Pico, *Deprecatoria*	Giovanni Pico della Mirandola, "Deprecatoria ad Deum," in *The Complete Works of St. Thomas More*, vol. 1, ed. Anthony S. G. Edwards, Katherine G. Rodgers, and Clarence H. Miller (New Haven, 1997), 378–80.
Poliziano, *Eleg.*	*Elegiae*. In Angelo Poliziano, *Prose volgari inedite e poesie latine e greche edite e inedite*, ed. Isidoro del Lungo (Florence, 1867), 227–56.
Poliziano, *Ep.*	*Epistolae*. In Angelo Poliziano, *Letters*, ed. and trans. Shane Butler (Cambridge, MA, 2006–).
Poliziano, *Epigr.*	*Epigrammata Latina*. In Angelo Poliziano, *Prose volgari inedite e poesie latine e greche edite e inedite*, ed. Isidoro del Lungo (Florence, 1867), 109–66.
Poliziano, *Silv.*	Angelo Poliziano, *Silvae*, ed. and trans. Charles Fantazzi (Cambridge, MA, 2004).
Pontano, *Am.*	Giovanni Pontano, *De amore coniugali*. In *Ioannis Ioviani Pontani carmina*, ed. Johannes Oeschger (Bari, 1948), 125–85.
Pontano, *Ecl.*	Giovanni Pontano, *Eclogae*. In *Ioannis Ioviani Pontani carmina*, ed. Johannes Oeschger (Bari, 1948), 1–62.
Pontano, *Eridanus*	Giovanni Pontano, *Eridanus*. In *Ioannis Ioviani Pontani carmina*, ed. Johannes Oeschger (Bari, 1948), 379–444.
Pontano, *Hendec.*	Giovanni Pontano, *Hendecasyllabi*. In *Ioannis Ioviani Pontani carmina*, ed. Johannes Oeschger (Bari, 1948), 277–342.
Pontano, *Hort.*	Giovanni Pontano, *De hortis Hesperidum*. In *Ioannis Ioviani Pontani carmina*, ed. Benedetto Soldati (Florence, 1902), 1:227–61.
Pontano, *Laud.*	Giovanni Pontano, *De laudibus divinis liber*. In *Ioannis Ioviani Pontani carmina*, ed. Johannes Oeschger (Bari, 1948), 259–76.
Pontano, *Lyra*	Giovanni Pontano, *Lyra*. In *Ioannis Ioviani Pontani carmina*, ed. Johannes Oeschger (Bari, 1948), 351–78.
Pontano, *Parthen.*	Giovanni Pontano, *Parthenopeus*. In *Ioannis Ioviani Pontani carmina*, ed. Johannes Oeschger (Bari, 1948), 63–121.
Pontano, *Tum.*	Giovanni Pontano, *De tumulis*. In *Ioannis Ioviani Pontani carmina*, ed. Johannes Oeschger (Bari, 1948), 187–258.
Pontano, *Urania*	Giovanni Pontano, *Urania sive de stellis*. In *Ioannis Ioviani Pontani carmina*, ed. Benedetto Soldati (Florence, 1902), 1:1–177.
Prud. *Amart.*	Aurel. Prudentius Clemens, *Amartigenia*.
Prud. *Apoth.*	Aurel. Prudentius Clemens, *Apotheosis*.
Prud. *Perist.*	Aurel. Prudentius Clemens, *Liber Peristefanon*.

Prud. *Tit. hist.*	Aurel. Prudentius Clemens, *Tituli historiarum* (*Dittochaeon*).
Ps.-Matt.	*Pseudo-Matthaei evangelium*, ed. Jan Gijsel. In *Libri de nativitate Mariae*, Corpus Christianorum. Series Apocryphorum 9 (Turnhout, 1997).
Sabell. *In natal.*	Marcantonio Sabellico, *In natalem diem divae virginis Mariae*. Cited according to the edition Deventer: R. Pafraet, 1490.
Sedul.	Caelius Sedulius, *Paschale carmen*, ed. J. Huemer. In *CSEL* 10:1–146.
Stella, *Boruss.*	Erasmus Stella, *De Borussiae antiquitatibus*, ed. Theodor Hirsch. In *Scriptores rerum Prussicarum: Die Geschichtsquellen der preussischen Vorzeit bis zum Untergange der Ordensherrschaft*, ed. Th. Hirsch, M. Töppen, and E. Strehlke, vol. 4 (1870; repr. Frankfurt am Main, 1965), 275–98.
Strozzi, *Eroticon*	Tito Vespasiano Strozzi, *Eroticon*. In Tito Vespasiano Strozzi, *Poesie latine tratte dall'Aldina e confrontate coi Codici*, ed. Anita della Guardia (Modena, 1916), 1–179.
Tifernate, *Carm.*	Gregorio Tifernate, *Carmina*. In *Hoc volumine haec continentur: P. Gregorii Tipherni poetae illustris opuscula. Francisci Octavii poetae elegiae* (Venice, 1498; quoted according to the reprint, Strasbourg, 1509).
Trebelius, *Carm.*	Hermann Trebelius, *Carmina* (Frankfurt an der Oder, 1509).
Trebelius, *Epigr.*	Hermann Trebelius, *Epigrammaton et carminum liber primus* [Frankfurt an der Oder, 1509?].
Vegius, *Aen.*	Mapheus Vegius Laudensis, *Aeneidos liber XIII*. In *Das Aeneissupplement des Maffeo Vegio*, ed. Bernd Schneider (Weinheim, 1985).
Ven. Fort. *Carm.*	Venantius Fortunatus, *Carmina*, ed. Friedrich Leo. In *MGH, Auctores antiquissimi*, 4.1.
Walter, *Alex.*	Walter of Châtillon, *Alexandreis*, ed. Marvin L. Colker (Padua, 1978).

B. Eobanus Hessus' Works

Accl.	*Divo ac invicto Imp. Caes. Carolo V. Augusto Germaniam ingredienti urbis Norimbergae gratulatoria acclamatio. Ad eundem de bello contra Turcas suscipiendo adhortatio* (Nuremberg, 1530); Eob. *Dichtungen*, 3:73–101.
Adnot.	*In P. Virgilii Maronis Bucolica ac Georgica adnotationes* (Haguenau, 1529).
Ama.	*De amantium infoelicitate, contra Venerem, de Cupidinis impotentia* (Erfurt, 1508); Eob. *Poetic Works*, 1:200–63.
Buc.	*Bucolicon* (Erfurt, 1509); Eob. *Poetic Works*, 1:272–381.
Calum.	*Descriptio Calumniae, ad doctissimum virum Philippum Melanthonem* (Marburg, 1539).
Coluth.	*Coluthi Lycopolitae Thebani vetusti admodum poetae de raptu Helenes ac iudicio Paridis poema* (Erfurt, 1534).
Consol.	*Ad optimum virum M. Philippum Nidanum, in morte Barbarae uxoris consolatio*. In *Helii Eobani Hessi descriptio Calumniae, ad doctissimum virum Philippum Melanthonem. Ad optimum virum M. Philippum Nidanum, in morte Barbarae uxoris consolatio, eodem authore* (Marburg, 1539).
Dial.	*Dialogi tres: Melaenus, Misologus, Fugitivi* (Erfurt, 1524).
Ebn.	*In funere clariss. quondam viri, D. Hieronymi Ebneri, Urbis Noribergae aerario praefecti supremi etc.* (Nuremberg, [1532]); Eob. *Dichtungen*, 3:485–99.
Eccles.	*Ecclesiae afflictae epistola ad Lutherum* (Haguenau, 1523).
Eleg.	*Elegiae tres* (Nuremberg, 1526).
Epic.	*Illustrium ac clarorum aliquot virorum memoriae scripta epicedia* (Nuremberg, 1531); Eob. *Dichtungen*, 3:103–81.
Epith.	*Epithalamion seu ludus gratulatorius in nuptiis et receptione insigniorum Doctoratus Iurium humanissimi et eruditissimi viri, D. Iusti Studaei* (Frankfurt am Main, 1539).

Eras.	*In funere clariss. et incomparabilis eruditionis viri, D. Erasmi Roterodami, epicedion* (Marburg, 1537); Eob. *Dichtungen*, 3:541–51.
Gen. ebrios.	*De generibus ebriosorum et ebrietate vitanda* [Erfurt, 1515].
Guil.	*Ad illustrissimum Principem Guilielmum, Ducem Brunsvigensem etc., apud hostes captivum . . . consolatio* [Erfurt, 1523].
Her.	*Heroidum libri tres* (Haguenau, 1532); Eob. *Dichtungen*, 3:269–483.
Her. Chr.	*Heroidum Christianarum epistolae* (Leipzig, 1514); Eob. *Poetic Works*, 2:126–435.
Hod.	*A profectione ad Des. Erasmum Roterodamum hodoeporicon carmine heroico* (Erfurt, [1519]).
Hymn.	*Hymnus paschalis nuper ex Erphurdiensi Gymnasio Christianae victoriae acclamatus* (Erfurt, 1515).
Hypocr.	*In hypocrisim vestitus monastici* [Nuremberg, 1527].
Icones	*Homericae aliquot icones insigniores, Latinis versibus redditae* (Nuremberg, 1533).
Idyl.	*Bucolicorum idyllia XVII.* In *Operum farr.*, vol. 1, fol. 1^r–55^r.
Ilias	*Poetarum omnium seculorum longe principis Homeri Ilias* (Basel, 1540).
In Ed. Leeum	Epigrams by Eobanus Hessus in *In Eduardum Leeum quorundam e sodalitate literaria Erphurdiensi Erasmiaci nominis studiosorum epigrammata* (Erfurt, 1520).
Laud.	*De laudibus et praeconiis incliti atque tocius Germaniae celebratiss. Gymnasii litteratorii apud Erphordiam . . . carmen succisivis horis deductum* (Erfurt, 1507); Eob. *Poetic Works*, 1:140–91.
Luth.	*Habes hic, lector: In evangelici Doctoris Martini Lutheri laudem defensionemque elegias IIII. Ad Iodocum Ionam Northusanum cum eodem a Caesare redeuntem elegiam I. Ad Udalricum Huttenum Equitem Germanum ac poetam nobilissimum de causa Lutheriana elegiam I. In Hieronymum Emserum Lutheromastiga conviciatorem invectivam elegiam I* (Erfurt, 1521).
Max.	*Responsio Maximiliani Aug.* In *Quae in hoc libello nova habentur: Epistola Italiae ad divum Maximilianum Caes. Aug. Ulricho Hutteno Equite Germano autore. Responsio Maximiliani Aug. Helio Eobano Hesso autore* (Erfurt, 1516).
Nob.	*De vera nobilitate et priscis Germanorum moribus. Ad Georgium Spalatinum libellus carmine elegiaco* [Erfurt, 1515].
Nor.	*Urbs Noriberga illustrata carmine heroico per Helium Eobanum Hessum anno M.D.XXXII* [Nuremberg, 1532]; Eob. *Dichtungen*, 3:183–267.
Nup.	*Encomium nuptiale divo Sigismundo, regi Poloniae, scriptum anno Christiani calculi M.D.XII* (Cracow, 1512); Eob. *Poetic Works*, 2:12–37.
Orat.	*Oratio sive praelectio in auspicio Officiorum M. Tullii Ciceronis et M. Accii Plauti comoediarum in Academia Erphurdiensi per Magistrum Eobanum Hessum in eadem Academia bonas litteras publice profitentem habita M.D.XV* [Erfurt, 1515].
Orat. Sylv.	*Oratio in praelectione Sylvarum, olim Lypsiae habita.* In *Epp. fam.*, 246–48; Eob. *Poetic Works*, 2:63–68 (introduction to *Sylv. duae*).
Pod.	*Ludus de podagra* (Mainz, 1537).
Praef.	*Praefatio in epistolas Divi Pauli Apostoli ad Corynthios Erphurdiae ad Christianae philosophiae studiosorum ordinem habita ab eximio viro D. Iodoco Iona Northusiano. . . . Huic addita est non multum dissimili argumento Eobani Hessi praefaciuncula in Enchiridion Christiani militis* (Erfurt, 1520).
Psalt.	*Psalterium universum* (Schwäbisch Hall, 1538).
Pug.	*De pugna studentum Erphordiensium cum quibusdam coniuratis nebulonibus* (Erfurt, 1506); Eob. *Poetic Works*, 1:122–33.
Rec.	*De recessu studentum ex Erphordia tempore pestilenciae* [Erfurt, 1506]; Eob. *Poetic Works*, 1:98–115.

Ruf.   *Ad Mutianum Rufum elegia.* In Harry Vredeveld, "A Forgotten Poem by
                 Eobanus Hessus to Mutianus Rufus," in *"Der Buchstab tödt – der Geist
                 macht lebendig": Festschrift zum 60. Geburtstag von Hans-Gert Roloff von
                 Freunden, Schülern und Kollegen,* ed. James Hardin and Jörg Jungmayr
                 (Bern, 1992), 1:1067–83.

Salom.   *Salomonis Ecclesiastes carmine redditus* (Nuremberg, 1532).

Sarmat.   *In poetam Sarmatam Germanos ignaviae insimulantem invectiva* [Erfurt,
                 1523/24].

Sylv.   *Sylvarum libri IX.* In *Operum farr.,* vol.1, fol. 179ʳ–340ʳ.

Sylv. duae   *Sylvae duae nuper aeditae: Prussia et Amor* [Leipzig, 1514]; Eob. *Poetic
                 Works,* 2:70–99.

Theoc.   *Theocriti Syracusani idyllia triginta sex, Latino carmine reddita* (Haguenau,
                 1531).

Tum.   *De tumultibus horum temporum querela. Priscorum temporum cum nostris
                 collatio. Omnium regnorum Europae mutatio. Bellum servile Germaniae. Haec
                 omnia carmine heroico. Ad Germaniam afflictam consolatio paraenetica, elegia
                 una. Roma capta, elegiae duae* (Nuremberg, 1528); Eob. *Dichtungen,* 3:7–71.

Val.   *Bonae valetudinis conservandae rationes aliquot. Simplicium ciborum facultates
                 quaedam. Medicinae encomion. Chorus illustrium medicorum. Novem Musae*
                 [Nuremberg, 1531].

Venus   *Venus triumphans, ad Ioachimum Cam. Qu. . . . In nuptiis Ioachimi Cam.
                 epithalamion seu ludus Musarum* (Nuremberg, 1527).

Vict.   *Victoria Christi ab inferis carmine heroico* (Erfurt, 1517).

Vitanda ebriet. *De vitanda ebrietate elegia, additis super eadem re aliquot epigrammatis*
                 (Erfurt, 1516).

Wirt.   *De victoria Wirtembergensi, ad illustrem et inclytum heroa Philippum,
                 Hessorum omnium ac finitimarum aliquot gentium principem, gratulatoria
                 acclamatio* (Erfurt, 1534); Eob. *Dichtungen,* 3:501–39.

C. Eobanus' Correspondence and Collected Works

Epp. fam.   *Helii Eobani Hessi, poetae excellentiss., et amicorum ipsius epistolarum
                 familiarium libri XII,* ed. Johann Drach (Marburg, 1543).

Epp. 1   *Narratio de H. Eobano Hesso . . . composita a Ioachimo Camerario
                 Pabebergensi. Epistolae Eobani Hessi ad Camerarium et alios quosdam,* ed.
                 Joachim Camerarius (Nuremberg, 1553).

Epp. 2   *Libellus alter, epistolas complectens Eobani et aliorum quorundam doctissi-
                 morum virorum, necnon versus varii generis atque argumenti,* ed. Joachim
                 Camerarius (Leipzig, 1557).

Epp. 3   *Tertius libellus epistolarum H. Eobani Hessi et aliorum quorundam virorum
                 autoritate, virtute, sapientia, doctrinaque excellentium,* ed. Joachim
                 Camerarius (Leipzig, 1561).

Epp. 4   *Libellus novus, epistolas et alia quaedam monumenta doctorum superioris et
                 huius aetatis complectens,* ed. Joachim Camerarius (Leipzig, 1568).

Operum farr.   *Operum Helii Eobani Hessi farragines duae, nuper ab eodem qua fieri potuit
                 diligentia contractae et in hanc, quam vides, formam coactae, quibus etiam
                 non parum multa accesserunt, nunc primum et nata et aedita* (Schwäbisch
                 Hall, 1539).

D. Other Abbreviations

Acta Sanctorum *Acta Sanctorum* (Antwerp and Brussels, 1643–1940). 68 vols.
add.   *addidit, addiderunt,* added (in)

AH	*Analecta hymnica medii aevi*, ed. Guido M. Dreves, Clemens Blume, and Henry M. Bannister (1886–1922; repr., New York, 1961). 55 vols.
app.	appendix
arg.	*argumentum*, argument, summary
Arnold	Udo Arnold, "Landesbeschreibungen Preußens." In *Landesbeschreibungen Mitteleuropas vom 15. bis 17. Jahrhundert*, ed. Hans-Bernd Harder (Cologne, 1983), 79–123.
ASD	Desiderius Erasmus, *Opera omnia* (Amsterdam, 1969–).
b.	born (in)
BHR	*Bibliothèque d'Humanisme et Renaissance*
bk.	book
BL	British Library
BNU	*Bibliothèque nationale et universitaire*, National and University Library
ca.	*circa*, approximately
Carm.	*Carmen, Carmina*
CCSL	*Corpus Christianorum. Series Latina* (Turnhout, 1953–).
CCCM	*Corpus Christianorum. Continuatio Mediaevalis* (Turnhout, 1971–).
cf.	*confer*, compare
chap.	chapter
col., cols.	column, columns
corr.	*correxit, correxerunt*, corrected (in)
CSEL	*Corpus scriptorum ecclesiasticorum Latinorum* (Vienna, 1866–).
Curtius, *ELLMA*	Ernst Robert Curtius, *European Literature and the Latin Middle Ages*, trans. Willard R. Trask (Princeton, 1990).
d.	died (in)
ded.	*dedicatio*, dedicatory letter
Dörrie	Heinrich Dörrie, *Der heroische Brief: Bestandsaufnahme, Geschichte, Kritik einer humanistisch-barocken Literaturgattung* (Berlin, 1968).
Ecl.	*Ecloga, Eclogae*
ed.	edited by; editor
eds.	editions; editors
e.g.	*exempli gratia*, for example
Ep., Epp.	*Epistula, Epistulae*
Epigr.	*Epigrammata*
et al.	*et alii, et alia*, and others; *et alibi*, and elsewhere
ex.	*exemplar*, copy
fol., fols.	folio, folios
Forstreuter	Kurt Forstreuter, *Vom Ordensstaat zum Fürstentum: Geistige und politische Wandlungen im Deutschordensstaate Preußen unter den Hochmeistern Friedrich und Albrecht (1498–1525)* (Kitzingen/Main, [1951]).
Gillert	See Mutian. *Ep.*
Häussler	Reinhard Häussler, ed., *Nachträge zu A. Otto: Sprichwörter und sprichwörtliche Redensarten der Römer* (Hildesheim, 1968). Cited by page number.
Höhle	Michael Höhle, *Universität und Reformation: Die Universität Frankfurt (Oder) von 1506 bis 1550*, Bonner Beiträge zur Kirchengeschichte 25 (Cologne, 2002).
introd.	introduction (to)
Kleineidam	Erich Kleineidam, *Universitas studii Erffordensis*, Erfurter Theologische Studien 14, 22, 42, and 47 (Leipzig, 1981–92). 4 vols.
Krause, "Beiträge"	Karl Krause, "Beiträge zum Texte, zur Chronologie und zur Erklärung der Mutianischen Briefe mit besonderer Berücksichtigung der Gillert'schen Bearbeitung," *Jahrbücher der Königlichen Akademie gemeinnütziger Wissenschaften zu Erfurt*, N.F. 19 (1893), 1–94.

Krause, *HEH*	Carl Krause, *Helius Eobanus Hessus, sein Leben und seine Werke: Ein Beitrag zur Cultur- und Gelehrtengeschichte des 16. Jahrhunderts* (1879; repr. Nieuwkoop, 1963). 2 vols.
Kühlmann and Straube	Wilhelm Kühlmann and Werner Straube, "Zur Historie und Pragmatik humanistischer Lyrik im alten Preußen: Von Konrad Celtis über Eobanus Hessus zu Georg Sabinus." In *Kulturgeschichte Ostpreußens in der Frühen Neuzeit*, Frühe Neuzeit 56, ed. K. Garber, M. Komorowski, and A. E. Walter (Tübingen, 2001), 657–736.
LB	Desiderius Erasmus, *Opera omnia*, ed. J. Clericus (1703–06; repr., Hildesheim, 1961–62). 10 vols.
lim.	liminary epigram, epigram on the title page
Mentzel-Reuters	Arno Mentzel-Reuters, "Von der Ordenschronik zur Landesgeschichte — Die Herausbildung der altpreußischen Landeshistoriographie im 16. Jahrhundert." In *Kulturgeschichte Ostpreußens in der Frühen Neuzeit*, Frühe Neuzeit 56, ed. K. Garber, M. Komorowski, and A. E. Walter (Tübingen, 2001), 581–637.
MGH	*Monumenta Germaniae Historica.*
ms., mss.	manuscript, manuscripts
n., nn.	(with) note, notes. When followed by a number, *n.* indicates "footnote"; without a following number, *n.* points to the Supplementary Notes.
n. p.	no place
no., nos.	number, numbers
om.	*omisit, omiserunt*, omitted (in)
ÖNB	*Österreichische Nationalbibliothek*, Austrian National Library
Otto	A. Otto, *Die Sprichwörter und sprichwörtlichen Redensarten der Römer* (1890; repr., Hildesheim, 1971). Cited by proverb number.
par.	paragraph
PL	J.-P. Migne, ed., *Patrologiae cursus completus. Series Latina* (Paris 1844–1902). 221 vols.
postscr.	*postscriptum*, postscript
praef.	*praefatio*, preface
r.	*regnavit*, reigned
Rener	Monika Rener, "Helius Eobanus Hessus, Heroides IV: 'Elisabeth Ludovico marito suo' oder: Die wundersame Einbürgerung des thüringi-schen Landgrafen in Hessen." In *Hundert Jahre Historische Kommission für Hessen 1897–1997*, Veröffentlichungen der Historischen Kommission für Hessen 61, ed. W. Heinemeyer (Marburg, 1997), 437–61.
repr.	reprinted
Salzer	Anselm Salzer, *Die Sinnbilder und Beiworte Mariens in der deutschen Literatur und lateinischen Hymnenpoesie des Mittelalters* (1886–94; repr., Darmstadt, 1967).
sc.	*scilicet*, namely
Schoenborn	Hans Joachim Schoenborn, *Lebensgeschichte und Geschichtsschreibung des Erasmus Stella: Ein Beitrag zur Geschichte des gelehrten Fälschertums im 16. Jahrhundert* (Düsseldorf, 1938).
sig., sigs.	signature, signatures
SB	*Staatsbibliothek*, State Library
StadtB	*Stadtbibliothek*, Municipal Library
s.v.	*sub verbo, sub voce*, under the heading
tit.	title, heading
t.p.	title page
trans.	translated (by), translator (of)
UB	*Universitätsbibliothek*, University Library

v., vv.	*versus,* verse, verses
VL	*Die deutsche Literatur des Mittelalters: Verfasserlexikon,* ed. Kurt Ruh et al., 2nd ed. (Berlin, 1978–).
VLDH	*Verfasserlexikon: Deutscher Humanismus 1480–1520,* ed. Franz J. Worstbrock (Berlin, 2005–). 2 vols.
vol., vols.	volume, volumes
Walther	*Proverbia sententiaeque Latinitatis medii aevi,* ed. Hans Walther (Göttingen, 1963–69). 6 vols.

INDEX OF MEDIEVAL AND NEO-LATIN WORDS

This index lists words that occur neither in *Thesaurus Linguae Latinae* nor in Forcellini's *Lexicon totius Latinitatis*. Words, in the sense indicated here, that are also found in dictionaries of later Latin are marked with an asterisk. For proper names and their derivatives see the Glossarial Index.

GLOSSARIAL INDEX

All references are to the Latin text. References to proper names that are alluded to in the text, but not explicitly mentioned, are enclosed in square brackets. The name *Helius Eobanus Hessus* is omitted when it occurs in the titles and headings of his own works. For a key to the abbreviations, see pp. 638–43 above.

ABANTIUS, a, um, *descended from Abas, King of Argos*: heros (*Acrisius, the father of Danaë*) *Her. Chr.* 10.121.

ACHELOIUS, a, um, *of the Achelous River; hence, filled with water*: pocula *Sylv. duae* 1.119.

ACHERONTAEUS *or* ACHERONTEUS, a, um, *of Acheron, a river in the underworld*: umbrae *Her. Chr.* 16.189; undae *Her. Chr.* 12.55.

ACHILLES, *the hero of the* Iliad, *son of Peleus and Thetis*: *Nup.* 57; iratus *Her. Chr.* 22.15; magnanimus *Nup.* 136; magnus *Nup.* 117. *See also* Aeacides.

ACHIVI, *the Greeks*: *Nup.* 172.

ACIDALIUS, a, um, *of Venus*: aves (*doves*) *Her. Chr.* 7.2; faces *Her. Chr.* 6.104.

ACONTIUS, *the wooer of the Athenian girl Cydippe*: *Her. Chr.* A 4.11; non aliquis *Her. Chr.* 17.141.

———, *Ovid's heroic letter "Acontius to Cydippe"*: *Her. Chr.*, ded. 16.1; [*Her. Chr.* A 4.11–12].

[ACRISIUS], *King of Argos, the father of Danaë*: *Her. Chr.* 10.121.

ADALBERTUS, *Albert of Prussia (1490–1568), Margrave of Brandenburg, last Grand Master of the Teutonic Order (1510–25), first Duke of Prussia (since 1525)*: [*Sylv. duae* 1.139]; *Her. Chr.*, ded. 17.4.

[ADALRIC], *the father of St. Ottilia (Odilia)*: *Her. Chr.* 9.143–44.

ADAMUS, *the first man*: *Her. Chr.* 1.49; 3.18.

ADRIACUS, a, um, *of the Adriatic Sea*: aestus *Her. Chr.* 21.155; ventus *Her. Chr.* 5.3.

AEACIDES, *Achilles*: *Her. Chr.* 17.139. *See also* Achilles.

AEDERA, *the Eder River in Hesse*: *Her. Chr.* 24.56.

AEGAEUS *or* AEGEUS, a, um, *of or in the Aegean Sea*: Pathmos *Her. Chr.* 16.9; aquae *Her. Chr.* 16.250.

AEGIPTUS *or* AEGYPTUS, *Egypt*: *Her. Chr.* [1.126; 4.34, 43, 48, 70–71, 207, 210; 9.91]; 15.145; 16.115; [20.148]; alma *Her. Chr.* 14.64; relligiosa *Her. Chr.* 4.26.

AEMILIANUS. *See* Maximus Aemilianus.

[AENEAS], *the Trojan hero*: *Her. Chr.* 5.94.

AENEIS, *Vergil's epic*: Vergiliana *Her. Chr.*, ded. 3.4.

AENEIS, idos, *married to Aeneas*: Creusa *Her. Chr.* 5.93.

AETHEREUS, *a British prince betrothed to St. Ursula*: *Her. Chr.* 17, tit.; [17, *passim*]; 17.232.

AETHNA, *Mount Etna, a volcano in Sicily*: ignipotens *Her. Chr.* 21.112.

AETHRUSCUS, a, um, *Etruscan*: Tybris *Her. Chr.* 12.235.

AETOLUS, a, um, *of Aetolia*: sus (*the boar of Erymanthus killed by Hercules*) *Sylv. duae* 2.102.

AFRICA. *See* Aphrica.

AGAPE, *virgin and martyr (d. 304), sister of Chionia and Irene, maidservant of St. Anastasia*: *Her. Chr.* 18.144.

AGAVE, *the mother of Alcyone*: *Her. Chr.* 12.19.

AGLAE, *the mother of St. Alexius*: *Her. Chr.* 7.87.

AGRIPPA, *the Roman general M. Vipsanius Agrippa (64/63–12 BCE), after whom Colonia Agrippinensis (Cologne) was supposedly named*: *Her. Chr.* 17.201, 266.

ALBINGUM, *Elbingen in the former East Prussia*: *Sylv. duae* 1.145.

ALCIDES, *the Greek hero Hercules*: *Her. Chr.* 9.104. *See also* Hercules.

ALCIONE *or* HALCIONE, *a princess rescued from a dragon by St. George*: *Her. Chr.*, ded. 15.7; *Her. Chr.* 12, tit.; [12, *passim*].

————, *her letter to St. George (Her. Chr. 12): Her. Chr.*, ded. 14.3.

ALEXANDER, *Alexander the Great (356–323 BCE): Nup.* 45; *Her. Chr.* 4.35; [4.55; 14.63].

————, *a King of Poland (1501–06):* [*Nup.* 69].

[ALEXANDRIA], *a city in Egypt, founded by Alexander the Great: Her. Chr.* 4.35, 55; 14.63–64.

ALEXIUS, *St. Alexius: Her. Chr.* 7, tit.; [7, *passim*]; 7.103, 153.

————, *the (imaginary) son of St. Alexius and Sabina:* parvus *Her. Chr.* 7.73.

ALPES, *the Alps:* altae *Her. Chr.* 7.29.

AMANS, *the Muse Erato: Sylv. duae* 2.161. *See also* Musa.

[AMAZONES], *a legendary race of warlike women whose right breast was removed so they would be better able to handle the bow: Her. Chr.* 16.46.

AMAZONIUS, a, um, *of the Amazons:* securis *Her. Chr.* 22.91.

AMMON. *See* Iuppiter Ammon.

AMOR, *the god of love: Sylv. duae* 2.99, 106, 250; *Her. Chr.* 23.6; imbellis *Sylv. duae* 2.108; timidus *Sylv. duae* 2.254. *See also* Cupido.

AMPHION, *a musician like the legendary harpist Amphion:* multi *Nup.* 299.

ANASTASIA, *St. Anastasia: Her. Chr.* 18, tit.; [18, *passim*]; 18.1, 118.

ANDROMACHE, *the wife of Hector: Nup.* 193.

[ANDROMEDA]. *See* Cepheis.

ANNA, *the mother of the Virgin Mary: Her. Chr.* 2.101, 111; 3.72; 13, tit.; [13, *passim*]; 13.1–2; 20.62, 151.

————, *her letter to St. Joachim (Her. Chr. 13): Her. Chr.*, ded. 13.1.

[ANNAS], *the Jewish high priest from CE 6 to 15: Her. Chr.* 16.196.

[ANTIOCHIA], *the ancient capital of Syria on the Orontes River: Her. Chr.* 21.123.

ANTIOCHUS, *the King of Syria after whom the city of Antioch was named: Her. Chr.* 21.123.

[ANUBIS], *an Egyptian god represented as having the head of a jackal or dog: Her. Chr.* 4.74.

AONIUS, a, um, *of Mount Helicon, Heliconian:* pulvis *Sylv. duae* 2.174; fontes *Nup.* 11.

[APELLES], *a celebrated Greek painter (fourth century BCE): Her. Chr.* 24.19.

APELLEUS, a, um, *like the credulous Jew Apella mentioned by Horace; Jewish, circumcised:* gens *Her. Chr.* 6.15. *See also* Iudaeus.

APHRICA, *North Africa:* tota *Her. Chr.* 12.232.

[APIS], *the sacred bull worshiped by the Egyptians at Memphis: Her. Chr.* 4.74; 9.92.

APOLLO, *the god of the sun, patron of poetry and the Muses:* crinitus radiis suis *Her. Chr.* A 3.14; melior *Nup.* 353; tuus *Her. Chr.* A 4.7. *See also* Phoebus.

AQUILO, *a north wind: Her. Chr.* 18.43.

AQUITANICUS, a, um, *in Aix-en-Provence (Aquae Sextiae):* templa *Her. Chr.* 22.121.

ARABS, *an Arab: Her. Chr.* 4.27; fuscus *Sylv. duae* 1.107; turilegus *Her. Chr.* 12.114.

ARABUS, a, um, *Arabian:* aes *Her. Chr.* 20.122.

ARACHNE, *a Lydian girl who was changed into a spider; hence, a spider: Her. Chr.* 17.117.

ARCADICUS, a, um, *Arcadian:* germen *Sylv. duae* 1.110.

ARCHIMAGISTER *or* MAGNUS MAGISTER, *Grand Master (of the Teutonic Order): Sylv. duae* 1.139; *Her. Chr.*, ded. 17.4 *(Albert of Prussia).*

ARCTOS, *the Great and Little Bear, constellations in the northern sky; hence, the lands of the North: Her. Chr.* 16.49; gelida *Nup.*, lim. 1; *Nup.* 258; Lycaonia *Nup.* 20; *Sylv. duae* 1.21; *Her. Chr.* 13.41. *See also* Ursa.

ARELATIUS, a, um, *of Arelate (Arles) in southern Gaul:* ager *Her. Chr.* 22.112; turres *Her. Chr.* 22.33.

[ARIADNE], *the daughter of King Minos of Crete; after she helped Theseus escape the Labyrinth, he abandoned her at Naxos: Her. Chr.* 17.136.

ARION, *a famous cithara player of Methymna in Lesbos (end of the seventh century BCE):* doctus *Her. Chr.* A 3.56.

————, *a musician like Arion:* non unus *Nup.* 298.

ARISTARCHI, *critics as severe as Aristarchus of Alexandria (second century BCE): Nup.*, ded. 15.

ARISTOPHANES, *the Athenian comic poet (late fifth century BCE): Her. Chr.*, ded. 8.4.

CLEANTES, *Cleanthes, a Stoic philosopher of Assos (ca. 331–ca. 232 BCE)*: *Her. Chr.*, ded. 8.4.

CODANUS SINUS, *the Kattegat and the westernmost part of the Baltic Sea*: *Her. Chr.* 17.170.

CODRUS, *a poet mentioned in Vergil's eclogues as bursting with envy; hence, an envious person*: *Her. Chr.* B 1.74; miser *Her. Chr.* A 2.29.

COLLUCIUS, THEODORUS, *pseudonym for Johannes Temonius, an amorous Hessian poet and priest*: *Sylv. duae* 2, tit.; [2, *passim*]; 2.12, 29.

[COLONIA AGRIPPINENSIS], *Cologne*: *Her. Chr.* 17.201, 266.

CONSTANTINUS, *Constantine the Great, Roman Emperor from 306 to 337*: *Her. Chr.* 6, tit.; [6, *passim*].

COPIA, *the goddess of plenty*: *Sylv. duae* 1.70; *Her. Chr.*, ded. 4.3.

CORINTHUS, *the city of Corinth*: alta *Sylv. duae* 1.173; dives *Her. Chr.* 19.84.

COSTIS, *St. Catherine of Alexandria, the daughter of King Costus*: *Her. Chr.* 4, tit.; 4.1, 120, 251; 21.189; indigna *Her. Chr.* 4.16; Niliaca *Her. Chr.* 11.56. *See also* Catharina.

COSTUS, *the father of St. Catherine of Alexandria*: *Her. Chr.* 4.33.

COUS. *See* Chous.

CRACOVIA, *Cracow*: *Nup.*, ded. 17; [*Nup., passim*]; *Her. Chr.*, ded. 10.1; docta *Nup.* 267, 349.

CRAETA *or* CRETA, *the island of Crete*: *Sylv. duae* 1.32; *Her. Chr.* 5.183; 9.87.

CRETICUS, a, um, *of Crete, Cretan*: musta *Sylv. duae* 1.124.

CREUSA, *the wife of Aeneas*: Aeneis *Her. Chr.* 5.93.

CUMAEUS, a, um, *of the Cumaean Sibyl*: carmen *Her. Chr.* 1.197.

CUPIDO, *the son of Venus, god of love*: *Sylv. duae* 2 [*passim*]; 2.167; *Her. Chr.* [17.88–97]; 17.101; [24.36]; B 1.28; aliquis *Sylv. duae* 2.23; atrox *Sylv. duae* 2.137; falsus *Her. Chr.* 4.93; gentilis *Her. Chr.* 17.94. *See also* Amor.

———, *Christ*: [*Her. Chr.* 17.89–98]; ille *Her. Chr.* 17.93.

CYDIPPE, *an Athenian girl wooed by Acontius; in Ovid's* Heroides *she responds to his letter with a letter of her own*: *Her. Chr.* A 4.11.

CYDNUS, *a small river that flows through Tarsus in Cilicia*: *Her. Chr.* 19.90.

CYMODOCAEA, *a Nereid*: glauca *Nup.* 184.

CYNTHIA, *the moon goddess Diana; hence, the moon*: *Her. Chr.* 12.282; nona *Her. Chr.* 5.7; 13.130; territa *Her. Chr.* 16.169. *See also* Diana; Phoebe; Trivia Luna.

CYPRIACUS, a, um, *Cyprian, belonging to Venus*: arma *Her. Chr.* 14.61.

CYPRIUS, a, um, *Cyprian*: aequor *Her. Chr.* 21.17.

CYPRUS, *the island of Cyprus*: aquosa *Her. Chr.* 5.183. *See also* Paphus.

CYRENE, *a nymph, mother of the mythical hero Aristaeus*: nuda *Nup.* 184.

CYRIACUS, *the Jew who told St. Helen where the True Cross was hidden; formerly called Judas, he was renamed Cyriacus [Quiriacus] after his conversion*: renatus *Her. Chr.* 6.123. *See also* Iudas.

———, *a legendary pope from Britain*: *Her. Chr.* 17.206; [17.223–24, 228].

CYRRHA, *Cirrha, the port of Delphi, at the foot of Mount Parnassus; also one of the twin peaks of Mount Parnassus*: Phocaica *Sylv. duae* 2.173.

CYTHERAEA, *Venus*: *Her. Chr.* 9.89.

CYTHERIACUS, a, um, *of Cythera, an island in the Aegean Sea, famous for the worship of Venus*: scortum *Her. Chr.* 6.99; aestus *Sylv. duae* 2.31. *See also* Citheraeus.

DACIA, *Denmark*: *Her. Chr.* 17.174.

DAEDALUS. *See* Dedalus.

DALMATICUS, a, um, *Dalmatian*: aurum *Her. Chr.* 1.105.

DAMASCUS, *city in Syria where St. Paul became a Christian*: clara *Her. Chr.* 19.67.

[DANAE], *the daughter of Acrisius, who confined her in a tower for fear that her son would kill him; she conceived a son after Jupiter visited her in a shower of gold*: *Her. Chr.* 10.121–22.

DANAI, *the Greeks*: *Her. Chr.* 5.93.

DANTISCUM, *Danzig (Gdańsk)*: [*Sylv. duae* 1.129–36]; nobile *Sylv. duae* 1.130.

DARDANIUS, a, um, *Trojan*: hostes *Nup.* 135.

DATIANUS, *a Roman prefect who had St. George arrested and martyred*: *Her. Chr.* 12.250.

DAVID, *the Psalmist and second King of the Jews (ca. 1000–ca. 962 BCE), the son of Jesse and father of Solomon and Absalom*: *Her. Chr.* [1.89; 6.56; 10.148, 161]; 13.159; nobilis ante alios *Her. Chr.* 1.81.

DEDALUS, *a mythical Athenian architect and inventor who escaped from Crete by making wings for himself and his son Icarus*: aliquis *Her. Chr.* 10.131.

DEITAS, *the Deity, God*: *Her. Chr.* 16.78. *See also* Deus.

DELOS, *an island in the Aegean Sea, the birthplace of Apollo*: *Her. Chr.* 9.87.

DELPHICUS, a, um, *Delphic, of Delphi where Apollo had a famous oracle*: pastor *(Apollo) Sylv. duae* 1.112.

DEUS, *the triune God, God the Father, Christ*: *Sylv. duae* 2.190, 195, 202, 211; *Her. Chr.* A 3.73; A 4.15; [1, *passim*]; 1.14, 19, 34, 81, 109, 118, 128–29, 204; [2, *passim*]; 2.30, 51, 80, 87–89, 114, 122; 4.12–13, 16, 75, 91–92, 192–93, 201–02; 5.20, 40, 78, 149, 165, 174; 6.26, 31, 51, 70, 80, 101, 122, 152–53, 175; 7.127; 8.22; [8.23]; 8.80, 85, 89, 92, 97; 9.13; [9.70]; 9.84; [9.122]; 10.67, 107–12]; 11.20; [11.30–31]; 11.35; [11.38]; 11.59, 106, 110; [11.163]; 12.54, 65, 110, 185; [13.70]; 13.72, 80, 139; [13.152–63]; 14.19, 27, 32, 52, 78, 122, 128; [14.129–30]; 15.86, 123, 137, 150; 16.1, 48, 115, 285, 288; 17.91, 99, 102–03; [17.241–53]; 18.66, 89, 99; [18.115–16]; 19.56; [19.137–39; 20.17–18]; 20.57; [20.87]; 20.100; [20.111–13]; 20.139; [21.229–32]; 22.66, 97, 111, 120, 162; aeternus *Her. Chr.* 9.121; 19.66; bonus *Nup.*, ded. 2; *Her. Chr.*, ded. 15.1; captus *Her. Chr.* 16.166; clausus *Her. Chr.* 21.230; exanguis *Her. Chr.* 21.188; flagellatus *Her. Chr.* 5.180; hic *Her. Chr.* 10.40; ille *Her. Chr.* 4.29; immensus *Her. Chr.* 1.138; 13.74; 21.60; immortalis *Her. Chr.* 4.66; ipse *Her. Chr.* 4.91; 6.84; 8.72; 18.141, 158, 179; mitis *Her. Chr.* 9.146; moriens *Her. Chr.* 15.158; mortalis *Her. Chr.* 3.20; motus *Her. Chr.* 11.176; nascens *Her. Chr.* 21.202; natus *Her. Chr.* 1.114; nescio quis *Her. Chr.* 4.116; noster *Her. Chr.* 9.142; 10.159; novus *Her. Chr.* 22.158; offensus *Her. Chr.* 11.16, 162; placatus *Her. Chr.* 15.218; 20.144; potens Her. Chr. 23.91, 97; praesens *Sylv. duae* 2.198; *Her. Chr.* 7.98; 17.66; 19.136; quis *Her. Chr.* 10.39; solus *Her. Chr.* 9.68, 80; 10.170; 17.102; summus *Her. Chr.* 4.80; 13.111; surgens *Her. Chr.* 19.108; suus *Her. Chr.* 21.224; tantus *Her. Chr.* 10.136; triformis *Her. Chr.* 17.11; tuus *Her. Chr.* 10.38; unus *Her. Chr.* 4.24, 200; 8.76; 10.56, 126; verus *Her. Chr.* 4.154; 6.172; 10.10; 12.12, 44; 17.28; 21.168; vester *Her. Chr.* 10.54. *See also* Christus; Deitas; Spiritus; Tonans; Trinitas.

[DIABOLUS], *the devil*: *Her. Chr.* 1.67–68, 92, 121, 180–81; 3.115, 117, 136; 6.125–36, 154; 8.12, 133; 9.145; 11.63, 72, 112; 12.107–08; 14.104, 111–12; 15.11; 16.44, 202; 17.19, 40; 22.71.

DIANA, *the moon goddess, identified with Artemis*: [*Her. Chr.* 21.205]; ipsa *Sylv. duae* 1.96. *See also* Cynthia; Phoebe; Trivia Luna.

DIDO, *mythical foundress and Queen of Carthage, lover of Aeneas, to whom she a writes a letter in Ovid's Heroides*: [*Her. Chr.* 17.138]; moritura *Her. Chr.* A 4.14.

[DIOCLETIANUS or MAXIMINIANUS], *Roman co-emperors (284–305 and 286–305)*: *Her. Chr.* 12.9, 23, 33, 40, 102, 237; 18.11, 35, 122, 137, 158.

DOBENECK. *See* Iobus de Dobeneck.

[DOMITIANUS], *a Roman Emperor (81–96)*: *Her. Chr.* 16.9.

DOROTHEA, *St. Dorothy of Caesarea in Cappadocia*: *Her. Chr.* 23, tit.; [23, *passim*]; 23.22, 112.

DRYIDAE, *the Druids, Celtic priests in Gaul*: *Her. Chr.* 22.131.

[DULCITIUS], *a Roman prefect who persecuted Christians*: *Her. Chr.* 18.151–60.

ECHO, *the echo (personified)*: *Her. Chr.* 4.166; [4.167–68].

EDERA. *See* Aedera.

EDESSA, *a city in Syria*: magna *Her. Chr.* 7.90.

ELISABETH, *the wife of Zechariah, mother of John the Baptist*: *Her. Chr.* 20, tit.; [20, *passim*].

———, *Elizabeth's letter to Zechariah (Her. Chr. 20)*: *Her. Chr.*, ded. 14.3.

———, *St. Elizabeth of Hungary (1207–31), married to Ludwig IV of Thuringia in 1221*: *Her. Chr.* 5, tit.; [5, *passim*]; mea dulcis *Her. Chr.* 5.31.

ELISAEUS, a, um, *of Carthage*: humus *Her. Chr.* 9.34. *See also* Punicus.

ELISIUM, *Elysium, the abode of the blessed after death*: *Her. Chr.* 17.51–52.

EMMANUEL, *"God with us," a name given to Christ*: *Her. Chr.* 1, tit.; 2, tit. *See also* Christus.

———, *the letter "Emmanuel to Mary" (Her. Chr. 1)*: *Her. Chr.*, ded. 13.1.

ENGADDI, *Engedi, an oasis on the west shore of the Dead Sea*: *Her. Chr.* 3.144.

[ENGLENDRUS, IOANNES], *Johann Englender (d. 1517), Chancellor of Hesse, to whom Eobanus dedicated his* Bucolicon *in 1509*: *Sylv. duae* 1.187.

EOBANUS HESSUS. *See* Hessus, Helius Eobanus.

EOUS, *the morning star, the East*: *Her. Chr.* 15.84; 16.191; surgens *Her. Chr.* 13.93. *See also* Lucifer; Phosphorus.

EOUS, a, um, *eastern*: hortus *(the earthly Paradise) Her. Chr.* 20.27; sylvae *Her. Chr.* 6.11, 197.

EPHESUS, *a city on the west coast of Asia Minor with a famous temple of Diana*: *Her. Chr.* [16.304]; 19.79; 21.205.

EPIPHANIUS, *Bishop of Salamis and Metropolitan of Cyprus from 367 to 403*: *Her. Chr.* 21.125.

ERASMUS, *Erazm Ciołek (ca. 1474–1522), Bishop of Płock from 1503 to 1522*: *Nup.* 269.

ERPHURDIA, *Erfurt*: magna *Her. Chr.* 24.107.

ETRUSCUS. *See* Aethruscus.

EUCLIO, *an old miser in Plautus' comedy* Aulularia: Plautinus *Her. Chr.*, ded. 5.2.

EUPHEMIUS, *the father of St. Alexius*: *Her. Chr.* 7.83.

EURIPIDES, *the Athenian tragic poet (480–ca. 406 BCE)*: *Her. Chr.*, ded. 6.2.

EURUS, *the east wind*: orientalis *Sylv. duae* 1.39.

EUSEBIUS, *Bishop of Caesarea in Palestine from ca. 314 to ca. 340 and church historian*: *Her. Chr.*, ded. 14.2.

EUSTOCHIUM, *one of St. Paula's daughters*: *Her. Chr.* [21.27–36]; 21.28; [21.135–42]; 21.146, 161; [21.177–82, 237]; pleno iam nubilis aevo *Her. Chr.* 21.135.

EVA, *the first woman*: *Her. Chr.* 1.75; 23.57.

FABIUS, *Q. Fabius Maximus "Cunctator," the famous Roman general and dictator in the Second Punic War*: *Nup.* 44.

FABRICIUS, *governor of Caesarea in Cappadocia*: *Her. Chr.* [23.18]; 23.28, 114.

FALERNA. *See* Phalerna.

FAMA, *Rumor (personified)*: garrula *Her. Chr.* 3.6.

FATUM, *Fate, destiny, death*: *Her. Chr.* 5.155; 8.21; 11.55; 14.49; 15.213; 16.101; 17.197, 273; 20.109; certum *Her. Chr.* 20.57, 139; grave *Her. Chr.* 16.145; caetera *Her. Chr.* 21.177; crudelia *Her. Chr.* 12.145; cruenta *Her. Chr.* A 3.58; improba *Her. Chr.* 17.39; meliora *Her. Chr.* 9.166; nostra *Her. Chr.* 20.95; sperata *Her. Chr.* 9.153; 18.83; superba *Her. Chr.* 20.108; talia *Her. Chr.* 12.249; tristia *Her. Chr.* 12.144; 16.117; 18.156; 20.36; turbato currentia ordine *Her. Chr.* 7.61. *See also* Fors; Parcae.

FAUSTA, *the mother of St. Anastasia*: *Her. Chr.* [18.59]; 18.63; [18.64–72, 166].

FEBRUA MARIAE, *Candlemas Day, the feast of the Purification of the Virgin Mary (2 February)*: *Nup.* 170.

FEBRUUS, a, um, *of February*: luna *Her. Chr.* 23.63.

FLAVIA, *a poetical name for Eobanus Hessus' sweetheart in Erfurt*: notissima Hessiaco versu *Sylv. duae* 2.33; nulla *Nup.* 12.

FLORALIS, e, *of Flora, the goddess of flowers*: opes *Her. Chr.* 4.64.

FOENIX. *See* Phoenix.

FORS, *Chance (personified)*: *Her. Chr.* 8.119. *See also* Fatum.

FORTUNA, *the blind goddess Fortune, Lady Luck, fortune*: *Sylv. duae* 1.18, 29, 166, [177–78]; *Her. Chr.* 5.152; [5.153–54]; 14.144; 17.29; 24.97, 153; alta *Her. Chr.* 17.27; mea *Her. Chr.* 20.91–92; saeva *Her. Chr.* 19.101; 22.27. *See also* Rhamnusia.

FORUM, *the Forum Romanum, the main square and center of public life in ancient Rome*: latum *Her. Chr.* 21.94; medium *Her. Chr.* 18.22; totum *Her. Chr.* 21.102.

[FRANCFORDIA], *Frankfurt an der Oder*: *Sylv. duae*, ded. 3; *Her. Chr.*, ded. 8.4; *Her. Chr.* 24.129–30.

FRANCOBERGA, *Frankenberg in Hesse, a town near which Eobanus Hessus was born*: [*Her. Chr.* 24.55–62]; parva *Her. Chr.* 24.57.

FRIDERICUS SECUNDUS, *Frederick II (1194–1250), Holy Roman Emperor from 1220*: *Sylv. duae* 1.49; [1.55].

FURIAE, *the Furies, who harry the guilty*: nocturna moventes insomnia *Her. Chr.* B 1.37.

GABRIEL, *the archangel who announced the conception of Jesus to the Virgin Mary*: *Her. Chr.* [1.3–8]; 1.161; [1.163; 2.31–32, 54–65; 16.82].

GALATAE, *the Galatians in Asia Minor*: feroces *Her. Chr.* 19.83.

GALILAEA *or* GALILEA, *Galilee in the north of Palestine*: *Her. Chr.* 13.126; tota *Her. Chr.* 13.27.

GALILAEUS, a, um, *of Galilee*: Petrus *Her. Chr.* 19.5; rex *(Herodes) Her. Chr.* 16.195; rura *Her. Chr.* 3.83, 129; 16.121.

GALLIA, *Gaul*: *Her. Chr.* 17.199; [bracata] *(transalpine Gaul, where the men wore breeches rather than togas) Her. Chr.* 22.34; tota *Her. Chr.* 22.129.

GALLUS, a *Gaul*: *Her. Chr.* 7.102; feri *Her. Chr.* 22.43; fortes *Her. Chr.* 7.101.

———, *a Frenchman*: fortis *Nup.* 37.

GAMMALIEL, *the Pharisee Gamaliel, a teacher of St. Paul*: tuus *Her. Chr.* 19.98.

GARAMAS, *a member of a tribe in the eastern Sahara, an African*: *Sylv. duae* 1.107.

GARGARICUS, a, um, *produced by the fertile fields of Gargara in the Ida range of mountains near Troy*: messis *Sylv. duae* 2.89.

[GEORGENTHAL], *a Cistercian abbey south of Gotha*: *Sylv. duae* 1.190.

GEORGIUS, *St. George, the dragon-slayer, said to have been martyred at Lydda in Palestine in the fourth century*: *Her. Chr.* 12, tit.; [12, *passim*; 22.82].

———, *a short epic poem about him by Baptista Mantuanus (1507)*: *Her. Chr.*, ded. 15.7.

GERASINA, *a legendary Queen of Sicily, aunt of St. Ursula*: *Her. Chr.* 17.225.

GERMANI, *the Germans*: *Sylv. duae* 1.24.

GERMANIA, *ancient Germany*: [*Her. Chr.* 7.98; 17.200, 260]; pugnax *Her. Chr.* 17.217.

———, *modern Germany*: [*Sylv. duae* 1.128, 182]; *Her. Chr.* [24.52]; 24.141; Martia *Her. Chr.* 24.51; nostra *Nup.* 365; *Her. Chr.* 24.87.

GERMANUS, a, um, *German*: Caesar *Her. Chr.* A 1.3; fama *Her. Chr.* A 4.17. *See also* Teutonicus; Teutonis; Teutonus.

GETA, *a Thracian*: *Sylv. duae* 1.108.

GNISNA, *the archdiocesan capital Gnesen in Poland*: *Nup.* 233.

GOLGATHA, *Calvary, where Jesus was crucified*: *Her. Chr.* [3.29; 6.37]; 6.38; [6.39–40; 16.217].

[GOLIATH], *the Philistine giant slain by David*: *Her. Chr.* 13.159.

GORGO, *Medusa, a snake-haired Gorgon killed by Perseus; anyone looking at her frightful head was turned to stone*: *Her. Chr.* 18.106.

GOTTHUS, *a Goth*: immanis *Her. Chr.* 17.169.

GRAECI, *the Greeks*: *Her. Chr.*, ded. 14.2.

GRAECUS, a, um, *Greek*: nomen *Her. Chr.* 17.218.

GRAIUS, a, um, *Greek*: scriptores *Her. Chr.*, ded. 3.4.

GRATIA, *one of the three Graces*: *Nup.* 67; omnis *Nup.* 303; ridens *Nup.* 87.

GREGORIUS, *Gregory the Great, pope from 590 to 604*: *Her. Chr.*, ded. 14.2.

———, *Gregory IX, pope from 1227 to 1241*: [*Sylv. duae* 1.55–56].

HAEBRAEUS. *See* Hebraeus.

HALCIONE. *See* Alcione.

HANNIBAL, *brilliant Carthaginian general (247–183/82 BCE) in the Second Punic War*: *Nup.* 42; [*Her. Chr.* 21.59].

HEBRAEUS *or* HAEBRAEUS, a, um, *Hebrew*: Christus *Her. Chr.* 6.213; dux *(Solomon) Her. Chr.* 6.176; manus *Her. Chr.* 22.5; orbis *Her. Chr.* 21.86; origo *Her. Chr.* 16.107; sanguis *Her. Chr.* 1.123; tyrannus *(Herod) Her. Chr.* 20.5; urbes *Her. Chr.* 7.93; vates *Her. Chr.* 4.25; 9.78; 10.91; 21.1. *See also* Iudaeus.

HEBRUS, *a river in Thrace that flows into the Aegean Sea, now called Maritsa*: *Nup.* 167.

HECALE, *Alcyone's nurse*: *Her. Chr.* 12.19.

HECTOR, *Trojan hero in Homer's* Iliad: *Nup.* 136.

HELENA, *Helen of Troy:* [*Nup.* 193–94]. *See also* Lacaena.

————, *the mother of Constantine the Great (ca. 257–ca. 337): Her. Chr.* 6, tit.; [6, *passim*]; 6.62.

HELIUS EOBANUS HESSUS. *See* Hessus, Helius Eobanus.

HELLESPONTUS, *the Hellespont, the Dardanelles: Her. Chr.* 7.95.

HENRICUS, *Henry II, Holy Roman Emperor from 1002 to 1024, saint, the husband of St. Cunegund: Her. Chr.* 8, tit.; [8, *passim*]; 8.71.

HERCINIA SYLVA *or* HERCINIUM NEMUS, *the Hercynian Forest in ancient Germany, stretching from the Black Forest to the Carpathians: Nup.* 161; *Sylv. duae* 1.104.

HERCULES, *mythical Greek hero, famous for his Twelve Labors; the abductor of Iole: Sylv. duae* 2.100; [2.101–06; *Her. Chr.* 9.115; 17.139–40; 20.45–46]. *See also* Alcides.

HERCULEUS, a, um, *of Hercules, Herculean:* manus *Her. Chr.* 9.66.

[HEREBORDUS MARGARITUS], *Herbord von der Marthen (ca. 1480–1529): Sylv. duae* 1.189–90.

HERMIONES, *women like Hermione, the daughter of Menelaus and Helen, wife of Neoptolemus and later of Orestes; she is one of the women who write letters in Ovid's* Heroides: *Her. Chr.* 17.41.

HERMON, *the highest mountain in Palestine, north of Caesarea Philippi: Her. Chr.* 16.94.

HERO, *a priestess of Aphrodite at Sestos, the mistress of Leander: Her. Chr.* 17.144.

HERODES, *Herod, King of Judea from 40 to 4* BCE: *Her. Chr.* [1.121–23]; 16.106; [16.195; 20.5, 13, 33, 79–80, 119–26, 143, 157].

HERODOTUS, *the earliest Greek historian (fifth century* BCE): *Her. Chr.*, ded. 14.2.

HESPERIDES, *daughters of Night who, on an island in the far West, watched over a garden with golden apples: Her. Chr.* 6.201; 23.7, 73.

HESPERIUS, a, um, *western:* aqua *Her. Chr.* 16.240.

HESSIA, *Hesse, Eobanus Hessus' homeland:* [*Sylv. duae* 1.114; 2.1; *Her. Chr.* A 1.8; A 3.62; 5, *passim*]; ipsa *Her. Chr.* 5.179; pugnax *Her. Chr.* 24.54; tota *Her. Chr.* 5.117.

HESSIACUS, a, um, *of Hesse, Hessian:* gens *Her. Chr.* A 1.7; solum *Her. Chr.* A 3.62; vir *(Ludwig IV of Thuringia) Her. Chr.* 5.2.

————, *of Eobanus Hessus:* versus *Sylv. duae* 2.33.

HESSUS, *a Hessian:* exiguus *(Eobanus Hessus) Nup.* 365.

HESSUS, HELIUS EOBANUS: *Sylv. duae,* lim. 5; *Sylv. duae* 1.1; [1, *passim*]; *Her. Chr.* [A 1, *passim*]; A 1.4, 7–8, 10, 16; [A 2, *passim*]; A 2.8; [A 3, *passim*]; A 3.10, 76; [A 4, *passim*]; A 4.18; 24, tit.; [24, *passim*]; 24.1, 104; B 1.62; enthea praestans arte *Her. Chr.* A 1.12; suus *Her. Chr.* A 3, tit.; A 4, tit.; tuus ille *Sylv. duae* 1.25.

HIBERNIA. *See* Hybernia.

HIBLA. *See* Hybla.

[HIEREMIAS], *the Hebrew prophet Jeremiah: Her. Chr.* 20.86–87.

HIERICHUS, *the city of Jericho in Palestine, on the west bank of the Jordan River:* alta *Her. Chr.* 3.140; hyperboreo usta gelu *Her. Chr.* 23.72.

HIERONIMUS *or* HIERONYMUS, *St. Jerome (ca. 347–419/20): Her. Chr.*, ded. 14.2; *Her. Chr.* 21, tit.; [21, *passim*]; 21.3, 65.

[HIEROSOLYMA]. *See* Solima.

[HIPPOCRENE], *a spring on Mount Helicon, sacred to the Muses: Her. Chr.* 24.104.

[HIPPOLYTUS], *the son of Theseus and Hippolyte, who preferred hunting to the advances of his stepmother Phaedra: Sylv. duae* 1.97.

HISPANUS, a, um, *Spanish:* sol *Her. Chr.* 7.100.

HOMERUS, *Homer (eighth century* BCE): Rhomanus *(Vergil) Her. Chr.*, ded. 3.2.

HORATIUS, *the Roman poet (65–8* BCE): *Her. Chr.*, ded. 3.1.

HOREB. *See* Oreb.

[HORLAEUS, IACOBUS], *Jakob Horle (Hurle) of Frankenberg (d. 1519), who taught Eobanus Hessus the art of versification: Her. Chr.* 24.97–99.

[HUNGARIA], *Hungary: Nup.* 160, 225.

HUNNUS, *a Hun:* atrox *Her. Chr.* 17.266.

HUTTENUS, ULRICHUS, *the German knight and humanist Ulrich von Hutten (1488–1523)*: Her. Chr. 24.143, 145.

HYBERNIA, *Ireland*: aeternis foeta pruinis Her. Chr. 17.165.

HYBLA *or* HIBLA, *a mountain in Sicily, famous for its honey*: florida Her. Chr. 23.68; redolens Nup. 49; Sicelis Sylv. duae 1.82; Sicula Her. Chr. 17.125.

HYBLEUS, a, um, *of Hybla*: favus Her. Chr. A 3.50.

[HYDRA], *the many-headed Lernean serpent. When one of its heads was cut off, two others grew in its place. But Hercules burned out their roots with firebrands and so killed the monster*: Sylv. duae 2.103; Her. Chr. 22.80.

HYMEN, *a nuptial song*: Nup. 114, 116, 256.

HYMENAEA, *wedding hymns*: Nup. 113–14, 243, 256; feralia Her. Chr. 18.95.

HYMENAEUS, *the god of marriage*: Nup. 366.

————, *a wedding hymn*: exultans Nup. 288.

HYPERBOREUS, a, um, *Hyperborean, arctic*: gelu Her. Chr. 23.72.

HYPSYPHYLES, *women like Hypsipyle, the Queen of Lemnos. She warmly welcomed the Argonauts on their return voyage and had twin sons by their leader Jason*: Her. Chr. 17.41.

HYRCANUS, a, um, *of Hyrcania, a country on the Caspian Sea*: saltus Sylv. duae 1.105.

[IACOBUS], *the Hebrew patriarch Jacob*: Her. Chr. 7.85.

————, *St. James the Greater, the brother of St. John the Evangelist. His body is said to have been translated to Compostela, Spain*: Her. Chr. 7.99.

IANUS, *the god of gates and doorways, to whom the month of January was sacred*: Her. Chr. 24.68.

IASON, *the leader of the Argonauts who set off in quest of the Golden Fleece*: malus Her. Chr. 6.203.

ICONIS, *an inhabitant of Iconium in Galatia*: Her. Chr. 19.4.

IDA, *mountain range in Phrygia, near Troy*: Phrygia Nup. 89, 115.

IDALIUM, *Idalium in Cyprus, sacred to Venus*: Sylv. duae 2.133.

IDALIUS, a, um, *of Idalium in Cyprus, associated with Venus; Cyprian*: lar Her. Chr. 23.6; nemus Her. Chr. 17, 90; luci Sylv. duae 1.94.

IDUMAEUS, a, um, *of Idumea (Edom), south of Judea, famed for its palm groves*: nemus Her. Chr. 3.142.

IESSAEUS, a, um, *begotten by Jesse*: senex *(King David)* Her. Chr. 10.148.

IESUS, *Jesus Christ*: Her. Chr. 3, tit.; [3, *passim*]; 3.81, 121, 147; 4.19; [20.147]; 21.63; 22.21; 23.13; desponsus Her. Chr. 4.167; florens Her. Chr. 19.97; infans Her. Chr. 1.115; magnus Her. Chr. 6.103; 7.151; ortus de Nazareth Her. Chr. 6.115; rite coronatus Her. Chr. 16.197; tuus Her. Chr. 19.85; vester Her. Chr. 4.85. *See also* Christus.

ILIACUS, a, um, *Trojan, founded by descendants of the Trojan Aeneas*: Rhoma Her. Chr. 9.5.

ILIAS, *the* Iliad *of Homer*: Her. Chr., ded. 3.4.

INDIA, *the subcontinent, homeland of Bacchus*: Her. Chr. 9.88.

INDUS, *an Indian*: decolor Sylv. duae 1.107; divites Her. Chr. 16.239; extremi Her. Chr. 13.39; imbelles Her. Chr. 12.233.

———— *the Indus River*: Nup. 151.

IOACHIMUS, *the husband of St. Anna, father of the Virgin Mary*: Her. Chr. 2.101; 13, tit.; [13, *passim*]; 13.1.

IOANNES, *John the Baptist*: [Her. Chr. 10.43; 20, *passim*].

————, *St. John the Evangelist and Apostle*: Her. Chr. 3.39; 16, tit.; [16, *passim*].

————, *Jan Laski (1455/56–1531), Archbishop of Gnesen since 1510*: Nup. [231–60], 233, [308–23].

IOBUS DE DOBENECK, *Job von Dobeneck, Bishop of Pomesania from 1501 to 1521*: Nup., ded. 3; [ded. 4–5, 13]; Nup. 227, [228–29]; Sylv. duae 1.155; Her. Chr., ded., tit.; ded. 1.1; [ded., *passim*]; ded. 4.2, 17.1, 19.1.

IOLE, *a daughter of King Eurytus of Oechalia, taken prisoner by Hercules*: Oechalia Her. Chr. 9.115.

IONIUS, a, um, *Ionian*: profundum Her. Chr. 15.179; aquae Her. Chr. A 3.56.

IOPAS, *a musician like Iopas, who played the cithara at Queen Dido's court*: non unus cythara spectandus Nup. 297.

IOPPAEUS, a, um, *of Joppa (Jaffa) on the Mediterranean Sea*: humus *Her. Chr.* 20.8.

IORDANES, *the Jordan River, formed by the confluence of the Jor and Dan*: *Her. Chr.* 14.86; [14.155–56]; fluctivagus *Her. Chr.* 14.1, 17; rapidus *Her. Chr.* 14.145.

IOSEPH *or* IOSEPHUS, *son of Jacob and Rachel, ruler of Egypt*: *Her. Chr.* [7.85]; 20.59; orbus *Her. Chr.* 13.87; Pharius *Her. Chr.* 6.79.

————, *husband of the Virgin Mary*: *Her. Chr.* 1.125; [16.119–20]; castus *Her. Chr.* 16.116.

IOVIANI, *Jovians, worshipers of Jupiter*: *Her. Chr.*, ded. 9.2.

IOVIS, *an Italian sky god identified with Zeus, chief god of the Romans*: *Nup.* 203; *Her. Chr.*, ded. 9.3; *Her. Chr.* 6.141; 9.64, 87; 10.106; 19.12; 20.45; falsus *Her. Chr.* 2.49; 12.228; 18.94; Latius *Her. Chr.* 21.204; mentitus *Her. Chr.* 6.168; non ullus *Her. Chr.* 18.98; vestras *Her. Chr.* 23.96; falsi *Her. Chr.* 4.73, 208. *See also* Iuppiter.

————, *god of the underworld; the devil*: infernus *Her. Chr.* 6.154; Stygius *Her. Chr.* 1.180. *See also* Diabolus.

[IRENE], *virgin and martyr (d. 304), the sister of Agape and Chionia*: *Her. Chr.* 18.145–46.

ISAAC, *the son of Abraham and Sarah*: *Her. Chr.* 13.86; 20.59.

[ISACHAR *or* RUBEN], *the high priest who told St. Joachim to leave the temple because he was childless*: *Her. Chr.* 13.17, 127.

[ISAIAH], *the Hebrew prophet*: *Her. Chr.* 1.35; 2.36, 38.

ISMARIUS, a, um, *Thracian*: orae *Her. Chr.* A 3.57.

ISRAEL, *the Israelites*: *Her. Chr.* 6.79; 13.158.

ISRAELITICUS, a, um, *begotten by the patriarch Jacob (Israel)*: fratres *Her. Chr.* 13.87.

ISTULA. *See* Vistula.

ITALUS, a, um, *Italian*: Lucania *Her. Chr.* 23.65; terra *Her. Chr.* 21.10.

IUDAEA, *Judea*: *Her. Chr.* 1.101; 3.32; [6.48]; potens *Her. Chr.* 13.126; sancta *Her. Chr.* 5.129. *See also* Palestina.

IUDAEI, *the Jews*: *Her. Chr.* [3.57–58; 6.15]; 6.115; [16.199–202].

IUDAEUS, a, um, *Jewish, of the Jews*: advena *Her. Chr.* 22.43; manus *Her. Chr.* 22.2; potentia *Sylv. duae* 1.175; pubes *Her. Chr.* 16.199; rex *(Jesus) Her. Chr.* 1.123; sceptrum *Her. Chr.* 5.19; vetustas *Sylv. duae* 2.213; vox *Her. Chr.* 6.38. *See also* Apelleus; Hebraeus.

IUDAS, *Judas Iscariot, the disciple who betrayed Jesus*: [*Her. Chr.* 6.129–30].

————, *a Jew who told St. Helen where the True Cross was hidden; called Cyriacus [Quiriacus] after his conversion*: *Her. Chr.* 6.91; [6.92–98; 6.121–36]; nequissimus *Her. Chr.* 6.127.

IULIUS, *Julius II, pope from 1503 to 1513*: [*Nup.* 219–22]; claviger *Sylv. duae* 2.3.

IUNO, *the sister and wife of Jupiter*: *Nup.* 91; improba *Her. Chr.* 9.89.

IUPPITER, *an Italian sky god identified with Zeus*: [*Nup.* 204; *Her. Chr.* 1.176; 4.114, 138]; bonus *Her. Chr.* A 3.35; nullus *Her. Chr.* 18.68; omnis *Her. Chr.* 1.202. *See also* Iovis.

IUPPITER AMMON, *Egyptian god represented as having ram's horns, identified with Jupiter*: *Her. Chr.* 12.49.

[KONARSKI, JOHANNES], *Bishop of Cracow from 1503 to 1523 (d. 1525)*: *Nup.* 267–68.

KUNEGUNDIS, *St. Cunegund (d. 1033 or 1039?), wife of Emperor Henry II*: *Her. Chr.* 8, tit.; [8, *passim*]; 8.31.

LACAENA, *a Spartan woman*: abducta *(Helen of Troy) Nup.* 130. *See also* Helena.

LACEDAEMONIUS, a, um, *Spartan*: ensis *Her. Chr.* 22.92.

LAETHAEUS, a, um, *of Lethe, a river in the underworld; drinking its water induced oblivion*: aquae *Her. Chr.* 18.78; undae *Her. Chr.* 15.187.

LAETICIAE, *Joys (personified)*: *Nup.* 303.

LANUS, *the Lahn River that flows through Marburg in Hesse*: piscosus *Her. Chr.* 5.79.

LAODAMIA, *the wife of Protesilaus*: *Her. Chr.* 22.16.

LAR, *a household god; hence, a house, home, hometown*: Idalius *Her. Chr.* 23.6; uterque *Her. Chr.* 21.74; mei *Her. Chr.* 22.38; patrii *Her. Chr.* 20.158; Stygii *Her. Chr.* 9.112.

[ŁASKI, JAN]. *See* Ioannes.

LATIALIS, e, *Latin*: iura *Her. Chr.* A 1.3.

LYDIA, *a country in western Asia Minor*: Moeonis *Her. Chr.* 23.69.

LYDIUS, a, um, *of Lydia in Asia Minor*: regna *Sylv. duae* 1.32.

LYMPURGK. *See* Schenck, Carolus, de Lympurgk baro.

LYPSIS, *Leipzig*: *Sylv. duae*, ded. 3, 10; *Her. Chr.*, ded. 19.5; Musis celebrata Latinis *Her. Chr.* 24.132.

LYRA, *a constellation that rises in the night from January 5 to 6*: *Her. Chr.* 24.65.

LYTHUANA [REGNA], *Lithuania*: *Sylv. duae* 1.40. *See also* Lithuania.

[MACAREUS], *a son of Aeolus, who committed incest with his sister Canace*: *Her. Chr.* 17.137.

MACARIUS MUTIUS. *See* Mutius, Macarius.

MACEDAE, *the Macedonians*: *Her. Chr.* 19.80.

MAEANDER, *a river of Phrygia in Asia Minor*: Phrygius *Her. Chr.* 23.39.

MAECENAS. *See* Moecenas.

MAENALOS, *a mountain in Arcadia, where Diana loved to hunt*: *Sylv. duae* 1.96.

MAEONIS. *See* Moeonis.

MAEOTIS, *the Sea of Azov*: *Nup.* 167.

MAGDALA, *a town in Galilee*: *Her. Chr.* 3.103.

MAGDALENA. *See* Maria Magdalena.

MAGDALIS, *Mary Magdalene*: *Her. Chr.* 15.146, 156. *See also* Maria Magdalena.

MAGDALIS, idos, *of Magdala in Galilee*: Martha *Her. Chr.* 22.1.

MAGI, *the three wise men from the East*: [*Her. Chr.* 21.211–12; 24.68]; adorantes *Her. Chr.* 1.120; tres *Her. Chr.* 16.84.

MAGNUS MAGISTER. *See* Archimagister.

MAHOMETIGENA, ae, *Mohammedan*: Turcae *Sylv. duae* 1.51.

MANTUANUS, BAPTISTA, *the Italian humanist Giovanni Battista Spagnolo of Mantua (1447–1516)*: *Her. Chr.*, ded. 15.5; [ded. 15.6–7].

[MARBURG], *the residence of the landgraves of Hesse*: *Her. Chr.* 5.79–80.

MARCELLA, *the servant of Martha of Bethany*: *Her. Chr.* 22.29.

MARCHIATICUS, a, um, *in the Mark Brandenburg*: Odera *Her. Chr.*, ded. 8.4.

[MARE GERMANICUM], *the Baltic Sea*: *Sylv. duae* 1.23.

MAREOTIS, *a lake near Alexandria*: piger *Her. Chr.* 4.56.

MARGARIS, *St. Margaret of Antioch, who was beheaded in the persecution of Diocletian*: *Her. Chr.* 11.55.

MARIA, *the Virgin Mary*: *Nup.* 170; [*Sylv. duae* 1.162]; *Her. Chr.*, ded. 13.1; *Her. Chr.* 1, tit.; [1, *passim*]; 1.183; 2, tit.; [2, *passim*]; 2.65; [3.35–40, 170, 173; 4.81–82, 107–23; 5.43; 6.26, 187; 7.152]; 8.84; [8.85–86, 93; 9.84; 13.77–81]; 13.79; [13.97, 131–40; 14.78–83]; 16.tit.; [16, *passim*; 17.91–92; 20.62–70, 147–54; 22.17–18; 24.55].

———, *Mary's letter to the Evangelist John (Her. Chr. 16)*: *Her. Chr.*, ded. 13.1.

———, *the Marys who stood by the Cross and wanted to anoint Christ's body on Easter morning*: *Her. Chr.* [3.71–84, 89–90]; 16.207; lugentes *Her. Chr.* 3.81.

———, *the three Marys, daughters of St. Anna by three different husbands*: tres *Her. Chr.* [13.131–32]; 13.133.

MARIA AEGYPTIA *or* AEGIPTIACA, *St. Mary of Egypt*: *Her. Chr.* 14, tit.; [14, *passim*]; 15.145.

———, *her letter to Zosimas (Her. Chr. 14)*: *Her. Chr.*, ded. 13.1.

MARIA MAGDALENA, *Mary Magdalene, identified with Mary of Bethany (the sister of Martha and Lazarus) and the sinning woman of Luke 7.36–50*: *Her. Chr.* 3, tit.; [3, *passim*; 22.25–26]; 22.133. *See also* Magdalis.

———, *her letter to Jesus Christ (Her. Chr. 3)*: *Her. Chr.*, ded. 13.1.

MARIEBURGUM, *Marienburg in East Prussia, the former residence of the Grand Master of the Teutonic Order*: *Sylv. duae* 1.147.

MARO, *the Roman poet P. Vergilius Maro (70–19 BCE)*: [*Her. Chr.*, ded. 3.2]; aliquis *Nup.* 214. *See also* Tytirus.

MARS, *god of war; hence also, war, battle*: *Sylv. duae* 2.163; diversus *Nup.* 26; durus *Her. Chr.* 24.122; falsus *Her. Chr.* 5.80.

MARSIAS, *the satyr Marsyas, who challenged Apollo to a flute-playing contest. The god defeated him and flayed him alive as punishment for his presumption*: Her. Chr., ded. 10.2; alter Her. Chr., ded. 10.2.

MARTHA, *the sister of Lazarus and Mary of Bethany (identified with Mary Magdalene)*: Her. Chr. 3.99, 101; 22, tit.; [22, *passim*]; Magdalis Her. Chr. 22.1.

MARTIGENA, ae, *descended from Mars (through his sons Romulus and Remus); hence, Roman*: manus Her. Chr. 9.6.

MARTIUS, a, um, *of Mars, martial, warlike*: Germania Her. Chr. 24.51; miles Her. Chr. 2.19; Rhoma *Sylv. duae* 1.171; Her. Chr. 17.68; terra *Nup.* 30; arma Her. Chr. 1.190; 12.165. *See also* Mavortius.

MARULLUS, *the Neo-Latin poet Michele Marullo (ca. 1453–1500)*: Her. Chr., [ded. 11.1–2]; ded. 11.3.

MASSILIENSIS, e, *of Massilia (Marseilles)*: tellus Her. Chr. 22.124.

MATHIAS, *Matthias Drzewicki (1467–1535), Chancellor of Poland, Bishop of Przemyśl from 1504 to 1513*: Nup. 265.

MAVORTIUS, a, um, *of Mars*: Rhoma Her. Chr. 6.145; arva Her. Chr. 12.235. *See also* Martigena; Martius.

MAXENTIUS, *Roman Emperor from 306 to 312*: Her. Chr. [4.209–36]; 6.6; [6.163]; impius Her. Chr. 4.209, 253.

MAXIMIANAEUS, a, um, *begotten by Emperor Maximian*: tyrannus (Maxentius) Her. Chr. 6.163.

[MAXIMIANUS], *Roman Emperor from 286 to 305*: Her. Chr. 6.166. *See also* Diocletianus.

[MAXIMILIAN I]. *See* Caesar; Maximus Aemilianus.

MAXIMINUS, *one of the seventy-two disciples of Jesus; after the Ascension he was set adrift on the Mediterranean with Martha, Mary Magdalene, Lazarus, and others, but eventually landed in Provence*: Her. Chr. 22, tit.; [22, *passim*].

MAXIMUS AEMILIANUS, *Maximilian I, King of the Romans from 1493 and Holy Roman Emperor from 1508 to 1519*: Nup. 35; Her. Chr. 24.121.

MAZOVITA, *an inhabitant of Mazovia, a territory in east-central Poland*: Sylv. duae 1.42.

[MEDEA]. *See* Phasias.

MEMPHIS, *a city of Middle Egypt, where the sacred bull (Apis) was worshiped*: Her. Chr. 9.92.

MEROE, *the capital of the ancient kingdom of Cush on the Nile, in present-day Sudan; according to Josephus it was formerly known as Saba (Sheba)*: potens Her. Chr. 6.174.

MEZENTIUS, *an Etruscan chieftain notorious for his atheism and cruelty*: impius Her. Chr. B 1.32.

MIGDONIUS, a, um, *from Bithynia, a Roman province on the northwest coast of Asia Minor*: gens Her. Chr. 10.5.

MINERVA, *the goddess of wisdom, learning, and the arts, identified with Athena*: [Her. Chr. 10.73]; invita *Nup.*, ded. 3; septemgeminum picta caput Her. Chr. 9.20; Suada Her. Chr. 19.28; tua Her. Chr. 21.117. *See also* Pallas.

MISENUS *or* MYSENUS, *the trumpeter of Aeneas; hence, a musician who plays a wind instrument*: non unus *Nup.* 295.

MOECENAS, *C. Maecenas (ca. 70–8 BCE), the patron of Horace and Vergil; hence, a patron of literature*: liberalissimus Her. Chr., ded. 17.2.

MOEONIS, idis, *Maeonian, Lydian*: Lydia Her. Chr. 23.69.

MOGA, *a corruption of Mazaca, an earlier name for Caesarea, the capital of Cappadocia and birthplace of St. Dorothy*: Her. Chr. 23.111. *See also* Caesarea.

MOISES, *Moses*: antiquus Her. Chr. 10.93. *See also* Mosaeus.

MONICA *(ca. 331–87), the mother of St. Augustine*: Her. Chr. 9, tit.; [9, *passim*].

MONSREGIUS, *Königsberg in Prussia, residence of the Grand Masters of the Teutonic Order from 1457*: Sylv. duae 1.137.

MORAVIA, *a province of Bohemia, now in the Czech Republic*: laudato generosa Baccho Nup. 156.

MORS, *Death (personified)*: Her. Chr. 3.7; atra Her. Chr. 18.56; 21.140; remorata Her. Chr. 14.48.

MOSAEUS, a, um, *of Moses*: manus Her. Chr. 21.190.

MOSCHI, *the Muscovites*: toties fugati *Nup.*, ded. 10.

[MOSES]. *See* Moises.

MUSA, *a Muse; hence, poem, song: Nup.* 6, 275, 342; *Sylv. duae* [2.1–44]; 2.6, 29, 34, 36, 136,
   [145–72], 152, 223, 248, [249–54]; *Her. Chr.* [A 2.12]; A 2.22; 24.101; inepta *Her.*
   Chr., lim. 2; mea *Her. Chr.* 24.133, 160; parca *Her. Chr.* 24.139; tua *Her. Chr.*
   A 3.64; Latiae *Nup.* 8; *Her. Chr.* 8.3; Latinae *Her. Chr.* 24.131; meae *Sylv. duae*
   1.153; steriles *Sylv. duae* 2.147. *See also* Amans; Calliopea; Camaenae; Pieris; Thalia.
MUSICUS, a, um, *of the Muses:* eques *Sylv. duae* 2.174.
MUTIANUS RUFUS, *the German humanist (1470–1526), close friend and mentor of Eobanus*
   Hessus: Sylv. duae 1, tit.; [1, *passim*]; 1.1, 159, 184; [*Her. Chr.* 24.103]; nobis charis-
   simus *Sylv. duae* 1.19.
MUTIUS, MACARIUS, *Macario Muzio, a Neo-Latin poet from Camerino (1440–1514?): Her. Chr.*,
   ded. 11.4.
MYRICIUS REGIOMONTANUS, SEBASTIANUS, *Sebastian Myricius (von der Heide) of*
   Königsberg (d. 1531): Sylv. duae, lim., tit.; ded., tit.; ded. 1; [ded., *passim*].
MYSNEUS, a, um, *of the Meissen region in Saxony, to which Leipzig belonged:* gens *Her. Chr.* 24.132.

NAEMAEUS, a, um, *of Nemea, a valley in Argolis, where Hercules killed the Nemean lion:* leo *Sylv.*
   duae 2.101.
NAIADES, *river nymphs, naiads: Her. Chr.* 4.113.
NAPEAE, *the nymphs of wooded valleys: Her. Chr.* 4.113.
NASO. *See* Ovidius Naso.
NATURA, *Nature (personified): Her. Chr.* 3.55; 20.23; facilis *Nup.* 88; fautrix *Her. Chr.* 24.83;
   territa *Her. Chr.* 3.45.
NAXOS, *largest of the Cyclades in the Aegean Sea:* barbara *Her. Chr.* 17.136.
NAZARETH, *town in Palestine: Her. Chr.* 6.115; 13.28.
NEMEUS. *See* Naemaeus.
[NEPTUNUS], *Neptune, god of the sea, identified with Poseidon: Sylv. duae* 2.143.
NERO, *a Roman Emperor (54–68):* [*Her. Chr.* 19.52, 55, 145–51]; magnus *Her. Chr.* 19.6; semideus
   Her. Chr. 19.31.
NESSAEUS, a, um, *of the centaur Nessus, killed by Hercules' envenomed arrow. His poisoned blood*
   eventually brought about Hercules' own death: mors *Her. Chr.* 17.140.
NESTOREUS, a, um, *Nestorian; of Nestor, a long-lived King of Pylos:* senex *Her. Chr.* A 3.49.
NILIACUS, a, um, *of Egypt:* Costis (*St. Catherine of Alexandria) Her. Chr.* 11.56.
NILUS, *the Nile: Her. Chr.* 4.210; comosus *Her. Chr.* 7.86; papyrifer *Her. Chr.* 9.91; tuus *Her.*
   Chr. 4.71.
NOGANUS, *the Nogat River, the eastern mouth of the Vistula:* amaenus *Sylv. duae* 1.151.
NONIUS, *Nonius (Nonnus), the Bishop of Heliopolis who converted St. Pelagia: Her. Chr.* 15, tit.;
   [15, *passim*]; 15.65.
NORICII, *the people of Nuremberg; hence, the city itself: Sylv. duae* 1.136.
NORVEGUS, a, um, *of Norway:* humus *Her. Chr.* 17.172.
NOTUS, *a south wind:* horrisonus *Her. Chr.* 17.186; celeres *Her. Chr.* 19.164; insani *Her. Chr.*
   8.128; 21.222.
NUMA, *Numa Pompilius, the legendary second King of Rome, proverbial for his devotion to religion:*
   Nup. 57.

OCEANITIS, *a daughter of Ocean:* multa *Her. Chr.* 19.154.
———, *Venus: Her. Chr.* 17.95. *See also* Venus.
OCEANUS *or* OCCEANUS, *the ocean that according to ancient belief surrounds the world: Nup.*
   283; *Her. Chr.* 2.33; 13.58.
OCEANUS, a, um, *of the ocean:* aqua *Her. Chr.* 2.56; 12.74; mare *Her. Chr.* 24.22.
ODERA, *the Oder River: Sylv. duae*, ded. 3; Marchiatica *Her. Chr.*, ded. 8.4; niger *Her. Chr.* 24.129.
ODILIA. *See* Otilia.
ODRYSIUS, a, um, *Thracian:* vates (*Orpheus) Her. Chr.* 21.39.
OECHALIUS, a, um, *of Oechalia:* Iole *Her. Chr.* 9.115.
OENONE, *a Phrygian nymph who fell in love with Paris when he was still a shepherd; she writes*
   a letter to him in Ovid's Heroides: Her. Chr. A 4.13.

OLENIUS, a, um, *Olenian, of Olenos*: capella (*the she-goat Amalthea*) *Her. Chr.* 10.69.

OLYMPIAS, *an Olympiad, a period of four years; poetically, a period of five years*: proxima *Her. Chr.* 14.3; quarta *Her. Chr.* 24.109.

OLYMPUS, *heaven*: altus *Her. Chr.* 13.73; excelsus *Her. Chr.* 1.5; patrius *Her. Chr.* 1.95.

ORAEAS, *a mountain nymph, Oread*: *Her. Chr.* 19.153.

ORCHADES, *the Orkney Islands north of Scotland*: terdenae *Her. Chr.* 17.167.

ORCUS, *the underworld*: *Sylv. duae* 2.141. *See also* Tartara.

OREAS. *See* Oraeas.

OREB, *Mount Horeb (Sinai), where God gave Moses the Ten Commandments*: *Her. Chr.* 5.16. *See also* Sinaius.

ORIGENES, *the Greek Christian writer Origen (early third century)*: *Her. Chr.* 10, tit.; [10, *passim*].

ORONTES, *the principal river of Syria*: gelidus *Her. Chr.* 19.99.

ORONTHAEUS, a, um, *of the Orontes River*: littus *Her. Chr.* 19.2.

ORPHEUS, *the legendary Thracian singer and lyrist, killed by the Bacchantes*: [*Her. Chr.* A 3.57–58; 21.39].

————, *a musician like Orpheus*: multus *Nup.* 299.

OTILIA, *St. Ottilia (Odilia), the patroness of Alsace (ca. 660–ca. 720)*: pia *Her. Chr.* 9.143.

OVIDIUS NASO, *the Latin poet Ovid (43 BCE–CE 17/18) of the Pelignian city Sulmo*: *Her. Chr.*, ded. 7.1, 13.4, 16.1; *Her. Chr.* A 1.2, 5–6, 9, 13; [A 1.17, 22]; A 3.43; [24.133]; fluidus *Her. Chr.* A 1.11.

PACTOLUS, *a river in Lydia, famed for its gold-bearing sands*: vagus *Nup.* 152.

PAESTUM. *See* Poestum.

PALATIA, *the imperial palace on the Palatine hill in Rome*: celebrata *Her. Chr.* 21.203.

PALESTINA, *Palestine*: [*Her. Chr.* 5.15–18, 166; 6.48; 21.13, 86]; rebellis *Her. Chr.* 12.253. *See also* Iudaea.

PALESTINUS, *a Palestinian*: coactus *Her. Chr.* 12.113.

PALESTINUS, a, um, *of Palestine*: colonus *Her. Chr.* 1.102; orbis *Her. Chr.* 6.48.

PALINURUS, *the helmsman of Aeneas. Overcome by the god of sleep, he fell overboard and was washed ashore in Italy, only to be murdered by the inhabitants and left unburied*: *Her. Chr.* 6.209.

PALLANTIAS, *Aurora, daughter of the giant Pallas*: *Nup.* 206. *See also* Aurora.

PALLAS, *a title of Athena, goddess of wisdom, learning, and the arts. She sprang fully armed from the head of Zeus*: *Nup.*, ded. 11; glauca *Nup.* 91. *See also* Minerva.

PALMARIA, *the Isle of Palms in the Gulf of Gaeta*: viridis *Her. Chr.* 18.3.

PANCHAEUS, a, um, *of Mount Pangaea in Macedonia*: rura *Sylv. duae* 1.87.

PANNONICUS, a, um, *of Hungary*: aurum *Nup.* 159; nurus *Nup.* 245; reges *Nup.* 93.

PANNONIS, idis, *of Hungary*: puella (*St. Elizabeth*) *Her. Chr.* 5.2.

PANNONIUS, a, um, *of Hungary*: rex (*Vladislav II*) *Nup.* 223; montes *Sylv. duae* 1.61.

PANTHULUS, *a legendary Bishop of Basel*: *Her. Chr.* 17.213.

PAPHIUS, a, um, *Paphian, of Paphos in Cyprus, sacred to Venus; hence, associated with or sacred to Venus*: aestus *Sylv. duae* 2.27; arundo *Nup.* 10; nox *Sylv. duae* 2.115; columbae *Nup.* 315; fores *Sylv. duae* 2.224.

PAPHNUCIUS *or* PAPHNUTIUS, *fourth-century Egyptian monk, Bishop of the Upper Thebaid, who converted St. Thais*: *Her. Chr.* 11, tit.; [11, *passim*]; 11.7.

PAPHUS, *a city in Cyprus with a famous temple of Venus*: *Sylv. duae* 2.168; *Her. Chr.* 9.89.

————, *the island of Cyprus*: *Sylv. duae* 1.32.

[PARADISE], *the earthly Paradise, believed to be located on a high mountain in the East*: *Her. Chr.* 1.49, 63; 6.170; 20.27; 23, *passim*.

PARADISIACUS, a, um, *of the earthly Paradise*: solum *Her. Chr.* 6.170; iuga *Her. Chr.* 23.42.

PARCAE, *the Fates*: *Her. Chr.* 8.19; 11.11. *See also* Fatum.

PARIS, *a son of Priam, King of Troy. While still a shepherd on Mount Ida he was chosen to judge a beauty contest between Hera, Athena, and Aphrodite. After deserting his lover Oenone, he seduced Helen and abducted her to Troy*: *Nup.* 89, 194; *Her. Chr.* 17.139.

————, *Ovid's heroic letter "Paris to Helen"*: *Her. Chr.*, ded. 16.1; *Her. Chr.* A 4.9.

PARNASSUS, *a twin-peaked mountain in Phocis, sacred to Apollo and the Muses*: Sylv. duae 2.135. See also Cyrrha.

PARTHENICAE, *a series of seven short epics about Christian women saints, written by Baptista Mantuanus*: Her. Chr., ded. 15.5.

PASCHA, *Passover*: Her. Chr. 1.182; [16.123]; 16.164; [16.294].

PATHMOS, *an island in the Aegean Sea, where St. John the Apostle lived in exile*: Aegea Her. Chr. 16.9.

PAULA, *St. Paula (347–404), a Roman lady of noble birth, wife of Toxotius. In 385 she and her daughter Eustochium followed St. Jerome to Palestine*: Her. Chr. 21, tit.; [21, *passim*]; 21.4.

PAULINUS, *a Bishop of Antioch*: Her. Chr. 21.123.

PAULUS, *St. Paul the Apostle*: Her. Chr. 19, tit.; [19, *passim*]; 19.41.

PAULUS DE SCHWARTZENBERGK BARO, *Baron Paul von Schwarzenberg (1498–1535), a friend of Eobanus Hessus in Leipzig*: Her. Chr. A 2, tit.

PELAGIA, *St. Pelagia, a dissolute actress of Antioch who became a penitent in Jerusalem*: Her. Chr. 15, tit.; [15, *passim*].

————, *her letter to Nonius (Her. Chr. 15)*: Her. Chr., ded. 13.1.

PELEUS, *a King of Phthia in Thessaly, father of Achilles, who possessed a magic sword*: Her. Chr., ded. 14.1.

PELIGNUS, a, um, *Pelignian, of the Peligni in central Italy*: poeta *(Ovid)* Her. Chr. 24.133; terra Her. Chr. A 1.5.

PELLAEUS, a, um, *of Pella in Macedonia, the birthplace of Alexander the Great*: iuvenis Her. Chr. 14.63; tyrannus Her. Chr. 4.55.

PENATES, *household gods; hence, home, homeland*: Her. Chr. 18.71; patrii Her. Chr. 10.11, 117; 20.31; Phrygii *Nup.* 131.

PERICLES, *Athenian orator and statesman (ca. 495–429 BCE)*: Her. Chr. A 3.51.

PERILLUS, *a sculptor who made a bronze bull for the tyrant Phalaris (d. ca. 554 BCE) in order to roast people alive*: aliquis Her. Chr. B 1.31.

PERINTHIACUS, a, um, *of Perinthos (later Heraclea) in Thrace*: ars *(of the painter Zeuxis of Heraclea)*: Her. Chr. 24.20.

PERSAE, *the three wise men from the East*: sapientes Her. Chr. 21.211. See also Magi.

PERSEUS, a, um, *founded by the legendary Greek hero Perseus*: Tharsus Her. Chr. 19.89.

PETREIUS, a, um, *of St. Peter*: limina *(of St. Peter's in Rome)* Her. Chr. 17.203.

PETRUS, *St. Peter*: Her. Chr. 3.84; 21.168; Galilaeus Her. Chr. 19.5.

[PHAEDRA], *the wife of Theseus, who attempted to seduce her stepson Hippolytus*: Sylv. duae 1.97.

[PHAETHON], *the son of Helios, who tried to drive the sun's chariot for a day, but lost control and was killed by Jupiter*: Her. Chr. 15.81–82.

PHALERNA, *Falernian wines; hence, fine wines*: nobilia Her. Chr. 5.141.

PHARIUS, a, um, *of Egypt*: Ioseph Her. Chr. 6.79; rex Her. Chr. 13.157.

PHAROS, *an island near Alexandria in Egypt with a famous lighthouse*: Her. Chr. 7.86; marmorea Her. Chr. 20.148.

————, *the lighthouse itself*: antiqua Her. Chr. 1.126.

————, *Egypt*: vario pisce superba Sylv. duae 1.78.

PHASIAS, *the sorceress Medea of Colchis*: callida magica arte Her. Chr. 19.130; non ulla Her. Chr. 8.100.

PHILEREMUS, *a pastoral name for Eobanus' friend Herbord von der Marthen (ca. 1480–1529)*: Sylv. duae 1.189.

PHILIPPI, *an ancient city in Macedonia*: Her. Chr. 19.75; [19.77].

PHILISTEUS or PHILYSTEUS, a, um, *Philistine*: gygas *(Goliath)* Her. Chr. 13.159; coloni Her. Chr. 5.17.

PHILOSTRATUS, *Flavius Philostratus (ca. 170–ca. 245), who composed a biography of Apollonius of Tyana and Lives of the Sophists*: Her. Chr., ded. 14.2.

PHLEGETHON, *a river of fire in the underworld; hence, the underworld*: Her. Chr. 9.162.

PHOCAICUS, a, um, *of Phocis in central Greece*: Cyrrha *(Mount Parnassus)* Sylv. duae 2.173.

PRUSSIA, *a German region on the southeast shores of the Baltic*: *Nup.*, ded., tit.; *Sylv. duae*, t.p.;
    lim., tit.; [lim., *passim*]; ded. 2; [ded. 6]; ded. 7; *Sylv. duae* 1, tit.; [1, *passim*]; 1.37,
    39, 50, 160–62; *Her. Chr.*, ded. 8.3, 17.4; *Her. Chr.* 24.127; mea dulcis *Sylv. duae*,
    lim. 7; tota *Her. Chr.*, ded. 17.3, 18.6.
PRUSSIACUS, a, um, *of Prussia*: orbis *Sylv. duae* 1.23.
PRUTHENICUS, a, um, *of Prussia*: tellus *Sylv. duae* 1.45.
PRUTHENUS, a, um, *of Prussia*: Lucas *(Lukas Watzelrode) Nup.* 274.
PTHOLOMAIS, *Acre, a port city in the Kingdom of Jerusalem, seat of the Grand Master of the
    Teutonic Order until 1291*: capta *Sylv. duae* 1.51.
PUNICUS, a, um, *of Carthage*: humus *Her. Chr.* 9.8; terra *Her. Chr.* 23.74; moenia *Sylv. duae*
    1.174. *See also Elisaeus; Poenus.*
PYLIUS, a, um, *of Nestor, the long-lived King of Pylos*: senecta *Her. Chr.* A 3.71.
PYRENAEUS, *the Pyrenees*: *Sylv. duae* 1.106.

[QUINTILIANUS, M. FABIUS], *M. Fabius Quintilianus (ca. 35–ca. 100)*: *Her. Chr.*, ded. 19.3.
QUIRINUS, *the name of Romulus after he was deified*: *Her. Chr.* 9.87; [19.21–22]; vetus *Her.
    Chr.* 21.7.

[RACHEL], *second wife of the patriarch Jacob, mother of Joseph and Benjamin*: *Her. Chr.* 13.88.
RHAMNUSIA, *the goddess worshiped at Rhamnus (Nemesis, identified with Fortuna)*: *Her. Chr.*
    8.7. *See also* Fortuna.
RHENUS, *the Rhine River*: *Her. Chr.* 17.200, 211, 262, [263–65], 269; celeber *Nup.*, lim. 3; mag-
    nus *Sylv. duae* 1.59; *Her. Chr.* 24.51.
RHODII, *the inhabitants of Rhodes*: *Her. Chr.* 19.85.
RHODIUS, a, um, *from the island of Rhodes*: cadi *Sylv. duae* 1.124.
RHODOPE, *mountain system in western Thrace*: *Sylv. duae* 1.87.
RHODOS, *an island and city in the Aegean Sea with a gigantic statue (Colossus) of the sun god*:
    Sylv. duae 1.32; *Her. Chr.* 5.183.
RHOMA, *Rome*: [*Nup.* 219]; *Her. Chr.* 1.199–200; [7.107, 145]; 9.155; [17.215, 220, 259;
    18.7, 13, 149, 161, 169; 19.5, 15–24]; 19.47, 88; [21.7]; 21.43; [21.93, 132, 149];
    21.167, 173; 23.111; caeca *Her. Chr.* 19.7; dulcis *Her. Chr.* 21.77; Iliaca *Her. Chr.*
    9.5; impia *Her. Chr.* 1.187; 12.240; infausta *Her. Chr.* 19.163; Martia *Sylv. duae*
    1.171; *Her. Chr.* 17.68; Mavortia *Her. Chr.* 6.145; maxima *Her. Chr.* 7.44; nova
    (Constantinople) Her. Chr. 6.149; potens *Her. Chr.* 19.15; sua *Her. Chr.* 9.87; vetus
    Her. Chr. 6.149; 21.203.
RHOMANI, *the Romans*: *Her. Chr.* 19.92.
RHOMANUS *or* ROMANUS, a, um, *Roman*: Caesar *(either Diocletian or Maximinian) Her.
    Chr.* 12.9; *(Domitian) Her. Chr.* 16.9; dux *(Fabricius) Her. Chr.* 23.18; elegantia *Her.
    Chr.* A 2.9; eques *Nup.* 133; grex *Sylv. duae* 1.182; Homerus *(Vergil) Her. Chr.*, ded.
    3.2; imperium *Her. Chr.* 1.171; manus *Her. Chr.* 21.2; navis *Her. Chr.* 21.19; nomen
    Her. Chr. 6.59; orbis *Her. Chr.* 6.83; 12.44; potentia *Her. Chr.* 6.75, 213; preses
    (Pontius Pilate) Her. Chr. 16.197; presul *(Pope Julius II) Nup.* 219; sermo *Her. Chr.*
    A 3.46; aquilae *Nup.* 37; arma *Her. Chr.* 6.161; 12.251; iura *Her. Chr.* 12.113; scrip-
    tores *Her. Chr.*, ded. 3.4; sedes *Her. Chr.* 17.203; volucres *Her. Chr.* 6.195.
RHOMULEUS, a, um, *Roman*: fascis *Her. Chr.* 12.27; securis *Her. Chr.* 12.221.
RHOMULIDES, *the Romans*: *Her. Chr.* 17.215; meliori sydere nuptae *Her. Chr.* 7.33.
RHOMULUS, a, um, *Roman, Latin*: manus *Her. Chr.* 22.6; Tybris *Her. Chr.* 18.4.
RHUSSI. *See* Russi.
RIPHAEUS, a, um, *arctic*: frigus *Her. Chr.* 18.44; nix *Her. Chr.* 23.68.
RISEBURGUM, *Riesenburg in Prussia, the residence of Bishop Job von Dobeneck*: [*Sylv. duae* 1.153–58];
    Her. Chr., ded. 18.7; meis nobile Musis *Sylv. duae* 1.153; tuum *Her. Chr.*, ded. 17.3.
ROMA; ROMANI, *etc. See* Rhoma; Rhomani; *etc.*
[RUBEN]. *See* Isachar.
RUBRUM AEQUOR, *the Red Sea*: *Her. Chr.* 13.157.

SILENUS, *Bacchus' tutor and companion*: *Sylv. duae* 1.89.

[SIMEON], *an aged Jew who told Mary in the Temple that a sword would pierce her soul*: Her. Chr. 16.100.

SIMOIS, *tributary of the Scamander in the Troad, rising on the Ida*: *Nup.* 116.

SIMON, *a leper in whose house Jesus was anointed by a woman (identified with Mary Magdalene)*: dolens Her. Chr. 3.111.

SINAIUS, a, um, *on Mount Sinai*: templa Her. Chr. 21.189.

SION, *Zion, the citadel of Jerusalem; hence, Jerusalem itself*: Her. Chr. 16.93; antiqua Her. Chr. 6.55; ipsa Her. Chr. 20.10; sanctus Her. Chr. 14.73; vetus Her. Chr. 7.93. *See also* Solima.

SIREN. *See* Syren.

SITHONIUS, a, um, *Thracian*: nix Her. Chr. 4.112.

SLESIA, *Silesia, a region in central Europe*: confini nimium vicina Polono *Nup.* 155.

SLESIUS, a, um: *Silesian*: tellus *Nup.* 154.

SOCRATES, *the Greek philosopher (469–399 BCE)*: Her. Chr., ded. 8.7.

SOL, *the sun god, the sun (personified)*: *Nup.* 125; Her. Chr. 2.33; 3.47; 14.36; 19.86; caelivagus Her. Chr. 21.74; fessus Her. Chr. 14.43; territus Her. Chr. 16.193. *See also* Phoebus.

SOLIMA, SOLYMA, *or* SOLIMAE, *Jerusalem*: Her. Chr. 1.122; 3.28; 5.5; [5.19–20; 17.66]; 19.79; 20.9. *See also* Sion.

SOLIMUS *or* SOLYMUS, a, um, *of Jerusalem*: urbs Her. Chr. 14.67; 16.122, 151; vates *(Isaiah)* Her. Chr. 1.35; 2.36; arces Her. Chr. 6.35; 21.186; colles Her. Chr. 3.139; 5.167; matres Her. Chr. 16.35; orae Her. Chr. 16.253; portae Her. Chr. 13.94.

SOLOMON, *King of Israel (tenth century BCE), son of David*: Her. Chr. [6.56, 176–78]; 6.179.

SOLOMONEUS, a, um, *built by King Solomon*: templa Her. Chr. 14.73.

SOLYMA; SOLYMUS. *See* Solima; Solimus.

SPIRITUS, *the Holy Spirit*: Her. Chr. 1.31; 2.65; 4.96; [4.203–04; 6.175; 10.67; 13.80]; 16.87; [17.91]. *See also* Deus.

[STAPHILEUS, JOHANNES], *Giovanni Stafileo (1472–1528), the papal nuncio at King Sigismund's wedding in 1512*: *Nup.* 218–20.

STATIUS, PAPINIUS, *the Roman poet P. Papinius Statius (latter half of the first century CE)*: *Nup.*, ded. 1; [ded. 3].

STEPHANUS, *Stephen Zápolyai (d. 1499), Palatine of Hungary since 1490, the father of Barbarba Zápolyai*: *Nup.* 104.

STOICUS, a, um, *Stoic*: virtus *Nup.* 270.

STYGIUS *or* STIGIUS, a, um, *Stygian, of the Styx; of the underworld*: aqua Her. Chr. 15.76; canis (Cerberus) Her. Chr. 11.70; domus Her. Chr. 3.16; 9.144; draco Her. Chr. 22.71; Iovis Her. Chr. 1.180; nox *Sylv. duae* 1.50; Her. Chr. 10.165; 11.17; pigricitas *Sylv. duae* 2.236; profundum Her. Chr. 3.3; lacus Her. Chr. 6.136; lares Her. Chr. 9.112.

STYMPHALIS, e, *of Stymphalus, a lake in northeastern Arcadia infested by man-eating birds*: unda *Sylv. duae* 2.104.

STYX, *the principal river in the underworld; hence, the underworld*: Her. Chr. 9.143; 15.128.

SUADA MINERVA. *See* Minerva.

SUEDI, *the Swedes*: humiles Her. Chr. 17.171.

SULMO, *a city in the Apennines, east of Rome, the birthplace of Ovid*: Her. Chr. A 1.6.

SYBILLA, *a Sibyl, a prophetess in ancient Greece and Rome*: Her. Chr. 1.173; [1.198]; 4.25; 9.77; tanta Her. Chr. 6.172.

SYREN, *one of the Sirens, female monsters who lived on the southern coast of Italy and lured sailors to their death with their enchanting voices*: *Nup.* 300; blandissima Her. Chr. 15.177.

SYRIA, *Syria (including Palestine)*: *Sylv. duae* 1.52.

SYRIUS, a, um, *of Syria*: arva Her. Chr. 12.115.

TAECLA. *See* Tecla.

TANAIS *or* THANAIS, *the Don River*: nivalis *Nup.* 83; undosus *Nup.* 167.

TARTARA, *Tartarus, hell*: [*Sylv. duae* 2.112]; Her. Chr. [3.3, 11–24; 6.184; 11.69, 118; 17.78]; 17.191; aethereo cassa die Her. Chr. 17.240; clausa Her. Chr. 1.38; ima Her. Chr. 23.94. *See also* Orcus.

TARTAREUS, a, um, *of Tartarus, hell*: rex *Her. Chr.* 3.117; tyrannus *Her. Chr.* 9.145; duces *Her. Chr.* 1.86.

TARTARUS, *a Tartar, inhabitant of the Tartar khanates on the Volga River and the Crimea*: audax *Nup.* 81; epoto satiatus equo *Nup.* 24; toties fusi *Nup.*, ded. 10.

TECLA *or* TAECLA, *legendary saint of Iconium*: *Her. Chr.* 19, tit.; [19, *passim*]; 19.119.

TERAPHNAEUS, a, um, *Corsican*: racemi *Sylv. duae* 1.121.

TEUTON, *a German*: cataphrattus *Nup.* 153.

TEUTONICI, *the Teutonic Knights, a military and religious order founded ca. 1190*: [*Nup.* 229]; *Sylv. duae* [1.36, 38, 47–64]; 1.54, [1.131–34, 139–40, 161].

TEUTONICUS, a, um, *Teutonic, German*: crux *Sylv. duae* 1.38, 52; iugum *Sylv. duae* 1.58; miles *Sylv. duae* 1.48; militia *Nup.* 229; milites *Sylv. duae* 1.161; nomisma *Her. Chr.* 8.1; ritus *Nup.* 162; solum *Her. Chr.* 17.260. *See also* Germanus.

TEUTONIS, idos, *German*: ora *Sylv. duae* 1.128; *Her. Chr.* 7.98; 24.52. *See also* Germanus.

TEUTONUS, a, um, *German*: pubes *Nup.* 29; arva *Sylv. duae* 1.182; *Her. Chr.* 17.200. *See also* Germanus.

THAIS, *St. Thais, an Egyptian courtesan converted by St. Paphnutius*: *Her. Chr.* 11, tit.; [11, *passim*]; 11.162; 15.145; vestra *Her. Chr.* 11.150.

THALIA, *the Muse of light verse*: blandiloqua *Her. Chr.* A 2.8; properata *Nup.* 216; reses *Sylv. duae* 2.11. *See also* Musa.

THARSUS, *the capital of Cilicia, said to have been founded by Perseus, the birthplace of St. Paul*: Persea *Her. Chr.* 19.89.

THEBAE, *Thebes in Boeotia, supposedly founded by Cadmus*: *Sylv. duae* 1.173; *Her. Chr.* 17.63.

THECLA. *See* Tecla.

THEOCHIUS, *the son of St. Paula*: *Her. Chr.* 21.146; [21.152].

THEOPHILUS, *a lawyer who mocked St. Dorothy as she was being led to her execution*: *Her. Chr.* 23, tit.; [23, *passim*]; 23.19.

THERAPNAEUS. *See* Teraphnaeus.

THESAEUS, a, um, *of King Theseus*: iuvenis (*Hippolytus*) *Sylv. duae* 1.97.

THESSALICUS, a, um, *of Thessaly, a region of northern Greece*: luci *Sylv. duae* 1.94.

THETIS, *a sea nymph, wife of Peleus and mother of Achilles*: formosa *Nup.* 118.

THISBE. *See* Thysbe.

THORONIA *or* THURONIA, *Thorn, a city on the Vistula River*: *Nup.* 239; *Sylv. duae* 1.141.

THRACES, *the Thracians*: *Her. Chr.* 4.27.

THUCIDIDES, *the Greek historian Thucydides (fifth century* BCE*), who composed* The History of the Peloponnesian War: *Her. Chr.*, ded. 14.2.

THURONIA. *See* Thoronia.

THUSCUS, a, um, *Tuscan, Etrurian*: Tybris *Her. Chr.* 19.2.

THYSBE, *Thisbe, the lover of Pyramus*: Babilonia *Her. Chr.* 17.133.

TIBERINUS. *See* Tyberinus.

TIBRIS. *See* Tybris.

TIBULLUS, *the Roman poet Albius Tibullus (55/48–19* BCE*)*: *Her. Chr.* A 3.46.

TIMANTES, *the famous Greek painter Timanthes (fifth century* BCE*)*: *Her. Chr.*, ded. 19.3.

TIPHYS. *See* Typhis.

TITAN, *the Titan Helios, the sun god*: pronus *Her. Chr.* 13.57. *See also* Phoebus.

TITYRUS. *See* Tytirus.

TMOLUS, *a mountain in Lydia, famous for its wines and saffron*: *Her. Chr.* 23.70.

TOMIS, *town on the west coast of the Black Sea, where Ovid lived in exile*: *Her. Chr.* A 3.43.

TOMYRIS, *a Scythian queen who defeated and killed Cyrus the Great*: *Her. Chr.* 6.61.

TONANS, *the Thunderer, the triune God, Christ*: *Her. Chr.* 1.157; 4.251; aeternus *Her. Chr.* 15.104; humanus *Her. Chr.* 21.187; iratus *Her. Chr.* 11.41; magnus *Her. Chr.* 2.7; 19.35; offensus *Her. Chr.* 11.171; verus *Her. Chr.* 17.241. *See also* Christus; Deus.

[TOXOTIUS], *husband of St. Paula*: *Her. Chr.* 21.122.

TRINACRIA, *Sicily*: potens *Her. Chr.* 17.225.

TRINITAS, *the Trinity*: *Her. Chr.*, ded. 13.1; [*Her. Chr.* 4.199–204; 10.61–68, 107–08]. *See also* Deus.

VISTULA *or* ISTULA, *the Vistula River in present-day Poland*: *Nup.*, lim. 3; *Sylv. duae* 1.2, 61, 129; vagus *Sylv. duae* 1.59, 144; *Her. Chr.* 24.128.

VITUS WERLERUS. *See* Werlerus, Vitus.

[VLADISLAV II], *King of Bohemia from 1471 and King of Hungary from 1490 to his death in 1516*: *Nup.* 223.

VRATISLAVIA, *Breslau (Wrocław), the chief city of Silesia*: celebris *Nup.* 224.

VULCANIUS, a, um, *of the blacksmith god Vulcan*: artificium *Her. Chr.*, ded. 18.9.

VULCANUS, *the god of fire, identified with Hephaestus, who made his home in Lemnos*: *Her. Chr.* 9.88.

[WARMIA]. *See* Varmia.

[WATZELRODE, LUKAS]. *See* Lucas.

WERLERUS, VITUS, *the German humanist Veit Werler of Sulzfeld (early 1480s–after 1535)*: *Her. Chr.* A 3, tit.; A 3.69; B 1, tit.; [B 1, *passim*]; B 1.56, 62; beatus *Her. Chr.* B 1.4.

[WILCZEK, BERNARDINUS], *Bishop of Lemberg from 1505 to 1540*: *Nup.* 262–63.

ZACHARIAS, *Zechariah, the father of John the Baptist*: *Her. Chr.* 20, tit.; [20, *passim*]; 20.1.

[ZÁPOLYAI]. *See* Barbara; Stephanus.

ZEBEDIDES, *St. James the Great, the son of Zebedee; he is said to be buried in Compostela, Spain*: divus *Her. Chr.* 7.99.

ZEPHYRUS, *the warm west wind, harbinger of spring*: *Her. Chr.* 1.154; meliores *Her. Chr.* 17.201.

[ZEUXIS], *a Greek painter of Heraclea (active in the late fifth century* BCE): *Her. Chr.* 24.20.

ZOILUS, *a sophist of the fourth century* BCE *who poked fun at Homer's errors and inconsistencies; hence, a malicious critic*: *Nup.*, postscr.; furens *Her. Chr.* B 1.14.

ZOZIMAS, *a monk who found St. Mary of Egypt beside the Jordan River*: *Her. Chr.* 14, tit.; [14, *passim*].

GENERAL INDEX

This index combines names and subjects. Names that do not appear in the text, or references to such names, are enclosed in brackets. All references are to the page numbers. References to the literary texts presented in this volume are to the English translation. For names in the Latin texts, consult the Glossarial Index.